William H. Powell

**Officers of the Army and Navy (regular)**

Who Served in the Civil War

William H. Powell

**Officers of the Army and Navy (regular)**
*Who Served in the Civil War*

ISBN/EAN: 9783337409326

Printed in Europe, USA, Canada, Australia, Japan

Cover: Foto ©ninafisch / pixelio.de

More available books at **www.hansebooks.com**

# OFFICERS

OF THE

# ARMY AND NAVY

(REGULAR)

WHO SERVED IN THE CIVIL WAR.

EDITED BY

MAJOR WILLIAM H. POWELL, U. S. ARMY,

AND

MEDICAL-DIRECTOR EDWARD SHIPPEN, U. S. NAVY.

# PREFACE.

The thought which inspired the publication of this volume was that of gathering together, in one work, the faces and life-sketches of as many as possible of the officers of the Regular Army and Navy who served during the Civil War, not that they themselves might view their own pictures and records, but that future generations might read with pride of the part their ancestors played, and look with pleasure on the faces of those who acted in the great tragedy for the preservation of our noble and powerful republic, at a time when its existence as a single government seemed about to terminate.

The volume contains not only the pictures and sketches of the greatest of our generals and admirals, but those of men who did their part in the great struggle, whether with sword or rifle, although of a minor character, and who will feel proud of occupying places beside those of such great distinction as Grant, Farragut, Sherman, Porter, Sheridan, and others.

Old comrades, who have not met for years, will also be pleased to see how Time is dealing with the living, and will gaze with fondness on the faces of those who no longer respond to the bugle's call, or have sailed to "unknown seas."

# OFFICERS OF THE ARMY AND NAVY

(REGULAR)

## WHO SERVED IN THE CIVIL WAR.

REAR-ADMIRAL JAMES ALDEN, U.S.N.

JAMES ALDEN was born in Maine. Appointed midshipman from same State April 1, 1828. Promoted to passed midshipman June 14, 1834; Navy-Yard, Boston, 1835; exploring expedition around the world 1838–42. Commissioned as lieutenant February 25, 1841; Naval Station, Boston, 1843; frigate "Constitution," around the world, second time, 1844–46; while attached to this vessel, commanded a boat expedition and cut out several war-junks from under the guns of the fort at Zuzon Bay, Cochin-China; Home Squadron during Mexican war; present at the capture of Vera Cruz, Tuspan, and Tobasco; Naval Station, Boston, 1847; Coast Survey, 1848–60; made a reconnoissance of all the West coast. In the winter of 1855–56, during the Indian war in Puget Sound, volunteered with the surveying steamer "Active," to cooperate with the army, and rendered important aid in bringing the war to a close; by his timely arrival in the spring of the same year, at San Juan Island, prevented a collision between the British naval forces and the United States troops; assisted in landing troops enough to hold the island in dispute against the threatened attack of the British. Commissioned as commander September 14, 1855; commanding the steamer "South Carolina," at the commencement of the Rebellion, May, 1861; reinforced Fort Pickens, while blockading Galveston, Texas; had a fight with the batteries in the rear of the city; while there, captured thirteen schooners laden with merchandise; commanded sloop "Richmond," at the passage of Forts Jackson and St. Philip, and the engagement with Chalmette batteries and defences of New Orleans; passage of Vicksburg batteries twice; Port Hudson, 1862–63. Commissioned as captain January 2, 1863; commanded

steam-sloop "Brooklyn," in the action with Forts Morgan and Gaines, and the rebel gunboats in Mobile Bay; commanded in two attacks on Fort Fisher. Captain Alden took a prominent part in all the great naval battles of the war, and was handsomely mentioned in the official reports. Commissioned as commodore July 25, 1866; commanding steam-sloop "Susquehanna," special service, 1867; commanding steam-frigate "Minnesota," special service, 1867–68; commandant Navy-Yard, Mare Island, California, 1868–69; chief of Bureau of Navigation and Detail, Navy Department, 1869–71. Promoted to rear-admiral 1871; commanding European Squadron 1872. Retired 1873. Died 1877.

### REAR-ADMIRAL JOHN J. ALMY, U.S.N.

JOHN J. ALMY was born in Rhode Island in 1815, and appointed a midshipman at fourteen. After a cruise in the Mediterranean, and another on the coast of Brazil, he was promoted passed mid-shipman 1835. After serving in the receiving ship "New York" he was attached to the "Cyane," in the Mediterranean, as acting-master and navigator, for three years. In March, 1841, he was commissioned as lieutenant, and served in the West Indies and on the coast of Africa. He was next attached to the "Ohio," 74, in the Gulf of Mexico and the Pacific, during the Mexican war. He was at the siege and capture of Vera Cruz, and the capture of Tuspan. In the latter part of the war, 1848, he commanded one of the forts at Mazatlan, during the occupation by the navy. Following this came a service of five years upon the coast survey; and then he was ordered to command the "Fulton," during the operations on the coast of Central America, consequent upon General Walker's doings in that region. Walker surrendered to Rear-Admiral Paulding on board the "Fulton," at Nicaragua. The admiral complimented Lieutenant Almy very highly, saying, "He performed his part of the work exceedingly well, and is an officer who can be relied upon at all times." Lieutenant Almy then commanded the "Fulton," in the Paraguay Expedition, and, upon her return, was attached to the New York Navy-Yard. He was made commander in April, 1861, as the civil war broke out. He was then constantly in command on the Atlantic coast. While commanding the "Connecticut," he captured and sent in four noted blockade-running steamers, with valuable cargoes. He ran ashore and destroyed four others.

Commissioned as captain March, 1865. Commanded the "Juniata," in a cruise to the coast of Africa and the coast of Brazil. While on the coast of Brazil he rescued the Brazilian brig "Americo" and her crew from shipwreck. The service was attended with great danger, and for it he was thanked by the Emperor of Brazil, the late Dom Pedro. In 1868–69 Captain Almy was on ordnance duty at Navy-Yard, New York. In December, 1869, he was commissioned commodore, and served for two years as chief signal officer of the navy, at Washington. Commissioned as rear-admiral August, 1873, and at once was ordered to the command of the U. S. naval forces in the Pacific. While at Panama, in October, 1873, a serious revolution occurred. The city of Panama and the Panama Railroad were in imminent danger of being destroyed. Admiral Almy landed a force of men, under competent officers, and afforded efficient protection to European as well as American citizens, and preserved the communication intact. At that time he had only the "Pensacola" and the "Benicia" at hand, in Panama. Passengers, freight, and specie passed over the road without molestation; and, when quiet was restored, Rear-Admiral Almy received the thanks of the Panama Company, the Pacific Mail Company, and of all the consuls and the foreign merchants at Panama. In 1875, while in command of the Pacific Squadron, Rear-Admiral Almy was presented by his Majesty King Kalakaua, of the Hawaiian Islands, with the Order of King Kamehameha I, in appreciation of courtesies and attentions bestowed upon his Majesty during his journey to the United States, when the king and his suite were conveyed to and fro in vessels of the squadron under the rear-admiral's command. Rear-Admiral Almy returned from his command of nearly three years, in the Pacific, in July, 1876. In April, 1877, he was retired, under the operation of law.

He performed, altogether, twenty-seven years and ten months sea-service,—the largest amount, up to this time, credited to any officer of the navy. His shore or other duty was fourteen years and eight months.

CAPTAIN LUTHER S. AMES.

CAPTAIN LUTHER S. AMES (Second Infantry) was born in Plattsburgh, New York, and entered the volunteer service during the war of the Rebellion, serving as private, quartermaster-sergeant, and sergeant-major from September, 1861, to December, 1863, participating in the campaigns of the Army of the West, and was engaged in the capture of New Madrid, Island No. 10, and Corinth, Mississippi, and the pursuit of the rebel General Beauregard; also the battles of Iuka and Corinth, Mississippi, October, 1862.

He was promoted first lieutenant and made regimental quartermaster of the Sixty-fourth Illinois Infantry, December 10, 1863. He was also acting adjutant of his regiment during the Atlanta campaign, and was engaged in the battles of Resaca, Dallas, Kenesaw Mountain, Nickajack Creek, Georgia, and those in front of Atlanta of the 22d and 28th of July, 1864.

He was promoted captain of his regiment July 17, 1864, and participated in the Atlanta campaign, being engaged in the battle of Jonesboro', Georgia, the capture of Atlanta, and the pursuit of the rebel General Hood into Northern Alabama. He also participated in General Sherman's "March to the Sea," and the Carolina campaigns, being engaged at Pocotaligo, Salkehatchie River, and the capture of Columbia, South Carolina, in February, 1865.

Captain Ames performed the duties of acting assistant adjutant-general of the First Brigade, First Division, Seventeenth Army Corps, from February, 1865, and was in the engagements at Cheraw, South Carolina, Bentonville, North Carolina, and the capture of Goldsboro' and Raleigh, North Carolina, and present at the surrender of the rebel General Johnston and his army. He accompanied the troops on the march from Raleigh to Washington, D. C., participating in the grand review at that place in May, 1865. He then occupied the position of commissary of subsistence of the First Division, Seventeenth Corps, to July 11, 1865, when he was honorably mustered out of the volunteer service, at Louisville, Kentucky.

Captain Ames was appointed to the regular service as a second lieutenant of the Sixteenth Infantry, to date from May 11, 1866, but did not accept the same until October 13, 1866, when he joined his regiment and served as acting assistant quartermaster and acting commissary of subsistence at Augusta, Georgia, until October, 1867. He was employed in Georgia, Alabama, and Florida during "reconstruction," and was transferred, upon the consolidation of regiments, to the Second Infantry April 17, 1869. He was promoted first lieutenant March 18, 1872, and was ordered with his regiment to the Department of the Columbia in July, 1877. While there he served as acting assistant quartermaster and acting commissary of subsistence at Fort Cœur d'Alene, Idaho, building the post, from January to October, 1879. Being transferred to Fort Spokane, Washington, he performed the same staff duties, and was engaged in the construction of that post from November, 1882, to April, 1885. He then commanded a company and the post of Fort Townsend, Washington, from August to November, 1885.

Captain Ames's regiment was transferred to the Department of the Platte in July, 1886, and was stationed at Omaha, Nebraska. While serving there he participated in the Sioux campaign in South Dakota during the winter of 1890–91. He was promoted captain February 27, 1887, and detailed on general recruiting service at Albany, New York, from October 1, 1891, at which place he is at present on duty.

### REAR-ADMIRAL DANIEL AMMEN, U.S.N.

REAR-ADMIRAL DANIEL AMMEN comes from Swiss lineage, but his ancestors emigrated to this country several generations ago. His parents went from Botetourt County, Virginia, to Brown County, Ohio, in 1816. The subject of this sketch was there born May 15, 1820, and entered the navy as a midshipman in 1836. In his book, "The Old Navy and the New," he gives some amusing reminiscences of his first experiences, so different from the present day when the Naval School moulds all into one form, at least externally.

Ammen served through the various grades to rear-admiral, and retired in 1878, by request, under the act authorizing such a step after forty years or more of consecutive service. His foreign service was in the Gulf of Mexico; on the coast of Labrador; in the Mediterranean; on the survey of the river Paraguay; on the coast of Brazil; on the Pacific station,—and twice on the Asiatic station,—making twenty-one years afloat.

In his long service Admiral Ammen has passed through many exciting and memorable scenes. During the civil war he was executive officer of the frigate " Roanoke ;" commanded the " Seneca" in the fight at Port Royal; at Tybee Island ; commanded at Port Royal Ferry ; in the expedition against Fernandina, Commander, February 21, 1863. Commanded monitor " Patapsco" against Fort McAllister, and attack on Sumter of April 7, 1863.

In May, 1864. Commander Ammen sailed for the Isthmus of Panama in the California passenger steamer " Ocean Queen" with a draft of two hundred and twenty seamen for the Pacific station. An organized mutiny by these men occurred on board a steamer with women and children on board, and a full passenger-list ; but Commander Ammen, assisted by Boatswain Bell, the only aid assigned him, and with the excellent co-operation of the captain of the " Ocean Queen," Tinklepaugh, put a sudden stop to the business. Commander Ammen shot one of the leading mutineers, and another was killed by his assistants in the repression of the mutiny. At the close of the civil war Captain Ammen designed the "Ammen balsa," for landing troops and field artillery on exposed beaches, and also a life-raft for steamers. As Chief of the Bureau of Navigation he had a signal-book compiled, of great excellence; and promoted the use of the dynamometer of Sir William Thomson, improved by the present Admiral Belknap, which, with the use of wire, instead of hemp, enabled correct soundings to be made in the deepest seas. Some years ago a Naval Advisory Board recommended the adoption of Admiral Ammen's plans and calculations for a marine ram, and, under a recent appropriation, one is now ready for launching, at Bath, Maine. When President Grant, in 1872, appointed a commission to examine into, and report upon, Isthmian Canal matters, Ammen was made the junior member. The committee reported in 1876, quite satisfied that the Nicaragua Canal route was preferable to any other. Further developments have only served to increase the estimate of its commercial value, and in regard to its economic maintenance. Under instructions from President Hayes, Ammen attended the (so-called) Paris Canal Congress, in May, 1879, a report of the proceedings of which he made to the State Department. In 1880 he wrote an article on the Panama Canal, which was published in the *North American Review*, contesting the position of M. de Lesseps in his article upon the subject in the previous number. The correctness of Ammen's assertions time has established. In January, 1890, Admiral Ammen visited Nicaragua, and was received there, by all parties and persons, with distinguished attention. In all his exertions in behalf of the construction of the canal there, he has endeavored to secure a rigid and honest management, and to protect both the government and the canal company against stock-gamblers and other persons disposed to make prey of it. Admiral Ammen is the author of " The Atlantic Coast during the Civil War" (Scribner's War Series), and " The Old Navy and the New" (Lippincott, Philadelphia), which is a history of the progressive changes in naval architecture, armament, and propulsion during the past half-century. It has an appendix containing a number of most interesting letters from General Grant, written while the latter was making the tour of the world. Admiral Ammen and General Grant were neighbors in boyhood, and always remained friends, widely as their paths in life diverged. When mere lads, Ammen saved Grant from drowning, and, years after, General Grant, in writing to Ammen from Nice, December, 1877, speaks of the incident, saying, jocosely, " . . . you rescued me from a watery grave. I am of a forgiving nature, however, and forgive you,—but is the feeling universal? If the Democrats get into full power, may they not hold you responsible?"

## CAPTAIN JOHN ANDERSON.

CAPTAIN JOHN ANDERSON (Eighteenth Infantry) was born in Monson, Massachusetts, and entered the military service as a private in Company E, of the First Michigan Sharpshooters, January 5, 1863, serving with that regiment until appointed a second lieutenant of the Fifty-seventh Massachusetts Volunteers, when his regiment was attached to the First Brigade, First Division of the Ninth Army Corps, participating in the campaign of the Army of the Potomac, and commanded Company E of his regiment through the Wilderness campaign, engaging in the battles of the Wilderness, Spottsylvania, North Anna River, Cold Harbor, and in the charge upon the rebel works around Petersburg, Virginia, June 16–18, 1864. He then served in the trenches before Petersburg during the siege, and participated in the Mine Explosion, July 30, 1864, where he was wounded.

He was discharged for disability arising from his wounds, January 21, 1865, but was appointed second lieutenant of the Twentieth Regiment of the Veteran Reserve Corps, March 25, 1865, serving at Wheeling, West Virginia, in connection with mustering out West Virginia volunteers to November, 1865, and in Tennessee, Georgia, and South Carolina during "reconstruction," until honorably mustered out of the volunteer service, June 30, 1866.

He was brevetted a first lieutenant of volunteers, March 13th, 1865, for gallant and meritorious services in the battles before Petersburg, and a captain of the same date for the same occasion.

Captain Anderson entered the regular service by appointment as second lieutenant of the Twenty-fifth U. S. Infantry, August 10, 1867, and served as quartermaster and commissary at Columbia, Newberry, and Greenville,

South Carolina, and was transferred to the Eighteenth Infantry, April 26, 1869. He was promoted first lieutenant, October 17, 1878, and served in his regiment until April, 1879, when he moved with it to Fort Assinaboine, Montana, participating in the campaign in Northern Montana against Sioux Indians under Sitting Bull and Gall, during the months of January and February, 1881. His regiment was transferred to the Indian Territory in 1885, and while on duty at Fort Gibson he was made regimental quartermaster, to date from November, 1889.

The regiment subsequently moved to Texas, and he was stationed with the head-quarters at Fort Clark until promoted a captain, June 21, 1890, when he was relieved as quartermaster and joined his company.

**BRIGADIER AND BREVET MAJOR-GENERAL ROBERT ANDERSON.**

BRIGADIER AND BREVET MAJOR-GENERAL ROBERT ANDERSON (deceased) was born in Kentucky, and graduated at the Military Academy, July 1, 1825. He was promoted brevet second lieutenant and second lieutenant Third Artillery the same day. He served as private secretary to the U. S. Minister Plenipotentiary and Envoy Extraordinary to the Republic of Columbia from October, 1825, to July, 1826, when he was ordered to the Artillery School at Fort Monroe, remaining there until 1828, and on ordnance duty to May 9, 1832. He was then appointed colonel of staff (assistant inspector-general) of Illinois volunteers, and was in the campaign against the Sac Indians, under Black Hawk, being engaged in the battle of Bad Axe, August 2, 1832. He was promoted first lieutenant, June 30, 1833, and was in garrison at Fort Constitution, New Hampshire, until 1835, when he was detailed at the Military Academy, as assistant instructor of artillery, to December, 1835, and instructor of artillery to November 6, 1837.

Lieutenant Anderson participated in the Florida War against the Seminole Indians in 1837–38, and was engaged in the action of Locha-Hatchee, January 24, capture of forty-five Indians near Fort Lauderdale (in command), April 2, and skirmish in the Everglades, April 24, 1838, for which services he was brevetted captain.

Captain Anderson served in the Cherokee Nation, as aide-de-camp to Major-General Scott, from May to July, 1838, while emigrating the Indians to the West. He was brevet captain of staff (assistant adjutant-general), from July 7, 1838, to November 30, 1841, and served as such in the eastern department. He was promoted captain Third Artillery, October 23, 1841, and was on a board of officers to examine his translation of "Instructions for Field-Artillery" to 1845, and then was stationed in South Carolina and Florida until the commencement of the war with Mexico, in which he participated, and was engaged in the siege of Vera Cruz, battle of Cerro Gordo, skirmish of Amazoque, and battle of Molino del Rey, September 8, 1847, where he was severely wounded in the assault of the enemy's works, and on account of wounds was granted sick-leave until 1848, when we find him on duty at Fort Preble, Maine. He was a member of a board of officers, in 1849–51, to devise "A Complete System of Instruction for Siege, Garrison, Sea-coast, and Mountain Artillery," which was adopted May 10, 1851, for the service of the United States.

Captain Anderson was brevetted major, for "gallant and meritorious conduct in the battle of Molino del Rey, Mexico." He was governor of the Harrodsburg Branch Military Asylum, Kentucky, in 1853–54; member of board for the armament of fortifications, 1854–55; inspector of iron-work manufactured at Trenton, New Jersey, for public buildings constructed under the Treasury Department, 1855–59; member of a board to arrange the programme of instruction at the Artillery School for Practice at Fort Monroe, Virginia, in 1859–60, and of the commission created to examine into the organization, system of discipline, and course of instruction at the Military Academy, to December 13, 1860, when he was ordered, as major of the First Artillery, to the command of the defences of Charleston Harbor, South Carolina.

At the commencement of the war of the Rebellion, Major Anderson transferred his garrison from Fort Moultrie to Fort Sumter, which was the first point of attack by the rebels, April 13, 1861. He sustained a heavy bombardment of the work, whose walls were crushed, interior buildings and quarters burned, and was so dismantled as to compel him to evacuate it. He was made brigadier-general U. S. Army, May 15, 1861, and placed in command of the Department of Kentucky, and subsequently of the Department of the Cumberland, which he retained until October 8, 1861. He was then on waiting orders until 1863, when he was given command of Fort Adams, Rhode Island, and on the 27th of October, 1863, he was retired from active service, for disability resulting from long and faithful service, and wounds and disease contracted in the line of duty.

General Anderson was brevetted major-general U. S. Army, February 3, 1865, for "gallant and meritorious service in defence of Fort Sumter, South Carolina."

General Anderson served, after being retired, on the staff of the general commanding the Department of the East, and died October 26, 1871.

General Anderson translated from the French "Instructions for Field-Artillery, Horse and Foot," for the service of the United States, in 1840; and "Evolutions of Field-Batteries," 1860.

## COLONEL THOMAS M. ANDERSON.

COLONEL THOMAS M. ANDERSON (Fourteenth Infantry) was born in Ohio, January 21, 1836. At the commencement of the war of the Rebellion he entered the military service as private of Company A, Sixth Ohio Infantry, April 20, 1861. He was discharged May 15, 1861, to accept the appointment of second lieutenant in the Second U. S. Cavalry, to date from May 7, 1861, but was in the mean time appointed a captain in the Twelfth U. S. Infantry, to date from May 14, 1861, which latter appointment, however, he did not accept until October 8, 1861. He was in the field with Pope's army and participated in the Cedar Mountain and second Bull Run campaigns, and was engaged in the battles of Cedar Mountain and second Bull Run; in the Maryland campaign, and engaged in the battle of Antietam, Maryland; in the Rappahannock campaign, and engaged in the battles of Fredericksburg and Chancellorsville, Virginia; in the Wilderness campaign of 1864, commanding the Twelfth Infantry, and engaged in the battles of the Wilderness, Laurel Hill, and Spottsylvania Court House, Virginia, at which latter place he was severely wounded and compelled to leave the field.

Upon his recovery for light duty, Colonel Anderson was occupied in organizing the First Battalion of the Invalid Corps. He also organized and mustered into service several regiments from rebel prisoners, known as the repentant rebel regiments, and mustered out sixteen thousand paroled prisoners at Camp Chase, Ohio.

At the conclusion of the war, he was brevetted major, August 1, 1864, "for gallant service in the battle of the Wilderness;" lieutenant-colonel, August 1, 1864, "for gallant services in the battle of Spottsylvania."

When the army was reorganized in 1866, Colonel Anderson was transferred to the Twenty-first Infantry, and was promoted major, March 26, 1868. He was then ordered to Texas, and served at Fort McIntosh and Ringgold Barracks, from August, 1869, to September, 1872, during which time he acted as attorney for the United States in the Mexican cattle-claims cases on the Rio Grande. In 1872 he was ordered to Vicksburg, Mississippi, and while there was disbursing officer for the United States until 1874.

In the consolidation of regiments in 1869, Colonel Anderson was unassigned from March 15 to June 24, 1869, when he was assigned to the Tenth Infantry, and

was second in command during MacKenzie's Kiowa campaign, in 1874. He was in command of Fort McKavett in 1876, and of the Tenth Infantry in 1877-78. He was then ordered on general recruiting service as commandant of Columbus Barracks, Ohio, where he remained until October, 1880.

Having been promoted lieutenant-colonel of the Ninth Infantry, March 20, 1879, he joined that regiment in Nebraska, and was in command of it from February, 1882, to June, 1883, at which time he was ordered to Fort McKinney, Wyoming, serving at that post, as well as at Forts Russell and Bridger, to 1885. He was then ordered in command of a battalion of the Ninth Infantry to Crisfield, Kansas, in the summer of 1885, at a prospective outbreak of Indians in the Indian Territory. Colonel Anderson was also on an expedition, sent to Evanston, Union Pacific Railroad, to protect Chinamen, during September and October of that year.

He was promoted colonel of the Fourteenth Infantry, September 6, 1886, and joined his regiment at Vancouver Barracks, Washington, where he has held station to the present time.

Colonel Anderson is the grandson of Brigadier-General Duncan McArthur, second in command to General Harrison in the Army of the Northwest during the war of 1812; his other grandfather was a lieutenant-colonel in the Continental army. He is, himself, the nephew of General Robert Anderson, of Fort Sumter fame.

### COLONEL GEORGE LIPPITT ANDREWS.

COLONEL GEORGE LIPPITT ANDREWS (Twenty-fifth Infantry) was born in Rhode Island, April 22, 1828. He was a private in the Fifth Ward City Guards at Providence, Rhode Island, during Dorr's Rebellion of 1842, and a private in the Providence Marine Corps of Artillery in 1844. He became a sergeant in the same in 1847, major from 1848 to 1852, and colonel (commandant) from 1853 to 1856. He was then made captain and commissary of the Second Brigade, Rhode Island militia, which he retained until appointed captain and quartermaster of the same troops. Removing to St. Louis, Missouri, he entered the militia service there as captain of Company B, Engineer Battalion, in 1860, and engaged in the Southwest expedition.

At the commencement of the war of the Rebellion, Captain Andrews, as a militia officer of the State of Missouri, was censured by the then governor of that State (Jackson) and the general of the First Military District for his fealty to the Union in preference to the State, "in case of a conflict between the State of Missouri and said government," which was considered "to amount to military insubordination in advance, and to be inconsistent with the law," to which Captain Andrews replied, under date of February 12, 1861, as follows:

"Finding my name has been brought to the notice of the public in a manner calculated to increase the bitterness of feeling now existing, and in the hope that positive information will do less harm than uncertain speculation, I herewith enclose copies of documents received by me on the 11th instant, with the request that they may find a place in the columns of your paper.

"I do not believe in mental reservations or quibbles of any description, particularly in connection with taking an oath; and when I swore to 'honestly and faithfully serve the State of Missouri against all her enemies, and that you will do your utmost to sustain the Constitution and laws of the United States, and of this State, against all violence of whatever kind and description; and you do further swear that you will well and truly execute and obey the legal orders of all officers properly placed over you, whilst on duty; so help you God,'—I did so in good faith, with a full, realizing sense of the moral and constitutional obligations I assumed. I still occupy the same position, and shall ever be found ready and willing to do my part to sustain 'the Constitution, the Union, and the enforcement of the laws,'

"Respectfully yours,
"GEO. L. ANDREWS.
"ST. LOUIS, February 12, 1861."

Captain Andrews was appointed lieutenant-colonel of the First Missouri Infantry, April 24, 1861, and was engaged at Camp Jackson, Booneville (of which he was military governor), Dug Spring, and McCullough's Store; and commanded the Second Brigade of General Lyon's column at the battle of Wilson's Creek, where he was wounded and his horse shot under him. He was appointed lieutenant-colonel of the First Missouri Light Artillery, September 1, 1861, and was discharged from the volunteer service September 5, of the same year, to enter the regular service,—he having been appointed major of the Seventeenth U. S. Infantry May 14, but did not receive the appointment until September 5. He joined his regiment at Fort Preble, Maine, where he remained until March, 1862, when he was ordered to the field with the Army of the Potomac, and his regiment became part of the Second Brigade, Second Division (regular) of the Fifth Army Corps. He participated in the operations and campaigns of the Army of the Potomac of 1862-63, and was engaged at the siege of Yorktown, battles of Gaines' Mill, Malvern Hill, Second Bull Run, Antietam, reconnoissances across the Potomac River below Sharpsburg, to Leetown, Snicker's Gap, battle of Fredericksburg, where he commanded the Second Brigade of regular infantry, and battle of Chancellorsville, Virginia. He was then ordered on regimental recruiting service at Fort Preble, Maine, and subsequently changed to Newport Barracks, Kentucky, October 14, 1864, on being promoted lieutenant-colonel of the Thirteenth Infantry.

Colonel Andrews received the brevets of lieutenant-colonel for Second Bull Run and colonel for Antietam, "for gallant and meritorious services," and was promoted colonel of the Twenty-fifth Infantry, January 1, 1871.

Since the close of the war he has been stationed in various parts of the country with his regiment, experiencing all the details of frontier life, such as falls to the lot of an army officer. His present station is with his regiment at Fort Missoula, Montana.

## COLONEL ABRAHAM K. ARNOLD.

COLONEL ABRAHAM K. ARNOLD (First Cavalry) was born in Pennsylvania, March 24, 1837. Retiring year, 1901; graduated from U. S. Military Academy, July 1, 1859. *Actual Rank.*—Brevet second lieutenant Fifth (old Second) Cavalry, July 1, 1859; second lieutenant, June 28, 1860; first lieutenant, April 6, 1861; captain, July 17, 1862; major Sixth Cavalry, June 22, 1869; lieutenant-colonel First Cavalry, June 11, 1886, and colonel, February 7, 1891. *Brevet Rank.*—Brevet captain, June 27, 1862, for gallant and meritorious service in the battle of Gaines' Mill, Virginia; brevet major, May 6, 1864, for gallant and meritorious service at the battle of Todd's Tavern, Virginia. *Honorably Mentioned.*—In the "Records of the Rebellion," Part I., Vol. XI., pp. 684, 86, 88, 691, 92, 711, 12, and 1007; Part II., Vol. XL, page 47, as far as published. *Service.*—In 1860 conducted a detachment of recruits from New York by sea to Indianola; marched by way of San Antonio to Fort Inge, Texas; joined December 2, in the field, 1861; marched from Fort Inge, March 19, 1861, for sea-coast; embarked at Indianola, on steamship "Empire City," just in time to escape capture, and sailed for New York; served in the defences of Washington and in the field during the winter of 1861 and 1862, until wounded at Gaines' Mill, which disabled him from service until September, 1862; appointed mustering and disbursing officer at New York and Boston until September, 1863; in the field 1863 and 1864; assistant instructor of cavalry tactics at U. S. Military Academy from August 23, 1864, to August 28, 1869; served at Fort Brown and Waco, and at Fort Richardson, Texas, and in Kansas from June 18, 1870, until September, 1872, on garrison and field duties; appointed a disbursing officer in the Freedmen's Bureau and served at New Orleans, Louisiana, until November, 1878; on duty in the West and South, part of the time in the field, from 1879 to 1892. *Staff Positions Occupied.*—Adjutant, assistant commissary of subsistence, acting assistant quartermaster at Fort Inge, Texas, winter and spring of 1860-61; adjutant of his regiment June 1, 1861; resigned May 9, 1862; acting inspector-general Department of Arizona from November, 1880, to August 2, 1884; acting assistant adjutant-general in the field during the Cibicu campaign of 1881. *Battles, Skirmishes, Etc.*—Operations against hostile Indians in Texas, winter and spring of 1860-61; participated in General Patterson's Shenandoah campaign; was engaged in the action at Falling Waters, and in the skirmishes near Martinsburg and Bunker Hill; in the defences of Washington during the winter of 1861-62; participated in the Manassas and Virginia Peninsula campaigns, and engaged in the siege of Yorktown, the battle of Williamsburg, and almost daily skirmishes during the advance towards Richmond; engaged with the enemy at the Hanover Court-

House; participated in the reconnoissance towards Ashland; severely wounded in the disastrous charge at Gaines' Mill; engaged in the combat at Bristoe Station, the operations at Mine Run, in the raid and action at Charlottesville, the action at Stannardsville, the skirmish near Morton's Ford, the battle of Todd's Tavern and Meadow Bridge, the skirmish near Mechanicsville, the battles of Cold Harbor and Trevilian Station; and marched to the relief of General Wilson at Ream's Station, when that officer made his raid on the South Side Railroad. Commanding field operations in Southeastern Arizona against hostile Apaches, raiding in New Mexico, spring of 1879; served with an expedition into old Mexico, in the neighborhood of Lake Guzman, and co-operated with the forces in New Mexico and Mexican troops, which resulted in destroying a large band of savages, until October, 1879; in the field during the Cibicu campaign in Arizona, 1881; against the disaffected Crows, November, 1887, in combat which resulted in killing their chief and bringing them to terms. *Commands Held.*—Commanded company during the last tour of field service performed in Texas by any part of regiment, 1861; in command of company May 9, 1862; in command of the regiment almost continuously from October 12, 1863, to July 24, 1864; in command of field operations in Southeastern Arizona from the spring until October, 1879; Fort Grant, Arizona, until November, 1880; Fort Bayard, New Mexico, and regiment until April 17, 1885; battalion of regiment in the field, November, 1887; post of Fort Maginnis, Montana, November 1, 1888, to March 4, 1889; Fort Custer, Montana, and First Cavalry, until September 25, 1889. *History.*—Grandson of Captain P. P. Walter, Thirty-second U. S. Infantry, War of 1812, and grandson of Peter Arnold, a soldier of the Revolutionary War.

### MAJOR ISAAC ARNOLD, JR.

Major Isaac Arnold, Jr., Ordnance Department, was born in Connecticut and graduated from the Military Academy, June 17, 1862. He was promoted second lieutenant of the Second Artillery the same date and was assigned to Battery F. He joined Battery K, Fourth Artillery, at Harrison's Landing, Virginia, and served with the same in the Army of the Potomac until after the battle of Chancellorsville, and was present at the following engagements: Second Malvern Hill, Chantilly, Fredericksburg, and Chancellorsville, and was wounded at the latter place.

He was transferred to the Ordnance Corps, April 27, 1863, but did not receive notice of transfer until after the battle of Chancellorsville. Having been promoted first lieutenant, April 27, 1863, he served at Washington Arsenal, District of Columbia, until about January 1, 1864, when he was transferred to St. Louis Arsenal, Missouri. From that point he was detached in the spring of 1864 and sent to Springfield, Illinois, to arm the one-hundred-day men. After three or four months he was relieved from that duty and ordered to Hilton Head, South Carolina, where he served as chief ordnance officer of the Department of the South until the close of the war.

Lieutenant Arnold served a short time as assistant at Allegheny Arsenal, Pennsylvania, and was then assigned to the command of the San Antonio Arsenal, Texas, and chief ordnance officer of the Department of Texas; was promoted captain of ordnance, March 7, 1867. From Texas he was ordered to Springfield Armory, Massachusetts, as an assistant, and moved from there to Allegheny Arsenal, Pennsylvania. He then took six months' leave of absence, on expiration of which he was ordered to Benicia Arsenal, California; being promoted major of ordnance, May 20, 1879, he was ordered to Indianapolis Arsenal, where he remained about eight years, and was then sent to command San Antonio Arsenal, Texas, and was chief ordnance officer, Department of Texas, per S. O. 230 and 261, respectively, H. Q. A. 1883, remaining there four years; he was then sent to Fort Monroe Arsenal, Virginia, per S. O. 222, H. Q. A. 1887, where he was stationed for two years, and then assumed command of Columbia Arsenal, December 1, 1889, per S. O. 272, H. Q. A. 1889, where he is at present.

## BRIGADIER-GENERAL AND BREVET MAJOR-GENERAL CHRISTOPHER C. AUGUR.

BRIGADIER-GENERAL AND BREVET MAJOR-GENERAL CHRISTOPHER C. AUGUR was born in Kendall, Orleans County, New York, July 10, 1821. His father dying when he was young, he went with his mother, in 1835, to friends in Michigan, and in 1839 was appointed a cadet to the U. S. Military Academy from that State. Graduated in 1843, and assigned a brevet second lieutenant to the Second Infantry. Served in that regiment until September, 1849, when promoted second lieutenant to Fourth Infantry, then serving with the "Army of Occupation," commanded by General Zachary Taylor, at Corpus Christi, Texas. Went with that army to the Rio Grande, and participated in all its operations, including battles of Palo Alto and Resaca de la Palma, and the capture and occupation of Matamoras, Mexico. Two companies of each regiment were here broken up, including his own company, and the officers sent North, recruiting. In March, 1847, he returned to Mexico as aide-de-camp to General Hopping. After that general's death went to the City of Mexico as aide-de-camp to General Cushing, and served with him until the end of the war. Then joined his regiment at Pascagoula, Mississippi, and went with it to Fort Niagara, New York. Remained there until July, 1852, when ordered with regiment to Pacific coast. Promoted to captain in August, 1852. Stationed at Fort Vancouver until February, 1856. Was in campaign against Yakima Indians in fall of 1855. In February, 1856, went to Port Orford, Oregon, against Rogue River and other hostile Indians in that vicinity. Engaged with Indians at Big Bend of Rogue River, and at Macamootney Hill. After campaign closed took first detachment of Indians by sea to Siletz Reservation. Established Fort Hoskins, Kings Valley, Oregon, in 1856. Commanded that post until July 1, 1861, when ordered with company to California. At San Francisco, found himself a major in the Thirteenth Infantry. Arrived in New York, he found orders sending him to West Point as commandant of cadets. November 14, 1861, was appointed a brigadier-general of volunteers. Joined new brigade in McDowell's division in Washington, D. C. Moved to front with Army of Potomac in March, 1862. Brought up at Catlett's Station, Virginia. In April, 1862, was sent with his brigade to capture Fredericksburg, Virginia, April 19, 1862. Was successful. In July promoted to division in Banks's corps operating about Little Washington, Virginia. Was in battle of Cedar Mountain, Virginia, August 9, 1862, where he was severely wounded. Was brevetted a colonel in the regular army, and appointed a major-general of volunteers for this battle. When able for duty, was put on court of inquiry to investigate surrender of Harper's

Ferry. Then applied for orders for the field, and was sent to report to General McClellan, then with his army at Warrenton, Virginia, and was assigned to command First Division First Army Corps. Received orders next day to report to General Banks. Accompanied him to New Orleans, and commanded district of Baton Rouge until advance upon Port Hudson. During siege commanded left wing of army. After surrender of Port Hudson, went North on sick leave in July, 1863. Was made president of military commission in Washington, D. C. While on that duty was assigned temporarily to command of the Department of Washington and Twenty-second Army Corps in October, 1863. Remained in that command until August, 1866. In September, 1866, appointed president of board to examine newly-appointed officers. January, 1867, was assigned to command of Department of the Platte, and remained there until assigned to command of Department of Texas in December, 1871, having in March, 1869, been appointed a brigadier-general in the regular service. Commanded the Department of Texas until March, 1875, when assigned to command Department of Gulf, at New Orleans. Commanded there until July, 1878, when that department was consolidated with Department of the South. Was assigned to command that department, head-quarters at Newport, Kentucky. Commanded that department until December, 1880, when again assigned to command Department of Texas. In October, 1883, was assigned to command Department of Missouri, head-quarters at Fort Leavenworth, Kansas. Commanded that department until July 10, 1885, when retired for age, after commanding important military departments continuously for twenty-two years, with the exception of four months. Since retirement has resided in Washington, D. C.

CAPTAIN WILLIAM AUMAN.

CAPTAIN WILLIAM AUMAN (Thirteenth Infantry) was born October 17, 1838, in Berks County, Pennsylvania. His father, Henry Auman, who was a non-commissioned officer in a Pennsylvania regiment in the war of 1812-14, removed to Union County, Pennsylvania, and again moved to Pottsville, in 1848. At the age of eighteen Captain Auman entered a general merchandise store in Pottsville as salesman, and continued in this occupation until the call of President Lincoln for troops in 1861, when he joined a local militia company (Washington Artillery), which had tendered its services to the government. The company left Pottsville on the 17th of April, 1861, and arrived at Harrisburg that evening. Early the next morning that company, with four others from the State, were sworn into the service of the United States, and left immediately (unarmed) for the national capital. At Baltimore these troops were surrounded by a howling mob of Secessionists. Threats and insults were heaped upon them, and some were injured by being struck with stones while marching through the streets. But as the mob was not organized, these unarmed troops managed to get through without loss of life, and arrived at Washington that evening, where they were temporarily quartered in the Capitol building. This was the day before the Sixth Massachusetts had their fight in Baltimore. After serving at Washington City and Fort Washington, Maryland, until July 29, 1861, Company H, Twenty-fifth Pennsylvania Volunteers, of which Captain Auman was a member, was honorably mustered out of service. But on the 9th of September, 1861, he enlisted in Company G, Forty-eighth Pennsylvania Infantry, and was appointed a corporal same date. He was promoted sergeant in the summer of 1862, second lieutenant of his company June 28, 1864, first lieutenant July 28, 1864, and captain March 3, 1865; and was brevetted captain of U. S. Volunteers, "for gallant and meritorious services before Petersburg, Virginia."

Captain Auman participated with his regiment in the battles of Fredericksburg, Virginia, Campbell's Station, Blue Springs, and siege of Knoxville, Tennessee. He was also engaged in the battle of the Wilderness, Spottsylvania, Tolepotomy, Bethesda Church, North Anna, Cold Harbor, and seven of the battles around Petersburg.

At the capture of Petersburg, April 2, 1865, while on the enemy's works, he was severely wounded in the face, having all the teeth on the left side of his upper jaw shot away, and his tongue so severely cut that he was unable to take any food for a number of days. On the eleventh day after he was wounded, a portion of the bullet was removed from his tongue. As soon as this was done he recovered rapidly, and soon afterwards he rejoined his regiment, and was mustered out with his company, July 17, 1865.

For his services in the war he was, on the 11th of May, 1866, commissioned second lieutenant of the Thirteenth U. S. Infantry; was promoted first lieutenant October 5, 1868, and captain March 26, 1879.

During a demonstration made by Crow Indians on the post of Camp Cook, Montana, May 17, 1868, he was severely wounded in the left foot. He served as regimental quartermaster from January 1, 1870, to August 1, 1871.

Captain Auman's service in the West has carried him to many different stations, his present one being Fort Supply, Indian Territory.

He received a medal of honor from the State of Pennsylvania for service as "First Defender of the National Capital, 1861."

## CAPTAIN AND BREVET MAJOR-GENERAL WM. W. AVERELL.

CAPTAIN AND BREVET MAJOR-GENERAL WM. W. AVERELL (retired) was born in New York and graduated from the Military Academy July 1, 1855. He was promoted brevet second lieutenant of the Mounted Rifles same day, and served at Jefferson Barracks, Missouri, until 1856, when he was ordered to the School for Practice at Carlisle, Pennsylvania, having been promoted second lieutenant Mounted Riflemen May 1, 1856. In 1857 he was on frontier duty, in command of an escort to the commanding general of the Department of New Mexico, and the same year was scouting, from Fort Craig, and engaged in a skirmish with Kiowa Indians near Fort Craig, December 7, 1857. He was on the Navajo expedition in 1858, and engaged in a skirmish in Chusca Valley, September 29; a skirmish with Kyatano's band, October 1; and skirmish at the Puerco of the West, October 8, 1858, where he was severely wounded in a night attack on the soldiers' camp. He was at Fort Craig until granted a sick leave, which separated him from his duties until 1861.

Lieutenant Averell was bearer of despatches to Colonel Emory, at Fort Arbuckle, Indian Territory, April and May, 1861, and on returning to Washington he was then promoted first lieutenant Third Cavalry. He was detailed on mustering duty at Elmira, New York, to July, when he was made acting assistant adjutant-general of General A. Porter, at Washington, participating in the Manassas campaign, and engaged at the battle of First Bull Run, July 21, 1861.

Having been appointed colonel of the Third Pennsylvania Cavalry, August 13, 1861, he was in command of a cavalry brigade in front of the defences of Washington (which was the first cavalry brigade of the war) to March, 1862, when he led the advance on Manassas, and subsequently participated in the Peninsula campaign, being engaged in the siege of Yorktown, battles of Williamsburg, Fair Oaks, Malvern Hill, where he commanded the rear guard (see "Battles and Leaders of the War"), and skirmishes at Sycamore Church, August 2, and at White Oak Swamp, August 5, 1862. On the 17th of July, 1862, he was promoted captain Third Cavalry.

Appointed brigadier-general of volunteers September 26, 1862. He was engaged in scouting and skirmishing on the Upper Potomac until the 31st of October, when he participated in the march back to the Rappahannock River, being engaged, en route, in skirmishes along the Blue Ridge, at Upperville, Markam, Corbins' and Gaines' Cross Roads, and Amissville. He then participated in the Rappahannock campaign of 1862-63, and was engaged in the battle of Fredericksburg, and as commander of the Second Cavalry Division in the skirmish at Hartwood Church, action at Kelly's Ford, the first considerable cavalry battles of the war. He commanded one of the two divisions of cavalry engaged in the Stoneman raid, and drove the enemy's cavalry towards Gordonsville, while Buford with Stoneman reached the enemy's rear.

General Averell was placed in command of the Fourth Separate Brigade May 16, 1863, and commanded in all the engagements of the brigade, which was increased to a division of three brigades cavalry and one infantry, in the West Virginia operations, defeating the intrenched rebel army of West Virginia at Droop Mountain, and driving the enemy out of the State. In the winter of 1863-64 he made the raid to the Tennessee Railroad, destroying it and General Longstreet's supplies, from December 8 to 25, 1863. He was in the West Virginia operations, commanding the Second Cavalry Division, in 1864, commanding in all the actions and combats, raids and skirmishes, and defeated Ramseur's division at Carter's Farm, July 20. He fought the combats at Winchester and Moorfield, and skirmishes at Bunker Hill and Martinsburg, and participated in the battles of Opequan and Fisher's Hill, and action at Mount Jackson, September 23, 1864.

He was brevetted for gallant and meritorious services, as follows: Major, for the battle of Kelly's Ford, Virginia; lieutenant-colonel, for the action at Droop Mountain, Virginia; colonel, for the Salem expedition in Virginia; brigadier-general, for the field during the war of the Rebellion; major-general, for the battle of Moorfield, Virginia. General Averell resigned from the army May 18, 1865, and was appointed United States Consul-General to British North America at Montreal in 1866. By act of Congress of August 1, 1888, he was restored to his grade of captain in the army and placed upon the retired list, August 17 of that year.

## LIEUTENANT-COLONEL ROBERT AVERY
### (RETIRED).

LIEUTENANT-COLONEL ROBERT AVERY was born in Tunkhannock, Pennsylvania, September 22, 1839. In September, 1861, he received authority from the governor of New York to raise a company, and in October, 1861, he was commissioned a captain of New York volunteers in the service of the United States, afterwards assigned first to the Twelfth, and then to the One Hundred and Second Regiment of New York Volunteers, in which regiment he was the senior captain, and frequently, for considerable periods, commanded his regiment. In December, 1862, he was promoted to be lieutenant-colonel of his regiment.

He participated in the battle of Cedar Mountain August 9, 1862; in the battles of the Second Bull Run campaign commanded his regiment, and during part of the time, at the battle of Chancellorsville, Virginia, May 3, 1863, his brigade. At this battle he was wounded by a musket-ball in the neck and lower jaw, severing the nerves on the left side, causing partial paralysis of the left side for several months. He rejoined his command, then a part of the Army of the Cumberland, in Tennessee, in October, 1863, having his left shoulder and neck bandaged, leading the advance line in the assault on Lookout Mountain November 24, 1863, where he received a wound which necessitated the amputation of his right leg close to the hip-joint. In this assault the major of the regiment, Gilbert M. Elliott, was killed by his side. For gallant and meritorious services at the battles of Chancellorsville and Lookout Mountain, he was brevetted colonel, brigadier-general, and major-general of United States volunteers.

In April, 1865, he was appointed a major in the Veteran Reserve Corps, and assigned to duty in Washington as assistant commissary-general of prisoners, serving as such under both Brevet Major-General W. Hoffman and Major-General E. A. Hitchcock, and won the earnest commendation of both those officers for the "prompt, energetic, and able performance of all the duties devolving upon him." In July, 1866, he was assigned to duty as inspector-general on the staff of Major-General John C. Robinson, commanding the District of North Carolina, and assistant commissioner of the Freedmen's Bureau. He was detailed as president of an important military commission and a court-martial, but, on account of his legal knowledge and skill in presenting evidence, was soon made judge-advocate of both the military commission and court-martial. Before the military commission there were tried many important cases,—murders, conspiracies, arson, rape, burglary, etc., —securing convictions in every case, winning the approval and commendation of General Grant and Secretary Stanton. On the 31st of December, 1870, he was placed upon the retired list, with the rank of lieutenant-colonel. General Hooker, in commending him to Secretary Stanton for promotion, said, " At the battle of Lookout Mountain his conduct was especially brilliant, as he led the line of skirmishers along the slope of the mountain, which resulted in the glorious achievement of that field." General George S. Greene, also commending him for promotion, said, " Colonel Avery was always distinguished for gallantry, intelligence, and energy in the discharge of his duties." He was twice recommended for promotion for gallantry by General Grant.

The importance of General Avery's services in North Carolina during the reconstruction period can hardly be over-estimated. The knowledge that there was one court constantly open, with a fearless and tireless prosecuting officer, to secure the conviction of criminals, no matter how great their political or social influence, soon made North Carolina as safe and as free from crime as any State in the Union. There can be little doubt that if the administration of justice in that State had remained in General Avery's hands, the crimes of the Ku-Klux Klans in North Carolina would not have been committed.

# LIEUTENANT-COLONEL LAWRENCE S. BABBITT.

LIEUTENANT-COLONEL LAWRENCE S. BABBITT (Ordnance Department, U.S.A.) was born in Boston, Massachusetts, February 18, 1839. Appointed cadet-at-large at West Point Military Academy July, 1857; graduated June, 1861, and appointed second lieutenant, Third Artillery, June 24, 1861. On October 26, 1861, he was transferred to Ordnance Department, and promoted to be first lieutenant of ordnance March 3, 1863, and captain of ordnance December 22, 1866; major of ordnance May 10, 1878, and lieutenant-colonel of ordnance September 19, 1890.

He was brevetted first lieutenant, July 21, 1861, for gallant and meritorious services at the battle of Bull Run, Virginia; is honorably mentioned in "Records of the Rebellion," series 1, vol. ii., pp. 312, 348, 380, 382, and in report of Nez Perces campaign, by General Howard, 1877. Saw service in field with Army of the Potomac, 1861-63. Took part in Virginia Peninsula campaign as assistant ordnance officer. Commanding Louisville Ordnance Depot, 1864 and 1865; commanding Vancouver Arsenal, 1865 to 1871; St. Louis Arsenal, 1871 to 1876; chief ordnance officer Department of Columbia, 1876 to 1879; in Nez Perces campaign, 1877; Bannock War, 1878; commanding Fortress Monroe Arsenal, 1879 to 1887; San Antonio Arsenal, 1887 to 1890; Benicia Arsenal, 1890 to present date. *Staff Positions Held.*—Assistant ordnance officer Army of the Potomac, 1862; aide-de-camp, 1868 to 1870; chief ordnance officer Department of Columbia, 1876 to 1879; chief ordnance officer Department of Texas, 1887 to 1890. *Battles, Skirmishes, Etc.*—Engaged in action at Blackburn's Ford, July 18, 1861; battle of Bull Run, July 21, 1861; siege of Yorktown, Virginia; skirmishes at Cottonwood Ranch, Idaho, July 3, 4, and 5, 1877; battle of the Clearwater, Idaho, July 12 and 13, 1877; skirmish at Muatella Agency, Oregon, July 13, 1888. Colonel Babbitt is the son of General E. B. Babbitt, U.S.A., deceased, who was a graduate of the U. S. Military Academy in the class of 1827.

## BREVET MAJOR AND CAPTAIN JOHN B. BABCOCK.

BREVET MAJOR AND CAPTAIN JOHN B. BABCOCK (Fifth Cavalry) was born in New Orleans, Louisiana, February 7, 1843. Major Babcock is descended from an old Rhode Island family. His great-great-grandfather, Joshua Babcock, was twice chief justice of Rhode Island, and major-general of Rhode Island militia during the Revolution. Major Babcock's great-grandfather, Henry Babcock, served five campaigns in the French and Indian War.

During the war he served as second lieutenant, first lieutenant, adjutant, captain, and major of New York State volunteers (One Hundred and Seventy-fourth and One Hundred and Sixty-second regiments), and was brevetted lieutenant-colonel; was present with his regiment in the battles of Plain's Store, Port Hudson, Sabine Cross-Roads, Pleasant Hill, Monett's Bluff, Mansura Plains, and Yellow Bayou, all in Louisiana; was with his regiment under General Grant at the siege of Petersburg, Virginia, and in the campaign of General Sheridan in the Shenandoah Valley; was, at the age of twenty-two, major and acting adjutant-general of the Military District of Savannah and inspector-general First Division, Nineteenth Army Corps.

Since the war, for twenty-five years, this officer has served continuously with his troop. For fifteen years after the war, Captain Babcock was almost constantly in the field, winter and summer, engaged in campaigns of the most severe character against hostile Indians.

The following is a brief statement of the campaigns and Indian fights in which this officer has been engaged:

Continuous campaign with his regiment, under General Carr, against the Kiowas and Southern Cheyennes, lasting from November, 1868, to August, 1869; without leaving the field, marching from Kansas to Texas and back to Nebraska, through the storms of a severe winter, driving the Indians eastward and fighting them at Beaver Creek and Spring Creek, Nebraska, and Summit Springs, Colorado. At Spring Creek his troop, then reduced to thirty-three men, was attacked by the whole village of Cheyenne and Sioux Indians under Tall Bull. Captain Babcock defended the position for two hours, until relieved by the regiment. At Summit Springs the regiment captured a camp of eighty-six lodges, killing seventy-two Indians, capturing five hundred ponies, and releasing two white women captives, and putting an end to the war with these bands.

From November, 1871, for three years, Captain Babcock served in Arizona under General Crook, and was almost constantly in the field. Having attracted the attention of General Crook by successful hard service in the mountains, he was kept in the field under general instructions to hunt up hostile Indians; was in many fights with Apaches; was twice thanked in general orders,—G. O. 14 and G. O. 24, Department of Arizona, 1873; was wounded in the breast by an arrow, and recommended for the brevets of lieutenant-colonel and colonel. Under date of November 28, 1874, General Crook writes of this officer as follows: "The official records of my department show that, since his first assignment to duty, Lieutenant J. B. Babcock has been one of the most *gallant, efficient,* and *distinguished* officers that have ever served in Arizona."

His last service in Arizona was the military control of the turbulent Apaches on the San Carlos Reservation.

Going north with his regiment, Captain Babcock was again in the field, in Northern Wyoming, during the winter of 1877, and again from June to December, 1878, and from January, 1879, to the spring of that year. In the latter campaign the regiment marched through the snows of Northern Nebraska against the Cheyennes.

In October, 1879, the famous Ute outbreak occurred. Captain Babcock marched with his troop, as part of General Merritt's command, one hundred and seventy miles in sixty-five hours,—in time to take part in the relief of Major Thornburg's command and the fight that followed, —remaining in the field until December.

In 1885 he marched six hundred miles, and took part in the protection of the Kansas border from the threatened raids of Southern Cheyennes, remaining in the field all the spring and until July.

From 1887 to 1889 Captain Babcock was assistant instructor in the Art of War at the U. S. Infantry and Cavalry School, Fort Leavenworth, Kansas. In the summer of 1889 he was adjutant-general of the Camp of Instruction for the troops in the Department of Missouri.

Since 1889 he has been assistant instructor in the Department of Cavalry at the U. S. Infantry and Cavalry School, which position he now holds, in addition to the command of his troop.

He was in the field with his troop at Pine Ridge Agency during the Ghost-Dance War last year.

# COMMODORE OSCAR C. BADGER, U. S. NAVY.

COMMODORE OSCAR C. BADGER was forty-three years and eleven months upon the active list of the navy. In this lengthened period he had twenty-one years and one month of sea-service, and one year and three months in vessels which were not sea-going. His shore duty extended to seventeen years and three months; and he was unemployed four years and four months. During one year and six months of this "unemployed" time, he was ill,—unable to perform duty,—the result of wounds received in the service.

This is a good record for any officer.

Commodore Badger was born in the township of Windham, Connecticut, August 12, 1823, and was appointed midshipman from Pennsylvania, September, 1841. He served for three years in the old razee "Independence," in the West Indies and Gulf of Mexico, and was then attached to the "Saratoga," on the west coast of Africa. Served in the attack on the Bereby tribes, when Commodore Perry punished them for piracy, and was in the different landing-parties. During the Mexican War he served in the steam-frigate "Mississippi," and was in the action at Alvarado. He then served on the Brazil Station in the frigate "Brandywine" and the brig "Perry." He was navigator of the "Perry," which vessel, during the cruise, captured and sent home three vessels engaged in the slave-trade. During this time he became a passed midshipman. He then served in the Pacific in various vessels,—"Supply," "Savannah," and "Vincennes,"—and upon his return home was in the Hydrographic Department of the Naval Observatory. Promoted master September 14, 1855, he was made lieutenant the next day. Serving on board the sloop "John Adams," in the Pacific, he was navigator, and commanded a party from that ship which attacked and destroyed the village of Vutia, in the Feejee Islands, on account of the piratical acts of its inhabitants. He was also engaged in successful skirmishes with the Feejeeans on other occasions. Lieutenant Badger afterwards served on the experimental cruise of the "Plymouth," the "Macedonian" in the Mediterranean, and the flag-ship "Minnesota."

When the Civil War occurred, he commanded the "Anacostia," of the Potomac flotilla, and was in the attack upon Cockpit Point, Aequia Creek batteries, and several others. He led with the "Anacostia," piloting the "Pensacola," under a heavy fire, past the entire line of batteries, and was favorably mentioned in despatches.

In the same vessel he was employed at the siege of Yorktown and Gloucester Point, and especially mentioned by General McClellan for his services there.

He became a lieutenant-commander in July, 1862, and was in charge of the ordnance for gunboats building on the Western waters, 1862-63. After this, as chief ordnance officer of the South Atlantic Blockading Squadron, he was engaged against the Morris Island batteries. He commanded the iron-clad "Patapsco" in the attack on Fort Wagner in July, and on Forts Wagner, Gregg, and Sumter on August 17 of that year. On the 22d of September, he commanded the "Montauk," in the night attack on Sumter. Lieutenant-Commander Badger was appointed fleet-captain of the squadron upon the death of Commander George W. Rodgers,—killed in battle,—and was serving in that capacity in the night attack upon Sumter, when he was dangerously wounded, his right leg being shattered by a metallic splinter. When he had partially recovered he served as inspector of ordnance at Philadelphia, and in the same capacity at Pittsburg.

Commander in July, 1866; and, as commander of the "Peoria," received thanks from the Assemblies of Antigua and St. Kitt's for services at the great fire at Basse-Terre. Upon his return, was upon equipment duty at Portsmouth; and from 1871 to 1873 commanded the "Ticonderoga," in the South Atlantic.

Captain, 1872. Commodore, 1881. As commodore he was commandant of the Boston Navy-Yard, 1882 to 1885. Retired, 1885.

MAJOR CLARENCE MITCHELL BAILEY.

MAJOR CLARENCE MITCHELL BAILEY (Fifteenth Infantry) was born in New York, and was appointed a second lieutenant in the Sixth U. S. Infantry August 5, 1861; promoted a first lieutenant July 14, 1863; a captain July 28, 1866; and major July 10, 1891, and assigned to the Fifteenth U. S. Infantry. His first military duty was at Newport Barracks, Kentucky where he arrived in September, 1861, and was almost immediately placed in command of Company A, permanent party. This position did not last long, as, on the 21st of the same month, he was ordered on duty with Company A, First Battalion Fifteenth Infantry, also directed to perform the duties of A. A. Q. M., A. C. S., and adjutant of the battalion then under orders to report to General Robert Anderson, U. S. Volunteers, at Louisville, Kentucky. Before leaving Newport he was given, on receipts and invoices, one thousand dollars quartermaster and three hundred dollars commissary funds. Asking an officer what he was to do with this money, he received the answer, "Keep it separate, and don't spend one fund in payment of the other's debts."

He arrived in Louisville, and was ordered by General Anderson to proceed in the direction of Elizabethtown, and report to General Sherman, wherever he might be. General Sherman was found at Rolling Forks. Lieutenant Bailey had provided the command with two days' fresh bread, and when he arrived at the river the general ordered rations issued; and as he desired the command to reach Muldrow's Hills as soon as possible, the lieutenant supposed he considered his way of giving out the bread too slow, so the general relieved him of this duty and did it himself. He would take a loaf and toss it to a man, saying, "Here, catch this." The lieutenant hired wagons of the farmers, and in due time joined the battalion with their tents, etc., etc. After being in camp a few days the commanding officer directed him to buy a saddle and bridle of a gentleman living near, and to draw a horse from the quartermaster's department. All this he did, thinking how kind the commanding officer was about his being mounted. Alas, for his hopes! As soon as they changed camp the commanding officer directed his servant to bring *that* horse saddled to his tent, and informed the lieutenant that in future he would use it. The latter can understand now the action of the former, but at that time thought he had been very badly treated.

The winter was spent on Green River, Kentucky, where the Thirty-second Indiana Volunteers had a skirmish with some Texas cavalry; some of the Indiana troops were killed. The dirge played over the graves of these men was the most doleful thing ever heard, and it was thought it had a very depressing effect. The troops suffered that winter greatly from poorly-cooked rations, bad bread, etc., and many a man died there who would have lived longer had the surroundings been different. The early spring found the battalion *en route* to the Tennessee River, going to the rescue of Grant's army. In May they occupied Corinth, Mississippi. The Fourth of July was spent at Huntsville, Alabama. Shortly after the army took up the march for Kentucky; reached Louisville in due time; got a new outfit, and started back. The battalion got a taste of Perrysville, and in December went into that memorable fight at Stone River, where so many good men gave up their lives.

Lieutenant Bailey was relieved from duty with the Fifteenth Infantry in 1863, and joined his own Company F, Sixth Infantry, in Washington Park, New York, and subsequently spent the winter at Fort Hamilton.

In May, 1864, he was detailed as judge advocate First Division, Department of the East. In May, 1865, he departed with his company for the Department of the Carolinas, and served on the staff of Generals Q. A. Gillmore and Chas. Devens as judge advocate. He was relieved by General Daniel Sickels. In 1869 he was ordered to Fort Gibson, Idaho Territory. He joined the Eighth Infantry by assignment in March, 1871, at David's Island. He spent the winter of 1871–72 at Chicago; went to Utah in May, 1872; to Arizona in July, 1874; on the Bannock campaign in 1878, and assigned to command of Fort Bidwell, California, the same year. He was on duty at Angel Island from September, 1881, to September, 1884; then at San Diego until January 2, 1886; in Arizona until the following November; then to Fort Robinson, Nebraska. Here he remained until March, 1891, when he was ordered to Pine Ridge, South Dakota, and remained there until he joined his new station, Fort Sheridan, Illinois.

## REAR-ADMIRAL THEODORUS BAILEY.

REAR-ADMIRAL THEODORUS BAILEY was born at Chateaugay, New York, in April, 1805. He came of good colonial stock, his grandfather, John Bailey, being the first to hoist the Revolutionary flag in New York. He also commanded the Second Dutchess County Regiment.

Theodorus Bailey witnessed the battle of Plattsburg, when he was nine years old, General Mooers, a relative, being engaged therein. Appointed midshipman, 1818. Served on the coast of Africa, the Pacific, and the West Indies. A lieutenant in 1827, he made a cruise round the world, in the "Vincennes." He was then transferred to the "Constellation," and made a second cruise round the world, being absent three years and eight months. In 1846 Lieutenant Bailey commanded the store-ship "Lexington," on the Mexican and Californian coasts. A company of artillery was taken out from New York as passengers,—Captain Tompkins in command; the late General Sherman, first lieutenant; and the second lieutenant was General E. O. C. Ord. General Halleck, then lieutenant of engineers, was also a passenger. The "Lexington" did good service on the west coast, especially at La Paz. She blockaded San Blas, and finally captured that town, after a brisk fight. Lieutenant Bailey was made commander, 1849. In 1855 commanded the "St. Mary's," in the Pacific. In the same year was commissioned captain. A long and useful cruise terminated with the settlement of serious troubles at Panama. In 1861 Captain Bailey was ordered to command the "Colorado," joining Farragut at the mouth of the Mississippi. It was found that the frigate, even if lightened, could not cross the bar; so Captain Bailey, although an invalid, and against the advice of the surgeon, obtained permission for himself and many of his guns, men, and officers to be transferred to other lighter vessels. Finally he obtained command of the leading division in the passage of the forts below New Orleans, hoisting his flag in the "Cayuga." His part in those events is too well known to require repetition. When the fleet arrived off New Orleans he went, accompanied by Lieutenant George Perkins, to demand an unconditional surrender from the mayor, a mission so hazardous as to be quoted as one of the most gallant acts performed during the whole war. The description of their reception by the mob of desperadoes is most thrilling, and how those two brave men escaped assassination will always be a wonder. His conduct as leader of the first division elicited the highest encomiums from both superiors and subordinates, which space forbids our placing here, even in condensed terms. What Farragut thought of him was shown by his selection of him to bear to the government at Washington the despatches and the reports of the successful operations. After his arrival at the capital, he described upon the floor of the Senate Chamber the capture of New Orleans.

In June, 1862, Captain Bailey was ordered to command the East Gulf Squadron, as acting rear-admiral. He was engaged in the important blockade of Florida, capturing prizes, destroying the illicit traffic so extensively carried on, at that time, between the Gulf ports and the West Indies, and securing supplies designed for the Confederate service. Admiral Porter remarks: "The command of this station, although a compliment to Admiral Bailey, was scarcely a reward commensurate with his character and services. He was not a man whose appearance would attract attention, except from those who could appreciate the honest and simple character of our old-time naval officer; but he was a man who had no superior in the navy in point of dash, energy, and courage; and if he had ever had the opportunity of commanding a fleet in action, he would have done it with the coolness and bravery of Nelson. No higher compliment could be paid him."

When Farragut was preparing for his attack on Mobile, he evinced his appreciation of Bailey by offering him the same position he had filled in the Mississippi. Bailey accepted with enthusiasm, asking "to be put down for two chances." But, unfortunately, a severe attack of yellow fever sent him North before the attack was made, and he passed a long convalescence in the peaceful command of the old naval station at Sag Harbor, instead of leading Farragut's van.

He was made rear-admiral in 1866, and commanded the navy-yard at Portsmouth, New Hampshire, from 1865 to 1867. His last service was as a member of the Examining Board at Washington, in which city he died in February, 1877.

BRIGADIER AND BREVET MAJOR-GENERAL ABSALOM BAIRD (RETIRED).

BRIGADIER AND BREVET MAJOR-GENERAL ABSALOM BAIRD was born in Pennsylvania August 20, 1824, and graduated at the U. S. Military Academy July 1, 1849. He was promoted brevet second lieutenant of the Second Artillery the same day, and second lieutenant of the First Artillery April 1, 1850. After serving at Fort Monroe and Fort Columbus, he participated in the Florida hostilities against the Seminole Indians until 1853, when he was detailed at the U. S. Military Academy as assistant professor of mathematics until September 9, 1856, when he was made principal assistant of the same branch. In 1859-60 he was on frontier duty at Fort Brown and Ringgold Barracks, Texas, and in 1860-61 in garrison at Fort Monroe.

He was promoted first lieutenant December 24, 1853, and served in command of a light battery in the defence of Washington from March 10 to May 11, 1861, when he was placed on duty as assistant in the Adjutant-General's Office at Washington and brevet captain of the staff. He was adjutant-general of General Tyler's division in the defence of Washington, and participated in the Manassas campaign of 1861, being engaged in the action at Blackburn's Ford and battle of First Bull Run, July 21 of that year. On the 3d of August, 1861, he was appointed captain and assistant adjutant-general, and until March, 1862, was assistant in the Adjutant-General's Department, and on inspection duty in the War Department.

Captain Baird was appointed major and assistant inspector-general November 12, 1861, and was assigned to duty as inspector-general and chief of staff of the Fourth Corps (Army of the Potomac), participating in the Virginia Peninsula campaign of 1862, being engaged in the siege of Yorktown, and battle of Williamsburg. He was appointed brigadier-general of volunteers April 28, 1862, and was in command of the Seventeenth Brigade (Army of the Ohio) from May to September, 1862, being engaged in the capture of Cumberland Gap, and its occupation until evacuated. Then he was assigned to command the Third Division (Army of Kentucky) about Lexington and Danville, Kentucky, to January, 1863, when he participated in the operations in Tennessee in 1863, being engaged in the defence of Franklin and repulse of Van Dorn's assault on the place.

General Baird took part in General Rosecrans's Tennessee campaign of 1863, and was in the advance on Tullahoma and capture of Shelbyville. Crossing the Cumberland Mountains and Tennessee River, was engaged in the action at Dug Gap, Pigeon Mountain, Georgia; battle of Chickamauga, where he especially distinguished himself; skirmish at Rossville, and occupation of Chattanooga, Tennessee, to October 10, 1863. He was in command of a division of the Fourteenth Army Corps in the occupation and operations about Chattanooga, Tennessee, and engaged in the battle of Missionary Ridge, and pursuit of the enemy to Ringgold. He made a reconnoissance towards Dalton, Georgia, skirmishes at Tunnel Hill April 29 and May 2, 1864. He pursued the enemy with constant skirmishing to May 28, 1864, and participated eventually in the Atlanta campaign, being engaged in all the battles and actions pertaining to that memorable march, terminating with the march through the Carolinas and the surrender of the rebel army under General Joseph E. Johnston, at Durham Station, North Carolina, April 26, 1865.

General Baird was brevetted lieutenant-colonel for "gallant and meritorious services at the battle of Chickamauga, Georgia;" colonel for the same, "at the battle of Chattanooga, Tennessee;" brigadier-general for the same, "in the capture of Atlanta, Georgia;" major-general for the same, "in the field during the Rebellion." He was also brevetted major-general of U. S. Volunteers September 1, 1864, for "faithful services and distinguished conduct during the Atlanta campaign, and particularly in the battles of Resaca and Jonesborough, and for general good conduct in command of his division against Savannah."

After the war closed, General Baird occupied many important positions too numerous to mention here. He filled the several grades of major, lieutenant-colonel, and colonel in the Inspector-General's Department, and was appointed brigadier-general (inspector-general) September 22, 1885, and on the 20th of August, 1888, was retired from active service by operation of law.

# LIEUTENANT-COLONEL JOHN W. BARLOW.

LIEUTENANT-COLONEL JOHN W. BARLOW (Corps of Engineers) was born in New York June 26, 1838, and graduated at the Military Academy May 6, 1861. He was promoted second lieutenant of the Second Artillery same day; promoted first lieutenant May 15, 1861, and transferred to the Topographical Engineers July 24, 1862. He served in the field with the Army of the Potomac, participating in the Peninsula campaign of 1862, and was engaged in the battles around Richmond, Virginia, especially at Malvern Hill, remaining with the rear-guard during the movement of the army to the James River, and the transfer of the army to the defences of Washington, D. C.

Colonel Barlow was detailed as assistant professor of Mathematics and Ethics at the Military Academy from September, 1862, to June 18, 1863, when he was ordered on duty with the Engineer Battalion of the Army of the Potomac to February 17, 1864, being engaged in constructing the bridge over the Potomac River at Berlin, Maryland, July 18, 1863; in laying, repairing, and guarding bridges over the Rappahannock River, August 1-23, 1863; over Bull Run, at Blackburn's Ford, October 17, 1863; and across the Rappahannock, at Kelly's Ford, November 7, 1863. He was engaged in the Mine Run operations from November 26 to December 3, 1863, and in making roads and reconnoissances, building blockhouses and erecting defensive works.

Colonel Barlow was again detailed as assistant professor of mathematics at the Military Academy from February 26 to June 20, 1864. He was promoted captain July 3, 1863, and in the summer of 1864 was ordered to the armies of the West, participating in the Georgia campaign from July 12 to August 27, 1864, as chief engineer of the Seventeenth Army Corps, and was at the latter date granted leave of absence to November 13, 1864, when he rejoined, and was placed in charge of the defences of Nashville, Tennessee, where he remained until October, 1865.

He participated in the Pennsylvania campaign, and was engaged at the battle of Gettysburg; and in the Georgia campaign, and engaged in the battle of Atlanta, July 22,

1864, and siege of Atlanta to August 27, 1864, including the repulse of the sortie of July 28, 1864.

He was brevetted captain May 27, 1862, for "gallant and meritorious services in the battle of Hanover Court-House, Virginia;" major July 4, 1864, for "gallant and meritorious services in the Atlanta campaign;" and lieutenant-colonel March 13, 1865, for "gallant and meritorious services in the battles before Nashville, Tennessee."

At the close of the war, Colonel Barlow was detailed as superintending engineer of the construction of Fort Clinch, Florida, from October 20, 1865, to November 19, 1867. He was at this time transferred to the same duty at Burlington, Vt., as Superintending Engineer of Fort Montgomery, New York, and harbor improvements on Lake Champlain to May 30, 1870. He was promoted major of Engineers April 23, 1869, and lieutenant-colonel March 19, 1884.

His duties as an officer of Engineers have required his services at Chicago, New London, Milwaukee, Chattanooga, Nashville, and other stations from 1870 to the present time, he being now employed as Commissioner and Engineer-in-Chief upon the relocation of the International Boundary between the United States and Mexico.

CAPTAIN AND BREVET COLONEL ALBERT BARNITZ.

CAPTAIN AND BREVET COLONEL ALBERT BARNITZ (retired) was born at Everett, Bedford County, Pennsylvania, March 10, 1835. At the breaking out of the war of the Rebellion he was pursuing the study of law, in the office of an eminent jurist, at Minneapolis, Minnesota, whither he had gone from Cleveland, Ohio, after some preparatory study at Kenyon College, and in a local law-school. But the importunate beating of war-drums, and the startling cry, "to arms!" caused him to relinquish his cherished opportunities and to hasten back to Cleveland, where, waiving all claims to immediate preferment, he at once enlisted as a private soldier in the Second Ohio Cavalry, then organizing on University Heights,—but was later enrolled as a sergeant.

The regiment with which he was now associated had a remarkable and altogether exceptional career. It served in five different armies, under twenty-four generals, and campaigned through thirteen States and the Indian Territory; fought in ninety-five battles and minor engagements, and marched an aggregate distance of twenty-seven thousand miles.

Captain Barnitz, meanwhile, won his way, step by step, to the rank of major. The command of the regiment, however, devolved upon him at a critical time, while he yet held the rank of captain, and throughout the entire Appomattox campaign, wherein the regiment under the eye of Custer, and justifying his enthusiastic commendation, habitually led the charge, or bore the brunt of onset, in every desperate crisis; and in the battles of Dinwiddie Court-House, Five Forks, Sailor's Creek, and Appomattox Station, well sustained its old time prestige, and fought with even more than its accustomed valor; crowning its achievements by the spirited repulse, at Appomattox Court-House, of the attempted sortie of a confederate cavalry brigade, while efforts towards capitulation were in progress.

It is historically stated that "from the 27th of March to the surrender of Lee" (Colonel Barnitz being meanwhile in command) "the Second captured, and turned over to the provost-marshal, eighteen pieces of artillery, one hundred and eighty horses, seventy army wagons, nine hundred prisoners, and small-arms not counted."

Upon the reorganization of the army, in 1866, Colonel Barnitz was commissioned captain of G Troop, Seventh U. S. Cavalry, and subsequently brevetted major, lieutenant-colonel, and colonel, in the regular army.

He served with the Seventh Cavalry, and in command of his troop and detachments, on independent scouts and other expeditions, in Indian campaigns in Kansas, Colorado, Texas, and the Indian Territory; marching many thousand miles, and participating in numerous engagements with the Cheyennes, Arapahoes, Apaches, Kiowas, Comanches, and Sioux. He was with General Hancock's Expedition on the Plains, in the spring of 1867, and participated in the seizure and destruction of the Cheyenne village. He was with General Sully in pursuit of the hostile tribes to the border of the Staked Plains, and in attendant engagements in 1868. He accompanied General Custer on the toilsome campaign, through blizzards and trackless snow, which culminated at the battle of Washita, Indian Territory, November 27, 1868, in which engagement Colonel Barnitz, at daybreak, led the attack from below the village, and later, while separated from his command, in an effort to head off a large party of Indians escaping to their ponies, killed, in a hand-to-hand encounter, three warriors, by one of whom he had been previously shot through the body, just below the heart,—the wound being pronounced mortal, at the time, by the surgeons present. The colonel was twice seriously wounded during the war of the Rebellion. He was retired from active service December 15, 1870, and makes his occasional home at Cleveland, Ohio. He was admitted to the bar in 1881, but has never engaged in active practice of the law, as he prefers to travel with his family, and meanwhile writes occasional letters for the Cleveland *Leader*. He has gained some celebrity as a poet, having written several war-poems of remarkable vigor, and others not less meritorious. His graphic war-correspondence for the Cincinnati *Commercial*, over the signature "A. B.," is still favorably remembered.

Colonel Barnitz is a son of Dr. Martin E. Barnitz and Martha McClintic, of Chambersburgh, Pa., who emigrated to Ohio in 1835. He is also a grandson of Captain John McClintic, renowned in the war of 1812.

## LIEUTENANT-COLONEL AND BREVET BRIGADIER-GENERAL JOHN W. BARRIGER.

LIEUTENANT-COLONEL AND BREVET BRIGADIER-GENERAL JOHN W. BARRIGER (Assistant Commissary-General of Subsistence) was born in Kentucky, and appointed a cadet at the U. S. Military Academy, from the same State, on the 1st of September, 1852. He was graduated, and appointed a second lieutenant in the Second U. S. Artillery, July 1, 1856.

Lieutenant Barriger served at the artillery school at Fort Monroe, Virginia, in 1857-59, and in Light Company A, of his regiment, in 1859-61. In May, 1861, being then on duty in the defences of Washington, he was assigned to the command of Fort Ellsworth, the principal earthwork in front of Alexandria, Virginia, which he armed and equipped. He served in the Manassas campaign of July, 1861, as first lieutenant of Light Company D, Second Artillery, commanded by Captain Richard Arnold, and was engaged with his battery in the battle of Bull Run, Virginia, fought on the 21st of July, 1861, for which he was brevetted captain, "for gallant and meritorious services," to date from July 21, 1861. On the 3d of August, 1861, Lieutenant Barriger was appointed a commissary of subsistence with the rank of captain, and ordered to Indianapolis, Indiana, for duty as chief commissary of subsistence for the volunteer troops being raised in the State of Indiana. On the 30th of November, 1861, he was relieved from duty at Indianapolis, and assigned as chief commissary of subsistence of the Department of Western Virginia, commanded by General W. S. Rosecrans. From July to November, 1862, after the discontinuance of the Department of Western Virginia, he was engaged in inspecting subsistence depots in the Middle Department, and in forwarding subsistence stores from Baltimore to Frederick, Maryland, for the use of the Army of the Potomac during the Antietam campaign. In December, 1862, he was ordered to report to General J. D. Cox, commanding the District of West Virginia, for duty as chief commissary of subsistence of that district. Upon the discontinuance of the District of West Virginia in April, 1863, he was ordered to report to General Ambrose E. Burnside, commanding the Department of the Ohio, for inspection duty. He was engaged in inspecting subsistence depots in the States of Ohio, Michigan, Illinois, Indiana, and Kentucky from April to November, 1863. In November, 1863, Captain Barriger was appointed a commissary of subsistence of volunteers with the rank of lieutenant-colonel, and ordered to report to General John G. Foster, at Cincinnati, Ohio, and accompany him to Knoxville, Tennessee, for duty as chief commissary of subsistence of the Department of the Ohio. Lieutenant-Colonel Barriger, upon arriving at Knoxville in December, 1863, just after the raising of the siege, found the Army

of the Ohio at a distance of one hundred and fifty miles from its depot of supplies, at Camp Nelson, Kentucky, which was accessible by mountain wagon-roads only, then nearly impassable for loaded wagons. It was quickly perceived that a better route of transportation must speedily be opened to, or the troops withdrawn from, East Tennessee. With the view of opening the route from Chattanooga to East Tennessee, Lieutenant-Colonel Barriger proceeded to Chattanooga, under the orders and instructions of General Foster, for conference with General George H. Thomas, commanding the Department and Army of the Cumberland. The result of this conference was an early opening of the railway to Loudon, and the occupancy of East Tennessee was thereby made possible and permanent. General Foster was the 1st of February, 1864, compelled by ill health to ask to be relieved of his command. He was succeeded by General Schofield, on whose staff Lieutenant-Colonel Barriger served as chief commissary of subsistence until the close of the Civil War, which found the command in North Carolina.

Since the close of the Civil War, General Barriger has performed duty as chief commissary of subsistence of the Department of Platte, Department of South, and Department of Missouri; as purchasing and depot commissary of subsistence at Louisville, Ky., Cincinnati, O., Chicago, Ill., and St. Louis, Mo.; and for six years as assistant to the commissary-general of subsistence at Washington, D.C. He attained his present grade—viz., assistant commissary-general of subsistence, with the rank of lieutenant colonel—March 12, 1892. In recognition of his services during the Civil War, he received, in addition to the brevet of captain heretofore mentioned, the brevets of major, lieutenant-colonel, colonel, and brigadier-general.

General Barriger is the author of "Legislative History of the Subsistence Department of the United States Army from June 15, 1775, to August 15, 1876," and is a companion of the Military Order of the Loyal Legion.

## MAJOR HENRY ANTHONY BARTLETT, U.S.M.C.

MAJOR HENRY ANTHONY BARTLETT was born in Pawtuxet, Rhode Island, and was appointed to the Marine Corps from that State. He served in the First Regiment Rhode Island Volunteers, under General A. E. Burnside; on its being mustered out of service he was appointed a second lieutenant in the Marine Corps September 8, 1861; Port Royal Marine Battalion, under Major John George Reynolds, which left Washington, October 16, 1861, on board the transport steamer "Governor," which foundered at sea, November 3, 1861, off the coast of North Carolina; all but seven of the four hundred marines were rescued by the frigate "Sabine," Captain Cadwalader Ringgold, commanding; Fort Clinch and Fernandina expedition, February, 1862; St. Augustine expedition, March, 1862.

Commissioned first lieutenant November 26, 1861; stationed at marine barracks, Boston, April, 1862, to July, 1862; commanding guard of the ironclad frigate "New Ironsides," from July, 1862, to August, 1864; in charge of after-division of two eleven-inch guns, manned by the marine guard, at bombardment of Morris Island, Sumter, and Moultrie, April 7, 1863, Flag-Officer Du Pont aboard "Ironsides" as his flagship; in twenty-six other engagements with Forts Wagner, Gregg, Sumter, Moultrie, Bee, and other forts and batteries in Charleston harbor; commanded a battalion of three hundred and twenty marines and one hundred and twenty sailors that landed at Morris Island, July, 1863, as a storming-party; in command of a battalion of marines on expedition to St. John's River and Jacksonville, February, 1864; marine barracks, Brooklyn, August, 1864, to March, 1865; 1864-65, commanded troops and assisted the revenue officers in breaking up whiskey distilleries; receiving-ship "North Carolina," from March, 1865, to September, 1865; marine barracks, Boston, September, 1865, to March, 1866; steam frigate "Chattanooga," special cruise, March, 1866, to September, 1866; steam sloop "Sacramento," special cruise, September, 1866, to November, 1867; aboard at the time she was wrecked on the Coromandel coast, Bay of Bengal, India.

Commissioned a captain November 29, 1867; marine barracks, Boston, December 6, 1867, to September, 1868; fleet marine officer flagship "Contoocook," September, 1868, to October, 1869; marine barracks, Boston, December 6, 1869, to February 4, 1870; receiving-ship "Vermont," February 10, 1870, to September 23, 1870; special duty on Tehuantepec surveying expedition, under command of Captain Shufeldt, September, 1870, to September, 1871; receiving-ship "Vermont," October, 1871, to June, 1872; fleet marine officer flagship "Hartford," Asiatic Station, October, 1872, to October, 1875; judge-advocate, Navy and Marine Corps, from November, 1875, to August, 1879; head-quarters Marine Corps, Washington, D. C., August, 1879, to February 26, 1880; training-ship "Minnesota," March 1, 1880, to August 8, 1881; commanding head-quarters Marine Corps, Washington, August 12, 1881, to November 21, 1881; special duty Navy Department, November, 1881, to March, 1882; receiving-ship "Colorado," March, 1882, to September 1, 1883; fleet marine officer flagship "Trenton," Asiatic Station, September 1, 1883, to September 22, 1886; commanding marine barracks, Norfolk, Virginia, January 1, 1887, to April 16, 1887; commanding marine barracks, Annapolis, Maryland, April 20, 1887, to April 1, 1891; graduated at the Torpedo School, Newport, Rhode Island, 1888.

Commissioned major January 29, 1891; commanding marine barracks, League Island, from April 1, 1891, to June, 1891; commanding marine barracks, Mare Island, August 1, 1891.

## MEDICAL-DIRECTOR NEWTON L. BATES.

Dr. Bates was born in New York, and appointed assistant surgeon from that State in July, 1861. His first service was at the Naval Hospital at New York. He then served in the "Seneca," in the South Atlantic Squadron, in 1861-62.

He was on duty at the Naval Laboratory at New York in 1862-63. That was then a very busy place, and to fill the requisitions required the devoted exertions of those on duty there,—while it is a kind of duty requisite for the completeness of naval outfits which seldom receives recognition.

Dr. Bates then went to the Mississippi, and served in the ironclad "Benton" in 1863-64, partaking in her work during that time. He was again stationed at the Naval Laboratory from 1864 to 1867. He was commissioned as surgeon September, 1865, and served in the "Portsmouth" during 1867-68, and the "Swatara" during 1868-69. He went directly to the "Miantonomah," and served in her in 1869-70. He was attached to the U. S. S. "Pawnee" in 1870-71, and to the navy-yard at Norfolk, Virginia, from 1871 to 1873. He was fleet-surgeon on board the flagship "Brooklyn," of the South Atlantic Squadron (Admiral Leroy), from 1873 to 1876. For two years after this he was attached to the "Minnesota." He was a member of the Board of Examiners, 1878-80.

Dr. Bates was made medical inspector in January, 1881, and was in charge of the Naval Hospital at Yokohama, Japan, for some time; after which he served in the flagship "Lancaster" as fleet-surgeon up to 1884.

Coming to the East again, he was for three years on special duty at Washington, where he made many friends by his skilful treatment and sympathy with his patients. He next served in three flagships,—the "Trenton" in 1887, the "Richmond" in 1888, and the "Pensacola" in the same year. He became medical director in September, 1888. Since then he has been in charge of the Naval Hospital at Mare Island, California.

CAPTAIN WILLIAM H. BECK.

CAPTAIN WILLIAM H. BECK (Tenth Cavalry) was born in Philadelphia, Pennsylvania. At the first call for troops by the President, at the breaking out of the war of the Rebellion, he entered the volunteer service as corporal of Company B, Tenth Illinois Volunteer Infantry, April 16, 1861, and was honorably discharged July 29, 1861. He then re-entered the service as quartermaster-sergeant of the Sixth Illinois Cavalry, September 21, 1861, and promoted first lieutenant October 21, 1862.

He served in the armies of the West, in the field, and was engaged in action at Coldwater, Mississippi, October 21, 1862, where he was severely wounded, and resigned his volunteer commission February 28, 1863.

Captain Beck did not again enter the service during the war, but was appointed to the regular service, as second lieutenant of the Tenth Cavalry, June 18, 1867, and was promoted first lieutenant December 11, 1867. He served in the field in Mexico and Arizona, participating in numerous campaigns, and was engaged in actions against numerous Apache Indians at Sierra Carmen, Mexico, November 1, 1877. He participated in action with Victorio, at Tenajos de los Palmos, Texas, July 30, 1880, and also with the same at Rattlesnake Cañon, August 6, 1880. He also participated in the capture of the Chiricahua Indians at Fort Apache, Arizona, August 30, 1886.

Captain Beck performed the duties of adjutant of the Sixth Illinois Cavalry from November 1, 1862, to February 28, 1863, and was acting assistant quartermaster of the district in 1880. He was promoted captain Tenth Cavalry December 23, 1887.

In 1892 his regiment was ordered to the Department of Dakota, and is now *en route* to stations therein.

## COLONEL AND BREVET MAJOR-GENERAL AMOS BECKWITH (RETIRED).

COLONEL AND BREVET MAJOR-GENERAL AMOS BECKWITH was born in Vermont on the 4th of October, 1825, and was graduated from the Military Academy July 1, 1850. He was promoted a brevet second lieutenant in the artillery, and served in the hostilities against the Seminole Indians, in Florida, from 1850 to 1853, in the mean time having been promoted to second lieutenant, First U. S. Artillery, February 22, 1851. He served at Forts Monroe and McHenry during the years of 1853-55, and was promoted to first lieutenant August 21, 1854.

After having served at Fort Monroe, Key West, and Barrancas, he was ordered on frontier at Fort Leavenworth, Kansas, from which place he was ordered, at the commencement of the Rebellion, to Washington, D. C., being a first lieutenant at the time in Colonel Magruder's battery of light artillery. In less than one year he and thirteen other officers were taken from that regiment for the Staff Corps, he being appointed captain and commissary of subsistence May 10, 1861, and performing the duties of chief depot commissary of subsistence at Washington, D. C., to January 15, 1864, having been, during that time, promoted major September 29, 1861, and colonel and additional aide-de-camp January 1, 1862, holding the latter appointment until May 31, 1866.

Colonel Beckwith was engaged on a tour of inspection of the commissary department in the Department of Ohio, the Cumberland, Tennessee, and the Gulf, from February 5 to April 13, 1864, and from April, 1864, to July, 1865, he was chief commissary of subsistence of the military division of the Mississippi, on the staff of Major-General Sherman, being present with his armies in their battles, marches, etc. His labors were not confined to his own duties, but he often aided others,—acting in the quartermaster's department when requested or necessitated to do so.

He was made brevet lieutenant-colonel and brevet colonel September 1, 1864, " for gallant and meritorious services in the campaign against Atlanta, Georgia;" brevet brigadier-general U. S. Volunteers, January 12, 1865; brevet brigadier-general U. S. Army, March 13, 1865, "for gallant and meritorious service in the campaign terminating with the surrender of the insurgent army under General Joseph E. Johnston;" brevet major-general U. S. Army, March 13, 1865, "for faithful and meritorious service in the subsistence department during the Rebellion."

After the close of field operations he went to St. Louis, Missouri, then served as supervising commissary of subsistence for the Department of the Gulf States and depot commissary of subsistence, New Orleans, Louisiana; as chief commissary of subsistence, Department of the Gulf, of the Fifth Military District (Louisiana and Texas), and in other important capacities in the Southern and Southwestern States. During his tour of duty in New Orleans, Louisiana, he passed through a disastrous yellow-fever epidemic which nearly terminated his career.

General Beckwith served as chief commissary, Department of the Gulf, to March 28, 1874. Having been promoted lieutenant-colonel and assistant commissary-general of subsistence June 23, 1874, he was ordered to Washington, D. C., in the office of the commissary-general of subsistence, and, after a few months, took station at St. Louis, Missouri, as purchasing and depot commissary, where he remained from June 7, 1875, to October 4, 1889.

On the 28th of August, 1888, he was promoted colonel and assistant commissary-general of subsistence, and was retired from active service, by operation of law, October 4, 1889.

The following is taken from an editorial in the *Army and Navy Journal* upon the retirement of General Beckwith:

"Although not connected directly with the Army of the Potomac, General McClellan, in his official report, handsomely refers to the valuable services of this officer. So highly was he regarded by the late President Lincoln, who knew him intimately, that a position in the adjutant-general's department, afterwards filled by General Drum, was tendered him, and also, about the same time, a position in the quartermaster's department. At the solicitation of prominent officials, he was induced to accept, in preference, a place in the subsistence department. Naturally of a meditative habit of mind, reserved and uncommunicative, General Beckwith's real ability was not always understood until necessity for action gave opportunity for the manifestation of his energy and persistence of purpose. Then difficulties seemed to intensify his force, and no temporary defeat could turn him from his purpose. Rising always to the greatness of the occasion, he never failed in the performance of his duties, whatever their magnitude. With his retirement from active service, the subsistence department loses one of the ablest officers of the United States Army, and one whose devotion to the obligations of duty and honor is an example to others."

REAR-ADMIRAL GEORGE E. BELKNAP.

REAR-ADMIRAL GEORGE E. BELKNAP was born in New Hampshire in January, 1832, and appointed midshipman from that State in October, 1847. After serving in the African and Pacific Squadrons, he went to the Naval Academy, and became passed midshipman in 1853. After serving on the Coast Survey, and as acting master of two sloops-of-war, he was promoted master in 1855, and lieutenant in the same year. After short shore-service, he went to China in the "Portsmouth;" commanded a howitzer-launch at the capture of the Barrier Forts, in the Canton River, November, 1856. The forts were four in number, and mounted one hundred and seventy-six guns of all kinds. He assisted in undermining and blowing up these works after capture. In 1861 he commanded the boats of the "St. Louis" at both reinforcements of Fort Pickens. While attached to the "Huron," in 1861-62, he was in the expedition against Fernandina, St. John's, St. Mary's, St. Augustine, etc.

Lieutenant-commander July, 1862. Executive-officer of the "New Ironsides" in twenty-seven engagements with Forts Wagner, Sumter, Moultrie, Batteries Bee, Beauregard, etc., of the defences of Charleston. After commanding gunboat "Seneca," he commanded the iron-clad " Canonicus" in two actions with the Howlett Horse-Battery in December, 1864, and at both battles of Fort Fisher, taking the advanced position. After the capture of Fort Fisher he proceeded to Charleston, and, after firing the last shot at its defences, was present at the evacuation. He then went to Havana, with Admiral Gordon, in quest of the ironclad "Stonewall."

Commanded "Shenandoah," in Asiatic Squadron, in 1866-67.

Commander July, 1866. Commanded "Hartford," Asiatic Squadron flagship, 1867-68. During this time commanded expedition against Formosan natives. After a tour of shore duty was ordered to command of "Tuscarora," and went to the Pacific. Co-operated with Selfridge's party in the Darien survey. In May, 1873, in command of "Tuscarora," went to make deep-sea soundings between the western coast of the United States and the coast of Japan, to test the feasibility of a submarine cable. His adaptation of Sir William Thomson's machine, and his success in obtaining soundings with wire at great depths, are well known. He ascertained the "true continental outline" from Cape Flattery to San Diego, and ran a line of soundings from San Diego to Yokohama, via the Hawaiian and Brown Islands, and from Yokohama to Cape Flattery, via the Aleutian Islands. Off the Japan coast he found the most extraordinary depths ever known,—more than five and one-fourth statute miles. He is the inventor of several cylinders for bringing specimens from ocean-bed, which are in use in the naval service and the coast survey.

For these successes he received the public and emphatic recognition of Sir William Thomson and many other scientific men.

Commander Belknap was senior officer present at Honolulu when serious political disturbances arose, and he landed a force from the "Tuscarora" and the "Portsmouth" which preserved order for several days. For this he had the thanks of the king, the chambers, and the consular corps. He then served as hydrographic inspector, and in command of "Ohio." With impaired health from exposure in deep-sea work, he was obliged to go South, and was ordered as captain of Pensacola Navy-Yard. During 1875 he was a member of the Board of Visitors to Naval Academy, and, later, member of the Board of Examiners of Midshipmen. In 1876 he was detached from duty at Pensacola and put on special duty in reference to deep-sea soundings. Afterwards he returned to Pensacola as commandant, and remained there three years. He then commanded the "Alaska" in the Pacific, and was attached to the navy-yard at Norfolk. In 1885 he was promoted to be commodore, and was superintendent of the Naval Observatory in 1885; was commandant of the navy-yard at Mare Island in 1886-90. He was promoted to be rear-admiral in February, 1889, and commanded the Asiatic Station until 1892.

## COLONEL AND BREVET MAJOR-GENERAL HENRY W. BENHAM.

COLONEL AND BREVET MAJOR-GENERAL HENRY W. BENHAM was born in Connecticut. Graduated first in his class at the Military Academy July 1, 1837; brevet second lieutenant Engineers July 1, 1837; assistant engineer on the improvement of Savannah River, Georgia, 1837-38; first lieutenant July 7, 1838; superintending engineer of repairs of Fort Marion and St. Augustine sea-wall, Florida, 1839-44; of repairs of defences of Annapolis Harbor 1844-45; repairs of St. Augustine sea-wall, Florida, 1845-46; Forts Mifflin and McHenry 1845; repairs of Forts Madison and Washington 1846-47; in war with Mexico, engineer on staffs of Generals Taylor and Wool; engaged and wounded in the battle of Buena Vista February, 1847; brevet captain February 23, 1847, for gallant and meritorious conduct in battle of Buena Vista, General Scott recommending a second brevet of major for "his great services" in that action; served on various engineer duties from 1847 to breaking out of Civil War, and part of the time was on duty in Europe. In 1855 was selected from the engineers for promotion in the new regiments, but declined to be major of the Ninth Infantry March 3, 1855; served during the rebellion of the seceding States 1861-66; as chief engineer of General McClellan, Department of the Ohio, May 14 to July 22, 1861, laying out and building fortifications at Cairo and Bird's Point; was temporarily on the staff of General T. A. Morris, in military operations at Laurel Hill, West Virginia, July 6-11, 1861; and in command of all the troops that pursued, routed, and killed General Robert S. Garnett, capturing his trains with artillery, and thus, as the general commanding reported, "Secession was dead in West Virginia." Was brevet colonel July 13, 1861, for gallant and meritorious services at the battle of Carrick's Ford, Virginia; this commission (the first battle-brevet of the war) made him the senior brevet major-general of the Corps of Engineers; and he was recommended to be brevet brigadier-general by the board of general officers for this action; major Corps of Engineers August 6, 1861; brigadier-general U. S. Volunteers August 13, 1861; in West Virginia campaign August to November, 1861; in command of brigade at New Creek August 16, 1861; commanded the leading and only brigade engaged in the action and rout of Floyd, at Carnifex Ferry, September 10, 1861; and on November 14 to 16, 1861, in the skirmishes and second rout of Floyd, from Cotton Hill to Raleigh, West Virginia, with great loss of baggage and trains, and his chief of cavalry, Colonel Croghan, killed. Was present and in command at the bombardment and capture of Fort Pulaski, Georgia, April 10-11, 1862; lieutenant-colonel Corps of Engineers March 3, 1863; reorganized and commanded engineer

brigade (Army of the Potomac), being engaged in throwing pontoon bridges across the Rappahannock for the passage and retreat of the army at Chancellorsville, April 29 to May 5, 1863; his horse shot under him at the "crossing" below Fredericksburg April 29, 1863; laid the pontoon bridges at Franklin's crossing in face of the enemy June 5, 1863; reorganized the pontoon trains at Washington July, 1863, to May, 1864; and laid most of the pontoon bridges for the Army of the Potomac from May, 1864, to May, 1865; one of them over the James River, at Fort Powhatan, June 13, 1864, was two thousand two hundred feet long, and built in five hours; in the mean time constructed and commanded the defences at City Point, Virginia, covering as a reserve the main depots and head-quarters of General Grant; and served with his command in the lines in front of Petersburg; brevet brigadier-general U. S. Army March 13, 1865, for gallant and meritorious services in the campaign terminating with the surrender of the insurgent army under General R. E. Lee; April 3, 1865, joined in taking possession of Petersburg, and was placed in command of that city, moving thence to Burkesville and towards the Roanoke River, to act against Johnston; repairing bridges across Appomattox and Staunton Rivers April 3-23, 1865; and on march to Washington, D. C., May to June, 1865; brevet major-general U. S. Vols. for faithful services during the Rebellion; brevet major-general U. S. A. March 13, 1865, for gallant and meritorious services during the Rebellion; mustered out of volunteer service Jan. 15, 1866, and took charge of the sea-walls in Boston Harbor; of the defences of Provincetown, Mass.; colonel Corps of Engineers March 7, 1867, and as member and president of the Board of Engineers June 20, 1865, to May 18, 1867; after July, 1877, in charge of inner defences of N. Y. Harbor, and of the forts at N. Y. Narrows, Sandy Hook, N. J., and Lake Champlain; retired June 30, 1882. He died at New York City June 1, 1884.

MAJOR AND BREVET COLONEL FREDERICK W. BENTEEN (RETIRED).

MAJOR AND BREVET COLONEL FREDERICK W. BENTEEN was born in Petersburg, Virginia, August 24, 1834. He entered the military service at the breaking out of the war of the Rebellion as a first lieutenant in the Tenth Missouri Cavalry, in which regiment he subsequently rose to the rank of lieutenant-colonel, and was appointed colonel of the One Hundred and Thirty-eighth U. S. Colored Troops July 15, 1863.

Colonel Benteen's service in the field during the war was with the Western armies, participating in the following engagements: Actions of Wet Glaze, Springfield, Salem, Second Springfield, Cane Creek, Sugar Creek; battle of Pea Ridge; actions of Batesville, Kickapoo, Cotton Plant; defence of Helena, Arkansas; actions of Milliken's Bend, Bolivar, and Greenville; engaged at the actions of Tuscumbia, Tupelo and Alabama Valley; the battle of Iuka, Mississippi; action of Florence; siege of Vicksburg; action of Brandon Station; capture of Jackson; raid to Meridian, and action of Bolivar; at the actions of Big Blue Osage, Charlotte Prairie, Pleasant Ridge, Montevallo; assault and capture of Selma, Alabama, and Columbus, Georgia.

Colonel Benteen commanded his regiment at the battle of Iuka and action of Montevallo, and a brigade at the action of Big Blue Osage, and at the close of the war was mustered out January 6, 1866, but subsequently appointed captain in the Seventh U. S. Cavalry, to date from July, 1866. He was then ordered to the plains and served at many posts and on campaign duty, participating in the engagement with hostile Indians on the Saline River, Kansas, and in the Big Horn and Yellowstone expedition of 1876, his company forming part of the ill-fated Custer's command.

He was made brevet major for gallant and meritorious services at the battle of the Osage, Missouri; brevet lieutenant-colonel for gallant and meritorious services in the charge on Columbus, Georgia; brevet colonel for gallant and meritorious conduct in the engagement with hostile Indians on the Saline River, Kansas.

He was promoted major of the Ninth U. S. Cavalry December 17, 1882, and retired for disability in the line of duty July 7, 1888.

## MAJOR EDWIN BENTLEY.

Dr. Edwin Bentley was born in New London County, Connecticut, and in the national contest, Dr. Bentley became incited by the fullest patriotism and devotion for the nation's cause, and he immediately took an active part, in season and out of season,—at all times engaged in caring for the sick and wounded, in which, for continued service and number of operations made, he was equalled by few and excelled by none. For years he had thousands of wounded men under his care, and at times more than a hundred medical officers under his charge. All this he conducted—with the vast property responsibility—without a controversy, or arrest of either officer or soldier subject to his orders. The following is gleaned from the official records, and is offered as a brief exhibit of his military service, which embraces an experience in the field, camp, post, general hospital, and Libby prison at Richmond in 1862.

Statement of the military service of Surgeon Edwin Bentley, of the U. S. Army, compiled from the records of the War Department, Washington:

He was mustered into the service as assistant surgeon, Fourth Connecticut Infantry, June 6, 1861. He was appointed surgeon, U. S. Volunteers, September 4, 1861, and honorably mustered out January 4, 1866. He received the brevet of lieutenant-colonel March 13, 1865, for faithful and meritorious service during the war. He served in the Army of the Potomac, in F. J. Porter's division, until the autumn of 1862; then in charge of General Hospital at Alexandria, Virginia, and subsequently as superintendent of hospitals at that place to April, 1866; was post-surgeon at Russell Barracks, D. C., until mustered out of the volunteer service.

Was appointed assistant surgeon, U.S.A., February 8, 1866,—service being continuous from the volunteer to the regular; captain and assistant surgeon July 28, 1866; major and surgeon July 12, 1876. He remained on duty at Russell Barracks, D. C., to December, 1868; at Lincoln Barracks, D. C., to April, 1869; at Camp Reynolds, California, to August, 1869; then as post-surgeon at Point San José, California, January, 1871; April 17, 1873, with Batteries B, C, and G, Fourth Artillery, to Modoc expedition,—in lava beds, at head-quarters of General Gillem, south side of Yula Lake, transporting wounded, at the conclusion of the war, from the field-hospital, of which he was in charge, to Fort Klamath, Oregon. He rejoined his proper station at Point San José, California, where he remained post-surgeon until 1874. Also on duty at Alcatraz Island, at the Presidio of San Francisco, California; at Camp Bidwell, California. February, 1875, recorder of Medical Examining Board and attending surgeon at San Francisco, California. In 1876 he was on leave of absence, to enable him to study mental diseases and morbid anatomy of the nervous system, being superintendent of the Napa Insane Asylum, California. February, 1877, on duty, with the Sixteenth Infantry, at New Orleans, Louisiana, where, finding an epidemic of small-pox producing much alarm among the troops of the command, he established a pest-hospital, by order of the commanding general, and for his success in its management and devotion to the patients he received a special letter of commendation from the medical director of the department. In 1887 he was on duty as post-surgeon at Little Rock Barracks; on duty in Pennsylvania during the labor strikes; also medical director of the Department of Arkansas. In 1884 he was post-surgeon at Fort Clark, Texas, and post-surgeon at Fort Brown, Texas, in 1886; was retired in 1888; was professor of anatomy in Pacific Medical College, California, and professor of surgery in the medical department of the Industrial University of Arkansas since its organization.

## CAPTAIN ERIC BERGLAND.

CAPTAIN ERIC BERGLAND (Corps of Engineers, U.S.A.) enlisted at the age of seventeen in Company D, Fifty-seventh Illinois Volunteer Infantry, September 14, 1861. In December, 1861, was mustered into service as second lieutenant, and in April, 1862, he was promoted to first lieutenant, in which capacity he served until the regiment was mustered out of service, the war being ended, July 7, 1865. During his connection with the Fifty-seventh Illinois Volunteer Infantry, he took part in the capture of Fort Donelson, and the battles of Shiloh, Corinth, and Resaca. While in the field at Rome, Georgia, in the autumn of 1864, he received an appointment as cadet at the U. S. Military Academy at West Point. On reporting to Superintendent of Military Academy November 10, he was informed that his class was already well advanced in their studies, and that it would require considerable previous knowledge of mathematics to be able to make up before examination for the time lost; as before enlisting in the army he had only enjoyed the advantages of a village school and knew nothing of the higher mathematics, he thought it highly improbable that he would be able to prepare for the first examination after being nearly two months behind his classmates. On the advice of the Superintendent, he therefore applied to the Secretary of War to have his appointment extended to the following June, when he could enter on equal terms with other members of his class. This request was granted, and he was in the mean time ordered to Johnson's Island, Ohio, for duty as assistant to Captain Tardy, Corps of Engineers, until June 1, 1865.

He graduated June 15, 1869, at the head of his class, and as the staff corps had just previously been closed by Act of Congress, he was commissioned second lieutenant Fifth Artillery, and stationed at Fort Warren, Massachusetts, and Fort Trumbull, Connecticut, and in the field on the Canada boundary during the Fenian raid in 1870. June 10, 1872, he was transferred to the Corps of Engineers, and promoted to first lieutenant; promoted to captain January 10, 1884.

Since his transfer to the Corps of Engineers, he has served with the Engineer Battalion, has been instructor of military engineering and mathematics, and assistant professor of ethics and law at the U. S. Military Academy; assistant engineer on Western explorations, under Captain George M. Wheeler, for three years in California, Arizona, Nevada, and Colorado; engineer in charge of river and harbor improvements in Tennessee, Mississippi, Arkansas, Louisiana, and Texas.

In command of Company C, Battalion of Engineers, and instructor of civil engineering U. S. Engineer School, located at Willett's Point, New York; was ordered to Johnstown, Pennsylvania, a week after the great flood, in charge of a detachment and bridge-train, and ordered to replace by pontoon-bridges those swept away by the flood; since November 13, 1891, stationed at Baltimore, Maryland, as engineer of Fifth and Sixth Light-House Districts.

## MAJOR AND BREVET COLONEL REUBEN F. BERNARD.

MAJOR AND BREVET COLONEL REUBEN F. BERNARD, Eighth Cavalry, was a private, farrier, corporal, sergeant, and first sergeant in the army from February 19, 1855, to January 5, 1862; then acting second lieutenant of the First Cavalry to July 17, 1862, when he was appointed a second lieutenant of that regiment. He served on the Pacific coast and in New Mexico before the war of the Rebellion, and participated in the following fights with Indians: On the head-waters of the Gila River, New Mexico, March 28, 1856; on the Mimbres River, New Mexico, April 5, 1856; in Pinal Mountains, Arizona Territory, December 25, 1858; on San Carlos River December 27, 1858; on San Pedro River, Arizona Territory, November 9, 1859; near Fort Buchanan, Arizona Territory, January 20, 1860; on San Carlos River, Arizona Territory, January 21, 1861; skirmish with rebel Texans near Fort Craig, New Mexico, February 19, 1862; battle of Valverde, New Mexico, February 21, 1862; fight with Indians in the mountains near Socorro, New Mexico, February 26, 1862; skirmish with rebels at Apache Cañon, New Mexico, March 28, 1862; battle of Pigeon's Ranch, New Mexico, March 30, 1862; skirmish at Albuquerque, New Mexico, April 25, 1862; skirmish at Peralto, New Mexico, April 27, 1862.

He was promoted to be first lieutenant June 23, 1863, and transferred to duty in the field with the Army of the Potomac, and participated in the following engagements:

Skirmishes near Culpeper Court-House, Virginia; Stevensburgh, Virginia; Mine Run, Virginia; Barnet Ford, Virginia; near Charlottesville, Virginia; on Rapidan River, Virginia; battle of Todd's Tavern, Virginia (wounded); battle of Spottsylvania Court-House, Virginia; skirmishes on road to Beaver Dam, Virginia; at Beaver Dam, Virginia; on road to Yellow Tavern, Virginia; battle of Yellow Tavern, Virginia; skirmishes at Meadow Bridge, Virginia; after passing Meadow Bridge, Virginia; at Tunstall's Station, Virginia; while crossing Mattapony River; battles of Hawes' Shop, Virginia; Old Church, Virginia; Cold Harbor, Virginia; skirmish at Chickahominy River, Virginia; battle of Trevilian Station, Virginia; skirmishes at White House Landing, Virginia; at Chickahominy River, Virginia; battles of Deep Bottom, Virginia; Darby's Farm, Virginia; skirmishes at Barnesville, Virginia; Stone Church, Virginia; New Town, Virginia; near Winchester, Virginia; near Front Royal, Virginia; Shepherdstown, Virginia; engagements at Smithfield, Virginia; skirmishes near Halltown, Virginia; Barnesville, Virginia; Opequan Creek, Virginia; battle at Winchester; skirmish at Cedarville; battle of Luray Valley, Virginia; skirmishes near Front Royal, Virginia; in Luray Valley, Virginia; near Staunton, Virginia; engagement at Waynesborough, Virginia; skirmishes at Rapidan River, Virginia; Warrenton, Virginia; Snicker's Gap, Virginia; Bunker Hill, Virginia; near Mount Jackson, Virginia; engagement at Waynesborough, Virginia; skirmish at South Anna Bridge, Virginia; engagement at White House Landing, Virginia; skirmish on Chickahominy River, Virginia; engagement at Dinwiddie Court-House, Virginia; skirmish at White Oak Road, Virginia; engagement near Dinwiddie Court-House, Virginia; battle of Five Forks, Virginia; engagement at Scott's Cross-Roads, Virginia; skirmish at Drummond's Mills, Virginia; battle of Sailor's Creek, Virginia; skirmish near Sailor's Creek, Virginia; skirmish at night near Appomattox Court-House, Virginia; engagement of Appomattox Court-House.

Colonel Bernard was brevetted captain May 6, 1864, for gallant and meritorious services in the battle of Todd's Tavern, Virginia; major August 28, 1864, for gallant and meritorious services in action at Smithfield, Virginia; lieutenant-colonel and colonel March 13, 1865, for gallant and meritorious services during the war.

He was promoted to the captaincy of Company G, First U. S. Cavalry, July 28, 1866, at which date he was serving with his company on the plains against the Indians, participating in nineteen fights, from 1866 to 1881, in Arizona, California, and Oregon. He thus has to his credit one hundred and three battles and skirmishes. He was recommended by General Ord for the brevet of brigadier-general, for gallantry in action with the Chiricahua Indians, October 20, 1869. On the 7th of Feb. 1886, marched Companies D and E, Sixteenth Infantry, from Fort McIntosh, Texas, to the city of Laredo, Texas, for the purpose of suppressing a local political riot that had been going on for several hours; some twenty odd persons having been killed, he took charge of the city, disarmed both parties, kept charge of the city for the night, restoring order. He was promoted major of the Eighth Cavalry November 1, 1882.

COLONEL CLERMONT L. BEST (RETIRED).

COLONEL CLERMONT L. BEST was born in New York, and graduated from the Military Academy in the class of 1847. He was appointed a brevet second lieutenant of the First U. S. Artillery, and served in the war with Mexico, during which time he received his appointment as second lieutenant, Fourth Artillery. On duty at Fort Monroe, Baton Rouge, Louisiana, and Jefferson Barracks, Missouri, in 1848–49, and was then engaged in Florida, in hostilities against the Seminole Indians, during the year 1850.

He was at this time promoted first lieutenant and ordered to Fort Hamilton, and served at that post and Fort Mifflin, Pennsylvania, from 1850 to 1853, when he was placed on frontier duty at Ringgold Barracks, Texas, serving there and at Fort Brown and Las Animas, Texas, to 1855. He was granted leave of absence at this time, and rejoined his command in 1856 in Florida, where he was engaged in hostilities against the Seminole Indians to 1857.

Lieutenant Best was again ordered on frontier duty, and engaged in quelling Kansas disturbances during the years 1857–58. He participated in the Utah expedition in 1858, and was on duty escorting recruits from New York to Kansas in 1859. He then served at Fort Randall, Dakota, to 1861.

In April, 1861, at the breaking out of the war of the Rebellion, he was promoted captain of his regiment, and ordered to the field in command of a battery in Major-General Banks's operations in Maryland and the Shenandoah Valley, Virginia, to August, 1862, then participated in the Northern Virginia campaign as chief of artillery of the Fifth Army Corps, being engaged in the battle of Cedar Mountain, August 9, 1862; in the Maryland campaign, Army of the Potomac, and engaged in the battle of Antietam, Maryland, September 17, 1862.

He was on the march to Falmouth, Virginia, during the fall of the same year, and subsequently participated in the Rappahannock campaign, being engaged in the battle of Chancellorsville, Virginia, May 2, 3, 1863, for which he was brevetted a major for gallant and meritorious services in said battle.

Captain Best was detailed as assistant inspector-general, Twelfth Army Corps, Army of the Potomac, May 16, 1863, which position he held to April 4, 1864, and during that time was engaged in the battle of Gettysburg, July 1–3, 1863, for which he received the brevet of lieutenant-colonel for gallant and meritorious services. He was then placed in command of the First Division of Artillery Reserve, Department of the Cumberland, from April to October, 1864, when he was detailed as instructor of artillery at Camp Barry, Washington, D. C., to February, 1865.

At the close of the war, Captain Best was brevetted a colonel for good conduct and gallant services during the Rebellion. He was placed on recruiting service at Philadelphia in February, 1865, where he remained to September, 1866, when he was ordered to garrison duty in the defences of Washington, remaining there to March, 1867.

Colonel Best was promoted major of the First Artillery February 5, 1867; lieutenant-colonel of the same regiment March 15, 1881, but subsequently transferred to the Fourth Artillery (October 27, 1881); and colonel of the Fourth Artillery October 2, 1883, from which he was retired from active service, by operation of law, April 25, 1888.

During the time that Colonel Best was a field-officer, he served at many of the artillery posts in different parts of the country, being commanding officer of most of them.

## COLONEL AND BREVET BRIGADIER-GENERAL JUDSON D. BINGHAM.

COLONEL AND BREVET BRIGADIER-GENERAL JUDSON D. BINGHAM (Quartermaster's Department) was born in New York May 16, 1831, and graduated from the Military Academy July 1, 1854. He was promoted second lieutenant of the Second Artillery same day, and served as assistant instructor of artillery tactics at the Military Academy from that time until the following August, and was then stationed at Fort Wood, New York harbor, and Barrancas, Florida, until March, 1856, when he was promoted first lieutenant and was placed on U. S. Coast Survey service to June, 1857. He was at the Artillery School of Practice at Fort Monroe from that time to 1861, in the mean time participating in an expedition to Harper's Ferry, Virginia, to suppress the John Brown raid of 1859.

Lieutenant Bingham was also engaged in an expedition from Fort Ridgely, Minnesota, to the Yellow Medicine, Minnesota, in the summer of 1860, and remained at that station until the opening of the Civil War in April, 1861, when he was transferred to Fort McHenry, Maryland. He was appointed a captain in the Quartermaster's Department May 13, 1861, and served in General Banks's command, in charge of trains and supplies, in the field in Maryland until February, 1862, when he was placed in charge of the quartermaster's depot at Nashville, Tennessee, and while there was appointed lieutenant-colonel of volunteers January 1, 1863.

He served as chief quartermaster of the Seventeenth Army Corps (lieutenant-colonel ex officio) to April 23, 1863, when General Grant appointed him chief quartermaster of the Department and Army of the Tennessee. He continued on duty, in the field, as chief quartermaster of that army up to the end of the siege of Atlanta, Georgia, August 25, 1864; was present as chief quartermaster of the Seventeenth Army Corps at Lake Providence and Milliken's Bend, Louisiana, at the siege of Vicksburg, Mississippi, at the surrender of the city, and during its occupation, to October, 1863; at Memphis, Tennessee, and at Bridgeport and Scottsborough, Alabama, until last of December, 1863; he joined General Sherman at Cairo, Illinois, January 1, 1864, and under his direction arranged for transporting troops from Memphis to Vicksburg for the expedition to Meridian, Mississippi; then as chief quartermaster of the Army of the Tennessee accompanied General Sherman on the march with the Sixteenth and Seventeenth Army Corps from Vicksburg to Meridian and return, February and March, 1864; was present as chief quartermaster at head-quarters, Army of the Tennessee, Huntsville, Alabama, and in the invasion of Georgia, including siege of Atlanta, 1864.

Colonel Bingham was appointed colonel of volunteers August 2, 1864, and was appointed inspector of the Quartermaster's Department (colonel ex officio), serving as such to December 31, 1866, being on duty in the quartermaster-general's office, Washington, D. C., at various times from September, 1864, to December, 1865; on duty with General Sherman at St. Louis, Missouri, as inspector of the Quartermaster's Department, to January, 1867; chief quartermaster, Department of the Lakes, at Detroit, Michigan, to March 31, 1870; in the spring of 1869 he made inspections at Forts Richardson, Griffin, Concho, Stockton, Davis, McKavett, and San Antonio, Texas.

He was promoted major in the Quartermaster's Department, U. S. Army, July 29, 1866, and lieutenant-colonel and deputy quartermaster-general March 3, 1875, serving as assistant in the office of the quartermaster-general at Washington, D. C., from April 4, 1870, to October, 1870, and in charge of the Bureau from October 25, 1873, to January 19, 1874, and from January 28 to February 20, 1875; he served as commissioner to audit Kansas war accounts, under act of Congress, from March 8 to April 5, 1871; as chief quartermaster of the Department of the Missouri, Fort Leavenworth, Kansas, from October, 1879, to November, 1883; as chief quartermaster, Division of the Pacific and Department of California, from November, 1883, to about May 30, 1886; as chief quartermaster, Division of the Missouri, Chicago, Illinois, from June 4, 1886, to present time, having been, on the 2d of July, 1883, promoted colonel and assistant quartermaster-general.

When the war terminated, Colonel Bingham had the following brevets conferred upon him: major, lieutenant-colonel, and colonel March 13, 1865, "for faithful and meritorious services during the war;" brigadier-general April 9, 1865, "for faithful and meritorious services in the field during the war."

### COMMANDER JOSHUA BISHOP, U.S.N.

COMMANDER JOSHUA BISHOP was born in Missouri in 1839, and appointed acting midshipman from that State. He graduated at the Naval Academy in 1858, and after the usual sea-service—in the "Saratoga," "Wabash," "Powhatan," and "Pawnee"—was made lieutenant in 1861.

The troublous time at the inception of the Civil War found him at his home in Missouri. He used all his influence to prevent an appeal to arms, and declared himself for the Union without hesitation. Being summoned to duty at Philadelphia, he had great difficulty in leaving the State, from the determined opposition shown by his rebel neighbors, who had stopped the running of the trains, and who pursued the stage in which he travelled. When he reached Philadelphia he was at first under Du Pont, but was soon sent West again, under Commander John Rodgers, to assist in fitting out gunboats. He reported to General McClellan at Cincinnati, and was thenceforth employed in various ways—fitting gunboats, commanding the receiving-vessel, and purchasing supplies—until August, 1861, when he went to St. Louis, recruited a number of men, and in September took them to Cairo, Illinois, for the gunboats. Naval officers reported to general officers, and until July, 1862, were part of army. Colonel Grant went down with him, in the same boat, to take command at Cairo. After that time events of importance occurred in rapid succession. Lieutenant Bishop became executive officer under Walke, in Foote's squadron, in which capacity he was present at several gunboat engagements, and at the battle of Belmont, which was Grant's first battle of the Civil War. His next duty was as aid to Foote at St. Louis. Then he was sent with Eads, the engineer and contractor for the "Benton," to get her down to Cairo at a very low stage of water. In the "Benton," Lieutenant Bishop was in the actions at Columbus, Island No. 10, Fort Pillow, and Memphis. On the way down he captured a rebel steamer in sight of the retreating fleet and out of sight of the Union fleet.

At Memphis he boarded the "General Bragg," saved her from being blown up by a train which had been laid to her magazine, and caulked the shot-holes in her, so that she was preserved as a prize. As a reward for his gallantry he was assigned to the command of the vessel. He commanded the "General Bragg" when the rebel ram "Arkansas" ran down through the fleet, and in the subsequent operations until the fall of Vicksburg. His health having become bad, he then applied for relief. The thanks of Congress were given to the officers and men of the squadrons of Rear-Admirals Foote and Davis for their long series of actions, beginning with Forts Henry and Donelson, in almost all of which Commander Bishop took part.

Commander Bishop was upon the blockade for a short time, and was also stationed at the Naval Academy. He has made extensive cruises in foreign waters, serving in the "Wyoming," "Saranac," "Pensacola," "Benicia," "Plymouth," and "Galena." His last cruise was in command of the "Iroquois" among the South-Sea Islands.

He is at present assistant to the Superintendent of the U. S. Naval Observatory.

## COLONEL Z. R. BLISS.

COLONEL Z. R. BLISS was appointed a cadet at West Point in 1850. Graduated in 1854. Was appointed brevet second lieutenant Sixteenth Infantry, and ordered to Fort Duncan, Texas. Served at various forts in Texas until 1861, part of the time in command of a company. On April 5, 1861, he left Fort Quitman with his company and joined the command of Colonel Reeve, and marched with that command six hundred and fifty miles to San Antonio, Texas. On May 9, 1861, when they were about fifteen miles from San Antonio, they were met by a large force of over two thousand men, under rebel General Earl Van Dorn, consisting of a regiment of infantry, one of cavalry, a battery of six pieces of artillery, and an independent company of about one hundred men. When met by the rebels, Colonel Reeve's command had only about a dozen rounds of ammunition per man and one day's rations; an unconditional surrender was demanded, and, after some parley, Colonel Reeve surrendered his command; but as Lieutenant Bliss was only a junior first lieutenant, and was not consulted in the matter, he was not responsible for the surrender. He remained a prisoner of war for nearly a year, most of the time confined in the negro jail at Richmond. In May, 1862, he was appointed colonel of the Tenth Rhode Island Volunteers and served with it till August, when he was appointed colonel of the Seventh Rhode Island Volunteers, and remained with it until honorably mustered out after the close of the war. Commanded the regiment during the Fredericksburg campaign, and after the first battle of Fredericksburg was recommended for promotion to rank of brigadier-general, but, in consequence of his having been present at the surrender in Texas, this recommendation was not carried out. In fact, no officer who was present with Colonel Reeve at the surrender was promoted during the war, although several of them were strongly recommended for advancement. In 1863 Colonel Bliss was transferred with his regiment to Kentucky, and thence to Vicksburg and Jackson in the campaign after Johnson, and at the conclusion was recommended, this time by General Grant, for promotion. Commanded the District of Middle Tennessee during the winter of 1863-64. It was an important command, including a large fort and several regiments, and protecting about two million rations for Sherman's army. In 1864 Colonel Bliss was again recommended for promotion to rank of brigadier-general. Colonel Bliss remained in command of District of Middle Tennessee until the regiment he commanded was transferred to the East, and he was assigned to the command of First Brigade, Second Division, Ninth Army Corps, and commanded it in the Wilderness, where he

was brevetted for gallant and meritorious services. He was in command of the brigade to Spottsylvania, where he was injured by his horse jumping on him in crossing a stream at night. He commanded the brigade in the mine which was constructed by a regiment of his brigade, and at the explosion of the mine and ensuing battle, and received a very complimentary letter from his division commander, General R. B. Potter. He remained in command of the brigade until the early fall, when he was obliged to take a sick-leave. After being absent some weeks he was placed on light duty on a board of officers, as president, and remained on that duty till the close of the war in the following spring, when he was mustered out of the volunteer service. Transferred with his company to South Carolina in 1866, and given command of the district of Chester. He was acting assistant commissioner of the Bureau of Freedmen, and had charge of all the civil and military business of that district. In August was ordered on recruiting service, receiving the detail for having served longer in the field during the rebellion than any other officer in the regiment. In August, 1867, promoted major of Thirty-ninth Infantry. Commanded part of Jackson Barracks, Forts Jackson and St. Philip, till 1870, when he was transferred with his regiment to Texas, commanding various forts there, and for more than a year the regiment. In 1878 he was ordered to command the principal depot for general recruiting service. In 1880 was promoted lieutenant-colonel of Nineteenth Infantry. In 1886 was made colonel of Twenty-fourth Infantry, of which he still remains in command. This officer has served longer on the Southwestern frontier than any other officer ever in the service.

MEDICAL DIRECTOR DELAVAN BLOODGOOD, U.S.N.

MEDICAL DIRECTOR DELAVAN BLOODGOOD, U.S.N., was born in Erie County, New York, in 1831. Commissioned as assistant surgeon March, 1857. Passed assistant surgeon December, 1861. Surgeon January 24, 1862. Medical inspector February 3, 1875. Medical director August, 1884.

His first service was on board the "Merrimac," on the Pacific station, from 1857 to 1860. Then attached to the "Mohawk," on special service in the West Indies, to intercept slaving vessels. The "Mohawk" made several captures, and then (without the sanction of the administration) aided in preserving the forts at Key West and Tortugas when the stormy days of the inception of the great rebellion were at hand. When the first secessions occurred, the "Mohawk" convoyed from Texas the troops involved in the Twiggs surrender, and then went upon the first blockade established during the war, off Pensacola. In November, 1861, Dr. Bloodgood was detached from the "Mohawk," and, on the way north, by transport steamer, arrived off Port Royal at the time of the battle there, and was ordered to the transport "Atlantic," in charge of a detachment of the sick and wounded for conveyance to the hospital at New York. He was next assigned for duty on board the steam-sloop "Dakota," and served on board that vessel till near the close of the war. In her he participated in the various operations about Hampton Roads, from the first appearance of the rebel ram "Merrimac" until her destruction, and then co-operated with the army during the first Peninsula campaign. For a short time the ship was in the Gulf of Mexico and the Mississippi, under Farragut, and next cruised through the West Indies and off the coast of Nova Scotia, in search of privateers; but she was mostly in service on the blockade off the Carolinas, and in numerous engagements with coast batteries. During this service, of nearly three years, there occurred on board an epidemic of yellow fever, and another of small-pox, each of which necessitated a visit to a Northern port, and the disinfection of the ship. In returning from service in this vessel, in 1864, Dr. Bloodgood happened to be one of those captured and plundered by rebel raiders in the railroad train taken near Gunpowder River. After service on board the "Michigan," and the receiving-ship "Vermont," he joined the sloop-of-war "Jamestown," in February, 1867, at Panama, when an extremely virulent type of yellow fever was raging on board. In consequence, the ship was sent to Sitka for disinfection, and remained there until the following spring, when she was put out of commission at the Mare Island Yard. He then joined the "Lackawanna," on the Mexican coast, and after that cruise had shore duty at New York. In May, 1872, was ordered to the "Plymouth," of the European Squadron, and thence, via India, to the China station, where he served on board the flag-ships "Colorado," "Lackawanna," and "Hartford," as fleet-surgeon for two years. Then he was transferred to Pacific station as fleet-surgeon, but soon detached and ordered home to duty at New York. Was fleet-surgeon of the European station, in flag ship "Trenton," 1877-79. On his return was in charge of the Naval Hospital at New York, and then of the Naval Laboratory, and next had charge of the Naval Hospital at Norfolk, Virginia. In 1887 he was ordered to the Naval Laboratory at New York, in which position he still continues. Dr. Bloodgood is an alumnus of Madison University, Hamilton, New York, and of Jefferson Medical College, at Philadelphia; member of the Phi Beta Kappa; the Military Order of the Loyal Legion of the United States; the Holland Society; the St. Nicholas Society, of Nassau Island; the University Club, of New York; the St. Nicholas Club, of New York, and Hamilton Club, of Brooklyn.

## REAR-ADMIRAL CHARLES S. BOGGS.

REAR-ADMIRAL CHARLES S. BOGGS was born in New Jersey January 28, 1811; appointed midshipman from the same State November 1, 1826; attached to sloop-of-war "Warren," Mediterranean Squadron, 1829-32. Promoted to passed midshipman April 28, 1832; receiving-ship at New York, 1832-35; rendezvous, New York, 1836. Commissioned as lieutenant September 6, 1837; sloop "Saratoga," coast of Africa, 1840-43. Was an active participant in the burning of five villages on the coast; Home Squadron, 1846-47; present at the siege of Vera Cruz; commanded the boat expedition from the "Princeton" that destroyed the U. S. brig "Truxton," after her surrender to the Mexicans; receiving-ship at New York, 1848-51; navy-yard, New York, 1852-54; inspector, etc., New York, 1855. Commissioned as commander September 14, 1855; commanding mail-steamer "Illinois," 1856-58; light-house inspector, 1860-61; commanded sloop-of-war "Varuna," at the passage of Forts Jackson and St. Philip, April 24, 1862. The "Varuna" was the only one of Farragut's squadron lost at the battle of New Orleans. She was attacked by two of the rebel rams and badly damaged, and her commander, finding his vessel sinking, ran her into the bank and made fast to the trees. Captain Boggs fought his vessel gallantly to the last. Commissioned as captain July 16, 1862; commanding steam-sloop "Juniata," 1863; special duty, New York, 1864-66. Commissioned as commodore July 25, 1866; commanding steamer "De Soto," North Atlantic Squadron, 1867-68; special duty, 1869-72. Promoted to rear-admiral July, 1870. He died in 1877.

Always an excellent and most reliable officer, his conduct in command of the "Varuna" elicited the praise even of his adversaries. Being in the First Division at the passage of the Mississippi forts, and having a fast ship, he outstripped his consorts, and chased the enemy alone until he was surrounded by them. At first, in the darkness, the Confederates did not attack him, thinking him one of their own squadron. But Boggs soon apprised them of his identity by a rapid fire from both sides.

Three of the enemy were driven ashore in flames, and one large steamer, with troops on board, drifted ashore with an exploded boiler, the result of this encounter. At daylight the "Varuna" was attacked by two vessels at the same time, the "Governor Moore" and the "Stonewall Jackson." The "Moore" was a ram, commanded by an ex-officer of the navy, and they treated the "Varuna" very badly, penetrating her below water, and killing and wounding a number of her crew. But the "Varuna's" people stuck to their guns, and finally drove off the two, completely disabled for further conflict, besides being on fire. The details of this encounter (most exciting) cannot be given. Admiral Porter says, in his account of the fight, "This ended the irregular fighting with the Confederate vessels; ten of them had been sunk or destroyed, while the 'Varuna,' with her two adversaries, lay at the bottom of the river, near the bank, evidence of the gallantry of Boggs."

Admiral Boggs had the respect of all who knew him, whether in the service or out of it. He was perfectly modest and unostentatious in deportment, while dignified and officer-like at all times.

### CAPTAIN EDWARD C. BOWERS, U.S.N.

CAPTAIN EDWARD C. BOWERS was born in Connecticut. Before entering the navy he served in the merchant service and in the Peruvian and Greek navies. The nautical experience thus gained proved of great value to him in his subsequent career as an officer of the U. S. Navy. Appointed from Connecticut to the grade of midshipman February 2, 1829. His first cruise was on the sloop-of-war "St. Louis," attached to the Pacific Squadron, 1829-31; served on schooner "Dolphin," Pacific Squadron, as acting lieutenant, 1832. He was then ordered to Navy-Yard, Boston, where he served during the years 1833-34. Promoted to passed midshipman July 3, 1835; was attached to frigate "Constellation," West Indies Squadron, 1836-38. His next cruise was on the flag-ship "Ohio," Mediterranean Squadron, in 1839; attached to receiving-ship "Boston," 1840. Commissioned as lieutenant April 26, 1841; receiving-ship, Boston, 1842-45. He was then ordered to the steamer "Princeton," and cruised on her in the Gulf of Mexico, 1846; transferred to ordnance transport "Electra," 1847; and from her again transferred, this time to sloop-of-war "Decatur," on which vessel he made a full cruise on the coast of Africa during the years 1847-50; at the expiration of his cruise on the "Decatur," he was at once ordered to the sloop "Plymouth," and went in her to the East Indies, where he served during the years 1851-52; receiving-ship, New York, 1852-54; retired, 1855. It will be seen from the foregoing statement of services that Captain Bowers, from the date of his original entry into the service, February 2, 1829, up to the time of his retirement in 1855, was almost constantly employed at sea, and in fact few officers of his date had so good a record of active and continuous service afloat. Rendezvous, Portsmouth, New Hampshire, 1861-63. Commissioned as commander July 21, 1861; commanding receiving-ship "Vandalia," Portsmouth, New Hampshire, 1864-65. Commissioned as captain 1867.

Captain Bowers was retired (in conformity with the Act of February 28, 1855, and its amendments, January 16, 1857, March 10, 1858, and May 11, 1858) on the 13th September, 1855, as stated above, but was on duty at Portsmouth, New Hampshire, during the Civil War.

Captain Bowers served in the Mexican and Seminole wars, and also under Commodores Hull, Bainbridge, Stewart, Perry, and Chauncey.

## COLONEL ALBERT GALLATIN BRACKETT (RETIRED).

COLONEL ALBERT GALLATIN BRACKETT was born in Otsego County, New York, on the 14th day of February, 1829. In 1846 he removed to Indiana, and in June, 1847, became second lieutenant in the Fourth Indiana Volunteers in the Mexican War, and was promoted first lieutenant during the same month. His regiment was attached to General Joseph Lane's brigade, and participated in the skirmishes at Paso de Ovejas and La Hoya, the battle of Huamantla, the siege of Puebla, and the bombardment of Atlixco in September and October, 1847. He served until the close of the war and was honorably discharged on the 16th of July, 1848.

On the 3d of March, 1855, he was appointed captain from Indiana, in the Second Regiment of Cavalry, and after raising a company in Indiana and Illinois, was sent to Texas to fight the Indians, who were then very troublesome. He met and defeated the Lipans on Guadalupe River in March, 1856, recapturing much valuable property; the Comanches at Arroyo de las Encinas February 1, 1857, and near Presidio de San Vincente, Chihuahua, May 2, 1859, for which he received the thanks of General Scott, commanding the army. He was engaged in suppressing the Cortinas troubles near Brownsville, and along the Rio Grande frontier in 1860.

When the Civil War broke out he went with his company to Key West, Florida, and thence to Havana, Cuba, and from there to New York and Carlisle Barracks, where he refitted and was sent to Washington, taking part in the battles of Blackburn's Ford and Bull Run in July, 1861. He became colonel of the Ninth Regiment of Illinois Cavalry in October, 1861, and participated in the actions at the Waddell Farm, Stewart's Plantation, and Cache Bayou, Arkansas, in June, 1862, being severely wounded at Stewart's Plantation, where he saved a valuable train from falling into the hands of the Confederates. He was promoted major in the First Cavalry on the 17th of July, 1862, and served as chief of cavalry, Department of Missouri, in 1862-63.

He was placed in command of the Second Brigade of the Cavalry Division, Sixteenth Army Corps (Army of the Tennessee), in West Tennessee in January and February, 1864, and was engaged in defending the Memphis and Charleston Railroad. As acting inspector-general of cavalry, he participated in the siege of Atlanta, Georgia, battle of Ezra Church, Georgia, and back to Nashville with General Thomas, taking part in the battle of Nashville, Tennessee, in December, 1864. Received the brevets of major, lieutenant-colonel, and colonel, for gallant and meritorious services during the war.

Commanded several posts in the Departments of California and Columbia, and the Districts of Nevada and

Summit Lake, assisting materially in quelling the hostile Pi Ute Indian disturbances in 1866-67 and 1868.

Went from Fort McPherson with four troops of the regiment to Montana in May, June, and July, 1869. Held a council with the Crow Indians and distributed goods to them on the Yellowstone River in December, 1869. While in command of Fort Steele he quieted disturbances among coal-miners at Carbon. Sent to Fort Sanders in Wyoming, and from there in 1877, with six more troops of the Second Cavalry, to Fort Custer, which post he helped to construct. He was promoted colonel of the Third Cavalry.

In the field operating against the Ute Indians, who had massacred Thornburg's command, a portion of which belonged to his regiment, from October to December, 1879. In command of Fort Laramie and of Fort Russell, Wyoming, from July, 1879, to May, 1882, when he was sent to Arizona with his regiment to operate against the hostile Apaches. Met the head men of the Apaches in council at Fort Thomas, Arizona, in May, 1882, when they made their grievances known. Was in command of field operations against the Apaches in July and August, 1882.

Superintendent Mounted Recruiting Service at Jefferson Barracks, Missouri, from October 1, 1882, to October 1, 1884. In command of his regiment at Whipple Barracks, Arizona, from 1884 to March, 1885, when he marched the Third Cavalry through Arizona, New Mexico, and a part of Chihuahua, Mexico, to Fort Davis, Texas, and in command of that post from May 12 to October 24, 1887, when he took command of Fort Clark, Texas, and remained there until January 9, 1890, when he marched to Fort McIntosh. Was retired February 18, 1891. Colonel Brackett is the author of "Lane's Brigade in Central Mexico," and "History of U. S. Cavalry."

## REAR-ADMIRAL D. L. BRAINE.

Rear-Admiral D. L. Braine was born in New York. Appointed midshipman from Texas, May 30, 1846. Served during the Mexican War in the Home Squadron, and present at capture of Alvarado, Tabasco, Tuspan, Laguna, Tampico, and Vera Cruz. In 1848 he was attached to the sloop-of-war "John Adams," of the Home Squadron. During 1849-50 served in the sloop-of-war "St. Mary's," of the East India Squadron. In 1850-51 in the steam sloop "Saranac," of Home Squadron. At the Naval Academy in 1852.

Promoted to passed midshipman June 8, 1852, and ordered to the sloop-of-war "St. Louis," of the Mediterranean Squadron, where he remained from 1853 to 1855. In 1855 he was promoted to the rank of master. Commissioned as lieutenant September 15, 1858. During 1856 and 1857 he had been employed upon the Coast Survey. During the period between 1858 and 1860 he served on the coast of Africa in the sloop-of-war "Vincennes."

When the Civil War occurred he was ordered to command the "Monticello," of the North Atlantic Blockading Squadron. Had an engagement with the rebel battery at Sewell's Point, Virginia, May 19, 1861, which lasted for more than an hour, and was the first naval engagement of the war. Present at the attack and capture of Forts Hatteras and Clark, August, 1861, and October 5, 1861. Lieutenant Braine engaged the enemy at Kinnekeck Woods, above Cape Hatteras, and, after exchanging shots with their gun-boats, dispersed two regiments of infantry, sank two barges, and rescued the Twentieth Indiana Regiment, which was surrounded. In November, 1861, Lieutenant Braine engaged and silenced a two-gun battery at Federal Point, North Carolina, and dismounted one of the guns. It must be remembered that his vessel was a purchased one.

Commissioned as lieutenant-commander July 15, 1862. During 1862-64 numerous engagements with Forts Fisher and Caswell. Besides the "Monticello," during this period, was in command of the "Vicksburg" and "Pequot." Commanded the "Pequot" during the attacks upon Fort Fisher, also at Fort Anderson, and at three other forts on the Cape Fear River, as the fleet advanced to Wilmington, North Carolina. Lieutenant-Commander Braine was on ordnance duty at the navy-yard at New York in 1866-67. Was commissioned commander July 25, 1866, and commanded the steamer "Shamokin," of the Brazil Squadron, during 1868. Was on equipment duty at the New York Navy-Yard, 1869-72. Commanded "Juniata," European station, 1874-75. Commissioned as captain December 11, 1874. Commanded receiving-ship "Colorado," 1875-78. Commanded "Powhatan," North Atlantic station, 1879-81. Member of Board of Inspection and Survey 1884-85. Promoted commodore March, 1885, and upon special duty at New York. Promoted rear-admiral September 4, 1887. Commanded the South Atlantic station 1886-88. After being again on special duty, Rear-Admiral Braine commanded the navy-yard at New York in 1889-91. He was retired by operation of law in 1891.

While Commander Braine was in the "Juniata," he went north to look for the "Polaris," and from this ship Lieutenant De Long went to Cape York (latitude, 76 north ) in the steam-cutter.

During the same commission, the "Juniata" received at Santiago de Cuba over one hundred of the "Virginius's" prisoners.

## COLONEL GEORGE M. BRAYTON.

COLONEL GEORGE M. BRAYTON was born in Massachusetts February 24, 1834; appointed from Ohio (civil life) as a first lieutenant Fifteenth Infantry May 14, 1861; promoted to captain January 3, 1863; transferred to Thirty-third Infantry September 21, 1866, and again transferred to Eighth Infantry May 3, 1869; commissioned major Fifteenth Infantry February 6, 1882; lieutenant-colonel Ninth Infantry September 6, 1886, and colonel Ninth Infantry in 1892.

He was on recruiting duty from July, 1861, to May, 1862; regimental quartermaster from May, 1862, to January, 1863, from whence he was ordered as mustering and disbursing officer at Harrisburg, Pennsylvania. In October, 1863, he joined his regiment, which was then in the field at Chattanooga, Tennessee, and with it was engaged in the battle of Missionary Ridge and the action at Taylor's Bridge, Georgia. For gallant and meritorious services at Missionary Ridge he was brevetted major U. S. A. He again acted as mustering and disbursing officer at Louisville, Kentucky, in October, 1864, and from December, 1864, to May, 1865, he was commanding Third Battalion, Fifteenth Infantry; provost-marshal District of Etowah from January to July, 1865; assistant inspector-general Department of Georgia from August to December, 1865. He was with his regiment from January to May, 1866. From May to July, 1866, he commanded Batteries Gladden and McIntosh, Mobile Bay, and from July, 1866, to January, 1867, he commanded Fort Morgan, Alabama. On being transferred to the Thirty-third Infantry he joined company at Macon,

Georgia, from whence he did service to Atlanta, and post at Augusta; in Montgomery, Alabama; Huntsville, Alabama; Selma, Alabama; Fort Macon, North Carolina; Columbia and Newbury, South Carolina. In October, 1870, he was ordered north to David's Island, New York harbor, and remained there until he was transferred West to Fort Rice, Dakota. From August to October, 1872, Colonel Brayton was on Yellowstone Expedition to escort surveying party of the Northern Pacific Railroad from Fort Rice west to Yellowstone River, Montana, and return. After completion of this he was ordered to Fort Russell, Utah, and then to join his regiment in Department of Arizona.

## LIEUTENANT-COLONEL AND BREVET BRIGADIER-GENERAL SAMUEL BRECK.

LIEUTENANT-COLONEL AND BREVET BRIGADIER-GENERAL SAMUEL BRECK (Adjutant-General's Department) was born at Middleborough, Plymouth County, Massachusetts, February 25, 1834 (eighth generation from Edward Breck, who came to Dorchester, Massachusetts, from Ashton, England, in 1635). He was graduated from the Military Academy July 1, 1855; promoted to brevet second lieutenant of artillery and second lieutenant, First Artillery, same day.

He served in the Florida hostilities against the Seminole Indians in 1855-56, and then was in garrison at Fort Moultrie, South Carolina, and Fort McHenry, Maryland, to 1859, when he was transferred to duty in the Southwest, and marched from Helena, Arkansas, to Fort Clark, Texas, during the same year. He then returned to duty at Fort Moultrie, South Carolina, where he remained until 1860, when he was detailed at the Military Academy as assistant professor of geography, history, and ethics to April 26, 1861, and then became principal assistant professor of geography, history, and ethics, which position he occupied to December 3, 1861, in the mean time having again been promoted first lieutenant, First Artillery, April 11, 1861, which grade he held to February 20, 1862. He was appointed captain and assistant adjutant-general November 29, 1861, and served in the war of the Rebellion from 1861 to 1866, being assistant adjutant-general of General McDowell's division (Army of the Potomac) in the defences of Washington, D. C., to March 24, 1862, when he took the field as assistant adjutant-general of the First Army Corps and of the Department of the Rappahannock, being engaged in the "occupation of Fredericksburg, Virginia," April 18, 1862, and in the "expedition to the Shenandoah Valley," to intercept the retreat of the rebel forces under General Jackson, May and June, 1862.

Captain Breck was appointed major and additional aide-de-camp May 23, 1862, and major and assistant adjutant-general July 17, 1862, and ordered to duty in the adjutant-general's office at Washington, D. C., where he remained until 1869, in charge of rolls, returns, books, blanks, and business pertaining to the enlisted men of the regular and volunteer forces, and of the records of discontinued commands and the preparation and publication of the "Volunteer Army Register."

At the close of the war he was made brevet lieutenant-colonel September 24, 1864, "for meritorious and faithful services during the Rebellion;" brevet colonel March 13, 1865, "for diligent, faithful, and meritorious services in the Adjutant-General's Department during the Rebellion;" brevet brigadier-general, U.S.A., March 13, 1865, "for diligent, faithful, and meritorious services in the Adjutant-General's Department during the Rebellion."

Since 1870 General Breck has had extended service throughout the country, his posts of duty having been in California, New York, Washington, D. C., Minnesota, Nebraska, and again at Washington, D. C., where he is now on duty.

He was appointed lieutenant-colonel and assistant adjutant-general February 28, 1887.

## BRIGADIER-GENERAL JOSEPH CABELL BRECKINRIDGE, INSPECTOR-GENERAL, U.S.A.

BRIGADIER-GENERAL JOSEPH CABELL BRECKINRIDGE was born at Baltimore January 14, 1842. The son of the eminent theologian, Robert Jefferson Breckinridge, and grandson of Senator John Breckinridge, attorney-general under Jefferson, he is, through his mother, descended from General Francis Preston and General William Campbell, "the hero of King's Mountain." Educated at the University of Virginia, he abandoned the study of law to join General Nelson, and August 26, 1861, became acting assistant adjutant-general of his force. General George H. Thomas, succeeding to the command, appointed him an aide-de-camp. He was present at the repulse and overthrow of Zollicoffer at Mill Spring, Kentucky, receiving mention from Thomas, and the campaign through Nashville to Shiloh. At Corinth he received, as a reward of gallantry at Mill Spring, a commission in Battery B, Second (regular) Artillery, dated April 14, 1862. With his battery he was at Forts Pickens and Barrancas, and Pensacola, and joined the Army of the Tennessee before Atlanta. When McPherson was killed, July 22, 1864, he was captured and sent to Charleston to be exposed to the fire of Union guns. Exchanged in a special cartel, he reached home broken in health, and served as mustering officer till the close of the war. He was brevetted captain July 26, 1864, and major March 13, 1865, "for gallant and meritorious conduct in front of Atlanta," and "during the war."

After the war he went with his regiment from Fort McHenry to California via the Isthmus of Panama. In 1870 he became adjutant of the Artillery School at Fort Monroe. Promoted to a captaincy June 17, 1874, he was assigned to the command of Fort Foote, and in 1877 of the artillery troops at Washington Arsenal. Promoted in 1881 major and assistant inspector-general, and ordered to the Pacific coast, where he served successively on the staffs of Generals McDowell, Schofield, and Pope, until 1885, when he was transferred to the Military Division of the Missouri, on the staffs of Generals Schofield and Terry. During the summer of 1884 he received leave for a year, which he spent in foreign travel and in the study of the armies of Europe. He was successively promoted to be lieutenant-colonel and colonel, and in 1889 inspector-general of the army, with the rank of brigadier-general.

Since he was senior inspector-general of the army an unusual number of changes have occurred, requiring great and exacting labor from him and improving the efficiency of the army. Thus, G. O. No. 30, A. G. O. 1889, forbids unnecessary military performance and inspection on Sunday; the Army Regulations of 1889 improve the post schools; G. O. No. 15, 1890, improve the instruction in colleges where officers of the army are detailed; a regular officer was named in 1891, for the first time, to inspect and instruct the militia camp of every State in the Union; all inspections were applied equally to every branch of the service; G. O. No. 11, A. G. O. 1891, reduced the delay in receiving post-inspection reports about one-half, and gave increased promptness and thoroughness to remedial action; every effort is being made to get younger and better men, and horses, and rations, and establish gymnasiums, riding-halls, and soldiers' institutes; and all unnecessary restrictions upon the legal rights of enlisted men have been removed, and the number of articles kept for sale at army posts has been doubled; the allowance of baggage has been increased, and an increased allowance of quarters has been recommended.

In personal appearance General Breckinridge is a typical Kentuckian, and well sustains the standard of the Inspector-General's Department for soldierly bearing; he is six feet in height, of athletic build and striking presence, possessing the conversational powers for which his family are justly famous, and his flow of wit and anecdote is unfailing.

## CAPTAIN KIDDER RANDOLPH BREESE, U.S.N.

CAPTAIN KIDDER RANDOLPH BREESE, U.S.N., was born in Philadelphia. Appointed midshipman November 6, 1846, from Rhode Island; February, 1847, was ordered to the "Saratoga," Commander Farragut, and served in her on the Mexican coast during the war. In the spring of 1848 ordered to the frigate "Brandywine;" served in the "Brandywine" until the expiration of her cruise, December, 1850. February, 1851, joined the frigate "St. Lawrence," then loading at New York with articles for the World's Fair, at London, and made that cruise in her, returning in September, 1851. Passed midshipman June, 1852, and was ordered to the "Mississippi," flagship of Commodore M. C. Perry, commanding Japan Expedition. On the return of the "Mississippi" to the United States, in June, 1855, was detached and granted leave. In July was ordered on Coast Survey duty, and was engaged on that work until August, 1858. Was then ordered to the "Preble," on the Paraguay Expedition, serving in that expedition and afterwards on the Mosquito coast, off Greytown, until September, 1859, when he was invalided home with Isthmus fever. December, 1860, was ordered to the "Portsmouth," on the coast of Africa. Served on board the "Portsmouth" until August, 1860, when he joined the "San Jacinto." Remained on board the "San Jacinto" until the expiration of her cruise, December, 1861, during which upward of fifteen hundred slaves were captured on the coast of Africa, and Messrs. Slidell and Mason were taken from the "Trent." December, 1861, was ordered to the command of the Third Division of Porter's Mortar Flotilla, and participated in the attack on New Orleans and Vicksburg, in 1862. Was recommended for promotion by Captain Porter for services at this time. July, 1862, was made lieutenant-commander upon the establishment of that grade. October, 1862, joined Admiral Porter in the Mississippi Squadron, and took command of his flag-ship, the "Black Hawk." Served in that capacity during Admiral Porter's command, and was present or connected with all the most important operations on the Mississippi River and its tributaries during that officer's command. At the close of the Red River Expedition was recommended, with certain other commanding officers, for promotion to commander. On Admiral Porter being ordered, in September, 1864, to command the North Atlantic Blockading Squadron, was selected by him as his fleet-captain, and served in that capacity until May, 1865, when hostilities ceased. As fleet-captain was in both engagements at Fort Fisher, and in the subsequent operations in Cape Fear River. Commanded the sailors and marines in the naval assault on Fort Fisher, and was recommended by Admiral Porter for immediate promotion for services on that occasion. August, 1865, was ordered to the Naval Academy, and served there until September, 1866, as assistant to the superintendent, Admiral Porter. June, 1867, to the Washington Navy-Yard, as inspector of ordnance. July, 1869, was detached from the navy-yard. June 29, 1870, ordered to the command of the "Plymouth," European Squadron. Detached from "Plymouth" in October, 1872. December, 1872, ordered to duty in the Bureau of Ordnance, Navy Department, and in June, 1873, to the Naval Academy, as commandant of midshipmen. Commissioned as captain August 9, 1874, and in November, 1874, was, at his own request, detached from the Naval Academy. In January, 1875, ordered to report to the superintendent of the Coast Survey for duty as hydrographic inspector, and in June, 1875, was detached and ordered to the command of Torpedo station, Newport, Rhode Island, where he served until 1879. Commanding "Pensacola," Pacific station, 1879–80. Died September 15, 1881.

## CAPTAIN HENRY F. BREWERTON.

CAPTAIN HENRY F. BREWERTON (Fifth Artillery) was born in New York June 30, 1838, and entered the military service from civil life, having been appointed second lieutenant of the Fifth U. S. Artillery May 14, 1861. He was assigned to Light Battery K, and was at the Light-Artillery School of Instruction at Camp Cameron, Pennsylvania, and with the Artillery Reserve of the Army of the Potomac until January, 1862, when he was made signal officer of the Artillery Brigade, and served in that capacity to March, 1862, at which time he was promoted first lieutenant. He was then detailed on recruiting service, and on mustering and disbursing duty, and assistant commissary of musters of the Department of the Susquehanna to July, 1864. Joining Light Battery B, Fifth Artillery, at Cumberland, Maryland, he served with it to October, 1866.

Captain Brewerton participated in the Peninsula campaign from Manassas (including siege of Yorktown, Williamsburg to Chickahominy), and in command of section of light artillery protecting passage of troops during battles of Fair Oaks and Seven Pines, and during battles of seven days (Gaines' Mill, Mechanicsville, and Malvern Hill) with Horse Battery C, Third Artillery, under General Stoneman. He commanded a section covering the retreat of the army with General Averell; he commanded a section of Horse Battery C, Third Artillery, at White Oak Swamp and White Oak Swamp Bridge; he was with General Sheridan in the Shenandoah campaign and commanded Light Battery B, Fifth Artillery, but was captured October 19, 1864, and prisoner of war in Libby Prison, Virginia, from October, 1864, to April, 1865, exchanged. At the termination of the war he received the brevet of captain, to date from October 19, 1864, "for gallant and meritorious services in the battle of Cedar Creek, Virginia," and was promoted captain September 18, 1868.

He served from 1866 to 1873 at Fort Monroe, Virginia; Camp Williams, Richmond, Va.; Fort Jefferson, Dry Tortugas, Fla.; Fort Preble, Maine; and St. Albans, New York, during the Fenian raid, and was on special duty at Newport, Rhode Island, under the orders of the major-general commanding the division, and was transferred, in 1873, to the light battery of the regiment at Fort Adams, Rhode Island. His station was changed in February, 1875, to Charleston, South Carolina, and in 1877 was detailed to proceed to Louisville, Kentucky, to purchase horses for light-artillery service. This kept him until July, 1878, when he was ordered to Atlanta, Georgia. In July, 1881, Captain Brewerton was detailed as a member of the Light-Artillery Board at Washington, D.C., which duty was completed in September of the same year, when he rejoined his battery at McPherson Barracks, Atlanta. On December 6, 1881, he was ordered to Fort Hamilton, New York, in command of Light Battery F, from which he was relieved and transferred to Battery C, at Fort Monroe, Virginia, as instructor at the Artillery School, December 19, 1882. He was transferred at his own request from Battery C to Battery K, January 10, 1883, at Fort Schuyler, New York, and assumed command of the last-named battery eight days later.

Upon the transfer of the Fifth Artillery to the Pacific coast in 1889, Captain Brewerton was stationed at the Presidio of San Francisco, in command of Battery K, and was recorder of a Retiring Board at New York City in 1891. He was placed on special duty in the Department of the East in 1892, where he is now located.

While a lieutenant, he was acting regimental quartermaster in 1861; adjutant of the Artillery Reserve of the Army of the Potomac to January, 1862; battalion adjutant of the Fifth Artillery, acting assistant adjutant-general, and inspector-general at Fort Monroe from 1867 to 1869. He commanded the post at Fort Preble, Maine, in 1870, and a battalion of the Fifth Artillery at St. Albans, Vermont, during the Fenian raids, as well as McPherson Barracks, Georgia, from November 12 to December 6, 1881.

## COMMANDER JOHN J. BRICE.

COMMANDER JOHN J. BRICE entered the volunteer navy in August, 1861, at the commencement of the Civil War. His first orders were to the U. S. steamer "Freeborn," Potomac flotilla; afterwards commanded the schooner "Bailey," the captured steamer "Eureka," the "Primrose," and at the end of the war commanded the U. S. steamer "Don." He was twice promoted for gallant conduct, and transferred to the regular navy in 1868. He took part in the following engagements and expeditions:

Engagement with the Shipping Point batteries on the Potomac River in 1861; expedition upon Yorktown in 1862; attack upon the Acquia Creek batteries; engagement with rebel batteries at Belle Plains; landing expedition at Matthias's Point, Potomac River; cutting-out expedition, Piankatank River, Virginia, 1862; Gloucester batteries, Rappahannock River, 1862; Jones's Bluff batteries, Rappahannock River, 1864; boat expedition on the Rappahannock River in 1864; at the capture of Fredericksburg, Virginia, in 1862; cutting-out expedition on Maddox Creek, 1864; landing expedition, Maddox Creek, and engagements with guerillas in 1864; cutting-out expedition to Mill Point; engagements with Cockpit Point batteries in 1861; running the Potomac River batteries at night in November, 1861, and January, 1862; attack upon Smith Point batteries on the Potomac River in 1862; attack of rebel rams, James River, 1865; cutting-out expedition, Wicomico River, in 1863; with Grant's army during the battles of the Wilderness and Spottsylvania, protecting the submarine telegraph and the wounded.

He joined the U. S. steamer "De Soto" in 1865, and made a cruise in the West Indies. In 1867 he was ordered to the U. S. steam-sloop "Quinnebaug," and served in that vessel in the South Atlantic Squadron until 1870. He was stationed at the Hydrographic Office, in Washington, after his return, but in August of that year was ordered to the U. S. steamer "Saco," of the European Squadron,—being afterwards transferred to the "Franklin." In 1872 he was at the Torpedo School at Newport. In 1873 he was attached to the U. S. steamer "Richmond," of the Pacific fleet, and was transferred to the U. S. steamer "Saranac," being attached to that vessel when she was wrecked, at Vancouver, in June, 1875. During 1876 he was on duty at the Naval Observatory, in Washington, and, in 1878, was ordered to the navy-yard at Mare Island. After making a cruise in the "Lackawanna" in the Pacific, he again returned to duty at Mare Island, whence he was sent to the Isthmus of Panama, during the operations of the U. S. forces in keeping the transit open. In 1885 he was ordered to the "Iroquois," of the Pacific Squadron. In 1888 he took the course at the Naval War College at Newport; and in 1889 was stationed at the navy-yard, Washington. In 1890 he was ordered to duty upon the United States Fish Commission.

## PAYMASTER-GENERAL HORATIO BRIDGE, U.S.N.
### (RETIRED.)

PAYMASTER-GENERAL HORATIO BRIDGE, U.S.N. (retired), was born in Augusta, Maine, April 8, 1806. He was educated at Bowdoin College, and graduated in the class of 1825. He studied law at the Northampton Law School, and practised it at Augusta for a few years; then left the legal profession and entered the navy February 19, 1838, as purser.

May 3, 1838, he was ordered to the sloop-of-war "Cyane," and made a cruise of three years in the Mediterranean. December 7, 1843, he was ordered to the sloop-of-war "Saratoga," and made a cruise of two years on the west coast of Africa, on returning from which he published the "Journal of an African Cruiser."

April 1, 1845, he was ordered to the navy-yard at Portsmouth, New Hampshire.

April 9, 1846, he was ordered to the frigate "United States," the flag-ship of Commodore Read, and made a three years' cruise on the African and European stations.

July 17, 1849, he was ordered to the navy-yard, Portsmouth, New Hampshire.

November 6, 1851, he was ordered to the sloop-of-war "Portsmouth," of the Pacific Squadron, from which vessel he was detached December 3, 1853, and ordered home.

September 21, 1854, he was appointed chief of the Bureau of Provisions and Clothing.

April 8, 1868, he was transferred to the retired list, with the title of paymaster-general and relative rank of commodore.

April 8, 1869, he resigned as chief of bureau.

July 6, 1869, he was appointed chief inspector of provisions and clothing.

February 8, 1873, he was detached from duty, under the provision of law prohibiting the employment of navy officers on the retired list except in time of war.

Paymaster-General Bridge now resides at "The Moorings," Athens, Pennsylvania.

He is well known as an accomplished writer and most capable officer, who enjoyed the intimacy and confidence of the different Presidents and Secretaries under whom he served so long in his most responsible position.

### CAPTAIN HENRY R. BRINKERHOFF.

CAPTAIN HENRY R. BRINKERHOFF (Fifteenth Infantry) was born in Ohio October 9, 1836. He entered the volunteer service in the early days of the Rebellion, as first lieutenant of the Thirtieth Ohio Infantry, August 29, 1861, and participated in the Vicksburg campaign of 1863, being engaged in the siege, assaults, and capture of Vicksburg, Mississippi, June, and July of that year.

He was honorably mustered out of the Thirtieth Ohio Infantry July 26, 1863, in order to accept the lieutenant-colonelcy of the Fifty-second U. S. Colored Troops July 27, and with his regiment participated in the Maryland campaign of the Army of the Potomac, being engaged in the battles of South Mountain and Antietam, Maryland, September 15, 16, and 17, 1862, and in the actions of Coleman's Cross-Roads, Mississippi, in 1864.

He was in the Department of the South, with colored troops, from this time until 1866. He resigned, June 20, 1865, but was reappointed lieutenant-colonel of the Fifty-second U. S. Colored Infantry September 16, 1865, from which he was honorably mustered out May 3, 1866.

Colonel Brinkerhoff then entered the regular service, by receiving the appointment of second lieutenant of the Fifteenth U. S. Infantry, June 3, 1867, and served with his regiment in the Department of the South, in Texas, New Mexico, and Dakota, at various stations. He was promoted first lieutenant November 7, 1867, and captain September 18, 1878. Since joining his regiment he has participated in its movements, both by rail- and wagon-road, and is at present stationed at Fort Sheridan, Illinois.

## CAPTAIN AND BREVET LIEUTENANT-COLONEL HENRY B. BRISTOL. (RETIRED.)

CAPTAIN AND BREVET LIEUTENANT-COLONEL HENRY B. BRISTOL was born in Detroit, Michigan, April 25, 1838. He was appointed second lieutenant of the Fifth Infantry, May 15, 1857, from civil life. He participated in the expedition to Utah under Colonel Albert Sydney Johnson in 1857. He was at Fort Bridger in 1858, and Camp Floyd, Utah, in 1859. He was promoted first lieutenant May 13, 1861, and captain June 1, 1861. He served during the war of the Rebellion, and was employed in scouting on the Spanish trail to New Mexico, and then stationed at Fort Marcy, Albuquerque, and Fort Defiance, when he participated in the Navajo campaign, and scouting the San Juan country and Chasco Valley. Then he was at Forts Craig and Union. He was engaged with Confederates at Los Perios. He pursued the hostile Texans down the Rio Grande to Fort Sumner.

He was appointed military superintendent of Navajo Indians at Bosque Redondo Reservation, and was acting commissary of subsistence and agent until 1866.

Captain Bristol was brevetted March 13, 1865, as major, for "faithful and meritorious services in New Mexico;" and lieutenant-colonel for "faithful and meritorious services in New Mexico, and particularly for his untiring zeal and energy in controlling the Navajo tribe of Indians at the Bosque Redondo Reservation, and for his praiseworthy efforts in advancing their condition from that of savages to that of civilized men."

In 1866 Captain Bristol was detailed on recruiting service in New York harbor, and Detroit, Michigan, in 1867. He was then stationed at Bedloe's Island, and was employed in conducting recruits to San Francisco, and returned to Chicago on recruiting duty in 1868. He was at Fort Reynolds, California, in 1869; Forts Harker, Larned, and Dodge to 1871, and then was employed along the line of the Atchison, Topeka and Santa Fé Railway, west to the Colorado line, engaged in the Comanche campaign. He was also engaged in the Sioux campaign, and at Fort Keogh, Montana, from 1877 to date of retirement, March 20, 1879.

**BRIGADIER-GENERAL JOHN R. BROOKE.**

BRIGADIER-GENERAL JOHN R. BROOKE was born in Pennsylvania July 21, 1838. He entered the military service at the commencement of the war of the Rebellion as captain in the Fourth Pennsylvania Volunteer Infantry April 20, 1861, and was appointed colonel of the Fifty-third Pennsylvania Volunteers November 7, 1861, serving in the field with the Army of the Potomac, 1861–65; he was in command of his regiment in the campaign commencing March 10, 1862, from the defences of Washington to the Rappahannock River, Virginia; returning to Alexandria, Virginia, thence by transport ships to Ship Point, York River Bay; was in the campaign culminating in the Seven Days' Battles before Richmond, Virginia; he was in the second Bull Run and Antietam campaigns, August and September, 1862; in advance of reconnoissance from Harper's Ferry to Charlestown, Virginia, October, 1862; in Fredericksburg campaign to December, 1862; in Chancellorsville campaign, May, 1863; in Gettysburg campaign to July, 1863; in campaign (October, 1863) resulting in the effort of Lee to turn the right of the Army of the Potomac, during which occurred the combats at Auburn Mills and Bristoe Station; following this, late in November, was the Mine Run campaign, with several combats and skirmishes; in camp at Harrisburg, Pennsylvania, from December 29, 1863, to March 26, 1864; in the Wilderness campaign of 1864 to Cold Harbor, Virginia, when he was severely wounded and granted leave of absence to September 16, 1864. Colonel Brooke then received the commission of brigadier-general of volunteers " for distinguished services during the recent battles of the Old Wilderness and Spottsylvania Court-House, Virginia." During the war he participated in the siege of Yorktown, battles of Fair Oaks (wounded), second Bull Run, Antietam, Fredericksburg, Chancellorsville, Gettysburg (wounded); skirmishes at Bank's Ford of the Rappahannock and Thoroughfare Gap, Virginia, as well as a skirmish at Falling Water, where part of Lee's army crossed the Potomac, after Gettysburg; combats at Auburn Mills and Bristoe Station; several combats and skirmishes in the Mine Run campaign, November, 1863; battle in the Old Wilderness; combats on the Po River; successful assault of "Salient" at Spottsylvania Court-House, and again May 16, 1864, capturing on May 12 a large number of prisoners and many pieces of artillery; combats at North Anna and Tolopotomy; assault of enemy's works at Cold Harbor, at daylight on June 3, 1864, during which Colonel Brooke's command penetrated the works and he was severely wounded. Colonel Brooke exercised the command of a brigade on numerous occasions during the war while a colonel, and commanded a special detachment of five regiments of infantry, three regiments of cavalry, and two batteries of artillery, the advance of a reconnoissance commanded by General Hancock, from Harper's Ferry, Virginia, to Charlestown, Virginia, October, 1862; camp of veteran volunteers at Harrisburg, Pennsylvania, December 29, 1863, to March 26, 1864; on recovering from the wounds received at Cold Harbor, Colonel Brooke was detailed on special duty to March 11, 1865, at which time he joined his command in the Army of the Shenandoah, where he remained until August 10, 1865, when he was placed on court-martial duty to February 1, 1866, when he resigned from the service.

On the 28th of July, 1866, General Brooke was appointed lieutenant-colonel of the Thirty-seventh U. S. Infantry, and was made brevet colonel, U. S. A., March 2, 1867, " for gallant and meritorious services in the battle of Gettysburg, Pennsylvania;" brevet brigadier-general U. S. A., March 2, 1867, " for gallant and meritorious services in the battle of Spottsylvania Court-House, Virginia;" brevet major-general of volunteers August 1, 1864, " for gallant and meritorious services in the battles of Tolopotomy and Cold Harbor, Virginia." Proceeding to the plains, he served at various stations in the West until transferred to the Third U. S. Infantry March 15, 1869, whereupon he joined his regiment at Holly Springs, Mississippi, serving in the neighborhood of New Orleans until ordered with his regiment to Pennsylvania during the labor riots of 1877, upon the completion of which duty his regiment was transferred to Montana. He was promoted colonel of the Thirteenth Infantry March 20, 1879, but transferred to the Third Infantry the following June; then appointed brigadier-general U. S. A. April 6, 1888, and assigned to the command of the Department of the Platte, which command he now holds. General Brooke took active part and was present in the Sioux campaign of 1890–91, at Pine Ridge Agency, South Dakota.

## COLONEL AND BREVET BRIGADIER-GENERAL HORACE BROOKS (RETIRED).

COLONEL AND BREVET BRIGADIER-GENERAL HORACE BROOKS was born in Massachusetts, and was appointed to the Military Academy through the application of General Lafayette, from which he graduated July 1, 1835, and was assigned to the Second United States Artillery, passing through all the various grades of that arm of the service to that of colonel of the Fourth Artillery, August 1, 1863.

His first war experience was with the Indians in Florida, being engaged in the combat of "Withlacoochie" and action of "Oloklikaha," March 31, 1836, for which he was brevetted first lieutenant. He was then ordered to duty as assistant professor of mathematics at the Military Academy, where he remained until 1839. He was then on frontier, recruiting, and garrison duty until the breaking out of the Mexican War, when he was sent to Tampico (old Mexico) with the first troops that occupied it, and was ordered to the neck, or only road by land to the city, which he was ordered to hold at all hazards.

During the Mexican War he was engaged in the siege of Vera Cruz, battles of Cerro Gordo, Amazoque, San Antonio, Contreras, Churubusco, Molino del Rey, Chapultepec, and capture of the City of Mexico. He was brevetted a major " for gallant and meritorious conduct in the battles of Contreras and Churubusco," and lieutenant-colonel " for gallant and meritorious conduct in the battle of Molino del Rey."

During the Canada War received a letter from the judge of the court (that tried McCloud) for handling his company with much discretion on the critical occasion, and he escorted McCloud to Montreal, with General Anderson, and turned him over to the civil authorities. Received the compliments of General Mansfield, inspector-general, for having one of the best-drilled companies in New Mexico in 1851; received the formal thanks of the citizens of Santa Fé, New Mexico, for cutting through the palace and placing a mountain howitzer in position to flank the plaza, there being fears of an insurrection of the Spanish population, which caused the Americans to stand guard night and day. On garrison and frontier duty, including the Utah expedition, Indian skirmishing, and the border troubles in Kansas, to 1861, having been engaged in a skirmish with Utah Indians April 28, 1855; also in a skirmish near the head-waters of the Arkansas River, while stationed at Fort Massachusetts, New Mexico.

At beginning of Civil War was in command of the Light-Battery School of Practice; transferred his command by way of Chicago to Baltimore, through a reception of artillery salutes as he passed through the States. February 22, 1861, passed his companies in review before

President Buchanan, the event causing some excitement; had a light battery stationed at the Treasury Department prepared for action on the inauguration of President Lincoln; soon after was placed in command of a steamer, sailing under sealed orders, which proved to be Fort Pickens, Pensacola, and took part in the council of war which was held to determine whether the fort should be held or abandoned; was in command at Tortugas at the time of the Mason and Slidell capture, and suppressed a strike by the New York Wilson Zouaves, which might result in consequence of the labor in mounting heavy guns; ordered by Secretary of War to the command of Philadelphia, Pennsylvania; superintendent of volunteer recruiting at Columbus, Ohio, at the time of the Morgan Raid; also chief mustering and disbursing officer; was for some time commissioner for the States of Maryland and Delaware on account of the Freedman's Bureau; was detached on the board to select officers from the volunteer service to appointments in the regular army. Relieved General Canby in the command of the Department of Washington; was in command of Fort Washington and the Fourth Regiment of Artillery at the time of the attack on Washington City by General Early.

At the close of the Civil War Colonel Brooks was honored with the brevet of brigadier-general in the United States Army for meritorious services during the war.

Title of A.B. conferred by the faculty of Geneva (New York) College in 1838; made an honorary member of the Literary and Historical Society of Sioux City, Iowa; and life-member of a rifle club at San Francisco, California.

General Brooks was retired from active service in 1877. His mother was Maria Gowen Brooks, the authoress of "Zophiel and other Poems;" and Doctor Southey, after quoting from "Zophiel," adds that "Maria del Occidente was the most imaginative and impassioned of all poetesses."

SURGEON-GENERAL JOHN MILLS BROWNE.

SURGEON-GENERAL JOHN MILLS BROWNE was born in Hinsdale, New Hampshire, May 10, 1831; graduated at the medical department of Harvard University in March, 1852, and appointed assistant surgeon from New Hampshire March 26, 1853.

His first duty was on board the store-ship "Warren," Lieutenant-Commanding Fabius Stanley, at Saucelito, opposite San Francisco. The naval station at Mare Island was just then in contemplation, and Commander Farragut had been sent out, to get the plans under way, as the first commandant. He was obliged to live on board the "Warren" until some sort of quarters could be provided on shore. Dr. Browne was medical officer of this naval establishment until May, 1855, a characteristic and critical period in the settlement of California. Dr. Browne was next ordered to the steamer "Active," which was engaged in the survey of the coasts and harbors of California, Oregon, and Washington Territories, and in the winter of 1855-56 (with the "Massachusetts" and "Decatur") in the Indian war in Puget Sound. In the summer of 1857 the "Active" was engaged, with H.M.S. "Satellite," in settling the northwest boundary.

After this long tour of duty on the Western coast, Dr. Browne came East, was promoted to passed assistant surgeon, and ordered to the "Dolphin," of the Home Squadron, in June, 1858. She was commanded by John N. Maffit, so well known afterwards as the commander of the Confederate "Florida." In August, 1858, the "Dolphin" captured the brig "Echo" off Cape Verde, Cuba, with over three hundred African slaves on board. The prize was sent to Charleston, South Carolina, and the negroes were taken to Liberia in the "Niagara."

When the Paraguay Expedition was sent out, Dr. Browne was ordered to the steamer "Atlanta," Captain Daniel B. Ridgely, and detached before sailing. After short service at the Naval Hospital at Norfolk, he was attached to the sloop-of-war "Constellation," flag-ship of the African Squadron, which we were at that time bound by convention to keep on the West Coast. During the cruise the "Constellation" captured, off the Congo River, the bark "Cora," with seven hundred and five slaves, who were sent to Liberia.

Dr. Browne was commissioned as surgeon June 19, 1861, and ordered to the steam-sloop "Kearsarge," a ship which will always be celebrated in the annals of our navy. She was sent on "special duty" to the European waters in 1861, visiting all the ports of the British and continental littoral where she was likely to find the Confederate corsairs. At last, when in command of Commander Winslow, she found the "Alabama" in Cherbourg. The preparations for the engagement which became necessary were like those for a battle "in the lists," and when the hour sounded the champions came forth. The "Kearsarge" destroyed the "Alabama" in one hour and two minutes. Special trains came from Paris to witness the fight. The "Kearsarge" then went to Brazil, to look for the "Florida," which was supposed to be about Fernando Noronha. Disappointed in the search, she returned to the United States.

After some temporary duty, Dr. Browne was, in April, 1865, ordered back to the scene of his original duty in California, where he superintended the building of the Naval Hospital at Mare Island, and was in charge there for nearly ten years, with the exception of a cruise as fleet-surgeon of the Pacific Squadron. This latter post he again filled, after he had been made medical inspector in the regular course of promotion. He was commissioned medical director October 6, 1878, and then came East again. During 1880-82 he served as president of the Medical Examining Board at Washington, and was a member of the Board of Visitors to the Naval Academy in 1881. In the same year he went to London, England, as the naval representative at the International Medical Congress; was a member of the National Board of Health in 1883, and in charge of the Museum of Hygiene at Washington from 1882 to 1885. During that time he also served on the Board of Naval Regulations. In 1884 Medical Director Browne was naval representative at the International Medical Congress at Copenhagen, and from 1885 to 1888 served as a member of the Naval Retiring Board. He became chief of Bureau of Medicine and Surgery, with the title of Surgeon-General of the Navy, April, 1888.

Surgeon-General Browne is said to wear the very highest honors of the Masonic fraternity, and is a distinguished member of club and official society in Washington.

## MEDICAL INSPECTOR GEORGE R. BRUSH, U.S.N.

MEDICAL INSPECTOR GEORGE R. BRUSH, U.S.N., was born at Smithtown, Suffolk County, Long Island, New York, on the third day of November, 1836, and his early youth was passed upon his father's farm in that town.

When at the proper age he took the course of academic study at the well-known Seminary of the Methodist Episcopal Conference at Pennington, New Jersey, then under the mastership of the Rev. J. Townley Crane, D.D.

Brush then entered the office of Lafayette Ranney, M.D., of the city of New York, as a student of medicine. His courses of lectures were taken at the College of Physicians and Surgeons (now the medical department of Columbia College), and in due course he was graduated from that institution in March, 1858.

Soon after graduation he began the practice of his profession at the village of Sayville, of the town of Islip, in Suffolk County, New York, which place has continued to be his usual residence.

The breaking out of the Civil War, however, altered his plans, and drew him, as well as so many thousand others, into embarking upon a very different career from that which they had contemplated.

Accordingly, on the 2d of September, 1861,—having passed the required examination before a board of naval surgeons at the Naval Hospital at Brooklyn, New York,—he was appointed an assistant surgeon in the U. S. Navy by the Hon. Gideon Welles, Secretary of the Navy. This appointment was confirmed by the Senate on the 24th of January following, and his commission issued.

During the war of the Rebellion he served on board the U. S. frigate "Potomac," of the West Gulf Blockading Squadron, and on board the U. S. receiving-ship "North Carolina," at New York,—a position of great responsibility for a medical officer, as that was the great naval recruiting-point.

Dr. Brush was promoted to the grade of passed assistant surgeon in April, 1865, and to that of surgeon in February, 1872; commissioned as medical inspector in November, 1889.

His service at sea, which aggregates sixteen years, was made on the Atlantic, Pacific, and Asiatic stations.

While attached to the U. S. S. "Wateree," he witnessed the bombardment of Callao, Peru, by the Spanish squadron, on May 2, 1866; was attached to the "Saranac" when she was wrecked in Seymour Narrows, British Columbia, in June, 1875.

His latest service afloat was on board the U. S. S. "Omaha," bearing the flag of Rear-Admiral George E. Belknap, on the Asiatic station.

His shore duty, of more than twelve years, has been mostly at the rendezvous in New York, and on board the receiving-ship at the same place.

It has included service at the U. S. naval hospitals at Norfolk, Virginia, and at Mare Island, California. He has also been stationed at the U. S. Naval Academy at Annapolis, and at the U. S. Naval Laboratory, Brooklyn, New York.

Dr. Brush is a son of Philetus Smith and Dorothy Ann Brush, and the eighth in descent from Thomas Brush, who settled at Southold, Long Island, about 1650. His paternal and maternal ancestors served as commissioned officers in the First Regiment of Suffolk County, State of New York, during the war of the American Revolution.

### REAR-ADMIRAL ANDREW BRYSON, U.S.N.

REAR-ADMIRAL ANDREW BRYSON was born in New York City, July 25, 1822. Was appointed a midshipman from New York December 1, 1837, by President Van Buren, his father's personal friend, and made his first cruises in the "Ontario," "Levant," and "Constellation," West India Squadron, until 1842, when he was ordered to the Naval School at Philadelphia, and on June 29, 1843, promoted to passed midshipman, serving on the frigate "Macedonian" and sloop "Decatur" on the coast of Africa. In 1845 he served on the "Michigan" on the great lakes, and in 1849 on the "John Adams." January 30, 1850, he was promoted to "master," and was executive officer on the store-ships "Erie" and "Relief." Promoted to lieutenant August 30, 1851; he was transferred to the brig "Bainbridge" at Montevideo, South America, September 2, to cruise off the coasts of Brazil and Africa. He was next attached to the receiving-ship "Ohio" at Boston, and in 1856 was on the "Saratoga." On this cruise the steamers "Gen. Miramon" and "Marquis de la Habana" were captured off the Mexican coast, in which affair Lieutenant Bryson, commanding the "Indianola," captured the former after a running fight. They also brought from San Juan Walker's filibustering party. In 1858 he was executive officer of the "Preble," Paraguay Expedition, returning late in 1860. In January, 1861, he was attached to the New York Yard, actively engaged fitting out vessels until October 10; he was then ordered to command the "Chippewa" one of the "ninety-day" gun-boats, and sent to the blockade, taking part in the capture of Fort Macon and action at Stony Inlet. July 16, 1862, he was commissioned commander, and, September 29, sent to Europe on special service, returning to blockade early in 1863. The "Chippewa," under his command, was the first gun-boat of the class to cross the Atlantic. June 23, 1863, he was detached, and August 4 ordered to command the monitor "Lehigh." On the way to Charleston, South Carolina, the ship was nearly lost off Hatteras, seas breaking over turret and pilot-house, washing away the ship's bell, which hung six and a half feet above the deck. On April 4, 1864, a medical survey was held without his request, and he was ordered home shattered in health. The work was severe. September 18, 1863, he reported, "up to this date the 15-inch gun has been fired forty-one times, the 8-inch rifle twenty-eight, and the ship has been struck thirty-six times." Again, November 4, "engaged for the past nine days, in company with the 'Patapsco' and shore-batteries, in bombardment of Fort Sumter, during which time I have thrown from the 8-inch rifle four hundred and eight percussion-shells, and from the 15-inch smooth-bore twenty-four." The actions were almost continuous; and his conduct on December 2, 1863, when he was slightly wounded, the ship being aground and subjected to the concentrated fire from nine separate batteries, was specially commended. May 24, 1864, he was again on duty at the New York Yard. October 13 ordered to command the "Essex," Mississippi fleet. October 24 to command the seventh, and on April 19, 1865, the eighth division. May 5 fleet-captain, and August 19 detached. April 6, 1866, to March, 1868, he commanded the "Michigan." On June 3, 1866, he captured the "Fenian" raiders on their return from Canada, and on July 25, 1866, was promoted to captain. 1868-71 he was at the Boston Yard, in command of the receiving-ship "Ohio," and on Board duty. September 19, 1871, to July 28, 1873, he commanded the "Brooklyn," European squadron, and was commissioned commodore February 14, 1873. September 15, 1874, to July 27, 1876, he commanded the Portsmouth, New Hampshire, Navy-Yard; was President of the Board to examine the class of 1876 at Annapolis, and engaged on Board and other duty to 1879. September 8, 1879, to July 25, 1881, he commanded the South Atlantic station, flag-ship "Shenandoah," and was promoted March 25, 1880, to rear-admiral. On January 30, 1883, he was retired at his own request, and spent the remainder of his days quietly at his home in the city of Washington.

"In all his long record there is not a blemish against his high character and honor, and he was greatly beloved by his fellow-officers. He was a man of a retiring disposition, excessively modest, but one of the best informed men of the navy." He was of Scotch ancestry, and his father, the late David Bryson, was prominent in New York City affairs. Died in Washington, D.C., February 7, 1892.

## LIEUTENANT-COLONEL HORACE BLOIS BURNHAM
(RETIRED).

LIEUTENANT-COLONEL HORACE BLOIS BURNHAM was born in Columbia County, New York, September 10, 1824. He was admitted to the bar at Wilkesbarre, Pennsylvania, August 12, 1844, and practised law in the courts of that State until 1861. He commenced the organization of a three-years' regiment of volunteers July 26, 1861, and entered the volunteer service as lieutenant-colonel of the Sixty-seventh Pennsylvania Infantry, October 31, 1861. He took station at Annapolis, Maryland, April 3, 1862, and accompanied the regiment to Harper's Ferry, Virginia, in February, 1863, and in April of the same year was stationed at Berryville, Virginia, from whence he joined the forces at Maryland Heights June 16, and escorted stores, ordnance, etc., from Harper's Ferry to Washington City.

Colonel Burnham joined the Army of the Potomac with his regiment in the following July, and participated in all its actions and campaigns during that year. He took part against the attack by General Early June 10; joined Milroy's forces and engaged in the affair at Opequan River, Virginia, and participated in the battle of Winchester, Virginia, during the 12th, 13th, and 14th of June, 1863. He was on temporary duty in New York City during the draft riots, and was ordered to Washington, D. C., December 26, 1863, as judge-advocate of a general court-martial.

Colonel Burnham was honorably mustered out of the line, October 31, 1864, to accept the position of a major and judge-advocate from that date, when he was detailed as judge-advocate of general courts-martial under orders of the War Department until 1866, when he was placed on duty in the Bureau of Military Justice until April 18, 1867, when he was assigned as chief judge-advocate of the First Military District, Richmond, Virginia, and continued so engaged until June, 1870; he was additionally assigned as judge of the Hustings Court, Richmond, Virginia, September 11, 1867, and was relieved and appointed one of the judges of the Supreme Court of Appeals of Virginia June 9, 1869, and elected president thereof; performed such duty until relieved June 1, 1870; June 3, 1870, he was assigned to the Department of the South; April 24, 1872, additionally assigned to temporary duty in the Department of Texas; from this he was relieved November 2, 1872, and assigned to duty in the Department of the Platte,

and judge-advocate, head-quarters, Department of the Platte, Omaha, Nebraska; he was relieved from duty September 10, 1880, and assigned to duty in the Department of California and Military Division of the Pacific, San Francisco, California, until retirement.

Colonel Burnham was transferred to the permanent establishment of the U. S. Army February 23, 1867, and received the brevets of lieutenant-colonel and colonel of volunteers March 13, 1865, "for faithful and meritorious services during the war." Upon being relieved from duty in the Department of the Platte, September 1, 1886, General Crook, department commander, in General Orders No. 11, Head-quarters Department of the Platte, I. 1886, said: "The department commander takes this occasion to express his appreciation of Colonel Burnham's conscientious fidelity to his duties during his long term of service in this department" (nearly fourteen years). In anticipation of his retirement, General Howard, the division commander, directed the following communication: "The division commander desires to express to you his esteem and his thanks for the faithful and zealous manner in which you have performed the duties of judge-advocate of this division and of the department of California. You will carry with you the best wishes of the staff officers for your welfare and happiness."

He was promoted lieutenant-colonel and deputy judge-advocate-general July 5, 1884, and was retired from active service by operation of law, September 10, 1888; and since retirement has occupied his farm, "Aspen Shade," near Richmond, in Henrico County, Virginia.

**AMBROSE E. BURNSIDE (DECEASED).**

AMBROSE E. BURNSIDE (deceased) was born in Indiana, and graduated from the Military Academy July 1, 1847. He was promoted brevet second lieutenant Second Artillery the same day, and second lieutenant of the Third Artillery September 8, 1847. He served in the City of Mexico during the winter of 1847-48, and when peace had been established with that republic he was stationed at Fort Adams, Rhode Island, from which point he was ordered to Las Vegas, New Mexico, and was engaged in a skirmish there with Jacarillo Apache Indians, August 23, 1849, in which he was wounded. During the years 1850-51 he was at Jefferson Barracks, Missouri; he was with the Mexican Boundary Commission from April, 1851, to March 16, 1852.

He was promoted first lieutenant December 12, 1851, and was at Fort Adams in 1852-53, and resigned October 2, 1853.

After leaving the army he became a manufacturer of fire-arms at Bristol, Rhode Island, from 1853 to 1858. He was major-general of Rhode Island militia in 1855-57. He invented the Burnside breech-loading rifle in 1856, and was member of the Board of Visitors to the Military Academy the same year. He was cashier of the Land Department of the Illinois Central Railroad Company in 1858-59, and treasurer of the same railroad in 1860-61.

At the commencement of the war of the Rebellion he was appointed colonel of Rhode Island Volunteers May 2, 1861, and served in defence of Washington in Patterson's operations about Cumberland, Maryland, and participated in the Manassas campaign, being engaged in the first battle of Bull Run, July 21, 1861. He was mustered out of service August 2, 1861.

On the 6th of August, 1861, he was appointed brigadier-general of volunteers, and served in command of Provisional Brigade near Washington, and was then employed in organizing a Coast Division at Annapolis, Maryland, to January 8, 1862.

General Burnside was then placed in command of the Department of North Carolina, and was engaged in the battle and capture of Roanoke Island; attack of New-Berne, North Carolina; attack on Camden and bombardment of Fort Macon, resulting in its capture April 26, 1862. For these affairs he received a sword of honor from the State of Rhode Island, in testimony of his services at Roanoke Island.

He was appointed major-general of volunteers March 18, 1862, and from July 6 to September 4, 1862, he was in command of the reinforcements to the Army of the Potomac, concentrated at Newport News, Virginia, and subsequently at Fredericksburg, constituting the Ninth Army Corps. General Burnside participated in the Maryland campaign, in command of the right wing of the Army of the Potomac, and of the Ninth Corps, and was engaged in the battles of South Mountain and Antietam. Afterwards he had general charge of Harper's Ferry, Virginia, and Second and Twelfth Corps, until November 10, 1862, and on this date, while marching towards Falmouth, he was assigned to the command of the Army of the Potomac, relieving General McClellan. He commanded the Army of the Potomac in the battle of Fredericksburg, December 11-13, 1862, and in March, 1863, was relieved and ordered to the West, where he commanded the Department of the Ohio. He participated in the capture of Cumberland Gap and occupation of East Tennessee, and was engaged in the actions of Blue Springs and Lenoir, combat of Campbell's Station, and siege of Knoxville. He was engaged in recruiting the Ninth Army Corps from January 12 to April 13, 1864, and then commanded that corps in the Richmond campaign with the Army of the Potomac, being engaged in the battles of the Wilderness, Spottsylvania, North Anna, Tolopotomy, Bethesda Church, and siege of Petersburg, including the Mine assault July 30, 1864. He was then on leave of absence and waiting orders to April 15, 1865, when he resigned his commission.

In 1864 General Burnside received the thanks of Congress for "gallantry, good conduct, and soldier-like endurance" in North Carolina and East Tennessee.

After leaving the service, General Burnside was director of the Illinois Central Railroad Company and in the Narragansett Steamship Company; president of the Cincinnati and Martinsville Railroad Company; of Rhode Island Locomotive Works at Providence; and of the Indianapolis and Vincennes Railroad Company. He was also governor and captain-general of Rhode Island and Providence Plantations. He was also U.S. senator from that State, and died September 13, 1881.

## LIEUTENANT-COLONEL ANDREW SHERIDAN BURT.
### U.S.A.

LIEUTENANT-COLONEL ANDREW SHERIDAN BURT (Seventh Infantry) was born in Cincinnati, Ohio, Nov. 21, 1839.

In April, 1861, he volunteered in the Sixth Ohio Infantry, and July, the same year, he accepted a first lieutenancy in the Eighteenth United States Infantry. The command was attached that fall to the Third Brigade, First Division, of the Army of Ohio, Colonel Robert L. McCook and Brigadier-General George H. Thomas commanding respectively.

Lieutenant Burt was detailed as aide-de-camp on the brigade staff. At the battle of Mill Springs he was wounded, and was brevetted for gallant services; he was appointed additional aide-de-camp on the staff of General Halleck and assigned to serve with Colonel McCook. The same year he was made assistant adjutant-general of the brigade, and continued as such until Colonel McCook's death.

In January, 1863, he reported to General Rosecrans, commanding the Army of the Cumberland, and by him was assigned to the inspector-general's department of his staff, serving so through Hoover's Gap and Tullahoma campaigns, advance beyond Chattanooga, and in the battle of Chickamauga. He was commended in reports by the commanding general for services in these campaigns and battle of Chickamauga. Captain Burt was specially mentioned for gallant service in that battle by Major-General Alexander McCook, commanding the corps. In the fall of 1883, at his own request, he relinquished his staff appointment and took command of his Company F, First Battalion, Eighteenth Infantry. He commanded that company in the charge on Missionary Ridge. General Palmer, on the Ridge, thanked the command.

Captain Burt commanded his Company F, Eighteenth Infantry, part of the Regular Brigade of the Fourteenth Army Corps, in the Atlanta campaign, and was in all the actions participated in by his regiment from Buzzard's Roost to Jonesboro', and received the personal thanks of the detachment commander for gallant services in the last battle. He was mentioned in reports for services in the Atlanta campaign by the detachment commander as well as by General Thomas. He was brevetted major 1864, for gallant services in Atlanta campaign and at the battle of Jonesboro'. Major Burt marched, in 1866, with his company, from Fort Leavenworth to Fort Bridger.

In the fall of 1877, while in command of a detachment of recruits *en route* to Fort McKinney, he was attacked by Indians under Red Cloud, at Crazy Woman's Fork, and the Indians were beaten off.

While in command of Fort C. F. Smith, Montana, in 1868, he had two successful skirmishes with hostile Indians. From 1865 until 1878 Major Burt, in command of his company, was nearly every year changing stations or on expeditions with all the difficulties of marching on the frontier in the hostile Indian days.

He was on Stanley's Yellowstone Expedition in 1873; with Colonel Dodge's command as escort to the Jenney expedition to the Black Hills in 1875; General Crook's expedition, 1876, and commanded a battalion of two companies in the attack by Indians on the command camped on Powder River.

At the battle of the Rosebud, General Crook having ordered the withdrawal of Colonel Royal's battalion of cavalry from a certain position on the field, the retreat became a rout under the Indians' hand-to-hand assault. Major Burt, with his company, and that of Major Burrows, was detailed "to stop those Indians," which the two companies did, and the hard-pressed cavalry battalion was rescued from a precarious position. At "Slim Buttes," same campaign, Major Burt commanded a battalion in the repulse of an Indian attack. In 1877 Major Burt, with his company, was part of General John King's command, sent to Chicago during the riots. In 1879 his company was especially selected to proceed to Hastings, Nebraska, to protect Judge Gaslin in holding court against the possible interference of hostile cowboys, some of their members being tried at the time for an atrocious murder. The major and his company received public thanks and commendation of Judge Gaslin and the officials for the manner in which the duty on this occasion was performed.

While in command at Fort Bidwell, California, in 1885, the citizens of that region, in a series of published resolutions, thanked Major Burt for his successful efforts in preventing an Indian outbreak.

He was promoted lieutenant-colonel of the Seventh Infantry, January 1, 1888.

Colonel Burt is the author of W. F. Cody's (Buffalo Bill) most successful play, "May Cody, or Lost and Won."

PAY INSPECTOR ARTHUR BURTIS, U.S.N.

PAY INSPECTOR ARTHUR BURTIS, U.S.N., was born in New York, and appointed assistant paymaster from that State by Mr. Lincoln in 1862, in accordance with the request of the Honorable Hamilton Fish and Senator Preston King. These gentlemen had been classmates of Assistant Paymaster Burtis's father,—a clergyman who was for many years a resident of Buffalo. His great-grandfather and great-great-grandfather both served in the Revolutionary War; the older being at the time sixty-four, and his son twenty-two years of age.

His first orders were to duty under Admiral Farragut in the "Sagamore," but on the way there in the supply steamer "Rhode Island" contracted yellow fever, and he was sent north. He was then, upon recovering his health, ordered to the "Connecticut," employed in convoying the California steamers through the Carribean Sea, rendered necessary by the fact that the "Alabama" had recently overhauled the "Ariel," with mails and passengers. The "Connecticut," of the North Atlantic Blockading Squadron, was next on the blockade, capturing four noted blockade-runners, all with valuable cargoes. She also caused the destruction of four more, in the course of which duty she was engaged with Fort Fisher.

From 1864 to 1866 Paymaster Burtis was attached to the "Muscoota," of the Gulf Squadron, and had the yellow fever a second time on board that vessel, off the Rio Grande, in 1866. The only medical officer died, and the vessel went to Pensacola, where she received a surgeon and other officers necessary to take the ship north. She proceeded to Portsmouth, New Hampshire, where the ship's company were landed and placed in quarantine.

While undergoing this unpleasant experience in the "Muscoota," he was promoted to paymaster May 4, 1866. From 1867 to 1869 he was stationed at League Island. From 1870 to 1873 was attached to the "Brooklyn," which ship brought the body of Admiral Farragut from Portsmouth, New Hampshire, to New York, and then went for a cruise in European waters. In 1871 he was appointed fleet-paymaster.

Upon his return home, after service at the Bureau of Provisions and Clothing, Navy Department, 1873, he became inspector of provisions and clothing at the navy-yard, Philadelphia, from 1874 to 1877. Most of the time he had the additional duty of paymaster of the receiving-ship "St. Louis." In 1878 he was a member of the Board of Examiners. He was again ordered to League Island, but after about a year's service there went to the practice-ship "Constellation" for her summer cruise with the cadets of the Naval Academy. After this he was for some time inspector of flour, etc., for the navy, at New York. From 1883 to 1886 he was attached to the "Galena," of the North Atlantic Squadron. The "Galena" was at Aspinwall in the spring of 1885. During the rebellion on the Isthmus, and when that city was burned, the officers and crew of the ship prevented much destruction of property and loss of life. The "Galena" also captured at St. Andrew's Island filibustering steamer "City of Mexico" in February, 1886. From June, 1866, to May, 1889, was the paymaster of the navy-yard, New York. He next went to the "Vermont," receiving-ship at New York, and in January, 1890, was ordered as fleet-paymaster of the Pacific Squadron in the flag-ship "Charleston." The "Charleston" brought King Kalakau from the Sandwich Islands to California and took his remains back to Honolulu in January, 1891. From the "Charleston" he was transferred to the flag-ship "San Francisco," 31st March, 1891. The "San Francisco" was in Chili during the revolution in 1891, and was in Valparaiso when Balmaceda's army was defeated and the Congressional forces captured that city August 28, 1891. Was promoted to pay inspector 21st September, 1891; was detached from the flag-ship "San Francisco" 30th January, 1892. He is at present general storekeeper at the navy-yard, Norfolk, Virginia.

## LIEUTENANT-COLONEL EDMOND BUTLER, U.S.A.
### (RETIRED).

LIEUTENANT-COLONEL EDMOND BUTLER (retired) was born in Ireland March 19, 1827. He was appointed second lieutenant Fifth Infantry at the outbreak of the war, and detailed to accompany General Baird (afterwards inspector-general) in inspection of Kansas and Missouri troops. In 1862, remustering and consolidating Kansas volunteers, and officially complimented by General Hunter for settling, without resort to force, "difficult and delicate" matters affecting Kansas troops. He was in New Mexico in 1862, and Texas 1864, and rebuilt Fort Bliss after reoccupation. Having been promoted captain, 1864, in 1865 he commanded an expedition against the Navajos, inflicting severe loss on them. In September, 1865, he received the formal surrender of Manoëlito Grande, and sent two thousand prisoners to the Reservation. He was recommended for brevet for gallantry and success. In letters from his head-quarters, November 16 and 17, 1865, General Carleton wrote, "To Captain Edmond Butler I owe many thanks." "To the efficiency and straightforward course and the energy and good sense of Captain B. I owe a great deal of the luck I get credit for as a commander."

In June, 1868, Captain Butler was ordered in attendance on General Sherman, and in December, with a small infantry force, he exhumed the bodies of the killed in the Forsyth affair, on the Arickaree Fork, under fire of main body of Sioux under Two Strike, and extricated his small force from a perilous position. In 1869, in the Indian operations on the Smoky Hill, with two soldiers he narrowly escaped capture. He volunteered for expedition against the Pawnees under General Woods, and commanded expedition after General Woods was disabled by illness. In 1874 he served through the expedition against the Kiowas and Comanches, under General Miles.

In September, 1876, Captain Butler cut a road through the Bad Lands north of the Yellowstone. In the campaign against Sitting Bull he commanded the centre at Cedar Creek, and in subsequent pursuit. He was shot at by Gall while relieving an outpost. He participated in campaign against the confederated Sioux and Cheyennes under Crazy Horse, and on January 8, 1877, led a charge against the Indians fortified on a high peak of the Wolf Mountains, and massing in rear of Miles's position. In his report General Miles said, "Captain Butler's horse was shot under him while gallantly leading a successful charge on the extreme left." He recommended Captain Butler for brevet, "for conspicuous gallantry in leading his command in a successful charge against superior numbers of hostile Indians strongly posted." This recommendation was approved by Gen-

erals Sherman, Sheridan, and Terry. At the close of the campaign General Miles wrote Captain Butler as follows: "In leaving the regiment, be assured you have the thanks and good-will of its commanding officer for your hard service in the field and fortitude in action."

Nothing in his service, however, touched him so deeply as a letter signed by every enlisted man of his company who was in the charge, thanking him "for the gallant manner in which he led the charge on the 8th of January, in which they had the honor of participating, and for the kindness he had shown them in so many different ways heretofore."

Captain Butler was promoted major in 1885. He commanded Fort Townsend, Washington. Commanded Bellevue Rifle Range three consecutive years; marksman, 1883, 1884, 1885. Sharpshooter marksman, 1888. He was recorder of Board of Visitors to School of Application in 1887, and was in Pine Ridge campaign, 1890–91, commanding troops in night march from Rushville, Nebraska, to the Agency, and his regiment during the campaign. At its close he received a copy of a letter to General Brooke, in which the Secretary of War and the General of the Army express a hope "that some opportunity may be presented for the promotion of this most deserving officer." He was promoted lieutenant-colonel in March, 1892.

Upon retirement from active service in March, 1891, after examination by the Bar Committee for the Seventh Judicial District of Montana, he was admitted to the Bar of that State.

Colonel Butler is the author of an "Essay on the Indian Question," honorably mentioned by the Board of Award of the Military Service Institution for 1880. After the fall of Sumter he wrote a series of articles in French for Parisian and Brussels papers, presenting the Union side of the question to Continental Europe.

### MAJOR JOHN G. BUTLER.

MAJOR JOHN G. BUTLER (Ordnance Department) was born in Pittsburg, Pennsylvania, January 23, 1842, and graduated from the Military Academy June 11, 1863. He was then promoted second lieutenant of the Fourth Artillery, but transferred to the Ordnance Department January 29, 1864. He served during the war of the Rebellion, in the Army of the Cumberland, from August, 1863, to January, 1864, participating in the campaign of that army, and engaged at the battle of Chickamauga, for which he received the following complimentary notice, in the report of first lieutenant F. L. D. Russell, Fourth Artillery: "Lieutenant Butler, the only officer with me, distinguished himself by his cool and gallant conduct and rendered me the most essential service." He was brevetted first lieutenant for "gallant and meritorious services in the battle of Chickamauga," September 20, 1863.

Lieutenant Butler was then stationed at Chattanooga, Tennessee, and Bridgeport, Alabama, until he was ordered on recruiting duty in January 1864, which duty he, by permission, declined. He was then ordered to appear at Washington, for examination for transfer to the Ordnance Department, and upon being transferred was stationed at Frankford Arsenal, Pennsylvania, as assistant ordnance officer, from February 1 to December 11, 1864, being detached May 19 to July 1, to arm and equip New Jersey troops. He sailed, under sealed orders, November, 1864, in charge of ordnance stores and material, to anticipate the arrival of General Sherman's army on the Atlantic coast.

After performing this duty, Lieutenant Butler was detailed as assistant to the inspector of ordnance in New York, Boston, Philadelphia, West Point, and Reading, to January, 1867, and assistant constructor of ordnance at Scott Foundry, Reading, Pennsylvania, to June, 1867. In the mean time he was promoted first lieutenant, to date from March 7, 1867. Upon being relieved at Reading, he was ordered as assistant at Fort Leavenworth Arsenal, Kansas, where he remained until May, 1870. He was then placed on detached duty in Philadelphia until the following September, when he was ordered to Fort Monroe Arsenal, Virginia, as assistant. From May to September, 1873, the lieutenant was on detached duty at the U. S. Ordnance Agency, New York, then assistant to the constructor of ordnance to April 22, 1876, in the mean time having been promoted captain June 23, 1874.

In May, 1876, captain Butler was ordered as assistant at Watervliet Arsenal, New York, and in May, 1880, transferred to Watertown Arsenal, Massachusetts, as assistant. On the 5th of April, 1883, his station was changed to Rock Island Arsenal, as assistant, and in September, 1886, to the National Armory at Springfield, Massachusetts; then to the St. Louis Powder Depot, in January, 1888, and subsequently to the command of the Augusta Arsenal, Georgia, his present station.

He was promoted major of ordnance September 15, 1890.

Major Butler is the son of John B. Butler, major and paymaster in Mexican War, on staff of General Taylor, and later in Ordnance Department, U.S.A., and grandson of John Butler, whose military records for three generations extend back through the four great wars in which the country has been engaged,—the war of the Revolution, the War of 1812, the Mexican War, and the war of the Seceding States, 1861-65. Major Butler is the author of "Projectiles and Rifled Cannon," and of various articles and publications upon the subjects of ordnance, the national defence, etc. He is also the inventor of the "Butler projectile," in use with rifled guns for the past ten or twelve years, and in the proof of both breech- and muzzle-loading guns adopted in U. S. service.

## BRIGADIER-GENERAL RICHARD N. BATCHELDER.

BRIGADIER-GENERAL RICHARD N. BATCHELDER (quartermaster-general, U.S.A.) was born in New Hampshire July 27, 1832. At the outbreak of the Rebellion he enlisted in the First New Hampshire Regiment, and was appointed regimental quartermaster April 30, 1861. In fifteen days after his appointment he had the regiment uniformed, armed, and equipped, and field-transportation provided for baggage, tents, and supplies. It was this comprehensive grasp of details and this energy of execution which early brought him to the attention of field-commanders, and secured for him rapid promotion until he became chief quartermaster of the Army of the Potomac, which position he filled with great credit to himself during the closing year of the war. No officer of the Quartermaster's Corps was complimented with more brevet rank, and few officers of the line or staff received higher encomiums in official reports. He was appointed captain and assistant quartermaster and assigned to duty as chief quartermaster, Corps of Observation, in August, 1861. He was made chief quartermaster, Second Division, Second Corps, Army of the Potomac, March, 1862; lieutenant-colonel and chief quartermaster, Second Corps, January, 1863; acting chief quartermaster, Army of the Potomac, June, 1864; and colonel and chief quartermaster, Army of the Potomac, August, 1864. He was brevetted major, lieutenant-colonel, and brigadier-general of volunteers, and major, lieutenant-colonel, and colonel, United States Army, for faithful and meritorious service during the war.

It was as chief quartermaster of the Army of the Potomac, however, that his great powers were fullest displayed, having charge of the immense baggage-trains of that great force, the duties of which position would have crushed the ordinary mind; yet he handled this great train of five thousand wagons and thirty thousand horses and mules on the campaign from the Rapidan to the James with a magical control. Some distinguished officer has said "that a man who can successfully handle the supply-trains of an army is capable of commanding that army."

In his "History of the Second Corps," General Francis A. Walker says, "Colonel Batchelder was one of the best, if not himself the very best, contribution made by the volunteer force to the supply department of the army. His subsequent promotion to be chief quartermaster of the Army of the Potomac and his present high position in the regular army are evidence of the manner in which his duties with the Second Corps were discharged. However exacting the demands of the infantry or the artillery, of the commissariat or the hospital service, they were always met, and met so easily that it seemed the simplest thing in the world to be done. It was impossible that the roads could become so bad as to keep the Second Corps trains back. No matter how the troops were marched about,—by day or by night, in advance or in retreat,—the inevitable six-mule wagon was always close behind. . . . The service rendered to the troops by this sagacious and efficient officer could hardly be over-estimated." "It is with officers of such qualifications that it is desirable we should fill up the standing army," wrote Grant, when he recommended Batchelder for appointment in the regular army. Said the gallant Hancock: "I consider him (Batchelder) the most efficient officer of the department in the volunteer service." Said General Meade: "General Batchelder's services for the two years I commanded the Army of the Potomac are well known to me. He not only managed his important department with great judgment and skill, but rendered me essential service on the battle-field as a staff-officer, showing high personal gallantry in the immediate presence of the enemy." "No officer," says Howard, "with whom I have had the fortune to serve ever had, at all times, my more complete confidence." "He has not a superior in ability and experience. Much of the success of my department is due to his untiring intelligence and faithful service. . . . He merits the high commendation awarded him by all his superiors," was the opinion of General Ingalls, who was Batchelder's superior officer in the Quartermaster's Corps. "He is one of the most intelligent and able officers of the Quartermaster's Department. I greatly relied upon his ability and zeal, and was never disappointed," wrote Quartermaster-General Meigs.

CAPTAIN LESTER A. BEARDSLEE, U.S.N.

CAPTAIN LESTER A. BEARDSLEE was born in Little Falls, New York, February 1, 1836. Appointed acting midshipman March 5, 1850; sloop "Plymouth," East Indies, May, 1851, to January, 1855; participated in one battle and several skirmishes with Chinese army at Shanghai; Naval Academy, October, 1855, to June, 1856.

Promoted to passed midshipman June 20, 1856; steam-frigate "Merrimac," special service, 1856–57; sloop "Germantown," East India Squadron, 1857–60. Promoted to master January 22, 1858. Promoted to lieutenant July 23, 1859; sloop "Saratoga," coast of Africa, 1860–63. Promoted to lieutenant-commander July 16, 1862; monitor "Nantucket," North Atlantic Squadron, January to May, 1863; participated in attack of the iron-clad fleet on the defences of Charleston Harbor, April 7, 1863; steam-sloop "Wachusett," special service, on coast of Brazil, cruising for rebel privateers, October, 1863, to January, 1865; participated in capture of rebel steamer "Florida" at Bahia, by "Wachusett," October, 1864; commanded prize steamer "Florida," from October, 1864, and brought her to Hampton Roads, Virginia; steam-sloop "Connecticut," special service, West Indies, 1865; commanded steam-gun-boat "Aroostook," 1867–68, taking her to East India Squadron from Philadelphia; commanded steamer "Saginaw," Pacific Squadron, October, 1868; executive of steam-sloop "Lackawanna," Pacific Squadron, 1868–69.

Commissioned as commander June 12, 1869; Hydrographic Office, Navy Department, 1869–70; steamer "Palos," April, 1870, to January, 1871; took her to East Indies; Hydrographic Office, January, 1871–72; Navy-Yard, Washington, May, 1872, to April 1, 1875; member of United States Board for testing iron, steel, and other metals, April, 1875, to April, 1879; commanding sloop "Jamestown," Alaska, April, 1879, to October, 1880.

Promoted to captain November, 1880; leave of absence, 1882–83; commanding receiving-ship "Franklin," 1883–84; commanding steam-frigate "Powhatan," June, 1884, to June, 1886; Torpedo Station, 1887; waiting orders, 1888; commanding receiving-ship "Vermont," July, 1888–91.

November 9, 1891, assumed command of Naval Station, Port Royal, South Carolina; and at this date—June, 1892—he remains in command at Port Royal.

## CAPTAIN JOHN H. CALEF.

CAPTAIN JOHN H. CALEF (Second Artillery) was born at Gloucester, Massachusetts, September 24, 1841. He is the great-grandson of Colonel Jeduthan Baldwin, of the Revolutionary army, first colonel of engineers of the U. S. Army; also, a great-grandson of Colonel John H. Calef, of Kingston, New Hampshire, an officer of the Revolutionary army.

Captain Calef graduated at the U. S. Military Academy June 17, 1862, and was promoted second lieutenant of the Fifth Artillery the same day. He was transferred to the Second Artillery October 6, 1862, and served in the field with the Army of the Potomac. He participated in the Peninsula campaign, and was engaged in the action of Malvern Hill August 5, 1862; in the Northern Virginia campaign, and engaged in the battle of second Bull Run August 29, 30, 1862; in the Maryland campaign, and engaged in the battle of Antietam September 17, 1862; skirmish at Sharpsburg September 19, 1862, and march to Falmouth, Virginia; in the Rappahannock campaign and engaged in Stoneman's raid towards Richmond; in the battle of Chancellorsville May 2-4, 1863, and several skirmishes; in the Pennsylvania campaign, in command of his battery, and engaged in the skirmish of Upperville, Virginia, June 21-22, 1863; battle of Gettysburg, Pennsylvania, July 1-3, 1863, and skirmishes at Williamsport, July 6, Boonesboro, Maryland, July 8-9, and Funkstown, Maryland, July 10, 1863; and in pursuit of the enemy to Warrenton, Virginia; in the Rapidan campaign and engaged in several skirmishes September, 1863, and wounded September 15 at Raccoon Ford.

He was promoted first lieutenant of the Second Artillery November 4, 1863, and was on leave of absence from February 14 to April, 1864, when he rejoined in the field and participated in the Richmond campaign, being engaged in the battle of Cold Harbor June 1, 1864; skirmished at Bottom Bridge June 3-4, 1864; battle of Trevilian Station June 11-12, 1864, and action of St. Mary's Church June 24, 1864. He was then on sick leave until the following September; but rejoining in the field, participated in the Richmond campaign and was engaged in the siege of Petersburg; combat of Boydton Plank Road October 27, 1864; destruction of Stony

Creek Station December 1, 1864, and skirmish at Bellefield December 9, 1864.

Lieutenant Calef was appointed adjutant of the Second Artillery November 6, 1864, and, after a short leave of absence, was with regimental head-quarters at Fort McHenry to July, 1865, when the regiment was transferred to the Pacific coast.

He was brevetted captain July 6, 1864, for "gallant and good conduct in the battle of Gettysburg, and in the campaign from the Rapidan to Petersburg, Virginia;" and major March 13, 1865, "for good conduct and gallant services during the Rebellion."

Lieutenant Calef served on the Pacific coast from 1865 to 1872. He was judge-advocate of a "travelling general court-martial" in 1868-69, making the tour of Arizona. His regiment being transferred to the Atlantic coast in 1872, he was on duty at Fort McHenry, Maryland, to May, 1875, when he was ordered to the Artillery School at Fort Monroe, Virginia, remaining there until April 8, 1888, during which time he was instructor in the "Art of War" and "Tactics," and compiled a work on "Military Policy and History of Ancient and Modern Armies," and one on "Description and Service of Machine-Guns."

He was promoted captain of the Second Artillery March 16, 1875, and is at present on duty in command of Fort Schuyler, New York.

CAPTAIN D. F. CALLINAN (RETIRED).

CAPTAIN D. F. CALLINAN (retired) was born in county Kerry, Ireland, July 24, 1839. He came to the United States when a boy. Enlisted in Company E, First Infantry, September 3, 1860. Served at Forts Arbuckle and Washita, Indian Territory. Left Indian Territory for Kansas May 1, 1861, the command consisting of six companies,—First (now Fourth) Cavalry and five companies First Infantry,—under command of Major Emory. During the first day's march were followed by Texan troops. When camp was reached line of battle was formed, Company E, First Infantry, as artillery; the cavalry were sent out and, without firing a shot, made the Texans prisoners. Next morning they were given back their arms and released. Arrived at Fort Leavenworth May 31.

In June assisted in the capture of a company of rebels at Liberty, Missouri, who were a few hours afterwards given back their arms (shot-guns and squirrel-rifles) and released. The command returned to Leavenworth, remaining a few days at Kansas City. He was appointed corporal August 1, 1861, and quartermaster-sergeant of post on September 15; appointed first sergeant in January, 1862, and scouted through Missouri in 1862. He was stationed at Fort Scott, Kansas, during the winter, and returned to Fort Leavenworth in February, 1863; resigned the position of first sergeant, and was appointed sergeant-major of post. He joined his regiment in the Army of the Tennessee, operating against Vicksburg; was acting sergeant-major of battalion for about two weeks; asked a volunteer officer who sat beside him one day what he thought of Vicksburg, etc.; the officer said he did not know, and inquired the sergeant's opinion. The sergeant said if Grant was the man they said he was, they would have it by the Fourth of July anyhow. After the officer left, the men informed him that it was General Grant to whom he was talking. A few days after this he was placed in command of a siege-gun within a short distance of Fort Hill, and remained in command until the surrender.

In August, 1863, he was appointed first lieutenant of colored troops, and reported to Brigadier-General J. P. Hawkins as aide-de-camp. October 2 he received the appointment of second lieutenant First Infantry, and was appointed commissary of musters, acting assistant adjutant-general, acting inspector-general, and acting ordnance officer. He was relieved at his own request in May, 1864, and joined his regiment in New Orleans, and promoted first lieutenant in 1866. He was almost constantly in command of companies until November, 1867, when he was appointed commandant of the New Orleans military prison. He turned the building over to the civil authorities in August, 1868, and again took command of his company. He was quartermaster and commissary at Fort Brady, Michigan, from July, 1869, to October, 1871, the last six months being also post-adjutant. He was in command of about one hundred recruits at Fort Wayne, Michigan, from January to May, 1874; post quartermaster and commissary of Fort Sully, Dakota, from July, 1874, to July, 1875; commanding detachment of recruits at Fort Randall during the winter of 1876–77; in Chicago during labor riots. In November, sent to New Spotted Tail Agency, to superintend construction of barracks; on leave of absence for four months, from September, 1878; promoted captain July 1, 1879, and stationed at Forts Sully and Meade from July, 1879, to May, 1880; employed with company in building road at mouth of Pecos River from December, 1880, to March, 1881; building road into pinery, near Fort Davis, Texas, December, 1881, and January, 1882; took part in Apache campaign in Arizona and New Mexico in 1882; on general recruiting from October, 1884, to October, 1886; on leave for four months; in command of Angel Island March and April, 1888; in summer camp at Santa Barbara; in command of Angel Island January to March, 1889; member of board to locate quarantine station; in summer camp at Monterey and Santa Cruz, California; on sick leave for six months from January, 1890; took part in Sioux campaign, 1890–91; on sick leave for two months from January, 1891; in command of company from April to October 29, 1891. Retired October 22, 1891.

## COLONEL JOHN CAMPBELL (RETIRED).

COLONEL JOHN CAMPBELL (retired) entered the United States service as an acting assistant surgeon June 11, 1847, and arrived at Vera Cruz, Mexico, July 20 following, when he was placed on duty at the Castle of San Juan d'Ulloa, from which duty he was relieved in October, and ordered to the command of Major-General Patterson. He arrived in the City of Mexico December 7, 1847, and on the 13th of the same month was appointed assistant surgeon U. S. Army. He was afterwards transferred to Tacubaya. He returned to Albany, New York, in July, 1848, and was ordered to New Orleans, where he reported October 24, 1848, and was then directed to proceed to San Antonio, Texas, where he remained, doing duty at various points, until the early part of 1850, when he was directed to proceed to California via the Isthmus of Panama. He arrived at Monterey, California, after a voyage of sixty-five days from Panama, and was subsequently stationed at Benicia and Sonoma.

In May, 1851, Dr. Campbell was detailed to accompany the escort to the Indian Commissioner, and in July arrived at Camp Bidwell, California, returning to Sonoma in September following. In October, 1851, he was ordered with two troops of the First Dragoons on an expedition to Port Orford, Oregon, and was engaged in a skirmish with Indians on the Coquilla River. He returned to Benicia December 12, 1851. After serving at various other stations, and having had six months' leave of absence, he was ordered to report to the head-quarters of the army at New York City, from Albany, New York, September 28, 1854, and was stationed successively at Fort Wood, West Point, Carlisle Barracks, Fort Crawford, Minnesota, Fort Ridgely, Minnesota, and was then assigned to duty with a battalion of the Second Infantry, August 22, 1856, on the march to the Missouri River, where they arrived, opposite Fort Pierre, September 23 of that year. On the 6th of November he was directed to proceed to Fort Leavenworth, and there received a leave of absence, rejoining for duty at West Point June 1, 1857.

At the commencement of the war of the Rebellion, Dr. Campbell was on duty at Plattsburg Barracks, New York, and on the 29th of January, 1861, accompanied the two companies stationed there to Baltimore, Maryland. On the 21st of July, 1862, he arrived at New York from Pensacola, Florida, and was stationed in and about that city until August, 1863, when the Board for Retirement of Officers, of which Dr. Campbell was a member, was transferred to Wilmington, Delaware.

On the 1st of October, 1863, he was transferred to Philadelphia, Pennsylvania, as medical director of the Department of the Susquehanna, which he retained until October 28, 1865, when he was detailed as attending surgeon-in-charge of invalid officers. He continued on this duty to November 23, 1865, when he was ordered to Augusta, Georgia, as medical director of the Department of Georgia. On the 26th of June, 1866, he was transferred to Madison Barracks, New York, remaining there until November 25, 1867, when assigned to duty at Fort Trumbull, Connecticut.

In 1870 he was ordered to the Department of Dakota, and assigned to duty temporarily as medical director, but subsequently ordered to duty at Fort Randall, Dakota, where he remained until 1872, when his station was changed to Fort Adams, Rhode Island. In 1878 he was ordered to Atlanta, Georgia, as medical director of the Department of the South. In 1880 he was at Newport Barracks, Kentucky, and remained on duty there until 1883, when he was ordered to New York City, where he was attending surgeon until retired from active service September 16, 1885.

Dr. Campbell was promoted captain and assistant surgeon December 13, 1852; major and surgeon May 21, 1861; lieutenant-colonel and surgeon November 8, 1877; and colonel and surgeon December 7, 1884.

## OFFICERS OF THE ARMY AND NAVY (REGULAR)

### BRIGADIER- AND BREVET MAJOR-GENERAL EDWARD R. S. CANBY (DECEASED).

BRIGADIER- AND BREVET MAJOR-GENERAL EDWARD R. S. CANBY was born in Kentucky and graduated from the U. S. Military Academy in the class of 1839. He was promoted upon graduation as second lieutenant, Second Infantry, July 1, 1839. During part of the Florida War (1839-42) he was on duty as quartermaster; 1840-42, assisted in conducting the emigrating Indians to Arkansas, after which he performed garrison duty at Fort Niagara, New York, to 1845, and was in recruiting service from 1845 to 1846. From March 24, 1846, to March 3, 1847, he was adjutant of the Second Infantry, and while serving in this capacity was promoted first lieutenant Second Infantry, June 18, 1846.

He was brevetted captain of staff and served as assistant adjutant-general from March 3, 1847, to March 3, 1855. During the war with Mexico, 1846-48, he was engaged in the siege of Vera Cruz, March 9-29, 1847; and participated in the battles of Cerro Gordo April 17-18, 1847; Contreras, August 19-20, 1847, and Cherubusco, August 20, 1847; and was brevetted major " for gallant and meritorious conduct in the battles of Contreras and Cherubusco, Mexico." He participated in the assault and capture of the City of Mexico September 13-14, 1847, and was " brevetted lieutenant-colonel September 13, 1847, for gallant conduct at the Belen Gate of the City of Mexico."

During 1847 and 1848 he was assistant adjutant-general of General Riley's brigade, and from February 27, 1849, to February 22, 1851, he served in the same capacity to the Pacific Division. On February 22, 1851, he was ordered to Washington, D. C., for duty in the adjutant-general's office, and remained on duty there until March 3, 1855, on which date he was promoted major Tenth Infantry.

While on duty in the adjutant-general's office he made a tour of inspection of the posts on the Arkansas and Red Rivers in Florida, and on the Gulf coast east of the Mississippi River, November 30, 1853, to July 15, 1854. He performed the usual garrison duties at Carlisle barracks, Pennsylvania, 1855, and frontier duty at the posts of Fort Crawford, Wisconsin, 1855-56; Fort Snelling, Minnesota, 1856-57; and at Fort Garland, New Mexico, 1860. He accompanied the Utah expedition, 1857-60, and commanded the Navajo expedition in 1860-61.

He was promoted lieutenant-colonel Nineteenth Infantry May 14, 1861, and was in command of the Department of New Mexico from June 23, 1861, to September 18, 1862. During January and February, 1862, he was engaged in the defence of Fort Craig, New Mexico, and participated in the combat of Valverde, February 21, 1862, and action of Pualta, April 15, 1862.

On March 31, 1862, he was commissioned brigadier-general U. S. Volunteers and was placed in command of the draft rendezvous at Pittsburg, Pennsylvania, March 7, 1862, to January 15, 1863; detailed on special duty in the War Department until May 7, 1864, and then took command of the city and harbor of New York, to suppress draft riots.

He was promoted major-general U. S. Volunteers May 7, 1864.

He was in command of the Military Division of West Mississippi May 16, 1864, to June 3, 1865, and while on a tour of inspection was severely wounded by rebel guerrillas on White River, Arkansas, November 4, 1864; and in command of the forces in the Mobile campaign, March to May, 1865, which resulted in the capture of Spanish Fort April 8, and of Blakely April 9, 1865. On March 13, 1865, he was brevetted brigadier-general U. S. Army for gallant and meritorious services at the battle of Valverde, New Mexico. On April 12, 1865, he occupied Mobile, Alabama; and Montgomery, Alabama, on April 27, 1865; and on March 13, 1865, he was brevetted major-general U. S. Army for gallant and meritorious services in the capture of Fort Blakely and Mobile, Alabama.

The rebel army under Lieutenant-General R. Taylor surrendered to him April 4, and also the rebel forces in the Trans-Mississippi Department, under General E. K. Smith, May 26, 1865.

Promoted brigadier-general U. S. Army July 28, 1866. He was mustered out of the volunteer service September 1, 1866.

General Canby twice received the thanks of the President for his services.

General Canby was in command of the Department of the Columbia, and took command of an expedition against the Modoc Indians in 1873, by whom he was basely murdered on the 11th of April of that year.

## COLONEL CALEB H. CARLTON.

COLONEL CALEB H. CARLTON (Eighth Cavalry) was born in Ohio September 1, 1836, and was graduated from the Military Academy in the Class of '59. He was promoted brevet second lieutenant of the Seventh Infantry July 1, 1859, and second lieutenant of the Fourth Infantry October 12, 1859. He served at Newport Barracks, Kentucky, until April, 1860, and was ordered to Jefferson Barracks, to participate in Blake's expedition from St. Louis, Missouri, to Fort Vancouver, via the head-waters of the Missouri River and Military Road, which occupied him until the following October. He was then stationed at Fort Hoskins, the Presidio, and San Bernardino, California, to October, 1861, when he was ordered East with his regiment. He was promoted first lieutenant May 14, 1861, and captain June 30, 1862.

Colonel Carlton was on provost duty with his regiment in the city of Washington until March, 1862, when he took the field with the Army of the Potomac, participating in the Peninsula campaign, and engaged in the siege of Yorktown, battles of Gaines' Mill, Malvern Hill, second Bull Run, and Antietam. He was then detailed on recruiting service to February, 1863, and then on mustering duty at Washington to June, 1863. He received the appointment of colonel of the Eighty-ninth Ohio Infantry July 7, 1863, and participated in the campaign of that year with the Western army, being engaged in the battle of Chickamauga, Kenesaw Mountain, and siege of Atlanta in 1864.

He was made prisoner of war September 20, 1863, and held by the enemy to March 7, 1864. After participating in the Atlanta campaign, he was placed in command of the post of Chattanooga, Tennessee, from October 17, 1864, to May 13, 1865, and was then commanding the Western District of Kentucky to June 23, 1865, when he was honorably mustered out of the volunteer service.

Colonel Carlton then joined his regiment in the regular service, and commanded the Fourth Infantry at Fort Wood, New York, from July 28 to September 28, 1865, when his regiment was ordered to the Lakes, and he took station at Fort Ontario, New York.

He was brevetted major July 4, 1862, for "gallant and meritorious services during the Peninsula campaign," and lieutenant-colonel September 20, 1863, for gallant and meritorious services at the battle of Chickamauga.

In March, 1867, Colonel Carlton's regiment was ordered to the Plains, and he served respectively in camp at Omaha, and in garrison at Forts Laramie and Fetter-

man until March 23, 1869, when he became unassigned. He was then detailed as professor of military science at Miami University, Ohio, and remained on that duty to October, 1871, he having in the mean time been assigned as captain of the Tenth Cavalry December 15, 1870. He was on leave in Europe from November, 1872, to June, 1873. He joined at Fort Sill, and was in the field in the Kiowa and Comanche expeditions from June, 1873, to March, 1875, and then was ordered to Texas, taking station at Fort McKavett, from which post he took the field, from April 17, 1875, to July 11, 1876. He was promoted major of the Third Cavalry May 17, 1876, and was in the field, and on the Cheyenne expedition in Dakota and Nebraska, from June to December 21, 1878, again in the field from October 8 to December, 1879, and again in June, 1880. He was on sick leave from July 8, 1880, to June, 1881, when he was appointed inspector of national cemeteries to April, 1882. He was again on leave to November, 1882, when he joined his regiment in Arizona, and marched with it to Texas in the spring of 1885, where he remained until September, 1886, and was at Forts Davis and Elliott until July 25, 1887. He then marched with a battalion of the Third Cavalry to Fort Brown, Texas, a distance of one thousand miles, arriving there October 20, 1887.

Colonel Carlton was promoted lieutenant-colonel Seventh Cavalry April 11, 1889, and ordered to Fort Sill, Indian Territory, September 5, remaining at that station until promoted colonel of the Eighth Cavalry, with head-quarters at Fort Meade, North Dakota. He is at present on leave of absence in California.

## OFFICERS OF THE ARMY AND NAVY (REGULAR)

### PAYMASTER JOHN RANDOLPH CARMODY, U.S.N.

PAYMASTER JOHN RANDOLPH CARMODY was born at Mohawk, New York, June 9, 1843. In July, 1862, the subject of this sketch enlisted in the navy, and served as paymaster's writer and clerk in the James and York Rivers, being present at many skirmishes and reconnoissances. As soon as he attained his majority he was appointed an acting assistant paymaster. He served in the "Cincinnati," on the Mississippi, under Admiral Porter, and was present at the operations on the Cumberland and Tennessee Rivers which resulted in the defeat of the Confederate army under Hood. During these operations he was employed in volunteer reconnoissance service on shore, which he performed so satisfactorily as to elicit a letter of special commendation from his commanding officer.

Paymaster Carmody participated in the siege and capture of Mobile in the spring of 1865, and was present at the surrender of the rebel naval forces on the Tombigbee River at the close of the war. He continued to serve in the West Gulf Squadron until July, 1866, when, in recognition of his good war record, he was appointed an assistant paymaster in the regular navy. During the next two years he was again in the Gulf of Mexico, while we were watching the events connected with Maximilian's assumption of the imperial crown under the auspices and with the support of Louis Napoleon.

Mr. Carmody was made passed assistant paymaster in 1868, and again went to Southern waters in the "Yantic," which vessel was for nearly a year constantly employed about Hayti, protecting American interests during a bloody revolution. The ship was then disabled by the serious outbreak of yellow fever, which carried off many of the officers and crew. Paymaster Carmody survived an attack of the disease, but never fully recovered his health.

After the Franco-Prussian War, when Congress authorized the conveyance to France in government vessels of contributions to aid the distressed people of that country, Paymaster Carmody was sent upon that business in the store-ship "Relief."

On returning from this duty he was stationed at New London and at New Orleans as disbursing officer. He was then ordered to the "Monocacy," on the China and Japan station, where he remained two years. From 1877 to 1879 he was in charge of the naval depot at Honolulu, Sandwich Islands, during which time he was promoted to be paymaster, with rank of lieutenant-commander. He was next attached to the receiving-ship "Independence," at the navy-yard, Mare Island, California, for three years.

In 1883 the Naval Mutual Aid Association selected Paymaster Carmody as their secretary and treasurer. The Navy Department assigned him to that duty, and he spent three years in managing its affairs and building up the association, to the expressed satisfaction of its members.

Having, in 1886, volunteered for duty in the "Vandalia," fitting out for the Pacific, he was ready to sail when he was detached and ordered to special duty as assistant to the paymaster-general of the navy. He was specially employed by the Secretary of the Navy in the work of bringing about the consolidation of the accounts of naval stores and the introduction of economic and business methods in the purchase and care of supplies. For this service he received a most complimentary letter from the paymaster-general.

Close confinement to office-work brought a renewal of ill health, and, in hope of improvement, he applied for sea-duty. Again he went, in the steam-corvette "Galena," to the Home Station and the West Indies until exposure to tropical climate brought on a recurrence of disease, and he was invalided home in 1888. In the following April, at his own request, he was placed upon the retired list, under the category, "through physical incapacity resulting from long and faithful service."

Since that period he has employed himself in journalistic writing, and has, beside, become actively identified with the financial circles of the capital city. Among the moneyed institutions of Washington, he was one of the organizers and directors of the West End National Bank, and is the treasurer and a director of the largest financial institution in that city,—the Washington Loan and Trust Company; also member of the Board of Directors of the Navy Mutual Aid Association and the Army and Navy Club, and is a companion of the Military Order of the Loyal Legion.

## MAJOR AND BREVET COLONEL L. H. CARPENTER.

MAJOR AND BREVET COLONEL L. H. CARPENTER (Fifth Cavalry) belongs to a family identified with the early history of Philadelphia. He is a lineal descendant of Thomas Lloyd, first governor of the province of Pennsylvania, and of Samuel Carpenter, first treasurer of that province and also a member of Penn's Provincial Council.

Colonel Carpenter was born at Glassborough, New Jersey, February 11, 1839. He was graduated at the Philadelphia High School, and remained for some time at the University of Pennsylvania. He was a student when the war broke out, and enlisted in the Sixth Cavalry November 1, 1861, and was commissioned second lieutenant, Sixth Cavalry, July 17, 1862. He served in the Army of the Potomac during a portion of the Peninsula campaign; was in the retreat to Yorktown, and in the cavalry covering Washington after the second battle of Bull Run, and was engaged in the cavalry operations and skirmishes connected with the advance of the army after Antietam. He participated at the battle of Fredericksburg, Stoneman's raid, and action at Beverly Ford June 9, 1863.

Colonel Carpenter was appointed acting adjutant, Sixth Cavalry, June 12, 1863, and served in the campaign of Gettysburg,—in various actions and combats, and in the battle of Gettysburg on July 3, 1863, and in pursuit of the enemy; and in the Mine Run expedition. May 4, 1864, he was detailed as acting aide-de-camp on the staff of Major-General Sheridan, commanding Cavalry Corps, and was engaged in the Richmond campaign,—battle of the Wilderness, Todd's Tavern, Sheridan's raid around Richmond, May 9-24, 1864; battles of Yellow Tavern, where Stuart was killed; combat of Meadow Bridge, May 27, 1864; guided advance of the Army of the Potomac from Chesterfield Station, on the North Anna, to Hanovertown, *en route* to Cold Harbor; engaged in preliminary actions and battle of Cold Harbor; in Sheridan's raid towards Gordonsville, June 7-28, 1864; battle of Trevilian Station, June 11-12, 1864; siege of Petersburg, and many actions in connection therewith. On August 10, 1864, he joined the Army of the Shenandoah as acting aide-de-camp on the staff of General Sheridan, commanding, and was engaged in many actions in the Shenandoah Valley and in the battles of Winchester and Fisher's Hill.

He was appointed lieutenant-colonel, Fifth U. S. Colored Cavalry, September 28, 1864 and on October 2, 1864 was ordered to Kentucky, commanding the regiment and post of Camp Nelson, Kentucky. He was promoted colonel, Fifth U. S. Colored Cavalry, October 28, 1865, and mustered out of the volunteer service at Helena, Arkansas, March 15, 1866.

Colonel Carpenter was appointed captain, Tenth Cavalry, July 28, 1866. He has served since the war on the plains, in the Indian campaigns of 1868 and 1874, against the Sioux, Cheyennes, Comanches, and Kiowas in Kansas and the Indian Territory,—that of 1868 being in relief of Colonel Forsythe's command by a forced march, and other Indian scouts.

Colonel Carpenter has been a member of numerous important boards, among which was the Cavalry Equipment Board at Fort Leavenworth and Watervliet Arsenal in 1873, and Board for Purchase of Cavalry Horses for the Department of Texas in 1876. He assisted in quelling a riot of Mexicans at San Martin, Texas, in 1877-78, and subsequently engaged in a campaign against the Apaches in Northwestern Texas in 1880. He was on leave of absence in Europe in 1881-82, and, after rejoining his regiment, marched with it down the Platte from Laramie to Kansas in 1885, and the same year was detached, with four troops, to Fort Reno, Indian Territory, to provide against an outbreak of Cheyennes.

Colonel Carpenter was brevetted during the war to lieutenant-colonel in the regular army and to colonel of volunteers for gallant services at Gettysburg, Winchester, and services during the war, and brevetted colonel in the regular army for gallant services in the action with Indians on Beaver Creek, Kansas, October 28, 1868. He was also mentioned in general orders for same engagement.

He received his promotion to major, Fifth Cavalry, February 17, 1883, and commanded Fort Robinson, Nebraska, 1883-85. He served at Fort Supply, 1885-87, and commanded Fort Myer, Virginia, 1887-91. He is now serving at Fort Reno, Oklahoma Territory.

MAJOR HENRY CARROLL.

MAJOR HENRY CARROLL (First Cavalry) was born in Copenhagen, Lewis County, New York, May 20, 1838. He moved to Minnesota in 1858, and enlisted as a private in Light Battery E, Third Artillery, January 13, 1859, at Fort Ridgely, Minnesota. He served through the grades of corporal, sergeant, and first sergeant to July 1, 1861. He participated in an expedition against the Sioux Indians in the summer of 1859 in Dakota Territory, and took part in the occupation of Alexandria, Virginia, in May, 1861, followed by a reconnoissance and engagement at Blackburn's Ford, July 18, and battle of Bull Run, July 21, same year. In October, 1861, he was in an expedition to Port Royal, South Carolina, and occupied Hilton Head in November. In 1862 he was at Fernandina and Jacksonville, Florida, in March; John's Island, South Carolina, May and June, and James Island same month, being engaged on James Island, June 10, in battle of Fort Lamar or Secessionville; in bombardment and capture of Morris Island, July 10, 1863; attack on Fort Wagner, July 10, and assaults on same position August 23 and September 7 following. He was under fire in an advanced battery alternate days during the siege of Forts Wagner, Gregg, and Sumter, and was presented a medal for gallant and meritorious conduct August 23, 1863. He was wounded the same day.

Having been discharged January 13, 1864, he re-enlisted in Light Battery G, Third Artillery, at Washington City, February 3, 1864, and joined Ninth Army Corps, participating in the battle of the Wilderness and the movements of the Army of Potomac to Spottsylvania until May 11, when he was ordered to Washington.

He was appointed second lieutenant Third U. S. Cavalry May 18, 1864, and joined his battery at Little Rock, then attached to the Seventh Army Corps. Participated in operations against Confederate cavalry in Arkansas in 1864-65, and was quartermaster of the Second Cavalry Brigade (Powell's) and depot quartermaster at Duval's Bluff, Arkansas, from June to November, 1865.

He was promoted first lieutenant April 14, 1866, and was *en route* to Fort Union, New Mexico, through the Indian Territory, from May to August of that year, performing the duties of adjutant and quartermaster. He then served at Fort Stevens, Colorado, and Los Pinos, New Mexico, to January, 1867, when he was promoted to a captaincy in the Ninth Cavalry, joining the latter at Fort Stockton, Texas. With the exception of a tour of recruiting service at St. Louis and Chicago from January, 1873, to October, 1874, Major Carroll's service was at numerous posts in Texas to 1876, where he was engaged in scouting after Indians, stock-thieves, and murderers; in affair with Comanche and Kiowa Indians in September, 1869, on the head-waters of the Brazos River, and in the reconstruction of civil affairs in Marion County during January and February, 1870. He was mentioned in orders from head-quarters Fifth Military District, Austin, Texas, in November, 1869, for the affair on the Brazos River.

Changing station to New Mexico in 1876, we find the major engaged in the following affairs: With Apache Indians at Florida Mountains, September 13, 1876, for which he was mentioned in orders, District of New Mexico; with Mescalero Apaches in Sacramento Mountains, July 22, 1878, and Dog Canyon, Sacramento Mountains, August 5, 1878; with Apaches in the San Andreas Mountains, February 3, 1880; with Victoria's Apaches, San Andreas Mountains, April 5-7, 1880, where he was twice seriously wounded on the 6th, and was mentioned in orders, District of New Mexico, and recommended for the brevet of lieutenant-colonel. After this affair the major was granted a sick leave of absence until March, 1881, when we find him again scouting after Ute Indians in Colorado and Utah in the summer of that year, for which he was mentioned in orders, Fort Lewis, Colorado. He was again in an affair with the Chiracahua Apaches at Dragoon Mountains, Arizona, October 4, 1881, for which he was mentioned in orders in the field, and especially mentioned by the department commander of Arizona, October, 1881.

It would be impossible to follow the major in his numerous changes of station in this short sketch, or the duties which have fallen to his lot. His field of duty was removed to the Indian Territory in 1881, to Nebraska in 1885, and in that year to Montana, having been promoted major of the First Cavalry July 3, 1885. He took part in the Sioux campaign of Dakota from November 24, 1890, to February 5, 1891.

## MAJOR-GENERAL SAMUEL S. CARROLL, U.S.A.
(RETIRED).

MAJOR-GENERAL SAMUEL S. CARROLL (retired) was born in Washington, D. C., September 21, 1832, and graduated from the Military Academy July 1, 1856. He was promoted brevet second lieutenant of the Ninth Infantry the same day. He was promoted second lieutenant of the Tenth Infantry October 1, 1856; to a first lieutenancy April 25, 1861, and to a captaincy November 1, 1861.

At the commencement of the Rebellion he was tendered a first lieutenancy in the Nineteenth Infantry May 14, 1861, which he declined. He was appointed colonel of the Eighth Ohio Infantry December 7, 1861, and commanded this regiment in Virginia under Generals Kelly, Lander, and Shields, until May, 1862, when, by the order of Secretary of War Stanton, he was made acting brigadier-general of volunteers, and nominated for the rank of brigadier.

General Carroll was assigned by General Shields to the command of a brigade, and served in Shields's division, Ricketts's division, McDowell's corps, and Whipple's division of the Third Corps until April, 1863, when he was assigned to the command of a brigade in French's division of the Second Corps, then commanded by General Couch, and subsequently by General Hancock. He commanded this brigade until May 13, 1864.

During this period of service General Carroll participated in the campaigns, battles, and skirmishes in West Virginia and the Shenandoah Valley under Generals Kelly, Lander, and Shields. Joining the Army of the Potomac in the fall of 1862, he participated in the Rappahannock campaign and was engaged in the battles of Fredericksburg, and afterwards in all the actions participated in by the Second Corps until May 13, 1864. He was wounded while making a reconnoissance at "Rapidan Station," just after the battle of Cedar Mountain in 1862; also wounded at Morton's Ford February 6, 1864; also wounded in the battle of the Wilderness, May 5 and 9, and again wounded at the battle of Spottsylvania Court-House May 13, 1864. He was appointed brigadier-general of volunteers May 12, 1864. In February, 1865, General Carroll was assigned to the command of the Department of West Virginia for about six weeks, then to the command of a division of the First Veteran Corps (Hancock's) in the Shenandoah Valley, and afterwards at Camp Stoneman, near Washington, until August, 1865, when the division was disbanded.

He received the following brevets: Major, May 3, 1863, for "gallant and meritorious services in the battle of Chancellorsville;" lieutenant-colonel, July 3, 1863, for "gallant and meritorious services in the battle of Gettysburg, Pennsylvania;" colonel, May 5, 1864, for "gallant and meritorious services in the battle of the Wilderness, Virginia;" brigadier-general, March 13, 1865, for "gallant and distinguished services in the eight days' battles in the old Wilderness and at Spottsylvania Court-House, Virginia;" major-general, March 13, 1865, for "gallant and meritorious services in the field during the war," and major-general of volunteers, March 13, 1865, for "gallant and meritorious services during the war."

In August, 1865, General Carroll was assigned to the command of the Military District in Virginia under General Terry, which he retained until January, 1866, when he was mustered out of the volunteer service. In consideration of his gallant conduct during the war, he was tendered the lieutenant-colonelcy of the Twenty-first United States Infantry January 22, 1867, which he accepted April 1, 1867, and on the 9th of June, 1869, he was retired for wounds in the line of duty on the rank of major-general. Since retirement he has lived in Montgomery County, Maryland, at what is now the suburban village of "Takoma Park."

### REAR-ADMIRAL AUGUSTUS LUDLOW CASE, U.S.N.

REAR-ADMIRAL AUGUSTUS LUDLOW CASE was born in Newburg, New York, in February, 1813, and appointed midshipman in 1828. After cruising in Brazil and West Indies, became passed midshipman in 1834. Served on the Coast Survey and on the United States South Sea Surveying and Exploring Expedition. While absent on latter duty commissioned acting lieutenant, and continued to serve in the expedition from 1837 to 1842.

Commissioned as lieutenant February 25, 1841; cruised in frigate "Brandywine," East Indies, 1843–45. During Mexican War, in schooner "Mahonese," brig "Porpoise," frigate "Raritan," sloops-of-war "John Adams" and "Germantown," Gulf of Mexico, 1846–48. He was present at and participated in the capture of Vera Cruz, Alvarado, and Tabasco. After the landing of the troops, on the first day, was in charge of the beach and superintended the landing of men, ordnance, and stores for the investment of Vera Cruz. After possession of Laguna was taken by the "Porpoise," he was despatched, in a "bungo" having one of the "Porpoise's" 42-pounder carronades mounted on the bow, with Passed Midshipman F. K. Murray and twenty-five men, up the Palisada River to the town of the same name, which was captured and held for a fortnight against a large body of cavalry which almost daily threatened an attack. The object of holding the town was to intercept and capture General Santa Anna, who, it was supposed, would endeavor to escape to Honduras via the Palisada passes. Cruising in sloop-of-war "Vincennes," Pacific Ocean, 1849–51; commanding sloop-of-war "Warren," Pacific Squadron, 1852–53; light-house inspector, third district, New York, 1853–57.

Commissioned as commander, September 14, 1855; waiting orders in 1858; commanding steamer "Caledonia," Brazil Squadron and Paraguay Expedition, in 1859; waiting orders in 1860. In March, 1861, just at the commencement of the Rebellion, Commander Case was ordered to Washington as assistant to (then) Commodore Stringham, in the Office of Detail; but on the assignment of the latter to the command of the North Atlantic Blockading Squadron, he was appointed fleet-captain of it, and with him joined the steam-frigate "Minnesota," at Boston, April 13. Subsequently served in the same position with Flag-Officer L. M. Goldsborough and Acting Rear-Admiral S. P. Lee, who were successively appointed to command the fleet, 1861–62. He took part in the capture of Forts Clarke and Hatteras, August 28 and 29, 1861; Roanoke Island, February 7 and 8, 1862; Sewell's Point (where, in passing the heavy fortifications on Craney Island, he landed from his "tug" and hauled down the large rebel flag there flying) and Norfolk, May 10, 1862; and all of the general active operations of the North Atlantic Fleet, until January, 1863, when, it being understood that active operations were over, and that the duty of the fleet would be mostly confined to blockading, he was assigned to the command of the steam-sloop "Iroquois," which was fitted to look after the "Alabama," but was afterwards attached to the North Atlantic Squadron. In charge of the blockade of New Inlet, North Carolina, 1863; cut out the steamer "Kate" from under Fort Fisher and the other batteries at New Inlet, aided by the steamers "James Adger" and "Mount Vernon," in August, 1863.

Commissioned as captain January 2, 1863; special duty, Washington, in 1864; navy-yard, New York, 1864–65; fleet-captain, European Squadron, 1865–66.

Commissioned as commodore December 8, 1867; light-house inspector, third district, New York, 1867–69. Chief of Bureau of Ordnance, 1869–73.

Commissioned as rear-admiral May 24, 1872; commanding European Squadron 1873–75, and combined European North and South Atlantic Fleets, assembled at Key West, Florida, 1874, for special service in connection with the steamer "Virginius" difficulties, and for ordnance, torpedo, and fleet-practice and tactics, etc. Total sea-service, twenty-four years ten months; shore or other duty, twelve years.

## COLONEL AND BREVET MAJOR-GENERAL SILAS CASEY, U.S.A.
(DECEASED).

COLONEL AND BREVET MAJOR-GENERAL SILAS CASEY (deceased), son of Elizabeth (Goodale) and Wanton Casey, and nephew of Dr. Lincoln Goodale, whom he succeeded in 1870, was born in East Greenwich, Rhode Island, July 12, 1807; died at Brooklyn, New York, January 22, 1882. His grandfather, Silas, an extensive importing-merchant before the Revolution, and his father, Wanton, who was educated in France during Franklin's residence there, were natives of East Greenwich. In his youth was educated at the academy in his native town and at West Point; on graduating July 1, 1826, was appointed brevet second lieutenant in Seventh Infantry, stationed at Fort Towson, Arkansas. His subsequent commissions are as follows: Second lieutenant, 1829; assistant commissary subsistence, February, 1836; first lieutenant, June, 1836; captain, July, 1839; brevet-major for Contreras and Churubusco, August 20, 1847; brevet lieutenant-colonel for Chapultepec, September 13, 1847; lieutenant-colonel Ninth Infantry, March 3, 1855; brigadier-general of volunteers, August 31, 1861; colonel Fourth Infantry, October 9, 1861; brevet brigadier-general U. S. Army and major-general volunteers for Fair Oaks, May 31, 1862; brevet major-general U. S. Army, March 13, 1865, for gallant and meritorious services during the Rebellion.

During the Florida War he was appointed captain in a regiment of Creek Indian volunteers. He distinguished himself in the battle of Pilaklikaha (April 19, 1842), and was recommended by Colonel Worth, his commander, for the brevet of major. He was engaged in Mexico in battles of Contreras and Churubusco; and at the storming of the castle of Chapultepec, while leading his men through a terrible fire, was severely wounded in the abdomen when near the Mexican batteries. For his services and conduct in the war with Mexico he received a beautiful silver vase from the inhabitants of his native town and a resolution of thanks from the Legislature of Rhode Island. In November, 1851, while stationed in California, Casey attacked and defeated the Coquille River Indians, whom he completely subdued.

In March, 1856, Lieutenant-Colonel Casey, in a campaign of twenty-five days, completely subdued the Puget Sound Indians in Washington Territory. Pending the controversy between the United States and the British government respecting the boundaries of each in that Territory, Lieutenant-Colonel Casey occupied and fortified San Juan Island, which place was, by agreement between General Scott and the British authorities, afterward occupied jointly by the two nations.

Was assigned at breaking out of Civil War to the duty

of organizing into brigades, disciplining, and instructing the volunteer troops arriving at Washington, D.C. On March 22, 1862, he was assigned to the command of a division in the Army of the Potomac, and accompanied it under General McClellan to the Peninsula. Having been, contrary to his advice and opinion, ordered to Seven Pines (Fair Oaks), where his division was within six miles of Richmond without support on either flank, he commenced work energetically, digging rifle-pits and cutting abatis to strengthen as much as possible his false position. Here, on May 31, Casey was attacked by an overwhelming force under Generals Longstreet and Hill, and after a severe conflict of three hours was driven from his position with a loss of fourteen hundred and thirty in killed, wounded, and missing, out of a total force of less than five thousand men. Says an eye-witness: " The veteran warrior Casey had been in the thickest of the fight, directing and animating . . . and nearly one-third of his command had found a soldier's death, or were maimed and helpless from the fight."

Besides his promotion, General Casey received the thanks of the Legislature of his native State for his bravery and skill in this battle. On June 30 he was relieved from the command of his division by General McClellan, and ordered to the White House on the " Pamunkey," where he successfully performed the duty of evacuating that depot, destroying supplies that could not be taken away. On August 11 he was again placed on duty to receive, organize, and instruct the volunteers arriving at Washington; and on this date the system of tactics for the United States Army by Casey was adopted by the government. During his period of duty in Washington General Casey equipped, organized, and in a preliminary manner instructed about three hundred thousand volunteer troops. He was, in July 18, 1868, retired at his own request.

### CAPTAIN SILAS CASEY, U.S.N.

CAPTAIN SILAS CASEY was born in Rhode Island upon a family place between Kingston and Narragansett Pier, on September 11, 1841. His father was General Silas Casey, of the U. S. Army, whose long service in the army, as well as his distinguished conduct in McClellan's Peninsula campaign, made his name well known to the country at large. Captain Casey's brother is now the chief of the Engineer Department of the U. S. Army; and another brother, Lieutenant Edward Casey, of the U. S. cavalry, was foully murdered only a short time ago by Western Indians, in whose interest he was endeavoring to make parley. It was a most lamentable thing, especially as Lieutenant Casey was a true friend of the Indians, and had succeeded—among the first—in drilling some of them into soldiers.

Captain Silas Casey was appointed an acting midshipman in September, 1856. After four years at the U. S. Naval Academy, he graduated in 1860, and was ordered to the steam-frigate "Niagara," then one of the remarkable naval vessels. The march of events was rapid in those days, and Casey found himself a master in the navy in 1861, at which time he was serving off Pensacola, in engagements with the Confederate batteries.

He was commissioned lieutenant in July, 1862, six years after his appointment as acting midshipman, and served as executive-officer of the gun-boat "Wissahickon," on the South Atlantic Blockading Squadron, in 1862–63. Was in several engagements with Fort McAllister during 1862. He served in the first attack upon Charleston under Admiral Du Pont, and then for a long time was executive-officer of the "Quaker City," in the North Atlantic Blockading Squadron, during which period he participated in the two attacks upon Fort Fisher.

After the war closed he was navigating-officer of the "Winooski," of the Atlantic Squadron, from 1865 to 1867. He was commissioned as lieutenant-commander in July, 1866, and was then stationed at the U. S. Naval Academy for three years. Lieutenant-Commander Casey was then ordered as executive-officer of the steam-frigate "Colorado," flag-ship of the Asiatic Squadron, where he remained from 1870 to 1873. He was in command of the battalion of sailors from the fleet in the Corean expedition, and the assault on Fort McKee (Elbow Fort), Seoul River, in June, 1872. Upon his return from this long and arduous cruise, he was upon ordnance duty at the Philadelphia Navy-Yard during 1873 and 1874. Commissioned as commander in June, 1874, and in 1875–76 was in command of the "Portsmouth," sloop-of-war. He was inspector of the Twelfth Light-House District from 1876 to 1879, and commanded the "Wyoming" and "Quinnebaug," of the European Squadron, in 1880–82. He then served a term as equipment-officer at the Navy-Yard, Washington, D. C., and was inspector of the Fifth Light-House District, and in command of the "Dale," up to 1889. In February, 1889, he was commissioned captain. He was ordered to the command of the U. S. S. "Newark," in July, 1890, which command he still retains.

### BRIGADIER-GENERAL THOMAS LINCOLN CASEY.

BRIGADIER-GENERAL THOMAS LINCOLN CASEY (Corps of Engineers) was born in New York. He is the son of General Silas Casey, deceased, who was retired as colonel of the Fourth Infantry. Young Casey was graduated at the U. S. Military Academy in the Class of 1852, and promoted brevet second lieutenant of the Corps of Engineers. He served at West Point, attached to the company of sappers, miners, and pontoniers, the year he graduated; and was then the assistant engineer in the construction of Fort Delaware and works of harbor and river improvement in Delaware River and Bay until 1854, when he was detailed at the U. S. Military Academy as assistant instructor of practical engineering, and serving with engineer troops to June 27, 1857; then made principal assistant professor of engineering, which position he occupied to August 31, 1859.

He was promoted second lieutenant June 22, 1854, and first lieutenant December 1, 1856.

Being ordered to the Pacific coast in 1859, he was in command of a detachment of engineer troops in Washington Territory, and in charge of the construction of a wagon-road from Vancouver to Cowlitz, Oregon, and in selecting and surveying military reservations on Puget Sound from 1858 to 1861.

He served during the rebellion of the seceding States as engineer at Fort Monroe, Virginia, on the staff of the general commanding the Department of Virginia, from June 11 to August 15, 1861; as superintending engineer of the permanent defences and field fortifications upon the coast of Maine, and on recruiting service for engineer troops; on special duty with the North Atlantic Squadron, during the first expedition to Fort Fisher, North Carolina, December 8-29, 1864, and as member of special board of engineers for work at Willett's Point, New York, from April 7 to June 20, 1865.

He was promoted captain of the Corps of Engineers August 6, 1861, and major October 2, 1863, and brevetted lieutenant-colonel and colonel March 13, 1865, for "faithful and meritorious services during the Rebellion."

Colonel Casey was member of the board of engineers

for work at Forts Preble, Scammel, Knox, and Popham, from August, 1865, to February, 1866, when he was granted leave of absence from July 26, 1866, to February 25, 1867. He was then detailed as superintending engineer of the construction of Forts Preble and Scammel, Portland harbor, Maine, and other important works, from March 1, 1867, to March 3, 1877, when he was appointed colonel and in charge of public buildings and grounds at Washington, D. C., retaining this position until April 1, 1881. He was placed in charge of the construction of the State, War, and Navy Department building, March, 1877, which building he completed March, 1888, of the Washington National Monument in 1878, which he completed December 6, 1884.

He was promoted lieutenant-colonel of Engineers September 2, 1874; colonel March 12, 1884, and brigadier-general and chief of engineers July 6, 1888. Since that time he has been stationed in Washington, D. C., at the head of his bureau. He has been a member of the Massachusetts Society of the Cincinnati since 1882, of the National Academy of Sciences since 1890, and an "Officer" of the Legion of Honor of France since January, 1890.

### COLONEL ISAAC S. CATLIN.

COLONEL ISAAC S. CATLIN (retired) was born at Oswego, New York, July 8, 1835. When the Rebellion was inaugurated, he was a member of the law-firm of Tracy and Catlin at Owego, New York, the senior member being the present Secretary of the Navy, Honorable Benjamin F. Tracy. Catlin was also mayor of Owego at that time, having been elected in November, 1860, without opposition. On the 17th of April, 1861, the date of Lincoln's first proclamation for volunteers, he officially approved a call for a meeting to raise a company of volunteers. On that evening he enrolled himself, with others, as an enlisted man, and before the meeting adjourned the minimum number of men for a company was enrolled, with himself unanimously elected as captain. It is claimed to have been one of the first, if not the very first, company of actual volunteers enlisted in this State. The company was attached to the Third New York Volunteers. He served with it at Big Bethel, Virginia. In March, 1862, he resigned for the purpose of raising a new regiment, and when General B. F. Tracy was assigned to the Twenty-fourth Senatorial or Regimental District by Governor E. D. Morgan, Catlin was first made adjutant of the post, then lieutenant-colonel of the One Hundred and Ninth New York Volunteers.

He served in the field with the Army of the Potomac during the war of the Rebellion; had separate command in 1863-64 at Falls Church, Virginia, which was kept in active service watching the predatory movements of Mosby and other guerillas; in May, 1864, his regiment joined the Ninth Corps, and was assigned to the First Brigade, Third Division; he was sick in hospital at Washington, D.C., with gastric fever, for several weeks after the action at Gaines' Farm, Virginia; he rejoined command in front of Petersburg, Virginia, July, 1864; and on July 30, while commanding a Provisional Brigade of three regiments at the battle of the "Crater," he lost his right leg and received other severe wounds. As soon as he recovered sufficiently to walk with crutches, the Secretary of War assigned him to duty as President of a Court-Martial and Military Commission at Washington, D.C., where he served with his brevet rank of major-general until mustered out June 4, 1865. In 1867, by reason of the severity of his wounds, he applied for a captaincy in the army, to which he was promptly appointed; and in May, 1870, he was retired as a colonel of infantry, being the lineal rank he held when wounded. He participated in the battle of Big Bethel, Virginia, March, 1862; Wilderness, and succeeding engagements; Spottsylvania, North Anna, Gaines' Farm, and other engagements from the Rappahannock to James River, and in the battle of the "Crater," in front of Petersburg, Virginia, 1864. After the wounding of Colonel Tracy, May 6, 1864, he commanded his regiment in all engagements up to Gaines' Farm, and commanded a Provisional Brigade at the battle of the "Crater," as stated above.

He was made brevet major U.S.A. May 6, 1867, for gallant and meritorious services in the battle of the Wilderness, Virginia; brevet lieutenant-colonel May 6, 1867, for gallant and meritorious services in the battle of Petersburg, Virginia; brevet brigadier-general of volunteers March 13, 1865, for gallant and meritorious services during the war; brevet major-general of volunteers March 13, 1865, for gallant and meritorious services in the battles before Petersburg, Virginia. In the report of Colonel Frederick Townsend, commanding One Hundred and Ninth New York, with regard to the battle of Big Bethel, Virginia, he said of him: "He was at Bethel, and I do not hesitate to say there was no man or officer more distinguished on that field than he."

After the war, in 1865, he was nominated for District Attorney of Tioga County, New York, and received the largest majority ever given a candidate in that county. In 1870 he was appointed assistant United States District Attorney, which position he held for two years, and then went into partnership with General Tracy, the present Secretary of the Navy, in the practice of the law. In 1874 he was nominated for District Attorney in Kings County, New York, but subsequently retired. In 1877 he was again, against his own protest, unanimously nominated by acclamation, and, overcoming an opposing majority of about 14,000, he was elected by about 3000 majority. He was unanimously renominated by acclamation in 1880, and, overcoming a normal opposing majority of 9600, he was elected by about 11,000. In 1885 he was nominated by the County Convention, by acclamation, for Surrogate, but declined peremptorily.

## LIEUTENANT-COLONEL HENRY L. CHIPMAN
(RETIRED).

LIEUTENANT-COLONEL HENRY L. CHIPMAN was born in Canandaigua, New York, February 23, 1823. He entered the volunteer service as lieutenant-colonel of the Second Michigan Infantry May 25, 1861, and resigned June 24, 1861, to accept the appointment of a captaincy in the Eleventh United States Infantry, to date from May 14, 1861. He joined head-quarters Eleventh Infantry at Fort Independence, Massachusetts, and remained there until October 14, assisting in organizing the regiment, and was then ordered to Perryville, Maryland; and was engaged doing guard duty here until March, 1862, when he joined the Army of the Potomac, and served continually with this army until April, 1864; went through the Peninsula campaign under General McClellan; on a reconnoissance from the Potomac River to Leetown, Virginia; the troops fording the river had continuous sharp skirmishing for two days, until the command recrossed the river, near Shepherd-town, Virginia, he being engaged on the skirmish-line the most of the time; March 21, 1863, he was appointed by Major-General Meade acting assistant inspector-general of the Second Division, Fifth Corps, (Sykes's regulars) and was on this duty until April 1, 1864, when, having been appointed colonel of the One Hundred and Second Regiment United States Colored Troops, he left the Army of the Potomac and went with regiment to Hilton Head, South Carolina. On the 30th of August, 1864, he went with regiment to Jacksonville, Florida, and was engaged in destroying the railroad leading from Jacksonville to Tallahassee, Florida; built an earthwork at Magnolia, on the St. John's River; and was then sent to Beaufort, South Carolina, with regiment, where he remained until November 30, 1864, in command of an extended picket line, taking in three of the Sea Islands. At the above date he started with five companies of regiment to join an expedition, under command of General John P. Hatch, at Boyd's Landing, South Carolina, for the purpose of capturing the Charleston and Savannah Railroad, the result was a severe battle at Honey Hill, South Carolina; he commanded a brigade a part of the time during this battle. Two days after he commanded a reconnoissance towards the railroad, about five miles from where the battle was fought, and had a sharp skirmish with the enemy. On the 9th of December, 1864, another attempt was made to capture the railroad, about thirty miles distant from Honey Hill, and in this affair, which was quite severe, he commanded a brigade composed of three regiments and a battalion of sailors and marines from the navy; he was with the first troops that entered Charleston, South Carolina. On April 1, 1865, left Charleston with two wagon-loads of ammunition and two hundred

and fifty men to join an expedition at Nelson's Ferry, on the Santee River, a command from Georgetown, South Carolina, under General Potter; on reaching the ferry learned that he had gone on towards Camden, some days before, so crossed the river and followed his command for five days, fighting his way through to him; one officer and nine men were wounded and one man killed while making this march. The day after joining General Potter he took his own regiment and five companies of another regiment to drive the enemy from a strong earthwork immediately in their front and across the road of the line of march; turned the enemy's flank and drove him out after a severe fight of thirty minutes. On the 17th of April, 1865, while on the march back to Georgetown, the enemy sent in a flag of truce with the intelligence of the surrender of Generals Lee and Johnston, and of the assassination of President Lincoln.

Colonel Chipman also participated in the siege of Yorktown, battles of Gaines' Mill, Malvern Hill, second Bull Run, Antietam, Fredericksburg, Chancellorsville, Gettysburg, and affair at Rappahannock Station. Was brevetted major for "gallant and meritorious services at Chancellorsville," and lieutenant-colonel for same at Gettysburg; and was also made brevet brigadier-general of volunteers for gallant and meritorious services during the war. Promoted major of the Third Inf. Oct. 1873, and lieutenant-colonel of the Seventh Inf. May 19, 1881.

When the Third Infantry, of which he was major, moved from Corinne, Utah, to Helena, Montana, it marched five hundred miles in thirty days over the Rocky Mountains, when the temperature at times was sixteen degrees below zero and the ground covered with snow, which had to be scraped away to pitch tents.

Colonel Chipman was retired from active service February 1, 1887, and now resides in San Antonio, Texas.

## CAPTAIN WM. H. CLAPP.

CAPTAIN WM. H. CLAPP (Sixteenth Infantry) was born in Ohio, September 7, 1836, and at the breaking out of the war of the Rebellion entered the volunteer service as a private in Company A, of the Seventy-first New York Infantry, April 19, 1861, from which he was discharged July 30, 1861. Feeling still the ambition to serve his country after his first three months' experience in that regiment in the battle of the first Bull Run, he again came into service September 25, 1861, as second lieutenant of the Forty-second Ohio Infantry, and was promoted first lieutenant March 14, 1862. He was an aide-de-camp of volunteers from December 19, 1861, to April 1, 1862, when he received the appointment of adjutant of the Forty-second Ohio Infantry, and was assistant adjutant-general of volunteers on the staff of Major-General Heron from May, 1862, to July, 1864, participating in the campaign in Eastern Kentucky, and engaged in the actions of Middle Creek and capture of Cumberland Gap. He then participated in the Mississippi campaign, and was engaged in the action of Tazewell, Tennessee. He followed the fortunes and misfortunes of the army in the investment of Vicksburg, being engaged in the first assault on the works about that city, the action of Chickasaw Bayou, the capture of Arkansas Post, and the siege of Vicksburg. He was also engaged in the capture of Yazoo City.

He was appointed captain and assistant adjutant-general of volunteers May 15, 1863. The captain's field of duty was subsequently transferred to Texas, and we find him present at the capture and surrender of Brownsville, Texas, and the Trans-Mississippi Department. He was honorably mentioned in General Orders, by Major-General Heron, for conduct at the siege of Vicksburg, and received the brevets of major and lieutenant-colonel of volunteers March 13, 1865, for "faithful and meritorious services during the war."

Captain Clapp entered the regular service as second lieutenant of the Eleventh United States Infantry February 23, 1866, and was promoted first lieutenant the same day. He was adjutant of the First Battalion of the Eleventh Infantry from August 9 to December 5, 1866, when he was appointed regimental adjutant. He occupied this position until April 14, 1869, when, by the consolidation of regiments, he was transferred to the Sixteenth Infantry. His services from that time have been connected with the movements of that regiment, of which he was appointed adjutant May 1, 1872, retaining the office until August 1, 1874, when he was made regimental quartermaster. He was promoted captain December 25, 1874. He served in various States and Territories, and finally became located at Fort Douglas, Utah, which is now his post of duty.

## MAJOR AND BREVET-COLONEL JOSEPH C. CLARK, JR.
### (RETIRED).

MAJOR AND BREVET-COLONEL JOSEPH C. CLARK, JR. (retired), was born at Mount Holly, New Jersey, November 28, 1825. He was graduated at the United States Military Academy in the Class of 1848, and was assigned as brevet second lieutenant to the Third United States Artillery and promoted to second lieutenant Fourth United States Artillery January 6, 1849; first lieutenant of the same regiment December 11, 1850, and captain May 11, 1861. He was assigned to duty in the Mathematical Department United States Military Academy August 28, 1849, and remained on this duty until August 28, 1851, when relieved at his own request. Was assigned to duty as assistant United States Coast Survey, 1854, and was engaged in the triangulation of the coast of Maine, New York Harbor, and Hudson River; in the survey of the Florida Reefs and Keys and approaches to Charlotte Harbor, Florida. Was relieved from this duty at his own request, 1858. At the commencement of the Rebellion was stationed at Camp Floyd, afterwards named Camp Crittenden, Utah, and on the withdrawal of the troops from this post for active service in the field was left in command of Fort Bridger. After several applications for active service he was relieved from duty at Fort Bridger and took command in January, 1862, of Light Battery "E," Fourth United States Artillery, in Lander's division in West Virginia. With this division, under General Shields in the Shenandoah Valley, took active part in the first Winchester battle March 23, 1862, and Port Republic June 8 and 9. As chief of artillery Reno's division Ninth Army Corps took active part in the battles of second Bull Run, Kettle Run, Chantilly, and South Mountain, and at Antietam had his horse killed under him, and received four severe wounds which completely disabled him from further active service. Was assigned to duty at the United States Military Academy, West Point, as principal assistant in the Philosophical Department August 29, 1863, and remained on this duty until February 21, 1870, when he was relieved under the Act of Congress which prohibited officers on the retired list being assigned to any military duty. He was retired from active service as captain May 11, 1864, and as major July 28, 1866, on account of wounds received in line of duty. Was appointed deputy governor of the Soldiers' Home, Washington, D. C., 1875, but was relieved from this duty May 1, 1877, on his own application on account of disability resulting from wounds received at Antietam. He was brevetted major for gallant and meritorious services in the campaign of the Shenandoah Valley, Virginia, June 9, 1862; lieutenant-colonel for gallant and meritorious services in the battle of Antietam, Maryland, September 17, 1862, and colonel for gallant and meritorious services during the war March 13, 1865.

### MEDICAL DIRECTOR CHRISTOPHER JAMES CLEBORNE, M.D., U.S.N.

CHRISTOPHER JAMES CLEBORNE, M.D., was born December 16, 1838, and was educated abroad at the Collegiate School of St. James and the Brunswick Academy, Bristol, England. He began the study of medicine at Edinburgh in 1856, and was graduated at the University of Pennsylvania in 1860, and the same year was made resident physician of the Pennsylvania Hospital for the unexpired term of the late Dr. Thomas B. Reed,—was *locum tenens* of Drs. Conrad and Lewis of that hospital. He was elected a member of the Academy of Natural Sciences July 31, 1860, and in 1861 was appointed an attending physician of the Moyamensing House of Industry.

At the outbreak of the Civil War, though most of his family joined the Confederacy, he entered the service of the United States as assistant surgeon May 9, 1861, and was attached to the sloop-of-war "Jamestown," North Atlantic Squadron, from May, 1861, to January, 1862, and participated in the destruction of the "Alvarado," under batteries at Fernandina, August 5, 1861. He was ordered, in 1862, to the sloop-of-war "Dale," South Atlantic Squadron, and was in expedition to Stono River, engagements on South Edisto, and saw temporary service with Forty-fifth Pennsylvania Regiment at Otter Island, South Carolina, 1862; ordered to gun-boat "Aroostook," West Gulf Squadron, 1863; in operations of Mobile, 1863. He was commissioned surgeon, with the rank of lieutenant-commander, November 24, 1863; at naval rendezvous, Philadelphia, 1864; ordered to the U.S.S. "Ticonderoga," South Atlantic Squadron, and coast of Brazil, 1864-65; present at both battles of Fort Fisher, December, 1864, when the "Ticonderoga," soon after going into action, lost, by the bursting of her Parrott-gun, twenty-one killed and wounded; present at the bombardment and capture of Fort Fisher January 15, 1865. He was ordered, as judge-advocate of the Naval Retiring Board, to Philadelphia in 1865; attached to the flag-ship "Rhode Island," West India Squadron, in 1866, and in charge of U.S.S. "Bienville" during epidemic of yellow fever in 1866; judge-advocate of Naval Retiring Board, 1867, and was elected a member of the Conchological Society of Philadelphia March 7, 1867; attached to sloop-of-war "Saratoga," 1868-69; flag-ship "Powhatan," 1870; a member of the Naval Medical Examining Board, Philadelphia, 1870; ordered to Naval Station, League Island, 1871; elected a member of the Pennsylvania Historical Society September 23, 1872; attached to sloops-of-war "Juniata," "Plymouth," "Brooklyn," and "Congress," in European Squadron, 1872-74; ordered to navy-yard, Portsmouth, New Hampshire, 1875-78; delegate to American Medical Association in 1876; commissioned medical inspector, with rank of commander, January 6, 1878; on special duty in Portsmouth from November, 1878, to April, 1879; ordered to flag-ship "Tennessee," as fleet-surgeon of the North Atlantic Squadron, 1879-81; attached to the navy-yard, Portsmouth, New Hampshire, 1881-84; elected a member of the Historical Society of Virginia in 1883; member of Medical Examining Board, Philadelphia, 1884-87; appointed one of the vice-presidents of the International Medical Congress June 4, 1886; chairman of the Medical Committee of the Constitutional Centennial in 1887, and organized the Volunteer Medical Corps of the Centennial in September, 1887; commissioned medical director, with the rank of captain, September, 1887; elected president of the Volunteer Medical Association of Philadelphia in 1887; director of Naval Hospital, Norfolk, Virginia, January, 1888, and director of Naval Hospital, Chelsea, 1891.

Dr. Cleborne is a grandson of the late William Cleborne, of Derinsolla,—representative of the Westmoreland family of that name, a branch of which was settled at Romancoke, Virginia, by Secretary William Claiborne, early in the seventeenth century.

The present station of Medical Director Cleborne is at Boston, where he is in charge of the Chelsea Naval Hospital, and is, *ex officio*, a trustee of the National Sailors' Home at Quincy, Massachusetts.

## CAPTAIN AND ASSISTANT QUARTERMASTER JOHN LINCOLN CLEM, U.S.A.

CAPTAIN AND ASSISTANT QUARTERMASTER JOHN LINCOLN CLEM was born in Newark, Ohio, August 13, 1851. He entered the volunteer service, at the breaking out of the Rebellion, as a drummer in May, 1861, but on account of his youth (not ten years old) was not enlisted, although he served as a drummer in Company C, Twenty-second Michigan Infantry until he was enlisted, May 1, 1863. He served in the field in the Army of the West; was promoted sergeant of Company C, Twenty-second Michigan Infantry at the battle of Chickamauga, and was honorably discharged from the volunteer service September 19, 1864.

Captain Clem is probably the youngest soldier on record, and began active service when about eleven years of age. Shortly after the death of his mother, he offered his services to the Third Ohio Regiment as drummer, but was rejected, being then not ten years of age. He afterwards offered himself to the Twenty-second Michigan Regiment, but was again rejected. He determined, however, to cast his fortunes with the Twenty-second Michigan, and April, 1862, found him beating the "long-roll" before Shiloh, where his bravery was so great that he was mustered in, and was known as "Johnny Shiloh." But it was on the 23d of September, 1863, at the battle of Chickamauga, that he won the name which will live long after he has passed away. Here, having just passed his twelfth year, he had laid aside the drum for the musket, and, after acting for a while as a marker, with a musket, the barrel of which had been cut down expressly for his use, he took his place in the ranks. As the day closed and the army retired to Chattanooga, his brigade was ordered to surrender by the enemy, and "Little Johnny" himself was covered by the sword of a Confederate colonel, but quickly bringing his gun into position he shot the Confederate colonel. His regiment was then fired into, and, falling as if shot, the juvenile soldier laid close until dark, when he went to Chattanooga and joined his command. For his bravery he was made a sergeant by General Rosecrans, and attached to the head-quarters of the Army of the Cumberland, and was presented with a silver medal by Miss Kate Chase, a daughter of the chief justice. He was afterwards captured and held prisoner for sixty-three days, and after his release was made orderly sergeant by General Thomas, who had succeeded General Rosecrans, and was attached to his staff. At the close of the war he went to school and graduated at the Newark High School. In 1871 General Grant, in recognition of his merits, appointed him second lieutenant of the Twenty-fourth U. S. Infantry, and served on signal duty at Fort Whipple, Virginia, during the years 1872–73; then ordered to the Artillery School at Fort Monroe, Virginia, from which he graduated in 1875; he was after this detailed as Professor of Military Science at Galesville University, where he served from June 8, 1879, to May 4, 1882.

Joining his regiment in Texas, he remained with it until appointed a captain and assistant quartermaster and ordered to Schuylkill Arsenal, Philadelphia, Pennsylvania, May 4, 1882, where he remained until transferred to Fort McHenry in 1883. In 1886 he was assigned to duty as depot quartermaster at Ogden, Utah, and in 1888 removed to Columbus, Ohio, doing duty as depot quartermaster at Columbus Barracks, his present station.

COLONEL DAVID RAMSAY CLENDENIN.

COLONEL DAVID RAMSAY CLENDENIN was born in Lancaster County, Pennsylvania, June 24, 1830, his family connection embracing the names of Colonel John Steele and David Ramsay. When but a youth, Colonel Clendenin visited Illinois and remained to complete his education at Galesburg Knox College, of which institution he is an alumnus.

In the summer of 1861 he raised a company of volunteers for the Eighth Illinois Cavalry (General Farnsworth) and at the organization of the regiment at St. Charles, Illinois, on September 18, 1861, he was made major of the regiment. For the next four years the Eighth Illinois Cavalry was identified with the Army of the Potomac, and the duties peculiar to cavalry brought them into scenes of danger and distress and gave opportunities of heroism.

He participated in the fatigue and exposure and fighting of the Peninsula campaign, taking his share of roughing it. At the battle of Upperville he had two horses shot under him. At one time (at Haxall's Landing), when alone with an orderly, inspecting pickets, a bullet from a rebel picket passed through his hat, the orderly also receiving some bullets through his clothes. When pushing ahead of the command with a squadron of the Eighth Illinois and a squadron of the Sixth Pennsylvania, as escort to the engineer officer, he captured a supply-train of the enemy, which had with it negro laborers, which he sent back to our lines as contraband of war.

General Hooker, in command of the Army of the Potomac, before the battle of Gettysburg, in the spring of 1863, when the army was in front of Fredericksburg, ordered him to take three days' rations and make a raid with his men along the fords of the James River and break up the contraband trade of ammunition and supplies. He was gone eleven days, and captured rebels and trains, three times as many men as under his command, and broke up the trade.

He was in the three-days' fight at Fredericksburg, at Coal Harbor, Kent Court-House, Cumberland, White House, Mechanicsville, First and Second Malvern Hill, and other battles of the Army of the Potomac.

Was made lieutenant-colonel of his regiment December 5, 1862, and brevetted colonel of volunteers and brigadier-general of volunteers for meritorious services during the war.

Most of the time after becoming lieutenant-colonel he was in command of his regiment.

In the summer of 1864, when the city of Washington was threatened and so nearly captured by General Jubal Early, Colonel Clendenin was with Major-General Lew Wallace in Maryland, fighting, with the six companies of his regiment, an overwhelming force of the enemy at fearful odds, delaying the progress of the rebel army until the Union army under General Grant, at Richmond, could send reinforcements for the defence of Washington. It is well to remember, says the historian, that but for the gallant stand at Monocacy, Maryland, the arrival of these troops would have been too late.

In the book "Story of Washington," page 154, we find him mentioned as follows: "Colonel Clendenin, who, as we have seen, had been fighting on the extreme left, proved himself a gallant officer. Finding himself cut off from the main body, he threw himself into the little village of Urbana, where he repeatedly repulsed the assaults of the enemy, and at last, by a bold charge, sabre in hand, cut through the hostile ranks, capturing the battle-flag of the Seventh Virginia. 'As brave a cavalry soldier as ever mounted horse,' said his commander, in his report of the battle."

After the surrender of General Lee and the cessation of hostilities, came the assassination of President Lincoln. The Eighth Illinois Cavalry, under Colonel Clendenin, was sent out as one of the search-parties to find the assassin Booth.

Colonel Clendenin was detailed on the commission to try the conspirators at Washington in 1865, and was a member of that court.

He was commissioned major of the United States Cavalry (Eighth) on January 22, 1867. Lieutenant-colonel of the Third United States Cavalry November 1, 1882, and colonel of the Second United States Cavalry October 29, 1888.

He has served on the frontier almost unremittingly since 1867, never having a detail except to harder duty, and never shirking the duty of his regular work. He was retired from active service on account of failing health April 20, 1891.

## COLONEL HENRY WHITNEY CLOSSON, U.S.A.

COLONEL HENRY WHITNEY CLOSSON (Fourth Artillery) was born in Whitingham, Vermont, June 6, 1832, and graduated from the Military Academy July 1, 1854. He was appointed second lieutenant in the First Artillery, and his first service was at Fort Yuma, California, from 1854 to 1855. While there he commanded the party which escorted Lieutenant Michler on the boundary survey of 1855. From Yuma he went to San Antonio, Texas, in 1856; from there to Fort Clark, Texas. The same year he took part in the scout to the head-waters of the Neuces, against the Lipan Indians, April 10 to 20, 1856, and was engaged in the pursuit and surprise of three parties of Lipans August 20, 1856, near the mouth of the Pecos River.

On October 31 of the same year he was promoted to first lieutenant in the First Artillery, and served the remainder of that year in garrison at Baton Rouge, Louisiana. In 1857 he served against the Seminole Indians of Florida, and from there went to Fort Adams, Rhode Island, where he remained until 1859. The conclusion of that year saw him again on the frontier at Fort Clark and Fort Duncan, Texas, and Fort Taylor, Florida, until 1861. He was offered a captaincy in the Nineteenth Infantry May 14, 1861, which was declined, and on the same date was promoted to be captain in his own regiment. He participated in the gallant defence of Fort Pickens, November, 1861, and January and May, 1862, distinguishing himself so much as to be selected for chief of artillery for the district of Pensacola, May 16 to December 24, 1862. From that time to March 13, 1863, he commanded his battery at Baton Rouge. He was chief of artillery of General Grover's division of the Nineteenth Army Corps in the Teche campaign, which lasted from March to August, 1863, being engaged in the following actions: Grand Lake Landing, April 13; Irish Bend, April 14; Vermilion Bayou, April 17, and the siege of Port Hudson, May 24 to July 8. He was brevetted major for gallant and meritorious services at the capture of Port Hudson. He was appointed chief of artillery Nineteenth Corps October 4, 1863, and served in the Red River campaign, being engaged at Sabine Cross-Roads April 8, 1864; Pleasant Hill April 9, and Crane River Crossing April 23; was chief of artillery of the Mobile Expedition, August, 1864, and participated in the siege of Fort Gaines and Fort Morgan, and for gallant and meritorious services at the latter place was brevetted lieutenant-colonel. November 1 of the same year he was transferred to the Army of the Potomac as chief of artillery and ordnance of the cavalry corps to December 31; was inspector of the horse artillery brigade from January until April, 1865. At the disbandment of the armies he returned to the command of his battery, at Winchester, Virginia, July, 1865; served at Fort McHenry, Maryland, July to October, 1865; Fort Schuyler, New York harbor, to June, 1866; Fort Porter, New York, to August, 1866, and on recruiting service, to November 30, 1867. Upon return to regimental duty he was stationed at Fort Hamilton, New York, until November 18, 1872. From there he went to Savannah, Florida, having been promoted to be major Fifth Artillery November 1, 1876.

He remained four years at Barrancas, and went in November, 1881, to Fort Niagara, where he was stationed until November, 1882. He then moved to Fort Wadsworth, New York, where he remained for six years, the longest tour of duty at one post. He was made lieutenant-colonel Fifth Artillery September 14, 1883, and colonel Fourth Artillery April 25, 1888. This transferred him to Fort Adams in May, 1888.

The regiment moved south in May, 1889, and Colonel Closson's head-quarters have been since then at Fort McPherson, Atlanta, Georgia.

January 5, 1890, he was a member of the board to examine the workings of the Artillery School at Fort Monroe, Virginia, and September 9, 1890, he was detailed upon another most important duty as member of a board to examine and report upon the capabilities of various sites for gun-foundries and factories, whereby the heavy steel rifled-guns can be made to put us upon an equality, to say the least, with other great nations of the world.

LIEUTENANT-COLONEL JOHN W. CLOUS, U.S.A.

LIEUTENANT-COLONEL JOHN W. CLOUS (Deputy Judge-Advocate-General) was born in Germany June 9, 1837. He entered the army February 2, 1857, serving as private, Company K, and in band, Ninth Infantry, to November 5, 1860, and as private and corporal, Company K, and quartermaster-sergeant, Sixth Infantry, from February 9, 1861, to December 7, 1862. In the fall of 1861 the Sixth Infantry was assigned to General Sykes's command of regulars and became part of the Army of the Potomac. Quartermaster-Sergeant Clous's "praiseworthy conduct during the movement" of that army "from the Chickahominy to the James River and his cool behavior at the battle of Malvern Hill in the performance of his duties" resulted in his being recommended for appointment as second lieutenant in the army. He was commissioned as such by President Lincoln on November 29, 1862, and assigned to the Sixth Infantry. He was on duty with his regiment during its entire service in the field with the Army of the Potomac, participating in the siege of Yorktown, seven days' battles in June, 1862, battles of Malvern Hill, second Bull Run, Antietam, Fredericksburg, Chancellorsville, and Gettysburg. He was brevetted first lieutenant and captain for gallant and meritorious services in the battle of Gettysburg. He was regimental quartermaster from February 1, 1864, to April, 1865, and regimental adjutant from the latter date to March 28, 1867. He was promoted first lieutenant, Sixth Infantry, March 28, 1865.

After a short term of service at Savannah, Georgia, and Hilton Head, South Carolina, in 1865, with his regiment, he took station at Charleston, South Carolina. While at this place Lieutenant Clous, in addition to his duties as regimental adjutant, was, in March, 1866, detailed as adjutant-general of the Department of South Carolina, continuing in that capacity upon the consolidation of the latter with the Department of the Carolinas and of the South, and subsequently into the Second Military District,—of all of which Major-General Daniel E. Sickles was the permanent commander. During the government and reconstruction of the States of North and South Carolina by this general officer, Lieutenant Clous rendered most valuable and efficient services. Having been appointed captain in the Thirty-eighth Infantry, he was, in September, 1867, at his own request, relieved from duty as adjutant-general.

In March, 1868, Captain Clous joined his company, in the Department of the Missouri, at once taking the field, escorting the construction forces of the Union Pacific Railroad, E. D. (now Kansas Pacific). In October, 1868, he was detailed as an acting aide-de-camp on the staff of Major-General Sheridan during the latter's winter campaign against the Indians of the Southwest. Upon his return, in March, 1869, he conducted a battalion of the Thirty-eighth Infantry from Fort Hays, Kansas, through the Indian country to Fort Richardson, Texas. Being, through consolidation, transferred to the Twenty-fourth Infantry, Captain Clous served with his company on the frontier of Texas at Forts Griffin, McKavett, and Brown, taking part, in 1872, as acting engineer-officer in General Mackenzie's expedition across the Staked Plains, and in the Indian engagement of the latter's command on September 29, 1872, at North Fork of the Red River, Texas.

For gallant conduct in that engagement, Captain Clous was specially mentioned in General Order No. 99, Headquarters of the Army, A. G. O., November 19, 1872; at Fort Brown—from 1873-77—his company was mounted, and performed scouting duty along the Rio Grande during the border disturbances.

He was admitted to the bar at San Antonio, Texas. He was judge-advocate in many important trials during his service in Texas, and served as judge-advocate of the Department of Texas, with the exception of a short interval, from January, 1881, to August, 1884. In April, 1886, upon the recommendation of Major-General Hancock and other prominent officers, as well as of the judges and lawyers of the bar of which he was a member, he was appointed major and judge-advocate. In May, 1887, he was admitted as an attorney and counsellor of the Supreme Court of the United States. From May, 1886, to August, 1890, he served in Washington as the assistant to the judge-advocate-general. On August 28, 1890, he became, by assignment of the Secretary of War, professor of law of U. S. Military Academy, West Point, New York, where he is now serving. On February 12, 1892, he was promoted lieutenant-colonel and deputy judge-advocate-general of the United States Army.

## MAJOR EDWIN M. COATES, U.S.A.

MAJOR EDWIN M. COATES (Nineteenth Infantry) was born in New York City January 29, 1836. He was a member of Ellsworth Chicago Zouaves in 1860, and entered the volunteer service as first lieutenant of the Eleventh New York Zouaves, Colonel E. E. Ellsworth, April 20, 1861, but the regiment was not mustered into the United States service until it arrived in Washington May 7, 1861. He was with the regiment in the advance of the army on Alexandria May 24, 1861, and assisted in taking possession of the Marshall House in that city, at six o'clock, A.M., May 24, with a squad of the regiment, a few moments after the shooting of Colonel Ellsworth by Jackson, the proprietor of the house. He accompanied the remains of Colonel Ellsworth to his former home at Mechanicsville, New York, where they were interred.

Lieutenant Coates resigned his volunteer commission August 4, 1861, and entered the regular service as second lieutenant of the Second Dragoons August 5, 1861. He was transferred to the Twelfth Infantry September 20, 1861, and joined his regiment at Fort Hamilton, New York harbor, where he served as battalion quartermaster until January, 1863, when he joined his regiment in the field with the Army of the Potomac at Falmouth, Virginia, where he was made adjutant of the first battalion, Twelfth Infantry. He served in the field with his regiment until September, 1864, when he left the field by being disabled from the fall of his horse, having participated in the battle of the Wilderness May, 1864, and the subsequent campaign.

He was then ordered on recruiting duty, where he remained until October, 1866, when he joined his regiment at Washington, D. C. He was promoted first lieutenant October 24, 1861, and was brevetted a captain August 1, 1864, "for gallant services in the battle of the Wilderness, and during the campaign before Richmond, Virginia."

He was promoted captain April 4, 1865, and upon the reorganization of the army, in 1866, was transferred to the Thirtieth Infantry. He left with his regiment for the plains in January, 1867, and passed the

remainder of the winter in camp on the South Platte River, opposite Fort Sedgwick, Colorado. He was afterwards in camp along the line of the Union Pacific Railroad during its construction, and at Fort D. A. Russell and Fort Sanders, Wyoming, until 1871. In the mean time Captain Coates with his company was transferred to the Fourth Infantry March 23, 1869, upon the consolidation of regiments. The station of his regiment was changed to Kentucky in 1871, and in 1872 to Little Rock, Arkansas, where he remained until May, 1873, when the regiment was ordered to California, to take part in the Modoc war; but upon arriving at Omaha, the necessity no longer existed for additional troops on the Pacific coast, and Captain Coates was sent with his company to Fort Bridger. He served subsequently at Forts Fetterman and Robinson, and was in the field against hostile Sioux Indians in the early part of 1876. Afterwards he was stationed at Fort Fred Steele and Fort Omaha, and was changed to Fort Sherman, Idaho, in July, 1886. From this post he was sent to Boise Barracks, Idaho, in 1890, when he was promoted major of the Nineteenth Infantry, to date from July 14, and ordered to the command of Fort Mackinac, Michigan, his present station.

## CAPTAIN JOHN NICHOLS COE, U.S.A.

CAPTAIN JOHN NICHOLS COE (Twentieth Infantry) was born in Portland, Maine, July 21, 1836. He entered the regular service as private of Company H, First Battalion Eleventh U. S. Infantry, and was subsequently appointed corporal, sergeant, and first sergeant of the same company. On the 14th of April, 1862, he was made quartermaster-sergeant of the Eleventh Infantry, which he retained until April 1, 1865, having been appointed second lieutenant of the Eleventh Infantry March 12, 1865, but not receiving the appointment until April. He was promoted first lieutenant the same day of his appointment.

Captain Coe served with his regiment in the field with the Army of the Potomac from December, 1862, to the close of the war of the Rebellion, and was then stationed with his regiment in Richmond, Virginia, from May, 1865, to January, 1867, and then in Louisiana to April, 1867. He was transferred to the Twentieth Infantry September 21, 1866, upon the reorganization of the army, and was promoted captain June 19, 1868.

He was stationed at various points in the Indian country (Dakota) most of the time from May, 1869, to December, 1877. His regiment was then transferred to Texas, along the Rio Grande, from January, 1878, to November, 1881. He then had two years' duty at Fort Leavenworth, Kansas, and rejoined his regiment at Fort Supply, Indian Territory, where he remained until May, 1885, when his regiment was ordered to Montana, and he took station at Fort Assinaboine, where he has been on duty to the present time.

Captain Coe was adjutant of the Second Battalion of the Eleventh Infantry from June 18, 1865, to October 4, 1865, when he was made quartermaster of the Second Battalion, which he retained until September 21, 1866. On the 6th of December, 1866, he was appointed regimental quartermaster of the Eleventh Infantry, and held that position until promoted captain.

## COMMANDER GEORGE W. COFFIN, U.S.N.

COMMANDER GEORGE W. COFFIN, U.S.N., is a native of Massachusetts, and was appointed from that State. He entered the Naval Academy in September, 1860, and graduated in 1863, during the height of the Civil War. He was promoted to ensign on October 1, 1863. While attached to the steam-sloop "Ticonderoga," North Atlantic Blockading Squadron, he was in both attacks upon Fort Fisher, and was wounded in the right leg by a Minie-ball during the land assault upon that stronghold. After the end of the Civil War he served in the "Shawmut," on the coast of Brazil. Commissioned as lieutenant July 25, 1866, and was attached to the steam-frigate "Franklin," of the European Squadron, in 1867-68. Was commissioned lieutenant-commander March 12, 1868. Upon his return from the European station he performed a tour of duty at the Naval Academy; and was then, in 1870-71, chief of staff of the North Atlantic fleet. He was next attached to the gunnery ship "Constellation," 1871-72, and was then at the Naval Academy again, 1873-74. Attached to the "Plymouth," North Atlantic Station, 1874-75; and the "Hartford," flag-ship of the same station, in 1875-77. Commanded the steamer "Hassler," on the Coast Survey, in 1877-80. Promoted to commander in November, 1878. Attached to Naval Observatory, 1880-81. On duty as light-house inspector from 1881 to 1884, and on ordnance duty at the New York Navy-Yard, 1884-86. In command of the "Alert," on the Greely Relief Expedition, in 1884. Commanded the steam-sloop "Quinnebaug," of the Mediterranean Squadron, 1886-87. Light-house inspector in 1888-89, and appointed secretary of the Light-House Board in 1889, which position he holds at present.

REAR-ADMIRAL NAPOLEON COLLINS, U.S.N.

REAR-ADMIRAL NAPOLEON COLLINS was a native of Pennsylvania, but was appointed midshipman from Iowa January 2, 1834; promoted to passed midshipman July 16, 1840; commissioned as lieutenant November 6, 1846; sloop "Decatur," Home Squadron, 1846-49; at Tuspan and Tabasco, Mexican War; steamer "Michigan," on the Lakes, 1850-53; commanding store-ship "John P. Kennedy," North Pacific Expedition, 1853-54; steam-frigate "Susquehanna," East India Squadron, 1854-55; navy-yard, Mare Island, California, 1856-57; sloop "John Adams," Pacific Squadron, 1857-58; steamer "Michigan," on the Lakes, 1858-60; commanding steamer "Anacostia," Potomac Flotilla, 1861; engagement at Acquia Creek, May 31 and June 1, 1861; commanding gun-boat "Unadilla," South Atlantic Blockading Squadron, 1861-62; battle of Port Royal, November 7, 1862; various expeditions on the coasts of South Carolina, Georgia, and Florida, 1861-62; commissioned as commander July 16, 1862; commanding steamer "Octorara," West India Squadron, 1862-63; commanding steam-sloop "Wachusett," special service, 1863-64. On the 7th October, 1864, Commander Collins, then in the "Wachusett," seized the rebel steamer "Florida," lying within the harbor of Bahia, Brazil; the capture was effected without loss of life. Commissioned as captain July 25, 1866; commanding steam-sloop "Sacramento," special service, 1867; navy-yard, Norfolk, 1869-70; commissioned as commodore 1871, and as rear-admiral 1874. Died in 1876.

Commander Collins's seizure of the "Florida" was a peculiar episode of the Civil War,—as much so as Wilkes's seizure of the Southern commissioners on board the "Trent." Mr. Seward disavowed the act, and insisted upon the trial of Collins by court-martial.

While negotiations were proceeding in regard to her return to the friendly neutral port from which she had been taken, she was run down by a steam-transport, at night, while moored at Newport News, Virginia, and sunk.

Commodore Collins was not long under technical punishment for this affair. He had the moral support of the service and of the country at large; the feeling being that so dangerous a vessel as the "Florida" must be disposed of when she could be laid hands on, even at the risk of international complications.

The case has since been often referred to by writers on such subjects, and it has been said that it might be brought up as a precedent in some future complication of a like nature. But our government placed itself rightly upon record by the arraignment of Collins, and by the express disavowal of his act.

The Brazilian government—the party really aggrieved—was satisfied with the explanations and the acts of our own government, and so the matter dropped. If the vessel had been actually delivered in the port of Bahia, it would have been when the civil war was near its end, and she would, no doubt, have been held by the Brazilian government until satisfactory evidence was given that she would not be used against a friendly state.

## CAPTAIN RICHARD S. COLLUM, U.S.M.C.

CAPTAIN RICHARD S. COLLUM was born in Indiana and appointed from that State to the U. S. Naval Academy as acting midshipman September 20, 1854. He resigned after remaining there about two years and a half. When the Civil War occurred he applied for service, and received a commission as second lieutenant in September, 1861. He served in the "St. Lawrence" frigate from September, 1861, to May, 1863, as his previous drill had rendered him an effective officer. During that service he was at St. Simon's, Georgia; Port Royal, South Carolina; the engagement with the Sewell's Point Battery, and the Confederate ram "Merrimac;" the bombardment of Sewell's Point and the capture of Norfolk. He was afterwards in the East Gulf Squadron, and in three boat expeditions on the Florida coast and in Indian River.

He was commissioned a first lieutenant on December 30, 1862, and while on leave of absence, in July, 1863, volunteered his services to Governor Morton, of Indiana, during the raid of the Confederate General Morgan to the north of the Ohio River. His services were accepted, and he was placed in command of a battalion of provisional troops. Lieutenant Collum was after this stationed at Cairo and Mound City, and attached to the Mississippi Squadron for a year. During that period he was actively engaged,—especially in expeditions into Kentucky in pursuit of guerillas. Afterwards member of a commission to investigate charges against certain active rebel sympathizers at Louisville, Kentucky; and was attached to the frigate "New Ironsides" from August, 1864, to April, 1865, during which time that vessel bore a prominent part in the two attacks upon Fort Fisher. He served at the Washington Navy-Yard next, being in temporary command at the barracks during the confinement of Paine and his associate conspirators. From November, 1867, to December, 1868, he was in command of Marine Barracks at Mound City, Illinois. His next service was on board the "Richmond" in the Mediterranean Squadron, from 1869 to 1871, being ordered to the Naval Academy upon his return to the United States.

Commissioned captain in March, 1872, and stationed at the marine barracks, Boston, from April, 1872, to January, 1875. During this tour of duty Captain Collum commanded the force of marines at the great fire in Boston, in November, 1872, and had charge of the removal of the treasure from the Sub-Treasury to the Custom-House, which was speedily and successfully accomplished, in spite of the circumstances, without the slightest accident or loss.

After a short term at head-quarters, upon leaving the

Boston Station, Captain Collum was made fleet marine-officer of the Asiatic Station and judge-advocate of the fleet, by special appointment of the Navy Department. He was attached to the flag-ship "Tennessee" from June, 1875, to July, 1878. From August, 1878, to November, 1881, member of the Board of Inspection. From 1881 to 1885, attached to the Marine Barracks at League Island.

In April, 1885, Captain Collum took part in the expedition to Panama. On the night of the withdrawal of the U. S. forces from the city and the occupation of the original lines, representations were made to the commanding officers that the insurgents were much excited; that drunkenness prevailed to an alarming extent, and that a violation of the armistice was in contemplation. At ten P.M. Captain Collum was ordered to enter the city alone, to endeavor to ascertain the truth of the report, and this most dangerous duty he successfully performed. Soon after he was commissioned captain and assistant quartermaster, which duty is performed in Philadelphia. Captain Collum is the author of "The History of the U. S. Marine Corps;" and the articles "Dai Nippon;" "The First Englishman in Japan;" "Notes on Duties in Camp and Garrison, Transportation of Troops by Rail, and Aid to Civil Powers;" and "Notes on Topography of Isthmus of Panama." He has also lectured on the "Heathen Chinee;" "An Historical Sketch of Small-Arms;" "The Story of a Great Crime,"—delivered before the United Service Club; "The American Marines during the War of the Revolution"—before the Historical Society; and "The Aborigines of North America and their Relation to Japan,"—before the Numismatic and Antiquarian Society of Pennsylvania.

**BREVET MAJOR-GENERAL CYRUS B. COMSTOCK, U.S.A.**

BREVET MAJOR-GENERAL CYRUS B. COMSTOCK was born in Massachusetts; appointed to Military Academy, from Massachusetts July 1, 1851, and graduated June, 1855, and on graduation was appointed brevet second lieutenant U. S. Engineers; served as assistant engineer in construction of Fort Taylor, Key West Harbor, Florida, 1855-56; in building Fort Carroll, Patapsco River, Maryland, 1856-59; promoted second lieutenant of Engineers April 1, 1855. In 1859 he was superintending engineer in construction of Fort Carroll; assistant professor of natural and experimental philosophy September 9, 1859, to July 27, 1861; July 1, 1860, was promoted first lieutenant of Engineers, and assistant engineer in the construction of the defences of Washington, D. C., August, 1861, to March, 1862; assistant to chief engineer of the Army of the Potomac March to June, 1862; senior engineer on staff of General Sumner; June-July, 1862, served in Virginia Peninsula campaign, being engaged in reconnoissance before and at siege of Yorktown; May to August, 1862, was senior engineer of defence works, making reconnoissance, and in various engineer operations on the advance towards Richmond and change of base towards James River; served in Maryland campaign (Army of the Potomac) September to November, being engaged in the battle of South Mountain September 14, 1862; took part in battle of Antietam September 17, 1862; was chief engineer, Army of the Potomac, from November 21, 1862, to March, 1863, and served in the Rappahannock campaign, taking part in the battles of Fredericksburg and Chancellorsville; March 3, 1863, he was promoted to captain of Engineers; served in the Department of Tennessee, and engaged in the siege of Vicksburg, June to July, 1863, for gallant and meritorious services in which battle he was brevetted major, U. S. Army; assistant inspector-general of the Military Division of Mississippi from November, 1863, to March, 1864; from that time he served as aide-de-camp on the staff of General Grant, with rank of lieutenant-colonel, until July, 1866; took part in the battle of the Wilderness May 5 and 6, 1864, and for gallant and meritorious services performed was brevetted lieutenant-colonel; served at the battle of Spottsylvania May 12, 1864; battle of Cold Harbor June 3, 1864; assault of Petersburg June 16 and 18, 1864, and of the Mine July 3, 1864, and the assault and capture of Fort Harrison September 29, 1864. He was chief engineer of expedition to Cape Fear River, North Carolina, in January, 1865, and was engaged at the assault and capture of Fort Fisher June 15, 1865. He was made brevet colonel, U. S. Army, and brevet brigadier-general, U. S. Volunteers, for gallant and meritorious services performed at capture of Fort Fisher; was senior officer on staff of General Canby in the Mobile campaign, taking part in the siege of Spanish Fort, March 27 to April 8, 1865, and storming of Blakely April 9, 1865. He was brevetted brigadier-general, U. S. Army, March 13, 1865, for gallant and meritorious services in the Mobile campaign, and brevetted major-general, U. S. Volunteers, March 26, for faithful and meritorious services during the campaign against the city of Mobile and its defences. December 28, 1865, was promoted to major of Engineers; served as aide-de-camp, with rank of colonel, to general-in-chief, at Washington, from July 26 to May 3, 1870; was superintending engineer of Geodetic Survey of the North and Northwestern Lakes, May 20 to July, 1874; January, 1874, to June, 1877, and June, 1878, until completion in 1882. In July, 1874, he was sent to Europe to examine the improvement of deltas of great rivers. Commencing in April, 1875, he was for two years superintending engineer to examine the progress of Ead's jetties at the mouth of the Mississippi; July 17, 1881, was made lieutenant-colonel of Engineers.

General Comstock, since 1871, has served as a member of the Engineer Board, and on Board on bridging the channels between Lake Huron and Lake Erie; on improvement of Buffalo harbor; improvement of mouth of Mississippi; on Cleveland Breakwater; of Board of Engineers for Fortifications, and River and Harbor Improvements. Since 1886 he has had charge of Fort at Willett's Point, commanded Engineer Battalion, in charge of Engineer School of Application at Willet's Point; was superintending engineer of repairs of Fort Schuyler May, 1886, to April, 1887. In 1888 he was detailed as division engineer for inspecting the engineer works in the Southeastern Territory of the U. S. He was made colonel of Engineers April 7, 1888. General Comstock is a member of the National Academy of Sciences, and author of "Report on Primary Triangulation."

## CAPTAIN JOHN CONLINE, U.S.A. (RETIRED).

CAPTAIN JOHN CONLINE was born at Rutland, Vermont, January 1, 1846, and entered the volunteer service at the breaking out of the war of the Rebellion as a private of Company E, First Vermont Infantry, May 2, 1861, from which he was discharged August 15, 1861. On September 5, 1861, he again entered the service as a private of Company E, Fourth Vermont Infantry, and participated in the various operations of the Army of the Potomac, being engaged in the battle of Big Bethel, Virginia, June 10, 1861; siege of Yorktown, Virginia, from April 5 to May 4, 1862; action at Lee's Mills, Virginia; battle of Williamsburg, Virginia; action of Garnett's Hill, or Golding's Farm, Virginia; battles of Savage Station, White-Oak Swamp, Malvern Hill, South Mountain, Antietam, Fredericksburg, Marye's Heights, action at Salem Heights and battle of Salem Church, and action at Franklin's Crossing. He was one of twenty volunteers who went across the Rappahannock River in the first boat, under fire, before the bridge was completed, in the last action mentioned, June 5, 1863; and subsequently participated in the battles of Gettysburg, Pennsylvania, July 1-3, and Funkstown Bridge, Maryland, July 10, 1863.

He accompanied the Vermont troops sent in August, 1863, to preserve order in the city of New York, where he was appointed a cadet at the U. S. Military Academy by President Lincoln, on the recommendation of the Secretary of War, for gallant and exemplary conduct as a private soldier in the Sixth Corps, Army of the Potomac.

Graduating June 15, 1870, he was appointed a second lieutenant of the Ninth Cavalry. On returning to duty from his graduating leave, he was on frontier duty at Forts Stockton, McKavett, and Concho, Texas, to August 23, 1874, when he was appointed engineer-officer of the second column of the Indian Territory expedition, remaining as such to November 27, 1874, and on temporary duty at Head-quarters Department of Texas to February 1, 1875.

After serving in Texas and Colorado to April 3, 1877, at Forts Clark and Garland, and having in the mean time been promoted first lieutenant of the Ninth Cavalry, January 27, 1876, he was placed in charge of the expedition to preserve order among Southern Utes at Parrott City, Colorado, to November, 1876, and at Los Pinos Agency, Uncompagre Utes, for a similar purpose from April 3 to June 16, 1877.

Lieutenant Conline was then stationed at Fort Bayard, New Mexico, to October 10, 1877, when he was granted a sick-leave of absence to August 20, 1878, and was then stationed successively at Fort Selden, Ojo Caliente, and Fort Union, New Mexico, performing various staff duties at each. Being transferred to Troop A, Ninth Cavalry, July 23, 1879, he was placed in command of it at Fort Stanton, and was in the field on Indian expeditions two hundred and seventy days in one year. He also commanded A and G Troops on scouting expeditions during part of 1880, and, with Company C, Fifteenth Infantry added to his command, he had charge of three hundred and eighty-four Indians at South Fork, New Mexico, in 1880.

The lieutenant was in an engagement with hostile Indians in Alamo Cañon, Sacramento Mountains, New Mexico, Sunday, February 28, 1880; he captured and burned their camp, all equipage and provisions, and captured all their stock,—twenty-one horses and mules. He was also in the engagement with Victorio's band of hostile Indians, in Mimbrillo Cañon, San Andreas Mountains, on the afternoon of April 5, 1880, which lasted two hours, the Indians being defeated. After the campaign was ended he went on sick-leave of absence, May 1, 1881, by authority of the Secretary of War, and remained until July, 1885, when he rejoined at Fort Robinson, Nebraska, serving there to June 17, 1887.

He was promoted captain of Troop C February 11, 1887, and, after a three months' leave of absence, joined his troop at Fort Robinson, Nebraska, from which station he was changed to Fort Du Chesne, June 5, 1888, marching six hundred and fifty-six miles, from which post he was retired, for disability in the line of duty, February 25, 1891.

Captain Conline was recommended for the brevet of major, for gallantry in action with hostile Indians, April 7, 1880, during the Victorio war. He has also received numerous letters and orders of commendation from his superior officers for ability and gallant conduct in engagements with hostile Indians. The captain's present residence is Detroit, Michigan.

### CAPTAIN CASPER HAUZER CONRAD, U.S.A.

CAPTAIN CASPER HAUZER CONRAD (Fifteenth Infantry) was born near the city of Kingston, Ulster County, New York, March 30, 1844. He enlisted in the One Hundred and Twentieth New York Volunteers August 18, 1862, and participated in all the battles and marches of the Army of the Potomac from November, 1862, up to the battle of Gettysburg. He was slightly disabled at the battle of Fredericksburg, Virginia, and while on the march to Gettysburg was sun-struck and sent to Fairfax Seminary Hospital; there he was found unfit for field-service and was transferred to the Veteran Reserve Corps. He was nearly two years recovering from disability.

When, during the battle of Chancellorsville, "a corporal of his regiment was severely wounded and would have been left on the field, he comprehended the situation, and, amid a storm of bullets, caught a riderless horse, threw the wounded man over the saddle, and succeeded in carrying him beyond range of the enemy." In April, 1864, he was detailed as clerk on duty at the headquarters of the district department of Washington, in connection with the provost-marshal's office. In June, 1865, he was detailed for duty at the office of the Executive Mansion, and while there was discharged June 19, 1865, and appointed executive clerk to President Johnson, remaining in that position until April 13, 1867, when he was commissioned first lieutenant in the Thirty-fifth U. S. Infantry. He reported for duty with Company I, July 1867, and commanded the company till April, 1869. He was then stationed at different posts in Texas.

At the consolidation of the Thirty-fifth and Fifteenth Regiments he became first lieutenant of the latter regiment, and marched with it to New Mexico, arriving September, 1869. He was stationed at Fort Stanton in command of company, and also as acting assistant quartermaster and acting commissary sergeant till February, 1871, when he was ordered on recruiting service; then stationed at Dayton, Marietta, Ohio, and Newport Barracks, Kentucky, where he remained as depot quartermaster, acting commissary sergeant and adjutant till April, 1873, when he was ordered to his regiment. From the time of rejoining until he received his captaincy in January, 1875, he was on duty as acting assistant quartermaster and acting commissary sergeant at different posts in New Mexico. He was promoted to Company C, and stationed with it at different posts in New Mexico until the regiment was ordered to Colorado, at which time he was absent on sick-leave.

While in command of Company C at Mescularo Indian Agency, New Mexico, in December, 1880, the regimental commander issued General Order, No. 13, complimenting Captain Conrad and his command for gallant and soldierly conduct in an engagement with hostile Indians December 2, 1880.

In November, 1882, he was ordered to Fort Randall, South Dakota, where he remained for nearly nine years, having been stationed with his company for one month in 1887 at Fort Sully, guarding the post during interchange of regiments. Captain Conrad commanded Fort Randall at different times, ranging from a month to nine months at a time, and was sent also at different times as special inspector of Indian agencies and distribution of annuity goods. He left Fort Randall for Fort Sheridan, Illinois, in May, 1891.

## CAPTAIN AUGUSTUS P. COOKE, U.S.N.

CAPTAIN AUGUSTUS P. COOKE was born in Cooperstown, New York, February 10, 1836; appointed to the Naval Academy in 1852, and graduated in 1856. During his first sea-service, in the Home Squadron, he participated in the capture of Walker, the filibuster, at Greytown, Nicaragua. In 1859 he received his warrant as passed midshipman, and made a cruise on the coast of Africa, in the "San Jacinto," assisting in the capture of several slavers. He was commissioned lieutenant in 1860. When the Rebellion occurred, the ship, then under the command of Captain Wilkes, returned to the United States, capturing, on the way, the rebel commissioners, Mason and Slidell.

In January, 1862, as executive-officer of the "Pinola," captured the blockade-runner "Cora," and then the "Pinola" proceeded to join Farragut's squadron. Lieutenant Cooke was several times under fire in the "Pinola" while that vessel was assisting in breaking the chain barriers which obstructed the Mississippi, and was present at the bombardment and passage of Forts Jackson and St. Philip, the destruction of the rebel flotilla, and the capture of New Orleans. He was also present at the first bombardment of Vicksburg; the passage of the batteries there, and the engagement with the rebel ram "Arkansas."

In August, 1862, he was made lieutenant-commander, and ordered to command a vessel in Buchanan's flotilla, to operate, in conjunction with the army, in the Bayou Têche. In January, 1863, he went up the Têche, supporting General Weitzel's brigade, and assisted in the destruction of the enemy's gun-boat "Cotton." Here Lieutenant-Commander Buchanan was killed, and the command of the flotilla devolved upon Lieutenant-Commander Cooke.

During the Red River expedition, in 1863, he crossed troops over Berwick Bay and transported General Grover's division through Grand Lake and landed it at Indian Bend, under fire, without accident. Next morning, at daylight, the flotilla under Cooke was attacked by the "Queen of the West" and another gun-boat armed with rifled cannon, and with sharp-shooters behind cotton-bales. Cooke very promptly went to meet them, and his shells soon set fire to the cotton-bales of the "Queen of the West," which was soon in flames, with her people leaping overboard to escape death from fire. Her consort, seeing this, turned, and, having superior speed and lighter draft than Cooke's vessels, escaped. The officers and ninety men of the "Queen of the West" were picked up. About twenty were lost. There were no casualties in the flotilla.

His next operation was the capture of Butte à la Rose, on the Atchafalaya, driving off the supporting gun-boat, and taking the garrison, with a large quantity of stores and ammunition, clearing the Atchafalaya from the Gulf to the Red River; and by this route he proceeded to join Admiral Farragut, then at the mouth of Red River. General Banks made special acknowledgment to Lieutenant-Commander Cooke for his success in these operations.

His next service was in the Red River, with Porter's fleet; followed, in the winter of 1863-64, by blockading Matagorda Bay and the coast of Texas.

In July, 1864, he was detached from duty in the Gulf, and ordered to the Naval Academy; serving in the practice ships "Marion" and "Savannah." In May, 1867, he was ordered as navigator of the steam-frigate "Franklin," Captain Pennock, which went to Europe as Admiral Farragut's flag-ship. This was a remarkable and interesting cruise, from the attentions shown the admiral in every country he visited, especially in Russia and Sweden. In October, 1868, he was detached from the "Franklin," and ordered as executive-officer of the "Ticonderoga," on the same station. Upon his return home he was, in 1869, appointed head of the department of ordnance at the Naval Academy, and published a text-book on gunnery, long used by the cadets.

Lieutenant-Commander Cooke was commissioned commander in 1870. Served at the Torpedo Station and in command of torpedo-boat "Intrepid," and afterwards the "Alarm." Later he commanded the steamer "Swatara." He was made captain in 1881, while stationed at Mare Island, California, and commanded the "Lackawanna," on the Pacific Station, in 1884-85. He next served at the navy-yard, Brooklyn, in command of the "Vermont," and afterwards as captain of the yard. In 1888 he took command of the "Franklin," at Norfolk. In 1890 he was relieved and ordered to New York as President of the Board of Inspection of Merchant Vessels.

COMMANDER PHILIP H. COOPER, U.S.N.

COMMANDER PHILIP H. COOPER is a native of New York, and was appointed to the Naval Academy from that State in September, 1860. The exigencies of the service at that period caused him to be sent forth from the Academy with his class, and with the rank of ensign, May 28, 1863. He saw war service at once, being attached to the steam-sloop "Richmond," of the West Gulf Blockading Squadron, up to 1865. He then served under the successive commands of Admirals Farragut and Thatcher, and participated in all the operations connected with the battle of Mobile Bay, August 5, 1864; the reduction of the forts at the entrance, and, later, the defences of the city of Mobile.

He was promoted to master November, 1865; made a cruise in the "Powhatan," South Pacific Squadron, 1865-67; during the cruise was commissioned as lieutenant November 10, 1866; served at the Naval Academy 1867-69; commissioned as lieutenant-commander March 12, 1868; made a special cruise in the frigate "Sabine" in 1869; served in the T. and N. surveying expedition in 1870-71; was then again stationed at the Naval Academy from 1872 to 1874; ordered to the Torpedo Station during 1875, and was then stationed at the Experimental Battery at Annapolis through 1876. During 1877-79 he was on duty at the Coast Survey Office. He was promoted to commander November, 1879, and was upon special navigation duty up to 1881.

Since then Commander Cooper's service has been in the regular order of detail by the Navy Department, including two periods of command of a vessel on the Asiatic Station.

## LIEUTENANT-COLONEL HENRY CLARK CORBIN, U.S.A.

LIEUTENANT-COLONEL HENRY CLARK CORBIN (Adjutant-General's Department) was born September 15, 1842, in Monroe Township, Clermont County, Ohio. His father's name was Shadrach Corbin, and his mother's Mary Ann. His father was of English descent. His parents were born in Ohio, and grandparents and great-grandparents were born in the State of Virginia, where many of the descendants yet reside. He attended the common schools of the neighborhood until fourteen years of age, when he entered Parker's Academy, situated in the southern part of the county of his birth. In 1860 young Corbin taught district school near Olive Branch, Ohio, and the following year at Newtown, Hamilton County, Ohio. In the mean time he studied law under the direction of Hon. Philip B. Swing, of Batavia. In response to President Lincoln's second call for volunteers, he entered the service in the Eighty-third Ohio Infantry. In July, 1862, he was transferred to the Seventy-ninth Ohio as a second lieutenant, and went with the regiment on its march and campaigns through Kentucky, serving with it until the 13th of November, 1863, on which day he resigned, to enable him to accept the appointment of major in the Fourteenth U. S. Colored Infantry, which regiment he joined at Gallatin, Tennessee, the following day, and assisted in its organization. On the 4th of March, 1864, he was promoted lieutenant-colonel of the same regiment, and on the 23d of September was raised to the rank of colonel. Six months later he was brevetted brigadier-general. Colonel Corbin participated with the regiment in all its marches, campaigns, and engagements, and was engaged in the battles of Pulaski, Decatur, and Nashville. He was made major by brevet for gallant and meritorious services in action at Decatur, Alabama, and lieutenant-colonel by brevet for similar services in the battle of Nashville, Tennessee. He was the first man in the State of Ohio to receive and accept a field-officer's position in a colored regiment. He was mustered out of the volunteer service March 26, 1866, and was appointed a second lieutenant in the Seventeenth U. S. Infantry, which regiment he joined at Fort Gratiot, Michigan, while the Fenian troubles were being settled. In September of the same year he went to Independence, Missouri, and participated in settling the troubles incident to enforcing the registration law in that State. After this he was ordered to Texas. In the mean time he had been appointed and confirmed as a captain of the Thirty-eighth Infantry, about to be organized at Jefferson Barracks, Missouri, to which station he immediately repaired, and until May of 1867 he was engaged in its organization. The latter part of May he joined his company at Fort Hays, Kansas. The command was there subjected to the cholera scourge, Colonel Corbin losing twenty per cent. of his company by the malady. During all the summer of 1867 he was engaged in guarding the overland stage, carrying the United States mail, from attacks of hostile Indians. After the Indian troubles in the Smoky Hill country were settled, he went, in command of a detachment of his regiment, across the plain over the old Santa Fé trail, and took station at Fort Craig, New Mexico, where he was engaged in scouting, and protecting the citizens from a roving band of hostile Apaches. In the spring of 1868 he marched with his company to Fort Bayard, New Mexico, and there engaged in like service until October, 1869, when he was given command of his regiment and ordered to march to Fort Davis, Texas, where it was consolidated with the Forty-first Infantry, and thereafter was known as the Twenty-fourth U. S. Infantry. He then served at several posts in that State, and commanded Ringgold Barracks until the autumn of 1876, when he was detailed on recruiting service, and ordered to Columbus Barracks, Ohio. On the 2d of March, 1877, on invitation of President-elect Hayes, he accompanied him to Washington. After his inauguration he was detailed for duty at the Executive Mansion. In August of that year he was appointed secretary of what was known as the Sitting Bull Commission, which was appointed to treat with the hostile Sioux Indians, then refugees in the British Dominion. Returning, he resumed duty in the city of Washington, where he remained until his appointment as assistant adjutant-general on the 16th of June, 1880. September, 1881, was ordered to the Department of the South, and in September, 1883, he was transferred to the Division of the Missouri, where he remained to 1891, and then changed to the Department of Arizona. During the celebration at Yorktown Colonel Corbin was made secretary of the Joint Congressional Committee, and by that committee made master of ceremonies. He was with General Garfield when he was assassinated, and was present at his death.

## COMMANDER CHARLES STANHOPE COTTON, U.S.N.

COMMANDER COTTON was born at Milwaukee, Wisconsin, February 15, 1843, and appointed acting midshipman, at the Naval Academy, from that State, September, 1858. The crisis of 1861 advanced the older midshipmen very rapidly, and in May of that year Commander Cotton was ordered to the frigate "St. Lawrence," which captured the privateer "Petrel" a few days afterwards, and he was sent to Philadelphia on duty in connection with the trial of the prisoners captured on that occasion. Then he served on board the frigate "Minnesota," flagship, and, as a midshipman, commanded the quarter-deck battery, comprising eight VIII inch guns during the Monitor-Merrimac action.

Commander Cotton was promoted to ensign November 11, 1862, and was attached to the steam-sloop "Iroquois," off Wilmington, North Carolina, and to the steam-sloop "Oneida," of the West Gulf Blockading Squadron, with a few weeks' service on board the "Hartford" and "Kineo," up to August, 1865. He was promoted lieutenant February 22, 1864, six years after his appointment as acting midshipman.

He served on board the "Oneida" during the battle of Mobile Bay, and the subsequent operations, up to the surrender of Fort Morgan. From November, 1865, to May, 1869, he was attached to the steam-sloop "Shenandoah" during a most interesting cruise which embraced South America, Africa, India, and China. For eight months of this cruise he was navigator as well as watch-officer. He was promoted to lieutenant-commander July, 1866, was on duty at the Naval Academy and at the Kittery Navy-Yard up to 1871. In April of that year he joined the frigate "Tennessee," which carried out the San Domingo commissioners, whose object was to examine into and report upon the contemplated project of securing the use of Samana Bay for a coaling station for the United States Navy. For a period after this service he was attached to the "Ticonderoga" as executive-officer, on the Brazil Station. Afterwards on duty at Kittery Navy-Yard, and under torpedo instruction at Newport, up to September, 1876. He was then stationed at Norfolk, Virginia, as the executive-officer of the "Worcester," and from October, 1876, to July, 1880, was attached to the New York Navy-Yard.

Promoted commander April 25, 1877, commanding "Monocacy," Asiatic Station, from September, 1880, to September, 1883, except during June and July, 1881, when he commanded the "Alert" on the same station. The "Monocacy" made several interesting visits to Corea, skirting the whole coast and entering several ports for the purpose of showing our flag and cultivating cordial relations. At one time the "Monocacy" was (summer of 1882) the only foreign ship-of-war present in Corean waters, during a crisis in the strained relations between Corea, Japan, and China. Her commander managed to maintain cordial relations and intercourse with the representatives of all three countries, and, as a mark of confidence and of esteem for the United States, he was furnished with a copy of the treaty between the three powers within an hour of its receipt from Seoul by the representative of one of them.

In the spring of 1883 Commander Cotton conveyed to Corea our minister, Mr. L. H. Foote, and the members of the legation, and accompanied them to Seoul, the capital, where ratifications of the treaty between Corea and the United States were formally exchanged, and the foreign delegation was received in state by the king. This was the first occasion upon which foreigners were presented to or received by his Majesty. The party were also entertained at a state dinner by the Minister of Foreign Affairs,—the first ever given by the Coreans in foreign style, with imported china, glass, and wines, and with the use of table-cloth, napkins, knives and forks, and so forth. These events will always be remembered as marking an important era in the intercourse with that remote country. The "Monocacy" was the first ship to salute the national flag of Corea, adopted prior to the ratification of the treaty. In the summer of 1883 Commander Cotton conveyed from Corea to Japan, en route to the United States, the first embassy accredited by Corea to a foreign power other than Asiatic.

These statements are chiefly of interest as marking the origin of a new era for the "Hermit Kingdom," and her emergence from the shell of seclusion and isolation, and entrance into the great brotherhood of nations. Commander Cotton has since been inspector of ordnance, light-house inspector; and is at present in command of the U. S. S. "Mohican," Pacific Station. Commanded five vessels in the Bering Sea, summer of 1891.

## CAPTAIN DAVID J. CRAIGIE, U.S.A.

CAPTAIN DAVID J. CRAIGIE (Twelfth Infantry) was born at Broomieside, Fifeshire, Scotland, December 6, 1840. Entered volunteer service from Oskaloosa, Mahaska County, Iowa, as first lieutenant Company H, Eighth Iowa Infantry, September 12, 1861. Honorably mustered out volunteer regiment and appointed captain and assistant adjutant-general July, 1864. Served in the field, etc., on the staff of Generals Curtis, Davies, Mitchell, and others until close of war of the Rebellion; was honorably mustered out of service September, 1865.

Volunteer service: Participated in the Springfield, Missouri, campaign, fall of 1861, under Generals McKinstry and Steele; thence to Pittsburgh Landing, Tennessee River, March, 1862; with regiment battle of Shiloh, Tennessee, 6th and 7th of April, 1862, commanding company; severely wounded, captured by enemy. Lay on battle-field until evening of the 7th April; rejoined regiment August same year near Corinth, Mississippi; was appointed aide-de-camp on the staff of Brigadier-General Thomas A. Davies, commanding second division Army of the Tennessee. Participated in the campaign battles and skirmishes at and near Corinth and Iuka, Mississippi, fall of 1862, and in pursuit of enemy after battle of Corinth, 3d and 4th of October, 1862. Thence to Columbus, Kentucky, and Rolla, Missouri, on staff-duty until January, 1864, and March, 1865; serving at Fort Leavenworth, Kansas, at the close of the war and there mustered out.

Commissioned second lieutenant Twelfth Infantry U. S. Army May, 1866. Appointed adjutant first battalion and regimental adjutant September and December, same year. Served in Washington, D. C., with regiment until April, 1869, a portion of the time as assistant to Adjutant-General Garrison, of Washington; thence to Pacific coast with regiment, serving on that coast at several stations in California, Nevada, and Arizona until June, 1879, when ordered to Washington, D. C.; assistant to Colonel R. N. Scott in preparation of Rebellion records of 1861-65, until March, 1881; rejoined company in Arizona April, 1881. Thence to Plattsburg and Madison Barracks, New York, till 1887, when regiment moved to Dakota Station, Fort Yates, North Dakota. Commanded company on Sitting Bull Sioux campaign winter of 1890-91; ordered to Fort Leavenworth with company March, 1891.

Promotion in regular army: First lieutenant, October, 1867; captain, December 16, 1880.

Brevet rank: First lieutenant U. S. Army for gallant and meritorious services in the battle of Shiloh, Tennessee, 6th and 7th April, 1862. Captain for gallant and meritorious services in the battle of Iuka, Mississippi, September, 1862.

Honorable mention: In records of the Rebellion in reports on battle of Shiloh, Tennessee, Volume X., battles of Iuka and Corinth, and in field-orders of division department and battalion commander, Sitting Bull Sioux campaign North and South Dakota, winter of 1890-91, Fort Yates battalion.

Staff-service in volunteers: Aide-de-camp from September, 1862, to July, 1864; assistant adjutant-general July, 1864, to September, 1865.

Staff appointments and staff services, etc., in the U. S. Army: Adjutant First Battalion and regimental adjutant September and December 1, 1866, to November, 1869; regimental quartermaster March 1, 1871, to January 31, 1876; depot quartermaster and commanding Yuma quartermaster depot, Arizona, June, 1870, to August, 1871, and from November, 1878, to April, 1879; commanding post, Fort Halleck, Nevada, June to October, 1877; commanding company and post, Whipple Banks, Arizona, April, 1879, to June, 1879; thence to Washington, D. C. War Department Rebellion records, to April, 1881; rejoined company same month, Fort Grant, Arizona.

Battles, skirmishes, etc., in which engaged: Skirmish crossing Osage River, Missouri, October, 1861, and near Springfield, Missouri, November, 1861; skirmish again near Sedalia, Missouri, November, 1861; battle of Shiloh, April 6 and 7, 1862, skirmish near Danville, Mississippi, September, 1862; battle of Iuka, Mississippi, September, 1862; skirmish again near Rienzi, Mississippi, same month, 1862; battle of Corinth, Mississippi, 3d and 4th October, 1862; skirmish near Davis's Mills, Hatchee River, Mississippi, October, 1862; again near "Bone Yard," Mississippi, October, 1862; skirmish near Bullock's Farm, Kentucky, December, 1862; again near same place, January, 1863; skirmish with bushwhackers at James's Mills, near Rolla, Missouri, August, 1863; skirmish near Weston, Missouri, October, 1864; again near Blue River, Kansas, November, 1864.

COMMANDER T. A. M. CRAVEN, U.S.N. (DECEASED).

COMMANDER TUNIS AUGUSTUS MACDONOUGH CRAVEN was born in Portsmouth, New Hampshire, and perished in the iron-clad "Tecumseh," of which vessel he was in command, and which was sunk by a torpedo during the passage of Farragut's fleet into Mobile Bay, on the 5th of August, 1864. He was appointed midshipman from New York in 1829; became a lieutenant in 1841; and commander in April, 1861. At the time of his death he had seen twenty years of naval sea-service, beside eight years on the coast survey, and was a most excellent and reliable, as well as a gallant officer.

At the outbreak of the Civil War he was in command of the steamer "Mohawk," in the Home Squadron; from which vessel he was transferred to the command of the steam-sloop "Tuscarora;" and in 1864, to the command of the monitor "Tecumseh," employed in the James River against Howletts' and other batteries, and the Confederate iron-clads from Richmond. He sunk in the main channel, at Trent's Reach, four hulks filled with stone, and completed other obstructions there.

He was afterwards ordered down to Farragut, in the Gulf, and by great exertion got there in time. When the fleet went in, under the fire of Fort Morgan, and at a critical moment, the "Tecumseh" was struck by a torpedo, and almost instantly went down. The "Brooklyn" stopped her engines, but Farragut ordered her to proceed in line, and hailed Jouett, in the "Metacomet," to drop a boat and save the few people seen struggling in the water. Acting Ensign Nields went in the boat and the fleet passed on. Within three hundred yards of the great fort, amidst pouring shot and shell, he picked up the survivors. One of the "Tecumseh's" boats, which floated, saved seven; and four swam on shore and were made prisoners.

Acting Masters Cottrell and Langley, who were among the saved, reported that, when the torpedo exploded, and blew a large hole in the bottom, and the vessel being instantly in a sinking condition, the order was passed to leave quarters and all to save themselves, if they could. "Commander Craven was in the pilot-house when the torpedo exploded, but his chivalric spirit caused him to lose his life. We know from the reports of the officers saved that he insisted on the pilots taking precedence in descending the ladder. They both reached the turret, but as the pilot passed through the port-hole the vessel keeled over and went down, taking with her as gallant an officer as there was in the American navy. One moment more and his life would have been saved to adorn the list of officers of which he was so bright a member. No more chivalrous event occurred during the four years' conflict. The example shown by Craven should be chronicled in every story of the war."

## MAJOR-GENERAL GEORGE CROOK, U.S.A.
(DECEASED).

MAJOR-GENERAL GEORGE CROOK was born in Ohio, and graduated at the Military Academy in the Class of 1852. He was promoted brevet second lieutenant of the Fourth Infantry, and was in garrison at Fort Columbus, New York, until his regiment sailed for California, when he accompanied it, and was stationed at Benicia, Humboldt, and Jones until 1857, participating in the escort of Topographical Party, 1855; Rogue River Expedition, 1856; and in command of Pitt River Expedition, 1857, being engaged in a skirmish, where he was wounded with an arrow. From Fort Terwaw he marched to Vancouver in 1858, and participated in the Yakima Expedition of that year.

He was promoted second lieutenant Fourth Infantry July 7, 1853; first lieutenant March 11, 1856, and captain May 14, 1861. Returning from the Pacific coast in 1861, he was appointed colonel of the Thirty-sixth Ohio Infantry September 12, 1861, and participated in the West Virginia operations in the early part of the war of the Rebellion, and commanded the Third Provisional Brigade from May 1 to August 15, 1862, participating in the action of Lewisburg, where he was wounded; in the Northern Virginia campaign; in the Maryland campaign with the Army of the Potomac, being engaged in the battles of South Mountain and Antietam, 1862. He was appointed brigadier-general of volunteers September 7, 1862, and continued to operate with his command in West Virginia until February, 1863, when he was ordered to the Western army, and was in command of an independent division at Carthage, Tennessee, until June of the same year, and subsequently participated in the Tennessee campaign of the Army of the Cumberland. He was placed in command of Second Cavalry Division July 1, 1863, and was engaged at Hoover's Gap Chickamauga; action at foot of Cumberland Mountains, McMinnville, and Farmington, and almost daily skirmishes.

General Crook was assigned to the command of the Kanawha District, West Virginia, in February, 1864, and was engaged in numerous raids and actions until the following July, when he was assigned to the command of the troops of the Department of West Virginia, and participated in several actions. He was in command of the Department of West Virginia, and participated in General Sheridan's Shenandoah campaign of 1864, being engaged in the action of Berryville, battles of Opequan and Fisher's Hill, action of Strasburg, and battle of Cedar Creek. He was appointed major-general of volunteers October 21, 1864, and was serving with his command in West Virginia when he was captured at Cumberland, Maryland, February 21, 1865. Returning to duty, he was placed in command of the cavalry of the Army of the Potomac

March 26, 1865, and held that command until the surrender of Lee, being engaged in the battle of Dinwiddie Court-House, action of Jetersville, battle of Sailor's Creek, combat of Farmville, and capitulation of Appomattox Court-House. He was then placed in command of the District of Wilmington, North Carolina, where he remained until January 15, 1866, when he was mustered out of the volunteer service.

General Crook had conferred upon him, for gallant and meritorious and distinguished services, the following brevets in the regular army: Major, for Lewisburg, Virginia; lieutenant-colonel, for Antietam; colonel, for Farmington; brigadier-general, for the campaign of 1864 in West Virginia; major-general, for Fisher's Hill. He was also brevetted major-general of volunteers for "gallant and distinguished services in West Virginia." He became major of the Third U. S. Infantry July 18, 1866, and lieutenant-colonel of the Twenty-third Infantry July 28, 1866, and was on a Board to Examine Rifle Tactics at Washington, D. C., and then awaiting orders until the following November, when he was placed in command of the District of Boisé, Idaho.

He was appointed brigadier-general U. S. A. October 29, 1873, and major-general U. S. A. April 6, 1888. He commanded the Department of the Platte on two different occasions, also the Department of Arizona and the Military Division of the Missouri, and, while holding the latter command, died suddenly at Chicago, Illinois, April 5, 1890.

While in command of the Departments of the Platte and Arizona, General Crook commanded the expedition against Sitting Bull and the hostile Sioux in the summer of 1876. In 1889 he was one of the commissioners appointed by the President of the United States to treat with the Indians on the subject of opening their lands to settlement.

REAR-ADMIRAL PEIRCE CROSBY, U.S.N. (RETIRED).

REAR-ADMIRAL PEIRCE CROSBY was born in Delaware County, Pennsylvania, and appointed midshipman from that State in June, 1838. Served in the "Ohio," 74, flagship in the Mediterranean; then in the "Experiment," and the steamer "Mississippi." He then went to the Mediterranean again, in the "Congress," was transferred to the "Preble," and came home, in 1843, to go to the Naval School at Philadelphia. Passed midshipman in 1844. For two years he was on the Coast Survey, and then, during the Mexican War, in the "Decatur," at the attack and capture of Tuspan and Tabasco, and in the "Petrel" until the peace. Served in the "Relief" in 1849-50, carrying stores to the Mediterranean and west coast of Africa.

Commissioned lieutenant in September, 1853, and made a long cruise on the coast of Brazil, in the "Germantown." He then made another cruise in the Gulf,—part of the time under Captain Farragut. While attached to the receiving-ship at Philadelphia, the Civil War began. Crosby was at once actively employed, in Chesapeake Bay, keeping open communications, and cutting off supplies and communications. He was then ordered to the frigate "Cumberland," and detailed for duty on shore, at Fortress Monroe. Transported the troops at Hampton Creek before and after the fight at Big Bethel. His services in the landing during the attack upon Forts Clarke and Hatteras were remarkable in the face of bad weather. Lieutenant Crosby's advice enabled the handful of troops left on the beach, when the squadron was driven to sea, to make such a show that their critical condition was not discovered by the enemy.

He was especially mentioned for his conduct on this occasion. In the winter of 1861 he took command of the "Pinola," one of the new steam gun-vessels. In the "Pinola" he joined Admiral Farragut, in the spring of 1862. On his way he captured a cotton prize, and sent her north. He commanded the "Pinola" on the memorable night when she co-operated with the "Itasca" in cutting the chain barrier of the Mississippi. The "Itasca" slipped the end of the cable on the opposite shore from Fort Jackson, but in doing so ran hard aground. By Crosby's exertions she was rescued from this position before daylight. The "Pinola" had to blow up the vessels holding the chains, directly under the guns of the fort. Three different attempts were made, under fire of the fort, but each time something went wrong with the wires. At last Lieutenant Crosby found that a way was opened, sufficient for the fleet to pass, and so reported. Lieutenant Crosby was engaged at the passage of the forts, the Chalmette batteries, and the capture of New Orleans. He was also at the passage and repassage of the batteries at Vicksburg, and the engagement with the "Arkansas." In the fall of 1862, he was ordered north to command the iron-clad "Sangamon." Promoted commander September, 1862. He was soon detached from "Sangamon" and made fleet-captain, North Atlantic Squadron, under Admiral Lee. Commanded an expedition up the York River, co-operating with General Dix.

In command of the "Florida," in the winter of 1863, destroyed two blockade-runners, at Masonborough Inlet, under the fire of the shore batteries. In 1864 commanded the "Keystone State," and captured five blockade-runners. He was then ordered to the "Muscoota," but soon detached and ordered to command "Metacomet." Blockaded Galveston in her, and was in command of her at the battle of Mobile Bay. Planned and directed the construction of torpedo-nets, and spread them in the Blakely River, removed one hundred and forty torpedoes, and cleared the way for the squadron to pass safely up to Mobile. He then occupied forts "Huger" and "Tracy" on the night the rebel forces evacuated. Especially commended in the official report of Admiral Thatcher. In September, 1865, he was ordered to command the "Shamokin," on the coast of Brazil, where he remained until 1868. He was made captain in May of that year. While in command of "Shamokin," conveyed Minister Washburn on his mission to Paraguay.

He was commissioned as commodore 1874. Rear-admiral March, 1882. Commanded South Atlantic Squadron. Commanded Asiatic Squadron. Retired, on his own application, 1883.

## CAPTAIN WM. H. H. CROWELL, U.S.A.

CAPTAIN WM. H. H. CROWELL (Sixth Infantry) was born in Ohio, January 25, 1841, and at the commencement of the war of the Rebellion entered the volunteer service as private of Company F, First Ohio Artillery, April 21, 1861, and served under General McClellan in West Virginia, and was engaged in the battles of Philippi, June 3, 1861 (which was the first contact of the hostile forces after the fall of Fort Sumter), and Laurel Hill, Virginia. He was honorably mustered out July 27, 1861, but re-entered the volunteer service December 12, 1861, as second lieutenant Fifteenth Ohio Battery, and served in the Western army during the campaign of 1862, participating in the battle of the Hatchie October 7, 1862. He was in the campaign against Corinth, Mississippi, and under General Grant in his Mississippi campaign of 1862.

He resigned December 15, 1862, for the purpose of recruiting a battery for the Second Ohio Heavy Artillery, and was appointed recruiting officer by the Governor of Ohio, with the rank of second lieutenant. He was promoted to the captaincy of the battery September 9, 1863, and served with it at Munfordville in the fall and winter of 1863. He also served with General Sherman in his East Tennessee campaign, returning to his command at Knoxville, Tennessee, from the north in December, 1864. On arriving at Nashville, he found the enemy in possession of the road and country generally between Nashville and Murfreesborough, and, being indefinitely detained and cut off from his command, he reported, by order of General George H. Thomas, to General Steadman for duty, and acted under his orders during the battle of Nashville. He was then stationed at Athens, Tennessee, where, by order of General Thomas, he fired one hundred guns in honor of the fall of Richmond.

He commanded Forts Willich and Terrill, at the crossing of Green River, at Munfordville, Kentucky, and commanded a battalion of the Second Ohio Heavy Artillery in 1864-65.

Captain Crowell was mustered out of the volunteer service on the 21st of August, 1865, but entered the regular service as second lieutenant of the Seventeenth Infantry January 22, 1867. He was promoted first lieutenant December 17, 1867, serving with his regiment until May 27, 1869, when he was placed on the unassigned list of officers. While unassigned Captain Crowell was engaged in reconstruction duty under General Canby in Virginia, and General Ames in Mississippi; in the former State he was made military commissioner and superintendent of elections for five counties, and in Mississippi for two; his duties were to appoint and instruct boards of registration in the counties under his control and recommend for appointment all county officers, and to conduct and report the result of the election as directed in orders.

He was assigned to the Sixth Infantry December 15, 1870, and promoted to captain October 31, 1883. He served with his regiment on frontier duty in the Departments of the Platte and the Missouri to April, 1889, having been adjutant of the Sixth Infantry from April 10, 1882, to October 31, 1883. In 1889 he was ordered to Fort Leavenworth, Kansas, and assigned to duty as assistant instructor in infantry tactics, in connection with the School of Application. Captain Crowell's present station is Fort Thomas, Kentucky.

COLONEL AND BREVET MAJOR-GENERAL GEORGE W. CULLUM, U.S.A. (DECEASED).

COLONEL AND BREVET MAJOR-GENERAL GEORGE W. CULLUM was born in New York, and graduated from the Military Academy July 1, 1833. He was promoted brevet second lieutenant of the Corps of Engineers the same day, and served as assistant engineer in the construction of several government works until April 20, 1836, when he was promoted second lieutenant. He was captain July 7, 1838, and continued as superintending engineer in the construction of important works along the Atlantic coast.

He was superintending engineer for devising and constructing sapper, miner, and pontoon trains for our armies in the war with Mexico, 1847-48; he was detailed on special duty at West Point, New York, preparing for publication a memoir on military bridges, with India-rubber pontoons, and construction of Cadet Barracks at West Point, New York, 1847-48, and at the same place as instructor in practical military engineering and commandant of sappers, miners, and pontoniers to July 5, 1850.

Captain Cullum then visited Europe, Asia, Africa, and the West Indies on a sick-leave of absence, 1850-52, when he returned to the Military Academy in his former position, retaining it to January 1, 1855. From that time until the commencement of the war of the Rebellion, Captain Cullum was superintending engineer in the construction of the New York assay-office, of Fort Sumter, Castle Pinckney, and Fort Moultrie, and other work in Charleston harbor; repairs to works at Forts Macon and Caswell, North Carolina; member of board to devise the defences of Sandy Hook, New Jersey; and superintendent of the construction and repair of many other works along the Atlantic seaboard.

Captain Cullum was appointed lieutenant-colonel (staff aide-de-camp to the general-in-chief) April 9, 1861, and colonel (staff, in same position) August 6, 1861. He was a member of the United States Sanitary Commission from June 13, 1861, to February 24, 1864, and an associate member of the Western Sanitary Commission from January 2 to July 11, 1862.

He was promoted major of Engineers August 6, and brigadier-general of volunteers November 1, 1861, serving successively as chief engineer of Military Departments and chief of staff to General Halleck, while commanding the armies and while chief of staff of the army, to September 5, 1864.

General Cullum was employed during this time in construction of fortifications in the field, organizing defences, etc., and was chief engineer in the campaign in Tennessee and Mississippi in 1862, being engaged in the advance upon and siege of Corinth and in fortifying Corinth until July 18, 1862, and then employed on many other duties connected with the Engineer Department of the army, which cannot be enumerated here for want of space, until the close of the war. He was promoted lieutenant-colonel of the Corps of Engineers March 3, 1863, and brevetted colonel and brigadier-general March 13, 1865, for "faithful and meritorious services during the Rebellion," and major-general March 13, 1865, for "faithful, meritorious, and distinguished services during the war of the Rebellion."

General Cullum was selected as superintendent of the U. S. Military Academy September 8, 1864, and retained the position until August 28, 1866. He was mustered out of the volunteer service September 1, 1866, and was awaiting orders to the November following, when he was detailed as a member of the Board of Engineers to carry out in detail the modifications of the defences in the vicinity of New York, as proposed by the board on January 27, 1864; and of Board of Engineers for Fortifications and River and Harbor Obstructions required for the defence of the Territory of the United States since May 18, 1867.

He was promoted colonel of the Corps of Engineers March 7, 1867.

General Cullum was retired from active service January 13, 1874, and died in 1892.

He was the author of a work on "Military Bridges, with India-rubber Pontoons," 1849; of "Register of Officers and Graduates of the United States Military Academy," from March 16, 1802 (when established) to January 1, 1850; translator and editor of Duparcq's "Elements of Military Art and History," 1863; author of "Systems of Military Bridges," 1863; of various military memoirs, reviews, and reports, 1863-67; and of "Biographical Register of the Officers and Graduates of the United States Military Academy," 1891.

## BREVET MAJOR HARRY COOKE CUSHING, U.S.A.

BREVET MAJOR HARRY COOKE CUSHING (captain Fourth Artillery) was born November 8, 1841, at Baltimore, Maryland. Went to Providence, Rhode Island, in 1849, and lived there until the breaking out of the war. Graduated 1860 at the Providence High School; undergraduate of Brown University, which he left to join Battery A, First Rhode Island Light Artillery. Corporal and sergeant therein from June 6 to November 5, 1861, participating in battle of Bull Run, July 21, 1861. Second lieutenant Fourth Artillery October 24, 1861, commanding section in Light Battery F, Fourth Artillery, and engaged in the following actions: Dam No. 5, December 11, 1861; Newtown, Virginia, May 24, 1862; Middletown, Virginia, May 24, 1862; Winchester, Virginia, May 25, 1862; Cedar Mountain, Virginia, August 9, 1862; (brevetted first lieutenant) Freeman's Ford, Virginia, August 23, 1862; Antietam, Maryland, September 17, 1862. First lieutenant Fourth Artillery September 17, 1862, and ordered to Army of the Cumberland. Commanding Light Battery H, Fourth Artillery, and engaged at Stewart's Creek, Tennessee, December 29, 1862; Stone River, Tennessee, December 31, 1862, to January 2, 1863; Woodbury, Tennessee, January 24, 1863; Chickamauga, Georgia, September 19-20, 1863 (brevetted captain), and siege of Chattanooga, Tennessee, October to November, 1863. Ordered, March, 1864, to Army of the Potomac; Inspector of Artillery, Cavalry Corps, Army of the Potomac, and engaged at Parker's Store, May 5; Wilderness, May 6; Todd's Tavern, May 8; Spottsylvania, May 9; Childsburg, May 9; South Anna, May 10; Yellow Tavern, May 11; Meadow Bridges, May 12; Hanover, May 27; Hawes' Shop, May 28; Old Church, May 30; Cold Harbor, June 1; White House, June 20; St. Mary's Church, June 23; siege of Petersburg, July; Smithfield, August 28; (brevetted major) Bunker's Hill, November 9; and Cedar Springs, November 12, 1864; with the Cavalry Corps, Army of the Potomac, and Sheridan's army in the Valley. On general recruiting service February, 1865, to October, 1866; rejoined regiment October, 1866, and served therewith continuously since. Captain Fourth Artillery August 22, 1874; in command of Battery C until November, 1887; since when he has commanded Light Battery B. Since the war he has served at various posts in the Division of the Atlantic and Division of the Pacific, and participated in the following Indian campaigns: Sioux campaign of 1876; Nez Perce campaign of 1877, and Apache campaign of 1881. During the Nez Perce campaign he was in command of a separate column of General Howard's army, and was specially and particularly mentioned by that officer for the energy and good judgment displayed by him in executing the duties imposed on him. He is a graduate of the Artillery School, Class of 1870. Brown University conferred upon him, June 16, 1871, the degree of Master of Arts. He is a member of the Military Order of the Loyal Legion.

For services in action during the war he was mentioned particularly in the reports of his brigade, division, corps, and army commanders of Banks's, Pope's, and Rosecrans's campaigns.

Major Cushing is a direct descendant of Nicholas Cooke, who was Governor of Rhode Island during the Revolution; of Colonel Samuel Barrett, one of the commanders at Lexington; of Captain Jarvis, of Massachusetts Line, and Colonel Benjamin Church, who commanded the Provincial army during King Philip's War, and who killed that celebrated Indian.

MAJOR SAMUEL T. CUSHING, U.S.A.

MAJOR SAMUEL T. CUSHING (Subsistence Department) was born in Rhode Island September 14, 1830, and was graduated from the Military Academy July 1, 1860. He was promoted acting second lieutenant of the Tenth Infantry, and served on the frontier in the Navajo campaign, and at Albuquerque and Santa Fé in the fall and winter of 1860-61. He was promoted second lieutenant of the Second Infantry January 19, and first lieutenant May 14, 1861, serving as such in the defences of Washington during that year. He served in the Manassas campaign as aide-de-camp to Colonel D. S. Miles, Second Infantry, commanding the reserve division; and as acting assistant inspector-general at the head-quarters of General McDowell, July and August, 1861.

He was then detailed as assistant signal-officer at Camp of Instruction, Georgetown, D. C., from September, 1861, to May, 1862, and then was placed in charge of the Signal Office at Washington, D. C., where he remained to October, 1862, in the mean time having been promoted captain February 15, 1862.

Captain Cushing was appointed captain and commissary of subsistence February 9, 1863, and made major in the Signal Corps May 29, 1863, which latter appointment he declined.

He was assigned to duty as instructor of signalling at the Military Academy July, 1863, which position he retained until January, 1864, when he was ordered on commissary duty in Tennessee, Kentucky, Indiana, and Mississippi from 1864 to 1866.

Captain Cushing was appointed brevet major March 13, 1865, " for faithful and meritorious services during the war."

He was at St. Louis in March and April; on inspector's duty from April 16 to August 23, 1866; on frontier duty in the latter part of that year, and again on inspection duty from March to May, 1867; then at Fort Laramie, Wyoming, until ordered again on inspection duty from September to November, 1867, and then stationed at Cheyenne, Wyoming, to December of the same year. He was chief commissary of the Department of the Platte to March 4, 1867, and in April, 1868, was ordered to Texas, where he held the position of chief commissary of the department until May, 1873, when his station was changed to New Mexico, where he was chief commissary of the district until July, 1874, at which time he was ordered to Louisville, Kentucky, as chief commissary of the Department of the South and purchasing commissary. From this post he was transferred to Atlanta, Georgia, September 20, 1876, remaining there to February 10, 1877.

Captain Cushing's field of action was changed to the Pacific coast February 22, 1877, where he performed the duties of purchasing commissary at San Francisco, California, remaining there until 1880, in the mean time having participated in the campaign against hostile Bannock Indians from June to September, 1878, serving as chief commissary of the Department of the Columbia during the campaign and until May, 1883, when he was placed on special duty in the office of the commissary-general of subsistence at Washington, remaining there to February 12, 1884. At this time he was detailed on duty at Pittsburg, Pennsylvania, distributing supplies to the sufferers from the flood on the Ohio River, which duty occupied him until March 17, 1884, when he was once more ordered to Texas, performing the duties of chief commissary of that department and purchasing and depot commissary of subsistence at San Antonio. Being relieved from this duty in August, 1886, he was ordered to Fort Leavenworth, Kansas, as purchasing and depot commissary of subsistence, part of the time being chief commissary of the Department of the Missouri.

Captain Cushing was promoted major in the subsistence department August 28, 1888, and is at present on duty at Fort Leavenworth.

## COMMANDER WILLIAM B. CUSHING, U.S.N.
(DECEASED).

COMMANDER WILLIAM B. CUSHING was born in Wisconsin, in November, 1842, and was appointed to the Naval Academy in September, 1857. He resigned in March, 1861, and went into the naval service afloat as an acting master's mate, as he was of that temperament which would not permit him to remain quietly at the Naval School when war was at hand. His was a disposition which could, under such circumstances, give no thought to theoretical studies,—fortunately for us, for we wanted just such men at that time. He served in the "Cambridge" for a short time, and was restored to his rank as midshipman in October, 1861. After a sick-leave he was ordered to the "Minnesota," and promoted to lieutenant in July, in common with a large number of young officers necessary to supply the demands of the service growing out of the Civil War. Henceforth, for a period of nearly three years, his service was eminently conspicuous in deeds of daring. While in command of a small steamer upon the blockade, he often visited the inland waters of the enemy at the risk of his life. He usually went at night, lying concealed during the following day, and always having in view some definite object. He had, in narrow waters, frequent fights with the field-batteries of the enemy. Once, while blockading off New Topsail Inlet, he reconnoitred a schooner lying inside, but was soon under the fire of a considerable force with a field-piece and small-arms. He retired; but, late that evening, he anchored his vessel close to the beach, abreast of the schooner, and several miles distant from the entrance to the inlet. Then he sent two boats on shore, the larger one to act as support. They hauled the smaller boat across the sand-beach, and launched her in the inlet beyond. Ensign Comey, with six men, then reconnoitred, and found that about twenty men and a small piece of artillery were guarding the vessel. In spite of this, an attack was made, the enemy routed, and ten prisoners, a howitzer, and eighteen small-arms captured. The schooner and adjacent salt-works were destroyed, and the expedition rejoined the vessel without loss.

Once, while blockading off Cape Fear River, Cushing went in his gig, with six men, up the river past Fort Caswell, to Smithville, two miles above, and got important information. Once he entered the river in the same way, captured the mail-rider for Fort Fisher, and possessed himself of his bag.

His most remarkable feat, however, was the destruction of the iron-plated ram "Albemarle," while that formidable vessel was secured to a wharf at Plymouth, North Carolina, with a guard of logs placed around her at a distance of thirty feet,—her crew on board to use her guns, and a company of soldiers on the wharf with small-arms and howitzers. Unfortunately, the reporters for the Northern press had found out that a torpedo-boat was preparing for those waters, and, of course, the information was transmitted to the enemy, so that they had ample time for preparation. The torpedo was of the early "boom" kind, carried in a steam-launch. The enemy was vigilant, and Cushing's approach was discovered after he had ascended the river, but before he came very near. But, nothing daunted by the fire of artillery and musketry, he put on steam, jumped his launch over the logs, lowered his torpedo in a most deliberate way, and blew the vessel up at the very moment when a shell from one of the heavy guns of the "Albemarle" and the column of water from the explosion of the torpedo sent the launch to the bottom. Cushing, Paymaster Swan, and others escaped, after much exposure in swimming down the ice-cold water and hiding in the swamps. But the terror of the "Sounds" was safely disposed of. For this act he was made lieutenant-commander, being then about twenty-two years of age. His entire career was a daring one, but he generally succeeded in his undertakings, because they were carefully planned and carried out with wonderful nerve.

When peace came Cushing seemed to suffer from a lack of purpose, but he could not reconcile himself to the perfunctory naval life. After the war he was executive-officer of the "Lancaster." He commanded the "Maumee," on the Asiatic Station, for three years. He was promoted to commander in the regular order in January, 1872, when he was about thirty years old. He then commanded the "Wyoming."

In the spring of 1874 he was ordered to the Washington Navy-Yard, but was soon detached at his own request. He soon showed symptoms of serious mental derangement, and was removed to the Government Hospital, where he died December 17, 1874, at the age of thirty-two years.

**CAPTAIN C. C. CUSICK, U.S.A. (RETIRED).**

CAPTAIN C. C. CUSICK was born in Niagara County, New York, August 2, 1835. He is the paternal grandson of Nicholas Cusick, an officer of the Revolutionary army of 1776, who was an intimate friend and co-laborer of Washington and Marquis de Lafayette; the maternal grandson of Captain Chew, of the British army, and the son of James Nicholas Cusick, who was for years the associate and companion of Catlin and Schoolcraft, the Indian historians, contributing largely to their work concerning the subject of "The Myths of the New World." His forest home in Western New York was honored by the frequent visits of Audubon. Captain Cusick is now the only representative of the Six Nations of New York favored with a commission in the regular army. As a hereditary official of the ancient Iroquois confederacy, he was installed to office September 6, 1860, as successor to William Chew, Sr., Sachem, and vacated the office June 20, 1866, he having received an appointment in the regular army.

He entered the volunteer service during the war of the Rebellion as second lieutenant of the One Hundred and Thirty-second Infantry August 14, 1862; was promoted first lieutenant July 1, 1863, and captain May 31, 1865, but owing to the long delay before the last commission was received was not mustered in to that rank. He was assigned to duty at Suffolk, Virginia, from October to the latter part of December, 1862, participated in several reconnoissances and engagements in the Blackwater region and vicinity of Suffolk, Virginia; served at New Berne, North Carolina, from January 2, 1863, until March 7, 1865, doing outpost duty, the defence of New Berne, and active field duty, during the month of March, 1865, the One Hundred and Thirty-second New York Infantry became a part of the Twenty-third Army Corps, and advanced with it into the interior of North Carolina under Major-General Schofield; commanded the large escort of infantry for General Sherman's supply-train from Goldsborough to Kingston, North Carolina, and return; pending the surrender of General Johnston's army near Raleigh, North Carolina, he was assigned to duty as acting assistant ordnance officer of the Second Division, Twenty-third Army Corps.

Captain Cusick led a charging force at night composed of two companies of the One Hundred and Thirty-second New York Infantry on works at Jackson's Mills, North Carolina; entire Confederate grand guard captured; Colonel Foulke, commandant of Kingston, North Carolina, attempted the rescue of prisoners the same night; he was also captured, together with his entire staff and escort; led a charging party on works at Southwest Creek, North Carolina, with one hundred and fifty selected men; works captured and colors planted; February, 1864, participated in the heroic defence of Bachelor's Creek Bridge, and other points of crossing, during the advance on New Berne by the Confederate forces under General Pickett; participated in the severe battle that was fought at Wise's Forks, near Kingston, North Carolina, March 9–11, 1865. He was recommended for brevet by the colonel of his regiment in 1867, for gallant and meritorious services during the war; but not acted on by the Senate of the United States owing to the order of 1867, suspending the granting of brevets.

Captain Cusick was appointed second lieutenant of the Thirteenth Infantry June 20, 1866; transferred to the Thirty-first Infantry September 20, 1866; transferred to the Twenty-second Infantry May 15, 1869; promoted first lieutenant August 5, 1872, and captain January 1, 1888. He joined his regiment in the West and aided in repelling an attack on Fort Stevenson, North Dakota, by hostile Sioux Indians August, 1867; repulsed a night attack of train escort by hostile Sioux Indians near Spring Lake, North Dakota, July 27, 1868; engaged with one hundred and seventy-five hostile Sioux Indians under Sitting Bull, near Fort Buford, Montana, August 20, 1868; captured Little Running Bear, a Brulé Sioux Indian, an associate of Sitting Bull, January, 1869, who was killed shortly afterwards while attempting to escape; engaged with a band of Indians under Crazy Horse, near Wolf Mountain, Montana, January 8–9, 1877; May 7–8, 1877, engaged with band of hostile Sioux Indians under Lame Deer; capture of four hundred horses and camp destroyed.

Captain Cusick was appointed by Director-General Davis, of the World's Columbian Exposition, as honorary and special assistant in the Department of American Archaeology and Ethnology September 25, 1891. Upon his own request, Captain Cusick was honorably retired from active service January 14, 1892.

## LIEUTENANT-COLONEL AND BREVET MAJOR-GENERAL GEORGE A. CUSTER, U.S.A. (DECEASED).

LIEUTENANT-COLONEL AND BREVET MAJOR-GENERAL GEORGE A. CUSTER was born in Ohio. He graduated at the Military Academy June 24, 1861, and was promoted second lieutenant of the Second Cavalry the same day. He was detailed to drill volunteers at Washington, and then participated in the battle of first Bull Run, July 21, 1861. He was absent, sick, from October, 1861, to February, 1862, and then participated in the Peninsula campaign of the Army of the Potomac, being engaged in the siege of Yorktown. He was promoted first lieutenant Fifth Cavalry July 17, 1862, and captain of staff (additional aide-de-camp) June 5, 1862, and served on the staff of Major-General McClellan in September and October, 1862, and was engaged in the battles of South Mountain and Antietam. He participated in Stoneman's raid towards Richmond, aide-de-camp to General Pleasonton in combat at Brandy Station, and on June 29, 1863, he was appointed brigadier-general of volunteers. As such, he commanded a cavalry brigade in the Pennsylvania campaign, and was engaged in the action at Aldie, battle of Gettysburg, various skirmishes in pursuit of the enemy, with constant fighting at Monterey, Smithsburg, Hagerstown, Williamsport, and Boonsborough; in fact, from this time to the end of the war his history is that of the Army of the Potomac, and the actions in which he was engaged are so numerous that it would require the space of this entire sketch to enumerate them. He commanded a brigade of cavalry in the Richmond campaign, cavalry corps in the Shenandoah campaign with Sheridan, and a division of cavalry in the Appomattox campaign of 1865, and was present at the capitulation of General Lee April 5, 1865. He then made a raid to Dan River, North Carolina, from April 24 to May 3, 1865, and was in command of a cavalry division in the Military Division of the Southwest from June 3 to July 17, 1865.

General Custer was appointed major-general of volunteers April 15, 1865, and was brevetted in the regular army, major, for Gettysburg, July 3, 1863; lieutenant-colonel, for Yellow Tavern; colonel, for Winchester; brigadier-general, for Five Forks; major-general, for gallant and meritorious services during the campaign ending in the surrender of the insurgent army of Northern Virginia. He was also brevetted a major-general of United States Volunteers, for "gallant and meritorious services at the battles of Winchester and Fisher's Hill, Virginia."

He served in the Military Division of the Gulf from July 17 to November 13, 1865, and was chief of cavalry of the Department of Texas to February 1, 1866, at which time he was mustered out of the volunteer service. He was then granted leave of absence, and was awaiting orders to September 24, 1866, when he was placed on frontier duty at Fort Riley, Kansas, October 16, 1866.

General Custer was promoted lieutenant-colonel of the Seventh Cavalry July 28, 1866, and served on the plains; in campaign against the Sioux and Cheyennes, on the South Platte and Republican Rivers, 1867-68; various other expeditions, scouts, and combats, and notably the Big Horn and Yellowstone expedition of 1876, where he and his gallant band were all massacred in the fight with Sitting Bull's village on the Little Big Horn River, Montana. The closing scene in Custer's history has been described by Horned Horse, an old Sioux chief, as follows: "Custer then sought to lead his men up to the bluffs by a diagonal movement, all of them having dismounted and firing, whenever they could, over the backs of their horses at the Indians, who had by that time crossed the river in thousands, mostly on foot, and had taken Custer in flank and rear, while others annoyed him by a galling fire from across the river. Hemmed in on all sides, the troops fought steadily, but the fire of the enemy was so close and rapid that they melted like snow before it, and fell dead among their horses in heaps. The firing was continuous until the last man of Custer's command was dead. The water-course, in which most of the soldiers died, ran with blood."

## MAJOR AND BREVET LIEUTENANT-COLONEL AARON S. DAGGETT, U.S.A.

MAJOR AND BREVET LIEUTENANT-COLONEL AARON S. DAGGETT (Thirteenth Infantry) was born in Maine June 14, 1839. He is the son of Aaron and Dorcas (Dearborn) Daggett, and married Rose, the daughter of Major-General Phillips Bradford, of Turner, a lineal descendant of Governor William Bradford, of Plymouth County.

At the breaking out of the war of the Rebellion, Major Daggett enlisted as a private April 29, 1861, and was commissioned second lieutenant May 1, 1861. He was promoted first lieutenant of Company E, Fifth Maine Infantry, May 24, and captain of the company August 4, 1861.

From the first engagement of the regiment (battle of first Bull Run) to the end of its three years' memorable service, Captain Daggett did faithful duty, and was promoted major April 14, 1863, and on January 18, 1865, was commissioned lieutenant-colonel of the Fifth Regiment U. S. Veteran Volunteers (Hancock's Corps).

Colonel Daggett was brevetted colonel and brigadier-general of volunteers March 2, 1867, for "gallant and meritorious services during the war," and received the brevets of major U. S. Army for "gallant and meritorious services at the battle of Rappahannock Station, Virginia, November 7, 1863," and lieutenant colonel for "gallant and meritorious services in the battle of the Wilderness, Virginia."

Immediately after the battle of Rappahannock Station, the captured trophies—flags, cannon, etc.,—were escorted to General Meade's head-quarters, Colonel Daggett being in command of the battalion of his brigade, he having been chosen by General Upton, the escort being selected from those who had taken the most conspicuous part in that battle. General Upton wrote as follows regarding Colonel Daggett:

"In the assault at Rappahannock Station, Colonel Daggett's regiment captured over five hundred prisoners. In the assault at Spottsylvania Court-House, May 10, his regiment lost six out of seven captains, the seventh being killed on the 12th of May at 'the angle,' or the point where the tree was shot down by musketry, on which ground the regiment fought from 9.30 A. M. until 5.30 P. M., when it was relieved. On all these occasions Colonel Daggett was under my immediate command, and fought with distinguished bravery. Throughout his military career in the Army of the Potomac he maintained the character of a good soldier and an upright man, and his promotion would be but a simple act of justice, which would be commended by all those who desire to see courage rewarded."

In recommending him to Governor Corry for promotion, General Upton said:

"Major Daggett served his full term in this brigade with honor both to himself and State, and won the reputation of being a brave, reliable, and efficient officer. His promotion would be a great benefit to the service, while the honor of the State could scarcely be intrusted to safer hands."

Generals Meade, Wright, and Russell concurred in this recommendation.

General W. S. Hancock also recommended him for promotion. He was twice slightly wounded during the war.

Colonel Daggett was appointed a captain in the Sixteenth U. S. Infantry July 28, 1866; was transferred to the Second Infantry April 17, 1869; was promoted major January 2, 1892, and assigned to the Thirteenth Infantry.

He was not an applicant for a position in the regular army. The appointment was made without solicitation, by recommendation of General Grant. In the regular army he has won the reputation of being a fine tactician, and also of being well versed in military law.

Colonel Daggett is not only a soldier, but has ability ouside of his profession. As a public speaker, the following is said by the Rev. S. S. Cummings, of Boston: "It was my privilege and pleasure to listen to an address delivered by General A. S. Daggett on Memorial Day of 1891. I had anticipated something able and instructive, but it far exceeded my fondest expectations. . . . The address was dignified, yet affable, delivered in choice language without manuscript, instructive and impressive, and highly appreciated by an intelligent audience."

A Vinton (Iowa) paper, August, 1889, thus says of Colonel Daggett: "In the evening a very interesting programme was carried out in front of regimental head-quarters, it being music and speaking combined. . . . Colonel Daggett proves to be an eloquent orator as well as a good soldier."

## REAR-ADMIRAL JOHN A. DAHLGREN, U.S.N.
### (DECEASED).

REAR-ADMIRAL JOHN A. DAHLGREN was born in Philadelphia, Pennsylvania, and appointed midshipman from that State in 1826, serving in the Brazil and the Mediterranean Squadrons, in the "Macedonian" and "Ontario;" passed midshipman in April, 1832, and was on duty on the Coast Survey until 1842; commissioned as lieutenant in March, 1837; served in the frigate "Cumberland," in the Mediterranean, during 1844-45. From 1847 to 1857 he was upon ordnance duty, during which time he perfected the invention of the famous Dahlgren heavy guns, introduced howitzers for use afloat and ashore, and wrote several works relating to ordnance. In September, 1855, he was commissioned as commander; commanded the ordnance practice-ship "Plymouth" in 1858-59, and was on ordnance duty at the Washington Navy-Yard in 1860-61. At this time his guns were in general use in the navy, and there were never better or more reliable ones of their kind.

On April 22, 1861, a few days after the attack of the Baltimore mob on the Massachusetts troops, all the officers of the Washington Navy-Yard resigned and left, except Commander Dahlgren, Lieutenant Wainwright (who was absent on sick-leave), and the boatswain. The officers who thus left were a commodore-commandant, a commander, two lieutenants, the surgeon, and paymaster. The command devolved upon Dahlgren, who took vigorous measures to defend the navy-yard. After the immediate emergency passed away, it was suggested that the law required that a captain should command a navy-yard, and applications were made for his position, but the President refused to disturb him, and Congress passed an act enabling him to retain the command. Commissioned captain June 16, 1862, and shortly afterwards appointed chief of the Bureau of Ordnance. Promoted to rear-admiral February 7, 1863, and relieved Rear-Admiral Dupont, in the command of the South Atlantic Blockading Squadron, July 6 of that year. A combined operation of naval and army forces, the latter under General Gillmore, was then begun for the possession of Morris Island, on the south side of the entrance to Charleston.

After a long and severe struggle the island was finally possessed, and the guns of the army and the fleet soon reduced Fort Sumter to a pile of ruins. The fort itself was assaulted by a boat expedition which failed. But Dahlgren's fleet thenceforth remained inside the bar and blockade-running at that port was at an end. In February, 1864, Admiral Dahlgren commanded in person an expedition to the St. John's River. In July, 1864, a concerted movement was made up the Stono River by General Foster and Admiral Dahlgren. This expedition, well conceived, failed for want of energetic carrying out on the part of some of the army subordinates. The column under Colonel Hoyt actually captured Fort Johnson, but, being unsupported, were made prisoners. On December 12, 1864, General Sherman having successfully accomplished his march to the sea, reached the vicinity of Savannah, and Admiral Dahlgren immediately established communication with him, and made the best possible disposition of the vessels under his command to assist the army in taking possession of Savannah, which was occupied by Sherman on December 21, 1864. On February 18, 1865, the movements of Sherman's army caused the evacuation of Charleston by the Confederate forces, and Admiral Dahlgren at once moved his vessels up and occupied that city. The evacuation of Charleston was followed by that of Georgetown, and on February 26 the admiral occupied that place. On March 1, immediately after the surrender, his flag-ship was blown up by a torpedo and sunk. In 1866 Rear-Admiral Dahlgren was ordered to the command of the South Pacific Squadron. On returning from that service, in 1868, he was for the second time appointed chief of the Bureau of Ordnance. In the fall of 1869 he was relieved from the charge of that bureau at his own request, and ordered to the command of the Washington Navy-Yard, where he died in 1870.

## COMMANDER WM. STARR DANA, U.S.N.
### (DECEASED.)

COMMANDER WILLIAM STARR DANA was born in New York April, 1843; and was the son of Richard P. Dana, whose ancestor Richard came from England to Massachusetts in 1640. Many of the members of the family have since been well known in the literary and scientific world. Commander Dana entered the Naval Academy in 1859, and graduated in 1863, becoming an ensign in the same year. After a short service in the North Atlantic Squadron, he was ordered to the West Gulf Squadron. Was attached to the flag-ship "Hartford" at the battle of Mobile Bay, and participated in all the events,—the taking of Forts Morgan, Gaines, and Powell and other operations of that epoch of the Civil War. He was one of those who received the thanks of Admiral Farragut; and was included in the thanks of Congress voted to the "officers, seamen, and marines of the fleet, for the unsurpassed gallantry and skill exhibited by them in the engagement in Mobile Bay on the 5th day of August, 1864." After the close of the war Commander Dana was executive-officer of the "Shenandoah," 1879-81,— the flag-ship of Rear-Admiral Andrew Bryson, on the South Atlantic Squadron. For two months, pending a change of captains, he was in command of the "Shenandoah." When the inspection of the ship was made, upon the new captain taking command he reported that the condition of the ship bore testimony to the vigilance and industry of those in authority,—" as near perfection as the exertions of the officers and crew could arrive at with the armament furnished by the government." Rear-Admiral Bryson endorsed the report very favorably, mentioning that Dana's "best energies have been given, as the executive, to the well-being of the vessel."

He was regarded as having most seamanlike qualities, and was favorably regarded for the order and discipline of the vessels in which he served. The late Admiral Nicholson, who was a competent judge in such matters, said, "He," Dana, "was a conscientious, painstaking officer."

Commander Dana was for a time a companion of the Military Order of the Loyal Legion of the United States. He was also a member of the Academy of Sciences of New York.

In 1889 he obtained a few months' leave of absence for the purpose of European travel, and was on his way home when he was taken with pneumonia, in Paris, and died there on January 1, 1890.

After his service with Admiral Farragut in the "Hartford," he served on the Pacific Station, being promoted to master while attached to "St. Mary's." "Aroostook," of Asiatic Squadron, 1866-68, and promoted lieutenant while serving in her. In the "Shenandoah," on same station, when promoted to lieutenant-commander; and then served in "Ashuelot." Attached to "Brooklyn" and "Plymouth," of the European Squadron, 1870-73. Executive-officer of "Ossipee," in the West Indies, 1874-75. Executive-officer of receiving-ship "Colorado," 1875-77. In 1878 he took a course of torpedo instruction at Newport. From 1879 to 1881 he was attached to "Shenandoah," as already mentioned.

Commissioned commander September, 1881. After some duty at the New York Navy-Yard, and in command of torpedo-boat "Alarm," he made a cruise in command of the "Nipsic," South Atlantic Squadron, returning home in June, 1886. His next station was the Naval War College, during a course lasting some weeks, in 1887. In 1888 he took another course at the Torpedo Instruction, and after that was ordered to duty at the Naval War College, Newport, from August to November, 1888. This terminated his active service.

## CAPTAIN AND BREVET MAJOR JOHN A. DARLING, U.S.A.

CAPTAIN AND BREVET MAJOR JOHN A. DARLING (First U. S. Artillery) was born at Bucksport, Maine, June 7, 1835. His ancestors settled in New England in 1632, and were ever quick to respond to all calls for support from the colonies and republic, rendering distinguished services. Major Darling graduated at the State Military Academy of Pennsylvania; was commissioned second lieutenant in Second U. S. Artillery, August 5, 1861.

His first service was at Fort McHenry. In the autumn of 1861 he was ordered to Sedalia, Missouri, to command Light Battery F of his regiment, well known as "Totten's Battery."

In the exceptionally severe winter of 1862, he marched, with his command, to St. Louis Arsenal, a distance of three hundred miles, arriving in February after a month's march. From there he proceeded at once to New Madrid, Missouri, and was engaged in active operations both there and at Island No. 10, resulting in their capture.

In addition to the command of his battery, he was specially detailed, in charge of two companies of volunteer engineer troops, to make gabions and fascines and to construct a field-work.

General Pope in his report says, "Lieutenant Darling's battery, Second Artillery, U.S.A., was frequently under the enemy's fire, and behaved in a very gallant and creditable manner."

Having been promoted to a first lieutenancy, he was appointed aide-de-camp to Major-General John A. Dix. While on this duty he made the first exchange of war prisoners, being associated with Judge Ould, commissioner of the Confederate States. He was also engaged in actual field-service before Suffolk, Virginia, and on the Peninsula. In March, 1863, was appointed major of Pennsylvania Heavy Artillery. Commanded regiment and Camp Hamilton, Virginia, until June. From there transferred to duty at Fort Monroe, Virginia, till October, 1864. At this date, having been detailed as acting assistant inspector-general for the Eastern District of Virginia, he served until June, 1865, in that capacity. Upon being relieved and returned to his regiment at Fort Monroe, Virginia, he remained there until September, 1865. During July and August, 1865, he held as prisoners in close confinement President Jefferson Davis, Senator C. C. Clay, and Editor John Mitchell (the Irish refugee), of the Southern Confederacy.

Brevetted captain and major for "gallant and meritorious services," he was honorably mustered out of the volunteer service, and ordered to join his regular regiment, the Second U. S. Artillery, at Alcatraz Island, San Francisco harbor, where he remained until December, 1867, commanding the post from July, 1866.

Placed in command of the post and his battery at Fort

Point San José, San Francisco, he remained there until February, 1868. Was promoted captain to date from December 9, 1867.

Removed to Fort Stevens, Oregon, he commanded the post and battery there until January, 1871.

Upon the reduction of the army in January, 1871, he was honorably mustered out of the service. By special act of Congress he was recommissioned as captain of artillery, with former rank and date of commission, and assigned to the First U. S. Artillery. The following is an extract from the united report of the Senate and House Committees on Military Affairs, unanimously adopted by both bodies: "His record during the war is that of a gallant, faithful, and efficient officer, who was constantly in the field, having command of artillery in active operations in Missouri, at New Madrid, Island No. 10, and, later, in the campaigns in Virginia. At the conclusion of the war he was brevetted captain and major for gallant and meritorious conduct."

From May, 1878, to July, 1879, he was on duty at the Artillery School at Fort Monroe, Virginia. Ordered to Fort Trumbull, Connecticut, in July, 1879, he commanded Battery M, First U. S. Artillery, at that point until November, 1881. Commanded post of Fort Mason, San Francisco, until February, 1889, nearly eight years. He was then removed to the Presidio of San Francisco, remaining until April, 1889. Ordered to Alcatraz Island, San Francisco harbor, he was on duty with his battery until May, 1890. At that date his regiment was ordered east, and he has been, up to the present time, in command of his battery at Governor's Island, New York harbor.

Major Darling is well known in the musical world as August Mignon, under which nom de plume have been published, both in this country and in Europe, many vocal and instrumental compositions of acknowledged high artistic merit.

REAR-ADMIRAL CHARLES HENRY DAVIS, U.S.N.
(DECEASED).

REAR-ADMIRAL CHARLES HENRY DAVIS, son of Daniel Davis, Solicitor-General of Massachusetts, was born in Boston January 16, 1807. He entered Harvard College in 1821, and on August 12, 1823, was appointed midshipman in the navy. His first cruise was in the Pacific, on board the frigate "United States," under Commodore Isaac Hull. He served temporarily on board the schooner "Dolphin," on a cruise to the Mulgrave Islands, in search of the mutineers of the whale-ship "Globe."

He was attached to the sloop "Erie," in the West Indies, in 1828; passed his examination in 1829, taking high rank in his class; served as sailing-master of the "Ontario," in the Mediterranean, until 1832; was commissioned lieutenant in 1831; sailed in the "Vincennes" as flag-lieutenant to Commodore Alexander Wadsworth, in 1833, on the Pacific Station; returned to the United States in 1835 in command of the American bark "Vermont," which had been condemned at Callao; and from 1837 to 1840 he served on board the razee "Independence," in Europe, and on the Brazil Station. In 1840 he began the serious study of mathematics. He was attached to the Coast Survey from 1842 to 1849. During this period he discovered Davis' New South Shoal, lying off Nantucket Shoals, and published his papers on the Geological Action of the Tidal and other Currents of the Ocean, and on the Law of Deposit of the Flood-tide, which gave him reputation as a hydrographer of skill. He also served on several harbor commissions. In 1849 he established the Nautical Almanac, and became its first superintendent. Commander in 1854, he commanded the "St. Mary's," in the Pacific, 1856-59. He raised the siege of Rivas, and received the surrender of Walker,

the filibuster, thereby saving his life, and took him out of Nicaragua. In 1857 he published a translation of Gauss's "Theoria Motus Corporum Cœlestium." This was the first presentation in English of this standard authority for astronomers. In 1861 he was member of the Board on Construction of New Vessels, and of the Commission on Southern Harbors, which planned the expedition to Port Royal, in which he sailed as fleet-captain, under Dupont.

In May, 1862, having been promoted to captain, he relieved flag-officer Foote, in command of the Mississippi Flotilla, off Fort Pillow. A few days after assuming command, he, with seven vessels, beat off a squadron of eight iron-clads in an action lasting an hour, the enemy's vessels avoiding capture under the guns of Fort Pillow. On June 5 Fort Pillow was evacuated, and on the 6th Davis brought on a general action with the Confederate iron-clads and rams off Memphis, won a signal victory, and received the surrender of the city. He then joined Farragut, and was engaged in operations near Vicksburg and on the Yazoo River until September, when he was forced, through ill health, to relinquish his command. He was made rear-admiral in 1863, and became the first chief of the Bureau of Navigation, and in 1865 was appointed superintendent of the Naval Observatory. In 1867 he hoisted his flag on board the "Guerriere," as commander-in-chief of the Brazil Station.

During this cruise he proceeded in force to Paraguay and demanded and obtained the surrender of two persons, one an American and the other a British subject, who had claimed protection of the American legation, and had been arrested by Lopez, when the minister left the country. This action involved Davis in a controversy with the ministers to Brazil and Paraguay, in which he was sustained by the Department. A congressional investigation followed, in which he was vindicated. He commanded the Norfolk Navy-Yard 1870-73. In 1874 he was again appointed superintendent of the Observatory, at which post he died February 18, 1877. Admiral Davis took the degree of A. B. at Harvard, and was made LL.D. by the same University in 1868. He was a member of the National Academy of Sciences, of the American Academy of Arts and Sciences, of the Massachusetts branch of the Society of the Cincinnati, and of the Military Order of the Loyal Legion, and was the author of many writings on scientific and other subjects. He received the thanks of Congress and his rear-admiral's commission for his victories at Fort Pillow and Memphis.

A stained-glass window in the Memorial Hall, at Harvard, commemorates the fact that he was the oldest representative of the University, and the senior in rank, who served during the Civil War.

## COLONEL JEFFERSON C. DAVIS, U.S.A.
### (DECEASED.)

COLONEL JEFFERSON C. DAVIS was born in Indiana, and appointed from the army. He was a private in the Third Indiana Volunteer Infantry June, 1846; engaged in Taylor's campaigns against Monterey and Saltillo, and the battle of Buena Vista, Mexico; sergeant Third Indiana Volunteer Infantry February, 1847; second lieutenant First U. S. Artillery June, 1848. He joined the regiment at Fort McHenry October, 1848, and was at Fort Washington, Maryland, and on the coast of Mississippi until the fall of 1852. First lieutenant First U. S. Artillery February, 1852, and in Florida in 1853. He was at Fortress Monroe, Virginia, until the fall of 1855 with a light battery; at Fort McHenry to 1857; on the east coast of Florida to summer of 1858, and at Fort Moultrie, South Carolina, till December, 1861, when it was evacuated and Fort Sumter occupied. Engaged in the defence of Fort Sumter, South Carolina. He was on staff duty, mustering and equipping troops for the field, Indianapolis, from May to August, 1861. Captain First U. S. Artillery May, 1861; colonel Indiana Volunteer Infantry August, 1861; commanding forces holding Jefferson City, Lexington, and Boonville; commanding brigade in the Army of the Southwest, and at the action of Springfield, Missouri; commanding Camp of Instruction at Otterville, Missouri. He commanded the forces engaged in the defeat and capture of the rebels on the Blackwater, Missouri, December, 1861. Commanded a division and was engaged in the action at Springfield and pursuit of Price. Commanded the troops in the action at Cross Timbers, Arkansas, and participated in the battle of Pea Ridge, Arkansas. He was in command of a division at the siege of Corinth, and in the pursuit of the enemy to Boonville. Made brigadier-general U. S. Volunteers May, 1862, to rank from December, 1861. Commanded troops in the engagement at Nolensville and Nole Gap in the advance on Murfreesborough. He was at the battle of Stone River, and commanded the forces in pursuit of the rebel General Wheeler. In the campaign against Tullahoma and Chattanooga; engaged at action of Liberty Gap, battles of Chickamauga, Missionary Ridge, pursuit of the rebels; actions of Chickamauga Station and Shepard's Farm; expedition for the relief of Knoxville; reconnoissance at Dalton; action of Buzzard's Roost (commanding forces); advance on Atlanta, battle of Resaca, capture of Rome; actions around Dallas, assault on Kenesaw Mountain, and capture of Marietta; in the actions of Nicojack Creek, Chatta- hoochie River, battle of Peach-Tree Creek, and operations around Atlanta, Georgia. Brevet major-general U. S. Volunteers August, 1864; commanding Fourteenth Army Corps; engaged at the battle and occupation of Jonesborough; pursuit of the rebel General Hood in rear of Atlanta. He was in Sherman's march to the sea and through the Carolinas, being engaged at the capture of Savannah, Georgia; battles of Avery-borough and Bentonville, capture of Raleigh, and surrender of the rebel army under General Johnston. In the march to Washington City via Richmond, Virginia, and transported the Fourteenth Corps to Louisville, Kentucky, when it was mustered out of service July and August, 1865; commanded Department of Kentucky 1866; commanded expedition to occupy Alaska, and in command of Department of Alaska September, 1867, to August, 1870. Brevet major U. S. Army for gallant and meritorious conduct at the battle of Rome, Georgia; brevet colonel U. S. Army for gallant and meritorious conduct at the battle of Pea Ridge, Arkansas; brevet lieutenant-colonel U. S. Army for gallant and meritorious conduct at the battle of Resaca, Georgia; brevet colonel U. S. Army for gallant and meritorious conduct at the battle of Rome, Georgia; brevet brigadier-general U. S. Army for gallant and meritorious conduct at the battle of Kenesaw Mountain, Georgia; brevet major-general U. S. Army for gallant and meritorious conduct at the battle of Jonesborough, Georgia. Colonel Twenty-third U. S. Infantry July, 1866. Eastern Superintendency General Recruiting Service, New York City, from January, 1871. Died November 30, 1879.

**COLONEL AND BREVET BRIGADIER-GENERAL HANNIBAL DAY, U.S.A. (DECEASED).**

COLONEL AND BREVET BRIGADIER-GENERAL HANNIBAL DAY was born at Montpelier, Vermont, February 17, 1804; he was the son of Dr. Sylvester Day, Surgeon U. S. Army, and grandson of Dr. Elkanah Day, of Westminster, Vermont,—one of the pioneers in the settlement of that State, who was active in establishing the State government, independent of the States of New York and New Hampshire.

General Day had an early experience in the military service, when in the beginning of the War of 1812 (15th July), at the age of eight years, he with his father and the garrison of Fort Michilimackinac, were taken prisoners by a British force of Canadians and Indians. The prisoners were paroled and sent to Detroit, where they were, a month later, at the surrender of the United States forces on 16th August, 1812, of which event and of the indignant expressions of the army officers, the general retained a vivid recollection.

After Hull's surrender the Michilimackinac paroled prisoners were all taken on board a sloop and carried to Fort Erie, on Lake Erie. Captain Elliot, of the navy, was at Buffalo with some boats; and the gallant Captain Lawson was there with the land forces; he volunteered to man the boats and rescue the prisoners, which was accomplished on a dark night without the loss of a man; no mention of the services of the army was made by Elliot in the report of the affair. After his rescue and his early experience of the incidents of war, young Hannibal Day returned to his native town and pursued his studies in the academic schools of his native State. In 1818 his father procured for him an appointment of cadet in the West Point Military Academy. Ill health prevented the successful pursuit of his studies, and he was allowed to enter the next class on September 1, 1819, and he was graduated on the 1st of July, 1823, and was at that date appointed second lieutenant Second Regiment U. S. Infantry, and served in the same regiment in the grades of first lieutenant, captain, major, and lieutenant-colonel. On the 7th of July, 1862, he was appointed colonel of the Sixth Regiment of Infantry. He was commissioned brigadier-general by brevet on March 13, 1865, for long and faithful service in the army.

He served forty years continuously: In garrison at Fort Brady, Michigan, 1823-28; on Topographical duty, 1828-31; in garrison at Fort Niagara, New York, 1832; Fort Dearborn, Illinois, 1832-33; Hancock Barracks, Maryland, 1833-36; Fort Independence, Massachusetts, 1836; on recruiting service, 1836-38; in the Florida War, 1838-39 and 1841-42; at Buffalo, 1842-45; and Detroit, 1845-46. In the Mexican War he was stationed at Tampico, 1846-47, and afterwards served in many places in California and on the Indian frontier. At the beginning of the Civil War he was at Fort Abercrombie, and was soon ordered to Georgetown, District of Columbia, in command of the Second Infantry.

Colonel Hannibal Day commanded the first brigade of Ayer's division, Fifth Army Corps, and was actively engaged at the battle of Gettysburg, rendering gallant service in the defence of Round Top, on the extreme left of the loyal line, where he had a horse killed under him. He held the same command during the march to Warrenton, Virginia, and until he was retired from active service, August 1, 1863, owing to want of sufficient physical strength to perform service in the field. He then commanded Fort Hamilton, New York, till July 8, 1864, and afterwards served on various military commissions and courts-martial till June 14, 1869, when he was relieved from duty.

He died at Morristown, New Jersey, March 26, 1891, at the age of eighty-seven years.

At the time of his death he was third in academic rank of the living graduates of the Military Academy, his seniors being Colonel William C. Young, of the Class of 1882, and brevet major-general Georget S. Green, of the Class of 1823.

General Day married, in 1831, Anna Maria Houghton, daughter of Thomas and Mary Leggate (Chase) Houghton, who died in 1881. He leaves one son, Sylvester Henry Day, of Carson City, Nevada, and one daughter, Mrs. Hoff, wife of Captain John Van Rensselaer Hoff, M.D., assistant surgeon U. S. Army.

## CAPTAIN SELDEN ALLEN DAY, U.S.A.

CAPTAIN SELDEN ALLEN DAY (Fifth Artillery) was born at Chillicothe, Ohio, July 22, 1838. His father, Demoval T. Day, was a native of Virginia, and his mother, Ruth Merriam, of Vermont. His grandfather, Samuel Day, and his great-grandfather, Leonard Day, were Virginia soldiers in the Revolutionary War, and both were at the capture of Yorktown and surrender of Cornwallis. In April, 1861, Captain Day obtained authority and raised a company of volunteers at Bowling Green, Ohio, for the war of the Rebellion. Owing, however, to the excess of troops enrolled under the first call, this company was not mustered, and was disbanded. Captain Day then enlisted as a private in Company C, Seventh Ohio Infantry, June 20, 1861, participating in the campaign in West Virginia, that year. After the action of Cross Lanes August 26, where his regiment suffered heavy loss, he was made corporal. He was present at Loop Creek, Paw-Paw, Romney, etc., in the winter of 1861-62.

At the battle of Winchester, Virginia, March 23, 1862, Corporal Day, though injured early in the fight, remained at the front; and in a charge of his brigade was one of the first over the stone wall forming part of the defence of the enemy, and was one of a small party following Major Casement into a battery and capturing the guns. At the close of the fight he had the good fortune, with the aid of a comrade, to capture and bring in a staff-officer of General Jackson. For his part in this action Corporal Day was promoted sergeant and recommended for a commission.

In the battle of Port Republic, June 9, 1862, Sergeant Day bore an active part, and, though again wounded, formed one of the rear-guard in the retreat after the battle.

At the battle of Cedar Mountain, where his regiment suffered terribly, August 9, 1862, Sergeant Day, though at one time "between two fires," escaped unhurt, and at the close of the action found himself in command of the remnant of three companies.

The fatigue and hardships of the campaign of 1862, however, brought about at last what shot and shell failed to accomplish, and at its close we find the subject of our sketch *hors de combat*. For several months he remained in hospital at Frederick, Maryland, where, having formerly studied medicine, as soon as able he performed efficient service in the care of the sick and wounded. During this time he was given the option of a discharge for disability or a transfer to the regular army as hospital steward. He chose the latter, and was ordered to Baltimore for duty. When that city was threatened in the summer of 1863, Steward Day, under the mayor, was instrumental in organizing and drilling companies

made up of members of the Union League and convalescents in the hospitals for special service.

After his health was restored, and on application for field service, Steward Day was called to Washington, D. C., appointed second lieutenant Fifth Artillery, and in the spring of 1864 ordered to the front. He joined Battery A in the battle of Cold Harbor, and was brevetted first lieutenant for that action. He served continuously in the field until the close of the war; entered Richmond with Battery F, Fifth Artillery, April 3, 1865, and was brevetted captain for "gallant and meritorious services during the war."

Since the war Captain Day has served in various parts of the country. He was detailed in charge of cholera quarantine at Craney Island, Virginia, and afterwards to command Battery F, Fifth Artillery, at Richmond, Virginia, in 1866, in which year he was promoted first lieutenant. He was made president of Board of Registration and Elections, and military commissioner in Virginia under the reconstruction acts in 1867-68. For several years he acted as ordnance officer, and was instructor in signalling and rifle practice at Fort Adams, Rhode Island. He graduated from the Artillery School in 1874, and from the Medical College of the State of South Carolina 1880. He was recorder of Board on Magazine-Guns 1881-82; promoted captain Fifth Artillery 1886; commanded Fort Wood, Bedloe's Island, New York harbor, March to June, 1887.

He travelled in Europe in 1888; was ordered to the Pacific coast in 1890, and assigned to the command of Fort Mason, San Francisco, California, where he is now serving.

Captain Day is a man in the prime of life, of medium height and weight, fair complexion, with brown hair, gray-blue eyes, and is a hard worker, an enthusiastic sportsman, and an expert rifle-shot.

CAPTAIN CHARLES C. DE RUDIO, U.S.A.

CAPTAIN CHARLES C. DE RUDIO (Seventh Cavalry) was born on August 26, 1832, in the city of Belleno, then the State of Venice. In 1845 he entered the Austrian Military Academy of Milan. At the revolution of 1848 he left the Austrian army and joined the Venetian Legion of the Cacciatori delle Alpi in Venice; served and participated at the siege and sorties till March, 1849, when he left Venice and entered the Legion of Garibaldi in Rome. He served and participated with that legion in the battles of April 30, 1849, against the French; at the battles of Palestrina and Velletri against the Neapolitan Bourbon army, and at the siege of Rome till its fall.

He entered the U. S. Volunteers August 25, 1864, in the Seventy-ninth New York Highlanders, and was sent to the front in Virginia. He joined his regiment at Fort Hays, near Petersburg, Virginia; served with his company (A) up to October 16, 1864, when he received a lieutenant's commission in the Second U. S. Colored Troops. He was discharged from the Seventy-ninth New York to enable him to accept the commission, and two weeks afterwards was sent to his company (D), stationed at Fort Meyer, Florida. He was then ordered to Punta Rassa, at the mouth of the Caloosahatchee, to guard a large depot containing over two millions of rations and ammunition, collected there for an expedition to capture Fort St. Mark, Florida, by General John Newton. The detachment was composed of sixteen men. During their absence a Confederate force attacked Fort Meyer. One of the videttes captured by the enemy near Fort Meyer escaped, and reported to Lieutenant De Rudio the circumstances of his capture and the attack on Fort Meyer. He immediately made preparations, in case he could not defend the depot, to destroy it by fire. The next morning the enemy made his appearance in the mangrove wood, about three miles off, but soon they were observed to be on a precipitate retreat, the gun-boat "Thunderer" happily making its appearance.

In a few days General Newton arrived with the Seventy-ninth, and De Rudio was complimented by the general for his conduct. Although he was anxious to participate in the expedition, he was ordered to remain at his post with thirty-sixty men, and ordered to fortify the place.

On the return of the expedition, De Rudio was ordered to Fort Meyer. On arriving there, he was informed that the post was to be abandoned, and that he had been picked out to remain with a detachment of thirty picked men, for the purpose of destroying the fort, after the troops, refugees, and property had safely arrived at Punta Rassa, as the enemy was supposed to be in the vicinity of the fort. The garrison left by land, and the refugees and property were transported by water. Finding that the fort could not effectually be destroyed, after demolishing all the barracks and buildings the block-houses were burned. After executing his orders, De Rudio, during the night, marched to Punta Rassa.

On January 5, 1866, he was mustered out at Key West, Florida.

Lieutenant De Rudio was recommended for the brevet of captain by General Newton, but he never received it.

On August 31, 1867, he was appointed second lieutenant Second U. S. Infantry by General U. S. Grant, while Secretary of War *ad interim*. He reported at Louisville, Kentucky, to his regiment. In March, 1868, he was selected by the major-general commanding the department to take charge of a detachment of fifty picked mounted infantry at Lebanon, Kentucky, for the purpose of assisting the U. S. Marshal to enforce the Civil-Rights Bill and the public-revenue law.

In April, 1869, he was relieved of that arduous duty, and ordered to his company at Louisville, then under orders to go to Atlanta, Georgia, for consolidation with the Sixteenth Infantry. On August 17 he was placed on waiting orders by reason of being a junior officer; but the same day received a telegram from the Adjutant-General of Department of Cumberland to report without delay to those head-quarters, and was ordered to Lebanon, Kentucky, to resume charge of the mounted detachment.

Lieutenant De Rudio was recommended by Major-General G. H. Thomas for transfer to the cavalry, and July 14, 1869, was transferred to the Seventh Cavalry; and the following month was relieved from Lebanon and ordered to join his new regiment in camp near Fort Hays, Kansas. He was assigned to H Troop, and participated in all the marches and campaigns with the regiment up to 1889.

## CAPTAIN GEORGE DEWEY, U.S.N.

CAPTAIN GEORGE DEWEY is a native of Vermont, and was appointed a midshipman from that State in September, 1854. He graduated from the Naval Academy in 1858, well up in his class, and served in the frigate "Wabash," in the Mediterranean, for the next two years. When the Civil War occurred he was ordered to the steam-frigate "Mississippi," and served at New Orleans, Port Hudson, and Donaldsonville, Louisiana, in that vessel, having been commissioned lieutenant in April, 1861. The episode of the destruction of the "Mississippi" (although a misfortune to the cause, in the unavoidable destruction of a fine vessel which was not only very serviceable, but dear to many officers and men who had sailed in her) brought forth Lieutenant Dewey's fine qualities as an officer in a more marked degree than any previous action. The destruction of the "Mississippi," which had served on stations all over the world, and bore Perry's broad-pennant at the opening of Japan to the world, appropriately occurred in the river from which she was named, and in consequence of a well-sustained action. The whole affair was creditable in the highest degree, and especially to Captain M. Smith and his first lieutenant, who had made the ship so efficient, and who were the last to leave her. Admiral Porter remarked, "It is in such trying moments that men show of what metal they are made, and in this instance the metal was of the very best."

After the destruction of the "Mississippi," Lieutenant Dewey was ordered to the steam-gun-boat "Agawam," of the Atlantic Blockading Squadron, and was engaged heavily with rebel batteries in August, 1864, for which Commander Rhind, his officers and men, received the highest praise in the report of the admiral commanding to the Navy Department.

Lieutenant Dewey served at both attacks upon Fort Fisher. He was commissioned lieutenant-commander March 3, 1865, eleven years after his entry as an acting midshipman. He served in the "Kearsarge," on the European Station, in 1866. He was transferred to the

"Colorado," frigate, flag-ship, in 1867, and, for some months, served on board the "Canandaigua," of the same squadron, showing executive ability of a high order at a time when it was needed.

During 1868-69 he was stationed at the Naval Academy, and then commanded the "Narragansett," on special service, in 1870-71. On duty at the Torpedo Station in 1872—just as he was made commander. For the next three years he was upon the Pacific Survey, in the "Narragansett," and followed this service by a term as lighthouse inspector. He was the secretary of the Light-House Board from 1877 to 1882. Then he made a cruise in command of the "Juniata," on the Asiatic Station, and was promoted captain in 1884. In that year he commanded the "Dolphin," and then was in command of the "Pensacola," the flag-ship of the European Station, from 1885 to 1888.

Captain Dewey is now the chief of the Bureau of Equipment and Recruiting, with the rank of commodore, having been commissioned, and approved by the Senate, in 1889.

CAPTAIN JOHN W. DILLENBACK, U.S.A.

CAPTAIN JOHN W. DILLENBACK (First Artillery) was born in New York; appointed from New York; enlisted in Company G, Tenth New York Heavy Artillery, August 7, 1862; served in the defences of Washington, D. C., until August, 1863; commissioned by the President captain in the Fourth U. S. Colored Infantry August, 1863; commanded battalion on recruiting and picket duty at Williamsburg, Virginia, to April, 1864; on duty at Point Lookout, Maryland, till May, 1864; engaged in the operations of the Army of the James for the capture of Petersburg, Virginia, till June 15, 1864; severely wounded while charging a battery in the defences of Petersburg, Virginia, June 15, 1864; engaged in repelling attack on Fort Harrison, Virginia, September 30, 1864; with first expedition under General Butler for the capture of Fort Fisher, North Carolina, December, 1864; engaged in the operations that resulted in the capture of Fort Fisher, North Carolina, January 15, 1864; wounded in charge on works on Sugar-Loaf, North Carolina, in the advance on Wilmington, North Carolina, February 11, 1865; with General Sherman's army at the capture of Raleigh and surrender of General Johnston's army; served in North Carolina till the autumn of 1865; commanded successively Forts Mahan and Stanton, near Washington, D. C., until April, 1866; was brevetted major and lieutenant-colonel of volunteers for gallant and meritorious services during the war, and honorably mustered out of volunteer service April 11, 1866; was appointed second lieutenant, First U. S. Artillery, February 23, 1866; first lieutenant May 1, 1866; was with light batteries of regiment in New Orleans, and Brownsville, Texas, to May, 1867; at Artillery School, Fort Monroe, Virginia, and graduated May, 1869; disbursing officer, Freedmen's Branch, Adjutant-General's Department, in Savannah, Georgia, and Charleston, South Carolina, from 1872 until October, 1874; appointed regimental quartermaster March 1, 1875, and served as such to June 30, 1882, when he was promoted to captain, First U. S. Artillery; stationed at Fort Adams, Rhode Island, from 1875 to December, 1881; on duty in the harbor of San Francisco, California, from 1881 to May 1890, when ordered to Fort Hamilton, New York harbor; assigned to command of Light Battery K, First Artillery, January 25, 1889, and still retains command of it at Fort Hamilton, New York harbor.

## CAPTAIN EUGENE D. DIMMICK, U.S.A.

CAPTAIN EUGENE D. DIMMICK (Ninth Cavalry) was born in Athens, New York, July 31, 1840. He entered the volunteer service at the commencement of the war of the Rebellion as a private in Company G, Second New Jersey State Militia, April 26, 1861, and was discharged July 31, 1861. He re-entered the volunteer service as first sergeant of Company M, Fifth New York Cavalry, October 7, 1861, and was appointed second lieutenant of that regiment May 9, 1862, and promoted first lieutenant October 10, 1862. He participated in the campaigns of the Army of the Potomac, and was engaged in the actions of Harrisonburgh and Culpeper, battles of Cedar Mountain (commanding company), second Bull Run (escort to General Banks), South Mountain, Antietam, Brandy Station, and Chantilly; actions of Warrenton Junction, Thoroughfare Gap, Beverly Ford, and Hanover Junction; battle of Gettysburg, and actions of Boonsborough and Hagerstown, where he was severely wounded, taken prisoner, and released.

He was promoted captain July 5, 1863, and in November he was discharged for disability arising from wounds. He again entered the service, as second lieutenant of the Eighteenth Regiment Veteran Reserve Corps, February, 1864, and served at Albany, New York, and on the Canada border during the Fenian raids, and was mustered out June 30, 1866.

Captain Dimmick entered the regular service as second lieutenant of the Ninth Cavalry August 9, 1867, and joined his regiment in Texas, where he served from 1867 to 1875, and was then ordered to change station with his regiment to the Department of the Missouri, he taking station first at Fort Wallace, Kansas. He was at Fort Lyon, Colorado, in 1876, and then was changed to Fort Union, New Mexico, where he served in 1877-78. He participated in the campaign against Victorio in 1879-80, through New Mexico, Arizona, and Old Mexico. He was after that detailed on recruiting service in 1882-84, subsequently returning to Fort Riley, where he was during the years 1884-85.

Lieutenant Dimmick was promoted first lieutenant Ninth Cavalry January 10, 1870, and captain October 25, 1883. He participated in the Boomer campaign, Indian Territory, and was then transferred to Fort McKinney, Wyoming, in 1885. He commanded a battalion (D and H Troop, Ninth Cavalry) at the affair at Crow Agency, Montana, November 5, 1887, when "Sword-Bearer" was killed.

COLONEL AND BREVET MAJOR-GENERAL ABNER DOUBLEDAY, U.S.A. (RETIRED).

COLONEL AND BREVET MAJOR-GENERAL ABNER DOUBLEDAY was born at Ballston Spa, New York, and graduated from the Military Academy in the Class of 1842. He was then promoted brevet second lieutenant of the Third Artillery, serving three years in this grade, when he was promoted second lieutenant of the First Artillery February 20, 1845, and first lieutenant March 3, 1847.

He served during the war with Mexico, being engaged in the battle of Monterey, September, 1846, and in the operations connected with the battle of Buena Vista, February 22-23, 1847.

At the close of the Mexican War the United States government purchased California for three million dollars, reserving from this sum sufficient money to compensate our merchants residing in Mexico whose property had been illegally confiscated by the authorities there. A Cuban, named George A. Gardner, of English descent, claimed to be an American citizen. He asserted that the President of Mexico had directed that the entrance to a mine belonging to him, worth eight hundred thousand dollars, should be blown up. He was awarded (in 1852) five hundred thousand dollars. After the money was paid, President Fillmore became convinced that Gardner never owned a mine in Mexico, but there was such a strong boom for him, and he was so strongly supported politically, that it became necessary to take extraordinary measures. A special commission was sent to Mexico, with a distinguished lawyer at the head. It included our secretary of legation, an expert in Spanish jurisprudence, one officer of the army, and one of the navy. Lieutenant Doubleday represented the army. In consequence of their report, Gardner was ultimately convicted, he having supported his claim by perjury and forged documents, and committed suicide in court by swallowing a roll of strychnine.

Lieutenant Doubleday was promoted to a captaincy March 3, 1855, and was engaged in hostilities with the Florida Indians in 1856-58. He was second in command at Fort Sumter, South Carolina, at the time of its first bombardment, April 12-14, 1861, on which occasion he aimed the first gun of the war on the side of the Union; he was appointed major of the Seventeenth Infantry May 14, 1861, and participated in the Shenandoah campaign, under General Patterson, in 1861; he was appointed brigadier-general of volunteers February 3, 1862, and participated in the campaign of the Army of the Potomac, being engaged in the battles of Groveton, second Bull Run, South Mountain, Antietam, Fredericksburg, Chancellorsville, and Gettysburg; having been promoted major-general of volunteers November 29, 1862.

While in camp near Fredericksburg, Virginia, he was sent with two regiments to make a demonstration against Port Conway, on the lower Rappahannock, with a view to attack the enemy in that direction, and thus facilitate the crossing of General Hooker's army above, April 29-21, 1863; on July 1 he went forward to Gettysburg, by order of General Reynolds, to reinforce Buford's cavalry, who were holding the ridge west of the Seminary, and General Reynolds being killed, General Doubleday took his place, acting for some hours in command of the field, when General Howard made his presence known. On this occasion the First Corps captured Archer's brigade, the greater part of Davis's brigade, and almost annihilated Iverson's brigade. The second day General Doubleday's division, with a brigade under General Stannard, was sent to assist in regaining the position which the enemy had taken; he followed them up and retook six guns which they had captured. When Pickett's grand charge advanced on the third day it exposed the right flank, and General Doubleday's front line, under General Stannard, wheeled, threw themselves upon the vulnerable point, and disordered the enemy's advance to such an extent that they were easily repulsed.

General Doubleday was promoted lieutenant-colonel Seventeenth U. S. Infantry September 20, 1863; honorably mustered out of volunteer service August 24, 1865; colonel Thirty-fifth U. S. Infantry September 15, 1867; assigned to the Twenty-fourth U. S. Infantry December 15, 1870. He was made brevet lieutenant-colonel September 17, 1862, for gallant and meritorious services in the battle of Antietam, Maryland; brevet colonel July 2, 1863, for gallant and meritorious services in the battle of Gettysburg, Pennsylvania; brevet brigadier- and major-general March 13, 1865, for gallant and meritorious services during the war.

He was retired from active service, at his own request, December 11, 1873.

## COLONEL HENRY DOUGLASS, U.S.A. (RETIRED).

COLONEL HENRY DOUGLASS was born in New York March 9, 1827, and graduated from the Military Academy in the Class of 1852, when he was promoted brevet second lieutenant of the Seventh Infantry. He was promoted second lieutenant of the Eighth Infantry December 31, 1853. Upon the organization of the Ninth Infantry, in 1855, he was transferred to that regiment March 3, and gained his first lieutenancy September 10, 1856. He served in garrison at Newport Barracks, Kentucky, Fort Monroe, Virginia, and on frontier duty.

He was detailed as assistant professor of drawing at the Military Academy January 16, 1858, and served there until July 2, 1861, having been promoted captain of the Eighteenth Infantry May 14, 1861. He entered the field during the war of the Rebellion, and participated in the battle of first Bull Run, July 21, 1861, and then served in the defences of Washington to October of that year. He joined his regiment in the Army of the West, participating in the Tennessee and Mississippi campaigns and the actions connected therewith from February until June, 1862. He then served with the army under General Buell, through Mississippi, Alabama, Tennessee, and Kentucky, from June to September, 1862, being engaged in the skirmish near Chaplin Hills, and in the battle of Perryville, October 8, 1862. He also participated in the actions under General Rosecrans, in his Tennessee campaign, from November, 1862, to April, 1863, and was engaged in the battle of Stone River, where he was wounded.

Captain Douglass was then detailed on the recruiting service from April to September, 1863, and on mustering and disbursing duty at Cleveland, Ohio, from December, 1863, to January, 1864, and was in charge of chief mustering and disbursing office of the State of Ohio from September, 1864, to June, 1866. He had the brevet of major conferred upon him December 31, 1862, for "gallant

and meritorious services in the battle of Murfreesborough, Tennessee."

He was promoted major of the Third Infantry July 28, 1866, upon the reorganization of the army, and served on frontier stations. Upon the consolidation of regiments, in 1869, he was unassigned, March 15, but placed on duty as superintendent of Indian affairs for the State of Nevada, which position he occupied until January 1, 1871, when he was assigned to the Eleventh Infantry. He was promoted lieutenant-colonel of the Fourteenth Infantry January 10, 1876, and served with his regiment at Fort Cameron, Utah, cantonment on the Uncompahgre, Colorado, and Fort Townsend, Washington, until promoted colonel of the Tenth Infantry July 1, 1885, when he joined his regiment in New Mexico, and served at Fort Union, Fort Bliss, Texas, and Santa Fé until retired, by operation of law, March 9, 1891.

Colonel Douglass is at the present time making his home at Barnegat Park, New Jersey.

## CAPTAIN PERCIVAL DRAYTON, U.S.N.
### (DECEASED).

CAPTAIN PERCIVAL DRAYTON, an officer of recognized ability and conduct in every position in which he was placed, was born in South Carolina, coming of a well-known and influential family. His father was the Honorable William Drayton, M.C.

Percival Drayton was appointed midshipman, from South Carolina, in December, 1827, and became a lieutenant in the navy on February 28, 1838.

After the usual varied service of the younger officers of his grade, including a period at the Naval Observatory at Washington, he was promoted to commander in 1855. When the Paraguay expedition was organized, in 1858, he became the aid, or fleet-captain, of Commodore Shubrick, returning with him to the United States when a satisfactory settlement was had. From 1860 to the outbreak of the Civil War, he was upon ordnance duty in Philadelphia, where many of his family resided. He was, however, strongly bound by family ties to the seceding States. He never wavered, however, but declared his allegiance to the flag under which he had served for a third of a century.

In the naval expedition which resulted in the capture of Port Royal he commanded the steamer "Pocahontas," of Dupont's squadron, while his brother, General T. F. Drayton, commanded the Confederate troops at Hilton Head Island, and fought the principal batteries opposed to the squadron. Such instances were not rare during that war.

After the capture of Port Royal he was transferred to the "Pawnee," and on July 16, 1862, upon his promotion to captain, was ordered to command the new Ericsson monitor "Passaic."

In this vessel he took part in the bombardment of Fort McAllister, and in Dupont's attack upon Fort Sumter.

He was next ordered as fleet-captain of the West Gulf Squadron under Farragut, and served in the flag-ship "Hartford" at the battle of Mobile Bay, August 5, 1864. He particularly distinguished himself as Farragut's chief of staff, as the detailed accounts of this remarkable action show.

He was appointed chief of the Bureau of Navigation on April 28, 1865, but died on August 4, 1865, at Washington.

# BRIGADIER-GENERAL RICHARD CAULTER DRUM,
## U.S.A. (RETIRED).

BRIGADIER-GENERAL RICHARD CAULTER DRUM was born at Greensborough, Westmoreland County, Pennsylvania, May 28, 1825. His military history commenced with his enrollment as a private in Company K, First Pennsylvania Volunteers, December 8, 1846, with which he served during the siege of Vera Cruz. He was appointed second lieutenant Ninth Infantry February 18, 1847, and served with that regiment during active operations in Mexico, participating in the battles of Contreras, Churubusco, Molino del Rey, Chapultepec, Garita Belen, and capture of City of Mexico.

He was transferred to Fourth Artillery March 8, 1848, and returned with that regiment at the close of the war, serving immediately after in Alabama, Florida, and Louisiana, when he was sent to the light battery at Fort Leavenworth September 30, 1850, and thence to Fort Columbus May 23, 1851. He conducted, by the overland route, recruits from New York to Jefferson Barracks, and thence to Fort Kearney, returning July 30, 1851, and joined his company at Governor's Island.

At the threatened secession of South Carolina in 1851 he went with his company to Fort Johnston, North Carolina, where he remained until June 6, 1852, when he was ordered to Fort Brady, Michigan, and was stationed there until October, 1853, at which time he was assigned to the light battery at Fort Leavenworth.

In May, 1855, he acted as quartermaster and commissary to the battalion of the Sixth Infantry in its march from Leavenworth to Kearney, in July; returned to Leavenworth and joined company temporarily armed as mounted riflemen, and served with it against hostile Sioux Indians, participating in the action of Blue Water September 3, 1855. On the 24th of October, 1855, he was appointed aide-de-camp to General W. S. Harney, commander of the expedition, to June 30, 1856. He commanded a detail of light artillery during the Kansas troubles in 1856, and was acting depot quartermaster at Fort Leavenworth. He was appointed aide-de-camp to General Persifor F. Smith, commanding Department of the West, and acting assistant adjutant-general at head-quarters of that department until the death of General

Smith, in May, 1858, when he joined his company at the Artillery School, Fort Monroe, Virginia, June, 1858. From September, 1858, to January, 1860, was adjutant of the school and ordnance officer until March, 1861, when he was appointed assistant adjutant-general, and assigned, at the request of General Sumner, to duty at the Head-quarters Department of the Pacific, where he continued to serve until October, 1866. He reported to General Meade November 1, 1866, and continued at Head-quarters Department of the East till January, 1868, when he accompanied General Meade to Head-quarters Third Military District, Atlanta, Georgia. On the 20th of March, 1869, he was assigned to the Division of the Atlantic, Philadelphia, where he continued to serve until the death of Major-General Meade, November, 1872, when he reported to Major-General Hancock at New York.

In November, 1873, General Drum was assigned to duty with Lieutenant-General Sheridan, and remained at Head-quarters Division of the Missouri until May, 1878, when he was assigned to duty in adjutant-general's office, Washington, D. C.

He was appointed adjutant-general of the army June 15, 1880, and was retired under the law May 28, 1889.

General Drum's present residence is at Washington, D. C.

LIEUTENANT-COLONEL WILLIAM F. DRUM, U.S.A.

LIEUTENANT-COLONEL WILLIAM F. DRUM (Twelfth Infantry) was born on Governor's Island, New York, November 16, 1833. He is the son of Captain Simon A. Drum, Fourth Artillery, who fell while commanding his battery at the Belen Gate, City of Mexico, September 13, 1847. He was at Owatonna, Minnesota, in the spring of 1861, and, at their request, drilled young men for the volunteer service; he then proceeded to Washington, D. C., in May, 1861, and made application for commission in regular army; he was commissioned by Governor of Ohio to raise a company of three years' volunteers; while so engaged at Springfield, Ohio, received appointment in regular army, and resigned State appointment.

He was commissioned second lieutenant of the Second United States Infantry August 5, 1861, having participated as a private of Company F, Second Ohio Volunteers, in the battle of first Bull Run, July 21, 1861, and discharged July 31, 1861. He joined the Second United States Infantry in Washington, and there was employed with his regiment on provost duty until his regiment took the field with the Army of the Potomac in 1862, and was engaged at the siege of Yorktown, battles of Gaines' Mill, Malvern Hill, second Bull Run, Antietam, action of Shepherdstown Ford, and battles of Fredericksburg and Chancellorsville; and with reserve at the battles of Hanover Court-House, Mechanicsville, and White Oak Swamp; engaged at the operations at Mine Run, and with reserve at the battles of Rappahannock Station and Bristoe Station. He was promoted first lieutenant October 9, 1861, and captain May 1, 1863.

Colonel Drum was detailed as acting inspector of the Provost-Marshal's Department of the State of Wisconsin in May, 1863, and remained on that duty until July of the same year, when he rejoined his company in the Army of the Potomac, but was shortly transferred with his regiment to New York City, where he participated in quelling the draft riots. He was then detailed on duty in New York harbor, and appointed inspector of the Prison Camp at Elmira, New York, until February, 1864, when he joined his regiment in the Army of the Potomac, and was present at the battles of the Wilderness, Spottsylvania, North Anna, Tolopotomy, Bethesda Church, Petersburg, Weldon Railroad, Poplar Grove Church, and First Hatcher's Run; he was appointed lieutenant-colonel of the Fifth New York Volunteers April 1, 1865, and was engaged at the battle of Five Forks, Virginia, and the subsequent capitulation of Lee's army at Appomattox Court-House April 9, 1865. He was made a brevet major U.S.A. for gallant services during the campaign of 1864 before Richmond, Virginia; brevet lieutenant-colonel U.S.A. for gallant and meritorious services at the battle of Five Points, Virginia.

At the close of the war Colonel Drum was on duty guarding mustered-out troops at Hart's Island, from June to August, 1865, when he was mustered out of the volunteer service and joined his company at Fort Hamilton, New York harbor. He was in November, 1865, transferred with his company to Louisville, Kentucky, where he was detailed as acting assistant adjutant-general, which position he occupied to March, 1869, and from that time to September, 1876, was on duty with his company in the States of Alabama, Georgia, Mississippi, and South Carolina.

He was then ordered on recruiting service duty at Boston, Massachusetts, from which he was relieved at his own request in July, 1877, and joined his regiment, then serving in the Department of the Columbia, where he participated in the campaigns incident to the Nez Perces and Bannock wars of 1877-78. He then returned to recruiting service in Boston, where he remained to October, 1880. On returning to his regiment he was at Fort Colville, Washington, and was transferred to the Department of the Platte, serving with the Fourteenth Infantry to August, 1883, having been promoted major of that regiment in June, 1882. He was at Fort Sidney, Nebraska, until June, 1884, when his regiment moved to the Pacific coast, where he was detailed as acting assistant inspector-general for the Department of the Columbia, but was transferred in that position to the Department of Arizona in June, 1885, and in August, 1888, again changed in the same position to the Department of Dakota, at St. Paul, Minnesota.

He was promoted lieutenant-colonel of the Twelfth Infantry in December, 1886, but was continued on duty as acting assistant inspector-general at St. Paul until the fall of 1890, when he was relieved and joined his regiment at Fort Yates, North Dakota, his present station.

# REAR-ADMIRAL SAMUEL FRANCIS DUPONT, U.S.N.
## (DECEASED).

REAR-ADMIRAL SAMUEL FRANCIS DUPONT was born at Bergen Point, New Jersey September 27, 1803 ; died in Philadelphia, June 23, 1865 ; grandson of P. S. Dupont Nemours. Midshipman in the navy at twelve ; lieutenant April 26, 1826 ; commander October 28, 1842. In 1845 he was ordered to the Pacific in command of the frigate "Congress," and during the Mexican War saw much active service on the California coast. In the "Cyane" he captured San Diego ; cleared the Gulf of California of Mexican vessels ; took La Paz, the capital of Lower California ; assisted in the capture of Mazatlan in November, 1847, and defended Lower California against the Indians and Mexicans. In February, 1848, he landed at San José with a hundred marines and sailors, and defeated and dispersed a Mexican force five times as great. Captain September 14, 1855. Having recommended the occupation of Port Royal as a central harbor or depot on the Southern coast, he was given the command of the South Atlantic Blockading Squadron, and intrusted with the attack on that place. Sailing from Fortress Monroe, October 29, 1861, in the "Wabash," with a fleet of fifty sail of war-vessels and transports, conveying General Sherman's troops, he arrived off Port Royal November 4 and 5, after a violent storm, and on the 7th attacked and captured two strong forts on Hilton Head and Bay Point, which defended the harbor. He followed up his advantage vigorously, and his operations along the Southern coast were invariably successful. He also succeeded in making the blockade more effective than before. July 16, 1862, he was made a rear-admiral on the active list. In April, 1863, he commanded the fleet which unsuccessfully attacked Charleston. He was soon after relieved of the command of the South Atlantic Blockading Squadron, and subsequently held no active command. Admiral Dupont aided in organizing the Naval School at Annapolis, and is the author of a report on the use of floating-batteries for coast-defence, which has been republished and highly commended in England by Sir Howard Douglas in his work on naval gunnery.

The history of Dupont de Nemours is a notable and interesting one. For three generations the name has been associated with the great powder-mills near Wilmington, Delaware, which are carried on upon a grand scale, with enlightened appreciation of the changes in explosives required by modern guns. The firm, yet benevolent, manner in which the employés of this exceedingly hazardous business are managed is worthy of all praise.

### COMMANDER GEORGE R. DURAND, U.S.N.

COMMANDER GEORGE R. DURAND was born in Connecticut. Appointed from Rhode Island, and rated master's mate, October 26, 1861; steamer "Mystic," North Atlantic Blockading Squadron, part of 1861-62. Appointed acting master April 14, 1862; executive, steamer "Mohawk," South Atlantic Blockading Squadron, part of 1862-63, and commanding same vessel latter half of 1863; executive, sloop "John Adams" and steamer "Paul Jones," part of 1864, same squadron; in July, 1864, while on an expedition up the Ogeechee River, Georgia, with two men and a guide, to endeavor to burn the steamer "Water-Witch," lately captured from us by the enemy, was captured by a company of Confederates, thirty-four men; was confined in Savannah and Macon, Georgia, Charleston, South Carolina, and Libby Prison, Richmond, Virginia; navigator, then executive, steamer "Muscoota," Gulf Squadron, 1865-66. Promoted to acting volunteer lieutenant June 27, 1866; executive, steamer "Penobscot," New York, latter part of 1866; navigator, then executive, steamer "Osceola," West Indies, 1867; executive, steamer "Maumee," 1867-68. Commissioned as master in regular navy from March 12, 1868; receiving-ship "New Hampshire," Norfolk, 1868; navigator, steamer "Ashuelot," Asiatic Squadron, 1869. Commissioned as lieutenant, from December 18, 1868; receiving-ships "Vermont," at New York, and "Vandalia," at Portsmouth, New Hampshire, 1870; commanding steamer "Speedwell," at Portsmouth, New Hampshire, 1871; executive, steamer "Nipsic," Gulf and West Indies, 1871-72; receiving-ships "Vermont," at New York, and "Ohio," at Boston, 1873; again commanding steamer "Speedwell," at Portsmouth, New Hampshire, part of 1873-74; receiving-ship "Ohio," 1874; commanding iron-clad steamer "Mahopac," North Atlantic Station, 1874-76; iron-clad steamer "Canonicus," New Orleans, part of 1874; receiving-ship "Wabash," Boston, 1877. Commissioned as lieutenant-commander, from November 25, 1877; commanding iron-clad steamer "Lehigh," North Atlantic Station, 1877-82; executive, "Alliance," North Atlantic Station, 1883-86; iron-clads, James River, 1886-89. Promoted to commander March, 1889; Light-House Inspector 1889-90.

## COMMANDER N. MAYO DYER, U.S.N.

COMMANDER N. MAYO DYER entered the volunteer navy in 1861 as a master's mate and served in that grade in the Western Gulf Squadron until he was, for gallant and meritorious conduct, promoted to acting ensign May 18, 1863, and appointed to command the "Eugenie," afterwards called the "Glasgow," blockading off Mobile and despatch duty. January 12, 1864, promoted to acting master in consideration of gallant and faithful service; July, 1864, granted two months' leave; but relinquished it upon arriving at New Orleans *en route* north, upon learning of the near prospect of an attack upon the Mobile forts. Returning off Mobile, and soliciting orders, he was assigned to the "Metacomet" July 19, 1864, in which vessel, as the consort of the "Hartford," took part in the passage of the forts and the capture of the rebel fleet, receiving the surrender of the "Selma" in person. Upon the surrender of Fort Morgan he accepted his leave, before relinquished, and upon his return therefrom, October 28, 1864, was ordered to the "Hartford," flagship of Admiral Farragut. Upon that vessel's return north, December, 1864, Master Dyer was appointed to the command of the U.S.S. "Rodolph," with which command he co-operated with the forces under General Granger during the winter of 1864-65, in their operation against Mobile from Pascagoula, rendering important service in this connection in Mississippi Sound and Pascagoula River. In the advance upon the defences of Mobile in the spring of 1865 via Blakely, his vessel, the "Rodolph," was sunk by a torpedo in Blakely River April 1, 1865.

April 22, 1865, Master Dyer was promoted to an acting volunteer lieutenant, and upon the surrender of the rebel fleet under Commodore Farrand, in the Tombigbee River, May 10, 1865, Lieutenant Dyer was selected to command successively two of the surrendered vessels, the "Black Diamond" and "Morgan;" appointed to command the "Elk" in June, 1865, and in July ordered to command the "Stockdale," and proceed to Mississippi Sound for the protection of the people along that shore, and to "cultivate friendly relations with the people lately in rebellion;" September, 1865, "Stockdale" was ordered to New Orleans to be sold, and Lieutenant Dyer was transferred to the "Mahaska" at Apalachicola, Florida; in October detached from the "Mahaska" and ordered to command the "Glasgow" at Pensacola; April, 1866, detached and ordered north to report to the Bureau of Navigation; on special duty in that bureau until May, 1868.

Commissioned a lieutenant in the regular navy March 12, 1868; July, 1868, ordered to the "Dacotah," South Pacific Squadron, joining at Valparaiso August 27. December 18, 1868, commissioned as lieutenant-com-

mander; the "Dacotah" being ordered to San Francisco, upon her arrival there Lieutenant-Commander Dyer was ordered, September, 1869, to command the "Cyane," and proceed to Sitka, Alaska, where he remained until March, 1870, from whence he was ordered to San Francisco to join the "Pensacola;" ordered to "Ossipee" July, 1870, on a short cruise to Lower California and the Mexican coast. While the "Ossipee" was proceeding north from the Mexican coast, she encountered a hurricane, which left the sea in a troubled state, and in the morning, whilst making a sail, a man fell overboard from the maintopsail-yard, the halyards carrying him away while hoisting topsails. Striking in the main-chains he was knocked senseless, and was drifting astern.

Commander Dyer was taking an observation on the poop-deck, and, immediately turning a bowline in the end of a boat-fall, jumped into the sea and saved the man from sharks or drowning. For this he was publicly thanked by Commodore W. R. Taylor, commander-in-chief, and received a medal, etc. In September to the South Pacific Station; detached and ordered home August 22, 1871; November 7, 1871, ordered to Boston Navy-Yard; September 1, 1873, to Torpedo School at Newport; November 24 to command torpedo-boat "Mayflower" at Norfolk, for duty on the North Atlantic Station; April 10, 1874, transferred to command of the "Pinta;" February, 1876, detached from the "Pinta" and ordered to the "New Hampshire" as executive-officer for permanent flag-ship at Port Royal. He was detached from the "New Hampshire" in December, 1876, and was next upon equipment duty at the Boston Navy-Yard. "Wabash," receiving-ship, 1880-81. "Tennessee," North Atlantic Station, 1881-83. Promoted commander April, 1883; light-house inspector 1883-87; commanded the "Marion," Asiatic Station, 1887-90.

### CAPTAIN AND BREVET MAJOR CHANDLER P. EAKIN, U.S.A. (RETIRED).

CAPTAIN AND BREVET MAJOR CHANDLER P. EAKIN was born in Philadelphia, Pennsylvania, December 26, 1836. He entered the volunteer service at the commencement of the war of the Rebellion as private of an independent company of Pennsylvania heavy artillery April 24, 1861, and was discharged June 25, 1861. He entered the regular service as second lieutenant of the First Artillery August 5, 1861, and was promoted first lieutenant October 26, 1861. He served with his company in Maryland to October, 1861. He participated in the campaigns of the Army of the Potomac in 1862-63, and was engaged at the siege of Yorktown and battles of Williamsburg (where he was severely wounded) and Gettysburg, where he was again severely wounded.

He joined his battery in January, 1864, and was on recruiting duty from April, 1864, to January, 1865, when he joined and commanded his battery in front of Petersburg, Virginia, and participated in General Sheridan's march to North Carolina. He was brevetted captain for "gallant and meritorious services in the battle of Williamsburg," and major for "gallant and meritorious services in the battle of Gettysburg."

On July 28, 1866, he was appointed captain of the Forty-second Infantry, which he declined, and eight years afterwards (October 1, 1874) became captain in the First Artillery.

Captain Eakin was at Fort Schuyler, New York, from October, 1865, to April, 1866, and then was detailed on recruiting duty at Philadelphia, and on court-martial duty in New York City, to January, 1868. He was at Fortress Monroe to November, 1868, and at McPherson Barracks, Georgia, to December of the same year, at which time he was ordered to the Artillery School of Fortress Monroe. Leaving here in May, 1869, his lot carried him to the posts of New York harbor until November, 1872, when a change of stations occurred, and he was stationed first at Key West, and subsequently at Barrancas, Florida, at which latter place he was in 1874, during the yellow-fever epidemic. Here his old wounds reopened, and he was taken to New Orleans, and thence to his home in Philadelphia, where he remained on sick-leave until December, 1875, when he rejoined his battery at Fort Adams. In July, 1876, he was sent to Fort Sill, Indian Territory, during the Sioux war of that year, and in December following was stationed at Washington Barracks, D. C.; and in 1877 was ordered to Fort Adams, from which point he moved to Philadelphia, thence to Reading, and finally to Mauch Chunk, taking part in quelling the mining riots of that year, after which he returned to Fort Adams.

Captain Eakin, with his battery, participated in the Yorktown celebration in 1881, and in the fall of that year changed stations to California, serving at Fort Point, Fort Canby, and the Presidio of San Francisco, from which point he was retired for disability in the line of duty January 14, 1888.

Major Eakin is the son of Lieutenant C. M. Eakin, Second Artillery, and grandson of Paymaster Samuel H. Eakin, U. S. Army.

## CAPTAIN FREDERICK H. E. EBSTEIN, U.S.A.

CAPTAIN FREDERICK H. E. EBSTEIN (Twenty-first Infantry) was born at Militsch, Prussia, April 21, 1847; educated at the Poughkeepsie (New York) Collegiate Institute. He entered the military service November 18, 1864, at the age of seventeen, as a private in Company H, Fourth United States Infantry. He joined his regiment in the field in Virginia, and served with it there till the close of the war. Subsequently, as a corporal and sergeant, he served at Battery Barracks, New York; Fort Schuyler, New York harbor, and Fort Wayne, Michigan. Later he became chief clerk at head-quarters of the Departments of the Ohio and of the Lakes.

He was appointed second lieutenant of the Eighteenth Infantry September 12, 1867, joining his regiment at Fort Fetterman, Wyoming; serving later at Fort Sedgwick, Colorado, and Atlanta, Georgia. While on the plains he participated in several scouts against hostile Sioux.

He was placed on waiting orders by the consolidation of regiments in 1869, but was in July of the same year assigned to the Twenty-first Infantry, joining Company H at Camp Date Creek, Arizona, and was engaged in post and scouting duty in that Territory during the three years following.

Being transferred to San Juan Island, Washington Territory, in 1872, he received, on behalf of the United States, the British property on that island, upon the withdrawal of the British troops.

He was promoted first lieutenant February 19, 1873, and served at Fort Klamath, Oregon, until June, 1876, when he was appointed regimental quartermaster, and ordered to Fort Vancouver, Washington Territory. In the summer and fall of 1877 he participated in the expedition against hostile Nez Perces, as chief quartermaster on the staff of General O. O. Howard, and was present at the engagements at Cottonwood (Ravine), Idaho, and Camas Meadows, Montana. On being relieved, he received the following complimentary order: "The general commanding takes this opportunity to express his satisfaction at the efficient manner in which Lieutenant Ebstein has discharged the duties of chief quartermaster of this expedition."

In the summer of 1878 he was again in the field against the Bannock Indians, serving as chief quartermaster on the staff of General O. O. Howard, and participated in the engagement at Umatilla Agency, Oregon. Returning to Fort Vancouver, he resumed duty at that post as regimental and post quartermaster until September 30, 1880, when he resigned his regimental staff appointment to accept the recruiting detail.

He served as depot adjutant, David's Island, New York

harbor, to October, 1882; then travelled in Europe during the winter of 1882-83, and subsequently served at Fort Canby and Vancouver Barracks, Washington, and was subsequently transferred with his regiment to Fort Sidney, Nebraska, in 1884.

He became captain April 1, 1885, and served in the field at Crisfield, Kansas, as acting assistant adjutant-general of the troops assembled there during the Cheyenne troubles in 1885, and again in the fall of the same year in command of his company at Rock Springs, Wyoming, during the anti-Chinese riots. He participated also in the camps of instruction at Kearney, Nebraska, 1888, and Fort Robinson, Nebraska, 1889.

In addition to the above-mentioned service, Captain Ebstein has performed duty as issuing commissary for the Apache-Mojave and Apache-Yuma Indians; as quartermaster, commissary, and adjutant at various posts; as acting assistant adjutant-general, District of the Lakes, and as disbursing quartermaster at head-quarters, Department of the Columbia. He has performed the duties of judge-advocate of numerous important courts-martial and courts of inquiry; was recorder of the court of inquiry appointed by the President at Jefferson Barracks, Missouri, to investigate the causes of desertions; was on duty under the War Department in connection with the establishment of canteens at military posts; member of boards of examination for promotion of non-commissioned officers, and president of board of officers at Fort Snelling, to prepare a system of book-keeping for post canteens. In the winter of 1890 he participated, in command of his company, in the Sioux campaign.

Captain Ebstein's present station is with his company at Fort Sidney, Nebraska.

MAJOR WILLIAM FRANCIS EDGAR, U.S.A. (RETIRED).

MAJOR WILLIAM FRANCIS EDGAR was born in Kentucky, and entered the regular service as first lieutenant and assistant surgeon March 2, 1849. His first duty was at Jefferson Barracks, Missouri, and he then accompanied the Second United States Dragoons on the march from that place to Fort Leavenworth, Kansas. He was next ordered with the Mounted Rifles on the march overland to Oregon, and subsequently in an expedition to Utah, and at Fort Hall (Cantonment Loring), Rocky Mountains, up to April, 1850. He served in Oregon and Washington Territories to April, 1851, and participated in an expedition against the Rogue River Indians, with the First Dragoons (Major Philip Kearney's expedition), and thence en route to California, to August, 1851.

The doctor was then stationed at Sonoma and Benicia, California, with the First Dragoons and Second Infantry, and at Camp Miller, head-waters San Joaquin River, with the Second Infantry. From this point he accompanied the Second Infantry in an expedition against hostile Indians in the Yosemite Valley and Sierra Nevada Mountains, to September, 1852. He was then stationed at Fort Reading, head-waters of the Sacramento River, with the Fourth Infantry, and took the field with the First Dragoons en route to establish Fort Tejon, in Southern California. The doctor was partially paralyzed on the left side, on returning to camp on the morning of December 6, 1854, after unusual exertion while being exposed all the previous night to the intense cold of a mountain snow-storm, and an injury of the left hip and lower part of the spine, from the falling of a horse while out searching, with a teamster, for a wounded soldier.

He was promoted captain and assistant surgeon March 2, 1854, and in April, 1855, was en route to Washington, and subsequently assigned to duty at Jefferson Barracks, with the Second Cavalry. His service here was of temporary duration, for, in September of the same year, he was en route to Texas by sea. In 1856 he was at the Head-quarters Department, Texas, from which he was ordered with the Second Artillery by sea and stationed with that regiment in Florida for a short while, when he was ordered to New York by sea, with the sick of the troops serving in Florida.

The doctor was stationed at Fort Wood, New York harbor, until 1857, when he was detailed for duty in the office of the medical purveyor at New York City. He was then ordered to accompany recruits to California, and was stationed at Fort Miller, with the Third Artillery, but was subsequently changed to the Presidio of San Francisco, and afterwards to Benicia. He participated in an expedition with the First Dragoons against the Mojave Indians on the Colorado River in 1858, and in an expedition against the same in Arizona in 1859, with the Sixth Infantry and Third Artillery, and then stationed at Camp Prentice, California, and San Diego, with part of the Fourth and Sixth Regiments of Infantry until November, 1861.

These regiments being ordered east, to take part in the war of the Rebellion, the doctor was ordered to accompany them by sea to New York, and thence to Washington, D.C. He was promoted major and surgeon May 24, 1861, and upon arrival at Washington was ordered to duty with General Buell's army in Kentucky, and was given charge of the General Hospital, Number 4, in Louisville. He was medical director of the district of Cairo, Illinois, to 1862, when he was taken sick on account of feeble health, resulting from former injuries. Upon replying to an inquiry regarding field duty at that time, " that a surgical operation was necessary first," he was ordered before a retiring board and retired from active duty " for disability in the line of duty." He was then placed on duty in the medical director's office of the Department of the East, as assistant medical director, and while there was member of the board examining applicants for admission to the medical corps of the army. The doctor performed various other duties, and was sent once more to California by sea, in March, 1866; but upon his own application was relieved from duty May 21, 1866, for one year, and in consequence of the act of Congress of 1870 was not again assigned to duty.

## COMMODORE HENRY ERBEN, U.S.N.

COMMODORE HENRY ERBEN is a native of the city of New York, and was appointed midshipman in June, 1848, from that city. He was ordered to the frigate "St. Lawrence," and served in that fine vessel from July, 1848, to July, 1853; was on duty on the Coast Survey in 1854, and at the Naval Academy in 1855. He became passed midshipman the same year. While serving in the "Potomac" frigate, in 1855, he was made master, and ordered to the prize filibuster bark "Amelia," which had been captured at Porto-Prince, Hayti. The officer in charge was ordered to take her to New York, but, after seventy days at sea, he arrived at St. Thomas, destitute of provisions and a wreck. During 1856-57 he was attached to the store-ship "Supply," employed in bringing camels for the War Department from Egypt to Texas. He was made lieutenant in December, 1856. For a part of 1857 he was in the steamer "Vixen," making deep-sea soundings for the Atlantic cable, and in August joined the U.S.S. "Mississippi," and served in her in the East,— bringing home the Chinese treaty in November, 1859. While serving in the Gulf of Mexico, in the "Supply," he was at Pensacola when the navy-yard there was surrendered to the troops of Alabama and Florida. He assisted in transferring the troops under Lieutenant Slemmer from Fort Barrancas to Fort Pickens on the night of January 9, 1861. On the previous day he had, with a boat's crew, spiked the guns at Fort MacRea, destroyed material and twenty thousand pounds of powder. He returned to New York with the sailors, marines, and workmen of the surrendered navy-yard.

In March, 1861, he returned to Fort Pickens in the "Release," and was transferred to the "Huntsville" on the blockade. In action with rebel gun-boats and batteries at Ship Island, and, in December, off Mobile with the rebel gun-boat "Florida," which, during the temporary absence of the "Huntsville," had come out in a calm to destroy the sailing-frigate "Potomac."

He was ordered to the Mississippi River fleet in April, 1862, and commanded iron-clad "St. Louis" at the siege of Fort Pillow and in action with rebel rams, May, 1862; capture of Memphis in June, 1862. Served on the admiral's staff. Commanded the "Sumter" at the siege of Vicksburg, and passed the batteries there with Farragut, July 15, 1862. At the battle of Baton Rouge August 6, 1862, and destruction of rebel ram "Arkansas" August 7, 1862. Lieutenant-commander on July 16, 1862.

He returned to the east to join the naval howitzer battery in Maryland, with General McClellan, during the Antietam campaign, and in October, 1862, joined the monitor "Patapsco" as executive-officer. Engaged at Fort McAllister in March, 1863, and attack on forts at Charleston in April, 1863. Steam-frigate "Niagara" on special

service on Atlantic coast from November, 1863, to May, 1864. In July, 1864, he was ordered to command monitor "Chimo" and then the monitor "Tunxis," which vessels were intended to destroy the ram "Albemarle," but were found unseaworthy and condemned. In October, 1864, ordered to command "Ponola," West Gulf Squadron, and captured, under the guns of batteries at Matagorda, Texas, the schooner "Dale" and the boats of the torpedo station, with twenty men; broke up the establishment. Engaged the batteries at Galveston in attempting the destruction of a blockade-runner, the "Let Her Be." In July, 1865, he was ordered home, and was on duty at the New York Navy-Yard during 1866. From 1867 to 1869 he commanded steamers "Huron," "Kansas," and "Pawnee" on South Atlantic Station. He was commissioned commander in 1868. During 1871-72 he was upon ordnance and rendezvous duty in New York, and in 1873 commanded the monitor "Manhattan" at Key West during the critical period of a serious misunderstanding with Spain.

In 1874-75 Commander Erben was in command of the "Tuscarora," of the North Pacific Squadron, and employed in running deep-sea soundings. He then had a term of shore-duty at the navy-yard, Portsmouth, New Hampshire; but went to sea again, from 1878 to 1882, in command of the nautical school-ship "St. Mary's." He was promoted captain in 1879, and commanded the "Pensacola," in 1883-84, in cruise around the world. He then had another turn of duty at the Portsmouth Navy-Yard, and then was on special duty at New York for three years.

In the early part of 1891 Captain Erben was ordered as governor to the Naval Asylum at Philadelphia, but, being promoted commodore in 1892, was soon transferred to the important command of the New York Navy-Yard, which he now holds.

## COMMANDER R. D. EVANS, U.S.N.

COMMANDER ROBLEY DUNGLISON EVANS was born in Virginia, but was appointed a midshipman from the Territory of Utah on September 20, 1860. He was at the Naval Academy when that institution was transferred, temporarily, from Annapolis to Newport, Rhode Island, on account of the war. The term of his class at the Academy was shortened on account of the pressing necessity for officers, and he became ensign on October 1, 1863. Being ordered to the steam-frigate "Powhatan," he first served in the West India Squadron, and then, in 1864-65, in the North Atlantic Blockading Squadron.

He landed with the force of seamen and marines for the land assault upon Fort Fisher, and received two severe wounds from rifle-shots, from the disabling effects of which he suffered for a considerable time.

On July 25, 1866, he was commissioned as lieutenant, and was, during that year, attached to the navy-yard at Philadelphia; being afterwards transferred to ordnance duty at the Washington Navy-Yard.

He next made a cruise in the flag-ship "Piscataqua," of the Asiatic Squadron, from 1867 to 1869. During this cruise, on March 12, 1868, he was promoted to be lieutenant-commander. He was attached, with this rank, to the Washington Navy-Yard, 1870-71; and to the Naval Academy in 1871-72.

From 1873 to 1876 he cruised in the "Shenandoah," second-rate, and the "Congress," second-rate, of the European Squadron; and, during 1877-78, was in command of the training-ship "Saratoga."

He was commissioned commander in July, 1878, and, after service at the Washington Navy-Yard, was light-house inspector from 1882 to 1886. In 1886-87 he was chief inspector of steel for the new cruisers. During 1887-89 he held the position of secretary of the Light-House Board.

During 1890 he was on leave of absence.

He was ordered to the command of the "Yorktown" in July, 1891, which command he holds at present.

## CAPTAIN AND BREVET MAJOR EVARTS S. EWING, U.S.A. (DECEASED).

CAPTAIN AND BREVET MAJOR EVARTS S. EWING was born in Giles County, Tennessee, March 25, 1841. He always had a strong desire to go through West Point, and at one time was offered an appointment, but bravely declined in accordance with the wishes of his parents. They hoped he might continue the work of his father in the Presbyterian ministry. However, within a week after the firing on Fort Sumter, Evarts Ewing was riding over the country, recruiting a company of volunteers to enter the war of the Rebellion. Southern born, yet his sympathies were with his country and the State which was at that time his home.

Through his efforts and those of a few others, Company D of the First Iowa Cavalry was soon formed, and Evarts Ewing lacked but five votes of being made the first lieutenant. He was then offered the position of second lieutenant, but refused it, saying he would carry a musket as a plain private. So he rode away only bugler and private of Company D, but before leaving the State was made quartermaster-sergeant of the regiment, and for a time had sole charge of that department, there being no commissioned officer over him. He became chief bugler and commissary-sergeant, and served in these grades until September 12, 1863. His campaigns were for the most part west of the Mississippi, in those many smaller engagements which, although less famous, were none the less heroically fought than the great battles with whose names we are more familiar. Perhaps his most marked gallantry was shown in the battle of Prairie Grove. He was appointed captain and commissary of subsistence January 13, 1865, and was honorably mustered out October 9, 1865. He was brevetted major, lieutenant-colonel, and colonel of volunteers, October 6 of the same year, for "faithful and meritorious services."

Colonel Ewing entered the regular service as second lieutenant of the Sixteenth Infantry, February 23, 1866, and was promoted first lieutenant March 19 the same year. The brevets of captain and major, U. S. Army, were conferred upon him March 2, 1867, for "gallant and meritorious services." He was transferred to the Thirty-fourth Infantry September 21, 1866, and upon the consolidation of regiments was transferred back to his old regiment, the Sixteenth, in which, to his last day, he always maintained the greatest pride and interest.

He was serving in Washington in 1867 as aide-de-camp to General O. O. Howard, when General Joseph A. Mower applied to the War Department for an especially efficient and responsible man to act as department quartermaster on his staff, and Major Ewing was relieved of his position on General Howard's staff to fill this place on General Mower's.

Since then he served with his regiment at the various posts where he was stationed. He was on duty in New Orleans in 1876 during the famous White League troubles, and later at different posts of the Indian Territory, Kansas, and Texas. He served as regimental quartermaster of the Sixteenth Infantry from March 9, 1880, to April 30, 1880, when he was promoted to captain of Company B.

Major Ewing was retired from active service the 3d of January, 1885, for disability in line of duty (see. 1251 rev. stat.).

In May, 1885, Major Ewing was honored by an invitation from the board of managers of the World's Fair in New Orleans to take command of the large interstate encampment of militia to take place at the close of the exposition. He accepted the offer, and won a most enviable reputation among all who understood military matters.

Among many other honors, Major Ewing might claim that of being the father of target practice in the U. S. Army, it being through his letters, written to the *Army and Navy Journal*, and the example he set by his untiring efforts in that direction in his own company, that the War Department first became interested in what is to-day so prominent a feature of our army. Major Ewing was the first commissioned officer in the Department of Texas to be given a marksman's button.

His nature was a remarkable combination of the poet and the soldier; from childhood his highest aims were in a military line, but next to this he hoped to achieve fame in the literary world.

Shortly after his distinguished services at the New Orleans encampment, he received an offer from the President of Honduras to take command of the armies of that republic. This offer, for various personal reasons, he reluctantly declined to accept. He died June 7, 1892.

## OFFICERS OF THE ARMY AND NAVY (REGULAR)

**LIEUTENANT-COLONEL J. P. FARLEY, U.S.A.**

LIEUTENANT-COLONEL J. P. FARLEY (Ordnance Corps, U. S. Army) was born in Washington, D. C., March 2, 1839. He was graduated at the U. S. Military Academy June 24, 1861; assigned to the Second U. S. Artillery, and transferred to the Ordnance Corps October 24, 1861.

Before and during the Bull Run campaign he served as aide on the staff of the general commanding the defences of Washington, and later, during the summer and fall of that year, with Horse Battery A, Second Artillery, covering the approaches to Washington and Alexandria, Virginia.

Special Order No. 174, Folly Island, South Carolina, July 8, 1863, was indorsed by Lieutenant-Colonel R. H. Jackson, Captain First U. S. Artillery, as follows: "Lieutenant Farley reported to me in obedience to the within order, and remained on duty in charge of one-half of the batteries of the front line until the capture by our troops of the south end of Morris Island on July 10, 1863.

"I take pleasure in testifying that to his ability, example, and gallant conduct in the action of the 10th of July, 1863, which resulted in the capture of Morris Island, the splendid practice, the admirable sighting, and the destructive effects of the artillery under his command were in a great measure due.

"This conduct was the more praiseworthy on his part, as he volunteered to command troops on that occasion out of the line of his duty as an ordnance officer.

"Lieutenant Farley's name received highly honorable mention in my report ('War of Rebellion Records,' Vol. XXVIII.) of the part taken by the artillery under my command in the capture of the south end of Morris Island."

Lieutenant Farley again volunteered his services as aide to General Truman Seymour during the bombardment and assault on Fort Wagner, South Carolina, July 18, 1863. The general in indorsing the foregoing order, No. 174, says: "Lieutenant Farley was a member of my staff during a considerable part of that summer (1863). He was one of the most active, intelligent, and useful of my right-hand assistants and advisers,—was always ready for any labor, however toilsome and disagreeable, and assuredly the work of the artillerist and ordnance officer on Folly and Morris Islands during that eventful summer was very trying; he was patient and persevering under unusual difficulties; he was, in fact, one of the comparatively few of whom, when charged with the accomplishment of any special duty, I was absolutely sure it would be conducted skilfully to its desired end."

General Seymour, in an official report, "War of Rebellion Record," Vol. XXVIII., referring to a successful engagement with the enemy on Morris Island, South Carolina, accords to Lieutenant Farley "no small share of the glory of this day."

The later service of Lieutenant Farley (1864-65) with Lieutenant General U. S. Grant was recognized by the general in the following terms: "I take pleasure in testifying to your efficiency as an ordnance officer while serving in the armies operating against Richmond.

"During the time you were in charge of the extensive and very important Ordnance Depot at City Point, Virginia, your duties were performed to my entire satisfaction, and, as far as my official and personal knowledge extend, to the perfect satisfaction of the armies you supplied."

In this connection, reverting to the field service of Lieutenant Farley, General Seymour says: "Approved, as it has been, by the greatest of our commanders, my own commendations are of little value in comparison; but they are the expressions of a profound appreciation of all that can confer honor and distinction upon one of the most worthy young officers I knew during the war."

Lieutenant Farley was brevetted captain "for meritorious services in the Ordnance Department during the war," and his field service is recognized in orders and reports, "War of the Rebellion Records," Vol. XXVIII.

Since the war he has served at the Military Academy; at arsenals, foundries, proving grounds, and on various boards, such as the Ordnance Board, the Experimental Testing Board, and a Board for the Selection of a Magazine Small-Arm for the Service. He is the author of "Professional and Scientific Papers," published by the War Department, and for which work he has received official commendation.

Colonel Farley is the son of Captain John Farley (Class of 1823, U. S. M. A.), First U. S. Artillery; grandson of Captain John Farley, U. S. Corps of Artillery, War of 1812; and great-grandson of Robert Breat, paymaster-general, U. S. A., 1819.

## CAPTAIN NORMAN H. FARQUHAR, U.S.N.

CAPTAIN NORMAN H. FARQUHAR is at present chief of the Bureau of Yards and Docks, Navy Department, with the rank of commodore. He was born in Pennsylvania April 11, 1840, and graduated from the Naval Academy in 1859. While still a midshipman, serving in different vessels of our African Squadron, he was detailed to bring to the United States a captured slaver, the "Triton," with a crew of ten men and no other officer. Still a midshipman at the breaking out of the great Rebellion, he became lieutenant in a very few months, and served on board the steamer "Mystic" and the steam gun-boat "Mahaska," of the North Atlantic Squadron; the steamer "Rhode Island," of the West India Squadron; and the "Santiago de Cuba," of the North Atlantic Squadron. Lieutenant Farquhar was present at both attacks upon Fort Fisher, and there and elsewhere was distinguished for his coolness and conduct under fire. General B. F. Butler, in his official report of the attack on Fort Fisher, North Carolina, dated January 3, 1865, speaks of Captain Farquhar (then lieutenant) as follows: "Lieutenant Farquhar, of the navy, having in charge the navy boats which assisted in the landing, deserves great credit for the energy and skill with which he managed the boats through the rolling surf."

In 1865 he was promoted to be lieutenant-commander, and then served for some time at the Naval Academy. He next served in the "Swatara," on the European Station, in 1868–69; and at the navy-yard, Boston, in 1870, being thence ordered as executive-officer of the United States steamship "Severn," from which ship he went to the command of the "Kansas," and was employed in surveying duties. After another tour of service at the Boston Navy-Yard, he joined the United States steamship "Powhatan" in 1872, and on December 12 of that year was made commander in the navy. He was then stationed at the Naval Academy, at Annapolis, in command of the "Santee," and in charge of buildings and grounds for about six years; commanding the "Portsmouth" in 1878, and in command of "Quinnebaug" and "Wyoming," European Squadron, from 1878 to 1881. He then became commandant of "cadets" at the Naval Academy, in which position he remained five years; commanding the "Constellation" on the practice cruise with the midshipmen in 1883 and 1884.

He was commissioned as captain March 4, 1886, and was ordered to command the flag-ship "Trenton," in the Pacific. The country will long remember the wreck of the "Trenton" and other vessels at Apia, Samoa, during a dreadful hurricane. On this occasion, by good seamanship, Captain Farquhar saved the lives of the four hundred and fifty officers and men who composed the ship's company.

For his services on this occasion the Humane Society of Massachusetts awarded Captain Farquhar its gold medal, with a letter couched in very complimentary terms. Captain Farquhar has probably commanded more vessels than any officer of his grade, but has held no command afloat since that of the "Trenton." In August, 1889, he was senior member of the Board of Visitors at the Torpedo Station, Newport, and was appointed a member of the Light-House Board in the latter part of the same year, but did not serve long in that capacity, as he was, on March 6, 1890, appointed chief of the Bureau of Yards and Docks at the Navy Department, as we have said above. Commodore Farquhar is the holder of a gold medal from the Naval Institute, given in 1885, for an essay entitled "Inducements for Obtaining Seamen in the Navy." Many of the suggestions contained in that paper have since been adopted by the department. "Captain Farquhar is universally regarded as one of the most accomplished, progressive, and trustworthy officers in the navy. Like all men of capacity and courage, he is considerate to those under him, while exacting prompt obedience to official orders."

ADMIRAL DAVID GLASGOW FARRAGUT, U.S.N.
(DECEASED.)

It seems hopeless, in the brief space allotted, to even mention the points in the career of this distinguished head of our navy; but, fortunately, the whole country, and the whole world, indeed, is familiar with them, and everywhere—from the Winter Palace at St. Petersburg to the fisherman's hut upon the shores of the Pacific—his likeness is to be found. Farragut was wounded in the bloody battle between the "Essex" and the British ships "Phoebe" and "Cherub," in March, 1814, when his commanding officer regretted "that he was too young for promotion." He lived to command at New Orleans, Vicksburg, and Mobile Bay, and yet was only sixty-nine when he died. But very much was compressed into those years. He served in three wars, as well as against the West Indian pirates, and he observed the military and naval operations of his time throughout the world with his native sagacity, all of which tended to ripen his mind for the great work before him. Admiral Farragut was a descendant of Don Pedro Ferragut, called "El Conquistador," from his successes in battle against the Moors of Spain. They had estates in Minorca, and his father was born there, and emigrated to America in 1776. He took part in the war of the Revolution, and was the friend and companion of General Jackson during his Indian campaigns. He married in North Carolina, settled in Tennessee, where his distinguished son was born, and finally entered the naval service as sailing-master.

Admiral Farragut, through Commodore David Porter, received his midshipman's warrant when less than ten years old, and in 1811 he went to sea with Porter. When the ship's company of the "Essex" returned to the United States in the cartel "Essex Junior" he was placed at school until the peace of 1815.

He then made two cruises to the Mediterranean, availing himself of favorable opportunities for study and travel. Under his old commander, Porter, he served during 1823-24, in the suppression of piracy in the West Indies, and always took pride in having obtained a command then at the age of twenty-two. In 1825 he was a lieutenant of the "Brandywine," when she took Lafayette home. He served on the coast of Brazil as executive-officer of the "Delaware," seventy-four, and in command of two vessels. While in command of the "Erie," in the Gulf, he noted carefully the French bombardment of Vera Cruz. Served in our own war with Mexico, in the "Saratoga;" then on ordnance, court-martial, and navy-yard duties. In 1854 he was sent to California to establish the navy-yard at Mare Island. During his four-years' service there his coolness and judgment in dealing with the delicate question of Federal and State jurisdiction, during the reign of the "Vigilance Committee" of 1856, not only saved the government from being drawn into a local quarrel, but also saved bloodshed. During 1859-60 Farragut commanded the "Brooklyn," and, at the breaking out of the great Rebellion, was living in Norfolk, Virginia, as he had done for many years. Local opinion and local pressure had no effect upon a man of his broad views, and he moved to the North, and took up his residence on the Hudson. In January, 1862, he was assigned to the command of the West Gulf Squadron, his mission being to unseal that great artery of commerce and travel, the Mississippi, and all that such an undertaking entailed. He seemed confident of success from the first, great as the task before him was. He wrote: "As to being prepared for defeat, I certainly am not. Any man who is prepared for defeat would be half-defeated before he commenced. I hope for success, shall do all in my power to secure it, and trust in God for the rest." The result of that continual strain of combat for so many months is a matter of common-school history, and need not be recounted here. The same may be said of his operations at Mobile Bay in 1864. He received the thanks of Congress, and was commissioned rear-admiral July 16, 1862; vice-admiral December 21, 1864, and was finally promoted to the rank of admiral July 26, 1866. In 1867 he went to the command of the European Squadron, and made an extended cruise, being everywhere received with the most marked attention. At this time, when past sixty-six, Admiral Farragut, with his rounded, active figure, and firm, clean-shaven face, gave one the impression of being a much younger man. He spoke several languages very fluently, and was a very close observer, and an indefatigable reader. Nothing escaped his keen eye, and when he felt himself among friends his observations were often very dry and even witty. He died on August 14, 1870.

## REAR-ADMIRAL JOHN C. FEBIGER, U.S.N.
### (RETIRED).

REAR-ADMIRAL JOHN C. FEBIGER was born in Pennsylvania and appointed from Ohio, his warrant as midshipman bearing date of September 14, 1838. His first service was in the frigate "Macedonian," of the West India Squadron, 1838-40. He was then attached to the sloop-of-war "Concord," mostly upon the Brazil coast, during 1841-43. In the latter year he was wrecked in the "Concord" on the east coast of Africa, and was then attached to the brig "Chippola," purchased by the government at Rio Janeiro and used to recover and dispose of the equipment of the "Concord." Engaged in this duty until 1844. On May 20 of that year he was made passed midshipman, and served in the frigate "Potomac," of the Home Squadron, for two years. He then made a cruise to the Pacific in the sloop-of-war "Dale," and was from her transferred to the "Columbus," 74, in which ship he came home.

Again attached to the sloop-of-war "Dale," he made a cruise upon the coast of Africa, and upon his return was employed upon the Coast Survey for several years.

He was promoted to master 1852, and was commissioned lieutenant in the navy April 30, 1853. In 1858-60 he was attached to the sloop-of-war "Germantown," of the East India Squadron, and upon his return, in 1861, was ordered to the sloop-of-war "Savannah."

Commissioned commander in the navy August 11, 1862. Commanded the "Kanawha," of the West Gulf Blockading Squadron, in 1862-63, and was in the engagement off Mobile Bay April 3, 1862.

During the year 1863 Commander Febiger commanded the "Osage," "Neosho," and "Lafayette," of the Mississippi Squadron; and in 1864-65 commanded the "Mattabeset," of the North Atlantic Blockading Squadron. During this period he participated in the spirited engagement with the rebel ram "Albemarle," in Albemarle Sound, May, 1864.

In the years 1866-68 he commanded the "Ashuelot," of the Asiatic Squadron.

Commissioned captain May 6, 1868, and commanded the steam-sloop "Shenandoah," of the Asiatic Squadron, in 1868-69. While commanding the "Shenandoah" he entered and surveyed Ping-Yang Inlet, on the west coast of Corea.

From 1869 to 1872 he was inspector of naval reserved lands. In 1872-74 he commanded the U. S. steamer "Omaha," of the South Pacific Squadron. He was promoted to commodore August 9, 1874. After this he became a member of the Board of Examiners, and then commandant of the navy-yard at Washington, D. C., for nearly four years. He was then upon special duty in Washington, D. C., and a member of the Retiring Board.

Promoted to rear-admiral February 4, 1882. Retired upon his own application July 1, 1882.

MAJOR E. G. FECHET, U.S.A.

MAJOR E. G. FECHET (Sixth Cavalry) was born July 11, 1844, in Michigan. He is the son of Alfred Edmond Fechet, M.D., a native of France, and graduate of the College of France, who came to the United States in 1840.

Young Fechet entered the volunteer service June 19, 1861, as sergeant of Company A, Seventh Michigan Infantry, and participated in the Maryland campaign of the Army of the Potomac, being engaged in the battle of Antietam, September 17, 1862, at which time he was shot through the right lung. He was promoted second lieutenant, to date from that battle, and first lieutenant June 18, 1863. He resigned June 31, 1863, on account of illness resulting from his wound. On recovery, he again entered the volunteer service as quartermaster-sergeant of the Tenth Michigan Cavalry, but was promoted second lieutenant January 23, 1864, and first lieutenant April 1, 1865. He was in several minor engagements in 1864, in East Tennessee, and commanded the Knoxville Depot of Ordnance November, 1865, and was honorably mustered out of service November 21, 1865. He was appointed to regular service as second lieutenant of Eighth Cavalry July 28, 1866, and brevetted first lieutenant and captain March 2, 1867, "for gallant conduct at the battle of Antietam." In February marched in command of Troop I from San Francisco to Fort Whipple, Arizona, and participated in a severe fight with the Hualapi and Tonto Apache Indians. He was promoted first lieutenant July 31, 1867, and captain May 23, 1870.

Rejoining his regiment in January, 1870, he took command of Troop G, and changed stations to New Mexico, arriving at Fort Selden in the March following. Captain Fechet commanded a detachment of troops in an engagement with the Mescalero Apaches, capturing their entire camp and herd, and forcing the tribe to return to Stanton reservation. He marched with his regiment to Texas, on change of department, arriving at Ringgold Barracks in March, 1876, where he remained to 1881, when he was transferred to Fort Clark, which post he did duty at until September, 1887. Then he commanded Camp Pena Colorado to May, 1888, when he marched with his regiment from Texas to Dakota. He left Pena Colorado on the 19th of May, and arrived at Fort Yates, North Dakota, September 17, the distance marched being two thousand one hundred miles.

While in command of his troop at Fort Yates, Captain Fechet became somewhat conspicuous in the Sioux campaign of 1890-91, by having been engaged in the affair which resulted in the death of the famous chief Sitting Bull, having on that occasion commanded the troops participating therein. The following extract from a communication from General Miles, in the field, on this subject, to General Thomas H. Ruger, commanding the department of Dakota, is here given:

"The division commander has received official report of Lieutenant-Colonel Drum, Twelfth Infantry, and Captain Fechet, Eighth Cavalry, regarding the arrest of Sitting Bull. He desires me to express his approval of the good judgment displayed by the officers and the assistance of agent, the fortitude of the troops and bravery of the Indian police. It required no ordinary courage to go into an Indian camp of well-armed warriors and arrest the chief conspirator on the eve of his departure to join the large body of his followers then in defiant hostility to the government, and engaged in robbing its citizens and looting their houses. It was from Sitting Bull that emissaries had been for months going to other tribes inciting them to hostility, and he died while resisting the lawful officials of the government. Even after he had been peaceably arrested, he raised the cry of revolt, and incited his men to shoot down the government police in the lawful discharge of their duty. The fearless action of Captain Fechet and his command entitles them to great credit, and the celerity of his movements showed the true soldierly spirit.

"The division commander desires that his sympathy be expressed to those who have suffered from wounds, and the families of the dead brave, loyal, Indian police, and his thanks to all who took part in the arrest that has already resulted in the surrender of more than one hundred defiant, lawless savages, and with other measures has done much to prevent the destruction of many peaceable homes and innocent lives. By command of Major-General Miles. (Signed)

M. P. MAUS, A.D.C."

Captain Fechet was promoted major of the Sixth Cavalry April 20, 1891.

## CAPTAIN EDWARD FIELD, U.S.A.

CAPTAIN EDWARD FIELD (Fourth Artillery) traces his lineage in unbroken thread from the distinguished astronomer and student, Sir John Field, to whose researches England was indebted for the explanation and introduction of the Copernican system. Emigrating from the mother-country long before the revolt of the infant colonies, his ancestors were among the first to take up arms against the sea of troubles which so crowded upon the young republic at its birth. Richard Stockton, member of the Continental Congress and signer of the Declaration of Independence, was his great-great-grandfather.

Richard Stockton Field, attorney-general of the State of New Jersey, United States Senator, and United States District Judge, was the father of Captain Field, and a resident of the classic old town of Princeton when, in 1841, the son was born who became the first of the family to permanently identify himself with the army of the nation. Naturally no Princeton lad thought of going elsewhere for education, and it was at the time-honored college of his native place that Edward Field was matriculated in 1857, and graduated in 1861, just at the outbreak of the war of the Rebellion. Always an enthusiastic horseman, he lost no time in seeking service with the cavalry, and was commissioned second lieutenant in the gallant First New Jersey that won such renown in the old Second Division of the Cavalry Corps in the Army of the Potomac. Early in 1862, however, he was tendered an appointment in the Fourth Artillery of the regular army, and within a month had joined Light Battery "C" of that regiment just in time to embark for the Peninsula.

Fair Oaks, Peach Orchard, and Savage Station gave him many an opportunity of testing the metal of which he was made. But White Oak Swamp was the fight that tried men's souls, so far at least as Battery "C" was concerned. For hours its eight guns were hotly engaged. Hazzard, its brave and impetuous commander, received his death-wound, and Field's comrade, Lieutenant Arthur Morris, was knocked *hors de combat*, while men and horses suffered severely from the deadly fire of the enemy.

Antietam, Halltown, Fredericksburg, and Chancellorsville were the next battles in order; and in the last named Field won high credit and the thanks of General Geary for fighting his battery, even after it was relieved, and hammering the rebel infantry an entire hour at close range despite heavy losses. This was at the Chancellor House salient.

In October, 1863, Lieutenant Field was transferred to Horse Battery "E" of his regiment, fighting with it at Buckland Mills and Raccoon Ford, following the

cavalry on Sheridan's raid, and backing them in all the stirring combats at Todd's Tavern, Spottsylvania, and Yellow Tavern, and winning another brevet at Meadow Bridge, not far from the field where his first was gained at White Oak Swamp.

The war over, the Fourth had a spell of rest and a hard time transforming horse-battery men into garrison gunners. They were sent to the Pacific coast just in time to be ordered into the lava beds against the Modocs, and to lose four gallant officers and a score of men in that thankless and inglorious warfare. Field took his full share of the campaign; had another touch of frontier duty in 1877, when sent after Chief Joseph and the Nez Percés, and still again was ordered down into Arizona, where the Apaches of the Sierra Blanca had their outbreak in 1881.

This concluded the frontier service of the Fourth, for the time being at least. But Field was of too active a temperament to stagnate in a stone fort, when once again they appeared on the Atlantic coast. In such time as his duties would permit he devoted himself to the instruction of the neighboring National Guardsmen, proving always a welcome visitor at their camps and armories. In 1882 he was detailed to visit and inspect the troops of Rhode Island; in 1884, of New York; in 1886, of Maine; and his reports on their condition and efficiency were widely read.

The captain has achieved literary honor in other fields, having been selected to deliver the Decoration Day address at Newport, Rhode Island, in 1882, and having subsequently addressed the National Guard Association of New York in 1884; the West Point Association in July, 1882, and the Military Service Institute, at Governor's Island, in 1885.

For some time past Captain Field has been stationed at the new Fort McPherson, close to Atlanta.

CAPTAIN M. J. FITZ GERALD, U.S.A. (RETIRED).

Captain M. J. Fitz Gerald was born in Athlone, County Westmeath, Ireland, September 24, 1837. He arrived in Baltimore, Maryland, about 1847 or 1848. He enlisted January 5, 1855, at Fort McHenry, Maryland, and was assigned to Company E, First Artillery, at Fortress Monroe, Virginia. He was ordered to Florida with his company in the winter of 1855-56, and served during the war against Billy Bowlegs and his tribe, part of the time as acting hospital steward in the field. He was then ordered with his company to Fort Moultrie, South Carolina, in the fall of 1858, and performed the duties of hospital steward during the epidemic of yellow fever at that post. He was promoted corporal Company E, First Artillery, in 1858, and discharged in November, 1859. He re-enlisted, and was transferred to the Ordnance Corps in January, 1860, and was assigned to duty at U. S. Arsenal, Charleston, South Carolina. He remained there until the surrender of the arsenal to the State of South Carolina, December 30, 1860, as artificer and acting first sergeant of the detachments. The disagreeable duty devolved upon him to lower—the first time in its history—our flag in the presence of traitors. He remained a prisoner in the arsenal until after the firing on the "Star of the West," when he proceeded to the U. S. Arsenal at Augusta, Georgia, reporting to Captain Elzie, late Second U. S. Artillery. He remained there until the surrender of the arsenal, and was then ordered to Washington, D. C.,

where he was discharged, at his own request, to enable him to accept a position under the State of South Carolina; but, instead, he proceeded to Fort McHenry, Maryland, and enlisted, and was then appointed hospital steward at that post. From there he was transferred, as chief hospital steward, to the general hospital at Frederick, Maryland, until appointed second lieutenant of the Ninth Infantry, and ordered to duty with his company, C, at San Juan Island, Washington Territory, June, 1863; he remained on duty, in joint military occupation of the group of islands with the British troops, until October, 1865, when he was relieved and ordered to the Presidio of San Francisco, California, and assigned to duty as post adjutant, acting commissary of subsistence, and acting assistant quartermaster until May, 1866, when relieved and ordered to Fort Bidwell, California, relieving companies of the Second California Cavalry. He commanded the post, consisting of Companies C, Ninth Infantry, and A, First Cavalry, and performed the duty of acting assistant commissary of subsistence and acting assistant quartermaster until the middle of 1867, when he was relieved and ordered to the command of Fort Crook, California. From this point he was ordered back to Fort Bidwell and placed on duty as acting assistant quartermaster and acting assistant commissary of subsistence until November, 1868, when detailed on general recruiting service, rejoining his regiment at Omaha Barracks, Nebraska, prior to its consolidation, in 1869, and assigned to Company C, but soon transferred to Company F, and changed station to Sidney Barracks to command company and post. From this he was relieved and ordered, with his company, to Omaha Barracks in 1871; to Fort Russell, Wyoming Territory, in 1872; to the Sioux Reservation, Camps Sheridan and Robinson, Nebraska, in 1875; to field duty on White River, Nebraska, in 1876.

Captain Fitz Gerald was wounded at Red Cloud Agency in 1876. He commanded his company in Chicago, Illinois, during the riots of 1877; after which he commanded the quartermaster's depot at Cheyenne, Wyoming Territory, until ordered to Fort McKinney, Washington Territory.

From there he was placed on the retired list in May, 1879, on account of wounds and injuries, at his own request.

He was promoted first lieutenant March 4, 1864, and captain December 31, 1873, and commanded companies from March 4, 1864, to 1868, and from 1869 to 1879.

## BRIGADIER-GENERAL DANIEL W. FLAGLER, U.S.A.

BRIGADIER-GENERAL DANIEL W. FLAGLER (Chief of Ordnance) was born in New York March 24, 1835, and graduated at the Military Academy June 24, 1861. He was promoted brevet second and second lieutenant of ordnance the same day, and first lieutenant August 3, 1861, and captain March 3, 1863. He served during the rebellion of the seceding States, 1861 to 1866; in drilling volunteers at Washington, D. C., July 1–13, 1861; in the Manassas campaign and in the defences of Washington July and August, 1861; assistant ordnance officer at Allegheny Arsenal, Pennsylvania, and on foundry duty at Fort Pitt Foundry, Pittsburgh, Pennsylvania, inspecting ordnance for fitting out the Mississippi River Flotilla, August to December, 1861; as chief of ordnance to General Burnside's Expedition to North Carolina, December, 1861, to August, 1862; in charge of transportation of siege-train across country, New Berne to Fort Macon, North Carolina, and of construction of approaches and batteries in front of Fort Macon, March and April, 1862; in the Maryland campaign (Army of the Potomac) as assistant ordnance officer and aide-de-camp September and October, 1862; as chief ordnance officer, November, 1862, to November, 1863; in hospital October and November, 1863; on inspection duty at the West Point Foundry, New York, November, 1863, to May, 1864; assistant to chief of ordnance, U. S. A., Washington, D. C., May, 1864, to June, 1865, and inspecting arms, Army of the Potomac, February, 1865; in charge of Tredegar Iron Works, Richmond, April and May, 1865.

General Flagler participated in the battle of Bull Run July 21, 1861; the battle and capture of Roanoke Island February 7–8, 1862; battle of New Berne, North Carolina, March 14, 1862, and in command of mortar batteries in bombardment of Fort Macon, resulting in capture April 26, 1862; engaged in the battle of South Mountain September 14, 1862; battle of Antietam September 17, 1862; engaged in the battle of Fredericksburg December 13, 1862; battle of Chancellorsville, Virginia, May 2–4, 1863, and battle of Gettysburg, Pennsylvania, July 1–3, 1863.

He was brevetted captain March 14, 1862, for gallant services at battle of New Berne, North Carolina; major April 26, 1862, for gallant services at siege of Fort Macon, North Carolina; lieutenant-colonel March 13, 1865, for distinguished services in the field during the war of the Rebellion.

After the war closed he was employed on a tour of inspection of Western arsenals, with chief of ordnance, U. S. A., May, 1865; in charge of receiving arms from disbanded volunteers from Delaware and Pennsylvania at Wilmington, Delaware, and Philadelphia and Harrisburg, Pennsylvania, May and June, 1865; on special ordnance inspection duty in Kentucky, Tennessee, Georgia, and Alabama, June to September, 1865; assistant ordnance officer, Watervliet Arsenal, New York, October to December, 1865; in command of Augusta Arsenal and Powder-Works, Georgia, January, 1866, to May, 1871, having charge also of Confederate ordnance establishments, depots, and stores, and disposal of same, at Atlanta, Macon, Athens, and Savannah, Georgia, January, 1866, to January, 1869; and on special ordnance inspection duty at Fort Fisher, North Carolina, December, 1866; Selma, Alabama, February, 1869; and Fort Pickens, Florida, February, 1871; in command of Rock Island Armory and Arsenal June, 1871, to May 31, 1886; member of Board on Heavy Gun-Carriages, at New York, January to March, 1873; special inspection of Fort Union Arsenal, New Mexico, with view of breaking up same, September, 1880; on Board at Indianapolis, Indiana, in regard to removal of Indianapolis Arsenal, January, 1883; on ordnance inspection duty, San Antonio, Texas, Fort Lowell, Arizona, and Benicia, California, February and March, 1883; in command of Frankford Arsenal, Pennsylvania, May 31, 1886, to November 11, 1889; president of Board on Site for Gun Foundry March 22 to May 14, 1887; president of Board on Comparative Merits of Morse and Service Reloading Cartridges, March 3 to May 1, 1888; on special duty to select site and make plans for Columbia Arsenal, Tennessee, May 29 to June 30, 1888; president of Board for Testing Rifled Cannon and Projectiles in 1889; in command of Watertown Arsenal, Massachusetts, from November 29, 1889, to 1891.

He was promoted major June 23, 1874; lieutenant-colonel August 23, 1881; colonel September 15, 1890; and was appointed brigadier-general and chief of ordnance January 23, 1891.

### COLONEL DELANCEY FLOYD-JONES, U.S.A. (RETIRED).

COLONEL DELANCEY FLOYD-JONES was born, 1826, in Queens County, State of New York. He was graduated at the U. S. Military Academy in the Class of 1846. Upon graduating he was appointed to the Seventh Regiment of Infantry, then serving in Mexico under General Taylor, which he proceeded to join in September of that year.

After a few months' service with General Taylor's army, he was promoted to the Fourth Regiment of Infantry, which was transferred to Worth's division of General Scott's army, and formed the advance in the landing, and at the siege of Vera Cruz. After the surrender of that city, his company formed a part of the garrison of San Juan d'Ulloa.

The regiment proceeded with the army en route for the City of Mexico, and for a time formed a part of the garrison of the Castle of Perote, and the city of Puebla. Lieutenant Floyd-Jones took part in the various engagements in the Valley of Mexico, notably in the battles of Molino del Rey, Chapultepec, and the taking of the City of Mexico. For his conduct at the battle of Molino del Rey, he was especially commended by Captain—afterwards General—Anderson, of Fort Sumter fame, on which he was brevetted first lieutenant.

At the close of the Mexican War he was assigned to duty on the Northern Lakes, and served for a time as aide-de-camp to General Brady. In 1852 his regiment was transferred to the Pacific coast, via the Isthmus of Panama; while serving in that department he took part in the war against the Rogue River Indians, a severe but successful campaign, lasting some six months.

On the breaking out of the Rebellion he was, at the instance of General Winfield Scott, made major of the Eleventh Infantry, and joined his regiment, which was being recruited at Fort Independence, Boston harbor.

The regiment was made a part of the Army of the Potomac, and under his command moved with that army in its advance upon Yorktown, his regiment being among the first to open the trenches in the siege of that place.

Colonel Floyd-Jones continued to serve with the Army of the Potomac and took part in the Peninsula, Manassas, Antietam, Fredericksburg, Chancellorsville, and Gettysburg campaigns.

He was frequently commended by his brigade commanders, and at the battle of Chancellorsville Colonel Burbank says, "Where all did so well it is difficult to discriminate, but I desire to mention by name the regimental commander, Major De Lancey Floyd-Jones, Eleventh Infantry, for the great coolness with which he commanded his regiment."

In February, 1868, General George Sykes, in recommending Colonel Floyd-Jones for the brevet of brigadier-general, says," This officer served under my command from March, 1862, until the fall of 1863, and was present with the division of regular infantry in the Peninsula, Manassas, Antietam, Fredericksburg, Chancellorsville, and Gettysburg campaigns of the Army of the Potomac. He was often favorably mentioned in the reports of his brigade commander, and in the fight on the Old Turnpike near Chancellorsville on the 1st of May, 1863, distinguished himself at the head of his regiment.

"As commander of the Fifth Corps I had the opportunity to observe the zeal of Colonel Floyd-Jones in the campaign and battle of Gettysburg, and for these special instances and his services during the Rebellion respectfully recommend him for the brevet of brigadier-general in the army.

"Colonel Floyd-Jones is one of the few officers of his grade who have not yet received this recognition of his services, and when so many have received it, whose duties in the field are not to be mentioned with those of Colonel Floyd-Jones, I think it should no longer be withheld from him.
(Signed) "GEORGE SYKES,
"Lieutenant-Colonel Fifth Infantry,
"Brevet Major-General U.S.A."

The colonel has been three times brevetted for gallant conduct in battle, viz.: First lieutenant for Molino del Rey, Mexico; lieutenant-colonel for the Peninsula campaign, Virginia, and colonel for the battle of Gettysburg, Pennsylvania. Much of Colonel Floyd-Jones's service has been on the Western frontier. He retired from active duty in 1879, after thirty-three years' service, nineteen of which was in the Indian country. He is a member of the well-known family of Floyd-Jones, of Long Island, and has his home at South Oyster Bay, Long Island. He has travelled extensively, and an outline of his journey around the world, made in 1885-86, has been published, under the title of "Letters from the Far East."

## LIEUTENANT-COMMANDER CHARLES W. FLUSSER, U.S.N. (DECEASED).

LIEUTENANT-COMMANDER CHARLES W. FLUSSER was a native of Maryland, but was appointed midshipman from Kentucky in July, 1847. Of this date, not a large one, three members were killed in battle during the Civil War,—Cummings, Gwin, and Flusser.

The latter was commissioned lieutenant in September, 1855, and lieutenant-commander in July, 1862.

During his early years of service on the Home Station, the Brazils, the East Indies, and elsewhere, his career was that usual to the junior naval officer. He was always noted for attention to duty, and a quiet, contained manner, approaching reticence in personal intercourse. But those who knew him well also knew that his quiet demeanor concealed a warm heart and a gallant spirit.

When the expedition to Roanoke Island was in course of preparation, Flusser was ordered there in command of the "Commodore Perry," a side-wheel steamer with four heavy guns. Roanoke Island was the grand strategic point for the North Carolina Sounds, and the preparations on both sides showed the importance attached to that position. The success was complete on both land and shore; and in the chase of the rebel flotilla their flag-ship "Sea-Bird" was run into and sunk by Flusser in the "Commodore Perry," who took as prisoners nearly all her officers and crew. In July, in command of three light-draught vessels with a company of soldiers on board, he made a reconnoissance of the Roanoke River, and fell under a sustained and galling fire of concealed riflemen on the banks. Flusser had been ordered to go to a certain point,—and he did it, in spite of the opposition of fire, which he could not return without delay. He reached his point and carried off the steamer "Nelson," belonging to the Confederacy. He returned with one killed and ten wounded, having accomplished his mission.

His fight at Franklin, on the Blackwater River, on the 3d of October, deserves to be read in full. After getting up the river, Flusser did not wait for the co-operating troops, but pushed on, to find a terrific fire from concealed riflemen on the banks, which made the working of the guns most difficult. Flusser was a particularly cool and daring man, and finding himself in a trap determined to fight it out until the troops came up. He threw XI.-inch shell into Franklin, and with his 32-pounder he poured grape and canister into the woods.

With another 32-pounder he fought on the other side, —and with his IX.-inch gun he shelled the strongest position of the enemy. Till this time his guns' crews were exposed to a hot rifle-fire which came from concealed positions. The enemy had cut trees down across the narrow river behind him, but, "neck or nothing," he got round, put on steam, and pierced his way through and over the obstruction. In all these enterprises in the Sounds he was a leading spirit. In many of them little was to be gained but hard knocks,—yet he was always ready. "He was a terror to the marauding troops of the enemy, who made a note of all his movements."

On the 18th of April, 1864, after a heavy fight about Plymouth, North Carolina, in which both army and navy were concerned, the "Miami" and "Southfield," being under Flusser's command, were anchored below the town to prevent a flank movement of the Confederates. Just then the news was received that the ram "Albemarle" was on her way down, and the two vessels were chained together to meet her. In less than five minutes the collision occurred. The ram struck the "Miami" on the port bow, and the "Southfield" on the starboard bow, causing the latter to sink rapidly. Both vessels were firing into the ram with their 100-pounder rifles, and XI.-inch Dahlgren guns, but apparently made no impression, although alongside. Flusser fired the first three shots himself, the third shot being a ten-second Dahlgren XI.-inch shell. Directly after this shot Flusser was killed by a fragment of a shell,—whether from the ram, or from the one from the "Miami" rebounding, is doubtful.

COMMANDER WILLIAM M. FOLGER, U.S.N.

COMMANDER WILLIAM M. FOLGER is a native of Ohio, and was appointed a midshipman from that State in September, 1861. He remained at the Naval Academy until November 22, 1864. He was then attached to the receiving-ship "North Carolina," at New York, and the school-ship "Sabine," New London, from February to July, 1865. He then made a three-years' cruise in the steam-sloop "Hartford," flag-ship of the Asiatic Squadron. Promoted to lieutenant March 11, 1868, and commissioned lieutenant-commander in December of the same year. After being stationed at the Norfolk Navy-Yard, he was ordered to the flag-ship "Franklin," of the European Squadron, and served in that vessel, and in others of that squadron, from 1868 to 1872. Upon his return to the United States he was upon ordnance duty for two years. In 1875-76 he was on leave of absence in Europe, and during 1877 was attached to the steam-sloop "Marion," on the European Station. From 1887 to 1889 he was on duty at the Naval Academy at Annapolis; and then made a cruise in the "Swatara," of the Asiatic Squadron. In 1882 he was attached to the Bureau of Ordnance, Navy Department; and was then for three years upon ordnance duty at Annapolis, when the naval proving and experimental ordnance work was carried on.

He was promoted to be commander in March, 1885, and commanded the "Quinnebaug," on the European Station, during 1886-88. After his return he was inspector of ordnance at the navy-yard at Washington from 1888 to 1890. In the last named year he was appointed and confirmed by the Senate as Chief of the Bureau of Ordnance, with rank of commodore, which office he fills at present. Commodore Folger has been for several years identified with the extensive and important work connected with the new ordnance provided for the navy, and the establishment of the plant necessary for making the same; as well as with the exhaustive trials of armor-plate of various descriptions. In this way his name has become familiar to scientific engineers, as well as to military and naval men of all countries.

## SURGEON-GENERAL JONATHAN M. FOLTZ, U.S.N.
### (DECEASED).

Surgeon-General Jonathan M. Foltz was born in Pennsylvania, and entered the service from Maryland, as assistant surgeon, in April, 1831. He first served in the frigate "Potomac," on the Pacific Station, and upon his return home was attached to the Medical Bureau, and to the navy-yard at Washington. He received his commission as surgeon in December, 1838, and was in charge of the United States Naval Hospital at Port Mahon during the years 1839-40. He afterwards made a three years' cruise on the Brazil Station, in the frigate "Raritan." He was attached to the Washington Navy-Yard in 1850; and from 1851 to 1854 served in the "Jamestown," on the coast of Brazil. His next service was at the Rendezvous at Philadelphia, and at the Naval Asylum in the same city.

After a short service in the steam-frigate "Niagara," he was, on the formation of Farragut's fleet for the capture of New Orleans, ordered as fleet-surgeon. During all Farragut's actions in 1862-63, he occupied the post of fleet-surgeon, a most responsible and onerous one.

In 1864-66 he was a member of the Board of Examiners, and president of the board in 1867. When Farragut went upon his European cruise in 1868-69, Foltz was again his fleet-surgeon. He was commissioned medical director in March, 1871, and was chief of the Bureau of Medicine and Surgery, 1871-73.

He died in Philadelphia in April, 1887. Dr. Foltz was a man who impressed all with whom he came in contact as a thorough-going and reliable person. He had no hobbies in his professional views, which were sound and sensible, without pretension. When President Buchanan was in the White House, and became indisposed or ill, his first act was to send for Foltz, who was stationed in Philadelphia at the time Mr. Buchanan was in the presidential chair; so Farragut came to rely upon him, and with reason. When the admiral became ill while on his travel in Europe, during his last cruise, he hastened back to the "Franklin," at Spezzia, for the care which he required. The estimation in which Dr. Foltz was held by his townsmen of Lancaster, Pennsylvania, was evidenced by an immense attendance upon his funeral in that ancient city, where his remains lie close to those of Reynolds, a townsman, and the hero and martyr of the first day of Gettysburg.

REAR-ADMIRAL ANDREW HULL FOOTE, U.S.N.
(DECEASED).

REAR-ADMIRAL ANDREW HULL FOOTE was born in Connecticut 12th September, 1806. He was a son of S. A. Foote, United States Senator. Foote entered the navy as a midshipman in 1822, and served under the elder Porter in breaking up the piratical haunts in the West Indies. He became lieutenant in 1830. In 1849-50-51, while in command of the "Perry," he did effective service in the suppression of the African slave-trade. In 1856 he was in China, in command of the "Plymouth," during hostilities between the Chinese and the English. While protecting American property he was fired upon by the forts on Canton River. He obtained permission from Commodore Armstrong to demand an apology, and, when this was refused, he attacked the forts, four in number, with the sloops "Portsmouth" and "Levant," breached the largest, and carried them by storm. His loss was forty, that of the enemy four hundred. When the Civil War began he was selected to command the flotilla forming upon the Western waters. It was most exacting duty, and he himself said the hardest he ever performed. In February, 1862, having a number of vessels in readiness, he moved against Fort Henry, in connection with General Grant's forces, had a hotly-contested engagement, and carried the fort before the army got up. His conduct on this, as on other occasions, was conspicuously fine. A few days after Fort Donelson was attacked by the united forces, and, during a prolonged engagement, had several of his vessels disabled and was himself wounded. In conjunction with General Pope he next operated against Island No. 10, the strong works there surrendering to him on April 7. His wound, which his impetuous spirit had caused him to neglect, now became so troublesome that he was forced to give up his command. In June he received the thanks of Congress, and was made a rear-admiral. He was also appointed chief of the Bureau of Equipment and Recruiting. In June, 1863, he was selected to succeed Rear-Admiral Dupont in command of the fleet off Charleston; but, while on his way to assume this command, he died at New York June 26, 1863. He was a man of a high type of Christian character, with most genial and lovable traits, but uncompromisingly firm in his principles, especially in regard to temperance reform in the navy, where he was the means of abolishing the spirit-ration. Admiral Smith said of him: "Rear-Admiral Foote's character is well known in the navy. One of the strongest traits was great persistence in anything he undertook . . . He was truly a pious man, severely an honest man, and a philanthropist of the first order. He was one of our foremost navy officers—none before him." By his being the first to break the Confederate line of defence, in an hour of great depression, he raised the hope and prestige of success. Courageous and successful, he was thoroughly devoted to his profession, and united the characteristics of both the new and old schools of the navy.

He wrote "Africa and the American Flag," which was published in 1854, and excited much attention at the time.

## LIEUTENANT-COLONEL JAMES FORNEY, U.S.M.C.

LIEUTENANT-COLONEL JAMES FORNEY (United States Marine Corps) was born in Lancaster, Pennsylvania, on January 17, 1844, the son of J. W. Forney.

Colonel Forney was commissioned a second lieutenant March 1, 1861, and served on board the flag-ship "Roanoke;" became a first lieutenant in September; was in command of the Marine Barracks at Washington; was in command of the Marine Barracks at Portsmouth, New Hampshire; ordered to the steam-sloop "Brooklyn," West Gulf Squadron, and in her participated in the capture of Forts Jackson and St. Philip, and the city of New Orleans. In the official report is stated, "Lieutenant James Forney, commanding marines, had two guns assigned him, and, with his men, fought most gallantly." Admiral Farragut detailed him to go on shore and raise the flag on the Custom-House of New Orleans. It was the first hoisted there, and he brought off the Confederate flag, and delivered it to Captain Craven, of the "Brooklyn." For these services he was brevetted a captain. While attached to the West Gulf Squadron he participated in the actions at Chalmette, Port Hudson, Grand Gulf, first and second attacks on Vicksburg, Donaldsonville, Bayou Sara, and Galveston, Texas. At Brazos Santiago he cut out and captured four vessels, with valuable cargoes, from under the rebel batteries. He was commissioned captain in April, 1864.

In July of that year, when a Confederate army under Early threatened the capital, Forney had command of the troops at Havre de Grace, Maryland. General French, in his report of the ensuing operations, writes thus: "The army of the Confederates, under Jubal Early, was at the gates of Washington; communication with the northern cities was cut off; Gilmore's cavalry had captured a passenger train (made prisoner of General Franklin) and then destroyed it, and burned the bridge over Gunpowder River. The War Department shared in these fears of disaster, and, by telegraph, all the available troops at the West were ordered to assemble at Havre de Grace, Maryland. At the same time a despatch requested me to assume command of them. In less than eight hours' time three thousand men had reported, of all arms of the service. Captain Forney was first on the ground, with a splendid battalion of troops of the Marine Corps, and eight field howitzers. These troops were at once advanced; a part covered the reconstruction of the bridges, and others were made to demonstrate upon the rebel rear and flanks, preparatory to an advance. The same day the travel through to Baltimore was opened. Early, threatened in every direction, fell back."

For this duty Captain Forney received the brevet of lieutenant-colonel, "for meritorious services in defeating a rebel raid at Gunpowder Bridge."

After the war Forney served in the flag-ship "Hartford," in the Asiatic Squadron, as fleet marine officer, from 1865 to 1868. During an unusually severe and exhausting expedition in the Island of Formosa, in June, 1867, he commanded the marines. The climate, the nature of the ground, and the bush-fighting of the natives rendered this service a particularly trying one. He was recognized by a brevet of major "for gallant and meritorious services in the action with the savages at Formosa, June 13, 1867."

In October, 1870, Colonel Forney commanded the marines in the riots which took place in Philadelphia in consequence of the enforcement of the Fifteenth Amendment, being the first vote of the colored population.

Aided the revenue officers in the task of breaking up illicit distillation in Philadelphia; and in September of 1873 joined the "Minnesota" steam-frigate.

In 1875 and 1876 he was fleet marine officer of the North Pacific Squadron; in August, 1876, assumed the command of the marines at League Island, and in 1877-78 commanded the marines at Norfolk, Virginia. In the summer of 1877, during the labor riots, he commanded the second battalion of marines, who were complimented in general orders by the Secretary of the Navy and by General Hancock. Colonel Barry, of the Second Artillery, brevet major-general commanding, says:

"On relieving the marines from further duty under my command, I shall express the opinion of Major-General Hancock, and shall find great pleasure in giving expression also to my own conviction, 'that the services and military appearance and conduct of the battalion of United States marines, commanded by Captain Forney, have been such, while serving in this command, as to entitle them to commendation and thanks.'"

In command at League Island, Pennsylvania.

## COMMANDER J. M. FORSYTH, U.S.N.

COMMANDER JAMES McQUEEN FORSYTH was born on Long Island, Bahamas, January 1, 1842. He came to Philadelphia when eleven years old, and was educated in the public schools of that city. At the age of fifteen he went to sea in the merchant service, and then, before he was twenty years of age, on August 1, 1861, entered the naval service as a volunteer, under Commander H. S. Stellwagen, who appointed him second-class pilot for the Hatteras Expedition, and who favorably mentioned him in his report of the capture of Forts Clark and Hatteras. In September, 1861, he was made acting master's mate, and served thenceforth in various grades through the war, in the North and South Atlantic and the West Gulf Squadrons. He was present in the engagements under Farragut from Forts Jackson and St. Philip to Vicksburg, the fight at Grand Gulf, and the engagements with the rebel ram "Arkansas." For good service in these actions he was made acting ensign in September, 1862; was then attached to the "Water-Witch," "Pawnee," and monitor "Nantucket," of the South Atlantic Squadron; took part in expeditions up St. John's River, and various engagements with Sumter, Moultrie, and other works at Charleston. Promoted to acting master August 1, 1864. He was one of the officers detailed to take north the captured rebel ram "Columbia," in May, 1865. From 1865 to 1868 served as navigator and executive-officer of the "Nyack," of the Pacific Squadron.

Commissioned as master in the regular navy March, 1868, and as lieutenant December 18, 1868. During 1868 and 1869 he was executive-officer of the "Purveyor," on special service. After duty on board the receiving-ship "Potomac," he became navigator and executive-officer of the iron-clad "Saugus," of the North Atlantic Squadron, and then executive-officer of the iron-clad "Ajax." He was next stationed at the navy-yard at Philadelphia from May, 1871, to December, 1872, and then joined the "Supply" as executive-officer. This vessel was employed on special service in connection with the Vienna Exposition from January to December, 1873. For some months after this, Lieutenant Forsyth was stationed at the Philadelphia Navy-Yard. From March, 1874, to February, 1877, he was navigating officer of the "Powhatan," North Atlantic Station. Ill health caused him to take three months' sick-leave, but he was ordered to the course in torpedo instruction that summer, and for the rest of 1877 and the whole of 1878 he was on duty at League Island. He was promoted lieutenant-commander May 9, 1878; served as executive-officer of the "Constellation" in her special service of Irish relief, March to June, 1880, and then was for some months upon "waiting orders." In 1881, after three months' service in the receiving-ship "Colorado," he was ordered to the "Lancaster," of the Mediterranean Squadron, as navigating and executive-officer, where he remained until September, 1884. The "Lancaster" was flag-ship during this period.

Lieutenant-Commander Forsyth was on leave from November, 1884, to April, 1885, when he was ordered to League Island as ordnance officer, and remained there until June, 1886. At that date he was ordered to the U. S. Naval Home as assistant to the executive-officer, and remained on that duty until July, 1889. He was promoted to be commander February 14, 1889.

Commander Forsyth was ordered to the command of the school-ship "Saratoga," but the orders were revoked at his own request, and he was then detailed for the command of the "Tallapoosa," of the Brazil Squadron. This vessel was condemned and sold on the station in the early spring of 1892, and Commander Forsyth returned to the United States by mail-steamer.

## LIEUTENANT-COLONEL ROYAL T. FRANK, U.S.A.

LIEUTENANT-COLONEL ROYAL T. FRANK (Second Artillery) was born in Gray, Cumberland County, Maine, May 6, 1836, his ancestors being among the pioneer settlers of that State. He was appointed to the Military Academy at West Point in 1854, and, graduating four years later, was assigned to the Eighth Infantry, which he joined in New Mexico in 1859. In the following summer he participated in a campaign against the Kiowa and Comanche Indians of that Territory, and on the 23d of July, while in command of Companies E and K of his regiment, was engaged in a severe skirmish with a largely superior number of those Indians near Hatch's Ranch, New Mexico. His prompt and soldier-like conduct in that affair was highly commended by the department commander, and was mentioned in orders from the head-quarters of the army announcing the operations of that year.

He was promoted first lieutenant May 14, 1861, and in May, 1861, while en route with a battalion of his regiment under the command of Brevet Lieutenant-Colonel J. V. D. Reeves, from El Paso, Texas, to the coast, he was surrendered a prisoner of war near San Antonio, and was held a prisoner in Texas until exchanged in February, 1862, when he rejoined his regiment in the defences of Washington, having been promoted captain February 27, 1862.

He was in the field with the Army of the Potomac, and during the Peninsula campaign was on provost duty at the head-quarters of that army. He commanded his regiment during the Maryland and Rappahannock campaign, and was on duty with it during the Gettysburg campaign. From 1864 to 1866 was acting assistant adjutant-general of the general recruiting service. He was made brevet major for gallant and meritorious services during the Peninsula campaign, and brevet lieutenant-colonel for gallant and meritorious services in the battle of Fredericksburg, Virginia.

After the war he was on duty in the South, and during the reconstruction period commanded the posts or districts of Wilmington, North Carolina, and Darlington, South Carolina, and subsequently was in command at several other posts until December, 1870, when he was transferred to the First Artillery. With that regiment he served at various points, North and South, and was engaged with it at different times in suppressing civil disturbances incident to the internal revenue laws, the political troubles in the South in 1876, and the labor troubles in Pennsylvania in 1877. In the performance of these duties he was in command at several important points, and was mentioned in the reports of General Hancock and others for especially valuable services. In 1881 his regiment was transferred to the Pacific coast, where he served until 1886, commanding the posts of Alcatraz Island and Fort Point, San Francisco harbor. In June he was ordered to Fort Monroe, Virginia, and assigned to duty at the Artillery School as superintendent of the departments of engineering, law, and military art; subsequently as senior instructor in the latter department. In November, 1888, he was assigned to the command of the Artillery School and of the post of Fort Monroe.

Colonel Frank was transferred from the Infantry to the First Artillery as a captain December 15, 1870. He was promoted major January 2, 1881, and lieutenant-colonel of the Second Artillery January 25, 1889.

### REAR-ADMIRAL SAMUEL R. FRANKLIN, U.S.N.
(RETIRED).

REAR-ADMIRAL SAMUEL R. FRANKLIN was born in Pennsylvania, and appointed midshipman from that State, February 18, 1841. First served on the frigate "United States," in the Pacific, and then in the "Relief," storeship. Present at the demonstration upon Monterey, when no resistance was offered, and the place was occupied without a battle. Midshipman Franklin was detained abroad by the event, and was not ordered to the Naval School until 1847. Passed midshipman August 10, 1847. Served in razee "Independence," Mediterranean, for three years, and on the Coast Survey for two years. Commissioned lieutenant September 14, 1855; Naval Academy, 1855-56; sloop "Falmouth," Brazil Squadron, 1857-59; sloop "Macedonian," Home Squadron, 1859-60; sloop "Dakota," Atlantic coast, 1861-62. When the "Merrimac" came out, on the 8th March, 1862, Lieutenant Franklin was a volunteer on board the "Roanoke" at the time the "Congress" and "Cumberland" were destroyed. The "Roanoke" was engaged with the batteries at Sewell's Point, but grounded soon after, and was not fairly in action with the rebel ironclad. July 16, 1862, was commissioned as lieutenant-commander, and ordered to command "Aroostook," gun-boat, James River Flotilla. In 1863 proceeded in same vessel to the West Gulf Blockading Squadron; was upon special duty in New Orleans in 1864; chief of staff of West Gulf Blockading Squadron, under Bell, Palmer, and Thatcher; was the naval representative in the demand for the surrender of the city of Mobile, in the spring of 1865. After the war commanded "Saginaw," North Pacific Squadron, 1866-67; on special duty in regard to laying a cable across Bering's Straits.

Commissioned commander September, 1866; ordnance duty, navy-yard, California, 1868-69. In 1869-70 commanded "Mohican," North Pacific Squadron, and took the scientific party to Plover Bay, Siberia, to observe the total eclipse of the sun.

Equipment duty, Mare Island Navy-Yard, 1870-72; commissioned captain August 13, 1872; commanded "Wabash," European Station, 1873; also served as chief of staff to Admiral Case. When the flag was shifted to the "Franklin," Captain Franklin commanded her, and was chief of staff to Rear-Admiral Worden; president of Board for Promotion of Officers, navy-yard, Norfolk, 1877; promoted to commodore May 1881; special duty, Washington, 1881-83; previous to which served as hydrographer to the Bureau of Navigation; superintendent of Naval Observatory, 1884-85. In that position represented United States of Colombia in the International Conference to establish a prime meridian; promoted rear-admiral January, 1885; ordered to command of European Station February, 1885, with "Pensacola" as flag-ship. Remained on that station until relieved, and retired, under operation of the law, in August, 1887.

Although Admiral Franklin was on the retired list, he was, in February, 1889, appointed by President Cleveland as one of the delegates on the part of the United States to the International Marine Conference, and was chosen president of that body upon its assembly at Washington, on October 16, 1889. Admiral Franklin had two brothers in the army. One was the very distinguished General William B. Franklin, the commander of an army corps of the Army of the Potomac. The other, younger, was in the Twelfth Infantry, and resigned, soon after the late war, to engage in the superintendence of extensive iron works.

## COLONEL AND BREVET MAJOR-GENERAL WILLIAM B. FRANKLIN, U.S.A.

COLONEL AND BREVET MAJOR-GENERAL WILLIAM B. FRANKLIN was born in Pennsylvania, and graduated at the Military Academy July 1, 1843. He was promoted brevet second lieutenant of the Topographical Engineers in 1843; he was detailed as topographical officer on General Kearney's expedition to the South Pass of the Rocky Mountains, in the same year.

Promoted second lieutenant in the same corps September 21, 1846, he served in the war with Mexico, participating in General Wool's march through Coahuila during 1846-47, being engaged in the battle of Buena Vista February 22-23, 1847, and brevetted first lieutenant for this engagement "for gallant and meritorious conduct."

On July 21, 1848, Lieutenant Franklin was ordered to the Military Academy as assistant professor of natural and experimental philosophy, which he retained until January 9, 1852.

He was promoted first lieutenant March 3, 1853, and captain in his corps July 1, 1857, was secretary of the Light-House Board from March 3, 1857, until November 1, 1859, when he was detailed as superintending engineer in charge of the extension of the capitol (including the new dome), and of the General Post-Office at Washington, D. C., until March 3, 1861, when he was made chief of the Construction Bureau of the U. S. Treasury Department and superintending engineer of the Treasury Building Extension until May 14, 1861, at which date he was appointed colonel of the Twelfth U. S. Infantry.

Colonel Franklin was appointed brigadier-general of volunteers May 17, 1861, and was engaged at New York City until June 30, 1861, in receiving and forwarding volunteers. He then entered the field, and was in command of a brigade in the Manassas campaign, being engaged in the battle of first Bull Run July 21, 1861. He was placed in command at Alexandria, Virginia, August 1, 1861, and from September 1, 1861, to March, 1862, was in command of a division in the defences of Washington. He entered the Peninsula campaign with the Army of the Potomac, in command of a division, in March, 1862, and was assigned to the command of the Sixth Army Corps in the following May, which he retained until August, 1862, being engaged in the siege of Yorktown, combat of West Point, Virginia (in command); action at Golding's Farm, battle of White Oak Bridge, battle of Savage Station, battle of Malvern Hill, and skirmish at Harrison's Landing.

Appointed major-general of volunteers July 4, 1862, and participated in the Maryland campaign, being engaged (in command) at the battle of Crampton's Gap, South Mountain; and was also engaged at the battle of Antietam, September 17, 1862. After McClellan's re-

lief from the command of the Army of the Potomac, he was placed in command of the Left Grand Division (First and Sixth Corps) of the Army of the Potomac to January 24, 1863, having been engaged in the battle of Fredericksburg, Virginia, December 11-14, 1862; was on waiting orders to June 27, 1863, when he was ordered to the Department of the Gulf, being in command of the troops in and about Baton Rouge, Louisiana, to August 15, 1863, when he commanded the expedition to Sabine Pass, Texas, and was in command of the Nineteenth Army Corps, and of the troops in Western Louisiana, and took part in the Red River Expedition, being engaged in the battle of Sabine Cross-Roads, April 8, 1864, where he was wounded, but, continuing on duty, was in the battle of Pleasant Hill, April 9, 1864, and action of Monette's Crossing of Cane River, April 23, 1864.

While on sick-leave from April 29 to December 2, 1864, he was captured by rebel raiders in the Philadelphia and Baltimore Railroad cars, July 11, 1864, but escaped during the next night; was president of board for retiring disabled officers, at Wilmington, to November 10, 1865, when he was granted leave of absence to March 15, 1866, when he resigned from the army, having resigned his volunteer commission November 10, 1865. March 13, 1865, he was brevetted major-general U. S. Army "for gallant and meritorious services in the field during the Rebellion."

Upon entering civil life, General Franklin became general agent of Colt's Fire-Arms Mf. Co., at Hartford, Conn., from November 15, 1865. He is the only citizen of the United States upon whom has been conferred the French decoration of "*Grand Officier de la Légion d'Honneur.*" Has been President of the Board of Managers of the National Home for Disabled Volunteer Soldiers since April 21, 1880.

## MAJOR HENRY BLANCHARD FREEMAN, U.S.A.

MAJOR HENRY BLANCHARD FREEMAN (Sixteenth Infantry) was born in Ohio January 17, 1837. At the commencement of the war of the Rebellion he entered the regular service as private in Company B, Second Battalion, Eighteenth Infantry, July 8, 1861; was promoted first sergeant, and was discharged November 4, 1861, to accept the appointment of second lieutenant of the Eighteenth Infantry to date from October 30, 1861.

He served in the Army of the Cumberland in 1862-63, and was engaged in siege of Corinth, Perryville, Kentucky, Hoover's Gap, Tennessee, Monroe Cross Roads, North Carolina, cavalry combat at Solemn Grove, North Carolina, and the battles of Murfreesborough and Chickamauga. He was made prisoner of war in September, 1863, and escaped from Libby prison, Richmond, through the famous tunnel, February 14, 1864, but was recaptured three days later on Appomattox River, above City Point. He was one of the officers placed under the fire from Union batteries at Charleston, South Carolina, in August, 1864. He again escaped from a railway train on the Savannah and Charleston Railroad, the same month, but surrendered to avoid starvation. In November, 1864, he escaped from prison, Camp Sorghum, near Columbia, South Carolina, in November, 1864, and was recaptured ten days later. For the fourth time he escaped from prison at Columbia, South Carolina, February 14, 1865, and joined General Sherman's army, and was with the Seventeenth Corps from that date to April, 1865, when he was on duty with the headquarters of Kilpatrick's Cavalry Corps, from Winsborough, South Carolina, to Fayetteville, North Carolina.

He was promoted first lieutenant May 30, 1862, and captain July 28, 1866, and received the brevets of captain December 31, 1862, for "gallant and meritorious services in the battle of Murfreesborough, Tennessee;" and major September 20, 1863, for "gallant and meritorious services in the battle of Chickamauga, Georgia."

Lieutenant Freeman was adjutant of the First Battalion of the Eighteenth Infantry from March 16, 1863 to November 1, 1865, and was acting assistant adjutant-general of the Seventeenth Army Corps from February 14, 1865 to April, 1865.

Captain Freeman served with his regiment on the frontier in the Department of the Platte at Forts Phil Kearney and Reno from 1866 to 1869, and was on the Republican River campaign of the latter year. Department of Dakota from April, 1870, to 1882. He commanded two companies and a detachment of the Seventh Infantry against the half-breeds on Milk River, Montana, in the fall of 1871, and then was stationed at Camp Baker, Montana, to July, 1875. He was in command of six companies of the Seventh Infantry in the Sioux campaign of 1876, and commanded the escort to the Sitting Bull Commission to Fort Walsh, Canada, in 1877. He was in command of the troops at Rock Springs, Wyoming, from July 13, 1887, to September 20, 1889, and was then detailed on special recruiting service at St. Paul, Minnesota, December 16, 1890, when he was detailed as a member of the board to select a magazine-gun for the army, on which duty he is at present in New York City.

He was promoted major of infantry June 19, 1891, and assigned to the Sixteenth Regiment.

## MAJOR-GENERAL JOHN CHARLES FREMONT, U.S.A., F.R.G.S. (DECEASED).

MAJOR-GENERAL JOHN CHARLES FRÉMONT, F.R.G.S., Chevalier of the Prussian "Order of Merit," etc., was of Huguenot parentage on his father's side, and connected with the Washington family on his mother's. He received from the Charleston College the degree of Bachelor and Master of Arts; his mathematical attainments especially fitted him for his after-life. In 1838 he was appointed second lieutenant Topographical Engineers, U.S.A., and was Nicollet's assistant in the two explorations north of the Missouri in 1838-39. After the second of these he married Jessie Benton, daughter of Senator Thomas H. Benton. In 1842 he made the first of the great explorations in the then unmapped West, and continued them through the years 1842, 1843-44, 1845-46-47, 1848-49, 1853-54. The third resulted in the conquest of California by Captain Frémont, to whom the government sent as special messenger Lieutenant Archibald Gillespie, with instructions that the President intended to take possession of California. Captain Frémont was the only army officer then in that Mexican province, and he acted for his government.

Later, General Kearney attempted to supersede Commodore Stockton, the provisional military governor. Failing this, he ordered Captain Frémont to desert Stockton. Captain Frémont refused, and was court-martialled, being thus kept from the command of his regiment during the Mexican War. He was sentenced to dismissal, but the President disapproved of and remitted the sentence. Colonel Frémont considered the sentence unjust, and resigned. He had previously received a double brevet at the instigation of General Scott, and had been appointed military governor of California. He then made the exploration of 1848-49, in which one-third of the party died from exposure and starvation. He was appointed by the government commissioner to run the boundary between the United States and Mexico; and, later, elected first U. S. Senator from California to Congress. In 1853 he made his last exploration across the Rocky Mountains; the last two explorations were made at his own expense. In 1856 he was nominated for the Presidency by the just-formed Republican party, which was defeated. He was in England at the breaking out of the war in 1861; offered his services, and commenced buying arms for the government on his own credit and responsibility; received his appointment as major-general in the regular army and was assigned to command the Western Department. He was given by President Lincoln unlimited powers in his own department. In three months he organized and equipped one hundred thousand men, having to buy and manufacture most of the weapons and clothing. He recognized the abilities of U. S. Grant, and gave him his first independent command, against the advice of those who had known Captain Grant, and after the War Department and General McClellan had refused to do so. He was the first to build iron-clad gun-boats. August 30, 1861, General Frémont issued his proclamation, emancipating the slaves of rebels in his department. He cleared Missouri of rebels, but, owing to political influences, General Frémont was superseded by Hunter on the eve of battle. Hunter immediately retreated from a far inferior force, his trains and rear-guard suffering severe loss at the rebels' hands. General Frémont was then placed in command of the Mountain Department, Virginia, and came in on Jackson's rear during the latter's retreat down the Valley of the Shenandoah in 1862, pursuing him for six days, and fighting a battle with ten thousand five hundred men against Jackson's seventeen thousand, the forces under Frémont remaining in the field.

Serious political and personal controversy between Frémont and Lincoln caused the latter to *refuse* Frémont another command, and Frémont resigned, to accept, June 4, 1864, the nomination to the Presidency, tendered him by the convention which met at Cleveland, Ohio. The division of the Republican party following the rival candidacy of Frémont and Lincoln would have resulted in the election of the Democratic candidate, and Lincoln sent Senator Zach. Chandler to Frémont, to ask him to withdraw, and General Frémont did so, to save the party.

General Frémont now embarked his large fortune in the building of a trans-continental railway, but through the dishonesty of agents lost every dollar. In March, 1878, a full release on all accounts and charges was given General Frémont, the courts having found that the charges made against him in 1872 by these agents were altogether false. In 1878 General Frémont was appointed Governor of Arizona Territory. In 1890 General Frémont was placed on the retired list of the army, with his former rank of major-general. Died July 13, 1890.

CAPTAIN J. H. GAGEBY, U.S.A.

CAPTAIN J. H. GAGEBY (Third Infantry) was born at Johnstown, Pennsylvania, September 5, 1836. He is of Scotch-Irish descent. His grandfather, James Gageby, was in Independence Hall when the Declaration of Independence was read, and fought through the entire Revolutionary War and afterwards settled in Westmoreland County, Pennsylvania.

Entered the army as sergeant of Company K, Third Pennsylvania Volunteers, April 19, 1861, and was actively engaged at the battle of Falling Waters, Virginia, July 2, 1861. He enlisted in the Nineteenth U. S. Infantry October 25, 1861, and was appointed first sergeant from the date of his enlistment. His company joined the Army of the Potomac at Harrison's Landing July 4, 1862, and was with it through the battles of South Mountain and Antietam, Maryland, and Fredericksburg, Virginia, when it was transferred to the Army of the Cumberland March, 1863.

He was appointed a second lieutenant of the Nineteenth Infantry June 1, 1863, and promoted first lieutenant December 28, 1863.

He was in command of Company G, Nineteenth Infantry, at the battle of Hoover's Gap, Tennessee, June 26, 1863, for which he was brevetted for "gallant and meritorious services in action."

He was actively engaged in several severe skirmishes during the march to the battle of Chickamauga, in which latter engagement he was wounded and made a prisoner of war September 20, 1863, and was again brevetted for gallant and meritorious services in this battle.

He remained a prisoner of war in the different Southern prisons,—Atlanta, Augusta, Libby Prison, Virginia; Danville, Virginia; Macon, Georgia; Charleston, South Carolina (under the fire of our own artillery in 1864); Columbia, South Carolina; Charlotte, Raleigh, Goldsborough, and Wilmington, North Carolina, from which place he was exchanged on parole March 1, 1865. Total length of imprisonment, seventeen months and ten days.

Lieutenant Gageby was one of Colonel Rose's party, when the latter commenced work on the second tunnel to escape from Libby Prison, at Richmond, Virginia. Although he did not actually work in the tunnel, he performed the necessary duty in the prison to prevent its discovery while in progress. He was Number 23, of the one hundred and ten who escaped by the famous tunnel in February, 1864, but he was, unfortunately, recaptured and confined in the dungeon at Libby Prison several days, and subsequently transferred to the prisons farther South.

Lieutenant Gageby was appointed a captain July 28, 1866, and assigned to the Thirty-seventh United States Infantry.

In the winter of 1868-69 he was in command of the Infantry column with Colonel Evans's expedition against the Comanches, and was actively engaged in the fight with those Indians all day of Christmas, 1868, in which their village of sixty lodges was destroyed. Colonel Evans's letter to him, concerning the fight, says, "The marching of your men was the talk and wonder of the column, and you held the line until their supplies were destroyed; and on no one did I place more dependence than yourself, and you are eminently deserving of a brevet for this fight,—certainly as much so as myself."

Captain Gageby participated also in the campaign of General Brooke against the Mesceleros and Sierra Diablo Lipan Apache Indians in April and May, 1869, and was then transferred to the Third Infantry August 11, 1869.

From 1874 to 1877, the captain was employed on "reconstruction duty" in the Bayou Têche district of Louisiana, and several letters commendatory of his service there are on file in the War Department, from Mr. Packard and others.

He was on leave at his home in Johnstown, Pennsylvania, at the time of the great flood in 1889, and was placed on duty there for several months by order of the Secretary of War.

## CAPTAIN FRANK DILLON GARRETTY, U.S.A.

CAPTAIN FRANK DILLON GARRETTY (Seventeenth Infantry) was born in Ireland February 4, 1829. He entered the military service as second lieutenant of Company G, Fifteenth Kentucky Infantry, December 14, 1861. He served with the Army of the West during the war of the Rebellion, and was with his regiment in the spring of 1862, at the capture of Bowling Green, Kentucky; Nashville, Murfreesborough, Shelbyville, and Fayetteville, Tennessee; and Huntsville, Alabama. He marched with his regiment, August 31, 1862, to Perryville, Kentucky, and engaged in the battle of Perryville, October 8, 1862, where he was wounded. He was honorably discharged June 27, 1863, for physical disability.

He received his commission as first lieutenant of the Veteran Reserve Corps October 2, 1863, and was guarding prisoners-of-war at Indianapolis, and Camp Douglas, at Chicago, during the years 1864-65. He was on duty in the State of Louisiana from January, 1866, to April, 1869, as agent and acting commissioner of the Freedmen's Bureau. While on this duty, he was commissioned as second lieutenant of the Forty-third Infantry July 28, 1866, and first lieutenant January 11, 1868. He was ordered on duty in the State of Iowa, as agent of the Sac and Fox Indians, 1869-70. On the 15th of December, 1870, Lieutenant Garretty was transferred to the Seventeenth Infantry, and was on duty

with his regiment in Dakota, from 1871 to 1886, participating with his company on the Stanley expedition in 1872, and also on the Custer campaign of 1876.

Lieutenant Garretty was promoted captain June 26, 1882, and moved with his regiment from Dakota to Fort D. A. Russell, Wyoming, in 1886. He was on recruiting duty at Chicago, Illinois, and St. Paul, Minnesota, from 1886 to 1888, and with his company and regiment during 1889-90, when he was again placed on recruiting duty in October, 1890.

### COLONEL AND BREVET MAJOR-GENERAL GEORGE W. GETTY, U.S.A. (RETIRED).

COLONEL AND BREVET MAJOR-GENERAL GEORGE W. GETTY was born in Georgetown, D. C., in 1819, and was graduated at the Military Academy in the Class of 1840. Receiving his appointment as second lieutenant of the Fourth U. S. Artillery, he was assigned to duty in the State of Michigan, and was engaged during the fall and winter of 1840-41 in removing the Pottawatomie tribe of Indians from that State to their reservation west of the Mississippi River, and on the Northern frontier during the Canada-border disturbances, 1841-42; served in the war with Mexico, 1847-48, and was in the battles of Contreras, Churubusco, and Molino del Rey; the storming of Chapultepec and assault and capture of City of Mexico, and received the brevet of captain for " gallant and meritorious conduct in the battles of Contreras and Churubusco;" was afterwards engaged in the Florida hostilities against the Seminole Indians, 1849-50 and 1856-57; on frontier duty, 1857-60, in quelling disturbances in that State. Served during the Rebellion, being engaged with Confederate batteries on the Potomac River near Budd's Ferry, Maryland; Virginia Peninsula campaign; engaged in the siege of Yorktown, battles of Gaines' Mill and Malvern Hill; in the Maryland campaign, Army of the Potomac, being engaged in the battles of South Mountain and Antietam, and the march to Falmouth, Virginia; served in the Rappahannock campaign, Army of the Potomac, being engaged in the battle of Fredericksburg, Virginia; in the operations about Suffolk, Virginia, on the line of the Nansemond River; in command of the Third Division of the Ninth Army Corps during the defence of Suffolk, April 11, May 3, 1863; in command of storming column in the assault of Hill's Point Works and Battery, April 19, 1863; in the Richmond campaign, being engaged in the battle of the Wilderness, where he was severely wounded while in command of the division; in the siege of Petersburg, and expedition to Reams' Station and Weldon Railroad, 1864; in the defence of Washington City, July 11-12, 1864, and in the pursuit of the army under General Early to the Shenandoah Valley, July 13 to August 9, 1864; in the Shenandoah campaign, being engaged in the action of Charlestown, battles of Opequan, Fisher's Hill, and Cedar Creek; served in the siege of Petersburg, being engaged in the assaults of March 25 and April 2, 1865, upon the enemy's works; in the pursuit of the Army of Northern Virginia, being engaged in the battle of Sailor's Creek, April 6, 1865, and was at the capitulation of General R. E. Lee, with that army. General Getty was appointed lieutenant-colonel and aide-de-camp in September, 1861; brigadier-general of volunteers September 25, 1862, in which latter grade he served until mustered out of the volunteer service October 9, 1866. He passed through the various grades in the regular service from lieutenant to major, and was made colonel of the Thirty-seventh U. S. Infantry July 28, 1866, and afterwards transferred to the Third Infantry, subsequently to the Third Artillery, and finally to the Fourth Artillery, from which he was retired for age October 2, 1883. General Getty was, for gallant and meritorious services, made brevet lieutenant-colonel during the siege of Suffolk; colonel, for battle of the Wilderness; brigadier-general, for capture of Petersburg; major-general, for services during the war; major-general of volunteers, for Winchester and Fisher's Hill, Virginia. The petition of General Getty to Congress to be retired on the grade of major-general received the following complimentary indorsement:

"HEAD-QUARTERS OF THE ARMY, WASHINGTON, D. C., January 26, 1883.— . . . George Getty as a boy and man, through a long, eventful life, has been a model gentleman and soldier, of unexceptional habits, of superior intelligence, and high professional acquirements. He has always been selected in war and peace for high and responsible commands. Modest to a fault, he has never pushed himself forward into undue prominence, but has done well all that he was appointed to do, and has always been sought for by his services for posts requiring high qualification and professional excellence. . . . I most respectfully represent that the principle of common justice seems to demand that General Getty should, during his few remaining years, have, for the support of himself and of his dependent family, the retired pay of a major-general. Even this will fall far short of compensation for the labor and responsibility imposed on him by superior authority in exacting from him the work of a major-general on the pay of a colonel.

(Signed) "W. T. SHERMAN, *General.*"

## REAR-ADMIRAL BANCROFT GHERARDI, U.S.N.

REAR-ADMIRAL BANCROFT GHERARDI is now the senior officer on the active list of the U. S. Navy, and is credited in the official register with nearly twenty-five years of sea-service, while his " shore duty" has comprised almost every variety of employment which can fall to the lot of a naval officer. He is the nephew of the eminent historian, George Bancroft, who was the Secretary of the Navy to whom the U. S. Naval Academy is indebted for its existence more than to any other one person; and who was for so many years, our excellent Minister at the Court of Berlin.

Admiral Gherardi was born in Louisiana November 10, 1832, but was appointed from Massachusetts in June, 1846. He made a cruise of nearly four years in the line-of-battle ship " Ohio" during the Mexican War, and afterwards. He then served in the " Saranac," of the Home Squadron, and, after a course at the U. S. Naval Academy, became passed midshipman in 1852; after a cruise in the Mediterranean, he was promoted master in 1855; and lieutenant in the same year. He next served in the " Saratoga," Home Squadron; the Boston rendezvous; and the steam-sloop " Lancaster," in the Pacific. He was commissioned lieutenant-commander July, 1862; and attached to the South Atlantic Blockading Squadron. In an engagement with Fort Macon, 1862; steam-sloop " Mohican ;" on special service in 1863. He was then ordered to the West Gulf Blockading Squadron, in which he commanded the " Chocura" and the " Port Royal ;" he took part in the battle of Mobile Bay, August 5, 1864, in the latter vessel. He next commanded the " Pequot," in the North Atlantic Squadron, until the close of the war.

He was commissioned as commander July 25, 1866, and was stationed at Philadelphia at the naval rendezvous and the navy-yard until 1870. He then took

command of the " Jamestown," in the Pacific, and of the receiving-ship " Independence" at Mare Island, after leaving the " Jamestown."

He was commissioned as captain in November, 1874, and commanded the flag-ship " Pensacola," of the North Pacific Station, for two years. From 1877 to 1880 he was in command of the receiving-ship " Colorado." After this he was for three years in command of the " Lancaster," flag-ship of the European Squadron. When the " Lancaster" came home he obtained a year's leave to travel in Europe, and during that time he received his promotion as commodore. In 1884-85 he was a member of the Examining Board, and in 1885-86 was governor of the Naval Asylum at Philadelphia. His promotion as rear-admiral dates from August, 1887, when he was ordered to the command of the navy-yard at New York. In 1889 he was ordered to the command of the North Atlantic Station, which he retains at this writing.

**BRIGADIER- AND BREVET MAJOR-GENERAL JOHN GIBBON, U.S.A. (RETIRED).**

BRIGADIER- AND BREVET MAJOR-GENERAL JOHN GIBBON was born in Pennsylvania April 20, 1827, and graduated from the Military Academy July 1, 1847. He was promoted brevet second lieutenant, Third Artillery, the same day, and second lieutenant, Fourth Artillery, September 13, 1847. He served in the war with Mexico, at the City of Mexico and Toluca, in 1847, and in garrison at Fort Monroe in 1848. He was then ordered to Florida, and participated in the hostilities against the Seminole Indians until 1850, when he was promoted first lieutenant and ordered to Texas, serving at Fort Brown and Ringgold Barracks until 1852. After availing himself of a leave of absence, he was employed in removing the Seminole Indians from Florida to the west of the Mississippi from May to August, 1854, upon the conclusion of which he was detailed at the Military Academy as assistant instructor of artillery, as quartermaster, and as a member of a board to test breech-loading rifles to 1857.

He was promoted captain November 2, 1859, and was on sick-leave of absence in 1859-60. In 1860-61 he was on frontier duty in Utah, and marched from Fort Crittenden, Utah, to Fort Leavenworth, Kansas, at the breaking out of the war of the Rebellion.

Captain Gibbon served as chief of artillery of General McDowell's division in the fall and winter of 1861-62, and was appointed a brigadier-general of volunteers May 2, 1862, and assigned to the command of a brigade in the Department of the Rappahannock. He took part in all the campaigns of the Army of the Potomac, and was engaged in the action of Gainesville, battles of second Bull Run, South Mountain, Antietam, Fredericksburg (wounded), Marye Heights, and Gettysburg, where he was severely wounded while commanding the Second Army Corps.

He was then on leave of absence, on account of wounds, to November 15, 1863, when he was placed in command of the draft depot at Cleveland, Ohio, for a short time, but subsequently transferred to Philadelphia, where he remained until March 21, 1864.

Upon rejoining for duty in the field, General Gibbon was assigned to the command of a division in the Second Army Corps, and participated in the Richmond campaign of 1864, being engaged in the battles of the Wilderness, Spottsylvania, North Anna, Tolopotomy, Cold Harbor, and the siege of Petersburg. He was appointed major-general of volunteers June 7, 1864, and was assigned to the command of the Twenty-fourth Army Corps (Army of the James), and while in command of that corps participated in the campaign of 1865, and was engaged in the assaults on the enemy's works April 1 and 2, and the pursuit of the enemy, terminating in the surrender of Lee's army at Appomattox Court-House April 9, 1865, he being one of the commissioners to carry into effect the stipulations for the surrender.

He was brevetted for gallant and meritorious services as follows: Major, September 17, 1862, for Antietam; lieutenant-colonel, December 13, 1862, for Fredericksburg; colonel, July 4, 1863, for Gettysburg; brigadier-general, March 13, 1865, for Spottsylvania; major-general, same date, for capture of Petersburg.

After being on various duties until January 15, 1866, General Gibbon was mustered out of the volunteer service, and was a member of the board to make recommendations for brevet promotions. He was appointed colonel of the Thirty-sixth Infantry July 28, 1866, and served with his regiment on the frontiers at various posts in the West and Northwest. He was, in the consolidation of regiments, transferred to the Seventh Infantry March 15, 1869, and participated with his regiment in the expedition against hostile Sioux Indians in 1876, and was also engaged with the Nez Percés Indians in 1877. Wounded at battle of Big Hole, Montana Territory, August 9, 1877.

General Gibbon was appointed brigadier-general U. S. Army July 10, 1885, and was assigned to the command of the Department of the Columbia, but in 1889 was placed in command of the Military Division of the Pacific, which command he retained until retired, by operation of law, April 20, 1891.

## MEDICAL DIRECTOR ALBERT LEARY GIHON, U.S.N.

MEDICAL DIRECTOR ALBERT LEARY GIHON was born in Philadelphia, Pennsylvania, September 28, 1833; received degrees of A.B. 1850, M.D. 1852, and A.M. 1854; was Professor of Chemistry and Toxicology in the Philadelphia College of Medicine and Surgery, 1853-54.

Entered navy as assistant surgeon May 1, 1855; first duty on board receiving-ship "Union," navy-yard, Philadelphia; attached to sloop-of-war "Levant," East India Station, 1855-58; was in the sloop-of-war "Portsmouth's" gig, November 15, 1856, when fired upon by the Chinese while attempting to pass the Barrier Forts on the Pearl River, near Canton, and participated as one of the landing party, in the subsequent engagements, which resulted in the capture of these forts, November 16, 20, 21, and 22, 1856; attached to brig "Dolphin," 1858-59, during Paraguay Expedition; and to sloop-of-war "Preble," 1859, on the coast of Central America and Panama.

Became passed assistant surgeon May 1, 1860; Naval Hospital, Brooklyn, New York, 1860-61; brig "Perry," 1861, on the blockade of Fernandina, Florida, and cruising off the Atlantic coast of the Southern States, capturing the rebel privateer "Savannah," the first Confederate letter-of-marque, May 1, 1861.

Promoted to surgeon, August 1, 1861; naval rendezvous, New York; sloop-of-war "St. Louis," 1862-65, on special service upon European Station and cruising among the Atlantic Islands after Confederate steamers "Alabama," "Florida," and "Georgia"; and in latter part of 1864 on blockade of coast of South Carolina; senior medical officer, navy-yard, Portsmouth, New Hampshire, 1865-68;

He was attached to United States ship "Idaho," 1868-70, anchored at Nagasaki, Japan, as hospital-ship for the Asiatic Station, and was on board during the memorable typhoon of September 21, 1869, when ship was wrecked by passing through centre of a cyclone, with barometer at 27.62 in.; for services rendered Portuguese colony at Dilly, Island of Timor, and the Portuguese men-of-war "Principe Dom Carlos" and "Sá da Bandeira," received from the King of Portugal, with the consent of Congress, the decoration of Knight of the Military Order of Christ; for services to H. B. M. ships "Flirt" and "Dawn," the thanks of the British government; and for similar services to the French gun-boat "Scorpion" those of the Commander-in-Chief of the French East India Station; special duty at New York, 1870; subsequently marine rendezvous, Phila.; and later member of Naval Medical Board of Examiners at Phila., 1870-72, and at Washington, 1872-73.

Promoted to medical inspector November 7, 1872; special duty at Bureau of Medicine and Surgery, Navy Department, 1873, and same year ordered to flag-ship "Wabash" as surgeon-of-the-fleet on the European Station; at Key West, Florida, with naval expedition of 1874, and returned to European Station as surgeon-of-the-fleet, on board the flag-ship "Franklin," 1874-75; head of medical department at Naval Academy, Annapolis, Maryland, 1875-80; at request of chief of Bureau of Medicine and Surgery designed and superintended construction of model of hospital-ship for Centennial Exhibition at Philadelphia, 1867, and at same Exhibition presented "Ambulance Cot," bearing his name, which was approved by Board of Officers, July 5, 1877, and adopted for use in the navy; appointed Inspector of Recruits and Recruiting Stations, November 20, 1878.

Commissioned medical director August 20, 1879; in charge of Naval Hospital, Norfolk, Va., 1880; member of Board of Inspection of the Navy, 1880-83; in charge of the Naval Hospital, Washington, D. C., 1883-86; of Naval Hospital, Mare Island, California, 1886-88; and of Naval Hospital, Brooklyn, New York, 1888-92.

Has represented the Medical Department of the Navy since 1876 to the present time in the prominent national medical, sanitary, and climatological associations and international medical congresses, and been honored by election to their highest offices; is member of various American and foreign historical and scientific societies, fellow and ex-president of the American Academy of Medicine, and member of the military order of the Loyal Legion of the United States.

He is the author of numerous papers and addresses on Naval Hygiene, Public Health, Sanitary Reform, State Medicine, Higher Medical Education, Vital Statistics, Medical Demography, and Climatology; contributor to literary magazines and other periodicals, and of articles on medical and surgical subjects to professional journals and other publications; and since 1887 one of the editors of the "Annual of the Universal Medical Sciences."

## CAPTAIN ERASMUS C. GILBREATH, U.S.A.

CAPTAIN ERASMUS C. GILBREATH (Eleventh Infantry) was born in Guernsey County, Ohio, May 13, 1840, and entered the volunteer service as first lieutenant of the Twentieth Indiana Infantry July 22, 1861. He was promoted captain December 7, 1862, and major of the same regiment July 27, 1863. He served in the First Brigade, First Division of the Third Army Corps, from June 8, 1862, to the breaking up of the Third Corps in March, 1864, participating in the campaigns of that corps with the Army of the Potomac, and engaged in the action at Chickamicomico, near Fort Hatteras, the "Merrimac" fight with the "Congress" and "Cumberland," action at Oak Grove, Virginia, Seven Days' Battles, skirmish at Rappahannock Station, battles of second Bull Run, Chantilly, Fredericksburg (where he was wounded), Chancellorsville (slightly wounded), Gettysburg, Kelly's Ford, Mine Run (especially Locust Grove), the Wilderness, Spottsylvania, Cold Harbor, siege of Petersburg,—including all the movements and operations of the Third Division Second Army Corps, from March to October, 1864.

Honorably mustered out of the Twentieth Indiana Infantry October 19, 1864, and was appointed captain and assistant quartermaster of volunteers January 23, 1865, from which position he was mustered out July 28, 1865, and appointed lieutenant-colonel in Hancock's Corps, on the approval of Major-General Hancock, February 14, 1865. He commanded the Twentieth Indiana during the battle of Gettysburg, from the time of the death of Colonel Wheeler, at the beginning of the action, to the close of the fighting on the 2d; Lieutenant-Colonel Taylor having been wounded, acted as major from the 4th of July, 1863, when commissioned, though not formally mustered into service as major until July 27, 1863. He commanded the Seventeenth Maine Infantry, by order of Major-General D. B. Birney, from June 17 to about June 30, 1864, and was in command of that regiment in the charge on the Confederate lines in front of Petersburg, June 17, 1864, and again in the charge at the Hare House, June 18, 1864.

Captain Gilbreath entered the regular service as first lieutenant of the Fifteenth Infantry February 23, 1866, was transferred to the Twenty-fourth Infantry September 21, 1866, and again transferred to the Eleventh Infantry April 25, 1869.

He was assigned to various complicated duties in connection with the reconstruction of the States of Mississippi and Texas; in Mississippi, sub-commissioner of Freedmen's Bureau in charge of that district, having charge of the counties now called Copiah, Simpson, Lincoln, Lawrence, Amite, Pike, and Marion,—eighteen thousand freedmen living in the district. He had charge of the registration and election in the counties named in October, 1867 (see testimony of Brevet Major-General A. C. Gillem, U.S.A., before the Committee on the Conduct of the War, given in 1868 in relation thereto). In Texas he had charge of the reconstruction and reorganization of Montgomery County from September, 1868, to May, 1869, promoted captain of Company H, Eleventh Inf. December 23, 1873. He was in command of Company H, Eleventh Infantry, in the campaign against hostile Comanche Indians, from November 8, 1874, to January 20, 1875, when he was compelled to go on sick report on account of wound received at Fredericksburg, Virginia, December 13, 1862, and on sick-leave of absence from same cause from May 17, 1875, to March 27, 1876. He was in command of company in the movement October 22, 1876, at Standing Rock, Dakota Territory, the result of which movement was the disarming of the Blackfeet and Yankton Indians at that Agency. He selected the site for and established the depot at Terry's Landing, Montana Territory, at the head of navigation on the Yellowstone River. He took the field with his company against hostile Bannock Indians from August 31 to September 13, 1878, and was then in charge of the construction of the military telegraph line from Fort Custer, Montana Territory, to the Yellowstone River—48 miles—from December 3 to 16, 1878. He was appointed inspector of Indian Supplies at the Crow Agency, Montana Territory, from September 5, 1879, to July 28, 1880. While inspector of Indian Supplies at the Crow Agency, Montana Territory, he assisted the agent for the three thousand three hundred Crow Indians in negotiating a treaty by which they gave up and sold two million acres of land at the west end of their reservation, and he signed this treaty in his official capacity.

Captain Gilbreath is a member of the G. A. R., Loyal Legion, and the Second and Third Corps societies.

## LIEUTENANT-COLONEL AND BREVET BRIGADIER-GENERAL GEORGE W. GILE, U.S.A. (RETIRED).

LIEUTENANT-COLONEL AND BREVET BRIGADIER-GENERAL GEORGE W. GILE was born in Bethlehem, N. H., January 25, 1830. His record of service was furnished by Adjutant-General R. C. Drum to a committee of Congress in 1884, and is given herewith:

"He entered the service April 23, 1861, as first lieutenant Twenty-second Penn. Inf., and served to August 7, 1861, upon which date he was honorably mustered out, his term of service having expired.

"He re-entered the service Sept. 16, 1861, as major Eighty-eighth Penn. Inf., and was promoted lieutenant-colonel Sept. 1, 1862, and colonel Jan. 24, 1863.

"He served with his regiment in the defences of Washington, the Army of Virginia, and the Army of the Potomac, from Oct. 1, 1861, to Sept. 17, 1862, upon which date he was wounded in the battle of Antietam, while in command of his regiment; was absent by reason of wound until honorably discharged on account of disability, March 2, 1863. Was appointed major in the Veteran Reserve Corps May 22, 1863, and colonel Sept. 29, 1863.

"He served as a member of a Board of Examiners for the Veteran Reserve Corps to some time in November, 1863; commanded a brigade engaged in the defences of Washington July 10 to 13, 1864, and for energy and good conduct in assisting to repel the attack on Fort Slocum, D. C., he was brevetted brigadier-general; commanded the garrison of Washington to September, 1865; on duty in the Bureau of Refugees, Freedmen, and Abandoned Lands in S. C. to Jan. 4, 1867; upon which date he was honorably mustered out of the volunteer service.

"He was appointed first lieutenant Forty-fifth U. S. Inf. to date from July 28, 1866, and promoted captain Feb. 4, 1868.

"He received the brevets of captain 'for gallant and meritorious services in the second battle of Bull Run;' major ' for gallant and meritorious services at the battle of South Mountain, Maryland;' and lieutenant-colonel ' for gallant and meritorious services at the battle of Antietam.'

"He served in the Bureau of Refugees, Freedmen, and Abandoned Lands in S. C. from Jan. 5, 1867, to Oct. 10, 1868; and in Florida with brevet rank to July 15, 1870; on duty at head-quarters Bureau of Refugees, Freedmen, and Abandoned Lands, Washington, until he was retired from active service, with the full rank of colonel, Dec. 15, 1870, for disability resulting from wounds received in line of duty, under section 32 of the act of Congress approved July 20, 1866, which authorized retirement in such cases with the full rank of the *command*

held by the officer when the disabling wounds were received; retired with the rank of lieutenant-colonel, the *actual rank* in the volunteer service held by him when wounded, March 3, 1875, under the provisions of an act of Congress approved that date."

Incidental to his field service he participated with his regiment in the battles of Cedar Mountain, three days at Rappahannock Station, Thoroughfare Gap, Bull Run, second Chantilly, South Mountain, and Antietam. Was in command from and during the battle of Bull Run to Antietam.

At the second battle of Bull Run, Major Gile commanded the Eighty-eighth Penn. Vol. This regiment was one of the four comprising Tower's brigade, and of the conduct of that brigade, General Pope, in his official report, speaks as follows:

"Tower's brigade, of Ricketts's division, was pushed forward into action into support of Reynolds's division, led forward in person by General Tower with conspicuous skill and gallantry.

"The conduct of that brigade in plain view of all the forces on our left was especially distinguished, and drew forth hearty and enthusiastic cheers. The example of that brigade was of great service and infused new spirit into all the troops who witnessed their intrepid conduct."

He was stationed in the city of Washington from November, 1863, to close of war; during this time he commanded a regiment, brigade, and the garrison of Washington, which consisted of two brigades of infantry, a battery of artillery, and a detachment of cavalry.

He commanded President Lincoln's second inaugural and funeral escort. Was general officer of the day on the occasion of the final review of the armies at the close of the war.

COLONEL AND BREVET MAJOR-GENERAL QUINCY
A. GILLMORE, U.S.A. (DECEASED).

COLONEL AND BREVET MAJOR-GENERAL QUINCY A. GILLMORE was born in Ohio and graduated from the U. S. Military Academy July 1, 1849. He was promoted brevet second lieutenant Corps of Engineers the same day; second lieutenant September 5, 1853; first lieutenant July 1, 1856, and captain August 6, 1861. He served on engineer duty in constructing Forts Monroe and Calhoun in 1849-52; was at West Point attached to company of sappers, miners, and pontoniers, from 1852 to 1856; was instructor of practical military engineering at West Point to September 15; treasurer to September 11, and quartermaster to September 15, 1856. He was then employed as assistant engineer in the construction of Fort Monroe, in charge of the engineer agency at New York for supplying and shipping materials for fortifications to 1861.

He served during the war of the Rebellion as chief engineer of the Port Royal Expeditionary Corps, 1861-62, being present at the descent upon Hilton Head, South Carolina, November 6, 1861, and engaged in the construction of fortifications on that island to January, 1862; then as chief engineer of the siege of Fort Pulaski, and in command during its bombardment and capture, April 10-11, 1862, being one of the commissioners to arrange the terms of capitulation.

He was appointed brigadier-general of volunteers April 28, 1862, and was on sick-leave of absence from May to July of that year. He assisted the Governor of New York in forwarding State troops until September 12, 1862, when he was assigned to the command of a division operating from Covington, Kentucky; of District of West Virginia; of First Division, Army of Kentucky; of District of Central Kentucky, and of the United States forces at the battle of Somerset, Kentucky, from September 18, 1862, to March 30, 1863. He was appointed major-general of volunteers July 10, 1863.

After a short leave of absence, he was placed in command of the Department of the South and of the Tenth Army Corps, from June 12, 1863, to June 17, 1864, being engaged in command of the operations against Charleston, South Carolina, comprising the descent upon Morris Island; bombardment and reduction of Fort Sumter; and siege and capitulation of Fort Wagner. He was then in command of the Tenth Army Corps in the operations on James River, near Bermuda Hundred, and engaged in actions of Swift Creek, near Chester Station; assault and capture of the right of the enemy's intrenchments in front of Drury's Bluff; battle of Drury's Bluff; defence of Bermuda Hundred; reconnoissance of the enemy's lines before Petersburg, and in command of two divisions of the Nineteenth Corps in defence of Washington, D. C., July 11, 1864, and in pursuit of the rebels under General Early until July 14, 1864, when he was severely injured by the fall of his horse, and was granted sick-leave of absence to August 21, 1864.

In October and November, 1864, General Gillmore was president of a board for testing Ames's wrought-iron cannon; and then on a tour of inspection of fortifications from Cairo, Illinois, to Pensacola, Florida, to January 30, 1865, at which time he was assigned to the command of the Department of the South, retaining that until the following November. He was brevetted for gallant and meritorious services, lieutenant-colonel April 11, 1862, in the capture of Fort Pulaski, Georgia; colonel March 30, 1863, at the battle of Somerset, Kentucky; brigadier-general March 13, 1865, in the capture of Fort Wagner, South Carolina; and major-general in the assault on Morris Island, South Carolina, and the bombardment and demolition of Fort Sumter. He resigned his volunteer commission December 5, 1865. He was promoted major of engineers June 1, 1863; lieutenant-colonel January 13, 1874; and colonel February 20, 1883; and was employed after the war closed as assistant to the chief engineer of the Third Division, Engineer Bureau at Washington City, D. C., to November 8, 1866; as member of a special board to conduct experiments in connection with the use of iron in the construction of permanent fortifications, and member of other boards; and was superintending engineer of the fortifications on Staten Island, New York, and engaged on other important engineer duty until he died at Brooklyn, New York, April 7, 1888. General Gillmore had the degree of Master of Arts conferred by Oberlin College, Ohio, 1856. He was the author of a work on the "Siege and Reduction of Fort Pulaski, Georgia, in 1862;" of a "Practical Treatise on Limes, Hydraulic Cements, and Mortars," 1863; and of "Engineer and Artillery Operations against the Defences of Charleston in 1863."

## REAR-ADMIRAL LEWIS M. GOLDSBOROUGH, U.S.N.
(DECEASED).

REAR-ADMIRAL LEWIS M. GOLDSBOROUGH was born in the city of Washington, in February, 1805. As was sometimes done in those days, he was appointed a midshipman when a mere child,—June 18, 1812. Of course, he went to school for some time after, but, by January, 1825, he attained the rank of lieutenant. He was attached to the schooner "Porpoise," of the Mediterranean Squadron, 1827-29. In 1827, while first lieutenant of the "Porpoise," took command of four boats, with thirty-five men and officers, and retook an English brig, the "Comet," which was in possession of two hundred Greek pirates. It was a desperate affair, but successful. There were three killed of the pirates to one killed of the boarding-party. The ward-room steward of the "Porpoise," a mulatto of herculean strength, a volunteer, killed eleven of the pirates with his own hand. Lieutenant John A. Carr, U.S.N., long since dead, killed the chief of the pirates, as well as several of his band. At that time no merchant vessel, unprotected by convoy, could go up the Greek Archipelago; and the pirates once succeeded in capturing an Austrian man-of-war brig. The action of Goldsborough and his little party had a most salutary effect, and they received thanks from several of the Mediterranean powers. After this Lieutenant Goldsborough made a full cruise in the frigate "United States" in the Pacific. He was commissioned commander in September, 1841; executive-officer of the "Ohio," 74, at the siege of Vera Cruz; commanded three hundred officers and men of the "Ohio" at the capture of Tuxpan; commanded the "Levant," in the Mediterranean, 1852-53. He was superintendent of the Naval Academy at Annapolis—having been commissioned captain in 1855—from 1854 to 1857. He commanded the flag-ship "Congress," of the Brazil Squadron, 1859-61. During the joint expedition to the North Carolina waters, in 1862, Flag-Officer Goldsborough commanded the naval force,—being present for duty far in advance of the army. He had seventeen light-draught vessels, which fought the battle of Roanoke Island, against the forts, the troops, and the flotilla, with defences, stationed there. On February 5, 1862, three columns, under the immediate command of Commodore Rowan,—afterwards vice-admiral,—formed for action. On the morning of the 7th the enemy's

vessels, eight in number, were found behind an extensive row of piles and sunken vessels, extending clear across the Sound. The engagement began at 10.30 A.M., and at 4 P.M. the batteries on the island were silenced enough to permit the landing of troops. By midnight over ten thousand troops had disembarked. On the following morning the army did the fighting, and in the afternoon the navy opened a passage through the obstructions, successfully accomplished by dark. On the 10th the remains of the rebel fleet were captured in the Pasquotank River by Commodore Rowan. On March 14, 1862, the town of New Berne, North Carolina, was occupied by a detachment of Flag-Officer Goldsborough's squadron. On May 10, 1862, Goldsborough engaged and silenced the batteries at Sewell's Point, opposite Fortress Monroe, and passed up to Norfolk, which had been evacuated by the rebels. He was commissioned as rear-admiral in July, 1862. At the close of the war he was ordered to command the European Station. He returned home in 1868, and from that time to the date of his death, in February, 1877, was on special duty at Washington.

Rear-Admiral Goldsborough was a man far beyond the usual size, and of a striking appearance in every way. He was a student all his life, and, in addition to his proficiency in professional matters, he was a fairly-good lawyer and an accomplished linguist. He wrote very well, and some of his letters were quite models of composition. He married a daughter of the celebrated William Wirt, and had two children, a son and a daughter, both of whom he survived.

MAJOR GREEN CLAY GOODLOE, U.S.M.C.

MAJOR GREEN CLAY GOODLOE, paymaster of the United States Marine Corps, was born at Castle Union, Madison County, Kentucky, January 31, 1845, on the plantation of his grandfather, Colonel J. Speed Smith, son of General D. S. Goodloe and Sally Clay Smith. Educated in the classics and law at Transylvania University, Lexington, Kentucky. Belongs to a family which has maintained a leading place in Kentucky for generations, by the distinction achieved by its members in civil and military positions. His ancestors were officers in the patriotic army of the Revolution. His great-grandfather, Green Clay, served in the wars of the Revolution and 1812. A noted achievement was marching a force to the relief of General W. H. Harrison, besieged by a superior force of British and Indians, at Fort Meigs, on the Maumee. General Harrison placed him in command of three thousand men. His grandfather, Colonel John Speed Smith, was aid to General W. H. Harrison in the war of 1812; Speaker of Kentucky House of Representatives, and member of Congress. An uncle is the veteran General Cassius M. Clay, captain in the Mexican War; wounded and taken prisoner; pioneer in abolishing slavery; a major-general in the army of the United States, minister to Russia. Another uncle is Major-General Green Clay Smith, United States Volunteers, shot in the knee in cavalry charge at Lebanon, Tennessee; veteran of Mexican War; lieutenant; member of Congress; governor. When the war became imminent, his family threw their powerful influence on the side of the Union, and no one thing did more to hold the State, which wavered, true to her allegiance. Major Goodloe, then a boy of sixteen, actuated by the soldiery traditions of his family, was then a member of the Lexington Chasseurs, which was loyal to the flag. Major Goodloe was a marker in the company, and carried the United States flag the last time it appeared in a parade of the Old Kentucky State Guard. He was ordered by Colonel R. W. Hanson, the colonel in command, to take it to the armory, and this precipitated the dissension which drew a sharp line between the Union and secession portion of the Guard, and broke it up. Major Goodloe, with the rest of his family, became active on the side of the Union, and he, with one other and a brother, were the first to arrive, armed with muskets, at depot, in Lexington, when it seemed inevitable that a fight must be made to secure for the troops the arms which had been sent them by the government. He joined the Fourth Kentucky Cavalry Regiment, which he reached at Wartrace, Tennessee, as it stood in line of battle to receive the attack of the enemy. He was in ten cavalry battles and skirmishes during his service. For his gallant conduct at the battle of Lebanon, Tennessee, General Dumont recommended his promotion, while still on the field, to first lieutenant. When promoted he was assigned to Company I, Twenty-third Kentucky Infantry, and detailed as aide-de-camp on the staff of General Green Clay Smith. He served in this capacity on brigade and division staffs during the campaign through Kentucky and Tennessee, participating in many engagements. At the cavalry battle of Little Harpeth, Forrest's men completely surrounded and cut him off, but he broke through them. Johnson's report says, "Lieutenant Clay Goodloe, of General Smith's staff, in returning from delivering an order, found himself surrounded by rebels, and had to run the gauntlet. After emptying his holster pistols, he laid flat on his horse, relying upon his spurs and his 'Lexington.' They brought him safely home, but he has a bullet-hole through his pants to remind him of the amiable intentions of his Southern brethren respecting himself." In the thorough rout of Morgan's cavalry command, on May 4, 1862, at Lebanon, Tennessee, Surgeon Adams reported, "Clay Goodloe kept in line with Colonel Smith, and was grazed on the third joint of the second finger by a bullet. He attempted to hold poor Piercefield on his horse after he received his fatal shot. He is a gallant and noble boy, yet beardless, but has the courage of a veteran." Every official report contained flattering mention of him.

In September, 1863, appointed cadet at West Point, but resigned in 1865; commissioned second lieutenant, United States Marine Corps April 21, 1869; promoted first lieutenant January 12, 1876; and made paymaster March 17, 1877. Married April 17, 1877, Miss Bettie Beck, daughter of United States Senator James Burnie Beck and Jane Washington Thornton. Mrs. Goodloe, his wife, is a great-great-great-niece of General George Washington, being related on both sides of her mother to the Father of our Country.

## LIEUTENANT-COMMANDER H. H. GORRINGE, U.S.N.
### (DECEASED).

LIEUTENANT-COMMANDER H. H. GORRINGE was a native of the West Indies, but was appointed a master's mate in the U. S. naval service from the State of New York on October 1, 1862. He was sent out to the Mississippi at once, and remained there during the whole of the Civil War. Owing to his courage, seamanship, and devotion to duty he obtained remarkable advancement. Three of his promotions were for gallantry in battle. He was made acting ensign in 1863, promoted to acting master in 1864, and to acting volunteer lieutenant in 1865.

Lieutenant-Commander Gorringe took part in nearly all the important battles of the Mississippi Squadron. He was promoted to be acting volunteer lieutenant-commander July 10, 1865.

In 1867 he commanded the steamer "Memphis," of the Atlantic Squadron, and on December 18, 1868, he was commissioned lieutenant-commander in the regular navy. He was attached to the navy-yard at New York during 1868, and then made a three years' cruise in the sloop-of-war "Portsmouth," of the South Atlantic Squadron, 1869–71. From 1872 to 1876 he was attached to the hydrographic office at Washington, and then commanded the "Gettysburg" (fourth rate), on special service in the Mediterranean, from 1876 to 1879.

In 1880 he was upon leave of absence, and was employed in conveying the Egyptian obelisk, now in Central Park, in New York, from Alexandria, Egypt, to its destination. A steamer, called the "Dessoug," was purchased for this purpose, and the ingenious and seaman-like manner in which he placed the huge monolith securely in her hold, and the safety with which he transported it, secured general admiration and approval.

After this he was engaged in a ship-building operation in Philadelphia, having been granted leave of absence for that purpose. He died in 1883.

Lieutenant-Commander Gorringe suffered much from a wound of the leg, received during the war, which never closed. This, with malarial troubles due to his long and continuous service in the Mississippi, no doubt hastened his death.

## ASSISTANT SECRETARY OF WAR LEWIS A. GRANT.

ASSISTANT SECRETARY OF WAR LEWIS A. GRANT was mustered into the service of the United States September 16, 1861, at St. Albans, Vermont, as major with the field and staff, Fifth Vermont Infantry Volunteers, to serve for three years; was mustered in as lieutenant-colonel, same regiment, to date September 25, 1861; as colonel, same regiment, to date September 16, 1862. The regiment was assigned to the Army of the Potomac, and participated in the advance of that army in the spring of 1862. During his service with the Fifth Vermont Infantry Volunteers, that regiment took part in the following battles: Yorktown, Virginia, April 4 and May 4, 1862; Williamsburg, Virginia, May 5, 1862; Golding's Farm, Virginia, June 28, 1862; Savage Station, Virginia, June 29, 1862; White Oak Swamp, Virginia, June 30, 1862; Crampton's Gap, Maryland, September 14, 1862; Antietam, Maryland, September 17, 1862, and Fredericksburg, Virginia, December 13–14, 1862.

He was honorably discharged as colonel to date May 20, 1864, to enable him to accept an appointment as brigadier-general of volunteers. He was appointed brigadier-general U. S. Volunteers April 27, 1864; accepted appointment May 21, 1864.

He commanded the Second Brigade, Second Division, Sixth Army Corps, from February 21, 1863, to December 29, 1863; from February 2, 1864, to September 29, 1864, and from October 8, 1864, to December 2, 1864; the Second Division, Sixth Corps, from December 2, 1864, to February 11, 1865, the Second Brigade, same division, from February 11, 1865, to February 20, 1865, and from March 7, 1865, to June 28, 1865.

The following is a list of the battles in which he participated as a brigade or division commander: Fredericksburg and Salem Heights, Virginia, May 3 to 5, 1863; Gettysburg, Pennsylvania, July 2 and 3, 1863; Fairfield, Pennsylvania, July 5, 1863; Rappahannock Station, Virginia, November 8, 1863; Mine Run, Virginia, November 27, 1863; Wilderness, Virginia, May 5 to 7, 1864; Spottsylvania Court-House, Virginia, May 8 to 21, 1864; Cold Harbor, Virginia, June 1 to 12, 1864; siege of Petersburg, Virginia, June 18 to July 10, 1864; Charlestown, Virginia, August 21, 1864; Gilbert's Crossing, Virginia, September 13, 1864; siege of Petersburg, Virginia, December, 1864, to April, 1865; assault on Petersburg, Virginia, April 2, 1865; Sailor's Creek, April 6, 1865.

At the close of the war General Grant was honored with the commission of brevet major-general U. S. Volunteers, to date from October 19, 1864, "for gallant and meritorious services in the present campaign before Richmond, Virginia, and in the Shenandoah Valley;" and was honorably discharged the service August 24, 1865. Under the provisions of the act of Congress approved June 3, 1884, and the acts amendatory thereof, he is considered as commissioned to the grade of major Fifth Vermont Volunteers, to take effect from September 7, 1861, to fill an original vacancy.

He was recommended August 22, 1866, by General U. S. Grant, commanding the army of the United States, for appointment as a field-officer in the regular army; was appointed August 29, 1866, lieutenant-colonel Thirty-sixth Regiment U. S. Infantry, to date from July 28, 1866, and declined the appointment November 6, 1866.

General Grant's field services were with or in command of the celebrated Vermont brigade whose fighting qualities were so well known in the Army of the Potomac, and whose soldierly dependence was of such character that it was transferred, with the regular division of the Army of the Potomac, in August, 1863, to New York City, to assist in quelling the riots occasioned there by the draft for men. As soon as this duty was completed, the troops were, in the fall of the same year, retransferred to the field with the Army of the Potomac.

General Grant was appointed Assistant Secretary of War in 1890, which office he now holds.

## GENERAL ULYSSES S. GRANT, U.S.A. (DECEASED).

GENERAL ULYSSES S. GRANT was born at Point Pleasant, Clermont County, Ohio, April 27, 1822, and graduated at the Military Academy July 1, 1843. He was promoted brevet second lieutenant of the Fourth Infantry the same day, and second lieutenant Fourth Infantry September 30, 1845. He served first at Jefferson Barracks, and then on frontier duty at Natchitoches (Camp Salubrity) in 1844-45, and then took part in the military occupation of Texas and the war with Mexico, being engaged in the battles of Palo Alto, Resaca de la Palma, Monterey, siege of Vera Cruz, battle of Cerro Gordo, capture of San Antonio, battle of Churubusco, battle of Molino del Rey, storming of Chapultepec, and assault and capture of the City of Mexico. He was regimental quartermaster of the Fourth Infantry from April 1, 1847, to July 23, 1848, and again from September 11, 1849, to September 30, 1853.

He moved with his regiment to the Pacific coast in 1852, and was at several different stations. He was promoted captain August 5, 1853, but resigned July 31, 1854.

Upon leaving the army Captain Grant retired to private life, and engaged in farming near St. Louis, Missouri. Then he became a real estate agent at St. Louis until 1860, and subsequently a merchant at Galena, Ohio, where he resided at the breaking out of the war of the Rebellion.

Entering the volunteer service he was in command of a company in April and May, and assisting in organizing and mustering volunteers into service until June 17, 1861, when he was appointed colonel of the Twenty-first Illinois Infantry. His first active service was to march on Quincy, Illinois, and then guarding the Hannibal and St. Joe Railroad. He was placed in command, first at Ironton, then at Jefferson City, and finally of the District of Southwestern Missouri, with headquarters at Cape Girardeau. This command was subsequently extended to embrace Southern Illinois and Western Kentucky. He had, in the mean time, been appointed brigadier-general of volunteers May 17, 1861.

General Grant commenced his operations by first seizing Paducah, Kentucky; then Belmont, and then invested and captured Fort Donelson, with fourteen thousand six hundred and twenty-three prisoners, and much material of war. This being the first real Union success of the war placed General Grant before the people of the country at large as a rising soldier; but many old officers who had known him in the regular service doubted his ability, and attributed his success on this occasion to "luck." He was, however, duly recognized, and the appointment of major-general of volunteers was conferred upon him, to date from February 16, 1862.

It would be impossible, in this limited sketch, to enumerate the campaigns, battles, and actions in which this illustrious general participated. He followed up his movements to Shiloh, then was placed in command of the District of West Tennessee, and was in immediate command of the right wing of General Halleck's army, and directed the operations about Corinth, the Hatchie, and Iuka. He was in command of the Army of the Mississippi, in the Vicksburg campaign, in all its various manœuvres, until he again electrified the country by the capture of the city of Vicksburg, July 4, 1863, with stores and garrison of thirty-one thousand five hundred men. For this brilliant affair he was made major-general of the U. S. Army.

General Grant was, on the 16th of October, 1863, placed in command of the Military Division of the Mississippi, including the Armies of the Ohio, Cumberland, and Tennessee, and continued his operations up to the battle of Chattanooga, for which he received the thanks of Congress December 17, 1863, and a gold medal.

On March 17, 1864, he was placed in command as general-in-chief of the armies of the United States, and was called to the East to supervise the operations of the Army of the Potomac, and commenced in the May following that celebrated campaign on the line which terminated on the 9th of April, 1865, in the surrender of the Army of Northern Virginia, under General Robert E. Lee.

He was by act of Congress made general of the U. S. Army July 25, 1866; but resigned this commission on March 4, 1869, having been elected President of the United States, and on that day was inaugurated as such. After holding this office for eight years, General Grant retired to private life, and died at Mt. McGregor, near Saratoga, N.Y., July 23, 1885.

BRIGADIER-GENERAL ADOLPHUS W. GREELY,
U.S.A.

BRIGADIER-GENERAL ADOLPHUS W. GREELY (Chief Signal-officer) was born in Massachusetts. He entered the volunteer service in the early part of the war of the Rebellion, as private of Company B, Nineteenth Massachusetts Infantry, July 26, 1861. He was afterwards promoted corporal and first sergeant of the same company, and served to March 18, 1863, in the field with the Army of the Potomac, participating in the Peninsula campaign, and was engaged at the siege of Yorktown, action of West Point, battles of Fair Oaks, Peach Orchard, Savage Station, White Oak Swamp, where he was wounded, and the battle of Malvern Hill, Virginia, in 1862. He participated in the Maryland campaign, and was engaged in the battle of Antietam, where he was again wounded. He also participated in the Rappahannock campaign, and was engaged at the battle of Fredericksburg, Virginia, in 1862.

On the 18th of March, 1863, he was appointed second lieutenant of the Eighty-first United States Colored Infantry, promoted first lieutenant April 26, 1864, and captain April 4, 1865. With this regiment Lieutenant Greely served in the field with the Army of the Southwest, and was engaged in the siege of Port Hudson, Louisiana. At the close of the war he was ordered on recruiting duty, and was honorably mustered out of the volunteer service March 22, 1867, having been appointed second lieutenant of the Thirty-sixth United States Infantry March 7, 1867. On the consolidation of regiments, in 1869, Lieutenant Greely was unassigned, but on the 14th of July, of that year, he was assigned to the Fifth Cavalry. He was brevetted major of volunteers for faithful and meritorious services during the war.

After joining the Fifth Cavalry he was on frontier duty in the West to 1869; on staff duty at Omaha to 1871; was assigned to duty in the office of the chief signal-officer of the army, where he served until June, 1881, and was employed as a station inspector, as superintendent of the construction of military telegraph lines in Texas, and as a general assistant in the Washington office.

He was promoted first lieutenant May 27, 1873, and captain June 11, 1886.

He was assigned to the command of the Arctic expedition of 1880, but the order was subsequently revoked, because of an unfavorable report made by a board of naval officers upon the vessel which had been selected for the service. The Lady Franklin Bay expedition was then organized during the spring and summer of 1881, and in July he sailed from St. John's, Newfoundland, in command, with the intention of remaining absent for two years. The object of the expedition was to establish a supply and meteorological station at Lady Franklin Bay and make explorations northward from that place. Lieutenant Greely was for six years a student of Arctic explorations, and his experiences of twelve years in the signal service in the army, particularly in compiling observations and forecasting the daily weather reports, were such as to qualify him for the scientific part of the work; the results of his researches have added valuable information to the subject of Arctic explorations, although his expedition met with the misfortune of being shipwrecked, and the entire party reduced to a state of starvation before the remnants of it were discovered by a naval expedition sent to their relief.

On the 3d of March, 1887, Captain Greely was appointed brigadier-general and chief signal-officer, and since that time has been on duty at Washington, D. C.

## COMMANDER JAMES G. GREEN, U.S.N.

COMMANDER JAMES G. GREEN was a native of Massachusetts, and entered the navy as master's mate May 18, 1861. He served in the U. S. S. "Mississippi" until November 27, 1862,—passing the forts at New Orleans.

He was promoted to acting ensign November 27, 1862, and transferred to U. S. S. "Katahdin," and served in that vessel on the blockade off Galveston until December, 1863.

He was ordered to U. S. S. "Wyalusing" in 1864, and served in the sounds of North Carolina and in the fight with the ram "Albemarle."

Promoted to acting master August 11, 1864, and was ordered to command the torpedo tug "Belle," serving on that vessel in the North Carolina sounds until the close of the war, being present at the final capture of Plymouth. Afterwards he was attached to the "New Hampshire," "Don," "Osceola," "Vermont," and "Constellation."

Having been transferred to the regular service, as master, March 12, 1868, he served on the Asiatic Station, in the "Aroostook" and "Ashuelot," from 1868 to 1871.

On December 18, 1868, he was promoted to lieutenant, and to lieutenant-commander July 3, 1870.

He was attached to the receiving-ship "Ohio" from 1871 to 1873, and to the Asiatic Station from 1873 to 1876.

While attached to the navy-yard at Norfolk he was sent to recover the dead washed ashore from the U. S. S.

"Huron," and, later, transferred them to the Naval Cemetery, Annapolis.

He was attached to the "Palos," Asiatic Station, 1878 to 1881.

At the hydrographic office, Washington, D. C., from 1881 to 1883.

He was on the "Galena" from 1883 to 1886; and promoted to commander March 6, 1887.

He commanded the "Alert" from 1888 to 1889, and the "Adams" in 1890.

He was light-house inspector, Sixth District, from 1890 to 1892.

CAPTAIN GEORGE GORDON GREENOUGH, U.S.A.

CAPTAIN GEORGE GORDON GREENOUGH (Fourth Artillery) comes of one of the oldest Boston families, and is descended from the ducal family of the Scottish clan Gordon. In one line he descends from the English Colonial Governor Treat, of Connecticut. His grand-uncle, Major Samuel Treat, was killed at Fort Mifflin, in the Revolutionary War. From his mother he is connected with Judge Cushing, of the U. S. Supreme Court, and with General Lincoln, of Revolutionary fame, and of the Burrs, of Massachusetts, of which Aaron Burr was a member.

Captain Greenough was born at Washington, D. C., December 8, 1844, and at eleven years old was placed at a French school in Paris, where he received his early education. In his sixteenth year he returned home and entered the West Point Military Academy June 1, 1861.

During his furlough year he had a great desire to see real active service with the army, which was strengthened by the invasion of the Confederates north of the Potomac, and hastening to the front he was placed upon the staff of Major-General W. H. French, commanding the Third Army Corps, in the extreme advance, and was sent forward with Colonel Julius Hayden, inspector-general Third Army Corps, to the front line of skirmishing on a tour of observation at Falling Waters, Virginia, on the slope near the river, where they were under a heavy artillery fire from the opposite bank. He remained with the army on General French's staff as long as his furlough permitted.

General French in his report of the actions of Wapping Height and Manassas Gap, July 23, 1863, says, "I would also mention Cadet Greenough acting aide-de-camp, who conveyed my orders with precision, and exhibited great coolness under fire."

Cadet Greenough graduated from the U. S. Military Academy June, 1865; was commissioned second lieutenant on the 23d in the Twelfth Infantry, his commission as first lieutenant is dated the 23d of June, 1865, and he was appointed acting regimental adjutant of the Twelfth at Washington, 1865-66. In September, 1866, he was transferred to the Twenty-first Infantry and was stationed at Fredericksburg, Virginia, in command of Company G. Lieutenant Greenough left the post July, 1868, to report for duty as instructor at West Point.

On the 15th of December, 1870, Lieutenant Greenough was assigned to the Fourth Artillery, and early in 1873 he joined Battery G at Black Point, California, with which he served in the field through the Modoc war. During the time the troops were in the Black Lava, near the Indians, Lieutenant Greenough went to his battalion commander, Colonel Mendenhall, and offered to take Battery G into the Black Lava at night, and attack the Indian camp early in the morning; his idea was that the remainder of the troops should be moved up in readiness to attack from different points as soon as the firing began. Later he volunteered to carry despatches alone, or with an escort of two men, through the Lava Beds; he was not permitted to carry out either of these projects on account of the extreme danger.

At the close of the Modoc war he was detailed with Captain Hasbrook to convey the Modoc prisoners to Camp McPherson, Nevada, in October, 1873. Subsequently he commanded Battery K, Fourth Artillery, in the Powder River winter campaign against the Sioux and Cheyenne Indians with General Crook.

On the 5th of September, 1875, he started for the field in the campaign against the Shoshones, his platoon with two field-pieces, as artillery, the rest as cavalry, and rendezvoused in Eastern Nevada, stopped the rising without fighting, and returned to the Presidio on the 4th of October.

He was detailed May 7, 1877, as professor of military science at the University of California, at Berkeley. In 1879 he went to Fort Canby. Then he went to Fort Monroe, Virginia, until May 1, 1882, and then went to Fort Adams.

On December 1, 1883, he was commissioned captain Fourth Artillery, and stationed at Fort Adams, Rhode Island, and Fort Warren, Massachusetts, from whence he joined the head-quarters of his regiment at Fort McPherson, Georgia, May 29, 1889.

Captain Greenough has made several important inventions, among which may be mentioned a reloading apparatus for reloading shells; a field gun-carriage, and a very complete range-finder for sea-coast defences, by which several vessels may be followed at once without confusion or delay. He has written on several important professional questions.

## REAR-ADMIRAL JAMES A. GREER, U.S.N.

REAR-ADMIRAL JAMES A. GREER was born in Ohio February 28, 1833, and appointed midshipman from that State January 10, 1848. He served in the "Saratoga" and "Saranac" of the Home Squadron up to 1850; sloop-of-war "St. Mary's," Pacific Squadron, 1850-52; frigate "Columbia," Home Squadron, 1853. Then went to the U. S. Naval Academy for the usual course of study. Passed midshipman June 13, 1854; served in the razee "Independence," in the Pacific, 1854-57; promoted to master September 15, 1855; commissioned as lieutenant September 16, 1855. After serving at the navy-yard at Norfolk made the Paraguay Expedition in the "Southern Star," 1858-59; steamers "Sumter" and "San Jacinto," coast of Africa, 1859-61; on return, assisted in the removal of Mason and Slidell from the English mail-steamer "Trent;" lieutenant-commander July 16, 1862; sloop "St. Louis," special service, 1862-63; Mississippi Squadron, 1863-65; commanded steamers "Carondelet" and "Benton," and a division of Admiral Porter's fleet; was at the passage of Vicksburg April 16, 1863; fought the batteries of Grand Gulf for five hours April 29, 1863,—an incident of this action was the killing and wounding of twenty-two persons on board the "Benton" by one projectile; in the Red River Expedition in May, 1863; was engaged in the combined attack on Vicksburg May 22, 1863, and was almost constantly under fire during the forty-five days of the siege of Vicksburg. Lieutenant Greer was engaged in the Red River Expedition during March and April, 1864, and frequently engaged with small bodies of Confederate troops and guerillas. In August and September, 1864, he was sent to Cincinnati, Ohio, to inquire into and correct abuses which existed at the Naval Recruiting Station at that place. He was then in command of the naval station at Mound City, Illinois, being transferred thence to the command of the flag-ship "Black Hawk." During this time he was charged by Admiral Lee with the selecting, purchasing, and contracting for the conversion into gun-boats of ten river steamers; also had charge of the convoying of army transports from Johnsonville up the Tennessee River.

During a portion of 1865 and 1866 was stationed at the Naval Academy, Annapolis, and commissioned as commander in July of the latter year. Commanded steamer "Mohongo," North Pacific Squadron, 1866-67. During his command of "Mohongo," he remained four months at Acapulco, Mexico, to protect American interests, which were endangered by the convulsion upon the fall of Maximilian; the State Department commended him for his course there.

He commanded the "Tuscarora," North Pacific Squadron, 1868; on ordnance duty, Philadelphia Navy-Yard, 1868-69; Naval Academy, 1869-73. In 1873 commanded purchased steamer "Tigress" on the "Polaris" Relief Expedition. In one month after sailing from New York found the wreck of "Polaris" at Littleton Island, latitude 78° 23', North Greenland. Cruised in search of the people, who had left in their boats, without success, in Baffin's Bay and Davis's Straits, until October 8, when it was deemed expedient to return.

He was upon the Board of Inspection in 1874-75; commanding "Lackawanna," Pacific Station, 1875-77; commissioned captain April 26, 1876; commanding training frigate "Constitution," 1877. In 1878 commanded sloop "Constellation," which took exhibits to France for the Paris Exposition; commanded steamer "Hartford," South Atlantic, in 1879; Board of Inspection, 1880-82; navy-yard, Washington, 1882-84; president of Naval Examining and Retiring Boards, 1885-87; commissioned as commodore, May 19, 1886; as acting rear-admiral, commanded the European Station, 1887-89; president of Board on Organization, Tactics, and Drills, 1889; president of Examining and Retiring Boards, 1890; member of the Board of Visitors of the Naval Academy, 1891; chairman of the Light-House Board, and now serving as such; April 3, 1892, commissioned as rear-admiral.

MAJOR STEPHEN W. GROESBECK, U.S.A.

MAJOR STEPHEN W. GROESBECK (Sixth Infantry) was born in Albany, New York, November 26, 1840. At the breaking out of the Rebellion he was teaching school in Iowa. Encouraged by his uncle, Stephen Walley, of Williamstown, Massachusetts, he had prepared himself to enter Williams College, but, like many young men of the period, he chose reluctantly to forego the advantages of school to enter the service. He enlisted as a private in the Fourth Iowa Cavalry on October 28, 1861; was mustered in as company quartermaster-sergeant, and in October, 1862, promoted to second lieutenant. On the 7th day of the following month he bore a conspicuous and most honorable part in the cavalry engagement at Marianna, Arkansas, and later in the same day received in a skirmish, among other wounds, a gun-shot wound in the left foot, the ball so lodging as to defeat the efforts of the surgeons to locate and remove it. Being wholly disabled he resigned his commission April 4, 1863. In justice to him the War Department, in subsequent orders, corrected his record to read "honorably mustered out April 4, 1863." A year later, in April, 1864, the ball was successfully removed at Albany, New York. While disabled, he took a course of instruction at a commercial school; but, with the restoration of a fair use of his foot, he entered Colonel Taggart's military school in Philadelphia,—a school designed to fit young men for commissions in the volunteer forces. Experience gained with troops in the field gave him an advantage at this school, and, stimulated by the offer of a commission in the Veteran Reserve Corps, he quickly accomplished the course of instruction, graduating ahead of students who had preceded him from six to eighteen months. He accepted a commission as second lieutenant in the Veteran Reserve Corps in November, 1864.

In January, 1866, he was assigned to duty in the Bureau of Refugees, Freedmen, and Abandoned Lands, at Nashville. Here he served a short time as aide-de-camp on the staff of Brigadier-General Clinton B. Fisk, commanding the District of Tennessee; and, later, as acting assistant adjutant-general to the assistant commissioner of the Bureau of Refugees, Freedmen, and Abandoned Lands until March, 1868. While stationed in Nashville he read law with D. W. Peabody, of the law-firm of Bradley & Peabody, with a view to better equip himself for the important and often very delicate duties devolving upon officers serving in the South during the reconstruction period; and of ultimately making the law his profession. He served as a volunteer until mustered out in January, 1867, to accept a commission in the regular establishment.

By consolidation of the Forty-second Infantry, V.R.C., with the Sixth Infantry, he became an officer of the latter regiment. He was promoted to first lieutenant in 1875, and was soon after appointed adjutant of his regiment, and served as such for five years. During the greater part of the years 1881-82 he served as acting judge-advocate of the Department of the Missouri, and for a short time in 1882 as instructor of law at the Fort Leavenworth School of Application. In 1883 he was again appointed adjutant of his regiment, serving in that capacity for three years, when he resigned the office to accept that of acting judge-advocate of the Department of Dakota; he served in this position from November 1, 1886, to April 28, 1891. He was promoted captain in July, 1889.

He is a member of the bar. His early reading in the law led to his special availability as a judge advocate of courts-martial, and as acting judge-advocate of military departments, in which fields he has established an enviable reputation for judicial fairness, and for able and accurate work, which led to his appointment as major and judge-advocate U. S. Army, at the death of Lieutenant-Colonel Curtis, on February 12, 1892.

An eye witness of the fight at Marianna expresses himself as follows:

"Lieutenant Stephen W. Groesbeck placed himself at the head of deponent's company, and appealed to them to follow him, and did lead it in a full charge in column upon the left of the enemy's line, broke the line, and, pursuing the advantages so gained, had put the whole force of the enemy to flight before the main command could come up to participate in the skirmish.

"Considering the fact that Lieutenant Groesbeck was compelled to assume command under fire, the inspiration his manner gave to the men of deponent's company, and the vigor and success of the charge, . . . he deems that this (then young) officer's conduct on that day was of unusual gallantry and merit."

## CAPTAIN FRANK C. GRUGAN, U.S.A.

CAPTAIN FRANK C. GRUGAN (Second Artillery) was born in Pennsylvania April 4, 1842, and early in the war of the Rebellion entered the volunteer service as a private in an independent company of heavy artillery, June 4, 1861, and served at Fort Delaware to August 5, 1861. He was appointed second lieutenant of the One Hundred and Fourteenth Pennsylvania Infantry August 15, 1862, and promoted first lieutenant September 1, 1863, serving in the campaigns of the Army of the Potomac, and engaged in the battles of Fredericksburg, Chancellorsville, action of Orange Grove, operations at Mine Run, actions of Auburn, Brandy Station, Kelly's Ford, battles of the Wilderness, Spottsylvania, North Anna, Cold Harbor, siege and capture of Petersburg, battle of Hatcher's Run, and the campaign ending in the surrender of General R. E. Lee April 9, 1865.

Lieutenant Grugan was appointed first lieutenant of the Third Pennsylvania Cavalry December 19, 1864, and was transferred to the Fifth Pennsylvania Cavalry May 8, 1865, from which he was honorably mustered out August 7, 1865. He then entered the regular service as a private of the general service August 18, 1865, and served first at Richmond, Virginia, and then was placed on duty in the War Department to May, 1866, having been appointed second lieutenant of the Second Cavalry April 25, 1866, and brevetted first lieutenant for "gallant and meritorious services at the battle of Hatcher's Run, Virginia," and captain for "gallant and meritorious services during the war."

Captain Grugan joined the Second Cavalry on the Plains, and served at Forts Laramie and Casper, Wyoming, and in the field during 1866-67; then at Camp Stambaugh, Wyoming; Fort Ellis, Montana; and in the field from 1870 to 1873. He was then detailed on signal duty, under the chief signal-officer of the army, from 1873 to 1879, when he was ordered to the Artillery School at Fort Monroe, Virginia, he having been transferred to the Second Artillery, April 11, 1879, as first lieutenant, he having reached that rank in the cavalry November 1, 1867.

After remaining at Fort Monroe until 1882, he was placed on special duty with the chief signal-officer of the army from June to October of the same year, when he was relieved, and served with a light battery at Washington City until March, 1885. He was promoted captain March 18, 1885, and commanded Battery B, Second Artillery, at Fort Barrancas, Florida, to March, 1889. At this time he was transferred to Light Battery A, and served with it at Little Rock Barracks, Arkansas, and Fort Riley, Kansas, to July, 1891.

Upon being relieved from light battery duty he was ordered to Fort Adams, Rhode Island, in command of Battery H, and is at the present time on duty at that station.

Captain Grugan filled the position of aide and acting assistant adjutant-general of the First Brigade, First Division, Third Army Corps, in the Army of the Potomac, to April, 1864. He was post adjutant at the head-quarters of the Army of the Potomac to December, 1864. He was adjutant of the Third Pennsylvania Cavalry to May, 1865, and regimental quartermaster of the Second Cavalry from November, 1867, to July, 1870.

### COMMODORE JOHN GUEST, U.S.N. (DECEASED).

COMMODORE JOHN GUEST was a native of Missouri, but was appointed midshipman from Arkansas in December, 1837. For several years he served in the West India Squadron, in the "Levant," "Constellation," "Boston," and "Warren." Having completed his sea-service as midshipman, he was ordered to the naval school, then at the Naval Asylum, at Philadelphia, and passed in June, 1843. For some time after he served in the "Poinsett," in the survey of Tampa Bay; and was then attached to the frigate "Congress," of the Pacific Squadron, for three years. This was during the Mexican War, and Commodore Guest took part in the battle of San Gabriel, January, 1848, and the battle at Mesa, California, January 9, 1848.

He was commissioned as lieutenant in December, 1850, when he served in the sloop-of-war "Plymouth," and the steam-frigate "Susquehanna," and was in the Japan Expedition, and at the first landing in that country, under Commodore Matthew C. Perry. During subsequent service in the East India Squadron, from 1851 to 1855, he boarded the Chinese man-of-war, "Sir H. Compton," at Shanghai, with a cutter from the "Plymouth," and liberated a pilot-boat's crew, who were under the protection of our flag. In April, 1854, was second in command of the "Plymouth," Captain John Kelley, in a severe and victorious action at Shanghai, to prevent aggression upon foreign residents.

Upon his return he was on duty at Washington, and then served in the "Niagara," which laid the first cable across the Atlantic, 1857-58. During 1859 he was on rendezvous duty in Philadelphia.

In 1860 he was again ordered to the frigate "Niagara," employed in taking home the first Japanese embassy which visited our country.

When the troublous times of 1861 came, Lieutenant Guest for some time commanded the "Niagara," of the West Gulf Blockading Squadron. During this period, in command of the boats of "Niagara," he cut out the schooner "Aid," which was under the protection of the guns of Fort Morgan, at the entrance to Mobile Bay.

In 1862 he was in command of the "Owasco," and in her participated in the passage of the forts below New Orleans, the capture of that city and the battles on the Mississippi River up to and including Vicksburg, 1862.

He was made commander in July, 1862, and served in the "Owasco" at the fight and capture of the Galveston forts.

In 1863 he was in command of monitor "Sangamon," of the South Atlantic Squadron. The "Sangamon" was the first United States vessel to be fitted with a spar torpedo, the invention of her commander. During 1864 he commanded "Galatea," on convoy duty in the West Indies. In the latter part of that year, and 1865, he commanded "Iosco," at both attacks upon Fort Fisher. He was commissioned captain in 1866, and commodore in December, 1872, when he became senior officer of the Board of Inspection, and continuing as such until 1876.

He became commandant of the navy-yard, Portsmouth, New Hampshire, in 1877, and died there, while still in command, January, 1879.

Commodore Guest was one of the most active and daring officers of the navy, and was repeatedly commended by commanders of squadrons on that account. At Fort Fisher the "Iosco's" fire twice cut away the flag-staff of the Mound Battery.

## LIEUTENANT-COLONEL PETER C. HAINS, U.S.A.

LIEUTENANT - COLONEL PETER C. HAINS (Corps of Engineers) was born in Philadelphia, Pennsylvania, July 6, 1840. He was graduated from the U. S. Military Academy in the Class of June, 1861, and appointed a first lieutenant in the Second Regiment of Artillery. Immediately on graduating he repaired, with other members of his class, to Washington, and was assigned to the drilling of volunteer troops, at that time assembling at the capital.

As an artillery officer he was engaged in the first battle of Bull Run, in the siege of Yorktown, in the battles of Williamsburg, Hanover Court-House, and Malvern Hill (July 1).

In July, 1862, he was transferred to the Corps of Topographical Engineers, but continued to serve with the artillery. In the second battle of Malvern Hill his battery commander, the gallant Captain Benson, was mortally wounded, and the command devolved on him. He continued in the command of the battery, being engaged in the battles of South Mountain and Antietam, as well as in several skirmishes prior and subsequent to those battles, until the latter part of September, 1862, when he was assigned as assistant topographical engineer at the head-quarters Army of the Potomac.

When the Army of the Potomac was organized into three grand divisions, he was assigned as chief topographical engineer of the Centre Grand Division, Major-General Hooker commanding, participating in the battle of Fredericksburg, Virginia, December 13, 1862, and continued with the Army of the Potomac until March, 1863, when he was transferred to the Army of the Tennessee, at that time about to begin the turning movement that resulted in the capture of Vicksburg, Mississippi.

He was assigned to duty as chief engineer of the Thirteenth Army Corps, and participated in the battles of Port Gibson, Champion Hills, Black River Bridge, the two assaults on Vicksburg, and conducted, throughout the entire siege, the operations in front of the Thirteenth Army Corps. After the surrender, he accompanied Sherman's army in its operations against Johnston, which resulted in the capture of Jackson, Mississippi.

In August, 1863, he was assigned to the duty of constructing an intrenched camp at Natchez, Mississippi, and remained there until April, 1864, when he was transferred to General Banks's army, at that time returning from the Red River campaign. He joined Banks's army at the mouth of the Red River, and in July, 1854, after the army had returned to New Orleans, he was assigned to duty as chief engineer of the Department of the Gulf.

Early in 1865 he was offered the command of a regiment of volunteers from New Jersey, the State from which he was appointed, but, owing to the scarcity of engineer officers at that time, was not allowed by the War Department to accept it. Subsequently—in June, 1865—he was appointed by Governor Parker, of New Jersey, colonel of the Tenth New Jersey Volunteers, but, as the war was about closed, he was not mustered into the volunteer service.

Lieutenant-Colonel Hains received the brevet of captain for "gallant and meritorious services in the battle of Hanover Court-House," of major for "gallant and meritorious services in the siege of Vicksburg," and of lieutenant-colonel for "gallant and meritorious services during the war."

Since the war Lieutenant-Colonel Hains has been engaged on various works of a civil and military nature. For three years he was in command of the Engineer Post of Jefferson Barracks, Missouri. Subsequent to that he served as engineer of the Fifth and Sixth Light-House Districts, and as engineer secretary of the Light-House Board.

In 1882 he was assigned to the charge of the reclamation of the Potomac Flats at Washington, D. C., and continued in charge till November, 1891, when that work was well advanced towards completion.

He constructed the new bridge on the piers of the old aqueduct at Georgetown, D. C.; a bridge across the Anacostia at the foot of Pennsylvania Avenue; a large iron pier at Fort Monroe, Virginia, and a bridge across Mill Creek.

Besides having served as a member of various boards of engineers, he had charge of the improvement of a number of rivers and creeks in the States of Virginia and Maryland, as well as the defensive works of Hampton Roads and the capital.

The present station of Lieutenant-Colonel Hains is Portland, Maine, where he has charge of all river and harbor works of improvement and the military works of defence of the States of Maine and New Hampshire.

MAJOR-GENERAL HENRY WAGER HALLECK, U.S.A.
(DECEASED).

MAJOR-GENERAL HENRY WAGER HALLECK was born at Waterville, Oneida County, New York, January 15, 1815. After studying a short time at Union College, he, in 1835, entered the West Point Military Academy, and graduated in 1839, when he was promoted to the army as second lieutenant in the corps of engineers, being at the same time appointed assistant professor of engineering at the Academy. In the following year he was made an assistant to the board of engineers at Washington, D. C., and from 1841 to 1844 was employed in connection with the fortifications of New York harbor.

In 1845, Lieutenant Halleck was sent by the government to examine the principal military establishments of Europe, and during his absence he was promoted to the rank of first lieutenant. After his return, he, in the winter of 1845-46, delivered at the Lowell Institute, Boston, a course of twelve lectures on the science of war, published in 1846, under the title of "Elements of Military Art and Science," and republished with additions, in 1861.

On the outbreak of the Mexican War, Lieutenant Halleck, in 1846, as military engineer, accompanied the expedition to California and the Pacific coast, where he distinguished himself not only as an engineer, but by his administrative skill as secretary of state, and by his presence of mind and bravery in several skirmishes with the enemy. In 1847, he was brevetted to the rank of captain. He continued for several years to act on the staff of General Riley, in California, holding at the same time the office of Secretary of State of the Province; and he took a leading part in framing the State Constitution of California, on its being admitted into the Union.

In 1852 he was appointed inspector and engineer of light-houses, and in 1853 was promoted captain of engineers. He, however, in 1854, resigned his commission in the army, in order to devote his chief attention to the practice of law, which he had already, for some time, carried on; and so great was his success in his profession that the firm of which he was senior partner soon obtained one of the largest legal businesses in the State. He was also, from 1850, a director of the New Almaden Quicksilver Mine, and in 1855 he became president of the Pacific and Atlantic Railroad, from San Francisco to San José.

At the outbreak of the Civil War, he was, in August, 1861, appointed major-general of the United States Army, and in the following November was appointed commander of the Western Department, where he conducted the campaign against the Confederates, which caused the evacuation of the strongly-fortified city of Corinth. In July, 1862, he was appointed general-in-chief of the armies of the United States,—a position he held until March, 1864, when he was succeeded by General Grant, and was appointed chief of the staff.

In April, 1865, General Halleck held the command of the Military Division of the James, and in August of the same year, of the Military Division of the Pacific, which he retained until March, 1869, when he was transferred to that of the South,—a position he held until his death, at Louisville, Kentucky, January 9, 1872.

Besides his work on the "Science of War," General Halleck was the author of "Bitumen: Its Varieties, Properties, and Uses," 1841; "The Mining Laws of Spain and Mexico," 1859; a translation of De Fooz, "On the Law of Mines," with an introduction, 1860; "International Law," 1861; a translation of Jomini's "Life of Napoleon," 1864; and a "Treatise on International Law and the Laws of War, prepared for the use of Schools and Colleges," 1866.

He was appointed professor of engineering in the Lawrence Scientific School of Harvard University, Massachusetts, September 28, 1848, which he declined. The degree of A.M. was conferred upon him by Union College, New York, in 1843, and that of LL.D. in 1862.

## MAJOR-GENERAL WINFIELD S. HANCOCK, U.S.A.
### (DECEASED).

MAJOR-GENERAL WINFIELD S. HANCOCK was born in Pennsylvania, and graduated from the U. S. Military Academy July 1, 1844. He was assigned to the Sixth Infantry as brevet second lieutenant July 1, 1844, and served on frontier duty at Fort Towson, Indian Territory, 1844-45, and at Fort Washington, Indian Territory, 1845-47. Promoted second lieutenant Sixth Infantry July 1, 1846. He participated in the war with Mexico, 1847-48, being engaged with the defence of convoy at the National Bridge August 12, 1847; the skirmish at Place del Rio August 15, 1847; the capture of San Antonio August 20, 1847; the battle of Churubusco August 20, 1847; the battle of Molino del Rey September 8, 1847, and the assault and capture of the City of Mexico September 13-14, 1847.

He was brevetted first lieutenant August 20, 1847, for gallant and meritorious conduct in the battles of Contreras and Churubusco, Mexico. He was promoted first lieutenant Sixth Infantry January 27, 1853, and from June 19 to November 27, 1855, he was on duty at headquarters Department of the West. He was appointed captain and assistant quartermaster November 7, 1855, and was with troops at Fort Leavenworth, Kansas, quelling the Kansas disturbances in 1857; was with the head-quarters of the Utah reinforcements in 1858, and with the Sixth Infantry on the march from Fort Bridger, Utah, to California, the same year.

He was appointed brigadier-general of volunteers September 23, 1861, and served during the war of the Rebellion, participating in the defence of Washington, D. C., and in the Virginia Peninsula campaign, Army of the Potomac; being engaged in the siege of Yorktown; in the battles of Williamsburg, Chickahominy, Golding's Farm, Savage Station, and White Oak Swamp. He conducted the retreat to Harrison's Landing July 1-4, and the movement to Centreville, Virginia, August to September, 1862. Was in the Maryland campaign, Army of the Potomac, being engaged in the battles of Crampton's Pass, South Mountain, and Antietam. He conducted the reconnoissances from Harper's Ferry to Charleston, Virginia, October 10-11, and the march to Falmouth, Virginia, October to November, 1862.

He was appointed major-general of U. S. Volunteers November 29, 1862. During the Rappahannock campaign he was engaged in the battles of Fredericksburg and Chancellorsville, and in the Pennsylvania campaign was in command of Second Corps of the Army of the Potomac, being engaged in the battle of Gettysburg, where he was severely wounded in the repulse of Longstreet's attack upon the left centre, which he commanded.

The thanks of Congress were tendered him May 30, 1866, "for his gallant, meritorious, and conspicuous share in the great and decisive victory."

He was promoted major and quartermaster U. S. Army November 30, 1863. Commanded and recruited Second Army Corps, January to March, 1864, and participated in the Richmond campaign, commanding Second Corps of the Army of the Potomac, being engaged in the battles of the Wilderness, Spottsylvania, North Anna, Tolopotomy, Cold Harbor, and operations in its vicinity; and the battle before Petersburg June 16-18, 1864.

During the operations in the vicinity of Petersburg, he was in command of the Second Corps Army of the Potomac, and engaged in the battles of Deep Bottom, Ream's Station, Boydton Plank Road, and the siege of Petersburg, Virginia, June 15 to Nov. 26, 1864. He was promoted brigadier-general U. S. Army August 12, 1864.

From November 27, 1864, to February 27, 1865, he was at Washington, D. C., organizing the First Army Corps of Veterans, and from February 27 to July 18, 1865, he was in command of Department of West Virginia, and temporarily of the Middle Division and Army of the Shenandoah.

He was brevetted major-general U. S. Army November 13, 1865, for gallant and meritorious services at the battle of Spottsylvania, Virginia. He was in command of the Middle Department from July 18, 1865, to August 10, 1866, and of the Department of Missouri from August 20, 1866. During part of 1867 he was engaged in an expedition against the Indians on the Plains.

General Hancock commanded also for many years the Department of the East, and was a candidate for the Presidency of the United States in 1880. He died February 9, 1886.

### BRIGADIER-GENERAL MARTIN D. HARDIN, U.S.A.
(RETIRED).

BRIGADIER-GENERAL MARTIN D. HARDIN was born at Jacksonville, Morgan County, Illinois, June 26, 1837. His great-grandfather, John Hardin, was an officer of Morgan's Rifles in the Revolutionary War; his grandfather, Martin D. Hardin, was a Senator from Kentucky, and served with distinction as an officer under General Harrison in the war of 1812; his father, John J. Hardin, was a prominent lawyer in Illinois, served in Congress as a member in 1843 and 1844, and was killed at the battle of Buena Vista, Mexico, while commanding the First Illinois Volunteers.

General Hardin graduated at West Point in 1859, and was attached to the Third Art.; served at the Artillery School at Fortress Monroe, and accompanied the force sent to recapture Harper's Ferry at the time of the John Brown raid. Joined Major Blake's expedition, which left St. Louis, Missouri, May 3, 1860. It ascended the Missouri River to its head-waters, crossed the Rocky Mountains by Mullan's Road, and reached Fort Vancouver in October. Lieut. Hardin was in command of Fort Umpqua, Oregon, when the late war began.

He came east with the Third Art. in the fall of 1861; served in the defences of Washington, and with McCall's Division of Pennsylvania Reserves until March, 1862; was aide-de-camp to Colonel Hunt, commanding the Art. Reserves, Army of the Potomac, at the siege of Yorktown, and "Seven Days' Battles" before Richmond.

He was colonel commanding the Twelfth Regiment Pennsylvania Reserves, July 8, 1862, and present in Pope's campaign; was slightly wounded at the battle of Groveton, and severely wounded at second Bull Run, whilst commanding Third Brigade of the Pennsylvania Reserves. Commanded his regiment at Gettysburg, and Third Brigade Pennsylvania Reserves at combats of Falling Waters, Rappahannock Station, Bristoe Station, and Mine Run campaign. He was severely wounded (losing left arm) whilst commanding troops guarding Orange and Alexandria Railroad, December 14, 1863.

On light duty January 12 to May, 1864, and then commanded First Brigade Pennsylvania Reserves, Third Division Fifth Corps, at battles of Spottsylvania, North Anna (when slightly wounded), Tolopotomy, and Bethesda Church. In this latter battle the First Brigade Pennsylvania Reserves was sent to the front to reconnoitre. Its skirmishers ran against the Confederate breastworks, a short distance in front of the church. When the brigade in line reached the church, it halted, tore down the fences, piled up the rails, and laid down behind these piles. Scarcely were the men in position when Ramseur's Confederate division charged down the pike. The Confederates came on in such large force, and with such an impetus, that the volley from Hardin's small brigade made no apparent impression. Soon the other brigades of Third Division Fifth Corps joined Hardin's, and a line of battle was formed across the country road. This line the Confederate division, after changing front, charged. The Confederates were repulsed with severe loss.

Colonel Hardin was appointed brigadier-general July 2, 1864, and assigned to the command of the defences of Washington, north of the Potomac. He was engaged in defence of the Capital against the Confederate General Early's army, July, 1864.

These defences had been stripped of the proper garrison to reinforce General Grant's armies. Two regiments of one-hundred-day men and a few dismounted batteries formed the garrison for fourteen miles of defences. The entire force was put on the picket-line, when, meeting Early's skirmishers and making a strong resistance, the Confederate advance force reported that the forts and outworks were fully manned, thus causing General Early to delay an attack in force. This attack would undoubtedly have been successful, had it been made before reinforcements to the garrison arrived.

General Hardin was relieved of the command of the defences of Washington, and assigned to command of District of Raleigh, North Carolina, August, 1865.

After the war he served in the Department of the Lakes as staff officer, and at times in command of Forts Wayne, Porter, or Gratiot.

Retired as brigadier-general December 15, 1870, for loss of left arm and other wounds. He practised law in Chicago, and has written a history of the Twelfth Regiment Pennsylvania Reserves, articles for magazines etc.

## PAYMASTER H. T. B. HARRIS, U.S.N.

PAYMASTER H. T. B. HARRIS entered the service as captain's clerk in March, 1863, on U. S. S. "Ino," and sailed to the South Atlantic Ocean as convoy to the ship "Aquila," with the monitor "Comanche" on board in sections, for San Francisco.

She was convoyed to about 10° south latitude, where the "Ino" parted with her and proceeded to cruise in search of the rebel cruiser "Alabama," reported in that locality. The "Ino" cruised for several months with quite a number of exciting incidents in the way of false alarms as to identity of different steamers sighted; but the "Alabama," with her well-known elusiveness, was soon reported on the United States coast,—so the "Ino" returned to New York, and the commanding officer and his clerk went to the steamer "Commodore Barney," serving on the rivers and bays of Virginia and North Carolina. In May, 1864, the "Barney" rendered very valuable assistance to the army in repelling Hoke's attack on New Berne, firing one hundred and twenty rounds with her IX.-inch Dahlgrens and 100-pounder Parrott guns. In July of the same year, while the "Barney" was at the head of Bachelor's Bay, guarding the mouth of Roanoke River, the ram "Albemarle" appeared and was hotly engaged by the "Barney" with her 100-pounder Parrott and two IX.-inch Dahlgrens, which compelled her to return to her moorings at Plymouth.

The subject of this sketch was at this time acting as signal-officer of the ship, and, in addition to that duty, on this occasion, commanded the forward battery of three IX.-inch guns with full crews of contrabands. After the return of the "Albemarle" to Plymouth, he volunteered to go with a boat's-crew at night up the Middle River to a point opposite Plymouth, cross the swamp to a point within two hundred feet of the ram, to observe and report upon the apparent damage to her from the shots of the "Barney." This duty was fraught with some danger, as two of the enemy's picket-stations were passed, and the trip through the cane brake was exceedingly difficult and fatiguing, but was successfully accomplished, and one prisoner taken,—a poor North Carolina conscript, going up the river in a canoe to visit his family, who,

having seen some of the reconnoitring party, was made prisoner to prevent his divulging their presence, which would have resulted in their capture.

Shortly after this the "Barney" returned to Norfolk, where the commanding officer and his clerk were transferred to the steamer "Emma," of the North Atlantic Blockading Squadron, and served on the Wilmington blockade, with much excitement in the chase of blockade-runners and frequent exchange of shots with the batteries, until October, 1864, when the subject of this sketch, who had been acting paymaster of the ship for two months, during the absence through sickness of the duly-appointed officer, was ordered to New York for examination for appointment as acting assistant paymaster, to which grade he was appointed November 1, 1864, and ordered to the monitor "Naubuc" at New York; afterwards to the "Napa," at Philadelphia. On February 21, 1867, was appointed assistant paymaster; February 17, 1869, passed assistant paymaster, and January 18, 1881, paymaster, having in the mean time served in every squadron and at the naval depots at the Sandwich Islands and Rio de Janeiro, Brazil; and at the time of writing is paymaster of the navy-yard, New York, where the disbursements exceed three millions of dollars per year.

FIRST LIEUTENANT JOHN C. HARRIS, U.S.M.C.

FIRST LIEUTENANT JOHN C. HARRIS was born near Philadelphia in 1840; admitted to the Bar in 1861; before entering the service, volunteered, in January, 1861, on an expedition (p. 111*) to take and hold Fort Washington, on the Potomac, and witnessed the first Bull Run disaster. He received a commission in 1861, in the Marine Corps, of which his uncle was then chief.

After some service about Washington, he was placed in command of the guard of the war-steamer, "Pensacola" (now, thirty years later, probably the only vessel of that date, still in active service). After much delay, in preparation, she passed down the Potomac (with President Lincoln and some of his Cabinet, until) under the fire of the rebel batteries, which failed, after repeated efforts, to seriously injure her. At Hampton Roads some time was spent in watching for the rebel iron-clad "Merrimac." In February, 1862, she continued South, to join Admiral Farragut's fleet; and, after almost a wreck on the Florida reefs, and getting off with difficulty, reached Key West, Florida; refitted, and proceeded to Ship Island, where were rendezvoused the fleet, Porter's mortar flotilla, and General Butler's army. In April, 1862, after heavy fighting at Forts St. Philip and Jackson, and the Chalmette batteries, (he being wounded, and, later, brevetted for "gallant and meritorious service" there,) (pp. 142–307*)—these naval forces captured New Orleans, where the "Pensacola" remained over a year; though he was for a time a volunteer at the siege of Port Hudson, with his friend, General Godfrey Weitzel, of the U.S. Engineers. Before General Butler's troops arrived, Lieutenant Harris was thrice landed, with his men, to carry out Admiral Farragut's different orders (pp. 141–142*).

In April, 1863, he was ordered North; and soon after the Union repulse, with great slaughter, at Fort Wagner, off Charleston, was made adjutant of a battalion (p. 146*)

of five hundred men, sent from New York, to lead a second storming-party against the Fort; which, with Fort Gregg, was soon after taken, and the rebels cleared off Morris Island. After these captures and the assault on Fort Sumter,—in which he was again a volunteer (p. 147*), in a picked body of one hundred men, called for by Admiral Dahlgren,—the command retired to Folly Island, where the long stay on the Mississippi and exposure off Charleston, with bad food and water, culminated in a severe fever, which sent him, successively, to the hospital-ship "Vermont;" to the hospital at Beaufort, South Carolina; and, when able to travel, back to the North.

A short service thereafter (in which he again volunteered) against the rebel cavalry raider, General Harry Gilmore (under Ewell) in Maryland (p. 154*), terminated his war experiences;—as the war about then ceased. Service on many courts-martial (in which he was generally Judge-Advocate) and at the Philadelphia Navy-Yard then occupied him, until the U. S. S. "Ticonderoga" (whose guard he commanded) sailed in November, 1865, for the European Squadron; where he spent some three years under Admirals Farragut and Goldsborough, visiting all the main ports of Europe, the East, and North and West Africa, with the Madeiras, Azores, Canaries, Balearics, etc.,—a cruise of unsurpassed interest; opportunity having been given for travelling, also, through the interiors of countries. On his return to the United States with Admiral Farragut, in 1869, on the frigate "Franklin," he resigned, and resumed business-life. The *Naval Register* of that year credits him with more "sea-service" than any of the corps of his date, or of the six preceding dates,—one officer excepted; who, however, was three dates ahead of him.

On both sides of his family he came from pre-Revolutionary Pennsylvania ancestry. His grandfathers, General William Harris, of Pennsylvania, whose monument is at the Great Valley Church, near Philadelphia, and Colonel Persifor Frazer on his maternal side, both served with the Pennsylvania troops under General Washington. His Frazer and Campbell ancestors evidence his partly Scotch origin, and the Harris name, (which is identified with Harrisburg, the capital of Pennsylvania) is English, being the family name of the Earls of Malmesbury.

As he only served when quite young, and in the *regular* Navy, where promotion awaited a vacancy ahead, there was no opportunity for other advance, as in the army. He was simply one of the million or more, whose course of life, was deflected by the war-call of the country, who did what occasion offered; and the survivors, when no more needed, returned whence they came. This modest record, therefore, he says, "must be of interest mainly to his fellow-officers and friends."

* Cullum's "Marine Corps."

## CAPTAIN MOSES HARRIS, U.S.A.

CAPTAIN MOSES HARRIS (First Cavalry) was born in New Hampshire September 6, 1839. Entering the regular army as a private soldier in Troop G, First Cavalry, he passed through the various grades to that of first sergeant, and then was appointed second lieutenant of the same regiment May 18, 1864.

Prior to the war of the Rebellion he served on the Indian frontier, and participated in an expedition against Cheyenne Indians in 1857, under General Sumner. In the summer of 1858 he marched with the troops to Sweetwater River, Nebraska, *en route* to Salt Lake City, and returned to Fort Riley. He again participated in an expedition against Kiowa Indians, under General Sedgwick, in 1860. He was at Fort Wise, Kansas, at the breaking out of the Rebellion, when the designation of the regiment was changed from First to Fourth Cavalry. After re-enlisting and being furloughed for two months, in 1862 he rejoined his troop in the field at Nashville, and participated in the various marches and campaigns of the Army of the Cumberland from March, 1862, to June, 1864, when he took part in the Atlanta campaign as far as Kenesaw Mountain, participating in various cavalry affairs and skirmishes. He was promoted first lieutenant August 15, 1864.

Captain Harris took part in the following engagements: Action at Solomon's Fork, Kansas, in 1857; affair at Blackwater Springs, Kansas, in 1860; battles of Shiloh, Corinth, Perryville, and Stone River, 1862; Spring Hill, Snow Hill, Franklin, Middleton, Shelbyville, Ringgold, and Chickamauga, 1863; Dallas, Georgia; Deep Bottom, Virginia; Newtown, Virginia; Shepherdstown, Virginia; Leetown, Smithfield, Winchester, Millford, Waynesborough, Tom's Creek, and Cedar Creek, Virginia, in 1864; and Appomattox Court House, April 9, 1865. He was brevetted a captain September 19, 1864, for "gallant and meritorious services at the battle of Winchester."

Shortly after the close of the war we find the captain on duty at New Orleans; and in 1866 he was transferred to the Pacific coast, with many changes of stations, numerous affairs with Indians, and disagreeable long marches. He was engaged in scouting operations against hostile Apaches from September, 1869, to March, 1870, taking part in several small engagements. He was engaged in constructing a wagon-road to the new post in the White Mountains, Arizona Territory, in 1870-71. He was then detailed for recruiting service, from which he returned to Benicia Barracks in the early part of 1873.

In the summer of 1874 the captain was camped in the Wallowa Valley, Washington Territory, watching restless Nez Perce Indians under Chief Joseph, and afterwards took station at Fort Colville. In 1878 he received a six months' leave of absence, but his troop being ordered into the field against the hostile Snake and Bannock Indians, he surrendered the unexpired portion and joined his troop in the field in August, and participated in that campaign under General O. O. Howard. After attending the usual round of post duties, member of boards, scouting, etc., he was in 1881 ordered to Arizona for field duty. On October 4 he left Lathrop with troop by rail for Arizona; on the 7th he took the trail of hostile Apaches at San Simeon Station, Arizona, and pursued them to the Mexican line. After being stationed at Fort Huachuca and Fort Bowie until January, 1882, he proceeded to and took station at the Presidio of San Francisco. In February of that year he was detailed on a board for the purchase of cavalry horses, and in April he was again ordered to Arizona, and was scouting against hostile Apaches until May 25, when he returned to the Presidio; but the station of his regiment was changed in 1884 to Montana, and his troop was assigned to Fort Custer, from which post he was detached, August 15, 1886, for duty in Yellowstone Park. He established the post of Camp Sheridan at Mammoth Hot Springs, and continued to perform the duties of superintendent of the park and commander of post of Camp Sheridan until June 1, 1889, when he took station at Fort Custer, Montana, remaining there until his regiment was ordered to Arizona in 1892.

## COMMANDER-IN-CHIEF BENJAMIN HARRISON, U.S.A.

COMMANDER-IN-CHIEF BENJAMIN HARRISON (President of the United States) is the son of John Scott Harrison, and grandson of General Wm. Henry Harrison, President of the United States from March 4 to April 4, 1841. He was born at North Bend, Indiana, in his grandfather's house, August 20, 1833, graduated from Miami University in Class of 1852; he subsequently passed through a legal course, and began practice of law at Indianapolis in 1854.

In the early part of the war of the Rebellion, Mr. Harrison tendered his services to Governor Morton, of Indiana, and the latter authorized him to raise a regiment. When the regiment was complete, Governor Morton voluntarily commissioned Mr. Harrison colonel of the Seventieth Regiment, Indiana Volunteers.

When Bragg was hastening with the main body of his army to Louisville, considerable excitement was created, and Colonel Harrison's regiment—although muskets had just been issued to them and they did not even know how to handle them—was hurried to Bowling Green, Kentucky, which was at that time fortified, and had become a Union outpost, below which everything had been broken by the Confederates.

Colonel Harrison's first experience as an independent commander was when he was sent on an expedition against a body of rebels lodged at Russellville. His command was put aboard a train at Bowling Green and hurried off. When within about ten miles of the town he was stopped by a burned bridge. Only a portion of a span was gone, however, and he made a pier of railroad ties in the centre, then cut down a couple of large trees and pushed them across the break. From a side-track near by, rails were torn up and laid upon the timbers. He pushed on with his train over the temporary bridge, and arriving at a proper point, after making his military dispositions he suddenly and with energy attacked the rebel camp. The surprise was complete. Forty rebels were killed and wounded, while only one Union soldier was killed. He captured ten prisoners and all the horses and arms, and then returned to Bowling Green.

Colonel Harrison's regiment was brigaded with the Seventy-ninth Ohio, and the One Hundred and Second, One Hundred and Fifth, and the One Hundred and Twenty-ninth Illinois, Brigadier-General Ward commanding; and, what is extraordinary, the organization thus effected was kept unchanged to the close of the war. From Bowling Green, Colonel Harrison, with his command, accompanied the brigade to Scottville, Kentucky, and thence to Gallatin, Tennessee, where he was occupied guarding the Louisville and Nashville Railroad. Four months were evenly divided between hunting guerillas and drilling his men. The brigade then marched to Lavergne and thence to Murfreesborough. There it became part of Granger's Reserve Corps. On the 2d of January, 1864, it became the First Brigade of the First Division of the Eleventh Army Corps, and Colonel Harrison was placed in command of it, General Ward taking the division.

Shortly after this the Eleventh and Twelfth Army Corps were consolidated into the Twentieth, whereupon Ward's old brigade became the First Brigade of the Third Division of the Twentieth Corps; and, as General Ward returned to the command of the brigade, Colonel Harrison resumed that of his regiment.

Colonel Harrison participated in the Atlanta campaign and was engaged in the battles of Resaca, where, in charging a battery, he was amongst the first to cross the parapet. He also assisted in the capture of Cassville; was engaged at New Hope Church, and commanded his brigade in the engagements at Gilgal Church, Kenesaw Mountain, Peach-Tree Creek, and Nashville. After the last-named, Colonel Harrison was occupied in the pursuit of Hood's army, and through many difficulties penetrated as far as Courtland, Alabama. He was then ordered to report to General Sherman at Savannah. At Pocotaligo he was assigned to a brigade, with which he joined Sherman at Goldsborough.

At the close of the war Colonel Harrison was made brevet brigadier-general of volunteers, to date from January 23, 1865, "for ability and manifest energy and gallantry in command of the brigade." He was honorably mustered out of service at Washington, D. C., on the 8th day of June, 1865, and at once entered upon his duties as reporter of the Supreme Court of the State of Indiana. He was elected United States Senator in 1881, and held that office for six years.

In 1888 General Harrison became the Republican candidate for President of the United States. He was duly elected, and took his seat March 4, 1889, which position he now holds, and by virtue of that position became commander-in-chief of the army and navy.

## CAPTAIN WILSON T. HARTZ, U.S.A.

Captain Wilson T. Hartz (Fifteenth Infantry) was born in Pottsville, Schuylkill County, Pennsylvania, September 9, 1836; received an academic education; embarked in life as a civil and mining engineer; served about one year at mining work, and then received an appointment as an assistant engineer on the Mine Hill and Schuylkill Haven Railroad, which position he held for about seven years, vacating it to answer the call of the President for volunteers. He was enrolled on the 16th day of April, 1861; mustered into service and appointed sergeant-major of the Sixth Pennsylvania Infantry April 22, 1861; and was mustered out of service July 27, 1861. He was then appointed first lieutenant First Regiment, Excelsior Brigade (Seventieth New York volunteers), August 30, 1861 (Hooker's Division, Third Army Corps), mustered to date October 22, 1861, and was adjutant of the regiment from February 1, 1862, to October 28, 1862, part of the time on duty as acting assistant adjutant-general of the brigade.

October 10, 1862, he was transferred to the First Army Corps for special assignment on the staff of General Nelson Taylor; was appointed captain and assistant adjutant-general of volunteers October 23, 1862. He received a bullet-wound in the right breast at Fredericksburg, Virginia, December 13, 1862; was assigned to duty as assistant to the commissary-general of prisoners February 17, 1863, and continued on that duty under the several administrative heads of the bureau—Generals Hoffman, Wessells, and Hitchcock—until the office was closed, and the records turned over to the adjutant-general of the army, August 22, 1867.

"OFFICE COMMISSARY-GENERAL OF PRISONERS,
"WASHINGTON, D. C., August 22, 1867.

"Special Orders: In compliance with an order of the adjutant-general of the 20th instant, the undersigned announces that he has delivered the books, papers, and property of this office to the control and direction of Brevet Brigadier-General Breck, of the Adjutant-General's Department, and it only remains for him to tender his thanks to the gentlemen in the office for their uniform fidelity and industry.

"To Brevet Major W. T. Hartz he feels particularly indebted, and desires to make his acknowledgment for his services and experience in the office, which have been of the highest value and importance, not merely to himself individually, but to the government.

(Signed) "E. A. HITCHCOCK,
"Major-General of Volunteers, Com.-Gen. Prisoners."

Captain Hartz was mustered out of service as a captain and acting adjutant-general of volunteers, to take effect September 1, 1867. He was commissioned major of volunteers by brevet to date from March 13, 1865, "for

faithful and meritorious service during the war." He then entered the regular service as second lieutenant Fifteenth U. S. Infantry, to date from May 11, 1866, and was promoted to first lieutenant June 17, 1867.

He was commissioned first lieutenant and captain by brevet to date from March 2, 1867, "for gallant and meritorious services in the battle of Fredericksburg, Virginia." On being mustered out of volunteer rank as captain and acting adjutant-general, he joined his company (D, Fifteenth Infantry) at Montgomery, Alabama, and commanded the company (the captain being absent) until January 25, 1868, when he was ordered to duty as acting assistant adjutant-general of the District of Alabama, and remained on that duty until the Fifteenth Infantry left the State, August 12, 1868. He marched and served with the regiment in Texas and New Mexico, on company and post duty as acting assistant quartermaster and acting commissary of subsistence; and as engineer officer of the regiment on its march from Texas to New Mexico in 1869, until the fall of 1874, when he was ordered on recruiting duty until October, 1876. He then took station at Fort Wingate, New Mexico, and was promoted captain August 23, 1877.

Captain Hartz was on detached service, building cantonment at Bagosa Springs, Colorado, during the winter of 1878-79; he was in the Ute campaign, winter of 1879-80; in the Victorio campaign, summer and fall of 1880; escorting engineers Atchison, Topeka, and Santa Fé Railroad, winter of 1880-81, in New Mexico and Arizona. On leave of absence, spring of 1881; thence to recruiting duty (special detail) until November, 1881; joined his company at Fort Lyon, Colorado, and served continuously with the regiment in Colorado, North Dakota, Louisiana, and Illinois. He was absent, with leave from November 15, 1891, to February 29, 1892, and has been on duty with regiment since.

### MAJOR WILLIAM L. HASKIN, U.S.A.

MAJOR WILLIAM L. HASKIN (First Artillery) was born at Houlton, Maine, May 31, 1844. He is the son of the late Brevet Brigadier-General Joseph A. Haskin, U.S.A., and is a graduate of the Rensselaer Polytechnic Institute of Troy, New York, Class of 1861, with the degree of Civil Engineer. He entered the regular service from civil life as second lieutenant, First Artillery, August 5, 1861, and was promoted first lieutenant the same day. He served during the war of the Rebellion, being stationed at Fort Washington, Maryland, to November, 1861, and was then ordered to Fort Pickens, Florida, where he remained until the occupation of Pensacola, Florida. He was stationed at Pensacola until July, 1862, and then served in the Department of the Gulf, Louisiana, until August, 1864. He participated in the campaigns pertaining to that locality, and was engaged in the battle of Fort Bisland, April 12 and 13, 1863; in a skirmish at Jennerets, April 14, 1863; in the siege of Port Hudson, Louisiana, from May 27 to July 8, 1863. He commanded Horse Battery F, First Artillery, during the second Red River campaign, and was engaged in a skirmish at Marksville, Louisiana, May 15, 1864, and in the action of Mansura, Louisiana, May 16, 1864, for which he was honorably mentioned to the Secretary of War by General Emory, in the following words:

"Lieutenant Haskin commanded a battery of the First Artillery in the Red River campaign of 1864, and greatly distinguished himself by the good order and discipline of his battery, and his gallantry and coolness upon all occasions; but particularly on the 16th of May, at the battle of Mansura, where he acted with conspicuous gallantry. I, therefore, respectfully recommend that he be brevetted captain of artillery, to date from May 16, 1864." At the close of the war he was brevetted captain (July 8, 1863) for "gallant and meritorious services in the capture of Port Hudson, Louisiana;" and brevet major, March 13, 1865, for "good conduct and gallant services during the war."

In September, 1864, Lieutenant Haskin was placed on recruiting service, and in February, 1865, was appointed aide-de-camp to General J. A. Haskin, chief of artillery Twenty-second Army Corps. In the following September he was ordered to Fort Trumbull, Connecticut, and there performed the duties of acting assistant quartermaster and assistant commissary of subsistence until June, 1866, when he was sent with his battery to Malone, New York, to assist in suppressing the Fenian raid.

Lieutenant Haskin was promoted captain July 28, 1866, and was at Fort Schuyler until 1870, when he was again sent to Malone, New York, in May, to assist in suppressing the second Fenian raid into Canada. He was then stationed at various posts on the Atlantic coast until 1876, when he was sent with his battery to South Carolina and Florida, during the contested election of that year. He was also sent to Pittsburgh and Reading, Pennsylvania, in 1877, during the labor riots.

Captain Haskin's station was changed to the Pacific coast in 1881, and he served at different posts until September, 1888, when he was in charge of the office of inspector-general, and inspector of target practice of the Department of California, in October, 1888. He was senior member of a board for reconnoissance of certain harbors on the Pacific coast from March to May, 1889, and commanded a battalion of light artillery at a summer encampment from July to September, 1889. He next served at Alcatraz Island, harbor of San Francisco, and then at other unimportant stations to the present time.

Captain Haskin was promoted major of the First Artillery August 11, 1887, and is now (May, 1892) in command of Fort Columbus, New York, and is the Secretary of the Military Service Institution of the United States, and one of the editors of its journal.

He is the author of the "History of the First United States Artillery," 1879.

## CAPTAIN CHARLES HAY, U.S.A.

CAPTAIN CHARLES HAY (Subsistence Department) was born in Holmes County, Ohio, August 23, 1840, and is, at the date of this record and portrait, in the fifty-second year of his age, and thirtieth of military service.

He first entered the service by enlistment at Cleveland, Ohio, April 23, 1861, for three months in the Eighth Ohio Volunteer Infantry, and served as a private; and, immediately on the expiration of this term, on July 24, 1861, he enlisted at Camp Chase, Columbus, Ohio, in the Twenty-third Ohio Volunteer Infantry for three years,— serving the full term in the ranks as a private, corporal, and regimental commissary sergeant. With the exception of about three months in 1862, his service with this regiment was in West Virginia, where it performed considerable scouting and marching, and had many minor engagements with the rebels, in nearly all of which he participated. August to October, 1862, his regiment was with the Army of the Potomac in the campaign through Maryland which culminated in the battles of South Mountain and Antietam, in both of which he was engaged. In the summer of 1863 he took part with his regiment in pursuing and intercepting the rebel raider, General John Morgan, in Eastern Ohio; and in June, 1864, was in General Hunter's campaign against Lynchburg, Virginia, which resulted disastrously, the Federal troops being obliged to retreat to the Kanawha Valley, a distance of over two hundred miles, through an unfriendly country and harassed by the rebels, suffering many hardships and privations because of insufficient supplies and a forced march of eleven days.

In May, 1864, Captain Hay passed examination at Washington City before the board presided over by General Silas Casey for a commission in the colored forces, and subsequently, in July, 1864, was commissioned a captain in the Forty-fifth Regiment U. S. Colored Volunteer Infantry, but declined the appointment.

Discharged by reason of expiration of service, July 24, 1864, he entered the office of the provost-marshal of the Fourteenth Ohio District, at Wooster, as a deputy, where he remained until February 20, 1865, when he was commissioned a captain in the First Army Corps of Veteran Volunteer Infantry, then being organized by General Hancock from volunteer soldiers who had served two years or more and been honorably discharged. After two months of recruiting duty in Ohio for the corps, he joined it at Washington City, and was assigned to the Fifth Regiment; and remained in camp near Washington until July, being present on duty with his regiment during the trial and execution of the Surratt conspirators. His remaining service with this regiment was at Providence, Rhode Island, and on Staten and Hart's Islands, New York harbor, until discharged May 28, 1866. Returning to Ohio, he entered the post-office

at Wooster as deputy, where he remained until March, 1867, when he was commissioned a second lieutenant in the Thirty-sixth U. S. Infantry, reporting for duty May 1, 1867, at North Platte, Nebraska. For the next two years he served with this regiment at posts and in the field in the vicinity of the line of the Union Pacific Railroad, then being constructed, protecting its workmen in what was then a hostile Indian country. At the reduction in 1869 of the infantry of the army from forty-five to twenty-five regiments, he was placed on "waiting orders," and so remained until July, when he was assigned to the Twenty-third Infantry, and, conducting a detachment of recruits from Carlisle Barracks to San Francisco in August, reported for duty September 1 at Boisé Barracks, Idaho, where he served until after his promotion to first lieutenant January, 1871, during which he performed considerable escort duty in Idaho and Oregon. His subsequent service of eighteen years in the Twenty-third Infantry was at posts in Oregon, Washington, and Arizona Territories, Nebraska, Kansas, Indian Territory, Colorado, Texas, and at Buffalo, New York, and comprised all of the garrison duties incidental to a subaltern line officer, of which, however, those of post-adjutant, quartermaster, and commissary were most frequent and almost constant. His last duty as post-quartermaster was the entire rebuilding of Fort Porter, at Buffalo, New York.

On December 10, 1888, Captain Hay was nominated by President Cleveland for commissary of subsistence with the rank of captain, and was confirmed January 15, 1889.

In September following he reported for duty at Denver, Colorado, where he is at present stationed as purchasing commissary of subsistence.

Captain Hay is a member of the Loyal Legion, Commandery of Colorado.

**BRIGADIER-GENERAL WILLIAM B. HAZEN, U.S.A.**
(DECEASED).

BRIGADIER-GENERAL WILLIAM B. HAZEN was born in Vermont, and graduated from the Military Academy July 1, 1855. He was promoted brevet second lieutenant of infantry the same day, and second lieutenant Eighth Infantry September 4, 1855. He first served on the Pacific coast, and was engaged in skirmishes at Applegate Creek January 3, and Big Kanyon February 12, 1856. He was then employed in conducting Rogue River Indians to Grand Ronde Reservation, Oregon, the same year. He was on leave of absence and awaiting orders from April to December, 1857. He rejoined in Texas, and was scouting against Apache Indians in 1858, being engaged in a skirmish at Guadalupe Mountains June 14. In 1859 he was engaged with Kickapoo Indians on the Nueces, May 10 and October 3, and with Comanche Indians on the Vanno November 3, where he was severely wounded, and went on sick leave of absence from 1859 to 1861. He was brevetted first lieutenant May 16, 1859, for "gallant conduct in two several engagements with Indians in Texas."

Lieutenant Hazen was promoted first lieutenant April 1, 1861, while assistant instructor of infantry tactics at the Military Academy. He was promoted captain May 14, 1861, and upon being relieved at the Military Academy, September 18, 1861, was appointed colonel of the Forty-first Ohio Volunteers, and, after recruiting and organizing his regiment at Cleveland, was engaged in the defence of the Ohio frontier, and in operations in Kentucky to February, 1862, when he commanded a brigade in the Army of the Ohio, and participated in the Tennessee campaign, being engaged in the battle of Shiloh, April 7, 1862, and the advance on Corinth. He was then on sick-leave from May 25 to July 4, 1862, when he returned, and was engaged with his troops in repairing railroads to August 4. After commanding at Murfreesborough for awhile, he participated in the retrograde movement on Louisville, Kentucky, and was engaged in the battle of Perryville and several skirmishes.

Colonel Hazen was appointed brigadier-general of volunteers November 29, 1862, and participated in the Tennessee campaign with the Army of the Cumberland, being engaged in a skirmish near Murfreesborough on Christmas Day, and battle of Stone River December 31, 1862. After a short leave of absence, General Hazen participated in the Tennessee campaign of 1863, and the campaigns which followed, including the march to the sea, and through the Carolinas, to the close of the war. He was engaged in numerous skirmishes, and in the battle of Chickamauga September 19 and 20, 1863; in operations about Chattanooga, in a movement with fifty-two pontoons to Brown's Ferry, with which a bridge across the Tennessee River was formed, Lookout Valley seized after a severe skirmish, and the line of supplies of the army reopened. He captured the Nineteenth Alabama Regiment at Orchard Knob November 23, and was in the battle of Missionary Ridge November 25, 1863. He was engaged also in the demonstration against Rocky-face Ridge, battle of Resaca, action at Adairsville, at Cassville, at Pickett's Mills, battle of Kenesaw Mountain, combat of Peach-tree Creek, siege of Atlanta, and, while in command of the Second Division, Fifteenth Army Corps, engaged in the battle of Jonesborough, the march to the sea, including numerous skirmishes, assault and capture of Fort McAllister, near Savannah.

While *en route* through the Carolinas, General Hazen constructed, with his troops, a trestle-bridge twelve hundred feet long, in eighteen hours, over Lynch's Creek, February 28, 1865, and was engaged in the battle of Bentonville, North Carolina, March 20-21, 1865, and was present at the surrender of Johnston's army April 26, 1865. He was appointed major-general of volunteers December 13, 1864, and was brevetted in the regular army from major to major-general, for gallant and meritorious services in the various general actions in which he had been engaged.

After holding several important commands, among them the command of the Fifteenth Army Corps during 1865-66, he was mustered out of the volunteer service January 15, 1866, and then was a member of the Board of Officers to Recommend Brevet Promotions. He was appointed colonel of the Thirty-eighth Infantry July 28, 1866, and while on duty in the West was transferred to the Sixth Infantry, upon the consolidation of regiments in 1869. He then served at various posts in the West with that regiment until December 15, 1880, when he was appointed brigadier-general and chief signal-officer, and stationed at Washington, D. C., at which place he died January 16, 1887.

## COLONEL CLEMENT D. HEBB, U.S.M.C.

COLONEL CLEMENT D. HEBB was born in Virginia, but was appointed a second lieutenant in the Marine Corps of the United States, from California, March, 1856. After going through his preliminary training at headquarters, and at the marine barracks at Philadelphia, where a large force of marines was always then kept, he was ordered in command of the marine guard of the sloop-of-war "Falmouth," and served in the Brazils for three years. During the year 1859 he was attached to the "Preble," of the Paraguay Expedition. After returning from the South American Station, Lieutenant Hebb served at head-quarters; at marine barracks, New York; at marine barracks, Pensacola; and at headquarters again in 1860-61. These were trying times, and people had to declare their sentiments very plainly. Lieutenant Hebb was ordered, with a detachment of marines, to occupy Fort Washington, on the Potomac, to prevent that fort from falling into the hands of the rebels. In June, 1861, he was commissioned a first lieutenant, and, after a short term at the marine barracks at Boston, was ordered to the frigate "Santee," of the West Gulf Squadron. He was promoted to captain while thus serving, and, being detached, served at the marine barracks at Norfolk, Virginia, and at Philadelphia. During a portion of the year 1863 he served with the battalion of marines at Morris and Folly Islands, South Carolina. During 1864 and 1865 he was on duty at New York, Portsmouth, New Hampshire, and at Washington; was attached to the flag-ship "Colorado," of the European Squadron, from April, 1865, to August, 1867.

Captain Hebb was, after this date, in command of the marine barracks at Washington; the marine barracks at Mound City; and again at Washington, D. C. Thence he went to the marine barracks at Boston, and was transferred to the command of the marine barracks at Pensacola, where he remained from October, 1869, to June,

1872. In 1872-73 he was stationed at Annapolis, afterwards serving in the flag-ship "Pensacola," Pacific Squadron. From July, 1874, to May, 1880, he commanded marines at the Mare Island Navy-Yard, California.

Commissioned major 1876. From May, 1880, to February, 1885, commanded marines at Boston Navy-Yard; commissioned lieutenant-colonel April, 1880; commanded marines at navy-yard, Portsmouth, New Hampshire, 1885, to August, 1889.

Commissioned colonel August, 1889, and stationed for a few months at League Island, Philadelphia. March 1, 1890, appointed to the command of the marine barracks at the navy-yard, Boston, Massachusetts.

Colonel Hebb was ordered by the Honorable Secretary of the Navy on September 7, 1891, to Washington, D.C., to command the Marine Corps while the commandant (McCawley) was sick, and until his retirement and successor was appointed in February, 1891, when he returned to the Boston Marine Barracks.

## CAPTAIN AND BREVET COLONEL HENRY B. HENDERSHOTT, U.S.A. (RETIRED).

CAPTAIN AND BREVET COLONEL HENRY B. HENDERSHOTT was born at Burlington, Kentucky, May 23, 1824. He was graduated at the United States Military Academy in the Class of 1847, and was assigned as a brevet second lieutenant to the Fifth U. S. Infantry, then serving in the war with Mexico. Shortly after graduation he proceeded to join his regiment at the seat of war in the City of Mexico; but, owing to a virulent attack of yellow fever in the Castle of San Juan d'Ulloa, off the coast of Vera Cruz, he did not reach his command until late in the fall of 1847. Shortly after joining his regiment he volunteered his services to act with a large force then fitting out in the City of Mexico by General Scott to open up the route between that city and Vera Cruz, which was then infested by large bands of guerillas under the noted guerilla chief Padre Jurata. He served with distinction, and was highly commended by his commanding officer, General Daniel Ruggles, Fifth Infantry, for his services on this occasion. On his return from Vera Cruz he was promoted to the rank of second lieutenant in the Second U. S. Infantry, and served creditably with this regiment until the close of the war. Immediately after this war, his regiment being ordered to California, he accompanied it to its destination, arriving at San Francisco on July 9, 1849, after a long and disastrous voyage of six months, via Cape Horn. On his arrival in California he was ordered with his company to cantonment Far-West, in the foot-hills of the Sierra Nevada, in the northern part of California. Whilst at this station he performed, in addition to the duties of company commander, all the staff duties incidental to a post command. While at Far-West he took an active part in numerous engagements with hostile Indians in the Sierra Nevada Mountains. On June 30, 1850, he was promoted to a first lieutenancy in his regiment, and joined his command, then on the Great Colorado Desert, en route to the junction of the Gila and Colorado Rivers. Here, again, in addition to his line command, he performed those of staff duties, and selected, with the approval of the commanding officer, General (then major) Samuel P. Heintzelman, the present site of Fort Yuma. He served three years at Yuma, and during this time was an active participant in many engagements against hostile Indians, notably the Yumas, Cocopas, Mohaves, etc. His services at this station were most arduous, and owing to these and exposure in tents to the heat of this excessively hot climate for nearly three years, frequently with an inadequate supply of provisions, his health was completely broken down. In the winter of 1854 he was ordered, with the officers of his regiment, to the Atlantic sea-board, to recruit his regiment. After three months' recruiting service, we find him again in active field service at Forts Ridgely and Randall, then in the Indian country.

In the spring and summer of 1859 he served in a campaign on the plains with W. T. Sherman's battery against hostile Sioux Indians; and in the winter of that year was ordered with his company to Fort Leavenworth, making an overland march of nearly six hundred and fifty miles.

It was while stationed at Leavenworth that he was transferred to the Second U. S. Artillery, and for the first time, in nearly fifteen years of hard service, availed himself of his first leave of absence. It was on his return from this leave, to join Barry's battery at Leavenworth, that he sustained at Hannibal, Missouri, serious and painful external and internal injuries. He was taken from there to Jefferson Barracks, and after a painful and lingering confinement of nearly two years to his post and quarters, again resumed such duties as he was able to perform, viz.: Chief commissary Department of the West, on the staff of General Frémont; superintendent of the recruiting service for the State of Iowa, and duty in the office of the provost-marshal general.

Believing that his usefulness as an officer for active field service had gone by, he reluctantly went upon the retired list near the close of the war; but continued to perform such duties as his health and condition would permit, until 1870, when, by a general order, all retired officers were relieved from duty.

He was successively brevetted a major, lieutenant-colonel, and colonel for faithful service during the war of the Rebellion. He was also appointed Register of the Virginia Land Office.

By the advice of his medical officer he took up his residence at Aiken, South Carolina, where he now resides, in very feeble health.

## LIEUTENANT-COLONEL AND BREVET COLONEL GUY V. HENRY, U.S.A.

LIEUTENANT-COLONEL AND BREVET COLONEL GUY V. HENRY was born at Fort Smith, Indian Territory, March 9, 1839. He was graduated at the U. S. Military Academy in the Class of 1861, at the breaking out of the war of the Rebellion, and assigned as a second lieutenant to the First U. S. Artillery. He served with distinction in that regiment until made colonel of the Fortieth Massachusetts Infantry, in the fall of 1863, and continued throughout the war with that command.

The attention of the commanding general was called "to the gallant and distinguished services of First Lieutenant Guy V. Henry" in the battle of Pocotaligo, South Carolina, October 22, 1862, and again to the advance led by Colonel Henry, of the Fortieth Massachusetts Infantry, into Florida, in 1864, in the following words by General Seymour: "I cannot commend too highly the brilliant success of this advance, for which great credit is due Colonel Henry and his command, and I earnestly recommend him to your [General Gillmore's] attention as a most deserving and energetic officer."

General Seymour again complimented Colonel Henry, in his report on the battle of Olustee, as follows: "Colonel Henry kept his cavalry in constant activity, watching and neutralizing that of the enemy, and by important and gallant services before and after, as well as during the battle, was eminently useful. I desire to recommend him to you [General Gillmore] as a highly deserving officer."

At the close of the war, when Colonel Henry was mustered out of the volunteer service, he was brevetted a colonel in the regular army, and had the honor conferred upon him of being made a brevet brigadier-general of volunteers.

Since the war Colonel Henry has had various positions of trust assigned him in the Indian country west of the Missouri River, and was transferred to the Third U.S. Cavalry in 1870, reaching the grade of major of the Ninth Cavalry in 1881. While in the cavalry service he has not only endured hard campaign duty, but has met with some sad misfortunes while in the performance of it. He has been engaged with different tribes of Indians in Arizona, Wyoming, Utah, Nebraska, and Dakota; and in the expedition to the Black Hills in the winter of 1874 and 1875 he, with his command, was badly frozen. Notwithstanding this misfortune, Colonel Henry is found again with his command in the Big Horn and Yellowstone expedition of 1876, where he was severely wounded through the face, losing the use of his left eye, in the battle of Rosebud Creek, Montana. He is honorably mentioned in General Orders by General Crook for this affair, and as "carrying on his person honorable marks of distinction in the severe wound he received at the hands of the enemy." Before thoroughly recovering from his wounds, he is found commanding a battalion in the capture of Crazy Horse Village of Sioux Indians in 1877.

After these arduous duties, and being much broken in health, Colonel Henry was granted leave of absence, and made an extended tour through Europe, returning in time, however, to take part in the White River expedition from September to December, 1879. In the winter of 1890 he commanded the Ninth Cavalry in the Sioux Indian troubles at Pine Ridge Agency, South Dakota.

In addition to his extensive field service, Colonel Henry was an instructor at the Fort Monroe Artillery School from 1867 to 1869; was a member of an artillery board to witness experiments with heavy guns at Fort Delaware in 1868; a member of a board of officers to determine and fix the cavalry accoutrements, equipments, and supplies at Fort Leavenworth in 1874; and member of a board of officers to determine and fix on cavalry accoutrements, equipments, and supplies at Washington in July, 1882. He also occupied important staff positions during and since the war.

Colonel Henry is a son of Major William Seaton Henry, Third U. S. Infantry, and grandson of Daniel D. Tompkins, who was twice Governor of New York and Vice-President of the United States; also of Smith Thompson, who was Secretary of the Navy and Judge of the Supreme Court.

Colonel Henry has furnished the profession with the following military works: "Records of Civilian Appointments U. S. Army," "Army Catechism for Non-Commissioned Officers and Soldiers," pamphlet on "Target Practice," and "Practical Information for Non-Commissioned Officers on Field Duty." He was promoted lieutenant-colonel Seventh Cavalry January 30, 1892, and is in command at Fort Myer, Virginia.

## MAJOR JAMES HENTON, U.S.A.

MAJOR JAMES HENTON (Twenty-third Infantry) was born in Liverpool, England, February 2, 1835. He enlisted in the Sixth U. S. Infantry November 22, 1853, and served at Jefferson Barracks and Fort Riley, Kansas, until August, 1854, when he marched with his company to Fort Laramie, then in Nebraska Territory, reaching that post in the subsequent October, where he remained until June 27, 1857. During this period he took part in several expeditions, under General Harney, against the Sioux and Cheyenne Indians. He participated in the expedition against the Cheyennes, under Colonel E. V. Sumner, and was engaged in the action at Solomon's Fork July 29, 1857. On the breaking up of this expedition he accompanied several companies of his regiment to Fort Leavenworth, Kansas, and did duty in that vicinity as *posse comitatus* during the political disturbances of that period, until April, 1858, when he left that post with his entire regiment as part of the Mormon expedition, under General Albert Sidney Johnston. In August, 1858, when this expedition was over, he marched with his regiment overland to Benicia Barracks, California, reaching the destination about the 6th of the following November, and on the 22d of the latter month he received his discharge for expiration of term of service, having been previously promoted corporal, sergeant, and first sergeant.

He re-enlisted at Newport Barracks, Kentucky, and became a lance-sergeant of the Permanent Party. In December, 1860, he was detached and placed in charge of a recruiting rendezvous at St. Louis, Missouri, under First Lieutenant J. D. O'Connell, Second Infantry. In September, 1861, he was transferred and made first sergeant of Company A, Second Battalion, Fourteenth Infantry, at Fort Trumbull. The regiment was transferred to Perryville, Maryland, soon afterwards, and while there he was appointed second lieutenant from October 5, 1861.

In March, 1862, Lieutenant Henton, with his regiment, proceeded to Washington, D. C., and formed part of the Army of the Potomac, participating in the campaigns of that army until August, 1863, being engaged in the siege of Yorktown, and in the battles of Gaines' Mill, Malvern Hill, second Bull Run, Antietam, Snicker's Gap, Fredericksburg, Chancellorsville, and Gettysburg.

From September, 1863, to March, 1865, he was detached on recruiting service, but rejoining his regiment at the latter date, in the field, he participated in the operations terminating with the surrender of General Lee, and at the close of the war was brevetted captain " for gallant and meritorious conduct at the battle of Gettysburg, Pennsylvania."

After a short tour of duty as provost guard in the city of Richmond, the regiment was concentrated at Hart Island, New York, preparatory to moving to the Pacific coast. While at this station Lieutenant Henton was appointed adjutant of the Second Battalion of the Fourteenth Infantry, and in that capacity proceeded, on the 16th of August, 1865, to San Francisco, California, *via* the Isthmus of Panama, reaching the former place on the 9th of the following September, but was transferred to Fort Vancouver, Washington, at which post he performed the duties of adjutant until promoted captain, November 4, 1865, but did not join his company until March, 1866, at which time he was relieved as adjutant, and took station at Fort Cape Disappointment, but soon afterwards was ordered to Fort Boisé, Idaho. During the year 1866 the Second Battalion of the Fourteenth Infantry became, under the reorganization law, the Twenty-third Infantry.

In October, 1866, Captain Henton's station was changed to Camp Warner, Oregon, at which point some field service was had, under General Crook, against the Piute and other Indians. He was then transferred to Arizona with his company in June, 1872, but was detailed on recruiting service in New York City from January, 1873, to October, 1874. Rejoining his company at Fort Omaha in April, 1875, then moving to Fort Dodge, Kansas, he served there and at Fort Hays and Fort Supply to 1880. In May of this year he participated in General Mackenzie's expedition against the Ute Indians.

After serving at Uncompahgre Cantonment, and at Fort Union, New Mexico, Captain Henton was transferred with his regiment to Michigan in 1884, and he took station at Fort Brady, where he was in command until May, 1890, when the regiment was transferred to Texas, the captain being ordered to Fort Davis, reaching that place May 14, 1890.

Captain Henton was promoted major January 31, 1891, and assigned to the Twenty-third Infantry, and in May, 1892, moved therefrom, in command of B and D companies, to Fort Bliss, Texas, his present station.

## CAPTAIN AND BREVET MAJOR FRANK W. HESS, U.S.A.

CAPTAIN AND BREVET MAJOR FRANK W. HESS (Third Artillery) was born in Fulton County, Pennsylvania, December 15, 1836. He was educated in the common schools of his county, at Milnwood Academy in Huntingdon County, and at Shryock's school in Chambersburg, Pennsylvania. He taught school and studied law, and was thus engaged when the war of the Rebellion commenced. He joined one of the companies that responded to the first call for troops as it passed through the village where he was teaching. On arrival at the rendezvous men enough had joined, while en route, to make two companies. Of one he was made captain, and ordered to duty with General Patterson's column in the valley of Virginia. He was honorably discharged, with this company in August, 1861, and re-entered the service as a lieutenant in the Third Penn. Cavalry in Sept., and served with it during the remainder of the war, being honorably mustered out in Aug., 1865, as its major.

He participated in thirty-eight battles and skirmishes. (For names of these, see "Powell's Record of Living Officers.") He was appointed a first lieutenant in the Eleventh Infantry February 23, 1866, and transferred in that year to the Twenty-ninth. In 1870 he was transferred to the artillery arm, and assigned to the Third Regiment, in which he attained his captaincy in 1886.

He was stationed in Texas during the reconstruction period, and served as mayor of the city of Marshall and military commissioner of Harrison County, and made decisions in many important cases of litigation, performing the delicate and difficult duties of a civil office so as to meet the approval of his superiors and gain the friendship of all law-abiding citizens.

Of his services, in the report of the operations of his brigade at Malvern Hill, General Warren says: "Lieutenant Hess, of the cavalry, reported to me with a platoon, was pushed forward till the enemy's pickets were reached. Throughout the day he continued to observe the enemy in front, while the fierce battle was going on to our right, and rendered most valuable service."

This day was spent under a severe shell-fire from our own gun-boats in the river, which were attempting to reach the enemy over the heads of this little command, in which one man and several horses were killed.

General Averell, reporting the result of a reconnoissance to and fight at White-Oak-Swamp Bridge, August 5, 1862, says: "I am particularly indebted to Lieutenant Hess, Third Pennsylvania Cavalry, my acting aide on the occasion, for his readiness in carrying orders and placing the squadrons and guns in position."

In a letter to the Secretary of War, General George G. Meade, commanding Army of the Potomac, says: "Major Hess served as major of the Third Pennsylvania Cavalry whilst that regiment was on duty at the head-quarters of the army. During this period it was frequently called on by me to perform picket, scouting, and other duties, giving me an opportunity to become personally acquainted with the manner in which Major Hess discharged his duties. I take pleasure in stating that he was active, intelligent, and faithful, and recommend him for appointment in the regular army."

General George P. Buell, on the 10th of August, 1868, in a letter to the War Department, says of him: "He is one of the most efficient officers of the regiment, of good education, zealous in discharge of his duty, proud of his profession, and deeply attached to his country."

Lieutenant Colonel Owen, who commanded the Third Pennsylvania Cavalry in the Antietam campaign, in a letter to the adjutant-general, said: "Captain Hess distinguished himself by his sound judgment and personal bravery, and at all times by his fidelity to the interests of the service. At Antietam, when Hooker was wounded and his command repulsed, Captain Hess was one of the last to leave the field, and principally through his exertions a section of artillery was removed when the enemy were within a few yards of it."

General J. B. McIntosh says, in an official paper: "I can testify to his gallant conduct in every action in which his regiment was engaged."

General A. S. Webb said, October 31, 1868, to the adjutant-general of the army: "Major Hess, when on duty with his regiment at head-quarters of the Army of the Potomac, was specially commended by Major-General Meade, commanding that army, and by myself as chief of staff, for distinguished gallantry, enterprise, and zeal in opening communications between corps in the vicinity of Hatcher's Run. General Meade will sanction this use of his name, since this was not the only occasion on which Major Hess distinguished himself."

### COLONEL-COMMANDANT CHARLES HEYWOOD, U.S.M.C.

COLONEL-COMMANDANT CHARLES HEYWOOD was born in Maine, 1839; appointed from New York, April, 1858. At the marine barracks, at Washington, and at Brooklyn, during that year, and served in the quarantine riots at Staten Island. On special duty in "Niagara," and in "St. Louis," of Home Squadron, looking after the filibusters, under Walker. Invalided from Aspinwall, January, 1860. Afterwards ordered to sloop-of-war "Cumberland," flag-ship of Squadron of Observation, at Vera Cruz. In March, 1861, the "Cumberland" returned to Hampton Roads, and there at the time of the destruction of the Norfolk Navy-Yard. Heywood was promoted to first lieutenant May, 1861; landed with marines at Hatteras Inlet, and present at the capture of Forts Clark and Hatteras.

Promoted to captain in the Marine Corps November, 1861; on a number of boat expeditions in the James River during winter of 1861-62; was on board the "Cumberland" during the fight with the ram "Merrimac" and consorts, March 8, 1862, and most favorably mentioned for gallant conduct. For some time after this Captain Heywood was actively employed, both on shore and in the search for the "Alabama," and then applied for duty on board the flag-ship "Hartford," and was ordered as fleet marine officer of West Gulf Squadron; served with the marines on shore, at Pensacola. On board the "Hartford" at the battle of Mobile Bay. Had command of two nine-inch guns, and was favorably mentioned.

Commanded Fort Powell, after its capture; marine barracks, Brooklyn, and Recruiting Rendezvous Philadelphia, 1865; brevets of major and lieutenant colonel for distinguished gallantry in the presence of the enemy. Ordered to command of marine barracks, navy-yard, Washington, 1865; fleet marine officer under Admiral Farragut, European Station, 1867; command of marine barracks at Washington, and at Norfolk; and fleet marine officer of the North Atlantic Squadron. In January, 1874, was attached to the flag-ship "Wabash," and commanded the marines during all the shore drills carried on by the navy at Key West and elsewhere. Was attached to the marine barracks at Brooklyn, when, in June, 1874, he was ordered to New Orleans to report to Admiral Mullany, as fleet marine officer of the North Atlantic Station; was attached to that admiral's staff during the troubles of that year in New Orleans. After serving in the "Worcester" and the "Hartford," was detached, and again ordered to Brooklyn Barracks, in September, 1876.

In November, 1876, he attained the substantive rank of major, to which he had been brevetted more than ten years before, and ordered to command the marine barracks at Washington. In July and August, 1877, had command of a battalion of marines at Baltimore, Philadelphia, and at Reading, Pennsylvania, during the very serious labor riots of that summer. Honorably mentioned by General Hancock, who was in general command. The state of the battalion for efficiency, neatness, and general soldierly bearing was commented upon by all who were capable of judging of such matters. Colonel and Medical Director Cuyler, of the Division of the Atlantic, in his official report, commended their condition in every respect, in spite of the hard duty they had suddenly imposed upon them. He said, "It is quite remarkable that men performing such service are able to keep themselves and their arms, etc., so clean." "The officers evidently take pride in looking after the health and comfort of the men."

In general orders, General Hancock, who knew what a soldier should be, bore testimony to this battalion's "soldierly bearing, excellent discipline, and devotion to duty" during a very trying time, and especially mentioned "Major Charles Heywood, of the marines." In 1880 Major Heywood went to the marine barracks at Mare Island, and returned to the command of the Brooklyn Barracks in 1883. In 1885, by telegraphic order, and within twenty-four hours, equipped two hundred and fifty men to go to Panama, to open the transit, and protect American lives and property. After reaching the Isthmus Colonel Heywood was reinforced, and had under his command nearly eight hundred marines, and a strong detachment of sailors, with artillery. For the arduous service there the admiral commanding asked Colonel Heywood to "receive his grateful acknowledgments."

Colonel Heywood is now the commandant of the Marine Corps of the United States.

## MAJOR JOHN HENLEY HIGBEE, U.S.M.C.

MAJOR JOHN HENLEY HIGBEE was born in New York City September 11, 1839. He is the son of the late Rev. Dr. Edward Y. Higbee, of Trinity Church, New York. On his mother's side he is descended from the Henley and Dandridge families of Virginia. Leonard Henley, Major Higbee's great-grandfather, married Elizabeth Dandridge, the sister of Martha Washington. Commodore John Dandridge Henley, U. S. Navy, grandfather of Major Higbee, and nephew of Mrs. Washington, received his warrant as midshipman from the hands of General Washington himself.

Major Higbee's grandaunt, Mrs. Francis Dandridge Lear, a niece of Mrs. Washington, married Colonel Lear, military secretary of General Washington, and lived for many years with General and Mrs. Washington at Mount Vernon. Major Higbee entered the Marine Corps as second lieutenant March 9, 1861. In June of the same year he was ordered to the U. S. S. "Vincennes," West Gulf Blockading Squadron. He was commissioned as first lieutenant September 1, 1861. While attached to the "Vincennes," he was sent upon a number of expeditions up the Blackwater River, Florida, in company with detachments of the army. Joined the U. S. S. flag-ship "Hartford," Admiral Farragut, September, 1862. Took part in the battles of Port Hudson, Vicksburg, Warrenton, and Grand Gulf, March 14, 19, 21, 23, and 28, 1863; bombardment of Port Hudson May 27, 1863, and was present at the surrender of the latter place; was brevetted captain for gallantry in battle May 25, 1863.

During the month of April, 1863, while the "Hartford" was blockading the mouth of the Red River, First Lieutenant Higbee was selected by Admiral Farragut to perform picket duty. The admiral expected a night attack by the rebel ram fleet, then at Alexandria, and after dark Lieutenant Higbee was sent, every other night, about three miles up river in a canoe paddled by two contrabands. He was provided with rockets to signal the "Hartford" in case of any movement on the part of the rebel fleet. In going up river, Lieutenant Higbee was obliged to pass close to a rebel picket, making the duty extremely hazardous. Lieutenant-Colonel Broome, then

Captain Broome, at the time in command of the marines of Admiral Farragut's fleet, states as follows: "I know there was no individual service rendered by any one more gallant and hazardous during the war of the Rebellion."

Lieutenant Higbee was ordered to marine barracks, New York, August, 1863. Commissioned captain June 10, 1864. Receiving-ship "North Carolina," 1864; marine barracks, Norfolk, Virginia, 1865; flag-ship "New Hampshire," 1865-66; marine barracks, New York, 1866; marine recruiting rendezvous, 1866-68; marine barracks, Portsmouth, New Hampshire, 1868-69; marine barracks, Philadelphia, Pennsylvania, 1869; fleet marine-officer, Pacific Station, 1870-73; marine barracks, Mare Island, California, 1874; marine barracks, Portsmouth, New Hampshire, 1873-78; fleet marine-officer, Asiatic Station, 1878-81; marine barracks, Boston, Massachusetts, 1881-82; marine barracks, navy-yard, Washington, D. C., 1883-86; commanded Second Battalion of marines on Isthmus of Panama, April, 1885; marine barracks, Norfolk, Virginia, 1886; marine barracks, Portsmouth, New Hampshire, 1888-92; commissioned as major 18th of August, 1889. At present, March, 1892, commanding marine barracks, Portsmouth, New Hampshire.

## CAPTAIN WILLIAM HOFFMAN, U.S.A.

CAPTAIN WILLIAM HOFFMAN was born in Maine February 18, 1839. As a soldier, he graduated on the battle-field in that distinguished and well-remembered regiment, the Fifth New York Volunteer Infantry (Duryea's Zouaves). He enlisted in the New York State service April 23, 1861, and was mustered into the United States service as sergeant, Company G, May 9, 1861.

He participated in the affair of Big Bethel, the affair at Pamunkey Bridge, the battles of Hanover Court-House, Gaines' Mill, White Oak Swamp, Charles City Cross-Roads, and Malvern Hill.

He was appointed second lieutenant, Fifth New York Volunteer Infantry, July 26, 1862, " for gallant and meritorious conduct upon the field of battle."

He participated in the battle of Manassas Plains (second Bull Run), where he received three severe rifle-ball wounds,—one through the left arm, grazing the bone; one under left shoulder-blade, glancing on ribs; and one through the fleshy portion of right thigh; and in this same battle his brother Edward was killed beside him (see " Rebellion Records," Series I., Vol. II., Part II., page 504).

He was promoted to first lieutenant, Fifth New York Volunteer Infantry, September 24, 1862, " for gallant services upon the field of battle."

He rejoined his regiment in ten weeks, and before his wounds were healed.

He participated in the battle of Fredericksburg; was promoted to captain, Company B, Fifth New York Volunteer Infantry, January 23, 1863; participated in the battle of Chancellorsville; and was mustered out with regiment, at expiration of term of service, May 14, 1863.

He was ever at the post of duty and danger with this celebrated regiment, and he still bears an enviable reputation among the few survivors of the brave comrades of those days.

As soon as he was mustered out he began recruiting in New York City, and raised Battery B, Thirteenth New York Artillery, and was mustered into the United States service as its captain August 29, 1863. He served about two years with this company in the defences of Portsmouth, Virginia, and participated in a successful raid upon Murphree's Station, Virginia. He commanded the infantry column of the expedition, numbering about three hundred men.

He did valuable service as chief of the military police at Norfolk, Virginia; and commanded Forts Reno and Cushing in the defences of Portsmouth,—about one year in each case.

About August 1, 1865, he took station at Washington, D. C., and was placed in command of Fort De Russy.

He was mustered out with his regiment, near New York City, August 24, 1865.

Upon his personal application alone, he was appointed second lieutenant, Eleventh U. S. Infantry, May 11, 1866. He was transferred to Twenty-ninth Infantry September 21, 1866, and promoted first lieutenant June 25, 1867; transferred to Eleventh Infantry April 25, 1869, and promoted captain April 24, 1886.

# BRIGADIER-GENERAL SAMUEL B. HOLABIRD, U.S.A.
## (RETIRED).

BRIGADIER-GENERAL SAMUEL B. HOLABIRD was born in Connecticut June 16, 1826, and graduated from the Military Academy July 1, 1849. He was promoted brevet second lieutenant First Infantry the same day, and second lieutenant June 10, 1850. He served on frontier duty, and was regimental quartermaster from July 1, 1852, to May 31, 1858. He was then detailed on recruiting service for two years, when he was ordered to the Military Academy, and was adjutant thereof from September 2, 1859, to May 13, 1861. He was promoted first lieutenant May 31, 1855. On May 13, 1861, he was appointed captain and assistant quartermaster; July 2, 1862, appointed major and additional aide-de-camp, and July 11, 1862, colonel and additional aide-de-camp. He was lieutenant-colonel of volunteers and inspector-general of General Dix's division (First Division of New York Volunteers), May 1–13, 1861.

General Holabird served during the war of the Rebellion as quartermaster at Harrisburg, Pennsylvania, from May 29 to June 10, 1861; in the field, at Hagerstown, Maryland, with Patterson's columns, to August 13, 1861; at Frederick, Maryland, to March 31, 1862; chief quartermaster of the division commanded by Major-General Banks to June, 1862; chief quartermaster Second Army Corps, under General Pope, to October, 1862, participating in the campaign of Northern Virginia and the subsequent Maryland campaign. He was then assigned to duty in New York City, engaged in fitting out the Banks Expedition, which he accompanied to Ship Island, Mississippi, and was then made chief quartermaster of the Department of the Gulf, which he retained until July, 1865, participating in the mean time in the siege of Port Hudson, Louisiana. He was then made depot quartermaster at New Orleans, and subsequently chief quartermaster of the Department of Louisiana, until March, 1866. He was honorably mustered out of the volunteer service May 31, 1866, and on the 29th of July of that year he was appointed lieutenant-colonel and deputy quartermaster-general, and ordered to Washington, D.C.

General Holabird was brevetted major, lieutenant-colonel, and brigadier-general March 13, 1865, for "faithful and meritorious services during the war."

He was relieved from duty in Washington in February, 1867, and assigned as chief quartermaster of the Department of Dakota, where he remained until April 18, 1872, and was then transferred as chief quartermaster of the Department of Texas to August 15, 1875. On October 31, 1875, he was chief quartermaster of the Military Division of the Missouri, and on May 6, 1878, became chief quartermaster of the Military Division of the Pacific and Department of California, serving at San Francisco to October 15, 1879, when he was ordered once more to Washington, D. C., and placed on duty in the quartermaster-general's office. He was promoted colonel and assistant quartermaster-general January 22, 1881.

On being relieved from duty in Washington April 30, 1882, he was placed in charge of the general depot of the Quartermaster's Department at Philadelphia, Pennsylvania, which he retained until July 2, 1883, when the President appointed him quartermaster-general, with the rank of brigadier-general, and he was ordered to Washington, where he remained on duty until retired, by operation of law, June 16, 1890.

General Holabird was ever alert to the needs of the army, and while occupying the position of quartermaster-general introduced many reforms to improve the condition of the enlisted men, supplying them with comforts and conveniences which soldiers could scarcely have dreamed of a quarter of a century before.

COMMANDER EDWARD HOOKER, U.S.N.
(RETIRED).

COMMANDER EDWARD HOOKER was born in Connecticut in 1822, and bred to the sea in the merchant marine, commanding a ship when twenty-three years old. One of the earliest volunteers for the naval service in the Civil War, he was appointed acting master in July, 1861. His first service was in the gun-boat "Louisiana," and, while attached to that vessel, he was severely wounded during a boat expedition October 5, 1861. He was the first officer of his grade wounded during the war, and, as years roll round, these wounds are causing him serious inconvenience.

He took an active part in the Burnside Expedition while in the "Louisiana." At New Berne that vessel fired the first and last shot of the action. Soon after the capture of New Berne he became the executive officer of the "Louisiana." At the time of the Confederate attack upon Washington, North Carolina, in September, 1862, the ship was fought by Commander Hooker, in the absence of the commanding officer, in a manner which caused high commendation from commanding officers of our own forces. The Confederate view of the matter we can give from the *Raleigh Standard*, although space requires us to condense the article. The paper speaks of the affair as "disgraceful" to some concerned on the Confederate side. "It is said that we lost three hundred, killed and wounded, among them four captains. Our forces held the town about two hours, but were forced to retire by the Yankee gun-boat 'Louisiana.' . . . Our forces engaged consisted of the Seventeenth and Fifty-fifth North Carolina Regiments, two artillery companies, and six companies of cavalry, amounting to some three thousand altogether. . . . Were

it not for the gun-boat the Union garrison would have been captured," for the town was surprised at daybreak, the fortifications captured, and the guns turned on the garrison. The rapidity and accuracy of fire of the "Louisiana" drove the Confederates off, after they were in full possession.

For gallantry on this occasion, Commander Hooker was made acting volunteer lieutenant, to date from the day of the action. He was then ordered to a command in the blockade off Wilmington, and soon after to the command of a division of the Potomac Flotilla, in which command he continued until the end of the war. In 1864 he was ordered, with his division, to co-operate with General Grant's army, and to clear the Rappahannock River, so that transports could reach Fredericksburg. This duty he performed, and he remained at Fredericksburg until it was evacuated by our forces. His ship being then in urgent need of repairs, Commander Hooker was sent by Commander Foxhall Parker, commanding the flotilla, to the Washington Navy-Yard, being then promoted to acting volunteer lieutenant-commander.

After the war closed he was at the New York Navy-Yard. He then took the store-ship "Idaho" to the Asiatic Squadron, and while there was transferred from the volunteer to the regular navy list. Commissioned lieutenant March, 1868, and lieutenant-commander December, 1868. He was, after this, captain of the yard at League Island, assistant light-house inspector, and other duties, until in February, 1884, while on duty at the Naval Home, at Philadelphia, he was promoted to commander. In December of that year he was placed upon the retired list by operation of law. Since then he has resided in Brooklyn, New York.

Commander Hooker is a lineal descendant of the Reverend Thomas Hooker, who founded the colony of Connecticut and the present city of Hartford, in 1636. He is also descended from the first mayor of the city of New York. His grandfather was a colonel of the Revolutionary War, and his grandmother was a daughter of Major Griswold, a noted cavalry officer in the French War. His father was a graduate of Yale, and, after a connection with Columbia College, South Carolina, devoted his life to scientific farming and to literature, in Connecticut.

Commander Hooker is a Companion of the Loyal Legion, member of Rankin Post, No. 10, Grand Army, Connecticut Society of Sons of the Revolution, the Brooklyn New England Society, Brooklyn Library Association, Long Island Historical Society, and Rhode Island Marine Society, and honorary member of other societies; a member of Aurora Grata Club, Brooklyn, and an active member of the Brooklyn Association of Masonic Veterans.

## BRIGADIER- AND BREVET MAJOR-GENERAL JOSEPH HOOKER, U.S.A. (DECEASED).

BRIGADIER- AND BREVET MAJOR-GENERAL JOSEPH HOOKER was born in Massachusetts and graduated from the Military Academy July 1, 1837. He was promoted second lieutenant of the First Artillery the same day, and first lieutenant November 1, 1838. He served in the Florida War of 1837-38, and then was on the Maine frontier at Houlton, pending disputed territory controversy in 1838; and afterwards, during the Canada border disturbances, at Swanton, Vermont, and Rouse's Point, lasting until 1840. After a short tour in garrison at Fort Columbus, he was adjutant of the Military Academy from July 1 to October 3, 1841. He was adjutant of the First Artillery from September 11, 1841, to May 11, 1846.

He participated in the war with Mexico on the staff of Brigadier-General P. F. Smith, and of Brigadier-General Harmar, in 1846, and aide-de-camp to Major-General Butler in 1847, and as assistant adjutant-general of Major-General Pillow's division in 1847-48, being engaged in the battle of Monterey; defence of the convoy at the National Bridge; skirmish of La Hoya; battles of Contreras and Churubusco, Molino del Rey, and storming of Chapultepec, for which he was brevetted captain, major, and lieutenant-colonel. He was appointed brevet captain of staff (assistant adjutant-general) March 3, 1847, and was assistant adjutant-general of the Sixth Military Department from September 13 to October 28, 1848; and of the Pacific Division June 9, 1849, to November 24, 1851. He was promoted captain of the First Artillery October 29, 1848, which he vacated. He was on leave of absence in 1851-53, and resigned from the army February 21, 1853.

Upon leaving the army Colonel Hooker went to farming near Sonoma, California; was superintendent of military roads in Oregon in 1858-59, and colonel of California militia in 1859-61. At the commencement of the war of the Rebellion he tendered his services to the government and was appointed brigadier-general of volunteers May 17, 1861. He served in the defences of Washington City, and in guarding the Lower Potomac to March 10, 1862, when he commanded a division in the Peninsula campaign with the Army of the Potomac. He was appointed major-general of volunteers May 5, 1862, and was engaged in the siege of Yorktown; battles of Williamsburg and Fair Oaks; combat on the Williamsburg Road; battles of Glendale, Malvern Hill, and reoccupation and action of the same place August 5, 1862. He commanded a division in the Northern Virginia campaign, and was engaged in the action of Bristoe Station; battles of second Bull Run and Chantilly. He commanded the First Army Corps in the Maryland campaign, and was engaged in the battles of South Mountain and Antietam, where he was severely

wounded, and was, in consequence, on sick-leave to November 10, 1862, when he rejoined the army, and was in command of the Fifth Corps to November 16; of the Centre Grand Division (Third and Fifth Corps) to January 26, 1863, and then of the Army of the Potomac, being engaged in the battle of Fredericksburg, action at Kelly's Ford, and battle of Chancellorsville; and then in pursuit of the enemy to Pennsylvania, to June 28, 1863, when he relinquished command of the army, which had been engaged in the action of Brandy Station and skirmishes at Aldie, Middleburg, and Upperville.

General Hooker received the thanks of Congress, January 28, 1864, "for the skill, energy, and endurance which first covered Washington and Baltimore from the meditated blow of the advancing and powerful army of rebels, led by General Robert E. Lee," and was appointed brigadier-general U. S. Army September 20, 1862.

From June 28 to September 24, 1863, General Hooker was on waiting orders at Baltimore, Maryland, and was then assigned to command the Eleventh and Twelfth Army Corps (consolidated afterwards into the Twentieth Corps), and participated in the operations of the Western army, being engaged in all the actions of that army from Chattanooga to the siege of Atlanta, in July, 1864. He was then placed on waiting-orders until the following September, when he was assigned to the command of the Northern Department. He was brevetted major-general U. S. Army, for "gallant and meritorious services at the battle of Chattanooga, Tennessee."

General Hooker was assigned to the command of the Department of the East July 8, 1865, and was then given the Department of the Lakes, where, after being mustered out of the volunteer service September 1, 1866, he remained to 1867, and he was retired upon the full rank of major-general U. S. Army October 15, 1868. He died at Garden City, Long Island, October 31, 1879.

MEDICAL DIRECTOR PHINEAS J. HORWITZ, U.S.N.
(RETIRED).

MEDICAL DIRECTOR PHINEAS J. HORWITZ was born in Maryland in March, 1822, and graduated in medicine at the University of Maryland in March, 1845. Appointed assistant surgeon in the navy November, 1847, and assigned to duty in the Gulf Squadron, then operating against Mexico. Dr. Horwitz was at once placed in charge of the Naval Hospital at Tabasco, and remained there until the close of the war. This duty was performed so energetically and efficiently as to receive the personal commendation and thanks of the commander-in-chief, Commodore M. C. Perry. Dr. Horwitz then made a cruise in the Mediterranean in the "Constitution," and was then ordered to the store-ship "Relief," bound to the Brazil Station. In January, 1853, he was examined and passed for promotion, and was then assigned to the steamer "Princeton," in which he served for two years. He next served in the store-ship "Supply," on the African and Brazil Stations. Upon his return to the United States, in 1859, he was offered the position of assistant to the Bureau of Medicine and Surgery, Navy Department, which office he held until he was appointed* chief of the Bureau of Medicine and Surgery, July 1, 1865. This position he retained until his term of service expired, July 1, 1869. Dr. Horwitz was promoted to surgeon on April 19, 1861, but his services in the bureau were considered so important that he was not permitted to vacate his appointment as assistant, and Congress, in acknowledgment of the immense amount of work he was performing, voted to give him the highest shore-pay of his grade. During the entire period of the war of the Rebellion the labor of the bureau fell almost wholly upon Dr. Horwitz, and his was the only bureau in which the clerical force was not increased. The whole system of tabulating the casualties of the war, of indexing books of reference, reports of survey, certificates of disability and of diseases, was designed and carried forward by Dr. Horwitz, so that there was probably no case of injury, disease, or disability that occurred during his connection with the bureau that will not be found in its appropriate place in the surgeon-general's office. The immense number of pension cases accruing during the war were all examined, adjusted, and prepared by him, and every official letter that left the bureau was written by him. All this was done without the aid of a single additional writer or clerk. On leaving the bureau, in 1869, Dr. Horwitz was placed in charge of the Naval Hospital at Philadelphia, and since that time has been assigned to various duties at that station. He was promoted to the grade of medical inspector March 3, 1871, and to that of medical director December 19, 1873. Was president of the Examining Board at Philadelphia, 1883-84. Retired in 1884.

* Surgeon-general with the rank of commodore.

## MAJOR-GENERAL OLIVER O. HOWARD, U.S.A.

MAJOR-GENERAL OLIVER O. HOWARD was born in Maine November 8, 1830, and graduated at the Military Academy July 1, 1854. He was appointed a brevet second lieutenant of ordnance the same day, and second lieutenant February 15, 1855. He served at various arsenals until 1856, and was ordered to Florida, where he participated in hostilities against the Seminole Indians in 1857. He was then detailed for duty at the Military Academy, as assistant professor of mathematics, September 21, 1857, having been promoted first lieutenant July 1, 1857. He resigned his commission in the army June 7, 1861.

General Howard was appointed colonel of the Third Maine Volunteers June 4, 1861, and served in the defences of Washington, and commanded a brigade in the Manassas campaign, being engaged in the first battle of Bull Run, July 21, 1861. He was appointed a brigadier-general of volunteers September 3, 1861, and made a reconnoissance in the early spring of 1862 from Washington to the Rappahannock River. He participated in the Peninsula campaign with the Army of the Potomac, and was engaged at the siege of Yorktown and battle of Fair Oaks, June 1, 1862, where he was twice severely wounded, losing his right arm. He was compelled to leave the field, and when convalescent devoted himself to raising volunteers. Returning to the field about August 27, 1862, he was engaged in a skirmish near Centreville September 1, following. He participated in the Maryland campaign, and was engaged in the battle of Antietam, Maryland, and in the subsequent march to Falmouth and battle of Fredericksburg, Virginia.

General Howard was appointed major-general of volunteers November 29, 1862, and served, in command of the Eleventh Army Corps, from April 1, 1863, and was engaged in the battles of Chancellorsville, Virginia, and Gettysburg, Pennsylvania, and in pursuit of the enemy to Warrenton, Virginia; then guarding the Orange and Alexandria Railroad until September, 1863. His corps was then put en route to Bridgeport, Tennessee, and took part in the operations about Chattanooga, being engaged in the action of Lookout Valley, battle of Missionary Ridge, and expedition for the relief of Knoxville, to December 17, 1863. He was then in occupation of Chattanooga to May 3, 1864, and was assigned to the command of the Fourth Corps April 10, 1864, when the Eleventh and Twelfth Corps were consolidated to form the Twentieth. He commanded the Fourth Corps until July 27, 1864, when he was assigned to the command of the Army of the Tennessee in the invasion of Georgia. He was engaged in the operations around Dalton, battle of Resaca, actions of Adairsville and Cassville, battle of Dallas, action of Pickett's Mill (May 27, 1864, where he was wounded), battles and skirmishes about Pine and

Kenesaw Mountains, actions of Smyrna Camp-Ground, combat of Peach-Tree Creek, siege of Atlanta, combat of Ezra Church, battle of Jonesborough, surrender of Atlanta and occupation of the place.

He pursued the rebels under General Hood into Alabama, with frequent engagements. He participated in the "march to the sea," and was engaged in numerous actions and skirmishes, including the combats and actions of General Sherman's army to the surrender of General Johnston, April 26, 1865.

General Howard was appointed a brigadier-general in the U. S. Army December 21, 1864, and was brevetted major-general, U.S.A., March 13, 1865, for "gallant and meritorious services at the battle of Ezra Church and during the campaign against Atlanta, Georgia."

At the conclusion of the war General Howard was appointed commissioner of the Bureau of Refugees, Freedmen, and Abandoned Lands, at Washington, D. C., May 12, 1865.

He commanded the Department of the Columbia from July, 1874, to 1880, and was superintendent of the Military Academy from June 21, 1881, to September 1, 1882, when he was ordered to the command of the Department of the Platte. He was appointed a major-general in the U. S. Army March 19, 1886, and assigned to the command of the Military Division of the Pacific, from which he was relieved, in 1888, and assigned to the Military Division of the Atlantic. Divisions having been discontinued, he now commands the Department of the East.

General Howard had the degree of A.M. conferred by Bowdoin College, Maine, in 1853; the degree of LL.D. conferred by Waterville College, Maine, in 1865; the same by Shurtleff College, Illinois, in 1865; and by Gettysburg Theological Seminary, Pennsylvania, in 1866.

CAPTAIN HENRY L. HOWE, U.S.A.

CAPTAIN HENRY L. HOWE (Seventeenth Infantry) was born in Massachusetts January 2, 1831. Prior to entering the volunteer service he was sergeant of Captain George C. Whitcomb's Company of State Militia of Minnesota, and participated in operations against Little Crow's band of hostile Sioux Indians from August 25 to October 17, 1862, participating in three engagements with said Indians.

He entered the volunteer service during the war of the Rebellion, and was private and first sergeant of Company B, Independent Battalion of Minnesota Cavalry, from July 1, 1863, to June 29, 1864, when he was appointed second lieutenant of the same battalion, and promoted first lieutenant July 6, 1865.

He was honorably mustered out of the volunteer service May 30, 1866, having been appointed second lieutenant in the Seventeenth U. S. Infantry February 23, 1866.

He joined his regiment at Hart's Island, New York, and has served with it at various stations in the several military departments.

He was promoted first lieutenant July 28, 1866, and captain June 1, 1875.

REAR-ADMIRAL JOHN C. HOWELL, U.S.N. (RETIRED).

REAR-ADMIRAL JOHN C. HOWELL was born in Pennsylvania November 24, 1819, coming of people who had always been distinguished in the colonial and warlike history of the States of New Jersey and Pennsylvania. He was appointed a midshipman from Pennsylvania on June 9, 1836, and made a cruise in the West Indies in the sloop-of-war "Levant," which extended to nearly four years. He was promoted to passed midshipman July 1, 1842, and served on board the frigate "Congress" in the Mediterranean for two years. He then went to the East Indies in the brig "Perry," served in her from 1844 to 1845, and then was naval storekeeper at Macao,—the most charming place in the East at that period,—from 1845 to 1848. He became a lieutenant in August, 1849, and made cruises in the frigate "Raritan," of the Home Squadron, and sloop "Saratoga," of the East India Squadron, returning home in 1854. After two years' service at the Philadelphia station he next made a cruise in the Mediterranean in the fine steamer "Susquehanna," and again came back to duty in Philadelphia. When the Civil War began, Lieutenant Howell was ordered to the "Minnesota" steam-frigate, and served in her at the battle of Hatteras Inlet.

He was commissioned as commander in the navy July 16, 1862, and commanded the steamer "Tahoma," of the East Gulf Blockading Squadron, in 1862-63. He was then transferred to the command of the "Nereus," of the North Atlantic Blockading Squadron, and in her was in the two actions at Fort Fisher in December, 1864, and January, 1865.

He was commissioned as captain July 25, 1866, and was in charge of recruiting duty at Philadelphia for two years. He next served as fleet-captain and chief of staff of the European Squadron from 1869 to 1871. Commanded the League Island Station in 1871-72.

Commissioned as commodore January 29, 1872, and commanded the Portsmouth Navy-Yard until 1875, when he was made chief of the Bureau of Yards and Docks, in the Navy Department, for the term of four years,—this being an office subject to the approval of the U. S. Senate.

He was commissioned as rear-admiral in 1877, and was in command of the European Station for two years. He was retired in 1881, under the operation of law.

### CAPTAIN RICHARD L. HOXIE, U.S.A.

CAPTAIN RICHARD L. HOXIE (Corps of Engineers) was born in New York City August 7, 1844, in the eighth generation from Lodovic Hanksie, who settled at Sandwich, Massachusetts, in 1650, and is the great-grandson of Lieutenant Pelig Hoxsie, of the First Rhode Island (Lippitt's) Regiment of the Revolutionary army. His early education was obtained in the public and private schools at New York and Pennsylvania, and in Europe, and at the outbreak of the Civil War he was a student in the State University of Iowa, at Iowa City. Here he enlisted in Company F, First Regiment Iowa Volunteer Cavalry, June 13, 1861, and marched to regimental rendezvous at Burlington, Iowa, where the regiment was soon after mustered into the service of the United States. Upon this occasion he was rejected by the mustering officer because of the fact that he was only sixteen years of age, but, continuing to serve with the company, he was mustered in a few months later. He served continuously with this regiment, which took the field in October, 1861, in Missouri and Arkansas, up to the taking of Little Rock, and the subsequent expedition to Camden in 1864. At this time the period of service of the regiment was about to expire. He was the first soldier to re-enlist in the regiment as a veteran volunteer, in January, 1864, and was followed by about six hundred more,—a very large proportion of the effective strength. He received honorable mention in official correspondence for conduct in action, and three separate tenders of a commission,—the latter declined,—and finally an appointment to the Military Academy at West Point from the veteran volunteers, to accept which he was mustered out of the volunteer service June 10, 1864. He was graduated from the Military Academy June 13, 1868, and promoted second lieutenant of Engineers June 15, 1868; served with the Engineer Battalion at Jefferson Barracks, Missouri, from October 1, 1868, to September 5, 1870, under General H. W. Benham; in charge of construction and repair of fortifications in Boston harbor, Massachusetts, from September 5, 1870, to July 3, 1872; promoted to first lieutenant September 22, 1870; on explorations and surveys in the Western Territories from July 3, 1872, to July 2, 1874; nominated by President Grant as member of the Board of Public Works of the District of Columbia, under the Territorial government, in 1874, and nomination confirmed by the Senate; detailed as engineer to the Board of Commissioners of the District of Columbia under the act of June 20, 1874, and continuously engaged upon the public works of the district until August 14, 1884; promoted to the rank of captain, Corps of Engineers, June 15, 1882; in charge of various works of river and harbor improvement and coast defences in the States of Georgia, Florida, and Alabama, from August 16, 1884, to January 17, 1889; member of Engineer Board on Selma Bridge in 1885; since January 17, 1889, has been in command of Company B, U. S. Engineer Battalion, stationed at Willet's Point, New York harbor, and instructor in military engineering and in field astronomy at the post-graduate U. S. Engineer School, at Willet's Point.

Captain Hoxie is a member of the American Society of Civil Engineers, of the Military Order of the Loyal Legion, U. S., and of the Order of Sons of the American Revolution.

## BRIGADIER- AND BREVET MAJOR-GENERAL ANDREW A. HUMPHREYS (DECEASED).

BRIGADIER- AND BREVET MAJOR-GENERAL ANDREW A. HUMPHREYS was born in Pennsylvania, and graduated from the Military Academy July 1, 1831, and was assigned as brevet second lieutenant Second Artillery, and promoted second lieutenant the same date.

He was on duty at Fort Moultrie, South Carolina, in 1831, and on special duty, making drawings at the Military Academy, from January 5 to April 18, 1832; in the Cherokee Nation 1832-33, and in garrison at Augusta Arsenal, Georgia, 1833; at Fort Marion, Florida, 1833-34, and on topographical duty August 12, 1834, to December, 1835, making surveys in West Florida and at Cape Cod, Massachusetts. He participated in the Florida War against the Seminole Indians in 1836, being engaged in the actions of Oloklikaha and Micanopy.

He was promoted first lieutenant Second Artillery August 16, 1836, and resigned the service September 30, 1836. After resigning from the army he was engaged as civil engineer, assisting Major Bache in the plans of Brandywine Shoal Light-house and Crow Shoal Breakwater, Delaware Bay, 1836-38.

On July 2, 1838, he was reappointed in the army as first lieutenant Corps of Topographical Engineers.

He served at Washington as assistant in the Topographical Bureau in 1840-41, and in Coast Survey Office, 1844-49.

He was promoted captain Corps of Engineers May 31, 1848, and in 1850 was detailed to make a topographic and hydrographic survey of the delta of the Mississippi River, with a view to its protection from inundation, and deepening the channels at its mouth. He continued on this detail, having general charge, till 1861. While engaged on this duty he visited Europe, examining means for protecting delta rivers from inundations, 1853-54, and upon return he was placed in general charge, under the War Department, of the office duties at Washington, D. C., connected with explorations and surveys for railroads from the Mississippi River to Pacific Ocean, and geographical explorations west of Mississippi, 1854-61.

During the war of the Rebellion, 1861-65, he served on the staff of Major-General McClellan, general-in-chief, at Washington, D. C., from December 1, 1861, to March 5, 1862, and in the Virginia Peninsula campaign as chief topographical engineer of the Army of the Potomac from March 5 to August 31, 1862, being engaged in the siege of Yorktown, April 5 to May 4, 1862.

He was promoted major Corps of Engineers August 6, 1862, and colonel, staff additional aide-de-camp, March 5, 1862, and April 28, 1862, brigadier-general U. S. Volunteers.

He served with distinction in the movements and operations against Richmond, Virginia, and on the James

River, May and June, 1862; in the Maryland and Rappahannock campaigns. He was brevetted colonel December 13, 1862, for gallant and meritorious services at the battle of Fredericksburg, Virginia, and promoted lieutenant-colonel Corps of Engineers March 3, 1863.

He participated in the Pennsylvania campaign, being engaged in the battle of Gettysburg, as chief of staff of General Meade, commanding the Army of the Potomac, from July 8, 1863, to November 25, 1864. On July 8, 1863, he was promoted major-general U. S. Volunteers.

He participated in the movements and operations during 1864-65 in Virginia, serving with distinction in the various battles, actions, and sieges, and in the pursuit of General Lee's rebel army (including the several actions of the Second Corps, April 6, 1865, terminating at Sailor's Creek, and actions at High Bridge and Farmville, April 7, 1865), till its surrender April 9, 1865.

He was brevetted brigadier-general U. S. Army March 13, 1865, for gallant and meritorious services at the battle of Gettysburg, Pennsylvania, and major-general U. S. Army March 13, 1865, for gallant and meritorious services at the battle of Sailor's Creek, Virginia. He was mustered out of the volunteer service May 31, 1866.

He was appointed brigadier-general and chief of engineers of the U. S. Army August 8, 1866, and was in command of the Corps of Engineers and in charge of the Engineer Bureau, August 8, 1866, until retired from active service June 3, 1879. He died December 27, 1883.

He was a member of the American Philosophical Society, Philadelphia, Pennsylvania, 1857, and American Academy of Arts and Sciences, Boston, Massachusetts, 1863. He was the corporator of the National Academy of Sciences since March 3, 1863; an honorary member of the Imperial Royal Geological Institute of Vienna, Austria, 1862, and of the Royal Institute of Science and Art of Lombardy, Milan, Italy, 1864.

COLONEL AND BREVET MAJOR-GENERAL HENRY J. HUNT, U.S.A. (DECEASED).

COLONEL AND BREVET MAJOR-GENERAL HENRY J. HUNT was born in Michigan, and graduated from the Military Academy July 1, 1839. He was promoted the same day to second lieutenant Second Artillery, and served on the Northern frontier during the Canada border disturbances. Afterwards he was stationed at posts on the Lakes, and was promoted first lieutenant June 18, 1846.

He participated in the war with Mexico, and was engaged in the siege of Vera Cruz, battle of Cerro Gordo, capture of San Antonio, battle of Churubusco, battle of Molino del Rey (where he was twice wounded), storming of Chapultepec, and assault and capture of the City of Mexico September 13, 14, 1847.

For this service Lieutenant Hunt was brevetted captain August 20, 1847, "for gallant and meritorious conduct in the battles of Contreras and Churubusco, Mexico;" and major September 13, 1847, "for gallant and meritorious conduct in the battle of Chapultepec, Mexico."

After the close of the Mexican War, Lieutenant Hunt was stationed at Fort McHenry, Fort Monroe, and Fort Moultrie, and was promoted captain Second Artillery September 28, 1852. Then he was ordered on frontier duty at Fort Smith, Arkansas, and Fort Washington, Indian Territory, until detailed as member of a board to revise the system of light-artillery tactics, which was adopted for the army March 6, 1860. He was at Fort Kearney, Nebraska, in 1858; Fort Brown, Texas, in 1860, and Harper's Ferry, Virginia, 1861. He was promoted major Fifth Artillery May 14, 1861, and participated in the defence of Fort Pickens, to June 28, and in the Manassas campaign of Virginia, being engaged in the battle of first Bull Run, July 21, 1861, when he was in command of the artillery on the extreme left.

Major Hunt was chief of artillery in the defences of Washington, south of the Potomac, until appointed colonel of staff,—additional aide-de-camp, September 28, 1861, and participated in the Peninsula campaign of the Army of the Potomac to August, 1862, in command of the Reserve Artillery, and was engaged in the siege of Yorktown, battle of Gaines' Mill, action of Garnett's Farm, action of Turkey Bend, battle of Malvern Hill, and various skirmishes.

Colonel Hunt was chief of artillery in the Maryland campaign, and was engaged in the battles of South Mountain and Antietam, and the subsequent march to Falmouth, terminating with the battle of Fredericksburg. He was in the mean time appointed brigadier-general of volunteers September 15, 1862.

As chief of artillery, General Hunt served in all the remaining campaigns of the Army of the Potomac to the end of the war, and was engaged in the battles of Chancellorsville, Gettysburg, Mine Run, Wilderness, Spottsylvania, Cold Harbor, siege of Petersburg, from June 15, 1864, to April 3, 1865, including the assaults on the enemy's works, combat at Fort Stedman, and pursuit of the enemy after the assault of April 2, 1865, until the capitulation of General Lee, at Appomattox Court-House, Virginia, April 9, 1865.

He was promoted lieutenant-colonel of the Third Artillery August 1, 1863, and was brevetted colonel, brigadier-general, and major-general for gallant and meritorious services in action. He was also brevetted major-general of volunteers July 6, 1864, for "gallantry and distinguished conduct at the battle of Gettysburg, and for faithful and highly meritorious services in the campaign from the Rapidan to Petersburg, Virginia."

At the close of the war General Hunt was in command of a camp of instruction for field artillery, near Bladensburg, Maryland, from June to August, 1865, and of the frontier district of Arkansas, at Fort Smith, from September, 1865, to April, 1866, when he was mustered out of the volunteer service. He then reverted to his rank of lieutenant-colonel Third Artillery, and was member of a board for the armament of fortifications, and in command of various posts, and was promoted colonel Fifth Artillery April 4, 1869. For a long time he was one of the prominent candidates for brigadier-general in the regular army; but the fates were against him, and he was retired for age September 14, 1883. He died while in command of the Soldiers' Home at Washington, D. C., February 11, 1889.

## CAPTAIN JAMES M. INGALLS, U.S.A.

CAPTAIN JAMES M. INGALLS (First Artillery) was born in the town of Sutton, Vermont, January 25, 1837. In his early youth his parents moved to Massachusetts, where he began his education in the public schools. After reaching manhood he went to the then West, and for four years was professor of mathematics in Evansville Seminary, Wisconsin. At the beginning of 1864 he enlisted in Company A, First Battalion, Sixteenth Regular Infantry, then stationed at Columbus, Kentucky, as head-quarters guard, having been promised by the captain of the company as rapid advancement to a commission as possible. In the latter part of January, 1864, Company A was ordered to join the remainder of the regiment at Chattanooga, Tennessee, in readiness for the opening of the Atlanta campaign. He was promoted to second lieutenant of his regiment May 3, 1865, and served with his company at various places in Tennessee, Georgia, and Alabama. He was promoted first lieutenant May 3, 1865, and upon the consolidation of regiments was transferred to the Second Infantry April 17, 1869, having performed the duties of quartermaster of the First Battalion of the Sixteenth Infantry from June 4, 1865, to September 21, 1866. During his tour of duty in the Southern States he was engaged in the extremely disagreeable service connected with reconstruction until January 1, 1871, when he was transferred to the First Artillery, his present regiment. He was assigned to Battery A (Silvey's), stationed at Fort Ontario, Oswego, New York, but was transferred to Battery G (Elder's) for a tour of duty at the Artillery School, Fort Monroe, May 1, 1871.

He was transferred, May 1, 1872, to Battery M (Langdon's), at Plattsburg Barracks, and followed its fortunes (including three yellow-fever epidemics at Forts Jefferson and Barrancas) until July 1, 1880, when he was promoted to a captaincy, and assigned to the command of Battery A, stationed at Governor's Island, New York harbor.

In September, 1881, his battery was selected by General Hancock to guard the Franklyn Cottage at Elberon, New Jersey, while it was occupied by President Garfield.

At the request of General Getty, commanding the Artillery School, Captain Ingalls was transferred to Battery G of his regiment, stationed at Fort Monroe, upon the promotion of Captain Elder, who had for many years been an instructor at the school. In December, 1882, at

the suggestion of Captain Ingalls, the Department of Ballistics was created at the Artillery School and placed in his charge, with the understanding that he should prepare a suitable text-book for the use of the school, which should embrace all the best modern methods employed in Europe. This work, printed at the Artillery School, was ready for use in September, 1883, and was the first treatise on Exterior Ballistics ever published in the United States. A second edition was published by the Artillery School in January, 1885, and a third edition from the press of D. Van Nostrand appeared in 1886.

Other professional works prepared by Captain Ingalls are: "Ballistic Machines," from the Artillery School press, 1885; "Hand-book of Problems in Exterior Ballistics," Artillery School, 1889; and a second edition by John Wiley & Sons, 1890; "Ballistic Tables for Direct, Curved, and High-Angle Fire," John Wiley & Sons, 1891; "Interior Ballistics," Artillery School press, 1891.

In addition to his ballistic work, Captain Ingalls was senior instructor of practical artillery exercises to the class of 1884; senior instructor of engineering to the class of 1888; senior instructor of electricity and defensive torpedoes to the classes of 1884, 1886, 1888, and 1890; senior instructor of telegraphy to the classes of 1884, 1886, and 1888; and senior instructor of signalling from 8th May, 1884, to 7th September, 1888.

### BRIGADIER- AND BREVET MAJOR-GENERAL RUFUS INGALLS, U.S.A. (RETIRED).

BRIGADIER- AND BREVET MAJOR-GENERAL RUFUS INGALLS was born in the State of Maine, and entered the Military Academy July 1, 1839. He was promoted brevet second lieutenant Rifles July 1, 1843, and served on frontier duty at Forts Jesup, Louisiana, and Leavenworth, Kansas, till the war with Mexico, 1846-47, in which he participated, being engaged in the skirmish of Embudo, January 29, 1847, and the assault of Pueblo de Taos, February 4, 1847. On March 17, 1845, he was promoted second lieutenant First Dragoons, and on February 4, 1847, brevetted first lieutenant, for gallant and meritorious conduct in the conflicts at Embudo and Taos.

After completing a tour of recruiting service, 1847-48, he accompanied the troops on the voyage to California, via Cape Horn, in 1848, and was on duty as quartermaster, and served at various posts in California till 1853, when he returned to Washington. He served with the Colonel Steptoe Expedition across the continent via Leavenworth, Kansas, and Salt Lake, Utah, to San Francisco, California, 1854-55; and at various posts till 1861, being on the commission to examine the war-debt of Oregon and Washington Territory, 1857-58, he having been, in the mean time, promoted first lieutenant, February 16, 1847; and captain (on staff, assistant quartermaster) January 12, 1848.

During the war of the Rebellion he served at Fort Pickens, Florida, from April 20 to July 15, 1861; and as chief quartermaster of the forces occupying the defences of Washington, D. C., south of the Potomac; and at Annapolis, Maryland, and Alexandria, Virginia, receiving transports and superintending the embarkation of the Army of the Potomac to the Virginia Peninsula campaign, March 1 to April 2, 1862.

On September 28, 1861, he was promoted lieutenant-colonel of staff, additional aide-de-camp, and major of staff, quartermaster, January 12, 1862, for fourteen years' continuous service as captain.

During the year 1862 General Ingalls had charge of the depots of Fort Monroe, Cheeseman's Creek, Yorktown, and White House, Virginia; and transferred stores to Harrison's Landing via York and James Rivers, after General McClellan's "change of base." He was then appointed chief quartermaster of the Army of the Potomac, and served in this capacity until the close of the war, being present at the battles of South Mountain, Antietam, Fredericksburg, Chancellorsville, Gettysburg, and in pursuit of the enemy to Warrenton, Virginia. He participated in the Mine Run operations, organized supply depots on the Orange and Alexandria Railroad, and participated in the campaigns of 1864-65, being present at the battles of the Wilderness, Spottsylvania, Cold Harbor, and siege of Petersburg and Richmond, and established the great army depot at City Point, Virginia.

He was appointed brigadier-general of volunteers May 23, 1863, and at the close of the war was brevetted lieutenant-colonel, colonel, and brigadier-general U. S. Army, for meritorious and distinguished services, and major-general of volunteers and U. S. Army, for faithful and meritorious services.

He was promoted lieutenant-colonel and deputy-quartermaster-general July 28, 1866; colonel and assistant quartermaster-general July 29, 1866.

While chief quartermaster of the Army of the Potomac, General Ingalls displayed great executive ability in supplying that vast army with stores always at the proper time and in the proper place.

Upon the disbandment of that army the general remained on duty at Washington City to May 4, 1866, when he was ordered on special inspection duty across the continent to Oregon, which occupied him until the following December. He was then on waiting orders to March 31, 1867, when he was detailed as chief quartermaster at New York City. He served there and at other stations until he was appointed brigadier-general and quartermaster-general February 23, 1882, which position he continued to fill until retired from active service, at his own request, July 1, 1883.

## MAJOR JAMES JACKSON, U.S.A.

Major James Jackson (Second Cavalry) was born near Deckertown, in Sussex County, New Jersey, November 21, 1833. After graduating from the Philadelphia High School, he moved to the West, and was living in Iowa when the war of the Rebellion broke out. In the fall of 1861 he recruited men for the Twelfth Regiment of Iowa Volunteers, under a recruiting commission from Colonel William B. Allison. But in November, 1861, he enlisted in the Twelfth U. S. Infantry, under Captain Newbury, of that regiment, and was placed on recruiting duty for the regular army.

In August, 1862, he went "to the field," in Virginia, a sergeant of Company C, Second Battalion, Twelfth Infantry, and was engaged in the battles of Antietam and Fredericksburg. In April, 1863, he was commissioned in the regular service as a lieutenant in the Twelfth Infantry, and as such took part in the battles of Chancellorsville, Gettysburg, Mine Run, the Wilderness, Spottsylvania, Bethesda Church, Cold Harbor, Petersburg, Weldon Railroad, Peeble's Farm, and Hatcher's Run, receiving the brevets of captain and major for "gallant services in battle."

In November, 1864, the Twelfth Infantry was sent from the field to Elmira, New York, to recruit and guard Confederate prisoners. While engaged in the latter duty Lieutenant Jackson was detailed on regimental recruiting service, and on expiration of this tour he joined the regiment at Russell Barracks, in Washington, D. C., being assigned to the Third Battalion of that regiment, now become the Thirtieth Infantry.

He accompanied the regiment to Nebraska in January, 1867, and was on duty at various places in the Department of the Platte, protecting the builders of the Union Pacific Railway from hostile Indians, until the consolidation of the infantry regiments in 1869, when, becoming an unassigned captain, the department commander, General C. C. Augur, placed him on duty as post quartermaster at Fort Steele, to complete the construction of that post.

In January, 1871, Captain Jackson was transferred to the First Cavalry, and joined his troop, B, at Camp Warner, in Oregon, changing station, soon after, to Fort Klamath, Oregon, and taking command of the post. In November, 1872, he was sent with a portion of his troop to place Captain Jack's band of Modoc Indians on their reservation, and in endeavoring to carry out these orders had a fight with them on Lost River, in Oregon, which commenced the "Modoc War." He was engaged in all

subsequent operations against these Indians until their surrender, and was recommended for the brevet of lieutenant-colonel by General Jeff. C. Davis, commanding the troops in the field.

During the Nez Perce war he was directed to join General Howard, with his troop, in Idaho. His timely arrival on the Clearwater, at Cottonwood Cañon, with reinforcements for the troops engaged in fighting Joseph's band of Nez Perces, broke the resistance of these Indians, and caused the defeat and evacuation of their fortified position. He joined in the pursuit of these Indians as far as the Judith Basin, in Montana, from which point the cavalry troops were directed to return to their stations. Captain Jackson was recommended by General Howard for a brevet for his services at Clearwater and during the campaign.

He was promoted major of the Second Cavalry December 28, 1889, and is at present on duty at Fort Wingate, New Mexico.

Major Jackson's great grandfather, Colonel Benjamin Loxley, of Philadelphia, organized and was captain of the "Philadelphia Light Horse," the first cavalry troop raised in Pennsylvania during the Revolutionary War. Colonel Loxley also raised and commanded "the First Artillery Company" of Philadelphia, which did such effective work during the war for independence, and was a volunteer aide on General Washington's staff at Valley Forge, and at other times until independence was achieved. He was also a lieutenant in the Pennsylvania division of Braddock's army, and assisted in bringing off the British troops after General Braddock's defeat.

### MEDICAL DIRECTOR SAMUEL JACKSON, U.S.N.
(RETIRED).

MEDICAL DIRECTOR SAMUEL JACKSON was born in Philadelphia, Pennsylvania. A graduate of the University of that State, he was appointed assistant surgeon in the navy, from North Carolina, in June, 1838. In January, 1839, he received orders for sea-duty, on board the United States frigate "Constitution," which vessel went, as flag-ship of the Pacific Squadron, for a term of three years. In those days the cruising was mostly in the South Pacific, California being seldom visited by any ships, except those which went there for trade, and to collect hides, the real currency of the country, in return. Returning to the East from this cruise, Dr. Jackson was, after a short leave of absence, ordered to the "Mississippi," the first steam-frigate of the United States navy. In that vessel he served during 1841 and a part of 1842. He was then ordered to the frigate "Congress," of the Mediterranean Squadron. He was afterwards detached upon the station, and served, in succession, in the "Preble," "Fairfield," and frigate "Cumberland," during the years 1843 to 1845.

The year 1846 found him on duty at the navy-yard at Philadelphia; but, the Mexican War impending, he was ordered to the razee "Independence," flag-ship of the Pacific Squadron, and served on board that ship until the conclusion of the peace, 1846-49.

In 1849-50 he was at the Philadelphia Navy-Yard, and then went to the receiving-ship "Franklin," at Boston, and thence to sea-service again in the "John Adams," and the "Decatur," of the Home Squadron.

He was commissioned as surgeon in September, 1852. During 1854-55 he was surgeon of the rendezvous at New York. He then made a long cruise on the coast of Africa, in the sloop-of-war "St. Louis," and on his return was stationed at the navy-yard at New York from 1858 to 1861.

During the early part of the Civil War he served in the frigates "Wabash" and "Cumberland," and participated in the bombardment and capture of the Confederate forts at Hatteras Inlet. Soon after he was ordered to the "Brooklyn," of the West Gulf Blockading Squadron, and served in her for nearly two years, on the blockade of Mobile and the passes, and then, under Farragut, made the passage of the Mississippi forts, the Chalmette batteries, and the other operations subsequent to the capture of that city. He was also present at the first series of operations against Vicksburg.

In 1863-64 he was the medical officer of the Naval Academy, and then went to the Boston Navy-Yard, during 1865-66.

In the three succeeding years he was fleet-surgeon of the North and South Pacific Squadrons. Upon his return he was, for about a year, at the Naval Hospital at Philadelphia, and then went to the Naval Hospital at New York, where he was on duty from 1879 to 1882.

He was commissioned as medical director in March, 1871.

From 1873 to 1875 he was in charge of the Naval Hospital at Norfolk, Virginia, and was thence transferred to the charge of the Naval Hospital at Chelsea, Massachusetts.

He was retired, by operation of law, April, 1879.

## REAR-ADMIRAL THORNTON A. JENKINS, U.S.N.
### (RETIRED.)

REAR-ADMIRAL THORNTON A. JENKINS was appointed midshipman from Virginia in November, 1828, and served five years in the West Indies, in "Natchez," "Vandalia," and the boat squadron in pursuit of the Cuban pirates. Passed No. 1, at his examination for promotion, in a class of eighty-two, June 2, 1834; on Coast Survey from 1834 to 1842, having been made lieutenant in 1839; served in the "Congress" in the Mediterranean, and was present at the capture of the Buenos Ayrean squadron off Montevideo in September, 1844; on special service, in Europe, 1845–46; executive-officer of "Germantown" during the Mexican War, and commanded store-ship "Relief" during the latter part of the war. He was actively engaged at Tuspan and Tabasco; Coast Survey from 1848 to 1852, and secretary of Light-House Board from 1853 to 1858. Commander, 1855; commanded the "Preble" in Paraguay Expedition and Gulf of Mexico; at San Juan d'Ulloa during the siege of General Miramon, and conveyed the prizes "Miramon" and "Marquis of Havana," with their crews and passengers as prisoners, to New Orleans. In 1861 secretary of Light-House Board. Captain in July, 1862; commanded "Wachusett" in the James and Potomac Rivers; senior officer present in the attacks at Coggin's Point and City Point. In the fall of 1862 in command of "Oneida," blockading off Mobile; was next appointed fleet-captain and chief of staff of Farragut's fleet; present at the passage of Port Hudson and fight with Grand Gulf batteries, Warrenton and Grand Gulf,— all in March, 1863; present at the siege and attack upon Port Hudson, May, 1863; wounded on board "Monongahela" during the engagement with enemy's batteries at College Point, Mississippi River, being in command of three armed vessels engaged in convoy duty. He was in command of the "Richmond," and senior officer in command of the naval forces below, at the time of the surrender of Port Hudson, July 9, 1863. In command of division, on the Mobile blockade, from December, 1863, to the battle of Mobile Bay, August 5, 1864, in which, and all the subsequent operations, he took part. He was left in command of the Mobile Bay division until February, 1865. He was then ordered to James River, and remained there until after Lee's surrender.

Admiral Farragut, in his detailed report of the Mobile affair, says, "Before closing this report, there is one other officer of my squadron of whom I feel bound to speak,— Captain T. A. Jenkins, of the 'Richmond,' who was formerly my chief of staff, not because of his having held that position, but because he never forgets to do his duty to the government, and takes now the same interest in the fleet as when he stood in that relation to me. He is also commanding officer of the Second Division of my squadron, and, as such, has shown ability and the most untiring zeal. He carries out the spirit of one of Lord Collingwood's best sayings,—'not to be afraid of doing too much; those who are, seldom do as much as they ought.' When in Pensacola, he spent days on the bar, placing buoys in the best position, was always looking after the interests of the service, and keeping the vessels from being detained in port one moment more than necessary. The gallant Craven told me, only the night before the action in which he lost his life, 'I regret, admiral, that I have detained you; but had it not been for Captain Jenkins, God knows when I should have been here. When your order came I had not received an ounce of coal.' I feel that I should not be doing my duty if I did not call the attention of the department to an officer who has performed all his various duties with so much zeal and fidelity."

Captain Jenkins was made commodore in 1866, while chief of the Bureau of Navigation. In 1869 he became secretary of the Light-House Board. Rear-admiral in 1870, he commanded the Asiatic Squadron, and was relieved on that station in 1873, having reached the age of retirement in December.

In March, 1874, he was appointed, by the President, commissioner to represent the Navy Department at the Centennial Exhibition of 1876, at Fairmount Park, Philadelphia.

COLONEL HORACE JEWETT, U.S.A.

COLONEL HORACE JEWETT was appointed first lieutenant of Fifteenth Infantry May 14, 1861, and ordered on the regimental recruiting service at Xenia, Ohio. He remained on that duty about four weeks, when he was transferred to Columbus, Ohio, to perform the same service at Newport, Kentucky. In October he was ordered to regimental headquarters, and in November was ordered from there to join that portion of the regiment serving in the field in Kentucky. From November, 1861, to August, 1863, he served constantly with his regiment in the field, taking part in the battles of Shiloh, siege of Corinth, Chaplain Hills, Stone River, and Hoover's Gap, and also campaigns of Buell and Rosecrans. During the greater portion of this service he commanded Company "A," First Battalion. While his army was in camp about Cowan, Tennessee, he was ordered to regimental headquarters, Fort Adams, Rhode Island, and detailed on recruiting service, stationed first at Boston, Massachusetts, and afterwards at Philadelphia, Pennsylvania. In March, 1864, upon his own application, he was ordered to take a company from Fort Adams, Rhode Island, to join that portion of his regiment then at Graysville, Georgia. He commanded Company B, Third Battalion, Fifteenth Infantry, from the commencement of the Atlanta campaign, until just before the battle of Utoy Creek, participating in all the engagements in which his regiment took part. When his commanding officer received a gunshot wound, he assumed command of the detachment, consisting of nine companies, First and Third Battalion, Fifteenth Infantry. In command of this detachment he took part in the battles of Utoy Creek, Jonesborough, and sundry skirmishes, and at the close of the campaign was ordered with it to Lookout Mountain, Tennessee. While on Lookout Mountain a detachment of cavalry was ordered to report to him, and he was ordered to make an exploration of the mountain, with a view to the defence of the same. In December was again ordered to regimental headquarters, Fort Adams, and reassigned to the Philadelphia recruiting service. January, 1866, Company D, First Battalion, being reorganized at Fort Adams, Rhode Island, he was ordered to join and take it to Mobile, Alabama September 1, he was detailed on the general recruiting service at Harrisburg, Pennsylvania, and remained until January 1868, when he rejoined his company in Montgomery, Alabama. In March he was assigned to the command of the post, embracing seventeen counties of the State, with from three to six companies of infantry and cavalry to assist him in their reconstruction, and he remained on this duty until the State was turned over to the civil authorities, when the regiment was ordered to Texas.

Upon orders for regiments to consolidate, he marched with his troops from Canton to Austin, and from there to Fort Concho, and then to Fort Seldon. In command of Fort Bascom, New Mexico, from October 17, 1869, until December 11, 1870. From December 19, 1870, until April 30, 1872, he served at Fort Union, in command of his company, and at times the post. From there he was ordered to Garland, Colorado, and in August 18, 1876, proceeded to Fort Wingate, New Mexico. While stationed there, in the fall of 1877, he arranged and secured the surrender of Victoria, Loco, and Nana, and three hundred and thirty other Warm Spring Apache Indians, who had been on the war-path in New Mexico and Arizona. In 1879 he marched across the Navajo Reservation to Farmington, New Mexico, and camped there a few weeks between the Navajo and Southern Ute Reservations. With two companies of infantry he marched from thence to Animas City, Colorado, and remained until the winter of 1880. In 1881 he returned with his command to Fort Wingate, New Mexico; was there but a few weeks, when he marched to Fort Cummings, New Mexico, to join a large body of troops that was concentrating there against the Apaches; marched from there, in pursuit of the Apaches, to near the city of Chihuahua, Mexico, when he was ordered to return to the United States as soon as practicable. Having been promoted a major of the Sixteenth Infantry January 31, 1882, he was ordered to headquarters, Department of Texas, and then to Fort McKavett, Texas. From there he marched to Fort Stockton, and then to Fort Concho. Promoted lieutenant-colonel Third Infantry August 1, 1885, and was immediately assigned to command Fort Missoula, Montana. In June, 1888, he was ordered to Fort Snelling, Minnesota, and remained there until his promotion as colonel of Twenty-first Infantry, when he was given command of Fort Huachuca, the present station.

## CAPTAIN STEPHEN PERRY JOCELYN, U.S.A.

CAPTAIN STEPHEN PERRY JOCELYN (Twenty-first Infantry) was born at Brownington, Vermont, March 1, 1843, and is directly descended, in the eighth generation, from Anthony Perry of the Plymouth colony, who, coming from Devonshire in 1638, founded in New England the family of his name, which, in its various branches, has furnished a line of soldiers and sailors alike distinguished in early Indian and colonial as well as the more recent wars of the United States.

Captain Jocelyn received an academic education in his native State, and when about to enter Dartmouth College was enrolled August 22, 1863, at the age of twenty, in the Sixth Vermont Infantry. The following year he was commissioned first lieutenant One Hundred and Fifteenth United States Colored Infantry, and served against guerillas in Kentucky until December, 1864, when his regiment was transferred to the Army of the James, where, in command of his company, he participated in the subsequent operations in front of Richmond, being present at the fall and occupation of that city, April 3, 1865.

Upon the transfer of General Weitzel's command to Texas, in June, 1865, Lieutenant Jocelyn accompanied it with his regiment, being soon after appointed quartermaster of the First Brigade, Second Division of the Twenty-fifth Army Corps, in which capacity, with station at Indianola, Texas, he continued to serve until mustered out of the volunteer service, February 10, 1866.

Arriving in Washington from Texas in April, 1866, Lieutenant Jocelyn found awaiting him a commission of second lieutenant in the regular army. He was assigned to the Sixth Infantry, and joining the regiment at Charleston, South Carolina, attained the grade of first lieutenant July 28, 1866, and was promoted captain Twenty-first Infantry May 19, 1874.

Beginning at Fort Gibson, Indian Territory, in 1867, Captain Jocelyn has had a wide experience of the varied vicissitudes of army service on the frontier, extending from Montana to Texas, and from Arizona to Alaska. For some time in 1869-70 he was detailed to assist General Hazen in the latter's duties of superintendent of Indian affairs for the Southern superintendency.

The year 1871, a culminating season of Apache atrocities, found Captain Jocelyn afield in Arizona, followed, during the years 1872-73 and '74, by service in Northern California and Southern Oregon, at the posts of Fort Bidwell, Camp Warner, and Fort Klamath.

Development of the gold-fields of Alaska caused the re-establishment of Fort Wrangel in 1875. Captain Jocelyn was assigned to and continued in command of this important and isolated post for a year and a half.

Captain Jocelyn participated in the harassing and

tedious war with the Nez Percés, throughout which he commanded his company, being engaged in the two-days' fight of the Clearwater and subsequent skirmish at Kamai. The summer of 1878 furnished another period of Indian hostilities, the recalcitrant Bannacks and Piutes being brought to their senses in the engagement near Umatilla Agency, in which Captain Jocelyn took part; after which a leave of absence was granted Captain Jocelyn, which he utilized by a year of travel and study in Europe, returning to Fort Townsend, on Puget Sound, in 1880, which continued to be his station for the next four years. He was, however, detached to command the Skagit River Indian expedition October-November, 1880, and again in 1881, to conduct the reconnoissance for a military telegraph-line between Port Angeles and Cape Flattery, Washington Territory.

Captain Jocelyn has given considerable attention to the subject of small-arms fire and drill. His company won the Nevada Trophy in 1882, and again the following year, and he was captain of Department of Columbia rifle-team in division contest at San Francisco, 1883.

In 1882 General Schofield, commanding Division of the Pacific, used the following commendatory language in orders: "It is a significant fact that the company in this division which has this year made the best average per cent. (87.42) in competition for the Nevada Trophy, is the one reported by the assistant inspector-general as by far the best instructed in the bayonet exercise."

The Twenty-first Infantry having been transferred to the Department of the Platte in 1884, Captain Jocelyn's service since that year, with exception of a tour of recruiting duty, has been in Wyoming, Utah, and Nebraska, at the posts of Fort Fred Steele, Fort Du Chesne, Fort Douglas, and Fort Sidney. At the latter he is now stationed.

## CAPTAIN JOHN BURGESS JOHNSON, U.S.A.

CAPTAIN JOHN BURGESS JOHNSON (Third Cavalry) was born at Rochester, Massachusetts, November 29, 1847. He entered the volunteer service during the war of the Rebellion as second lieutenant of the Sixth U. S. Colored Infantry September 8, 1863, and served with the Army of the James in the Tenth and Eighteenth Army Corps, and was engaged in front of Petersburg, at the explosion of the mine, and action of New Market Heights, Virginia, where he was wounded and promoted first lieutenant. He was honorably mustered out of the service January 20, 1865, on account of wounds received in action; but was reappointed and mustered to his promotion as first lieutenant February 15, 1865, and joined his regiment at Fort Fisher, North Carolina. He participated in the engagement at Cox's Bridge, North Carolina, and at the surrender of General Johnston and his army, acting as aide and assistant adjutant-general. He was honorably mustered out of the volunteer service September 20, 1865.

Lieutenant Johnson entered the regular service as second lieutenant of the Seventh Infantry April 23, 1866, and was promoted first lieutenant October 12, 1867. He joined his regiment in Florida, and served as post adjutant at Fernandina. He served there and in Georgia until May 19, 1867, when he became unassigned by reason of the consolidation of regiments. While unassigned, Lieutenant Johnson was placed on reconstruction duty in Mississippi until January 1, 1871, when he was assigned to the Third Cavalry. On joining his regiment he served in Arizona, and was adjutant of his regiment from May, 1871, to April, 1878.

The Third Cavalry having been transferred to the Department of the Platte, Lieutenant Johnson was in command of Troop E, and participated in the capture and destruction of Crazy Horse Sioux village, on Powder River, Montana, March 17, 1876. He was promoted captain of the Third Cavalry April 4, 1878, and was in command of the battalion of the Third Cavalry which captured Dull Knife's band of one hundred and forty-nine Cheyenne Indians October 24, 1878, in the sand-hills of Northern Nebraska.

In 1881, while his troop was on duty at Fort Leavenworth, Captain Johnson was instructor at the U. S. Infantry and Cavalry School, which position he retained until 1886, when he was transferred to Texas, and was in command of a battalion of the Third Cavalry on the march from San Antonio to Brownsville. He has been in command of Fort Brown, Texas, since October 18, 1890.

## CAPTAIN AND BREVET LIEUTENANT-COLONEL LEWIS JOHNSON, U.S.A.

CAPTAIN AND BREVET LIEUTENANT-COLONEL LEWIS JOHNSON (Twenty-fourth Infantry) was born in Rostock, Germany, March 30, 1841. He entered the volunteer service at the commencement of the war of the Rebellion, as private of Company E, Tenth Indiana Infantry, April 18, 1861, and was discharged August 6, 1861, having participated in McClellan's West Virginia campaign, and engaged in the battle of Rich Mountain. He re-entered the volunteer service as first lieutenant of the Tenth Indiana Infantry September 18, 1861, and was promoted captain August 29, 1862. He participated in the battles and campaigns of the West, and was engaged in the battle of Mill Springs, Kentucky, where he was wounded. He was in the advance upon and siege of Corinth, Mississippi, where he was again wounded. He then participated in the battle of Perryville, Kentucky; action on Salt Run, Kentucky; advance on Tullahoma, Tennessee; battle of Chickamauga, Georgia; action at Rossville, Georgia; siege of Chattanooga, Tennessee; battle of Missionary Ridge, Tennessee; engagements of Tunnel Hill, Georgia; Rocky-Face Ridge, Georgia, and Dalton, Georgia, where he was captured.

He was honorably mustered out of the Tenth Indiana Infantry September 15, 1864, and was appointed colonel of the Forty-fourth United States Colored Troops September 16, 1864. He was in command of troops in the action on Mill Creek, Tennessee, December 2 and 3, 1864, and commanded his regiment in the battles of Nashville, Tennessee (where he was wounded), and succeeding pursuit of Hood's routed army. He occupied various positions on the staff of brigade, division, and corps commanders,—on the staff of Brigadier-General J. M. Brannan, at Chickamauga, and Brigadier-General A. Baird, at Missionary Ridge. He was in command of the First Colored Brigade, Army of the Cumberland, Second Brigade, District of East Tennessee, District of Northern Alabama, and District and Post of Huntsville, Alabama. He commanded the Exchange Barracks, Nashville, Tennessee, when mustered out of the volunteer service.

Colonel Johnson had the following brevets conferred upon him: captain March 13, 1862, for "gallant and meritorious services in the battle of Mill Springs, Kentucky;" major March 22, 1867, for "gallant and meritorious services in the siege of Corinth, Mississippi;" and lieutenant-colonel for "gallant and meritorious services in the battle of Missionary Ridge, Tennessee." He was also brevetted brigadier-general of volunteers March 13, 1865, for "gallant and meritorious services during the war."

Colonel Johnson entered the regular service as first lieutenant of the Forty-first United States Infantry July 28, 1866, was promoted captain December 12, 1867, and, on the consolidation of regiments, was transferred to the Twenty-fourth Infantry November 11, 1869. He was on regimental recruiting service in Alabama, Tennessee, Ohio, and Michigan, from 1866 to 1868, and then served with his regiment on frontier duty in Texas from 1868 to 1880, at which time his regiment was transferred to the Indian Territory, where the colonel was stationed until 1883, when he was detailed on general recruiting service in St. Louis and Harrisburg, Pennsylvania. In 1885 he rejoined his regiment in the Indian Territory, and commanded a battalion of the Twenty-fourth Infantry during the transfer of the regiment to Arizona, in 1888. He commanded the post of San Carlos, Arizona, from May, 1889, to October, 1891, when he was appointed Indian agent of the White Mountain (Apache) Indian Reservation at the San Carlos Agency, on which duty he is at the present time.

CHIEF ENGINEER DAVID PHILLIPS JONES, U.S.N.

CHIEF ENGINEER DAVID PHILLIPS JONES was born in Philadelphia in 1841, and was educated at the Central High School of that city when the celebrated scholar and educator, Professor John S. Hart, was at its head.

In 1858, when but a youth, he was appointed one of the principal examiners of the Utah Surveys. The duty of the examiners was to test the accuracy of the surveys of the public lands in that Territory. After the completion of this work he was appointed resident engineer of the surveyor-general's office.

At the breaking out of the Civil War he returned East, and in 1862 entered the navy as assistant engineer, and was ordered to duty on the gun-boat " Cimmerone." This vessel was attached to the James River fleet, and afterwards was assigned to Admiral Wilkes's Flying Squadron, and thence transferred to Admiral Dupont's fleet, where she participated in various engagements on the St. John's River, Florida.

His next service was on the iron-clad " Sangamon." This was the vessel that received the Confederate commissioners, Stephens and Campbell, upon their memorable mission to secure an interview with President Lincoln.

The arduous duties and close confinement on the iron-clad undermined Engineer Jones's health, and he was condemned by medical survey and detached.

In a short time he again reported for duty and was ordered to the " Mendota." The " Mendota" was attached to the James River fleet, and participated in many actions on that river preceding the fall of Richmond.

While this vessel was stationed at Hampton Roads, Engineer Jones was detailed to carry the despatches from Admiral Porter informing General Grant of the capture of Fort Fisher. Army head-quarters were at that time at City Point. The dangerous journey was made at night, and the despatches safely delivered to General Grant in the early morning. For this service he was highly complimented by his commanding officer.

His next duty was on the flag-ship " Powhatan," on the South Pacific. While on this vessel he witnessed the bombardment of Valparaiso and Callao by the Spaniards in 1866. After leaving the " Powhatan" he was attached to the " Gettysburg" and " Michigan," and to the Portsmouth Navy-Yard. He was stationed at the latter place when Admiral Farragut died there, and was one of the officers' guard-of-honor selected to watch over the remains. He was afterwards on duty in the Bureau of Steam-Engineering, and was thence assigned to the Naval Academy, where he aided in perfecting the system of mechanical drawing and machine design for the cadet engineers. He was retained on this duty for five years, which was the best comment upon his usefulness.

Beside the duties enumerated, Engineer Jones has been attached to various vessels and stations, and also as professor of mechanical engineering at the Kansas Normal College. While upon extended leave he became the engineer of the St. Louis and Southeastern Railway, and designed and built the great railway transfers at Evansville, Indiana, and Henderson, Kentucky.

Of his ability and the esteem in which he is held, Commander, now Rear-Admiral, John Irwin, wrote, " With his professional ability and scholarly attainments, I consider him one of the most accomplished officers in the service." The lamented Captain Shoemaker, in a special report to the Navy Department, says, " This method of repairing the defect in the machinery (of the ' Nipsic') was the design of Passed Assistant Engineer Jones, and is very creditable to the designer, showing knowledge, skill, and ingenuity."

Chief Engineer Jones is a member of many prominent scientific societies, and has a broad and comprehensive grasp of engineering subjects. He has always been identified with the progressive element of the Naval Engineer Corps, and has never failed to retain the confidence and esteem of the engineers-in-chief. The law authorizing the detail of naval engineer officers as instructors in technical schools was his conception.

As a writer he has contributed much to establish the importance and define the responsibilities of his corps, while his official reports upon professional topics are regarded as models. He is also the author of many well-known navy songs. He has considerable reputation as a public speaker. His witty and eloquent responses to the toast of " The Navy," at the inaugural banquet given to Governor Davis, of Rhode Island, in 1890, and at the thirtieth anniversary of the Rhode Island Artillery at Newport in 1891, will long be remembered.

Chief Engineer Jones's present duty is at the Naval Training Station, Newport, Rhode Island.

## MEDICAL INSPECTOR WILLIAM H. JONES, U.S.N.

Medical Inspector William H. Jones was born in Northampton County, Pennsylvania, December 15, 1840.

He was appointed acting assistant surgeon in the U. S. Navy in April, 1863, and ordered on duty at the Naval Hospital, Norfolk, Virginia.

He was appointed assistant surgeon August 12, 1863.
Served on U. S. S. "Pensacola," West Gulf Blockading Squadron, 1863-64.
U. S. S. "Marblehead" (practice cruiser), 1864.
U. S. Naval Academy, practice ships, 1864.
U. S. ram "Tennessee," West Gulf Blockading Squadron, 1864-65.
U. S. Naval Hospital, New Orleans, Louisiana, 1865.
U. S. Naval Hospital, Pensacola, Florida, 1865-66.
U. S. S. "W. G. Anderson," West Gulf Blockading Squadron, 1866.
Navy-yard, Washington, D. C., 1866-67.

He was promoted to passed assistant surgeon December 24, 1866.
U. S. S. "Maumee," Asiatic Squadron, 1867-69.
Navy-yard, Washington, D. C., 1870-71.
U. S. S. "Jamestown," South Pacific Station, 1871.
U. S. S. "Saranac," North Pacific Station, 1871.
U. S. S. "Pensacola," Pacific fleet, 1871-73.
U. S. S. "Portsmouth," survey of the Pacific, 1873-75.
He was commissioned as surgeon in July, 1873.
U. S. training-ship "Portsmouth," San Francisco, California, 1875.
U. S. receiving-ship "Potomac," Philadelphia, Pennsylvania, from December, 1875, to 1877; then transferred to U. S. S. "Constitution," at Philadelphia, Pennsylvania, in 1877.

U. S. S. "Constitution," European Station, 1878-79.
U. S. Naval Hospital, Brooklyn, New York, 1879-80.
U. S. S. "Michigan," on the Lakes, 1881.
U. S. S. "Franklin," Norfolk, Virginia, 1881.
U. S. S. "Wachusett," Pacific Station, 1884-85.
U. S. Navy-Yard, League Island, Pennsylvania, 1885-88.
U. S. S. "Pensacola," New York Navy-Yard, 1888.
U. S. S. "Richmond," New York Navy Yard, 1888.
U. S. S. "Pensacola," navy-yard, Norfolk, Virginia, 1888-89.
U. S. S. "Swatara," Asiatic Station, 1889-91.
U. S. Navy-Yard, League Island, Pennsylvania, 1891-92.

Surgeon Jones was promoted to medical inspector in November, 1891.

**REAR-ADMIRAL JAMES E. JOUETT, U.S.N.**
(RETIRED.)

REAR-ADMIRAL JAMES E. JOUETT was born in Kentucky in 1828, and appointed midshipman from that State in 1841. His first service was in the West Indies and Home Squadron on the razee "Independence," and he next served on the coast of Africa in the "Decatur;" engaged in the Berriby War. Passed midshipman in 1847. During the Mexican War he served in the Gulf Squadron in most of the operations incident to the war, so far as the east coast was concerned. He occupied Point Isabel with sailors from the squadron for some time. Master September, 1855, and lieutenant the same month. Landed with detachment at Panama to keep transit open and protect Americans. In 1857 went out in the "Chapin," a chartered vessel, on the Paraguay Expedition. Upon his return he was ordered to the "Crusader," employed on special service in suppressing the slave-trade in Cuban waters. The "Crusader" captured three slavers. In 1861, while at Pensacola, awaiting the return of the "Crusader," the navy-yard was captured by the Confederate forces, and Jouett was placed on parole. After exchange he was ordered to the frigate "Santee," on blockade of Galveston, Texas. Here he commanded the party which cut out the "Royal Yacht," being severely wounded. Captain Eagle, commanding the "Santee," in his official report, says: "It is with pleasure that I would call the attention of the Department to the gallantry of Lieutenant Jouett. He was seriously wounded in the arm and side at the commencement of the contest. Although suffering from wounds and loss of blood, he showed great firmness throughout, and after setting fire to the vessel he was three hours in the launch pulling for the ship, and had the care of twelve prisoners and six of his wounded men. I can, with confidence, recommend him for a command of any vessel in the service suitable to his rank, although I should much regret his detachment from this ship, as he is a very efficient officer."

He was made lieutenant-commander August, 1862, and ordered to command the "Cuyler," off Mobile. He captured four blockade-runners while on this duty. He was soon ordered to the command of the "Metacomet." In this command his vessel was lashed alongside of Farragut's flag-ship at the battle of Mobile Bay, August 5, 1864. After passing Fort Morgan and the torpedoes, the rebel gun-boats inside the bay began to rake the flag-ship. Farragut ordered the "Metacomet" to cast off and go in pursuit. Jouett promptly pursued, and, after a desperate conflict, captured the Confederate war-steamer "Selma," and also rendered other gallant service during that fight, of which Farragut reported: "Lieutenant-Commander Jouett's promptness and coolness throughout the fight merited high praise, received his warmest commendation, and was worthy of his reputation." For this occasion, the board, of which Farragut was president, in 1865 recommended Jouett to be promoted thirty numbers. This advancement was not made. *The war was over.*

During the action in Mobile Bay, it is related by Commodore Parker, the "Metacomet" ran into *less water than she drew* in pursuit of the rebel gun-boats. When this happened, Jouett called in the leadsman from the chains, saying, "The admiral has directed me to follow these gun-boats, and I am going to do it!" Fortunately, the "Metacomet" only stirred up the mud, and accomplished her mission. Had it been otherwise, they might have turned upon her, as they drew less water.

In July, 1866, he was commissioned as commander, and for two years commanded the "Michigan," on the Lakes. In January, 1874, he was commissioned as captain. From June, 1880, to January, 1883, he had command of the Port Royal Naval Station. Commissioned commodore January 11, 1883. Ordered to command North Atlantic Squadron as acting rear-admiral in September, 1884. He commanded the squadron for two years, and during that time, "by his prompt, firm, and judicious course in the spring of 1885, during the rebellion on the Isthmus of Panama, restored order, re-established transit, prevented great destruction of property and loss of life, and was instrumental in bringing about the surrender of the insurgent forces in the United States of Colombia, and reflected credit on the United States of America."

In June, 1886, he was detached and ordered as president of the Board of Inspection and Survey, and chief of Admiral Porter's staff, having been commissioned as rear-admiral from February 19, 1886.

He was retired from active service by operation of law in February, 1890.

## CAPTAIN ALBERT KAUTZ, U.S.N.

CAPTAIN ALBERT KAUTZ was born in Ohio January 29, 1839. Appointed acting midshipman September, 1854. Graduated at Naval Academy, Annapolis, June 11, 1858. Served in several vessels of the Home Squadron, and in January, 1861, was promoted to passed midshipman; in the February following to master, and in April to lieutenant. This rapid promotion was due to the many vacancies in the navy-list caused by the imminence of the Civil War. Served in the steamer "Flag," North Atlantic Squadron. In June, 1861, placed in command of prize-brig "Hannah Balch," off Charleston, South Carolina, with orders to proceed to Philadelphia; and on June 25 was captured, in sight of Cape Hatteras, by the privateer "Winslow," Captain Thomas M. Crossan. Lieutenant Kautz was on parole in North Carolina for two months, at the end of which time the parole was revoked and he was incarcerated in Henrico County Jail, Richmond, Virginia, by order of Jefferson Davis, as a retaliatory measure consequent on the imprisonment of privateers in the Tombs, at New York. On the last day of October, 1861, Lieutenant Kautz was released on parole for the purpose of going to Washington to procure an exchange. He had an interview with the Confederate Secretaries Benjamin and Mallory before he left Richmond, and then with President Lincoln and Secretaries Seward and Welles, in Washington. He succeeded in negotiating an exchange, by means of which Lieutenant (the present admiral) Worden, the late Lieutenant George L. Selden, and himself were released from prison and restored to duty, on condition that Lieutenants Stevens, Loyall, and Butt should be sent South under flag of truce. There were also three hundred and fifty prisoners, captured at Hatteras Inlet in August, 1861, sent South under the same negotiation, for which were received three hundred and fifty of the Bull Run prisoners, captured in July, 1861.

This was the first exchange of prisoners authorized by President Lincoln and his Cabinet, and marks a distinct phase in the conduct of the war.

In January, 1862, Lieutenant Kautz was ordered to the "Hartford," Admiral Farragut's flag-ship, and served upon his staff; but commanded the first division of great guns in the engagements with Forts Jackson and St. Philip, the Chalmette batteries, and the capture of New Orleans, in April, 1862. He had command of the howitzers, under Captain Henry Bell, at New Orleans, and hauled down the "Lone-Star" flag in person from the City Hall. This was the flag which the mayor re-

fused to strike. He then hoisted the Stars and Stripes on the Custom-House. (The hauling down of the "Lone-Star" flag has been erroneously attributed to Captain Bell in some accounts of those exciting times.)

Lieutenant Kautz continued to serve in the "Hartford" during the engagements with the batteries at Vicksburg in June and July, 1862. In August he was seized by malarial fever, condemned by medical survey, and sent North. His next service was on board the steam-sloop "Juniata," of the West India Squadron, in 1863; and in 1864-65 he served as first lieutenant of the sloop-of-war "Cyane" in the Pacific. Promoted lieutenant-commander in May, 1865. Served in the "Winooski," of the Home Squadron, and flag-ship "Pensacola," of the Pacific Squadron, up to August, 1868. Then on board the receiving-ship at Norfolk, and at the navy-yard, Boston, up to August, 1871, at which time he was appointed inspector of light-houses, with head-quarters at Key West, Florida. During his service in this capacity he was promoted to commander September 3, 1872. Commanded the "Monocacy," on the Asiatic Station, from 1872 to 1873. Light-house inspector, with station at Cincinnati, from January, 1876, to July, 1880. Commanded the steamer "Michigan," on the Lakes, from August, 1880, to August, 1883. In 1884 Commander Kautz was on duty in the Bureau of Equipment, Navy Department. Equipment officer, Boston, 1884-87. Promoted captain June 2, 1885, and on duty at navy-yard, Portsmouth, since June, 1890. Captain Kautz has had command of the U. S. S. "Pensacola," cruising in the Atlantic, and then in the Pacific Ocean.

**BRIGADIER-GENERAL AUGUST VALENTINE KAUTZ, U.S.A. (RETIRED).**

BRIGADIER-GENERAL AUGUST VALENTINE KAUTZ was born in the Grand Duchy of Baden on the 5th of January, 1828. His parents emigrated the same year, and in 1834 settled in Brown County, Ohio. In a company of young men from Georgetown, he went to the Mexican War as a volunteer in the First Ohio, which served on the Northern campaign under General Taylor. He participated in the battle of Monterey, and upon his discharge he was appointed a cadet at the Military Academy, graduating in 1852, and assigned second lieutenant of the Fourth U. S. Infantry. He joined his regiment in Oregon soon after graduation, and served in Oregon and Washington Territory until the Civil War. He participated in the Rogue River Wars, 1853 and 1855, and was wounded in the latter, and again wounded in the spring of 1856, in the Indian War on Puget Sound, for which action he was commended for gallantry in general orders No. 14, from the head-quarters of the army, dated November 13, 1857, by General Scott. Promoted first lieutenant in 1854.

He was appointed captain Sixth U. S. Cavalry in 1861, and served with the regiment from its organization through the Peninsula campaign of 1862, and commanded the regiment during the seven days, and up to South Mountain, September 10, when appointed colonel Second Ohio Cavalry, and joined the regiment in Kansas.

His regiment was subsequently ordered to Camp Chase, Ohio, and Colonel Kautz commanded that post from December, 1862, to April, 1863. Early in April, 1863, he took the field with his regiment, and served in Kentucky, his regiment forming a part of General Carter's Division. He participated in a number of engagements until the Morgan raid, which he joined from the Cumberland River to Portland, Ohio. His judicious attack on Morgan's rear early in the morning with simply the advance of Hobson's force, which was fifteen miles in the rear, prevented Morgan from recrossing the Ohio, and led to the capture on that day and the day following.

Upon the organization of the Twenty-third Corps for the campaign into East Tennessee, Colonel Kautz was assigned as chief of cavalry of the corps, and served in that capacity to the capture of Knoxville, and through the subsequent siege by the rebel forces.

In the spring of 1864 Colonel Kautz took the field, having been appointed brigadier-general, and assigned to the command of the cavalry division of the Army of the James. This command was an independent command under General Butler, and was used to cut the railroads south of Richmond and Petersburg while Bermuda Hundred was being occupied. He served alternately with the Army of the James and the Army of the Potomac throughout the year 1864. He entered Petersburg with his small cavalry command on the 9th of June, 1864, and had he been properly supported by the infantry it might have been held, and the long siege that followed have been avoided. He led the advance of the Wilson raid, which cut the roads leading into Richmond from the south for more than forty days.

During the winter of 1864-65 he held and picketed the right flank of the Army of the James with his cavalry command. When the dispositions were made for the final campaign in the last days of March, 1865, General Kautz was assigned to the First Division, Twenty-fifth Army Corps, as brevet major-general, and he marched his division of colored troops into Richmond on the 3d of April. Soon after the death of Mr. Lincoln he was detailed as a member of the Military Commission for the trial of the conspirators implicated in the assassination.

When the army was reorganized, in 1866, General Kautz was appointed lieutenant-colonel of the Thirty-fourth Infantry. He served with his regiment in Mississippi on reconstruction duty, and in 1869, on the reduction of the army, was assigned lieutenant colonel of the Fifteenth Infantry, and commanded the regiment for several years on the New Mexican frontier.

In June, 1874, General Kautz was promoted colonel of the Eighth Infantry, and joined his regiment in Arizona. In March, 1875, he was placed in command of the Department of Arizona, and relieved General Crook. General Kautz was brevetted major-general in the volunteers as well as the regular service.

General Kautz, as colonel of the Eighth Infantry, commanded the post of Fort Niobrara, Nebraska, from December, 1886, to December, 1890, when he was appointed the president of the Magazine-Gun Board. On the 20th of April, 1891, he was appointed brigadier-general, and assigned to the command of the Department of the Columbia. He commanded the department until the 5th of January, 1892, when he was retired in accordance with law.

## MAJOR E. R. KELLOGG, U.S.A.

MAJOR E. R. KELLOGG (Eighth Infantry) was born at Newfield, Tompkins County, New York, March 25, 1842. He began the study of law early in April, 1861, at Norwalk, Ohio, but enlisted (in what afterwards became Company "A," Twenty-fourth Ohio Volunteer Infantry), April 15, 1861, at Norwalk. He was mustered to date from April 22, 1861. He was a private, corporal, and sergeant in this company, and was made sergeant-major of the regiment in June, 1861, and second lieutenant July 8, 1861. (He has his commission to prove this. It has been twice sent to the War Department, but the officials there refused to correct the Army Register, because the muster-roll of Company "A," Twenty-fourth Ohio Volunteer Infantry, gives his commission a different date.) Lieutenant Kellogg served in West Virginia from July until October, 1861, and was in action at Greenbrier River in September of that year. He resigned October 28, 1861, and enlisted in Company "B," First Battalion Sixteenth U. S. Infantry, November 29, 1861, and immediately joined the Army of the Ohio, in Kentucky. He was appointed a sergeant of Company "B," Sixteenth Infantry, on the day following his enlistment; was made sergeant-major about a week later, and was soon recommended for a commission; but this recommendation was lost in the adjutant-general's office before it was acted upon. He was again recommended immediately after the battle of Shiloh, in which he participated with his battalion, and was commissioned a second lieutenant in the Sixteenth Infantry from that date, April 7, 1862. He was promoted to first lieutenant May 3, 1862, and to captain February 16, 1865.

He served constantly with his regiment in the field in Kentucky, Tennessee, Mississippi, Alabama, and Georgia, until the close of the Atlanta campaign, in 1864; was in the battle of Shiloh, actions before Corinth, Mississippi, and at Dog Walk, Kentucky; battle of Murfreesborough, or Stone River, Tennessee; combat at Hoover's Gap, Tennessee; at Rocky Face and Buzzard Roost, Georgia, in February, 1864; again in the Atlanta campaign, at Rocky Face and Buzzard Roost, Resaca, New Hope Church, Kenesaw Mountain, Neal Dow Station, Peach-Tree Creek, Utoy Creek, Atlanta, and Jonesborough, Georgia, in which last battle, September 1, 1864, he commanded the two left companies of his regiment, and was dangerously wounded by a musket-ball through his right hip. In the charge at Jonesborough his regiment was checked by the enemy's fire when near his works, but Lieutenant Kellogg took his two companies forward, drove the enemy from the intrenchments in his front, and, although enfiladed and wounded by his fire, held the position until the rest of his regiment joined him.

In January, 1866, he took command of a company of his regiment at Madison Barracks, Sackett's Harbor,

New York. From there he went to Nashville, and then to Memphis, Tennessee. He was transferred to the Twenty-fifth Infantry September 25, 1866, and was on general recruiting service in Toledo, Ohio, about one year, in 1866-67, and then was stationed at Paducah, Kentucky, from January, 1868, until April, 1869, when he went to Atlanta, Georgia, with his regiment, and was there transferred to the Eighteenth Infantry, in which he served until December 26, 1888. He served at various places in the Southern States from April, 1869, until April, 1879. He commanded the post of Chattanooga, Tennessee, from July, 1877, until April 1879, when he went to Montana. He served at Fort Assinaboine from May, 1879, until May, 1885, and was in the field from July until October, in 1882, in command of three companies of the Eighteenth Infantry and three troops of the Second Cavalry.

He was stationed at Fort Hays, Kansas, from June, 1885, until September, 1887, when he was detailed on general recruiting service at Cleveland, Ohio. He was promoted major of the Eighth Infantry December 26, 1888, Nebraska, in April, 1889; serving at Fort Robinson, Nebraska, from April, 1889, until September, 1890, when he went to Fort Washakie, Wyoming, which post he commanded until December, 1891, when he was ordered to Fort McKinney, Wyoming.

Major Kellogg was acting assistant adjutant-general to Lieutenant-Colonel J. V. Bomford, Sixteenth Infantry, for a few weeks in 1862, while he commanded the Fifteenth, Sixteenth, and Nineteenth Regiments U. S. Infantry, in Buell's army, and was battalion quartermaster from January until March or April, 1864.

He was brevetted captain for "gallant and meritorious services in the battle of Murfreesborough, Tennessee," and major for "gallant and meritorious services in the Atlanta campaign, and in the battle of Jonesborough, Georgia."

### BRIGADIER-GENERAL JOHN C. KELTON, U.S.A.

BRIGADIER-GENERAL JOHN C. KELTON (adjutant-general) was born in Pennsylvania June 24, 1828, and graduated at the Military Academy July 1, 1851. He was promoted brevet second lieutenant of the Sixth Infantry the same day, second lieutenant December 31, 1851, and first lieutenant May 9, 1855. He served at Fort Snelling, Minnesota, from September 29, 1851, to November 15, 1852; at Traverse de Sioux, Minnesota, to December 4, 1852; at Fort Snelling, Minnesota, to April 26, 1853; at Fort Ridgely, Minnesota, to July 26, 1854; on an exploring expedition to August 21, 1854; at Fort Ridgely, Minnesota, to September 30, 1854; at Jefferson Barracks, Missouri, to November 4, 1854; on recruiting service to December 1, 1854; at Jefferson Barracks, Missouri, to April 16, 1855; at Fort Leavenworth, Kansas, to June 9, 1855; on the march to and at Fort Laramie, Nebraska, to November 21, 1856; at Fort Leavenworth, Kansas, to January 3, 1857. He was then detailed at the U. S. Military Academy, as assistant instructor of infantry tactics, from March 6, 1857, to February 28, 1858, and as instructor in the use of small-arms and military gymnastics, etc., to April 24, 1861, having been on leave from June 15, 1859, to April 24, 1861.

He was appointed brevet captain and assistant adjutant-general May 11, 1861, and captain and assistant adjutant-general August 3, 1861. He was also appointed colonel of the Ninth Missouri Infantry September 19, 1861, which he held until March 1, 1862, having been appointed colonel and additional aide-de-camp January 4, 1862, which position he held until May 31, 1866.

At the commencement of the war of the Rebellion General Kelton was detailed as purchasing commissary of subsistence at St. Louis, Missouri, from May 11 to August 5, 1861, and assistant adjutant-general of the Department of the West from June 13 to September 19, 1861. He was in command of a brigade in military operations in Missouri from September 21 to November 21, 1861. He was then placed on duty as assistant adjutant-general of the Department of the Missouri from November 24, 1861, to March 11, 1862, and of the Department of the Mississippi from March 11, 1862, to July 11, 1862, participating in the advance upon and siege and occupation of Corinth, Mississippi, April 19 to July 17, 1862. Then he was assistant adjutant-general on the staff of Major-General Halleck, while general-in-chief of the armies of the United States, from July 11, 1862, to March 12, 1864, while chief of staff to the army, March 12, 1864, to April 19, 1865, and while at Richmond, Virginia, commanding the Military Division of the James, April 22 to July 1, 1865.

He was promoted major and assistant adjutant-general July 17, 1862, and was brevetted lieutenant-colonel and colonel March 13, 1865, "for most valuable and arduous services both in the field and at head-quarters," and brigadier-general March 13, 1865, "for valuable and arduous services during the war, both in the field and at head-quarters."

After the war closed, General Kelton was on duty in the adjutant-general's office at Washington, D. C., from July 6, 1865, to February 10, 1870; on special service in Europe to July 21, 1870; assistant adjutant-general of the Division of the Pacific from August 3, 1870, to September 26, 1885; on duty in the adjutant-general's office at Washington, D. C., from October 13, 1885, to June 7, 1889; and adjutant-general of the army since that date.

He was promoted lieutenant-colonel and assistant adjutant-general March 23, 1866, and colonel and assistant adjutant-general June 15, 1880. On June 7, 1889, he was appointed brigadier-general and adjutant-general of the army, which position he now occupies.

## CAPTAIN FREDERIC A. KENDALL, U.S.A. (RETIRED).

CAPTAIN FREDERIC A. KENDALL was born in New Hampshire August 28, 1838. He graduated from Bowdoin College, Maine, in 1860; degree of M.A. conferred by same college in 1868.

He entered the volunteer service early in the war of the Rebellion as private of Company B, Eleventh Indiana Infantry, June 18, 1861; was transferred to Company I, First New Hampshire Infantry, July 23, 1861, and was discharged August 9, 1861. He was appointed second lieutenant of the Fourth New Hampshire Infantry September 18, 1861; promoted first lieutenant November 2, 1862, and captain September 27, 1864.

He took part in the Port Royal expedition, and was in the Department of the South to April, 1864, participating in the operations against Forts Sumter and Wagner, and in the expedition to Florida in January, 1864, and was engaged in the action at Pocotaligo, South Carolina. He was then transferred to the Army of the James, and was engaged in the actions of Bermuda Hundred, Drury's Bluff, Cold Harbor, Mine Explosion, and battle of Fussel's Mills, Virginia; he was also engaged at the capture of Fort Harrison, and in the operations terminating in the surrender of General Lee. He was on duty as assistant commissary of musters of the Third Division, Tenth Army Corps, from September, 1864, and on mustering duty at Richmond and Petersburg, Virginia, until August 17, 1865, when he resigned his volunteer commission to accept commission as captain.

Captain Kendall again entered the volunteer service as captain of the Eighth U. S. Colored Troops October 9, 1865, and was ordered to duty in Texas, where he served as assistant commissary of musters of the district of the Rio Grande until mustered out, February 10, 1866. He then entered the regular service July 28, 1866, as second lieutenant of the Fortieth Infantry, and served in Texas as acting assistant U. S. marshal of Western Texas until 1870.

After entering the regular service Lieutenant Kendall was, on March 2, 1867, brevetted first lieutenant and captain U. S. Army " for gallant and meritorious services at

Fort Harrison, Virginia." He was promoted first lieutenant July 31, 1867; transferred to the Twenty-fifth Infantry April 20, 1869, and promoted captain March 22, 1879. He remained on duty with his regiment until 1874, when he was detailed on the recruiting service, being relieved from that duty in October, 1876. He was then detailed on college duty in Ohio, and while on that duty was assigned to duty by the Governor of Ohio in connection with the National Guard, being appointed special aide-de-camp, with the rank of colonel in the State militia, by Governors Young and Bishop,—in all three years.

Captain Kendall was relieved from duty in 1879, and was retired from active service December 4, 1884, for disability in the line of duty.

In February, 1886, appointed general agent of the Penn Mutual Life Insurance Company of Philadelphia for Northern Ohio, with head-quarters at Cleveland, which position he still occupies.

In 1887 was elected first president of the Cleveland Life Underwriters' Association, and was re-elected for a second term in 1890.

In 1890 elected a vice-president of the National Life Underwriters' Association at Boston.

MAJOR WM. B. KENNEDY, U.S.A.

MAJOR WM. B. KENNEDY (Fourth Cavalry) was born in Ireland, August 12, 1834, and brought to the United States in 1841. He entered the volunteer service March 3, 1863, as first lieutenant of Company I, First California Cavalry, and was promoted captain of the same company June 26, 1863. He was first ordered to duty at Benicia Barracks, California, December 10, 1863, and remained on duty at that station, under Colonel H. M. Black, then colonel of the Sixth California Infantry, to March 10, 1864, when he was ordered to proceed to the Department of Arizona. After a delay at Fort Yuma of about three weeks, he arrived at Tucson, Arizona Territory, May 4, 1864. He was then ordered to take station at El Riventon, where he remained until June 24; and was then transferred to Tithar, Arizona Territory.

On the 10th of July, 1864, Captain Kennedy was detached from his company and ordered to conduct a supply train, with a guard of twenty cavalrymen and five infantrymen. He conducted this train of forty wagons, from Tucson, Arizona Territory, to Fort Goodwin, Arizona Territory, through a country almost unknown, and seemingly unsuited for wagon travel; the march was toilsome and dangerous, owing to unbroken roadways, July heat, presence in close proximity of large forces of Cayotan Apaches. On this trip he found and named Eureka Spring, which name it bears to this date and possibly for all time. He reached Goodwin about July 20, 1864, when the wisdom and provision of the then post commander saved his command and animals from exhaustion from heat and thirst, by causing a water-wagon, with a large force of mules attached thereto, to be dragged through the sand some six miles, where his command was halted, the tired men and animals getting a share of the life-giving fluid. This was not war, but was hard, dangerous work at the time. On his return to Tucson and station at Frebace he was ordered, on or about August 4, 1864, to proceed to Fort Goodwin with his company and there take station, where he was in command from June 1, 1865, to November 1, 1865, when ordered to Fort McDowell, Arizona Territory, then in course of construction. He was at this point to March 31, 1866, when he marched to California, and was mustered out with his company at the Presidio of San Francisco, May 22, 1866. There is no records of wars or fights during this time, but unadulterated work of scouting and marching after the nomad, where a possible show was given for his pursuit or punishment.

On the 22d of January, 1867, Captain Kennedy was appointed first lieutenant of the Tenth United States Cavalry, and promoted captain June 7, 1870. He organized Troop G at Fort Leavenworth, Kansas, and was ordered with the troop to guard the grading parties of the Kansas Pacific Railway, then in course of construction, and while thus engaged his command was attacked with the cholera, July 24, 1867, which carried off twelve men in seven days, thus losing one-seventh of his available strength. He took station at Fort Riley, Kansas, December 10, 1867, where he remained until April 15, 1868, when he was ordered with his troop, with a battalion of the Tenth Cavalry, for duty in the field, continuing on that duty until the December following, and then was granted sick-leave to June, 1869.

The captain was at Fort Dodge until August 20, 1870, when he joined Troop F, as captain by promotion, and remained on duty with this troop in all the work of scouting and frontier duty, including all campaigns against Indians in Kansas, Indian Territory, Texas (length and breadth), New Mexico, and Arizona. He commanded Troop F, in all its wanderings and changes, through twenty-one years and seven months, quitting its command by promotion to the Fourth Cavalry as major, January 1, 1892, surrendering the actual command January 31, 1892.

## MEDICAL INSPECTOR EDWARD KERSHNER, U.S.N.

Dr. Kershner's ancestors were early settlers of Washington County, Maryland, where they bought land from the Indians. He was born in Hagerstown, Maryland, and graduated in medicine at the University of the City of New York in 1861. All the young men were then going into either military or naval service, and he entered the navy as assistant surgeon, being stationed at the Washington Navy-Yard for a short time, and where he had an opportunity of seeing Lincoln and other persons who were to be prominent in our history. He was then attached to the "Cumberland," and in that vessel experienced the fierce fight and sudden destruction which often characterized naval warfare. It is not necessary to repeat here the story of the "Cumberland,"—it suffices to say that Surgeon Charles Martin and Assistant Surgeon Kershner attended the many dreadfully wounded until they had to leave them, or go down with them. They were among the last to leap from the ports of the sinking ship, and were fortunately assisted by boats to the shore, close by. Lieutenant George Morris, in his report of the action, says: "Among the last to leave the ship were Surgeon Martin and Assistant Surgeon Kershner, who did all they could for the wounded." Dr. Kershner reached Fortress Monroe, and then Assistant Secretary Fox ordered him to take charge of Lieutenant Worden, of the "Monitor," who had been injured in action with the "Merrimac," and accompanied him to Washington. This duty performed, he was summoned by the Secretary of the Navy, and gave the first verbal account of the actions in Hampton Roads, by an eye-witness, to persons at the seat of government.

Dr. Kershner was then ordered to the Washington Navy-Yard again, and as soon as the "New Ironsides" was finished, at Philadelphia, he was ordered to her. She was the most powerful ship in the navy, and one of the most powerful in the world at that time. She went to Hampton Roads, to cover the movements of McClellan's army, and then was ordered to Charleston. The services of that ship, in storm and battle, are well known. She succeeded, in spite of gloomy predictions by certain people. Her history is a most remarkable and interesting one.

In February, 1864, Dr. Kershner was transferred to the monitor "Passaic," and served in her in all the operations until the June following, when he was ordered North. In August he went to the Mississippi, serving in the iron-clad ram "Choctaw," one of the most actively employed of all Porter's squadron. Here he remained until the close of the war.

Although in bad health from long exposure to malaria

in the Southern rivers, he passed the examination for passed assistant surgeon in September, 1865. In January, 1866, he was ordered to the "Tacony," and was on the Atlantic coast until October, when the officers and ship's company were transferred to the "Osceola," which vessel cruised in the West Indies,—suffering much from fever, and escaping, by a very few days, the great earthquake at Santa Cruz, which threw the "Monongahela" on shore.

He was next most commendably employed in the cholera epidemic of the receiving-ship "Potomac," at Philadelphia; and when that was over he went to the receiving-ship at New York. He was then ordered to the "Richmond," and cruised in Europe for three years. He afterwards served at the Naval Hospital, and on the receiving-ship at New York, being made surgeon in 1872. In 1874 he sailed in the "Swatara," upon the Transit of Venus Expedition, acting as photographer and naturalist, and bringing to the "Smithsonian" many specimens new to science. He remained attached to the "Swatara" until 1877, when he was ordered to special duty in New York. After this he was on duty in the "Minnesota" training-ship, and, after his tour there, was again on "special duty" in New York, acting at the same time as professor in the post-graduate school. In 1883 he went to China in the "Omaha," having several epidemics to encounter. On his return home he served in New York, being promoted to medical inspector in 1891. Here he superintended the building and fitting of the new medical and surgical office at the navy-yard, where every facility is offered for professional work, as well as for chemical examinations of supplies and materials. At present Dr. Kershner is "waiting orders."

CAPTAIN H. H. KETCHUM, U.S.A.

CAPTAIN H. H. KETCHUM (Twenty-second Infantry) was a son of Henry and Mary A. Ketchum, who were born in Vermont in 1806. He received an academic education. Enlisted in 1861 in the Sixteenth New York Volunteers, at the age of seventeen. He participated in the Peninsula campaign of the Army of the Potomac, and was slightly wounded at Gaines' Mill. He continued in the field with that army through the Maryland campaign, and was discharged after the battle of Antietam, broken down in health, owing to his youth. When he regained his health again he enlisted in the First New York Engineers, and was mustered out of service June 1, 1865.

He was appointed second lieutenant in the Thirteenth Infantry on the 23d of February, 1866, and served at Fort Buford during the summer of 1866, fighting Indians almost daily during that time. He then served at Fort Dakota until July, 1867. He was promoted first lieutenant and served at Fort Sully until 1874, when he was appointed adjutant Twenty-second Infantry, by General Stanley. He served in that capacity over twelve years.

Lieutenant Ketchum was adjutant-general of the Yellowstone expeditions under General Stanley during the years 1871 and 1873; had his horse killed under him in an Indian fight in August, 1873, at the mouth of Big Horn River, Montana, while serving with General Custer in the capacity of aide. General Stanley, in a report to the adjutant-general of the army, says, " I have the honor to state that on the 11th of August, 1873, the troops under my command had a severe engagement with the Sioux Indians on the Yellowstone River, near the mouth of the Big Horn. The principal fight was between seven troops of the Seventh Cavalry, commanded by Lieutenant-Colonel G. A. Custer, in repelling the attack of at least fifteen hundred Sioux warriors. First Lieutenant H. H. Ketchum, adjutant of the Twenty-second Infantry, was in the thickest of the fight and had his horse killed under him. His services were gallant and important." General Custer, in a report to General Stanley, says, " I desire to commend to the brevet major-general commanding First Lieutenant H. H. Ketchum, adjutant Twenty-second Infantry, acting assistant adjutant-general of the expedition, but temporarily serving with me, who rendered me great assistance in transmitting my orders on the battle field. He had his horse killed under him, and I had my horse shot at the same time."

In 1874 Lieutenant Ketchum was ordered with his regiment to the Department of the Lakes. In 1877 he was adjutant-general of the troops serving under the command of Lieutenant-Colonel E. S. Otis, Twenty-second Infantry, in quelling riots in Pennsylvania. He was ordered to Texas with his regiment in the spring of 1879, and served at Fort McKavett and Fort Clark until the fall of 1881, when he was ordered on recruiting service for two years. He rejoined his regiment in the fall of 1883, at Fort Lewis, Colorado. He was ordered with his company to quell troubles with the Utes, Navajos, and settlers on San Juan River, Colorado, in 1883-85. In 1888 he was ordered with his regiment to Fort Keogh, Montana, and participated in the Sioux campaign of 1890-91. Upon promotion to captaincy, in 1882, General Stanley paid Captain Ketchum the following compliment:

" I was absent on leave when you resigned the adjutancy and left for other duty last year. Upon my return I intended to write you a letter expressing my thanks to you, but have kept putting it off until now. But if it is late, it is earnest. Through twelve eventful years you served me faithfully and well as adjutant of the Twenty-second Infantry. On long and weary marches, in the field, in the excitements of Indian attacks, during watchful nights, under burning suns and frosty skies, in many hours of office drudgery, you were always prompt, always ready, and always faithful to your commanding officer and to your duty. Twelve years is a long space in the lifetime of any one, and especially in the prime of life, and the intimate relations of colonel and adjutant during that period must lead to a pretty thorough acquaintance of each other. I hope that in your case it has left upon you the same feeling of respect and affection for me that in my case I entertain for you."

Captain Ketchum has been recommended for brevet rank for Indian campaigns, and has been favorably mentioned by department inspectors to the inspector-general of the army for efficiency as company commander.

## CAPTAIN AND BREVET MAJOR-GENERAL JUDSON KILPATRICK, U.S.A.

CAPTAIN AND BREVET MAJOR-GENERAL JUDSON KILPATRICK was born in New Jersey, and graduated at the Military Academy May 6, 1861. He was promoted second lieutenant, First Artillery, the same day, and was appointed captain of the Fifth New York Infantry May 9, 1861. He joined his volunteer regiment at Fort Schuyler, and was ordered to Fort Monroe, Virginia, from which point he participated in the expedition to Big Bethel, and was engaged in the action at that place June 9 and 10, 1861, where he was wounded. He was on sick-leave of absence to July 30, and then on recruiting service to August 14, 1861, when he resigned his volunteer commission.

He was promoted first lieutenant of the First Artillery May 14, 1861, and again appointed to the volunteer service September 25, 1861, as lieutenant-colonel of the Second New York Cavalry, which regiment he assisted in organizing and commanding, and in February, 1862, was ordered to accompany Brigadier-General Lane's expedition to Texas, as chief of artillery; but, it being abandoned, he returned to his regiment at Arlington, Virginia.

He was appointed lieutenant-colonel (staff aide-de-camp) January 29, 1862, and participated in the operations of the Department of the Rappahannock, 1862, being engaged in skirmishes near Falmouth, Virginia; movement to Thoroughfare Gap, raids on railroads, and skirmish at Carmel Church July 23, 1862. Following this, he participated in all the campaigns with the Army of the Potomac until 1864, when he was transferred to the Western army.

He was promoted colonel of the Second New York Cavalry December 6, 1862, and brigadier-general of volunteers June 13, 1863, and was in command of a cavalry brigade, after participating in the battle of Manassas, in an expedition to Leesburg September 19, 1862. He was on leave of absence and on recruiting service to January 27, 1863, when he rejoined his command (the cavalry brigade) and participated in Stoneman's raid towards Richmond, and engaged in the combat of Beverly Ford.

In the Pennsylvania campaign General Kilpatrick commanded a cavalry division, and was engaged in the action of Aldie, skirmishes at Middleburg, Upperville, Hanover, Hunterstown, and battle of Gettysburg; and, while pursuing the enemy back to Virginia, constant fighting at Monterey, Smithsburg, Hagerstown, and Falling Waters, in July, 1863.

After a short leave of absence he commanded a cavalry division in the operations in Central Virginia, being engaged in the expedition to Hartwood Church, to

destroy the enemy's gun-boats "Satellite" and "Reliance," in the Rappahannock, August 14, 1863, with actions at Culpeper, Somerville Ford, Liberty Mills, James City, Brandy Station, and Gainesville, in September and October, 1863. He was in command of a cavalry division in the spring of 1864, and participated in the raid to Richmond and down the Virginia Peninsula, being engaged in the action at Ashland and numerous skirmishes, with much destruction of the enemy's property.

General Kilpatrick was then transferred to the Western army, and assigned to the command of the Third Cavalry Division, Army of the Cumberland. He participated in the invasion of Georgia, and was engaged in the action of Ringgold and operations about Dalton, where he was severely wounded, and compelled to leave the field. But he returned July 22, 1864, and, in command of his division, was engaged in guarding General Sherman's communications and making raids, with constant heavy skirmishes with the enemy; and in the "march to the sea," in actions at Lovejoy, Walnut Creek, Sylvan Grove, Rocky Creek, Waynesborough, Salkehatchie, Monroe's Cross-Roads, Raleigh, and Morristown, April 13, 1865.

He was promoted captain, First Artillery, November 30, 1864, and was brevetted from major to major-general in the regular army for gallant and meritorious services, and was appointed major-general of volunteers June 18, 1865. He was in command of the Third Division of the Cavalry Corps, Military Division of the Mississippi, from April 26 to June 13, 1865, and on leave of absence and awaiting orders until he resigned.

He resigned his volunteer commission January 1, 1866, having been appointed United States Envoy Extraordinary and Minister Plenipotentiary to Chili in 1865. He resigned his commission as captain, First U. S. Artillery, October 15, 1867.

## OFFICERS OF THE ARMY AND NAVY (REGULAR)

GENERAL RUFUS KING, U.S.A. (DECEASED).

GENERAL RUFUS KING was born January 26, 1814, New York City. His father, Charles King, afterwards editor of the New York *American*, and for many years President of Columbia College, was second son of Rufus King, who for twenty years represented New York State in the U. S. Senate, and was twice minister resident at the Court of St. James. The first of the family to reach America was Richard King, who came to Boston from Kent, England, in 1710. Rufus King, the subject of this sketch, was educated in New York, and thoroughly prepared for West Point, which he entered in 1829, when less than sixteen, and was graduated in 1833, standing fourth in a large class, and being assigned to the Engineer Corps. General King's first duty was as assistant to Lieutenant Robert E. Lee, in the construction of Fortress Monroe. A year later he was employed on the survey of the boundary-line between Ohio and Michigan, and then in the improvement of the navigation of the Hudson River to September, 1836, when he was induced to resign and enter into the service of Erie Railway, then in course of construction. On the entry into office of William H. Seward as governor of New York, in 1839, he appointed King adjutant-general of the State. For four years King served as adjutant-general, and I mean time, inheriting his journalistic tastes and talents from his father, he became associate editor of the Albany *Evening Journal*, with Thurlow Weed as his chief and mentor. In 1845, he removed with his wife and infant son to Milwaukee, Wisconsin, and became editor, and later proprietor, of the Milwaukee *Sentinel*, which at once took rank as the leading newspaper of Wisconsin. King remaining at the helm almost to the outbreak of the war of the Rebellion. He was a member of the Constitutional Convention of Wisconsin in 1847-48.

Regent of the University of Wisconsin from 1848 to 1861; superintendent of the public schools of Milwaukee from 1849 to 1861; member of the Board of Visitors to West Point in 1849; was associated with Wisconsin militia, as captain of the long famous Milwaukee Light-Guard, colonel of the First Regiment, and major-general of the State troops. In March, 1861, appointed by President Lincoln minister resident to the Court of Rome, he was in New York City with his family awaiting the sailing of the steamer, when the news came of the attack on Sumter, and he at once begged for service in the field; was sent to Wisconsin to organize the regiments tendered for the war; commissioned brigadier-general of the Wisconsin volunteers May 7, and brigadier-general of the U. S. Volunteers May 17, and in July was ordered to Washington as president of a court-martial, and then in the organization of the first brigade of Western troops serving in the Army of the Potomac, a brigade which later became famous as the "Iron Brigade of the West." A month was spent in drill at Camp Kalorama; then the brigade marched to Chain Bridge, and later to Arlington, where it consisted of the Second, Sixth, and Seventh Wisconsin, and the Nineteenth Indiana, and where King was promoted to the command of a fine division, with J. P. Hatch, Doubleday, Patrick, and Gibbon as his brigade commanders.

He accompanied the advance on Manassas, was later ordered to Fredericksburg, and, as the Third Division of McDowell's corps, guarded the line of Rappahannock while McClellan was battling on the Peninsula. In August the division hurried forward to the support of Pope at Cedar Mountain; took part in the ill-starred campaign of second Bull Run; was swung to and fro from one flank to the other along the Rapidan; was heavily engaged, all unsupported, with Jackson's Corps on the evening of August 28, a fight in which the Iron Brigade lost forty per cent. in killed and wounded; and on the following day, as the result of exposure and fatigue, King was prostrated by severe illness and sent in to Washington. After his sick-leave he commanded a division in the defences of the Capital to November 25, 1862, when detailed member of the court for the trial of Fitz John Porter; commanded the defences of Yorktown from March until after Gettysburg, 1863; was then ordered to Fairfax, Virginia, commanding division until October 20, when, his health being grievously impaired, and upon notification from the President that his services were urgently needed at Rome, he resigned his generalship and went at once to his post near the Papal Court, retaining it until the abolition of the mission in July, 1867, when he returned to the United States. He died October 13, 1876.

## CAPTAIN ADAM KRAMER, U.S.A.

CAPTAIN ADAM KRAMER (Sixth Cavalry) was born in Germany October 15, 1837; came to America while quite young and settled in Philadelphia, Pennsylvania. He enlisted in the mounted service, at Philadelphia, May 16, 1857, and remained at the recruiting depot, Carlisle Barracks, Carlisle, Pennsylvania, until July, 1857, when he was assigned to Company F, Second Dragoons, then stationed at Fort Leavenworth, Kansas. He served with the regiment in Kansas until September of that year, when it was ordered to Utah. He served in Utah during the Salt Lake Expedition and in Nebraska until 1861, at which time the regiment was ordered to Washington, D. C. He was with the Army of the Potomac until discharged, May 16, 1862.

Captain Kramer re-enlisted in Philadelphia August 25, 1862, in Company I, Fifteenth Pennsylvania Cavalry; he was made a sergeant October 30, 1862, and first sergeant November 1, 1862. He was promoted first lieutenant March 1, 1863, and became a captain May 8, 1863, and was with the regiment until the close of the Rebellion. He participated in the following battles and engagements, viz.: Siege of Yorktown, Virginia; battles of Antietam, Maryland; Murfreesborough, Tennessee; Chickamauga, Georgia, and numerous minor engagements of the regiment. He was mustered out with his regiment, the Fifteenth Pennsylvania Cavalry, June 21, 1865.

The following indorsement on Captain Kramer's application for a commission in the regular army was made by Colonel William J. Palmer:

"Captain Adam Kramer enlisted in my regiment (the Fifteenth Pennsylvania Cavalry) in August, 1862, after already serving out a five-years' enlistment in the regular cavalry. He continued to serve in my regiment, brigade, and division until the end of the war. . . . I had occasion frequently to select him to command separate expeditions of importance, in several of which he greatly distinguished himself, so as to earn the special commendation of Major-General George H. Thomas, as is shown in the accompanying highly laudatory letter of that officer. Captain Kramer is very brave, faithful, and experienced, and should not be lost to the cavalry service."

General Garfield indorsed this as follows: "I cheerfully concur in the above recommendation. Such a man as Captain Kramer ought not to be lost to the service."

Major Morrow, the President's private secretary, indorsed as follows: "Having been on the staff of Major-General Stoneman during the time the Fifteenth Pennsylvania Cavalry was under his command, I can bear testimony to Captain Kramer's excellent reputation as a brave and skilful officer, and I would be glad to learn of his appointment in the regular service."

Captain Kramer was appointed a second lieutenant of the Second U. S. Colored Cavalry December 7, 1865, and was stationed at Brazos Santiago, Texas. He was mustered out February 12, 1866. He then received his appointment as second lieutenant, Sixth U. S. Cavalry, to date from April 27, 1866; was promoted first lieutenant December 12, 1866, and captain August 1, 1874.

He was stationed in Texas until 1870, when he availed himself of a leave of absence from September, 1870, to February, 1871, during part of which time he was with the German army in the Franco-Prussian War.

He was engaged in the following affairs with the Indians (with his troop): At Ash Creek, Arizona Territory, May 7, 1880; also at Chevalon's Fork of the Little Colorado River, Arizona Territory, the campaign against the Sioux of 1891 and 1892, and various others.

Captain Kramer received special commendation from Brevet Major-General Grierson, commanding the District of New Mexico, in his special report on the removal of the intruders from the Jicarillo Indian Reservation of New Mexico, in these words:

"It is a pleasure to acknowledge my indebtedness to Captain Adam Kramer, commanding Troops E and F, Sixth Cavalry, and the officers and soldiers under his command, for the alacrity with which the important duties devolving upon them were carried out. Detachments were carefully and promptly furnished, and Lieutenants Cruse and Gallagher, and the men sent out under their charge, endured without a murmur the hardship of long marches and arduous work required in the removal of intruders and their stock from the Jicarillo Reservation. The efficient and valuable service rendered while under my command, by these well-disciplined and deserving troops, is worthy of the highest praise."

## MAJOR JOHN ALEXANDER KRESS, U.S.A.

Major John Alexander Kress (Ordnance Department) was born in Pennsylvania November 4, 1839, and was appointed a cadet at the Military Academy from Laporte, Indiana, in June, 1858, but he resigned October 18, 1861, to serve as aide-de-camp on the staff of Brigadier-General James S. Wadsworth, in the Army of the Potomac. He was appointed first lieutenant of the Twenty-fifth New York Infantry for that purpose November 1, 1861, and performed duty in that position until July 9, 1862, when he was promoted major of the Ninety-fourth New York Infantry, and participated with that regiment in General Pope's campaign of 1862, being engaged at the battle of Cedar Mountain and Rappahannock Crossing, Virginia. He commanded the regiment at the battle of Fredericksburg, Virginia, December 11-14, 1862, it forming part of General Gibbon's division.

Major Kress was promoted lieutenant-colonel of the Ninety-fourth New York Infantry November 1, 1862, and made acting inspector-general of the First Division of the First Army Corps, serving in that capacity during the Rappahannock and Pennsylvania campaigns of 1863, having been engaged in the battles of Chancellorsville, Virginia, and Gettysburg, Pennsylvania.

Colonel Kress entered the regular service as a second lieutenant of ordnance November 24, 1863, and resigned his commission in the volunteer service to accept his appointment December 11, 1863. He was first stationed at Fortress Monroe, Virginia, where he remained until September, 1864, when he was assigned as chief ordnance officer of the Army of the James and of the Department of Virginia and North Carolina, and performed the duties of that office until June, 1865. He was promoted first lieutenant of ordnance July 16, 1864, and served as acting inspector-general of the Twenty-fifth Army Corps from April to May, 1865.

He was honorably mentioned by the major-general commanding the First Corps, in his official report, for meritorious conduct at the battle of Gettysburg, Pennsylvania, July 1-4, 1863, and at the close of the war was made brevet captain April 2, 1865, for "gallant and meritorious services during the siege of Richmond and Petersburg, Virginia," and brevet major April 3, 1865, "for meritorious and distinguished services as chief ordnance officer."

After the fall of Richmond he was ordered in June, 1865, to Rock Island Arsenal, Illinois, where he remained until July, 1867, when he was transferred to the Allegheny Arsenal, at Pittsburg, Pennsylvania. Serving at this post until April, 1871, his field of duty was changed to the Pacific coast, and while commanding at Vancouver Arsenal, Washington, was chief ordnance officer of the Department of the Columbia, retaining this position until 1882. While on this duty he commanded a gunboat, with sixty men, on the Upper Columbia River in July, 1878, and was engaged skirmishing with hostile Indians, preventing their escape from the forces commanded by General Howard.

Lieutenant Kress was promoted to a captaincy July 16, 1874, and, upon being relieved from duty in the Department of the Columbia in 1882, was ordered to San Antonio Arsenal, which he commanded, and was also chief ordnance officer of the Department of Texas. On November 5, 1883, he was relieved and ordered to Indianapolis, where he commanded the arsenal at that point until July, 1886. On January 3, 1887, he was promoted major, and he commanded the St. Louis powder-depot from July, 1886, to December, 1887, when he was again ordered to the Pacific coast, doing duty at Benicia Arsenal to September, 1890, at which time he was transferred to Rock Island Arsenal, Illinois, where he remained until November 18, 1890, when he was assigned to the command of the St. Louis powder-depot, which is now his present station.

## COLONEL LOOMIS L. LANGDON, U.S.A.

COLONEL LOOMIS L. LANGDON (First Artillery) was born in New York, and graduated from the Military Academy July 1, 1854, when he was promoted brevet second lieutenant of artillery, and served in garrison at Fort Monroe, Virginia. He was promoted second lieutenant of the First Artillery August 21, 1854, and participated in the Florida hostilities against the Seminole Indians during the years 1854-56, being engaged in action, in command of the advanced guard attacking Billy Bowlegs in his village (" Billy's Town"), in the heart of the Big Cypress Swamp, April 7, 1856.

From 1857 to 1860 Lieutenant Langdon was on frontier duty in Texas, and was at Fort Brown during the yellow-fever epidemic, which carried off half the command, in the latter part of 1858. He was also in the yellow-fever epidemic of 1859 at Brownsville. In 1859-60 he received the public thanks of the citizens of Brownsville, for organizing them into a defensive force, and assisting them "to defend their lives and property" from the attacks of the outlaw Cortinas and his band.

He was promoted first lieutenant July 13, 1860, and captain Aug. 28, 1861, serving in defence of Fort Pickens, Florida, from Feb. 7, 1861, to Jan. 7, 1862, being engaged in the repulse of the attack on Santa Rosa Island, and in command of the mortar battery at Fort Pickens during the two bombardments of that place, Nov. 22, 23, 1862.

Captain Langdon's field of duty was changed to South Carolina, and he participated in the operations about Charleston from June 20, 1862, to Feb. 5, 1864, and was engaged (commanding field and siege batteries) in the descent on and capture of Morris Island from Folly Island. He also participated in the siege of Fort Wagner in command of siege and field batteries, and commanded the artillery brigade and his own light battery (M), First Artillery, in the expedition under General Seymour to Florida, being engaged in the battle of Olustee, Feb. 20, 1864, for which he was made brevet major " for gallant and meritorious services." As chief of artillery, First Division, Tenth Army Corps, Captain Langdon participated in the operations on James River, Virginia, from Bermuda Hundred, from May 5 to Sept. 28, 1864, and was engaged in the actions at Howlett's House and Weir Bottom Church, assault and capture of the enemy's defences near Chester Station, and the capture of the right of the enemy's intrenchments; he was also engaged in the battle of Drury's Bluff, in defence of the Bermuda Hundred intrenchments, and siege of Petersburg. He was in command of Battery M, First Artillery (light), in the operations before Richmond, from Sept. 29, 1864, to March 27, 1865, being engaged in the assault and capture of New Market Heights, and in the repulse of the attack on the Federal position on the New Market Road. He was chief of artillery of the Twenty-fifth Army Corps (Army of the

James) from Feb. 14 to June 18, 1865, participating in the capture of Richmond April 3, 1865, and superintended the batteries of the Twenty-fourth and Twenty-fifth Corps in collecting the field artillery abandoned by the enemy—over three hundred guns—in the earthworks around Richmond. Captain Langdon was made brevet lieutenant-colonel Sept. 29, 1864, " for gallant and meritorious services in the attack on Fort Gilmer, Virginia." At the conclusion of the war of the Rebellion, Captain Langdon, as chief of artillery, accompanied General Weitzel's expedition to the Rio Grande, as chief of artillery and assistant inspector-general, to recover munitions of war sold to the Imperialists under Maximilian, in Mexico, by the Confederates, from June to August, 1865, on the conclusion of which duty he was granted a sick-leave of absence, though he rejoined his command at Brownsville, Texas, in November of that year. His station was changed to New York harbor in Jan., 1866, and from April 21 to Oct. 20, 1867, he was on leave of absence in Europe. From 1867 to the present time Colonel Langdon's duty has called him to numerous important positions, and his service has been at posts in various parts of the country, mainly in the Southern States. He was promoted major of the Second Artillery March 20, 1879, and lieutenant-colonel of the same regiment Dec. 1, 1883. He has been engaged in the suppression of election disturbances, the suppression of railroad riots, and has been on several occasions inspector of militia encampments, as well as a member of important courts and boards, all of which are too numerous to detail in this limited sketch. He was promoted colonel of the First Artillery Jan. 25, 1889, joining it at San Francisco, and with his regiment was transferred to New York harbor in May, 1890. He took station at Fort Hamilton, where he is now in command of his regiment, that garrisons all the forts in New York harbor.

### REAR-ADMIRAL JAMES L. LARDNER, U.S.N.
(DECEASED).

REAR ADMIRAL JAMES L. LARDNER, belonging to a well-known Pennsylvania family, entered the navy from that State in May, 1820. As midshipman he made a long cruise in the Pacific,—first in the schooner "Dolphin," and then in the "Franklin," eighty-gun ship, and flag-ship of Commodore Stewart. His next service was in the appropriately-named new frigate "Brandywine," which carried home General La Fayette, the "nation's guest." The vessel afterwards went to the Mediterranean, but came back in 1826, and became the flag-ship of Commodore Jacob Jones in the Pacific. In that ship, in the schooner "Dolphin," and in the "Vincennes," he served until June, 1830, nearly three years of that time being navigator of the "Vincennes," in which he circumnavigated the globe. Commissioned lieutenant May 17, 1828. In 1832 was attached to the schooner "Experiment," and in 1833-34 served in the "Delaware," eighty-gun ship, flag-ship of Commodore Patterson, in the Mediterranean. In 1837-38 served in the razee "Independence" (sixty), Commodore Nicholson, and in her went to Russia, England, and Brazil. He went to the Pacific in the sloop "Cyane" in 1841; was transferred to the frigate "United States," and served in her as first lieutenant for nearly three years. He then commanded the receiving-ship at Philadelphia, and in 1850 went out to the coast of Africa in command of the brig "Porpoise." He was made commander in 1851, and transferred, on the station, to the sloop-of-war "Dale." He came home in her in 1853. He next served as fleet-captain of the West India Squadron, and in 1860 was attached to the Philadelphia Navy-Yard. In May, 1861, he was commissioned as captain, and in September of that eventful year was ordered to the command of the steam-frigate "Susquehanna," of the North Atlantic Blockading Squadron. He blockaded the coasts of South Carolina and Georgia, and was at Port Royal, for which his name was included by President Lincoln in the recommendation for a vote of thanks by Congress. This vote passed the House, but was thrown out in the Senate. Port Royal was one of the first naval successes, and Flag-Officer Dupont addressed Captain Lardner a letter upon his conduct then, of which the following is an extract: "I enclose a general order, to be read to the officers and men of the 'Susquehanna,' and I take the occasion to say that your noble ship, throughout the whole of the battle, was precisely where I wanted her to be, and doing precisely what I wanted her to do, and that your close support of this ship (flag-ship 'Wabash') was a very gallant thing."

In May, 1862, Captain Lardner assumed command of the East Gulf Blockading Squadron, but was obliged to return home in December, invalided by a severe attack of yellow fever at Key West. In the previous summer he lost, from yellow fever, forty gallant officers and men from his flag-ship alone. In May, 1863, as acting rear-admiral, he took command of the West India Squadron, and retained it until the squadron was withdrawn in October, 1864. He was commissioned commodore in July, 1862; commissioned rear-admiral July, 1866; on special duty from 1864 to 1869; and governor of the Naval Asylum at Philadelphia, 1869-71. He died in Philadelphia April 12, 1881.

Admiral Lardner was a particularly handsome man, with high-bred look and manner. He retained a youthful figure and alert and active manner until his death. He was a noticeable person, whether in uniform or in plain clothes, and an excellent exemplar of the best class of officers of the "old navy."

## CHIEF ENGINEER EDWARD B. LATCH, U.S.N.
### (RETIRED).

CHIEF ENGINEER EDWARD B. LATCH was born in Montgomery County, Pennsylvania, November 15, 1833. Having a taste for mechanics, he entered the locomotive works of the well-known firm of Norris Brothers, of Philadelphia, and passed five years there in the machinery and draughting departments. By the recommendation of Mr. Richard Norris, he was appointed a third assistant engineer in the navy in September, 1858, and was ordered to the steamer "Atalanta," which vessel formed part of the Paraguay Expedition. On her return, Engineer Latch was ordered to the steamer "Sumter," in which he served on the west coast of Africa, in 1860-61. In the latter part of 1861 he was promoted to second assistant engineer.

He next served in the celebrated flag-ship "Hartford," under Admiral Farragut, and was present at the engagements of Forts Jackson and St. Philip, and the Chalmette batteries, which led to the capture of New Orleans. He was also present on the two occasions when the "Hartford" ran the gauntlet of the Vicksburg batteries; at the affair of the ram "Arkansas;" and at the passage of Port Hudson. Before Port Hudson fell, the chief engineer of the "Hartford" was detached, and Engineer Latch was ordered to take charge of the "Hartford's" machinery. When we consider the difficulty of maintaining machinery in fighting order, without having access to machine-shops or repairing stations, this showed an unusual mark of confidence in the ability of an officer of junior grade. Engineer Latch retained his charge until the "Hartford" steamed into New York harbor, bearing Admiral Farragut's flag. Of all the ships of his fleet, the "Hartford" was—as he said himself—the home of the admiral; and when he went South again, for the Mobile campaign, the "Hartford" bore his flag at her mizzen-top-mast head. In the "Hartford" Engineer Latch again fought under Farragut at Mobile Bay, and the numerous minor engagements in that quarter. After the capture of the ram "Tennessee," Engineer Latch was ordered in temporary charge of her machinery.

After the war he served in the East India Squadron, and at the Naval Academy. Promoted chief engineer 1870; "Congress," special service, 1870-72; Board of Inspection, 1873-75; sick-leave, 1876-77; and retired in 1878.

Chief Engineer Latch's forefathers took up land in Montgomery County nearly two hundred years ago, and his grandfather served in the Revolution, rising to the rank of major. Another branch settled nearer to Philadelphia, and were allied with the De Monseaus, who, after the revocation of the edict of Nantes, settled at Frankford, near Philadelphia.

Since his retirement, Mr. Latch has been engaged in writing upon Biblical subjects, principally, much of which has been published.

He now resides at Overbrook, Pennsylvania, on a portion of an estate which has been in his family for five generations.

CAPTAIN PETER LEARY, JR., U.S.A.

CAPTAIN PETER LEARY, JR. (Fourth Artillery), was born September 15, 1840, in Baltimore, Maryland. When the Civil War began he was a student of law. He was commissioned second lieutenant in the Baltimore Battery of Light Artillery, Maryland Volunteers, in August, 1862, and continued in service until honorably mustered out in June, 1865, having been engaged in the actions which inaugurated the Gettysburg campaign at Berryville, June 12; Opequan Creek, June 13; Winchester, June 14, and Martinsburg Pike, June 15, 1863. He participated in the Maryland campaign of 1864, and was present in action on Catoctin Mountain, July 7; at Frederick, July 8, and Monocacy, July 9, and was engaged in the pursuit of the Confederate army under Early from Washington to Leesburg in July and August of that year.

He was appointed second lieutenant Fourth U. S. Artillery July 2, 1867, and assigned to Light Battery B, which he joined September 6 at Fort Harker, Kansas. In November the battery marched to Fort Leavenworth, where it remained until the spring of 1869, when it was ordered to Fort Riley. In April, 1869, he was placed on special duty on the Sac and Fox Reservation in Kansas, under instructions from Major-General Schofield, concerning the removal of settlers from that reservation. Rejoining the battery early in June, he immediately joined Light Batteries K, First Artillery, and C, Third Artillery, mounted as cavalry, under command of Captain William M. Graham, First Artillery, scouting the valley of the Republican River for hostile Indians, performing the staff duties of the expedition.

He was promoted first lieutenant to date from January 24, 1873, and on April 1 joined Miller's battery in the field against the Modoc Indians, taking part in the engagements in the Lava Beds of April 15. He commanded an escort of nineteen men in an engagement in the pedregal April 20, in which he had one man killed and one wounded, repulsing the attack and assuring the safety of the convoy. For good conduct in this campaign he was nominated by the President to be captain by brevet.

On June 17, 1877, he went into the field again with Miller's battery in the campaign against the hostile Nez Perces, under their able war-chief Joseph, and was appointed field-quartermaster and acting chief commissary of subsistence of General Howard's command. On July 13, Major George H. Weeks, quartermaster, having reported for duty, he was relieved as field-quartermaster, continuing on duty as acting chief commissary until the end of the campaign. He was in the engagements of July 11 and 12 on the Clearwater, and in the skirmish of July 13, 1877, at Kamiah, and was honorably mentioned in General Howard's report of the campaign in the following terms: "I wish to make special mention of the following officers who have served under my command during the late expedition against the hostile Nez Perces, . . . First Lieutenant Peter Leary, Jr., Fourth Artillery. He discharged the duties of chief commissary officer to the forces in the field, operating under my immediate command, during the entire campaign. He was always active and energetic, giving his entire attention to his important duties, and deserves commendation for the very satisfactory manner in which they were performed."

In garrison at Fort Point, California; Fort Canby, Washington Territory; Madison Barracks, New York; Fort Warren, Massachusetts (part of the time ordnance officer and acting assistant quartermaster and acting commissary subsistence of post), from May, 1880, to September 20, 1885. On October 1, 1885, assigned to and on duty with Light Battery F at Fort Snelling, Minnesota, from October 1, 1885, to March, 1887.

Captain Leary was graduated from the Artillery School in 1880. He has twice, under orders from the Secretary of War, inspected the National Guard of Vermont in their summer encampments of 1888 and 1889. In February, 1890, he was detailed as professor of military science and tactics in the Agricultural College of South Dakota, and was promoted captain August 28, 1891.

Captain Leary is the eldest son of Cornelius L. L. Leary, of Baltimore, who represented the Third Congressional District of Maryland in the Thirty-seventh Congress from 1861 to 1863, and is a brother of Commander Richard P. Leary, U. S. Navy.

Captain Leary was appointed private secretary to Thomas Swann, Governor of Maryland, in January, 1866, and was subsequently commissioned aide-de-camp to the governor, with the rank of colonel, from May 20, 1867, to July 31, 1867, when he resigned to enter the U. S. Army.

## REAR-ADMIRAL SAMUEL PHILLIPS LEE, U.S.N.
### (RETIRED).

REAR-ADMIRAL SAMUEL PHILLIPS LEE, born in Virginia, was appointed midshipman in 1825. Commanding the "Vandalia" under orders to the East Indies, and learning at Cape Town of the Rebellion, he brought his command back to the support of the Union. His services in the early blockade of Charleston in that ship were valuable. Under Farragut, in the "Oneida," he commanded the guard division, was in the gun-boat action with the forts, and at the passage of the forts captured "Kennon" and officers and men, the only captures from the rebel fleet that day; was second on both passages of the Vicksburg batteries. Ordered to command the North Atlantic Blockading Squadron, September 2, 1862. Secretary Welles, in his two next annual reports, states, "Acting Rear-Admiral Lee, in command, has faithfully and ably discharged his duties in a position of great responsibility, and in some respects of great embarrassment. All intercourse with the rebels has been cut off, with the single exception of the port of Wilmington, of two inlets forty miles apart, flanked with extensive batteries, where some of the fastest steamers have run by under cover of darkness. This port could not be closed without a co-operating land force, and there has been no time within the last two years when the navy has not been ready and anxious to perform its part. There were ninety-one affairs and expeditions in co-operation with the army or independently; fifty-four steamers were captured or destroyed during his command." Lee's system of steam-blockade, original and effective, was adopted by his successor, and will be an instruction for the future. De Joinville says, "Many persons believe the rigor of the blockade the primary cause of the subjection of the South." Lee, assigned to the Mississippi Squadron, took command November 1. Hood with a large army was moving to attack Thomas before he could concentrate. Lee promptly stationed the vessels on the Mississippi to prevent Kirby Smith's forces from joining Hood's.

Sent two iron-clads to the Cumberland to support Thomas, and protect his communications, and followed in the hastily-prepared iron-clad "Cincinnati;" was stopped, by low water on Harpeth Shoals, at Clarksville, where Thomas and Fitch had asked an iron-clad should be stationed, to prevent Hood from crossing for the Ohio, about which Grant was anxious. The river rose barely enough to allow Fitch to move the gun-boats and assist the army to turn the enemy's left in the battle of the 15th, but not enough to make Harpeth Shoals passable until three days later. Fitch desired to remain on the Cumberland and retain an iron-clad. Lee hurried up the Tennessee to cut off Hood's escape at Duck River, or at Florence, at the foot of the shoals heretofore considered the head of steamboat navigation, where Hood had crossed last fall. All visible means of crossing were destroyed. The operations of the squadron forced Hood to cross six miles up on Muscle Shoals, where the iron-clads could not reach the enemy. Hood says he crossed Duck River on the 19th, "proceeded on different roads," and "entertained but little concern in regard to being further harassed by the enemy." "Therefore continued to march leisurely, and arrived at Bainbridge on the 25th." His army mostly restored itself to citizenship. The defeat of Hood's army by the Army of the Cumberland, with the co-operation of the Mississippi Squadron, virtually ended the war, and left only ceremonial proceedings for the custom-house selvage of the Southern States and the Trans-Mississippi. General Lee was unable to hold or leave his trenches, and General Sherman wrote that Fort Fisher would fall with his advance. Charleston, strongly fortified, so fell. General Thomas telegraphed to Admiral Lee, "Your co-operation on the Tennessee River has contributed largely to the demoralization of Hood's army, and it gives me great pleasure to tender to you, your officers and men, my hearty thanks for your cordial co-operation during the operations of the last thirty days." The war was over; Admiral Lee closed up all the affairs of the Mississippi Squadron except selling the vessels. Secretary Welles wrote, June 19, "Acting Rear-Admiral Lee is so correct and accurate a business-man, that I know he would wish himself to close up the final affairs of the squadron he has commanded with so much ability and with such indefatigable industry." Detached August 14. Promoted to commodore July 25, 1866. Promoted to rear-admiral April 22, 1870. Commanded North Atlantic Squadron two years. Retired February 13, 1873. He was devoted to duty and just in command.

### REAR-ADMIRAL WILLIAM E. LE ROY, U.S.N.
(DECEASED).

REAR-ADMIRAL WILLIAM E. LE ROY was born in New York March 24, 1818. Appointed from New York January 11, 1832; attached to frigate "Delaware," Mediterranean Squadron, 1833-36; brig "Dolphin," Brazil Squadron, 1837-38. Promoted to passed midshipman June 23, 1838; frigate "Constitution," Pacific Squadron, 1839-40; store-ship "Erie," 1842-43. Commissioned as lieutenant July 13, 1843; steamer "Mississippi," Home Squadron, 1846; steamer "Princeton," Home Squadron, 1847; engagement with Mexican soldiers at Rio Aribiqua, while assisting to water the "Princeton;" sloop "Savannah," Pacific Squadron, 1849-51; waiting orders, 1852; frigate "Savannah," Brazil Squadron, 1853-55; Naval Station, Sackett's Harbor, New York, 1857-58; frigate "Sabine," Brazil Squadron, 1859; commanding steamer "Mystic," coast of Africa, 1861. Commissioned as commander July 1, 1861; commanding steamer "Keystone State," South Atlantic Blockading Squadron, 1862-63; capture of Fernandina, 1862; engagement with iron-clads off Charleston, South Carolina, January, 1863; commanding steam-sloop "Oneida," Western Gulf Squadron, 1864; commanding steam-sloop "Ossipee," Western Gulf Squadron, 1864-65; commanded the "Ossipee" at the battle of Mobile Bay, August 5, 1864; his vessel was struck many times, but, fortunately, not disabled. When about running down the "Tennessee," that vessel displayed a white flag, and Captain Le Roy received her surrender from Captain Johnson, her commander, the rebel Admiral Buchanan being wounded; naval rendezvous, New York, 1866-67.

Commissioned as captain July 25, 1866; fleet-captain European Squadron, under Admiral Farragut, 1867-68. Commissioned as commodore July, 1870; special duty, New London, 1871; senior officer Board of Examiners, 1872-73. Commissioned as rear-admiral April 5, 1874; commanding South Atlantic Station, 1874-76; commanding European Station, 1878-80. Died, 1888.

Admiral Le Roy was a man of such singularly happy temperament and urbane manners, that every one who came in contact with him became fond of him. There were few men in the navy more generally beloved. At the same time he was a strict disciplinarian, and a fine type of the naval officer, impressing foreigners, as well as our own people, by his correct and courteous bearing on all occasions.

## CAPTAIN BENJAMIN C. LOCKWOOD, U.S.A.

CAPTAIN BENJAMIN C. LOCKWOOD (Twenty-second Infantry) was born in Kentucky February 28, 1844. He entered the military service as a private in Company F, Sixth Kentucky Infantry, October 2, 1861, and served during the war of the Rebellion in the armies of the West.

He was appointed second lieutenant of the Fifty-fourth Kentucky Infantry September 30, 1864, and was honorably mustered out September 1, 1865. He was engaged during the war of the Rebellion in the battles of Shiloh, Cumberland Gap, Charlestown, Chickasaw Bayou, Arkansas Post, siege of Vicksburg, Pound Gap, Saltville, Marion Heights, Aberdeen, Zollicoffer, Leadville (North Carolina), Bardstown (Kentucky), and with guerillas in the remainder of his war-service.

Captain Lockwood entered the regular service as a second lieutenant of the Thirty-first Infantry March 7, 1867, and joined his company, and was engaged in skirmishes with Indians in 1868 at Fort Totten; in 1868-69 at Fort Buford; and in 1869 at Fort Stevenson; also on Yellowstone River in 1876, and Tongue River in 1877.

He was transferred to the Twenty-second Infantry May 15, 1869, and served at Fort Rice, Dakota, 1869; at Fort Randall, Dakota, 1872-73; with his company to reinforce General Terry at the mouth of Rosebud Creek in 1876; participated in the campaigns of General Terry and General Miles against hostile Indians during the years of 1876-77; on sick-leave from June, 1877, to November, 1877, when he joined Company G at Fort Porter, New York. He moved with his company to Texas in 1879; served at Fort McKavett until July, 1880, when he was transferred to command Company B, and served there until January, 1881. He was at Fort Duncan until October, 1881; at Fort Clark until October, 1882; on leave until May, 1883; and rejoined his company at Fort Lewis, Colorado, 1884. He was then detailed on recruiting service from 1887 to 1889; and was promoted captain June

2, 1889, when he joined Company I at Fort Abraham Lincoln, Dakota, in October, 1889.

Captain Lockwood was post adjutant at Fort Totten, Dakota, from July, 1867, to December, 1867; acting assistant quartermaster and acting commissary of subsistence at Fort Buford, Dakota, from October, 1868, to June, 1869; post adjutant at Fort Stevenson from June, 1869, to October, 1869; post adjutant at Fort Randall, Dakota, from August, 1870, to July, 1871; post adjutant at Lower Brule Agency from July, 1871, to September, 1872; post adjutant at Fort Randall, Dakota, from May, 1873, to June, 1874; acting assistant quartermaster and acting commissary of subsistence at Fort Brady, Michigan, from May, 1875, to May, 1876; acting commissary of subsistence at Fort Lewis, Colorado, 1884-85; post adjutant at Columbus Barracks, Ohio, from 1887 to June 2, 1889.

Upon the consolidation of Company I, Twenty-second Infantry, Captain Lockwood was ordered to Fort Keogh, Montana (his present station), and subsequently assigned to Company D, Twenty-second Infantry.

### EX-PAYMASTER-GENERAL THOMAS H. LOOKER.
### U.S.N. (RETIRED).

EX-PAYMASTER-GENERAL THOMAS H. LOOKER was born in Ohio, and has been for many years a resident of the District of Columbia. He originally entered the navy as a midshipman in November, 1846, and served with credit throughout the Mexican War in several expeditions on the coast and up rivers. On account of ill health, incident to hard service, he resigned in 1852.

Paymaster Looker's record while serving as a line-officer in the navy was most creditable, and his standing in his class rendered it certain that, had his health not broken down, he would have been just as successful in the line as he had been in the staff. However, later in his career, the knowledge gained as a line-officer proved of great benefit to him and to the service.

In August, 1853, he was appointed a purser in the navy. Attached to brig "Bainbridge," Brazil Squadron, 1853-56; sloop-of-war "Portsmouth," East India Squadron, 1857-58; steamer "Brooklyn," Home Squadron, 1858-60; and in the same ship in 1861, in the Atlantic and Gulf Squadrons, conveying troops and assisting in saving Fort Pickens, and instituting the blockade off the mouths of the Mississippi.

From 1861 to 1863 he was paymaster in charge of supplies North Atlantic Blockading Squadron, and was, as a volunteer, in the memorable action between the "Merrimac" and the "Monitor" and squadron at Hampton Roads, Virginia, in 1862.

During 1864, Paymaster Looker was temporarily on important duty in Baltimore. It will thus be seen that Paymaster Looker was actively engaged during the entire period of the Civil War, and his creditable services then had much to do with his appointment afterwards to the head of his corps.

In 1865 he was ordered to the "Powhatan," on the South Pacific Station, and became fleet-paymaster to 1868. From 1869 to 1872 he was in charge of the Naval Pay-Office at Baltimore, and then served a term at the navy-yard at Washington. Then he was ordered to the Pay-Office in Baltimore again. In 1877-78 he was "Assistant to the Secretary of the Navy." From 1878 to 1882 he was general inspector of the pay corps of the navy. He was then stationed at the Pay-Office at Washington, and was again general inspector of the pay corps in 1889 and 1890. In March, 1890, he was appointed paymaster-general of the navy, and chief of the Bureau of Provisions and Clothing, Navy Department, with the relative rank of commodore. He was retired with that rank in November, 1891, by reason of age and length of service, together with ill health caused by the great strain which at that time devolved upon the incumbent of the office of the paymaster-general.

## MAJOR JAMES H. LORD, U.S.A.

MAJOR JAMES H. LORD (Quartermaster's Department) was born in Pennsylvania February 27, 1840, and graduated from the Military Academy June 17, 1862. He was promoted brevet second lieutenant of the Second Artillery the same day, and on July 24 of the same year was promoted second lieutenant of the same regiment. He served in the Peninsula campaign of the Army of the Potomac during the war of the Rebellion, and in the Northern Virginia campaign in 1862, and was engaged at the battles of Malvern Hill, second Bull Run, Chantilly, and several skirmishes. He participated in the Maryland campaign, and was engaged in the battles of South Mountain and Antietam, and then took part in the march back to the Rappahannock River, and was engaged in the battle of Fredericksburg, Virginia.

Having been transferred to the Western army, he was at Covington, Kentucky, in April, 1863, and at Lexington to June 4, 1863, when he took part in the movements of the Ninth Army Corps to Young's Point, Louisiana. He then participated in the Vicksburg campaign, being engaged in the siege of that place from June 17 to July 4, 1863, and capture of Jackson, Mississippi, July 16, 1863. He was then granted a leave of absence, on account of sickness, from August 10 to September 26, 1863. He was detailed as mustering and disbursing officer at Cincinnati, Ohio, from March 15 to May 2, 1864, and at Boston, Massachusetts, to December 25, 1864. In the mean time he was promoted first lieutenant, to date from March 30, 1864.

In February, 1865, Lieutenant Lord took command of his battery, and participated in the operations about Petersburg, Virginia, and was engaged in the battle of Dinwiddie Court-House, March 31, 1865; battle of Five Forks, April 1, 1865, and, while in pursuit of the enemy, in the actions at Lisbon Centre, High Bridge, Farmville, and Appomattox Court-House, at the surrender of Lee. He was brevetted first lieutenant July 1, 1862, for "gallant and meritorious services at the battle of Malvern

Hill, Virginia;" captain, September 17, 1862, for "gallant and meritorious services at the battle of Antietam, Maryland," and major, April 9, 1865, "for gallant and meritorious services in action at Appomattox Court-House, Virginia."

Lieutenant Lord was at the head-quarters of the Second Division, Cavalry Corps, as aide to General Crook, from June 22 to August 25, 1865, having been appointed captain on the volunteer staff. He then took command of a company at Fort McHenry, Maryland, and in the fall of that year was transferred to the Pacific coast, serving at the Presidio, San Diego, and in garrison at the Presidio of San Francisco, as quartermaster of the Second Artillery, from May 1, 1867, to April 28, 1875.

He was appointed captain and assistant quartermaster April 24, 1875, and since that time has served in various sections of the country, until promoted major, October 4, 1889, when, shortly afterwards, he was ordered to San Francisco as depot quartermaster, which position he is filling at the present time.

CAPTAIN GEORGE G. LOTT, U.S.A. (RETIRED).

CAPTAIN GEORGE G. LOTT was born July 2, 1843, in Pennsylvania. He is the son of Dr. Geo. W. Lott, for many years practising physician and surgeon of Columbia County, in that State, eminent in his profession, distinguished for conspicuous and consistent loyalty to the national government, ever active in maintaining the supremacy of the same. A second son, Dr. John H. Lott, late acting assistant surgeon United States Army, and practising physician and surgeon of Buffalo, Wyoming.

Captain Lott was a cadet at the Military Academy from July 1, 1861, to June 23, 1862, when he was appointed captain and aide-de-camp of volunteers, and reported for duty to Brigadier-General S. D. Sturgis, at Alexandria, Virginia. He served with that officer from that time to March, 1864; with Reserve Army Corps, comprising troops garrisoning the defences of Washington, July 8 to August 22, 1862; General Pope's army during the second Bull Run campaign, August 22 to September 2, 1862; with Second Division, Ninth Corps, Army of the Potomac, through the Maryland campaign, September, 1862, and its march to and battle of Fredericksburg, Virginia, December 13, 1862; its transfer to and services in Central and Eastern Kentucky to June, 1863; with Central Division of Kentucky to September, 1863; with Cavalry Corps, Army of the Ohio, operating in Eastern Kentucky and East Tennessee, to March, 1864. In April, 1864, he was assigned to duty with Brigadier-General E. H. Hobson, and served with that officer as member of his personal staff until May, 1864.

He was with the Mounted Brigade and Second Division, Department of Kentucky, throughout the length and breadth of that State and in West Virginia. Taken prisoner at Keller's Bridge, Licking River, near Cynthiana, Kentucky, in engagement with Confederate forces under General John H. Morgan, June 10, 1864, and recaptured by United States forces two days later.

October 2, 1864, he was in an engagement at Saltville, West Virginia, with Confederate forces under General John C. Breckenridge. In May, 1865, he was assigned to duty with Brigadier-General Louis D. Watkins, commanding at Louisville, Kentucky, and served with that officer as member of his personal staff until mustered out of volunteer service, May 31, 1866.

On the 7th of March, 1867, he accepted the appointment of second lieutenant Twenty-fourth U. S. Infantry. He appeared before the Board at Louisville, Kentucky, for examination, March 27, 1867, and being duly commissioned, reported, under orders for duty at Newport Barracks, Kentucky, and subsequently joined his regiment June 3, 1867, at Vicksburg, Mississippi, and served with regiment in Mississippi to March, 1869, when the regiment was transferred to Texas, where, April, 1869, the Twenty-fourth and Twenty-ninth Regiments were consolidated and afterwards known as the Sixteenth Infantry.

He was promoted first lieutenant Twenty-fourth U. S. Infantry October 14, 1868, transferred to the Eleventh U. S. Infantry by reorganization of the army, April 25, 1869; regimental adjutant Eleventh U. S. Infantry November 11, 1874, to May 30, 1886; promoted captain Eleventh U. S. Infantry June 1, 1886.

Lieutenant Lott was judge advocate of a general court-martial at Galveston, Texas, April and May, 1869; with company at Jefferson, Texas, June, 1869, to June, 1870; commanding company and on the march to Fort Concho, Texas, June 6 to July 17, 1870; Fort Concho, Texas, July, 1870, to November 11, 1874; at Fort Richardson, Texas (regimental adjutant), to November, 1876; en route to Department of Dakota, November and December, 1876; at Cheyenne Agency, Dakota, to December, 1879; at Fort Sully, Dakota, to July, 1880; on general recruiting service at David's Island, New York harbor, July, 1880, to October, 1888; at Sackett's Harbor, New York, October, 1888, to July, 1889; at Plattsburgh Barracks, New York (commanding post and company), July, 1889, to December, 1889, when, as a result of examination by Retiring Board, was ordered home to await retirement, and he was retired from active service February 25, 1891. Residence, Covington, Kentucky.

## REAR-ADMIRAL STEPHEN BLEEKER LUCE, U.S.N.
### (RETIRED).

REAR ADMIRAL STEPHEN BLEEKER LUCE has been upon so many stations, and in so many different kinds of duty, that it would be impossible, within our limited space, to enumerate them. He was born in New York; entered the naval service as midshipman in 1841, when thirteen years and a half old. In 1889, by operation of law, he was placed upon the retired list, having then a total sea-service of thirty-three years; other duty, twelve years and three months; and "unemployed," one year, eleven months. While a midshipman he served in the Mediterranean and on the coast of Brazil; and, from 1845 to 1848, in the "Columbus," 74, circumnavigating the globe, visiting Japan, and serving on the coast of California during the Mexican War. He next went to the Naval Academy, becoming passed midshipman in 1848. After a three years' cruise in the Pacific, he was upon astronomical duty, the Home Squadron, and the Coast Survey, up to September, 1855, when he was promoted to be master, and to lieutenant the day after. After a cruise in the Gulf of Mexico and the West Indies, he went to the Naval Academy as assistant instructor. While there the Civil War broke out. Lieutenant Luce was ordered to the frigate "Wabash," on the Atlantic blockade, and in her took part in the actions at Hatteras Inlet and Port Royal. He commanded a howitzer launch of the "Wabash," in a reconnoissance in force, and an engagement at Port Royal Ferry, by combined military and naval forces. In January, 1862, he was ordered to the Naval Academy, which had been removed to Newport during the war, and in July of that year was commissioned lieutenant-commander. In the summer of 1863 he commanded the "Macedonian," on her practice cruise to Europe, and, upon his return, was ordered to the command of the monitor "Nantucket," of the North Atlantic Blockading Squadron.

While in command of "Nantucket" he engaged Forts Moultrie and Sumter a number of times. In August, 1864, he was ordered to command the "Sonoma," double-ender, of the North Atlantic Squadron, but was almost immediately transferred to the command of the "Canandaigua," and from her to the "Pontiac," where he remained until June, 1865. While in command of "Pontiac" engaged Battery Marshall. In January, 1865, reported to General Sherman, at Savannah, for duty in connection with army operations. With great difficulty got the "Pontiac" up to Sister's Ferry, forty miles above Savannah, and guarded the pontoon bridge there, while Slocum's wing passed into South Carolina. Lieutenant-Commander Luce next served as commandant of midshipmen at Annapolis; commanding, in 1866, the practice squadron of six vessels. In 1867 he commanded the practice cruise, which extended to European waters, with three ships. In 1868 he took the same squadron on a practice cruise, visiting West Point, and then going to Europe. He had been commissioned as commander in 1866; commanded the "Mohongo," in the Pacific, and the "Juniata," of the European Squadron. In September, 1872, he was serving as equipment officer at the Boston Navy-Yard, and was commissioned captain in December of that year. During the "Virginius" excitement he was ordered to command the "Minnesota," but returned to his former duty in a short time. His next duty was the command of the "Hartford," from which he went to that of inspector of training-ships, in which he has always shown an enlightened interest and fostering care. From January 1, 1878, to January 1, 1881, he was in command of the "Minnesota" training-ship, on our coast. From April, 1881, to January, 1884, he was in command of the Training Squadron, constantly cruising. Commodore in 1881, he was, the next year, ordered as president of the Commission on the Sale of the Navy-Yards. In July, 1884, he was ordered to the command of the North Atlantic Squadron, as acting rear-admiral; and in September of the same year made president of the U. S. Naval War College, at Coaster's Harbor, Rhode Island. He was promoted to rear-admiral in October, 1885. From June, 1886, to February, 1889, he was in command of the North Atlantic Station.

**BRIGADIER-GENERAL RANALD S. MACKENZIE,
U.S.A. (DECEASED).**

BRIGADIER-GENERAL RANALD S. MACKENZIE was born in New York. He was a son of Commodore Slidell Mackenzie, U. S. Navy. He graduated at the Military Academy June 17, 1862, and was promoted second lieutenant Corps of Engineers the same day. He served during the war of the Rebellion as assistant engineer of the Ninth Army Corps in the Northern Virginia campaign, and was engaged in the action of Kelly's Ford and battle of Manassas, where he was wounded, and for which he received the brevet of first lieutenant August 29, 1862, for gallant and meritorious services.

He left the field on account of wounds, and was on leave to October 19, 1862, when he was attached to the Engineer Battalion in the Maryland campaign of the Army of the Potomac, and was engaged in constructing, repairing, and guarding bridges. He was in the Rappahannock campaign, and engaged in the battles of Fredericksburg and Chancellorsville. He was promoted first lieutenant March 3, 1863, and was in the Pennsylvania campaign, in command of an engineer company, and was engaged in laying bridges over the Occoquan, and across the Potomac at Edwards' Ferry, and took part in the battle of Gettysburg. He participated in the subsequent campaigns of the Army of the Potomac as captain of engineers, laying and guarding bridges, making roads and reconnoissances, building blockhouses, constructing rifle-trenches, and was engaged in the battle of the Wilderness, combat at Todd's Tavern, and battles about Spottsylvania, and while in command of his regiment was wounded in front of Petersburg June 22, 1864.

Captain Mackenzie was appointed colonel of the Second Connecticut Heavy Artillery July 10, 1864, and, joining his regiment in the Sixth Army Corps, was engaged in defence of the national capital July 11-12, 1864. He commanded a brigade in the Sixth Army Corps in the Shenandoah campaign, and was engaged in the battle of Opequan, Fisher's Hill, and Cedar Creek, where he was wounded, and was on sick-leave from October 19 to November, 1864. He then rejoined and commanded a brigade in the siege of Petersburg. He was appointed brigadier-general of volunteers October 19, 1864, and commanded a cavalry division in the Army of the James during March and April, 1865, and was engaged in the battle of Five Forks, pursuit of General Lee's army, and skirmish and capitulation of Appomattox Court-House April 9, 1865.

General Mackenzie was brevetted for gallant and meritorious services as follows: First lieutenant August 29, 1862, for Manassas; captain May 3, 1863, for Chancellorsville; major July 4, 1863, for Gettysburg; lieutenant-colonel June 18, 1864, for Petersburg; colonel October 19, 1864, for Cedar Creek; brigadier-general March 13, 1865, for services during the Rebellion. He was also brevetted major-general of volunteers March 31, 1865, for "gallant and meritorious services during the Rebellion."

At the close of the war he was stationed at Richmond, Virginia, commanding a cavalry division until August, 1865; then he was placed on waiting orders to January 15, 1866, at which time he was mustered out of the volunteer service. He was on leave of absence to February 8, 1866, when he was detailed as assistant engineer in the construction of the defences of Portsmouth harbor, New York, to May, 1867.

He was appointed colonel of the Forty-first U. S. Infantry March 6, 1867, and transferred to the Twenty-fourth Infantry March 15, 1869. He was transferred to the Fourth Cavalry December 15, 1870. He was appointed a brigadier-general, U. S. Army, October 26, 1882, and while in command of the Department of Texas was retired for disability March 24, 1884. He died January 19, 1889, at New Brighton, Staten Island, New York.

## CAPTAIN AND BREVET MAJOR JUNIUS W. MAC-MURRAY, U.S.A.

CAPTAIN AND BREVET MAJOR JUNIUS W. MACMURRAY (First Artillery) was born near Carondelet, Missouri, May 1, 1843. He was educated for a civil engineer. He volunteered as a substitute in Company B, Engineer Battalion National Guard, State of Missouri, during the campaign of the Kansas border in Missouri, October, November, and December, 1860, under order of the Governor of the State. At the commencement of the war of the Rebellion, during the bombardment of Fort Sumter, South Carolina, he commenced recruiting volunteers in the State of Missouri, under the call of the President of the United States, but in opposition to the Governor of the State of Missouri. He recruited a company, which was accepted for defence of the U. S. Arsenal at St. Louis, Missouri, and was sworn in with this company after midnight of April 20, 1861, in St. Louis Arsenal, by Captain Nathaniel Lyon, Second U. S. Infantry. Brigadier-General Harney, commanding the Department of the West, refused to recognize the swearing in of volunteers for this purpose by Captain Lyon, without authority from the Governor of Missouri; but the men and officers were retained in the arsenal, armed for its defence, and performing the duty of guards. On April 25, 1861, the command was sworn in by Lieutenant Rufus Saxton, Fourth Artillery, as Company B, Rifle Battalion, First Missouri Volunteers. Lieutenant Saxton not being a regularly-designated mustering officer, the company was again duly sworn into service April 29, 1861, by Lieutenant John M. Schofield, First U. S. Artillery, mustering officer (major First Missouri Infantry Volunteers), as Company B, Saxton Rifle Battalion of the First Missouri Volunteers, of which MacMurray was second lieutenant. He was transferred to the First Missouri Light Artillery June 10, 1861, and was promoted first lieutenant September 1, 1861. He served in the Western army, and was engaged in the blockade of the Mississippi River against steamers bringing munitions of war captured by Confederates at Baton Rouge Arsenal to St. Louis. He participated in the expedition to Southwest Missouri, and was afterwards on recruiting service and with his regiment at Camp of Instruction near St. Louis. He participated in Frémont's expedition to Southwest Missouri, and was in the regular brigade from October, 1861, to February, 1862, when he was transferred to the Army of the Mississippi, and assigned to a cavalry division. He was engaged in the capture of Camp Jackson, with twelve hundred rebel prisoners, May 10, 1861; at the capture of Jefferson City, Missouri, June 15, 1861, and participated in the following actions, battles, and skirmishes: Booneville, Missouri; Blackwater, Missouri; New Madrid and Island No. 10; with gun-boats at Point Pleasant, Fort Pillow, Farmington, siege of Corinth,

Hatchie River, Jacinto, Rienzi, Blackland, Booneville, Tuscumbia, Holly Springs, Iuka, Corinth, Davis's Bridge, The Hatchie, Ripley, Waterford, Lumpkin's Mills, Tallahatchie Bridge, Lamar, Coffeeville, Fort Hindman, Port Gibson, Bayou Pierre, Hankinson's Ferry, Raymond, Clinton, Jackson, Champion Hills, Big Black; assault, siege, and surrender of Vicksburg.

Lieutenant MacMurray was promoted captain of First Missouri Light Artillery Nov. 1, 1863; was at St. Louis to Feb., 1865; in charge of reconstruction of fortifications at New Madrid, and served with the Powder River Indian Expedition, on the march from Franklin, Missouri, to the valley of the Powder River, Montana, from June 1 to Nov. 12, 1865, having been engaged with Sioux, Cheyennes, and Arapahoes near Yellowstone River, in September. He was honorably mustered out of the volunteer service Nov. 20, 1865.

Captain MacMurray entered the regular service February 23, 1866, as second lieutenant of the First Artillery; was promoted first lieutenant March 20, 1866, and was brevetted captain for "gallant and meritorious services" in the siege of Corinth, and major for "gallant and meritorious services" in the siege of Vicksburg. He was also brevetted major of volunteers for "gallant and meritorious services," and lieutenant-colonel of volunteers for "gallant and meritorious services" during the war.

Since entering the regular army, Major MacMurray's service has been of both varied and important nature. His education as a civil engineer fitted him for many duties to which he has been assigned. He was professor of military science and tactics at the University of Missouri, at Columbia and Rolla, Missouri; at Cornell University, New York, and at Union College; he made plans and estimates for sanitary system for Vancouver Barracks, and designed water system for that and other posts. Now on recruiting service at Binghamton, New York.

CHIEF ENGINEER DAVID B. MACOMB, U.S.N.
(RETIRED.)

CHIEF ENGINEER DAVID B. MACOMB was born near Tallahassee, Florida, February 27, 1827. He was appointed third assistant engineer in the navy January 11, 1849, from Pennsylvania. His first duty was in the office of the engineer-in-chief, Navy Department, Washington, D. C., 1849–50; coast-survey steamer "Bibb," 1850–51; promoted to second assistant engineer February 26, 1851, remaining attached to the coast-surveying steamer "Bibb," as her senior engineer, until December, 1852, and was then ordered to the steamer "John Hancock," attached to the squadron of the U. S. Exploring Expedition to the North Pacific Ocean, China and Japan Seas, under Acting Commodore Cadwalader Ringgold, U.S.N., which acted in conjunction with Commodore M. C. Perry, U.S.N., in concluding the treaty of amity and commerce with Japan, 1853–55; promoted to first assistant engineer June 26, 1856, and ordered to the steam-frigate "Wabash," flag-ship of Commodore Paulding, U.S.N., commanding the Home Squadron, 1856–57; ordered to duty on frigate "Saranac," attached to the Pacific Squadron, 1858–59; promoted to chief engineer September 21, 1860; ordered to the steam-frigate "Niagara," which conveyed the Japanese ambassadors back to Jeddo, now Tokio, Japan, 1860. Returned to Boston April 23, 1861, and then first learned that Fort Sumter had been fired upon and surrendered to the South Carolina State forces, and that several other States had seceded from the Union. The "Niagara" was immediately ordered to New York Navy-Yard, and, after taking on board some fresh stores and outfits, she left New York May 3, 1861, for blockade duty off Charleston, South Carolina, and Savannah, Georgia, being the first war-vessel ordered on that service. The "Niagara," being the flag-ship of Flag-Officer William W. McKean, was the leading vessel in the bombardment and reduction of Fort McRae and Pensacola Navy-Yard, October, 1861; detached from the "Niagara," February 23, 1862, and March 9, 1862; ordered to special duty in superintending the building and fitting out of the iron-clad monitors "Nahant," "Nantucket," and "Canonicus," 1862–63, and upon the completion of the latter vessel was ordered as her chief engineer, and in May, 1863, she was sent to Norfolk, Virginia, to join the James River fleet of iron-clads and gun-boats, and North Atlantic Blockading Squadron, under Acting Rear-Admiral S. P. Lee, U.S.N., 1863–64. The "Canonicus" was at the reduction of "Howlett's House" batteries, June 21, 1864; and at battles of Dutch Gap and Deep Bottom, August 13, 1864; and before Fort Fisher December 23 and 25, 1864; and at the final reduction and surrender of that place January 13–15, 1865; and immediately after the surrender (that night) the "Canonicus" and "Monadnock" were ordered off Charleston, South Carolina, to assist in the blockade of that place, and participated in the bombardment and occupation of Charleston by the Union forces, February 18, 1865, the "Canonicus" throwing the last hostile shot at the retreating rebels on Sullivan's Island in the early morn of that day. After the evacuation, the "Canonicus" was sent in pursuit of the rebel iron-clad and ram "Stonewall," and went to Havana, Cuba, in company with other vessels of that squadron, Commodore Sylvanus W. Godon, commanding; the "Canonicus" being the first American iron-clad to enter a foreign port. The "Canonicus" returned to the United States June 26, 1865; inspection duty in laying up the iron-clads at League Island, Philadelphia, and of government work and machinery at Baltimore, Maryland, 1865–66; duty at navy-yard, Pensacola, Florida, 1866–67; and at navy-yard, Portsmouth, New Hampshire, 1868–1870; steam-frigate "Tennessee," having on board the United States Commissioners sent by President Grant to San Domingo, 1871; fleet-engineer of the North Atlantic Fleet, 1871–73; again at navy-yard, Portsmouth, New Hampshire, 1874–77. Again fleet-engineer of the North Atlantic Station, 1877–79; and duty at Portsmouth, New Hampshire, 1879–82; president of the Board organized under Act of Congress, August 5, 1882, for survey and appraisal of the great amount of accumulated stores and material during and since the war, 1882–83; on duty at the navy-yard, Boston, Massachusetts, 1884–89. Retired February 27, 1889, with the relative rank of commodore, having arrived at the age of sixty-two and served forty years and over in active service.

The residence of Commodore Macomb is in North Cambridge, Massachusetts, where, in the society of his wife, daughters, and grandchildren, and with his books and papers, he endeavors to enjoy the remainder of a life spent in the service of his country.

## CAPTAIN WILLIAM R. MAIZE, U.S.A. (RETIRED).

CAPTAIN WILLIAM R. MAIZE was born in Indiana, Pennsylvania, February 14, 1844. At the commencement of the war of the Rebellion he entered the volunteer service as private of Company K, Nineteenth Pennsylvania Infantry, April 18, 1861, and was discharged August 9, 1861. He re-entered the volunteer service August 27, 1861, as second lieutenant of the Seventy-eighth Pennsylvania Infantry; was promoted first lieutenant September 1, 1863, and mustered out November 4, 1864.

He served in the field as aide-de-camp to the brevet brigadier-general commanding the Third Brigade, Second Division, Fourteenth Army Corps, during the campaign from Murfreesborough, Tennessee, to Chickamaugua and Chattanooga, in 1863; and was on the staff of the First Division Fourteenth Army Corps, with Brevet Major-Generals R. W. Johnson, John H. King, and William P. Carlin, during the campaign from Chattanooga, Tennessee, to Atlanta and Jonesborough, Georgia, in 1864.

He entered the regular service as second lieutenant of the Second Infantry, April 23, 1866; was promoted first lieutenant January 22, 1867, and transferred to the Twentieth Infantry April 2, 1870. He was brevetted captain March 2, 1867, for "gallant and meritorious services in the battle of Stone River, Tennessee."

Captain Maize served at Carlisle Barracks, as adjutant, quartermaster, and commissary, until 1870, when he joined at Fort Ransom, Dakota Territory. His station was changed to Fort Abercrombie, where he remained until 1871, when he was transferred to Fort Wadsworth, Dakota Territory, where he did duty as commissary and quartermaster until 1873.

He was then ordered to Fort Pembina, where he was post adjutant to May, 1875. Then he was stationed at Fort Seward, Dakota Territory, where he was depot and post quartermaster and commissary to August, 1876.

Captain Maize's regiment being transferred to Texas, we find him at Fort Brown to January, 1879; at Fort Ringgold in the summer of 1880; at Fort Hays, Kansas, to May, 1882, performing, while there, the duties of quartermaster and commissary. He was then at Fort Riley, Kansas, during the balance of the year 1882. His regiment was then transferred to the Department of Dakota, and the captain was stationed at Fort Maginnis until August, 1886, when he was ordered to Camp Poplar River, Montana, remaining there to 1887. He was then made inspector of Indian supplies at Fort Peck, Indian Agency.

He was promoted captain Twentieth Infantry, May 6, 1882, and on March 19, 1888, was ordered to his home to await retirement on account of disability, having been examined and recommended for retirement by a Retiring Board, but he was not placed on the retired list until February 24, 1891.

### CAPTAIN AND BREVET LIEUTENANT-COLONEL GARRICK MALLERY, U.S.A. (RETIRED).

CAPTAIN AND BREVET LIEUTENANT COLONEL GARRICK MALLERY was born in Pennsylvania April 23, 1831. He is the son of the President Judge of Circuit Court of Pennsylvania, and in direct line from Peter Mallery, who arrived in Boston, from England, in 1638. Several ancestors were military officers in the Colonial service and in the Revolutionary War. Through his mother he was descended from William Maclay, first U. S. Senator from Pennsylvania. He was graduated at Yale College in 1850; in 1853 was admitted to the bar of Philadelphia, where he practised law until the first call for troops in the Civil War.

He entered the volunteer service as captain of the Seventy-first Pennsylvania Infantry June 4, 1861, and was engaged in the actions of Lewinsville, Munson's Hill, Falls Church, and Ball's Bluff, Virginia, and was detailed as acting assistant adjutant-general of brigade October 23, 1861. In the early part of 1862 he returned to the command of his company, and was engaged in the battles of Fair Oaks, Seven Pines, Peach Orchard (where he commanded the left wing of his regiment), and Savage Station. He was there taken prisoner, having received two severe wounds and left on the field, from whence he was taken to Libby Prison. He was honorably mustered out February 16, 1863, to accept the appointment of lieutenant-colonel of the Thirteenth Pennsylvania Cavalry, and commanded the regiment in the engagements of Winchester, Culpeper, and others, in 1863–64, and was honorably mustered out July 15, 1864, having been appointed lieutenant colonel in the Veteran Reserve Corps July 1, 1864. He commanded a Provisional Regiment in July, 1864, in the defence of Washington against Early, and was engaged near Fort Stevens.

Colonel Mallery next served on various duties, and commanded his regiment in Maine and Vermont to January, 1866, and then was acting inspector-general, assistant adjutant-general, and assistant commissioner of Bureau of R., F., and A. L., in Virginia. Was appointed captain of the Forty-third U. S. Inf. July 28, 1866, and was brevetted major, U. S. Army, for "gallant and meritorious services in a skirmish at Garnett's Farm, Virginia;" and lieutenant-colonel, U. S. Army, for "gallant and meritorious services at battle of Peach Orchard, Virginia." He was also brevetted colonel of U. S. Volunteers for "gallant and meritorious services during the war."

From September, 1867, to March, 1868, he commanded his company, and part of the time the regiment, at Fort Wayne, Michigan, then was detailed as judge-advocate of First Military District, State of Virginia, and also secretary of state and adjutant-general of Virginia, with the rank of brigadier-general, until February 15, 1870, some of the time being acting governor of Virginia. In August, 1870, he reported to the office of chief signal-officer, U. S. Army, at Washington, and was for long periods acting chief signal-officer, until August, 1876, when, having been assigned to the First U. S. Infantry (December 15, 1870), he was ordered to Fort Rice, Dakota, where he made investigations into the sign-language, pictographs, and mythologies of the North American Indians, resulting in an order of the Secretary of War (June 13, 1877) to report to Major J. W. Powell, in charge of the Survey of the Rocky Mountain region. On July 1, 1879, he was retired for wounds received in line of duty, and accepted appointment of ethnologist of the Bureau of Ethnology, Smithsonian Institution, which he now (1892) holds.

Colonel Mallery is an honorary or active member of several scientific and literary societies in Europe as well as the United States, and was a founder and president of the Anthropological Society and of the Cosmos Club, both of Washington; also president of the Philosophical Society and of the Literary Society of Washington, and vice-president of the American Association for the Advancement of Science, and is now president of the joint commission of the five scientific societies of Washington. He has contributed largely to periodical literature, but his most important works, some of which have been translated, are the following: "A Calendar of the Dakota Nation" (1877); "The Former and Present Number of our Indians" (1878); "A Collection of Gesture-Signs and Signals of the N. A. Indians, with some Comparisons" (1880); "Sign Language among N. A. Indians compared with that among Other Peoples and Deaf Mutes" (1881); "Pictographs of the N. A. Indians" (1886); "Manners and Meals" (1888); "Philosophy and Specialties" (1889); "Israelite and Indian, a Parallel in Planes of Culture" (1889).

## COMMANDER H. DE HAVEN MANLEY, U.S.N.
### (RETIRED.)

COMMANDER MANLEY was born in Chester, Pennsylvania, December 20, 1839, being the son of the late Hon. Charles D. Manley. Appointed to the Naval Academy in September, 1856, and graduated in June, 1860, as a midshipman. He was then ordered to the U. S. S. "Brooklyn," and was detailed as assistant hydrographer to Lieutenant Jeffers, U.S.N., in the survey of the Chiriqui Lagoon. This duty was completed in the fall of 1860.

The war of the Rebellion was then imminent, and naval vessels had been so scattered that, when the government wished to reinforce Fort Pickens, Florida, the "Brooklyn" was almost the only vessel available. She was sent on this duty, in which Midshipman Manley bore an active part. After this the "Brooklyn" went to the "passes" of the Mississippi, being the first vessel on the blockade of New Orleans. Midshipman Manley was made prize-master of her first capture, which he took to Key West, Florida.

After delivering his prize, Midshipman Manley was ordered to the frigate "Congress," at Newport News, Virginia, having been promoted to the rank of master. The "Congress" was quite short of officers, and during the memorable fight with the rebel iron-clad "Merrimac," on March 8, 1862, Manley commanded the three gun divisions on the "Congress's" main-deck, and was slightly wounded. His commanding officer, the survivor of the fight, Lieutenant Austin Pendergrast, expressed in his letter his appreciation of his (Manley's) noble behavior on that occasion, and praised highly his "bravery, coolness, and skill" in the performance of his duties.

Midshipman Manley was next ordered to the navy-yard at Philadelphia, to recuperate from the strain of such a murderous engagement, and from his labors in landing the survivors. But, desiring active service afloat, he was ordered to the steam-sloop "Canandaigua," then on the blockade off Charleston; about which time he was promoted to a lieutenancy.

Lieutenant Manley commanded the howitzer, boats, and landing party from the "Canandaigua" at the capture and occupation of Morris Island, via Stono Inlet, and was engaged in all the fights which occured during the operations of Admirals Dupont and Dahlgren with Forts Sumter, Wagner, and Moultrie, and the Confederate batteries on Morris and Sullivan's Islands which contributed to the defence of Charleston. While attached to the "Canandaigua" he had temporary command of that vessel and of the "Nipsic," and for several months was commanding and senior officer of the offshore blockade at Charleston, having four vessels under his command.

After two years of this hard service he went North on a short furlough, and was then ordered to the "State of Georgia," on the same blockade.

While in temporary command of this ship he was ordered to Fortress Monroe to convey to the government the news of the evacuation of Charleston by the Confederates.

Upon returning to the station he was transferred to the U. S. monitor "Canonicus," which was one of the squadron which went to Havana to seize the Confederate ram "Stonewall," then in that port.

When the war closed, Lieutenant Manley returned to Philadelphia in the "Canonicus," which was put out of commission.

Lieutenant Manley became a lieutenant-commander in 1866, and commander in April, 1874. Under these commissions he was assigned to varied and responsible duties.

In 1865-66 he was executive officer of the frigate "Sabine," and in 1867-68 was attached to the "Franklin," the flag-ship of Admiral Farragut, in Europe. He afterwards served in the flag-ship "Lancaster," Brazil Station, under Admiral Lanman, and was in command of the "Wasp." Was both pupil and instructor at the Newport Torpedo Station, and on ordnance duty at Washington.

Commanded the U. S. S. "Ranger" on the Asiatic Station, and returned thence in command of the "Alert" to San Francisco,—having thus circumnavigated the globe.

He returned in impaired health, and was then ordered to duty at the War Records Office in the Navy Department. Here he remained until January, 1883, when he was retired from active service on account of ill-health and loss of hearing, induced by exposure in the line of duty.

CAPTAIN MATTHIAS C. MARIN, U.S.N. (RETIRED).

CAPTAIN MATTHIAS C. MARIX is a native of Florida, and was appointed a midshipman from that State in January, 1832. He served in the schooners "Spark" and "Porpoise" on the coast of Florida, and in the West Indies, and, afterwards, in the sloop-of-war "John Adams," in the Mediterranean, until 1837. In June, 1838, he was promoted passed midshipman, and, after some duty at the Naval Rendezvous at New York, served in the Florida war, in the schooner "Flirt," 1839-40; and in the sloop-of-war "Vandalia," Home Squadron, 1841-43. Commissioned a lieutenant in March, 1844. Served, for two years, in the "Yorktown," on the coast of Africa, and in 1846-47, in the steamer "Scourge," during the Mexican War. Was present at the capture of Alvarado and Tlacotalpam, the capture of Tuxpan, and the capture of Tabasco. After the Mexican War he was for some time upon the Coast Survey, and in 1852-53 served in the sloop-of-war "Levant," in the Mediterranean. After this he was stationed at the navy-yard, Pensacola; and, about the breaking out of the Civil War, was attached to the "Macedonian."

Commissioned commander October, 1861, and commanded the sloop-of-war "St. Louis," on special service, in 1862-63. In 1864-65, he was upon ordnance duty at the navy-yard at Boston. Was commissioned captain, on the retired list, March, 1867. Was upon special duty at Malden, Massachusetts, in 1869-70.

## COMMODORE W. P. McCANN, U.S.N. (RETIRED).

COMMODORE W. P. McCANN was born in Kentucky on May 4, 1830, and appointed midshipman from that State in 1848; was attached to frigates "Raritan" and "Columbia," in the Gulf and West Indies, and in the Pacific, until 1853, when he was ordered to the Naval School. Passed midshipman June, 1854, and made a cruise of three years and three months in the Pacific; commissioned lieutenant in September, 1855; served in the frigate "Sabine," as lieutenant and navigator, in the Paraguay Expedition, and afterwards in the West Indies and Gulf of Mexico. At breaking out of Rebellion the "Sabine" (April 14-15, 1861) reinforced Fort Pickens with marines and sailors, and afterwards assisted in landing the force under Colonel Harvey Brown; afterwards, during blockade of South Carolina coast, the "Sabine" rescued the battalion of marines from the steamer "Governor," which vessel foundered; in the gun-boat "Maratanza," from April to October, 1862, during which time saw constant and exciting service in co-operating with the Army of the Potomac, from Yorktown to Malvern Hill; made capture of rebel gun-boat "Teaser" and several blockade-runners, and other most important service. Made lieutenant-commander July, 1862; severe engagement with Whitworth battery, at Fort Caswell; ordered to command "Hunchback," in Sounds of North Carolina, October, 1862. In the following March the "Hunchback" performed distinguished service at the battle of New Berne, for which Lieutenant-Commander McCann received special commendation in the official reports. In April, 1863, he had command of five gun-boats, and was frequently engaged with batteries in the Sounds, and other duties.

In November, 1863, he was ordered to command the "Kennebec," West Gulf Blockading Squadron. While serving on blockade of Mobile had frequent engagements with batteries and Fort Morgan, while attacking stranded blockade-runners; mentioned in congratulatory order by Admiral Farragut, for the destruction of the "Ivanhoe," under the guns of Battery G and Fort Morgan. The "Kennebec" captured at sea three loaded blockade-runners, with valuable cargoes, and rebel officers on board. At the battle of Mobile Bay, August 5, 1864, the "Kennebec" was lashed to the "Monongahela," fifth in line of battle, and in that position ran by the fort and engaged the enemy's vessels. Had several men wounded by shell from the "Tennessee," while in contact with that vessel, after ramming her in conjunction with the "Monongahela." The "Kennebec's" anchor carried off the "Tennessee's" boat, davits, and falls. Soon after a 10-inch shell from Fort Morgan struck the "Kennebec's" quarter, but did little harm, except knocking down one man. That night she pursued the "Morgan," which had escaped, and got into shoal water at "Dog River Bar."

From February to August, 1865, Lieutenant-Commander McCann was in command of the "Tahoma," which was disabled in a gale in the Gulf Stream; Naval Academy, 1866; command of "Tallapoosa;" naval rendezvous, and navy-yard, Philadelphia, to 1870; light-house inspector, and commanding "Nipsic" up to August, 1872.

July 2, 1872, commissioned commander, from July, 1866; advanced sixteen numbers; navy-yard, Norfolk, and light-house inspector up to November 1, 1876. Commissioned captain September 21, 1876; commanding "Lackawanna," in Pacific; receiving-ship "Independence," California; and flag-ship "Pensacola," Pacific, up to August, 1882. Court-martial duty at Washington, Hong-Kong, China, Panama, and Boston, 1883; member of Light-House Board from 1883 to 1887, and, in addition, president of Naval Advisory Board from 1885 to 1887. Promoted to commodore January 26, 1887. Served full term as commandant of Boston Navy-Yard, and in addition as president of the Navy-Yard Site Commission, and president of a Board on the Policy for the Increase of the Navy.

Our space prevents more than a glance at Commodore McCann's part in recent events which brought his name prominently before the country.

In August, 1890, he was ordered to command the South Atlantic Station, with rank of acting rear-admiral. When the revolution in Chili occurred in 1891, the South Pacific was embraced in his command. Upon his arrival there he was engaged in protecting American interests; at the same time initiating negotiations for peace between the contending parties in the civil war, which, unfortunately, had no result. We can only say that his course throughout was approved by the Navy Department and by the government. In May, 1892, Commodore McCann was retired by operation of the law governing the retirements.

### REAR-ADMIRAL E. Y. McCAULEY, U.S.N.
#### (RETIRED.)

REAR-ADMIRAL EDWARD YORKE McCAULEY was born in Pennsylvania November 2, 1827, and was appointed a midshipman from that State in September, 1841. He served in the Mediterranean Squadron from 1841 to 1845, and then in the frigate "United States," on the African Station, from 1846 to 1848.

He was promoted to passed midshipman August 10, 1847, and was again in the Mediterranean, in the frigate "Constitution," for three years. Passed Midshipman McCauley had a great facility in the languages spoken on the shores of the Mediterranean, and was a most useful officer there, on that account, in addition to his naval acquirements. He served in the steam-frigate "Powhatan," in East Indies and China, 1852–56, and present at the attack on pirates, in China Sea, in 1855.

He was commissioned lieutenant September 14, 1855. During 1856–57 he was attached to the receiving-ship at Philadelphia. When the memorable "cable expedition" took place, in 1857–58, he served on board the steam-frigate "Niagara."

On August 19, 1859, while on duty at the Naval Observatory at Washington, he resigned from the service; but upon the breaking out of the war of the Rebellion, in 1861, he re-entered, with the rank of acting lieutenant, and was attached to the steamer "Flag," of the South Atlantic Blockading Squadron, during 1861–62.

He was commissioned lieutenant-commander in the regular service on July 16, 1862, and commanded the steamer "Fort Henry," of the East Gulf Blockading Squadron, 1862–63. During this time he made a boat attack upon Bayport, Florida, and two skirmishes with the enemy. In 1863–64 he commanded the gun-boat "Tioga," of the East Gulf Blockading Squadron, and in 1864–65 the gun-boat "Benton," of the Mississippi Squadron.

In 1866–67 he was on "special duty" in Philadelphia, having been commissioned as commander in 1866. During a part of the years 1867–68 he served as fleet-captain of the North Atlantic Squadron, and then was at the navy-yard at Portsmouth, New Hampshire, for two years. After this he was stationed at the Naval Academy, Annapolis, during 1871–72.

He was commissioned captain September 4, 1872, and commanded the steam-sloop "Lackawanna," on the Asiatic Station, from 1872 to 1875. From 1875 to 1878 he was on duty at the Boston Navy-Yard, and from 1878 to 1880 at the Naval Asylum at Philadelphia.

He was promoted to commodore August 1, 1881, and was commandant at League Island in 1884–85.

He was promoted to rear-admiral in March, 1885, and commanded the Pacific Station during 1885–86.

He was retired on his own application, under the law, in January, 1887.

# COLONEL-COMMANDANT CHARLES G. McCAWLEY, U.S.M.C. (DECEASED).

COLONEL-COMMANDANT CHARLES G. McCAWLEY was born in Pennsylvania, but appointed from Louisiana; commissioned as second lieutenant March 3, 1847; in June ordered to join battalion of marines for service with army in Mexico; participated in the storming of the Castle of Chapultepec and taking of the City of Mexico; brevetted first lieutenant, for gallant and meritorious conduct in these actions, September 13, 1847; in August, 1848, was ordered for duty at marine barracks, Philadelphia; December, 1848, marine barracks, Boston; July, 1849, "Cumberland," Mediterranean Squadron; March, 1850, at Naples, to razee "Independence;" August, 1852, marine barracks, Philadelphia; June, 1853, "Princeton," Home Squadron. Promoted first lieutenant January 2, 1855; July, 1855, marine barracks, New York; December, 1855, marine barracks, Boston; July, 1857, "Mississippi;" detached and ordered to Philadelphia; December, 1857, "Jamestown," at Philadelphia, for Home Squadron; March, 1860, marine barracks, Philadelphia; December, 1860, "Macedonian," Home Squadron, Atlantic coast, West Indies, and Spanish Main; January, 1862, marine barracks, Boston; detached immediately and ordered to join battalion of marines at Bay Point, South Carolina; April, 1862, returned with battalion to Washington. Received commission as captain July 26, 1861; ordered in command at head-quarters; May, 1862, ordered with detachment of two hundred men to reoccupy the Norfolk Navy-Yard; hoisted the flag again on the part of the navy; October, 1862, ordered to head-quarters, Washington, D. C.; in command until July, 1863; ordered to join battalion of marines, for service in South Atlantic Squadron; served with same on Morris Island during bombardment and destruction of Fort Sumter, and capture of Forts Wagner and Gregg; commanded a detachment of one hundred men and officers in the boat attack on Fort Sumter September 8, 1863; received a brevet as major for gallant and meritorious conduct in this action; served on Folly Island, and, in December, 1863, battalion returned to Philadelphia; marine barracks, Philadelphia. Promoted major June 10, 1864; ordered to marine rendezvous, Philadelphia; March, 1865, ordered to command marine barracks, Boston. Promoted to lieutenant-colonel December 5, 1867; August, 1871, ordered to command marine barracks, Washington, D. C.; June, appointed superintendent of recruiting, in addition to other duty; ordered to New York to attend to organizing the recruiting service; returned to Washington November, 1872. Promoted colonel-commandant of the U. S. Marine Corps November 1, 1876; head-quarters U. S. Marine Corps, 1876–90.

Colonel McCawley was retired, by operation of law, on account of age, in 1891. He died, soon after his retirement, at Rosemont, Pennsylvania, on October 13, 1891.

## MAJOR-GENERAL GEORGE B. McCLELLAN (DECEASED).

MAJOR-GENERAL GEORGE B. McCLELLAN was born in Pennsylvania, and graduated from the Military Academy July 1, 1846. He was promoted brevet second lieutenant Corps of Engineers the same day, and second lieutenant April 24, 1847. He served in the war with Mexico, attached to the company of sappers, miners, and pontoniers, participating in opening the road from Matamoras to Tampico, and engaged in the siege of Vera Cruz, battle of Cerro Gordo, skirmish of Amozoque, battles of Contreras and Churubusco, constructing batteries against Chapultepec, and assault and capture of the City of Mexico, September 13-14, 1847. He was brevetted first lieutenant August 20, 1847, for "gallant and meritorious conduct in the battles of Contreras and Churubusco," and captain September 8, 1847, for "gallant and meritorious conduct in the battle of Molino del Rey," which he declined. He was then brevetted captain September 13, 1847, for "gallant and meritorious conduct in the battle of Chapultepec, Mexico."

Captain McClellan was ordered to West Point, New York, at the close of the Mexican War, attached to the company of engineer troops, part of the time in command, and then was assistant engineer in the construction of Fort Delaware to 1852. He was then detailed as engineer of an exploring expedition to the sources of the Red River of Texas; after which he was chief engineer of the Department of Texas, and in charge of surveys of rivers and harbors on the Gulf coast to 1853; was engineer for exploring and survey of the Western Division of the Union Pacific Railroad through the Cascade Mountains in 1853-54.

He was promoted captain First Cavalry March 3, 1855, and was detailed as a member of the military commission to the "Theatre of War in Europe," in 1855-56, his official report being published by order of Congress in 1857, embracing his remarks upon the operations in the Crimea. He resigned from the army January 16, 1857.

Captain McClellan then became chief engineer of the Illinois Central Railroad, and subsequently vice-president of the same; and in 1860 was president of the St. Louis and Cincinnati Railroad. When the Rebellion began he was made major-general of Ohio volunteers April 23, 1861, and major-general U. S. Army May 14, 1861. He served in the Department of the Ohio, and was engaged in the action of Rich Mountain, West Virginia, July 11, 1861, and, by a forced march upon the rebel camp, compelled General Pegram's surrender July 12, 1861.

The thanks of Congress were tendered General McClellan, July 16, 1861, for "the series of brilliant and decisive victories" achieved by his army over the rebels "on the battle-fields of West Virginia."

General McClellan was then called to the command of the Division of the Potomac August 17, of the Army of the Potomac August 20, and as general-in-chief of the Armies of the United States November 1, 1861. He participated in the advance on Manassas, in command of the Army of the Potomac, and in the Virginia Peninsula campaign, being engaged in the siege of Yorktown, occupation of Williamsburg, battle of Fair Oaks; the battles of the Seven Days, with change of base to the James River, from June 26 to July 2, 1862. He was in command of the defences of Washington, and in the Maryland campaign, in command of the Army of the Potomac, from September 7 to November 10, and was engaged in the battles of South Mountain, Antietam, and march to Warrenton.

At this time he was relieved of his command, and was waiting orders at New York City November 8, 1864, during which time he was nominated by the Chicago Convention as a candidate for President of the United States, but was defeated at the election in 1864 by President Abraham Lincoln. He resigned November 8, 1864, and resided in New York City for a time, but subsequently established himself in a home at Orange, New Jersey.

General McClellan translated from the French a "Manual of Bayonet Exercises," adopted for the U. S. Army in 1852. He edited his own "Personal Memoirs," which were not published until after his death, which took place on October 29, 1885, at Orange, New Jersey.

## CAPTAIN AND BREVET LIEUTENANT-COLONEL SAMUEL McCONIHE, U.S.A.

CAPTAIN AND BREVET LIEUTENANT-COLONEL SAMUEL McCONIHE (Fourteenth Infantry) was born in New Hampshire, September 8, 1836. He graduated at the Union College, Schenectady, New York, in the Class of 1856, as Bachelor of Arts and Master of Arts, and during the war of the Rebellion entered the volunteer service as captain of the Ninety-third New York Infantry, January 9, 1862; he was promoted major December 3, 1863, and colonel of the same September 7, 1864. Although he was commissioned as colonel by the Governor of New York, he could not muster-in, owing to the reduced numbers in his regiment, but he exercised the command of his regiment as colonel from the time appointed until he was mustered out, February 15, 1865, and his rank was acknowledged in the Army Register of 1867, but not since.

Colonel McConihe was in the field with the Army of the Potomac, and participated in all its campaigns, from the commencement of the year 1862 to the close of the war, and was engaged at the siege of Yorktown and battle of Williamsburg; the battles of Antietam, Fredericksburg, and Chancellorsville; the battles of the Wilderness (commanding regiment), Spottsylvania, North Anna, Tolopotomy, Cold Harbor; action at Strawberry Plains; battles of Deep Bottom, Poplar Spring Church, Petersburg, and first Boydton Road; the battles of Hatcher's Run and second Boydton Road; and was brevetted colonel and brigadier-general of volunteers March 13, 1865, for "conspicuous gallantry in the battles of the Wilderness and Spottsylvania, and for gallant and meritorious services during the war."

He was guard at the head-quarters of the army in September, 1862, and served at Richmond, Virginia, in 1865.

Colonel McConihe entered the regular service as second lieutenant of the Fourteenth Infantry February 23, 1866, and was promoted first lieutenant the same day. He joined his regiment on the Pacific coast, and served with it there until 1870, when the regiment was transferred to the Department of the Platte, he serving there and in the Department of the Missouri to 1885, when he was sent to the Department of the Columbia, remaining there until September 8, 1890, at which time he was ordered to the Department of the Missouri, and stationed at Fort Leavenworth, Kansas, where he is at the present time.

He was promoted captain of the Fourteenth Infantry February 25, 1876.

Upon entering the regular service, he was brevetted captain March 2, 1867, for "gallant and meritorious services in the battle of the Wilderness, Virginia;" major March 2, 1867, for "gallant and meritorious services in the battle of Spottsylvania, Virginia;" and lieutenant-colonel March 2, 1867, for "gallant and meritorious services during the war."

### BRIGADIER- AND BREVET MAJOR-GENERAL ALEXANDER McD. McCOOK, U.S.A.

BRIGADIER- AND BREVET MAJOR GENERAL ALEXANDER McD. McCOOK was born in Ohio April 22, 1831, and graduated at the Military Academy July 1, 1852. He was promoted brevet second lieutenant Third Infantry the same day; second lieutenant June 30, 1854; first lieutenant Dec. 6, 1858; and captain May 14, 1861. He served at Newport Barracks and Jefferson Barracks until 1853, when he was ordered on frontier duty at Fort Fillmore, New Mexico, and was scouting against Apache Indians in 1854. He was stationed at Fort Union, and participated in an expedition against Utah and Apache Indians, on commissary duty, in 1855, being engaged in the actions of Sanwatchie Pass and Arkansas River. Was at Cantonment Burgwin, New Mexico, in 1855-56; on the Gila Expedition, as chief of guides, and engaged in action on the Gila River, June 27, 1856; on leave of absence 1857-58, and at the Military Academy, as assistant instructor of infantry tactics, from Feb. 12, 1858, to April 24, 1861.

At the commencement of the war of the Rebellion he served as mustering and disbursing officer at Columbus, Ohio, and in the defences of Washington City, May to July, 1861, and was engaged in the action of Vienna, June 17, and in the battle of Bull Run, July 21, 1861.

He was appointed colonel of the First Ohio Volunteers, to date from April 16, 1861, and was employed in recruiting and organizing his regiment at Dayton. He was mustered out of the volunteer service August 2, 1861, and reappointed colonel of the First Ohio Volunteers August 10, 1861, and appointed brigadier-general of volunteers September 3, 1861. He commanded a brigade in the Department of the Cumberland, and participated in the operations in Kentucky, October to December, 1861. He was then assigned to the command of a division in the Army of the Ohio, participating in the movement to Nashville and Pittsburg Landing, in the battle of Shiloh, advance upon and siege of Corinth, operations in North Alabama, and movement through Tennessee to Louisville, Kentucky, June to September, 1862.

General McCook was appointed major-general of volunteers July 17, 1862, and was assigned to the command of the First Corps, Army of the Ohio, and participated in the advance into Kentucky in October, 1862, and was engaged in the battle of Perryville and march to the relief of Nashville, October, 1862. He was in command of Nashville, Tennessee, November and December, 1862, and was then placed in command of the right wing of the Fourteenth Corps from December 14, 1862, to January 12, 1863; and of the Twentieth Corps from January to October, 1863. He was in the Tennessee campaign, and was engaged in several skirmishes on the march to Murfreesborough, in the battle of Stone River, combat of Liberty Gap (in command), advance on Tullahoma, crossing the Cumberland Mountains and Tennessee River, and in battle of Chickamauga. He was awaiting orders from October, 1863, to November, 1864, being engaged, while at Washington City, in the defence of the Capital, July 11-12, 1864; and in the Middle Military Division from November, 1864, to February, 1865. Commanded the District of Eastern Arkansas from Feb. to May, 1865.

He was brevetted for gallant and meritorious services: lieutenant-colonel March 3, 1862, at the capture of Nashville, Tennessee; colonel April 7, 1862, at the battle of Shiloh, Tennessee; brigadier-general March 13, 1865, at the battle of Perryville, Kentucky; and major-general March 13, 1865, in the field during the Rebellion.

General McCook was with a joint committee of Congress, investigating Indian affairs, from May to October, 1865; was then on leave of absence and awaiting orders to March 27, 1867. He resigned his commission as major-general of volunteers October 21, 1865, and was promoted lieutenant-colonel of the Twenty-sixth Infantry March 5, 1867, transferred to Tenth Infantry in 1869, and promoted colonel of Sixth Infantry December 15, 1880. He served with his regiment in various departments, and was acting inspector-general of the Department of the Missouri from December, 1874, to June, 1875, and then colonel and aide-de-camp to the general of the army to December, 1880.

He was in command of the post of Fort Leavenworth and the Infantry and Cavalry School of Application from May 13, 1886, to August 28, 1890; appointed brigadier-general July 11, 1890, and assigned to command the Department of Arizona, which position he now occupies.

General McCook is the son of Major Daniel McCook, who was born in 1796, and killed in battle by Morgan's guerillas near Buffington Island, Ohio, July 19, 1863. Seven of his brothers took part in the war for the Union, three of whom, like their father, were killed. Four of the eight McCook brothers attained the rank of general,

## MAJOR TULLY McCREA, U.S.A.

MAJOR TULLY McCREA (Fifth Artillery) was born in Mississippi July 23, 1839, and graduated at the Military Academy in the Class of 1862. He was promoted second lieutenant of the First Artillery June 17, 1862, and first lieutenant November 4, 1863. He served in the field with the Army of the Potomac, participating in the Maryland, Rappahannock, and Pennsylvania campaigns, and was engaged in the battles of Antietam, Fredericksburg, Chancellorsville, and Gettysburg, and in the operations incident thereto. He also participated in the campaign in Florida, and was engaged in the battle of Olustee, where he was severely wounded, and compelled to leave the field, remaining on sick-leave from February to October, 1864. He was then detailed at West Point, as assistant professor of geography, history, and ethics, until August 31, 1865; and as assistant professor of mathematics to June 23, 1866.

He was brevetted first lieutenant September 17, 1862, for gallant and meritorious services at the battle of Antietam; captain, July 3, 1863, for gallant and meritorious services at the battle of Gettysburg; major, February 20, 1864, for gallant and meritorious services at the battle of Olustee, Florida (where he was severely wounded). He was also honorably mentioned in the "Records of the Rebellion," in the report of the chief of artillery, Second Army Corps, Army of the Potomac, on the battle of Gettysburg, as follows:

"Honorable mention should be made of . . . Second Lieutenant Tully McCrea . . . for their distinguished coolness and bravery."

Lieutenant McCrea was quartermaster of the First Artillery from June 20 to November 20, 1866, at Fort Hamilton, New York. He was appointed captain of the Forty-second Infantry July 28, 1866; and was detailed on recruiting service at Newark, New Jersey, and Harrisburg, Pennsylvania, from September, 1866, to April, 1867, when he was ordered to Madison Barracks, New York, where he commanded his company until August, 1867, and then was transferred to Fort Porter, New York. In June, 1868, he was on waiting orders and conducted recruits to California. In October, 1868, he was detailed at West Point as quartermaster of the Military Academy, remaining there until August, 1872, at which time he was ordered to Washington, D. C., as deputy governor of the Soldiers' Home.

Upon being relieved from duty at the Soldiers' Home in July, 1875, having been assigned to the First Artillery, December 15, 1870, he took station at St. Augustine, Florida, but was transferred to Fort Trumbull, Connecticut, the following December, remaining there until July, 1876, when ordered to Fort Sill, Indian Territory. In November, 1876, Captain McCrea was ordered to Washington, D. C., and in April, 1877, again took station at Fort Trumbull, from which point he was sent to assist in suppressing the railroad disturbances in Pennsylvania. Returning to Fort Trumbull in the following November, he remained there until November, 1881, when his regiment was transferred to the Pacific coast, and he took station at the Presidio of San Francisco. He afterwards served at Fort Winfield Scott, California, the Presidio, and Vancouver Barracks, Washington, until February, 1889.

He was promoted major of the Fifth Artillery December 4, 1888, and joined his regiment at Governor's Island in February, 1889, but had hardly become settled, when he was again transferred to the Pacific coast with his regiment, and is now serving on that station.

## COMMANDER FELIX McCURLEY, U.S.N.

COMMANDER FELIX McCURLEY was born in Baltimore, Maryland; appointed an acting master in the navy November 13, 1861, at the request of the Honorable Reverdy Johnson, of Baltimore, Maryland, and ordered to the U. S. S. "Winona," West Gulf Blockading Squadron, 1861-62; engaged in several skirmishes with Forts Jackson and St. Philip, and in the attack on April 24, 1862.

Engaged in the attack on and passage of Vicksburg batteries June 28, 1862; also in the engagement with the iron-clad "Arkansas," on the Mississippi River above Vicksburg, July 15, 1862. Again engaged and passed the batteries at Vicksburg in U. S. S. "Winona." Engaged, also, in the destruction of Grand Gulf City, in U. S. S. "Winona," and in numerous skirmishes and fights on the Mississippi River.

October 12, 1863, engaged in fights with Fort Morgan, while in command of U. S. steamer "Eugenia" (Glascow); 1863 and 1864 attached to U. S. S. "Lackawanna," and in her engaged in the attack and passage of Forts Morgan and Gaines, and subsequent engagement in Mobile Bay with iron-clad "Tennessee" and other vessels of Confederate fleet. Afterwards promoted to acting volunteer lieutenant, and during latter part of 1864 and first part of 1865 commanded U. S. S. "Selma" and U. S. S. "Chocura." From 1867 to 1870 attached to U. S. S. "Quinnebaug," South Atlantic Squadron. Stationed at Hydrographic Office, 1870. Attached to U. S. S. "Worcester," European Station, 1871.

On duty at Hydrographic Office, 1871-73.

Commissioned as master March 12, 1868; as lieutenant December 18, 1868; as lieutenant commander March 2, 1870.

Attached to U. S. S. "Alaska," European Station, from August, 1873, to July, 1876; at Torpedo Station, Newport, Rhode Island, 1877. Commanding U. S. S. "Fortune," North Atlantic Station, 1878-79; U. S. S. "Wabash," 1881-82; U. S. S. "Franklin," 1883-86.

Commissioned commander January, 1887; commanding U. S. iron-clads "Wyandotte," "Ajax," "Canonicus," "Catskill," "Mahopac," "Lehigh," and "Manhattan," in James River, 1889-90.

Commanding U. S. S. "Nipsic," Pacific Station, 1890, 1891, and 1892; commanding U. S. S. "Alliance," Asiatic Station, during which time rescued the crews of two shipwrecked Chinese vessels at sea, receiving letters of thanks from Chinese authorities on both occasions.

Commander Felix McCurley is a son of James McCurley and Elizabeth Wallace Graham, a grandson of Felix McCurley and Mary Pierpont, and a great-grandson of Morgan Pierpont and Mary Chew. His great-grandfather fought in the Revolution, and both his grandfathers in the war with England in 1812.

Commander McCurley married Miss Anna B. Fowble, of Baltimore, and has two children,—James Wallace and Edith Lisle McCurley.

## CAPTAIN JOHN McDONALD, U.S.A. RETIRED.

CAPTAIN JOHN McDONALD was born in Ireland, and entered the regular service at Boston, Massachusetts, as a private, August 18, 1857, and was assigned to Company K of the First Dragoons. He joined his regiment at Fort Buchanan, Arizona, and participated in several campaigns against hostile Indians in Arizona and California. He was ordered with his troop to the seat of war in November, 1861, and served in the Army of the Potomac as first sergeant of his troop during the Peninsula campaign, for which he was complimented by his troop commander, Captain B. F. Davis, for his conduct at Williamsburg, Virginia, May 4, 1862.

He was appointed second lieutenant of the First Cavalry July 17, 1862, and sent to Carlisle, Pennsylvania, the following August, to recruit his troop to one hundred men. He rejoined his regiment in February, 1863, and was in the battle at Kelly's Ford, March 17 following, being severely injured by his horse having been wounded and falling with him while commanding the rear-guard. He was complimented by General Averell, through his regimental commander, for the part he bore in that action. He had to be sent to Washington, D. C., in April, for medical treatment; after which he was ordered to Carlisle, and in the November following to Harrisburg, Pennsylvania, where he was assigned to recruiting and mustering duty.

Lieutenant McDonald was promoted first lieutenant December 29, 1863, and rejoined his regiment at Winchester, Virginia, in November, 1864. He participated in the cavalry raid to Gordonsville, Virginia, in December, 1864.

He was then sent to the general hospital for officers at Annapolis, Maryland, in February, 1865, until May 15, 1865, when he was assigned to mustering duty in Baltimore, Maryland; after which he joined his regiment at New Orleans, Louisiana, in June. Then he was or-

dered to California, with his regiment, in January, 1866, and from there to Arizona, in command of Troop G, in March.

In July, 1867, Lieutenant McDonald was on sick-leave, and ordered to report to the medical director of the Department of California, who recommended a change of station.

While at Fort McDermitt he was assigned to the command of Fort Halleck, Nevada, from which he was relieved in October, and ordered to return to Fort McDermitt as quartermaster and commissary.

A short while after this Captain McDonald was required to appear before a retiring board, at San Francisco, in November, 1867. He was commanding Drum Barracks, California, when ordered to his home, in Maryland, January 15, 1868. He was promoted to captain July 1, 1868, and retired the same day.

Captain McDonald was assigned to court-martial duty in Texas from November, 1868, to March, 1869.

CAPTAIN ROBERT McDONALD, U.S.A. (RETIRED).

CAPTAIN ROBERT McDONALD was born in New York May 12, 1822. He joined the U. S. Army July 21, 1856, and was assigned to the Fifth Infantry, in Florida, participating in General Harney's Seminole campaign.

In 1856-57 ordered to compose the second column of the Utah forces in General Johnston's Mormon campaign, only to arrive within fourteen miles of the city to have a pardon proclamation by President Buchanan announced in orders.

In 1857 to 1860 ordered to march to New Mexico to engage in General Canby's Navajo campaign, and from 1860 to 1867 were occupied in subjugating and civilizing that tribe (ten thousand strong), and in defeating the Army of the Trans-Mississippi, preserving to the Union New Mexico, Arizona, and possibly California. In 1862-63, though only a non-commissioned officer, he was given charge of the defences of the Fort Union field-works, ordnance, and ordnance stores, with orders to allow no one inside the magazine, where the ammunition for the whole Territory was stored. In 1864 he was ordered to Annapolis, Maryland, for examination for promotion. He was assigned to duty as acting assistant quartermaster and assistant commissary subsistence and provost-marshal at El Paso, Texas, in 1865; ordered to Fort Sumner, New Mexico, and assigned to duty as acting assistant quartermaster, assistant commissary subsistence, and assistant commissary subsistence for the Navajo Indians, in 1866, transferring them, by order of General Grant, to the Department of the Interior. He was regimental quartermaster from 1866 to 1869, and assigned to duty as acting assistant quartermaster and assistant commissary subsistence twice at Fort Hays, Kansas; once at Fort Riley, Kansas, and again at Fort Harker, Kansas, 1868-69. He was then ordered to join his company at Fort Reynolds, Colorado. He was detailed on recruiting service at Louisville, Kentucky, from 1871 to 1872, and then joined his company at Fort Larned, Kansas, and assigned to duty as acting assistant quartermaster and assistant commissary subsistence. He was on duty guarding the line of the Atchison, Topeka, and Santa Fé Railway, 1873-74. He was assigned as chief commissary of subsistence on the staff of General Miles in his operations against the hostiles of the Southwest, and on duty as acting assistant quartermaster and assistant commissary subsistence, camp North Fork of Red River, Texas, 1874-75. He joined his company at Fort Riley, Kansas, and took station at Fort Reno, Indian Territory, in 1876. His company was ordered to join the regiment in the field in General Terry's campaign against the hostiles of the Northwest, and afterwards, with great success, under General Miles, commanding the District of the Yellowstone; on duty as assistant commissary subsistence at Fort Keogh, Montana. He was assigned to duty as chief commissary of subsistence on the staff of General Miles in the operations resulting in the defeat and capture of the Bannocks, Nez Perces, Cheyennes, and Sioux of the West and Northwest, assuring peace to the harassed settlements of Montana from 1877 to 1879. Captain McDonald was recommended for the brevets of captain and major in 1867; again as captain in 1877. He experienced a few conflicts with Indians, beginning in the palms of Florida, continuing on the alkaline plains of Kansas and Texas, the arid wastes of New Mexico and Arizona, and ending amid the dreary, frozen wilds of Montana,—once leading the Navajos against the Comanches, fighting from early dawn unto the afternoon, the captain being the only white person in the fight. Again, when, contrary to advice, the temporary post commander brought on a conflict between the troops and the Navajos, in which three successive detachments of cavalry, with fatal casualties, were whipped and chased into the post, a general assault being imminent, declining any escort, he undertook to quell the disturbance. He was deserted on the way by the two principal chiefs. He sought the hostile leaders and succeeded, though not until twelve arrows in the hands of so many horsemen, each bowstring at the ear, were pointed at his breast.

Captain McDonald was retired from active service, by operation of law, May 12, 1886.

## CAPTAIN THOMAS M. McDOUGALL, U.S.A. (RETIRED).

CAPTAIN THOMAS M. McDOUGALL was born at Fort Crawford, Prairie du Chien, Wisconsin, May 21, 1845. He is the son of Brevet Brigadier-General Charles McDougall, surgeon U. S. Army, deceased. He served as second lieutenant and aide-de-camp of volunteers, when only seventeen years of age, at Milliken's Bend and Goodrich Landing, Louisiana, until January 22, 1864. He was appointed second lieutenant Forty-eighth U. S. Colored Infantry February 18, 1864, and was aide-de-camp to General John P. Hawkins, commanding the First Division of U. S. Colored Troops. He was relieved from this duty October 17, 1864, and made assistant commissary of musters of the post and defences of Vicksburg, from which he was relieved and appointed aide-de-camp and commissary of musters, February, 1865; afterwards appointed commissary of musters of the Division of Colored Infantry. He was also on the staff of General Emory Upton, as provost-marshal, District of Colorado, and assistant commissary of musters, October 16, 1865.

Captain McDougall, while on duty in Louisiana, participated in the engagements at Haines' Bluff, Yazoo City, Port Gibson, and Grand Gulf, Mississippi, and while in Florida those of Perdido River, Florida, siege and assault of Fort Blakely, Alabama, and the capture of Mobile.

He was honorably mustered out of the Forty-eighth U. S. Colored Infantry June 1, 1865, to enable him to accept a captaincy in the Fifth U. S. Volunteer Infantry; and, having joined that regiment, proceeded with it to the Plains, marching from Missouri to Selina, Kansas, thence to Fort Riley, Kansas; and from that place to Denver, Colorado, arriving there October 16, 1865, having been engaged in an affair with Indians near Fort Ellsworth, Kansas. He was at Camp Collins, Colorado, June 11, 1866, to muster out the Twenty-first New York Cavalry, and a few days later was ordered to Fort Columbus, New York harbor, and was honorably mustered out of the volunteer service August 10, 1866.

Captain McDougall entered the regular service as second lieutenant Fourteenth Infantry May 10, 1866; was transferred to the Thirty-second Infantry September 21, 1866; was promoted first lieutenant November 5, 1866; was again transferred to the Twenty-first Infantry April 19, 1869; was unassigned October 21, 1869; was assigned to the Seventh Cavalry December 31, 1870; and was promoted captain December 15, 1875.

When first assigned to the regular service, he was ordered to take recruits by sea from New York to Cali-

fornia, and after accomplishing that duty he served at numerous posts until August, 1867, when he was changed to Arizona, and subsequently, in 1869, his station was changed to Fort Vancouver. After being transferred to the cavalry, he was with Stanley's Yellowstone Expedition, escorting the Northern Pacific Railroad Survey, from May 7 to October 1, 1873. He was in the field almost every summer while in the cavalry service, scouting, protecting construction trains, etc., etc. He participated in engagements with Indians at Aravipa Cañon, Tonto Basin, Point of Mountain, and Rock Springs, Arizona, and in action at the mouth of the Big Horn with hostile Indians, August 11, 1873. While on Ku-Klux duty in the South, he had a skirmish with illicit distillers at McGownsville, and Limestone Springs, South Carolina, in 1871.

Captain McDougall took part in the Big Horn and Yellowstone Expedition of 1876, and with his troop was rear-guard and in charge of the pack-train of Custer's command in the battle of the Little Big Horn, Montana Territory, June 25 and 26. He also commanded the Third Battalion of the Seventh Cavalry, as part of the escort to Chief Joseph and his band of Indians to camp opposite Fort Abraham Lincoln, North Dakota, and took station at Fort Yates, January 2, 1883. He marched with Troop B, Seventh Cavalry, to Fort Meade, South Dakota, arriving there October 17, 1886, and remained until May 17, 1888, when he was granted leave of absence on account of sickness, after which he was ordered to appear before a retiring board at San Antonio, Texas, June 11, 1889, and, having been found incapacitated for active service, was retired July 22, 1890.

## OFFICERS OF THE ARMY AND NAVY (REGULAR)

### MAJOR-GENERAL IRWIN McDOWELL, U.S.A.
(DECEASED).

MAJOR-GENERAL IRWIN McDOWELL was born in Ohio, and graduated from the Military Academy July 1, 1838. He was promoted to brevet second lieutenant the same day, and second lieutenant, First Artillery, July 7, 1838. He served on the Northern frontier during the Canadian Border disturbances, and on the Maine frontier, pending the "Disputed Territory," until 1841, when he was detailed at the Military Academy as assistant instructor of infantry tactics, and as adjutant, to October 8, 1845; then as aide-de-camp to Brigadier-General Wool to May 13, 1847, when the war with Mexico occurred, and he was employed in mustering in volunteers. He was promoted first lieutenant October 7, 1842, which he retained to February 22, 1851.

Lieutenant McDowell was acting assistant adjutant-general of the army commanded by Brigadier-General Wool, on the march for Chihuahua, from August, 1846, to January, 1847, and was engaged in the battle of Buena Vista, for which he was brevetted captain February 23, 1847. He was then made brevet captain of staff (assistant adjutant-general) May 13, 1847, and was adjutant-general to Brigadier-General Wool's division in the Army of Occupation, to May 22, 1848. He was then on duty mustering out and discharging troops.

In 1848-49 he was on duty as assistant adjutant-general at the War Department, and at the head-quarters of the army at New York City until 1851, when he was on duty at various head-quarters until 1858, having been made brevet major of staff (assistant adjutant-general) March 31, 1856. From November 17, 1858, to November 14, 1859, he was on leave of absence in Europe, and on returning from leave was assistant adjutant-general at the head-quarters of the army to January 11, 1860, when he was transferred to Texas. After two months' service there he was on leave of absence from April 8 to August, 1860, when he made a tour of inspection in Minnesota, Missouri, and Kansas, to February, 1861. He was then employed in inspecting troops in Washington City to April, 1861. He assisted in organizing and mustering District of Columbia volunteers into the service at Washington, and was in command of the Capitol building to May, 1861, when he was made brigadier-general United States Army, and placed in command of the Department of Northeast Virginia, and of the defences of Washington south of the Potomac, and subsequently in command of the Army of the Potomac to July 25, 1861. He organized the Manassas campaign, and commanded in the battle of Bull Run, July 21, 1861. He was, on July 25, placed in command of a division in the defences of Washington, D. C., which he retained until March 13, 1862, when he was appointed major-general of volunteers.

He was then assigned to the First Corps of the Army of the Potomac, and commanded the Department and Army of the Rappahannock from April 4 to August 12, 1862, at which time he was assigned to the command of the Third Corps, Army of Virginia, and was in the Northern Virginia campaign (Pope's), being engaged in the battle of Cedar Mountain, action of Rappahannock Station, and battle of second Bull Run, August 29-30, 1862.

After this campaign General McDowell was detailed as president of a court for investigating alleged cotton frauds, from May to July, 1863, and of Board for Retiring Disabled Army Officers, at Wilmington, Delaware, to May 21, 1864, when he was assigned to the command of the Department of the Pacific to June 27, 1865, and of the Department of California from that date.

He was brevetted major-general, United States Army, March 13, 1865, for "gallant and meritorious services at the battle of Cedar Mountain, Virginia," and was mustered out of the volunteer service September 1, 1866. He was appointed major-general, United States Army, November 25, 1872, and commanded the Military Division of the Pacific up to the date of his retirement from the army, by operation of law, October 15, 1882. He died at San Francisco, California, May 4, 1885.

## COMMANDER CHARLES McGREGOR, U.S.N.
### (DECEASED).

COMMANDER CHARLES McGREGOR was born in Ohio, but was appointed a midshipman from Illinois in September, 1860. He remained at the Naval Academy until 1863, when the advanced classes were sent to war-service. But while on leave of absence, in 1862, he volunteered against Kirby Smith, and was assigned to duty,—at first with the army, and afterwards transferred to the gun-boat flotilla, under Commander Duble, of the gun-boat service, and received commendations from that officer and General Wallace for services rendered. In 1862 he also acted as acting assistant professor at the Naval Academy. He was promoted to ensign May, 1863; steam-gun-boat "Tuscarora," North Atlantic Blockading Squadron, 1863-64; steam-sloop "Juniata," North and South Atlantic Blockading Squadrons, 1864-65; in both attacks upon Fort Fisher, and in the land assault on the same, and received the commendation of his commanding officer. Ensign McGregor was in the expedition to Bull's Bay at the time of the capture of Charleston.

He was attached to the "Juniata" during her service in Brazil, 1865-67; promoted master January 10, 1865; commissioned lieutenant July, 1866; and served in the flag-ship "Powhatan," South Pacific Squadron, 1867-69; commissioned as lieutenant-commander March, 1868, and served during the next year in the "Powhatan" once more, when flag-ship of the West India Squadron. After service at the Naval Observatory and the Naval Academy, he was ordered to the flag-ship "Wabash," European Squadron, and was afterwards attached to the "Shenandoah," on the same station. From 1875 to 1878 he was on duty at Boston and at Washington upon equipment duty, being promoted commander in 1878. In 1880-81 commanded the "Despatch," upon special service. In 1882 he was in command of the "Nantucket." From 1885 to 1888 he commanded the U. S. S. "Alliance" on the South Atlantic Station, and was light-house inspector of the Fourteenth District in 1890.

Commander McGregor died at Cincinnati, Ohio, on August 1, 1891.

## MAJOR G. W. McKEE, U.S.A.
### (DECEASED).

MAJOR G. W. McKEE was graduated at the Military Academy June 11, 1863, and promoted first lieutenant of ordnance. He was engaged in active operations at Forts Gregg and Wagner, South Carolina, and in mounting guns in the Swamp Angel and other batteries on Morris Island, South Carolina, for the bombardment of Charleston, from September, 1863, until February, 1864.

He organized the ordnance department of the Shenandoah Valley, and was engaged in the combat of New Market, Virginia, and several skirmishes from Mount Jackson to Cedar Creek, in May, 1864, and as chief ordnance officer, Department of West Virginia, and on the staff of Major-General Sheridan, from 1864 to 1865. He was brevetted captain and major "for efficient and valuable services during the Rebellion," and was promoted successively from first lieutenant to major of ordnance, which latter rank he held at the time of his death, December 30, 1891, at which date he was in command of Frankford Arsenal and a member of the Magazine-Gun Board.

Major McKee served as assistant instructor of ordnance and gunnery, and as assistant professor of chemistry, mineralogy, and geology at the U. S. Military Academy; assistant at Watertown, Benicia, St. Louis, and Rock Island Arsenals, and at the National Armory; in command of the Washington, Allegheny, and Frankford Arsenals; in charge of the manufacture of heavy rifled cannon; as a member of the Ordnance Board; of the board for testing rifled cannon of the Magazine-Gun Board, 1891, and on various boards for the determination of important questions concerning ordnance material, etc.

The chief of ordnance, General D. W. Flagler, in announcing to the Ordnance Corps the death of Major McKee, and after reciting in detail his valuable services, adds:

"In addition to Major McKee's important military services as briefly sketched above, he is the author of many valuable professional papers which have appeared in ordnance publications, and the department is indebted to him for much valuable scientific investigation and research.

"The department, the service, and the country have suffered a serious loss in the death of an officer whose abilities and service were much needed.

"Few officers have ever been so widely known and have had so many devoted friends, both in the army and throughout the country, as Major McKee.

"His eminently great and good qualities of mind, heart, and character; his affection for and stanch loyalty and devotion to his friends; his contempt and hatred of whatever was wrong or mean; his unselfishness, charity, and gentleness, won for him the high admiration and friendship of all who knew him. His talents and many entertaining qualities made him a most welcome and agreeable companion. But above all else, the man won the love of all those who knew him well, and it is in this last which now causes the deep sorrow for his loss.

"Major McKee's father, Colonel William R. McKee (Class of 1829, U. S. Military Academy), was killed at Buena Vista, Mexico; his brother, Hugh McKee, of the navy, was killed at Corea. . . ."

Both of these gallant officers, father and son, laid down their lives in the service of their country at the head of assaulting columns.

To the friends of Major McKee the wish was often expressed, that he, too, like that father and son, might find a grave on the battle-field.

## BRIGADIER-GENERAL JAMES B. McPHERSON, U.S.A.
### (DECEASED).

BRIGADIER-GENERAL JAMES B. McPHERSON was born in Ohio in 1829, and graduated at the Military Academy July 1, 1853. He was promoted brevet second lieutenant, Corps of Engineers, the same day, and second lieutenant December 18, 1854. He served at the Military Academy as assistant instructor of practical engineering to September 6, 1854, and was assistant engineer in the construction and repairs of the defences of New York harbor; as superintending engineer of the building of Fort Delaware; of the construction of the defences of Alcatraz Island, San Francisco harbor; in charge of the engineer operations at Boston harbor, Massachusetts, and recruiting sappers, miners, and pontoniers, from 1854 to 1861. He was promoted first lieutenant December 13, 1858, and was appointed captain of the Nineteenth Infantry May 14, 1861, which he declined, and received his promotion as captain of engineers August 6, 1861. He was appointed lieutenant-colonel of staff November 12, 1861, and colonel of staff May 1, 1862. He served as aide-de-camp to General Halleck, and as chief engineer on the staff of General Grant from November 12, 1861, to the date of his appointment as brigadier-general of volunteers, May 15, and major-general of volunteers, October 8, 1862.

No better sketch of his military life can be furnished than that given by General Grant, when recommending him for promotion, as follows:

"He has been with me in every battle since the commencement of the Rebellion, except Belmont. At Forts Henry and Donelson, Shiloh and the siege of Corinth, as a staff-officer and engineer, his services were conspicuous and highly meritorious. At the second battle of Corinth his skill as a soldier was displayed in successfully carrying reinforcements to the besieged garrison when the enemy was between him and the point to be reached. In the advance through Central Mississippi, General McPherson commanded one wing of the army with all the ability possible to show,—he having the lead in the advance and the rear retiring.

"In the campaign and siege terminating with the fall of Vicksburg, General McPherson has filled a conspicuous part. At the battle of Port Gibson, it was under his direction that the enemy was driven, late in the afternoon, from a position they had succeeded in holding all day against an obstinate attack. His corps, the advance always under his immediate eye, were the pioneers in the movement from Port Gibson to Hawkinson's Ferry. From the north fork of the Bayou Pierre to Black River it was a constant skirmish, the whole skilfully managed. The enemy was so closely pressed as to be unable to destroy their bridge of boats after them. From Hawkinson's Ferry to Jackson the Seventeenth Army Corps marched on roads not travelled by other troops, fighting the entire battle of Raymond alone; and the bulk of Johnston's army was fought by this corps, entirely under the management of General McPherson. At Champion Hills the Seventeenth Corps and General McPherson were conspicuous. All that could be termed a battle there was fought by the divisions of General McPherson's corps and General Hovey's division of the Thirteenth Corps. In the assault of the 22d of May, on the fortifications of Vicksburg, and during the entire siege, General McPherson and his command took unfading laurels. He is one of the ablest engineers and most skilful generals. I would respectfully, but urgently, recommend his promotion to the position of brigadier-general in the regular army."

As a result of the above letter, General McPherson was appointed brigadier-general U. S. Army August 1, 1863, and he was awarded—October, 1863—a medal of honor, by the officers of his corps, for "the gallant manner in which he had led them during the campaign and siege of Vicksburg."

General McPherson was killed July 22, 1864, in the repulse of a sortie from Atlanta, Georgia. Soon after his death, General Grant addressed the following letter to General McPherson's aged grandmother:

"I am glad to know the relatives of the lamented Major-General McPherson are aware of the more than friendship existing between him and myself. A nation grieves at the loss of one so dear to our nation's cause. It is a selfish grief, because the nation had more to expect from him than from almost any one living. I join in this selfish grief, and add the grief of personal love for the departed. He formed for some time one of my military family. I knew him well. It may be some consolation to you to know that every officer and every soldier who served under your grandson, felt for him the highest reverence. Your bereavement is great, but cannot excel mine."

MAJOR-GENERAL GEORGE GORDON MEADE, U.S.A.
(DECEASED).

MAJOR-GENERAL GEORGE GORDON MEADE was born at Cadiz, Spain, December 31, 1815; his father, Richard W. Meade, being at that time U. S. naval agent there. His grandfather, George Meade, a wealthy merchant of Philadelphia, had contributed liberally for the support of the Revolutionary army. The grandson graduated at the Military Academy in 1835, and entered the artillery service. He participated in the war against the hostile Seminole Indians, in Florida, but resigned in October, 1836, and became a civil engineer. He was engaged in a survey of the mouths of the Mississippi; and afterwards on the boundary line of Texas, and on that of Maine.

In 1842 he re-entered the army as second lieutenant of topographical engineers, and during the Mexican War he served with distinction on the staffs of Generals Taylor and Scott. He was afterwards employed in light-house construction, and on the geodetic survey of the great lakes.

In August, 1861, he was appointed brigadier-general of volunteers, and commanded the Second Brigade of the Pennsylvania Reserve Corps.

In McClellan's Peninsula campaign, Meade fought at Mechanicsville, Gaines' Mill, and Glendale, being severely wounded in the latter engagement, second Bull Run. He afterwards commanded a division at Antietam, and when General Hooker was wounded there, succeeded temporarily to the command of the First Corps of the Army of the Potomac.

General Meade was appointed major-general of volunteers, and in December, 1862, led the attack which broke through the right of Lee's line at Fredericksburg, but, not being supported, was obliged to fall back. He was placed in command of the Fifth Corps, and, though much esteemed by General Hooker, was not called into action at Chancellorsville.

On the 28th of June, 1863, after Lee had crossed the Potomac, on his way to Pennsylvania, President Lincoln placed General Meade in chief command of the Army of the Potomac, then hastening to oppose Lee, wherever the two armies should strategetically meet. This occurred at the town of Gettysburg, Pennsylvania, and after three days of severe fighting, the Confederate army, under its ablest leader, was forced to retreat into Virginia. For this victory he was made a brigadier-general in the regular army.

In the spring of 1864, Lieutenant-General Grant being placed in command of all the Union armies, General Meade entered the field with the Army of the Potomac. He, however, still retained the immediate command of this army till the close of the war, discharging the duties of his difficult and delicate position to the entire satisfaction of General Grant. In the bloody battle of the Wilderness, and the subsequent campaign, the Army of the Potomac suffered severely.

In June, 1864, it was transferred to the south side of the James, in order to capture Petersburg, the main defence of Richmond on that side; but General Lee saved the place by prompt reinforcements. The siege of Petersburg lasted ten months, and at its close Richmond had to be evacuated, and General Lee, after being pursued from Petersburg to Appomattox Court-House, with constant and severe fighting, surrendered April 9, 1865.

General Meade was appointed major-general U. S. Army August 18, 1864.

After the war, General Meade had command of the Military Division of the Atlantic until August, 1866, when he took command of the Department of the East.

He received the thanks of Congress, January 28, 1866, "for the skill and heroic valor which, at Gettysburg, repelled, defeated, and drove back—broken and dispirited—beyond the Rappahannock, the veteran army of the Rebellion."

General Meade was subsequently placed in command of the military district comprising Georgia, Florida, and Alabama, with head-quarters at Atlanta. He died in Philadelphia November 6, 1872. His fellow-citizens of that city had presented him with a house, and after his death raised a fund of one hundred thousand dollars for his family.

General Meade had the degree of Doctor of Laws conferred on him by Harvard College, Massachusetts, in 1865. He was a member of the Historical Society of Pennsylvania, and of the Philadelphia Academy of Natural Sciences.

# LIEUTENANT-COLONEL FREDERICK MEARS, U.S.A.
## (DECEASED).

LIEUTENANT-COLONEL FREDERICK MEARS was born in New York City January 1, 1836, and was a member of an old and influential family. He practised law before the war, and in 1861 went to Washington and tendered his services to General C. P. Stone, then assistant adjutant-general for the District of Columbia. He served as drill instructor at Washington, and rendered valuable and important services to the country at a trying period in the nation's history. He was appointed second lieutenant of the Ninth Infantry in 1861, and reported to General Mansfield, then in command at Washington. Lieutenant Mears instructed a force of fourteen thousand men in company, battalion, and skirmish drill, working chiefly on Tyler's brigade; afterwards on Baker's (of Oregon) regiment, at Hampton Creek; and taking it to Washington, he was assigned as acting assistant adjutant-general to the Provisional Brigade Office. He was promoted to first lieutenant May 17, 1861, and soon after was made lieutenant-colonel of the First Regiment of Sharpshooters. In 1862 he joined his regiment at Fort Vancouver. Later he served as aide and assistant adjutant-general to General Alvord, then commanding the District of Columbia.

He was promoted to captain the same year, and for his good service at Point San José harbor, San Francisco, was commended in orders by the division commander, General McDowell.

Captain Mears served in San Francisco during the trouble arising from the assassination of President Lincoln, and had a long period of service with General Crook on the frontier during the Indian troubles. Afterwards he served in the Yellowstone campaign under General Stanley, Custer and his regiment forming part of the command. In 1874 he assisted in building Camp Robinson, Red Cloud Indian Agency, being in command of the post when flag-staff troubles broke out, and what may be termed the Sioux struck the first blow that brought on the war that lasted during 1875-77. Captain Mears was also active in restoring quiet amongst Spotted Tail's band. Except for a few weeks' service in Chicago during the riots, and a brief period in San Francisco harbor and at Fort Omaha, his services were for twenty-one years with his company west of the Missouri River, always discharging the duties assigned him with alacrity, zeal, and ability. He devoted his best thoughts to the interests of the service, endeavoring to better it by writing on such subjects as "Target Practice," "Cooking," "The Army Register," "The Muster-Rolls," etc., his suggestions being accepted, and many of them being enforced to-day.

On March 13, 1865, Captain Mears was brevetted major for faithful and meritorious services, and his nomination sent to the Senate for a brevet as lieutenant-colonel.

In 1883 he was promoted to major of the Twenty-fifth Infantry, and in October, 1887, was promoted to be lieutenant-colonel of the Fourth Infantry. Lieutenant-Colonel Frederick Mears died at his post of duty, at Fort Spokane, Washington, on January 2, 1892, after a brief illness.

He was a member of the Loyal Legion, Grand Army of the Republic, Army of the Potomac, and a Veteran of the Seventh New York Regiment.

BRIGADIER- AND BREVET MAJOR-GENERAL MONTGOMERY C. MEIGS, U.S.A. (DECEASED).

BRIGADIER- AND BREVET MAJOR-GENERAL MONTGOMERY C. MEIGS was born in Augusta, Georgia, May 3, 1816. He was a son of Charles D. Meigs, M.D., and of Mary Montgomery Meigs, who removed with him to Philadelphia when he was three months old. His father was of an old Connecticut family, and his mother a daughter of William Montgomery, merchant, of Philadelphia.

On graduating at the U. S. Military Academy at West Point in 1836, he entered the artillery, but within one year was transferred to the Engineer Corps of the army.

His first engineering work was the repairing of Fort Mifflin, on the Delaware River, and later in building Fort Delaware, and the improvement of the Delaware River and Bay and other places along the coast.

In 1850 he was in charge of building Fort Montgomery, Lake Champlain.

From 1852 to 1860 he was engaged in the designing and construction of Washington Aqueduct, and superintending construction of the new wings and great dome of the Capitol; also the new halls of Congress. His work on the aqueduct included building the Cabin John Bridge, with its largest stone arch in the world.

He became captain of engineers in 1853. His other work included extension of General Post-Office in Washington, and completion of Fort Madison, Annapolis.

In 1860, on declining to obey an order given by Secretary-of-War Floyd, because it plainly violated a law of Congress, he was sent to Florida, to take charge of the completion of Fort Jefferson, Dry Tortugas, where he remained until his recall to Washington just before the inauguration of President Lincoln, one of whose first active war-measures was ordering him to plan and accompany as its engineer an expedition for the relief and reinforcement of Fort Pickens, Pensacola, then besieged by the rebel forces; and a few weeks later Mr. Lincoln, on opening a telegram in the presence of some visitors to the White House, exclaimed, " Here is the first good news I have yet had: Captain Meigs telegraphs Fort Pickens is reinforced!" He also largely contributed to the holding of Forts Jefferson and Taylor by the government; and Mr. Seward, Secretary of State, said the retaining of those three forts was of the greatest importance to the Union cause, especially as at one period of the war this action had great influence in preventing a recognition of the Confederacy by foreign governments.

He returned to Washington and on May 14 was made colonel of the Eleventh Infantry; on the next day was made quartermaster-general of the U. S. Army, with the rank of brigadier-general, which position he held until his retirement in 1882. During the Civil War the expenditure of over nineteen hundred million of dollars was intrusted to his direction, and history records how this great duty was discharged.

He was present at the first battle of Bull Run and at the battle of Lookout Mountain. During Grant's Richmond campaign he had personal charge of the base of supplies of his army at Fredericksburg and Belleplaine; and when Washington was threatened by Early in 1864 he was placed in charge of the defences of that city, and at that time he was brevetted major-general U. S. Army.

He met Sherman at Savannah, after his march to the sea, with a fleet loaded with supplies for his army.

When he visited Europe in 1867, on account of illhealth, Mr. Seward, Secretary of State, while giving him a letter to our ministers and consuls abroad, wrote: " The prevailing opinion of this country sustains a firm conviction which I entertain, and on all occasions cheerfully express, that without the services of this eminent soldier the national cause must either have been lost or deeply imperiled in the late Civil War."

He visited Europe in 1875-76 on special service.

In 1882 he designed the Pension Bureau Building, which he completed a few years later.

He was a Regent of the Smithsonian Institution and a Fellow of the National Academy of Science.

He died January 2, 1892, and was buried at Arlington Cemetery with military honors. A general order from head-quarters, by command of General Schofield, says: " General Meigs was personally a man of kind and amiable character, of strict probity and sense of right, and of great breadth of intellect. The army has rarely possessed an officer who has combined within himself so many and valuable attainments, and who was intrusted by the government with a greater variety of weighty responsibilities, or who proved himself more worthy of confidence. There are few whose character and career can be more justly commended, or whose lives are more worthy of respect, admiration, and emulation."

## ENGINEER-IN-CHIEF GEORGE W. MELVILLE, U.S.N.

It is rare to find high professional ability and the capacity to attend scrupulously to office-work and details combined in the same individual with the daring spirit and dauntless courage which lead to gallant deeds in the face of the most distressing conditions under which men can be placed. The "sound body" enabled the "sound mind" to do such things as Melville has accomplished,—for his life has been one of strange and stirring adventure.

Although his name will ever be associated with the "Jeannette" Expedition, he was a volunteer for two other well-known similar ventures to the far North, each of which accomplished their mission " *tuto, cito, jucunde*,"—owing, in great measure, to the knowledge which he had of the things to be provided,—a complete outfit being the necessary adjunct of success in undertakings of this nature.

De Long, in his journals, bears full testimony to his cheerful and steady co-operation during that trying drift through entirely unknown seas. When the supreme moment came, and with their own resources cut down to the lowest amount, the party had to make for an unknown shore, over a vast extent of ice and water, Melville was equal to the occasion. He commanded one of the three boats engaged in the retreat, and accomplished the feat of bringing that whole boat's-crew out alive,—while the others perished, either in the icy waters of the Arctic or the equally inhospitable waste about the Lena delta. Most men would have thought that they had done enough; but, after a few days of rest to recuperate his forces, he again took his life in his hands and led a party which discovered, far down in that lonely, wintry waste, the bodies of De Long, Dr. Ambler, and their ill-starred companions. One boat, he rightly judged, had been lost during a night of storm, as they were approaching the land. In searching for the other boat's-crew "he fought his perilous and painful way, mile by mile, through the rigors of perpetual winter and floating archipelagoes of ice along the Arctic coast for over five hundred miles, surviving the privations which had been fatal to so many, and persevered until his search was rewarded by the recovery of all the records of the 'Jeannette' Expedition." In the face of obstacles presented by the worst season, he penetrated to the mouth of the Lena in his search, and left no doubt that the unfortunate crew of the third boat had not succeeded in reaching the shore. As it was, he contributed to the geography of the world a new and important chart of that region.

It was under his charge that the rude but massive tomb was built which sheltered the poor remains of the lost, "and the rites of Christian burial were performed over these martyrs to science and humanity, where perpetual winter had embalmed them." They were, however, subsequently exhumed by order of the United States government and brought home, to be laid among the dust of their kin, with impressive ceremonies. The Russian government offered every assistance to the officers who accomplished this pious mission, while our own government conferred substantial rewards upon those who had aided Melville in his extremity. For his Arctic services Engineer Melville afterwards received special promotion, with the approbation of the whole navy and of the country at large.

Engineer-in-chief Melville was born in New York, of Scottish lineage, on January 10, 1841, and his education was acquired in the public schools, the school of the Christian Brothers, and the Brooklyn Polytechnic School.

He entered the navy at the outbreak of the Civil War, and served well and faithfully, both during that trying period and afterwards,—when peace came,—on our own coast, in the West Indies, in Brazil, and on the East India Station; beside duty at navy-yards. He was everywhere a favorite, on account of his cheerful, modest, and unostentatious deportment, as well as for the zeal, bravery, and endurance which he showed on all occasions which were calculated to bring forth those qualities,—and they are not few, even in the ordinary course of service. Melville was made engineer-in-chief of the navy and chief of the Bureau of Steam-Engineering in August, 1887, and in January, 1892, was recommissioned in the same office, with the entire approbation of the whole navy, as well as that of the great industrial establishments with which he necessarily comes in contact in conducting a vast business.

As an instance of his ability to accomplish unusual feats, and his capacity for extraordinary effort, we may mention the fact that in the summer of 1887 he himself prepared the general designs of the machinery of five vessels of the new navy.

COLONEL HENRY C. MERRIAM, U.S.A.

COLONEL HENRY C. MERRIAM (Seventh Infantry) was born at Houlton, Maine, and educated at Colby University with degrees of A.B. and A.M., and member of the American Institute of Civics. He entered the volunteer service as captain Twentieth Maine Volunteers, and mustered into service August 29, 1862. He participated in the battles of Antietam, Shepardstown Ford, and Fredericksburg. He then went to Louisiana with General Ullmann's expedition, March, 1863, to organize colored troops, and served with them to the end of the war, commanding the oldest of all the colored regiments, the First Louisiana Native Guards, later known as the Seventy-third U. S. Colored Infantry.

Colonel Merriam participated in the siege of Port Hudson, where the colored troops gained their first distinction, in the assault of May 27, 1863, celebrated in George H. Boker's song, "The Charge of the Black Brigade." He commanded this regiment in the Mobile campaign of 1865, leading the assault on Fort Blakely, April 9, 1865, at his personal request. This assault was described by the Confederate commander, General Liddell, as follows: "I had placed my very best troops, General Cockrell's Missouri Veterans, to oppose the colored troops, yet they were first to break my lines, and first over my parapet." This was the last assault of the war. It resulted in the capture of more than six thousand prisoners, and the occupation of Mobile with all its defences. He was mustered out of service October 24, 1865, and resumed the study of law. He was appointed to the regular army as major Thirty-eighth Infantry, July 28, 1866; commanded the infantry reserve battalion during Custer's Indian campaign in Kansas, April and May, 1867; marched for New Mexico in June; pursued and defeated Kiowa Indians under Satanta, on the Upper Arkansas, July 11; commanding expedition against Indians and captured an Apache village, in the Mogollon Mountains, June, 1869. He was transferred to the Twenty-fourth Infantry at reorganization of the army. While in command at Fort Ringgold, in 1873, he was operating against marauders on lower Rio Grande. He commanded at Fort McIntosh in 1876, during the Diaz revolution in Mexico; bombarded Mexican Federal force of Colonel Pablo Quintana, April 10; redressing outrages against American flag and citizens. He crossed the Rio Grande, August 22, and rescued U. S. commercial agent, J. J. Haines, who had been captured by the revolutionary force of Colonel Estrada.

He again crossed the Rio Grande on the night of September 6, capturing Nueva Larado, and holding it in military possession for protection of American merchants for seven days, until assurance was given by responsible Mexican authorities for their safety.

Colonel Merriam had been promoted, June 10, 1876, to lieutenant-colonel Second Infantry, but was retained by the War Department on the Mexican border until the complications arising from the Mexican revolution were settled, and was recommended by General Ord for a brevet, in recognition of the ability and energy displayed in that important and difficult duty.

He joined Second Infantry and went to Idaho during the Nez Perce war of 1877; commanding depot of supplies and communications at Lewiston, Idaho, relieving General Sully. He established, planned and built Fort Sherman, Idaho, 1878-79; commanding battalion in Bannock campaign, 1878; established Camp Chelan, Washington Territory, 1879; established Fort Spokane, Washington Territory, 1880. While in command of Fort Spokane, 1883-85, planned and built the permanent post. Accorded special credit by Generals Howard and Miles for administrative ability displayed in building Forts Sherman and Spokane, and for successful management of the neighboring tribes of Indians, resulting in their peaceful settlement on the Spokane and Colville Reservations; promoted to colonel Seventh Infantry July 10, 1885; in command of Fort Logan, Colorado, from 1889 to date (1892); commanding all troops operating on Cheyenne River, South Dakota, including Forts Sully and Bennett, during General Miles's winter campaign of 1890-91. On this line the Sitting Bull Indians were intercepted on their way to the hostile camp, after the killing of their chief on Grand River. They were successfully disarmed and held as prisoners to the number of two hundred and twenty-seven.

Colonel Merriam received the following brevets-colonel U. S. Volunteers " for faithful and meritorious services in the Mobile campaign;" lieutenant-colonel U. S. Army "for gallant and meritorious services in the battle of Antietam;" colonel U. S. Army "for conspicuous gallantry in the capture of Fort Blakely, Alabama."

## BRIGADIER- AND BREVET MAJOR-GENERAL WESLEY MERRITT, U.S.A.

BRIGADIER- AND BREVET MAJOR-GENERAL WESLEY MERRITT was born in New York December 1, 1836, and graduated from the Military Academy July 1, 1860, when he was promoted brevet second lieutenant Second Dragoons, and second lieutenant of the same regiment January 28, 1861. He was appointed captain of the Second Cavalry April 5, 1862, and brigadier-general of volunteers June 29, 1863. He served in the field with the Army of the Potomac, during the war of the Rebellion, on the staff of General Cooke, until September, 1862, when he was transferred to the head-quarters of the defences of Washington until April, 1863; he again entered the field as an aide-de-camp for General Stoneman, and served with him in April and May during his raid towards Richmond; rejoining his regiment, he commanded it in the cavalry engagement at Beverly Ford, where, June 9, 1863, the national forces crossed the Rappahannock, surprised the enemy's pickets, and maintained for hours an obstinate battle with a superior force; he narrowly escaped capture, being at one time almost, if not quite, surrounded by the enemy; he won the highest commendation from General Buford for conspicuous gallantry on that field; commanded regiment in engagements at Upperville and Aldie, and was assigned to the command of the Reserve Cavalry Brigade, Army of the Potomac, during the Pennsylvania campaign.

General Merritt succeeded General Buford in the command of the First Division of Cavalry, and participated in the operations in Central Virginia; in the Richmond campaign of 1864; accompanied General Sheridan on the cavalry raid towards Charlottesville, and in the battle of Trevilian Station he rescued the Third Division of Cavalry from impending capture when almost surrounded by the enemy. He was transferred, in August, 1864, from the Army of the Potomac to the Shenandoah Valley, where he arrived about the 8th. His division (First) was then composed of seventeen regiments of cavalry, organized into three brigades (commanded by Custer, Devin, and Gibbs), and two batteries of artillery. Then came the struggle with General Early's army for the possession of the Valley, during which General Merritt was continuously employed with his command, and at the battle of Winchester, where the turning column of cavalry at a critical moment, when the result of the battle was uncertain, repeatedly charged the left of the enemy's line, and, together with the rallied infantry, swept down upon General Early, and sent him whirling through Winchester. The affair at Cedarville, near Front Royal on the Shenandoah, was a brilliant success for General Merritt, being gained unaided and against odds; he defeated General Kershaw's division of infantry and two brigades of cavalry in an attempt to force a passage of the Shenandoah, and inflicted upon the enemy a loss of six hundred men; then followed the movement to Front Royal, the engagement at Milford, and the skilful manœuvring of the cavalry in front of Bunker Hill, until the Sixth and Nineteenth Corps seized an advanced position in front of Fisher's Hill, which they held until the Eighth Corps turned General Early's flank and forced him to abandon his fortifications, when the cavalry joined the pursuit; and on the 19th of October General Merritt won for himself and his division an enduring fame at the battle of Cedar Creek, where he confronted the enemy from the first attack in the morning until their retreat that night, and held his position on the pike, just north of Middletown, all day, although entirely unassisted by the infantry, until the enemy gave up the contest, when he charged with his cavalry, and, crossing the stream below the bridge, continued the pursuit to Fisher's Hill, capturing and retaking a large number of guns and colors and much material of war. Then followed the action at Middletown. In November General Merritt was detached, with his division, to the east side of the Blue Ridge, by the way of Ashby's Gap, to operate against Mosby's guerillas.

He was in command of the cavalry of the Army of the Shenandoah, and participated in all the attendant actions of 1865, resulting in the surrender of Lee's army, and then was designated as one of the three commissioners to carry out the terms. He was appointed major-general of volunteers, and was brevetted from major to major-general in the regular army for his gallantry.

At the close of the war he was appointed lieutenant-colonel of the Ninth Cavalry, and promoted colonel of the Fifth Cavalry, and served with much distinction in numerous campaigns and actions with Indians on the frontier, and was finally rewarded with the appointment of brigadier-general, U. S. Army, April 16, 1887, and is at present in command of the Department of Dakota.

## LIEUTENANT-COLONEL EVAN MILES, U.S.A.

LIEUTENANT-COLONEL EVAN MILES (Twenty-fifth Infantry) was born in McVeytown, Pennsylvania, March 28, 1838. He entered the regular service as first lieutenant of the Twelfth Infantry August 5, 1861, and was promoted captain January 20, 1865. He served at Fort Hamilton to December 3, 1861; and was on regimental recruiting service to June, 1862, when he was returned to duty at Fort Hamilton, New York, until August, 1862. He was then ordered to the field, serving with the Fifth Corps, Army of the Potomac, and was engaged in the battles of second Bull Run, Antietam, Fredericksburg, Chancellorsville, and Gettysburg. He was then, with the regular division, sent to New York during the draft riots of 1863. He returned to the field with his regiment in November, 1863, and was placed on special duty, in charge of a detachment of volunteer cavalry, to prevent marauding, and to arrest stragglers, from May to June, 1864, after having participated in the battle of the Wilderness. He was engaged at the battle of the Weldon Railroad as volunteer aide to General Ayres, August 18, 19, and 21; and Peeble's Farm, September 30 and October 1, 1864. His regiment was then transferred to Elmira, N. Y., where he served with it to February, 1865, having been promoted captain Jan. 20, 1865.

Captain Miles was brevetted captain August 18, 1864, "for gallant services during the operations on the Weldon Railroad, Virginia."

After a tour of duty at Washington, D. C., the captain was ordered to the Pacific coast with his regiment, he having been transferred to the Twenty-first Infantry, and served at different stations in Arizona and the Department of the Columbia, to September 8, 1883. He was in the field operating against the hostile Nez Perce Indians, commanding six companies of the Twenty-first Infantry, one of the Eighth, and one of the Twelfth, and was honorably mentioned by the commanding general of the Department of the Columbia, for gallantry and efficiency during the battle of Clearwater, Idaho, on the 11th and 12th of July, 1877. He commanded seven companies of the Twenty-first Infantry, two companies of the Fourth Artillery, and one troop of the First Cavalry, in the field operating against the hostile Bannock-Piute Indians; with this command he attacked and defeated them near Umatilla Agency, Oregon, July 13, 1878, for which he was honorably mentioned by the department commander, by members of Congress, by the Governor of Washington Territory, and citizens of Umatilla, Oregon, to the Secretary of War, for his efficient services.

While serving in the Twenty-first Infantry, Major Miles was very energetic in endeavoring to have canteens (or what is now termed post exchange) established in the army, as the following extract from the report of Colonel H. A. Morrow, Twenty-first Infantry, to the adjutant-general U. S. Army, dated Fort Sidney, Nebraska, December 31, 1889, shows:

"In closing this brief history of the canteen in the American service, and particularly of its operations at Fort Sydney, I should be unjust to myself if I did not acknowledge my obligations to certain officers of the Twenty-first Infantry for many valuable recommendations and suggestions.

"Captain Evan Miles, then of the Twenty-first Infantry, by his zealous co-operation and faithful and intelligent administration of the affairs of the Twenty-first Infantry Canteen, deserves, perhaps, a larger share of credit than any other officer for making a great success of what was at first an experiment."

Captain Miles was also a zealous officer on the subject of target practice in the army. He was superintendent of it at Fort Vancouver from 1877 to 1884; was range officer at Fort Sidney, Nebraska, in 1885–86; was executive-officer of the division rifle competition, Division of the Pacific, in 1880; was commander of camp and executive-officer of the Department of the Platte Rifle Competition, in 1882; was in charge of the Department of Dakota Rifle Competition in 1888; commanded the Department of Dakota Rifle Camp, and in charge of competition, in 1889; and commanded the Division of the Missouri Rifle Camp the same year.

Captain Miles was promoted major of the Twenty-fifth Infantry April 24, 1888, and, upon joining in the Department of Dakota, was detailed as inspector of rifle practice at the head-quarters, which he retained until December, 1890, when he joined his regiment at Fort Missoula, Montana, his present station. He was promoted lieutenant-colonel April 23, 1892, and assigned to the Twentieth Infantry.

## MAJOR-GENERAL NELSON A. MILES, U.S.A.

MAJOR-GENERAL NELSON A. MILES was born in Westminster, Massachusetts, August 8, 1839. He entered the volunteer service during the war of the Rebellion as captain of the Twenty-second Massachusetts Infantry September 9, 1861, from which he was honorably mustered out May 31, 1862, to accept the lieutenant-colonelcy of the Sixty-first New York Infantry.

He was promoted colonel of the same regiment September 30, 1862; appointed brigadier-general of volunteers May 12, 1864, and major-general of volunteers October 21, 1865.

General Miles served in the Army of the Potomac during the Manassas, Peninsula, Northern Virginia, Maryland, Rappahannock, Pennsylvania, Mine Run, Wilderness, Petersburg, and Appomattox campaigns, and was engaged in all the battles of the Army of the Potomac, with one exception, up to the surrender of General Lee, with the Confederate Army, at Appomattox Court-House, April 9, 1865, and was wounded three times during the war.

He was honorably mustered out of the volunteer service September 1, 1866, having been appointed colonel of the Fortieth U. S. Infantry July 28, 1866, and he was brevetted brigadier-general March 2, 1867, for "gallant and meritorious services in the battle of Chancellorsville, Virginia," and brevet major-general March 2, 1867, for "gallant and meritorious services in the battle of Spottsylvania, Virginia." He was also brevetted major-general of volunteers August 25, 1864, for "highly meritorious and distinguished conduct throughout the campaign, and particularly for gallantry and valuable services at the battle of Ream's Station, Virginia."

General Miles's service since the war has been of note, to which many of the nomadic tribes of the great West could readily testify. He was transferred to the Fifth Infantry as colonel March 15, 1869, and joined that regiment shortly afterwards, making a history for it in the annals of the country. He defeated the Cheyenne, Kiowa, and Comanche Indians on the borders of the Staked Plains in 1875, and in 1876 subjugated the hostile Sioux and other Indians in Montana, driving Sitting Bull across the Canada frontier, and breaking up the bands that were led by him and by Crazy Horse, Lame Deer, Spotted Eagle, Broad Trail, Hump, and others. In September he captured the Nez Perces, under Chief Joseph,

in Northern Montana, and in 1878 captured a band of Bannocks near the Yellowstone Park. After a difficult campaign against the Apaches under Geronimo and Natchez, he compelled those chiefs to surrender on September 4, 1886.

He received the thanks of the Legislatures of Kansas, Montana, New Mexico, and Arizona for services in campaigns against the Indians in the West, and the citizens of Arizona presented him a sword of honor at Tucson on November 8, 1887, in the presence of a large gathering of citizens of the Territory.

General Miles was appointed a brigadier-general in the U. S. Army December 15, 1880, and was assigned to the command of the Department of the Columbia; from this he was transferred to command the Department of the Missouri in July, 1885. In April, 1886, he was ordered to command the Department of Arizona, and he remained in that department until ordered to command the Division of the Pacific in 1888. He was appointed major-general, U. S. Army, April 5, 1890, and ordered to command the Military Division of the Missouri at Chicago, Illinois.

In the winter of 1890-91 an Indian war of considerable magnitude seemed imminent in the Dakotas and other Western States. General Miles took the field in person, and proceeded to Pine Ridge Agency, the scene of the greatest trouble. By his disposition of troops and clear judgment a serious war was averted.

## LIEUTENANT-COMMANDER FREDERICK A. MILLER, U.S.N. (RETIRED).

LIEUTENANT-COMMANDER FREDERICK A. MILLER was born in Maryland, June 12, 1843, and was educated at Episcopal Academy, Philadelphia, Pennsylvania, and at the Military Academy at Port Chester, after which he entered Trinity College, but, being rusticated, went to sea. When the Civil War broke out he was in Peru, and, hastening home, was offered a position in the Pacific Mail Company and an appointment to the Naval Academy. Thinking the war would be short, and wishing to see service, he preferred to volunteer, and was made a master's mate September 11, 1861. This was changed to an appointment as acting master's mate a few days later. For three months was under instructions at Washington, and was then ordered to the "Tuscarora," and made drill-master of her 11-inch gun. Went to the European Station in that ship, on the lookout for Confederate privateers. She blockaded the "Nashville" in Southampton, and the "Sumter" at Gibraltar. Chased the "Alabama," and came near catching her on the west coast of England. By her presence she destroyed the availability of Madeira and the Azores as recruiting stations for these vessels.

Upon his return to the United States he was made acting ensign, and ordered to the "Princess Royal." In her he served at Donaldsonville, when the Confederates, under Generals Green and Monton, were prevented from capturing Fort Butler and crossing the Mississippi. He received the warm commendation of his commanding officer for his gallant behavior on this occasion, and reported that much of the success in repulsing five thousand of the enemy with artillery was due to the spirited manner in which he commanded the 9-inch gun of the "Princess Royal."

After this he was promoted to acting master, and served on board the "Arizona" when that vessel was burned off Poverty Point, Mississippi River, leaving her in the last boat. He was then ordered to superintend her wrecking. After this he applied for and was ordered to the "Cincinnati."

In this vessel he bore part in the operations against Spanish Fort and the defences of Mobile, and in the surrender of that city. Was then employed, under Captain Crosby, in sweeping for torpedoes in the bay. These were so numerous that the monitor "Milwaukee," casemate iron-clad "Osage," tin-clad "Rudolph," tug "Althaea," and tug "Ida" were all destroyed by them; and his own boat, the "Cincinnati's" launch, was also blown up and had three of her crew killed. At the moment he was on board an abandoned rebel torpedo-boat. During his service on board the "Cincinnati" she convoyed General Steele's division to Selma, Alabama, and was present at the surrender of the Confederate flotilla at Nauna Hubba Bluff, on the Tombigbee.

After the war he served on the European Station, the South Atlantic, and the Pacific Station. Then in the North Atlantic, and again in the Pacific, besides going to the French Exposition in the "Portsmouth," and round the world in the "Ticonderoga." Then had shore duty at Boston, New York, and New Orleans, and in the Bureau of Equipment at Washington.

March 12, 1868, was made an ensign in the regular navy, and made lieutenant in 1870. Lieutenant-commander in 1882; and, after being some time on sick-leave, was retired, with that rank, November 30, 1885.

Lieutenant-Commander Miller is the author of several valuable articles; among others, one upon "The Advantages of Entering the Naval Service;" and an "Address to American Seamen," which was published by the Bureau of Equipment and Recruiting, Navy Department. He was a member of the Board which revised the Equipment Allowance Book, and also wrote several reports upon the Naval Apprentice System.

## LIEUTENANT-COLONEL ANSON MILLS, U.S.A.

LIEUTENANT-COLONEL ANSON MILLS (Fourth Cavalry) was born in Boone County, Indiana, August 31, 1834. He was a cadet at the Military Academy from July 1, 1855, to February 18, 1857. He then went to Texas and taught school in McKinney, Collin County, Texas, 1857 and 1858, studying law during the time with Colonel R. L. Waddell, the district judge of that district.

During the winter of 1858-59, in anticipation of the construction of the Memphis, El Paso, and Pacific Railroad, he projected and surveyed the present city of El Paso, Texas, the plat of which is now in use.

Surveyor for the State of Texas on the boundary survey between Texas and New Mexico, 1859.

In February, 1861, on the submission to the popular vote of the State of the question of separation from the Union, he cast one of the lonely two votes in the county of El Paso "against separation," against nine hundred and eighty-five "for separation."

At the commencement of the war of the Rebellion he was a sergeant of the Clay Guards, Washington Volunteers, from March to May, when he entered the regular service as first lieutenant of the Eighteenth Infantry, and was ordered on recruiting and mustering duty in Ohio to February, 1862, when he joined a detachment of the three battalions of his regiment at Nashville, Tennessee. He participated in the Corinth, Chickamauga, and Atlanta campaigns with the Army of the West, and was engaged in the battles of Corinth, Mississippi; Stone River, Tennessee; Hoover's Gap, Chickamauga, Georgia; Missionary Ridge, Tennessee; Resaca, New Hope Church, Kenesaw Mountain, Neal Dow Station, Utoy Creek, Atlanta (where he was wounded), and Jonesborough, Georgia; Nashville, Tennessee, and Decatur, Alabama. He was then on recruiting duty from Feb. to Nov., 1865.

Inventor of the looped, or woven, cartridge-belt for metallic cartridges, adopted by the U. S. Army.

He was brevetted captain December 31, 1862, for "gallant and meritorious services in the battle of Murfreesborough, Tennessee;" major, September 1, 1864, for "gallant and meritorious services in the battle of Chickamauga, Georgia, and during the Atlanta campaign;" and lieutenant-colonel December 16, 1864, for "gallant and meritorious services in the battle of Nashville, Tennessee."

Lieutenant Mills served as adjutant of the Eighteenth Infantry from February to October, 1862; was acting commissary of subsistence of the Regular Brigade to April, 1863, and was acting inspector-general of the District of Etowa in 1864.

Member of the Board of Visitors to the U. S. Military Academy from Texas, June, 1866.

Colonel Mills was *en route* in command of troops in Kansas in 1865, and commanded Fort Bridger, Wyoming, from November, 1866, to September, 1867, and then was stationed at Fort Sedgwick, Colorado, and other posts from 1867 to 1876. He was transferred to the Third Cavalry December 31, 1870, and participated in various Indian expeditions, particularly the one against Sitting Bull's band of hostile Sioux Indians in 1876-77. It was on this campaign that General Crook's command, on the Hart River, about one hundred and eighty miles from the nearest point of supplies, gave out of rations, and on the march to Deadwood, North Dakota, subsisted alone on the broken-down cavalry horses. In order to facilitate the getting of supplies, one hundred and fifty picked men of the Third Cavalry were detailed to go forward as rapidly as possible and send out supplies to meet the troops. Colonel Mills was given the command of this force, and starting south, with Frank Gruard, the scout, as his guide, he marched from camp in the midst of a cold, disagreeable rain, and proceeded, without a road or trail to guide him, through a night as black as ink, and the following day, until his scout informed him that he was in the neighborhood of an Indian village. Colonel Mills halted his command until daylight next day, and charged the village, driving therefrom every Indian, and held the ground until General Crook came upon the field with the entire command. This was the capture of the village at Slim Buttes.

Military attaché to the International Exposition at Paris, France, 1878.

Colonel Mills was promoted major of the Tenth Cavalry April 4, 1878, and was stationed at posts in Texas. After a tour of duty in Arizona, from 1885 to 1888, he was at Fort Bliss, Texas, surveying an international dam and reservoir of his own projection in the Rio Grande at El Paso del Norte. He was promoted lieutenant-colonel of the Fourth Cavalry March 25, 1890, and is stationed in command of his regiment at Fort Walla Walla, Washington.

## CAPTAIN AND BREVET MAJOR WILLIAM HOWARD MILLS, U.S.A. (RESIGNED).

CAPTAIN AND BREVET MAJOR WILLIAM HOWARD MILLS was born at Bangor, Maine, April 8, 1838. At the outbreak of the war of the Rebellion he was in business at St. Louis, and was appointed from Missouri a first lieutenant of the Fourteenth U. S. Infantry March 6, 1862.

He was appointed a captain by brevet, in the army of the United States, "for gallant and meritorious services at the battles of Chancellorsville, Virginia, and Gettysburg, Pennsylvania, to date from July 3, 1863," and a major by brevet, "for meritorious services in the campaign terminating with the surrender of the insurgent Army of Northern Virginia, to date from April 9, 1865."

He was appointed adjutant of the First Battalion—eight companies—of his regiment January 10, 1865, and received "the thanks of the commanding officer for the able and efficient manner in which he performed his duties as adjutant," "having been officially informed of his promotion to a captaincy," to date from December 23, 1865, at Fort Yuma, California, June 30, 1866.

The Fourteenth Infantry, having been placed at the head of the Army of the Potomac by Major-General Meade upon the day of its grand parade through the city of Richmond, upon arrival at the pontoon bridges over the James River to Manchester, received orders to remain in the city for duty, and he was selected by Brigadier-General M. R. Patrick, provost-marshal-general, to "proceed at once to Danville, for the purpose of carrying out certain verbal instructions." Having been directed to call upon Brevet Brigadier-General Thomas W. Hyde, colonel of the First Maine (Veteran) Infantry, stationed there, for such assistance as might be needed, the general courteously placed the entire regiment, including himself, at his disposal. With a carefully-selected corporal's guard, he received a large sum of money that had been taken from Union prisoners while in confinement there.

He was then appointed assistant commissary of musters by Major-General Ord, commanding the Department of Virginia and Army of the James, and ordered to report to Brevet Major-General Miles, commanding the District of Fort Monroe, for the purpose of establishing a large muster-out camp. General Miles, after announcing him upon his staff, left the rest to him.

Such mutually-advantageous arrangements were made with Assistant-Surgeon Ely McClellan, U.S.A., in charge of the general hospital at Fort Monroe, for the issuance, cooking, and serving of rations,—more than rations,—that the thousands of survivors, who there answered to the last roll-call by the government's representative and received honorable discharge from the military service, cannot have forgotten the pleasures of Camp McClellan.

In September, by command of Lieutenant-General Grant, he joined his regiment at Hart's Island, New York harbor, and soon afterwards proceeded with it to California. He served as regimental and post adjutant at the Presidio of San Francisco, was stationed awhile at Drum Barracks, Wilmington, and made the march across the desert to Fort Yuma.

Upon his promotion to the rank of captain, by direction of Brevet Major-General McDowell, commanding the Department of California, he was placed in charge of the depot of supplies—for the District of Arizona—at Fort Yuma, at a time when the supplies were nearly exhausted at all the posts, and, when ordered to join his company at Fort McDowell, Arizona, in the following January, left quartermaster and commissary stores sufficient for six months at every post in the district.

In the fall of 1867 he was directed by the department commander to establish, with two companies of infantry, a new post, at a place northeast from Fort McDowell, "in the midst of the hostile Apaches, and inaccessible to wagons."

After considerable opposition and several attacks by the Indians, the post was established, but soon abandoned on account of the difficulty of getting supplies over mountains where, when the best road possible was constructed, wagons had to be let down with ropes.

Major Mills resigned his commission December 12, 1868, and was at the time of this publication a resident of Washington, D. C.

CAPTAIN GEORGE MITCHELL, U.S.A.

CAPTAIN GEORGE MITCHELL (Second Artillery) was born in Ireland March 11, 1845. At the commencement of the war of the Rebellion he was a student at the Collegiate and Commercial Institute, New Haven, Connecticut. He entered the volunteer service as first sergeant of Company B, Fifty-seventh New York Infantry, September 24, 1861, and was promoted second lieutenant of that regiment January 24, 1862. He served during the war with the Third Brigade, First Division, Second Army Corps, Army of the Potomac, acting as aide and assistant adjutant-general of the consolidated brigade before Petersburg, Virginia, and aide to General Neill, in the summer of 1865. He was wounded at the battle of Fair Oaks, Virginia, June 1, 1862. He was promoted first lieutenant August 2, 1862, and appointed major Nov. 15, 1864. He was honorably mustered out of service November, 1864. He re-entered the volunteer service as first lieutenant and adjutant Seventh Regiment U. S. Veteran Volunteers June 9, 1865, and was promoted to captain September 27, 1865. He was again mustered out of the volunteer service April 24, 1866.

Captain Mitchell was brevetted major and lieutenant-colonel of volunteers March 13, 1865.

He was appointed second lieutenant of the Thirteenth U. S. Infantry April 30, 1866; was transferred to the Thirty-first Infantry September 21, 1866. He was promoted first lieutenant June 10, 1868, and became unassigned May 15, 1869, upon the consolidation of regiments.

On December 15, 1870, Lieutenant Mitchell was assigned to the Second Artillery, and was regimental adjutant from May 21, 1875, to March 24, 1877, and from January 24, 1881, to March 22, 1885.

Captain Mitchell served at Forts Rice, Buford, Abercrombie, and Sully, Dakota, from 1866 to 1871; at Sitka, Alaska, in 1871-72; at the Presidio of San Francisco in 1872; Fort McHenry, 1872-74; at Charleston, South Carolina, 1874-75; at Fort McHenry, 1875 to 1877; Fort Foote, Maryland, 1877-78; Fort Monroe, Virginia, 1878 to 1880; at Washington Barracks, District of Columbia, 1880 to 1885; at St. Francis Barracks, Florida, to 1889; and at Fort Adams, Rhode Island, from 1889 to present date.

COLONEL HENRY R. MIZNER, U.S.A. (RETIRED).

COLONEL HENRY R. MIZNER was born in Geneva, New York, August 1, 1827. He entered the service from civil life, having been appointed a captain in the Eighteenth U. S. Infantry May 14, 1861, and was employed on recruiting duty, and mustering and disbursing officer, quartermaster and commissary for the State of Michigan to October, 1861, and continued on recruiting duty to May, 1862, when he joined his regiment in the field with the Western army, participating in the battle of Perryville, Kentucky, October 8, 1862, pursuit of the rebel General Bragg, and the battle of Stone River, Tennessee.

He was appointed colonel of the Fourteenth Michigan Infantry Volunteers December 22, 1862, and served with the Western armies to the close of the Atlanta campaign. He commanded the regiment as mounted infantry, securing horses from the country, being furnished cavalry equipments, revolvers, and one hundred Spencer rifles, and employed in scouting duty in Tennessee.

At Jonesborough, Georgia, September 1, 1864, the Fourteenth Michigan charged the earthworks on the run, capturing with the bayonet Swett's Battery of Cleburne's division, Hardee's corps; four twelve-pounder Napoleon guns; Brigadier-General D. C. Govan (with the sword of Major Sidney Cooledge, Sixteenth U. S. Infantry, lost at Chickamauga); Captain Williams, assistant adjutant-general; Major Weeks, Second Arkansas; the battle-flag of the First Arkansas, and three hundred other prisoners.

Major-General Jefferson C. Davis, commanding the Fourteenth Corps, referring to the Fourteenth Michigan Infantry Volunteers, wrote the Secretary of War as follows:

"Colonel Mizner and regiment joined my command early in the campaign against Atlanta, and served with distinction to its close. This regiment was one of the best in the corps under my command, and upon every occasion where the enemy was met invariably signalized its courage and discipline. In the assault of the corps upon the enemy's works at Jonesborough, which resulted in the fall of Atlanta, the colors of this regiment were among the first carried over the works. Colonel Mizner had been long in command of this regiment, and without doubt much was due his exertion and skill in promoting that excellent discipline and spirit of gallantry for which his regiment was conspicuous throughout the war. Colonel Mizner's personal bearing on the field was no less conspicuous than that of his regiment."

At the close of the war he was honored with the brevet of major U. S. Army for "gallant and meritorious services in the battle of Stone River;" brevet lieutenant-colonel for "gallant and meritorious services during the Atlanta campaign, and in the battle of Jonesborough, Georgia ;" brevet brigadier-general volunteers for gallant and meritorious services during the war.

He was transferred to the Thirty-sixth U. S. Infantry September 21, 1866, and ordered to duty on the plains in Wyoming, locating and constructing Fort Sanders, Wyoming, 1866-67; and at Fort Bridger, Wyoming, from April, 1866, to April, 1869.

He was promoted major of the Twentieth Infantry February 22, 1869, and transferred to the Twelfth Infantry March 15, 1869; again transferred to Eighth Infantry May 14, 1877.

He was on duty in California and Arizona from April, 1869, to August, 1880, participating in the Bannock Indian campaign in Oregon and Washington, July to September, 1878; acting chief commissary Department of Arizona, from November, 1877, to March, 1878; at Fort Porter, New York, from March, 1881, to June 1, 1884; at Fort Union, New Mexico, June 5, 1884, to August 10, 1885; Fort Stanton, New Mexico, 1885; at Fort D. A. Russell, Wyoming, from February 9, 1888, to May, 1891.

Colonel Mizner was promoted lieutenant-colonel of the Tenth Infantry December 15, 1880, and colonel of the Seventeenth Infantry January 2, 1888, and retired August 1, 1891.

## COLONEL J. KEMP MIZNER. U.S.A.

COLONEL J. KEMP MIZNER (Tenth Cavalry) entered the army as a graduate from the U. S. Military Academy July 1, 1856, and was assigned as a brevet second lieutenant to the Second Dragoons. He reached a captaincy in the same regiment November 12, 1861, and on March 7, 1862, was appointed colonel of the Third Michigan Cavalry, joining Pope's command at New Madrid, Missouri; he moved with that army to Hamburg Landing, on the Tennessee River, in April, 1862.

He commanded a brigade of cavalry from May 20, in front of Corinth, and during the subsequent pursuit of the enemy; and continued to cover the front of the troops near Corinth until late in June. Early in July he was sent with his brigade to occupy the line of the Memphis and Charleston Railroad, from Iuka, Mississippi, to Decatur, Alabama, having an independent command, and reporting direct to General W. S. Rosecrans, commanding the Army of the Mississippi. He was appointed chief of cavalry of the Army of the Mississippi, and commanded the Cavalry Division of that army in all its operations in Northern Mississippi, and in the battles of Iuka, September 19, and the battle of Corinth, October 3 and 4, 1862, both of which were brilliant victories for our army. Colonel Mizner moved from Corinth to La Grange, Tennessee, with troops under General Grant, and took part in the campaign against Pemberton's rebel troops, to Grenada, Mississippi, November and December, 1862. He commanded a cavalry brigade at Jackson, Tennessee, during January, 1863, and later, all the cavalry in the left wing of the Sixteenth Army Corps, under Major-General R. J. Oglesby, at La Grange, and then all the troops serving on the line of the Memphis and Charleston Railroad, from White's Station to Grand Junction, including a division of cavalry of nine regiments, organized into three brigades, until midsummer, 1863. Later, and after this, the cavalry was reorganized under General B. H. Grierson, and Colonel Mizner commanded a brigade at Corinth, Mississippi.

The Third Michigan became a veteran volunteer regiment by the re-enlistment of three-fourths of its strength in February, 1864, and when ready to return to the field was sent to Little Rock, Arkansas, where they became a part of the Seventh Army Corps, under Major-General Steele.

During most of his stay in Arkansas Colonel Mizner commanded the troops at Duvall's Bluffs (some seven thousand in number), the base of supplies for the Seventh Army Corps.

Early in 1865 he was sent with his brigade to New Orleans, to take part in operations against Mobile, and after the fall of the enemy's works at that place the Third Michigan Cavalry moved to Baton Rouge, where it was joined by the Fourth Wisconsin and Third Il-

linois Cavalry. These three regiments constituted a brigade in General Merritt's division, and was moved by water to Shreveport, Louisiana, and from there was marched by Colonel Mizner to San Antonio, Texas, where it took part in the demonstrations made by General Sheridan along the Mexican frontier.

Colonel Mizner succeeded General Custer (upon his muster out) in command of the Central District of Texas, which he exercised until February 12, 1866, when his regiment was mustered out and returned to Michigan. In 1867, as a captain of the Second Cavalry, he made the entire tour of the Department of the Platte with his troop, as escort to General Augur, commanding the department, and then accompanied General G. M. Dodge, chief engineer Union Pacific Railroad, to Salt Lake and Ogden, Utah, and return, making the distance marched over two thousand miles. In 1888, as lieutenant-colonel of the Eighth Cavalry, Colonel Mizner marched his entire regiment of twelve troops and band from Fort Concho, Texas, to Fort Meade, Dakota, a distance of fifteen hundred miles, being the longest march ever made by so large a body of troops in the history of this country.

In earlier days, with a small party, he rode three hundred miles in five days without change of horses, and without forage, depending solely upon grazing. Individually he has ridden thirty-five miles before breakfast, and sixty-five miles after a one o'clock dinner, and has frequently marched a battalion of cavalry thirty-five miles after three P.M., before making camp.

Colonel Mizner has been promoted through all the grades, from brevet second lieutenant in 1856 to colonel of cavalry in 1890, the rank he now holds, and has had a varied frontier experience as a post commander in Texas, New Mexico, Arizona, and Indian Territory, as well as in Nebraska and Dakota.

### LIEUTENANT-COMMANDER WILLIAM AUGUSTUS MORGAN, U.S.N.

LIEUTENANT-COMMANDER WILLIAM AUGUSTUS MORGAN was born at Newport, Monmouthshire, England, August 10, 1836, and commenced a seafaring career August 14, 1850, by being bound as an apprentice for five years to a Maine ship-master and owner. He continued in that employ in the European and general freighting business until 1856, and from that time until the breaking out of the late war sailed out of the ports of Portland (Maine), New York, and Boston.

On June 2, 1863, he entered the U. S. Navy as acting ensign, and became instructor in gunnery on board the frigate "Savannah" on July 7, 1863; was ordered to the gun-boat "Tulip," of the Potomac flotilla, and in August was transferred to the schooner "Hope," of the South Atlantic Blockading Squadron. From that time until October, 1865, he served on board the sloop-of-war "John Adams," ships-of-the-line "Vermont" and "New Hampshire," and temporarily on board the steamer "Pawnee," and several other vessels of the South Atlantic Blockading Squadron, and on expeditions on shore with the forces of that squadron.

He was promoted to acting master October 27, 1864, and discharged January 14, 1866.

He was reappointed acting master April 13, 1866, and was on duty on board the receiving-ship "Vermont" until July, 1868. He was transferred to the regular navy, as ensign, March 12, 1868, under the Act of Congress approved July 25, 1866, and served in the Pacific Squadron from July, 1868, to July, 1869; on board the flag-ship "Powhatan;" under orders to the ill-fated "Fredonia;" steamer "Wateree" (after the earthquake of 1868 on the coast of Peru); steamer "Tuscarora," and store-ship "Onward."

He was promoted master December 18, 1868, and returned to the North Atlantic Station on board the "Powhatan;" on board port admiral's flag-ship "New Hampshire," at Norfolk, in 1870.

He was promoted to lieutenant March 21, 1870; attached to the steamer "Shawmut," North Atlantic Squadron, 1871-74; at navy-yard, Boston, 1875; monitor "Montauk," North Atlantic Squadron, 1875-77; navy-yard, Boston, 1877-78; flag-ship "Shenandoah," South Atlantic Squadron, 1879; steamer "Wachusett," South Atlantic and Pacific Squadrons, 1880-81; instruction at torpedo station, Newport, 1882; monitor "Miantonomah," special service, 1882-83; receiving-ship "Wabash," 1884-86.

He was promoted to lieutenant-commander July 28, 1884; corvette "Ossipee," North Atlantic Squadron, and on sick-leave, 1887-88; at the United States nitre depot, Malden, 1889-90.

## CAPTAIN AND BREVET MAJOR ARTHUR MORRIS U.S.A. (RETIRED).

CAPTAIN AND BREVET MAJOR ARTHUR MORRIS was born in Virginia, but entered the regular army from Maryland, by appointment from civil life, as second lieutenant of the Fourth Artillery, March 24, 1862, and was promoted first lieutenant November 12, 1863. He served during the war of the Rebellion with the Second Army Corps, in the field with the Army of the Potomac, and was engaged at the siege of Yorktown and in the battles of Williamsburg, Fair Oaks, Savage Station, White Oak Swamp, Glendale, Malvern Hill, second Bull Run, Antietam, action at Charlestown, and in the battle of Fredericksburg.

In the action at Charlestown he volunteered for the occasion, and was personally congratulated on the field of battle for bravery in action by General Hancock, who was in command.

He was brevetted first lieutenant for "gallant and meritorious service" at the battle of White Oak Swamp, Virginia, and captain for "gallant and meritorious service" at the battle of Antietam, Maryland; major, for "gallant and meritorious service" during the war. The latter was confirmed by Congress; commission not issued by War Department. He has been recommended for brevet major for Nez Perce Indian campaign (commission not yet issued by War Department).

After a period of recruiting duty, Captain Morris was stationed at Fort McHenry, Maryland, from October, 1867, to June, 1869, when he was transferred to Fort Riley, Kansas, and while there was sent with Light Battery B, Fourth Artillery, serving as cavalry on the Salmon River Indian campaign, and was scouting all the summer of 1870. He was then at Fort McHenry,

Maryland, 1871-72, and at Fort Monroe (Artillery School) from May, 1872, to June, 1873. In June, 1873, he was transferred to the Pacific coast, and was stationed at Alcatraz Island, Black Point, Fort Canby, Sitka, Alaska, and Alcatraz Island the second time.

While on the Pacific coast Captain Morris participated in the Modoc campaign in 1873, and the Nez Perce campaign of 1877, being engaged at the battle of Clearwater, Idaho, July 11 and 12.

He was promoted captain Fourth Artillery January 10, 1877, and the regiment being ordered East in 1881, the captain took station at Fort Warren, Massachusetts, where he remained until September, 1882, and was then stationed at Fort Adams, Rhode Island, until retirement. He was retired from active service, on account of disability, October 5, 1887.

## COMMANDER GEORGE UPHAM MORRIS, U.S.N.
### (DECEASED).

COMMANDER GEORGE UPHAM MORRIS was born in Massachusetts, June 3, 1830, and died at the Jordan Alum Springs, in Virginia, in August, 1875. He was the son of Commodore Charles Morris, one of the best known and most respected of our older naval officers, both on account of personal character and professional ability.

Commander Morris entered the navy as midshipman in August, 1846; became lieutenant in September, 1855; and was promoted commander July 25, 1866.

When the iron-clad ram "Merrimac" came out from Norfolk, on the 8th of March, 1862, and attacked the "Congress" and "Cumberland" at Newport News, Morris, who was executive-officer of the last-named ship, was in temporary command, and distinguished himself in the highest degree by his conduct on that occasion. "As her guns approached the water's edge," said the Secretary of the Navy in his annual report, "her young commander, Lieutenant Morris, and the gallant crew stood firm at their posts and delivered a parting fire, and the good ship went down heroically, with her colors flying."

It was but a very few minutes from the time the "Merrimac's" ram struck the vessel until she was at the bottom. A large number perished with the vessel, but many of the officers and men, Lieutenant Morris among them, managed to reach the shore, where they manned the batteries in the intrenchments, to resist Magruder's force, coming from Yorktown to co-operate with the "Merrimac."

In May, 1862, Commander Morris was ordered to the command of the steam gun-vessel "Port Royal." In her he had an engagement with a nine-gun battery on the James River, and was subsequently wounded during an engagement with Fort Darling.

In February, 1864, he was engaged with Fort Powell, at Grant's Pass, in the "Port Royal."

Commander Morris was retired less than a year before his death,—the date of which is given above.

## COLONEL ALBERT P. MORROW, U.S.A.

COLONEL ALBERT P. MORROW (Third Cavalry) was born in Illinois, March 10, 1842. He entered the volunteer service from Pennsylvania as sergeant of Company K, Seventeenth Pennsylvania Infantry, April 18, 1861, and was honorably discharged August 1, 1861. He re-entered the volunteer service September 9, 1861, and was sergeant of Company C, first sergeant of Company I, and sergeant-major of the Sixth Pennsylvania Cavalry. He served with his first regiment in the defences of Washington, at the beginning of the war of the Rebellion, in the Rockville expedition, and Patterson's operations in the Shenandoah Valley, and with the cavalry regiment in the Army of the Potomac, until captured by the enemy near White House, Virginia, June 13, 1862. He was a prisoner of war at Richmond, Virginia, until August 12, 1862, and, upon rejoining his regiment, served with it until the battle of Chancellorsville, when he was again captured, May 3, 1863, and remained a prisoner of war until the 25th of May, when he rejoined his regiment, and remained with it to July 13 following.

He was appointed second lieutenant Sixth Pennsylvania Cavalry March 27, 1862; first lieutenant November 20, 1862; and in July of 1863 was aide-de-camp to General John Buford, remaining on his staff to December 16, 1863. He then served with his regiment in the Army of the Potomac to July, 1864. He was promoted captain February 2, 1864; major February 10, 1865; and lieutenant-colonel March 29, 1865. He participated in the Shenandoah campaign to March, 1865, and in the operations against Richmond, Virginia, to March 31, 1865, when he was wounded in the action at Dinwiddie Court-House, Virginia. He was honorably mustered out of the volunteer service August 6, 1865.

Colonel Morrow entered the regular service as captain of the Seventh Cavalry July 28, 1866, and was promoted major of the Ninth Cavalry March 6, 1867, and served with his regiment on frontier duty at Fort Hays, Kansas, until promoted major, when he joined the Ninth Cavalry in Texas, and served at various posts to March, 1869. He participated in an expedition in 1870, and in another against hostile Indians in 1871. He served at various posts in Texas to 1876, having, in the mean time, been member of a board to purchase cavalry horses in 1874, and with a battalion in the field under General Macken-

zie, in the Indian Territory, to January, 1875. He commanded a battalion *en route* to New Mexico, in the summer of 1876, and participated in a campaign against Indians to Sept. 1, 1876, after which he was granted leave of absence, on account of sickness, to Sept. 3, 1877. Returning to Fort Union, he participated in an expedition against the Ute Indians in 1878; and on scouts in the field in 1879, from Fort Bayard; and again in 1880, when, on August 22, 1880, he proceeded to Washington, D. C., to receive instructions, having been designated as one of the officers to witness the manœuvres of the French army during that autumn; and on the completion of that duty he was granted a delay in returning to the United States until January, 1881, when he was appointed colonel and aide-de-camp to the general of the army. He served till June 1, 1883, when he was relieved at his own request, and joined his regiment in the Department of Arizona, he having been promoted lieutenant-colonel of the Sixth Cavalry December 17, 1882.

Colonel Morrow was brevetted colonel of volunteers, March 13, 1865, for conspicuous gallantry in action, and was commended by Colonel Hatch, commanding District of New Mexico, in 1880, for his persistent pursuit of Indians, in which he exerted himself to such an extent as to produce a dangerous hemorrhage.

He was promoted colonel of the Third Cavalry February 18, 1891, and is at present stationed at Fort McIntosh, Texas.

CAPTAIN ALFRED MORTON, U.S.A.

CAPTAIN ALFRED MORTON (Ninth Infantry) was born in Maine on January 16, 1834. He entered the volunteer service from California during the war of the Rebellion as sergeant of Company F, and commissary sergeant of the Second California Cavalry, September 13, 1861, and served in the last-named grade until January 6, 1862, when he was appointed a first lieutenant of the same regiment, and was promoted captain February 14, 1863.

Captain Morton's regiment was kept upon the Pacific coast during the war, and he was on duty in California most of the time. He participated in an expedition against the Indians in the Humboldt Military District in the summer of 1863, and he was subsequently provost-marshal of San Francisco, and of the State of California. He was mustered out of the Second California Cavalry November 25, 1864, having been appointed major of the Seventh California Infantry. He retained the latter rank until finally mustered out of the volunteer service on March 17, 1866.

Captain Morton entered the regular service as second lieutenant Ninth Infantry March 3, 1866, and was promoted first lieutenant July 28, 1866. He joined his regiment, then on duty in California, and served with it until 1869, when it changed station to the Department of the Platte, at Fort Russell, Wyoming. The captain's station was changed a number of times, he serving at many posts. He was then ordered to Texas, and in 1891 to the Northern Lakes.

Captain Morton was regimental quartermaster from June 1, 1866, to March 20, 1879, at which time he was promoted captain. He is now on the recruiting service at Chicago, Illinois.

## COMMANDER DENNIS W. MULLAN, U.S.N.

COMMANDER DENNIS W. MULLAN was born in Maryland, and appointed midshipman from Kentucky September, 1860. Under the pressure of the war, his class was graduated from the Naval Academy in 1863; ensign, October 1, 1863; attached to steam-sloop "Monongahela," West Gulf Blockading Squadron, from 1863 to 1865. In attacks on various batteries on the coast of Texas, and at the battle of Mobile Bay, August 5, 1864; in both attacks upon and the surrender of Fort Morgan; served in the steamer "Malvern," North Atlantic Station, in 1865; and the "Mohongo," Pacific Station, 1865-67; promoted to master November 10, 1865; steam-sloop "De Soto," North Atlantic Squadron, 1867-68; commissioned lieutenant February 21, 1867; commissioned lieutenant-commander March 12, 1868. While attached to the "De Soto," he was selected by Commodore Charles S. Boggs to command the steamer "Glasgow," then at the Pensacola Navy-Yard, to co-operate with him in suppressing an expedition against Mexico, then fitting out in New Orleans. "Monocacy," on the Asiatic Station, from 1868 to 1871. Present at the two attacks upon the batteries on the river, at Corea, on June 1 and 10, 1871. In 1872-73, attached to the receiving-ship "Independence," at Mare Island; "Saco," on the Asiatic Station, from 1873 to 1876; and navigation-duty at Norfolk Navy-Yard, 1877-78; executive-officer of the "Adams," in the Pacific, from 1879 to 1881. While attached to the "Adams," Lieutenant-Commander Mullan was detailed to accompany the staff of General Baquedano, the Chilian commander-in-chief, in his operations against Lima, Peru. He was present at all the engagements at Chorillos, Miraflores, and other places near Lima, and made a report of these operations to the Navy Department.

He was promoted to commander in July, 1882, and was in command of the seven iron-clad vessels at City Point, James River, Virginia, from 1884 to 1887. On October 1, 1887, he was ordered to command the U.S.S. "Nipsic," and went via the Straits of Magellan to the Pacific Station. Was in command of the "Nipsic" at Samoa during the troublous times with the Germans there. At that time he gave protection to the American correspondent, whom the Germans wished to be sent on board the German man-of-war "Adler," their flag-ship there, to be tried by court-martial for alleged offences. Commander Mullan's firm stand put an end to that. He was in command of the "Nipsic" during the great Samoan hurricane of March 16, 1889, and the "Nipsic" was the only American man-of-war that was saved.

Commander Mullan, upon his return from the Pacific, was on leave of absence for some months, and was then ordered to duty as light-house inspector, with headquarters at New Orleans, where he is at present.

The City Council of Annapolis, Maryland, where Commander Mullan was born, voted him thanks for his conduct at the Samoan Islands; and the Legislature of Maryland, in its session of 1890, presented him with a gold watch, in appreciation of his conduct during the Samoan complications.

REAR-ADMIRAL J. R. M. MULLANY, U.S.N.
(DECEASED).

REAR-ADMIRAL J. R. M. MULLANY was born in New York, and appointed from that State, as midshipman, in January, 1832. He passed through the ordinary course of service upon the Mediterranean and the African Squadrons, the Coast Survey, the Mexican War, and the West Indies.

In 1861 he was commanding the "Wyandotte," in the Gulf Squadron, and was commissioned commander in October of that year. In command of the "Bienville," he was frequently engaged with the forts at Charleston and elsewhere on the South Atlantic coast. Shortly before the battle of August 5, 1864, at Mobile Bay, he volunteered his services, but the "Bienville" not being considered by Admiral Farragut a fit vessel to engage the forts, he was assigned to the command of the "Oneida," which vessel, on passing Fort Morgan, occupied the side exposed to the fire of that fort; the "Galena," which was lashed on the port side, being under his control by virtue of his seniority. He lost an arm in this action. While commanding the "Bienville," off Charleston, in 1862, he captured the blockade-running steamers "Stettin" and "Patras," under the English flag, and loaded with munitions of war,—the vessels and cargoes being valued in the aggregate at $500,000. He also captured nine schooners from Nassau, all under the English flag. From April to September, 1863, he commanded, while in the "Bienville," a division of the West Gulf Blockading Squadron. Off Galveston, he sent in a boat expedition, and captured and brought off two schooners, with five hundred and seventy-six bales of cotton.

After the end of the Civil War he was inspector of ordnance at the New York Navy-Yard for three years. He was commissioned captain in July, 1866. Commanded steam-sloop "Richmond," of the European Squadron, from December, 1868, to November, 1871. Commissioned as commodore in August, 1870, and was in command of the Mediterranean Squadron of the European Fleet after that for nearly a year. He was stationed at the Philadelphia Navy-Yard during the time the station was changed to League Island, 1872-74. Commissioned as rear-admiral June, 1874, and commanded the North Atlantic Station from that time until February, 1876. During a part of this time he was in New Orleans, with a portion of the squadron, to support General Emory, and afterwards General Sheridan, during the political turmoil of the period. September and October of 1875 he spent at Aspinwall, with two vessels of the squadron, to protect American interests on the Isthmus of Panama, then menaced by the rebellion in that State. He was also, for the time being, placed in command of the vessels of the Pacific Squadron which were in the Bay of Panama. He was governor of the Naval Asylum at Philadelphia from 1876 to 1879. Died in 1887.

## PAY-DIRECTOR JAMES D. MURRAY, U.S.N.
### (RETIRED.)

PAY-DIRECTOR JAMES D. MURRAY was born in Maryland, and was appointed purser in the navy from Minnesota June 3, 1858. In 1860 the title was changed to paymaster, and as such he dates from June 22, 1860. He served on board the sloop-of-war "Cyane," of the Pacific Squadron, from August, 1858, to February, 1861.

In July, after the breaking out of the Rebellion, he was ordered to the frigate "Potomac," Atlantic Blockading Squadron. The "Potomac" was afterwards made storeship at Pensacola, Florida. In April, 1863, he was ordered to the iron-clad "Roanoke," North Atlantic Blockading Squadron, and served in her until August, 1864. After a leave of absence he joined the receiving-ship "Princeton," at Philadelphia, and remained there three years. During this term he was also the paymaster of the United States Naval Asylum. In 1858-59 he was fleet-paymaster on board the U. S. S. "Contoocook." After a tour of duty at the Washington Navy-Yard, which extended over two years, he next was paymaster of the Naval Academy at Annapolis, from July, 1871, to January, 1873. At the latter date he joined the flag-ship "Franklin," as fleet-paymaster of the European Squadron, and was detached from her in September, 1876, with permission to remain abroad. After some months of travel, under these orders, he returned to the United States, and served three years at the Naval Asylum, and then another term of three years at the Naval Academy, Annapolis.

During 1884-85, Pay-Director Murray was on general court-martial and board duty, and, for a period, at the Navy Pay-Office, Washington, D. C., but in September, 1885, was ordered to the Navy Pay-Office at Baltimore, where he remained until April, 1889.

In August of that year he reported to the Bureau of Navigation for special duty in connection with the promotion of pay officers and other cognate matters. While upon this duty (August, 1890) he was again ordered to the Naval Academy, and remained there until September 20, 1891, when he was detached to make a settlement of accounts, as he was then retired from active service in conformity with chapter iii., section 1444, of the Revised Statutes.

### REAR-ADMIRAL J. W. A. NICHOLSON, U.S.N.
(DECEASED).

REAR-ADMIRAL J. W. A. NICHOLSON was born in Massachusetts, and appointed from New York February 10, 1838. He was attached to the sloops "Natchez" and "Warren," West India Squadron, 1838-41; to the frigate "Brandywine," Mediterranean Squadron, 1841-42; on special service, 1842-43.

He was promoted to passed midshipman June 20, 1844, and was with the steamship "Princeton" from 1844-46; Pacific Squadron, 1846-47; store-ship "Fredonia," 1848; frigate "Raritan," 1849-50; store-ship "Southampton," Pacific, 1851-52.

He was promoted to lieutenant April 24, 1852; with sloop "Vandalia," Japanese Expedition under Commodore Perry, from 1853 to 1855; participated in all of the official meetings with the Japanese on that expedition; stationed on shore, with a guard from the "Vandalia," at Shanghai, China, for several months, to protect the foreign settlement, while the contending Chinese were encamped near by; at navy-yard, New York, 1856-57; with sloop "Vincennes," on the African coast, 1857-60; in 1861 was attached to steamer "Pocahontas," which vessel started for the relief of Fort Sumter, but arrived too late, as the fort capitulated, a short time after the arrival of the "Pocahontas," on April 13, 1861; stationed in Potomac River until October, 1861; in engagement with rebel batteries at Acquia Creek; in command of the steamer "Isaac Smith," 1861, and participated in actions with rebel fleet, November 5 and 6, and battle of Port Royal, November 7, 1861; also participated in the capture of Jacksonville, Fernandina, and St. Augustine, Florida; held the towns of Jacksonville and St. Augustine for several months; while in command of St. John's River, was attacked by rebel infantry, and defeated them with considerable loss; in engagement with rebel flotilla in Savannah River in February, 1862.

He was commissioned as commander July 16, 1862; on ordnance duty in New York in 1863; with South Atlantic Blockading Squadron in 1864; in command of monitor "Manhattan," Western Gulf Squadron, in 1864; in battle of Mobile Bay forts, and capture of rebel ram "Tennessee," August 5, 1864; bombarding of Fort Morgan from August 9 until the surrender, on the 21st; commanding the steamer "Mohongo," Pacific Squadron, 1865-66; commanding the steam-ship "Wampanoag," 1867-68.

He was commissioned as captain July 25, 1866; at the navy-yard, New York, 1868-70; commanding the "Lancaster" (second-rate), South Atlantic fleet, 1871-72.

He was commissioned as commodore November 8, 1873; a member of the Board of Examiners, 1873-74; president of Board of Examiners, 1875-76; commandant at navy-yard, 1879; commanding European Station, 1880-83.

He was promoted rear-admiral in 1881, and died in 1887.

## CAPTAIN AND BREVET LIEUTENANT-COLONEL JOHN B. NIXON, U.S.A. (RETIRED).

CAPTAIN AND BREVET LIEUTENANT-COLONEL JOHN B. NIXON was born near Boothsville, Harrison County, Virginia, April 6, 1828. His education was obtained in the private schools of that locality, and at Rector College, Pruntytown, Virginia.

In 1855 he removed to Henry County, Illinois, where he held several subordinate county positions, including justice of the peace and postmaster.

After the breaking out of the war of the Rebellion, he enlisted June 30, 1862, and was mustered into the U. S. service as second lieutenant of Company D, One Hundred and Second Illinois Infantry, September 2, 1862, and promoted first lieutenant April 20, 1863.

He served with his regiment in the Army of the Ohio and of the Cumberland, under Generals Buell, Rosecrans, and Thomas, until November 23, 1863, when he was appointed captain of the Seventeenth U. S. Colored Infantry, and mustered into service December 3, 1863.

He participated in all the important services of that regiment, including the battle of Nashville, where, in command of his company, A, he took part in the first assault on the enemy's works on the morning of December 15, 1864, in which the casualties in his company were nineteen in an enlisted strength "present" of forty-two; following Hood's retreating army to Tuscumbia, Alabama, through an arduous campaign of hardship, suffering, and exposure.

In March, 1865, he was given the position (unsolicited) of assistant-inspector general, on the staff of Brigadier-General John F. Miller, U. S. Volunteers (late U. S. Senator from California), and served as such until November 3 of that year, when he was relieved to join and assume command of his regiment, of which he was the senior captain during its entire service.

He was retained in service some six months after the muster-out of his regiment on general court-martial duty, and was honorably discharged by special orders number 550, War Department, A. G. O., November 3, 1866.

After the close of the war, upon the recommendations of Generals Grant, Thomas, Fisk, and others, on June 12, 1867, he received the appointment of first lieutenant Thirty-eighth U. S. Infantry, and served in that and the Twenty-fourth U. S. Infantry for seventeen years in Kansas, New Mexico, Colorado, Texas, and the Indian Territory. He was promoted captain Twenty-fourth Infantry January 5, 1877.

During his long and active duties in the Southwest, Colonel Nixon saw much arduous service. His company changed station twelve times during ten years.

He participated in the campaign against the Apache chief Victorio, in 1880, and commanded a battalion of his regiment from Fort Davis, Texas, to Fort Sill, Indian Territory, in the winter of 1880-81, marching over five hundred miles, encountering severe "northers," causing great suffering from cold and frost-bites.

He was regimental quartermaster of the Twenty-fourth Infantry for six years under Generals Potter, Doubleday, and Colonel Shafter.

Colonel Nixon descended from a long line of ancestry, all branches of the family originally emigrating from Scotland, some from Edinburgh, others from Dundee, in the seventeenth century, and settling in New Jersey and Pennsylvania.

Colonel John Nixon, of Philadelphia, who, on the 8th of July, 1776, read to the people of that city the Declaration of Independence, and the late Judge John T. Nixon, of New Jersey, a graduate of Princeton College, in the Class of 1841, formerly member of Congress, and legatee of the late John C. Green, are of the ancestral stock.

Brevet Lieutenant-Colonel John B. Nixon is a son of George Nixon, who was born on the 9th of May, 1776, near Winchester, in Frederick County, Virginia, and served in the Indian wars in 1792, at the age of sixteen, at a "block-house" on the Monongahela River, having emigrated with his parents in 1786 to Harrison County, Virginia, and where he afterwards resided on his estate of several hundred acres until his death in 1844, and where still remain members of the family, nine of whom saw service on the Federal side in the war of the Rebellion, though all native-born Virginians.

Colonel Nixon is now residing at his country-seat, Belle Mead, Somerset County, New Jersey, having been retired from the army, November 26, 1884, for disability in the line of duty.

CAPTAIN HENRY B. NOBLE, U.S.A. (RETIRED).

CAPTAIN HENRY B. NOBLE was born August 17, 1837, and graduated at the Military Academy May 6, 1861, when he was promoted second lieutenant of the Eighth Infantry, and first lieutenant of the same regiment June 11, 1861. He was ordered to Washington immediately after graduating, and assigned the duty of assisting in drilling and mustering the Sixty-ninth New York Volunteers. He participated in the Manassas campaign, and was engaged in the first battle of Bull Run, July 21, 1861, with two companies of the Eighth Infantry. Upon returning to Washington, after that battle, he was on duty as part of the provost guard until October of the same year, when he was ordered to Fort Hamilton, New York, to assist in reorganizing the Eighth Infantry, which had previously been surrendered by General Twiggs, in Texas. He was ordered to the field again in May, 1862, and served in the valley of Virginia, in command of a company of his regiment, until the battle of Cedar Mountain, August 9, 1862, where he was wounded by a bullet going through the left leg below the knee. He was then granted sick-leave of absence until November 19, 1862.

Upon recovering from his wounds, he was detailed at the Military Academy as assistant professor of geography, history, and ethics to March 20, 1863, and then as assistant instructor of infantry tactics to September 9, 1865.

Lieutenant Noble was brevetted captain for "gallant and meritorious services at the battle of Cedar Mountain, Virginia," August 9, 1862. He was promoted captain of the Eighth Infantry February 13, 1866.

At the close of his tour of duty at West Point, Captain Noble was on duty with his company at Baltimore, Maryland, to January 12, 1866, when he was ordered to North Carolina, and served at Raleigh, Salisbury, Morgantown (where he commanded the post), and then was sent to Charleston, South Carolina, where he was stationed for a few months, when he was ordered North on sick-leave, and afterwards was retired from active service February 18, 1869.

## COLONEL BASIL NORRIS, U.S.A. (RETIRED).

COLONEL BASIL NORRIS was born in Maryland on March 9, 1828. He was appointed to the regular service as first lieutenant and assistant surgeon October 11, 1852, and was promoted captain October 11, 1857. He accompanied recruits to Texas in November, 1852. He reported to General P. F. Smith, at Fort Leavenworth, February 8, 1858, for duty with the expedition fitting out for the Utah campaign, and after arrival in Utah was assigned to duty at Camp Floyd. In May, 1860, he accompanied the Seventh Infantry and a detachment of the Second Dragoons, changing station from Utah to New Mexico. He was at Fort Craig and Albuquerque from September, 1860, to December, 1861, as medical purveyor of the department and post surgeon, and then was ordered to report to Colonel E. R. S. Canby, at camp near Belin, New Mexico, as medical director and purveyor of troops in the field, and was engaged at the battle of Val Verde, New Mexico, in his report of which Colonel Canby uses these words: " Higher thanks than any I can bestow are due to the medical officers of the command," etc.

Having reported to the surgeon-general, under orders, in 1862, Dr. Norris became medical inspector of hospitals, and December 6, 1862, he reported to General Franklin's head-quarters, in the field with the Army of the Potomac, as medical director of the Left Grand Division, having received his promotion to a majority April 16, 1862.

On February 23, 1863, Dr. Norris was ordered to report to the surgeon-general in person as attending surgeon at Washington, remaining there until October 15, 1884. He was then ordered to the Pacific coast, and was medical director of the Department of California, when he was retired March 9, 1892.

At the close of the war Dr. Norris was brevetted lieutenant-colonel for " faithful and meritorious services during the war," and colonel for " meritorious services and diligent discharge of duties during the war." He was promoted lieutenant-colonel December 14, 1882, and colonel, November 14, 1888.

During his long period of service Dr. Norris performed numerous difficult surgical operations. At Fort Clark, Texas, in 1854, he amputated the thigh of Private Kinney, for accidental gun-shot wound through knee-joint; in 1855 amputated arm of Corporal Ives for gun-shot wound through elbow-joint, received in attack of Indians on paymaster's escort at crossing of Devil's River; in 1856 ligated brachial artery of Lieutenant Crosby, U.S. Mounted Riflemen, for cure of aneurism from arrow-wound received fighting Indians at Lake Trinidad; in 1859, at a time of great excitement, was despatched from Camp Floyd to Salt Lake City to attend Sergeant Pike, Tenth U. S. Infantry, who, when in uniform and present in obedience to summons of U. S. Court, was waylaid at noon in the public street, shot and mortally wounded by Spencer, in front of the public hotel. He was post surgeon at Albuquerque, New Mexico, in the summer of 1861 during the prevalence of small-pox; in Washington, in May, 1863, amputated thigh of Lieutenant Kirby for gun-shot fracture of the femur by two bullets from spherical case-shot at Chancellorsville; in 1864 amputated thigh of General John C. Robinson for gun-shot wound of knee-joint from rifle-ball received in battle in the Wilderness; in Washington, amputated leg of Lieutenant Smedburg, for disease of bone after primary amputation for gun-shot wound of foot from shell explosion, battle in the Wilderness.

In Washington, he attended Hon. William H. Seward, Secretary of State, for double fracture of the inferior maxillary bone caused by a fall from his carriage, April 4, 1865, and for wounds inflicted by Payne at ten o'clock on the evening of April 14, 1865. It was by authority of Mr. Stanton, Secretary of War, that Surgeon-General Barnes directed a daily detail from Douglas Hospital of two enlisted men to keep watch by turns in the sick chamber at night; from that circumstance the assassination of Mr. Seward was prevented by George F. Robinson, Eighth Maine Volunteers; in Washington, in 1878, amputated arm of Sergeant Penrod, Signal Service, for injury to elbow from fall on roof of station on Broadway, New York, in 1877; in Washington, had charge of medical and surgical practice in all its departments, including officers and general service men on duty in the War Department and their families and others.

The duty of attending surgeon in Washington included medical attendance at the Executive Mansion from May, 1865, to March, 1877,—including the terms of office of President Andrew Johnson and General U. S. Grant.

## CAPTAIN AND BREVET MAJOR THOMAS H. NORTON, U.S.A. (RETIRED).

CAPTAIN AND BREVET MAJOR THOMAS H. NORTON was born at Pittsburg, Pennsylvania, April 29, 1840. He received an academic education at the Linsly Institute, at Wheeling, West Virginia, founded by Noah Linsly, a former philanthropic and public-spirited citizen of that State. In 1859 young Norton served as a non-commissioned officer in a company of Virginia militia, which was called upon by the Governor of Virginia to attend the execution of John Brown, at Charlestown, Virginia, in that year, but Corporal Norton refused to respond to the summons, and immediately thereafter severed his connection with the Virginia militia. At the beginning of the war of the Rebellion he occupied the position of paymaster at the Belmont Iron-Works, at Wheeling, Virginia, and under the first call of President Lincoln for seventy-five thousand volunteers, he raised a company of men, principally from among the employés of the iron-mills, of which his father was part owner.

On the 11th of May, 1861, he was elected second lieutenant of this company, and was mustered into the United States service by Major James Oakes, U.S.A. A few days thereafter the First Regiment of loyal Virginians, fully organized, but without uniforms, and only partially armed and equipped, took the field in defence of the Union. While serving with this regiment, Lieutenant Norton took part in the engagement at Philippi, Virginia, on June 3, 1861, in which Colonel Kelly, commanding the First Virginia Volunteers, with the co-operation and support of a brigade of Ohio and Indiana troops, defeated and dispersed the Confederate forces under Colonel Porterfield; and in recognition of his services in this affair, Lieutenant Norton was on August 5, 1861, appointed captain in the Fifteenth U. S. Infantry, and reported for duty at Newport Barracks, Kentucky, in September following. Being at that time but little over twenty-one years of age, it is believed that Captain Norton was the youngest officer who then held the rank of captain in the regular service.

During the remainder of 1861 and part of 1862, Captain Norton was on recruiting, mustering, and disbursing duty at Columbus, Ohio, and Harrisburg, Pennsylvania. At the latter capital he mustered in many of the famous Pennsylvania regiments that afterwards achieved distinction in the Civil War. Being relieved of this duty in November, 1862, he joined the Second Battalion Fifteenth U. S. Infantry, at Memphis Tennessee, which command, after the battle of Chickamauga, in September, 1863, was attached to the Regular Brigade, Second Division, Fourteenth Corps, Army of the Cumberland. Captain Norton remained on duty in the field with this command until the end of the war, participating in the battles of Missionary Ridge, Tennessee, on November 25, 1863, and all the battles of the Atlanta campaign, including those of Resaca, New Hope Church, Kenesaw Mountain, Neal Dow Station, Peach-Tree Creek, the siege of Atlanta, and battle of Jonesborough, Georgia.

He was brevetted major for gallant and meritorious services in the above actions, and at the end of the war was awarded a medal of honor by the Legislature of the State of West Virginia, for his services while connected with the Virginia volunteers.

During the campaign in Georgia, ending with the capture of Atlanta by the army under General Sherman, the company commanded by Captain Norton was reduced by battle and disease, from a full complement of one hundred officers and men, to one captain, one corporal, and eight men.

From 1865 to 1870, Major Norton continued to serve in Alabama, Mississippi, and Texas, performing duty under the reconstruction laws of Congress, and in 1868 and 1869 was military mayor of the city, and commanding officer of the post of Jackson, Mississippi. He was retired from active service December 17, 1870, for disability incurred in the line of duty, and is now engaged in the banking business at his former home, at Wheeling, West Virginia, and in carrying on mining operations in Colorado and West Virginia.

## CAPTAIN AND BREVET MAJOR JOHN M. NORVELL, U.S.A. (RETIRED).

CAPTAIN AND BREVET MAJOR JOHN M. NORVELL was born in Michigan July 22, 1832. Early in the war of the Rebellion he entered the volunteer service as second lieutenant of the Second Michigan Infantry, May 25, 1861, and was honorably mustered out August 31, 1861. He was appointed captain and acting assistant adjutant-general of volunteers August 30, 1861, and promoted major and assistant adjutant-general of volunteers August 22, 1862.

He participated in the campaigns of the Army of the Potomac from 1861 to 1865, in the Manassas campaign, and engaged at the action of Blackburn's Ford, and the first battle of Bull Run, in 1861; with the First Division, Second Army Corps, in the Peninsula campaign; and engaged in the battle of Fair Oaks and the Seven Days' fights, in 1862; in the Maryland campaign, and engaged in the battle of Antietam, 1862; in the Rappahannock campaign, and engaged in the battle of Chancellorsville, Virginia, 1863; in the Pennsylvania campaign, and engaged in the battle of Gettysburg, Pennsylvania, 1863.

Major Norvell was assigned to the Third Corps, Army of the Potomac, from September, 1863, to March, 1864, when he was transferred to the Second Division, Second Corps, serving with it to the close of the war, and engaged in all its battles, from the Wilderness to the surrender of General Lee.

Major Norvell resigned from the volunteer service June 21, 1865, and was appointed first lieutenant of the Thirty-first U. S. Infantry July 28, 1866. He was brevetted captain March 2, 1867, for "gallant and meritorious services in the battle of Gettysburg, Pennsylvania;" and major for "gallant and meritorious services in the battle of the Wilderness, Virginia." He was also brevetted lieutenant-colonel of volunteers April 9, 1865, for "meritorious services in the recent campaign terminating with the surrender of the insurgent army under General R. E. Lee."

Major Norvell served on the Upper Missouri River in 1866, and was at Fort Buford, Dakota Territory, for two years, and constructed most of the post. Upon the consolidation of regiments he was unassigned May 15, 1869, but on the 1st of January, 1871, he was assigned to the Twelfth Infantry. He served at Angel Island, California, and at various other posts in other departments from 1871 to 1890. He was promoted captain January 31, 1874. His last station was at Fort Yates, North Dakota, from which he went on sick-leave of absence, and was retired for disability in the line of duty December 29, 1890.

MEDICAL INSPECTOR A. S. OBERLY, U.S.N.
(RETIRED).

MEDICAL INSPECTOR A. S. OBERLY was born near Easton, Pennsylvania, on April 7, 1837, and graduated in medicine at Yale College in 1860. At the outbreak of the Civil War he was engaged in the practice of medicine at New Haven, Connecticut, and after refusing several flattering offers to join the volunteer army as surgeon, he answered a call of the Secretary of the Navy to appear before an examining board; after which he was appointed an assistant surgeon, and assigned to the receiving-ship "Ohio," at Boston, and later was commissioned an assistant surgeon July 30, 1861.

His next duty was on the frigate "Sabine," off the South Carolina coast, and while en route for an attack on Port Royal, the rescuing of about four hundred marines from the foundering steamer "Governor" detained the ship until too late for action.

In January, 1862, he was transferred to the gun-boat "Kineo," and participated with Flag-officer Farragut in his attacks and passage of Forts Jackson and St. Philip, and Port Hudson, and was present during the attack on Baton Rouge, where he assisted the army in caring for the wounded.

During the siege of Port Hudson he was on duty ashore, at the request of the medical director of the army, but, owing to weeks of prolonged arduous service and loss of rest in a malarious locality, his health became greatly impaired.

About the same time he was called upon by the army to assist in taking care of the Union and Confederate wounded, during an attack on Fort Butler, at Donaldsonville, Louisiana.

After the opening of the Mississippi River, he was ordered to the Naval Academy at Newport, Rhode Island, and the following autumn was sent to the North Atlantic Squadron, and by Admiral Porter assigned to the steamer "Santiago de Cuba," participating in both attacks on Fort Fisher.

After the fall of Fort Fisher that vessel conveyed the wounded to the Naval Hospital at Norfolk, and subsequently carried cabinet officers and their friends to visit the different battle-fields along the Atlantic coast and the James River.

His next service was at the Naval Hospital at New York, and a few months afterwards on the steamer "Rhode Island," which brought the Confederate steamer "Stonewall" from Havana to Washington.

Following this duty came orders to the navy-yard, New York, to remain until June 19, 1866, when he was promoted to surgeon, after which he was transferred to the Naval Station at Mound City, Illinois. Leaving here, he was ordered to the steam-sloop "Narragansett," but from a long stay at Havana and Matanzas during a sickly season, yellow fever appeared on the ship, causing her to be sent North to be put out of commission.

A few months later he went to Rio de Janeiro to join the sloop "Portsmouth," cruising on the Brazilian and African coasts, and touching at the different islands in the South Atlantic. Here he had a varied experience with small-pox and yellow fever on board ship. The next assignment was to the receiving-ship at Boston, but in a few months he was detached and ordered as surgeon of the navy-yard.

In the winter of 1873, while trouble was pending between the United States and Spain, he was ordered to the iron-clad "Dictator" for duty in the West Indies, and from her he was transferred to the navy-yard and hospital at Pensacola, Florida, to pass the next three and a half years.

Leaving here, he was sent to the Torpedo Station, and in the fall of 1880 to the steamer "Powhatan."

Early in 1881 he was detached from this vessel and ordered to the Asiatic Station for duty as fleet-surgeon, a duty he performed until the return of the flag-ship "Richmond" in 1884, making, during this cruise, a circuit around the earth.

On his return to the United States he was promoted to the grade of medical inspector, with the relative rank of commander, from March 4, 1884, and then ordered to the navy-yard and hospital at Portsmouth, New Hampshire, where he remained until the spring of 1888, when, with his family, he set apart a six months' trip to visit the various places of interest in Europe.

Returning to the United States, he was ordered again to the steamer "Richmond," but failing health, dating back to his last cruise, compelled him to accept the alternative of the retired list, and on which he was placed January 24, 1889.

## CAPTAIN JAMES O'KANE, U.S.N.

CAPTAIN JAMES O'KANE is a native of Indiana, and was appointed midshipman in the navy from that State on October 30, 1856. Upon graduating from the Naval Academy in 1860 he was ordered to the frigate "Niagara." When the Civil War broke out in the succeeding year, and officers were in demand, the graduate of only a year's standing was made acting lieutenant of the "Niagara," and in her participated in the stirring events in connection with Fort Pickens. He was promoted to master in 1861, and with that rank was second lieutenant of the "Brooklyn," and present at the passage of Forts Jackson and St. Philip, the Chalmette batteries, and the capture of New Orleans. At the passage of the forts he was wounded. He was present at the various attacks upon and at the passage of Vicksburg.

He was commissioned as lieutenant July, 1862, and became executive-officer of the "R. R. Cuyler" in the fall of 1862. He was executive-officer of the gun-boat "Paul Jones," and of the monitor "Sangamon," on the South Atlantic Blockading Squadron, in 1863. In the latter vessel he participated in various attacks upon Fort Moultrie, and batteries Bee and Beauregard. He also commanded the marine battalion in an expedition up Broad River, South Carolina, in connection with the army. He took part in the battles of Honey Hill, Tullifinny Cross-Roads, and in an engagement on the Charleston and Savannah Railroad. After this expedition, Lieutenant O'Kane served upon the staff of Admiral Dahlgren, and continued to do so until the close of the war. During this duty upon the staff, he commanded two expeditions of tugs and launches up the Santee, into the Congaree and Wateree Rivers, with the object of communicating with Sherman's army, which was expected to pass through Columbia, South Carolina. After the close of the Civil War, Lieutenant O'Kane served in the West Indies on board the "Rhode Island," and was commissioned as lieutenant-commander in April, 1866. He was executive-officer of the "Swatara," European Squadron, in 1866–67, and then executive-officer of the "Lancaster," of the South Atlantic Squadron. In 1870-71 he was in command of the "Wasp," of the last-named squadron. After some service on ordnance duty at Pittsburg in 1872, he became executive-officer of the "Powhatan," and was in command of the iron-clad "Mahopac," North Atlantic Squadron, in 1873. He was commissioned as commander in January, 1874, and was head of the department of ordnance and gunnery at the Naval Academy from 1875 to 1878. His next service was in command of the "Galena," European Squadron, in 1880-82. From 1883 to 1886 he was inspector of light-houses. From 1887 to 1889 he was on duty at the navy-yard, Portsmouth, New Hampshire. From February, 1889, to February, 1891, he commanded the cruiser "Boston," Squadron of Evolution.

Captain O'Kane is at present in command of the receiving-ship "Wabash."

## OFFICERS OF THE ARMY AND NAVY (REGULAR)

MAJOR-GENERAL EDWARD OTHO CRESAP ORD, U.S.A. (DECEASED).

MAJOR-GENERAL EDWARD OTHO CRESAP ORD was born in Cumberland, Maryland, October 18, 1818, and died in Havana, Cuba, July 22, 1883. He showed in his youth great mathematical ability, which attracted attention and gained for him an appointment to West Point, where he graduated in 1839. He was assigned to the Third Artillery, and served in the Florida War against the Seminole Indians, 1839-42, winning his promotion as first lieutenant in 1841. He was one of two lieutenants selected by General Harney to attack the Indians in the Everglades, and on one occasion went back to his wounded sergeant, whom his companions had deserted, and, taking his musket, held the Indians off until they returned to the rescue. In 1847, with Lieutenants H. W. Halleck and W. T. Sherman, he was ordered to California, via Cape Horn, where he served during the Mexican War, and at its close was stationed at Monterey, where, by his individual efforts, he did much to preserve law and order. Once, following a party of desperadoes several hundred miles, his men deserted him; he then continued alone, overtook, and, by the aid of the inhabitants, succeeded in capturing and executing them. In September, 1850, he was promoted captain; on December 3, 1852, he was assigned to Coast Survey duty; in 1855 he was on the Yakima Indian Expedition; in 1856 he was on the Rogue River Expedition, being in command in the action of Macknyhootney Villages on March 26. Of this fight he said, " It was the first defeat in pitched battle these Indians had ever experienced." During that night he carried in his arms on his saddle one of his worst-wounded men, for several hours, through the thick underbrush to the river, amid the groanings and pleadings of the poor fellow to be put out of his misery. He was also in command of the action at Cheeto Creek, April 28, 1856. He was then stationed at Benicia until 1858, when he was on frontier duty at Fort Miller, California, and participated in the Spokane Expedition; was engaged in the combat of Four Lakes, September 1, 1858; combat of Spokane Plain, September 5, 1858; skirmish of Spokane River, September 8, 1858,—the celebrated chief, Rogue River John, surrendering to him. In 1859 he was stationed at Fort Monroe, and was in the Harper's Ferry Expedition to suppress the John Brown raid. He was commissioned brigadier-general of volunteers, "for services in the war," September 4, 1861, and commanded the Third Brigade, Pennsylvania Reserves. His first engagement of the war was at Dranesville, where he defeated the Confederates, under General Jeb. Stewart, after a sharp contest lasting several hours. In this fight he pointed and fired the first cannon himself, the shell causing great havoc among the enemy. General John F. Reynolds said at the time, " I knew, if there was a fight to be scared up, Ord would find it." He was brevetted lieutenant-colonel for gallantry in that battle. In May, 1862, he commanded a division in the Army of the Rappahannock; in June and August, Corinth, Mississippi. In May he was promoted major-general of volunteers, and commanded left wing, Army of Tennessee; was engaged in the battle of Iuka; fought the battle of the Hatchie. He was severely wounded, and had to be carried from the field. After his recovery he was given the 18th Army Corps, before Vicksburg. He was with Gen. Grant during the conference and surrender of Gen. Pemberton. He was engaged in the capture of Jackson, Miss.; Feb. 16, 1864, commanding the 18th Army Corps and all troops in the Middle Department. He was then given the Eighteenth Army Corps, and took part in the movements before Petersburg; and, crossing his army to the north side of the James on the 29th of September, led the forces that carried the strong fortifications and long line of intrenchments below Chapin's Farm known as Fort Harrison. During the assault he was severely wounded. In January he was given the Army of the James and Department of Virginia. With this command he was engaged in the various operations terminating in the evacuation of Richmond and surrender of General Lee.

He was twenty years a general,—commanding, after the Rebellion, the Departments of Ohio, Arkansas, 4th Military District, Departments of California, Platte, and Texas. He was retired with the rank of major-general.

On one occasion he saved a worthless member of his company from drowning, in San Francisco Bay, by jumping from the deck of the steamer into the bay after him.

The War Department order that announced his death closed with these words: " As his intimate associate since boyhood, the general (Sherman) here bears testimony of him that a more unselfish, manly, and patriotic person never lived."

## CAPTAIN GILBERT E. OVERTON. U.S.A. (RETIRED).

CAPTAIN GILBERT E. OVERTON was born in New York City March 18, 1845. At the breaking out of the war he was attending school in New York City, and it was intended by his parents to educate him for the law. He entered the service as second lieutenant of the Fourth New York Cavalry September 26, 1861, when but sixteen years old, and was consequently one of the youngest officers in the service. He was honorably mustered out April 29, 1862, but re-entered the volunteer service as first lieutenant and adjutant of the Twelfth New York Cavalry October 25, 1862, from which he was honorably mustered out March 2, 1863. He then, for the third time, entered the service as first lieutenant and adjutant Twelfth New York Cavalry September 21, 1863, and at the close of the war he was honorably mustered out July 19, 1865.

During his volunteer service he participated in the Shenandoah Valley campaign of 1862, and in campaigns in North Carolina in 1863 to 1865. He was appointed in the regular army as second lieutenant of the Sixth U. S. Cavalry October 2, 1867; was promoted first lieutenant May 22, 1872, and captain December 30, 1881.

He was, for over twenty years, on active duty on the plains of the Southwest, during which period he operated against most of the powerful savage tribes of that section. Fourteen years of his service were passed in the territories of Arizona and New Mexico. In his report to the War Department of a fight with the Cheyenne Indians, August 30, 1874, Colonel Nelson A. Miles, Fifth Infantry, commanding, stated, " A splendid charge was made by the First Battalion. . . . companies D, F, and G, Sixth Cavalry . . . Lieutenant Overton . . . respectively, as commanding officers . . . up a steep crest, and the position carried in fine style ;" and at the conclusion of that hard campaign the same officer, under date of March 11, 1875, recommended to the War Department, " that First Lieutenant G. E. Overton, Sixth Cavalry, be brevetted captain U. S. A., for distinguished service in leading a cavalry charge in the engagement on McClellan Creek, Texas, November 8, 1874, and for faithful services during the campaign." This brevet was not granted, owing to the fact that brevets for Indian service are not granted in the U. S. Army. Major George B. Sanford, First Cavalry, commanding, in his report (dated October 5, 1881), to the department commander, of a fight between his (Sanford's) battalion and Chiricahua Indians (near Fort Grant), Arizona, states, " The officers engaged were Lieutenant G. E. Overton, Sixth Cavalry, . . . all of whom are deserving of the highest commendation."

Under date October 22, 1881, Adjutant-General J. C. Kelton (Military Division, Pacific), states, in an indorsement on a communication from Lieutenant G. E. Over-

ton, reporting the results in practical tests of recent improvements in arms, " Lieutenant Overton, Sixth Cavalry, has always shown himself a brilliant young cavalry officer, very observant and progressive. The troop he commands is one of the best drilled and most enterprising of his regiment."

Colonel James W. Savage, who commanded the Twelfth New York Volunteer Cavalry during the war of the Rebellion, states, in a communication to the President (Andrew Johnson), dated Omaha, Nebraska, February 1, 1868, and after referring to Lieutenant Overton's original entry into the volunteer service, and his having twice declined promotion in order that he might retain the adjutancy of his (Savage's) regiment, " at the organization of the First Florida (loyal) Cavalry, he was offered a majority in that regiment, but he preferred to remain with the Twelfth New York Cavalry. He distinguished himself for bravery at the two attacks upon New Berne, North Carolina, in the early part of 1864 ; at the attack on Kinston, North Carolina, in December of the same year; at the battle of Wise's Forks, in March, 1865 ; and in numerous other affairs of minor importance during the war. On the 8th of March, 1865, at Wise's Forks, he led a most brilliant and successful charge, bringing in more prisoners than were taken by the remainder of the Federal forces (in an entire division) engaged during the entire day. His ability in the position of adjutant became well known in the department where the regiment served."

In July, 1889, Captain Overton left his post—Fort Stanton, New Mexico—on sick-leave, and after spending two years in Europe for his health, he was finally retired from active duty (in February, 1891), in consequence of permanent disability contracted in the line of duty. In May, 1891, he returned from Europe and established his permanent home in Washington, D. C.

### LIEUTENANT-COLONEL JOHN H. PAGE, U.S.A.

LIEUTENANT-COLONEL JOHN H. PAGE (Twenty-second Infantry) was born in Delaware, March 26, 1842. He is the son of Captain John Page, 4th Inf., who was horribly wounded by a cannon-shot in the battle of Palo Alto, May 8, and died of his wound July 12, 1846. Colonel Page entered the military service as a private in Company A, First Illinois Light Artillery, August 25, 1861, and while serving as a volunteer he was appointed a second lieutenant in the Third U. S. Infantry, to date from August 5, 1861. This appointment he accepted October 24, 1861, and was, in consequence, honorably discharged from the volunteer service on that date.

Joining his regiment, he served with it in Washington during the winter of 1861, and was promoted first lieutenant March 12, 1862, taking the field with the regular brigade in the Army of the Potomac, and participating in the Peninsula campaign, being engaged in the siege of Yorktown, battles of Gaines' Mill, Malvern Hill, and second Bull Run. He also participated in the Maryland campaign, and was engaged in the battle of Antietam; in the Rappahannock campaign, and engaged in the battle of Fredericksburg, Virginia, and the subsequent movements, terminating with the battle of Chancellorsville, Virginia; in the Pennsylvania campaign, and engaged in the battle of Gettysburg and subsequent march back to the Rappahannock River, from whence his regiment was despatched to assist in quelling the draft riots in New York City, encamping in Washington Square.

Returning to the Army of the Potomac in September, he was engaged in the Rappahannock Station and Mine Run fights. He wintered at Bristol Station, Virginia, guarding the railroad bridges, when his regiment was ordered again to duty in New York City. He was promoted captain 6th of May, 1864, and was in command of Fort Wadsworth, New York harbor, serving as instructor of heavy artillery to the Sixty-ninth New York militia during the scare produced by the privateer "Alabama," for which service he was appointed chief ordnance-officer of the city and harbor of New York, serving until the spring of 1865, when, with his regiment, he again joined the Army of the Potomac, serving with the Provost Brigade attached to the head-quarters of the army, and commanded the Third Infantry at the surrender of Lee at Appomattox. At the close of the war he was made brevet captain December 13, 1862, for "gallant and meritorious services in the battle of Fredericksburg, Virginia;" brevet major July 2, 1863, for "gallant and meritorious services in the battle of Gettysburg, Pennsylvania."

In the fall of 1865 he, with his regiment, started for the frontier, wintering at Jefferson Barracks, Missouri. In the spring of 1866 he was at Leavenworth, Kansas, from which post he marched to the Smoky Hill River, and aided in building Fort Harker, Kansas. In November of the same year he marched to Fort Dodge, Kansas, wintering in dug-outs on the banks of the Arkansas. Indian hostilities had been uninterrupted since his arrival at Fort Dodge, of which he had his fair share, and when the troops for the campaign of 1868 were assembled, General Alfred Sully, commanding, placed him in command of the infantry column, leaving him after the campaign was over to build Camp Supply, Indian Territory, and gather the hostile Indians there until such time as the Interior Department was ready to assume control of them. In 1871 he changed station to Fort Lyon, Colorado, and in July, 1874, was ordered South with his regiment, serving at Holly Springs, Mississippi, and New Orleans, Louisiana (during White League troubles), Jackson Barracks, McComb City, and Holly Springs, from which place he was ordered to duty in Indiana and Pennsylvania during the railroad riots of 1877. The regiment, being concentrated at Wilkesbarre, Pennsylvania, was ordered by telegraph to Montana, via Corinne, Utah, from which point it marched to Helena, building log-houses on its arrival. The spring found his regiment again on the march to Milk River region, his company reaching Frenchman's Creek November, 1878, when, after arresting the Canadian Indians trespassing on the Assinaboine hunting-grounds, he took station at Fort Shaw, Montana. In 1884 he was at Fort Missoula, where he received, on the 12th of September, 1885, his majority in the Eleventh Infantry. He joined his new regiment at Fort Abraham Lincoln, Dakota; 1886 found him in command of Fort Yates, Dakota. In August, 1887, his regiment was ordered to Fort Niagara, New York, which post he commanded until 1889, when he was ordered to Madison Barracks.

He was promoted lieutenant-colonel February 24, 1891, and assigned to duty with the Twenty-second Infantry at Fort Keogh, Montana.

## COLONEL AND BREVET BRIGADIER-GENERAL INNIS N. PALMER, U.S.A. (RETIRED).

COLONEL AND BREVET BRIGADIER-GENERAL INNIS N. PALMER was born in New York, and graduated from the Military Academy July 1, 1846. He was promoted brevet second lieutenant Mounted Rifles the same day, second lieutenant July 20, 1847, and first lieutenant January 27, 1853. He served during the war with Mexico, and arrived at Vera Cruz March 9, 1847; participated in the siege of Vera Cruz, the battles of Cerro Gordo, Contreras, Churubusco, Chapultepec (severely wounded), and in the assault upon and capture of the City of Mexico; commanded Company B of the police in the City of Mexico from December 18, 1847, to June 5, 1848; returned to Jefferson Barracks in July, 1848; served as acting adjutant of his regiment to March 25, 1849, when he was on regimental recruiting service at St. Louis until May; then he rejoined his regiment near Fort Leavenworth and marched with it to Oregon City, where he arrived about the 15th of October; he served as acting adjutant of his regiment from October 14, 1849, to May 1, 1850, and held the position until July 1, 1854; returning East, served at Jefferson Barracks in 1851, and during the years 1852-54 was employed in Indian campaigns in Texas, and had stations at Forts Merrill, Ewell, and Inge; he was on recruiting service in Baltimore when appointed a captain in the Fifth (old Second) Cavalry, to date from March 3, 1855; joined at Jefferson Barracks August 27, 1855; marched with the regiment to Texas, and arrived at Fort Mason January 14, 1856, where he served until July, when he was assigned to the command of Camp Verde, which he retained until May, 1858, and was employed during January and February, 1858, in operations against hostile Indians near the head-waters of the Brazos and Colorado Rivers; returned to Fort Mason in May, 1858, and about one month later proceeded to Fort Belknap, where the regiment was ordered to concentrate for the march to Utah; but the order was revoked, and he was assigned to duty at that post, where he served until January, 1859. He returned to duty in October, 1860, and conducted a detachment of recruits to Texas, and rejoined his company at Camp Cooper January 5, 1861. He marched his company to Green Lake, where he was joined by five other companies; then conducted the battalion to Indianola, and there embarked on the steamship "Coatzacoalcos," and arrived in New York harbor April 11, 1861, proceeding directly to Washington, where he was employed in guarding the Treasury building and served in the defences of the city; commanded the regular cavalry in the Manassas campaign; served as a member of a board convened at Washington in August, 1861, for the examination of officers who were reported to be unable to perform field-service; commanded the regiment in the defences of Washington from August 28, 1861, until March, 1862, when he participated in the Virginia Peninsula campaign as a brigade commander in the Fourth Corps, Army of the Potomac, having been appointed brigadier-general of volunteers September 23, 1861, and was engaged in the siege of Yorktown, in the battles of Williamsburg, Fair Oaks, Glendale, and Malvern Hill; he was then employed in organizing and forwarding to the field New Jersey and Delaware volunteers, and in superintending camps of drafted men at Philadelphia, until December, 1862, when he was transferred to North Carolina, where he served until June, 1865; commanded at different periods the First Division of the Eighteenth Army Corps, the Department of North Carolina, the District of Pamlico, the Eighteenth Army Corps, the defences of New Berne, the Districts of North Carolina and Beaufort, and participated in March, 1865, in General Sherman's movements, and was engaged in the action of Kinston; joined his regiment at Fort Ellsworth, Kansas, on the 21st of May, and commanded it until September; he was on leave of absence until December, and rejoined the regiment at Fort Laramie, Wyoming, and commanded it until August, 1867, and again from November, 1867, to July, 1868; served as a member of a board convened at Washington to pass upon a system of cavalry tactics from July, 1868, to June, 1869. He served at Omaha Barracks and Fort Sanders, Wyoming, until retired from service March 20, 1879.

Colonel Palmer was brevetted major-general of volunteers, and also lieutenant-colonel, colonel, and brigadier-general U. S. Army, for gallant and meritorious services. He was promoted major Second Cavalry April 25, 1861; lieutenant-colonel Second Cavalry September 23, 1863; and colonel Second Cavalry June 9, 1868.

LIEUTENANT-COLONEL DAINGERFIELD PARKER,
U.S.A.

LIEUTENANT-COLONEL DAINGERFIELD PARKER (Thirteenth Infantry) was born in New York May 23, 1832. He is the great-grandson of Richard Parker, of Westmoreland County, Virginia, the first judge of the Court of Appeals, and signer of the "Protest to the Stamp Act;" great nephew of Colonel Richard Parker (killed at the head of his regiment at the siege of Charleston, South Carolina, during the Revolutionary War); of Colonel Alexander Parker, an officer of the Revolutionary army, and afterwards colonel of the Fifth Regiment of Infantry (regular army), 1808; of Thomas Parker, an officer of the Revolutionary army, and afterwards colonel of the Twelfth (regular) Infantry, in 1812, and promoted (1813) brigadier-general; grandson of William Harmar Parker, a lieutenant in the Virginia State Navy during the war of the Revolution.

The subject of this sketch entered the regular service at the commencement of the war of the Rebellion, as second lieutenant Third Infantry, April 26, 1861. He was promoted first lieutenant May 30, 1861, and served in General Patterson's Virginia campaign, 1861. He was with the Army of the Potomac, and engaged at the battles of first and second Bull Run, Antietam, Fredericksburg, Chancellorsville, and Gettysburg, where he was slightly wounded. He was with his regiment enforcing the draft in New York City, and then on recruiting duty in Washington, D. C. He commanded Fort Slocum during the attack of the rebel General Early upon Washington, D. C., in the autumn of 1864. Lieutenant Parker was promoted captain in October, 1863, and was at Governor's Island, New York harbor, and commanding three companies of his regiment in Washington, D. C., to 1865. He was brevetted major for "gallant and meritorious services at the battle of Gettysburg, Pennsylvania." He commanded his regiment at the head-quarters Army of the Potomac in the spring of 1865; commanded the Military Prison, St. Louis, Missouri, from October, 1865, to April, 1866, when he was ordered to Fort Leavenworth, Kansas, and commanded a detachment engaged in an expedition against hostile Indians to October, 1866. He was then stationed at Fort Harker, Kansas, and commanded a battalion engaged in an expedition against hostile Indians to September, 1867, and was then at Fort Leavenworth, Kansas, to September, 1868.

Major Parker was at Fort Larned, Kansas (commanding post), from September, 1868, and from February, 1869, to October, 1870; then stationed at Fort Leavenworth, Kansas, to July, 1874, when the Third Infantry changed station to the Department of the Gulf. He was stationed at Holly Springs, Mississippi, in July and August, 1874; in command of post at Shreveport, Louisiana, from September, 1874, to July, 1876; at Baton Rouge, Louisiana, for a few weeks, when, after a four months' leave, he was stationed at New Orleans, Louisiana, until the early part of 1877; then for a brief period in command at Holly Springs, Mississippi, and afterwards at Jackson, Mississippi.

He was ordered North during the labor riots of 1877, stopping for brief periods at Louisville, Indianapolis, and Pittsburg, eventually conducting seven companies of the Third Infantry to Scranton, and afterwards to Wilkesbarre, Pennsylvania. He was ordered West to Montana Territory the same year with the regiment, going by rail to Corinne, Utah, and marching thence to Helena. He was stationed in Montana at various posts (alternating with field-service) until August, 1880, when he established Fort Maginnis, Montana. He was then on leave for eight months the following year, returning to Montana (Fort Shaw) in May, 1882. He was then ordered on recruiting service in Philadelphia until September, 1883, and then stationed at David's Island, New York harbor, to April, 1884.

He was promoted major Ninth Infantry April 14, 1884, and was stationed at Fort D. A. Russell, Wyoming, from June, 1884, to July, 1886; thence at Fort Wingate, New Mexico, until February, 1887; at Whipple Barracks, Arizona, until October, 1887; thence to San Diego Barracks, California (in command), until July, 1889; then on leave for four months. He was promoted lieutenant-colonel May 15, 1889, and was in command of Depot General Recruiting Service, New York harbor, from October, 1889, to October, 1891. Thence, after one month's leave, to Fort Supply, Indian Territory, remaining there from November 3 to December 3; thence to Fort Sill, Oklahoma Territory, assuming command of that post February 13, 1892.

## COMMODORE FOXHALL A. PARKER, U.S.N.
### (DECEASED.)

COMMODORE FOXHALL A. PARKER was a son of Commodore F. A. Parker, of the United States Navy, and was born in New York. Appointed from Virginia March 11, 1839; attached to sloop "Levant," West India Squadron, 1840; served in Florida against the Indians. Promoted to passed midshipman June 29, 1843; steamer "Michigan," on the Lakes, 1844-45; Coast Survey, 1848; Mediterranean Squadron, 1849-50. Commissioned as lieutenant September 28, 1850; steam-frigate "Susquehanna," East India Squadron, 1851-53; Coast Survey, 1854-55; unemployed, 1856-59; Pacific Squadron, 1859-61; navy-yard, Washington, as executive-officer, 1861-62; doing duty with the navy on the Potomac, and with the army at Alexandria; while attached to the navy-yard at Washington, was ordered, two days after the battle of Bull Run, to Fort Ellsworth, with two hundred and fifty seamen and marines, to protect it from the attack of General Beauregard, who was expected to storm it, and by his prompt and vigorous action contributed greatly to the safety of Alexandria, and to rallying the men from their demoralization after the defeat at Bull Run. Commissioned as commander July 16, 1862; commanding steam-gun-boat "Mahaska," 1863; in command of the naval battery on Morris Island, at the bombardment of Fort Sumter, from the 17th to the 23d of August, 1863; engaged with skirmishes with batteries on the Potomac and Rappahannock Rivers, and off Wilmington, North Carolina, with rebel troops on shore, while commanding the "Mahaska," in 1863, and the Potomac Flotilla, in 1864-65; on one occasion, at the head of a small detachment of soldiers and marines, with two howitzers manned by seamen, Commander Parker marched some distance into Virginia and drove a force of over one hundred cavalry out of Matthew's Court-House, which he took possession of; Bureau of Navigation, 1866. Commissioned as captain July 25, 1866; special duty, Hartford, Connecticut, 1867-68; navy-yard, Boston, 1869-70; commanding frigate "Franklin," European Squadron, 1870-71; member Board of Examiners, 1872. Commissioned as commodore November 25, 1872; was chief of staff to the North Atlantic Fleet, 1872; ordered to special duty at Washington August 7, 1872, to draw up a code of signals for steam tactics, and chief signal-officer of the navy, 1873-76. In 1863 he prepared, by order of the Navy Department, systems of "Fleet Tactics under Steam," and "Squadron Tactics under Steam;" in 1865, "The Navy Howitzer Afloat;" and in 1866, "The Naval Howitzer Ashore," all of which works are text-books at the Naval Academy. Was one of the founders of United States Naval Institute, organized October 9, 1873, at Annapolis, "for the advancement of professional and scientific knowledge in the navy." In December, 1874, Commodore Parker was appointed chief of staff of the united fleets under command of Admiral Case, which were assembled for instruction in tactics in the Florida waters; commanding navy-yard, Boston, Massachusetts, 1877-78; superintendent Naval Academy, 1878-79. Died June 10, 1879, while in command of the Academy.

Commodore Parker was the author of several works, most of them on professional subjects.

SURGEON JOSEPH B. PARKER, U.S.N.

SURGEON JOSEPH B. PARKER was born June 20, 1841, in Bloomfield, Perry County, Pennsylvania. His father died the year after the birth of the subject of this notice, and the family removed to Carlisle, Pennsylvania, where he was brought up, being educated at the public schools, and then to Dickinson College, from which, in due course, he received the degrees of Bachelor of Arts and Master of Arts. While in college he had been much attracted by the course in physiology, and this had an influence in determining him to pursue the study of medicine. His family had by this time moved to Martinsburg, now in West Virginia, the home of his mother's ancestors, and circumstances rendered it expedient for him to study at the medical college at Richmond, in that State, but he afterwards studied in New York, and received his degree of medical doctor in that city.

He intended to settle in Virginia, to practise his profession, but the breaking out of the Civil War interfered with his plans, and he repaired to Baltimore, Maryland, and offered his services to the surgeon in charge of the United States hospital on Camden Street, which, in 1862, was crowded with wounded and sick. Here, under competent superior officers, young Parker had a valuable experience, which prepared him for the responsibility involved in his subsequent position, and gave him, in addition, the habit of prompt decision. As the military hospitals of Baltimore increased in number, Dr. Parker was transferred to the one in Calvert Street, to take part in its organization.

In the autumn of 1862 he left this place to become one of the seventy-five medical cadets provided for by Act of Congress, for service in hospitals and in the field. He was immediately ordered to assist in the organization of the Campbell Hospital, Washington, with a capacity of one thousand beds. He was afterwards, at his own request, transferred to the Lawson Hospital at St. Louis, Missouri, devoted to surgical cases alone.

The government at that time needed medical officers for service in the Mississippi Squadron, and made an appeal for competent ones. Dr. Parker therefore left the Lawson Hospital, and was appointed acting assistant surgeon in the navy, in March, 1863.

He reported to Admiral Porter, whose flag-ship was then lying at the mouth of the Yazoo, and received orders assigning him to the hospital transport "Red Rover." From the hospital-boat he was temporarily ordered to the gun-boat "Forest Rose," at her station in sight of Vicksburg, on account of an epidemic of small-pox on board that vessel. When she was pronounced clear, he returned to the "Red Rover," and, after some months, was transferred to Naval Hospital, Memphis, Tennessee. Here he remained until the termination of the war and the reduction of the naval forces. After two months' leave he was "honorably discharged, with the thanks of the Department," October, 1865. After some months of professional study, Dr. Parker settled in Baltimore, as a practitioner, and was fairly successful; but years of public service had rendered the new and exacting conditions of private practice hard to accept. In October, 1866, he appeared before the Examining Board at Philadelphia, and, having passed, was appointed an assistant surgeon in the regular service. His first orders were to the Naval Academy at Annapolis, where he remained until his promotion to passed assistant surgeon. This occurred quite soon, on account of an Act of Congress, applicable in all cases where service in the volunteer navy had been rendered. In August, 1876, he was promoted to be surgeon.

During his service of more than twenty-five years in the regular navy, he has served at sea on all foreign stations, except the European. He has been employed on shore at most of the Eastern naval establishments.

Surgeon Parker was for some time on special duty at the Bureau of Medicine and Surgery, at Washington, and was then assistant to the bureau. During an interregnum he acted as chief of the bureau.

He was lately, for three years, surgeon of the navy-yard at Boston.

# REAR-ADMIRAL THOMAS PATTISON, U.S.N.
## (RETIRED.)

REAR-ADMIRAL THOMAS PATTISON was born in New York in 1822; appointed midshipman March, 1839; served in the Pacific Squadron from 1839 to 1842; attached to the receiving-ship "Ohio" in 1843, and at the Naval School, Philadelphia, from 1844 to 1845; promoted to passed midshipman July 2, 1845. From 1846 until 1848, during the Mexican War, served on board the following ships as passed midshipman and sailing-master: The steamer "Princeton," "Raritan" and "Cumberland" frigates, the ordnance-ship "Electra," steamer "Scorpion," and gun-boat "Reefer." Coast Survey in 1850 and 1851; sailing-master of the sloop "Portsmouth," in the Pacific, from 1851 to 1853. Promoted to master in 1854. Commissioned a lieutenant September 12, 1854; served on board the "Ohio," receiving-ship at Boston, in 1855 and 1856; navy-yard, Boston, in 1857; steam-frigate "Mississippi," East India Squadron, 1857 to 1860; Naval Station, Sackett's Harbor, Lake Ontario, from 1860 to 1861. At the breaking out of the war, ordered executive-officer of the "Perry;" in June, 1861, the "Perry" had an engagement off Charleston with the rebel privateer "Savannah," and captured her after an engagement of forty minutes; commanded the steamer "Philadelphia," the heaviest armed vessel in the Potomac flotilla, in 1861; had several engagements with the Acquia Creek and Potomac River batteries; the ship injured in the last fight with the Potomac batteries. Commissioned as lieutenant-commander July 16, 1861; commanded steamer "Sumter," South Atlantic Blockading Squadron, in 1862. In 1863 ordered to Admiral Porter's Fleet on the Mississippi River; commanded the "Dolson" in 1863; ordered same year as commandant of Naval Station at Memphis, Tennessee, and served until 1865. Commissioned as commander March 3, 1865; commanded steamer "Muscota," Atlantic Squadron, during 1866 and 1867; navy-yard, Norfolk, in 1867 to 1870. Commissioned as captain July 3, 1870; commanded steam-frigate "Richmond" during the years of 1872 and 1873, serving in the North Atlantic Squadron and in the Pacific Squadron; also commanded the steamer "Saranac," of the Pacific Squadron, in 1874; commanded the receiving-ship "Independence," at Mare Island, California, in 1874 to 1877. Commissioned a commodore December 11, 1877, and ordered to command the Naval Station at Port Royal, South Carolina, 1878 to 1880; July 1, 1880, ordered to command navy-yard, Washington, and continued in command until July 1, 1883.

Promoted to rear-admiral November 1, 1883, and placed on the retired list February 8, 1884, having reached the prescribed age for retirement.

COLONEL AND BREVET BRIGADIER-GENERAL
GABRIEL R. PAUL, U.S.A. (DECEASED).

COLONEL AND BREVET BRIGADIER-GENERAL GABRIEL R. PAUL was born in Missouri. He was promoted brevet second lieutenant and assigned to the Seventh Infantry upon his graduation at the Military Academy, July 1, 1834, and was on duty at the frontier posts of Red Fork, Indian Territory, 1834; Fort Gibson, Indian Territory, 1834 to 1836; camp Nacogdoches, Indian Territory, 1836, and again at Fort Gibson, Indian Territory, 1836 to 1839.

He was promoted second lieutenant Seventh Infantry December 4, 1834, and first lieutenant Seventh Infantry October 26, 1836. He participated in the Florida War in 1839, serving against the Seminole Indians, a camp of whom he surprised near Tampa Bay in 1842.

He was on duty at the various garrisons in the South from 1842 to 1845, and during the war with Mexico (1846 to 1848) he was engaged in the defence of Fort Brown May 3 to 9, and participated in the battle of Monterey September 21 to 23, 1846.

He was promoted captain Seventh Infantry April 19, 1846.

From March 9 to 29, 1847, he was engaged in the siege of Vera Cruz, and participated in the battles of Cerro Gordo, April 17-18, where he was wounded; Contreras, August 19 to 20; Churubusco, and of Molino del Rey, September 8, 1847.

He participated in the storming of Chapultepec, September 13, 1847, with much distinction and bravery, and in recognition of the services rendered he was " brevetted major September 13, 1847, for gallant and meritorious conduct in the battle of Chapultepec, Mexico," and in 1848 he was presented, by citizens of St. Louis, Missouri, with a sword for his services in Mexico.

From 1848 to 1850 he was on recruiting service, and in garrison at Fort Leavenworth, Kansas, and in 1851 on duty at Jefferson Barracks, Missouri. He was on frontier duty at Corpus Christi, Texas, 1851-52, and accompanied the expedition on the Rio Grande, Texas, 1852, in which he captured Caravajol and his gang of desperadoes, April 1, 1858.

He served in garrison at different posts till 1858, when he accompanied the Utah Expedition, 1858 to 1860, being engaged in the surprise and capture of a camp of hostile Indians on Spanish Fork, Utah, October 2, 1858. He marched with his company to New Mexico in 1860, serving at Albuquerque and Fort Fillmore, New Mexico, to 1861.

On April 22, 1861, he was promoted major of the Eighth Infantry, and served during the war of the Rebellion, 1861 to 1865. He was appointed colonel of the Fourth New Mexico Volunteers December 9, 1861, and participated in the operations in New Mexico, 1861-62, being engaged as acting inspector-general of the Department of New Mexico from July 13 to December 13, 1861, on which date he assumed command of Fort Union, New Mexico, and of the Southern Military District of New Mexico, to March, 1862.

He was promoted lieutenant-colonel Eighth Infantry, U. S. A., April 25, 1862, and participated in the Rappahannock campaign (Army of the Potomac), December, 1862, to May, 1863, being engaged in the battles of Fredericksburg, December 13, 1862, and Chancellorsville, May 2 to 4, 1863. He was appointed brigadier-general U. S. Volunteers April 18, 1863, and participated in the Pennsylvania campaign, Army of the Potomac June-July, 1863, being engaged in the battle of Gettysburg, July 1, 1863, where he was severely wounded by a rifle-ball, which deprived him of the sight of both eyes. He was on leave of absence from July 1, 1863, to February 16, 1865, disabled by the Gettysburg wound.

On September 13, 1864, he was promoted colonel Fourteenth Infantry, and from February 16 to June 13, 1865, he was deputy governor of the "Soldiers' Home," near Washington, D. C. From June 13, 1865, to December 20, 1866, he was in charge of the Military Asylum at Harrodsburg, Kentucky.

He was retired from active service February 16, 1865, for disability resulting from wounds received in the line of duty, and on February 23, 1865, he was brevetted brigadier-general U. S. Army for gallant and meritorious services at the battle of Gettysburg, Pennsylvania.

On September 1, 1866, he was mustered out of the volunteer service.

He was the recipient, in November, 1863, of a magnificent jewelled sword, the present of the Twenty-ninth New Jersey Volunteers, as a recognition of his gallant services. He died May 5, 1886.

## REAR-ADMIRAL HIRAM PAULDING, U.S.N.
(DECEASED).

REAR-ADMIRAL HIRAM PAULDING was born December 11, 1797, at Cortlandt, New York, on the farm which New York gave his father, John Paulding, in recognition of his services in the capture of André. In 1811 he was appointed midshipman, and, as he was then not fourteen years of age, was permitted to continue his studies until war was declared against England the next year, when he was ordered to Lake Ontario. From here he was transferred to Lake Champlain, and when the "Ticonderoga" was put into commission was assigned to her, and here he was on September 11, 1814 (a midshipman not seventeen years old doing duty as lieutenant), when McDonough gave battle to the British fleet, and achieved one of the most signal victories of the war. Paulding's courage and intelligence received favorable mention from his commanding officer, and he was voted a sword by Congress. His next service was on the frigate "Constellation," in the war with Algiers; and after a cruise in the Pacific of three years, he obtained leave of absence and secured admission to the private Military Academy of Captain Partridge at Norwich, Vermont.

In 1822, his health failing from study, he went to Boston, and under an assumed name, in the garb of a common sailor, entered a rigging-loft that he might become familiar with that work of his adopted profession. His leave of absence ended, he was ordered to the West Indies, and in 1824 joined the frigate "United States," and was absent in the Pacific Ocean for nearly five years.

Returning from this long cruise, he was permitted a short respite from sea-duty, and it was at this time he was married to the devoted wife who, for nearly fifty years, gave new happiness to his life,—a daughter of Jonathan W. Kellogg, of Flatbush, Long Island.

After a cruise in the Mediterranean, he commanded successively the "Shark," "Levant," "Vincennes," and "St. Lawrence," and in 1855 was appointed to command the West India Squadron.

In returning to the United States the filibuster Walker, he incurred the hostility of the Southern "fire-eaters," and at their behest was relieved of his command. This adventurer had fitted out an expedition in the United States for the purpose of seizing Nicaragua, the intention being to found there a slave government in sympathy with the Southern States. Walker had already landed when Commodore Paulding arrived at Greytown, and the question arose whether to invade the territory of a friendly government for its protection from desperadoes from our shores, or assume that, as he had landed, the United States government had no further responsibility in the matter. It was not Paulding's habit to hesitate between right and wrong, and Walker was seized and returned to the United States. Commodore Paulding was censured by Mr. Buchanan, but he was fully sustained by the people of the country, who, three years later, were called to save their own government from destruction at the hands of those who had been friendly to Walker.

The Congress of Nicaragua voted Commodore Paulding a large tract of land and a sword. Our government permitted the acceptance of the sword, but the land was declined.

In 1861, Commodore Paulding was ordered upon special duty in the Navy Department, to assist the Secretary of the Navy in the reorganization rendered necessary by the defection of many officers of Southern birth. At this time his patriotism, intelligence, and energy were of inestimable value to the country, as also when afterwards he was transferred to command the navy-yard in New York. While attached to the Navy Department, Commodore Paulding was ordered by President Lincoln to destroy the navy-yard at Norfolk, Virginia, and bring from there such vessels as could be removed. This service was performed in a manner which elicited the President's strong commendation, although its success was much impeded by the failure of officers, because of disloyalty, to render assistance expected of them. Some of the vessels had been scuttled and could not be removed.

Great interest was taken by Admiral Paulding in the construction of the "Monitor," and to his foresight was due the fact that the "Monitor" was at Fortress Monroe to meet the "Merrimac."

The labor and anxieties of the war, at his advanced age, told seriously upon his health, and the Rebellion being ended, he was glad to retire to the quiet of his farm at Huntington, Long Island, where, on October 20, 1878, he passed to the better life, mourned by all who knew him.

MEDICAL DIRECTOR GEORGE PECK, U.S.N.
(RETIRED).

MEDICAL DIRECTOR GEORGE PECK is a native of New Jersey, and graduated at the College of Physicians and Surgeons, at New York, afterwards receiving the honorary degree of A.M. from the College of New Jersey, at Princeton; commissioned assistant-surgeon February, 1851. His first duty was on board the "Cyane," in the Gulf and the West Indies,—a most interesting cruise. He crossed the Isthmus of Panama before the construction of the railroad; assisted the survivors of Strain's Darien Expedition; went to the Pacific via the San Juan River and Lake Nicaragua, carrying despatches to the U. S. Minister at Leon, and other important duty; present at the bombardment of San Juan del Norte. He served for a year at the Naval Rendezvous at New York; was then examined and promoted, and ordered to the frigate "St. Lawrence," of the Brazil Squadron, serving in the Paraguay Expedition during the cruise. Upon his return he was attached to the "North Carolina," and then went to the Brazils again in the steam-sloop "Seminole." When that vessel was ordered home, on account of the breaking out of the Civil War, he was commissioned surgeon May, 1861. He served in the "Seminole" against the batteries on the Potomac, and was present at the capture of Port Royal, Fernandina, and Norfolk. He was then detached from that vessel, and was for some time upon marine recruiting duty in New York. After this he served for a year in the "Dictator," of the North Atlantic Blockading Fleet. In September, 1865, he was ordered to the "Vanderbilt," which vessel was the convoy of the "Monadnock" to San Francisco via the Straits of Magellan. En route these vessels witnessed the bombardment of Valparaiso and Callao by the Spanish fleet. He volunteered in aid of the wounded at Callao, and assisted the medical officers on board the "Villa de Madrid" of the Spanish fleet. Tendered his services, also, to the Peruvian medical officers. In June, 1866, he was detached from the "Vanderbilt," and accompanied Commodore John Rodgers from San Francisco across the continent to the Atlantic coast. It was before the railway was completed, and they were escorted a part of the way by a squadron of U. S. cavalry.

Upon his return he was ordered to the navy-yard, New York, but, after about a year's service there, he was ordered to the frigate "Sabine," which took the graduated class of midshipmen from the Naval Academy on a cruise to Europe and the Brazils. They returned in July, 1870, and he was again ordered to the New York Navy-Yard.

Commissioned as medical inspector May, 1871. In May, 1872, he was ordered as fleet-surgeon of the North Atlantic Fleet. Joined the flag-ship "Worcester" at Key West. In February, 1874, he was ordered as a member of the Retiring Board, and for Examination of Officers for Promotion, at Washington. In 1877 he was detached, and ordered as member of the Naval Medical Examining Board.

Commissioned medical director of the grade of captain January 7, 1878. He then, for nearly two years, served on the Retiring Board, and as president of the Medical Examining Board; and then as president of the Board of Physical Examination of Officers for Promotion. On February 29, 1880, he was detached from these duties, and ordered to the Medical Examining Board at Philadelphia. In July of that year he was detached, and ordered to the charge of the Naval Hospital at Mare Island, California. He served there over three years, and then came East on leave, and in December, 1883, was ordered to duty on the Board of Inspection and Survey. After this he was a member of a Court of Inquiry at Washington, and then delegate from the Medical Department of the Navy to the American Medical Association at Washington, 1884, and at New Orleans, Louisiana, in 1885.

Medical Director Peck was again a representative of the Medical Department of the Navy, at Washington, in 1887. Finally, he was ordered as member of the Examining Board, Navy Department, Washington, on November 5, 1887, and detached on July 9, 1888, when, by operation of law, he was transferred to the retired list of officers of the navy.

He is a member of the American Medical Association, American Academy of Medicine, American Public Health Association, New York Academy of Medicine, Society for the Relief of Widows and Orphans of Medical Men, Military Order of the Loyal Legion of the United States, New Jersey Historical Society, and Washington Head-Quarters Association of Moorestown, New Jersey.

## MAJOR AND BREVET COLONEL ALEXANDER C. M. PENNINGTON, U.S.A.

MAJOR AND BREVET COLONEL ALEXANDER C. M. PENNINGTON (Fourth Artillery) was born in New Jersey, January 8, 1838, and graduated at the Military Academy July 1, 1860. He was promoted brevet second lieutenant Second Artillery the same day; second lieutenant February 1, and first lieutenant May 14, 1861. He served in garrison at Fort Monroe, Virginia, until the commencement of the war of the Rebellion, and then was in the defences of Washington to April 4, 1861, being attached to a light battery of the First Artillery (Magruder's). In the defence of Fort Pickens, Florida, in Battery H, Second Artillery, April 19, and was engaged in the bombardments of November 22-23, 1861, and January 1, 1862.

Lieutenant Pennington was then transferred to the Army of the Potomac, and served in the Peninsula, Maryland, and Rappahannock campaigns, with horse batteries, and was engaged in the siege of Yorktown, battle of Williamsburg, action of Mechanicsville, and battles of Gaines' Mill and Malvern Hill, Virginia; action of Boonesborough, battle of Antietam, being with Horse Battery A, Second Artillery (Tidball's). Assumed command of Horse Battery M, Second Artillery, September 23, 1862, and was engaged in action of Shepardstown Ford, Maryland (attached to Pleasanton's Cavalry Brigade), Martinsburg, Nolan's Ford, Philomont, Upperville, Barber's Cross-roads, Corbin's Cross-roads, battles of Fredericksburg and Chancellorsville, Beverly Ford, Hanover, Pennsylvania (attached to Custer's brigade of cavalry), Hunterstown, Pennsylvania; battle of Gettysburg; pursuit of the rebel army, with skirmishes at Monterey Springs, Williamsport, Boonsborough, Hagerstown, and action at Falling Waters. He commanded Horse Battery M, Second Artillery, with Custer's brigade in the Rapidan campaign, and engaged in the actions of James City, Virginia; Brandy Station, Buckland Mills, and Morton's Ford; in the Richmond campaign with the same battery, attached to Wilson's Cavalry Division, and engaged in the battle of the Wilderness; in Sheridan's raid to Haxall Landing, and returning to Newcastle, Virginia, participating in the combats of Yellow Tavern and Meadow Bridge; in Sheridan's raid towards Gordonsville, and engaged in the battle of Trevilian Station.

Lieutenant Pennington was promoted captain March 30, 1864, and was appointed colonel of the Third New Jersey Cavalry October 1, 1864. He participated in Sheridan's Shenandoah campaign, in command of the First Brigade, Third Cavalry Division (Custer's), and was engaged in all the battles, actions, and combats of that army; and was in the Richmond campaign, and engaged at the battles of Five Forks and Sailor's Creek, and action at Appomattox Station, and present at the capitulation of General Lee, April 9, 1865. He then marched to Danville, Virginia, returned to Petersburg, and thence to Washington, D. C., in May, 1865. He was mustered out of the volunteer service July 31, 1865.

He was brevetted "for gallant and meritorious services," captain, June 9, 1863, for Beverly Ford; major, July 3, 1863, for Gettysburg; lieutenant-colonel, Oct. 19, 1864, for Cedar Creek, Virginia; colonel, March 13, 1865, for during the war. He was brevetted brigadier-general of volunteers, July 15, 1865, for faithful and meritorious services. Promoted major Fourth Artillery Nov. 8, 1882.

Colonel Pennington commanded during the war Light (Horse) Battery M, Second Artillery, from Sept., 1862, to Oct., 1864, and then commanded the First Brigade, Third Cavalry Division (Custer's), to Aug. 1, 1865.

At the close of the war, in the fall of 1865, Colonel Pennington was ordered with Light Battery M, Second Artillery, to California, where he remained until 1872, and then his regiment was transferred to the Atlantic coast, where he occupied various stations until 1877, when he participated in suppressing the riots of that year, being in garrison at the Pittsburg Arsenal until October, 1877, when he was ordered to Fort McHenry, Maryland, remaining there until 1881. He was transferred to Light Battery A, Second Artillery, March 18, 1879, and was in garrison at Washington Barracks until November, 1882. He marched with his battery to Yorktown, Virginia, and returned in November, 1881; also to Antietam and Gettysburg in 1882. He was in garrison at Fort Trumbull, Connecticut, from 1882 until September 1, 1885, when he was detailed for duty at U. S. Artillery School, Fort Monroe, Virginia, from September 1, 1885, to June 1, 1892, as director departments of artillery, chemistry, and explosives, callisics, artillery practical exercises, instructor of photography, etc. Inspector of Artillery Department of East since June 2, 1891.

REAR-ADMIRAL A. M. PENNOCK, U.S.N. (DECEASED).

This excellent officer was best known to the navy during the war of the Rebellion for his work at Cairo, at the junction of the Ohio and the Mississippi. This command required a man of courage, of firm will, and, above all, of incessant industry, activity, and vigilance. These were found combined in the subject of this sketch.

ALEXANDER M. PENNOCK was born in Norfolk, Virginia, and was appointed a midshipman from Tennessee April 1, 1828. The custom of appointing lads from the older States as midshipmen from Western States was quite common at that time. Pennock's first cruise was in the frigate "Guerriere" in the Pacific, and he then sailed in the sloop-of-war "Natchez," of the Brazil Squadron. Passing in June, 1834, he served successively in the frigate "Potomac," in the Mediterranean, and the frigate "Columbia," in the East Indies. Promoted lieutenant in March, 1839. Served in 1843-46 in the "Decatur," coast of Brazil; then at the Norfolk Navy-Yard; in the store-ship "Supply," and was first lieutenant of the sloop "Marion," of the East India Squadron. For many months the "Marion" was the only American man-of-war in China, and much devolved upon her. Her "smartness" and general fine condition reflected the greatest credit upon her executive-officer, who, often for months at a time, did not leave the ship.

The "Marion," when lying in the Typa, near Macao, had the experience of having a small frigate to blow up close to her. The ships were moored, and just cleverly swung clear. The scene was appalling, and the destruction of the Portuguese complete. A rain of débris followed, and a pall of smoke drifted over the "Marion." In the midst of it Lieutenant Pennock (who was in temporary command) called to quarters, the decks and bunts of sails were set down, and boats lowered to rescue survivors. These were few. Nine living men were picked up, but six of them died soon after being brought on board the "Marion." He received the thanks of the Portuguese government, but was more pleased with the conduct, in a sudden emergency, of the ship's company he had drilled. During this cruise he had an illness which resulted in the loss of sight of one eye.

He was light-house inspector during the years 1853-56. Commissioned commander in December, 1855, and was on special duty in connection with the steam-frigate "Niagara" in 1857. He was in command of the steamer "Southern Star" in the Paraguay Expedition, 1859-60, and was light-house inspector for the second time, when in 1862 he was ordered to duty as fleet-captain of the Mississippi Squadron, where he remained for two years, gaining, as we have said, a reputation for executive ability of the highest order. He was commissioned as captain January 2, 1863.

In 1866-67 he was captain of the yard at New York. During Admiral Farragut's cruise in European waters, in 1868, he was selected to command his flag-ship, the "Franklin." He was commissioned commodore in May of that year, and he had command of the European Squadron in 1869-70.

From 1871 to 1873 he was in command of the navy-yard at Portsmouth, New Hampshire.

He received his commission as rear-admiral in 1872, and commanded the Pacific Squadron from 1873 to 1875. He was upon special duty when he died, in 1876.

## COLONEL AND BREVET MAJOR-GENERAL GALUSHA PENNYPACKER, U.S.A. (RETIRED).*

COLONEL AND BREVET MAJOR-GENERAL GALUSHA PENNYPACKER is a native of Pennsylvania, belonging to one of its oldest families, whose names are written in the annals of the State and nation. The appointment to West Point from the Sixth Congressional District having been tendered him, he would, but for the war, have probably entered the Military Academy in 1861 or 1862.

General Pennypacker entered the service in April, 1861. Declining, on account of his youth, the appointment of first lieutenant in his company, A, of the Ninth Regiment Pennsylvania Volunteers, he was made a non-commissioned staff-officer of that regiment, and served with it, during its three months of service, in Major-General Patterson's column, in the Shenandoah Valley, Virginia.

He entered "for the war" as captain of Company A, Ninety-seventh Pennsylvania Volunteers, August 22, 1861, and was promoted major October 7 following. The Ninety-seventh Regiment joined the Tenth Corps in the Department of the South, and during the years 1862 and 1863 participated in all the various movements, engagements, and sieges, in which that corps took part, on the coasts of South Carolina (Forts Wagner and Gregg, James Island and siege of Charleston), Georgia (capture of Fort Pulaski), and Florida (taking of Fernandina and Jacksonville).

General Pennypacker commanded his regiment and the post of Fernandina, Florida, in April, 1864, when the regiment was ordered with the Tenth Corps to Virginia, and became part of the Army of the James. Promoted to lieutenant-colonel April 3, 1864, and to colonel June 23 following.

In action in command of his regiment at Swift Creek, May 9; Drury's Bluff, May 16; and Chester Station, May 18. On May 20 he led his regiment in an assault upon the enemy's lines at Green Plains, Bermuda Hundred, receiving three severe wounds, losing one hundred and seventy-five men killed and wounded out of two hundred and ninety-five taken into the charge.

Returned to duty in August, and in action at Deep Bottom on the 16th, and Wierbottom Church on the 25th of same month. In the trenches before Petersburg in August and September.

Assigned to command the Second Brigade, Second Division, Tenth Corps, in September, and on the 29th led his brigade in the successful assault upon Fort Harrison, where he was again wounded, and his horse shot under him.

In action October 7 at Chaffin's Farm, and on the 29th at Darbytown Road. With the first Fort Fisher Expedition under General Butler, December 1 to 31.

General Pennypacker's brigade (composed of New

York and Pennsylvania regiments) formed a portion of the expeditionary corps which, under command of Major-General Terry, made the successful (and perhaps most brilliant of the war) assault upon Fort Fisher, North Carolina, January 15, 1865.

For his distinguished personal gallantry in this assault, when he was most severely (and it was thought for a time mortally) wounded, and "for gallant and meritorious services during the war," Pennypacker received six brevets or promotions as follows: Brevet brigadier-general U. S. Volunteers, January 15, 1865; brigadier-general U.S. Volunteers, February 18, 1865; brevet major-general U. S. Volunteers, March 13, 1865; colonel Thirty-fourth (designation changed to Sixteenth) Infantry, U.S.A., July 28, 1866; brevet brigadier-general U.S.A., March 2, 1867, and brevet major-general U.S.A., March 2, 1867.

The Congressional medal of honor was awarded General Pennypacker for "bravery at the battle of Fort Fisher." He was one of the youngest (if not the youngest) general officers of the war, and was the youngest man in the history of the regular army to be commissioned a colonel and brevet major-general. His commanding general emphasized to the writer of this sketch the declaration that Pennypacker and not himself was the real hero of Fort Fisher, and that his "great gallantry was only equalled by his modesty."

Since the war (with the exception of two years on leave in Europe), General Pennypacker has served in the Southern, Southwestern, and Western States, performing the duties incident to a regimental and post commander. He was temporarily in command of the District of Mississippi in 1867, the Fourth Military District in 1868, the Department of Mississippi in 1870, the United States troops in New Orleans in 1874, and the Department of the South in 1876.

Placed on the retired list of the army in 1883, on account of wounds, he has since resided in Philadelphia.

---
* Condensed from a sketch by Colonel Isaiah Price, U. S. Volunteers, in the *United Service* magazine for January, 1892.

## MEDICAL INSPECTOR THOMAS N. PENROSE, U.S.N.

MEDICAL INSPECTOR THOMAS N. PENROSE was born in Philadelphia, Pennsylvania. His preliminary education was received at the Protestant Episcopal Academy and other schools in Philadelphia, and he was graduated in the Medical Department of the University of Pennsylvania, in the Class of 1858. He has received also (in course) the degree of Doctor of Philosophy from the same university.

He entered the U. S. Navy, November 11, 1861, as assistant surgeon, and soon thereafter was ordered to the United States Navy-Yard at Washington, D. C. Early in 1862 he was ordered to the U. S. S. " Harriet Lane," then preparing for sea, and which afterwards successfully ran the batteries in the Potomac to become the flag-ship of the mortar flotilla, commanded by then Commander, afterwards Admiral, D. D. Porter, attached to Flag-Officer D. G. Farragut's fleet. He was present at the attack and surrender of Forts Jackson and St. Philip, commanding the approach to New Orleans. He was present and took part in the attack on Vicksburg, June 28, 1862, made by the fleet under command of Flag-Officer, afterwards Admiral, David G. Farragut. In the autumn of 1862 he was present at the attack and capture of Galveston, Texas, and on January 1, 1863, was made prisoner-of-war in that desperate engagement which resulted in the capture of the " Harriet Lane." On this occasion the " Harriet Lane" engaged the enemy's vessels, " Bayou City" and " Neptune," in the harbor of Galveston, Texas, sinking the " Neptune," but was finally captured by " boarding," by the " Bayou City," at the third attempt made by that vessel.

After his release he was attached to the U. S. S. " Massachusetts" for several months before the close of the war. After the war, having been promoted to passed assistant surgeon, he was ordered to the China Station, serving on board of the U. S. flag-ship " Hartford" and U. S. S. " Wachusett."

He has made several cruises in the West Indies, being attached on different occasions to the U. S. ships " Swatara," " Marion," and " Ticonderoga," and has cruised in European waters attached to the U. S. S. " Marion." He was promoted to surgeon in May, 1871, and to medical inspector January, 1889.

His last cruise was in the U. S. S. " Richmond," flag-ship of the South Atlantic Station. His shore duty has been at the Philadelphia Navy-Yard; Naval Hospital, Philadelphia; navy-yard, Boston; and member of the Naval Medical Examining Board. At present he is officer in charge of U. S. Naval Hospital at Norfolk, Va.

## CAPTAIN GEORGE HAMILTON PERKINS, U.S.N.
### (RETIRED.)

Of Perkins, as a young lieutenant,—and holding a place which many a man twenty years his senior would have coveted,—Admiral Farragut said, "He was young and handsome, and no braver man ever trod the decks of a ship. His work in the 'Chickasaw' did more to capture the 'Tennessee' than all the guns of the fleet put together." "Praise from Sir Hubert Stanley is praise indeed." Farragut was not lavish of his praises, when fighting was in question, nor did he distribute commendation lavishly when the fight was over,—as some commanders are wont to do. If not another word about Perkins was to be said, Farragut's estimate of him might stand for his epitaph.

CAPTAIN GEORGE HAMILTON PERKINS was born in New Hampshire, October 20, 1836, of most worthy parentage, and entered the Naval Academy at Annapolis in 1851. Here he distinguished himself, especially in gunnery. When he graduated he first served in the "Cyane," at a period when the disturbances on the Isthmus of Panama, about 1856, served to show him some of the duties of a naval officer. Passing over that remarkable time, for the want of space, we may say that, in the same ship, he visited all the British provinces, and then made a cruise in the West Indies, full of interest from the state of things then existing. After this cruise, Midshipman Perkins served in the Paraguay Expedition; came home in the frigate "Sabine," and was at once ordered to the steamer "Sumter," as acting master, for a cruise on the West Coast of Africa. Here he passed through the various scenes familiar to those who have had the same experience, and not of great interest to those who have not. But about the end of that cruise came the mutterings of the Rebellion. The South rushed on their suicidal course as if truly mad, and now "a wall, as of fire, rose up between the officers; every mess in every ship was divided against itself; brothers-in-arms of yesterday were enemies of to-day; and no one spoke of the outlook at home except in bated breath and measured speech, from fear that the bitter cup would overflow then and there, and water turn to blood." God grant that no officers in our time may ever experience the anxiety and distress of those who were on foreign stations in 1860-61!

The young lieutenant at last reached home, to find the country in the throes of war, indeed; and, after a brief leave to recover his health, somewhat shattered by exposure on the African coast, he was ordered as the executive-officer of the "Cayuga," one of the new gun-boats, carrying a battery of an 11-inch gun, a 20-pounder Parrott, and two 24-pound howitzers. She was commanded by Lieutenant N. B. Harrison, a stalwart, loyal Virginian, and afterwards became the bearer of the divisional flag of Captain Bailey, leading the fleet through the obstructions and past the forts at the time of the well-known ascent of

Farragut's fleet towards New Orleans. Such confidence had Harrison acquired in Perkins that he gave in his charge the piloting of the vessel past the forts. He noticed that St. Philip's guns were all aimed at mid-stream, and so coolly steered right under the walls of the fort,—suffering much in masts and rigging, but little in the hull. Once past the last battery, the officers looked back to find themselves alone and in the presence of the enemy's gun-boats and the ram "Manassas." They sustained an unequal combat until the rest of the division arrived. This was carried on muzzle to muzzle for a few moments. When relieved from this entanglement the "Cayuga" pressed on, and at daylight captured the Chalmette regiment, encamped close to the river-bank.

On arriving before New Orleans, Bailey and Perkins went on shore to demand the surrender and the hoisting of the flag. How they escaped the fiendish mob which surrounded them on their way to the mayor's office is a wonder. The story has been told many times, and by none better than by George W. Cable, the well-known author.

After many exciting scenes on board the "Cayuga" and the "New London," Perkins at last found himself in command of the "Scioto," and was about to be relieved after arduous service in that vessel, when the preparations for the capture of Mobile induced him to apply for any duty connected with the enterprise. Farragut knew his man, and appointed Perkins to the command of the "Chickasaw," a double-turretted monitor,—a command much above his rank. Not really completed, and with a green crew, the "Chickasaw" gave ample opportunity for energy, and, although short time for preparation was allowed, he managed to join Farragut off Mobile bar on August 1, and on the 5th the battle was fought, with imperishable fame for the subject of this sketch, then not twenty-eight years of age.

Captain Perkins voluntarily retired in 1891.

## LIEUTENANT-COMMANDER S. LEDYARD PHELPS, U.S.N.

LIEUTENANT-COMMANDER S. LEDYARD PHELPS was one of the "date of 1841," which was so large that it blocked the appointment of midshipmen for several years; but, in time, it produced some of the most creditable and valuable officers the service has ever had. He was appointed midshipman on October 19, 1841; became passed midshipman August 10, 1847; master June 30, 1855, and lieutenant September, 1855. He became a lieutenant-commander in 1862, when that grade was established, and resigned his commission October 29, 1864,—after performing arduous and valuable services during the war of the Rebellion.

Up to that time his service had not differed materially from that of most officers of his grade; but, during the long period for which he served on the Western waters, he had an opportunity of showing his ability in many ways.

When first ordered to Admiral Foote's squadron he was put in command of the "Conestoga," a wooden gun-boat of the river type, with three heavy guns, which vessel rendered a good account of herself at Foote's first fight at Fort Henry, when the navy took the extensive earthworks before the army, delayed by swamps, could get up.

Lieutenant Phelps made some celebrated reconnoissances up the rivers Tennessee and Cumberland,—doing away with the idea that gun-boats would find great obstacles from the operations of the enemy. He afterwards commanded the "Benton" at the battle in front of Fort Pillow, on the Mississippi, when a shot from that vessel exploded the boiler of one of the leading vessels of the rebel naval force. This was really the first purely naval battle of the war; the two squadrons being fairly pitted against each other. But the unwieldy Union iron-clads were so slow that they could barely maintain themselves against the rapid current, and therefore, with the chance of drifting under the enemy's batteries, could not possess themselves of the disabled rebel steamers.

The "Benton" became the flag-ship of Rear-Admiral C. H. Davis, and bore a great part in the naval fight at Memphis, which resulted in a decisive victory,—almost breaking up the Confederate naval force on the great river.

Lieutenant-Commander Phelps afterwards performed most valuable service in the Tennessee River. His command extended from Fort Henry as far up stream as the vessels under his command could go. He chose command of this district to enable him to attend to the reconstruction of the "Eastport," a vessel captured by him in the Tennessee River after the fall of Fort Henry. At the time of the capture, the Confederates were converting her into an iron-clad ram. She afterwards did good service on the Union side.

Lieutenant-Commander Phelps was very active in breaking up the depots whence the rebel conscription officers harried the region of the river Tennessee, and he was most vigilant and useful in assisting the army on many occasions,—in one of which the troops, through his energetic assistance, were enabled to cross the river in good form and push on to Florence, Alabama, where they destroyed about two million dollars' worth of Confederate stores, and captured a number of prisoners.

## REAR-ADMIRAL THOMAS STOWELL PHELPS. U.S.N.

REAR-ADMIRAL THOMAS STOWELL PHELPS was born in Maine in 1822. He is a descendant of General Israel Putnam, and of Colonel Thomas Nixon, of the Revolutionary Army.

He was appointed midshipman from his native State in 1840, and served in the Mediterranean and on the Brazil Station until 1846, when he went to the Naval School, and became passed midshipman. He was then ordered to the "Boston," which ship was wrecked on the island of Eleuthera, West Indies, in November, 1846. He was then ordered to the steamer "Polk," but that vessel, being unseaworthy, returned, and Midshipman Phelps was ordered to the Coast Survey, where he served until 1849. In that year he went to the Mediterranean in the razee "Independence," and served in her and in the "Constitution" until 1851. Upon his return home he was again upon the Coast Survey; ordered to the sloop "Decatur," Pacific Squadron, in December, 1853. In this ship he served in the Indian war in Washington Territory, and was present at the battle of Seattle; was promoted master during this cruise, and lieutenant in September, 1855. In January, 1856, Lieutenant Phelps was ordered to ordnance duty at Norfolk, from whence he went upon the Paraguay Expedition. In 1860 he joined the "Crusader," of the Home Squadron, and, after a few months in her, had command of the "Vixen," on the Coast Survey. While in command of this vessel he took part in the expedition for the relief of Fort Sumter, in March, 1861. As an officer skilled in surveying, and with intimate knowledge of the coast and its inlets and rivers, he was then selected for special service in that direction. This was done by ballot of a board, consisting of chiefs of departments,—a high compliment. From the destruction of buoys and marks for navigation, and the erection of heavy rebel batteries on the Potomac, the river was rendered almost impassable, and the safety of the capital was in jeopardy. A chart and survey of the river became of the first necessity. Selecting two steamers, of several placed at his disposal, Lieutenant Phelps successfully executed this work, although almost continually within range of the enemy's guns, to the full satisfaction of the government. His next service was in command of the "Corwin," on secret service. In her he buoyed the shoals and the entrance to Hatteras Inlet, in preparation for the expedition to that region. He was often under fire in carrying out this duty, and received the thanks of the department for the manner in which it was accomplished.

In December, 1861, he was attached to the North At-

lantic Blockading Squadron, and was in March, 1862, commanding a division at Yorktown and its neighborhood. Destroyed five of the enemy's vessels. In May, by preventing destruction of White House Bridge, and later, at the battle of West Point, and by the ascent of the Mattapony River, he rendered the greatest assistance to the army. Lieutenant-commander in 1862, he was ordered to make another complete survey of the Potomac, which he did, though continually opposed by the enemy with artillery and infantry fire. He continued to serve in the "Corwin," making surveys, in anticipation of naval and military movements. He commanded the iron-clad "Saugus" for a short time, and was then transferred to the command of the sloop "Juniata," in which vessel he served at Fort Fisher. Promoted to commander in August, 1865, he was ordered to command the "Lenapee," in the North Atlantic Squadron; and in April, 1867, he was sent to California, where he served in various capacities. Then he commanded the flag-ship "Saranac" until June, 1883, when, then holding the rank of commodore and the command of the navy-yard at Mare Island, he was detached, and ordered to command the Brazil Squadron, with his flag, as acting rear-admiral, on the "Brooklyn." He was promoted to rear-admiral March 1, 1874. There is no man in the naval service more beloved and respected than Rear-Admiral Phelps. "Perfectly unassuming, and even modest, he has always shrunk from publicity, which has prevented the knowledge—outside of the service—of his cool bravery, his devotion to duty, his seaman-like qualities, and his justice in the execution of authority." In the navy these attributes are well understood.

CAPTAIN JOHN W. PHILIP, U.S.N.

CAPTAIN JOHN W. PHILIP was born in New York August 26, 1840, and appointed to the Naval School from that State in September, 1856. Midshipman January 1, 1861, and attached to the frigates "Constitution" and "Santee." Promoted acting master June 1, 1861, and ordered as executive-officer of the sloop-of-war "Marion," Gulf Blockading Squadron. Was attached to the "Sonoma," James River Fleet, and commissioned lieutenant on July 16, 1862. Was executive-officer of the "Chippewa," "Pawnee," and monitor "Montauk," of the South Atlantic Blockading Squadron, from September, 1862, to January, 1865. In the "Pawnee" was engaged with the rebel batteries in the Stono River, and wounded in the leg. In the "Montauk" in the various actions during the siege of Charleston. Executive-officer of the "Wachusett," Asiatic Squadron, from January, 1865, to September, 1867. Commissioned lieutenant-commander in July, 1866. Executive-officer of flag-ship "Hartford," Asiatic Station, September, 1867, to August, 1868. December, 1868, ordered as executive of the "Richmond," European Station. Detached November, 1871. September, 1872, ordered executive of the "Hartford;" detached, and ordered to command the "Monocacy," on the Station, June, 1873. Was detached from the latter vessel January 8, 1874, and granted leave of absence by the Navy Department for the purpose of taking command of one of the steamers of the Pacific Mail Company, plying between San Francisco and Hong-Kong, China. He commanded the "China," and then the "City of New York." The trip of the latter vessel is one of record, for she made the passage from New York to San Francisco without stopping for coal or repairs. He was commissioned commander December 18, 1874. His leave from the department was revoked in July, 1876, and he was then ordered to command the "Adams." Detached from the "Adams" in April, 1877, and granted leave to command the "Woodruff Scientific Expedition around the World." In December, 1877, he was ordered to the command of the "Tuscarora," engaged in surveying the west coast of Mexico and Central America; was transferred from the "Tuscarora" to the "Ranger" in August, 1880, and detached from the command of the latter vessel in October, 1883. Commander Philip was light-house inspector of the Twelfth District from April, 1884, to April, 1887, and in command of the U. S. receiving-ship "Independence," at the Mare Island Navy-Yard, from May, 1887, to May, 1890. He was commissioned captain March 31, 1889.

From May, 1890, to December, 1890, Captain Philip was a member of the Board of Inspection at San Francisco, and was then ordered to command the "Atlanta," of the Squadron of Evolution. He was detached by order of the Secretary of the Navy in December, 1891, and detailed to superintend the fitting out of the armored cruiser "New York," with the intention of commanding her when she is ready for sea.

## MAJOR DE WITT C. POOLE, U.S.A.

MAJOR DE WITT C. POOLE (Pay Department) was born in New York September 28, 1828. He entered the volunteer service as first lieutenant of the First Wisconsin Infantry May 16, 1861, and participated in the campaign of the Upper Potomac River in that year, and was honorably mustered out October 21, 1861. He re-entered the volunteer service as lieutenant-colonel of the Twelfth Wisconsin Infantry October 31, 1861, and served with his regiment in the campaign of Southwestern Missouri in the winter of 1862; participated in the expedition sent to reinforce the army in New Mexico, from Fort Riley, Kansas; joined the expedition into Central Mississippi in the winter of 1863, and was in advance on the Tallahatchie River, Mississippi. He then returned to Memphis, and was ordered to Vicksburg, in 1863. He was engaged in the action at Falling Waters, Virginia, in 1861; engagement on the Coldwater and at Hernando, Mississippi, May, 1863; and was at the siege and capture of Vicksburg, Mississippi, June and July, 1863.

Major Poole resigned his volunteer commission July 3, 1863, and was appointed lieutenant-colonel of the Veteran Reserve Corps November 15, 1863, and was ordered to duty at Washington, D. C., June, 1864, subsequently joining his regiment at White House Landing, Virginia. In July, 1864, he was ordered to Washington, as acting provost-marshal of the District of Columbia. He performed duty in charge of the provost-marshal's office at Utica, New York; then at Baltimore, Maryland; at Scranton, Pennsylvania; and then with the chief mustering officer of the State of Wisconsin, 1864-65. In December, 1865, he was detailed as commissioner of the Freedmen's Bureau, at Atlanta, Georgia, from which post he resigned his commission in the Veteran Reserve Corps.

Major Poole was appointed to the regular service as captain of the Twenty-fifth Infantry January 22, 1867, and joined his regiment at Memphis, Tennessee. He was then placed on reconstruction duty with his company in Western Tennessee, and afterwards in Georgia,

in 1867-68. He was unassigned April 26, 1869, and performed the duties of Indian agent for the Sioux Indians in Dakota, from June, 1869, to December, 1870, having been assigned to the Twenty-second Infantry the previous October.

Captain Poole participated with his company in expeditions to the Yellowstone country in 1871-73; then employed in suppressing riots at New Orleans in 1874-75. He took part in the Big Horn and Yellowstone expeditions of 1876-77 against Sitting Bull, and was engaged in suppressing the labor riots at Chicago and Wilkesbarre, Pennsylvania, in July, 1877. He was then on garrison duty in 1878, and transferred to Texas, where he served during 1879-80. Then he was detailed for two years on recruiting service at New York.

He was appointed major and paymaster July 5, 1882, and has served at different stations throughout the country, his present station (1891-92) being at Cincinnati, Ohio.

Major Poole performed the duties of adjutant of the First Wisconsin Infantry from June 24, 1861, to August 21, 1861.

ADMIRAL DAVID D. PORTER, U.S.N. (DECEASED).

ADMIRAL DAVID D. PORTER was born in Chester, Pennsylvania, and, as a mere lad, accompanied his father, Captain David Porter, United States Navy, on a cruise in the West Indies for the suppression of piracy. This was in 1824. In 1826 his father was given command of the Mexican Navy, and his son accompanied him, being appointed midshipman in that service, and sent to the City of Mexico to learn the Spanish language. He saw service in cruising against Spanish commerce, and also in operations against Spanish men-of-war, and was finally a prisoner of war in Havana. In February, 1829, young Porter was appointed midshipman in the United States Navy, and, after serving in the Mediterranean, in the frigates "Constellation" and "United States," and the ship-of-the-line "Delaware," was made passed midshipman in 1835; lieutenant in 1841. In the Mediterranean; the Naval Observatory; and commissioner to San Domingo. In the Mexican War served in "Spitfire;" bombardment of Vera Cruz; Lieutenant Porter buoyed out the passage to the flanking forts, and acted as pilot for the flotilla, when a heavy action took place, until withdrawn by Commodore Perry's order. As first lieutenant of "Spitfire" took an active part in the capture of Tuspan and that of Tabasco. Lieutenant Porter, after the obstructions were forced, landed and captured Fort Iturbide. Soon after, Lieutenant Porter received command of the "Spitfire," and was in several other engagements. He was, after the Mexican War, much in command of mail steamers, and some supply duty. Just before the surrender of Fort Sumter, President Lincoln sent him to see if Fort Pickens could be saved. The history of this operation is too long to be given here. Captain Meigs, of the army, accompanied the expedition, and, in twenty-four hours after arrival, the fort was rendered secure against any attack from General Bragg's army, then at Pensacola. The first hostile guns fired by the navy, during the Civil War, were from the 11-inch gun of the "Powhatan," by Lieutenant Porter. He next blockaded the mouths of the Mississippi, until he accidentally learned of the escape of the "Sumter." He then pursued her for a long time, but she succeeded in eluding him, over a wide extent of sea.

Lieutenant Porter was made commander April, 1861, and was at once put in charge of the organization of a mortar flotilla for the purpose of regaining control of the Mississippi, and was consulted on the organization of the fleet for that purpose. He commanded the Mortar Flotilla, and to him the Forts Jackson and St. Philip surrendered, after the passage of Farragut's fleet. After the capture of New Orleans, Admiral Farragut ordered the Mortar Flotilla to Vicksburg, and, under their fire, passed the celebrated batteries. In October, 1862, Commander Porter took command of the Mississippi River Squadron, as acting rear-admiral. Then followed the long history of operations (which cannot be given here) in co-operation with General Sherman. For the capture of "Arkansas Post" Porter received the thanks of Congress. Then came Vicksburg, with Grant in command. The story of the fights there is a matter of history. After Vicksburg, Porter again received the thanks of Congress. The Red River expedition was one of the most curious and picturesque incidents of the great war, and must be read at length by those who are not familiar with it. Lieutenant-Colonel Bailey, by his great engineering ability, rescued Porter's fleet from certain destruction, and saved to the government an immense sum.

Porter was next ordered to the command of the North Atlantic Fleet in September, 1864. A powerful force was collected at Hampton Roads. After much delay, from various causes, the fleet sailed for Fort Fisher. It would be impossible, in this space, even to touch upon the events which followed; an account of them is to be found everywhere. After the fall of Wilmington, Admiral Porter was next at the operations in James River, and accompanied President Lincoln when he entered Richmond. Porter's guns, fired at Richmond, April 2, 1865, were about the last fired by the navy during the war, as his was the first gun of the war at Pensacola.

He was superintendent of the Naval Academy from September, 1865, to December, 1869. Commissioned vice-admiral July, 1866. In that year he was sent to San Domingo, with a large sum in hand, to purchase a lease of Samana Bay and the adjacent peninsula; but, finding the Dominican government hard to deal with, gave up the project and returned to the United States. He was upon special duty in the Navy Department in 1869-70. Was commissioned admiral August 15, 1870; and was upon special duty, at Washington, from 1870 until his death, in that city, on February 13, 1891.

## COLONEL AND BREVET BRIGADIER-GENERAL FITZ-JOHN PORTER, U.S.A. (RETIRED).

COLONEL AND BREVET BRIGADIER-GENERAL FITZ-JOHN PORTER was born in New Hampshire in 1822. He graduated from the Military Academy July 1, 1845, and was promoted the same day brevet second lieutenant Fourth Artillery; second lieutenant June 18, 1846, and first lieutenant May 29, 1847. He is a son of Captain John Porter, U.S.N., and nephew of Commodore David Porter, of "Essex" renown. He served at West Point as an assistant in the Department of Artillery and Cavalry, and engaged in instructing the cadets during encampment, and was later sent to join his regiment at Fort Monroe. In July, 1846, he joined the army operating against Mexico at Point Isabel, Texas, and saw active service at Saltillo in the same year. In January, 1847, he embarked at Brazos and accompanied General Scott's army, performing more or less service during the siege of Vera Cruz and the battles of Cerro Gordo, Contreras, Molino del Rey, and the siege of Chapultepec and the capture of Mexico. At Contreras, Porter's company recaptured two guns belonging to his regiment which had been taken at Buena Vista. General Scott then mounted the company. At the last action during the war,—the sanguinary fight at the capture of the Garita of Belen,—Porter was wounded, while the other two officers of his company were killed, and twenty-seven out of thirty non-commissioned officers and privates were killed or wounded. In 1849 he was assigned to duty at the Military Academy, where he remained until 1855. Here he occupied the positions successively of assistant instructor of natural and experimental philosophy, assistant instructor of artillery, adjutant of the Military Academy, and, finally, instructor of artillery and cavalry. He served during the Kansas troubles. In 1857, while on duty at the head-quarters of the army in New York City, Porter was assigned to duty on the staff of General Albert Sidney Johnston, and accompanied that officer to Utah, enduring with him the hardships and annoyances of that campaign in the Rocky Mountains, and of two years' residence among the resentful and murderous Mormons.

In the autumn of 1860 Porter was assigned to duty at the head-quarters of the army in New York City as assistant inspector-general, in which capacity in November he inspected, by order of the War Department, the defences in Charleston harbor, and recommended that they should be strengthened and supplied with additional force, ammunition, and provisions. As a result of this inspection and of Major Porter's recommendations, Major Robert Anderson was placed in command of Fort Moultrie, and carried out the plans recommended by Porter and arranged between them, to, at the proper time, abandon Moultrie and take possession of Sumter. The secession of the Southern States now began, and

Major Porter was sent to Texas and to reinforce the garrison at Key West and Dry Tortugas, a task requiring great judgment, patience, and tact. In April, 1861, Porter was on duty in the Adjutant-General's Office in Washington, when he was chosen by the Secretary of War, Hon. Simon Cameron, and General Scott, to superintend the protection of the railroad between Baltimore and Harrisburg against Baltimore rioters, and maintain communication through Baltimore to Washington.

Major Porter was now appointed colonel of the Fifteenth Infantry, and shortly afterwards brigadier-general of volunteers. He served with the Army of the Potomac (commanding the Fifth Corps), in the Peninsula, Northern Virginia, and Maryland campaigns, and engaged in all the actions connected therewith. After passing through the latter campaign, and returning with the army to Falmouth, Virginia, he was relieved from his command November 12, 1862, and tried at Washington, D. C., by a general court-martial for disobedience of orders and general misconduct on the battle-field,—offences said to have been committed in the Northern Virginia campaign under General Pope the previous August in connection with the battle of second Bull Run, Virginia.

The court-martial convicted General Porter and sentenced him to be cashiered and forever prohibited from holding any office of profit or trust from the government. For fifteen years General Porter languished under the stigma of this sentence. At last he obtained a Board of General Officers to examine the matter by order of President Hayes, and this board fully exonerated him from all blame. In 1885 a bill passed by Congress authorized the President to restore General Porter to the army, and he was restored and retired as a colonel in the army, with his original commission dated May 14, 1861.

COMMODORE WILLIAM DAVID PORTER, U.S.N.
(DECEASED).

COMMODORE WILLIAM DAVID PORTER, son of Commodore David Porter and brother of Admiral David D. Porter, was born in New Orleans in 1809, and died in New York in 1864. After being educated in Philadelphia, he was appointed midshipman in the navy in January, 1823. He became a lieutenant in 1833. He performed the usual service and made the usual cruises, but was retired by the Retiring Board of September, 1855. Like many others retired by that board, he was restored to the active list (in his case with the rank of commander) September, 1859. When the Civil War broke out he was in command of the sloop-of-war "St. Mary's," in the Pacific. He was ordered home, and then to the Mississippi, to assist in fitting out the gun-boat flotilla for service in those waters. He afterwards commanded one of them, named "Essex" after his father's ship, in which he fought the famous battle with the "Phoebe" and the "Cherub," in which Farragut served as junior midshipman. In the attack upon Fort Henry a shot went through one of the boilers of the "Essex," wounding and scalding twenty-eight officers and men and the commanding officer. He recovered sufficiently to command his vessel at Fort Donelson, February, 1862.

In his favorite "Essex" he ran past the batteries on the Mississippi River, to join the fleet at Vicksburg. He had an engagement with the Confederate iron-clad ram "Arkansas," above Baton Rouge, on July 15, 1862, in which the "Essex" soon destroyed her. At least she was set on fire and blew up; whether this was done by the "Essex's" shells, or by the officers of the "Arkansas" to escape capture, can never be known. At any rate, the Union forces were rid of one of their most formidable enemies. It was a great relief to Farragut, for the "Arkansas" had been a regular *bête noire*. After her destruction he could go to the Gulf and arrange for blockading off Galveston.

The captain of the "Essex" was made commodore in July, 1862. In September, 1862, in an account of an engagement off Port Hudson, Louisiana, he reported that the "Essex," since the 6th of the previous July, had, in her different encounters with the enemy, been struck by heavy shot, perceptibly, one hundred and twenty-eight times, "glancing shot having left no record." "Three have broken the iron, and but one through, and that at a distance of a few feet from the battery delivering it." The "Essex" had been much improved since her first experiences at Forts Henry and Donelson.

Although a man of robust physique, Commodore Porter's health failed from his constant service in a malarious climate, and the effects of his scalds from steam. After the bombardment of Natchez and the Port Hudson batteries, he was obliged to come East an invalid, and never served again. The year of his death is mentioned above.

Commodore W. D. Porter had two sons in the Confederate service,—as happened often during the Civil War,—father arrayed against son, and brother against brother.

## CAPTAIN EDWARD F. POTTER, U.S.N.

CAPTAIN EDWARD F. POTTER was born in New York, and was appointed a midshipman from the State of Illinois on February 5, 1850; first served on board the sloop-of-war "Decatur," of the Home Squadron, and then made a cruise on the coast of Africa, in the frigate "Constitution." Upon his return from this cruise, 1856, he was ordered to the Naval Academy, and was promoted to the rank of passed midshipman in June of that year; made a cruise on the coast of Brazil in the frigate "St. Lawrence," in the years 1857 to 1859, having been commissioned as a lieutenant in July, 1858, during his service in the "St. Lawrence."

In May, 1860, he was ordered to the steam-frigate "Niagara," which vessel had the mission of conveying home the first Japanese embassy, an interesting episode in our relations with that country, which was opened to the world by the American navy.

When the "Niagara" reached home in April, 1861, it was to find the war of the Rebellion fairly begun. Lieutenant Potter was detached from the "Niagara," and ordered to the "Wissahickon," one of the new "ninety-day" gun-boats, so called from the very short time in which they were built. They were schooner-rigged screw vessels, of about five hundred tons, and carrying four guns. They were efficient vessels. In the "Wissahickon" Lieutenant Potter was present at the capture of the forts below New Orleans, and of that city. He became a lieutenant-commander in July, 1862, and afterwards served in the steam-sloop "Lackawanna," the steam-frigate "Wabash," and other war duty. In 1867-68 he was executive-officer of the steam-frigate "Franklin," the flag-ship of Admiral Farragut during his European cruise. Made commander in June, 1869, and was stationed at the navy-yard, Boston. During his next cruise in command of the "Shawmut" he ascended the river Orinoco to Ciudad Bolivar, and recovered from revolutionists there two steamers belonging to an American company. The "Shawmut" was the second American man-of-war to visit Ciudad Bolivar.

In 1880 Commander Potter commanded the U. S. ship "Constellation," which conveyed supplies to Ireland for the sufferers by famine in that island.

He was promoted captain in the navy on the 11th of July of that year. During the years 1881-83, he was attached to the Brooklyn Navy-Yard, and in November, 1883, went to the European Squadron as captain of the "Lancaster." There he remained until 1885, when the ship was sent to the Brazil Station. Captain Potter was in command of the station from December, 1885, until September, 1886, when he was detached and ordered home.

In December, 1886, he was ordered to the command of the League Island Navy-Yard, but was soon after transferred to the Naval Asylum at Philadelphia, as governor of that institution. Then he was ordered to the command of the U. S. S. "Minnesota," training-ship at New York, his present station.

GENERAL JOSEPH HAYDN POTTER, U.S.A.
(RETIRED).

GENERAL JOSEPH HAYDN POTTER was born at Concord, New Hampshire, October 12, 1822. He graduated at West Point Military Academy, July 1, 1843; was promoted in the army to brevet second lieutenant First Infantry July 1, 1843; second lieutenant Seventh Infantry October 2, 1845; brevet first lieutenant September 23, 1846, for gallant and meritorious services in the battle of Monterey, Mexico; first lieutenant Seventh Infantry October 30, 1847; captain Seventh Infantry January 9, 1856; colonel Twelfth New Hampshire Volunteers September 27, 1862; major Nineteenth U. S. Infantry July 4, 1863; brevet lieutenant-colonel December 13, 1863, for gallant and meritorious service at the battle of Fredericksburg, Virginia; brevet colonel May 3, 1864, for gallant and meritorious services at the battle of Chancellorsville, Virginia; brevet brigadier-general U. S. Army, March 13, 1865, for gallant and meritorious services in the campaign terminating with the surrender of the Confederate army under General R. E. Lee; brigadier-general U. S. Volunteers May 1, 1865; mustered out of volunteer service January 15, 1866; lieutenant-colonel Thirtieth Infantry July 28, 1866; transferred to Fourth Infantry March 15, 1867; colonel Twenty-fourth Infantry December 11, 1873; brigadier-general U. S. Army April 1, 1886; retired from active service October 12, 1886.

He served in garrison at Fort Des Moines, Iowa, 1843-45; and Jefferson Barracks, Missouri, 1845; in military occupation of Texas, 1845-46; in the war with Mexico, being engaged in the defences of Fort Brown, May 3-9, 1846; and battle of Monterey September, 1846, where he was wounded in storming the enemy's works; on recruiting service, 1846-48; in the war with Mexico, 1848; in garrison at Jefferson Barracks, Missouri, 1850; on frontier duty at Fort Gibson, Indian Territory, 1850-53; Fort Smith, Arkansas, 1853-55; as adjutant Seventh Infantry, November 16, 1853, to January, 1856; on frontier duty at Fort Gibson, Indian Territory, 1855-56; Fort Arbuckle, Indian Territory, 1857-58; on frontier duty in Utah expedition, 1858-60; marched to New Mexico, 1860, and Fort Webster, New Mexico, 1860; on court-martial duty at Fort Bliss, Texas, 1860-61; on frontier duty at Fort McLane, New Mexico, 1861, and was captured by Texas insurgents at San Augustine Springs, Texas, July 27, 1861, and was not exchanged until August 27, 1862.

He served during the rebellion of the seceding States, 1862-66, in the Maryland campaign (Army of the Potomac), October-November, 1862, being engaged in the march to Falmouth, Virginia, November, 1862; in the Rappahannock campaign (Army of the Potomac), December, 1862, to May, 1863, being engaged in the battle of Fredericksburg, Virginia, December 13, 1862, commanding a brigade; and battle of Chancellorsville, Virginia, May 2-3, where he was severely wounded and captured; as prisoner-of-war May 3 to October, 1863 (paroled May 17, 1863); on special duty October 18, 1863, to February, 1864; as assistant provost-marshal general of Ohio, February to September, 1864; in command of brigade, Eighteenth Corps (Army of the James) September 16 to December 2, 1864, being in command of Bermuda Hundred front during the attack on Fort Harrison, September 29, 1864; in command of brigade of the Twenty-fourth Army Corps December 2, 1864, to January 16, 1865; as chief of staff of Twenty-fourth Army Corps, January 16 to July 10, 1865, being engaged in the attack on the rebel lines at Hatcher's Run, and south of Petersburg, April 2, 1865, and pursuit of the rebel army, with several skirmishes, terminating with the capitulation of General Lee at Appomattox Court-House, April 9, 1865; awaiting orders July 10, 1865, to January 15, 1866; as superintendent of regimental recruiting service at Newport Barracks, Kentucky, February 3, 1866, to January 4, 1867; in command of regiment in Department of the Platte, January 15, 1867. From 1866 to July, 1877, in garrison at Fort Sedgwick, Colorado; Fort Sanders, Wyoming; Little Rock, Arkansas, and Fort Brown, Texas. From July, 1877, to July, 1881, governor of the Soldiers' Home, Washington, D. C.; 1881 to April 1, 1886, in garrison at Fort Supply, Indian Territory. Assigned command of Department of the Missouri, retaining command until retirement, October 12, 1886.

## CAPTAIN CHARLES F. POWELL, U.S.A.

CAPTAIN CHARLES F. POWELL (Corps of Engineers) was born August 13, 1843, at Jacksonville, Illinois. He is a great-grandson of a Revolutionary soldier, and was educated at private and public schools at Milwaukee, Wisconsin. Early in 1861 he joined a newly-formed military company of young men whose services at the outbreak of the Civil War were successively offered for the Second, Third, and Fourth Regiments of Wisconsin Volunteers, but rejected on account of the youth of its members. After most efficient service in aiding to quell the "bank riot" at Milwaukee in the spring of 1861, and upon a renewal of tender of service it was accepted, and the subject of this sketch with his comrades was enrolled, May 10, 1861, in Company B, Fifth Regiment Wisconsin Volunteer Infantry, which regiment was assigned to Hancock's brigade, Smith's division, Army of the Potomac, subsequently incorporated in the Sixth Army Corps, and during its organization in the Light Division of the same corps.

He saw active service in the marches, engagements, and battles of the campaigns of the advances from Washington, 1861-62; Peninsula, second Bull Run, Antietam, Fredericksburg, and Gettysburg, and was promoted to be corporal, sergeant-major, and cadet at the U. S. Military Academy, which he entered from the field September 29, 1863, having been recommended for such cadet appointment by company, regimental, and brigade commanders for "soldierly courage and ability," faithful and "brave conduct," and "gallantry on the field of battle."

He was graduated from the Military Academy June 17, 1867, and promoted to be second lieutenant Corps of Engineers; first lieutenant April 23, 1869, and captain June 17, 1881.

He served as company officer and as battalion quartermaster and battalion recruiting officer of the Battalion of Engineers, and as post quartermaster and commissary, Engineer Department, to May 1, 1871; as assistant engineer on the survey of the North and Northwestern Lakes and the Mississippi River; resident engineer at the Cascades Canal, Oregon; as engineer-in-charge of the same, and of certain river and harbor works in Oregon, Washington, and Idaho; as engineer of the Thirteenth Light-house District; as secretary of the Mississippi River Commission, and assistant to its Construction Committee, and in charge of the survey of the Mississippi River; as engineer-in-charge of the improvements of the Missouri River between the Great Falls and Sioux City, and of the Yellowstone River, and in charge of the survey of the Missouri River from Fort Benton to Sioux City; also on certain boards and commissions concerning public works.

His present station is Sioux City, Iowa.

### LIEUTENANT-COLONEL WILLIAM H. POWELL, U.S.A.

LIEUTENANT-COLONEL WILLIAM H. POWELL was born in the city of Washington September 21, 1838. He is a descendant, on his father's side, of Captain William Powell, who was one of the colonists named in the charter granted by King James I. to the Virginia colony in 1609, and on the mother's side of the Gough family, who accompanied Leonard Calvert, the brother of Lord Baltimore, to this country, and settled in St. Mary's County, Maryland, in 1632.

Colonel Powell's first military service was as a member of Company E, Fourth Battalion District of Columbia Militia, which company tendered its services to the government for the protection of the national capital at the earliest outbreak of the Rebellion, and was mustered into the United States service on the 17th of April, 1861, and was employed guarding the National Treasury and State Department. Having been discharged from this service at the end of three months, he was appointed a second lieutenant of the Fourth U. S. Infantry October 24 of the same year, entering upon duty at once at Governor's Island, New York, where he awaited the arrival of his regiment from California.

He served in the field with the Army of the Potomac during the entire war, and was never absent from duty with his command but ten days on two occasions from the beginning to the end, being engaged in the siege of Yorktown, battles of Gaines' Mill, Malvern Hill, second Bull Run, Antietam, Snicker's Gap, Fredericksburg, Chancellorsville, Gettysburg, Cold Harbor, Petersburg, June 16–18, 1864; battle of the Crater, assault and capture of Petersburg, April 2, 1865, and Appomattox Court-House at the surrender of Lee.

General Buchanan, commanding First Regular Brigade, in his report on the Seven Days' battles, says: "It now becomes my agreeable duty to bring to the especial notice of the commanding general the names of the following officers, whose gallant conduct entitles them to that distinction; . . . Second Lieutenant William H. Powell, adjutant Fourth Infantry, acting assistant adjutant-general of First Brigade."

In report of same, on the second Bull Run, he says: "I would particularly mention my staff, Second Lieutenant William H. Powell, acting assistant adjutant-general. . . . These officers behaved with the utmost coolness and gallantry, and carried my orders to every part of the field to which they were sent with cheerfulness and alacrity."

In report of same on battle of Antietam, he says: "To my staff . . . Second Lieutenant William H. Powell, Fourth Infantry, acting assistant adjutant-general, my thanks are due for the cheerful alacrity and coolness with which they carried my orders to the different portions of the brigade."

In report of same on the battle of Fredericksburg, he says: "My staff, consisting of First Lieutenant William H. Powell, Fourth Infantry, acting assistant adjutant-general, . . . carried my orders with zeal and alacrity, and discharged their duties to my entire satisfaction."

General Ayres, commanding Regular Division, in his report on the battle of Gettysburg, says: "My staff performed their duties with intelligence and gallantry, and have my sincere thanks. I name them in the order of rank; . . . First Lieutenant William H. Powell, Fourth Infantry, aide-de-camp."

Lieutenant Powell was also honorably mentioned in reports for "gallantry in front of Petersburg, June 16–18, 1864," and was recommended by General Grant for the brevet of lieutenant-colonel, for "gallantry at the battle of the Crater," July 30, 1864.

At the close of the war, he was brevetted a captain for "gallant and meritorious conduct" at the battle of Antietam, and major for that of Petersburg, April 2, 1865.

Colonel Powell was promoted to a captaincy in the Fourth Infantry February 2, 1865, and, with the exception of two years on the recruiting-service and three leaves of absence, served continuously with his company for twenty-three years, when he was promoted major of the Twenty-second Infantry. Over twenty-two years of his life have been spent at various posts and on campaign duty west of the Missouri River, the last campaign being that of the Big Horn and Yellowstone, of 1876.

Colonel Powell's literary efforts are to be found in regular contributions to the *United Service Magazine*, in "Battles and Leaders of the Civil War," and in the publication of "Tactical Queries for the Infantry," "Records of Living Officers, U. S. Army," "Hand-book and Guide for Boards of Examination," and "Officers of the Army and Navy (regular) who served in the Civil War." Promoted lieutenant-colonel May 4, 1892.

## REAR-ADMIRAL GEORGE HENRY PREBLE, U.S.N.
(DECEASED).

REAR-ADMIRAL GEORGE HENRY PREBLE, a relative of the Commodore Preble who was distinguished in our early naval service, was a native of Maine, and was appointed midshipman from that State in 1835. He served in the Mediterranean and in the West Indies; was at the naval school at Philadelphia, and warranted passed midshipman in June, 1841. He then served in Florida, as acting lieutenant, in the course of which service he went on several canoe expeditions into the Everglades. After a year of this work he was taken ill, and was sent North and stationed on the receiving-ship at Boston. His health being re-established, he sailed in the "St. Louis," as acting master and acting lieutenant, in May, 1843, for a circumnavigation of the globe. He had charge of the first American armed force ever landed in China,—which was in June and July, 1844,—for the protection of the American consulate and residents at Canton. He was acting master of the "Petrel," in the Gulf of Mexico, during the war with that country, and took part in the operations at Alvarado, Laguna, Tampico, Panuco, and the siege and capture of Vera Cruz, etc. Invalided home, he was made master in July, 1847, and lieutenant in February, 1848. He returned to the Gulf in 1848, but had to be invalided again in 1849. His next service was in the "Legaré," a Coast Survey steamer, and next in the frigate "St. Lawrence," which conveyed American contributions to the World's Fair at London in 1851. He then was in command of the "Gallatin," of the Coast Survey, and attached to the "Vermont," 74. He then joined the "Macedonian," and took part in the Japan Expedition, and served in China from 1853 to 1856. He commanded the chartered steamer "Queen," and assisted in the surveys of Jeddo and Hakodadi Bays, and surveyed the harbor of Kealing in the island of Formosa. He was upon several expeditions after Chinese pirates, which were successful, and received the thanks of our own commander-in-chief and the English admiral for the one to Kulan. In the American steamer "Confucius," he destroyed several pirate junks at Foochow-foo.

On his return home, he was light-house inspector on the coasts of Maine and New Hampshire; at the Boston Navy-Yard, and made a cruise in the "Narragansett" in the Pacific. When the Civil War broke out he was ordered East, at his own request, and took command of "Katahdin," in which vessel he joined Admiral Farragut, passed the forts below New Orleans, and was in all the operations up to Vicksburg and Grand Gulf. In August, 1862, he was transferred to the command of the steam-sloop "Oneida," having been commissioned as commander in the previous month. While on the blockade off Mobile, he was left senior officer present, on August 29, 1862, with three vessels, the other four of that station having gone for supplies.

On September 4, a steamer, having every appearance of a British gun-vessel and flying English colors, came in about six P.M. When she did not come to, the "Oneida" fired three shots ahead of her, and then, finding that she did not bring to, fired a broadside, but the vessel's superior speed enabled her to run in over the shoals and reach the shelter of the guns of Fort Morgan. This vessel proved to be the "Oreto," which was built and fitted out by the English, and under the command of John N. Maffitt. She was afterwards rechristened "Florida." For not preventing the "Oreto's" running into Mobile, Preble was summarily dismissed the service, without a true understanding of the circumstances. These were war times, and all classes were excited, so that cool judgment was not always possible. Maffitt, who was a well-known officer of our old service, did full justice to Preble, saying, "The superior speed of the 'Florida' alone saved her from destruction, though not from a frightful mauling. . . . The damage done to her"—the "Oreto"—" was so great that we did not get to sea again for over three months." By recommendation of the Naval Committee, the President renominated him in February, 1863, and he was confirmed by the Senate,—as every one recognized the injustice which had been done him,—and he was at once ordered to a command. In November, 1864, he had command of the fleet brigade on shore at Port Royal, and co-operated with the army in the severe battles of Honey Hill and De Vaux's Neck, and was daily under fire for three weeks. After much important service as commander, he was made captain in March, 1867, and commodore in 1871. He commanded the Philadelphia Station for three years. He was commissioned rear-admiral in September, 1876, and commanded the South Pacific Station in 1877-78. He was retired in February, 1878, and died March 1, 1885.

Admiral Preble's "History of the American Flag" is standard, and he wrote much valuable magazine matter.

MAJOR CURTIS E. PRICE, U.S.A.

MAJOR CURTIS E. PRICE (Medical Department) was born in Ohio, but when a child went with his parents to Illinois, which has since been his residence. After going through college and receiving the degree of Bachelor of Arts, he studied medicine under the direction of his father, a physician in extensive practice. At the breaking out of the Rebellion he was in Philadelphia, studying medicine. After finishing his medical course he went to Kansas, and entered the service by appointment as assistant surgeon, but was not commissioned. In 1863, he accepted a contract as acting assistant surgeon U. S. A., and went to Nashville, Tennessee. His duties here were various, including service with the Twelfth Indiana Battery; medical charge of detachments serving the siege-guns in the fortifications; in charge of Fort Negley; in charge of Exchange Barracks (now the Maxwell House); attending surgeon at the penitentiary and military prison, and for awhile in charge of a gun-boat, while it was lying at Nashville.

Regiments of loyal Tennesseeans were then being raised and mustered into the U. S. service, and the subject of this sketch was commissioned assistant surgeon of the Twelfth Tennessee Cavalry, and as soon as a vacancy occurred was promoted to major and surgeon, although he was the junior assistant surgeon of his regiment.

He joined his regiment at Charlotte, Tennessee, and from that time till the close of the war was constantly in active field service in Tennessee, Alabama, Georgia, and Mississippi, with the Army of the Cumberland, and Military Division of the Mississippi. He was engaged in the skirmishes and battles of Lebanon, Dechard, Triune, Richland Creek, Taylorsville, Hollow-Tree Gap, Laurenceburg, Fayetteville, Taylor's Creek, Campbellsville, Bainbridge, Florence, Pulaski, Spring Hill, Columbia, Franklin, Nashville, and the retreat of Hood.

After Hood's army had been driven back across the Tennessee River, the brigade went to Eastport, Mississippi, where it was at the time of Lee's surrender, Major Price being brigade surgeon of the Second Brigade, Fifth Division, Cavalry Corps, Military Division of the Mississippi. His regiment was then ordered West on an Indian expedition, Major Price accompanying it. The summer was spent scouting in Western Kansas and Nebraska. The regiment returned to Fort Leavenworth, was mustered out of service, and finally discharged at Nashville, Tennessee, October 25, 1865. Major Price was brevetted lieutenant-colonel for "valuable and meritorious services during the war, and more especially for gallant conduct in the battle of Nashville."

He again entered the service as acting assistant surgeon U. S. Army, September 1, 1867, at Vicksburg, Mississippi, at the request of his old commander, General Gillem. His first duty was to quarantine against and treat yellow fever. He served at Columbus, Woodville, and Natchez, Mississippi; Louisville and Lebanon, Kentucky; and Little Rock, Arkansas, till February, 1873, when he was sent to San Francisco, California. He was commissioned assistant surgeon, U. S. Army, June 25, 1875, having passed an examining board second in a class of twenty-three. He went as medical officer with a battalion of artillery to the Department of the Platte in August, 1876, and was surgeon of the artillery and infantry battalions in the "Powder River Expedition," during the fall and winter campaign which General Crook conducted against the hostile Sioux and Cheyennes.

Since then his stations have been Angel Island, Alcatraz, and Fort Gaston, California; Fort Niagara, New York; Fort Custer, Montana; Fort Du Chesne, Utah; and Fort Wadsworth, New York harbor.

He was promoted to captain and assistant surgeon in 1880, and to major and surgeon in 1892. He received the degree of Master of Arts from his alma mater in 1865.

## COLONEL JOHN PULFORD, U.S.A. (RETIRED).

COLONEL JOHN PULFORD was born in New York City July 4, 1837. He was educated in the public schools and afterwards read law, and is now a member of the Detroit Bar, in which city he has resided since 1850. When the war of the Rebellion broke out in 1861 he was proprietor of a hotel and foreman of Engine Company No. 3 in said city, and on April 20 he, in conjunction with Mr. E. T. Sherlock, proprietor of the Metropolitan Theatre, reorganized said fire company into a military company and offered their services to the general government, and on June 19, 1861, he was commissioned first lieutenant Fifth Michigan Infantry. He was stationed at Fort Wayne, Michigan, to September 11, 1861, when he, with his regiment, left to join the Army of the Potomac, and was actively engaged with said army in all its campaigns and battles up to Malvern Hill, where he was severely wounded by a ricochet cannon-ball, which fractured his temporal bone and also broke his jaw and collar bones. He was taken prisoner and retained at Richmond until July 18, 1862. He was promoted captain May 15, 1862, and major January 1, 1863. He did not recover from his wounds until September 12, 1862, when he again took the field, and participated in the battle of Fredericksburg. In this battle his company and regiment suffered severely.

The regimental commander having been killed, Captain Pulford, although one of the junior captains, was soon after appointed major of the regiment, the officers of the regiment having petitioned to the governor for his promotion, on account of his efficient services as an officer. At the battle of Chancellorsville, May 2, 1863, he assisted in the capture of the Twenty-third Georgia Infantry, and the next day, May 3, assumed command of the regiment, after Lieutenant-Colonel E. T. Sherlock had been killed, and remained in command of the regiment (though suffering severely from a wound received at Chancellorsville) up to and including the battle of Gettysburg, Pennsylvania, where he was twice wounded, but did not leave the field or his command.

Major Pulford was promoted lieutenant-colonel of the Fifth Michigan May 3, 1863, and in August of that year was sent to New York City with his regiment on account of the draft riots, and from there to Troy, New York, for the same purpose, returning to the Army of the Potomac September 18, 1863. On December 29, 1863, he went on veteran furlough, and returning to the field in February, 1864, he participated in the actions and movements of the Army of the Potomac to the surrender of Lee, April 9, 1865.

At the battle of the Wilderness Colonel Pulford was severely wounded, having his back broken and both arms partially disabled from an injury to the brachial plexus and loss of part of the first and second dorsal vertebrae.

He was promoted colonel of his regiment July 12, 1864, and brevet brigadier-general of volunteers March 13, 1865, "for good conduct and meritorious services during the war," and was honorably mustered out July 5, 1865.

Colonel Pulford held on various occasions command of a brigade and division during the war, and of several Western regiments at its close, in Louisville, Kentucky.

He has to his credit the following battles and actions: Siege of Yorktown, Williamsburg, Fair Oaks, Peach Orchard, Glendale, Malvern Hill, Fredericksburg, Chancellorsville, Gettysburg, Wapping Heights, Auburn Heights, Kelly's Ford, Locust Grove, Mine Run, Wilderness, siege of Petersburg, Deep Bottom, Strawberry Plains, Poplar Springs Church; also the first line of battle at Boydton Plank Road, October 27, 1864; Hatcher's Run, Boydton Plank Road, capture of Petersburg, Sailor's Creek and New Store, the surrender of the insurgent armies at Appomattox Court-House.

On February 23, 1866, Colonel Pulford entered the regular army as second lieutenant of the Nineteenth Infantry, and was promoted first lieutenant the same day. He joined his regiment at Newport Barracks, Kentucky, and served with it in the Southwest and West, and engaged in General Hancock's expedition across the Plains against hostile Indians to April, 1867. Subsequently he was placed on reconstruction duty in the South, and on recruiting duty at Newport Barracks, Kentucky, and was retired from active service with the rank of colonel, on account of wounds received in the line of duty, December 15, 1870.

Colonel Pulford is the seventh son and ninth child of Edward and Sarah Lloyd (Anis) Pulford, the former a native of Norwich, and the latter of Bristol, England. They emigrated to New York City in 1833.

## MAJOR GEORGE A. PURINGTON, U.S.A.

MAJOR GEORGE A. PURINGTON (Third Cavalry) was born in Athens, Athens County, Ohio, July 21, 1838; removed to Rock Island, Illinois, in 1847; entered Rock Island High School in 1856. Prepared for college at Twinsburg and Hudson, Ohio. In 1861 assisted in organizing Company G, Nineteenth Ohio Volunteer Infantry (three months' service). Was appointed first sergeant of the company April 16, 1861. In May uniformed and acted as second lieutenant, but was not mustered in as such. Participated in the battle of Rich Mountain, Virginia. After the muster out and discharge of the regiment in August, 1861, Sergeant Purington reorganized the company into a troop of cavalry, and was mustered in as captain of Troop A, Second Ohio Volunteer Cavalry, August 16, 1861, at Cleveland, Ohio. Promoted major September 10, 1861. Was engaged in actions at Independence, Lone Jack, Sarcoxie, Fort Wayne, Rhea's Mills, Cane Hill, Missouri; Mount Sterling, Fishing Creek, Steubenville, Kentucky; pursuit and capture of John Morgan; Cumberland Gap, Waterga Bridge, Blountsville, Bristol, siege of Knoxville, Bean's Station, Blue Springs, Walker's Ford, Clinch River, Cheek's Cross-Roads, Russellville, Burnt House, Blain's Cross-Roads, and Mossy Creek, Tennessee. Commissioned lieutenant-colonel Second Ohio Cavalry June 25, 1863. Commanded the regiment or a brigade until mustered out of service.

He was commissioned colonel Second Ohio Cavalry June, 1864, but was not mustered as such, the regiment being below the minimum, caused by casualties of the battles of the Wilderness, Spottsylvania, Cold Harbor, actions of St. Mary's Church, Piney Branch Church, Hanover Court-House, Ashland Station, Shady Grove, Nottaway Court-House, through which battles Colonel Purington commanded the regiment; also in the battles of Stony Creek, Ream's Station, and action at Summit Point; commanded the First Brigade of the Third Division, Cavalry Corps, at the battles of Winchester, Fisher's Hill, actions of Luray Valley, Waynesborough, Bridgewater, Reamstown, Charlestown, and Berryville; commanded his regiment at the battle of Cedar Creek, and in the action of Back Road, Virginia. Was honorably mustered out November, 1864.

He was commissioned captain in the Ninth Regiment of Cavalry July 28, 1866. Was with his troop in all the Indian campaigns in Texas, New Mexico, and Arizona, from April, 1867, until 1881, the war with the Indian chief Victoria included. During this campaign the battalion in which Colonel Purington served, consisting of less than two hundred and fifty-men, lost two officers and sixteen men killed, one officer and sixty-four men wounded.

In October, 1883, was promoted major Third U. S. Cavalry, serving since then in Arizona, Texas, and Indian Territory. Commanded the battalion of the Third Cavalry that was present during the threatened Indian troubles, in 1885, in the Indian Territory.

Brevet major U. S. Army for gallant and meritorious services at the battle of the Wilderness, Virginia.

Brevet lieutenant-colonel U. S. Army for gallant and meritorious services at the battle of Winchester, Virginia.

Brevet colonel U. S. Army for gallant and meritorious services at the battle of Cedar Creek, Virginia.

Is now in command of Third U. S. Cavalry and stationed at Fort Clark, Texas.

## REAR-ADMIRAL STEPHEN P. QUACKENBUSH, U.S.N.
### (DECEASED).

REAR-ADMIRAL STEPHEN P. QUACKENBUSH was born in New York. Appointed from New York February 15, 1840; attached to sloop "Boston," East India Squadron, 1841-42; frigate "Raritan," Brazil Squadron, 1843-45; Naval School, 1846; sloop "Albany," Home Squadron, 1846-47; was actively engaged in operating against Vera Cruz, and on blockading duty during the Mexican War. Promoted to passed midshipman July 11, 1846; storeship "Supply," Mediterranean, 1847-48; Coast Survey, 1849-50; mail-steamer "Pacific," 1850-51; mail-steamer "Illinois," 1852; brig "Perry," coast of Africa, 1853-54. Commissioned as lieutenant September 4, 1855; Home Squadron, 1856; steam-frigate "Wabash," Home Squadron, 1857-58; navy-yard, Philadelphia, 1859; frigate "Congress," Brazil Squadron, 1859-61. Commissioned as lieutenant-commander July 16, 1862; commanding steamer "Delaware," North Atlantic Blockading Squadron, 1862; covered the retreat of General Burnside's army at Roanoke Island, and scattered a large body of the enemy who were preparing to resist them; commanding the "Delaware," flying the divisional flag of Commander S. C. Rowan, at the battles of Roanoke Island, Elizabeth City, and New Berne, 1862; at Winton, N. C., in same vessel, engaged a rebel battery and a regiment of infantry at short range; engagements with Sewell's Point battery and a flying battery at Wilcox Landing, and a battery on Malvern Hill, James River; engagement with a battery at Point of Rocks, Appomattox River, 1862; covered the rear-guard of the army at the retreat to Harrison's Landing, 1862; commanded the steam-gun-boat "Unadilla," South Atlantic Blockading Squadron, 1863; commanding steam-gun-boat "Pequot," North Atlantic Blockading Squadron, 1863-64; commanded the iron-clad "Patapsco," South Atlantic Blockading Squadron, 1864, and while engaged in ascertaining the nature and position of the obstructions in Charleston harbor and dragging for torpedoes, was struck by one, and sunk in twenty seconds,—this occurred within three hundred and fifty yards of Fort Sumter; commanded the steamer "Nungo," South Atlantic Blockading Squadron, Georgetown, South Carolina, for the protection of that place, and, with a force of light-draught vessels under his command, prevented the re-erection of the fort by the enemy, which had been previously destroyed by our fleet. Commissioned as commander July 25, 1866; commanding steamer "Conemaugh," Atlantic Squadron, 1866-68; navy-yard, Norfolk, 1868-70; commanding steam-sloop "Tuscarora," 1871. Commissioned as captain July, 1871; commanding "Terror" (third-rate), North Atlantic Station, 1872; commanding receiving-ship "New Hampshire," 1873-75. Commodore in 1880; commanding Naval Station, Pensacola, 1880-82. Promoted to rear-admiral in July, 1884. Died in 1890.

COMMODORE F. M. RAMSAY, U.S.N.

COMMODORE FRANCIS MUNROE RAMSAY was born in the District of Columbia, and is the son of General George Douglas Ramsay, of the U. S. Army, who was for some years chief of ordnance, and was brevetted major-general for "meritorious services during the Civil War."

Commodore Ramsay entered the navy as midshipman from Pennsylvania October, 1850. He was at the Naval Academy on board the practice-ship "Preble," and the frigate "St. Lawrence," of the Pacific Squadron, until 1855. Then he went to the Naval School again, and became passed midshipman in June, 1856. Serving in the sloop "Falmouth," on the Brazil Station, he was made acting master, and became master in January, 1858, while attached to the steam-frigate "Merrimac," of the Pacific Squadron.

He was made lieutenant the same month, in 1858, and, after his return from the Pacific, was, for a time, on ordnance duty at the Washington yard. During 1860-62 he made a cruise on the coast of Africa, in the sloop-of-war "Saratoga."

The Civil War was now in full progress, and Commodore Ramsay, having been commissioned lieutenant-commander in July, 1862, was ordered to the command of the iron-clad "Choctaw," of the Mississippi Squadron, where he was to be actively and conspicuously employed for the next two years.

Among his services were the engagements at Haines's Bluff, Yazoo River, April 30 and May 1, 1863; the expedition up the Yazoo River to Yazoo City in May, 1863, when the rebel naval building-yard and the vessels there were destroyed. The same month he was in the engagement at Liverpool Landing, on the Yazoo. In June, 1863, he was engaged with a heavy force of the enemy at Milliken's Bend,—the capture of which his heavy fire prevented, and thereby saved a disaster of great importance.

He was engaged at the siege of Vicksburg, and commanded a battery of three heavy guns, mounted on scows, from June 19 to July 4, 1863, when the capitulation occurred.

After this event, Lieutenant-Commander Ramsay commanded the Third Division of the Mississippi Squadron for some fourteen months. He had many engagements with field batteries and guerillas, commanded an expedition up the Black and the Ouachita Rivers, and had engagements with the enemy at many points on those water-courses. He was in the celebrated Red River Expedition, when the dam was made by the army to allow the iron-clads that had been caught by the falling waters to pass. At Simmsport, Louisiana, he had the pleasure, in his trip up the Atchafalaya, of recapturing, in a battery which attacked him, some rifled guns which had been taken from General Banks.

He went East with Admiral Porter, and commanded the "Unadilla" at the engagements at Fort Fisher, Fort Anderson, and the other forts on the Cape Fear River. He was present at the capture of Richmond. After the peace, he was in charge of the Department of Gunnery at the Naval Academy.

Promoted commander July, 1866, and on navigation duty at Washington, and then fleet-captain, and in command of "Guerriere," 1867-69, on South Atlantic Station. After more duty in the line of ordnance at Washington, he became the naval attaché at London in 1872-73. After that he commanded the "Ossipee," of the North Atlantic Squadron, 1873-74, and the "Lancaster" in 1874-75. The next two years were spent as the executive-officer of the Naval Asylum at Philadelphia, and then he went for the same term as inspector of ordnance at New York.

He was commissioned captain in 1878, and had charge of the Torpedo Station for three years after that. During the year 1881 he commanded the "Trenton," flag-ship of the European Station. His next duty was upon the Board of Examination, and, during 1887-89, he commanded the "Boston" upon special service.

He received his commission as commodore in March, 1889, and was appointed chief of the Bureau of Navigation in the Navy Department in the same year, which position he still retains.

## MAJOR JACOB B. RAWLES, U.S.A.

MAJOR JACOB B. RAWLES (Fourth Artillery) was born in Michigan August 4, 1839, and graduated at the Military Academy May 6, 1861. He was promoted second lieutenant Third Artillery the same day, and first lieutenant Fifth Artillery May 14, 1861. He served during the war of the Rebellion, and was engaged from May 7 till about July 15, 1861, in drilling volunteers in and about Washington, D. C.; he was thus occupied with the Sixty-ninth New York Infantry (Irish), the Second Connecticut Infantry (General Terry's regiment), and the Sixth Maine Infantry. He was then detailed on recruiting service in connection with the organization of the Fifth Artillery from about July 5 until October, 1861, serving at Camp Greble, Harrisburg, Pennsylvania, and at Fort Hamilton, New York harbor, till November, 1862; joined Light Battery G, Fifth U. S. Artillery, December 1, 1862; he sailed from New York, on the clipper-ship "Jennie Beals," with Banks's Expedition, bound for New Orleans, Louisiana, December 9, 1862, and served in the Department of the Gulf from date of arrival at New Orleans, December 25, 1862, until after the surrender of Fort Morgan, Mobile Bay, Alabama, in August, 1864. He participated in the first attack upon Port Hudson, Louisiana, operations about Baton Rouge, Louisiana, in the spring of 1863, and the final siege of the former-named place, terminating July 8, 1863,—returning to New Orleans with the battery in the fall of the same year. In the spring of 1864 he participated in the Red River campaign, being present and actively engaged with Light Battery G, Fifth Artillery, at the battle of Sabine Cross-Roads, or Mansfield, Louisiana, April 8, 1864. After the retreat of the Army of the Gulf, returned to New Orleans, remaining there until the operations of the army about Mobile Bay, Louisiana, and the siege of Fort Morgan. He took part in all those operations which culminated in the surrender of the latter place. After the surrender of Fort Morgan he returned to New Orleans, Louisiana, and from there, in the month of August, 1864, was transferred with Light Battery G, Fifth Artillery, to the Army of the Potomac. The winter of 1864-65 was passed with the Artillery Reserve of the Fifth Corps, occupying winter-quarters on the Jerusalem Plank Road, rear defensive line of the Army of the Potomac.

In the spring campaign of 1865 he participated in most of the actions, skirmishes, and battles of the Fifth Corps, terminating with the surrender of the rebel Army of Northern Virginia, April 9, 1865.

He was made brevet captain July 8, 1863, for "gallant and meritorious services in the siege of Port Hudson, Louisiana;" brevet major April 9, 1865, for "gallant and meritorious services during the campaign terminating

with surrender of the insurgent forces under General R. E. Lee." He was regimental quartermaster of the Fifth Artillery from November, 1861, to November, 1862.

After the Rebellion, he was with Light Battery G, Fifth Artillery, at Camp Bailey, Bladensburg, Maryland, and at Little Rock, Arkansas, until July 28, 1866, when he was promoted captain, and served at Fort Warren, Massachusetts, with Battery D, Fifth Artillery, from March, 1869, until December, 1875; at Oglethorpe Barracks, Savannah, Georgia, until 1879; McPherson Barracks, Georgia, from April 1, 1879, until February, 1880; at Key West Barracks, Florida (second time), and Fort Brook, Tampa, Florida, until July, 1881; on leave of absence from July 1881, till December, 1881; at Fort Schuyler, New York harbor, from December, 1881, to September, 1882; left Fort Schuyler for Omaha, Nebraska, with Battery D, Fifth Artillery, September 10, 1882; during the fall of that year the battery was mounted, equipped, and organized as a mounted battery; absent from Fort Omaha during the months of October, November, and December, 1882, as a member of a Horse Board for purchasing horses for the battery and for the cavalry service; ordered with battery to Fort Douglas, Utah, in December, 1885; serving there till November, 1886; during sojourn at that post built large, commodious stables for battery, capable of accommodating eighty horses; from Fort Douglas took station, in December, 1886, at Fort Schuyler, New York, having been transferred to Battery E; in May, 1887 ordered to duty with battery at Fort Hamilton, New York; ordered to Fort Preble, Maine; served at Fort Preble until the Fourth Artillery was transferred South, to Fort McPherson, Georgia, May 28, 1889, having been promoted major of the Fourth Artillery August 10, 1887.

### BREVET MAJOR-GENERAL J. A. RAWLINS, U.S.A.
(DECEASED.)

BREVET MAJOR-GENERAL J. A. RAWLINS was born in East Galena, Illinois, February 13, 1831. Died at Washington, D. C., Sept. 9, 1869. He was of Scotch-Irish extraction. His father, James D. Rawlins, removed from Kentucky to Missouri, and then to Illinois. John passed his early years on the family farm, and attended the district school in winter. Studied law with Isaac P. Stevens at Galena, and in Oct., 1854, was admitted to the bar, and taken into partnership by his preceptor. In 1855 Mr. Stevens retired, leaving the business to Rawlins.

In 1860 he was nominated for the electoral college on the Douglas ticket. He was outspoken for the Union and for the war to maintain it, and at a mass meeting at Galena, on April 16, 1861, Rawlins was called on to speak; but instead of deprecating the war, as had been expected, he made a speech of an hour, in which he upheld it with signal ability and eloquence. Among those of the audience that had acted with the Democrats was Captain Ulysses S. Grant. He was deeply impressed by the speech, and thereupon offered his services to the country, and from that time forth was the warm friend of Rawlins. The first act of Grant after he had been assigned to the command of a brigade, August 7, 1861, was to offer Rawlins the post of aide-de-camp on his staff, and soon after the position of captain and assistant adjutant-general, to date from August 30, 1861. He joined Grant at Cairo, Illinois, September 15, 1861, and from that time was constantly with the latter till the end of the war, except from August 1 to October 1, 1864, when he was absent on sick-leave. He was promoted major April 11, 1862; lieutenant-colonel November 1, 1862; brigadier-general of volunteers August 11, 1863; brevet major-general of volunteers February 24, 1865; chief of staff to Lieutenant-General Grant, with the rank of brigadier-general United States Army, March 3, 1865; and brevet major-general United States Army March 13, 1865. Finally, he was appointed Secretary of War March 9, 1869, which office he held till his death. Before entering the army, Rawlins had never seen a company of uniformed soldiers, nor read a book on tactics or military organization; but he soon developed rare executive abilities. Early after joining Grant, Rawlins acquired great influence over him. He was bold, resolute, and outspoken in counsel, and never hesitated to give his opinion upon matters of importance, whether it was asked or not. His relations with Grant were closer than those of any other man, and so highly did the latter value his sterling qualities and his great abilities that, in a letter to Henry Wilson, chairman of the Senate Military Committee, he declared that Rawlins was more nearly indispensable to him than any other officer in the army. He was a man of austere habits, severe morals, aggressive temper, and of inflexible will, resolution, and courage. He verified, re-arranged, and rewrote, when necessary, all the statements of Grant's official reports, adhering as closely as possible to Grant's original drafts, but making them to conform to the facts as they were understood at head-quarters. At Chattanooga he became an ardent advocate of the plan of operations devised by General Wm. F. Smith, and adopted by Generals Thomas and Grant, and for the relief of the army at Chattanooga, and for the battle of Missionary Ridge, where his persistence finally secured positive orders from Grant to Thomas directing the advance of the Army of the Cumberland that resulted in carrying the heights. He accompanied Grant to the Army of the Potomac, and was his devoted and loyal friend all through this campaign. Rawlins, as Secretary of War, was the youngest member of the Cabinet, as he was the youngest member of Grant's staff when he joined it at Cairo in 1861. Soon after entering the Cabinet he suffered much from pulmonary consumption, which he had contracted during the war, and up to the time of his death he performed all the duties of his office, and exerted a commanding influence in the counsels of the President to the last.

## CAPTAIN WILLIAM C. RAWOLLE, U.S.A.

CAPTAIN WILLIAM C. RAWOLLE (Second Cavalry) was born in Prussia August 28, 1840. In childhood he became a resident of New York, and in July, 1861, he was appointed junior second lieutenant of a light battery of the New York National Guard, subsequently known as Battery L, Second New York Artillery. He was commissioned in the same October 26, 1861, and was promoted first lieutenant March 4, 1862.

On June 21, 1862, he was promoted captain and additional aide-de-camp, and attached to the staff of General Samuel D. Sturgis, serving in the field with the Army of the Potomac, and being engaged in the battles of second Bull Run, South Mountain, Antietam, Warrenton, Sulphur Springs, and Fredericksburg, in 1862.

In March, 1863, he was detailed on the staff of Major-General John E. Wool, commanding the Department of the East, where he remained until General Wool's retirement, when he was returned to duty with General Sturgis, then commanding the Cavalry Corps of the Army of the Ohio, operating in East Tennessee, and later on in West Tennessee and Mississippi. He remained on this duty until the close of the war of the Rebellion, participating in the campaigns of Tennessee and Mississippi, and battle of Brice's Cross-Roads, Mississippi.

He was brevetted major of volunteers March 13, 1865, for gallant and meritorious services in the Army of the Potomac from August, 1862, to January, 1863, including the battles of second Bull Run, South Mountain, Antietam, Warrenton, Sulphur Springs, and Fredericksburg; and lieutenant-colonel of volunteers March 13, 1865, for services in the West, including the cavalry campaign in East Tennessee and expeditions to Northern Mississippi, and for gallant, daring, and good conduct at the battle of Brice's Cross-Roads, Mississippi.

Captain Rawolle resigned his volunteer commission August 11, 1865, and remained out of service until June 6, 1868, when he was appointed second lieutenant of the Second U. S. Cavalry.

He was promoted first lieutenant April 26, 1869, and captain December 20, 1880. He served on frontier duty in Colorado, Wyoming, Montana, Idaho, and Washington, from 1868 to 1890, participating in the Big Horn and Yellowstone Expedition in 1876 against Sitting Bull's band of Sioux Indians.

He was regimental quartermaster of the Second Cavalry from July 15, 1870, to September 15, 1874, and adjutant of the Second Cavalry from March 31, 1878, to August 31, 1880.

In 1890 the Second Cavalry was transferred to Arizona, and Captain Rawolle is at this date on duty at Fort Huachuca, Arizona.

## CAPTAIN P. HENRY RAY, U.S.A.

CAPTAIN P. HENRY RAY (Eighth Infantry) was born in Wisconsin May 8, 1842. Upon the breaking out of the Civil War he entered the volunteer service and served as private, corporal, sergeant, and first sergeant of companies K and A, Second Wisconsin Infantry, from May 7, 1861, to July 12, 1863, participating in the Manassas campaign of the Army of the Potomac, and was engaged in the action at Blackburn's Ford, July 18, 1861, and the first battle of Bull Run, July 21, 1861.

He was appointed second lieutenant of the First Wisconsin Heavy Artillery July 13, 1863; promoted captain September 13, 1864, and honorably mustered out June 26, 1865. He became captain of the Sixth U. S. Veteran Infantry August 9, 1865, and honorably mustered out April 12, 1866. He then entered the regular service as second lieutenant of the Thirty-third Infantry March 7, 1867, and served on special duty, constructing McPherson Barracks, Alabama, to November, 1867; then at Huntsville, Tuscaloosa, Mobile, and Montgomery, Alabama, to May, 1869, when he was transferred to the Eighth Infantry, and served at Fort Johnson, North Carolina; Columbia, South Carolina; and Raleigh, North Carolina, to October 27, 1870, when he was ordered to David's Island, New York.

In July, 1872, the Eighth Infantry was transferred to Dakota, and Lieutenant Ray participated with General Stanley's first expedition to the Yellowstone in the summer of that year. He was then stationed at Omaha Barracks until May, 1873, when he took the field with the second expedition of General Stanley to the Yellowstone. Serving then at Fort Russell until February 22, 1874, he participated in an expedition against the Sioux Indians, under General John E. Smith, until July of the same year, and then the station of his regiment was changed to Arizona. Lieutenant Ray was promoted first lieutenant Dec. 31, 1875, and afterwards stationed at Yuma Depot, Fort Lowell, and Fort Apache to 1878.

Lieutenant Ray was acting signal officer from May, 1881, to June, 1885. He was assigned to the command of the International Polar Expedition to Point Barrow, Alaska, June, 1881; organizing and outfitting expedition in San Francisco, California, to July, 1881; sailed from San Francisco, California, and landed at Plover Bay, Siberia, August 21, 1881, and at Point Barrow, Alaska, September 8, 1881; established and commanded meteorological station at Uglaamie, Alaska, to August 22, 1883, when the station was abandoned; during 1882 and 1883 he made two expeditions into the interior, travelling over one thousand miles in an unexplored region with dogs and sledge; discovered and partly surveyed Meade River; sailed from Uglaamie, Alaska, August 23, 1883; picked up Lieutenant Schwatka and party at Redoubt Michaelofsky September 13, 1883; landed in San Francisco, California, October 7, 1883, and disbanded the expedition October 15, 1883. He was then on duty in the office of the chief signal officer, Washington, D. C., preparing report of the International Polar Expedition to June, 1885. He was appointed United States delegate to International Polar Congress at Vienna, Austria, from March, 1884, to July, 1884, and on duty in Washington, D. C., from July, 1884, to April, 1885.

As to Lieutenant Ray's Arctic work, it is believed that more was accomplished than his instructions required. Of all the expeditions sent out by the United States government officially, his was the only one that passed two years in the Arctic without losing a single life, or that did not come to grief. In July, 1882, he personally piloted through the moving pack, and safely brought to land, the crew of the whaler "North Star" (fifty-two officers and men), when that vessel was crushed in the ice and sunk six miles off shore.

In 1885, Lieutenant Ray was stationed on the Pacific coast, and served at various posts until the fall of 1886, when he was transferred to the Department of the Platte; was acting judge-advocate (captain) from April, 1887, until 1891, then ordered to Fort Washakie, where he raised the first Indian company of infantry.

He was promoted captain May 27, 1889; was elected Fellow of Royal Geographical Society in June, 1884.

In January, 1871, Lieutenant Ray, with six men of the Eighth Infantry, while on duty at David's Island, New York, perilled their lives in a fearful storm to save the lives of two citizens discovered helplessly drifting in the vicinity of this island, and who, notwithstanding their inability to return without assistance, knowing none could be afforded at the time, still persevered, and succeeded in the object for which they had endangered their lives, for which a highly complimentary order was issued by the commandant of the post.

## CAPTAIN ALLEN VISSCHER REED, U.S.N.

CAPTAIN ALLEN VISSCHER REED was born at Oak Hill, New York, July 12, 1838. When very young, he moved to Lockport, New York, and resided there till sixteen, receiving a primary-school education, supplemented by three years in the Union School, an academic institution.

Graduated from Naval Academy 1858, number one of the class, and received the first sword presented to a graduate, which was engraved, "The U. S. Naval Academy to Allen V. Reed, as a testimony of highest academic merit." Warranted midshipman; joined the " Macedonian" at Key West, where all available ships had reinforced the Home Squadron on account of threatened trouble with Spain, arising from filibustering expeditions to assist Cuban insurgents. Cruised in Mediterranean till May, 1860, when ship returned, leaving him dangerously sick at Spezzia; promoted to passed midshipman; joined " Pawnee" as watch-officer; promoted to master in February; transferred to " Water-Witch" in March, as navigator and watch-officer. The " Water-Witch" was ordered to Fort Pickens when Sumter was invested, then joined Gulf Squadron. Promoted to lieutenant April, 1861; joined "Colorado" on blockading duty in September; transferred to "Potomac" in December, and on detachment of Lieutenant-Commander Kimberly was executive-officer for one year; joined "Lackawanna," on the Mobile blockade, August, 1863; ordered North in November, and to "Tuscarora," North Atlantic Blockading Squadron, February, 1864. The "Tuscarora" went out of commission in June, and he took the crew by rail from Baltimore to the receiving-ship at New York without losing a man, although it was in the height of bounty-jumping. Joined the "Pawtuxet" and returned to the Wilmington blockade; engaged in both attacks on Fort Fisher, where, according to the report of Admiral Porter, this vessel did good service; in the second attack was in temporary command. After Fort Fisher was captured, was in Cape Fear River working through the obstructions there, at the bombardment of Fort Anderson and to the capture of Wilmington. This river being cleared, the "Pawtuxet" was ordered to the James River, where she co-operated with the army in the vicinity of Fort Darling and Dutch Gap Canal in the closing scenes of the war; then he commanded the vessel for two months at various points on the James till matters quieted down, when it went to New York and out of commission.

Promoted to lieutenant-commander, 1865; joined double-turreted iron-clad "Miantonomoh" in September; detached April, 1866; was assistant to executive-officer at Norfolk Navy-Yard July to September; then to "Resaca;" ordered to North Pacific Station. On arrival at Panama was detained there on account of the unsettled state of affairs till yellow fever broke out, when ship went

north; stopped at San Francisco, but was hurried on to Alaska to disinfect by freezing out. This fever was very fatal, as the " Resaca" lost over one-seventh of her total complement. At Sitka during winter of 1867; assisted in the ceremonies transferring the territory to the United States. "Resaca," being free from fever, returned south, and he was transferred to "Saranac," and in January, 1869, to the "Jamestown;" ordered home in July.

On shore duty at New York yard 1869-72, on receiving-ship, in equipment and navigation. Promoted commander 1872; in command of "Kansas," 1872 to 1874, connected with Nicaragua Surveying Expedition; while on this duty met the steamer "Virginius" at Aspinwall, June, 1873, which it was claimed had been employed by the insurgents in running arms into Cuba. The Spanish war-steamer "Bazan," in search of the "Virginius," arrived next day, and her captain inquired of Commander Reed the status of the "Virginius," and informed him that he would "resolutely oppose" her departure. On inquiry, the papers of the "Virginius" being found regular and in order, he so informed the commander of the " Bazan," and that he should afford her protection as an American vessel. When the "Virginius" was ready for sea, the "Kansas," with shotted guns, placed herself between the two vessels, and so proceeded till the "Virginius" was well at sea and beyond the reach of the " Bazan," when the "Kansas" returned to port and resumed the duties of the canal survey.

From 1874 to 1880 in Hydrographic Office; after September, 1875, as assistant hydrographer. Commanding "Alliance," North Atlantic Station, 1882-84; promoted to captain July, 1884; commanding apprentice training-ship "Minnesota," 1884-86; commanding "Richmond," South Atlantic Station, 1888-90; commandant of the Pensacola Naval Station from December, 1890.

CAPTAIN GEORGE C. REMEY, U.S.N.

CAPTAIN GEORGE C. REMEY is a native of Burlington, Iowa, and was born on August 10, 1841. His father, W. B. Remey, was a Kentuckian, while his mother, whose maiden name was Howland, was a native of Vermont.

Captain Remey graduated from the U. S. Naval Academy in June, 1859, and immediately joined the U. S. flagship "Hartford,"—of New Orleans and Mobile fame,— and sailed for the Asiatic Station. The "Hartford" returned to the United States in December, 1861, and Remey was at once ordered as executive-officer of the "Marblehead," one of the gun-boats built in ninety days. He served in the "Marblehead" until April, 1863, when he was transferred to the "Canandaigua," steam-sloop, as executive-officer. During his service in the "Marblehead" he commanded that vessel for a short period. While attached to these two vessels he took part in several engagements with the enemy's batteries. From August 23 to September 8, 1863, he commanded the naval battery on Morris Island during the siege of Fort Wagner and the bombardment of Fort Sumter. In the night attack on Sumter, September 8, he commanded the second division of boats. The attack was a bold one, and well pushed, but was unsuccessful, and resulted in great loss in killed, wounded, and prisoners. Remey landed on the fort, but his boat was sunk, and he was made a prisoner.

Thirteen months were then passed by him in the jail of Columbia, South Carolina, and a short time in the jail of Charlotte, North Carolina, and in Libby Prison, in Richmond, Virginia, from which latter point he was exchanged, and came North.

In February, 1865, he was ordered as the executive-officer of the U. S. S. "De Soto," and from April, 1865, to August, 1867, was executive-officer of the U. S. S. "Mohongo," on the Pacific Station. Having accomplished this long tour of service, he became instructor in gunnery at the Naval Academy, and in 1869-70 was executive-officer of the U. S. frigate "Sabine," on special service.

At the time of the expedition for the survey of the Tehuantepec and Nicaragua routes for a canal in 1870-71, Remey was one of the staff, being employed during the intervals at the Naval Observatory.

For a few months of 1872 he commanded the U. S. S. "Frolic," and from August of that year to May, 1873, was upon staff-duty on board the U. S. flag-ship "Worcester," of the North Atlantic Squadron.

From 1874 to 1877 he was in the Bureau of Yards and Docks, Navy Department, Washington, excepting three months, during which he commanded the naval force during the troubles upon the Rio Grande.

In 1877-78 he commanded the "Enterprise," North Atlantic Station; going from thence to Newport for torpedo instruction. The course completed, he returned to the Bureau of Yards and Docks, and in 1881 was ordered as commander to the flag-ship "Lancaster," of the European Squadron, where he remained until 1883. Upon his return he was ordered to the navy-yard at Washington, during which time he received his promotion to a captaincy. He served three years in this grade at the navy-yard, Norfolk, Virginia, and was then, in November, 1889, ordered to the command of the "Charleston," fitting out at San Francisco. This fine ship, a protected cruiser of modern type, with twin screws, two military masts, and eight guns, had been, during this commission, the flag-ship of Acting Rear-Admiral George Brown, and her active service in connection with the Chilian business made her name well known to the country at large.

Captain Remey's tour of duty on board the "Charleston" expired before the settlement of the extraordinary action of the Chilians. He was retained in the command while there was a prospect of hostile action; but that period having passed, was relieved in regular course.

Captain Remey had a younger brother in the service, E. W. Remey, who rose to the rank of lieutenant, and was a most capable and energetic officer, liked by all with whom he came in contact, whether officer or man. He graduated at the Naval Academy in the class of 1867.

Another brother is Colonel W. B. Remey, of the U. S. Marine Corps, who has been the judge-advocate-general of the navy for a number of years.

Captain Remey is a Companion of the Military Order of the Loyal Legion, and was made a Knight Companion of the Royal Order of Kalakaua by his late Majesty King Kalakaua, of the Hawaiian Islands. It is well, in this connection, to state that no foreign order can be accepted by an American without permission of Congress. Captain Remey's connection with the political disturbances in Hawaii renders his recognition in this manner quite proper.

## COLONEL WM. B. REMEY, U.S.M.C. (RETIRED).

COLONEL WM. B. REMEY is a native of Iowa, and entered the Marine Corps as second lieutenant in November, 1861, when the whole country was in a ferment, and all the young men, North and South, were taking up arms. During the years 1862-63 he performed his first service in the "Sabine," a well-known frigate of the old school.

After receiving promotion to be first lieutenant, he was ordered to the navy-yard at Norfolk, where he was stationed during 1864 and a part of 1865, a period when vigilance on the part of the marine guard was particularly necessary.

For two years after this he served in the "Vanderbilt," in the Pacific. Upon his return home his orders changed rapidly. He was on board the "North Carolina" and the "New Hampshire," receiving-ships; at the marine barracks at Philadelphia; on special duty at Washington; and at head-quarters at Washington.

He was commissioned captain in 1872, and was ordered to the frigate "Colorado," of the North Atlantic Squadron. In 1875 he returned to head-quarters, being soon after detailed as fleet-marine-officer of the South Pacific Station. There he remained until 1876, when he was ordered to the same position on the South Atlantic Station. He came home in 1877, and was attached to the Norfolk Navy-Yard during 1878. In 1880 he became the acting judge-advocate-general of the United States Navy, with the rank of colonel, from June, 1880.

In this position he continued to serve until May, 1892, having been the law-officer of the department for fourteen years, during which time he won many friends, not only in the service itself, but among those having business with the department, owing to his devotion to the duties of his office and the signal ability with which he accomplished the immense amount of work devolving upon him. By assiduous study and industry he became thoroughly able to decide questions of naval law as well as to advise competently in the large contracts for building, in which the Navy Department was engaged.

During his administration of the office of judge-advocate he gained the respect and esteem of all the different secretaries under whom he served. Personally a very genial and companionable man, it was with unfeigned regret and sorrow that his friends learned, in May, 1892, that his health had suddenly and utterly broken down. In consequence of this state of things he was retired on June 4, 1892, with the full rank of colonel.

## COLONEL JOHN F. REYNOLDS, U.S.A. (DECEASED).

COLONEL JOHN F. REYNOLDS was born in Pennsylvania, and graduated at the Military Academy July 1, 1841. He was promoted brevet second lieutenant Third Artillery the same day; second lieutenant October 23, 1841; first lieutenant June 18, 1846, and captain March 3, 1855. He served at Fort McHenry, Maryland; Fort Pickens, Florida; Fort Marion, Florida, and Fort Moultrie, South Carolina, until 1845, when he participated in the military occupation of Texas in 1845-46, and in the war with Mexico, 1846-48, being engaged in the defence of Fort Brown, Texas; battle of Monterey and battle of Buena Vista, for which he was brevetted, for "gallant and meritorious conduct," captain September 23, 1846, in the battle of Monterey, and major February 23, 1847, in the battle of Buena Vista, Mexico.

After the war closed, he was in garrison at Fort Trumbull, Connecticut; Fort Preble, Maine; Fort Adams, Rhode Island (as regimental quartermaster), to 1852. He was aide-de-camp to Major-General Twiggs to November 30, 1853, and then at Forts Lafayette and Wood, New York, until 1854, when he participated in the march to Salt Lake City, Utah, 1854-55. Upon his promotion to a captaincy he was ordered to Fort Yuma, and subsequently served at Benicia and Fort Oxford during 1855-56. He participated in the Rogue River Expedition of 1856, and was engaged in several skirmishes with Oregon Indians. He was transferred to Fort Monroe in 1856, and served there until 1858, when he was ordered on frontier duty at Fort Leavenworth, Kansas, subsequently joining in the Utah Expedition of 1858-59, after which he took part in the march to the Columbia River in 1859, and was stationed at Fort Vancouver, Washington, during 1859-60. He was at the Military Academy as commandant of cadets (*ex-officio* lieutenant-colonel), and instructor of artillery, infantry, and cavalry tactics, from September 8, 1860, to June 25, 1861.

He was appointed lieutenant-colonel of the Fourteenth Infantry May 14, 1861, and was in command of his regiment at Fort Trumbull, Connecticut, from July 6 to September 8, 1861. Having been appointed brigadier-general of volunteers, August 20, 1861, he was in command of a brigade of the Pennsylvania Reserve Corps, on the right of the lines before Washington City, from September 16, 1861, to June 9, 1862, when he joined in the Virginia Peninsula campaign with the Army of the Potomac, and was engaged in the battles of Mechanicsville, June 26; Gaines' Mill, June 27, and Glendale, June 30, 1862, where he was captured, and remained as prisoner-of-war until the 8th of August following. On rejoining the army he was assigned to the command of a division, participating in the Northern Virginia campaign, and engaged in the second battle of Bull Run August 29-30, 1862.

General Reynolds was placed in command of the Pennsylvania Volunteer Militia, in defence of the State, during the Maryland campaign, from September 14 to 26, 1862, and, upon being relieved, Governor Curtin, September 26, 1862, tendered him his thanks, in behalf of the State of Pennsylvania, in the following terms: "Having relieved you from duty as commander of the Pennsylvania Volunteer Militia, recently called for the defence of the State, I deem it proper to express my strong sense of the gratitude which Pennsylvania owes for the zeal, spirit, and ability which you brought to her service at a period when her honor and safety were threatened. That for her security you left the command of your brave division, the Pennsylvania Reserves, thus losing the opportunity of leading this gallant corps at South Mountain and the Antietam, is a just demonstration of the true affection you bear for your native State, which, be assured, her freemen reciprocate, and for which, in their behalf, I am happy to make you this acknowledgment."

General Reynolds was appointed major-general of volunteers November 29, 1862, and was assigned to the command of the First Corps, Army of the Potomac, participating in the Rappahannock campaign, and engaged in the battles of Fredericksburg, December 13, 1862, and Chancellorsville (in reserve), May 2-4, 1863. He was promoted colonel of the Fifth U. S. Infantry June 1, 1863. He participated in the Pennsylvania campaign, June and July, 1863, and, while in command of the engaged forces at the opening of the battle of Gettysburg, while urging on his men with animating words, was killed July 1, 1863, at the age of forty-two years. He was struck with a rifle-shot that caused almost instant death,—a grievous loss to the Army of the Potomac, one of whose most distinguished and best-beloved officers he was.

## LIEUTENANT-COMMANDER WILLIAM WARLAND RHOADES, U.S.N.

Lieutenant-Commander William Warland Rhoades was born in Boston, Massachusetts, October 2, 1837. He was appointed an acting ensign in the navy on August 19, 1864. He was ordered to the frigate "Susquehanna," and was present during the attacks upon Fort Fisher, December 24 and 25, 1864, and January 13 and 15, 1865. Commodore Godon, who commanded the division, as well as the "Susquehanna," reported to Admiral Porter: "From my position on the wheel-house, overlooking my entire battery, I had every officer and man under my observation, and I have sincere pleasure in testifying to the fine bearing, zeal, and gallantry of the division officers, and of Acting Ensign Rhoades, of the First Division."

On January 15 the "Susquehanna" landed a body of about one hundred sailors and marines, for the assault upon Fort Fisher, under Lieutenant-Commander Blake, Lieutenant Bartlett, and Acting Ensign Rhoades. Lieutenant-Commander Blake's report states: "I sent Mr. Rhoades, with ten men, to report to Lieutenant Preston, who was engaged at the front in digging rifle-pits. Mr. Rhoades rendered most valuable service in the rifle-pits, which were dug under the fire of the enemy's sharp-shooters, and occasionally a discharge of grape, and when the army made the assault, accompanied by one brave fellow, James Shannon, he followed into the fort. Shannon carried a flag and placed it on the parapet."

Immediately after the capture of the fort the ships' boats returned to their respective vessels, leaving Acting Ensign Rhoades with the army. He reported to General Terry, and during the night was placed on picket-duty with the troops. On the following morning, by order of the general, he went into the fort to collect the stragglers from the navy, and, as he was passing out with these men, was thrown violently to the ground by the concussion caused by the explosion of the magazine of the fort, by which over two hundred men lost their lives.

Acting Ensign Rhoades was promoted to acting master April 2, 1866, and was commissioned as ensign in the navy March 12, 1868, being one of the sixty-four who qualified, before the Board of Examiners, out of three hundred and five applicants. Ensign Rhoades reached the grade of lieutenant-commander in February, 1884.

He has served in the following-named United States vessels-of-war: "Savannah," "Susquehanna," "Nipsic," "Pensacola," "Independence," "Cyane," "Resaca," "Powhatan," "Kansas," "Ossipee," "Sabine," "Mahopac," "Jamestown," and "Dale."

During the time he was attached to the "Ossipee," the steamer "Virginius," while being towed and manned by a crew from the "Ossipee," foundered off Frying-Pan Shoals. When it was discovered that she was sinking, he immediately called for a volunteer crew for the ship's cutter, and went to the rescue of his shipmates. He rescued forty-five officers and men; the execution of this necessitated him to make five trips, because of the heavy gale and rough sea it was unsafe to bring off more than nine persons at any one trip of the cutter.

He has served as a member of two Nicaraguan surveying expeditions; also in charge of the Bellevue magazine, and had instruction at the Torpedo Station. He is now United States light-house inspector, Thirteenth District.

CAPTAIN AND BREVET LIEUTENANT-COLONEL
EDMUND RICE, U.S.A.

CAPTAIN AND BREVET LIEUTENANT-COLONEL EDMUND RICE (Fifth Infantry) was born in Cambridge, Massachusetts, December 2, 1842. He is descended from Edmund Rice (born 1594), of Berkhamstead, County of Hertfordshire, England, who came to this country and settled in Sudbury, Massachusetts, in 1639. Several of his descendants were engaged in Indian and French colonial wars, and during the Revolution many of their children fought at Lexington, Concord, Bunker Hill, Bennington, Crown Point, and in other battles of the war. Two of his ancestors, Major Nathan Rice, of Sturbridge, Massachusetts, and Lieutenant Oliver Rice, of Sudbury, Massachusetts, were original members of the Massachusetts Society of Cincinnati. His grandfather, Edmund Rice, was an officer of the war of 1812. The subject of this sketch was educated at Norwich University, Vermont, which conferred on him the degree of Bachelor of Arts.

His first active service was in driving off pirates from the ship "Snow-Squall" while it was becalmed in the China Sea in 1859. From his knowledge of gunnery he was given charge of one of the small swivels with which the ship was provided; by judiciously charging it with lead pipe and nails the attack was repulsed.

At the age of nineteen he entered the volunteer service as captain of the first Fourteenth Massachusetts Infantry April 27, 1861, and remained with it until disbanded in June following. He immediately re-entered as captain of the Twentieth Massachusetts, and was captain of the Nineteenth Massachusetts Infantry July 25, 1861, rising in the grade of major and lieutenant-colonel to that of colonel of the same regiment in July, 1864.

Colonel Rice served in the field with the Army of the Potomac, and was engaged in the battles of Ball's Bluff, Myron's Mills, siege of Yorktown, West Point, Fair Oaks, Oak Grove, Peach Orchard, Allen's Farm, Savage Station, White Oak Swamp, Glendale (commanding regiment), Malvern Hill, second Malvern Hill, Bull Run, Fairfax Court-House, South Mountain, and Antietam, where he was severely wounded.

He rejoined his regiment at Falmouth, and engaged in the second attack on Fredericksburg, and action at Thoroughfare Gap, battle of Gettysburg (wounded twice), in the repulse of Pickett's charge.

On this occasion, when a portion of Webb's men gave way and the rebels were exultingly sweeping through our line, he had the honor to lead the counter-charge, which resulted in their overthrow. In the hand-to-hand conflict that followed, Colonel Rice was twice severely wounded and fell inside their lines, the foremost man in the Union line at that point. A large number of those shot on both sides had their clothes burned by the discharge of the guns, so near were the men together.

He was presented by Congress with a medal of honor for leading the advance of his regiment, and the Forty-second New York, in the charge made to repel Pickett's assault. "The Congress to Lieutenant-Colonel Edmund Rice, Nineteenth Massachusetts Volunteers, for conspicuous bravery on the third day of the battle of Gettysburg."

Colonel Rice commanded his regiment in the Rapidan and in the Richmond campaigns, and was engaged in the battles of Bristoe Station, Blackburn's Ford, Robinson's Cross-Roads, Mine Run, the Wilderness, Spottsylvania, Laurel Hill, and was captured in the assault at the death angle, Spottsylvania, on the morning of the 12th of May, 1864, and in North Carolina, while being conveyed South, escaped by cutting through the door of a freight car in which the prisoners were confined, and jumping from it while the train was under full headway, reached the Union lines near the Ohio River, after travelling twenty-three nights (resting by day), having walked between three and four hundred miles.

Colonel Rice rejoined his regiment in front of Petersburg in August, 1864, and participated in the closing scenes of the war, being engaged in the battles of Second Deep Bottom, Weldon Railroad, Ream's Station, Second Hatcher's Run, and present at the surrender of Lee's army.

On the 28th of July, 1866, Colonel Rice was appointed first lieutenant in the Fortieth U. S. Infantry, and was brevetted captain, major, and lieutenant-colonel U.S.A., for gallant and meritorious services in action. He was assigned to the Fifth Infantry in 1871, and promoted captain March 10, 1883. He is at present commandant of the Columbian Guard, World's Columbian Exposition, at Chicago.

Colonel Rice is the inventor of the celebrated "stacking swivel and knife-intrenching bayonet," of which ten thousand were ordered by the government.

## CHAPLAIN I. NEWTON RITNER, U.S.A.

CHAPLAIN I. NEWTON RITNER, son of George A. and Mary T. Ritner, was born in Chester County, Pennsylvania, February 22, 1841. In April, 1850, he removed to Juniata County, where outside of school hours and during vacations he clerked in a store and transacted the business of various offices of responsibility. Before he was eighteen years old he taught, with signal ability, one of the largest public schools in that county, and two years later became associate principal of a select academy.

While thus engaged he enlisted, September 3, 1861, as private in Company I, Forty-ninth Pennsylvania Volunteers, and was soon afterwards promoted to sergeant. He passed through the entire Peninsula campaign with the Army of the Potomac, to which his regiment belonged, including the battle of Williamsburg, the siege of Yorktown, the action at Golding's Farm, the engagements at White Oak Swamp, and Malvern Hills, and the general vicissitudes of the "Seven Days' retreat."

While at Harrison's Landing he was prostrated by the prevailing fever, the result of constant exposure in the line of duty, and in August, 1862, was ordered to his native State on recruiting service. While thus engaged at Lewistown he secured an unusually large number of recruits, and was commissioned second lieutenant of Company A. Early in December he was promoted to first lieutenant and ordered to Harrisburg, to superintend the payment of bounty to volunteers and substitutes. Soon after this he was made adjutant of "Camp Curtin," and, when it became necessary to cut off all communication with the camp on account of the ravages of the small-pox, he was placed in command. Under his personal supervision the process of renovation was prosecuted with such vigor and thoroughness, that within three weeks the entire camp had been purified, the disease eradicated, the convalescents transferred to isolated quarters, and the quarantine removed.

On January 27, 1863, he was appointed adjutant Volunteer Recruiting Service for the State of Pennsylvania, and filled that office with exceptional efficiency until November 27, 1863, when, because of the depletion and consolidation of his regiment, he was honorably mustered out as a supernumerary officer. In recognition of his special fidelity he was commissioned captain by brevet "for faithful and meritorious services during the war."

While arranging for immediate return to active service in the field, he visited his parents in Philadelphia, and while there was persuaded to accept the appointment as chief clerk of recruiting service, which had been proffered by Major C. C. Gilbert, acting assistant provost-marshal general, Eastern Division, Pennsylvania. He resigned this position in November, 1864, and accepted a

clerkship under Major W. B. Lane, chief marshal and division officer, under whom he had served at Harrisburg, and was placed in charge of the disbursing records of that office. Having completed this work in March, 1866, he resigned and settled in Philadelphia, where he engaged as a book-keeper, and subsequently as the manager of a large sewing-machine office, the business of which increased sevenfold under his administration. In November, 1873, in compliance with an intense conviction, he withdrew from secular pursuits, and on the 12th of the succeeding February was ordained as a gospel minister in the denomination (Baptist) to which he belonged. At the time of this change he was offered, with an enticing salary, the general management of a prominent manufacturing establishment, which he declined, and ten days after his ordination he entered upon the pastorate of the Eleventh Baptist Church, where he labored for nearly eighteen years until September 3, 1891, when he started for Fort Niagara, New York, as an army chaplain, having been appointed to that office July 20. After seven months' temporary service at Niagara, he was transferred to Fort Keogh, Montana, where he now is, having arrived there April 11, 1892.

While in civil life Chaplain Ritner was frequently honored by his denomination, having in 1882 been elected moderator of the oldest and largest (Philadelphia) Baptist association in the United States, of which body, also, he had been associate clerk for thirteen years. For nearly eighteen years he was secretary of the "Philadelphia Conference of Baptist Ministers;" for five years secretary of the ".American Baptist Historical Society;" and for long terms served as a member of the board of managers of four of the leading denominational societies; and this, in addition to his duties as chaplain of George G. Meade Post 1, G. A. R., of Philadelphia, for the nine years preceding his present appointment.

## CAPTAIN HENRY P. RITZIUS, U.S.A.

CAPTAIN HENRY P. RITZIUS (Twenty-fifth Infantry) was born in Prussia on January 3, 1839. Early in the war of the Rebellion he entered the volunteer service as private of Company A, Fifth New York State Militia, May 1, 1861, and was honorably discharged, after serving in the defences of Washington, August 7, 1861. He re-entered the volunteer service as first sergeant of Company G, Fifty-second New York Infantry, September 17, 1861, and was discharged June 30, 1862, in order to accept the appointment of second lieutenant in the same regiment, in which he was promoted first lieutenant August 23, 1862, and captain September 16, 1863. He was honorably mustered out August 2, 1864, but was appointed major of the Fifty-second New York Infantry December 8, 1864, and was promoted lieutenant-colonel of the same regiment in May, 1865, but was not mustered as such, owing to the regiment being reduced below the number of men required.

He served in the field with the Army of the Potomac in the Peninsula campaign, and was engaged in the battles of Fair Oaks, Peach Orchard, Savage Station, White Oak Swamp, and Malvern Hill, Virginia; in the Maryland campaign and engaged in the battle of Antietam, and the march of the army back to the Rappahannock River; in the Rappahannock campaign, and engaged in the battles of Fredericksburg and Chancellorsville, Virginia; in the Pennsylvania campaign, and engaged in the battle of Gettysburg, Pennsylvania; in the operations at Mine Run, Virginia; in the Richmond campaign, and engaged in the battles of the Wilderness, Po River, Spottsylvania, North Anna, Tolopotomy, Cold Harbor, siege of Petersburg, action of Strawberry Plains, and battles of Deep Bottom and Ream's Station, Virginia.

Captain Ritzius was provost-marshal of the First Division of the Second Corps from September, 1862, to March, 1863. He was honorably mustered out of the Fifty-second New York July 1, 1865, and was appointed first lieutenant Seventh U. S. Veteran Infantry (Hancock's Corps) August 10, 1865, and served with his company and on court-martial duty at Philadelphia, Fort Delaware, and Harrisburg to April 30, 1866, when he was honorably mustered out of the volunteer service.

On October 23, 1867, he entered the regular service as second lieutenant of the Thirty-ninth Infantry, and served in Louisiana, Texas, Dakota, and Montana. On the consolidation of regiments, Captain Ritzius was transferred to the Twenty-fifth Infantry April 20, 1869, promoted first lieutenant March 3, 1875, and captain September 1, 1887. His present station is at Fort Missoula, Montana.

## COLONEL AND BREVET BRIGADIER-GENERAL JOSEPH ROBERTS, U.S.A. (RETIRED).

COLONEL AND BREVET BRIGADIER-GENERAL JOSEPH ROBERTS was born in Delaware, and graduated from the Military Academy July 1, 1835. He was promoted brevet second lieutenant Fourth Artillery the same day, second lieutenant June 10, 1836, first lieutenant July 7, 1838, and captain Fourth Artillery August 20, 1848. He served at Fort Hamilton in 1835-36, and then took part in the operations in the Creek Nation in the latter year. He participated in the Florida War in 1836-37, being captain of a regiment of Mounted Creek Volunteers September 1 to November 13, 1836. He was on duty at the Military Academy, as assistant professor of natural and experimental philosophy, from September 29, 1837, to September 1, 1839, and as principal assistant professor of the same branch until August 17, 1840.

He afterwards participated in the Florida hostilities against the Seminole Indians, and was in garrison at Key West, Florida, until 1850; at Fort Mifflin, Pennsylvania, until 1853, when he was ordered to Ringgold Barracks, Texas, where he remained until 1855. He was then transferred to Fort Wood, New York, and again sent to Ringgold Barracks, Texas, in 1856, but was shortly changed to stations in Florida, serving at Forts McRea, Jupiter, and Capron, and engaged in hostilities against the Seminole Indians until 1857. His field of duty was changed to Fort Leavenworth, Kansas, in 1857, and he served at Platte Bridge, Nebraska, during 1858-59, after which he was detailed on recruiting service to recruit a company for the Artillery School.

From 1859 to 1861 Captain Roberts was in garrison at Fort Monroe, Virginia (Artillery School of Practice), being a member of the board to arrange the programme of instruction for the school.

He served during the war of the Rebellion from 1861-65. He was promoted major of the Fourth Artillery September 3, 1861, and was in command of Fort Monroe, Virginia, from October 19, 1861, to September 13, 1862; then was chief of artillery of the Seventh Army Corps to March 19, 1863, when he was appointed colonel of the Third Pennsylvania Heavy Artillery, and promoted lieutenant-colonel of the Fourth U. S. Artillery August 11, 1863.

Colonel Roberts was in command of Fort Monroe from June 10, 1863, to November 9, 1865, and at the close of the war was brevetted colonel March 13, 1865, and brevet brigadier-general of volunteers April 9, 1865, for faithful and meritorious services during the Rebellion. He was also brevetted brigadier-general United States Army March 13, 1865, for faithful and distinguished services during the Rebellion. He was mustered out of the volunteer service Nov. 9, 1865, and assigned to the command of Fort McHenry, Maryland, continuing there in garrison until Nov. 16, 1866, when he was detailed on court-martial duty at Washington, D. C., to April 30, 1867.

General Roberts performed the duties of acting assistant inspector-general of the Department of Washington from May 1, 1867, to April 1, 1868. He was then assigned as superintendent of theoretical instruction at the Artillery School, Fort Monroe, and occupied this position until February 14, 1877. He was promoted colonel of the Fourth Artillery January 10, 1877, and retired from active service July 2, 1877, being at the time on duty at the Presidio of San Francisco.

General Roberts is the author of "Hand-Book of Artillery," 1861.

MAJOR-GENERAL JOHN C. ROBINSON, U.S.A.
(RETIRED).

MAJOR-GENERAL JOHN C. ROBINSON was born in New York. He was a cadet at the U. S. Military Academy from July 1, 1835, to March 14, 1838. He was appointed second lieutenant of the Fifth Infantry October 27, 1839. He served at Madison Barracks, New York, to May, 1840, and at Green Bay, Wisconsin, to 1841, when he was en route to Florida. After serving at Fort Brady and at Mackinac, Michigan, until 1845, he joined the Army of Occupation of Mexico, and was at Corpus Christi, Texas, to September, 1845. He participated in the Mexican war, and was engaged at Palo Alto, Resaca de la Palma, and Monterey, and then on the march to and occupation of the City of Mexico via Saltillo, Point Isabel, and Vera Cruz. He was promoted first lieutenant June 18, 1846. While in Mexico, Lieutenant Robinson applied for the appointment of assistant quartermaster. His application was indorsed by General Worth as follows:

"I take special pleasure in cordially recommending Lieutenant Robinson as qualified in every respect by habits, services in the field, experience in the department, and gallant conduct in action, for the appointment he desires. Indeed, I know of no young officer with higher claims or better qualifications.

"(Signed) W. S. WORTH,
"Brevet Brigadier-General, Commanding Division."

After the war closed, Lieutenant Robinson was stationed at Fort Smith, Arkansas, and Fort Gibson, C. N., in 1848-50, at which time he was promoted captain. After two years' recruiting duty he was commanding recruits for the Seventh Infantry, en route from Fort Columbus, New York, via Newport, Kentucky, to Fort Arbuckle, C. N., in the fall of 1852. He then joined his company at Phantom Hill, Texas, and was engaged against hostile Indians in 1853-54. He then served at various stations in the West until the commencement of the war of the Rebellion, when he was employed on mustering duty until September, 1861. He was promoted major of the Second Infantry February 20, 1862, and appointed brigadier-general of volunteers April 28, 1862.

General Robinson participated in the campaigns of the Army of the Potomac, and was engaged in the battles of Peach Orchard, Savage Station, Glendale, Malvern Hill, action of Bristoe Station, battles of second Bull Run, Chantilly, and Fredericksburg. He was also at the battles of second Fredericksburg, Chancellorsville, and Gettysburg, operations at Mine Run, action of Mitchell's Station, battles of the Wilderness, Spottsylvania, and Todd's Tavern, and, while leading his division, was wounded in the knee, resulting in the loss of his left leg.

At the battle of Glendale, General Robinson's brigade repulsed repeated attacks of a superior force. The following is an extract from General Kearney's report:

"I have reserved General Robinson for the last. To him this day is due above all others in this division the honors of this battle. The attack was on his wing. Everywhere present, by personal supervision and noble example, he secured to us the honor of victory. . . . Our loss has been severe, and when it is remembered that this occurs to mere skeletons of regiments, there is but one observation to be made, that previous military history presents no such parallel."

Extract from a letter of Major-General G. K. Warren to the adjutant-general U. S. Army, dated April 16, 1866, relating to Spottsylvania Court-House:

"In the flank movement to the left, begun at dark of the 7th of May, the Fifth Corps again had the lead, with General Robinson's division in the advance. Delayed as we were by darkness and bad roads, crowded with troops, until it was probable the enemy had anticipated us in reaching the desired point, yet urged by the importance of time to our success, General Robinson marched rapidly on, driving the light troops of the enemy before him, till charging directly the desired position, himself animating the advance by leading in person, he fell dangerously wounded, and his command was repulsed by the opposing infantry, already arrayed in strong force."

At the close of the war General Robinson was brevetted lieutenant-colonel, colonel, brigadier-general, and major-general, U. S. Army, for " gallant and meritorious services in action."

General Robinson served in North Carolina, 1866, and other like duties in 1867-68, and was commanding the Department of the Lakes. Retired from active service, with the rank of major-general, May 6, 1869.

## COMMANDER C. H. ROCKWELL, U.S.N.

COMMANDER C. H. ROCKWELL was born in Chatham, Massachusetts, April 29, 1840, and entered the naval service as acting master July 5, 1862. Attached to the "North Carolina," and then ordered to the steamer "Penguin," East Gulf Squadron, as executive-officer. In May, 1863, ordered to the U. S. schooner "Wanderer." In July of the same year he was ordered to command the U. S. schooner "Two Sisters." During the time he held this command active and important services were performed on the west coast of Florida, calling forth a commendatory letter from the commander-in-chief, who recommended Rockwell for promotion. On December 16, 1863, the Navy Department promoted him to acting volunteer lieutenant, "in consideration of good service," and a few days afterwards Lieutenant Rockwell was detached from the "Two Sisters" and ordered to command the bark "Gem of the Sea." This command he retained until November, 1864, when he was ordered to the command of the U. S. steamer "Hendrick Hudson." While in this command, and of the force blockading St. Mark's, Florida, he organized and directed an expedition against rebel salt-works, dispersing the armed force at the entrance of the river, and destroying a large amount of property. This called forth another letter of commendation from the commander-in-chief. On February 22, 1865, an expedition under Brigadier-General John Newton was organized to operate about St. Mark's, and at the request of General Newton, Lieutenant Rockwell was ordered to the expedition as naval aid on the staff of the general, being placed in charge of the transportation of the troops. The forces landed at St. Mark's, and had an engagement at Newport, followed by a bloody battle at Natural Bridge, eight miles below Tallahassee. Upon the return of the expedition, Lieutenant Rockwell received a letter of thanks for his services from General Newton. He resumed command of the "Hendrick Hudson," and on March 27, 1865, was promoted to the grade of acting volunteer lieutenant-commander. Remained in command until August 8, 1865, when he was granted four months' leave of absence, and was honorably discharged from the naval service December 8, 1865. In November, 1866, Lieutenant-Commander Rockwell was examined for the regular service, and appointed acting master at once. He served for nearly a year on board the "Osceola," in the West Indies, and then went to Brazil as a passenger in the "Idaho," joined the flag-ship "Guerriere," and served in her until her return home in July, 1869. In 1868 he was made master, and in December of the same year commissioned as lieutenant. After a short service in the receiving-ship "Vandalia," at Portsmouth, New Hampshire, he was ordered to the U. S. S. "Palos," and proceeded in her to China, commanding her until October, 1872, when he returned to the United States in the "Alaska." During his command of the "Palos" participated in the actions with the Corean forts, in Admiral John Rodgers's expedition. From March, 1873, to September, 1874, he was on duty at the Portsmouth Navy-Yard; then served some months on the "Plymouth" and "Colorado," and in June, 1875, became light-house inspector of the Fourteenth District. On June 1, 1876, was ordered as executive-officer of the U. S. S. "Adams." On February 26, 1878, was promoted to lieutenant-commander, and served at the Torpedo School. In May, 1878, joined the "Jamestown" as executive, and served in Alaska in that ship until September, 1881. Then he was on duty at the Boston Navy-Yard until October, 1882. In 1883 attached to the receiving-ship "Franklin," at Norfolk, Virginia. In Sept., 1884, took a large draft of men to the Isthmus for the Pacific Squadron. Was at the Torpedo School again in 1885, and at the War College. From April, 1886, to Oct., 1888, served on the training-ship "Minnesota," at New York. On Oct. 31, 1888, was promoted to commander, and in Feb., 1889, took command of U. S. S. "Yantic."

Commander Rockwell is at present in command of the receiving-ship "St. Louis," at the navy-yard, League Island, Pennsylvania.

COLONEL AND BREVET BRIGADIER-GENERAL THEOPHILUS FRANCIS RODENBOUGH, U.S.A.
(RETIRED).

COLONEL AND BREVET BRIGADIER-GENERAL THEOPHILUS FRANCIS RODENBOUGH was born at Easton, Pennsylvania, November 5, 1838. He attended private schools, had special tutors, and took a course of mathematics and English literature at Lafayette College (1856-57).

Upon the outbreak of the war for the Union, President Lincoln appointed him (March 27, 1861) a second lieutenant in the Second U. S. Dragoons. He served (1861-62) as post adjutant and quartermaster U. S. Cavalry School of Practice, Carlisle, Pennsylvania, and with his regiment in all the campaigns of the Army of the Potomac (1862-64).

He was promoted first lieutenant in 1861, and captain July 17, 1862; he was slightly wounded and had two horses shot under him at Beverly Ford, Virginia, June 9, 1863, the great cavalry fight in which nearly twenty thousand Union and Confederate cavalry crossed sabres. He commanded his regiment at Gettysburg, having two horses killed during the campaign; was severely wounded at Trevilian Station, Virginia, June 11, 1864, and, while in command of his regiment, lost his right arm and had his horse killed at the battle of the Opequan, Virginia, September 19, 1864; after which General Sheridan made the following recommendation: "I have the honor to request the promotion of the following-named officers: Captain T. F. Rodenbough, Second U. S. Cavalry, to the rank of brevet brigadier-general for gallant and meritorious conduct at Trevilian Station, June 11, 1864, at which engagement he was wounded while charging at the head of his regiment. At the battle of Opequan he was again wounded (losing his arm) while charging at the head of his regiment. He is a gallant and meritorious young officer, and would do honor to the grade asked for him."

Upon the recommendation of General Sheridan, he was granted leave of absence from the regular army to accept the colonelcy of the Eighteenth Pennsylvania Cavalry, and in July, 1865, by direction of the President, was specially assigned, with the rank of brigadier-general, to command a brigade (consisting of regulars and volunteers) and the District of Clarksburg, West Virginia. He was honorably mustered out of the volunteer service October 31, 1865. He served during the winter of 1865 as inspector-general "U. S. forces in Kansas and the Territories," with headquarters at Fort Leavenworth, and, later, with the Second Cavalry at Fort Ellsworth, Kansas.

Upon the reorganization of the army he was appointed major (July 28, 1866) of the Forty-second U. S. Infantry, commanding it and the posts of Plattsburg and Madison Barracks, New York, 1866-69; and also serving on various boards: for the selection of a magazine-gun, the examination of officers, and the investigation of the case of the first colored cadet at West Point.

He received brevets to the rank of brigadier-general U. S. Army, "for gallant and meritorious services" at the battles, respectively, of Trevilian Station, Opequan, Todd's Tavern, and Cold Harbor, Virginia, and was, at his own request, retired from active service, December 15, 1870, "with full rank (colonel of cavalry) of the command held when wounded."

In recommending this officer for his highest brevet, General Sheridan wrote to the War Department as follows: "Colonel Rodenbough was one of the most gallant and valuable young officers under my command in the Cavalry Corps, Army of the Potomac. He was constantly in the field with his regiment, the Second U. S. Cavalry (a portion of the time in command of it), from the spring of 1862 up to the time of his being wounded, while gallantly leading his regiment at the battle of Opequan, September 19, 1864."

After retirement, General Rodenbough was deputy governor of the U. S. Soldiers' Home, Washington, D. C., 1870-71; general eastern agent of the Pullman Car Company, 1872-73; associate editor Army and Navy Journal, 1876-77; corresponding secretary, Society of the Army of the Potomac, 1878; secretary and editor of the Journal (1878-90) and vice-president (1891-93) Military Service Institution of the United States; chief of the Bureau of Elections, city of New York, 1892; author of several essays, sketches, and the following books: "From Everglade to Cañon with the Second Dragoons," 1875; "Afghanistan, or the Anglo-Russian Dispute," 1882; "Uncle Sam's Medal of Honor," 1887; "The Bravest Five Hundred of '61'," 1891; and "Autumn Leaves from Family Trees," 1891.

REAR-ADMIRAL C. R. P. RODGERS, U.S.N.
(DECEASED).

REAR-ADMIRAL C. R. P. RODGERS was born November 14, 1819, in Brooklyn, New York. Appointed midshipman from Connecticut October 5, 1833; attached to frigate "Brandywine" and sloop "Vincennes," Pacific Station, 1834-36; navy-yard, New York, 1837; sloop "Fairfield" and brig "Dolphin," Brazil Squadron, 1837-39. Promoted to passed midshipman July 8, 1839; schooner "Flirt," coast of Florida, 1839-40; and in command of schooner "Phœnix," 1841-42, being actively employed in the Seminole War during those three years. Sloop "Saratoga," coast of the United States, 1842-43. Commissioned as lieutenant September 4, 1844; served in Mediterranean Squadron in frigate "Cumberland," 1843-45, and in store-ship "Lexington," 1845; Coast Survey, 1846; frigate "Potomac" and sloop "Albany," blockading Mexican coast, 1847; present and in the trenches at the reduction of Vera Cruz, and at the capture of Tuspan and Tabasco; Coast Survey, 1848-49; frigate "Congress," Brazil Squadron, 1850-51; frigate "Constitution," coast of Africa, 1852-55; Coast Survey, commanding steamer "Bibb" and schooner "Gallatin," 1856-57; steam-frigate "Wabash," Mediterranean Squadron, 1858-59; commandant of midshipmen at Naval Academy, 1860-61. Commissioned as commander October 15, 1861; served in steam-frigate "Wabash" as captain and fleet-captain, 1861-63, commanding that ship at the battle of Port Royal, November, 1861, and the naval force in the trenches at the reduction of Fort Pulaski, January 27, 1862. While in the "Wabash," much employed on detached service, in command of a division of gun-boats, in retaking the coast and inlets of Georgia and Florida, and South Carolina south of Port Royal; fleet-captain in the "New Ironsides," in the attack on Charleston, April 7, 1863. Rear-Admiral Dupont, in his official report of that engagement, says: "On this, as on all other occasions, I had invaluable assistance from the fleet-captain, C. R. P. Rodgers, who was with me in the pilot-house directing the movements of the squadron. For now over eighteen months in this war this officer has been afloat with me, and in my opinion no language could overstate his services to his country, to this fleet, and to myself as its commander-in-chief." Commanded steam-sloop "Iroquois," 1863-65, on special service. Commissioned as captain July 25, 1866; navy-yard, Norfolk, 1865-67; commanded steam-frigate "Franklin," Mediterranean Squadron, 1868-70. Commissioned as commodore August 28, 1870; special service in Europe, 1871; chief of Bureau of Yards and Docks, October, 1871-74; Commissioned as rear-admiral June 14, 1874; superintendent Naval Academy, 1874-78; commanding Pacific Squadron, 1878-80; superintendent Naval Academy, 1881. Retired 1881. Died 1892.

In 1884 Rear-Admiral Raymond Rodgers was president of the International Meridian Conference.

## COMMANDER GEORGE W. RODGERS, U.S.N.
### (DECEASED).

COMMANDER GEORGE WASHINGTON RODGERS, a brother of C. R. P. Rodgers, was born in Brooklyn, New York, October 30, 1822, and died off Charleston harbor, South Carolina, August 17, 1863. Entered the navy as midshipman April 30, 1836. In July, 1842, he became passed midshipman, and during the Mexican War served in the steamer "Colonel Harney," and the sloop-of-war "John Adams," participating in the operations at Vera Cruz, Tuspan, Alvarado, and other points on the coast of the Gulf of Mexico, which were captured by our forces. During much of the time he served as acting master.

After being attached to the Coast Survey in 1849 and 1850, he was commissioned lieutenant in June of the latter year. Made a cruise in the "Germantown" on the home station, and in the "Falmouth," on the coast of Brazil.

When the Civil War occurred he was stationed at the Naval Academy at Annapolis, and was chiefly instrumental in saving the frigate "Constitution" from a threatened attack of the rebels at Annapolis. He afterwards took the ship to Newport, at which place the Naval Academy remained during the war.

In January, 1862, he was commissioned commander, and in October was ordered to the command of the monitor "Catskill," in which he took part in many of the attacks upon the defences of Charleston. On April 7, in the "Catskill," he took her almost under the walls of "Sumter." Rear-Admiral Dahlgren appointed Rodgers chief of staff in July, 1863, principally on account of the cool and deliberate manner in which he fought his vessel on all occasions; but he did not relinquish command of the "Catskill."

During the attack on Fort Wagner, August 17, 1863, he took command of the vessel as usual, and, while in action, was instantly killed by a shot that struck the top of the conning-house, and broke it in, scattering fragments in all directions.

It was of Commander Rodgers that Miles O'Reilly wrote one of his most admired stanzas:

> "Ah, me! George Rodgers lies
> With dim and dreamless eyes;
> He has ably won the prize
> Of the striped and starry shroud."

He was noted as an excellent executive officer and navigator, and generally beloved for his amiable disposition and his devotion to duty.

## REAR-ADMIRAL JOHN RODGERS, U.S.N. (DECEASED).

REAR-ADMIRAL JOHN RODGERS'S record is so extensive that we fear we shall have to condense it very materially. He was born in Maryland, and appointed midshipman from the District of Columbia in March, 1828. Served in the Mediterranean; passed at the Naval School at Norfolk, 1834. Served on the Brazilian Station, and on special service. Commissioned as lieutenant January, 1840. Served in the Home Squadron, special service, Mediterranean, and Coast Survey up to 1852. He commanded the steamer "John Hancock" on the surveying and exploring expedition to the North Pacific and the China Sea, in the years 1853-56. During this cruise he was made commander. Upon his return he was on special duty. In 1861 Commander Rodgers was ordered to special duty in superintending the construction of the "Benton" class of iron-clads, for the Western waters. In 1862 he was assigned to the command of the iron-clad "Galena," and in May left Hampton Roads with a squadron of gun-boats, and went up the James River. After silencing two rebel batteries, the fleet reached Fort Darling, a casemated battery on the crest of a hill, which, with vessels sunk in front, obstructed the channel. On May 15 Rodgers took the "Galena" within five hundred yards of the fort, and anchored there. Two wooden gun-boats were some hundred yards below. For four hours the fight went on, when, having expended all ammunition, the vessels retired. The "Monitor" of the squadron could not sufficiently elevate her guns, while the rifle-gun of the "Naugatuck," or "Stevens Battery," burst at the first fire. Their crews did service as sharpshooters. The so-called armor of the "Galena" proved of no service. She was hit one hundred and twenty-nine times, and lost in killed and wounded two-thirds of her crew. Rodgers was commissioned captain July 16, 1862. Commanded the monitor "Weehawken" in 1863, and sailed from New York in that vessel for the South Atlantic Blockading Squadron. On the passage south, and while off the Delaware, he encountered a heavy gale. He was urged to run in to the Breakwater and remain until the storm was over. This he declined, saying that he wished to test the sea-going qualities of the monitors. The "Weehawken" rode out the gale, and reached Port Royal in safety. On June 17, 1863, Captain Rodgers, in the "Weehawken," encountered the very powerful rebel iron-clad "Atlanta," of much greater tonnage than the "Weehawken." The "Atlanta" came down Wassaw Sound, and so confident of victory were the Confederates, that she was accompanied from Savannah to the scene of conflict by boats freighted with gay parties, eager to witness the triumph of their vessel.

Only five shots were fired by the "Weehawken." In fifteen minutes the "Atlanta" surrendered, overwhelmed by the fifteen-inch guns of the "Weehawken." This action settled the question as to their use. Captain Rodgers was made commodore June 17, 1863, the date of this action. In 1864-65 he commanded the iron-clad "Dictator," on special service. In 1866-67 he commanded the monitor "Monadnock," which he took around to the Pacific. He reached Valparaiso in time to witness the bombardment of that city by the Spanish fleet. From San Francisco, when he left the "Monadnock," he came home overland before the completion of the railroad. He was then ordered to the command of the Boston Navy-Yard, where he remained three years. He was commissioned as rear-admiral on December 31, 1869, and commanded the Asiatic Squadron 1870-72. He then commanded the Mare Island Navy-Yard from 1873 to 1877; and was superintendent of the Naval Observatory from 1877 to 1882, in which latter year, in May, he died at Washington.

Lieutenant Rodgers performed a remarkable piece of work in the surveying expedition of 1853 to 1856. The "John Hancock" was a small steam-vessel, built upon, with light upper works, to enable her to contain in some fashion the material and personnel of the expedition. When she sailed from Boston, there were grave doubts expressed by experienced seamen as to whether she would ever reach her destination. Yet in this craft, by dint of sheer pluck and perseverance, he accomplished some of the most valuable exploratory and hydrographic work ever done.

Dignified, but unassuming in deportment, he always obtained the regard and respect of all with whom he came in contact.

PAYMASTER ROBERT BURTON RODNEY, U.S.N.
(RETIRED).

PAYMASTER ROBERT BURTON RODNEY'S ancestors numbered among them a signer of the Declaration of Independence, and senators and representatives, and attorneys-general of the United States, with governors of Delaware. He is of the same family as Lord Rodney, whose naval exploits are known to readers of history.

Paymaster Rodney was born in Philadelphia, where his parents were temporarily residing, on October 11, 1840. He was appointed acting paymaster from Delaware October 26, 1862; served on board the ordnance-ship "Dale" at Key West during 1862-63; attached to the blockader "Chambers," of the East Gulf Squadron, 1863-64; attached to the supply steamer "Massachusetts," 1864-65, and the double-ender "Conemaugh" in 1865-66.

In 1867 he was ordered to Annapolis, and served on board the training-frigates "Constitution" and "Santee." During the years 1868-69 he was attached to the store-ship "Cyane," lying in Panama Bay. He then served on board the iron-clad "Terror," in the Cuban waters, during 1870 and a part of 1871.

During the latter year he was placed upon the retired list on account of broken health, dating back to his service in the "Chambers" in 1864. This vessel had a notably bad experience. While moored off Indian River, Florida, in August and September, almost all the ship's company, numbering eighty persons, were stricken with yellow fever of the worst type at about the same time. No such mortality had been ever known in any ship of the navy. About one-fourth of the men and one-half of the officers died, including the commanding officer. The only medical officer became violently deranged, and had to be confined. Paymaster Rodney's clerk and steward being both dead, he had to issue provisions and clothing, serve as watch-officer, chaplain, and nurse. He was the last one to be affected, nearly dying from the malady at the Lazaretto, below Philadelphia, to which the vessel had by that time been brought.

In July, 1866, Paymaster Rodney was commissioned in the regular service as passed assistant paymaster, and was promoted to paymaster, with the relative rank of lieutenant-commander, June 30, 1869, and with this rank he was retired.

Paymaster Rodney is the author of "Alboin and Rosamond," and several lesser poems.

## REAR-ADMIRAL F. A. ROE. U.S.N. (RETIRED).

REAR-ADMIRAL F. A. ROE is a native of New York, and after appointment as midshipman, in 1841, served in the Brazil and West African Squadrons; was in the "Boston" when she was wrecked on Eleuthera; then attached to the "Allegheny" until ordered to Naval School in 1847; passed midshipman from August, 1847; dismissed by sentence of court-martial for disobeying an illegal order, October, 1849; reappointed to original rank and place in navy list, September, 1850; served two years in the mail-steamer "Georgia," which employed naval officers; next in Behring Sea and the Pacific Exploring Expedition,—a most valuable and interesting service, including a battle with heavily-armed Chinese pirates. In the Arctic, and along north coast of Siberia, the Kurile Islands, Japan, etc. Promoted master October, 1855, and lieutenant in September, 1855; Coast Survey; a cruise in the Mediterranean; ordnance duty, New York, until July, 1861, when he applied for service afloat; was ordered to the "Pensacola," but temporarily sent, at the time of "Bull Run," to occupy Fort Ellsworth, Virginia, with five hundred seamen; occupied the fort until General McClellan moved. He then, having returned to the "Pensacola" as first lieutenant, made the memorable passage, in that ship, down the Potomac, past nine miles of batteries. The "Pensacola" led the starboard column of Farragut's fleet past the forts below New Orleans, and past the Chalmette batteries. Lieutenant Roe was especially commended, and recommended for promotion for these services; ordered to command the "Katahdin," August 5, 1862, and the same day fought the battle of Baton Rouge, against Breckenridge. He had been promoted to the new grade of lieutenant-commander from August, 1862; detached and ordered North on account of ill health, February, 1863. During his service in the Mississippi in many engagements; September 4, 1863, commanding "Sassacus," on Wilmington blockade, when he destroyed two English blockade-runners. Then went into the North Carolina Sounds until July, 1864, when he was sent North as an invalid.

During his service in the Sounds he was engaged with the rebel ram "Albemarle," and the "Bombshell." The attack was by broadside of shot at close quarters, and by ramming. The ram was disabled and retreated in bad condition. The "Bombshell" surrendered to the "Sassacus," and was taken possession of. Roe received the thanks of the Secretary of the Navy, and an advancement of " five numbers in his grade for gallant and meritorious conduct before the enemy." He next commanded the "Michigan," on the Lakes. Suppressed insurrection of miners at Marquette and Houghton,

and caused a privateer to be captured by the English authorities at Collingwood, Canada; ordered to "Madawaska."

Commander, July, 1866; ordered to "Tacony," and commanded Gulf Division of Palmer's squadron at Vera Cruz; was in this command at the time of the execution of Maximilian, the evacuation by the French, and the establishment of a republic under Juarez. Roe took the famous Santa Anna out of an American steamer, and sent him out of Mexico. His services in Vera Cruz at this juncture were very many and great, but space forbids more than to say that he received the surrender of the city and of San Juan d'Ulloa from Gomez, who refused to surrender to Juarez; preserved order and established provisional government. Our President thanked and congratulated him for his many services at this critical period. His next service was as fleet-captain, Asiatic Fleet, under Admiral Rowan, where he served three years. Captain, April 1, 1872; Naval Rendezvous at San Francisco; captain of the yard, Boston, to June, 1873; then in command of "Lancaster," as chief of staff, also on a cruise on the coast of Brazil; at the Naval Station, New London; member of Board of Examiners at the Naval Academy in April, 1879; served as president of a board to revise the allowance books of the Bureaus of the Navy Department; received letters of commendation from Department, and from Admiral Le Roy; torpedo station, as president of the Board of Examiners, 1883; governor of the U. S. Naval Asylum, Philadelphia, October, 1883; commissioned a rear-admiral in the navy, October, 1885; detached from the command of the Naval Asylum, and transferred to the retired list, under the operation of the law, having reached sixty-two years of age.

## CAPTAIN WILLIAM PENNOCK ROGERS, U.S.A.

CAPTAIN WILLIAM PENNOCK ROGERS (Seventeenth Infantry) was born in Maryland September 10, 1842. He entered the volunteer service early in the war of the Rebellion as corporal of Company H, of the Seventh Maryland Infantry, August 21, 1862, and served with his regiment in the operations of the Army of the Potomac from that time to 1865. He was engaged in the battle of Sharpsburg, Maryland, July, 1863; Haymarket, Virginia, October, 1863; the Wilderness, Virginia, and Spottsylvania, Virginia, 1864, in which he was wounded and lost his left arm. He was discharged from the volunteer service May 4, 1865, and was appointed in the regular service, second lieutenant Forty-fourth Infantry, July 28, 1866.

He was at Fort Greble, Maryland, from December, 1866, to October, 1867, guarding public property; then at Washington City until 1869, when he was transferred to the Seventeenth Infantry. He served on reconstruction duty at Lynchburg, Richmond, and Raleigh until March, 1870, when he joined his regiment in Dakota, serving at Cheyenne Agency and Fort Rice to October, 1873. He participated with an expedition to and up the valley of the Yellowstone River, Montana, guarding engineers of the Northern Pacific Railroad, from July to October, 1872; and again in the following year on the same duty from June 23 to September 27. He was engaged in an affair with a band of Sioux Indians, under Chief "Gall," on Heart River, Dakota, October 3, 1872, and was promoted first lieutenant (incidentally) the same day.

Lieutenant Rogers was stationed at Fort Abercrombie, Dakota, from October 10, 1873, to August 15, 1876, when he was ordered to Standing Rock Indian Agency (Fort Yates), and was engaged with forces disarming and dismounting Sioux Indians. He changed station to Fort Totten, Dakota, November 11, 1878, and returned to Fort Yates May 24, 1879, and served at that post and at Fort Abraham Lincoln, Dakota, to July, 1886, when his regiment was ordered to the Department of the Platte, and he took station at Fort D. A. Russell. He was promoted captain December 23, 1884.

Captain Rogers was detailed on recruiting service from October 1, 1888, to October 1, 1890, at Baltimore, Maryland, York, Pennsylvania, and Hagerstown, Maryland. He rejoined his regiment at Fort D. A. Russell, Wyoming, October 15, 1890, and was in command of his company, with the regiment, forming part of General Miles's forces in the Sioux Indian campaign, through the bad lands of Dakota to Pine Ridge Agency, during the winter of 1890-91, until the surrender of the hostile Indians, returning to Fort Russell at the close of the campaign.

Captain Rogers has occupied numerous staff positions. In addition to the ordinary post-staff, he was acting assistant adjutant-general of the Middle District, Department of Dakota, from June, 1877, to February, 1878, and from July 28, 1879, to August 12 of the same year. He was adjutant of the battalion of the Seventeenth Infantry in the field on the Yellowstone expedition in 1872; adjutant, quartermaster, and commissary in the expedition of 1873, and adjutant of the Seventeenth Infantry from July, 1874, to December 23, 1884.

## CAPTAIN HENRY ROMEYN, U.S.A.

CAPTAIN HENRY ROMEYN (Fifth Infantry) was born in New York June 1, 1833. His first military service began at the breaking out of the war of the Rebellion, and was in the grades of private, corporal, and sergeant of Company G, One Hundred and Fifth Illinois Volunteers, serving in the field to November 15, 1863, at which time he was appointed a captain of the Fourteenth U. S. Colored Infantry.

He served as chief of scouts at Gallatin, Tennessee, from January to June, 1863, and then was occupied in recruiting the Forty-second and Forty-fourth U. S. Colored Troops until April, 1864, after which he was detailed as provost-marshal at Knoxville, Tennessee, which position he occupied to December, 1865.

He was brevetted major of volunteers for "gallant and meritorious services at the battle of Nashville;" was honorably mustered out of volunteer service March 26, 1866.

During the war of the Rebellion Captain Romeyn was engaged at the action of Frankfort, Kentucky; engaged at the action of Dalton; defence of Decatur; action of Shoal Creek, Alabama; battle of Nashville, and action of Decatur, Alabama.

Captain Romeyn entered the regular service as first lieutenant of the Thirty-seventh Infantry January 22, 1867, and subsequently assigned to the Fifth Infantry August 14, 1869. Upon his entrance into the regular army he was brevetted a captain for "gallant and meritorious services at the battle of Nashville, Tennessee." He joined his regiment and was with it on frontier duty at Fort Larned, Kansas, May to September, 1867; Fort Garland, Colorado Territory, October, 1867, to November, 1868; Fort Union, New Mexico, and Cimarron Agency, New Mexico, November, 1868, to April, 1869; at Fort Wallace, Kansas, September, 1869, to October, 1871. He was then ordered in field against hostile Indians, where he remained from August to November, 1874; at Fort Gibson, May, 1875, to June, 1876; in field, Sioux campaign, Montana Territory, July to November, 1876; also May, July, and August, 1877; cantonment, Tongue River (Fort Keogh), June and July, 1877; escort duty, September, 1877; in campaign against Nez Perces, September, 1877. He was then granted a sick-leave on account of wound to March, 1878; on leave (surgical certificate) to April, 1882; at Fort Keogh, Montana Territory, April to October, 1882; at Fort Brown, Texas, December, 1882, to November, 1883; at Fort Keogh, Montana, from February, 1884, to June, 1888; at Fort Ringgold, Texas, from June, 1888, to May, 1891; Mount Vernon Barracks, Alabama, from that date to present time. He was promoted to a captaincy in the Fifth Infantry July 10, 1885. He filled the position of post adjutant, acting assistant quartermaster, and assistant commissary of subsistence at Fort Larned, Kansas, May to September, 1876; post adjutant, acting assistant quartermaster, and assistant commissary of subsistence at Fort Wallace, Kansas, September, 1869, to October, 1871; post adjutant, acting assistant quartermaster, and assistant commissary of subsistence, post Southeast Kansas (Fort Scott, Kansas), to May, 1873; acting assistant quartermaster and assistant commissary of subsistence, Fort Gibson, Indian Territory, May, 1873, to July, 1874; post adjutant, cantonment Tongue River, June and July, 1877. Captain Romeyn participated in action against Cheyennes, Cheyenne Agency, Indian Territory, April 6, 1875; in action with Nez Perces Indians September 30, 1877, and was shot through the lungs, the wound thought at the time to be mortal.

He was then detailed as professor of military science and tactics at Hampton Institute, Virginia, from March, 1878, to November, 1881. Joining his regiment at Fort Keogh, Montana, he remained until September, 1882, when he was ordered to Fort Brown, Texas, where he remained to December, 1883; then rejoining at Fort Keogh, accompanied his regiment to Texas in 1888.

The first of the name of Romeyn in this country (1661) had been an officer in the army of Prince Maurice, of Holland, and in the Brazils.

One of Captain Romeyn's great-grandfathers, John Moore, of New York, was a member of the first Provincial Congress of that colony, and of the " Council of Safety" of Tryon County. His maternal great-grandfather, Captain Henry Shoemaker, of Pennsylvania, was a prisoner on board the old hulks in New York harbor, from which he escaped in irons by dropping from a port and floating out with the tide at night. His paternal grandfather served against the Indians in the Mohawk Valley on different occasions. Several of the name served during the War of 1812, and one was killed at the storming of the gates of the City of Mexico, while thirty-seven participated in the war of the Rebellion.

VICE-ADMIRAL STEPHEN CLEGG ROWAN, U.S.N.
(DECEASED).

VICE-ADMIRAL STEPHEN CLEGG ROWAN was born in Ireland, on Christmas-day, 1808. While still an infant his parents came to America, he being left behind on account of an accident. A few years later, while still a child, he joined his parents in Ohio, and was sent to Oxford College, Ohio. He was appointed a midshipman February 21, 1826, and was attached to the sloop-of-war "Vincennes" during her cruise round the world,—the first of our navy to do so. She was absent nearly four years. Promoted to passed midshipman in April, 1832, he served in several vessels of the West Indian Squadron for the next four years; in several boat expeditions on the Withlacoochee during the Florida War, and at Charlotte Harbor, with a boat's crew of twelve men, he attacked and captured an Indian village for the purpose of rescuing a collector believed to be in their hands. When a South Polar Expedition was arranged, he volunteered for that service in 1836; but, as the scheme came to naught, he was detached in December, 1837. He had been made lieutenant March 8, 1837. For three years after that he served in the Coast Survey, under Gedney. But, with great regret, he went on a cruise again, "because he thought it due to himself and the service" to give up home and emoluments for "improvement in my profession." He was ordered to the "Delaware," 74, which ship went to Brazil and to the Mediterranean. He afterwards served in the "Cyane," on California coast, taking part in five engagements during the Mexican War. In one of these he was wounded. He always took great pleasure in telling how he built a stockaded fort at Monterey by the assistance of the "Cyane's" crew. He has published in the "Proceedings of the Naval Institute" some reminiscences of those times. Commanded "Relief" and commissioned commander in September, 1855.

On receiving-ship and ordnance duty at New York when, in January, 1861, "believing war inevitable," he applied for duty. Assigned to the command of the "Pawnee," he had the first naval engagement of the war with a battery at Acquia Creek, and was struck nine times. Commanded the same ship at the battle of Hatteras Inlet.

In October, 1861, ordered to the "Brooklyn," but soon after ordered to command a flotilla in the Sounds of North Carolina, and received the thanks of Congress "for distinguished service in the waters of North Carolina, and particularly in the capture of New Berne."

In July, 1862, he was made captain and ordered to the "Powhatan," but was detached from her in the following September. In December, 1862, he was ordered to the command of the monitor "Roanoke" (the frigate of that name, cut down, with three turrets), which vessel was fitting out at the Brooklyn Navy-Yard. In June, 1863, Captain Rowan was ordered to command the iron-clad "New Ironsides," in which ship he participated in the capture of Morris Island. He was engaged with Forts Wagner and Gregg, and other forts in Charleston harbor, seventeen times. To rescue the "Weehawken," which was aground, he engaged Fort Moultrie, September 8, 1863, and silenced that work, after three hours, and then withdrew for want of ammunition. In this fight the "New Ironsides" was hit seventy times. On October 15, 1863, this ship was attacked by a torpedo-boat, but, owing to the place where the torpedo exploded, less damage was done than might have been expected. Captain Rowan was made commodore in July, 1863, and in October detached from the "Ironsides." In May, 1864, he was presented with a handsome sword by the United States Sanitary Commission.

Promoted to rear-admiral, by selection, in July, 1866, he hoisted his flag on board the "Madawaska," then on her trial trip. In command of Norfolk Navy-Yard from August, 1866, to July, 1867. Commanded the Asiatic Squadron from 1867 to 1870. Was promoted to vice-admiral August 15, 1870, and first learned of it when he anchored in New York, on his return. In 1871 he commanded the fleet which received the Grand Duke Alexis, of Russia. He was commandant of the Brooklyn Navy-Yard from May, 1872, to August, 1877; president of the Retiring and Examining Boards for three years; governor of the Naval Asylum at Philadelphia for about a year; was superintendent of the Naval Observatory, and then appointed chairman of the Light-House Board.

He retired voluntarily in February, 1889. By special Act of Congress he was permitted to retire, on his own application, with full pay of his grade. He died in Washington, D. C., March 31, 1890, in the eighty-second year of his age, having served sixty-four years in the navy. He was buried at Oak Hill, District of Columbia.

## COLONEL WM. A. RUCKER, U.S.A.

COLONEL WM. A. RUCKER (Pay Department) was born January 17, 1831, on Grosse Isle, Wayne County, Michigan. He was educated at an academy at Romeo and at select schools at Ypsilanti and Grosse Isle. In August, 1853, he went to New Mexico, arriving at Fort Union October 13 of the same year, and remained in that country until February, 1859, when he returned to Detroit, entered into business, and was so engaged until September 16, 1862, when he was appointed captain and commissary of subsistence of volunteers and stationed in Washington; and on November 26, same year, was appointed additional paymaster, U. S. Army, serving as such in Washington, in the paymaster-general's office and in the field, making payments to the Army of the Potomac, in Virginia. In December, 1863, he was ordered to Hilton Head, South Carolina, and took station there, and was employed in making payments to the troops on Folly and Morris Islands, and at Jacksonville, Fernandina, and St. Augustine, Florida.

In August, 1864, he was ordered to New York for funds, and waited there until about October 1, when seven hundred and fifty thousand dollars was placed to his credit with the assistant treasurer there, which he had just time to get before the sailing of the steamer "Fulton" for South Carolina. The money was counted and put into two portable safes, and deposited in the steamer's mail-room. On arriving at Hilton Head he was ordered to make payments on one of the islands, and when nearly completed, received orders to report himself at Washington, D. C., which he did after having finished his payments in the South. On November 1 was again assigned to paying troops in the Army of the Potomac, and in the Shenandoah Valley. He was ordered to Louisville, Kentucky, and thence to Tennessee, and paid troops at and near Chattanooga and Knoxville on two occasions. On March 13, 1865, he was brevetted lieutenant-colonel of volunteers for faithful and meritorious services during the war, and on April 16, 1866, received the appointment of major and paymaster U. S. Army, and was ordered in July of same year to New Mexico, with station at Santa Fé, and to take five hundred thousand dollars with him to pay off California and New Mexican volunteers, which he did, making the journey from Fort Leavenworth to Santa Fé in wagons, with an escort of about twenty soldiers, through a country infested with hostile Indians. He arrived there September 23. His duties in that country required him to make long and fatiguing journeys as far south as Fort Quitman, Texas, and west to near the Arizona line, in a country then full of bloodthirsty Indians. Colonel Rucker was ordered to change stations and report at Washington in May, 1868, and, in July of that year, was changed to St. Louis, Missouri, where he served until March, 1873, and was then ordered to Portland, Oregon. During his service there he visited Alaska five times, paying troops stationed there. In June, 1876, he was ordered to San Francisco, California, and on leaving Portland, Oregon, received from Major-General O. O. Howard an order from which this extract is taken: "It is no passing formal compliment to express, as the department commander now does, his sincere regret at losing the services of Major Rucker, who has not only given him entire satisfaction in the faithful performance of his laborious and responsible duty as paymaster, but has done it in a manner to give eminent satisfaction to this command." He remained in the Department of California, stationed at San Francisco, making payments to troops stationed from Camp Gaston to San Diego and the interior posts until April, 1878, when he was ordered to Fort Leavenworth, Kansas, and was assigned the payment of several posts in Western Kansas, Colorado, Indian Territory, and New Mexico, and remained on that duty until August, 1880, when he was transferred to St. Paul as chief paymaster of the Department of Dakota. After serving there and at Fort Snelling nearly five years, he was ordered in July, 1885, back to Fort Leavenworth as chief paymaster of the Department of the Missouri, where he served to May, 1890, when the head-quarters of the department were moved to St. Louis. In July, 1891, head-quarters having been abolished at St. Louis, he was directed to take station at Chicago, Illinois.

Major Rucker was promoted lieutenant-colonel and deputy paymaster-general October 1, 1882; and colonel and assistant paymaster-general Dec. 30, 1888. Colonel Rucker is the son of John Anthony Rucker, one of the first settlers of Michigan; his mother was Sarah Macomb, and came from one of the representative military families of the United States. In 1812 Colonel Rucker's father was a partner of Decatur, the firm being Rucker, Bullis & Decatur, manufacturing powder for the government.

**BRIGADIER-GENERAL THOMAS H. RUGER, U.S.A.**

BRIGADIER-GENERAL THOMAS H. RUGER was born in New York, and graduated from the U. S. Military Academy July 1, 1854, when he was appointed brevet second lieutenant Corps of Engineers. He served at New Orleans, La., in 1854-55, and resigned from the service April 1, 1855.

In civil life he was counsellor-at-law at Janesville, Wisconsin, from 1856 to 1861, when he again entered the service as lieutenant-colonel of the Third Wisconsin Volunteers, serving in command of his regiment in operations in Maryland and the Shenandoah Valley from July, 1861, to August, 1862, in the mean time having been promoted colonel of his regiment, to date from August 20, 1861.

Colonel Ruger was engaged in the movement to Harrisonburg, Virginia, February, 1862; combat of Winchester, May 25, 1862; retreat to Williamsport, Md., May, 1862, and advance to Little Washington, Va., July, 1862; in the Northern Virginia campaign, being engaged in the battle of Cedar Mountain, August 9, 1862; in the Maryland campaign (Army of the Potomac), being engaged in the battle of Antietam, and subsequent march to Falmouth, Va.

He was appointed brigadier-general U. S. Volunteers November 29, 1862, and commanded a brigade in the Twelfth Corps, Army of the Potomac, in the Rappahannock campaign, being engaged in the battle of Chancellorsville, May 2-4, 1863; in the Pennsylvania campaign, being engaged in the battle of Gettysburg (where he commanded a division), July 1-3, 1863, and subsequent march to Warrenton, Va. He participated in suppressing the draft-riots in New York City, August to September, 1863, and when that trouble ceased was on duty in Tennessee, October, 1863 to April, 1864. He was then assigned to the command of a brigade of the Twentieth Corps in the invasion of Georgia, being engaged in the battles of Resaca, May 15, 1864, and New Hope Church, May 25, 1864; action of Kulp House, June 22, 1864; combat of Peach-Tree Creek, July 20, 1864, and in numerous skirmishes on the march from May to July, 1864; siege of Atlanta, July 22 to September 2, 1864, and occupation of Atlanta, September 2 to November 8, 1864. He commanded a division of the Twenty-third Corps in the Tennessee campaign against the rebel army of General Hood, November 15 to December 8, 1864, being engaged in operations about Columbia and battle of Franklin, Tennessee, November 30, 1864.

He then organized the First Division of the Twenty-third Corps, and was in command of his division in the operations in North Carolina, being engaged in the movement up the Neuse River, February to March, 1865; action at Wier's Fork, near Kinston, March 10, 1865; surrender of the insurgent army under General J. E. Johnston at Darien Station, April 26, 1865, and in command of the Department and District of North Carolina, June 27, 1865, to September 1, 1866, when he was mustered out of the volunteer service, having been reappointed in the U. S. Army, with the rank of colonel of the Thirty-third Infantry, July 28, 1866.

General Ruger was brevetted major-general U. S. Volunteers November 30, 1864, for gallant and meritorious services at the battle of Franklin, and brevet brigadier-general U. S. Army, March 2, 1867, for gallant and meritorious services at the battle of Gettysburg. While in command of his regiment at Atlanta, he was made provisional governor of the State of Georgia from January 13 to July 4, 1868, and was in command of the District of Alabama to February 1, 1869. He was transferred to the Eighteenth Infantry March 15, 1869.

General Ruger commanded the Department of the South from March 5 to May 31, 1869, and after serving with his regiment until September 1, 1871, was detailed as superintendent of the U. S. Military Academy, where he remained until September 1, 1876; he was then placed in command of the Department of the South to July 1, 1878. He commanded Fort Assinniboine, together with the District of Montana, to October 1, 1879, and then commanded the District of Montana to May 13, 1885. He commanded his regiment and the post of Fort Leavenworth, Kansas, and the Infantry and Cavalry School of Application from June 29, 1885, to April 8, 1886, when he was appointed brigadier-general U. S. Army March 19, 1886, and assigned to the command of the Department of the Missouri, remaining to May 4, 1886, and then transferred to the Department of Dakota, which command he retained until April, 1891, when he was transferred to the command of the Military Division of the Pacific. The military divisions being discontinued in July, 1891, General Ruger was assigned to the command of the Department of California, which he now retains.

## COLONEL AND BREVET BRIGADIER-GENERAL GEORGE D. RUGGLES, U.S.A.

COLONEL AND BREVET BRIGADIER-GENERAL GEORGE D. RUGGLES (Adjutant-General's Department) was born at Newburgh, New York, September 11, 1833, and graduated from Military Academy, June, 1855. Appointed brevet second lieutenant First Infantry July 1, 1855. Promoted second lieutenant Second Infantry the same day. He served in the Sioux Indian country; at Fort Ridgely, Minnesota, 1855 and 1856; with column marching from Fort Ridgely to Fort Randall, Dakota, 1856; at Fort Randall, Dakota, 1856 and 1857; adjutant Second Infantry September 10, 1857, to July 1, 1861; at Fort Ridgely, Minnesota, 1857 and 1858. At St. Louis, Missouri, 1858, as acting adjutant-general, Department of the West. In Sioux Indian country at Fort Randall, Dakota, 1859; in the Chippewa Indian country at Fort Ripley, Minnesota, 1859; at St. Louis, Missouri, 1859 and 1860; Jefferson Barracks, Missouri, 1860; in the Sioux Indian country at Fort Kearney, Nebraska, 1860 and 1861; at Fort Leavenworth, Kansas, 1861. He was promoted first lieutenant May 2, 1861. He served during the rebellion of the seceding States from 1861 to 1866; acting assistant adjutant-general, Miles's brigade, Patterson's army, three months' service, June, 1861; in garrison, Washington, D. C., June 20 to July 1, 1861; appointed assistant adjutant-general (brevet captain) July 1, 1861; on special duty, Adjutant-General's Office, in War Department, in charge of organization of volunteer army, July 1, 1861, to June 28, 1862; captain, assistant adjutant-general, August 3, 1861; colonel, additional aide-de-camp, June 28, 1862, to May 31, 1866; major, assistant adjutant-general, permanent establishment, July 17, 1862; chief of staff, and adjutant-general, Army of Virginia, commanded by Major-General John Pope, June 28 to September 6, 1862, being engaged in the battle of Cedar Mountain, August 9, 1862; in retreat from the Rapidan; the two days' fight on the Rappahannock, August 22 and 23, 1862; the battle of Waterloo Bridge, August 23, 1862; and battles of Gainesville and Groveton (second Bull Run), August 29 and 30, 1862; and battle of Chantilly, September 1, 1862; as assistant chief of staff, Army of the Potomac, commanded by Major-General George B. McClellan, in the Maryland campaign, September 7 to November 10, 1862; being engaged in the battle of South Mountain, September 14, 1862; battle of Antietam, September 17, 1862; skirmish at Snicker's Gap, November 2, 1862; on special duty, immediately under the orders of Hon. E. M. Stanton, Secretary of War, in his office, December 27, 1862, to March 19, 1863; as first assistant to the provost-marshal-general, War Department, Conscription Bureau, March 19, 1863, to August 16, 1864; on inspection duty August 16, 1864, to January, 1865; as adjutant-general of the

Army of the Potomac, commanded by Major-General George G. Meade, February 1 to June 30, 1865; being engaged in the affair at Hatcher's Run, February 5 to 7, 1865; assault and capture of Petersburg, Virginia, March 29 to April 3, 1865; and campaign in pursuit of the Confederate Army, terminating in General Lee's capitulation at Appomattox Court-House, April 9, 1865. He was brevetted lieutenant-colonel March 13, 1865, "for gallant and meritorious services during the Rebellion." Colonel, March 13, 1865, "for gallant and meritorious services during the Rebellion." Brigadier-general U. S. Army, March 13, 1865, "for gallant and meritorious services during the campaign, terminating with the surrender of the insurgent Army of Northern Virginia." Brevet brigadier-general U. S. Volunteers, April 9, 1865, "for gallant and meritorious services during the operations resulting in the fall of Richmond, Virginia, and the surrender of the insurgent army under General R. E. Lee." General Ruggles was adjutant-general of the Military Div. of the Atlantic, July 1, 1865, to Feb. 9, 1866; of the Dep. of the East, to Aug. 11, 1866; of the Dep. of the Lakes, to Jan. 15, 1868; of the Dep. of the East, Feb. 14 to June 1, 1868; of the Dep. of the Platte, June 30, 1868, to Jan. 1, 1876; of the Dep. of Dakota, to Sept. 23, 1880. Promoted lieutenant-colonel, assistant adjutant-general, June 15, 1880; and on duty in the Adjutant-General's Office, War Department, October, 1880, to June 1885; as adjutant-general of the Dep. of Texas, to Oct. 1, 1888; with leave, to Jan. 9, 1889; *en route* to California, to Jan. 18, 1889; adjutant-general, Div. of Pacific and Dep. of California, Jan. 19, 1889, to Oct. 1, 1890; as adjutant-general of the Div. of Atlantic and Dep. of East, Oct. 13, 1890, to July 8, 1891, and then adjutant-general Dep. of East to present date, March, 1892. Colonel, assistant adjutant-general, June 7, 1889.

### MAJOR AND BREVET COLONEL BENJAMIN PIATT RUNKLE, U.S.A. (RETIRED).

MAJOR AND BREVET COLONEL BENJAMIN PIATT RUNKLE was born on September 3, 1836; is a great-grandson of Colonel Jacob Piatt, of the Revolutionary Army. He was educated at Miami University, Oxford, Ohio, graduating in July, 1857; was admitted to the bar, July, 1859; was nominated for the Ohio State Senate by the Democracy in 1860; was captain of the Douglas Guards, Ohio Militia, which company furnished the first volunteers for the war from Champaign County, Ohio; he was commissioned captain, Thirteenth Ohio Infantry, April 22, 1861, and promoted major, November 8, 1861. He served in the West Virginia campaign under General William S. Rosecrans.

Major Runkle was serving in Smith's brigade, Crittenden's division, Army of the Ohio, at the battle of Shiloh, when he was severely wounded, and left for dead on the field. His obituary, written by the Hon. Whitelaw Reid, appeared in the New York *Tribune*. He recovered, however, and was commissioned colonel of the Forty-fifth Ohio Infantry, which he raised and led to the field, August 19, 1862; served in the Department of Kentucky under Generals Wright, Burnside, and Gillmore during the remainder of 1862 and part of 1863; commanding at this time a brigade of mounted infantry. He was thanked on the field at Somerset, Kentucky, March 30, 1863, for the conduct of his command and himself in breaking the Confederate lines. General Gillmore afterwards wrote, "I shall always remember with pleasure your conduct at Somerset, for to the charge of your command, so gallantly led by yourself, was due the victory of that day."

Colonel Runkle's wounds breaking out afresh, and incapacitating him for active service, he was ordered to report to Governor Tod, of Ohio, for duty. The Governor ordered him to Washington, D. C., as his confidential aid and agent, sending a letter to President Lincoln in the following words: "The bearer hereof commands my full confidence, and is worthy of yours." He transacted business for the State of Ohio with the Departments at Washington, D. C., until the Atlanta campaign, when he joined his command, which had been dismounted and were serving as infantry, and remained with the same till July 21, 1864, when he was mustered out " on account of disability occasioned by wounds received in action."

Colonel Runkle was appointed lieutenant-colonel Veteran Reserve Corps (volunteers), August 22, 1864; commanded the Twenty-first Regiment of that corps until September, 1865. He was a member of the committee appointed by that corps to secure its recognition in the regular army, and spent the winters of 1865–66 in Washington on that business. Largely as a result of the labors of that committee, four Veteran Reserve Corps regiments were authorized for the regular army. Colonel Runkle was commissioned major of the Forty-fifth Infantry, U. S. A., July 28, 1866.

From 1866 to 1870, Colonel Runkle served under Major-General O. O. Howard, being assigned to duty in Tennessee, South Carolina, and Kentucky. He was brevetted lieutenant-colonel and colonel U. S. Army, to date from March 2, 1867, upon the recommendations of General Gillmore and others, " for gallant and meritorious services at the battle of Shiloh, and during the war." He was also brevetted major-general of volunteers, November 9, 1865.

Colonel Runkle was retired "on account of disability occasioned by wounds received in action," December 15, 1870. He now resides in San Francisco, California.

PAY-DIRECTOR A. W. RUSSELL, U.S.N. (RETIRED).

PAY-DIRECTOR A. W. RUSSELL was born in Maryland, and first served in the navy as captain's clerk of the sloop "Saratoga," on the coast of Africa, 1842-44. In the operations against Berehy and adjacent towns,—a three days' engagement involving the destruction of six towns,—under Commodore M. C. Perry, December, 1843. During the Mexican War he served in the mounted rifle regiment,—Captain Samuel H. Walker, the distinguished Texan Ranger,—Company C. Was clerk to the Committee of Naval Affairs of the United States Senate in 1858-61. Commissioned paymaster in the navy from the District of Columbia in February, 1861. Was then attached to the "Pocahontas," in the Potomac River and Chesapeake Bay, for a short time, when he was transferred to the sloop-of-war "Savannah," on the blockade of the Atlantic coast, and was present at the capture of Tybee Island. He was then ordered to the "Colorado," and was at the mouth of the Mississippi during the operations in that river leading to the capture of New Orleans. Paymaster Russell was next attached to the iron-clad steamer "New Ironsides," on special service in 1862, and in the South Atlantic Squadron during 1863-64, when he was especially thanked by Commodore (afterwards Vice-Admiral) Rowan, commanding the "New Ironsides," in his official despatches, "for great zeal and ability in command of the powder and shell division," during the various engagements (twenty-seven) with the forts and batteries of Charleston harbor.

Paymaster Russell was attached to the receiving-ship "North Carolina," at New York, 1864-65, and to the "Chattanooga," on "special service," in 1866. Then sailed in the steam-sloop "Sacramento" on a special cruise, but the cruise was finished by the wreck of the vessel in the Bay of Bengal. Paymaster Russell, although losing his personal belongings in the wreck, saved all his official books, accounts, vouchers, public money, and was thus enabled to settle his accounts with the Treasury Department without the difference of a penny. In 1868-70 he was inspector of provisions and clothing at the navy-yard at Washington, and on duty at the Navy Pay-Office at Philadelphia from 1870 to 1873.

He had been promoted to pay-inspector in March, 1871. Was inspector of provisions and clothing at the Philadelphia yard for some months. He then went again to the Pay-Office at Philadelphia from 1874 to 1877.

Promoted pay-director in February, 1877. Navy Pay-Office, Baltimore, March 31, 1877, to January, 1882. At the Navy Pay-Office at Philadelphia, from May, 1882, to February, 1886. Was retired, by operation of law, February 4, 1886.

MAJOR GERALD RUSSELL, U.S.A. (RETIRED).

MAJOR GERALD RUSSELL was born in Ireland, and entered the military service as a private in July, 1851. He was assigned to Company F, Mounted Riflemen, U.S.A. He served at Carlisle and Jefferson Barracks, and after assignment went with his company to Indianola, Texas. He scouted almost continuously through the State of Texas during the period of his first enlistment, and was engaged in action with Indians on the Rio Grande, above Fort Ringgold, in 1853. On this occasion he volunteered to swim the Rio Grande, and, with the assistance of two other volunteers, recovered forty head of stolen horses. He was honorably discharged in 1856, and six months later re-enlisted, and joined his old regiment in New Mexico.

In February, 1858, he participated, with thirty men, under Lieutenant H. M. Lazelle, in a fight in Dog Cañon, New Mexico, against Mescalero Apache Indians, for which he was honorably mentioned in General Orders of the War Department of 1859. In the latter part of 1860 he participated in the attack on a large camp of Comanche and Kiowa Indians at Cold Springs, New Mexico. In the memorable year of 1861 he was stationed at Fort Stanton, New Mexico, when the news of the fall of Fort Sumter was received at that post. The commanding officers stationed at Fort Stanton at the time were Southern men, with one or two lukewarm exceptions. The news caused great commotion among the Southern officers, and extensive preparations were commenced to take the entire garrison, which consisted of three companies of mounted rifles and two companies of infantry, into Texas. In fact, the movement was fully determined upon; for Russell received orders, as first sergeant, to have his company (D) in complete order to march. But the movement was frustrated by an anonymous letter received by Captain Thomas Claiborne, who was conspicuous in creating disaffection among the troops, warning him not to proceed one step further at his peril. The letter had the desired effect. All preparations immediately ceased, and the officers, once sanguine of taking the formidable garrison of Fort Stanton to swell the ranks of the Confederacy, took their departure two days later with a modest escort, all of whom returned in due time, except one man, who cast his lot with the South. The writer of the anonymous letter referred to hopes not to be accused of egotism for relating the above facts, for the first time, after a lapse of thirty-one years. On February 22, 1862, he participated in the battle of Val Verde, and served in all the campaigning in Southern New Mexico from the day the invaders first entered the Territory until they were driven from it. In May, 1862, while in command of sixty men of his regiment (Third Cavalry), he fought a hostile band of Navajo Indians, killing several of them, and capturing three thousand head of sheep, some burros, mules, and oxen, at Sierra Caballo, New Mexico. In the fall of 1862 he was transferred to the Western Army, and in May, 1863, was on mustering duty with the Fourth Division, Sixteenth Army Corps, serving during the siege of Vicksburg, not only as mustering-officer, but as aide-de-camp to the general commanding.

He was appointed second lieutenant Third U. S. Cavalry July 18, 1862, and promoted first lieutenant August 4, 1864. He continued to serve with the Western Army, participating in the battle of Jackson, Mississippi, and was captured by the enemy a few days subsequently while en route to Vicksburg, under orders. Lieutenant Russell was exchanged in October, 1863, and was ordered to Natchez, but here met with an accident, which interrupted his duties in the field, and he was placed on mustering duty at Louisville, Kentucky, until the close of the war, when he rejoined his regiment, and marched with it from Little Rock, Arkansas, to New Mexico, and in 1869 was transferred to Arizona, where he participated in numerous engagements with Indians in the Pelonica, Chiricahua, and Dragoon Mountains. He was transferred to the Department of the Platte in 1871, and in 1875-77 participated in the campaigns against hostile Sioux Indians, under Generals Crook and Mackenzie.

He was promoted captain August 4, 1864, and major Fifth Cavalry October 29, 1888. He was retired from active service December 17, 1890.

## FIRST LIEUTENANT AND BREVET CAPTAIN ROBERT GEDNEY RUTHERFORD, U.S.A. (RETIRED).

FIRST LIEUTENANT AND BREVET CAPTAIN ROBERT GEDNEY RUTHERFORD was born in New York City, New York. His first service was as second lieutenant, Ninth Regiment, New York State Militia (Eighty-third New York State Volunteers), from May 20, 1861. He was detailed on recruiting duty in New York City from May 27 to November 17, 1861, during which time he conducted a detachment of recruits to the regiment on the Upper Potomac. (This service of nearly six months was performed at an officer's own expense, and he is not credited with it in the official record.) He was not mustered into the service of the United States until November 19, 1861. Entering on duty with regiment from November 19, 1861, he was detailed on staff of brigadier-general commanding Second Brigade, Third Division, Banks's Army Corps, afterwards Third Brigade, First Division, Twelfth Army Corps, serving successively with Generals Charles S. Hamilton, George H. Gordon, and George S. Green, and performing the duties of brigade quartermaster from January 18, 1862, to August 18, 1862. He then became aide-de-camp to Brigadier-General A. S. Williams, commanding First Division, Twelfth Army Corps, in which capacity he served from August 18, 1862, to September 14, 1862.

He was taken sick at Frederick City, Maryland, and sent to New York City, where he remained until February 26, 1863, suffering from effects of contused wounds of right knee-joint. He was honorably discharged and mustered out of service on surgeon's certificate of disability February 26, 1863, at New York City.

On September 19, 1863, he reported for duty with Veteran Reserve Corps at department camp, near Washington, D. C., having been appointed a captain in that corps by President Abraham Lincoln. At Washington, D. C., he did duty as officer of the guard, every second or third day, at the "Old Capitol Prison," where the rebel prisoners were confined, and at the "Carroll Prison," where the prisoners of the State were kept. March 5, 1864, commanded the expedition sent from Washington, D. C., for the relief of Cherrystone, on the eastern shore of Virginia, which had been raided by the rebels.

He commanded a company at Washington, D. C., and was doing duty as field-officer of the day for the defences of Washington at the time the rebel General Early made his attack on the national capital in July, 1864; participated in the fight with General Early's forces in front of Fort Stevens, and in the campaign which followed.

On August 16, 1864, assumed command of the "Central Guard-House," then used as a military prison, and remained on this duty until July 12, 1865, when, the war having terminated, the prison was turned over to the

civil authorities July 12 to October 4, 1865; he was on sick-leave to December 7, 1865, and then on duty at Camp Carrington, Indianapolis, Indiana, commanding detachment of two companies of the Twenty-second Regiment, Veteran Reserve Corps, and engaged in mustering out volunteer troops.

Lieutenant Rutherford received contused wound of right knee-joint at Rappahannock Station, Virginia, and contracted rheumatism in the field, causing great and continuous suffering, and resulting in the distortion of both feet.

He took part in the Shenandoah Valley campaign of 1862, and General Pope's campaign from Culpeper Court-House to Washington, and was present at Winchester, Rappahannock Station, Beverly's Ford, Sulphur Springs, second Bull Run, and Fort Stevens.

Captain Rutherford was mustered out of the volunteer service as brevet lieutenant-colonel April 30, 1867, and was appointed second lieutenant of the Forty-fifth Infantry, to date from March 7, 1867, and was the same day brevetted first lieutenant and captain for "gallant and meritorious services in the battle of Rappahannock Station," and "gallant and meritorious services during the war."

During the years of 1866–68 he was on "reconstruction duty."

On July 30, 1869, reported for duty at Fort Columbus, New York harbor, as post quartermaster; was also post commissary of subsistence, and for part of the term depot treasurer. In addition, commanded a company during the last two years of his tour.

Having been examined by retiring board and recommended for retirement for disability resulting from causes incident to the service, he was, June 28, 1878, retired from active service. Since retirement he has resided at Washington, D. C.

## CAPTAIN WILLIAM THOMAS SAMPSON, U.S.N.

CAPTAIN WILLIAM THOMAS SAMPSON, the eldest son of James and Hannah Sampson, was born in Palmyra, New York, on February 9, 1840. He entered the Naval Academy in September, 1857, and graduated at the head of his class at the outbreak of the war, in April, 1861. After serving for a short time in the Potomac flotilla, he was ordered to join the frigate "Potomac" as watch and division officer, under the command of the late Rear-Admiral Levin M. Powell. The "Potomac" was stationed off Mobile on blockade duty. From her he was transferred to the "Water-Witch," as executive-officer, and saw service on all parts of the Gulf.

In 1862 he returned to the Naval Academy, then at Newport, for a short tour of duty as an instructor. In 1864 he became executive-officer of the "Patapsco," then stationed in the South Atlantic Squadron. On the night of January 15, 1865, the "Patapsco" was the advance monitor for the night in Charleston Roads, protecting the picket-boats that were dragging for torpedoes and examining the obstructions between Forts Sumter and Moultrie. She was kept under way, being allowed to drift towards the obstructions, and then steamed down the channel when sufficiently near them. The third time, while steaming down-stream, a torpedo struck her under the port bow, and she went down in less than a minute. Lieutenant Sampson, who was running the ship, was standing on the ridge-rope around the turret, and was picked up while in the water by one of the picket-boats. He was mentioned in the report of the commanding officer for the cool intrepidity which he displayed. After the sinking of the "Patapsco," Lieutenant Sampson joined the "Colorado," the flag-ship of the European Station, Rear-Admiral L. M. Goldsborough in command. While on that station, in 1866, he was commissioned as lieutenant-commander.

In the fall of 1867, Lieutenant-Commander Sampson was ordered to the Naval Academy at Annapolis as an instructor in the Department of Natural Philosophy. In 1869 he became head of that department, and was mainly instrumental in introducing the present system of monthly examinations.

In January, 1871, he joined the "Congress" as executive-officer. The "Congress" first carried coal and stores to Disco, Greenland, for Hall's Polar Expedition, and on her return joined the European Station. He received his commission as commander in 1874, and was ordered to the Naval Academy as head of the Department of Physics and Chemistry. During this tour of duty the instruction in applied science was greatly developed to meet the modern requirements, and several of our most distinguished electricians acquired the groundwork of their knowledge at the Naval Academy since 1874.

In 1878, Commander Sampson was sent in charge of a party to observe the total eclipse of the sun from a station at Creston, Wyoming. In 1879 he was ordered to command the "Swatara" for a cruise on the Asiatic Station. Both the "Congress," of which he was executive-officer, and the "Swatara," which he commanded, were noted throughout the service for being in fine condition, under excellent discipline, and thoroughly drilled. The present chief of the Bureau of Ordnance—Commander Folger—was executive of the "Swatara" during this time.

In 1881, Commander Sampson returned to the United States, and in 1882 was ordered as assistant superintendent at the Naval Observatory. During his tour of duty at the observatory many of the instruments, that had been neglected for some years, were put in thorough repair and placed under the charge of naval officers who were competent observers. The system of time-signals was extended, and the testing, care, and rating of chronometers were thoroughly systematized.

He was superintendent of the Naval Academy at Annapolis for a considerable period, having been promoted captain in March, 1889. This is one of the most important posts a naval officer can fill. Since November, 1890, he has been in command of the "San Francisco," on the Pacific Station.

### CAPTAIN EGBERT B. SAVAGE, U.S.A.

CAPTAIN EGBERT B. SAVAGE (Eighth Infantry) was born February 2, 1843, at Saratoga Springs, New York. He entered the volunteer service as first lieutenant of the One Hundred and Fifteenth New York Infantry, August 26, 1862, and was promoted captain August 30, 1862. He served in the field during the war of the Rebellion, and was engaged in the battle of Maryland Heights, Maryland, and Bolivar Heights, Virginia, and was taken prisoner at Harper's Ferry, Virginia, September 15, 1862. He was then in the parole camp at Chicago, Illinois, until November, 1862, when he was exchanged, and joined his regiment in the field in Virginia.

He was transferred to the Department of the South, and served at Hilton Head and Beaufort, South Carolina; then participated in the expedition to Florida, commanded by General Seymour, and was engaged at the capture of Jacksonville, Camp Finnegan, and battle of Olustee (also Ocean Pond and Silver Lake), February 20, 1864.

Captain Savage was then transferred to the Army of the James, in Virginia, and was engaged in the battle of Chesterfield Heights, Virginia, May 18, 1864; action of Drury's Bluff, Virginia, May, 1864; and was on duty at Bermuda Hundred, from May 25-30, 1864. He was then attached to the Army of the Potomac, and was engaged in the battle of Cold Harbor, Virginia, in June, 1864, where he was wounded. He was in the siege of Petersburg, Virginia, from the commencement until about September 26, 1864, and was engaged in the mine explosion, July 30, 1864; battle of Deep Bottom, Virginia, August 16, 1864; commanded the One Hundred and Fifteenth New York in action near Deep Bottom, August 18, 1864; battle of Chapin's Farm, Virginia, September 29, 1864, where he was wounded and sent to hospital near Fort Monroe.

Captain Savage rejoined his regiment in the field in November following, and participated in the first expedition to Fort Fisher, North Carolina, commanded by General Butler, in December, 1864. He also participated in the second expedition to the same place under General Terry, in January, 1865. He was engaged in the assault and capture of that place January 15, and at the explosion of the magazine of Fort Fisher on the 16th. He then joined General Sherman's army in North Carolina, and was honorably mustered out August 30, 1865, having been transferred to the Forty-seventh New York Infantry on the muster-out of the One Hundred and Fifteenth, June 17, 1865. Captain Savage was commissioned major of the One Hundred and Fifteenth, April 29, 1865, but was not mustered into service. He was acting ordnance officer of the Second Division, Tenth Army Corps, and department ordnance officer at Raleigh, North Carolina, from May to August, 1865.

Captain Savage entered the regular service as second lieutenant of the Fifteenth Infantry, February 23, 1866, and promoted first lieutenant the same day. He was transferred to the Thirty-third Infantry September 21, 1866; transferred to the Eighth Infantry May 3, 1869; and promoted captain May 30, 1877. From 1866 to 1871 he was on duty in the South, and stationed at Mobile, Montgomery, Huntsville, Selma, and Jacksonville, Alabama, and Charleston, South Carolina; in 1871-72 he was at David's Island, and his regiment was transferred to the West. He participated in General Stanley's Yellowstone Expedition in 1872-73, and for two years was stationed at Fort Omaha and Fort D. A. Russell. He was then transferred to Arizona, where he remained until 1879, when he was detailed on recruiting service until 1882, rejoining his company at Fort Gaston, California.

From 1882 to 1886 he served at Angel Island and Fort Halleck, Nevada; and from January to May of that year was in the field in Arizona, taking station at Fort Grant, and remaining there until 1890, when his regiment was transferred to the Department of the Platte, and he took station at Fort Niobrara, but was changed to Fort McKinney, in 1891, where he is now serving.

## LIEUTENANT-COLONEL AND BREVET BRIGADIER-GENERAL CHARLES G. SAWTELLE, U.S.A.

LIEUTENANT-COLONEL AND BREVET BRIGADIER-GENERAL CHARLES G. SAWTELLE (Quartermaster's Department) was born in Maine, May 10, 1834; was a cadet at the U. S. Military Academy July 1, 1850, to July 1, 1854, when he graduated and was promoted a brevet second lieutenant of infantry, and second lieutenant of the Sixth Infantry March 3, 1855. He served on frontier duty at Fort Ripley, Minnesota, 1854-55; on Sioux expedition in 1855; Fort Laramie, Dakota, 1855-56; Fort Pierre, Dakota, 1856; Fort Leavenworth, Kansas, 1856-57. Regimental quartermaster, Sixth Infantry, February 15, 1857, to May 17, 1861; quelling Kansas disturbances, 1857-58; Utah expedition, 1858, and on march to California, 1858; in garrison at Benicia, California, 1858, and Presidio of San Francisco, California, 1858-59; as quartermaster on Mojave expedition to Arizona, 1859; at Benicia, California, 1859-61, being acting regimental adjutant, April 29 to July 10, 1861.

Served during the rebellion of the seceding States, 1861-66; in charge of the Quartermaster Depot at Perryville, Maryland, August, 1861, to March, 1862; in the Virginia Peninsula campaign, in the Army of the Potomac from March to May, 1862, to September 7, 1862; as acting chief quartermaster of the Army of the Potomac, September 7 to November 12, 1862, during the Maryland campaign; as chief quartermaster of the Second Corps in the Rappahannock campaign (Army of the Potomac), November 12, 1862, to January 24, 1863.

He was promoted first lieutenant June 5, 1860, and appointed captain, staff-assistant quartermaster, May 17, 1861, and lieutenant-colonel, staff, U. S. Volunteers, November 12, 1862, being present at the battle of Fredericksburg, December 13, 1862, as chief quartermaster of the Right Grand Division; as chief quartermaster of Cavalry Corps (Army of the Potomac), January 24 to June 13, 1863, being engaged on "Stoneman's Raid" towards Richmond, May, 1863; as assistant chief quartermaster of the Army of the Potomac, June 21 to August 6, 1863, being engaged in the Pennsylvania campaign; as chief quartermaster of the Cavalry Bureau at Washington, D. C., August 6, 1863, to February 15, 1864; as chief quartermaster at Brownsville, Texas, of the forces on the Rio Grande, February to April 30, 1864; in charge of transports and supplies, May 15-19, 1864, for the relief of General Banks's army returning from Red River, which he met at Atchafalaya, and constructed a bridge of nine hundred feet across the river, using twenty-one large steamboats as pontoons; as chief quartermaster of the Military Division of West Mississippi, June 6, 1864, to June 2, 1865, being engaged in the Mobile campaign and expedition terminating in the surrender of the rebel forces under General Taylor.

He was brevetted major, lieutenant-colonel, and colonel, March 13, 1865, for "faithful and meritorious services during the Rebellion;" and brigadier-general, March 13, 1865, for "faithful and meritorious services in the quartermaster's department during the Rebellion." He was lieutenant-colonel, staff, U. S. Volunteers, from May 27, 1864, to May 25, 1865; and colonel, staff, U. S. Volunteers, from May 25, 1865, to January 1, 1867, and served as chief quartermaster of the Military Division of the Southwest, June 3 to July 17, 1865; of the Military Division of the Gulf, July 17, 1865, to August 15, 1866; of the Department of the Gulf, August 15, 1866, to April 1, 1867; and of the Fifth Military District, April 1 to August 31, 1867.

On January 18, 1867, he was promoted major, staff-quartermaster, and served in charge of clothing depot, and assistant to the depot quartermaster at New York City, September 9, 1867, to April 10, 1869; as chief quartermaster of the Department of California, May 4, 1869, to August 15, 1872; quartermaster in the Department of the East, August 23, 1872, to November 10, 1877; and as chief quartermaster, Department of the East, November 10, 1877, to March 25, 1878; and of the Department of the Columbia, May 14, 1878, to April 12, 1881; having been promoted lieutenant-colonel, staff, deputy quartermaster-general, January 24, 1881, and then served as chief quartermaster of the Department of the South, April 27, 1881, to April 27, 1882; and of the Military Division of the Atlantic and Department of the East, May 1, 1882, to October 29, 1883; in office of quartermaster-general, Washington, D. C., from October 29, 1883, to September 16, 1890. In charge of the general depot of the quartermaster's department in Philadelphia, Pennsylvania, October 1, 1890, to this time.

## COLONEL AND BREVET MAJOR-GENERAL RUFUS SAXTON, U.S.A. (RETIRED).

COLONEL AND BREVET MAJOR-GENERAL RUFUS SAXTON was born in Massachusetts in 1824. Graduating at the Military Academy in 1849, he was appointed a lieutenant of artillery. In 1853 he was assigned to duty on the Northern Pacific Railroad Exploration and Survey, and made a barometric profile of the route across the Rocky Mountains on which that railroad was afterwards built. The following order is in recognition of this service:

"NORTHERN PACIFIC RAILROAD EXPLORATION AND SURVEY,
"CAMP DOBBIN, NEAR FORT BENTON, September 18, 1853.

"ORDER NO. 18.

"The chief of the expedition congratulates Lieutenant Saxton and his party upon their safe arrival at Fort Benton from the mouth of the Columbia. For indomitable energy, sound judgment, and crowning accomplishment, Lieutenant Saxton has the thanks of all his associates, and deserves honorable mention at the hands of all men who seek to advance the honor and renown of their country.

"ISAAC I. STEVENS,
"Governor of Washington Territory."

From this time until the war, Lieutenant Saxton was on the Coast Survey, and also instructor of tactics at the Military Academy. In 1861 he was chief quartermaster on the staff of General Lyon in his Missouri campaign, of General McClellan in Western Virginia, and General Sherman's Port Royal expedition. In 1862 he was promoted brigadier-general and assigned to the command of Harper's Ferry, Virginia. In May, Mr. Stanton wrote General Saxton: "By special assignment of the President, you are assigned to the command of the forces at Harper's Ferry without regard to seniority of rank, and will exercise your own discretion with regard to its defence." The defence was successful, and General Jackson was driven up the valley. Mr. Stanton telegraphed General Saxton: "I have reserved to say to you personally what I feel concerning the important service you have rendered the government, and the high sense I have of the skill and ability you have shown in the performance of your arduous duties, which have fulfilled my expectations." He also wrote:

"WAR DEPARTMENT, WASHINGTON, D. C., June 17, 1862.

"TO BRIGADIER-GENERAL RUFUS SAXTON:

"The thanks of this department are cordially tendered to you for your late able and gallant defence of Harper's Ferry against the rebel forces under command of General Jackson. You were placed in command at that point at a moment of extreme danger, and under circumstances of extraordinary difficulty. By your skill and gallantry great service was rendered to the country, which I feel it to be the duty of this department to acknowledge and place on record, assuring you at the same time of my personal confidence and regard.

"Yours truly,
"EDWIN M. STANTON,
"Secretary of War."

Afterwards General Saxton was appointed by the President, upon the request of Secretary Chase, military governor of the Department of the South, and also superintendent of the recruiting of colored troops. He also commanded a division of the Tenth Army Corps, the Beaufort district, and also of the forces on Morris and John's Islands in the attack on Charleston. He was also commissioner of the Freedmen's Bureau for South Carolina, Georgia, and Florida until the end of the war.

At this time he received the following from the war-governor of his native State:

"BOSTON, Feb. 15, 1866.

"MAJOR-GENERAL RUFUS SAXTON, BEAUFORT, S. C.:

"GENERAL,— . . . But more than all, I thank you for the fidelity to liberty and justice and to every duty, and the zeal and ability which have distinguished your service of the country and mankind during the Rebellion. Among the sons of Massachusetts none will leave behind them a more gracious memory or a more honorable name than yours. Believe me always,

"Your friend and servant,
"JOHN A. ANDREW."

After the war General Saxton was chief quartermaster of the Department of the South, of the Lakes, of the Missouri, of the Columbia, and of the Military Division of the Pacific. He was brevetted major, lieutenant-colonel, colonel, brigadier-general, and major-general. After forty-three years of service he was retired by action of law.

### REAR-ADMIRAL JAMES FINDLAY SCHENCK, U.S.N.
(DECEASED).

REAR-ADMIRAL JAMES FINDLAY SCHENCK was born in Ohio, June 11, 1807. Appointed from Ohio, March 1, 1825; sloop "Hornet," West India Squadron, 1829; frigate "Brandywine," 1830. Promoted to passed midshipman June 4, 1831; sloop "John Adams," Mediterranean Squadron, 1833-34.

Commissioned as lieutenant December 22, 1835; sloop "St. Louis," West India Squadron, 1837; brig "Dolphin," Brazil Squadron, 1840; razee "Independence," Home Squadron, 1843; frigate "Congress," Pacific Squadron, 1846-47.

During the war with Mexico, Lieutenant Schenck, as chief military aid to Commodore Stockton, landed and took possession of Santa Barbara and San Pedro, in California; serving in same capacity, marched on and was at the first capture of Los Angeles. As second lieutenant of the frigate "Congress," was at the bombardment and capture of Guaymas, and the taking of Mazatlan. Frigate "Congress," East India Squadron, 1848; commanding mail steamship "Ohio," 1848-52.

Commissioned as commander September 14, 1855; commanding receiving-ship, New York, 1848; commanding steamer "Saginaw," East India Squadron, 1860-61. On June 30, 1861, the "Saginaw" was fired upon by a fort at Quin Hone, Cochin-China; the fire was returned and the fort silenced.

Commissioned as captain, 1861; commanding frigate "St. Lawrence," Blockading Squadron, 1862.

Commissioned as commodore July 2, 1863; commanding steam-sloop "Powhatan," North Atlantic Squadron, 1864-65; commanded "Powhatan" and Third Division of Porter's Squadron in the two attacks on Fort Fisher; commanded Naval Station, Mound City, Illinois, 1866.

Commissioned as rear-admiral July, 1880. Died in 1882.

## CAPTAIN WINFIELD SCOTT SCHLEY, U.S.N.

CAPTAIN WINFIELD SCOTT SCHLEY belongs to a well-known family of western Maryland. He was born in that State, near Frederick, in 1839, and was appointed an acting midshipman in 1856. He was at the Naval Academy until 1860, when he graduated. He served in the U. S. frigate "Niagara," in China and Japan, after carrying the embassy from Japan back to their own country in 1860–61.

The exigencies of war at that time brought officers forward very rapidly, and he was promoted to master in 1861, and ordered to the U. S. frigate "Potomac." While serving in her he was present at the occupation of Mexico, early in 1862, by the combined powers of England, France, and Spain. When the "Potomac" was turned into a store-ship he was ordered to the gunboat "Winona," of the West Gulf Blockading Squadron, and, after several months of service in the Mississippi River, was ordered to the steam-sloop "Monongahela," and subsequently to the steam-sloop "Richmond." He was engaged in several operations with field-batteries in the river, and subsequently in all the engagements which led to the capture of Port Hudson, in Louisiana, from March 16 to July 9, 1863. He was engaged in several skirmishes, and in cutting out, under heavy fire, two schooners engaged in supplying the rebels.

He was commissioned as lieutenant on July 18, 1862,— only two years after leaving the Naval Academy. From 1864 to 1866 he was attached to the steam-gun-boat "Wateree," as executive-officer, in the Pacific Squadron, and suppressed an insurrection among the Chinese coolies on the Chincha Islands in 1864. In 1865 he landed with one hundred men at La Union, San Salvador, to protect the custom-house and U. S. Consulate during a revolution.

He was commissioned as lieutenant-commander in July, 1866, and, upon his return from the Pacific, was ordered to the U. S. Naval Academy, where he remained until 1869, when he was ordered to the U. S. ship "Benicia," and served in her on the Asiatic Station until 1872. He was present at and participated in the attack upon and complete overthrow of the forces defending the forts on the Salee River, in Corea, in 1871, when Lieutenant Hugh McKee was killed at his side. After his return to the United States in the fall of 1872 he was ordered to the Naval Academy as head of the Department of Modern Languages.

He was commissioned a commander in 1874, and was ordered to command the U. S. ship "Essex" in 1876, and served in her on the North Atlantic, West Coast of Africa, and South Atlantic Stations until 1879. He was inspector of the Second Light-House District at Boston from 1880 to 1883, when he was ordered to the Bureau of Equipment and Recruiting at Washington.

When the "Greely Relief Expedition" was organized in 1884, he was sent in command of it to the North Polar regions, and rescued Lieutenant Greely and six survivors at Cape Sabine and brought them home with great promptitude. Partly as a reward for this service he was promoted by President Arthur to chief of the Bureau of Equipment and Recruiting in the Navy Department, where he served until 1888, when he was reappointed to the same position by President Cleveland, and resigned the position in 1889. While in the bureau he was promoted to captain, and in leaving this position he was ordered the same year to command the new cruiser "Baltimore," and served with her in the North Atlantic, European, and South Pacific Stations.

During his command of the "Baltimore," he carried back to Stockholm, Sweden, the remains of the late John Ericsson, the distinguished inventor of the "Monitor." He was in command of the "Baltimore" during the complications and troubles at Valparaiso, Chili, in 1891.

He is at present on light-house duty as inspector of the Third Light-House District at Tompkinsville, New York. Captain Schley has received two gold medals for his services, and from his native State, Maryland, a gold chronometer watch for services in the expedition which found and rescued Lieutenant Greely and the survivors of the "Lady Franklin Bay" in the Polar regions.

MAJOR-GENERAL JOHN M. SCHOFIELD, U.S.A.

MAJOR-GENERAL JOHN M. SCHOFIELD (commanding the army) was born in New York September 29, 1831, and graduated at the Military Academy July 1, 1853. He was promoted brevet second lieutenant of artillery the same day, and second lieutenant First Artillery, August 31, 1853. He served at Fort Moultrie in 1853, and in Florida in 1854-55, as acting assistant professor of philosophy, and assistant professor of the same at the Military Academy from 1856 to 1860. He was on leave of absence as professor of physics, at Washington University, St. Louis, Missouri, in 1860-61, and when the war of the Rebellion commenced was made mustering officer for the State of Missouri, from April 20 to May 20, 1861. He was major of the First Missouri Infantry, April 26; captain, First U. S. Artillery, May 14; brigadier-general of volunteers, November 21; brigadier-general of Missouri State Militia, November 26, 1861; and major-general U. S. Volunteers, November 29, 1862.

He joined our forces near Fredericktown, Missouri; organized and equipped a battery, and took part in the battle of Fredericktown, October 21, 1861; he commanded the District of St. Louis, November 27, 1861, to February, 1862, and District of Missouri from February 15 to September 26, 1862, and organized and commanded the Missouri State Militia during this period. He was member of the Army and Navy Board to examine the condition and fitness of the Mississippi Gun and Mortar-boat Flotilla, December 9 to 31, 1861; from September, 1862, to April, organized 1863, and commanded the Army of the Frontier, in Southwest Missouri and Northwest Arkansas, forcing the Confederates south of the Arkansas River; in command of the Third Division, Fourteenth Army Corps, Army of the Cumberland, April 20 to May 13, 1863; in command of the Department of the Missouri (*ex-officio* major-general, commanding Missouri State Militia), May 13, 1863, to January 31, 1864, during which time the forces under his command operated with success in Missouri and Arkansas as far south as Little Rock. He commanded the Department and Army of the Ohio, January 31, 1864, to January 29, 1865, forming the left wing of General Sherman's army (opposing Johnston), participating in all the operations and movements thereof, including the Atlanta campaign. In October, 1864, he was sent with the Twenty-third Corps to report to General Thomas, at Nashville, Tennessee, and commanded the troops in the field opposed to the Confederate General Hood, from November 13 to December 1, 1864, including the battle of Franklin, November 30. In the decisive victory gained by General Thomas near Nashville, December 15-16, General Schofield participated with the Twenty-third Army Corps; in pursuit of the army under General Hood, to January 14, 1865. At this time the Twenty-third Army Corps, Army of the Ohio, General Schofield commanding, was transported from Clifton, Tennessee, to Washington, D. C., and transferred to North Carolina by the 8th of February, 1865. Commanded the Department of North Carolina and Army of the Ohio, February 8, 1865, forming a junction with General Sherman at Goldsborough, March 22, 1865; present at Durham's Station, North Carolina, April 26, 1865, and intrusted with the execution of the terms of capitulation of Johnston's army.

General Schofield was appointed brigadier-general U. S. Army November 30, 1864, and brevetted major-general March 13, 1865, and on the 4th of March, 1869, was advanced to the grade of major-general U. S. Army.

He was sent on special mission to Europe, November, 1865, to May, 1866, and successively commanded the Department of the Potomac, Richmond, Virginia, the First Military District (State of Virginia), and was Secretary of War from June 1, 1868, to March 11, 1869. He commanded the Department of the Missouri, and the Military Division of the Pacific until July, 1876; was on special mission to the Hawaiian Islands, December 30, 1872, to April, 1873; superintendent U. S. Military Academy, July, 1876, to January 21, 1881; in command of the Military Division of the Gulf, which was discontinued May 9, 1881, and General Schofield then spent a year in travel in Europe. He then commanded the Military Division of the Pacific, the Division of the Missouri, and the Division of the Atlantic, and was then assigned to the command of the army of the United States, by order of the President, August 14, 1888. He is at present in command, and president of Board of Ordnance and Fortifications, created by Act of Congress, approved September 22, 1888.

## LIEUTENANT-GENERAL WINFIELD SCOTT, U.S.A.
### (DECEASED).

LIEUTENANT-GENERAL WINFIELD SCOTT was born near Petersburg, Virginia, June 13, 1786, the grandson of a Scottish refugee from the field of Culloden. He was a student at William and Mary College in 1805, and was admitted to the bar at Richmond, Virginia, in 1807. One of the sudden war excitements of the time changed the course of his life, and he obtained a captain's commission in the United States Army in 1808. He served on the Niagara frontier throughout the war of 1812-15, and became one of its leading figures, rising rapidly through all the grades of the service, to that of major-general, which was then the highest. Among other curious testimonials to his valor and conduct, he received from Princeton College, in 1814, the honorary degree of Doctor of Laws, a distinction on which he never ceased to look with peculiar satisfaction. In 1841 he became the senior major-general of the army, and in 1855, after he had passed out of political life, the exceptional grade of lieutenant-general was created for him. His most noteworthy military achievement was his conduct of the main campaign against Mexico in 1847. Landing (March 9) at Vera Cruz with but five thousand five hundred men, he fought his way through a hostile country to the capital city of Mexico, which he captured September 14, thereby practically ending the war. His service, however, was not confined to the army; from 1815 until 1861 he was the most continuously prominent public man of the country, receiving and justifying every mark of public confidence in his integrity, tact, and reasonableness. At a time (1823) when duelling was almost an imperative duty of an officer, he resisted successfully the persistent efforts of a brother-officer (Andrew Jackson) to force him into combat; and the simple rectitude of his intentions was so evident, that he lost no ground in public estimation. In 1832, when ordered to Charleston by President Jackson during the "nullification" troubles, he secured every advantage for the government, while his skilful and judicious conduct gave no occasion to South Carolina for an outbreak. In like manner, in the Black Hawk Indian troubles of 1832-33; in the Canadian "Patriot War" of 1837-38; in the boundary dispute of 1838 between Maine and New Brunswick; in the San Juan difficulty in 1859,—wherever there was imminent danger of war and a strong desire to keep the peace, all thoughts turned instinctively to Scott as a fit instrument

of an amicable settlement, and his success always justified the course. Such a career seemed a gateway to political preferment, and his position was strengthened by the notorious fact that, as he was a Whig, the Democratic administration had persistently tried to subordinate his claims to those of officers of its own party. In 1852 his party nominated him for the Presidency; but, though his services had been so great, and his capacity and integrity were beyond question, he had other qualities which counted against him. He was easily betrayed into the most egregious blunders of speech and action, which, drawing additional zest from his portly and massive form and a somewhat pompous ceremoniousness of manner, destroyed his chances of election in the North. The Southern Whigs, believing him to be under the influence of the Seward or anti-slavery wing of the party, cast no strong vote for him, and he was overwhelmingly defeated in both sections, completing the final overthrow of his party. In 1861 he remained at the head of the United States armies, in spite of the secession of his State, until November, when he retired on account of old age and infirmities. After travelling for a time in Europe, he published, in 1864, his autobiography, a work which reveals the strong and weak points of his character,—his integrity and complete honesty of purpose, his inclination to personal vanity, his rigid precision in every point of military precedent and etiquette, and his laborious affectation of an intimate acquaintance with belles-lettres. He died at West Point, New York, May 29, 1866.

## MAJOR AND BREVET COLONEL JAMES WALL SCULLY, U.S.A.

MAJOR AND BREVET COLONEL JAMES WALL SCULLY (Quartermaster's Department) was born in Ireland, February 19, 1837, of the Tipperary family of Scullys, who have been members of the British House of Commons for many years.

An ancestor, Captain James Cantwell (cavalry), served in the British army in the war of the American Revolution, and another, Captain Joseph Cairns (infantry), served on the American side in the same war.

From his seventh to tenth year he was a student at Saint Kieran's College, in Kilkenny; came to the United States in 1848, and attended school at, Albany, New York. He left school and enlisted in the U. S. Cavalry, and was attached to the "permanent party" at Carlisle Barracks, Pennsylvania, and in February, 1857, he was transferred to Light Battery K, First Artillery. He served on the Texas frontier until the breaking out of the war of the Rebellion, when he marched with his battery from Fort Duncan, Texas, to Brazos Santiago, in February, 1861, being part of the command that refused to surrender to the rebels under the orders of General Twiggs. He commanded the detachment that hauled down the rebel flags from the court-house and other buildings at Key West, Florida, in 1861. He was discharged, on account of expiration of term of service, September 20, 1861.

He entered the volunteer service as first lieutenant and regimental quartermaster of the Tenth Tennessee Infantry July 14, 1862; was appointed lieutenant-colonel August 21, 1863, and promoted colonel June 6, 1864. He served with his regiment in the Army of the Cumberland, commanding regiment and troops on Nashville and N. W. Railroad to June, 1864; special service with regiment and disbursing officer of quartermaster and commissary departments of expedition against General Morgan in Tennessee. He was aide-de-camp to General George H. Thomas in the Mill Spring and Shiloh campaigns, and was second in command to General A. C. Gillem in the campaign against the rebel General John H. Morgan when that officer was killed.

Colonel Scully was quartermaster-general of the State of Tennessee from August to November, 1864, and commanded his regiment in the field. He was honorably mustered out May 25, 1865, and was appointed captain and assistant quartermaster of volunteers September 25, 1865, and two days later appointed to the same office in the regular service. He was made brevet major September 27, 1865, for "gallant and meritorious services in the battle of Mill Spring, Kentucky;" lieutenant-colonel September 27, 1865, for "gallant and meritorious services in the battle of Shiloh, Tennessee;" colonel September 27, 1865, for "gallant and meritorious services in the battle of Nashville, Tennessee."

Colonel Scully served as depot quartermaster, Natchez, Mississippi, from January to May, 1866; depot quartermaster, Vicksburg, Mississippi, to June, 1867; inspector of the Freedmen's Bureau, State of Mississippi, from December, 1867, to February, 1868; depot quartermaster, Vicksburg, Mississippi, to March, 1869; inspecting duty in Texas from April to July, 1869; depot and post quartermaster, Corpus Christi, Texas, to June, 1870; Ringgold Barracks, Texas, August, 1871; Sioux City, Iowa, December, 1871, to April, 1872; Fort Rice, Dakota, 1872 to 1878; Camp Thomas, Arizona Territory, from 1879 to 1882; Fort Adams, 1883; and at various other stations till 1890; present station, Atlanta, Georgia.

He was promoted major in the Quartermaster's Department January 25, 1883.

## CAPTAIN CLINTON B. SEARS, U.S.A.

CAPTAIN CLINTON B. SEARS (Engineer Corps) was born in New York June 2, 1844, and graduated at the Military Academy June 17, 1867, and promoted first lieutenant the same day. He entered the volunteer service as private of Company G, Ninety-fifth Ohio Infantry, July 24, 1862, and was promoted corporal subsequently.

He participated in Buell's campaign after Bragg, and in the Stone River campaign, where he was on detached duty. He rejoined his regiment in February, 1863, at Memphis, Tennessee, and participated in the Vicksburg campaign, and in several minor actions, having been engaged in the battle of Richmond, Kentucky; battle of Perryville, Kentucky; both assaults on Vicksburg, Mississippi, and two attacks on Jackson, Mississippi. He was honorably mentioned in general orders from the head-quarters of his regiment, and "specially commended for gallantry in volunteering to carry the regimental colors," and was appointed color-sergeant April 25, 1863.

He has meritorious mention by name in General Order No. 66, 1863, head-quarters Fifteenth Army Corps, and recommended to the Secretary of War for appointment as cadet at the U. S. Military Academy. He was recommended for the same position, also, by Generals Grant and Sherman, and was so appointed September 16, 1863.

After graduating in 1867, he was promoted first lieutenant of the U. S. Corps of Engineers, and was detailed as assistant instructor of artillery tactics and practical military engineering at the Military Academy from July 5 to August 31, 1867, when he was placed on duty with the Engineer Battalion to February 1, 1869; then was assistant instructor of practical military engineering, signalling, and telegraphy at the Military Academy to February 1, 1870.

He then entered upon regular engineering duty, as assistant engineer on Lake Erie harbor improvements, to March 23, 1870; engineer officer on the general staff, Military Division of the Pacific, to July 21, 1870; chief engineer on staff of General Canby, Department of the Columbia, to May 6, 1871; assistant engineer on the defences of San Francisco harbor to August 14, 1871; executive engineer in charge of improvement of Wilmington harbor, California, to September 3, 1875; temporarily detached, February, 1873, to make a survey for the improvement of Estero Bay, at Moro, California; on leave October 1, 1875, to January 1, 1876; assistant engineer defences of Boston harbor to August 28, 1876; at the U. S. Military Academy as principal assistant professor of civil and military engineering to August 25, 1877; principal assistant professor of geography, history, and ethics, to July 1, 1878; and principal assistant professor of natural and experimental philosophy and astronomy to April 13, 1882; also during the last year in charge of the construction of the new Astronomical Observatory at West Point; executive-officer Construction Department, Mississippi River Commission, with station at St. Louis, Missouri, from April, 1882, to April, 1884; in charge of Third District, improving Mississippi River, with station at Vicksburg, Mississippi, and afterwards at Memphis, Tennessee, to May 14, 1886; temporarily in charge of the Second District from August 31, 1884, to March 10, 1885; and of the First and Second Districts from July 6 to October 6, 1885; on leave of absence to September 14, 1886; in charge of the improvement of Upper Missouri and Yellowstone Rivers, and from March 28, 1887, of the improvement of roads and bridges, Yellowstone National Park, to April 16, 1888, with station at Bismarck, Dakota Territory, and afterwards at St. Paul, Minnesota; assistant to the chief of engineers in charge of the First and Second Division of the office at Washington, D. C., to June 18, 1890. On duty with the Battalion of Engineers, in command of Company A, and instructor of submarine mining, U. S. Engineer School, Willet's Point, New York, at the present time; on special duty in June, 1889, at Johnstown, Pennsylvania, in charge of construction of pontoon bridges in aid of the survivors of the great flood. He was promoted captain April 9, 1880.

Captain Sears is the author of "Principles of Tidal Harbor Improvements" and "Ransom Genealogy." He is a member of the New York Society of the Sons of the Revolution and D. C. Society Sons of the American Revolution, and of the American Institute of Civics; Fellow National Academy of Design; member Military Order Loyal Legion, U. S.; honorary degrees of A. B. from Ohio Western University, 1881; of A. M., 1884.

CAPTAIN FRANCIS W. SEELEY, U.S.A.

CAPTAIN FRANCIS W. SEELEY entered the regular army February 15, 1855, as private in Battery E, Third Artillery, and was promoted brevet second lieutenant Third Artillery September 19, 1860; second lieutenant Fourth Artillery February 4, 1861; first lieutenant Fourth Artillery May 14, 1861, and captain Fourth Artillery July 11, 1864. He was on duty in the Adjutant-General's Office from February 21 to March, 1861, and joined Battery H, Second Artillery, April 1, serving with it at Washington, D. C., to April 5, 1861, when ordered to Fort Pickens, Florida. Here the lieutenant served as adjutant-general of the department, under Col. Harvey Brown, from July, 1861, to Jan. 18, 1862, and was present at the action of Santa Rosa Island, Florida, and bombardments of Forts McRae and Barrancas, Nov. 22, 1861, and Jan. 1, 1862.

He then left to join his own battery and regiment, which he served with at Washington City to March 10, when he took the field with the Army of the Potomac, participating in the siege of Yorktown, Virginia; Oak Grove, Virginia; Malvern Hill, Virginia (July 1, 1862); Malvern Hill (August 5, 1862); Fredericksburg, Virginia; Chancellorsville, Virginia, and Gettysburg, Pennsylvania (where he was twice wounded),—having commanded his battery in all the above engagements. On account of his wounds, Lieutenant Seeley was forced to leave the field until August 15, 1863, when he rejoined the Army of the Potomac and commanded his battery to October 1, 1863. He was appointed regimental quartermaster, and reported at Fort Washington, Md., remaining on duty there until he resigned, August 31, 1864.

The following is an extract from the Report of the Congressional Committee on the Conduct of the War:

" . . . At the conclusion of the battle of Sunday, Captain Seeley's battery, which was the last battery that fired a shot in the battle of Chancellorsville, had forty-five horses killed, and in the neighborhood of forty men killed and wounded; but being a soldier of great pride and ambition, and not wishing to leave any of his material in the hands of the enemy, he withdrew so entirely at his leisure that he carried off all the harness from his dead horses, loading his cannoneers with it; he even took a part of a set of harness on his own arm, and so moved to the rear. . . . "

And from an extract from the official report of Major-General Humphreys on the battle of Gettysburg, and referring to the occasion of Longstreet's attack:

"Seeley's battery (K, Fourth U. S. Artillery) was placed at my disposal. . . . The firing of Seeley's battery was splendid, and excited my admiration, as well as that of every officer who beheld it. His loss in men and horses was heavy,—including himself, severely wounded."

In Walker's "History of the Second Army Corps" his battery is mentioned in most favorable terms (referring to Malvern Hill): "The regular batteries of Kingsbury, Seeley, and Ames, and the volunteer battery of Weeden, far surpassed the ordinary achievements of artillery; they fairly smashed the artillery which the Confederates sought to bring into action; battery after battery, on that side, was driven from the field, without being able to get a single shot out of one of their guns; while upon the daring infantry lines which pressed forward in the hope of carrying the crest they rained a fire which, for destructiveness, has seldom, if ever, been exceeded in the history of the war." In regard to Chancellorsville: "One of General Sickles's batteries, K, of the 4th U. S., holds its post after all the infantry has passed to the rear, exchanging fire with the advancing enemy; only when these are close upon his guns does the gallant commander, Seeley, condescend to retire, carrying along everything that might serve the enemy as a trophy."

In "Historical Sketches of the U. S. Army," the historian writes of his battery as follows: "May 3 it fought at Chancellorsville, losing Lieutenant I. Arnold (Ordnance Department, attached), wounded, and forty-four men and fifty-nine horses killed and wounded. It was in this battle, on the height at Fairview, at the extreme left of the crest, while under the most terrific fire, that K Battery won the admiration of all who beheld it; and its record at Chancellorsville under Lieutenant F. W. Seeley, that prince of battery commanders, must always form one of the brightest pages in the history of our light artillery. Its work may be equalled, but it cannot be surpassed."

Captain Seeley resigned Aug. 31, 1864, on account of physical disability resulting from wounds, since which time he has been a resident of Minn., in which State he has held prominent civil positions, and has served one term as adjutant-general, with the rank of brigadier-general. He was recommended for several brevets, but his early separation from the service prevented action on them.

## CAPTAIN T. O. SELFRIDGE, JR., U.S.N.

CAPTAIN T. O. SELFRIDGE, JR., was born in Boston, Mass.; he entered the Naval Academy in October, 1851, and graduated in June, 1853, at the head of his class. Was the first naval officer to receive a diploma of graduation under the present organization of the Naval Academy. Served in the Pacific on board the "Independence." Promoted passed midshipman, November, 1856. On coast survey, and master of the "Vincennes," coast of Africa, until April, 1860. He had been commissioned lieutenant, February, 1860. Ordered to flag-ship "Cumberland," of the Home Squadron, he was present at the destruction of the Norfolk Navy-Yard in April, 1861; the bombardment and capture of the Hatteras forts in September, 1861. Volunteered for the command of a cutting-out expedition from the "Cumberland," at Newport News, February, 1862. Second lieutenant of the "Cumberland," and in command of gun-deck battery, when that vessel went down, with her flag flying. He jumped from a port, and swam to a boat. Ordered to command the "Monitor," after Captain Worden was wounded. Then served as flag-lieutenant of the North Atlantic fleet. Present at recapture of Norfolk, and the destruction of defences in Virginia waters. Volunteered for service in a submarine torpedo-boat which proved a failure for want of speed. Was next ordered to the "Mississippi," having been commissioned lieutenant-commander in July, 1862. Commanded the iron-clad "Cairo," and, while in command of a flotilla of gun-boats, forcing the passage of the Yazoo, was blown up by a torpedo. Then commanded the gun-boats "Conestoga" and "Manitou." Commanded a battery at the siege of Vicksburg, with guns and men from the "Manitou." After capture of Vicksburg commanded flotilla of gun-boats in the Red and Tensas Rivers. While in the "Conestoga," had many engagements, and was sunk, March 8, 1863, in that vessel, by collision with rebel ram, "General Price." Commanded the iron-clad "Osage," in the Red River expedition. On its return brought up the rear, and, in company with "Lexington," while aground, was attacked by a battery and a brigade of dismounted cavalry, but defeated them, with loss of their general and four hundred men. Then commanded "Vindicator," and the Fifth Division of the Mississippi fleet. When Admiral Porter was ordered to the East, Lieutenant-Commander Selfridge was one of the officers selected to accompany him, and was assigned to the command of the gun-boat "Huron," in which he took part in both bombardments of Fort Fisher, and volunteered for and commanded the third division of the assaulting columns of seamen and marines. Took part in the bombardment of Fort Anderson, and the subsequent capture of Wilmington. He was three times recommended for promotion by Admiral Porter, and

was selected for a promotion of thirty numbers by the Board of Admirals assembled at Washington, at the close of the Civil War. He then next served at the Naval Academy, and commanded the "Macedonian," in the practice cruises of 1867-68. He then went to the command of the "Nipsic," in the West Indies. Commissioned commander in December, 1869. Was in charge of the expedition for the surveys of the Isthmus of Darien in 1869, having four vessels under his command,—" Guard," " Penobscot," " Nyack," and " Resaca." These important surveys continued until 1874. Explored and reported upon all the country south of Panama to the head-waters of the Atrato River, in South America. After home service at Boston, was selected to make a survey of the Amazon and Madeira Rivers, in South America. He ascended these rivers, in the "Enterprise," thirteen hundred miles, and completed the survey, returning to the United States, October, 1878. Commanded the "Enterprise" in the European Squadron in 1879-80. Was invited as special delegate by Ferdinand de Lesseps to the International Canal Congress at Paris, in May, 1879. Received from the French government the Decoration of the Legion of Honor, in recognition of the work performed in the survey of the Isthmus of Darien, and was made an honorary member of the Royal Geographical Society of Belgium. From 1880 to 1884 was in charge of the Torpedo Station at Newport, Rhode Island; captain, 1881. Commanded "Omaha," Asiatic Squadron, 1885-87. Was tried by court-martial for alleged carelessness and neglect of duty in conducting target-practice on the coast of Japan, and wholly and honorably acquitted by the court, June, 1888.

He was a member of Board of Inspection, 1889-90. Detailed as commandant of the Boston Navy-Yard, June, 1890.

## CAPTAIN R. G. SHAW, U.S.A.

CAPTAIN R. G. SHAW (First Artillery) was born in Rhode Island, June 29, 1832. He entered the volunteer service, early in the war of the Rebellion, as captain of the Third Rhode Island Artillery, August 27, 1861, and participated in General W. T. Sherman's Port Royal, South Carolina, expedition at Hilton Head and Bay Point, South Carolina, in command of Company D, Third Rhode Island Artillery, and was engaged in the operations resulting in the capture of Morris Island, South Carolina. He commanded his battery in the assault and capture of the Confederate batteries on the lower end of the island.

Captain Shaw commanded the 30-pounder siege battery at the siege of Fort Wagner, South Carolina, and commanded the same battery in the operations against Fort Gregg, at Cumming's Point, South Carolina. He commanded Battery "Hayes" (200-pounder guns) at the siege of Fort Sumter, South Carolina.

After the capture of Fort Wagner by the Union forces, he was assigned to the command of the latter battery, which, in connection with other Union batteries, was continuously engaged with the Confederate batteries in Charleston harbor until the date of the capture of the city by General W. T. Sherman's army.

Captain Shaw remained in command of Battery Gregg until January 13, 1864; then he accepted the appointment of major of the Fourteenth Rhode Island Artillery (colored), and took command of the second battalion of that regiment at English Turn, Louisiana. He was soon afterwards assigned to the command of the troops and post of Plaquemine, Louisiana. He remained in command of that post and military district until the close of the war. He was honorably mustered out of the volunteer service October 2, 1865.

Captain Shaw entered the regular service as second lieutenant First Artillery, May, 1866, and was brevetted captain U. S. Army for "gallant and meritorious services on Morris Island, South Carolina," March 2, 1867.

He was promoted first lieutenant July 28, 1866, and captain September 20, 1883. He has served continuously in the First Artillery since date of appointment, and is at present on duty at Fort Hamilton, New York harbor.

## COLONEL AND BREVET BRIGADIER-GENERAL OLIVER L. SHEPHERD, U.S.A. (RETIRED).

COLONEL AND BREVET BRIGADIER-GENERAL OLIVER L. SHEPHERD was born in New York, and graduated at the Military Academy July 1, 1840. He was promoted brevet second lieutenant Fourth Infantry the same day, second lieutenant Third Infantry October 2, 1840, and first lieutenant November 3, 1845. He served at Fort Gibson, Indian Territory, 1840-41; in the Florida War, 1841-42; at Fort Stansbury, Florida, 1842-43; at Jefferson Barracks, Missouri, 1843-44, and at Fort Jesup, Louisiana, 1844-45. He participated in the military occupation of Texas, and in the war with Mexico, and was engaged in the battles of Palo Alto, May 8, and Resaca de la Palma, May 9, 1846. He was then ordered on recruiting service, but rejoined the army in Mexico in time to take part in the skirmish at the National Bridge, August 12; Plan del Rio, August 15; Ocalaca, August 16; battle of Contreras, August 19-20; battle of Churubusco, August 20; storming of Chapultepec, September 13; and assault and capture of the City of Mexico, September 13-14, 1847. He was brevetted captain for gallant and meritorious conduct in the battles of Contreras and Churubusco, and major for gallant and meritorious conduct in the battle of Chapultepec, and was promoted captain Third Infantry, December 1, 1847.

After the war with Mexico he served at East Pascagoula, Mississippi, and San Antonio, Texas, until 1849, when he marched to El Paso, and was then stationed at Fort Bliss, Texas, Doña Ana, Fort Conrad, Camp Vigilance, Fort Defiance, and Albuquerque, New Mexico, until 1856, when he participated in a scout against Apache Indians, and was engaged in a skirmish on the Sierra del Amagre, New Mexico, in March of that year. He was at Fort Defiance and Albuquerque until 1857, when he took part in the Gila Expedition, and was engaged in a skirmish at the Cañon de los Muertos Carneros, New Mexico, against Mogollan Indians, May 24, 1857. He was again stationed at Fort Defiance in 1858-59, and participated in the Navajo Expedition of 1859, returning to Fort Defiance, where his able defence of that post from an attack of Navajo Indians just before daybreak, April 30, 1860, is spoken of in General Scott's orders of that year. Subsequently in the same year he marched to Texas, and occupied stations at Forts Clark and Duncan, until early in 1861, when he moved to Fort New York.

Captain Shepherd was appointed lieutenant-colonel Eighteenth Infantry, May 14, 1861, serving in command of a battalion of the Third Infantry during May and June, 1861. He was then on mustering duty in New York City to December, 1861, when he participated in the Tennessee and Mississippi campaign of the Army of the Ohio, being engaged in the advance upon and siege of Corinth, Mississippi, April and May, 1862, routing a rebel camp May 17, 1862, and pursuit to Baldwin, Mississippi, to May 31, 1862. He then participated in Major-General Buell's movement through Alabama and Tennessee, to Louisville, Kentucky, from July to September, 1862. After serving as a member of a court of inquiry at Allegheny Arsenal, Pennsylvania, in October and November, he participated in Major-General Rosecrans's Tennessee campaign with the Army of the Cumberland, from November, 1862, to April 17, 1863, commanding the brigade of regulars in the battle of Stone River, December 31, 1862.

He was brevetted colonel May 17, 1862, for gallant and meritorious conduct at the siege of Corinth, Mississippi, and promoted colonel of the Fifteenth Infantry, January 21, 1863, when he was assigned as superintendent of Regimental Recruiting Service at Fort Adams, from May 7, 1863, to February 13, 1866.

Colonel Shepherd was brevetted brigadier-general U.S. Army, March 13, 1865, for gallant and meritorious services at the battle of Stone River, Tennessee.

At the close of the war, General Shepherd was ordered to Georgia, and served in command of his regiment in the reconstruction of the State of Alabama, until December 31, 1867. The first assembly under the new constitution was held during that time. He was then on leave of absence and awaiting orders until March 6, 1868, when he was again in command of his regiment and sub-district of Alabama until August 12, and the post of Marshall, Texas, to September 3, 1868. After this he was awaiting orders before Sub-Judiciary Committee of the House of Representatives, and on court of inquiry, until 1869. He was then in command of his regiment to Nov. 13, 1869, and on leave of absence to Dec. 15, 1870, when he was retired from active service on his own application, after thirty consecutive years of service.

**GENERAL PHILIP HENRY SHERIDAN, U.S.A.**
(DECEASED).

GENERAL PHILIP HENRY SHERIDAN was born in Albany, New York, in March, 1831. He graduated from the U. S. Military Academy in July, 1853. He was appointed brevet second lieutenant of the Third Infantry. After serving in Kentucky, Texas, and Oregon, he was made second lieutenant of the Fourth Infantry November 22, 1854, first lieutenant March 1, 1861, and captain Thirteenth Infantry May 14, 1861. In December of that year was chief quartermaster and commissary of Army of Southwest Missouri; served in Mississippi campaign from April to September, 1862; was appointed colonel of the Second Michigan Cavalry May 20, 1862; on July 1 was sent to make a raid on Booneville, Mississippi. He did excellent service in pursuit of the enemy from Corinth to Baldwin, and in many skirmishes during July and at battle of Booneville. Appointed brigadier-general of volunteers, and on October 1 was placed in command of the Eleventh Division of the Army of the Ohio. He was distinguished for his services at Perryville on October 8, having driven back the enemy.

Marched with army to relief of Nashville, October and November. Was placed in command of Army of Cumberland, and took part in the two days' battle of Stone River, December 31, 1862, and January 3, 1863. Division after division was driven back by Bragg's army until Sheridan was reached, and the fate of the day seemed to be in his hands. He resisted vigorously, then advanced, and drove the enemy back; held the overwhelming force in check, and retired only at the point of the bayonet. This brilliant work enabled General Rosecrans to form new lines in harmony with his overpowered right. He was appointed major-general of volunteers, to date from December 31, 1862. Was with army crossing Cumberland Mountains and Tennessee River, August and September 6, and in battle of Chickamauga, September 19 and 20. At this battle he rendered valuable assistance to General Thomas, when a gap occurred in the centre of his line through the misconception of an order. Took part in the battles of Lookout Mountain and Missionary Ridge. In this latter action he first attracted the attention of General Grant, who saw that he might be one of his most useful lieutenants in the future.

He was transferred to Virginia by Grant, and on April 4, 1864, placed in command of Cavalry Corps of Army of Potomac, all the cavalry being consolidated to form that command. He took part in the bloody battle of the Wilderness, May 5 and 6, 1864, being constantly engaged in raids against the enemy's flanks and rear. His fight at Todd's Tavern was an important aid to the movements of the army, and his capture of Spottsylvania Court-House added to his reputation for dash and daring. Was in battle of Cold Harbor, on May 31 and June 3. After cutting the Virginia Central and Richmond and Fredericksburg Railroads, capturing five hundred prisoners, he joined the Army of the Potomac for a short period, and took part in their battles till the end of July. In August, 1864, he was placed in command of the Army of the Shenandoah. On the 19th of September Sheridan drove Early's army through Winchester and captured five thousand prisoners and five guns. Early, on October 19, attacked Sheridan's army. They gave way, and soon the whole army was in retreat. Sheridan had been in Washington, and at this juncture had just returned to Winchester, twenty miles from the field. Hearing the sound of the battle, he rode rapidly and arrived on the field at ten o'clock. As he rode up, he shouted, " Face the other way, boys; we are going back." A succession of attacks was made, and Early's army was driven back as far as Mount Jackson. The Confederates lost in the campaign sixteen thousand nine hundred and fifty-two killed or wounded and thirteen thousand prisoners. Between Feb. 27 and March 24, 1865, he conducted, with ten thousand cavalry, a colossal raid from Winchester to Petersburg. His battle of Five Forks was one of the most brilliant and decisive of the engagements of the war, and compelled Lee's evacuation of Petersburg and Richmond, leaving in Sheridan's hands six thousand prisoners.

After the war Sheridan had command of several of the departments. In 1867 he conducted a winter campaign against the Indians. In 1870 he visited Europe to witness the Franco-Prussian war. On the retirement of Sherman, in 1883, he was made lieutenant-general. In May, 1888, while he was ill, President Cleveland signed a bill commissioning him a full general, and on August 5, 1888, he died. Sheridan never was defeated, and often plucked victory out of the jaws of defeat. He bore the nickname of " Little Phil;" he was below middle height, and very powerfully built.

## GENERAL WILLIAM T. SHERMAN, U.S.A.
### (DECEASED).

General William T. Sherman was born in Ohio February 8, 1820, and graduated from the Military Academy July 1, 1840. He was promoted second lieutenant Third Artillery the same day, and first lieutenant November 30, 1841. He served in the Florida War, 1840-41; on duty in various Southern States and in Pennsylvania, 1842-46; on breaking out of war with Mexico applied for duty in the field, and was assigned to Company F, Third Artillery, then under orders for California; he was bearer of despatches from General Smith to War Department, and, after six months' leave of absence, joined Company C, Third Artillery, at Jefferson Barracks, Missouri. He was appointed captain and commissary of subsistence September 27, 1850, and stationed at St. Louis and New Orleans, but resigned from the army September 6, 1853, and entered upon a civil career as a banker in San Francisco and New York until 1857; was major-general of California Militia in 1856; counsellor-at-law at Leavenworth, Kansas, 1858-59; superintendent of the La. State Seminary of Learning and Military Academy, 1859-61.

At the breaking out of the war of the Rebellion, he was reappointed in the U. S. Army, colonel of the Thirteenth Infantry, May 14, 1861, and brigadier-general of volunteers May 17, 1861. He served in the defences of Washington, and was in command of a brigade in the Army of the Potomac, in the Manassas campaign, until July 23, being engaged in the battle of Bull Run, July 21, 1861. He was then assigned to duty in the Department of the Cumberland until November, 1861, when he was transferred for duty to the Department of the Missouri, and ordered to report to Major-General Halleck at St. Louis; on inspection duty at Sedalia, Missouri, and commanding camp of instruction at Benton Barracks, Missouri, 1861-62; at post of Paducah, Kentucky, expediting and facilitating operations in progress up the Tennessee and Cumberland Rivers, and organizing a division to be commanded by himself; bore a distinguished part in the battle of Shiloh and in the operations against Corinth; commanding District of Memphis and an expedition against Vicksburg, 1862; assigned to command of Fifteenth Army Corps in January, 1863; participated in capture of Arkansas Post; took part in operations preceding and attending siege of Vicksburg; assigned to command of Department of the Tennessee October 27, 1863; joined his forces to the army under General Grant at Chattanooga, Tennessee, and bore a conspicuous part in the battle of that name; moved with great energy to the relief of General Burnside at Knoxville, Tennessee, and returned to Chattanooga, 1863; made an expedition from Vicksburg to Meridian, Mississippi, destroying much railroad and war material thereabouts, and returned to Vicksburg; assumed command of Military Division of the Mississippi March 18, 1864; captured Atlanta, Georgia, and made his march to the sea which terminated in the capture of Savannah, Georgia, December 21, 1864; marched northward from Savannah, captured Columbia, South Carolina, compelling the evacuation of Charleston; repulsed the enemy under General J. E. Johnston at Bentonville, and joined his forces with those of General Schofield at Goldsborough; moved against General Johnston, who, on April 26, 1865, surrendered his army on the same terms as had been granted General Lee.

General Sherman was appointed major-general of volunteers May 1, 1862, and brigadier-general U. S. Army July 4, 1863. He had conferred on him the commission of major-general, August 12, 1864, for "gallant and distinguished services as commander of the Mississippi Division in the conduct of the campaign in Georgia," and was further honorably mentioned by Congress in the following joint resolution of thanks, February 19, 1864:

"To Major-General W. T. Sherman and the officers and soldiers of the Army of the Tennessee for their gallant and arduous services in marching to the relief of the Army of the Cumberland, and for their gallantry and heroism in the battle of Chattanooga, which contributed in a great degree to the success of our arms in that glorious victory." June 10, 1865 : "To Major-General W. T. Sherman and officers and soldiers of his command for their gallantry and good conduct in their late campaign from Chattanooga to Atlanta and the triumphal march thence through Georgia to Savannah, terminating in the capture and occupation of that city."

General Sherman, after the war closed, commanded several of the most important military divisions, and was appointed lieutenant-general, U. S. Army, July 25, 1866. Appointed general of the army, March 5, 1869, and retained that position until retired from active service, Feb. 8, 1884. He died Feb. 14, 1891, at New York City.

## MEDICAL DIRECTOR EDWARD SHIPPEN, U.S.N.
(RETIRED).

MEDICAL DIRECTOR EDWARD SHIPPEN was born in New Jersey, but belongs to a family long settled in Philadelphia, and numbering among its members the first mayor (under the proprietor), a colonel of Colonial troops, the first public lecturer on anatomy in this country,—who was afterwards a surgeon-general of the Revolutionary army,—and a chief justice, both under the Crown and the State.

Medical Director Shippen is Bachelor of Arts and Master of Arts, of Princeton; Doctor of Medicine, of the University of Pennsylvania; a member of the Historical Society, and Fellow of that venerable institution, the College of Physicians of Philadelphia; president of the Genealogical Society of Pennsylvania; and Companion of the Military Order of the Loyal Legion.

He was appointed from Pennsylvania, August 7, 1849. Entered the service as assistant-surgeon; attached to sloop "Marion," and was on board that vessel when the Portuguese frigate " Donna Maria Segunda" was torn to fragments by the explosion of her magazines, when within a cable's length of the "Marion." Of the large number of people on board, nine were rescued alive by the "Marion's" people, of whom only three survived,—one white man and two Lascars. The only person seriously injured on board the "Marion" was a boat-keeper on the side away from the explosion. Some of the frigate's guns and one of her lower masts went clear over the "Marion." East India Squadron, 1849-52; receiving-ship "Ohio," Boston, 1852-53; steamer "Fulton," Fishing-Banks Squadron, 1853; steamer "Hetzel," Coast Survey, 1854; brig "Dolphin," coast of Africa, 1855-57. During his cruise in the "Dolphin," he was present at the bombardment of a native town; at two landings for the protection of white traders and other interesting proceedings. The "Dolphin" ascended the river Congo for many miles, at a time when it was an unknown stream, except to slave-traders. Rendezvous, Philadelphia, 1857; Naval Asylum, Philadelphia, 1858; steamer "Caledonia," Paraguay Expedition, 1859; flagship "Congress," Brazil Squadron, 1859-61.

Commissioned as surgeon April 26, 1861; frigate "Congress," North Atlantic Blockading Squadron, 1861-62; in the "Congress" when attacked by the rebel ram " Merrimac," at Newport News, and injured by shell; recorder of Medical Examining Board, Philadelphia, 1862; receiving-ship and special recruiting duty, New York, 1862-64. During this time frequently employed, in the dearth of line officers, in carrying drafts of men to Philadelphia and Washington. Frigate "New Ironsides," North Atlantic Squadron, 1864-65; at both battles of Fort Fisher, and at Bermuda Hundred; steam-sloop "Canandaigua," European Squadron, 1866-68; during which made the Russian cruise, under Admiral Farragut; member of Naval Retiring Board, Philadelphia, 1868; surgeon of the Naval Academy, Annapolis, Maryland, from 1869 to 1871; fleet-surgeon, European Station, 1871-73; Navy-Yard, Philadelphia, 1873; Naval Hospital, Philadelphia, 1874-79.

Commissioned as medical director, 1876; president of the Naval Medical Examining Board, Philadelphia, 1880-81; president Board of Examiners, March, 1881-83; Naval Hospital, Philadelphia, 1883-86; special duty, Philadelphia, 1886-88. Retired, 1888.

## CHIEF-ENGINEER WILLIAM H. SHOCK, U.S.N.
### (RETIRED).

CHIEF-ENGINEER WILLIAM H. SHOCK was born in Maryland, and appointed third assistant engineer from that State in January, 1845. Served during the Mexican War in the "General Taylor," "Princeton," "Spitfire," and frigate "Mississippi," in which vessels he participated in the capture of Tampico, under Commodore Conner, and Alvarado, Tuxpan, Tlacotalpan, and Vera Cruz, under Commodore Perry. Promoted second assistant engineer July 10, 1847. Served in the steamer "Engineer," of the Home Squadron. Promoted to first assistant engineer October 31, 1848, and in 1849 was senior engineer of the steamer "Legaré," on the Coast Survey. The next two years were spent upon special duty at Philadelphia, superintending the construction of the machinery of the steam-frigate "Susquehanna." Promoted chief engineer in March, 1851, and was ordered to Boston to superintend the construction of the new machinery for the "Princeton," where he spent two years. In 1853 and 1854 he was inspecting engineer of ocean steamers for United States mail service, and chief engineer of the steamer "Princeton," of the Home Squadron. During 1854-55 he was at the West Point Works, superintending the construction of machinery for the steam-frigate "Merrimac." In 1855-56 he served as chief engineer of the "Merrimac," on the Home Station. That ship was then one of the most formidable afloat in any navy. From 1857 to 1860 he was chief engineer of the steam-frigate "Powhatan," of the East India Squadron. In 1860-62 he was president of the Examining Board of Engineers, and for the next two years was on special duty at St. Louis, superintending the construction of river monitors. From 1863 to 1865 he was fleet-engineer of the West Gulf Squadron, participating in the capture of Forts Gaines and Morgan, under Admiral Farragut, and the Spanish Fort and city of Mobile, under Admiral Thatcher. After the war he served two years as chief engineer of the Boston Navy-Yard, and a similar term at the Washington yard. During 1868-69 he was fleet-engineer of the European Squadron; in 1869-70 inspector of machinery afloat, and member of the Board of Visitors to the Naval Academy at Annapolis. In the summer of 1870 he was appointed acting chief of the Bureau of Steam-Engineering, retiring from that office with the written thanks of the department for the efficient manner in which the duties of the bureau were discharged. In 1871 he was again called to take temporary charge of the Bureau of Steam-Engineering, and upon retiring from the position was actively employed on other duty in the United States until 1873, at which time he was ordered to Europe, on a tour of inspection of public and private dock-yards, and to represent the Bureau of Steam-Engineering at the International Exhibition at Vienna. By direction of the President he was appointed one of the American judges of awards.

When he returned from Europe he was again employed actively until March 3, 1877, when he was appointed and confirmed engineer-in-chief of the U. S. Navy. After serving a full term of four years under his commission, he was reappointed and confirmed for a second term. He was placed upon the retired list June 15, 1883, with the rank of commodore, under an Act of Congress, approved March 3, 1871.

CAPTAIN AND BREVET MAJOR GEORGE SHORKLEY, U.S.A. (RETIRED).

CAPTAIN AND BREVET MAJOR GEORGE SHORKLEY was born in New York, and entered the military service as a volunteer in 1861.

Recruited a volunteer company, and it was assigned as Company B, of the Fifty-first Pennsylvania (Hartranft's) regiment, which he joined as first lieutenant, September 22, 1861, and was with the regiment with Burnside's expedition at Roanoke Island, Fort Brown, etc., 1861-62; with the Ninth Army Corps in Virginia in 1862, as regimental adjutant.

At the battle of Antietam he led the regiment in the flank charge, which took the bridge, receiving a severe gun-shot wound in the left arm.

At the time of Lee's move into Pennsylvania he reported, with his arm in a sling, to General Couch, at Harrisburg, and was ordered on his staff and assigned to duty organizing militia regiments and sending them to the front. After the battle of Gettysburg he was in command of parole camp at West Chester, Pennsylvania.

The Ninth Army Corps having been ordered to Mississippi, he received orders to report to General Hartranft, commanding division, his left arm still of little use. He was with the Ninth Army Corps in East Tennessee as inspector for General Hartranft. Served with his regiment in the winter of 1863-64, and with the Ninth Army Corps, and returned East to Annapolis, when he was ordered to duty as assistant adjutant-general to General Hartranft, commanding depot, and reorganization of Ninth Army Corps. Was designated to be colonel of one of the new Pennsylvania regiments to be assigned to the corps; but upon the command being ordered for duty with General Grant in Virginia, this was thrown up, and he went to the field as assistant adjutant-general for General Hartranft. In the Wilderness, where Hartranft's command had joined lines with General Hancock's corps in a woods. The enemy's artillery and musketry fire had sent one of Hancock's Pennsylvania regiments back, endangering the whole line. Knowing the regiment, and seeing this, and being well mounted, he dashed across the wood, took the flag from the color-bearer, advanced the regiment to its position, receiving the thanks of its commander, and returned to his command.

While serving before Petersburg, Virginia, he was ordered as the officer to relieve the Ninth Corps from the line of works for the assault at the explosion of the mine, July 30, 1864; this had been done, the assault made, the crater reached, when all were hemmed in by enfilading fires from the enemy's works. Seeing this, he ran across the field between the lines to our troops on the left, secured a fire that checked the enemy's fire from that flank, and in returning he was struck by a shell, tearing away the front of his coat and sleeve and carrying away the fingers of his right hand. After partially recovering from this wound he returned again to the field, when the appointment of assistant adjutant-general was offered him, but declined, having lost the ability to write rapidly in losing his fingers. He was then assigned to duty in the inspector-general's department in accordance with his brevet rank, by the President, and ordered to duty with General Hartranft's Third Division, Ninth Army Corps.

At the assault on Fort Steadman he was again seriously wounded, the ball lodging in his right thigh.

He was with the corps, and acting as inspector-general for the grand review; and with General Hartranft in charge of conspirators in the assassination of President Lincoln. He was mustered out of the volunteer service July 27, 1865, having participated in thirty-seven battles and affrays, and six times wounded in action,—three times slightly, and three times seriously,—in left arm at Antietam, Maryland, ball extracted; at mine, Petersburg, Virginia, fingers of right hand carried away by cannon-ball; and at Fort Steadman, Virginia, in right thigh, ball extracted.

Captain Shorkley was appointed second and first lieutenant Fifteenth Infantry, February 23, 1866, and on March 2, 1867, was brevetted captain and major in the regular army "for gallant and meritorious services at Antietam and Fort Steadman," he having previously received the volunteer brevets of major, lieutenant-colonel, and colonel for his gallant services before Petersburg and Fort Steadman.

He joined the Fifteenth Infantry in Alabama and served on reconstruction duty in 1866-68, and was then transferred with his regiment to Texas. He was promoted captain October 13, 1867, and was retired, for disability in the line of duty, September 23, 1885.

## REAR-ADMIRAL ROBERT W. SHUFELDT, U.S.N.
### (RETIRED).

REAR-ADMIRAL ROBERT W. SHUFELDT was born in Dutchess County, New York, February, 1822; appointed midshipman from New York May 11, 1839; first cruise in frigate "Potomac," 1839-41; Brazil Station; in brig "Bainbridge," Home Squadron, as acting master, 1842-44; at Naval School, Philadelphia, 1844-45; promoted to passed midshipman July 2, 1845; on Coast Survey, 1845-46; in sloop "Marion" and frigate "United States," West Coast of Africa and Mediterranean, 1846-48; in U. S. mail steamers "Atlantic" and "Georgia," as chief officer, 1849-51; promoted to master February 21, 1853; commissioned as lieutenant, 1854; resigned June 21, 1854. (While out of the navy he was active in the organization of the steam commercial marine of New York, and after serving two years in the Collins line of steamers between New York and Liverpool, superintended the building of and commanded the steamers "Black Warrior" and "Cahawba" between New York and New Orleans.) Was engaged for a year in the effort to open a transit route across the Isthmus of Tehuantepec. At the commencement of the war, was commanding the steamer "Quaker City" between New York and Havana, when he was appointed consul-general to Cuba by President Lincoln; but when the war broke out he volunteered for the navy, and was appointed lieutenant and ordered to command the "Quaker City," that ship having been turned over to the government. Mr. Seward, the Secretary of State, insisted, however, upon his going at once to Havana, where there were very important duties to be performed, for which he was thought to be peculiarly qualified. At the end of two years, having, under very trying circumstances, fulfilled the object for which he was sent to Cuba, he resigned his commission of consul-general and accepted a commission in the navy as commander, which had been previously tendered to him. In 1862, while consul-general, was sent to Mexico on a special mission. At this time the French troops were in possession of Vera Cruz, and it required some discretion to reach the capital and perform the duty required. This, however, was accomplished.

His commission as commander was dated November 19, 1862. In May, 1863, commanded the "Conemaugh," South Atlantic Squadron. Was present and participated in the capture of Morris Island, and in several of the attacks on Fort Wagner. Commanded the "Proteus," East Gulf Squadron, 1864-65, and was senior naval officer in the attack upon St. Mark's, Florida; commanding flag-ship "Hartford," Asiatic Squadron, 1865-66, and steam-sloop "Wachusetts," 1866-68, on the Asiatic Station; commanding Naval Rendezvous, New York, 1868-69; commissioned as captain December 31, 1869; commanding monitor "Miantonomah," 1870; commanding "Tehuantepec," Surveying Expedition, 1870-71; commanding flag-ship "Wabash," "Congress," and "Plymouth," European Squadron, 1871-72; Navy-Yard, New York, 1872-74; chief of Bureau of Equipment and Recruiting from February 1, 1875, to November, 1878. While there he reorganized the Naval Apprentice System upon its present basis.

Commissioned as commodore September 21, 1876; went to New Orleans to take command of the naval forces there, and, in conjunction with General Sheridan, to maintain the peace and order of that city, then much disturbed by the result of the Presidential election. In 1878 he had as his flag-ship the steam-sloop "Ticonderoga," and made a commercial and diplomatic cruise around the world, under the auspices of the State Department; was appointed arbitrator by the English and American governments to settle the Liberian boundary question, and also authorized to open negotiations with the kingdom of Corea for the protection of American life and property; was naval attaché at Peking, China, 1881; was appointed special agent, with full power, by President Arthur, to negotiate a treaty with Corea. This was accomplished, and the treaty signed, May, 1882. This was the first treaty made by that country with any Western power, and opened it to the commerce of the world. Was president of the Naval Advisory Board which designed the first steel cruisers of the new navy, 1882-84, and superintendent of Naval Observatory, 1883-84. Promoted to rear-admiral, 1883; retired February 21, 1884.

In 1860 he wrote a thesis on the African slave-trade with Cuba which attracted the attention of the government, and led to a treaty with Great Britain, which caused the extirpation of that traffic between Africa and the island of Cuba.

## FIRST LIEUTENANT AND BREVET CAPTAIN EDMUND R. P. SHURLY, U.S.A. (RETIRED).

FIRST LIEUTENANT AND BREVET CAPTAIN EDMUND R. P. SHURLY was born in England, and entered the volunteer service as second lieutenant of the Twenty-first New York Infantry April 15, 1861, and was first lieutenant Twenty-sixth New York Infantry May 21, 1861; promoted captain August 7, 1861, and honorably mustered out April 25, 1863.

He served in the field during the war of the Rebellion, participating in the Shenandoah operations in 1862; and at Front Royal, with his own and two companies of the Second Maine Infantry, constructed a rope-ferry across the Shenandoah River, thereby saving from capture by Jackson's corps the Twenty-sixth New York Infantry and a section of Hall's battery, the bridge washing away soon after they had passed over.

Captain Shurly participated in the battles of Pohick Church, Virginia; first Bull Run, Cedar Mountain (General Tower's brigade covering the retreat of General Pope), Rappahannock Station, Thoroughfare Gap, second Bull Run, Chantilly, South Mountain, Maryland; Antietam, Maryland, and Fredericksburg, Virginia, where he was severely wounded, and compelled to leave the field, being subsequently mustered out.

On August 28, 1863, he was appointed a captain in the Veteran Reserve Corps, and served until October 7, 1865, when he was honorably mustered out of service. He was brevetted major of volunteers March 13, 1865, for "gallant and meritorious services in the battle of Fredericksburg, Virginia," and lieutenant-colonel of volunteers, same date, for "gallant and meritorious services during the war."

On May 11, 1866, he was appointed a second lieutenant of the Eighteenth U. S. Infantry, and transferred to the Twenty-seventh Infantry September 21, 1866, which commission he resigned February 12, 1867. On March 15, 1867, he was again appointed second lieutenant of the Twenty-seventh Infantry, and was promoted first lieutenant September 29, 1868.

While on duty at Camp Douglas, Chicago, Illinois, in the fall of 1864, Captain Shurly aided in suppressing the conspiracy to release prisoners-of-war and destroy Chicago. He was the last commanding officer of that post, from which he was relieved in the fall of 1865.

After being appointed to the regular service, he was brevetted first lieutenant, March 15, 1867, for "gallant and meritorious services in the battle of Fredericksburg, Virginia," and captain for "gallant and meritorious services during the war." He served on the Plains at Forts McPherson, D. A. Russell, Laramie, Fetterman, Phil Kearney, and C. F. Smith,—most of the time on escort duty. He was engaged in action with hostile Indians near Fort Reno, Wyoming; on Goose Creek, near Fort Phil Kearney; Hayfield, near Fort C. F. Smith; Clark's Fork, Montana, and in various skirmishes while on escort duty. While in command of a detachment of Company A, Second Cavalry, he rescued a detachment of fifteen mounted men from Indians. He was also in an expedition with the same detachment after a band of Indians through Little Powder River Mountains to Little Horn River. He was severely wounded at the battle of Goose Creek, Wyoming.

While in command of a detachment of forty men of the Twenty-seventh Infantry, he successfully defended a train of forty-six wagons against a force estimated at one thousand Indians under Red Cloud.

Captain Shurly was retired from active service, on account of wounds received in the line of duty, December 2, 1868.

## REAR-ADMIRAL EDWARD SIMPSON, U.S.N.
(DECEASED).

REAR-ADMIRAL EDWARD SIMPSON was born in New York, and appointed midshipman from that State in February, 1840. After serving on the Brazil Station, in the "Decatur" and "Potomac," he came home in the frigate "Constitution." He was next attached to the "Independence," Home Squadron; the "Congress," of the Mediterranean and Brazil Squadrons; and the receiving-ship "North Carolina," at New York. Went to the Naval Academy in 1845, and graduated passed midshipman, 1846. His was the first class at Annapolis. He was then ordered to the steamer "Vixen," and was present, in her, at the attacks on the forts at Alvarado; the two attacks upon Tabasco; at the capture of Tampico; at the capture of Tuspan; at the capture of Coatzacoalcos, and that of Laguna de Terminos. At the siege of Vera Cruz the "Vixen" assisted in covering the landing of the army of the United States, and took part, with the rest of the smaller vessels, in the bombardment of the city, and of the Castle of San Juan d'Ulloa. After the war, was upon the Coast Survey, the Brazil Station, and assistant instructor of gunnery and infantry tactics at the Naval Academy, until 1854, when he was promoted to master, and was on Coast Survey duty again. In April, 1855, was commissioned lieutenant, and went to China in the Portsmouth, where he participated in the capture of the Barrier Forts, under Foote. From 1858 to 1862 he was attached to the Naval Academy, in charge of instruction in the theory and practice of naval gunnery. He was then, for a year, the commandant of midshipmen. He was commissioned lieutenant-commander in July, 1862. Commanded the iron-clad "Passaic" in 1863-64. Engaged with Fort Wagner, June 29, 1863; Fort Sumter, August 17, 1863; Fort Wagner, August 18, 1863; Fort Sumter, August 23, 1863; Fort Moultrie, August 31, 1863; Fort Sumter, September 1, 1863; Battery Bee, September 8, 1863; Fort Moultrie, November 16, 1863. Commanded steamer "Isonomia," on the Wilmington blockade, in the East Gulf Squadron, and on the Bahama Banks, in 1864. Fleet-captain of the blockading squadron, 1865-66. Engaged in the operations before Mobile in March and April, 1865, and until the city capitulated. Commissioned commander March, 1865, and then commanded the "Mohican" and the "Mohongo," on the North Pacific Station, 1866-68. Upon his return, he was in charge of the Hydrographic Office, Washington; and then assistant to the chief of Bureau of Ordnance, Navy Department, Washington, 1869-70. Commissioned as captain in August, 1870, and was sent to Europe on special duty in regard to ordnance. In 1873 he was in command of the torpedo station at Newport. In the next two years he commanded the steam-frigate "Frank-

lin," of the North Atlantic Station, and the steam-frigate "Wabash," of the same station. Commanded torpedo station again in 1874-75; and the steam-sloop "Omaha," of the South Pacific Station, in 1875-77. He was stationed at the navy-yard at New York, next; and, upon being made commodore, in April, 1878, commanded the naval station at New London for three years. He was promoted rear-admiral in 1884. President of the Advisory Board; and then president of the Board of Inspection and Survey. He never ceased to show his warm and active interest in the navy until his death at Washington, December 1, 1888. His total sea-service was twenty-one years and six months, and his shore duty twenty-one years and four months.

Admiral Simpson was remarkable for his urbane and officer-like manner, his fidelity to duty and promptness of decision. He exercised a large and wholesome influence upon succeeding generations of officers, and upon the scientific development of the navy, especially in gunnery and torpedo-work. His true kindness of heart can be vouched for by hundreds, and his death was looked upon as a personal misfortune to many, as well as a great loss to the service. At one time Simpson's "Ordnance and Gunnery," and his translation of Le Page's "Théorie du Pointage," were the principal text-books at the Naval Academy in that department. His enlarged edition of "Ordnance and Gunnery," of 1862, was a text-book for many years. He wrote many professional reports and magazine articles, and in 1873 he published "The Naval Mission to Europe," and "Report of the Gun-Foundry Board." Several of his articles are republished in "Modern Ships of War" (New York, 1887).

Admiral Simpson was president of the U. S. Naval Institute in 1886-88. He was also the president of the Naval Academy Graduates' Association from its organization until his death.

## CAPTAIN JAMES F. SIMPSON, U.S.A. (RETIRED).

CAPTAIN JAMES F. SIMPSON was born in Massachusetts October 25, 1841. He entered the volunteer service during the war of the Rebellion as second lieutenant of the Fourteenth Connecticut Infantry August 10, 1862; promoted first lieutenant February 4, 1863, and captain October 20, 1863. He served in the field with the Army of the Potomac, and was engaged in the battles of Fredericksburg and Chancellorsville, Virginia, where he was taken prisoner, confined in Libby Prison at Richmond, paroled, and exchanged. He then took part in the Richmond campaign, and was engaged in the battles of the Wilderness, Spottsylvania, Cold Harbor, North Anna River, Bristoe Station, and in the actions in front of and near Petersburg, Virginia, in 1864. He was severely wounded in the battle of Ream's Station, Virginia, and was honorably mustered out of service November 14, 1864. He was appointed second lieutenant of the U. S. Veteran Infantry (Hancock's Corps) February 16, 1865, and was honorably mustered out March 26, 1866. He was appointed second lieutenant of the Fortieth U. S. Infantry August 17, 1867, and brevetted the same day first lieutenant for "gallant and meritorious service in the battle of the Wilderness, Virginia," and captain for "gallant and meritorious service in the battle of Ream's Station, Virginia."

Captain Simpson was transferred to the Twenty-fifth Infantry April 20, 1869, and again transferred to the Third Cavalry March 15, 1871. He served in the South after the war, and was stationed at Hilton Head, South Carolina; Goldsborough and Raleigh, North Carolina; Baton Rouge, Louisiana; Ship Island, Mississippi; Jackson Barracks, Louisiana, and Fort Duncan, Texas, to 1871, when he joined the Third Cavalry in Arizona; but his regiment was soon ordered to the Department of the Platte, serving at Fort McPherson, Camp Sheridan, Fort Robinson, Fort Laramie, and Fort D. A. Russell. He took part in the Big Horn and Yellowstone Expedition under General George Crook, from May to October, 1876, and after Colonel Guy V. Henry received his severe wound in the engagement with hostile Indians, June 25, 1876, he was assigned to command his troop (D, Third Cavalry), which command he retained until the close of the expedition. Captain Simpson was also engaged with hostile Indians at Slim Buttes, Dakota, in September, 1876, and in the Cheyenne Indian outbreak at Fort Robinson, Nebraska.

He was promoted first lieutenant December 14, 1877, and captain November 26, 1884.

In 1882 the Third Cavalry was transferred to the Department of Arizona, and Captain Simpson served at Whipple Barracks and Whipple Depot, and was regimental quartermaster of the Third Cavalry from July 24, 1879, to September 1, 1883. He was retired from active service, November 25, 1887, for disability in the line of duty.

Captain Simpson performed the duties of acting assistant quartermaster and acting commissary of subsistence at nearly every post in which he served.

## LIEUTENANT-COLONEL AND BREVET BRIGADIER-GENERAL MICHAEL P. SMALL. U.S.A.

LIEUTENANT-COLONEL AND BREVET BRIGADIER-GENERAL MICHAEL P. SMALL (Subsistence Department) was born in York, Penn., August 9, 1831, and graduated at the Military Academy July 1, 1855. He was promoted brevet second lieutenant of artillery the same day, and second lieutenant Second Artillery September 21, 1855. He served on frontier duty at Benicia, Cal., 1855; in Florida against the Seminole Indians, 1856-57; in garrison at Fort Lafayette, New York, 1857, and Fort McHenry, Maryland, 1857; frontier duty at Fort Leavenworth, quelling Kansas disturbances, 1857-58; march to Utah, 1858, and Fort Leavenworth, 1858-59; in garrison at Fort Monroe, 1859; on Harper's Ferry expedition to suppress John Brown's raid, 1859; in garrison at Fort Monroe (Artillery School for Practice), 1859-61, and as quartermaster 2d Art., July 10 to Aug., 1861.

He was promoted first lieutenant April 27, 1861, and appointed captain of staff (commissary of subsistence) August 3, 1861, and served during the Rebellion of the seceding States (1861-66) as chief commissary and quartermaster at Rolla, Missouri, Southwestern District of Missouri, September 4, 1861, to January 31, 1863; as mustering officer and depot commissary and quartermaster at Rolla, Missouri, January 21, 1862, to January 31, 1863; colonel of the Missouri volunteers and aid to the governor of the State; as inspecting commissary of subsistence of the Department of the Missouri, February 1 to March 31, 1863; as chief commissary of the District of Minnesota, Department of the Northwest, and depot and purchasing commissary at St. Paul, Minnesota, April 10 to August 22, 1863; as chief commissary of the 13th Army Corps, and of the army in the field in the Têche campaign (Dept. of the Gulf), Sept. 15 to Nov. 9, 1863.

He was promoted lieutenant-colonel (staff) U. S. Volunteers September 15, 1863, and colonel and commissary of subsistence May 25, 1865, and was on duty as purchasing and depot commissary at Chicago, Illinois, and supervising commissary of the States of Illinois and Indiana, December 30, 1863, to February 15, 1864; as chief commissary of the Department of Virginia and North Carolina at Fort Monroe, Virginia (supplying the "armies operating against Richmond" on the James River). February 22, 1864, to February 21, 1865; of the Army of the James and Department of Virginia, February 21 to June, 1865; chief commissary of the Army of the James in pursuit of the rebel army, terminating in the capitulation at Appomattox Court-House, April 9, 1865; supplied the rebel army with rations from the subsistence train of the Army of the James after the surrender; of Military Division of the Southwest and Military Division of the Gulf (*ex officio* colonel U. S. Vol.), May 25 to Dec. 29, 1865, and as purchasing and depot commissary of subsistence at New Orleans, July 25 to Dec. 1865. He was made brevet colonel U. S. Volunteers January 1, 1865, for "distinguished and meritorious services in the campaign of 1863 and 1864;" brevet major, brevet lieutenant-colonel, and brevet colonel, March 13, 1865, for "meritorious services in the Subsistence Department during the Rebellion;" and brevet brigadier-general April 9, 1865, for "faithful and meritorious services in the Subsistence Department during the Rebellion."

After the war terminated, he served at Nashville, Tenn., and supervising commissary of subsistence of the States of Kentucky, Tennessee, and portions of Alabama and Georgia, February 17 to November 6, 1866; as chief commissary Department of the Tennessee, November 6, 1866, to March 16, 1867, and of the Cumberland, March 16, 1867, to July 26, 1869, and purchasing and depot commissary at Louisville, Kentucky, December 1, 1866, to July 26, 1869; in settling accounts at Washington, D. C., to September, 1869; as chief commissary Department of California, and purchasing and depot commissary at San Francisco, California, September 30, 1869, to December 12, 1872; as chief commissary Depart. of Arizona, Feb. 20, 1873, to May 25, 1875, and acting chief quartermaster, June 23 to May 10, 1874; as purchasing and depot commissary, Chicago, June 25, 1875, to Dec. 22, 1880; as chief commissary Dept. of Texas, and purchasing and depot commissary at San Antonio, Dec. 26, 1880, to Aug. 31, 1883; as purchasing and depot commissary at New York City, Sept. 20, 1883, to Oct. 31, 1884; as purchasing and depot commissary at Baltimore, from Nov. 1, 1884, to Aug. 30, 1889, and chief commissary, Div. of the Atlantic and Dept. of the East from Sept. 1, 1889. He was promoted major, staff, commissary of subsistence, June 23, 1874, and lieutenant-colonel, assistant commissary-general of subsistence, Oct. 4, 1889.

CAPTAIN AND BREVET LIEUTENANT-COLONEL WILLIAM RENWICK SMEDBERG, U.S.A. (RETIRED).

CAPTAIN AND BREVET LIEUTENANT-COLONEL WILLIAM RENWICK SMEDBERG was born in New York City on the 19th of March, 1839; he entered Columbia College, New York, in 1853, graduating in June, 1857. He enlisted in Company F of the New York Seventh Regiment in July, 1858, remaining with it until 1860, when he was honorably discharged on account of his removal to Washington, D. C., where he joined the National Rifles in 1861, and resided until the breaking out of the war.

He enlisted in the U. S. service on the 15th of April, 1861, as a private in Company A, Third Battalion, District of Columbia Volunteers; was promoted corporal, served in Stone's Brigade on the Potomac, and throughout Patterson's campaign, and was honorably discharged on the 4th of July, 1861, on acceptance of a commission in the U. S. Army as first lieutenant Fourteenth U. S. Infantry, with rank from May 14, 1861. He was adjutant Second Battalion, Fourteenth U. S. Infantry, from August 30 to October 25, 1861, when he was promoted captain Fourteenth Infantry, and commanded his company from that time until March, 1864, in First Brigade, Second Division, Fifth Army Corps, participating in the Peninsula campaign, siege of Yorktown, battles of Gaines' Mills, White Oak Swamp, Malvern Hill, second Bull Run, Antietam, Leetown, Snicker's Ferry, Fredericksburg, and campaign of Mine Run.

In March, 1864, he was appointed division inspector, First Division, Fifth Army Corps, on staff of Brigadier-General Charles Griffin, and at the battle of the Wilderness, May 5, 1864, was struck by a piece of shell, which carried away his right foot, resulting in amputation just below the knee.

From April, 1861, until May 5, 1864, he served in the field continuously with the Fifth Corps, Army of the Potomac, excepting a brief period on sick-leave and recruiting service in 1863, and he received the brevets of major and lieutenant-colonel for gallant and meritorious services in battle.

He was assistant inspector of the Department of California from December, 1865, to May 26, 1866, on the staff of General Irwin McDowell; aide-de-camp of the Military Division of the Pacific from that period to the 31st of May, 1869; on the staff of Major-General H. W. Halleck, and acting assistant adjutant-general on the staffs of Major-Generals George H. Thomas and J. M. Schofield from June, 1869, to December 15, 1870, when he was retired from active service, with rank of mounted captain, on account of the loss of his right leg from a wound received at the battle of the Wilderness.

Had he remained on the active list, he would have become colonel Twenty-first U. S. Infantry, January 31, 1891.

Colonel Smedberg joined the National Guard of California in September, 1874, when he was commissioned lieutenant-colonel and division inspector on the staff of Major-General D. W. C. Thompson; brigade inspector on the staff of General John McComb, Second Brigade, January 19, 1876, and was elected colonel of the Second Infantry (now the Second Artillery Regiment) October, 1876, being successively re-elected in 1880 and 1884, but resigned the position in December, 1885, after serving eleven years.

He was repeatedly tendered the positions of brigadier- and major-general, but declined, preferring to command a regiment.

Colonel Smedberg joined Lincoln Post, No. 1, Department of California, Grand Army of the Republic, in 1875; was a charter-member of George H. Thomas Post, No. 2; adjutant-general Department of California, February, 1885, and was elected department commander in February, 1886. To his energy and efficiency was largely due the success of the National Encampment held in San Francisco in August, 1886.

At the Twenty-fifth National Encampment of the Grand Army of the Republic, in Detroit, August, 1891, he was a prominent candidate for commander-in-chief Grand Army of the Republic.

Upon the organization of the Commandery of California, Military Order Loyal Legion, U. S., May, 1871, he was elected recorder; re-elected twenty times successively. He will complete his twenty-first year as recorder in May, 1892.

Since his retirement from the army in 1870, Colonel Smedberg has been well and favorably known as a business man in San Francisco, and is the senior partner of a prominent fire-insurance firm.

## COLONEL AND BREVET MAJOR-GENERAL CHARLES H. SMITH, U.S.A. (RETIRED).

COLONEL AND BREVET MAJOR-GENERAL CHARLES H. SMITH was born in Hollis, Maine, November 1, 1827. He entered the volunteer service as captain of the First Maine Cavalry October 19, 1861, and was sent to Augusta, Maine, in charge of a squad for the regiment, soon after enlistment. He was subsequently ordered to Washington City, and was sent with his company from there to Upton Hill, Virginia, to take charge of the camps abandoned by the Army of the Potomac, on its departure for the Peninsula, in March, 1862. He participated in the campaign of 1862, including the reconnoissance to Front Royal, the battle of Cedar Mountain (after which he was detailed with company to collect wounded and bury dead on battlefield, under a flag of truce), the retreat of General Pope; the second battle of Bull Run, and the engagement at Frederick City. He was with regiment on Stoneman's raid, and participated in the battle of Brandy Station, June 9, and, after the charge, rallied and conducted the regiment from enemy's rear; at Middleburg he had a horse shot under him; at Upperville he led the charge through the town; he was in skirmish with the enemy's rear-guard at Westminster, Pennsylvania; in battle of Gettysburg and the pursuit of the enemy that followed; in skirmish at Halltown, and in the battle of Shepardstown; commanded First Maine and Sixteenth Pennsylvania Cavalry on reconnoissance from near Auburn to White Plains, through Thoroughfare and Hopewell Gaps, August 16 and 17; he was on a reconnoissance to the Blue Ridge as far as Sperryville, October 12 and 13.

He was promoted major February 16, 1863; lieutenant-colonel March 1, 1863, and colonel June 18, 1863. He conducted a reconnoissance from Centreville to Manassas, fighting the enemy, October 14, 1863; he was through the Mine Run campaign, and conducted the rear-guard of the left column of the army on its retreat from Mine Run to and across the Rapidan, November 26 to December 1; commanded four regiments from Bealton Station to Luray, encountering the enemy at Little Washington, Sperryville, and Luray, December 21 to 24, 1863; was part of a reconnoissance in force from Bealton Station to Front Royal and return, fighting the enemy at Salem, January 1 to 4, 1864. He commanded regiment in the campaign of 1864 from April 29 to June 24; reconnoissance from Chancellorsville to Fredericksburg and return, participating in the fight at Todd's Tavern, May 5–8; conducting the advance from Beaver Dam Station to Ground Squirrel Bridge, fighting part of the way, May 10, and was rear-guard of the corps, having a severe fight and skirmish near Ground Squirrel Bridge (having a horse shot under him), May 11; fighting all day, in front of Richmond, May 12; conducting the regiment and the pioneers of the division from Haxhall's Landing to the Chickahominy to build bridges, and driving off the enemy, May 16–18; fighting at Hawes's Shop, May 28, and at Trevilian Station, June 11; conducting a reconnoissance to Louisa Court-House and skirmishing with the enemy, June 12; fighting at White House Landing, June 21, and in the battle of St. Mary's Church, June 24, where he had two horses shot under him, and was himself shot through the thigh, about two o'clock in the afternoon, but did not relinquish command of the regiment till the day was done. He commanded Second Brigade in the severe engagement west of Ream's Station, August 23 (where he was wounded in the ankle), as well as in the battle of Ream's Station, August 25; in the fight at Wyatt Farm, September 29; commanded Third Brigade in the battle of Boydton Plank-road, October 17; charged and drove the enemy at Rowanty Creek, and again at Gravelly Run; formed on the right of infantry on the plank-road to repel an assault, and afterwards protected the rear of the Second Corps against Hampton's cavalry in a hard fight; in reconnoissance and skirmish down Weldon Railroad, November 7; in movement to Stony Creek, where he fought and defeated the enemy, December 1, and in movement to Bellefield, December 7–12, skirmishing with enemy continuously; in Appomattox campaign, March 29 to April 9, 1865; engaged at Dinwiddie Court-House (where he was hit in the leg by a bullet which had passed through his horse); fight at Jettersville; in the battles of Sailor's Creek, Briery Creek, Farmville, and at Appomattox, April 9, and in movement against Johnston's army, April 24 and following days.

Colonel Smith was appointed colonel, Twenty-eighth U. S. Infantry, July 28, 1866, and was brevetted brigadier- and major-general U. S. Army March 2, 1867. He was transferred to the Nineteenth Infantry in 1869, and served with his regiment until retired, November 1, 1891.

### MAJOR FRANK G. SMITH, U.S.A.

MAJOR FRANK G. SMITH (Second Artillery) was born in Pennsylvania February 16, 1840. He graduated as a civil engineer at Rensselaer Polytechnic Institute, Troy, New York, in the Class of 1859. He entered the regular service as second lieutenant of the Fourth Artillery August 5, 1861, and was promoted first lieutenant the same day. He served at Camp Duncan until December, 1861, and then with Battery I, Fourth Artillery, in the field from January, 1862, throughout the war of the Rebellion, except the last campaign, and was engaged in the siege and capture of Corinth, Mississippi, April and May, 1862; in the campaign of Buell against Bragg, ending in the battle of Perryville, Kentucky, October 8, 1862; in the operations of the same army under Rosecrans, through the Murfreesborough, Tullahoma, and Chickamauga campaigns, to October 10, 1863; in the siege of Chattanooga and battle of Missionary Ridge, November 23–25, 1863; in the battle of Nashville, Tennessee, December 15–16, 1864; in pursuit of Hood's army to the Tennessee River in December, 1864. He was then with Wilson's Cavalry Corps (his battery equipped as a horse-battery) at Gravelly Springs, Mississippi, Atlanta, and Augusta, Georgia, to October, 1865.

He was brevetted captain December 31, 1862, for "gallant and meritorious services in the battle of Stone River, Tennessee," and major, September 20, 1863, for "gallant and meritorious services in the battle of Chickamauga, Georgia," and was honorably mentioned in reports on the battle of Perryville and Chickamauga.

Major Smith was adjutant of Camp Duncan in December, 1861, and was on the staff of Major-General D. C. Buell, at Louisville, Kentucky, in December, 1861, and January, 1862.

At the close of the war, Major Smith's battery was ordered to garrison duty at Fort McHenry, Maryland, where he remained on duty to February, 1867, when he was promoted captain, and was transferred to Fort Whipple, Virginia, but soon returned to Fort McHenry, where he remained until July, 1870. He was then stationed at Raleigh, and other places in North Carolina, until November, 1872, when his regiment changed station to the Pacific coast, he taking station at Fort Canby, Washington Territory, remaining there until July, 1876.

During the year 1876 the Sioux Indian war required so many troops in the field that the artillery was called upon for frontier service, and Major Smith with his battery was in the field in Nebraska and Dakota from August, 1876, to January, 1877. Returning to the Pacific coast, he was stationed at Alcatraz Island, California, to July, 1878, when he again took the field against hostile Bannock Indians in Nevada, Oregon, and Idaho, to October, 1878. He was at Angel Island and the Presidio of San Francisco until September, 1881, when he took the field, and participated in the campaign in Arizona during the months of September and October, 1881, where he had command of a battalion of three batteries of the Fourth Artillery.

The Fourth Artillery was transferred to the Atlantic coast in the fall of 1881, and Major Smith served with it at Plattsburg Barracks, New York, and Madison Barracks, New York, to September, 1882, when he was transferred to Fort Snelling, Minnesota, where he was employed in organizing Light Battery F, Fourth Artillery, and doing duty with it there until November, 1886. He was at Fort Adams, Rhode Island, from November, 1886, to May, 1889, and then at Fort McPherson, Georgia, until he was promoted major Second Artillery, August 28, 1891, when he was assigned to duty at Fort Adams, Rhode Island, which is now his station.

## COMMANDER FREDERICK R. SMITH, U.S.N.

COMMANDER FREDERICK R. SMITH is a native of Maine, and was appointed a midshipman from that State in 1858, and left the Naval Academy in 1861, at the time when the classes were advanced on account of the war. He served in the "Colorado," flag-ship, West Gulf Blockading Squadron, and then in the steamer "Flambeau," as acting master and navigator, 1862. Then on the South Atlantic Blockade, 1862-63. Became lieutenant and executive-officer August 1, 1862. Engagement with Fort McAllister; on boat expedition to Bull's Island, South Carolina; present, but not participating, in Admiral Dupont's first fight at Charleston, 1864. Served as flag-lieutenant and senior watch-officer in the "Ticonderoga," in Admiral Lardner's West India "flying squadron." Was executive-officer of the "Rhode Island," of the North Atlantic Blockading Squadron, 1864-65. At both attacks upon Fort Fisher, and commanded a detachment of seamen in the assault.

In the Selnave revolution at Cape Haytien, commanded the landing party from the "Rhode Island," which, with the men landed from H. B. M. gun-boat "Lily," afforded protection to the foreign merchants of that city. Commissioned lieutenant-commander July, 1866. Served in "Ashuelot" a full cruise. Was navigator while convoying the iron-clad "Miantonomah" across the Atlantic to Queenstown, Ireland. Navigator of "Ashuelot" until her arrival at Hong-Kong. Was then made executive-officer, and finally commanded that vessel until detached in 1870. After being on equipment duty at the Boston Navy-Yard, he was ordered as executive-officer of the U. S. flag-ship "Severn," of the North Atlantic Squadron. Commanded U. S. iron-clad "Ajax" on her voyage from Key West, Florida, to League Island Navy-Yard, 1872. The same year he served as executive-officer of the "Iroquois," of the North Atlantic Squadron, during the ceremonies of the reception of the Grand Duke Alexis, of Russia. Was upon ordnance duty at Boston in 1873, and inspector of ordnance, Key West, in 1874. Executive-officer of the "Lancaster," flag-ship of South Atlantic Squadron, in 1875. Afterwards senior aid to Commodore Cooper,

commanding navy-yard, Pensacola. Commander April 6, 1875. Commanded iron-clad "Saugus," on voyage from Pensacola to Port Royal, South Carolina.

Commander Smith received the following letter from the late Admiral D. D. Porter:

"WASHINGTON, D. C., February 3, 1875.

"SIR,—Having applied to me for a letter stating what I know about your services and your reputation as an officer, I take pleasure in saying you served under my command on board the U. S. S. 'Rhode Island,' and was handsomely mentioned by your commanding officer, Captain Trenchard, in both attacks on Fort Fisher, in one of which you led a detachment of men in the assault.

"I also made a passage in the 'Rhode Island,' and had an opportunity to witness the most excellent discipline that was maintained throughout that ship, and have reason to *know* that your duties were always performed with ability.

"I believe your moral character is beyond reproach.

"Very respectfully,

"DAVID D. PORTER, *Admiral.*

"To LT.-COMM'R F. R. SMITH, U. S. N.,

"Washington, D. C."

### CAPTAIN AND BREVET MAJOR HENRY EAGLE SMITH, U.S.A.

CAPTAIN AND BREVET MAJOR HENRY EAGLE SMITH was born in Brooklyn, New York, August 8, 1842. At the commencement of the war of the Rebellion he entered the volunteer service as a private in the Seventy-first New York Militia, April 19, 1861; was promoted color-sergeant April 21, and with the regiment proceeded to Annapolis, Maryland, and marched to Washington City, April 25, when he did duty at the navy-yard until June 21, when he was discharged to accept the appointment of first lieutenant in the Twelfth U. S. Infantry, to date from May 14, 1861.

He was on duty at Fort Hamilton, New York, organizing Company D, First Battalion, Twelfth Infantry, from July 6, 1861, to March 5, 1862, when ordered to join the Army of the Potomac in the field. He then served in the Infantry Reserve to May, 1862, when attached to First Brigade, Second Division, Fifth Army Corps, to latter part of July, 1863.

He participated in the siege of Yorktown; reconnoissance to Hanover Court-House, Virginia; support at battle of Mechanicsville; and engaged in the battles of Gaines' Mill and Malvern Hill, Virginia. After marching from Harrison's Landing to Fort Monroe, he was taken sick, and was absent from August to October, 1862, when he rejoined his regiment at Sharpsburg, Maryland, and participated in the march to the Rappahannock, being engaged in action at Snicker's Gap, Virginia, battles of Fredericksburg and Chancellorsville. He participated in the Pennsylvania campaign, and was engaged in the battle of Gettysburg. Returning to Virginia with his regiment, he was ordered to New York with his regiment during the draft riots, and did duty at police head-quarters in command of two companies from August, 1863, until the troubles in the city had ended, when he was detached on recruiting service and mustering duty in New York City, from September 1, 1863, to March, 1865. He was guarding prisoners at Elmira to May, 1865; on mustering duty at Albany to September, 1865, and then ordered to join his regiment at Richmond, Virginia. In December, 1865, he was ordered to Fort Hamilton, and organized Company A, Third Battalion.

He was commissioned captain Sept. 9, 1863, and then changed to Aug. 31, 1863, and was brevetted captain June 27, 1863, for gallant and meritorious conduct at battle of Gaines' Mill; and major, July 2, 1863, for gallant and meritorious services at battle of Gettysburg.

Captain Smith moved with Companies A and B to Richmond in March, 1866, and was in command of the battalion at that point for some months, when ordered to Washington City, where he remained to September, 1866, when he was transferred to the Twenty-first Infantry, April 21. He was then on duty at City Point, Virginia, closing up the affairs of the Army of the Potomac, until April, 1867, when ordered to Norfolk, and assigned to command the post; also acting as military commissioner for eight counties, including the cities of Norfolk, Suffolk, and Portsmouth, till December, 1868; on leave of absence, May, 1869, in Europe; rejoined command at Omaha, Nebraska, before expiration of leave, and was on duty there till May 10, when he moved to Sacramento, California. He was on duty at the Presidio and Drum Barracks till June 19, 1869, crossing the Colorado desert, a continuous march of fifty miles; Gila Desert, fifty miles; Maricopa Desert, fifty-five miles; in heat of summer, no shade, little water, and that mostly in water-holes, not fit to drink; on the march to Camp Goodwin, Arizona, via Fort Yuma (one thousand miles), commanding battalion of four companies during the entire march; arrived August 24, 1869; and on duty at that point, participating in numerous scouts against the Coyoteros Apache Indians in Sierra Blancas, till December, 1870; constructed wagon-road from Fort Goodwin to Fort Apache, seventy-five miles due north, and over three ranges of mountains; at completion of road, located present post of Fort Apache, Fort Goodwin having been abandoned because of its unhealthy location; on duty at Fort Apache till December, 1870, during which time explored from Fort Apache to Fort Wingate, via Zuni villages, for a new freight-route, about one hundred and twenty-five miles. He was honorably discharged, at his own request, December 31, 1870.

Captain Smith is a member of the following army societies: Military Order Loyal Legion, Commandery State of New York; George Washington Post, 103, G. A. R., Department of New York; society Army of Potomac; society Fifth Army Corps.

## COLONEL AND BREVET MAJOR-GENERAL JOHN EUGENE SMITH, U.S.A. (RETIRED).

COLONEL AND BREVET MAJOR-GENERAL JOHN EUGENE SMITH was born in the canton of Berne, Switzerland, August 3, 1816. His father, John Bauder Smith, in his early life a soldier, followed the fortunes of Napoleon,—shared the rigor of the Russian campaign, and was one of the few survivors of the fatal retreat from Moscow. He was severely wounded at Waterloo. Leaving his native land, he arrived in Philadelphia, Pennsylvania, November 30, 1816, where he died September 22, 1848, a respected and distinguished member of the Pennsylvania Horticultural Society.

General Smith received an academic education, and learned the trade of a jeweller. He went to St. Louis, Missouri, in the spring of 1833, and removed to Galena, Illinois, in 1838, where he followed his avocation until 1860, having in the meantime served two terms in the City Council and one term as a member of the County Board of Supervisors. He was elected county treasurer for Jo Daviess County in 1860, and the same year appointed aide-de-camp to the Honorable Richard Yates, Governor of the State of Illinois, reporting for active duty April 15, 1861, assisting in organizing the three months' troops; also with General Grant and others in organizing the ten provisional regiments authorized by the special session of the Legislature, known as the Ten-Regiment Bill.

After the first battle of Bull Run he recruited and organized the Forty-fifth Regiment Illinois Volunteers, known as the Washburne Lead-Mine Regiment, and was commissioned its colonel, ranking from July 23, 1861. This regiment followed the fortunes of the Army of the Tennessee, and participated with honor in all the marches and battles of that army to the end of the Rebellion.

Colonel Smith was promoted brigadier-general of volunteers November 29, 1862, and assigned to the command of the Eighth Division, left wing, Sixteenth Army Corps, March 25. Being junior commanding a division, was succeeded by Brigadier-General Tuttle, and assigned to First Brigade, Third Division, Seventeenth Army Corps, June 3, 1863. He was assigned to the command of Third Division, Seventeenth Army Corps, October, 1863. On the march to the relief of Chattanooga, this division was designated as the Third Division, Fifteenth Army Corps, participating in all the marches, including the great "march to the sea," and battles of the Army of the Tennessee, to the close of the war.

After the surrender of the Confederate forces he was

relieved from duty with the Army of the Tennessee, and assigned to the command of the District of West Tennessee, head-quarters at Memphis.

He was honored with the brevet of major-general of volunteers, January 12, 1865, for "faithful and efficient services and for gallantry in action," and subsequently mustered out of the volunteer service April 30, 1866. In June, 1866, he was appointed United States assessor for the District of Utah. July 28, 1866, he was appointed colonel of the Twenty-seventh U. S. Infantry. March 2, 1867, he was brevetted brigadier-general U. S. Army, for "gallant and meritorious services in the siege of Vicksburg," and brevet major-general U. S. Army, for "gallant and meritorious services in action at Savannah, Georgia, December, 1864."

During the consolidation of regiments in 1869, he was assigned to duty in the War Department, Washington, D. C., in connection with Generals McK. Dunn and Wager Swayne, investigating claims for depredations during the war. Dec. 20, 1870, he was assigned to the Fourteenth Infantry, and retired for age May 19, 1881.

General Smith served on the Western plains, commanding the Mountain District, comprising Forts Phil Kearney, C. F. Smith, and Fort Reno, until they were abandoned in compliance with treaty with the Sioux Indians, 1867-68; at Fort Laramie, 1870-74.

During his service on the plains he has encountered the Sioux, Cheyenne, Arrapahoe, and Bannock Indians, always successfully, and acquired their confidence by his justice in dealing with them. His various missions to them have always proved satisfactory.

COLONEL JOSEPH ROWE SMITH, U.S.A.

COLONEL JOSEPH ROWE SMITH (Medical Department) is of an army family. His father, General J. R. Smith; his uncle, Major Henry Smith, aid to General Scott, afterwards in charge of Northern Lake Improvements, and dying at Vera Cruz during the Mexican War; his cousin, W. C. DeHart, of court-martial fame,—all distinguished themselves, and were well and favorably known in the army.

Colonel Smith was born at Madison Barracks, New York, April 18, 1831. He was liberally educated, receiving the degrees of A.B. and A.M. at the University of Michigan, in 1848 and 1881.

He then was employed as engineer under the Topographical Bureau, determining the boundary between the Cherokees and Creeks in 1850, and laying out territorial roads in Minnesota in 1851.

He graduated in medicine at the University of Buffalo in 1853, soon passed the Army Medical Board, and was commissioned assistant surgeon in 1854.

After constant frontier service, including many Indian and the Utah expeditions, he was captured by rebels in Texas in April, 1861. He was paroled and proceeded North, and, under the agreement between the United States and the Confederate States, was soon after released from his parole.

He was at once selected by the surgeon-general to organize general hospitals, to be prepared for the wounded from the approaching first battle of the war, Bull Run, and thereupon organized Seminary Hospital and the hospitals later organized in Georgetown, which he administered until selected by Surgeon-General Hammond for executive officer in the Surgeon-General's Office in July, 1862, having been promoted to a majority in June.

In August, 1862, he was appointed by President Lincoln acting surgeon-general.

In November, 1863, he went to Little Rock, and served as medical director, Department and Army of Arkansas and Seventh Army Corps, with rank of lieutenant-colonel, under Act of February 25, 1865, until assigned as medical director, Fourth Military District, Vicksburg, in 1867.

While so serving he was brevetted lieutenant-colonel, U.S.A., for "superior ability and excellent management of the affairs of his department" (being the only officer in whose case this language was used), and also colonel for "meritorious services and devotion to the sick during the prevalence of the cholera," etc.

The department commander, General Ord, urged that he be brevetted brigadier-general.

After 1867 he served successively as post-surgeon at Jefferson Barracks, Fort Wayne, and Fort Monroe, and as medical director, Department of Texas, from 1879 to 1885, being promoted to a lieutenant-colonelcy in January, 1885.

Until 1887 he served as attending surgeon, New York City; then as medical director Department of Dakota till December, 1888, and thence to the present time as medical director Department of Arizona, being promoted colonel in February, 1890.

Besides performing full share of duty on routine boards and courts-martial, he was selected by General Twiggs for special duty, travelling to various posts in the Department of Texas, and as judge-advocate, trying cases, and when, in 1861, retiring boards were organized under the new retirement law, he was selected as member of the early boards.

He was assigned in 1862-63 as member of board for examination of assistant surgeons for promotion, and in 1867 as president medical board for examination of candidates for appointment as assistant surgeons U.S.A., and of assistant surgeons for promotion.

In 1887 he was selected by the War Department as a member of the board for preparing rules and regulations for the then recently-organized Hospital Corps.

He was selected and detailed by the Secretary of War to represent the Medical Department of the army at the meetings of the American Medical Association in 1874-77, and 1882-85; of the Public Health Association in 1880; of the International Medical Congress in 1876 in Philadelphia, and in 1887 in Washington.

He was elected vice-president of the American Medical Association in 1877-78, and of the Ninth International Congress, as well as of its section of military and naval medicine and surgery, in 1887, and is member of many medical societies.

Besides purely official reports, he has published many papers on various subjects.

A large and influential number of army officers and physicians in civil life desire to see Colonel Smith appointed surgeon-general of the army.

## REAR-ADMIRAL MELANCTHON SMITH, U.S.N.
(RETIRED.)

REAR-ADMIRAL MELANCTHON SMITH.—This veteran officer comes of good fighting stock, as his father, of the same name, served as colonel in the War of 1812, and commanded Fort Moreau, at the battle of Plattsburg. Sidney Smith, his uncle, who was a captain in the U. S. Navy, served under McDonough at the same time. His grandfather, also named Melancthon, was a leader in Revolutionary times, sheriff of Dutchess County, New York, in 1777, and a delegate to the convention of the State to take into consideration the Constitution of the United States.

Admiral Smith was born in New York, May, 1810, and appointed a midshipman March, 1826. Our space only enables us to state that after the usual service he was sent to the Naval School, and became a passed midshipman in June, 1832. After active employment he was promoted master in 1836, and lieutenant in 1837. He then served in the Florida war, commanding a fort and a twenty-oared barge a part of the time. He then served at New York; the Mediterranean Squadron; and in various other service until 1846. He was then executive-officer at Pensacola for two years, and served in the frigate "Constitution," in the Mediterranean, a full cruise.

Commander in September, 1855. After various commands, during which, in the "Massachusetts," he engaged the fort at Ship Island, July 9, 1861, and three Confederate steamers and a revenue cutter off Ship Island, he had also an engagement with the rebel steamer "Florida," in Mississippi Sound, in October, 1861. He grappled and cut the telegraph wire between Shieldsborough and Pass Christian, and captured a two-gun battery at Biloxi, during this service. He was then ordered to command of the "Mississippi," and served at the passage of the forts below New Orleans, and the destruction of the rebel ram "Manassas." Admiral Farragut said, in his report of these operations, "Just as the scene appeared to be closing, the ram 'Manassas' was seen coming up under a full head of steam to attack us. I directed Captain Smith, in the 'Mississippi,' to turn and run her down. This order was instantly obeyed by the 'Mississippi' turning and going at her at full speed. Just as we expected to see the ram annihilated, when within fifty yards of each other, she put her helm hard-a-port, dodged the 'Mississippi,' and ran ashore. The 'Mississippi' poured two broadsides into her, and sent her drifting down the river a total wreck. Thus closed our morning's fight." The details of this particular fight are most thrilling, but we cannot introduce them. Chalmette batteries were passed with the rest; and in July, 1862, Commander Smith became captain, remaining in the stanch old "Mississippi," and in all the engagements up to March, 1863, when, in attempting to pass the batteries at Fort Hudson, she grounded in twenty-three feet of water, and heeled to port. In spite of every effort of her veteran officers and crew, she could not be moved. The enemy got the range, and were hulling her at every shot. At last Captain Smith gave the order to set the ship on fire, which was done in four different places between decks. When the flames had obtained sufficient headway, the ship was abandoned under a most heavy fire, in the most orderly way, quietly, and without confusion, Captain Smith being the last to leave her. By his cool and courageous bearing under such trying circumstances, Captain Smith won universal admiration, and his course was approved by Admiral Farragut and by the Navy Department. He was then ordered to command the "Monongahela," and was in the attacks upon Port Hudson upon many occasions.

After temporary command of the "Onondaga," iron-clad, he served in the Albemarle Sound, engaging the ram "Albemarle," and capturing her consort, the "Bombshell."

He returned to the "Onondaga," as divisional officer in James River, and was transferred to the command of the frigate "Wabash," which vessel he commanded in both the bombardments of Fort Fisher.

After the war Captain Smith was attached to the Washington Navy-Yard, and on July 25, 1866, was commissioned as commodore. He then held the position of chief of the Bureau of Equipment and Recruiting in the Navy Department for four years. This is an office which requires confirmation by the Senate of the United States.

He was commissioned as rear-admiral in July, 1870, and was commandant of the New York Navy-Yard until his retirement, by operation of law, in 1872.

## CAPTAIN JAMES A. SNYDER, U.S.A. (RETIRED).

CAPTAIN JAMES A. SNYDER was born March 12, 1837, at Alexandria, D. C., and at the age of sixteen (in 1853) he became a member of the scientific party (assistant topographer) in an exploration and survey for a Pacific railroad, under the command of Captain J. W. Gunnison, Topographical Engineers, U.S.A., and during this expedition, in addition to his other duties, was employed in the collection of botanical specimens. Again, in 1858, he became a member of the Pacific Wagon-road Expedition, under charge of Colonel F. W. Lander, C. E., in the construction of a wagon-road from the South Pass, Rocky Mountains, to the Pacific coast, serving as quartermaster and commissary of the expedition, in addition to his duties as assistant engineer. He remained on this work until its completion, in 1860. At the breaking out of the war he was appointed by President Lincoln a second lieutenant in the Third U. S. Infantry, to date from August 5, 1861. He joined his regiment in Washington City, August 10, 1861, and performed patrol-duty in that city up to February, 1862, when he was appointed aide-de-camp of volunteers and assigned to the staff of Brigadier-General George Sykes, who commanded the regular infantry, Army of the Potomac, serving with that officer from February, 1862, to November, 1864.

He was promoted first lieutenant December 3, 1863.

He then rejoined his regiment in Washington, serving with it but a short time, when he was placed on duty in the Judge-Advocate-General's Office, under the immediate direction of Adjutant-General Nichols, remaining on this duty until his regiment was ordered to St. Louis, Missouri, in 1865, when he accompanied it to that place, and on January 1, 1866, was appointed regimental adjutant, serving in that capacity until August, 1866, when he received a detail for recruiting service, and was assigned to duty in New York City in September, 1866. He was relieved in September, 1868, and assigned to duty at David's Island, New York, as assistant quartermaster and post adjutant, serving until July, 1869.

He was promoted captain December 31, 1867.

Captain Snyder served with his regiment in New Orleans and Natchitoches, Louisiana, being in command at the latter place; and, on being relieved from that duty (the last named), received the following complimentary letter from the citizens of that place:

"The undersigned citizens of the parish of Natchitoches, having learned with regret that at your own request your command is about to be removed from our midst, take this occasion to express their high appreciation of your character as a gentleman and as an officer of the United States Army. While you have so faithfully discharged your duties as an officer during your stay among us, your conduct as a citizen has fully convinced us that you made it a point to be always guided by the adage, 'Cedant arma togae.' In expressing their views, we feel confident that we but reflect the sentiments of our people. Be assured, sir, that our good wishes attend you wherever your duty as a soldier may demand your services."

Captain Snyder served with his regiment in Pennsylvania during the railroad riots, and accompanied it to Montana in the winter of 1877, serving with it in that Territory at Helena, Fort Shaw, Fort Ellis, and Fort Custer. In 1879 he accompanied the Eighteenth Infantry from the Coal Banks, Montana, to Fort Assinniboine, Montana, and made the survey of the military reservation of that post, and, on finishing the work, received from Colonel (now General) Ruger the following complimentary letter:

"The commanding officer desires me to express his thanks and approbation to Captain Snyder for services rendered the command on the movement from the Coal Banks and at this place, and especially for the faithful and efficient manner in which he has performed the duty of making the surveys for the military reservation at the post."

In August, 1877, received a leave of absence on account of sickness, and reported to Washington, D. C., for medical treatment, and on November 13, 1889, was retired, "for disability in line of duty." His present place of residence is Washington, D. C.

Captain Snyder served as adjutant Third Infantry from January 1 to August 6, 1866, and was recommended for promotion, by General George Sykes, for services at the battle of Chancellorsville, Virginia, in May, 1863.

During his tour of services, Captain Snyder participated in siege of Yorktown, Virginia; battles of Gaines' Mills and Malvern Hill, Virginia; Antietam, Maryland; engagement at Shepherdstown, Virginia; skirmish at Snicker's Gap, Virginia; battles of Fredericksburg and Chancellorsville, Virginia; Bristoe campaign, and battle of Rappahannock Station.

## MEDICAL INSPECTOR JOHN C. SPEAR, U.S.N.
(RETIRED).

MEDICAL INSPECTOR JOHN C. SPEAR was born near Middletown, Delaware, March 12, 1839; was graduated at the University of Pennsylvania as Doctor of Medicine, 1861. Commissioned assistant surgeon in the U. S. Navy May 9, 1861; joined U. S. frigate "Roanoke," May, 1861; engaged blockading Charleston and Wilmington; participated in the engagement between the United States vessels-of-war and the rebel ram "Merrimac," Hampton Roads, March 8 and 9, 1862; was ordered on board the "Monitor" directly after the fight to help to dress wounds of Captain John L. Worden, aiding Acting Assistant Surgeon Logue of the "Monitor;" joined the U. S. steamer "Mahaska," April, 1862, and was employed on the blockade of the Atlantic coast for several months; present at the battle of Malvern Hill, and aided there in caring for wounded soldiers both on board ship and on shore; present at the shelling of Ruggle's Point and other minor engagements with rebel batteries on the James and the York Rivers; served as surgeon and adjutant of a land expedition under Commander Foxhall A. Parker, U.S.N., to Matthews' Court-House, Virginia; engaged with rebel batteries, mouth of Cape Fear River, North Carolina; ordered to U. S. flag-ship "Minnesota" in the autumn of 1862, and served on board of her, North Atlantic Blockading Squadron, till the summer of 1863. Promoted to passed assistant surgeon October 26, 1863; on duty at navy-yard, Philadelphia, 1863-64. Commissioned surgeon June 23, 1864; attached to the U. S. S. "Seminole," West Gulf Blockading Squadron, 1864; present at the bombardment and surrender of Fort Morgan, Mobile Bay; transferred to U. S. S. "Monongahela," November, 1864, and served on blockade off the coast of Texas until spring of 1865, when ship was ordered home to New York at close of the war; was attending surgeon in the city of Washington, 1865, and also did duty as assistant to the chief of Bureau of Medicine and Surgery in the Navy Department at the same time; ordered to U. S. S. "Swatara," October, 1865; cruised in West Indies, 1865-66; in Europe and West Coast of Africa, 1866-68; "Swatara" captured John H. Surratt in Alexandria, Egypt, and brought him to Washington; autumn of 1868, detached from "Swatara" and transferred to flag-ship "Franklin," Admiral Farragut, and returned to United States; on duty at Naval Rendezvous, Philadelphia, 1869-70; in the winter of 1870-71 served as geologist of the Tehuantepec Surveying Expedition, and wrote a report of the geology and general resources of the Isthmus with reference to the construction of a ship-canal there; ordered to Naval Hospital in Philadelphia, 1871; served on the U. S. S. "Omaha," 1872-74, cruising on coast of Brazil, and in the South Pacific; went as one of the boat's crew of volunteers to pick up an officer and man overboard at sea, off east coast of Patagonia, heavy sea running at the time; attached to the U. S. receiving-ship "Potomac," 1874-75; served on the U. S. monitor "Dictator," North Atlantic Squadron, for eighteen months, from June, 1875; had charge of quarantine measures to protect U. S. vessels-of-war in Port Royal waters from yellow fever, during an epidemic in the vicinity; commander-in-chief of station officially commended services to Navy Department, under date of September 29, 1876; on duty in Washington, 1877-78, as member of Examining Board for admission and promotion of medical officers. Promoted to medical inspector, with relative rank of commander, October, 1878; ordered to U. S. flag-ship "Trenton" as fleet-surgeon, European Station, September, 1879, serving till 1881; member of Medical Examining Board, Navy Department, 1881-82; and member of Examining Board in Philadelphia, 1882-83, for admission and promotion of medical officers; served as surgeon of the navy-yard, New York, 1883-86; was ordered as director of U. S. Naval Laboratory, Brooklyn, New York, September, 1886, serving till July, 1887, when was granted leave for one year on account of ill health. Placed on retired list, September 14, 1888. Member of the Military Order of the Loyal Legion of U. S., No. 7353; member of the Academy of Natural Sciences of Philadelphia (1869).

Medical Inspector Spear was retired in consequence of disability incurred in the line of duty.

**BRIGADIER-GENERAL DAVID S. STANLEY, U.S.A.**
(RETIRED).

BRIGADIER-GENERAL DAVID S. STANLEY was born in Ohio June 1, 1828, and graduated at the Military Academy in the Class of 1852. He was promoted brevet second lieutenant of the Second Dragoons the same day; second lieutenant September 6, 1853; second lieutenant of the First Cavalry March 3, 1855, and captain of the Fourth Cavalry March 16, 1861, up to this time having served on the frontier with distinction against the Indians, especially the Comanches. He also participated in several actions in Missouri in 1861.

He was commissioned brigadier-general of volunteers September 28, 1861, and major-general November 29, 1862.

He commanded a division of the Army of General Rosecrans at the battle of Corinth, and distinguished himself as commander of all the cavalry at the great battle of Stone River in 1863. He participated in the Tullahoma, Chickamauga, Missionary Ridge, and Atlanta campaigns of 1863-64. About August 1, of the latter year, the command of the Fourth Corps, in General Sherman's army, devolved upon him, and in October, 1864, he was ordered with his corps to Nashville, to report to General Thomas. He had been engaged in the battle of Stone River, actions of Guy's Gap and Shelbyville, Tenn., battles of Chickamauga, Missionary Ridge, Taylor's Ridge, Resaca, Jonesborough, Adairsville, and on to Atlanta, and in the battle of Franklin, Tenn., November 30, 1864, of which General Thomas, in a letter to the Secretary of War, September 14, 1865, says,—

"In the discharge of his duties in the various positions held by him as a division and corps commander, as well as in less responsible positions, he has given entire satisfaction. By his personal attention to the wants and necessities of the troops subject to his orders, he was enabled to report more than the usual proportion as being fit for duty, and, though a strict disciplinarian, his just and impartial treatment of all won for him the respect and high esteem of his entire command. Careful and skilful in the handling and management of troops, both in putting them in proper positions, and in directing movements under fire, he at all times exhibited before his troops those sterling qualities of a true soldier, which they were but waiting to adopt as their own and with their leader breast the storm of battle. A more cool and brave commander would be a difficult task to find, and, although he has been a participant in many of the most sanguinary engagements in the West, his conduct has on all occasions been so gallant and marked that it would be almost doing an injustice to him to refer particularly to any isolated battle-field.

"I refer, therefore, only to the battle of Franklin, Tenn., November 30, 1864, because it is the more recent, and one in which his gallantry was so marked as to merit the admiration of all who saw him.

"It was here that his personal bravery was more decidedly brought out, perhaps, than on any other field, and the terrible destruction and defeat which disheartened and checked the fierce assaults of the enemy is due more to his heroism and gallantry than to any other officer on the field."

Badeau, in his "History of the Life of General Grant," thus alludes to the operations of General Stanley at Spring Hill, just prior to the battle of Franklin:

"Thus one of the most difficult and dangerous operations in the war was executed with equal success and skill; the army was extricated from a situation of imminent peril, in the face of greatly superior numbers, and the opportunity for which Hood had labored so long was snatched from his grasp."

General Stanley was twice wounded during the war, at Jonesborough and Franklin, in the last-named having led the brigade which restored the break in the main line of battle, which had just been penetrated by the Confederate force.

He was brevetted brigadier- and major-general U. S. Army March 13, 1865, for gallantry, and appointed colonel of the Twenty-second Infantry July 28, 1866.

It would be impossible in this short sketch to enumerate the subsequent career of General Stanley in his various duties. His life has been that of the officer on the frontier, in garrison, on expeditions, campaigns, and encounters with Indians of various tribes in different sections of the country.

He was appointed brigadier-general U. S. Army March 24, 1884, and assigned to the command of the Department of Texas, which he now holds, but will be retired by operation of law June 1, 1892.

# COMMODORE OSCAR F. STANTON. U.S.N.

COMMODORE OSCAR F. STANTON is a native of New York, and appointed midshipman from that State in December, 1849. Served on board the U. S. steam-frigate "Susquehanna" in the East Indies, China Seas, and Japan Expedition under Commodore M. C. Perry, December, 1850, to June, 1853; U. S. sloop-of-war "Saratoga," China and Japan Seas, June, 1853, to September, 1854; Naval Academy, September, 1854, to June, 1855; U. S. ship "Constellation," Mediterranean Squadron, August, 1855, to August, 1858; U. S. steamer "Memphis," Paraguay Expedition, October, 1858, to June, 1859; U. S. store-ship "Supply" and U. S. sloops-of-war "Portsmouth" and "Marion," West Coast of Africa, September, 1859, to October, 1860; U. S. sloop-of-war "St. Mary's," Pacific Squadron, December, 1860, to March, 1862; U. S. steamer "Tioga," James River and Potomac Flotilla and West India Flying Squadron, May, 1862, to November, 1863; U. S. steam gun-boat "Pinola," West Gulf Blockading, December, 1863, to November, 1864; ordnance duty, New York Navy-Yard, December, 1864, to March, 1865; U. S. frigate "Powhatan," March to August, 1865, East Gulf Blockading Squadron; navy-yard, New York, August to November, 1865; Naval Academy, November, 1865, to May, 1867; U. S. steamer "Tahoma," Gulf Squadron, May to September, 1867; U. S. store-ship "Purveyor," Gulf of Mexico and West Coast of Africa, July, 1868, to May, 1869; U. S. receiving-ship "Vandalia," Portsmouth, New Hampshire, February, 1870, to April, 1871; U. S. steamer "Monocacy," China and Japan Seas, January, 1872, to June, 1873; U. S. steamer "Yantic," China and Japan Seas, June, 1873, to October, 1874; navy-yard, Norfolk, Virginia, November, 1874, to

March, 1877; Torpedo Station, June to September, 1878; U. S. frigate "Constitution," training-ship, October, 1879, to June, 1881; U. S. Naval Asylum, November, 1881, to October, 1884; U. S. steamer "Tennessee," November, 1884, to October, 1885; Naval Station, New London, Connecticut, October, 1885, to April, 1889. Naval Training Station at Newport, Rhode Island, July, 1890, to July, 1891. Promoted to passed midshipman, June, 1855; promoted to master in line of promotion, September, 1855; promoted to lieutenant, April, 1856; promoted to lieutenant-commander, July, 1862; promoted to commander, December, 1867; promoted to captain, June, 1879; commissioned commodore, May, 1891.

At present governor of the U. S. Naval Home at Philadelphia.

### REAR-ADMIRAL CHARLES STEEDMAN, U.S.N.
### (DECEASED.)

REAR-ADMIRAL CHARLES STEEDMAN was born in parish of St. James, Santee, South Carolina. Appointed midshipman in the navy April 1, 1828; first duty at the New York Navy-Yard; served in the West Indies as midshipman in the sloops-of-war "Natchez" and "Fairfield," and schooner "Grampus." Promoted to passed midshipman January 14, 1834. In the Mediterranean, on board of the frigates "Constitution" and "United States," and schooner "Shark," in the years 1836-38; and in the West Indies, on board the "Macedonian," up to 1840,—the last six months as acting lieutenant. Promoted as lieutenant February 25, 1841; served in the brig "Dolphin," on the Home Station and West Indies; invalid and sent home, 1842; Coast Survey, 1843-44; served in the West Indies and Gulf of Mexico on board of the "St. Mary's," 1845-47; commanded the eight-inch gun on naval battery at the bombardment of Vera Cruz, and commanded the "St. Mary's" launch in an attempt to surprise and capture Mexican gun-boats inside of Tampico bar; attached to Naval Observatory from latter part of 1847 to first of 1849; served on board frigate "Cumberland," in the Mediterranean, 1850-51; attached to Naval Observatory, 1853-55. Commissioned as commander, September 14, 1855; special duty in Washington, 1857-58; revising signal code and framing station bills for ships of the navy; commanded brig "Dolphin," Paraguay Expedition, 1859-60, and was left in command of Brazil Squadron when Flag-Officers Shubrick and Forrest returned home; remained in command for nine months, until the arrival of Flag-Officer Sands; returned home December, 1860; when Rebellion broke out was on leave; volunteered to Admiral Dupont for any service; was by him sent to take command of the Baltimore Railroad Company's steamboat "Maryland;" kept communication open between Havre-de-Grace and Annapolis until the railroad bridges were repaired, and communication opened between Baltimore and Philadelphia; was first to telegraph from Havre-de-Grace to General Patterson that General Butler had landed at Annapolis with Massachusetts regiment and Seventh New York Regiment, and had opened communication with Washington; in 1861, ordered to join Commodore Foote on the Mississippi; soon detached and ordered to take command of "Bienville;" attached to Port Royal Expedition, under Flag-Officer Dupont; led the second column in the attack and capture of Port Royal; in the "Bienville," brought north Flag-Officer Dupont's despatches reporting the capture; after this blockaded the coast of Georgia in the "Bienville," and participated in the capture of all the ports on that coast south of Savannah; after this returned north; was detached from "Bienville" and ordered to "Paul Jones;" joined Admiral Dupont's Squadron with "Paul Jones" and other gun-boats; engaged Fort McAllister, on the Ogeechee River, in August, 1862; on the 17th of September following, engaged and silenced the batteries of St. John's Bluff, on the St. John's River, Florida; considered it necessary to have troops to co-operate in capturing the forts and getting possession of the river; applied to Admiral Dupont for the same, on the 30th of the same month; with the co-operation of General Brannon captured the forts on St. John's Bluff, and with the gun-boats opened and held the St. John's River to Lake Beaufort. Commissioned as captain September 13, 1862. Transferred to the steam-frigate "Powhatan," and employed in her blockading off Charleston for several months; with the "Powhatan," towed the captured ram "Atlanta" to Philadelphia; soon after was detached and took command of "Ticonderoga;" in her was employed on various detached service; returned in her in November, 1864, with engines disabled from an unsuccessful search of the rebel vessel "Florida," on the coast of Brazil; volunteered to join Admiral Porter's command; vessel temporarily repaired.

After the fall of Fort Fisher and Wilmington, he joined Dahlgren off Charleston, but "Ticonderoga," being unfit for service, was ordered to Philadelphia for repairs. When she was once more fit for sea, he joined the European Squadron, under Admiral Goldsborough.

He was promoted to be commodore in July, 1866; exchanged commands with Captain Wyman, of the flag-ship "Colorado," and returned home in that ship in September, 1867. On special duty in 1868-69; and commanded the Boston Navy-Yard, 1869-72. Was commissioned rear-admiral in May, 1871. Commanded the South Pacific Squadron, 1872-73. Died at Washington, 1890.

# REAR-ADMIRAL R. N. STEMBEL, U.S.N. (RETIRED).

REAR-ADMIRAL R. N. STEMBEL was born in Maryland. Appointed a midshipman from the State of Ohio on March 27, 1832. For five years after appointment he served in the West India Squadron in the schooner "Porpoise," and the sloop-of-war "Vandalia." During part of 1837-38 he was at the Naval School at New York. (At that time the naval schools were attended by old midshipmen for a few months. They were at Norfolk, Virginia, New York, or elsewhere. For several years before the establishment of the present Naval School at Annapolis, it had its seat at Philadelphia, in a part of the Naval Asylum building.) Promoted to passed midshipman, 1838. Stationed at the Depot of Charts and Instruments, at Washington. Midshipman Stembel next served in the frigate "Brandywine," on the Mediterranean Station, from 1839 to 1842. He was commissioned lieutenant in 1843, and was attached to the Coast Survey for several years. In 1849-50 he served in the sloop-of-war "Germantown," on the Home Squadron; and from 1851-54 in the sloop "Jamestown," of the Brazil Squadron. Special duty at Washington from 1855-57, and then attached to the steam-frigate "Mississippi," China and East India Squadron, for three years. Lieutenant Stembel was attached to the Naval Asylum, at Philadelphia, when the Civil War broke out, and was ordered to special duty at Cincinnati, Ohio, in connection with the Western Gun-boat Flotilla.

Just at this time he was commissioned as commander, and in active service in the Mississippi Flotilla; engagements at Lucas's Bend, September 9, 1861; Belmont, November 7, 1861; Fort Henry, February 6, 1862; bombardment and capture of Island No. 10, from March 16 to April 7, 1862; the fight with the rebel rams at Craig-

head's Bend, near Fort Pillow, May 10, 1862, and several minor affairs. At the engagement at Craighead's Bend he was seriously wounded by a rifle-ball. He was invalided in consequence of this wound in 1863, and the peculiar nature and effects of the ball's passage were the subject of great interest to medical men.

During 1864 he was stationed at the Recruiting Rendezvous at Philadelphia, and afterwards on special duty at Pittsburg. He was commissioned as captain in 1866, during his command of the steam-sloop "Canandaigua," on the European Station. Returned to the United States in 1867. Commanded the Naval Rendezvous at Boston, 1869-71. Commissioned commodore 1870, and commanded Northern Squadron of the Pacific Fleet, 1871-72, and, for a time, the Pacific Fleet. He was retired as a commodore in 1872, and commissioned as rear-admiral on the retired list in 1874.

## LIEUTENANT-COLONEL GEORGE M. STERNBERG.
### U.S.A.

LIEUTENANT-COLONEL GEORGE M. STERNBERG (Medical Department) was born in New York on January 8, 1838, and was appointed assistant surgeon, U. S. Army, May 28, 1861. He served with General Sykes's regular division of the Army of the Potomac, and participated in the battles of first Bull Run, July 21, 1861, Gaines' Mill, June 27, 1862, and Malvern Hill, July 1, 1862, and was brevetted captain and major for "faithful and meritorious services during the war."

Dr. Sternberg was on hospital duty at Portsmouth Grove, Rhode Island, until November, 1862, when he was assigned to duty with the troops in the Department of the Gulf, and participated in General Banks's expedition, and subsequently on duty in the office of the medical director until January, 1864, when he was transferred to the office of the medical director at Columbus, Ohio, and in charge of the U. S. General Hospital at Cleveland, Ohio, to July, 1865. He was then ordered to Jefferson Barracks for duty with the Thirteenth U. S. Infantry, but his station was subsequently changed to Kansas, where he passed through a severe epidemic of cholera at Fort Harker, in 1867. He was promoted captain and assistant surgeon May 28, 1866.

Dr. Sternberg was at Fort Riley, Kansas, and in the field during the campaign of 1868-69 against the Cheyenne and Arapahoe Indians, and was then ordered to Fort Columbus, New York, serving at that post and at Fort Warren, Massachusetts, to August, 1872. At that time he was transferred to the Department of the Gulf, and was in the medical director's office at New Orleans, Louisiana, to October, 1872, when ordered to Fort Barrancas, Florida, where he passed through a severe epidemic of yellow fever in 1873-75. He was on sick-leave to May, 1876, at which time he was assigned to duty in the Department of the Columbia, and was present at the battle of the Clearwater, Idaho (with Chief Joseph, of the Nez Perces), in 1878.

Dr. Sternberg was appointed a member of the "Havana Yellow Fever Commission" in 1879, and was ordered to the Department of California August 10, 1881, being assigned to duty at Fort Mason to May, 1884. He was then ordered East, and was attending surgeon and examiner of recruits at Baltimore, Maryland, and was delegate from the United States to the International Sanitary Conference of Rome in 1888. Was detailed, under an Act of Congress (by the President of the United States), to make investigations relating to the cause and prevention of yellow fever in Brazil and in Mexico in 1887; in Decatur, Alabama, during the epidemic of 1888, and in Havana during the summers of 1888 and 1889.

He was promoted major and surgeon December 1, 1875, and lieutenant-colonel and surgeon January 2, 1891.

Dr. Sternberg is a Fellow of the American Association for the Advancement of Science; a Fellow of the Royal Microscopical Society of London; late Fellow, by courtesy, in Johns Hopkins University; member and ex-president of the American Public Health Association; member of the American Medical Association, of the Association of American Physicians, of the American Microscopical Society; honorary member of the Epidemiological Society of London, of the Royal Academy of Medicine of Rome, of the Academy of Medicine of Rio de Janeiro, of the American Academy of Medicine, etc.; author of "Bacteria" (William Wood & Co., New York, 1884); of "Photo-Micrographs, and how to make them" (James R. Osgood & Co., Boston, 1884); of "Malaria and Malarial Diseases" (William Wood & Co., New York, 1884), and of numerous scientific papers published in various medical and scientific periodicals.

At present on duty as attending surgeon, New York City.

## REAR-ADMIRAL THOMAS HOLDUP STEVENS, U.S.N. (RETIRED).

Rear-Admiral Thomas Holdup Stevens was born in Connecticut, and is a son of Commodore Thomas Holdup Stevens, who at the age of eighteen commanded the "Trippe," one of Perry's squadron at the battle of Lake Erie. Upon the old navy lists Lieutenant T. H. Stevens appears as the second of the "date of 1836," a notable one for the ability of those who composed it.

Thomas H. Stevens was appointed a midshipman from Connecticut in 1836, and after varied service became a lieutenant in 1849, and, after serving on board the "Michigan," some Coast Survey vessels, and the steam-frigate "Colorado," was ordered to the command of the "Ottawa," early in 1862. In this vessel he took part in the actions of the squadron at Port Royal, capture of Forts Beauregard and Walker, battle of Port Royal Ferry, and the different engagements with Tatnall's fleet. After that the "Ottawa" was constantly employed for many months in the waters of Florida, under fire many times. Stevens commanded the naval forces on these waters.

Lieutenant Stevens received his commission as commander in July, 1862, and commanded the "Maratanza" during the exciting period of the battle of Malvern Hill. Then, for a short time, he was in command of the celebrated "Monitor," covering McClellan on his withdrawal from the Peninsula. He next commanded the "Sonoma," in the West India Squadron, and captured several blockade-runners. Commanded the monitor "Patapsco," during which period that vessel took part in numerous attacks on the defences of Charleston, and on the night of September 8, 1863, Stevens commanded the boat-assault on Fort Sumter. He next took command of the steam-sloop "Oneida." During the operations before Mobile, in Aug., 1864, to enable Commander Mullany (late rear-admiral), who had volunteered for the occasion, to take part in the fight, Stevens consented to take command of the double-turretted monitor "Winnebago," and Mullany took the "Oneida," so that both those officers could command fighting-ships. In the "Winnebago" Stevens took part in the battle of Mobile Bay, and the capture of the "Tennessee" and her consorts, as well as Forts Powell, Gaines, and Morgan, in all which operations he was conspicuous for the handling of his command and for his personal daring. Resuming command of the "Oneida," he remained in command of the Texas Division of the West Gulf Blockading Squadron, participating in the final operations of the war, and returned North in that vessel in August, 1865.

During these stirring four years Stevens received testimonials in regard to his zeal and conduct from every superior officer under whom he served, including Rear-Admirals Dupont, Wilkes, John Rodgers, Dahlgren, Rowan, Farragut and Le Roy. All of these speak in the highest terms, both in official reports and in special letters, of the judgment and discretion, the gallantry and unfaltering determination of the subject of this sketch. No service was too arduous, no mission too perilous for him to undertake, and his only failures to accomplish what he undertook, were in capturing the "Florida," because he could not overtake her, and in the boat-assault on Sumter. After making an earnest protest against the plan of attack arranged by the admiral in command, he took charge of the expedition as it was; otherwise the attempt would have been abandoned. He had just returned from an all-day engagement with the harbor forts, when he was sent for to assume the command of the boat expedition which made the attack that same evening.

Admiral Dahlgren, in his farewell order, said, in regard to the night attack on Sumter, "When I began to perceive that the enemy was not likely to be driven out of Sumter, except by assault, and saw that the force which I had could not of itself go farther, unless he was driven out, I ordered the assault. It failed, but never was more gallantry displayed than in the attempt."

Admiral Rowan says, "I witnessed, upon one occasion, the gallant and intelligent conduct of this officer while engaged with Fort Moultrie and its other defences. I also witnessed his gallant bearing on occasion of the 'Ironsides's' attack on Fort Moultrie, when he passed from his monitor to the 'Ironsides,' and back to his vessel in a boat, while the fire of Moultrie and its surrounding batteries was concentrated on that ship."

Similar comments were made upon his conduct at Mobile Bay by his superior officers. After the war he commanded the frigate "Guerriere;" then the navy-yard at Norfolk; commanded, as rear-admiral, the Pacific Squadron; and, upon arriving at the prescribed age, hauled down his flag while in that command.

PAY-INSPECTOR JOHN H. STEVENSON, U.S.N.

PAY-INSPECTOR JOHN H. STEVENSON entered the navy as acting assistant paymaster of the "Satellite," in September, 1862, and was in the first battle of Fredericksburg, in Hooker's Division. In December, 1862, Stevenson, with the approbation of the commanding officer of the "Satellite," captured the party of a rebel signal-station, and broke it up. He then left the boats with keepers, and penetrated ten miles inland, and captured Captain Lawson, of the rebel cavalry, who had a recruiting-station established and cavalry pickets out. He broke up the station, secured Captain Lawson, and brought him to the "Satellite," from whence he was sent to the Old Capitol Prison.

The commanding officer of the "Satellite" wrote, "To the bravery and energy of Acting Assistant Paymaster Stevenson the success of the expedition was due. Mr. Stevenson frequently volunteered his services for other hazardous duty, and always performed it to my entire satisfaction." Rear-Admiral Harwood, who was in command of the Potomac Flotilla, wrote warmly upon Paymaster Stevenson's "gratuitous patriotic services," but says that those at Donaldsonville eclipsed his earlier ones. It was in June, 1863, while attached to the "Princess Royal" gun-boat, that that vessel was detailed to protect the town of Donaldsonville, and a small fort, manned by one hundred and twenty-five sick and convalescent soldiers. It was the only fortified position held by the Union forces between Port Hudson and New Orleans, and the necessity of holding it was supreme. The rebel Generals Taylor, Mouton, and Green, with a force of several thousand men, sent in a demand for the surrender of the fort and town. This was refused. They then sent a notification to remove the women and children. At this critical juncture, Paymaster Stevenson went as a spy into the enemy's camp, in the rôle of a refugee from New Orleans. He acted thus entirely upon his own responsibility. He was obliged to run the Union pickets, and narrowly escaped being shot in doing so. But he got safely through, entered the enemy's camp, learned when and how they were to make the attack, and returned with full information to the "Princess Royal." In returning, he was obliged to run the enemy's pickets, and again narrowly escaped being shot. The information he obtained, with the heroism of the defenders, saved the place, for the enemy were beaten off after four hours' desperate fighting, with an acknowledged loss of fifteen hundred. Captain Woolsey, U. S. Navy, says, "for the information" (which enabled preparation to be made) " I am indebted to A. A. Paymaster Stevenson, who was out for three days . . . reconnoitring in and about the enemy's camp."

In July, 1863, when the steamer "New London," with important despatches, was aground and under the enemy's fire, Paymaster Stevenson went to the vessel, got the despatches and took them to New Orleans, through a hostile country, seizing horses as he wanted them, and dashing through the enemy's pickets and suspicious places. Admiral Farragut bore testimony to his great service on this occasion. Admiral Porter testifies, "General Sherman had not heard of the capture of Fort Fisher," and to prevent his possible divergence in that direction, "Mr. Stevenson volunteered and carried the despatches safely to General Sherman, through the enemy's country, at the risk of his neck; for had they caught him, they would have hung him."

From the character of the vessels to which Paymaster Stevenson was attached, he was present at very many of the battles and skirmishes on the Potomac and Rappahannock Rivers, from November, 1862, to April, 1863; and on the Mississippi River, from June, 1863, to September, 1863; and all the fights on the James River during the last year of the war. He was also present at the capture of Petersburg and Richmond. In June, 1870, the President, by advice and consent of the Senate, advanced Paymaster Stevenson fifteen numbers in his grade, and again, in 1879, he was advanced fifteen numbers "for gallant and conspicuous conduct in battle, and extraordinary heroism." He became pay-inspector in January, 1881, and has since performed routine service abroad and at home.

## PAYMASTER-GENERAL EDWIN STEWART, U.S.N.

PAYMASTER-GENERAL EDWIN STEWART was born in New York City, May 5, 1837. He is a graduate of Phillips Academy, Andover, Massachusetts, and of Williams College, from which institution he has received the degrees of B.A. and M.A. Had it not been for the war he would have followed a profession; in fact, had already commenced the study of law, when, in September, 1861, he was appointed an assistant paymaster in the navy. His first duty was on board the gun-boat "Pembina," then fitting out at New York. The "Pembina" joined the expedition against Port Royal, and on November 7, 1861, took part in the bombardment and capture of the forts at that place.

In April, 1862, Assistant Paymaster Stewart was promoted to the grade of paymaster, and ordered to the "Richmond," in the South Atlantic Squadron. The "Richmond," in company with the "Hartford," participated in that series of brilliant naval engagements which made the name of Farragut famous.

Paymaster Stewart was attached to the "Richmond" during the three most eventful years of her career, and saw memorable service, both on the blockade and in the battles in which she was engaged, notably at Port Hudson and at the passage and capture of the forts in Mobile Bay.

At the close of the war he was assigned to duty on the Lakes, being attached to the steamer "Michigan" from 1865 to 1868. Much of the duty of the "Michigan" during those years was in watching and endeavoring to frustrate the persistent and repeated efforts of the Fenians to effect a landing in Canada.

The "Michigan" finally succeeded in capturing the whole party as they were making their way across the Niagara River.

In 1869 Paymaster Stewart was ordered to Washington, where for three years he was in charge of the Purchasing Pay-Office.

In the spring of 1872 he was appointed a member of the Board of Visitors to the Naval Academy.

In the fall of 1872 he was ordered to the "Hartford" as fleet-paymaster on the Asiatic Station. The "Hartford" went to China by way of the Mediterranean and the Suez Canal, stopping at various places of interest en route. The cruise lasted three years, a large portion of the time being spent in the seaport cities of China and Japan.

When homeward bound in 1875 the "Hartford" received at Messina telegraphic orders to go to Tripoli and settle a difficulty growing out of an alleged indignity offered to the United States consul. On her arrival at Tripoli she found the "Congress" already there under similar orders. An apology for the indignity was demanded from the Pasha, and forty-eight hours named as the time within which it must be made.

The two ships steamed into position before the city, and in this menacing attitude awaited the Pasha's reply. It came within the time specified. A full and satisfactory apology was made, and the "Hartford" steamed away on her homeward voyage.

Paymaster Stewart was commissioned "pay-inspector" March 8, 1880, and for three years was on duty as inspector at the navy-yard, New York. In 1882 he was ordered to the "Lancaster," and for nearly three years was fleet-paymaster on the European Station, visiting during the cruise most of the seaport cities of Europe from St. Petersburg to Alexandria and Palestine. An interesting feature of this cruise was the visit to Russia, the "Lancaster" having been ordered to Cronstadt to represent the United States on the occasion of the coronation of the Czar.

In 1886 Pay-Inspector Stewart was assigned to the important position of purchasing pay-officer in New York City, on which duty he was continued until May 16, 1890, when he was made paymaster-general of the navy. He was selected for this position while he was still a pay-inspector, with thirteen pay-directors senior to him on the list.

The bureau of which he is chief directs all purchases for the navy, has custody of all supplies, keeps account of all appropriations for the navy, and is the financial and business bureau of the department.

General Stewart is a member of the Loyal Legion, of the University Club in New York, and of the Metropolitan and Army and Navy Clubs in Washington.

He has for many years been a Sunday-school superintendent, and is a ruling elder in the Presbyterian Church.

COMMANDER YATES STIRLING, U.S.N.

COMMANDER YATES STIRLING is a native of Maryland, and was appointed to the Naval Academy from that State in September, 1860. The services of all were in demand soon after, and on May 28, 1863, he left the academy with the rank of ensign in the navy. He was assigned to the sloop-of-war "Shenandoah." Was detached from "Shenandoah" in April, 1864, while that vessel was undergoing repairs at Philadelphia. Ordered back to the "Shenandoah" in June following; but, in the mean time, had served the two months in the monitor "Onondaga," then the flag-ship of the North Atlantic Blockading Squadron, in James River. Served in both attacks upon Fort Fisher. After the close of the Civil War he went to the "Mohongo," in the Pacific, and was attached to her from 1865–67. In 1866 he received his lieutenant's commission. He was commissioned lieutenant-commander March 12, 1868. Was attached to the "Wampanoag" during her trial-trip in that year; and then served in the "Contocook," flag-ship, North Atlantic Squadron, 1868–69. He was attached to the receiving-ship "Independence" during 1871–72. During the years 1873–75 Lieutenant-Commander Stirling was upon sick-leave. Upon his recovery he was ordered to the receiving-ship "Worcester," during 1875–76; torpedo duty in 1877; ordnance duty at the navy-yard, Washington, 1877–78.

From 1878–81 he served in the steam sloop-of-war "Lackawanna," in the Pacific. Was promoted to commander November 26, 1880. From 1882–84 he was stationed at the Washington Navy-Yard. From 1884–86 he commanded the steam-sloop "Iroquois," on the Pacific Station. From 1887–90 he commanded the receiving-ship "Dale," at Washington. In 1890–91 he was in command of the U. S. S. "Dolphin."

## CAPTAIN EDWIN J. STIVERS, U.S.A. (RETIRED).

CAPTAIN EDWIN J. STIVERS was born in Bolivar, Ohio, June 14, 1836. He entered the volunteer service early in the war of the Rebellion, and was fifer and private of Company K, and fife-major and sergeant-major of the Eighty-ninth Illinois Infantry from August 7, 1862, to December 1, 1863, when he was appointed second lieutenant of the Seventeenth U. S. Colored Infantry.

He served in the field with the armies of the West, and was engaged in the battles of Stone River, Liberty Gap, Chickamauga, Missionary Ridge, and Nashville.

In the report of the battle of Chickamauga, made by the commander of the Eighty-ninth Illinois Infantry, he says, "Sergeant-major E. J. Stivers deserves special mention for brave and intrepid conduct." He was also referred to by General Rosecrans in his report of the same battle. He was captured by four guerillas in Alabama during the Hood campaign, but escaped after a few hours' captivity.

He was promoted first lieutenant February 5, 1864, and captain August 2, 1865, and honorably mustered out of service November 3, 1866. He was appointed second lieutenant of the Fortieth U. S. Infantry July 28, 1866, but did not accept the appointment until February 5, 1867. He was then brevetted first lieutenant March 2, 1867, for "gallant and meritorious services in the battle of Nashville, Tennessee."

Lieutenant Stivers was promoted first lieutenant September 15, 1868, and transferred to the Twenty-fifth Infantry, on the consolidation of regiments, April 20, 1869. He performed garrison duty at various posts until 1879, when he was examined by a retiring board on account of injuries incidental to the service, and, after nearly two years' absence on account of disability, returned to active service, which continued until May 4, 1888, when he was ordered by the Secretary of War to his home, on account of disability incurred in the line of duty, and was finally placed on the retired list February 24, 1891.

Lieutenant Stivers was promoted captain February 19, 1883. During his active service in the regular army he filled the positions of quartermaster and commissary at Fort Macon, North Carolina; Raleigh, North Carolina; and Fort Pike, Louisiana.

## CAPTAIN AND BREVET LIEUTENANT-COLONEL
## EBENEZER W. STONE, U.S.A.

CAPTAIN AND BREVET LIEUTENANT-COLONEL EBENEZER W. STONE (Twenty-first Infantry) was born at Boston, Massachusetts, October 23, 1837. He was commissioned captain, First Massachusetts Infantry, May 24, 1861, and served with the regiment until mustered out, May 25, 1864.

The regiment was the first three years' organization to leave the State, and was engaged at first battle of Bull Run. It was assigned to Army of the Potomac, and engaged in all battles and campaigns of that army until mustered out, except the Antietam campaign.

In September, 1864, he was commissioned lieutenant-colonel Sixty-first Massachusetts, and mustered as such February 28, 1865. He served with the regiment until mustered out, July 16, 1865. The regiment was assigned to the Army of the Potomac, and served with it until mustered out.

He was commissioned second lieutenant, Twelfth U. S. Infantry, May 11, 1866, and in the reorganization of the army in 1866 he was transferred to the Twenty-first Infantry (Second Battalion, Twelfth Infantry), and promoted first lieutenant, Twenty-first Infantry, March 26, 1868. He was promoted captain, Twenty-first Infantry, November 11, 1879. He then became unassigned from April 19, 1869, to December 15, 1870.

He served as chief quartermaster for the garrison of Washington, under command of Brevet Major-General William H. Emory, from October, 1866, to March, 1867. He was adjutant of the Artillery School from October, 1867, to March, 1868; assistant adjutant-general, Sub-District of Fort Monroe and Norfolk (First Military District), from September, 1867, to July, 1868.

He was military commissioner, Division of Reconstruction, comprising the counties of Accomac and Northampton, Virginia, from July to September, 1868; aide-de-camp to Brevet Major-Generals George Stoneman and A. S. Webb, commanding First Military District (Virginia), from September 25, 1868, to May 1, 1869; acting assistant adjutant-general, Department of California, from May, 1869, to May, 1870, Brigadier-General E. O. C. Ord commanding; acting assistant adjutant-general, Department of Arizona, from May, 1870, to June, 1871, Brevet Major-General George Stoneman commanding; depot and purchasing quartermaster and commissary in the field, with the Modoc campaign, from November, 1872, to August, 1873, Brigadier-General E. R. S. Canby and Brevet Major-General J. C. Davis commanding; chief commissary in the field during the Bannock campaign of 1878, Major-General O. O. Howard commanding.

Upon being appointed to the regular army he was brevetted first lieutenant and captain, U.S.A., for "gallant and meritorious services at battle of Williamsburg, Virginia;" major, U.S.A., for "gallant and meritorious services at battle of Chancellorsville, Virginia;" lieutenant-colonel, U.S.A., for "gallant and meritorious services at battle of Gettysburg, Pennsylvania."

He was also brevetted colonel of volunteers, for "gallant and meritorious services during the campaign resulting in the fall of Richmond, Virginia, and the surrender of insurgent army under General R. E. Lee."

# REAR-ADMIRAL S. H. STRINGHAM, U.S.N.
### (DECEASED).

REAR-ADMIRAL S. H. STRINGHAM, in his day and generation, stood among the very foremost in our service. Born in Orange County, New York, he entered the service as a midshipman in June, 1810, and first served in the frigate "President," in 1811-12. While attached to the "President" he took part in the engagement with H. M. S. "Little Belt" and the English frigate "Belvidere."

In December, 1814, Midshipman Stringham was commissioned as lieutenant, and he took part in the capture of the Algerine privateers in 1815. It was not until 1831 that he was made commander,—having for a long time been employed on various naval duties, ashore and afloat. During the years 1836-37 he commanded the "John Adams," and was stationed at the New York Navy-Yard when he was commissioned as captain, in 1841. He then commanded the razee "Independence;" was in command of the navy-yard at New York; commanded the ship-of-the-line "Ohio," in the Pacific, during the Mexican War; was commandant of the navy-yard at Norfolk. His next duty was the command of the Mediterranean Squadron from 1852 to 1855. From 1856 to 1860 he was in command of the Boston Navy-Yard. When the Civil War broke out he was made flag-officer of the North Atlantic Blockading Squadron. His limits of command were from the easternmost line of Virginia to Cape Florida. The small force which the department was then able to afford him was skilfully disposed of, and a very fairly effective blockade instituted. At that period forays of privateers, so-called, became seriously annoying, and as most of them came from the Great Sounds of North Carolina, it became necessary to seize and possess their mode of exit to the high seas. This pass was Hatteras Inlet. Stringham, at an age when he would be subject to retirement a year or two later, commanded the naval forces in person, and a military force of eight hundred men co-operated with him. Forts Clark and Hatteras were speedily captured, and the entire garrisons, under Captain Barron, who had been fifty years in the U. S. Navy, surrendered, after great loss. Not a man of the attacking force was killed or wounded. The military force sent was not sufficient to follow up the success. At that period we were only learning, slowly, how to conduct war. In September, 1861, at his own request, he was relieved from a command too arduous for a person of his age. He was commissioned as rear-admiral July 16, 1862, and ordered to special duty. Was commandant of navy-yard, 1864-66; port-admiral, at New York, 1868. Died in 1869.

Admiral Stringham was of very strong, square build, and of medium height. His countenance was most firm, while pleasant and mild in expression. He wore no beard, and was always careful to be clean-shaven, and was especially neat in his dress. He was a martinet, but he always scrupulously obeyed "regulations" himself,—at whatever personal inconvenience,—and always took care that every one under his command did so.

CAPTAIN AND BREVET LIEUTENANT-COLONEL
SHELDON STURGEON, U.S.A. (RETIRED).

CAPTAIN AND BREVET LIEUTENANT-COLONEL SHELDON STURGEON was born in Sparta, New York, February 7, 1838, and graduated from the Military Academy May 6, 1861. He was promoted second lieutenant of the First Infantry the same day; first lieutenant June 24, 1861; and captain April 25, 1862. He served during the war of the Rebellion drilling the Sixty-ninth New York Infantry, Second Maine Infantry, and Second Connecticut Infantry until July 1, 1861; then he was on duty with the battalion of the Third U. S. Infantry until September, 1861, participating with it in the battle of Bull Run, when he joined his company at Governor's Island, New York, on its return from Texas on parole. He was then detailed on recruiting service, and was mustering and disbursing officer at Buffalo, New York, from 1861 to 1863. At that time he joined his company at New Orleans, Louisiana, and was attached to the staff of Major-General Banks and Major-General Hurlburt; commissary of musters and superintendent of the recruiting service, Department of the Gulf. He was also attached to the staff of Major-General Canby, January 7, 1864. He was chief mustering officer and acting assistant provost marshal-general for the Military Division of West Mississippi, conducting the enrollment and draft. He held the same position under Major-General Sheridan in 1865–66.

He was brevetted major and lieutenant-colonel, March 13, 1865, "for gallant and meritorious services during the war." He was appointed colonel of the First New Orleans Infantry April 25, 1865, and honorably mustered out of the volunteer service August 15, 1865. He joined his company at Jackson Barracks, Louisiana, and served with it until November, 1868, being detached, in the mean time, for several months, as supervising officer of registration for the nine southern parishes of Louisiana, including New Orleans, under the direction of Major-General Sheridan, until attacked with yellow fever. He was then granted leave of absence for five months, rejoining his company at New Orleans, in April, 1869.

His regiment was transferred to the Department of the Lakes, and Captain Sturgeon served at Fort Wayne, Michigan, and Fort Porter, New York, until January 1, 1871, when he was transferred to the Sixth Cavalry, and served with Troop H, at Fort Richardson, Texas; Fort Hayes, Kansas; Aberdeen, Mississippi; Fort Riley, Kansas, and scouting in the Indian country until October, 1872. From that time he was on leave of absence, and was retired from active service, May 17, 1876, for disability.

# COLONEL SAMUEL D. STURGIS, U.S.A. (DECEASED).

COLONEL SAMUEL D. STURGIS was born in Pennsylvania, and graduated at the Military Academy July 1, 1846. He was promoted brevet second lieutenant, Second Dragoons, the same day, and second lieutenant, First Dragoons, Feb. 16, 1847. He served in the war with Mexico, and was captured, Feb. 20, 1847, while reconnoitring near Buena Vista, and not released until Feb. 28, 1847, after the battle. He was on frontier duty in California, 1848-51, and then served at Jefferson Barracks; Fort Leavenworth; and Albuquerque, New Mexico, until 1854.

He was promoted first lieutenant July 15, 1853, and was scouting against Jicarilla Apaches, being engaged in the action of Cienega, New Mexico, April 6, 1854. He was at Moro, Fort Fillmore, and Santa Fé, New Mexico, until 1855, and from the latter place was scouting and engaged against Apache Indians in a skirmish, January 16, 1855. He was on frontier duty and Fort Leavenworth, 1855-57; on Cheyenne Expedition, and engaged in the combat on Solomon's Fork of the Kansas River, July 27, 1857, and skirmish against Kiowa and Comanche Indians near Grand Saline, August 6, 1857. He then served in Kansas, Nebraska, Indian Territory, Missouri, and Fort Cobb, Indian Territory, until 1860, when he was in command of the southern column of Kiowa and Comanche Expedition from June to Oct., 1860, being engaged in a severe action on Prairie Dog Creek, Aug. 9, 1860, and in several skirmishes.

He was promoted captain March 3, 1855. During the years 1860-61 he was employed in adjusting difficulties between Cherokee Indians and white settlers, and afterwards at Fort Smith, Arkansas, at the breaking out of the war of the Rebellion. He evacuated this post April 23, 1861, to prevent being captured by a formidable expedition, and marched to Fort Leavenworth, via Wichita, Kansas. He was promoted major, May 3, 1861, and was engaged on an expedition to Southwest Missouri, June 24, 1861, uniting with General Lyon, July 5, 1861, on Grand River, Missouri, and was engaged in the action of Dug Spring and battle of Wilson's Creek, where he commanded after the fall of General Lyon, and conducted the retreat to Rolla, Missouri.

Made brigadier-general of volunteers Aug. 10, 1861, and participated in an expedition to northeast Missouri; was on the march to Kansas City, October, 1861, forming the right of General Frémont's movement on Springfield; chief of staff to Major-General Hunter, November, 1861; on tour of inspection of Ohio and Mississippi River posts in Dec., 1861; in command of the District of Kansas from April 10 to May 5, 1862; in command of the defences of Washington from May 25 to Aug. 24, 1862; and then participated in the campaigns of the Army of the Potomac, being engaged in the battle of Bull Run, Aug. 29, 1862, South Mountain, battle of Antietam, and several skirmishes while pursuing the enemy, and battle of Fredericksburg.

General Sturgis was transferred to the Western armies, and participated in the operations in central Kentucky from April to July, 1863, and was chief of cavalry, Department of Ohio, to April 15, 1864. He was promoted lieutenant-colonel, Sixth Cavalry, October 27, 1863, and subsequently engaged in organizing the militia of Cincinnati during Morgan's rebel raid; in operations in East Tennessee, and action of Mossy Creek, Dandridge; capture of General Vance and his rebel command; rout of General Martin's rebel cavalry, and destruction of camp of rebels and Indians near Quallatown, North Carolina; in expedition from Memphis, May, 1864, and engaged in the combat at Bolivar, Tennessee, and pursuit of rebels under Forrest, to Ripley, Mississippi: and in the second expedition against Forrest, being engaged in the combat near Gun Town, Mississippi, June 10, 1864. Aug. 24, 1865, he was mustered out of the volunteer service.

He was brevetted lieutenant-colonel, August 10, 1861, for "gallant and meritorious services in the battle of Wilson's Creek, Missouri," and colonel, December 13, 1862, for "gallant and meritorious services at the battle of Fredericksburg, Virginia."

He then served in command of the Sixth Cavalry at Austin, Texas; Camp Wilson, Texas; and on Board on System of Cavalry Tactics, July 3, 1868, to April 24, 1869.

He was promoted colonel, Seventh Cavalry, May 6, 1869, and at Fort Leavenworth and Louisville, Kentucky, to 1873; superintendent of general recruiting service, 1874-76; at Fort Lincoln, Dakota, 1876-77; on Yellowstone Expedition, 1877-78; and then served in various other capacities, commanding posts, etc., to 1881. He was governor of the Soldiers' Home at Washington to May, 1885, and then at Fort Meade, Dakota. Was retired from active service June 11, 1886. He died at St. Paul, Minnesota, Sept. 28, 1889, aged sixty-seven years.

MAJOR-GENERAL EDWIN V. SUMNER, U.S.A.
(DECEASED).

MAJOR-GENERAL EDWIN V. SUMNER was born in Boston, Massachusetts, January 30, 1797; died in Syracuse, New York, March 21, 1863. Young Sumner was educated at Milton (Massachusetts) Academy, and entered the army in 1819 as second lieutenant of infantry. He served in the Black Hawk War, became captain of the Second Dragoons in 1833, and was employed on the Western frontier, where he distinguished himself as an Indian fighter. In 1838 he was placed in command of the School of Cavalry Practice at Carlisle, Pennsylvania. He was promoted major in 1846, and in the Mexican War led the cavalry charge at Cerro Gordo, in April, 1847; commanded the reserves at Contreras and Churubusco, and at the head of the cavalry at Molino del Rey checked the advance of five thousand Mexican lancers.

He was governor of New Mexico in 1851–53, when he visited Europe to report on improvements in cavalry. In 1855 he was promoted colonel of the First Cavalry, and made a successful expedition against the Cheyennes. In command of the Department of the West, in 1858, he rendered efficient service during the Kansas troubles. In March, 1861, he was appointed brigadier-general in the regular army, and sent to relieve General Albert Sidney Johnston, in command of the Department of the Pacific, but was recalled in the following year to the command of the First Corps of the Army of the Potomac. He commanded the left wing at the siege of Yorktown. At Fair Oaks, where McClellan's army was divided by the Chickahominy, and the left wing was heavily attacked, the orders of Sumner to cross the river and reinforce that wing found him with his corps drawn out and ready to move instantly. In the Seven Days' battle he was twice wounded. In 1862 he was appointed major-general of volunteers, led the Second Corps at the battle of Antietam, where he was wounded, and commanded one of the three grand divisions of Burnside's army at Fredericksburg, his division being the first to cross the Rappahannock. At his own request he was relieved in 1863, and being appointed to the Department of the Missouri, he was on his way thither when he died. He was brevetted lieutenant-colonel for Cerro Gordo, colonel for Molino del Rey, and major-general in the regular army for services before Richmond. Major-General Sumner's last words, as he, with great effort, waved a glass of wine above his head, were, "God save my country, the United States of America." His son, Edwin Vose, served with merit through the Civil War, and was appointed major of the Fifth Cavalry in 1879, and inspector of rifle practice, Department of the Missouri.

## BRIGADIER-GENERAL CHARLES SUTHERLAND, U.S.A.

BRIGADIER-GENERAL CHARLES SUTHERLAND (Surgeon-General) was born in Philadelphia, Pennsylvania, May 29. 1830. He was appointed assistant surgeon August 5, 1852, and was promoted captain and assistant surgeon August 5, 1857, and major and surgeon April 16, 1862. He was assigned to duty as acting assistant surgeon at Fort Monroe, Virginia, and in New Mexico from November, 1851, to April, 1852; served with troops on the plains, also at Fort Webster, Fort Fillmore, Fort Craig, Santa Fé, and Fort Stanton, New Mexico, to September, 1857; Fort Moultrie, South Carolina, to January 18, 1858; on leave until September, 1858; Forts Davis and Duncan, Texas, to February, 1861; not taken prisoner on the secession of Texas, and left that State with artillery and infantry troops for New York City; reported for duty to surgeon-general in March, 1861; sailed in April, 1861, on secret expedition to Fort Pickens, Santa Rosa Island, Florida; at Fort Pickens to March, 1862, and participated in the two bombardments of Fort Pickens and in the assault on Wilson's camp on the island of Santa Rosa, Florida. He was then stationed at Fort Warren, Massachusetts, until June, 1862, when he joined the armies of the West in the field, and was medical purveyor to the armies under Major-General Halleck, Pittsburg Landing, Tennessee. He established a large depot at Columbus, Kentucky, and fitted out nine general hospitals and a second purveying depot at Memphis, Tennessee. He was then appointed medical inspector of camps and transports of the Army of the Tennessee in and about Vicksburg, Mississippi; was with the Army of the Tennessee in the campaign and siege of Vicksburg, and participated in the surrender of that place July 4, 1863. He then became medical director, Department of Virginia and North Carolina, to November, 1863; member Retiring Board, Wilmington, Delaware, to January, 1864; medical director of hospitals, Annapolis, Maryland, to May, 1864; and purchasing medical purveyor, Washington, D. C., until the close of the Rebellion.

He was brevetted lieutenant-colonel, March 13, 1865, for "faithful and meritorious services during the war;" and colonel, March 13, 1865, for "meritorious services and diligent discharge of duties during the war." He was promoted lieutenant-colonel and assistant medical purveyor July 28, 1866, and remained on duty in Washington, D. C., to June, 1870; then was member of Retiring Board, in New York City, from October, 1870, to March, 1871. He was acting chief medical purveyor, New York City, to June, 1876; acting assistant medical purveyor, New York, to July, 1878; on leave to September, 1879; on duty as medical director of the Military Division of the Pacific, Presidio of San Francisco, October 27, 1879, to May, 1884; member of Retiring Board; member of a board convened by President Arthur to locate a site for a quarantine station at San Francisco, California; medical director, Division of the Atlantic, from May, 1884, and member of Retiring Board, at Governor's Island, New York, 1890.

Colonel Sutherland was appointed brigadier-general and surgeon-general December 23, 1890, taking station at Washington City.

### BRIGADIER-GENERAL DAVID G. SWAIM, U.S.A.

BRIGADIER-GENERAL DAVID G. SWAIM (Judge-Advocate-General) was born in Salem, Columbiana County, Ohio. His family has been represented in the active operations of every war in which the United States has been engaged, and conspicuously during the War of 1812 in the person of Commodore (Captain) Lawrence, of the navy. His father was the friend of Joshua R. Giddings, Salmon P. Chase, and other advanced political thinkers of that day, and was one of the few who organized the Free-Soil party in Ohio.

General Swaim received an academic education in his native State, studied law, and was admitted to the bar in 1859. He has always been a Republican in politics, and, although young in years, took an active part in the Presidential campaign of 1860. In 1861 he entered the army as first lieutenant of the Sixty-fifth Ohio Volunteers (Sherman's brigade), and soon after taking the field was promoted adjutant of the regiment, and acting adjutant-general of the brigade to which his regiment was attached in the Army of the Ohio (afterwards the Army of the Cumberland), commanded successively by Generals Buell, Rosecrans, and Thomas. He participated in the campaigns and battles of those armies, among others the battles of Shiloh (where he was slightly wounded), Perryville, Kentucky; Chickamauga (where he was injured by the killing of the horse on which he was mounted), and Missionary Ridge. For his services at the battle of Shiloh he was promoted captain and assistant adjutant-general of volunteers; and after the battle of Stone River he was assigned to the staff of the general commanding the Army of the Cumberland. He served through the entire period of the war of the Rebellion, and was several times promoted, and was retained on staff duty more than a year after the actual close of the war, and was mustered out in October, 1866, as assistant adjutant-general, with the rank of major and brevet colonel of volunteers. In February, 1867, he was commissioned in the permanent military establishment, and on account of his legal abilities and successful services on military courts, he was assigned to duty as judge-advocate of the Fourth Military District at Vicksburg, Mississippi, where, as counsel for the government, he successfully argued against eminent counsel the celebrated *habeas corpus* case of *ex parte* McCardle, involving the constitutionality of the Reconstruction Acts of Congress, before the Circuit Court of the United States for the District of Mississippi; and was of counsel in arguing the case on appeal in the Supreme Court of the United States. In 1869 he was appointed major and judge-advocate in the U. S. Army, and was assigned to duty at headquarters of the Military Department of the Missouri, which position he filled for more than ten years, and on many occasions during that period he was, by special detail of the Secretary of War, designated to officiate as judge-advocate of courts-martial in the trial of important cases in different parts of the country. He also appeared as counsel for the government before the ordinary courts of law in matters affecting military jurisdiction and administration.

In December, 1879, President Hayes appointed him judge-advocate-general of the army, with the rank of brigadier-general, which he now holds. Upon his assignment to duty as judge-advocate-general, thus severing his connection with the Department of the Missouri as its judge-advocate, the commanding general of the department issued the following in a general order:

"Official notice having been received of the appointment of Major D. G. Swaim, judge-advocate, to be judge-advocate-general of the army, the immediate connection of that officer with this department is terminated. This appointment is so public and splendid a recognition by the highest officials of the government of the ability and efficiency with which he has, during a period of more than ten years, discharged the duties of judge-advocate of this department, that it would be superfluous, and perhaps unbecoming, in the department commander to add the commendation which he so deeply feels.

"The appointment, however, involves the disruption of personal and official ties which have been cemented by so many years of intimate intercourse, and the department commander cannot fail to regret this, while he congratulates General Swaim on his deserved promotion."

It will be remembered that General Swaim was the devoted friend of the late President Garfield; and was his trusted friend and companion all through the fatal hours that attended the close of that noble life.

## COLONEL PETER T. SWAINE, U.S.A.

COLONEL PETER T. SWAINE (Twenty-second Infantry) was born in New York City, Jan. 21, 1831; in military service since Sept. 1, 1847; a graduate of U. S. Military Academy; a commissioned officer since July 1, 1852.

He was on continuous frontier duty prior to the war of the Rebellion. At the breaking out of the war was engaged in the preparatory work of advancing the efficiency of regular and State troops in Cincinnati and vicinity, compiling for their instruction several military works.

Commanded a battalion Fifteenth U. S. Infantry, and joined the volunteer force (the nucleus of the Army of the Cumberland), at Louisville, September 20, 1861, proceeding under Sherman to Muldraugh's Hill. Advanced with his army (the battalion enlarged to eight companies), through Kentucky into Tennessee, participating in the battle of Shiloh and the siege of Corinth. Was favorably mentioned in Rousseau's report of the battle as "conspicuous for good conduct, and strongly recommended as a soldier by profession who has shown himself fit for higher offices of usefulness." Was favorably mentioned in King's report of battle as "entitled to special notice for the discipline and manœuvring of his command."

Was called to the aid of General Lew Wallace in the defence of Newport, Covington, and Cincinnati, against the forces of General Kirby Smith, and appointed colonel of the Ninety-ninth Ohio Infantry September 2, 1862; constructed rifle-pits, strengthened fortifications, and commanded the volunteers and irregular riflemen assembling there. Upon the withdrawal of the enemy was assigned to the command of a large force of the combined arms of the service for the relief of Lexington, which was effected. Subsequently commanded the Second Brigade, First Division, Department of the Ohio, and upon reorganization was assigned to the command of the Second Brigade, Third Division, Army of Kentucky, October, 1862. Voluntarily relinquished command of brigade to command his regiment on learning that it was badly in need of instruction, serving in command of it in Third Brigade, Third Division, left wing Army of the Cumberland, in the Stone River campaign, and was severely wounded in that battle. The brigade commander, Price, in his report of that battle, states, "that officers and men of the Ninety-ninth Ohio commanded by him deserve special praise for their gallantry."

Was assigned the command of three regiments of infantry, a battery, and a section of another battery, Sept. 18, 1863, in the Chickamauga campaign, and directed to occupy a commanding position on the front, which was accomplished. This position was maintained until two o'clock P.M., of the 19th, when the elements composing this temporary command were returned to their proper brigades, and he assigned to command of two regiments of infantry during rest of the battle, that day and the next, doing valiant service, as noted in the reports of his military superiors. Received favorable notice in Rosecrans's report of battle of Chickamauga, which quotes the special remarks of his two immediate commanders.

Was mentioned in the report of General A. Baird, commanding a division, as "an officer from another division, commanding two regiments, brought into action near his own, whom he was glad to mention to the commanding general."

The report of General H. P. Van Cleve, his division commander, referring to his assignment to the special command on the 18th and 19th, states that "in posting his troops he displayed, as I have noticed on other occasions, much judgment and skill; that his conduct on the field received the commendations of his brigade commander, and he commends him to the notice of the general commanding."

Was frequently alluded to in the report of his brigade commander in favorable terms, the report closing with the remark that "he acted well his part and gave evidence of undoubted courage and ability to command."

Was placed in command of all brigades and regiments occupying Missionary Ridge the day after the battle, and retained in command of all outposts and pickets of the left wing of the army when it was drawn within the fortifications of Chattanooga until late in the fall of 1863.

Was transferred with his regiment to the Twenty-third Army Corps, to command the Second Brigade of the First Div. during the invasion of Georgia by Sherman, participating in all the engagements to and including siege of Atlanta, leading the corps and army in the flank attack on Kenesaw Mountain, and capture of Decatur in front of Atlanta by a charge in line of this brigade. He received three brevets. Has commanded various districts and posts in Southern States and on the frontier since the war.

### GENERAL WAGER SWAYNE, U.S.A. (RETIRED).

GENERAL WAGER SWAYNE was born in Columbus, Ohio, 10th of November, 1834; was graduated at Yale in 1856, and at the Cincinnati Law School in 1859. On his admission to the bar he practised in Columbus. He was appointed major of the Forty-third Ohio Volunteers on August 31, 1861; became lieutenant-colonel December 14, 1861; colonel on October 18, 1862; served in all the marches and battles of the Atlanta campaign; lost a leg at Salkehatchie, South Carolina, and was brevetted brigadier-general U. S. Volunteers on February 5, 1865, becoming full brigadier-general on March 8, 1865, and major-general on June 20, 1865. He was made colonel of the Forty-fifth Regular Infantry on July 28, 1866, and on March 2, 1867, was brevetted brigadier-general, U. S. Army, for gallant and meritorious services in the action of River's Bridge, South Carolina, and major-general for services during the war. He was mustered out of the volunteer service on September 1, 1867. General Swayne was a commissioner of the Freedmen's Bureau in Alabama, where he commanded the U. S. forces, and was also intrusted with the administration of the reconstruction acts of Congress, organizing an extensive system of common schools for colored children, who had none, and establishing at Montgomery, Selma, and Mobile, important high schools, which still remain, and also Talladega College. He retired on July 1, 1870, and practised law in Toledo, Ohio, but in 1880 he removed to New York City, where he is counsel for railroad and telegraph corporations. His ancestor, Francis Swayne, came to this country with William Penn, and the farm on which he settled is still in possession of his descendants. Wager's father, Noah Haynes Swayne, was an eminent jurist in Culpeper County, Virginia. The trial of William Rossane and others, in the U. S. Circuit Court, at Columbus, in 1853, for burning the steamboat "Martha Washington" to obtain the insurance, was one of his most celebrated cases.

## BRIGADIER-GENERAL THOMAS W. SWEENY, U.S.A.
(DECEASED)

BRIGADIER-GENERAL THOMAS W. SWEENY was born in Cork, Ireland, December 25, 1820, and came to the United States in 1832, settling in New York, where he was apprenticed as a printer. When a young man he joined the Independent Tompkins Blues, then one of the crack military organizations of the metropolis.

At the breaking out of the Mexican War he joined Colonel Ward B. Burnett's First Regiment of New York Volunteers, being elected second lieutenant.

Lieutenant Sweeny participated in the campaign under General Scott to the storming of Churubusco. He was severely wounded at Cerro Gordo. At Churubusco he was twice wounded, receiving a ball in the groin and another in his right arm, "but nevertheless continued to lead and animate his men till he sank from exhaustion and loss of blood and had to be carried to the rear." The wound in his arm proved so serious that amputation was deemed necessary, and was accordingly performed.

On his return to New York, in 1848, he received a brevet of captain and a silver medal from the city of New York. He was also given a grand reception ball at Castle Garden by the printers of the city, which was a notable affair, the guests comprising ex-President of the United States Martin Van Buren, Major-General John A. Quitman, Hon. Simon Cameron, United States Senator William B. Maclay, and representatives of the city and State government.

He was soon after commissioned second lieutenant in the Second U. S. Infantry, and served in California and in the Western States, engaging in frequent actions with hostile Indians.

He was made captain January 19, 1861. At the outbreak of the Civil War he was ordered to St. Louis and given the command of the United States Arsenal.

He was second in command of the Union troops at the surrender of Camp Jackson, and, in consequence of General Lyon being disabled, conducted the final negotiations. Subsequently he was instrumental in the organization of the Missouri three months' volunteers, and was appointed brigadier-general of the Fourth United States Reserve Corps, May 20, 1861.

In the battle of Wilson's Creek he led the Second Kansas Regiment, General Lyon leading the First Iowa. Of General Sweeny's conduct in this engagement, General Sturgis, in his official report, says, "This gallant officer was especially distinguished by his zeal in rallying broken fragments of various regiments (even after receiving a severe wound in his leg) and leading them into the hottest of the fight."

He afterwards accepted the command of the Fifty-second Illinois Volunteers, and was attached to the army of General Grant, participating in the capture of Fort Donelson, after which he took six thousand prisoners to Alton, Illinois.

At Shiloh he was again wounded, receiving a bullet in his leg, and another in his remaining arm. Toward the close of the first day's battle, a gap existed between the right flank of Sweeny's brigade and General William T. Sherman's left. The defence of this position, which was the key of the situation, was intrusted to him by Sherman, who has since said, "He held it, and I attach more importance to that event than to any of the hundred achievements which I have since heard saved the day."

General Sweeny was commissioned brigadier-general November 29, 1862, and thereafter commanded a division of the Sixteenth Army Corps.

He was promoted major of the Sixteenth U. S. Infantry October 20, 1863, and in the Atlanta campaign commanded the Second Division of the Sixteenth Corps of the Army of the Tennessee. At Snake Creek Gap his command took possession of the Gap twenty-four hours in advance of the cavalry, and held it, in spite of the desperate efforts of the enemy to dislodge him. He took part in the battle of Resaca, and forced a passage across the Oostenaula River at Lay's Ferry, where he fought a successful battle, which resulted in General Joseph E. Johnston's retreat southward.

He also participated in the battles of Dallas and Kenesaw Mountain; and at the battle before Atlanta, July 22, 1864, his division drove the enemy back with great loss, capturing four battle-flags and nine hundred prisoners.

General Sweeny was mustered out of the volunteer service August 24, 1865. He afterwards was placed in command of various posts in the Southern States. He received an elegant gold sword from the city of Brooklyn for his services in the Rebellion. General Sweeny was retired with the full rank of brigadier-general May 11, 1870, and died at Astoria, Long Island, April 10, 1892.

CAPTAIN OWEN J. SWEET, U.S.A.

CAPTAIN OWEN J. SWEET (Twenty-fifth Infantry) was born in Kent, Connecticut, September 4, 1845. He entered the service as second lieutenant of the One Hundred and Thirty-seventh New York Infantry, September 6, 1862. He served in the Third Brigade, Second Division, Twelfth Army Corps, Army of the Potomac. During the year 1862, in skirmishes at Bolivar Heights, Hallstown, Charlestown, Berryville, and near Winchester, Virginia; March 19, 1863, promoted first lieutenant One Hundred and Thirty-seventh New York Infantry; 1863, in skirmishes at Occoquan Creek, Dumfries, Snicker's, and Manassas Gaps, Virginia; Fairfield, Maryland; battles of Fredericksburg and Chancellorsville, Virginia, and Gettysburg, Pennsylvania, where, when seventeen years of age, on the night of July 2, after his regiment, which had been holding a brigade front against repeated assaults by General Ewell's corps, was compelled to change its position; and orders being given to hold Culp's Hill to the death, he called for volunteers and advanced against the flank, and finally into the works in his front, and from an angle there directed such a persistent attack and destructive fire as to drive the rebels outside of the intrenchments, keeping them there until their force was spent, and they were compelled to retreat. Of the four officers with him, two were killed, one wounded, and one taken prisoner, and he narrowly escaped death, a bullet grazing his forehead. For his good judgment, energy, and conspicuous gallantry in this affair, he received on the field the special thanks of his immediate commander, Colonel David Ireland.

He was promoted captain, One Hundred and Thirty-seventh New York Infantry, March 12, 1864, and joined with the Army of the Cumberland (Twentieth Army Corps), 1864, in skirmishes at Villanow, Gordonsville, Snake Creek Gap, Pumpkin-Vine Creek, Big Shanty, Adairsville, Nickajack Creek, Smyrna Church, Steep Banks, Pace's and Turner's Ferry, Chattahoochee River, Macon Railroad, Decatur, and Stone Mountain; battles of Rocky-faced Ridge and Resaca (where, when commanding a division of his regiment, in the front line, in a charge on the rebel position, he gallantly aided in the capture of a four-gun intrenched battery), New Hope Church, Dallas, Allatoona, Lost Mountain, and Pine Mountains (where, being among the first to enter the enemy's breastworks, he was wounded in the shoulder), Nose's Creek, Culp's Farm, Marietta, Kenesaw Mountain, Peach-Tree Creek, and fighting in front, siege, and capture of Atlanta, Georgia.

Captain Sweet was also in the Army of Georgia, and participated in Sherman's "march to the sea;" in skirmishes at Davisborough, Milledgeville, Louisville, Sandersville, Millen, Buckhead Creek, Williamson Plantation; fighting in front, siege, and capture of Savannah, Georgia, where he was the first officer to enter the enemy's fortifications; in 1865, in Sherman's campaign through the Carolinas; in a skirmish at Blackville, Big and Little Edisto Rivers. Maxwell's, Meadow's, and New Bridges on the Blackwater; at the latter bridge he was in command of several hundred of "Sherman's Bummers;" he forced a passage under a destructive cavalry and artillery fire, crossing his command on fence-rails laid on the bridge timbers, turned and drove the enemy before him and from the upper bridges, enabling his division and corps train to cross. For his activity, skill, and marked gallantry in this affair, he received the special thanks of Brevet Major-General John W. Geary, commanding Second Division, Twentieth Army Corps. Lexington Court-House, Williams's Mill, McDaniel's, Evans's, and Sikes's Plantation, Fayettville, Cheraw, Jackson's Cross-Roads, Winsborough, Wadesborough, on Little River, Goldsborough, Smithfield, Raleigh, and Jones's Cross-Roads; battles of Averysborough and Bentonville, North Carolina.

Commissioned brevet major New York Volunteers by the governor of New York, for "gallant and meritorious services during the Rebellion," March 13, 1865. Since the war, Capt. Sweet has served in N. C., in expeditions against Indians in Cal. and Texas, and Indian Territory.

He was promoted captain, Twenty-fifth U. S. Infantry, October 10, 1886. In May, 1890, he was charged with the supervision of marking the boundary-lines of the Custer Battle-field National Cemetery, and the erection of the head-stones designated to mark the places on the battle-field of the Little Big Horn, Montana, where General Custer and five troops of his command, Seventh U. S. Cavalry, fell in battle with the Sioux Indians, June 25, 1876. Present station, Fort Custer, Montana, where he is commanding Company D, Twenty-fifth U. S. Infantry.

## COLONEL AND BREVET BRIGADIER-GENERAL NELSON B. SWEITZER, U.S.A. (RETIRED).

COLONEL AND BREVET BRIGADIER-GENERAL NELSON B. SWEITZER was born in Pennsylvania, December 12, 1828, and graduated from the Military Academy July 1, 1853. He was promoted brevet second lieutenant of the Second Dragoons the same day; second lieutenant July 25, 1854, and first lieutenant First Dragoons September 24, 1855. He served at the cavalry depots until 1854, and then joined his regiment in New Mexico. He was at Fort Lane, Oregon, from the spring of 1855 to the summer of 1856, and was engaged campaigning against and fighting Pacific coast Indians, the last of which ended by surrender and removal of all Indians in Southern Oregon to reservations in Northeastern Oregon.

Joined Troop " E" at Walla Walla, W. T., as first lieutenant, fall of 1856, and commanded escort to Wagon-road Expedition, from Fort Dallas, Oregon, to Salt Lake, Utah, during summer and fall of 1859. He was promoted captain, First Cavalry, May 7, 1861, and was appointed lieutenant-colonel and additional aide de-camp, September 28, 1861, on the staff of General McClellan, with whom he took the field, and participated in all the campaigns under that officer and others. He was engaged in so many actions, skirmishes, combats, and battles that it is impossible to find room for them in this sketch. He accompanied General McClellan to New York on his being relieved from command of Army of the Potomac, November 10, 1862, and assisted writing report of operations of Army of the Potomac until July, 1863; applied to join Army of the Potomac; took command First United States Cavalry, Cavalry Corps Army of the Potomac.

He was selected by order of General Sheridan to take First and Second U. S. Cavalry and dislodge, at any cost, enemy from ridge commanding Meadow Bridge, General Custer reporting his being unable to dislodge them with his brigade; the two regiments dislodged the enemy.

Colonel Sweitzer was with General Sheridan in the Shenandoah campaign, and in combats at Berryville, Stone Church, New Town, Front Royal, Shepherdstown, at Smithfield, made a sabre charge with the First Cavalry on the advance of the enemy, consisting of a regiment and battalion, and drove them back on the main body of the enemy, disabling and capturing a number. He was appointed colonel of the Sixteenth New York Cavalry, November 12, 1864, and he was, on the assassination of President Lincoln, with his regiment ordered to Washington, April 16, 1865; patrolled Southern Maryland and Virginia, between Potomac and James Rivers, for assassins of the President; Booth, the assassin, killed, and Harold and Mudd, conspirators, were arrested by a detachment of the regiment.

At the close of the war he was brevetted in the regu-

lar service from major to brigadier-general, for " gallant and meritorious services;" and was also brevetted brigadier-general of volunteers. He was in command of the District of the Northern Neck, Virginia, from May to September, 1865; proceeded to New York with regiment, and honorably mustered out of volunteer service September 21, 1865. Commanded battalion Fifth Cavalry and Sedgwick Barracks, Washington, D. C.; joined Second Cavalry as major, dating July 28, 1866, at Fort Laramie, Wyoming; scouted North Platte and Sweet-water country to South Pass; re-established telegraph stations and lines destroyed by Indians; selected location for Fort Fetterman; established route for road from proposed site of Fort Fetterman on North Platte south to projected line of Union Pacific Railroad on Laramie Plains; sent with battalion of Second Cavalry to patrol road and protect supply trains from Sioux Indians on road leading from North Platte to Forts Reno, Phil. Kearney, and C. F. Smith, in Powder River and Big Horn country, until October 20, 1867; inspector-general, Department of the Platte, April, 1868, to March, 1871; engaged in scouting country of Platte and Loup Rivers until October, 1872; March, 1873, at Fort Ellis, Montana, to September, 1875; guarding Gallatin Valley and scouting country from Yellowstone to Musselshell and Missouri Rivers; took command of Fort Sanders, Feb. 1877, and regiment; joined Eighth Cavalry as lieut.-col. June 1877; took command of regiment and District of the Rio Grande, from Fort Brown to Fort McIntosh, Texas; served in Department of Texas to March, 1886. Promoted colonel Second Cavalry, to date from January 9, 1886.

On Retiring Board, detailed by authority of the President, Dec. 18, 1885, to April, 1886; at Fort Walla Walla, Washington Territory, May 1, 1886, to Oct. 29, 1888.

Retired on his own application October 29, 1888.

PAYMASTER JOHN F. TARBELL, U.S.N.

PAYMASTER JOHN F. TARBELL received his appointment as acting assistant paymaster, U.S.N., January 28, 1862, and was immediately ordered to join the U. S. S. "Kensington," then fitting out at the Boston Navy-Yard. In February sailed for Port Royal, towing the U. S. S. "Vermont." During a gale had to cut loose from the "Vermont" in the night, she losing her rudder and being adrift for some time before arriving at Port Royal. In May joined Admiral Farragut's squadron off the Passes of the Mississippi, and went up with the fleet to New Orleans. Went to Vicksburg with Porter's bomb flotilla; was attacked by rebel batteries at Grand Gulf and lost several men; was chased down the river by rebel ram "Arkansas," when she passed our fleet at Vicksburg. Present at the capture of Sabine Pass, Texas, in which action he commanded a boat, and was favorably mentioned by his commanding officer. Blockading off Galveston and coast of Texas. In 1864 and 1865 was attached to the U. S. S. "Neptune," convoying the California steamers from New York to Aspinwall. In 1867 was attached to U. S. S. "Marblehead," in the West Indies. Had been commissioned, February 21, 1867, an assistant paymaster in the regular navy.

On September 16, 1868, was promoted to a passed assistant paymaster, and in January, 1870, joined the U. S. S. "Wasp," South Atlantic Station, where he served three years. From 1873 to 1876 was paymaster of the Torpedo Station at Newport. From 1876 to 1879 was attached to U. S. S. "Gettysburg," on the European Station. On April 3, 1879, was promoted to paymaster, and from 1881 to 1885 was paymaster of the Portsmouth and Boston Navy-Yards.

From 1885 to 1887 was attached to the U. S. S. "Juniata," on South Pacific Station. From 1887 to 1890 was paymaster of the Boston Navy-Yard and U. S. receiving-ship "Wabash." At present time is upon sick-leave.

Paymaster Tarbell was born at Pepperell, Massachusetts, on January 8, 1840; and before entering the service was a clerk in a merchant's office in Boston.

## FIRST LIEUTENANT ALEXANDER H. M. TAYLOR, U.S.A.

FIRST LIEUTENANT ALEXANDER H. M. TAYLOR (Nineteenth Infantry) entered the military service as a recruiting officer, at New York City, April 22, 1861, and was mustered in as a private of Company B, Eighty-third New York Volunteer Infantry (Ninth New York State Militia), November 30, 1861.

He was commissioned as second lieutenant of Company F, President's Life Guard (afterwards Company A, Fifty-ninth New York Volunteers), August 19, 1861, but the appointment was revoked on the consolidation of regiments. He had recruited some sixty men for the regiment.

Lieutenant Taylor then enlisted in the regular army, and was made a sergeant of the general service September 10, 1862, but was honorably discharged, April 30, 1863, on account of having been appointed chief clerk of the Volunteer Bureau of the War Department. He remained on this duty until commissioned as second lieutenant of the Seventeenth U. S. Infantry. He was promoted first lieutenant of the same regiment September 1, 1867, and, on the consolidation of regiments, was honorably discharged December 1, 1870.

He re-entered the service as hospital-steward on May 24, 1872, and was appointed a second lieutenant of the Nineteenth U. S. Infantry October 1, 1873. He was promoted first lieutenant November 24, 1879, and has served with his regiment in various parts of the country up to the present time.

Lieutenant Taylor's duties have been varied and responsible,—adjutant, quartermaster, and adjutant-general of a district, aide-de-camp to the late Major-General Charles Griffin, and a variety of public demands in the service,—all of which have given him a valuable experience, and rendered him an officer capable of meeting expectations of his superiors, no matter what the exigency or nature of the duty upon which placed.

Lieutenant Taylor, though born in England, is an American, his father belonging to the Taylors of Saratoga County, New York, of which John W. Taylor was such a distinguished representative. On his mother's side he is descended from the Pelham family of Suffolk, England, one member of which, Herbert, was prominent as a member of the Massachusetts Company in England in colonial times.

## MEDICAL DIRECTOR JOHN Y. TAYLOR, U.S.N.
### (RETIRED)

MEDICAL DIRECTOR JOHN Y. TAYLOR was born January 21, 1829, at East Nottingham, Chester County, Pennsylvania, and is a graduate of Jefferson Medical College, Philadelphia, Pennsylvania. He entered the United States naval service, appointed from Delaware, as an assistant surgeon, September 26, 1853, and was ordered, in December of that year, to the U. S. S. "Decatur," at Boston, Massachusetts.

After refitting at Norfolk, Virginia, the "Decatur" joined the Pacific Squadron via the straits of Magellan. The ship was nearly three months contending with adverse weather in the straits, and was reported in the United States as lost.

During this cruise in the Pacific, the Indian war in Washington Territory broke out, and the "Decatur" was sent to Puget Sound to co-operate with the small force of regular troops then in the Territory. In addition to duty performed on shore with the seamen and marines belonging to the ship, Assistant Surgeon Taylor served as a volunteer, with the Fourth U. S. Infantry and Washington Territory Volunteers, in a winter campaign (1855-56) through the region occupied by the hostile Klikitats, Yakimas, and Klalams, and portions of other tribes in alliance with them. Several indecisive encounters took place with the hostiles, as at the Ford of the Puyalup River, Brannan's Prairie, and Seattle, then an insignificant settlement.

He was promoted to passed assistant surgeon, September 26, 1858, while attached to the U. S. S. "Preble," school-ship, and later detailed as one of the vessels of the Paraguayan Expedition.

He was promoted to surgeon, August 1, 1861, and in December following ordered as medical officer of the U. S. S. "Oneida," fitting out at New York for the West Gulf Blockading Squadron. The "Oneida" participated (April, 1862) in the attacks upon and passage of Forts Jackson and St. Philip, the destruction of the enemy's flotilla on the lower Mississippi, and the silencing of the Chalmette batteries, below New Orleans.

After the fall of that city she proceeded with the advance division of gun-boats to Vicksburg, Mississippi, and was engaged with the Confederate ram "Arkansas" (July 15) and the Vicksburg batteries at various times, running these fortifications twice in company with other vessels of the fleet.

On the 5th of August, 1864, the "Oneida" was a part of the naval force which attacked Forts Morgan and Gaines, and the Confederate vessels "Tennessee," "Morgan," "Gaines," and "Selma," in Mobile Bay. In passing Fort Morgan, the wooden ships were lashed together in pairs, and the "Oneida's" position being at the rear of the line, she suffered severely after the others had ceased firing. Her casualties in killed and wounded on this occasion amounted to thirty-eight, out of a complement of one hundred and ninety-six officers and men, or nearly twenty per cent. She was struck thirty-two times in hull and rigging; the starboard boiler was exploded by a shell, scalding seventeen men; many of her guns, including the eleven-inch after-pivot, were dismounted or disabled, and the ship was twice on fire.

Detached from the "Oneida" and returned home in September, 1864, and having applied for sea-duty, received immediately telegraphic orders to the U. S. S. "Tuscarora," of the South Atlantic Blockading Squadron. This vessel took part in the bombardment of Fort Fisher, North Carolina, December 25, 1864, and the attack of January 15, 1865; and at the close of the war was sent North to be put out of commission, convoying on the way the steamer "W. P. Clyde," with the ex-president of the Southern Confederacy, to Fortress Monroe, and carrying as passengers to Fort Warren, Boston harbor, the ex-vice-president and ex-postmaster-general of the Southern Confederacy.

The next service was a tour of duty at the United States Naval Hospital, New York, followed by orders to the U. S. S. "Kenosha," afterwards named "Plymouth," for a cruise of forty-two months in European waters, and on the coast of Africa. Promoted to medical inspector, June 29, 1882, and subsequently ordered as fleet-surgeon of the North Atlantic Squadron, flag-ship "Powhatan." Promoted to medical director April 20, 1879. In charge of the United States Naval Hospital, Washington, D. C., May 1, 1879. In charge of United States Naval Hospital, Norfolk, Virginia, June 20, 1883. In charge of United States Naval Hospital, New York, October 1, 1886. President of Naval Examining Board and Naval Medical Board, November 26, 1889. Retired January 21, 1891.

## MAJOR-GENERAL ALFRED H. TERRY, U.S.A.
### (RETIRED).

MAJOR-GENERAL ALFRED H. TERRY was born in Hartford, Connecticut, November 10, 1827. He was educated in the schools of New Haven, and at the Yale Law School. He began the practice of his profession in 1849, and was clerk of the Superior and Supreme Courts of Connecticut from 1854 to 1860. He was in command of the Second Regiment of Connecticut militia when the Civil War began. In response to President Lincoln's call for three months' troops, he was appointed colonel of the Second Conn. Vol., and with that regiment was present at the first battle of Bull Run. At the expiration of the term of service he returned to Connecticut, organized the Seventh Connecticut Volunteers, of which he was appointed colonel, and on September 17 he was present at the capture of Port Royal, South Carolina, and also at the siege of Fort Pulaski, of which he was placed in charge after its capitulation. On April 25, 1862, he was promoted brigadier-general of volunteers, and he served at the battle of Pocotaligo, and in the operations against Charleston. He commanded the demonstration up Stono River during the descent on Morris Island and at the action on James Island, and he was assigned by General Q. A. Gillmore to command the troops on Morris Island, which post he held during the siege of Forts Wagner and Sumter.

After the reduction of Fort Wagner he was assigned to the command of the Northern District of the Department of the South, including the islands from which operations against Charleston had been carried on. General Terry commanded the First Division of the Tenth Army Corps, Army of the James, during the Virginia campaign of 1864, and at times the corps itself. He was brevetted major-general of volunteers on August 20, 1864, became permanent commander of the Tenth Corps in October, and held that place until the corps was merged in the Twenty-fourth the following December, when he was assigned to head the First Division of the new corps. He commanded at the action of Chester Station, and was engaged at the battle of Drury's Bluff, the various combats in front of the Bermuda Hundred lines, the battle of Fussell's Mills, the action of Deep Bottom, the siege of Petersburg, the actions at Newmarket Heights on the Newmarket Road, the Darbytown Road, and the Williamsburg Road. On January 2, 1865, after the failure of the first attempt to take Fort Fisher, which commanded the sea approaches to Wilmington, North Carolina, General Terry was ordered to renew the attack with a force numbering a little over eight thousand men. On the 13th he debarked his troops about five miles above the fort, and finding himself confronted by General Robert F. Hoke's Confederate division, proceeded to throw a line of strong intrenchments across the peninsula between the sea and Cape Fear River, facing toward Wilmington, and about two miles north of the fort. After the landing of the troops, the co-operating fleet under Admiral David D. Porter, numbering forty-four vessels, and mounting upward of five hundred guns, opened fire upon the work, and from 4.30 to 6 P.M., four shots a second, or twenty thousand in all, were fired. This was the heaviest bombardment of the war. On the 14th the line of intrenchment was completed, and General Charles J. Paine's division of infantry was placed upon it. While this was in progress, General Terry made a reconnoissance of the fort, and in view of the difficulty of landing supplies for his troops and the materials for a siege upon an open, unprotected beach in midwinter, he determined to carry the work by assault the next day, and the plan of attack was arranged the next day with Admiral Porter. At 11 A.M. on the 15th, the entire fleet opened fire, silencing nearly every gun in the fort. Admiral Porter landed two thousand sailors and marines; gained the parapet by hand-to-hand fighting of the most obstinate character, and by five o'clock nine of the traverses of the fort which had been constructed were carried, and General Terry ordered up reinforcements, consisting of a brigade and the sailors and marines, taking their places there; by nine o'clock two more traverses were carried, and one hour later the occupation of the work was complete, and the Confederate force surrendered. For this General Terry was promoted to be brigadier-general in the regular army and major-general of volunteers, and received the thanks of Congress. He was brevetted major-general in the regular army on March 13, 1865, for his services at the capture of Wilmington. He was promoted to the rank of major-general March 3, 1866, serving in charge of the Division of the Missouri until his retirement in April, 1888.

### COMMANDER SILAS WRIGHT TERRY, U.S.N.

COMMANDER SILAS WRIGHT TERRY was born in Kentucky, December, 1842; entered the Naval Academy, September, 1858. Ensign September, 1862. Commissioned lieutenant February, 1864. Lieutenant-commander, July, 1866. Commissioned commander July, 1877. At the outbreak of the Rebellion, before completing his academic course, this officer was ordered into active service. Was in "Dale" and "Wabash" on Atlantic coast, and engagements with sharp-shooters in "Edisto" during boat expedition. Aid to Rear-Admiral Lee for some time, then attached to "Dacotah," blockading Cape Fear River. Thence he went to the flag-flag-ship "Black Hawk," on the Mississippi. Took part in the Red River expedition, and at Alexandria, Louisiana, was placed in command of transport "Benefit," with fifty men and two howitzers, to carry despatches and supplies to Porter. We regret that space does not allow the full recountal of how he fought his way up the river; he had his river-captain and three men killed in reaching Admiral Porter, who handsomely acknowledged this service. Lieutenant Terry was advanced five numbers in his grade " for gallant conduct on expedition up Red River." In May, 1864, he was appointed detail officer on the staff of Admiral Porter, and served in that capacity until the close of the war. He was present at the operations at Forts Fisher and Anderson, and the capture of Wilmington, as well as at the fall of Richmond, accompanying President Lincoln and Admiral Porter on the morning that city was occupied by General Grant's forces. After the close of the Civil War he made a cruise in the " Ticonderoga," on the European Station, and then served at the Naval Academy for two years. He was executive officer of the flag-ships " Severn" and " Worcester;" and then was attached to the Naval Observatory for one year, passing to the Naval Academy, and thence to the inspectorship of the Fifth Light-House District.

He was next in command of the " Marion," South Atlantic Station, during which cruise he was ordered to Heard's Island, latitude 53° 20′ south, longitude 73° 30′ east, to rescue the crew of the bark " Trinity." He reached the island, after coaling at Cape Town, on January 15, 1882, and rescued thirty-three of the " Trinity's" crew, who had been there since October, 1880. The men were on the point of starvation. The " Marion" returned to Cape Town on February 20, 1882, and Commander Terry's despatch announcing the rescue was received in Washington the same day. Commander Terry was at once requested by Lloyd's agents to assist the English ship " Poonah," on the beach a few miles off. The English commodore had declined to render assistance, but the " Marion" was successful in getting the vessel off. Sir Hercules Robinson, the governor of Cape Colony, tendered to Commander Terry and his officers and crew official thanks; and the British government, on representations made by the governor of Cape Colony, wrote a letter of thanks to Commander Terry, through the British Minister at Washington and the Department of State.

From April, 1883, to October, 1884, Commander Terry was stationed at the League Island Navy-Yard. From October, 1884, to May 26, 1886, he commanded the Training Squadron, comprising the " Portsmouth," " Jamestown," and " Saratoga." In October, 1885, the vessels of the squadron were inspected, at Newport, Rhode Island, by the chief of the Bureau of Equipment and Recruiting, who addressed an official communication to Commander Terry, after the inspection, in which he says, "The zeal and interest shown by the officers, the skill and knowledge of their duties shown by the apprentices, and the excellent condition of the several vessels, alike reflected the greatest credit on all concerned."

In October, 1887, Commander Terry was appointed member of the Naval Examining and Retiring Boards, where he is at present.

# REAR-ADMIRAL HENRY KNOX THATCHER, U.S.N.
### (DECEASED).

REAR-ADMIRAL HENRY KNOX THATCHER was born in Maine, at the seat of his grandfather, Major-General Henry Knox,—who was one of the most remarkable men the Revolutionary War produced,—the organizer of the artillery of the Continental troops, and the recipient of the surrender of New York City, by the British, when they took their final departure. His other functions, including a service of eleven years as Secretary of War, are well known to all Americans who read.

His grandson, Henry Knox Thatcher, was appointed midshipman in March, 1823. He served in the equipment of the elder Porter's "Mosquito Fleet," and then in the "United States," frigate, under Commander Isaac Hull. Passing, in 1829, he served on board the "Independence," 74, and as master, in two vessels of the West India Squadron, under Commodore Elliot.

He was made lieutenant in February, 1833. Served at Boston Navy-Yard, and in a few months went to the West Indies again,—in the "Falmouth" and then in the "Erie." After some shore service at Boston, he went to the Mediterranean in the "Brandywine," frigate, and returned from that cruise to be stationed in Boston again. He then, on going to sea again, served, from 1847 to 1853, in the African, the Mediterranean, and the Brazil Squadron,—in which latter he commanded the "Relief."

In 1854 he was ordered to duty at the Naval Asylum at Philadelphia, but, being promoted to commander in February, 1855, he went to the command of the sloop-of-war "Decatur" in the Pacific. In 1860-61 he was executive-officer of the Boston Navy-Yard, and in 1862-63 commanded the "Constellation" on the European Station.

He was promoted to commodore during this command, and relieved, in July, 1863, and ordered home to command the steam-frigate "Colorado" and a division of the Southern blockade. He commanded the First Division of the squadron in the attacks upon and capture of Fort Fisher and its dependencies, in December, 1864, and January, 1865. He was, after that, ordered to command the West Gulf Squadron, as acting rear-admiral, and at once commenced active operations for the capture of Mobile, and the possession of the coast of Texas, in co-operation—in the former case—with the land-forces under General Canby. There was a vigorous bombardment at Mobile of Fort Alexis and of Spanish Fort, after which they were carried by assault by the army on the night of April 9, 1865, which success left the minor works a comparatively easy prey to the forces.

In May, 1866, Commodore Thatcher was relieved from the command of the Gulf Squadron, and ordered to that of the North Pacific, in which command he remained until relieved, in August, 1868.

During his Pacific cruise he had been commissioned as rear-admiral, to date from July 25, 1866. He was post-admiral at Portsmouth, New Hampshire, from 1869 to 1871. He died in 1881.

### MAJOR-GENERAL GEORGE H. THOMAS, U.S.A.
(DECEASED).

MAJOR-GENERAL GEORGE H. THOMAS was born in Virginia, and graduated from the Military Academy July 1, 1840. He was promoted second lieutenant and assigned to the Third Artillery. He served in garrison at Fort Columbus, N. Y., until the Florida War, in which he participated. He assisted in Major Wade's capture of seventy Seminole Indians on Nov. 6, 1841, and was "brevetted first lieutenant, Nov. 6, 1841, for gallantry and good conduct against the Florida Indians."

From 1842 to 1845 he served in garrisons in the South and Southeast, and in 1845 participated in the military occupation of Texas; and when war was declared with Mexico he participated in the operations and movements thereof, being engaged in the defence of Fort Brown, in May, 1846, and the battles of Monterey and Buena Vista.

He was promoted first lieutenant April 30, 1846, and was brevetted captain, September 23, for gallant conduct in the several conflicts at Monterey, Mexico, and major, February 23, 1847, for gallant and meritorious conduct in the battle of Buena Vista, Mexico.

After the cessation of hostilities with Mexico the Seminole Indians again took the war-path, in which he participated. On December 4, 1853, he was promoted captain, and served in various sections of the country until the war of the Rebellion; being during the interim promoted major, Second Cavalry, May 12, 1855; April 25, 1861, he was promoted lieutenant-colonel, Second Cavalry; colonel, Second Cavalry, August 3, 1861, and on August 17, 1861, brigadier-general U. S. Volunteers. From June 1 to August 26, 1861, he participated in the operations in the Shenandoah Valley, being engaged in the various actions and skirmishes in that vicinity; and until May 30, 1862, he participated in the various movements and operations in the march to Nashville, Tennessee, and Corinth, Mississippi, being engaged in the actions and combats during the march.

He was appointed major-general, U.S. Volunteers, April 25, 1862, and was in command at Corinth, Mississippi, from June 5-22, 1862. During the operations in North Alabama, Tennessee, and Kentucky, from June 26 to November 7, 1862, he was with the Army of the Ohio, and participated in the many skirmishes, actions, and battles. From November 7, 1862, to October 19, 1863, he was with Major-General Rosecrans in the Tennessee campaign, in command of the Fourteenth Army Corps (Army of the Cumberland), and during the many hotly-contested encounters, from Nashville to Chattanooga, in which he participated, he was conspicuous for daring and gallantry on the field of battle. He was in command of the Department and Army of the Cumberland from October 19, 1863, being engaged in opening communications by the Tennessee River and Lookout Valley to November 26, 1863, participating in the battle of Missionary Ridge, the pursuit of the enemy, and combat at Ringgold, Georgia. He was promoted brigadier-general, U.S.A., October 22, 1863.

During the invasion of Georgia, May 2 to September 7, 1864, he was in command of the Army of the Cumberland, composed of the Fourth, Eleventh, and Twentieth Army Corps and three cavalry divisions, and with this command participated in the demonstrations and operations, in which were daily skirmishes and actions, to Atlanta, Georgia, occupying that city after a long siege. He was engaged in organizing the defences of Tennessee against the invasion of General Hood's army during the fall of 1864, and during the hotly-contested battles in the vicinity of Nashville, Tennessee. He was promoted major-general, U.S.A., December 15, 1864. He was in command of the Military Division of Tennessee, embracing the Departments of Kentucky, Tennessee, Georgia, Alabama, and Mississippi, with head-quarters at Nashville, from June 27, 1865, to Aug. 13, 1866, and of the Dept. of Tennessee from Aug. 13, 1866, to March 11, 1867, with head-quarters at Nashville, Tenn., and Louisville, Ky., when he was assigned to the Third Military District (Georgia, Florida, and Alabama), from which he was relieved at his own request, and of the Dept. of the Cumberland, March 16, 1867.

The Senate and House of Representatives of the United States, in Congress assembled, resolved, March 3, 1865,—

"That the thanks of Congress are due and are hereby tendered to Major-General George H. Thomas, and the officers and soldiers under his command, for their skill and dauntless courage, by which the rebel army under General Hood was signally defeated and driven from the State of Tennessee."

General Thomas died March 28, 1870.

## MAJOR AND BREVET BRIGADIER-GENERAL HENRY GODDARD THOMAS, U.S.A. (RETIRED).

MAJOR AND BREVET BRIGADIER - GENERAL HENRY GODDARD THOMAS was born April 5, 1837, at Portland, Maine. He is the son of William Widgery Thomas, Portland's war-mayor. Descends, on his father's side, from Isaiah Thomas, publisher of the first Bible in New England, and William Widgery, judge and member of Congress from Maine. On his mother's side he descends from Timothy Pickering, Washington's Postmaster-General, Secretary of War and State, etc. He graduated at Amherst College, Massachusetts, in 1858, Φ B K of that college; first assistant, Boys' High School, Portland, Maine, 1858–59; read law from October, 1859, to April, 1861; member Cumberland bar. Enlisted April 27, 1861; elected captain of his company (G, Fifth Maine), May 4, 1861.

First "smelled powder" at first Bull Run. His colonel, Mark H. Dunnell, since member of Congress from Minnesota, in his report of this battle, says of him: " . . . Captain Thomas exhibited a coolness and courage not surpassed by any other on the field." General O. O. Howard, commander of brigade, endorses this: " . . . On the day of battle I found you working hard to rally a broken line." From this and other recommendations, Captain Thomas was appointed captain, Eleventh U. S. Infantry, August 5, 1861.

In December, 1862, he was offered by Governor Andrew, of Massachusetts, who had the nomination thereto, the coloneley of one of the five colored regiments about to be raised in Louisiana. This he accepted, and was commissioned early in 1863, being the first regular officer to accept a colored regiment. In Louisiana he contracted a malarial fever, which developed, first, into a gastric and afterwards a typhoid fever. His youth and fine constitution enabled him to take the field again with the Eleventh Infantry in September, 1863,—serving with them through the campaign of 1863. In the winter of 1863–64, he was again appointed colonel, this time of the Nineteenth U. S. Colored Troops. After raising his regiment in Maryland, he was placed in command of Camp Birney, Baltimore, the largest post in the department. Taking the field (Army of the Potomac) at the head of three regiments, at the commencement of hostilities in April, 1864, he was assigned to command the Second Brigade, Fourth Division, Ninth Corps. He took part in all the battles of his command, from the Wilderness to the taking of Richmond, when he was assigned to the only separate command, that of Manchester, Virginia, where he extinguished the fires set by their own people and saved millions of property; saved the mills, operated them, and fed the people. He was transferred to the Army of the James, Twenty-fifth Corps, about New-Year's, 1865, and commanded the First Division of that corps for a short period, as also the corps temporarily in the absence of General Weitzel.

General Thomas was made brigadier-general Dec. 9, 1864, at the age of twenty-seven. In recommending him, General Burnside says, " His uniform good conduct, particularly his *conspicuous gallantry* before Petersburg, July 30, entitle him to the favorable consideration of the department." General Weitzel, taking leave of him at the close of the war, says, " His brigade is and always has been one of the finest in my corps." General B. F. Butler, recommending him for colonel (regular) at the close of the war, says, " His record as a gallant soldier and a true-hearted and attentive officer stands among the highest on every report of action or inspection."

He was appointed major Forty-first Infantry and declined it, because his medical advisers held that a return to the extreme South in his case would bring death or permanent invalidism. Since the war his service has been in the Indian country on our Western frontier, except a detail in Philadelphia during the Centennial of 1876. He received the brevets of major, lieutenant-colonel, colonel, and brigadier-general, U.S.A., and that of brevet major-general, volunteers. In 1878 he was transferred into the Pay Corps, U. S. A.

General Thomas has contributed somewhat to current literature in newspapers and magazines.

In 1884 he was present at the military manœuvres in Sweden and Norway, unaccredited, but as the guest of the king, and has contributed the military chapter to the late work on Sweden and the Swedes, by his brother, W. W. Thomas, Jr., minister to Sweden and Norway. Also the chapter on the " Colored Troops at Petersburg," in the *Century* War History, entitled " Battles and Leaders." His health having failed him, he was retired, July 2, 1891, after a continuous service of over thirty years.

## CAPTAIN J. M. THOMPSON, U.S.A.

CAPTAIN J. M. THOMPSON (Twenty-fourth Infantry) was born in Lebanon, New Hampshire, August 1, 1842. He enlisted as a private in Company E, Seventh New Hampshire Volunteers, November 7, 1861, and served with this regiment at Fort Jefferson, Florida, and Beaufort, South Carolina, until appointed second lieutenant, First South Carolina Volunteers, November 28, 1862. He was promoted first lieutenant January 27, 1863, and captain November 7, 1863. Designation of the regiment was changed to Thirty-third U. S. Colored Troops February 8, 1864. He was present during the siege of Charleston and minor operations from June, 1862, until capture of the city, in the command known as Department of the South, and designated as Tenth Army Corps. He was with expedition up St. Mary's River, Florida, January and February, 1863; in command of detachment in action with cavalry at Township, January 26, 1863; in expedition up St. John's River, Florida, for recapture of Jacksonville, March and April, 1863, participating in the engagement of Jacksonville, March 29. He was acting aide-de-camp of Kozlay's Brigade, June, 1864, and relieved to lead his company in the assault on Fort Lamar (front of Charleston). The First South Carolina Volunteers was the first colored regiment ever mustered into the United States service. Its officers were proclaimed outlaws and felons by the President of the Confederate States, in General Order No. 60, dated at Richmond August 21, 1862. (Its first colonel was Thomas Wentworth Higginson, of Massachusetts.) Commanding company at engagement on James Island, South Carolina, July 1 and 2, 1864; commanding company in assault on Fort Lamar, same dates and place.

After serving as brigade adjutant-general, provost-marshal, provost-judge, and commanding forces at Abbeville Court-House, and provost-marshal and treasurer of Charleston, from 1864 to 1866, he was honorably mustered out of service as captain, January 31, 1866.

Captain Thompson then entered the regular service as second lieutenant, Thirty-eighth Infantry, July 28, 1866, and was brevetted first lieutenant, March 2, 1867, for "gallant and meritorious services at James Island, S. C."

He joined his regiment at Jefferson Barracks in November, 1866, and was acting regimental adjutant from December 15, 1866, to May 4, 1867. He was promoted first lieutenant November 4, 1867. His regiment being transferred to Kansas in 1867, he served in various capacities at Forts Hays and Harker, and in the field until April, 1869, when he left Fort Harker in command of Company B, Thirty-eighth Infantry, en route to Fort Richardson, Texas, via Forts Hays, Dodge, Sill, Arbuckle, and Sherman, Texas, reaching Fort Richardson June 22, 1869, having marched six hundred and eighty-seven miles. He was transferred to the Twenty-fourth Infantry, August 23, 1869, on the consolidation of regiments, and served at Forts Richardson, Griffin, Clark, and McKavett, Texas. He was employed in scouting in the vicinity of San Saba River and Manardsville, after hostile Indians, in October and November, 1871; on expedition to the "Staked Plains" against hostile Indians in June, 1872, and on escort duty from August to October, 1872, returning from which was attacked by Indians in Sept. of that year, and in Dec. was ordered to Fort Brown, Texas.

Lieutenant Thompson was detailed on general recruiting service from March, 1875, to March, 1877, and was stationed at Newport Barracks, Kentucky, and Columbus Barracks, Ohio, and on leave of absence to May 1, 1877, when he rejoined his regiment at Ringgold Barracks, Texas, and was promoted captain December 23, 1878, which carried him to Fort McIntosh, Texas, from which post he was relieved October 27, 1880, and marched to Fort Sill, Indian Territory, a distance of eight hundred and fifteen miles. He was on detached service at Fort Leavenworth, Kansas, as executive-officer, in connection with the Department and Division Rifle Contest, in September and October, 1883, and rejoined his company at Fort Supply, Indian Territory. He was on detached service in the vicinity of Rodger's Ranche, New Mexico, hunting, fishing, and taking observations, in August, 1888, and at Fort Wingate, New Mexico, in July and August, 1889, as chief range-officer, and in command of competitors in the department rifle competition.

Capt. Thompson was again detailed on general recruiting service from Oct. 1, 1889, to Oct. 1, 1891, and stationed at Providence, R. I. He was on leave of absence to Jan. 2, 1892, when he rejoined his regiment at San Carlos, Arizona, his present station. Capt. Thompson is a member of the Military Order of the Loyal Legion, of the New York Society of the Sons of the American Revolution, and New Hampshire Society of the same order.

## COLONEL AND BREVET BRIGADIER-GENERAL JOHN C. TIDBALL, U.S.A. (RETIRED).

COLONEL AND BREVET BRIGADIER-GENERAL JOHN C. TIDBALL was born in Ohio County, Virginia, but at an early age emigrated with his parents to Belmont County, Ohio, from which place he entered the Military Academy in 1844, graduating in 1848; shortly afterwards assigned as second lieutenant to Second Artillery. From the summer of 1849 to the winter of 1851 he served in Florida, assisting in the suppression of Indian hostilities; after that, until the spring of 1853, in Charleston harbor, South Carolina.

In March, 1853, he was promoted first lieutenant, and joined his company at Fort Defiance, New Mexico. Shortly afterwards he was detailed to accompany Captain (subsequently General) Whipple, of the engineers, in his exploration for a railroad route to the Pacific through New Mexico, Arizona, and Southern California, a route since realized as the Atlantic and Pacific Railroad. This duty occupied the winter and spring of 1853-54. In the following fall he was assigned to Coast Survey duty at Washington, where he continued until the fall of 1859, when he rejoined his company at Fort Monroe, Virginia; soon after which he accompanied the troops sent to Harper's Ferry to suppress John Brown's raid.

The war of the Rebellion having broken out, Lieutenant Tidball accompanied his battery with the expedition that sailed, in April, 1861, to the relief of Fort Pickens. In July the battery returned to Washington, and was at once hurried to the front to participate in the Manassas campaign of that year, in which he commanded his battery, having been promoted to it as captain.

Soon after the Manassas campaign Captain Tidball organized his light battery into a horse battery, the first battery of the kind ever organized on this continent. With his battery thus equipped, he accompanied the Army of the Potomac to the Peninsula. He was in the campaigns of the Army of the Potomac, being engaged in the siege of Yorktown, battle of Williamsburg, actions at New Bridge and Mechanicsville; battles of Gaines' Mill, Malvern Hill, skirmish of Harrison's Landing, skirmish at Boonsborough, battle of Antietam, skirmish at Shepherdstown and march to Falmouth, Virginia, being engaged in the skirmishes of Upperville, Markham, and Amisville, 1862; in the campaign of 1863, being engaged in Stoneman's raid toward Richmond, and battle of Chancellorsville; in command of Second Brigade Horse Artillery, battle of Gettysburg, Pennsylvania; in the defences of Washington, D. C., August, 1863, to March, 1864; he was appointed colonel, Fourth New York Volunteer Artillery, August 28, 1863, and was in command of the artillery of the Second Corps, in the campaigns of 1864-65, being engaged in the battles of the Wilderness, Spottsylvania, North Anna,

Tolopotomy, Cold Harbor, and siege of Petersburg. He was at the Military Academy as commandant of cadets and instructor of artillery, infantry, and cavalry tactics, July 10 to September 22, 1864; in command of the artillery of the Ninth Corps, being engaged in the siege of Petersburg, including the repulse of the attack on Fort Steadman, and assault from Fort Sedgwick upon the rebel works; pursuit of the rebel army, terminating in the capitulation of General R. E. Lee at Appomattox Court-House, April 9, 1865. He was mustered out of the volunteer service September 30, 1865.

The war having closed, he returned to the command of his battery at the Presidio of San Francisco. He was brevetted through the various grades to that of brigadier-general U. S. Army, and major-general of volunteers. In 1867 he was selected as one of the new majors of artillery, being appointed as such to his old regiment, the Second. Served in command of the District of Astoria, Oregon, 1867-68; of District of Kenai, Alaska, 1868-70; on leave of absence, October 7, 1869, to March, 1870; in command of District of Alaska, 1870-71; of Depot Guard at Yerba Buena Island, California, November 1, 1871, to November 1, 1872; and of post of Raleigh, North Carolina, November 16, 1872, to April 29, 1874; and as superintendent of artillery instruction at the U. S. Artillery School, Fort Monroe, Virginia, to January 1, 1881; aide-de-camp (colonel) to General of the Army, January 1, 1881, to February 8, 1884; he was promoted lieutenant-colonel, Third Artillery, June 30, 1882, and transferred to First Artillery, November 10, 1882; transferred to Third Artillery, January 25, 1884; and promoted colonel, First Artillery, March 1, 1885; he was in command of the U. S. Artillery School and post of Fort Monroe, Virginia, from November 1, 1883, to January 25, 1889, when, having arrived at the legal age, he was retired from active service.

COLONEL JOSEPH GREENE TILFORD, U.S.A. (RETIRED).

COLONEL JOSEPH GREENE TILFORD, son of Colonel Alexander Tilford, a veteran of the War of 1812, was born in Georgetown, Kentucky, November 26, 1828. He graduated at West Point, July 1, 1851; was assigned to the mounted rifles, and ordered to Carlisle Barracks. He served there until the fall of 1853, then joined his regiment in Texas, doing duty against the hostile Comanche and Kiowa Indians, until 1856, when his regiment was ordered to New Mexico to operate against the Navajoes and Apaches.

In 1858, with a detachment of his regiment, he accompanied Captain Marcy with a supply train to Utah; entered Salt Lake City with General Albert S. Johnston's army, remained in Utah a few weeks, then returned to New Mexico, where he engaged in active warfare for three years against the Navajoes and Apaches. The opening of the Civil War found him at Fort Fauntleroy, New Mexico, where he bade good-by to many an old friend who espoused the Southern cause, and left for Fort Union, New Mexico. From there he marched with General Canby's army to Fort Craig, New Mexico, and there engaged in many skirmishes against the rebel forces from Texas. He was promoted captain in the Third Cavalry, July 30, 1861, and commanded his troop at the battle of Val Verde, February 21, 1862, for which he was brevetted major for gallant service in action.

In May of 1862, whilst commanding an outpost of General Canby's army (separated by the Rio Grande from the army), he was attacked by an overwhelming force of the rebels. By parleying with them for awhile he succeeded in getting his small command in such a position as to enable it to repulse the superior force. From that time on he was engaged in many skirmishes against the rebels until July, when they were driven from the country. In August his regiment was ordered to Fort Leavenworth, from there to St. Louis, where it remained for a few weeks, and was then ordered to Memphis. It remained there until October, 1863, and was then detailed as part of the body-guard of General Sherman to Chattanooga. He was present at the battles of Lookout Mountain and Missionary Ridge; also engaged in the battle of Cherokee Station and the capture of Tuscumbia, Alabama, where he led the advance. He was then ordered to Huntsville, Alabama, and from there to St. Louis. The regiment was remounted and recruited at that place, and then ordered to Little Rock, Arkansas. At that point it was actively engaged. He then served on General Reynolds's staff as acting assistant inspector-general.

In November, 1865, he was detailed on general recruiting service, but after a short tour at Carlisle, Pennsylvania, he applied to be relieved from duty and rejoined his regiment in New Mexico. He was there assigned to command the post of Fort Selden, where he remained until promoted major of the Seventh Cavalry, November 14, 1867. He joined the Seventh in Kansas, and was ordered with it to the South in 1869, he being assigned to command the District of Chester, South Carolina. From there he was ordered to command the post of Mount Vernon, Kentucky, then the post of Crab Orchard Springs, Kentucky. From there he was ordered, with two troops of the Seventh, to New Orleans. In 1873 was sent with his regiment to the Department of Dakota, and was assigned to the command of Fort Rice, garrisoned by four troops of his regiment. In July, 1874, was ordered to report to General Custer, in the expedition to explore the Black Hills. He commanded the left wing of General Custer's forces. He returned to Fort Rice, and from there to the command of Fort Lincoln, to which he had been assigned in 1877. In November, 1878, he was ordered, in command of eleven troops of the Seventh Cavalry and three companies of infantry, to Nebraska, to intercept the hostile Cheyennes, who were endeavoring to make their way North. He returned to Fort Lincoln, where he remained until 1882, when he was ordered to Fort Buford.

In September, 1883, he was promoted lieutenant-colonel of the Seventh Cavalry, and ordered to take command of the regiment, with head-quarters at Fort Meade, Dakota. He remained there until June 10, 1888, when he was ordered to take command of eight troops of the Seventh across the country, four troops to be left at Fort Riley, four at Fort Sill, Indian Territory, which post he commanded until April 11, 1889, when he was promoted colonel of the Ninth Cavalry. He remained as colonel of the Ninth until July 1, 1891, when he was retired, on his own application, after forty years of service.

## BREVET BRIGADIER-GENERAL FREDERICK TOWNSEND, U.S.A. (RESIGNED).

BREVET BRIGADIER-GENERAL FREDERICK TOWNSEND was born in Albany, New York, September 21, 1825. His parents, Isaiah and Hannah Townsend, were natives of New York, and both descended from English ancestors of same name, who came to this country in 1640. He was graduated at Union College in 1844, and admitted to the practice of law in 1849. He was appointed, January 1, 1857, by Governor John A. King, adjutant-general of the State, and was reappointed by the succeeding governor, Edward D. Morgan, January 1, 1859, thus holding the office for four years, until January 1, 1861.

General Townsend effected noted results in the consolidation and reorganization of the militia. At the beginning of the Civil War he promptly tendered his services to his country; organized immediately the Third Regiment of New York State Volunteers, of which he was commissioned colonel in May, and which he commanded at the battle of Big Bethel, June 10, 1861. He was appointed major of the Eighteenth Infantry (regular army), August 19, 1861, by President Lincoln, and assigned to duty in the West. His command first joined the army of General Buell, and then that of General Rosecrans. He participated in the reconnoissance to Lick Creek, Mississippi, April 26, 1862. He took part in the siege of Corinth, April 30, and in its occupation. On the 6th of October he was in the advance of the Third Corps, Army of the Ohio, driving the rear-guard of the enemy from Springfield to near Texas, Kentucky, and took part in the battle of Perryville, or Chaplin Hill, Kentucky, on the 8th of October. After the first day of the battle of Stone River, Tennessee, December 31, 1862, to and including January 3, 1863,—all of his senior officers of the regular brigade having been shot, except the commander,—he was placed by the latter in command of the left wing of the brigade. He was also in the affair at Eagleville, Tennessee, March 2, 1863, with a large force supporting a foraging party. In May, 1863, he was detailed for duty at Albany, New York, as acting assistant provost-marshal-general.

In 1867, on his return from Europe, on the expiration of a leave of absence, being then lieutenant-colonel of the Ninth U. S. Infantry, he was ordered to California, and placed by General McDowell on his staff as acting assistant inspector-general of the department, and in

which capacity he made an inspection of all the government posts in Arizona.

He resigned his commission in the army in 1868. For his services he received, successively, the brevets of lieutenant-colonel, that of colonel, and that of brigadier-general, all in the regular army. He is a member of the Society of the Army of the Cumberland, of the Grand Army of the Republic, and of the Military Order of the Loyal Legion.

On the 1st of January, 1880, General Townsend was again appointed, by Governor A. B. Cornell, adjutant-general of the State of New York. He held the office for three years. He again consolidated the National Guard, made extensive reforms, established a service uniform, and organized the "State Camp of Instruction" at Peekskill-on-the-Hudson, New York. He was nominated by the Republican State Convention in 1880 for the office of elector of President and Vice-President; was elected, and cast his vote for James A. Garfield and Chester A. Arthur for those offices, respectively.

General Townsend is a director or trustee of the following-named institutions:

New York State National Bank, Albany, New York.
Albany and Bethlehem Turnpike Company, Albany, New York.
Union College, Schenectady (since resigned).
Vassar College, Poughkeepsie, New York.
The Dudley Observatory, Albany, New York.
The Albany Academy, Albany, New York.
The Albany Orphan Asylum, Albany, New York.

MAJOR AND BREVET COLONEL ALBERT TRACY,
U.S.A. (RETIRED).

MAJOR AND BREVET COLONEL ALBERT TRACY is a native of Western New York, having been born in the then village of Buffalo, in the year 1818. Removing in earlier life to the State of Maine, he was, in February, 1847, appointed therefrom to a first lieutenancy in the Ninth Infantry,—one of the regiments added to the regular establishment for service in the Mexican War. Marching with the Ninth, in July, 1847, from Vera Cruz, in the command under General Pierce, Lieutenant Tracy saw service in the various encounters with guerillas along the route to the interior, notably in an affair of decided severity at Puente Nacional. By the "Official List of Officers who were engaged in the Battles of Mexico," published by General Scott (Mexico, February 7, 1848), Lieutenant Tracy stands further accredited as present in the several battles of Contreras, Churubusco, Molino del Rey, Chapultepec, and the Garita Belen. "For gallant and meritorious conduct in the battle of Chapultepec," Lieutenant Tracy received the brevet of captain.

With the close of the Mexican War, Captain Tracy was, with his regiment, disbanded. Upon the increase of the army, however, in 1855, this officer was reappointed to the grade of captain by President Pierce, his former commander, and assigned to the Tenth Infantry.

In the spring of 1857, Captain Tracy was engaged in an expedition out from Fort Snelling, Minnesota, against the Sioux, and later on in the same year marched with his regiment in the expedition against the Mormons in Utah, the latter an undertaking which, for its privations and starvations among the snows of the mountains in the winter of 1857-58, has scarcely a parallel in the history of the army. In October, 1858, Captain Tracy commanded an expedition to check incursions of the Utes upon inhabitants of Salt Lake Valley.

Prior to the actual outbreak of the Rebellion, Captain Tracy, then on leave in the East, proceeded under orders to Jefferson Barracks, Missouri, whence, moving at night, he reinforced with some three hundred and fifty men and officers Captain Lyon, at St. Louis Arsenal,—this post being virtually in a state of siege, and threatened with capture by armed organizations of St. Louis City. Following upon his tour with Lyon, and also one of detached command, guarding magazines near Jefferson Barracks, Captain Tracy accompanied, as acting chief commissary of subsistence, the column of General Frémont, in its autumn campaign to southwest Missouri.

Under appointment by the President, in 1862, as additional aide-de-camp, with volunteer rank of colonel, Colonel Tracy took part with General Frémont, as his acting assistant adjutant-general, in the campaign up Shenandoah Valley, in pursuit of Jackson, being present at the battle of Cross-Keys.

Promoted in 1863 from his captaincy in the Tenth to be major in the Fifteenth Infantry, and joining at Chattanooga, Colonel Tracy accompanied with his battalion the demonstration of General Thomas, in February, 1864, towards Mill-Creek Gap, becoming engaged, in common with the body of the advance, in a prolonged and obstinate skirmish with the enemy at Rocky-Face Ridge.

With the command of his regiment at Lookout Mountain, during the winter of 1864-65, terminated the more conspicuous service of the subject of this sketch, his retirement from the active list of the army taking place in November, 1865, for disability in the line of duty.

"For meritorious services during the campaign of 1862, under General Fremont, in Virginia," Colonel Tracy received the brevet of lieutenant-colonel. "For faithful and meritorious services during the war," the brevet of colonel.

In the interval between his disbandment in 1848 and his re-entry into service in 1855, Colonel Tracy was appointed to, and held for the period of nearly three years, the position of adjutant-general of Maine,—rewriting, compiling, and procuring to be established, the initiatory laws resuscitating the decayed volunteer system of the State, and affording thus a proportion of fairly-trained men to meet the exigencies of a broad-spread civil war.

As a writer, Colonel Tracy has contributed much to the press, while to his attainment as an artist are due the pictures of "Molino del Rey" and "Churubusco," painted in Mexico, at the instance and under the immediate eye of General Worth, and now in possession of the United Service Club at Governor's Island. Colonel Tracy resides at present at Portland, Maine.

## BENJAMIN FRANKLIN TRACY
### (SECRETARY OF THE NAVY).

BENJAMIN FRANKLIN TRACY was born in Owego, New York, April 2, 1830. His father was a man of marked integrity and enterprise, a pioneer in the settlement of the southern tier of counties in that State. His son was fond of study, and was educated at the Owego Academy. When of the proper age he entered a law-office in his native town, and was admitted to the bar in May, 1851. He soon won local distinction, for he was pitted against men who afterwards became distinguished. In 1853 he was, as the Whig candidate, elected district attorney for Tioga County, at that time a Democratic stronghold. He was re-elected in 1856, beating the Democratic candidate, Hon. Gilbert C. Walker, afterwards governor of Virginia. Although on opposite sides, they were friends, and soon after this election formed a law partnership. In 1861 Tracy took an active and prominent part in the exciting politics of the time, and filled important offices in the State Legislature. In the spring of 1862, under appointment of the governor of New York, he recruited two regiments of State troops, the One Hundred and Ninth and the One Hundred and Thirty-seventh, and became the colonel of the former. This regiment first went to Baltimore, and then to Washington, D. C., where it remained on duty until the spring of 1864. Then, with the general advance under Grant, it joined the Ninth Army Corps of the Army of the Potomac, and took part in the battle of the Wilderness. Near the close of the battle he fell, exhausted by his exertions, and was carried from the field; but refused to go to the hospital, and continued to lead his regiment during the three days' conflict at Spottsylvania, when he utterly broke down, and was forced to surrender his command to the lieutenant-colonel. He then went North, to recruit his health, and, in the following September, was made colonel of the One Hundred and Twenty-seventh U. S. Colored Troops, and soon after was assigned to the command of the military post at Elmira, New York, where was a prison camp and the draft rendezvous for Western New York. In this camp there were at one time as many as ten thousand prisoners.

In March, 1865, Colonel Tracy was brevetted brigadier-general of volunteers, for gallant and meritorious services during the war. On June 13, 1865, he was honorably discharged, on tendering his resignation.

Colonel Tracy then entered the law-firm of Benedict, Burr & Benedict, in New York City, and in 1866 was appointed U. S. district attorney for the Eastern District of New York, during which time he drew an internal revenue bill which more than trebled the revenue of the United States, at the period when our credit was being established by the rapid payment of the huge war-debt.

In 1873 Colonel Tracy resigned his position, and again entered upon the general practice of his profession, being engaged in many notable cases.

In December, 1881, he was appointed by the governor of New York an associate justice of the State Court of Appeals, the appointment being to fill a vacancy. This he held for two years, and then returned to the practice of the law with Mr. William De Witt, and his son, F. F. Tracy, their office being established in Brooklyn. While thus engaged in business he was, on March 5, 1889, appointed by President Harrison, Secretary of the Navy, and was confirmed on the same day by the Senate. The Secretary entered very zealously upon the prosecution of the plans for the rehabilitation and increase of the naval force,—an object which meets the approval of administrations of widely different opinions in other matters.

In April, 1891, he reported that the department was then engaged in the construction of twenty-five vessels, in addition to eleven completed and put in service since the spring of 1889; that the Washington gun-foundry for heavy artillery had been brought to high perfection, and that a reserve naval militia was in process of formation, fostered by the department. The principle of Civil Service Reform has been applied to the administration of our navy-yards in a most gratifying way during his service.

Secretary Tracy is a companion of the Loyal Legion, and a member of the Grand Army of the Republic.

### REAR-ADMIRAL STEPHEN DECATUR TRENCHARD, U.S.N. (DECEASED).

REAR-ADMIRAL STEPHEN DECATUR TRENCHARD was descended from the Trenchard family of Dorset, England. His great-grandfather, George Trenchard, was attorney-general of West Jersey under the Crown, but he drew his sword in favor of the Colonies. The admiral's father, Captain Edward Trenchard, served in the war with Tripoli, and was one of the commanders of Commodore Chauncey's flag-ship "Madison," in the War of 1812. Admiral Trenchard was born in Brooklyn, New York, in 1818. He received his appointment as midshipman on October 23, 1834, having previously made a cruise as acting midshipman under Commodore Downes. His first cruise was on board the "Constitution." In 1836 he served in the West Indies and Florida War. He was promoted to master in 1842, and served in the Coast Survey from 1845 to 1846. While on this duty he was aboard the brig "Washington" when she was wrecked off the coast of North Carolina. During the Mexican War he was lieutenant on board the U. S. S. "Saratoga." In 1856, while in command of the U. S. surveying-steamer "Vixen," he rescued the crew of the British bark "Adieu," of Gloucester, Massachusetts, for which service he received a sword from Queen Victoria. Admiral Trenchard was flag-lieutenant to Commodore Tatnall, in the East India Squadron, in 1858, and was wounded when the commodore visited Sir Admiral Hope, at the battle of the Pei-ho River. He had just returned from China when the war was declared. On April 19, 1861, he sailed under sealed orders from the Navy Department in command of the "Keystone State," destined for Norfolk, where she rendered much assistance with the tug-boat "Yankee" in towing out the "Cumberland," and taking the loyal officers and men of the Norfolk station to Washington. Lieutenant Trenchard received a letter of thanks from Secretary Welles for this service. On May 25 following he assumed command of the "Rhode Island," which was first used as a special despatch and supply steamer, but was afterwards converted into a heavily-armed cruiser, and ordered to the North Atlantic Squadron on November 28, 1862. While taking the "Monitor" from Fort Monroe that noble vessel foundered off Cape Hatteras. The "Rhode Island's" boats, notwithstanding the heavy sea, succeeded in rescuing nearly all the "Monitor's" crew. On February 12, 1863, Commander Trenchard received orders to cruise after the "Alabama" and other privateers. On May of the same year the "Rhode Island" was attached to Admiral Walke's squadron, and a short time to the South Atlantic Blockading Squadron. In November following she was ordered to the North Atlantic fleet, and became one of Admiral Porter's squadron before Fort Fisher. The "Rhode Island" was one of the vessels that assisted in landing General Terry's siege-guns, and General Abbott sent a letter of thanks for this service to Commander Trenchard and officers. In the engagement at Fort Fisher the "Rhode Island's" guns were trained on Battery Lamb, and shot away the flag-staff of the mound. After the reduction of Fort Fisher, Commander Trenchard was ordered, as senior officer, to command the convoy fleet which protected the Pacific Mail steamers going through the Southwest Pass. The "Rhode Island," as a cruiser, captured five blockade-runners.

After the war Commander Trenchard was on duty at the Brooklyn Navy-Yard. As captain he commanded the flag-ship "Lancaster," of the South Atlantic Squadron, 1869-71. Returning to the United States, he received his promotion to the grade of commodore, and served as a member of the Board of Examiners at Washington. His next duty was in charge of the Light-house Department, head-quarters at Staten Island. In 1875 he was promoted to rear-admiral, and, after serving as chairman of a special board at San Francisco, he was ordered to command the North Atlantic Squadron, the historic "Hartford" being his flag-ship. After serving on a special board at Washington, he was retired, according to the U. S. N. regulations, in July, 1880, having seen twenty-eight years' sea-service out of forty-five years in the navy.

Admiral Trenchard was senior vice-commander of the New York Commandery, Loyal Legion, 1879-80. He died in November, 1883.

## COMMODORE WILLIAM TALBOT TRUXTUN, U.S.N.
(DECEASED).

COMMODORE WILLIAM TALBOT TRUXTUN was born in Philadelphia, Pennsylvania, March 11, 1824; appointed midshipman from Pennsylvania, February 9, 1841; attached to brig "Dolphin" and sloop-of-war "Falmouth," Home Squadron, 1841-44; brig "Truxtun," west coast of Africa, 1844-45; Naval School, 1846-47. Passed examination August 10, 1847, and warranted as passed midshipman, Flag-ship "Brandywine" and brig "Perry," Brazil Station, 1847-48; returned from Brazil as an acting master on the prize-brig "Independence" (slaver), captured by the "Perry," off Rio de Janeiro, January, 1848; navy-yard, Norfolk, and steamer "Alleghany," 1848-49; store-ship "Supply," Pacific Squadron, 1849-52; special service in the "Dolphin," 1853, when the bank on which the first transatlantic cable is laid was discovered, and the first specimens of the bottom brought up; special duty, 1854, on the Strain Expedition to find a route for a ship-canal across the Isthmus of Darien.

The complete history of this expedition was never given to the world by any of those who experienced all of its vicissitudes. No Arctic Expedition ever went through more hardship and suffering than these explorers of a tropical wilderness. The survivors always had a horror of speaking of the incidents of their journey. The diary is, probably, only a partial record of starvation, struggle, and death to many. Truxtun's iron constitution caused him to be one of the survivors; but he never entirely recovered from the strain.

Promoted master September 14, 1855; promoted lieutenant September 15, 1855; Coast Survey, 1855-57; ordnance-ship "Plymouth," 1857-58; brig "Perry," Brazil Squadron, 1858-60; sloop "Dale," 1861, as executive; commanded the "Dale," North Atlantic Blockading Squadron, 1862. Promoted lieutenant-commander July 16, 1862; remained attached to the North Atlantic Blockading Squadron till the close of the war, during which time commanded the steamers "Alabama," "Chocura," and "Tacony," and took part in the capture of Plymouth, North Carolina, 1864, the two attacks and capture of Fort Fisher, North Carolina, 1864-65, and in various engagements with batteries along the coast of North Carolina; superintendent of coal shipments for the navy at Philadelphia, 1866-67. Promoted commander July 25, 1866; commanded "Jamestown," Pacific Squadron, 1868-70; inspector ordnance, navy-yard, Boston, 1871-73. Promoted captain September 25, 1873; commanding "Brooklyn" (second-rate), North Atlantic Squadron, 1873-74, and flag-ship, South Atlantic Squadron, 1874-75; member of Board of Inspectors, 1876; navy-yards, Boston and Norfolk, 1877-81. Commodore, May 11, 1882. Died, February 25, 1887.

### MAJOR TULLIUS C. TUPPER, U.S.A.

MAJOR TULLIUS C. TUPPER (Sixth Cavalry) was born in Strongsville, Ohio, September 23, 1838. He is the son of Charles Tupper, a soldier of the War of 1812; grandson of Samuel Tupper, a militiaman at the age of sixteen in the American Revolution; and a lineal descendant of Thomas Tupper, one of the original proprietors in 1637 of the town of Sandwich, Plymouth Colony.

He enlisted in the Third (now Sixth) Cavalry in July, 1861. Upon the organization of Captain D. McM. Gregg's company, E, he was made first sergeant. At White House Landing, Virginia, he was appointed sergeant-major, which position he held when appointed second lieutenant, in 1862. He participated in all the battles and affairs in which his regiment was engaged until January 1, 1865, when he was ordered on recruiting service.

Major-General Stoneman "particularly" invited the attention of the commanding general to Lieutenant Tupper "for driving in and capturing the enemy's pickets, and a staff-officer of General Stuart," during the raid made in connection with the battle of Chancellorsville. He commanded the squadron detailed as rear-guard at Beverly Ford, and which suffered greater loss than any other squadron of his regiment in that battle. He was adjutant of his regiment from October, 1863, to November, 1864, when relieved at his own request.

In the Shenandoah Valley, Lieutenant Tupper was frequently verbally assigned to duties as acting aide-de-camp. He accompanied various commands upon different occasions under special instructions from General Sheridan or his chief of staff, and carried the general's despatches from the battle-field of Cedar Creek, during the night after the close of that battle, and delivered them at Martinsburg at sunrise the next morning. After the war he was brevetted first lieutenant, captain, and major.

He was promoted captain of Troop G, and commanded that troop while on duty as personal escort to Generals Hancock and Rousseau, while those officers commanded the Fifth Military District.

During a scout, in 1870, he successfully repulsed a night attack by hostile Indians upon his camp, near Little Wichita, Texas. In 1874, with twenty men, he overtook and routed a band of Cheyennes, who had raided the settlement of Medicine Lodge, Kansas, recovered the stolen stock, and captured that of the Indians, with their camp equipment.

In August, 1874, his troop made the final charge in an engagement between the forces of General Miles and confederated bands of hostile Indians, relative to which General Miles used the following language to the War Department in recommending a brevet: "For distinguished services in successfully leading a cavalry charge across Red River and up the steep bluffs held by hostile Indians."

During the summer of 1876, Captain Tupper was placed in charge of "scouting operations in Southeastern Arizona." In September, with his troop, other detachments, and Indian scouts, he overtook and punished Loco's band of Apaches, led by chief Victorio. The results were the killing and capture of a portion and the surrender of over three hundred at Fort Wingate, whence they were subsequently returned to San Carlos.

In 1882, Captain Tupper, in command of two troops and forty-three Indian scouts, by forced night marches, overtook a large band of Apaches in the Sierra Madre Mountains, Mexico; the Indian herd was captured, from seventeen to twenty-five warriors killed, and a large number wounded. Concerning this affair General Sherman directed the following telegram, addressed to the department commander: "The general of the army desires Captain Tupper to be congratulated in his name for his success in an engagement with the Apaches, April 28." In subsequent orders the following appeared: "The department commander expresses to Captain T. C. Tupper, Sixth Cavalry, and the officers and men of his command, his appreciation of their untiring energy and perseverance while pursuing the renegade Chiricahuas, and the skill and gallantry displayed by them in action on the 28th of April, 1882."

During the Sioux troubles in 1890-91, Major Tupper, with two troops, guided by the firing, marched to the relief of Troop K, which had been attacked on the march and enveloped by a superior force. After the campaign the members of Troop K, Sixth Cavalry, presented him an elegant service sabre inscribed: "As a testimonial of their appreciation of his gallant action in battle with Sioux Indians on White River, South Dakota, January 1, 1891."

He was promoted major, Sixth Cavalry, October 19, 1887.

## REAR-ADMIRAL THOMAS TURNER, U.S.N.
### (DECEASED).

REAR-ADMIRAL THOMAS TURNER was a native of Virginia, and appointed a midshipman in the navy from that State, April, 1825. He was attached to the frigate "Constellation," and to the sloop-of-war "Warren," of the Mediterranean Squadron, for several years; coming home for his examination and being promoted to passed midshipman, in June, 1831. He then went out to the Mediterranean again, serving in the frigate "Constellation" and the line-of-battle-ship "Delaware" until 1835. He was commissioned as lieutenant December 22, 1835, and made a cruise to the East Indies and China, in the "Columbus," 74. Upon his return, he was upon shore duty in Philadelphia, which city had become his permanent residence. He served in the sloop-of-war "Albany," of the Gulf Squadron, and was actively engaged in the war with Mexico, being present at the capture of Tuspan and other operations. After the war he served a term of duty on board the receiving-ship at Philadelphia.

During 1851–53 he was executive-officer of the frigate "Congress," the flag-ship of Commodore McKeever, on the Brazil Station, and, upon his return from that cruise, was upon ordnance duty for several years. He was commissioned as commander in September, 1855, and commanded the sloop-of-war "Saratoga," of the Home Squadron, during 1859–60.

Commander Turner was in command of that vessel in the engagement with the "Marquis of Havannah" and the "General Miramon," two Spanish steamers, in the harbor of Anton Lezardo, Mexico, capturing them at midnight of March 6, 1860.

He received his commission of captain July 16, 1862; and was commissioned commodore, December 13, 1863, while in command of the U. S. iron-clad frigate "New Ironsides." In this very fine fighting-ship he took part in the attack upon Forts Sumter, Moultrie, and Beauregard, in Charleston harbor, April 7, 1863. Rear-Admiral Dupont was on board the "New Ironsides," and commended Turner for the judgment and ability with which he handled his vessel.

In 1864–65 Commodore Turner was employed upon special duty in New York; and in 1866–67 upon special duty in Philadelphia. He was afterwards upon ordnance duty in Philadelphia.

He was commissioned as rear-admiral in May, 1868, and commanded the South Pacific Station during 1869, 1870, and 1871.

After being for several years on the retired list, he died in 1883.

Rear-Admiral Turner was well known throughout the service of his day for his elegant deportment and his invariably kind and courteous manner; while he was an excellent and gallant officer.

### COLONEL JOHN J. UPHAM, U.S.A. (RETIRED).

COLONEL JOHN J. UPHAM was born in Delaware July 23, 1837, and graduated from the Military Academy in the Class of 1859, when he was promoted brevet second lieutenant of the Ninth Infantry, and second lieutenant of the Sixth Infantry, December 2, 1859. He was again promoted first lieutenant, May 4, 1861; captain, September 9, 1861, and transferred to the Sixth Cavalry December 31, 1870. He was promoted major of the Fifth Cavalry, August 1, 1874; lieutenant-colonel, Third Cavalry, October 29, 1888; and colonel, Eighth Cavalry, January 14, 1892.

On the expiration of his graduating leave he was assigned to Governor's Island, where he had station until after his transfer to the Sixth Infantry; he then proceeded to California and served at Fort Crook and Benicia Barracks during 1860–61. He served during the war of the Rebellion in the defences of Washington during the winter of 1861–62; participated in the Virginia Peninsula campaign, and was engaged in the siege of Yorktown and the battle of Malvern Hill, and served in the defences of Washington during the summer of 1862; participated in the Pennsylvania campaign, and was engaged in the battle of Gettysburg and in pursuit of the enemy to Warrenton. He was stationed in New York harbor from August, 1863, to January, 1864, when assigned to duty as mustering and disbursing officer, and served in that capacity until April, 1865, and had stations at Elmira, Philadelphia, and Detroit. He was brevetted major, July 2, 1863, for "gallant and meritorious services in the battle of Gettysburg, Pennsylvania."

After the war had terminated, Colonel Upham was on duty in Georgia and South Carolina until June, 1866; on leave of absence and visited Europe in 1866; returned in April, 1867, and served in the Carolinas until March, 1869, and had stations at Charleston, Wilmington, and Florence. He was then ordered to the frontier, and served at Fort Gibson, Indian Territory; Fort Smith, Arkansas, and Crawfordsville and Girard, Kansas, until January 1, 1871, when he was transferred to the Sixth Cavalry, and continued to serve in Kansas, Texas, and the Indian Territory, where he had field service, until August 13, 1874. He was at Fort Leavenworth from January to April, 1874, as a member of a board of officers convened to report upon changes, if any, to be made in horse-equipments, and continued on duty in the Department of the Missouri until the regiment arrived at Fort Lyon, Colorado, and the companies were assigned to stations. September 7, 1875, he assumed command of Fort Gibson, Indian Territory, where he served until June 6, 1876, when he was ordered to field service in the Department of the Platte; he joined the head-quarters of the regiment June 10, and served in the District of the Black Hills, and with the Big Horn and Yellowstone Expedition until the following October, and was engaged in the combat at War Bonnet (Indian Creek), Wyoming; the skirmish at Slim Buttes, Dakota, and commanded the rear guard (a battalion of the regiment) in the second skirmish at Slim Buttes on the morning of the 10th of September, 1876.

He was assigned at the end of the campaign to Fort D. A. Russell, Wyoming, where he served until November 24, and was then on leave of absence until January 24, 1877, when he was detailed on special duty in the Indian Department for the purpose of investigating the management of the Union Agency in the Indian Territory, being thus employed until June 26, when he resumed his leave of absence and again visited Europe. He returned in June, 1878, and commanded Fort Washakie, in Northwestern Wyoming, from August, 1878, to April, 1880, when he was transferred to Fort Niobrara, Nebraska, where he exercised the command until June, 1881. On leave of absence till December, 1881, and then assigned to Fort Leavenworth, Kansas, School of Instruction as executive-officer.

He served at various other stations till 1892, when he was retired, on his own application, after thirty years' service,

## LIEUTENANT-COLONEL AND BREVET MAJOR-GENERAL EMORY UPTON, U.S.A. (DECEASED).

LIEUTENANT-COLONEL AND BREVET MAJOR-GENERAL EMORY UPTON was born in New York, and graduated from the Military Academy on May 6, 1861. He was promoted second lieutenant, Fourth Artillery, the same day, and first lieutenant, Fifth Artillery, May 14, 1861. He served in drilling volunteers at Washington, D. C., May 7-27, 1861; as aide-de-camp in the defences of Washington and during the Manassas campaign, and was engaged in the action at Blackburn's Ford, July 18, and battle of Bull Run, Virginia, July 21, 1861, where he was wounded. He was on sick-leave, on account of wounds, to August 14, 1861, and then served in the defences of Washington to March 22, 1862, at which time he participated in the Virginia Peninsula campaign with the Army of the Potomac, commanding a battery, and was engaged in the siege of Yorktown, action at West Point, battle of Gaines' Mill, and Glendale, 1862. Commanded artillery brigade of the First Division of Sixth Corps in the Maryland campaign, and engaged in the battles of South Mountain and Antietam.

Lieutenant Upton was commissioned colonel of the 121st N. Y. Inf., on Oct. 23, 1862, and participated in the Rappahannock campaign, being engaged in the battle of Fredericksburg and Salem Heights. He participated in the Pennsylvania campaign, and was engaged, after a forced march of thirty-five miles, in the battle of Gettysburg and the pursuit of the enemy to Warrenton, in command of a brigade; was in the Rapidan campaign, commanding a brigade of the Sixth Corps, and engaged in the capture of the rebel works at Rappahannock Station, Nov. 7, 1863, and was in the operations at Mine Run, from Nov. 26 to Dec. 3, 1863; was in the Richmond campaign, in command of a brigade of the Sixth Corps, and engaged in the battles of the Wilderness and Spottsylvania, where he was wounded on May 10, 1864, while commanding the assaulting column of twelve regiments of the Sixth Corps.

Colonel Upton was commissioned brigadier-general of volunteers on May 12, 1864, and was engaged in the battles and actions of Cold Harbor, June 1-23, 1864, and siege of and battles about Petersburg to July 10, 1864, when he was transferred with his command to Washington, and participated in the defence of the national capital, July 11-12, 1864. He participated in the Shenandoah campaign, August and Sept. 1864, and was engaged in the battle of Winchester, Sept. 19, where he was wounded while commanding the First Division of the Sixth Corps, which compelled him to leave the field, and was absent sick until Dec. 13, 1864. He commanded the Fourth Cavalry Division in General J. H. Wilson's operations in Alabama and Georgia, from March to May, 1865, and was engaged

in the actions at Montevallo and Plantersville, and assault and capture of Columbus, Georgia, April 16, 1865. He was then at the Nashville Cavalry Depot, in command of the First Cavalry Division, District of East Tennessee, and of the District of Colorado, to April 30, 1866, when he was mustered out of the volunteer service. He was brevetted major-general of volunteers, Oct. 19, 1864, for gallant and meritorious services at the battle of Winchester. He was also brevetted in the regular army for gallant and meritorious services, as follows: Major, November 8, 1863, at the battle of Rappahannock Station; lieutenant-colonel, May 10, 1864, at the battle of Spottsylvania; colonel, Sept. 19, 1864, at the battle of Winchester; brigadier-general, March 13, 1865, at the battle and capture of Selma, and major-general, March 13, 1865, in the field during the Rebellion.

He was promoted captain, Fifth Artillery, February 22, 1865, and appointed lieutenant-colonel of the Twenty-fifth Infantry, July 28, 1866, but transferred to the Eighteenth Infantry, March 15, 1869. He served, after the war, with a board of officers at West Point, New York, in examining his System of Infantry Tactics, from June 25, 1866, to February 4, 1867, which were adopted for the army. Sept. 1867, assigned to the command of Paducah, Kentucky, until November 12, 1867. He was then in garrison at Memphis, Tennessee, and Atlanta, Georgia, to May 30, 1870, when he was assigned to duty at the Military Academy as commandant of cadets, which position he retained until June 30, 1875. Was assigned to the First Artillery, December 15, 1876, and transferred to the Fourth Artillery, March 20, 1877. He was on professional duty in Europe and Asia from July, 1875, to March, 1877. Was at Fort Monroe and Presidio of San Francisco, California, from April, 1877, to March, 1881, when he died at the last-named post, aged forty-two years.

### COLONEL JAMES J. VAN HORN, U.S.A.

COLONEL JAMES J. VAN HORN (Eighth Infantry) was born at Mount Gilead, Ohio, February 6, 1835. He was graduated at the U. S. Military Academy in the Class of 1858, and promoted brevet second lieutenant, First Infantry, the same day.

He served in garrison at Fort Columbus, New York, 1858-59; and was promoted second lieutenant, Eighth Infantry, July 19, 1858. He was then on frontier duty at Fort Davis, Texas, in 1859-61; and also at San Antonio, where he was made prisoner-of-war, May 8, 1861, and not exchanged until April 4, 1862. He was promoted first lieutenant, Eighth Infantry, May 14, 1861, and served during the Rebellion of the seceding States, 1861-66. He was promoted captain, Eighth Infantry, February 19, 1862, and served as aide-de-camp to the provost-marshal-general of the Army of the Potomac, from June 6, 1862, to July 4, 1863. He participated in the Virginia Peninsula and Maryland campaigns, and was engaged at the battle of South Mountain, September 14, 1862, and battle of Antietam, September 17, 1862.

He was then detailed as mustering and disbursing officer at Trenton, New Jersey, from July 4, 1863, to April 27, 1864; when he rejoined the Army of the Potomac and was engaged at the battle of Bethesda Church, June 3, 1864. He was an aide-de-camp to Major-General W. F. Smith, commanding Eighteenth Army Corps, from July 3, 1864, to November 4, 1865.

He was brevetted major, June 4, 1864, for "gallant and meritorious services at the battle of Cold Harbor."

At the close of the war he was detailed as recorder of Tactics Board (Upton's) at West Point, New York, from June 27, 1866, to February 4, 1867, after which he joined his regiment and was in command of the military post of New Berne, Second Military District, at New Berne, North Carolina, comprising the counties of Hyde, Beaufort, Craven, Carteret, Onslow, Pitt, and Jones, from February 16, 1867, to January 29, 1868.

During the reconstruction of the Southern States, he served at various posts in North and South Carolina, from 1867 to August 27, 1870. Since July, 1872, he has served almost continuously on the frontier, at posts in Arizona, New Mexico, Montana, and Wyoming.

He was with the Yellowstone Expeditions of 1872-73; on escort duty to the Northern Pacific Railroad engineers in their surveys of the present route of that railroad, and was promoted major, Thirteenth Infantry, June 7, 1879.

Colonel Van Horn received the thanks and commendation of the department commander for his conduct "in disarming of Mescalero Apache Indians, at their agency in New Mexico," September 12, 1882.

He was promoted lieutenant-colonel, Twenty-fifth Infantry, June 28, 1885; and colonel of infantry (Eighth), April 20, 1891, taking station at Fort McKinney, Wyoming, where he is now serving.

## COLONEL AND BREVET MAJOR-GENERAL STEWART VAN VLIET, U.S.A. (RETIRED).

COLONEL AND BREVET MAJOR-GENERAL STEWART VAN VLIET was born in New York and graduated from the Military Academy July 1, 1840, when he was promoted second lieutenant Third Artillery. He first served at Fort Columbus, New York, and participated in the Florida War, 1840-41, being engaged against the Seminole Indians in several skirmishes. He was detailed at the Military Academy as assistant professor of mathematics from September 20 to November 15, 1841, when he again participated in the Florida War of 1841-42. Afterwards he served at Fort Pike, Louisiana; Fort Macon, North Carolina; and Savannah, Georgia, to 1843, when he was promoted first lieutenant November 19, 1843. He then was on duty at Fort Moultrie, South Carolina, and Savannah, Georgia, until 1846, when the Mexican War occurred, and in which he participated, being engaged in the battle of Monterey, September 21-23, 1846, and siege of Vera Cruz, March 9-29, 1847. He was then appointed quartermaster Third Artillery, March 28, and served in that capacity until June 4, 1847, when he was appointed captain, staff-assistant quartermaster, and was on duty with Missouri Mounted Volunteers, building posts on the Oregon route, from 1847-51; Fort Kearney, Nebraska, 1847-49, and Fort Laramie, Dakota, 1849-51. He was ordered to St. Louis, Missouri, and stationed there to 1852, and then transferred to Fort Brown, Texas, serving at that post and Brazos Santiago, Texas, until 1855. He participated in the Sioux Indian expedition from April 3, 1855, to July 17, 1856, and was engaged in the action of Blue Water, September 3, 1855.

Captain Van Vliet was detailed on special service in Utah, in 1857, and was on duty in New York City in 1857-58, from which point he was transferred to Fort Leavenworth, Kansas, and served there until the commencement of the war of the Rebellion. He was promoted major, staff-quartermaster, August 20, 1861, for fourteen years' service as captain, and appointed brigadier-general of volunteers September 23, 1861, and served as chief quartermaster of the Army of the Potomac from August 20, 1861, to July 10, 1862, participating in the Virginia Peninsula campaign. He was then ordered on duty at New York City, furnishing supplies and trans-

portation to the armies in the field until March 31, 1867. He was brevetted major-general of volunteers, March 13, 1865, for faithful and meritorious services during the Rebellion, and received the following brevets in the regular service: lieutenant-colonel, colonel, and brigadier-general, October 28, 1864, for faithful and meritorious services during the Rebellion. He was re-commissioned brigadier-general of volunteers, March 13, 1865, and brevetted major-general U. S. Army the same date, for "faithful and distinguished services in the quartermaster's department during the war."

He was promoted lieutenant-colonel, staff, deputy quartermaster-general, July 29, 1866, and mustered out of the volunteer service September 1, 1866. He served as depot quartermaster at Baltimore from April 18, 1867, to May 13, 1869; was in charge of Schuylkill Arsenal, Pennsylvania, and chief quartermaster in the Division of the Atlantic to June 1, 1872, and then on leave of absence to October 28, 1872.

General Van Vliet was promoted colonel, staff-assistant quartermaster-general, June 6, 1872, and was chief quartermaster of the Division of the Missouri from October 28, 1872, to July 13, 1875, and of the Philadelphia depot of quartermaster's stores to November 8, 1875. He was then detailed as inspector of the Quartermaster's Department, with head-quarters at Washington City, to January 22, 1881, when he was retired from active service, being over sixty-two years of age.

### CAPTAIN S. C. VEDDER, U.S.A. (RETIRED).

CAPTAIN S. C. VEDDER was born in New York, and appointed from New York as first lieutenant, Sixteenth New York Volunteer Infantry, April, 1861. He served in the field with the Army of the Potomac, and was engaged at the first battle of Bull Run, Virginia. He commanded company, and was engaged at the action of West Point, Virginia, battles of Mechanicsville, Gaines' Mill, Golden's Farm, and Charles City Cross-Roads. He was adjutant of his regiment, and engaged at the second battle of Bull Run, Virginia, and was honorably discharged (resigned), September 13, 1862, on account of sickness.

He was then connected with the Subsistence Department, U. S. Army, Department of Washington, D. C., part of 1863-64. He commanded a company of one hundred clerks in Subsistence Department at Alexandria, Virginia, during part of 1863-64, the company doing duty in the defences of Washington, D. C., and Alexandria, Virginia.

He was appointed a captain and commissary of subsistence, U. S. Volunteers, July, 1864 ; in Department of Washington, D. C., to June, 1865, when he was honorably mustered out, having been brevetted major for meritorious services. He was appointed second lieutenant, Twenty-eighth Infantry, U. S. Army, March 7, 1867, and brevetted first lieutenant, captain, and major for gallant and meritorious services at the battles of Gaines' Mills, Virginia (commission as captain and major not issued). He was detailed on duty as acting signal officer, under orders of chief signal officer U. S. Army, doing duty in Washington, D. C., New Mexico, Arizona, Washington Territory, and Idaho, from February 20, 1875, to December 1, 1880, when he was promoted first lieutenant, Nineteenth Infantry, March 18, 1878. He was regimental quartermaster from February 24, 1882, to March 31, 1887, and relieved as regimental quartermaster, March 31, 1887, but remained on duty as acting assistant quartermaster, and in charge of construction of public buildings at Fort Clark, Texas, until June 30, 1887, after which he was on duty as assistant commissary of subsistence, and as officer in charge of construction of public buildings at Fort Clark, Texas, from July 1, 1887, to August 1, 1888. He was also on duty as officer in charge of construction of public buildings at San Antonio, Texas, from August 10, 1888, to January 31, 1889, when he was detailed as recruiting officer at Washington, D. C., from February 7, 1889, to October 24, 1889, being then granted leave of absence (surgeon's certificate of disability), to February 20, 1891, at which time he was retired on account of disability in line of duty, with rank as captain.

## COMMANDER JONATHAN M. WAINWRIGHT, U.S.N.
(DECEASED).

COMMANDER JONATHAN MAYHEW WAINWRIGHT was born in the city of New York in July, 1821, and was killed in battle at Galveston Bay on January 1, 1863. He was a son of the well-known prelate of the same name, so long the Protestant Episcopal Bishop of New York.

Commander Wainwright entered the navy as a midshipman in June, 1837, and performed the usual sea-duty of his grade until, in 1842, he was ordered to the Naval School, then at Philadelphia. He became a passed midshipman in 1843, in 1849 an acting master, and was commissioned as lieutenant in September, 1850. His service in the "Lexington," "San Jacinto," "Saratoga," "Dolphin," and other vessels did not differ from that of most junior lieutenants. Never very robust, he managed always to do his duty well, and was a great favorite with his messmates and shipmates on account of his pleasant manners and officer-like conduct. The outbreak of the Civil War found him engaged in special duty at Washington. He was ordered to the command of the "Harriet Lane," the well-known revenue-steamer which had been transferred to the navy. She became the flag-ship of Commander (afterwards Admiral) Porter, of the Mortar Flotilla, during the operations against the forts below New Orleans, and the capture of that city and the mouths of the Mississippi. He also, in the same vessel, took part in the first operations against Vicksburg. In October, 1862, the "Harriet Lane" took part in the capture of Galveston, as a part of Commander Renshaw's little squadron. Their tenure was not long, for on New Year's Day, 1863, the small squadron, some of which were ashore at low tide, was attacked by a Confederate force, which soon resumed control of the town and the bay. General Magruder had, for the water attack, fitted out three steamers with cotton-bale defences, and placed on board as many riflemen as could find room to act. They came down the bay at four A.M., and, as the "Harriet Lane" was the highest up, she was first attacked. Boarded by these vessels, swarming with sharp-shooters, the decks were swept by a shower of balls. Wainwright fell almost immediately, at the head of his men, endeavoring to repel boarders. The executive-officer, Lea, was mortally wounded, and the next officer severely so. Half of those

on deck were shot down, and in ten minutes the vessel was in the enemy's possession. A curious incident of the fight was, that young Lea's father was an officer on the Confederate side, and found his son in a dying condition after possession was taken.

To complete the tragedy, Commander Renshaw, of the "Westfield," and the senior officer present, was summoned to surrender under favorable conditions, which he might have done, as his vessel was unmanageable from the state of water at that time. This he refused, sending most of his crew on board an army transport which was afloat, and remaining, with a few people, to destroy the "Westfield." Unfortunately the flames spread so fast that she blew up just as they got into the boat, and Renshaw, his first lieutenant, Zimmerman, Chief Engineer Green, and about a dozen men, lost their lives.

Commander Wainwright had a son, also named Jonathan Mayhew, who was appointed a midshipman the year his father was killed, and who graduated from the Naval Academy in 1867. This young officer also lost his life by rifle-shot only three years after graduation. He had attained the rank of master, and was attached to the Pacific Squadron. In command of a boat expedition against the piratical steamer "Forward," in the lagoon at San Blas, he was shot in leading the boarders at her capture, and died the next day. The attack was successful, and the vessel was captured and burnt.

## OFFICERS OF THE ARMY AND NAVY (REGULAR)

REAR-ADMIRAL HENRY WALKE, U.S.N.
(RETIRED).

REAR-ADMIRAL HENRY WALKE'S services have been so many and so various, that limited space will compel the passing over many of them. Born in Virginia, 1808, he was appointed midshipman from Ohio, February 1, 1827. During his service in this grade he passed through a frightful hurricane in the "Natchez," and in another in the "Ontario," where, with the vessel almost on her beam-ends, Midshipman Walke and seven or eight men struggled aloft, furled the main-topsail, and, no doubt, saved the ship. In 1833 he was promoted to passed midshipman, continuing to serve on all stations. Present at the surrender of Vera Cruz, Tabasco, Tuspan, and Alvarado. After other foreign service, promoted commander, September 14, 1855, and commanded the "Supply" on the coast of Africa and the West Indies.

When the Civil War broke out Walke was in Florida, and secured Fort Pickens from capture, which important service had far-reaching results, and resulted in the recapture of Pensacola, Forts Barrancas and McCrea, and the navy-yard. Although censured by the Secretary of the Navy for neglect of orders on this occasion, he was upheld in his course by the Board of Rear-Admirals, who reported that his course had a marked and important bearing on the success of our arms.

On November 7, 1861, Walke commanded the gunboat "Taylor," of the Mississippi Flotilla, at the first battle of General Grant during the Civil War, protecting his rear at Belmont, and preventing the Confederates from cutting off a portion of our troops on their retreat to the transports, for which he was highly commended in the general's report. He then commanded the "Carondelet," partially iron-clad, of thirteen guns, at the battle of Fort Henry, under Flag-Officer Foote, for which he and his officers received the thanks of the Secretary of the Navy and of the State of Ohio. Commanded the "Carondelet" at three days' battle of Fort Donelson, being thrice as long under fire as any other gun-boat, and losing more, in officers and men, than all the rest of the flotilla. In the "Carondelet" at the bombardment of Island No. 10, and voluntarily ran the gauntlet of the enemy's batteries with the "Carondelet" alone, a remarkable feat, and the first time it had been attempted. It ultimately resulted in the capture of the island and its batteries, and the achievement broke the enemy's line of fortifications which blockaded the great river, producing far-reaching results. The Secretary wrote in glowing words of the "daring and heroic act, well executed, and deserving special recognition." In May, 1862, at the river battle at Fort Pillow, Commander Walke again distinguished himself very greatly in the "Carondelet." At Memphis his vessel was second in line of battle, at the time of the destruction or capture of the rebel flotilla, and the capture of Memphis, with the navy-yard and public stores. The "Carondelet" was one of the gun-boats engaged with the formidable and famous Confederate ram "Arkansas."

Walke was commissioned a captain on July 16, 1862, and commanded the ram "Lafayette," when Porter's flotilla passed the batteries at Vicksburg, April 16, 1863. At Grand Gulf, a fortnight later, the "Lafayette" again bore a distinguished part, being longer under severe fire for many consecutive hours, but having very few wounded herself, although as frequently struck by shot and shell as the rest. "It is worthy of record that his officers and crew were always required 'to remember to keep holy the Sabbath day,'" according to our naval regulations. Captain Walke's next service was in dispersing the Confederate camps at Simsport, Louisiana, and in blockading the mouth of the Red River.

On July 24, 1863, after a long and arduous service on the Western rivers, he was ordered East to command the "Fort Jackson," but was soon transferred to the steam sloop-of-war "Sacramento," which he commanded on special service in search of the "Alabama." He was close upon her track when that notorious vessel was sunk by the "Kearsarge," off Cherbourg.

The "Sacramento" blockaded the Confederate steamer "Rappahannock" at Calais, France, until the end of the war, and "intercepted her when she escaped into British waters under British colors."

Captain Walke was commissioned as commodore on July 25, 1866, and, after commanding the naval station at Mound City for eighteen months, was promoted to be rear-admiral June 13, 1870.

He retired voluntarily, under the provisions of the law, in April, 1871.

## COMMODORE JOHN GRIMES WALKER. U.S.N.

COMMODORE JOHN GRIMES WALKER was born in New Hampshire, on March 20, 1835, of Scotch-Irish parentage. One of his ancestors was a defender of Londonderry at its famous siege, and his great-grandfather was a lieutenant in the Continental army. Having upon the death of his mother gone to Iowa, to his uncle, Governor Grimes, he was appointed a midshipman from that State in October, 1850, when he served, for a long cruise, on board the "Portsmouth," in the Pacific. After a course at the Naval Academy, he became a passed midshipman in 1856, and served in the "Falmouth" and the "St. Lawrence," of the Brazil Squadron. Made lieutenant in 1858. Attached to the steamer "Connecticut" at the breaking out of the Civil War, but was transferred to the gun-boat "Winona," in which vessel he took part in the passage of Forts Jackson and St. Philip, and the capture of New Orleans; and, later, in the operations before Vicksburg. Commissioned lieutenant-commander in July, 1862. Commanded the iron-clad steamer "Baron de Kalb," of the Mississippi Squadron, and in her took part in the operations about Vicksburg, the attacks upon Haines's Bluff, and the capture of Arkansas Post. The "De Kalb" formed part of the Yazoo Pass expedition in the endeavor to get into the rear of the defences of Vicksburg. Later, the "De Kalb" reached Haines's Bluff, which was found with the works evacuated. They were occupied and destroyed. Then the "De Kalb," with three gun-boats, was sent to dislodge the Confederates engaged in fortifying Yazoo City as a depot of military supplies for the Confederates. General Herron, with five thousand troops, co-operated with the naval force. By a combined attack the enemy was driven off, leaving everything (but four steamers, which were destroyed) in the hands of the Union forces. One gun-boat was captured by the navy. During the attack the "De Kalb" was blown up by a torpedo. Lieutenant-Commander Walker afterwards commanded the naval battery of the Fifteenth Army Corps at the siege of Vicksburg.

When Admiral Porter was transferred to the Atlantic coast he took several of his officers with him, and among them Walker, who was ordered to command the "Saco," and later the "Shawmut." In the latter vessel he participated in the capture of Wilmington, North Carolina.

After the cessation of hostilities he was ordered to the command of the "Shawmut," on the Brazil Station. In the "Naval Register" for January, 1866, Lieutenant-

Commander Walker stood No. 84 on the list of that grade. In August of that year he appeared on the list of commanders as No. 89, having been advanced, by the recommendation of the Board on Promotion, for meritorious services during the Civil War.

In 1866, Commander Walker was chief of staff to Admiral Porter at the Naval Academy, and served there with much ability up to 1869. He was then selected to command the frigate "Sabine," on a special cruise for the instruction of the graduated midshipmen from the Naval Academy. In 1871 he became light-house inspector, and in 1873 secretary of the Light-House Board, which he held until 1878, showing great administrative ability. While on this duty he was commissioned as captain.

During a leave of absence, in 1879-81, he was engaged in duty connected with the Chicago, Burlington, and Quincy Railroad, which gave him a good insight into the business methods of railroad corporations.

In March, 1881, he was ordered to the command of the steam-frigate "Powhatan," and in October of the same year became chief of the Bureau of Navigation, which position he held until the fall of 1889, when he resigned to command the "Squadron of Evolution," with his flag, as an acting rear-admiral, on board the "Chicago." He was promoted to the grade of commodore February 12, 1889.

To the energy and firmness of purpose of this officer, and to his enlightened ideas, are due much of the improvement which has taken place in the *personnel* and *materiel* of the navy.

## OFFICERS OF THE ARMY AND NAVY (REGULAR)

CAPTAIN G. S. LUTTRELL WARD, U.S.A. (RETIRED).

CAPTAIN G. S. LUTTRELL WARD was born in Philadelphia, Pennsylvania, educated for the bar, and admitted to practice January 17, 1863. He was commissioned as second lieutenant, Third Pennsylvania Cavalry, May 17, 1863, and served with his regiment in the First Brigade, Second Cavalry Division, Army of the Potomac, in the battle of Brandy Station, Virginia, June 9, 1863; as acting aide-de-camp on the staff of Colonel Taylor, in action of Aldie, June 21, 1863; as acting aide-de-camp on the staff of General J. B. McIntosh, in the battle of Gettysburg, July 2-3, 1863, and action of Shepherdstown, July 16, 1863. He returned to duty with his regiment and with it in the action of Culpeper Court-House, September 13, 1863; in battles of Occoquan, (detached with regiment in General Buford's first cavalry division), October 15, 1863, and New Hope Church (Mine Run), November 27, 1863; and action of Parker's Store, November 29, 1863. In February, 1864, his regiment was assigned to duty at the head-quarters of the Army of the Potomac, and engaged in the battles of the Wilderness, Spottsylvania, North Anna, Cold Harbor, and siege of Petersburg, from June 16, 1864.

He was promoted first lieutenant and mustered in October 3, 1864, and engaged in the battle of Boydton Plank-Road, October 7, 1864; again promoted captain, mustered in October 31, 1864, and engaged in battle of Hatcher's Run, Virginia, December 9, 1864, when he was severely wounded and absent on one month's sick-leave, at the expiration of which was on court-martial duty at Harrisburg, Pennsylvania, until after Lee's surrender, when he joined his regiment at Burkesville Junction, Virginia, and served there and at Richmond until his regiment was consolidated with the Fifth Pennsylvania Cavalry, June 7, 1865, when he was mustered out.

He was appointed second lieutenant, Thirteenth U. S. Infantry, May 11, 1866, and ordered to Newport Barracks, Kentucky, from which post he conducted a detachment of recruits to Nashville, Tennessee, and was assigned to Company H, Third Battalion, Thirteenth Infantry, September 13, 1866, and transferred to the Thirty-first Infantry September 21, 1866. He was in command of a battalion, en route to the site of Fort Stevenson, Dakota, June and July, 1867, where he was adjutant and acting assistant adjutant-general of the Middle District of Dakota to August 7, 1867. With his company he participated in the construction of Fort Stevens, 1867-68, and was engaged with Sioux Indians opposite that place in October, 1867.

Captain Ward was on leave of absence to August 22, 1868, at which time he was appointed aide-de-camp to Major-General Hancock, from which duty he was relieved at his own request, to be present with his regiment when it was consolidated with the Twenty-second Infantry. He therefore rejoined at Fort Stevens in April, 1869, and served there until May 27, 1869, when ordered to Fort Sully, Dakota, where he served, after two months' leave of absence, until June 12, 1870, when he was assigned to duty at the head-quarters, Department of Dakota, as acting ordnance officer, acting chief signal officer, and acting assistant quartermaster, to February 7, 1871. He was on temporary duty at Fort Snelling, Minnesota, to April, 1871, and then rejoined his company at Fort Randall, Dakota, and was in command of a detachment at Old Ponca Agency, Dakota, protecting settlers on the Niobrara River, to June 28, 1871. He was at Fort Randall to September, 1871; on Yellowstone Expedition, commanded by Major J. N. G. Whistler, September and October, 1871, as escort to surveyors of the Northern Pacific Railroad. He was then appointed aide-de-camp to Major-General Hancock, November 1, 1871, and served in that capacity to October, 1885, in the mean time having been promoted first lieutenant, July 1, 1872, and captain, April 24, 1883. He was on four months' sick-leave from January 15, 1880, and four months from December 22, 1880. He was on duty at Fort Lyon, Col., from Oct. 25, 1885, to Feb. 12, 1886; on special duty at New York City to May, at Fort Lyon to July, and on sick-leave to August, 1887; again on sick-leave from October, 1887, to April, 1888; then served at Fort Crawford, Col., Fort Lyon, Col., and Fort Keogh, Montana, to March 13, 1889; then on sick-leave to April 18, 1891, when he was retired on account of disability incident to the service.

Captain Ward was brevetted first lieutenant for the battle of Hatcher's Run, and captain for gallant and meritorious services in the campaign terminating in Lee's surrender, for which no commissions were issued in consequence of an Act of Congress, March 1, 1869, abrogating brevets.

## LIEUTENANT-COLONEL AND BREVET MAJOR-GENERAL GOUVERNEUR K. WARREN. U.S.A.
### (DECEASED.)

LIEUTENANT-COLONEL AND BREVET MAJOR-GENERAL GOUVERNEUR K. WARREN was born in New York, and graduated from the Military Academy July 1, 1850. He was promoted brevet second lieutenant Topographical Engineers the same day; second lieutenant September 1, 1854, and first lieutenant July 1, 1856. He served on topographical and hydrographical survey of the delta of the Mississippi; on board for the improvement of the canal around the falls of the Ohio; on surveys for the improvement of Rock Island and Des Moines rapids, Mississippi River; compiling general map and reports of Pacific Railroad explorations; on Sioux Expedition of 1855, and engaged in the action of Blue Water; preparing maps of Dakota and Nebraska, and at the Military Academy as assistant and principal assistant professor of mathematics, to April 27, 1861.

He was appointed lieutenant-colonel of the Fifth New York Infantry (Zouaves) May 14, 1861, and colonel of the same August 31, 1861. He served in the Department of Virginia from May to July, and was engaged in the action at Big Bethel, Virginia, June 10, 1861. He was then in the defences of Baltimore, and constructing fort on Federal Hill to March, 1862, being temporarily detached on an expedition to Northampton and Accomac Counties, Virginia, in November and December, 1861. He then participated with his regiment in all the campaigns of the Army of the Potomac until May 1, 1863, and was engaged in the siege of Yorktown, skirmish on Pamunkey River, capture of Hanover Court-House, battle of Gaines' Mill (wounded), Malvern Hill, and skirmish at Harrison's Landing; battle of second Bull Run, skirmish near Centreville, battle of Antietam, and skirmish with the enemy's rear-guard on the Potomac.

He was appointed brigadier-general of volunteers September 26, 1862, and was engaged with his brigade in the march to Falmouth and the battle of Fredericksburg. On the 4th of February, 1863, he was chief topographical engineer of the Army of the Potomac, and was engaged in action on Orange Pike, storming of Marye Heights, and battle of Salem. He was appointed major-general of volunteers May 3, 1863, and was engaged in the battle of Gettysburg (wounded). Then he was employed in the construction of bridges and making reconnoissances while pursuing the enemy from that place. He was in temporary command of the Second Army Corps from August 12, 1863, to March 24, 1864, and participated in the movement to Culpeper and the Rapidan, and engaged in the combat at Auburn and Bristoe Station, skirmish at Bull Run and Kelly's Ford, operations of Mine Run, and demonstration upon the enemy across Morton's Ford, until February 6, 1864, when he was placed in command of the Fifth Army Corps, with which he was engaged in the battles of the Wilderness, Spottsylvania, North Anna, Tolopotomy Creek, Bethesda Church, Cold Harbor, White Oak Swamp, assaults on Petersburg, siege of Petersburg, Mine Explosion, actions for the occupation of the Weldon Railroad, combat of Peeble's Farm, Chapel House, skirmish near Hatcher's Run, destruction of Weldon Railroad to Meherrin River, combat near Dabney's Mill, movement to White Oak Ridge, and battle of Five Forks, Virginia, April 1, 1865, and then in command of the defences of Petersburg to May 1, 1865.

General Warren resigned his volunteer commission May 27, 1865, and was brevetted, for "gallant and meritorious services," lieutenant-colonel, June 27, 1862, at the battle of Gaines' Mill; colonel, July 4, 1863, at the battle of Gettysburg, Pennsylvania; brigadier-general, March 13, 1865, at the battle of Bristoe Station; and major-general, March 13, 1865, in the field during the Rebellion.

General Warren's career had been a remarkable one, and he rose gradually in rank and trusted position until relieved of his command by General Sheridan, just after the battle of Five Forks, regarding which General Abbot, in the summary of his case as established by testimony before a court of inquiry, says:

"This charge had put an end to all resistance. Surrounded by his captures and flushed with victory, Warren sent back a staff officer to report to General Sheridan, and asked for further orders. These orders came in writing. They relieved him from the command of his corps, and ordered him to report to General Grant."

General Warren was promoted lieutenant-colonel of engineers, March 4, 1879, and served from the time the war closed until his death upon many important duties connected with the Corps of Engineers. He died August 2, 1882, at Newport, Rhode Island, aged fifty-two.

## CAPTAIN J. CRITTENDEN WATSON, U.S.N.

CAPTAIN J. CRITTENDEN WATSON is a native of Kentucky, and born August 24, 1842. He was appointed a midshipman from that State, September 29, 1856, being then just fourteen years old. He remained at the Naval Academy until his graduation, in 1860. In those days Kentuckians were much divided in their allegiance, but young Watson remained true to his flag. He was promoted to the grade of master in 1861, while serving in the frigate "Sabine." From the "Sabine" he was ordered to the "Hartford," Farragut's flag-ship, and in her he served for over two years, being commissioned as lieutenant in July, 1862, when not twenty years of age.

He was at the bombardment and passage of Forts Jackson and St. Philip, and of the Chalmette batteries; at the passage of the Vicksburg batteries, June and July, 1862; passage of Grand Gulf, March 19 and 30, 1863; passage of Port Hudson. Was present at the battle of Mobile Bay, August 5, 1864, and was wounded by a fragment of a shell from a rebel battery at Warrington.

During the years 1865-67 he was attached to the steam-frigate "Colorado," the flag-ship of the European Squadron.

Commissioned as lieutenant-commander on July 25, 1866, and continued to serve in the European Squadron until 1869,—being in the "Franklin," Farragut's flag-ship, and then in the steam-sloop "Canandaigua."

The year 1870 he passed upon special duty in Philadelphia. In 1871 he went to the Asiatic Station in the "Maska," second rate, and during the years 1872-73 commanded the store-ship "Omaha," at Yokohama.

During the year 1874 he was on ordnance duty at New York.

He received his commission as commander in the navy in January, 1874, and was stationed at the Mare Island Navy-Yard, 1875-77.

In 1877 he was ordered to command the "Wyoming," on the European Station, where he remained three years.

Upon his return he was appointed light-house inspector, which position he occupied from 1880 to 1886.

He was promoted to captain in March, 1887, and spent the succeeding three years upon special duty in San Francisco, California. His last duty was that of captain of the yard at Mare Island.

## MAJOR WILLIAM GEORGE WEDEMEYER, U.S.A.
(RETIRED.)

MAJOR WILLIAM GEORGE WEDEMEYER was born in Hilperdingen, Kingdom of Hanover, February 15, 1836. In 1850 his parents came to this country, and settled near Watertown, Wisconsin. He studied surveying and engineering, practising that profession until 1861. He studied law during the latter year, and was admitted to the bar. He took an active part in the Presidential campaign of 1860. In June, 1861, he, with others, began to raise a company. He had no experience as a soldier, but knew a little drill, and had some notions of discipline. These, however, were totally at variance with the inclinations of his associates. Believing that an organization of men ignorant of soldiers' duties, commanded by persons of no more knowledge of them than the privates, and owing or expecting their rank to the votes of their subordinates, would be a very unsatisfactory place to serve, he abandoned the squad he had raised, leaving it to join another company. In the mean while he had become acquainted with Lieutenant P. T. Keyes, Sixteenth U. S. Infantry, then on recruiting service at Watertown. He learned much from him, and, although not encouraged to do so, concluded to enter the regular army, and enlisted in that regiment on November 16, 1861; and on December 1 was sent to its recruiting depot at Columbus, Ohio. He was at once appointed a sergeant, and ordered to duty as acting sergeant-major. The duties were onerous, particularly to one ignorant of them, and with little help and instruction.

On December 25 Major Sidney Coolidge, commanding Sixteenth Infantry, recommended him for the appointment of second lieutenant. It was a great surprise, as he had so high an opinion of the necessary qualifications for an officer of the regular army.

In March, 1862, Lieutenant Dykeman, the regimental adjutant, was promoted; he organized his company, H, First Battalion, and took Lieutenant Wedemeyer with him. In May, 1862, the company went to the field, via the Ohio and Tennessee Rivers. His first picket-duty was on the Tennessee River bank, the steamer tied up for the night. Quiet it was, but the major will always remember it. He joined the battalion in the Fourth Brigade, Second Division, just before the evacuation of Corinth. Then followed the march to Stevenson, Alabama, the retreat to Nashville, where, on September 7, 1862, he received his appointment as second lieutenant in the Sixteenth U. S. Infantry. Then came the tiresome march to Louisville, the advance to Perryville, where the regiment arrived after the battle, it having in the mean time a lively brush with Kirby Smith's forces at Dogwalk, south of Lawrenceburg, Kentucky. After many delays and countermarchings, the regiment again found itself in Nashville. The battle of Stone River followed. At

Murfreesborough, in April, 1863, Lieutenant Wedemeyer was detailed to command the provost-guard of the First Division, Fourteenth Army Corps. He remained in that charge during the campaign on Tullahoma and Chattanooga, acting as topographical engineer on the latter, in addition to his regular duties.

At the battle of Chickamauga he had charge of a large number of prisoners, which he had considerable difficulty in getting from the field and to Chattanooga. On October 1 he was assigned to duty as assistant commissary of musters of the department. After the fall of Atlanta he was sent to the Cavalry Division of Sherman's army in the same capacity. He left Chattanooga on the last train going south, and only got to Ackworth, when Hood struck the road, sending him back to Allatoona, where he witnessed the fight for the hard-bread stored there. He joined General Kilpatrick and made with him the memorable campaign through the South. The march through Georgia was pleasant, with sufficient excitement in the fights with Wheeler's cavalry to break the monotony. The Carolina campaign was less so, on account of the weather. When General Kilpatrick was surprised at Monroe's Cross-Roads, North Carolina, Lieutenant Wedemeyer was with one of the brigades thirteen miles in the rear, stuck in the mud. After mustering out the cavalry at the close of the war, Lieutenant Wedemeyer joined his regiment at Sackett's Harbor, New York; there he was promoted captain, and proceeded with his company to Nashville, Tennessee, in January, 1866. Then followed the years of reconstruction, wherein he participated in various capacities. The crisis of 1876-77 found him in New Orleans. Thereafter he served in Kansas and Colorado; on recruiting service at Columbus, Ohio; in Texas and Utah, where, at Fort Duchesne, on February 24, 1891, he was retired as a major. He now resides at Los Angeles, California.

## CAPTAIN CHARLES WHEATON, U.S.A. (RETIRED).

CAPTAIN CHARLES WHEATON was born in Rhode Island May 31, 1835. He entered the volunteer service early in the war of the Rebellion as first lieutenant, Second Massachusetts Infantry, May 25, 1861, from which he was honorably mustered out July 26, 1862, after having served in the field in Virginia and the Shenandoah Valley, and engaged in the actions at Newtown, Bartonsville, Kernstown Heights, and Winchester, Virginia, March to May, 1862. He was appointed captain and commissary of subsistence of volunteers, July 17, 1862, and participated in the battles of Cedar Mountain, Rappahannock Station, South Mountain, Antietam, and Chancellorsville. He was inspector of subsistence, Department of the South, from August, 1863, to February, 1864; then chief commissary of subsistence in the field in Florida, in 1864, and was engaged in the battle of Olustee and action of King's Road. He was then transferred to the Army of the James, and was chief commissary in the field, from July, 1864, to January, 1865, being present at the attack on Fort Darling and actions of Deep Bottom, Laurel Hill, Fort Harrison, New Market Heights, siege of Petersburg and Richmond, operations about the latter and occupation of the same on the morning of April 3, 1865.

He was appointed lieutenant-colonel and commissary of subsistence of volunteers June 9, 1865, and honorably mustered out of the volunteer service May 31, 1866. He was brevetted major of volunteers, March 13, 1865, for meritorious services in his department during the war; and lieutenant-colonel and colonel of volunteers, December 1, 1865, for faithful and meritorious services in the subsistence department; and was honorably mentioned in reports on the battle of Antietam, Maryland.

Colonel Wheaton was acting chief commissary of subsistence of the Twenty-fifth Army Corps from January to June, 1865, and lieutenant-colonel and chief commissary of subsistence of the same corps to January, 1866.

He entered the regular service, as captain of the Thirty-third Infantry, July 17, 1867, and joined his regiment in Atlanta, Georgia, and was on company and garrison duty in that State to December, 1867, when he was Provisional Secretary of State and Comptroller-General of the State of Georgia to August, 1868, under the reconstruction laws. He was stationed at Huntsville and Jacksonville, Alabama, to May 3, 1869, and at Columbia, South Carolina, to May, 1869.

He then became unassigned, and served on reconstruction duty in Virginia and recruiting at Boston, Massachusetts, to February, 1871. Having become assigned to the Twenty-third Infantry, December 15, 1870, he joined it at Fort Colville, Washington, May 21, 1871, where he served to June, 1872, when he was ordered to the Department of Arizona, and stationed at Camp Hualpai to May, 1873; then at Yuma to July, 1874. His regiment being transferred to the Department of the Platte, he was at Omaha Barracks to May, 1875; at camp on Pawnee Reservation, Nebraska, to August, 1875; at Omaha Barracks to May, 1876, and en route for and at Fort McPherson, Nebraska, to October, 1876. He then participated in a winter campaign under General Crook, against Sioux Indians, to January, 1877, returning to Omaha Barracks, where he remained to February, 1877, when ordered to Fort Leavenworth, Kansas. In February, 1879, he was en route for camp on the North Fork of the Canadian River, Indian Territory, and in camp and cantonment at that place from March, 1879, to September, 1880. He was then detailed on recruiting service at Buffalo, New York, for two years, to October, 1882, rejoining his regiment at Fort Bliss, Texas.

In June, 1884, his regiment was transferred to the Lakes, and he was stationed at Fort Wayne, Michigan, to February, 1889, being present at the International Encampment at Chicago, Illinois, in October, 1887. He was in camp with the State troops of Michigan, at Mackinac Island, in July, 1888.

He was retired from active service, June 22, 1889, for disability contracted in line of duty.

## MAJOR AND BREVET LIEUTENANT-COLONEL LLOYD WHEATON, U.S.A.

MAJOR AND BREVET LIEUTENANT-COLONEL LLOYD WHEATON (Twentieth Infantry) was born in Michigan, July 15, 1838. He entered the volunteer service to participate in the war of the Rebellion, as first sergeant of Company E, Eighth Illinois Infantry, April 20, 1861, and was discharged, July 24, 1861, to accept the appointment of first lieutenant of the same regiment. He was promoted captain March 25, 1862; major, August 28, 1863; lieutenant-colonel, December 2, 1864; and colonel (but not mustered), March 8, 1866.

He served in the field, in the Western armies, as aide-de-camp and engineer-officer to Brigadier-General E. A. Paine, from October, 1861, to February, 1862; was then with his regiment and engaged in the battle of Shiloh, April 6, 1862, where he was wounded; was in the campaign of Vicksburg, and participated in the battles of Raymond, Jackson, Champion Hill, and the siege of Vicksburg, being acting assistant inspector-general of Logan's Division, Seventeenth Army Corps, from April 19, 1863. He was acting assistant inspector-general of the Seventeenth Corps during August, 1863, and aide-de-camp to Major-General Logan, November, 1863, and senior aide-de-camp to General Logan, while in command of the Fifteenth Army Corps, from December, 1863, to April, 1864. He was engaged in action at Jackson, Mississippi, July, 1864, and participated in the campaign against Mobile and defences, and present at the siege of Spanish Fort, and in assault on Fort Blakely, Alabama, April 9, 1865. Colonel Wheaton then served in Western Louisiana and Eastern Texas, until mustered out of the volunteer service, May 4, 1866.

On July 28, 1866, he was appointed captain of the Thirty-fourth U. S. Infantry, and was brevetted major and lieutenant-colonel, March 2, 1867, for gallant and meritorious services in the siege of Vicksburg, and in the assault on Fort Blakely, Alabama. He also received the brevet of colonel of volunteers, March 26, 1865, for faithful and meritorious services during the campaign against the city of Mobile and its defences.

Colonel Wheaton served at Nashville and Chattanooga, Tennessee, and Grenada, Mississippi, from November, 1866, to May, 1867; on reconstruction duty in Mississippi, May, 1867, to October, 1867; at Corinth, Mississippi, until April, 1869; at Head-quarters, Department of Mississippi, until September, 1869; at Fort Ripley, Minnesota, October and November, 1869; at Fort Abercrombie, Dakota, November, 1869, to May, 1870; established post of Fort Pembina, Dakota; at post, 1870-73; suppressed Fenian raid and captured raiders on the Province of Manitoba, October, 1871; in Custer's expedition to the Black Hills, July and August, 1874; at Fort Pembina, Dakota, until September, 1876; on recruiting service to November, 1878; at San Antonio, Texas, to April, 1879; at Fort Brown, Texas, to November, 1881; at Fort Hays, Kansas, to July, 1883; at Fort Leavenworth, Kansas, instructor infantry tactics, School of Infantry and Cavalry, until May, 1885; at Fort Assinniboine, Montana, until August, 1886; at Camp Poplar River, Montana, from 1886 to present time, 1892.

He was promoted major October 14, 1891, and assigned to the Twentieth Infantry.

He was honorably mentioned in the "Records of Rebellion," in report on battle of Shiloh, vol. x., part i., p. 127; capture of Vicksburg, vol. xxiv., part i., p. 649, as far as published; for services in suppressing Fenian raid and capture of raiders on the Province of Manitoba, October, 1871; received the thanks, officially, of Major-General W. S. Hancock, commander Department of Dakota, and of the British government, conveyed by the British Minister at Washington, through the Secretary of War, also thanks of the lieutenant-governor of Manitoba.

**MAJOR AND BREVET MAJOR-GENERAL AMIEL WEEKS WHIPPLE, U.S.A. (DECEASED).**

MAJOR AND BREVET MAJOR-GENERAL AMIEL WEEKS WHIPPLE was born in Greenwich, Massachusetts, in 1818. His parents were of English origin, his father being a descendant of Matthew Whipple, who received a grant of land in Ipswich in 1638, and his mother, Abigail Pepper, a descendant of an equally old New England family. He studied at Amherst College, but left before graduation to enter the U. S. Military Academy. In spite of ill health, which necessitated absence from West Point during parts of the scholastic course, he graduated, in 1841, number five in a class of fifty-two members.

He was assigned to the First Artillery, but shortly after joining his regiment was transferred to the Topographical Engineers. He was at once assigned to duty in connection with the hydrographic survey of the Patapsco River, and from that date until 1856 was continuously employed on important surveys.

In 1842 he was engaged in surveys connected with the approaches to New Orleans and of Portsmouth harbor. In 1844 he was detailed as assistant astronomer upon the Northeastern Boundary Survey, and the following year in determining the northern boundaries of New York, Vermont, and New Hampshire. In 1849 he was appointed assistant astronomer of the Mexican Boundary Commission, and, until the spring of 1853, was constantly in the field on this arduous duty. At all times in command of independent parties, he was frequently acting as chief astronomer and principal surveyor, and in that latter capacity signed the document establishing the initial point of the survey. His journal was published by order of Congress, and his services were highly commended by all of his superior officers. On the completion of this duty, he was assigned to the command of the survey for a railroad route to the Pacific near the thirty-fifth parallel.

His party left Fort Smith, Arkansas, July 13, 1853, consisting of a number of scientific assistants and an escort of troops. The Pacific coast was reached March 25, 1854, the route followed between Albuquerque and Los Angeles being very near that adopted by the Atlantic and Pacific Railroad.

Like all such expeditions in those early days, the dangers from hostile Indians and from exposure were very great, and the work exceedingly difficult; but the results obtained were highly successful, and his final report, published by order of Congress, was almost literally republished in Germany, and led to a correspondence with Baron Von Humboldt, which continued till his death.

In 1856 he was appointed engineer for the Southern Light-House District, and placed in charge of the improvements of the St. Clair Flats and St. Mary's River.

At the commencement of the Civil War he at once applied for service in the field, and was assigned as chief topographical engineer on the staff of General McDowell. In this capacity he was the author of the first maps of that part of Virginia, and their preparation necessitated most hazardous service and participation in many of the earlier engagements of that campaign. He was present at the first battle of Bull Run, and upon the second advance of the army was attached to the staff of General McClellan as chief topographical engineer. In May, 1862, he was appointed brigadier-general of volunteers, recalled from the Army of the Potomac, and assigned to the command of the defences of Washington south of the Potomac, his command extending from Alexandria to the Chain Bridge.

In October, 1862, his division was assigned to the Ninth Corps, and took part in the movement down the eastern base of the Blue Ridge, upon the skirts of Lee's retreating army.

At Waterloo his division was attached to the Third Army Corps, and he led it at the battle of Fredericksburg. At the battle of Chancellorsville it was, with the rest of the Third Corps, much exposed, and suffered as severely as any division of the army.

He was shot on Monday, May 4, 1863, when the battle was practically at an end. He was carried to Washington, where he died, May 7, without the knowledge that he had been appointed major-general of volunteers "for gallantry in action."

He had received brevets in the regular army of lieutenant-colonel for the Manassas campaign; colonel for Fredericksburg; brigadier-general for Chancellorsville, and major-general, "for distinguished services during the war."

The fort in Virginia opposite Washington, and the barracks at Prescott, Arizona, were both named in his honor.

## COLONEL AND BREVET MAJOR-GENERAL WILLIAM DENISON WHIPPLE, U.S.A. (RETIRED).

COLONEL AND BREVET MAJOR-GENERAL WILLIAM DENISON WHIPPLE was born in New York, and graduated July 1, 1851, when he was promoted brevet second lieutenant, Third Infantry, the same day, and second lieutenant, Third Infantry, July 1, 1851.

His first duty was at Newport Barracks, Kentucky, and in the spring of 1852 was ordered to conduct a detachment of recruits from Bedloe's Island, New York, to Jefferson Barracks, Missouri, where the detachment joined a larger command, which proceeded by steamer to Fort Leavenworth, and thence marched to New Mexico.

Reaching New Mexico, Lieutenant Whipple joined his company in Camp Vigilance, at Albuquerque, assisted in the construction of Fort Fillmore, and served there until 1857; participated in the Gila expedition, was engaged with Apache Indians on the Gila River, New Mexico, June 27, 1857; at Fort Defiance, New Mexico, in 1858; participated in the Navajo expedition of that year, and was engaged in a skirmish near Fort Defiance, May 30, 1858. He was engaged in the defence of Fort Defiance, when it was attacked by Indians just before daybreak, April 20, 1860; was transferred to Texas, and served at San Antonio, Fort Clark, Fort Duncan, and on quartermaster duty at Indianola, until 1861.

Lieutenant Whipple was promoted first lieutenant December 31, 1856, and appointed brevet captain, staff, assistant adjutant-general, May 11, 1861. He served as assistant in the Adjutant-General's Office, at Washington, from May to July, 1861; and as assistant adjutant-general of Colonel Hunter's division in the Manassas campaign, being engaged in the battle of Bull Run, July 21, 1861; then in the Department of Pennsylvania to September 16, 1861; the Department of Virginia to June 1, 1862; and in the Middle Department and Eighth Army Corps to March 10, 1863.

He was appointed captain, staff, assistant adjutant-general, August 3, 1861; lieutenant-colonel, staff, additional aide-de-camp, February 10, 1862; promoted major, staff, assistant adjutant-general, July 17, 1862; and appointed brigadier-general of volunteers July 17, 1863. He was in command of the post of Philadelphia, Pennsylvania, from March 11 to July, 1863; and of Second Division of Lehigh District, Pennsylvania, from July 31 to September 21, 1863.

General Whipple was then transferred to the West, and served as assistant adjutant-general of the Department and Army of the Cumberland, and as chief of staff, from November 12, 1863, to May 6, 1864, participating in the operations about Chattanooga, engaged in the battle of Missionary Ridge, demonstration on Rocky-Face Ridge, Buzzard's Roost, battle of

Resaca, action at Adairsville, battles and skirmishes near New Hope Church, battles and skirmishes of Pine Top and Kenesaw Mountain, combat of Peach-Tree Creek, siege of Atlanta, assault of the enemy's intrenchments at Jonesborough, assault at Lovejoy's Station, and occupation of Atlanta, September 8-27, 1864. He was on duty at the head-quarters of the Department of the Cumberland, from October, 1864, to June, 1865, being engaged in the battle of Nashville, and pursuit of the rebel army under General Hood, to December 31, 1864, and as assistant adjutant-general and chief of staff of the Military Division of the Tennessee to August 16, 1866.

General Whipple was brevetted lieutenant-colonel, colonel, and brigadier-general, March 13, 1865, for gallant and meritorious services in the Atlanta campaign, and in the battles before Nashville, Tennessee; and brevet major-general, U. S. Army, the same date, for gallant and meritorious services in the field during the Rebellion. He was mustered out of the volunteer service January 15, 1866.

He then served as assistant adjutant-general of the Department of Tennessee to March 16, 1867; of the Department of the Cumberland to May 8, 1869; and of the Division of the Pacific to June 15, 1870; as assistant in the Adjutant-General's Office to January 1, 1873, when he was appointed colonel, staff, aide-de-camp to the general-in-chief. He served as such in Washington and St. Louis to May 1, 1878. He was promoted lieutenant-colonel, staff, assistant adjutant-general, March 3, 1875, and served as assistant adjutant-general of the Division of the Missouri, the Division of the Atlantic, and Department of the East, from May 1, 1878, to August 2, 1890; was promoted colonel, staff, assistant adjutant-general, February 28, 1887, when he was retired from active service by operation of law.

### MEDICAL INSPECTOR CHARLES HENRY WHITE, U.S.N.

MEDICAL INSPECTOR CHARLES HENRY WHITE was born November 19, 1838, in the town of Sandwich, New Hampshire. His father was Dr. Charles White, and his mother the daughter of Ezekiel French, one of the early settlers of Sandwich. He studied civil engineering for a year, and was in the office of J. B. Henck, of Boston, Massachusetts, but gave up this course, and applied himself to medicine in the office of Dr. D. T. Huckins, of Watertown, Massachusetts, and graduated from Harvard Medical School in March, 1860. He entered the naval service as assistant surgeon in December, 1861, and was ordered for his first duty to the Chelsea Naval Hospital, then under the charge of Surgeon John L. Fox. His first sea-duty was in the U. S. S. "Huron," on the blockade off Charleston, South Carolina, and in the sounds and rivers of the coasts of South Carolina and Georgia.

From the "Huron" he was transferred to the monitor "Lehigh," and engaged in the close blockade of Charleston. Returning North in 1864, he was sent to the navy-yard at Portsmouth, New Hampshire, as assistant to Surgeon Dulaney, during the prevalence of yellow fever at that place. Thence he was ordered to the Naval Academy at Newport, Rhode Island, and put on detached duty at the recruiting rendezvous in Brooklyn, New York.

In the fall of 1864 he joined the U. S. iron-clad "Roanoke," at Point Lookout, Maryland, and remained on this vessel to the close of the war, when he was promoted to passed assistant surgeon, and attached to the navy-yard, New York. In the spring of 1866 he was ordered to the U. S. S. "Ashuelot," and made a cruise on the Asiatic Station. Returning to the United States in 1869, he was first sent to the Boston Navy-Yard, and then to the Naval Laboratory, Brooklyn, as assistant to Medical Director Benjamin F. Bache. In 1872 he returned to the Asiatic Station, and joined the U. S. S. "Benicia," but was shortly afterwards transferred to the U. S. S. "Idaho," and when that vessel was sold he went to the U. S. S. "Monocacy" to complete his cruise. On his return to the United States, he was again on duty at the Naval Laboratory, Brooklyn, and afterwards at the Naval Hospital, Mare Island, where he joined the U. S. S. "Lackawanna," and spent three years on the coast of South America and cruising among the South Sea Islands.

In 1883 he was ordered to the Museum of Hygiene at Washington, and in 1888 was sent to join the U. S. S. "Trenton," at Callao, Peru. He remained on the "Trenton," as fleet-surgeon of the Pacific Station, till that vessel was wrecked at Samoa. He continued on duty at Samoa till the officers and crew were sent back to the United States, when he went to join the U. S. S. "Pensacola," at Norfolk, Virginia, and in that vessel went to the coast of Africa with the expedition for the observation of the eclipse of December, 1889.

On the return of the "Pensacola," he was detached and sent to join the U. S. S. "San Francisco," at Mare Island, California, and in that vessel sailed for the coast of Chili, where he was transferred to the U. S. S. "Baltimore," and shortly after to the U. S. S. "Pensacola." The "Pensacola" soon after went to Honolulu, where he was detached and ordered to the "Charleston," and returned in that vessel to Mare Island, at which place he was detached on the completion of his sea-duty. He is now awaiting orders.

## CAPTAIN JOHN CHESTER WHITE, U.S.A. (RETIRED).

CAPTAIN JOHN CHESTER WHITE was born in New York City, March 8, 1841. He is the grandson of Dr. Samuel White, an eminent physician of Hudson, New York. After the death of his father, at a very early age, he became the ward of his uncle, Arthur G. Coffin, President Insurance Company of North America, Philadelphia, into whose office he entered after leaving the University of Pennsylvania, but which he left to respond to the President's call for troops, enlisting, April 18, 1861, in the Washington Grays, Company A, Seventeenth Pennsylvania Volunteers (First Pennsylvania Artillery), and serving in the field with the regiment until mustered out, Aug. 2, 1861. He returned to the insurance company until President's call for troops, prior to Antietam, when he enrolled again with the Washington Grays, forming part of Twenty-first Regiment, Pennsylvania Militia (see Bates, vol. v., p. 1195), serving with same at Camp Curtin (Harrisburg) and Camp McClure (Chambersburg), as sergeant, until discharged, September 30, 1862 (service not recognized in War Department records).

After recruiting some time as captain from One Hundred and Eightieth Pennsylvania Volunteers, Eighteenth Cavalry, he was mustered in as regimental adjutant, and extra first lieutenant, November 10, 1862, and performed all the duties as such, until formal muster out, February 26, 1863, on consolidation, the War Department since refusing to recognize in its records said service on muster-rolls.

Unwilling to lose a war record by accepting a cadetship at West Point, he enlisted to get his commission, May 8, 1863, in Eleventh U. S. Infantry. He served in the field with Company B, First Battalion, as private, corporal, and sergeant; receiving commission, May 18, 1864, as second lieutenant, Tenth U. S. Infantry, upon examination by board at Washington, his discharge reading, "His own conduct has made him an officer in the army." He served with his regiment in the Ninth and Fifth Corps until August 19, when he was captured by the enemy while in temporary command of the Fourteenth U. S. Infantry, to which he had been attached. He was confined at Petersburg and Libby Prison, Richmond, Virginia, and exchanged, December, 1864, when he rejoined his regiment at Fort Porter, New York, and returned to the field with it for the last campaign against Lee.

Captain White was engaged in the battles of the Wilderness, Laurel Hill, Spottsylvania, North Anna, and Bethesda Church, Virginia; in the assault on and siege of Petersburg, and capture of the Weldon Railroad, Virginia. He was brevetted first lieutenant, June 18, 1864, for gallant and meritorious services in front of Petersburg, Virginia, and captain for gallant and meritorious services in the battle on the Weldon Railroad, Virginia.

He was promoted to first lieutenancy, September 13, 1864, and served with his regiment in Washington; at Fort Ridgely, Minnesota, as post quartermaster and commissary; at Fort Ransom, Dakota Territory, and Fort Snelling, Minnesota, in same capacities, in addition to other duties. He was acting regimental quartermaster, Tenth Infantry, and chief quartermaster and commissary of subsistence, District of Minnesota, to March 15, 1869; awaiting orders by reason of sickness in service, May 19, 1869, until May, 1870, when detailed on recruiting service for cavalry at Cincinnati, Columbus, and Toledo, Ohio. He was then assigned to the First U. S. Artillery, January 1, 1871, and served with his regiment continuously; at Fortress Monroe, graduate Artillery School; at Fort Ontario; Fort Hamilton, Light Battery; Charleston, South Carolina; Savannah, acting assistant quartermaster and assistant commissary of subsistence, and post adjutant and temporary commandant Oglethorpe Barracks, Plattsburg Barracks, in field at Columbia, South Carolina, Edgefield Court-House, and Tallahassee, as quartermaster and commissary for all the troops there employed in political troubles of 1876-77; in command, Plattsburg Barracks, February to April, 1877; post adjutant, Fort Independence; in field with battery during labor riots, 1877, at Philadelphia, Pittsburg, and Reading, Pennsylvania; in command, Fort Wood, New York harbor, from July, 1878, to July, 1879; captain, July 18, 1879. In temporary command, Fort Warren, serving with his battery (I) there until November, 1881. In command, post and battery at Fort Canby, Washington Territory; Fort Stevens, Oregon, December, 1881, to April, 1883. Retired by reason of disabilities received in service, September 20, 1883.

Captain White now resides at 25 Lambert Avenue, Boston Highlands, Massachusetts.

PAYMASTER E. N. WHITEHOUSE, U.S.N.

PAYMASTER EDWARD NORMAN WHITEHOUSE is the second son of the late Right Reverend H. J. Whitehouse, Bishop of Illinois. He was born in New York, December 12, 1840; his family being a well-known one both in New York and Chicago, and connected with literary and educational public movements in both cities.

Paymaster Whitehouse graduated from Columbia College, in New York, in 1860.

With a strong liking for the sea, the Civil War, which occurred while he was still in doubt as to the choice of a profession, led him to seek an appointment as acting assistant paymaster, July, 1862.

He served in the "Tyler," one of the first of the celebrated Mississippi gun-boats, and afterwards in the "Tuscumbia" and "Choctaw," iron-clads of the same squadron. He was present at the first operations before Vicksburg, and the passage of the batteries there, in 1862. In the "Choctaw" he participated in much hard fighting and endless activity of movement. He participated in the two attacks upon Haines's Bluff, in the Yazoo, and was present at the capture and destruction of the navy-yard and vessels at Yazoo City; the engagements at Liverpool landing, and at Milliken's Bend. Serving at the siege of Vicksburg, May, June, and July, 1863, he was, after the surrender of that stronghold, in the expeditions up the Black and Ouachita Rivers; the Red River expedition; the severe engagement with guerillas at Fort de Russy, Louisiana; and was with the expedition in the Atchafalaya and the engagement at Simsport.

His next service was in the steamers "James Adger"

and "Corwin," on the South Atlantic blockade, 1865–66. He became assistant paymaster in July, 1866; and was commissioned passed assistant paymaster September 6, 1867. In 1867–68 he was attached to the sloop-of-war "Dale," on the North Atlantic Station, and in 1869–70 made a special cruise in the "Sabine," to the Mediterranean and Brazil. He afterwards served in the Practice Squadron, the Pacific Surveying expedition, and the "Supply." From 1876–79 he was attached to the "Monocacy," in Chinese and Japanese waters, and made an interesting cruise up the Yang-tse River, more than a thousand miles, on the occasion of the opening of the port of Ichang. The American flag was the first ever recognized, officially, so far in the interior of that country. Mr. Whitehouse was commissioned as paymaster April, 1877. For a year he was on shore duty at New York, and then went to the Asiatic Station again, being wrecked in the "Ashuelot," on the Lamock rocks, Formosa Channel. Twelve of the ship's company were lost. Mr. Whitehouse remained two and a half months on the island in charge of those who were recovering treasure from the wreck. After that he was fleet-paymaster of the station, returning home in the "Richmond," via the Suez Canal, in 1884. For about a year after this he was inspector of provisions at New York, and then, from June, 1885, to November, 1886, was in the important post of chief of the Bureau of Provisions and Clothing, at Washington, introducing beneficial reforms at a time when they were much needed. Mr. Whitney, who was then Secretary of the Navy, acknowledged Paymaster Whitehouse's efficient control of the Bureau in a letter couched in the most gratifying terms, saying that "the good judgment and energy you have displayed in putting the reforms in practice appear to me to call for special commendation."

From 1886–89 Paymaster Whitehouse was paymaster of the receiving-ship at the New York Station, and in May, 1889, he was ordered to the new cruiser "Chicago," flag-ship of the "Squadron of Evolution." In her he visited all the great European naval stations of the Mediterranean, and then went to the Brazils to convey the congratulations of the President of the United States to the Republic of Brazil.

Paymaster Whitehouse was next on the South Atlantic Station, in the "Chicago," whither Acting Rear-Admiral Walker was ordered in December, 1891, to be ready to force and hold the Straits of Magellan in case of war with Chili, and returned to the United States in May, 1892. Up to the present time Paymaster Whitehouse has performed more than twenty years of sea-service.

## MAJOR S. MARMADUKE WHITESIDE, U.S.A.

MAJOR S. MARMADUKE WHITESIDE (Seventh Cavalry) was born in Canada, January 9, 1839, and was a private of the general mounted service; and sergeant-major of the Sixth Cavalry, from November 10, 1858, to November 1, 1861, when he was appointed second lieutenant of the Sixth Cavalry; he was promoted first lieutenant January 25, 1864, and served during the war of the Rebellion in the field, with the Army of the Potomac, as acting aide-de-camp to Major-General McClellan, and engaged in all the battles of the Army of the Potomac while said army was under his command.

He also served as acting aide-de-camp to General Banks, and engaged in the operations before Port Hudson, Louisiana, and performed the duties of acting assistant quartermaster. He was aide-de-camp to General Martindale, commanding the district of Washington, D. C., and aide-de-camp to General Pleasonton, in the Army of the Potomac, and was severely injured at Culpeper Court-House, Virginia.

He was brevetted captain and major, March 13, 1865, for faithful and meritorious service.

On the 4th of April, 1864, he was assigned to duty as mustering and disbursing officer of the State of Rhode Island at Providence, remaining there until February, 1865, when he became chief commissary of musters of the Army of the Shenandoah, mustering out of service thirty thousand men. He then joined his regiment and served with it in Texas from November, 1865, to January, 1871, at which time he was detailed on recruiting service at Philadelphia, Pennsylvania, and remained there until January, 1873. He was with his regiment in Arizona from December, 1875, to July, 1882, when he was again on general recruiting service at Washington, D. C.

He served at that place and at various other stations until promoted major, Seventh Cavalry, April 14, 1884, and served at Fort Riley until 1890.

He participated in the Indian campaign at Pine Ridge Agency, South Dakota, in the winter of 1890–91; and participated in the capture of Big Foot's band of four hundred Indians, December 28, 1890, on the Porcupine; in the battle and destruction of the band on the following day; and in the fight, on December 30, with the Indians near Drexel's Mission, in which eight troops of the Seventh Cavalry were engaged.

On the 4th of January, 1891, Major Whiteside was assigned to the command of the regiment, which command he held until the close of the trouble. At the end of the campaign the command returned to Fort Riley, where the major is at present stationed, having had leave of absence, which expired April 20, 1892.

CAPTAIN AND BREVET MAJOR THOMAS WILHELM, U.S.A.

CAPTAIN AND BREVET MAJOR THOMAS WILHELM (Eighth Infantry) was born in Northampton County, Pennsylvania. He organized a company of one hundred men at the breaking out of the Rebellion; was appointed its captain, and reported with it at the capital of his State, where he was assigned to the Sixth Pennsylvania Infantry, and at once participated in the campaigns on the Upper Potomac.

On the conclusion of the service of the troops first called into activity, Major Wilhelm, upon being mustered out in July, 1861, found a second company prepared for him for the three-years call, of which he was appointed captain, and became a part of the Second Pennsylvania Heavy Artillery, which regiment was soon ordered into field-duty. He attained the rank of major in November, 1862, and was placed in command of one of its battalions. In 1864 was appointed by the War Department colonel of the Second Provisional Pennsylvania Heavy Artillery, retaining the grade of major in his former regiment. He was ordered with his new command to report for duty with the Army of the Potomac.

He served in all the battles of Grant's campaign of 1864, viz.: Those of the Wilderness, Spottsylvania Court-House, Cold Harbor (where he was wounded), and in the battles establishing the lines at Petersburg. He commanded the First Brigade, First Division, Ninth Corps, Army of the Potomac, and was complimented by General Burnside for the handsome advance of his command in the first attacks upon the enemy's lines at Petersburg. He was assigned to the command of the Second Brigade, First Division, Twenty-second Corps, in the defences of the national capital, 1864, and then as assistant inspector-general of the defences of Washington, south of the Potomac, in 1864. In addition to this duty, he was appointed recorder of a board of officers organized at Washington, D. C., for the examination of officers as to their fitness for promotion. In July, 1865, he was honorably mustered out of the service, and appointed captain of the Seventh U. S. Veteran Volunteers, and ordered to Philadelphia, where he was appointed provost-marshal of that city for a short period.

His regiment being mustered out of the service in April, 1866, he was appointed lieutenant in the Eighth U. S. Infantry on the 11th of the following month. He at once joined his regiment in South Carolina, where it was on duty performing the difficult task of passive interposition under the reconstruction laws. He was, however, soon detached from his regiment to make the survey and contracts for the improvements of the National Cemetery at Salisbury, North Carolina. From here, in March, 1868, he was appointed adjutant of his regiment, and joined the head-quarters at Raleigh, North Carolina, in which position he continued over eleven years, when he was appointed captain on June 7, 1879. During this period he was assigned to many responsible and difficult duties pertaining to the service,—among them, acting assistant adjutant-general of the District of South Carolina in the days of reconstruction; acting assistant adjutant-general of the Department of Arizona, and judge-advocate of the same department.

After his regiment was ordered to California he was selected as judge-advocate of the Military Division of the Pacific, on the staff of Major-General McDowell, serving in this capacity until the retirement of that officer.

With this enviable record, he was twice brevetted for gallant and meritorious services in action,—receiving the brevet of captain in the battles of the Wilderness, and that of major in the battles of Cold Harbor.

In the early part of the major's staff duty he saw the importance of supplying his profession with various military works; among them he produced the laborious work known as "Wilhelm's Military and Naval Encyclopædia." This work contains in the neighborhood of twenty thousand subjects; is the first book precisely of its kind in the English language, and has taken nearly ten years of the major's time in its production.

Soon after he put into the book world a revised edition of the "Encyclopædia," known as "Wilhelm's Military Dictionary and Gazetteer." This work has not only a wide circulation, but has long been one of the most useful works to the profession. This officer has also put into book form the biographies of the officers of his regiment; has written the history of his regiment in two volumes, embracing reminiscences of his corps. "Wilhelm's Military Pocket-Book" is another of his publications.

Throughout his military career, Major Wilhelm has taken many opportunities to devote his pen to the defence and improvement of the soldier.

## REAR-ADMIRAL CHARLES WILKES, U.S.N.
### (DECEASED).

REAR-ADMIRAL CHARLES WILKES was born in the city of New York on the 3d of April, 1798. His family were English, his great-uncle being John Wilkes, or "Liberty" Wilkes, as he was called. In character he was energetic, fearless, and unflinching; when acting for his country's good, never afraid to assume responsibility when assured that it was the best thing to do.

On the 1st of January, 1818, he received his appointment as midshipman; promoted to lieutenant April 28, 1826. In 1830 he was ordered to duty in the Department of Charts and Instruments. It was then that he set up fixed astronomical instruments in a small house on the grounds of his home on Capitol Hill, Washington, D. C., and he was the first in the United States to observe with them.

In 1838 he was ordered as commander of the United States Exploring Expedition, and sailed from Norfolk, Virginia, on the 18th of August of that year with five vessels under his command. During the expedition he visited the islands of the Pacific, explored and surveyed the Samoan group, and then turned southward, where they discovered the Antarctic Continent, coasting westward along it for more than seventy degrees.

In 1840 the northwestern coast of North America was visited, also the Columbia and Sacramento Rivers. In November, 1841, the expedition turned its face homeward, via the Cape of Good Hope, and cast anchor in New York harbor June 10, 1842.

The contributions of this expedition constitute part of the world's history. In acknowledgment of his services to science in this connection, the Geographical Society of London presented Lieutenant Wilkes with a gold medal.

After this expedition charges were preferred against Lieutenant Wilkes and a court-martial held. He was acquitted of all charges save that of illegally punishing some of his crew. He served on the Coast Survey in 1842–43.

He was promoted to commander July 13, 1843, and was sent to bring home the African Squadron. He was then employed in the report of the expedition until 1861. When the Civil War opened, having received his commission as captain September 14, 1855, he was placed in command of the cruiser "San Jacinto." He then sailed in pursuit of the Confederate privateer "Sumter."

On the 8th of November, 1861, he intercepted the rebel commissioners bound for England on board Her Majesty's steamer "Trent." Sending Lieutenant D. M. Fairfax on board, Messrs. Mason and Slidell were brought to the "San Jacinto," and the "Trent" proceeded on her way. The officials were taken to Fort Warren, Boston harbor. Wilkes was the hero of the North. Congress passed a resolution of thanks, and the Secretary of the Navy sent an emphatic commendation. It resulted, however, in an international complication, and the Confederate ambassadors were released at England's request. It has been claimed that Captain Wilkes should have made the case impregnable by sending the "Trent" to the United States as a prize. He was, however, justified in the course which he pursued by English precedent, according to Major George B. Davis's work on "International Law." Cf., note, pp. 361–362.

In 1862 Captain Wilkes commanded the James River Flotilla, and shelled City Point. He was promoted to commodore July 16, 1862, and placed in command of the Flying Squadron in the West Indies.

Of the officers under his command, Rear-Admiral Stevens is among the few remaining. Commodore Wilkes was placed on the retired list, June 25, 1864, from age, and promoted to rear-admiral, on the retired list, July 25, 1866. His contributions to literature were the narrative of the expedition (four volumes), and the volumes on meteorology and hydrography. He is also the author of "Western America," 1849, and "The Theory of the Winds," 1856.

Admiral Wilkes lived until February 8, 1877. He died at his home in Washington. His latter years were spent in retirement, but up to a few days of his death his one thought was his country, and his regret that his time of serving her was ended.

**BRIGADIER- AND BREVET MAJOR-GENERAL ORLANDO B. WILLCOX, U.S.A. (RETIRED).**

BRIGADIER- AND BREVET MAJOR-GENERAL ORLANDO B. WILLCOX was born in Mich., April 16, 1823, and graduated from the Military Academy in the Class of 1847, when he was promoted second lieutenant of the Fourth Artillery, and first lieutenant April 30, 1850. He served with Light Battery G, in the war with Mexico, from Sept., 1847, to June, 1848, and in the Summer Expedition on the Plains, 1850; served with troops, Fourth Artillery and marines, in the Anthony Burns Riot, Boston, May 17 to June 3, 1854, and with company in Florida, Billy Bowlegs's War, 1856-57. He resigned from Fourth Artillery Sept. 10, 1857, and settled at Detroit, Mich., in the practice of the law until May, 1861.

At the commencement of the war of the Rebellion he was appointed colonel of the First Mich. Infantry, May 1, 1861, and brigadier-general of volunteers July 21, 1861; commanded in the capture of Alexandria and Ball's Bluff, May 21, 1861; captured Fairfax Station, July 18; served in command of Second Brigade, Third Division (Heintzelman's), at battle of Bull Run, July 21, 1861, where he was severely wounded in a charge and captured; prisoner of war in Richmond, Charleston jail (hostage for privateers), Castle Pinckney, and Columbia jail, and at Salisbury and Libby Prisons, one year and twenty-four days; exchanged in August, 1862; commanded First Division, Ninth Corps, Army of the Potomac, in the battles of South Mountain and Antietam, September 14-17, 1862; commanded Ninth Corps in October and November, 1862; supporting Pleasonton's cavalry operations in the advance of Army of the Potomac (skirmish at Sulphur Springs, Warrenton, November 15), and Burnside's crossing and battle of Fredericksburg, December 11-14, 1862; commanded Ninth Corps and District of Central Kentucky from April 10 to June 9, 1863, and District of Ind. and Mich., during the enrollment riots, from June 10 to September 11, 1863; marched in command of division of reinforcements for East Tennessee from Nicholasville, Ky., Sept. 17, 1863, with which he served in Burnside's battle, Blue Springs, East Tennessee, Oct. 10, 1863, and in command of left wing on retreat from Bull's Gap; occupied Cumberland Gap, holding open communications with Kentucky during siege of Knoxville, and operated successfully at Mulberry Gap, Jonesville, Jacksonborough, and Maynardsville in November, 1863, and defeated Wheeler's cavalry at Walker's Ford, Clinch River, December 2, 1863; commanding District of the Clinch until Jan. 15, 1864; commanded Second Division and the Ninth Corps in skirmishes at Strawberry Plains, rear-guard of the Army of the Ohio, Jan. 21, and near Knoxville, Jan. 22, retreating from Dandridge, and in subsequent operations in East Tennessee, from Jan. 26 to March 16, 1864; commanded Ninth Corps en route to Annapolis, Maryland, March and part of April, 1864; commanded Third Division, Ninth Corps (reorganized under Burnside), battles of Wilderness, May 6, North Anna River, May 9 (commanding two divisions); Third Division, Spottsylvania, May 12; skirmishes on Tolopotomy, May 31 and June 1; battle of Bethesda Church, June 3; at Petersburg, June 17-18, and July 30; in action on Weldon Railroad, August 19, 21, and 25; commanding First Division (consolidated), Ninth Corps, in action, Pegram House, September 30; in skirmishes near same, Oct. 2 and 8, and at Hatcher's Run, Oct. 27, 1864; commanding division in the trenches, siege of Petersburg, from Nov. 29, 1864, to April 3, 1865; engaged in action Fort Steadman March 25, and the lines of Petersburg, from March 29 to April 3, when the city fell. He accepted surrender of Petersburg from civil authorities, and took command of city and vicinity until April 5; marched in command of division to Burksville, Virginia, April 5, and thence to Washington, on the assassination of the President; commanded District of Lynchburg, Va., from Sept., 1866, to March, 1869, reconstruction difficulties; transferred as colonel to the Twelfth Infantry, March 15, 1869, and moved with regiment to Pacific coast; superintendent general recruiting service from August, 1873, to Oct., 1874; commanded Department of Arizona on brevet commission of major-general from March, 1878, to Sept., 1882; in command of regiment at Madison Barracks until retirement, April 16, 1887; military governor of the Soldiers' Home at Washington, D. C., in 1890-92.

General Willcox was brevetted brigadier-general, March 2, 1887, for Spottsylvania Court-House, and major-general same date for the capture of Petersburg. He was also brevetted major-general of volunteers, August 1, 1864, for the " several actions since crossing the Rapidan."

He was appointed brigadier-general, Oct. 13, 1886.

## PAY-DIRECTOR W. W. WILLIAMS, U.S.N.

PAY-DIRECTOR W. W. WILLIAMS was born in Ohio, and appointed assistant paymaster from that State in August, 1861. His first duty was on board the "Louisiana," and he was in her at the battles of Roanoke Island, Elizabeth City, and New Berne, in 1862. In 1863, while still attached to the "Louisiana," he volunteered his services to General Foster during the three weeks' siege of Washington, commanding the army gun-boat "Eagle," and, for his services at that critical juncture, received a warm letter of thanks from General Foster, which is on file in the Navy Department. For the same service he received a letter of thanks "for brave and gallant conduct," from Commander Renshaw, of the "Louisiana," which is also on file in the Navy Department; and one highly commendatory, and going more into detail, from Acting Volunteer Lieutenant-Commander Saltonstall, also on file.

He was promoted to paymaster March 2, 1864, and ordered to the steam-sloop "Wachusett," on the Brazil Station. Was attached to her at the time the "Florida" was taken at Bahia, in October, 1864. Captain Collins, of the "Wachusett," gave him a letter, which is on file, in regard to his conduct on that occasion, in which he says, among other things, "Your coolness, at a time of considerable confusion, served me to execute many details of the surrender of the 'Florida,' while we were still under the range of the guns of the shore forts and batteries. Had the equanimity of others been equal to your own, and my orders, transmitted through you, been fully carried out, I have no doubt we should have sunk the 'Florida' within five minutes from the time we struck her, and should have avoided the useless noise and disgrace of firing needlessly shotted guns in a neutral port. I can state that your services to me in making the capture were more valuable than that of any one person that night, etc."

Commander Alexander Murray also bore written testimony to Paymaster Williams's gallantry on boat expeditions and other occasions. He was promoted ten numbers in his corps," for gallant and meritorious service" at Wallop's Island, and Washington, North Carolina. In 1864-65 he was inspector of clothing in the Mississippi Squadron; and was attached to the store ship "Fredonia," at Callao, 1867-68. He was one of the three surviving officers of that vessel when she was wrecked by an extraordinary tidal wave at Arica, Peru, on August 13, 1868. He was attached to the navy-yard, Portsmouth, New Hampshire, in 1870-73. Promoted to pay-inspector in October, 1871, and at that date received the advancement in his grade alluded to above. He served as fleet-paymaster of the North Atlantic Station in 1874-75; and was in charge of the pay-office at Washington, 1875-78. After a service as inspector of provisions at the Washington Navy-Yard—1878-80,—he was for three years fleet-paymaster of the European Station. From 1884 to 1887, he was in charge of the pay-office at San Francisco. Since then he has been general storekeeper at the navy-yard at Mare Island, California.

## CAPTAIN BYRON WILSON, U.S.N.

CAPTAIN BYRON WILSON was born in Ohio, December 17, 1837, and appointed midshipman from that State in January, 1853. After four years at the Naval Academy, Annapolis, he made a cruise in the steam-frigate "Mississippi," in the East Indies, and in the steam-sloop "Richmond," which ship was attached to the West Gulf Squadron in 1861. He was commissioned lieutenant in April of that year, and ordered to the Mississippi Squadron, where he had command of the "Mound City," and, from 1863 to 1865, command of a division of the squadron. He served in almost all the important events of the war upon the river. At the passage of the Vicksburg batteries, April 16, 1863; Deer Creek, 1863; Red River Expedition, 1864. He was commissioned as lieutenant-commander in 1863. Served in the steam-sloop "Saranac," Pacific Squadron, 1866-68; steam-sloop "Plymouth," European Squadron, 1868-69. Commanded the "Nipsic," on the Darien Expedition of 1870-71. Commissioned as commander, January, 1872; and commanded the receiving-ship "St. Louis," from 1875 to 1878. Commanded the "Wachusett," Pacific Station, 1879-80. From 1881 to 1883 in charge of Naval Rendezvous at Philadelphia. Commissioned captain in April, 1883. At present in command of the "Independence," at Mare Island, California.

The operations at Deer Creek, mentioned above, were among the most curious of the whole war. It was an attempt to get in the rear of Vicksburg with the gunboats, by way of the Yazoo, through passes so overhung with trees and bushes that they had to be cut away in many places for the boats to pass. The latter were compared, with their iron-clad casemates, to great mud-turtles crawling through their native swamps. Trees were run down, made fast to, and hauled out of the way, and saws and axes employed upon others, which stood in many feet of water. The details of this romantic expedition of vessels of six hundred tons among the primeval forests of the swamps must be read in detail to be understood and appreciated. The retreat, made necessary by the physical difficulties, is even more remarkable and more interesting than the advance. Fortunately, General Sherman and his army had been detached to the assistance of the beleaguered fleet, and arrived in time to succor them, when caught in a sort of trap. The expedition, though not entirely successful, had a great effect upon the operations of the Confederacy.

The wonderful work of the "dam" on the Red River, by which the fleet of gun-boats was saved, is much better known to the public at large than this extraordinary bayou expedition.

After the surrender of Vicksburg, the "Mound City," under Lieutenant-Commander Wilson, "gave the enemy a severe lesson." Confederate raiders, under McNeil, made a descent upon Lake Providence, for the purpose of carrying off mules, horses, and wagons belonging to the Federal army. Much to their surprise,—as they naturally did not expect to find an iron-clad on Lake Providence,—Wilson opened upon them, and they retreated, leaving many dead and wounded, and never troubled that part again.

The night-passage of the Vicksburg batteries, in which Captain Wilson bore a prominent part, is well known. Fortunately, the results were commensurate with the daring displayed.

## MAJOR AND PAYMASTER CHARLES I. WILSON, U.S.A.

MAJOR AND PAYMASTER CHARLES I. WILSON was born in Washington, D. C., May 3, 1837. Retiring year, 1901. Appointed from New York,—civil life. Assistant surgeon, May 28, 1861; accepted, May 31, 1861; captain and assistant surgeon, May 28, 1866; resigned, January 1, 1867; captain Sixteenth Infantry, January 22, 1867; accepted, March 23, 1867; unassigned, April 17, 1869; honorably discharged, December 31, 1870; major and paymaster, March 3, 1875; accepted, March 22, 1875. Brevet captain, March 13, 1865, for meritorious and distinguished services in the battle of Todd's Tavern and Yellow Tavern, Virginia; brevet major, March 13, 1865, for highly meritorious and distinguished services in his department in twelve engagements in the Shenandoah Valley, Virginia; brevet major, March 2, 1867, for meritorious services in the battle of Todd's Tavern. On duty as post-surgeon at Fort Leavenworth and Fort Larned, Kansas, from September, 1861, to September, 1862; on duty at Frederick, Maryland, from September, 1862, to December, 1862, in charge of Confederate hospitals; reported for duty in Army of the Potomac, December, 1862; assigned to duty with regular cavalry, and was successively regimental surgeon Second United States Cavalry, surgeon-in-chief Regular Cavalry Reserve Brigade, surgeon-in-chief First Cavalry Division, and acting medical director Cavalry Corps, Middle Military Division (Shenandoah Valley), until early spring of 1865; as assistant surgeon U. S. A., with rank of first lieutenant, participated in all the cavalry engagements from spring of 1865; was on duty in Washington as hospital surgeon, surgeon-in-chief of the defences of Washington, and post-surgeon at Fort Washington, Maryland, until January 1, 1867, when he resigned the service; appointed captain Sixteenth Infantry, to date January 22, 1867, and served with regiment until April, 1869; was then unassigned and shortly after ordered on duty on recruiting service; appointed major and paymaster U. S. A., March 3, 1875; was assigned to duty in the Department of Texas, and served there until May, 1881; then ordered to the Department of the East, station New York City, and served there until June, 1885; was then ordered to the Department of the Platte, station Omaha, Nebraska, and served there until July, 1887; was then ordered to Department of the Missouri, station St. Louis, Missouri, where he has been since, and is at present serving. Participated in the first battle of Bull Run and in all the cavalry engagements of the Army of the Potomac and Shenandoah Valley. In command of Bedloe's Island, a sub-depot of recruits, and also at David's Island, New York harbor, until December 31, 1870, when he was honorably discharged the service at his own request.

COLONEL JOHN M. WILSON, U.S.A.

COLONEL JOHN M. WILSON (Corps of Engineers) was born in the District of Columbia, and graduated at the Military Academy July 1, 1860, when he was promoted brevet second lieutenant of artillery the same day. He was transferred to the ordnance October 9, 1860, transferred to the First Artillery January 17, 1861, and promoted second lieutenant, Second Artillery, January 28, 1861. He was promoted first lieutenant May 14, 1861, having served as assistant ordnance-officer at Fort Monroe and at Washington Arsenals until April, 1861, when he was in the defences of Washington to July, and participated in the Manassas campaign, being engaged in battle of Bull Run, July 21, 1861. He was then in the defences of Washington to March, 1862, when he participated in the Virginia Peninsula campaign, and was engaged in the siege of Yorktown, April 5 to May 4, 1862; battle of Williamsburg, May 4–5, 1862; action of Slatersville, May 9, 1862; skirmish at Gaines' Mill, May 23, 1862; action of Mechanicsville, May 23–24, 1862; battle of Gaines' Mill, June 27, 1862; battle of Malvern Hill, June 30 to July 1, 1862; skirmish at Harrison's Landing, July 2, 1862; action at Malvern Hill, August 5, 1862.

He was transferred to the Topographical Engineers July 24, 1862, and was in the Maryland campaign, and participated in the battles of South Mountain and Antietam, Maryland, and was superintending engineer of construction of defences of Harper's Ferry, Virginia, November 1, 1862, to March 20, 1863; assistant professor of Spanish at United States Military Academy, March-June, 1863; assistant engineer of the construction of defences at Baltimore, Maryland, June–July, 1863; superintending engineer of the defensive works at Memphis, Vicksburg, and Natchez, August, 1863, to May, 1864; inspector-general, Military Division, West Mississippi, May, 1864, to September, 1865; in the Mobile campaign, March–May, 1865; detailed to present to the Secretary of War the Confederate flags captured in the Mobile campaign, May, 1865; in charge of the construction of fort at Ship Island, Mississippi, and defences of New Orleans, September 16, 1865, to January 10, 1866.

He was engaged in the skirmish at Charlestown, Va., Oct. 17, 1862; in the siege and capture of Spanish Fort, March 28–April 8, 1865; storming of Blakely, April 9, 1865; occupation of Mobile, April 12, 1865; and surrender of General Dick Taylor's army at Citronelle, May 4, 1865.

He was promoted captain, June 1, 1863; major, June 3, 1867, and lieutenant-colonel, March 17, 1884. He was made brevet captain, June 27, 1862, for gallant and meritorious services in the battle of Gaines' Mill, Virginia; major, July 1, 1862, for gallant and meritorious services in the battle of Malvern Hill; lieutenant-colonel, April 8, 1865, for gallant and meritorious services in the capture of Spanish Fort, Mobile harbor; colonel, April 8, 1865, for gallant and meritorious services at Spanish Fort and Fort Blakely; colonel of volunteers, March 26, 1865, for faithful and meritorious services during the campaign against the city of Mobile and its defences.

At the close of the war Colonel Wilson was at Jefferson Barracks, Missouri, and in charge of disposition of engineer property in Ark. and Missouri, Jan. 28, 1866, to Sept. 4, 1866; assistant engineer in the improvement of the Hudson River, Sept. 4, 1866, to Jan. 21, 1871; superintending engineer of Forts Ontario and Niagara, of harbor improvements on Lake Ontario and St. Lawrence River, and of the survey of the Third Subdivision of the Northern Transportation route, from the Great Lakes to tide-water, Jan., 1871, to Dec., 1875; superintending engineer of Forts Stevens and Canby, of river and harbor improvements in Oregon and Washington Territories, including Columbia, Willamette and Snake Rivers and Cascade Canal, and engineer, Thirteenth Light-House District, Dec., 1875, to Oct. 21, 1878; superintending engineer of the river and harbor improvements of Lake Erie west of Dunkirk, Dec., 1878, to Oct. 24, 1882, and engineer of the Tenth Light-House District, July, 1881, to Dec., 1881; in charge of the First and Second Divisions, office of the chief of engineers, U. S. A., October, 1882–86; on duty in California connected with proposed restraining barriers on the Yuba, American, and Bear Rivers, August 2–29, 1883; in charge of public buildings and grounds, in the District of Columbia, with the rank of colonel, June 1, 1885, to September 7, 1889. On August 17, 1889, he was assigned to duty as superintendent of the Military Academy, which position he now occupies. Degree of LL.D. conferred by Columbia University, Washington, D. C., 1890.

## COMMODORE THEODORE D. WILSON, U.S.N.

COMMODORE THEODORE D. WILSON (Chief Constructor) was born in Brooklyn, New York, May 11, 1840. Served a regular apprenticeship as shipwright under Naval Constructor B. F. Delano, U.S.N., at the navy-yard, Brooklyn, New York. Served for three months at the outbreak of the Civil War as a non-commissioned officer in the Thirteenth Regiment, New York State Militia.

On the return of the regiment he was appointed a carpenter in the navy, from August 3, 1861. Served afloat in the North Atlantic Blockading Squadron, aboard the U. S. steamship "Cambridge," William A. Parker, commander, commanding, until 1863, during which time he took part in the first day's fight with the "Merrimac," and was in several minor engagements on the coast.

On December 15, 1863, he was ordered to special duty under Rear-Admiral Gregory, general superintendent of all works outside of navy-yards, and by his order was intrusted with the building, repairing, and alterations of scores of vessels, involving the exercise of great judgment and skill.

Commodore Wilson remained on this important duty until May 17, 1866, when he was examined for, and appointed, an assistant naval constructor in the navy, and ordered to duty in charge of the Construction Department of the navy-yard, Pensacola, Florida. Detached December 28, 1867, he was ordered to the navy-yard, Philadelphia, Pennsylvania. While attached to this station as assistant to Naval Constructor S. M. Pook (deceased), he finished and launched the "Omaha," completed the rebuilding of the "Juniata," commenced the rebuilding of the frigate "Brooklyn," and repaired the "Sangamon" and "Dictator."

Detached on the 3d of July, 1869, he was ordered to the Naval Academy as instructor in ship-building and naval architecture, where he remained for a period of four years, giving great satisfaction.

During the summer of 1870 he was ordered by the Secretary of the Navy to England and France, on special service, for the purpose of observing, personally, the improvements in the construction of iron vessels-of-war. This duty was satisfactorily performed, and much reliable information obtained for the naval service.

Detached from the Naval Academy, July 16, 1873, he was ordered in charge of the Department of Construction and Repair, at the navy-yard, Washington, D. C., and while there rebuilt the sloop-of-war "Shawmut," fitted her for sea, and laid down and put the sloop-of-war "Nipsic" in frame.

He was promoted and commissioned as naval constructor from July 1, 1873; detached, and ordered to the navy-yard, Portsmouth, New Hampshire, June 1, 1874, where he was stationed until March 3, 1882. While there he had the supervision of the work on the "Plymouth," "Kearsarge," and "Wachusett;" finished the "Enterprise;" launched the sloop-of-war "Essex;" completed and fitted for sea the sloop-of-war "Marion;" rebuilt and fitted out the sloop-of-war "Ticonderoga;" rebuilt and fitted for sea the corvette "Lancaster," the latter vessel being almost entirely rebuilt from his own designs.

In 1881 he was appointed a member of the First Naval Advisory Board, of which Rear-Admiral John Rodgers was president, organized for the purpose of determining and recommending the number and classes of new vessels to be constructed for the naval service.

On the 3d of March, 1881, he was nominated by President Arthur, and confirmed by the Senate, as chief constructor of the navy and chief of the Bureau of Construction and Repair. On the 15th of December, 1886, he was renominated by President Cleveland and confirmed by the Senate, and for the third time he was renominated by President Harrison on the 15th of December, 1890, his present term expiring December, 1894.

During the period that he has been chief constructor, plans have been made for thirty-two of the new steel vessels now in the service, or in course of construction, and plans prepared for completing the five double-turretted iron monitors, aggregating eighty-nine thousand three hundred and sixty-three tons displacement.

## CAPTAIN GILBERT C. WILTSE, U.S.N.

CAPTAIN GILBERT C. WILTSE is a native of the State of New York, and born November 29, 1838. He was appointed a midshipman from his native State on September 20, 1855. From that time until 1859 he was at the Naval Academy. Upon graduation he was ordered to the frigate "Congress," the flag-ship of Admiral J. R. Sands, on the Brazil Station. The "Congress" was recalled from that station upon the breaking out of the Civil War, arriving in Boston in August. The officers of that ship (two midshipmen and the two marine officers) who resigned upon arrival, with the expressed intention of going South, were the first naval officers held for exchange, being arrested and placed in Fort Warren.

Wiltse was detached from the "Congress" and ordered to the frigate "St. Lawrence," in which ship he was present at the engagement between the "Merrimac," the "Congress," and the "Cumberland," in Hampton Roads, March 8 and 9, 1862. He was also in the engagement with Sewell's Point batteries in May, 1862. He had been commissioned as lieutenant April 19, 1861.

He was detached from the "St. Lawrence" and ordered to the steam-sloop "Dacotah," in which ship he served in the West Indies during 1862-63, and in the South Atlantic Blockading Squadron from 1863 to 1865. He participated in the engagement of the monitors with Forts Sumter and Moultrie in November, 1863. He was commissioned lieutenant-commander in March, 1865. In 1866-67 he served in the "Agawam," of the North Atlantic Squadron, and was then ordered to the apprentice-ship "Sabine," where he remained two years.

Upon his return from this cruise he was upon shore duty at the navy-yard, New York, and went thence to the monitor "Saugus," of the North Atlantic Squadron, where he remained during 1869-70. From 1870 to 1872 he was on duty at the navy-yard, Pensacola.

On November 8, 1873, he was commissioned a commander in the navy, and during 1875-76 commanded the "Shawmut" (third rate) in the North Atlantic Squadron. From 1878 to 1881 he had a tour of shore duty at the New York Navy-Yard, and during 1884-85 he commanded the steam-sloop "Swatara," of the North Atlantic Squadron.

He was promoted to captain January 26, 1887, and commanded the receiving-ship "Franklin" and the U. S. training-ship "Minnesota" in succession.

Captain Wiltse is at present in command of the cruiser "Boston," of the Pacific Squadron.

## COMMANDER GEORGE E. WINGATE, U.S.N.

COMMANDER GEORGE E. WINGATE was born in Portsmouth, New Hampshire, July 10, 1837. First cruise in clipper-ship "Reporter," North Atlantic, October 4, 1853-55; clipper-ship "Storm King," China, 1855-57; North Atlantic Ocean, 1857-60; China Sea and East Indies, 1860-63. Entered the naval service of the United States as an acting ensign, October 31, 1863; served in the East and West Gulf Blockading Squadrons during the Rebellion; commissioned master, U.S.N., March 12, 1868; promoted to lieutenant, December 18, 1868; U. S. S. "Quinnebaug," South Atlantic Station, 1867-68; transferred to U. S. flag-ship "Guerriere," and served on board until her return to the United States in 1869. Commissioned lieutenant-commander, July 13, 1870; U. S. S. "Saugus" and "Ajax" (iron clads), North Atlantic Station, 1869-70; Torpedo Station, 1871-72; U. S. S. "Richmond" (second rate), 1872-73; U. S. receiving-ships "New Hampshire" and "Sabine," 1874; commanding U. S. S. "Ajax," 1875-76; "Adams," North Atlantic and Pacific Stations, 1877-79; Boston Navy-Yard, 1880-82; U. S. flag-ship "Brooklyn," 1882-84; in charge of Nitre Depot, Malden, Massachusetts, December, 1884-88. Promoted to commander, May 26, 1887; commanding U. S. store-ship "Monongahela," Pacific Station, 1888-89; U. S. S. "Ranger," Pacific Station, 1890-91; U. S. S. "Michigan," Northwestern Lakes, December 1, 1891.

**PASSED ASSISTANT SURGEON GEORGE F. WINSLOW, U.S.N.**

PASSED ASSISTANT SURGEON GEORGE F. WINSLOW was born at New Bedford, Bristol County, Mass., on May 8, 1842. Graduated at Harvard University in March, 1864. Appointed an acting assistant surgeon on July 26, 1862, at that time not having arrived at the age of twenty-one, the limit of age-requirement established by the regulations governing the navy; and having successfully passed the Board of Medical Examiners for admission, his age was waived by Hon. Gideon Welles, the then Secretary of the Navy, and his appointment was issued on the above date. Attached to U. S. S. "Morse," North Atlantic Blockading Squadron, until January, 1864. Different engagements on James River, protecting flanks of Army of the Peninsula, under General McClellan; White-House Landing, Malvern Hill, Brick-House Point, West Point, Pamunkey, and Mattapony engagements; Nansemond River and Suffolk against General Longstreet, C.S.A. Ordered to "Osceola," February 24, 1864. Detached August 25, 1865. Commissioned assistant surgeon, May 28, 1864. On detached duty with army in front of Petersburg during the summer of 1864. Detailed on operating surgical staff; both battles at Fort Fisher, North Carolina. Engagements in Cape Fear River, Forts Strong and Buchanan; taking of Wilmington, N. C., and Richmond, Va.

Ordered by Admiral D. D. Porter to take charge of the Confederate hospital at Fort Fisher the day after its surrender. Without trained nurses or surgical assistance, performed all operations on Confederate and Union wounded. In a letter addressed to Admiral Porter, dated January 21, 1865, head-quarters U. S. forces, Fort Fisher, North Carolina, Surgeon-General Barnes, U.S.N., wrote as follows: "In behalf of the commanding general and the officers of this command, I have the honor of thanking Assistant Surgeon Winslow, of the navy, for his professional services rendered to the wounded within the fort (particularly the Confederate wounded) immediately after the battle of the 15th instant. His promptness and skill saved many a poor fellow, who otherwise would have suffered. For myself I cannot sufficiently thank him for his noble conduct on that occasion." U. S. frigate "Sabine," apprentice system, September 5, 1865; detached June 25, 1867. Promoted to passed assistant surgeon, May, 1867. Ordered to South Pacific Squadron, July, 1867; detached in December, 1869. During his service in the Pacific he was attached to the "Wateree," "Nyack," and "Powhatan." On August 13, 1868, the U. S. S. "Wateree," then at anchor in the harbor of Arica, was washed up and wrecked by an earthquake wave, landing her three hundred and ten yards beyond the sea-coast line. The prefect of the province of Arica requested the admiral of the station to detail an officer to aid the medical officers of the province, after the catastrophe, and Passed Assistant Surgeon Winslow was ordered to remain at Arica for that purpose. In recognition of his services the Colonel Minister of War and Navy of Peru made his services matter of official and commendatory report, which lack of space prevents repeating here.

Subsequent to this recognition the Congress of Peru in Lima voted the thanks of the nation to Dr. Winslow for his philanthropic surgical aid rendered to the suffering inhabitants of Arica after the earthquake of August 13, 1868. The following letter explains itself:

" WASHINGTON, D. C., October 14, 1869.
" TO THE HONORABLE SECRETARY OF THE NAVY:

" SIR,—I take much pleasure in complying with an instruction which I have received from Her Majesty's Principal Secretary of State for Foreign Affairs to request you to cause to be conveyed to Passed Assistant Surgeon George F. Winslow, U.S.N., the thanks of Her Majesty's Government for his great kindness to distressed and frozen seamen in the Straits of Magellan during the winter of 1868.

" I have the honor to be, with the highest consideration,
[Signed] " EDWARD THORNTON."

Ordered to navy-yard, Boston, April 9, 1870. Naval Hospital, Chelsea, Mass., June 8, 1871. Practice-ship "Saratoga," May, 1871. Flag-ship " Wabash," European Squadron, October 5, 1871; detached April 17, 1874. Portsmouth Navy-Yard, apprentice-ship " Sabine," November 16, 1874, to November 13, 1875. Promoted to surgeon April 2, 1875. U. S. Torpedo Station, Newport, Rhode Island, 1876-78; " Vandalia," North Atlantic Station, 1879-82; navy-yard, Boston, 1882-86; "Atlanta," North Atlantic Station, 1886-88; marine rendezvous, Boston, 1889-90; navy-yard, Norfolk, Virginia, 1891-92; still on duty at that station, May 31, 1892.

## REAR-ADMIRAL JOHN A. WINSLOW, U.S.N.
(DECEASED).

REAR-ADMIRAL JOHN A. WINSLOW'S name will always be associated with the capture of the notorious privateer "Alabama." He was a native of North Carolina, born in 1811, and was appointed midshipman from that State in 1827. After service in the West India Squadron, he became passed midshipman in 1833. Attached to the navy-yard at Boston, and served at sea in the Brazils. Commissioned as lieutenant in December, 1839, and from 1840 to 1846 served in the Home Squadron, in the "Missouri" and the "Cumberland." Present at the attack upon Tabasco, and in various skirmishes from the Rio Grande down the Mexican coast. He next went to the Boston Navy-Yard, and from 1852 to 1855 was attached to the frigate "St. Lawrence," in the Pacific. Was commissioned commander in 1855. Service at Boston rendezvous and as light-house inspector until the Civil War broke out. He was then ordered to the Mississippi Flotilla, and was present at Fort Pillow; engaged in various attacks and skirmishes with guerillas; and was in command of the expedition up White River, in June, 1862, for the relief of General Curtis's army.

He was commissioned as captain July 16, 1862. During 1863-64 he commanded the steam-sloop "Kearsarge," on special service. This service took him to the port of Cherbourg, France, where he found the "Alabama." That a marine duel would be fought between these ships was so certain, excursion trains were run from Paris, to enable people to see it from the cliffs north of Cherbourg. On Sunday, June 19, 1864, the "Alabama" stood out from the port, accompanied by an English steam-yacht, called the "Deerhound." Captain Winslow cleared for action, and ran off to be without the limits of the neutral zone. When the "Alabama" was about seven miles from the shore, and about nine hundred yards from the "Kearsarge," the action began. Captain Winslow fearing that if his adversary received serious damage, he would steam within the line of jurisdiction for protection, determined to run under her stern and rake her. To avoid this, Semmes, the commander of the "Alabama," sheered, and so keeping broadside on to the "Kearsarge," the vessels were forced into a circular track.

At the seventh rotation the "Alabama" was disabled and made for the shore, but another shot brought down the rebel flag, and a white one was run up. An officer

from the "Alabama" came alongside the "Kearsarge" and surrendered his vessel, reporting her in a sinking condition. In twenty minutes after this the "Alabama" sank. In spite of the surrender and demand for assistance, Semmes, and many of his officers and crew, escaped in the "Deerhound." The remainder were picked up by the "Kearsarge's" boats. Only three men of the "Kearsarge" were wounded in this remarkable combat. The number of killed and wounded on board the "Alabama" has never been given. Seventeen men, who were wounded, were picked up by the victors. The battery of the "Kearsarge" consisted of seven guns—two eleven-inch Dahlgren, one 30-pounder rifle, and four light 32-pounders. That of the "Alabama" consisted of eight guns,—one heavy 68-pounder, weighing nine thousand pounds; one 100-pound rifle, and six heavy 32-pounders. For this gallant action, the only action at sea during the war, when the conditions were not those of surprise, Winslow was promoted to be commodore from July 19, 1864.

In 1866 he was ordered to command the Gulf Squadron, which he retained until 1867. He was commandant of the Portsmouth Navy-Yard from 1868 to 1871. Commissioned as rear-admiral March 2, 1870. Commanded the Pacific Fleet in 1871-72. Died, September, 1873.

Whenever the action of the "Alabama" and the "Kearsarge" is mentioned, naval men will bear in mind his first lieutenant, James S. Thornton, who died, a captain in the navy, on the 14th of May, 1875, at Philadelphia.

## COMMANDER WILLIAM CLINTON WISE, U.S.N.

COMMANDER WILLIAM CLINTON WISE was born at Lewisburg, Greenbrier County, Virginia (which county is now embraced in the State of West Virginia), on the 8th of November, 1842.

He was appointed an acting midshipman from the State of Kentucky, and entered the Naval Academy in September, 1860. Those were times which proved what men were, and young Wise remained firmly loyal. The Naval Academy was removed, temporarily, to Newport, Rhode Island; and, as the war assumed a more and more serious nature, the midshipmen were advanced in their studies as rapidly as possible. Wise was one of those who were sent out, with the rank of ensign, just three years after he had entered the Academy.

His first ship was the "New Ironsides," off Charleston, where he served on picket and signal duty, and in the general bombardments, as divisional-officer. He also served in the expedition to Jacksonville. When the "Ironsides" was ordered North for repairs in 1864, he was detached and ordered to the "Canandaigua," and was aid to Captain J. F. Green, commanding the in-shore squadron flag-ship "John Adams."

In August, 1864, he was detached and ordered, as aid to Commodore Stephen C. Rowan, for duty in the great Sounds of North Carolina, but, those operations having been put an end to, he was next ordered to the steam-frigate "Minnesota," the flag-ship of Commodore Lanman, commanding the Second Division of Admiral Porter's fleet. In that ship he participated in both bombardments of Fort Fisher, and the final capture of that stronghold. After the fall of Fort Fisher, Wise was detached from the "Minnesota" and ordered to the command of the steamer "Malvern," Admiral Porter's flag-ship, being then twenty-two years of age. He commanded that vessel during the attacks upon Forts Anderson and Strong, and the various batteries on the Cape Fear River, which resulted in the evacuation of Wilmington, North Carolina, the "Malvern" being the first vessel to reach that city.

After the Cape Fear River was closed to the blockade-runners, which had so freely availed themselves of that safe and convenient resort, the "Malvern" went up the James River, and participated in the exciting events attending the close of the war.

She was the first vessel to reach Richmond after the evacuation, and was then honored by the presence of President Lincoln.

Lieutenant Wise was recommended for promotion by the board of 1866. In the mean time—June, 1865—he joined the flag-ship "Hartford," Admiral H. H. Bell, on the Asiatic Station, and from her was transferred to the "Wachusett," Commander Townsend, on the same station. Here he served in a landing party, in Northern China, in breaking up a band of land-pirates which the native authorities were afraid to attack. In the same vessel he served, under Commander Shufeldt, in investigating the circumstances of the massacre of the crew of an American schooner by the Coreans. That vessel was afterwards employed in surveying the almost unknown Corean coast.

Upon his return from the East, Lieutenant Wise was employed at the Naval Academy during the practise cruise of 1869, and in 1870 was the navigating-officer of the monitor "Miantonomah."

His next service was in the U.S.S. "Brooklyn," on the European Station, where he remained nearly three years, visiting a great number of English and Continental ports. After his return he was ordered to the "Ajax," West India Station; the receiving-ship "Vermont," where he was on duty in 1874-75; the flag-ship "Tennessee," on the Asiatic Station, in 1875-76; and commanded the "Palos," on the same station, in 1877-78.

Commander Wise has since commanded the "Portsmouth" and "Juniata," and served on several shore stations.

## CAPTAIN FRANCIS WISTER, U.S.A. (RESIGNED).

CAPTAIN FRANCIS WISTER was educated at the University of Pennsylvania, and graduated from that institution in the Class of 1860.

August 5, 1861, in the early part of the Civil War, he was appointed from State of Pennsylvania as captain of Twelfth U. S. Infantry. At the time this appointment was made Captain Wister was barely of age; as soon as the appointment reached him, Captain Wister hastened to join his regiment. He took part in the battles of Gaines' Mill, Turkey Bend (here supporting the batteries), Malvern Hill, second Bull Run, Antietam, Fredericksburg, Chancellorsville, and Gettysburg. Captain Wister was brevetted major of U. S. Army, January 3, 1863, for gallant and meritorious services at the battle of Chancellorsville, Virginia, and brevetted lieutenant-colonel, July 2, 1863, for gallant and meritorious services at the battle of Gettysburg, Pennsylvania. In this battle he was second in command of his battalion, and gave all the orders during the battle.

In September, 1863, Captain Wister was ordered on recruiting service as one of the officers of his regiment, having seen the longest service in the field.

After serving on this duty for a year, he, in September, 1864, again returned to the army and took command of his regiment, which took part in several affairs in the vicinity of Hatcher's Run. Soon after this his regiment, the Twelfth U. S. Infantry, was ordered to New York, and Captain Wister was appointed senior aide-de-camp on the staff of Major-General A. A. Humphries. Serving in that capacity, he remained in the field until after the surrender of General Lee.

Immediately after Lee's surrender to General Grant, Captain Wister was, on April 21, 1865, appointed colonel of the Two Hundred and Fifteenth Pennsylvania Volunteers, and by selection of General Parke was given command of a provisional brigade at Washington, this brigade consisting of an Ohio regiment, an Indiana regiment, and the Two Hundred and Fifteenth Pennsylvania Volunteer Infantry.

On July 31, 1865, he was honorably mustered out of volunteer service, and took command of his company in the Twelfth Infantry. He only served with his regiment eight months after this, for, on April 17, 1866, he resigned his commission and was honorably discharged. He, since 1866, has been engaged in commercial pursuits.

Colonel Wister is an active and enthusiastic member of the Pennsylvania Commandery of the Military Order of the Loyal Legion of United States. He was one of the first officers to join the Loyal Legion, and has always taken a warm and active interest in the success of the order. He is also a member of the United Service Club of Philadelphia.

CAPTAIN AND BREVET MAJOR CHARLES TRIPLER WITHERELL, U.S.A.

CAPTAIN AND BREVET MAJOR CHARLES TRIPLER WITHERELL, (Nineteenth Infantry) was born in Maine, October 11, 1837. He entered the volunteer service as sergeant of Company K, Sixth Maine Infantry, May 7, 1861, and was discharged March 10, 1862, to accept the appointment of second lieutenant in the same regiment. He was promoted first lieutenant February 12, 1863, and captain August 13, 1863. He served in the Army of the Potomac during the War of the Rebellion, and participated in the Rappahannock campaign, being engaged in the battle of Marye's Heights, Virginia, May 2, 1863. He also participated in the Shenandoah campaign of 1864, and was present in all its operations and engagements, being wounded four times.

Captain Witherell was transferred to the First Maine Veteran Infantry, August 21, 1864, and honorably mustered out of the volunteer service June 28, 1865.

He entered the regular service by appointment from civil life as first lieutenant of the Twenty-eighth Infantry, July 28, 1866, and was brevetted captain, March 2, 1867, for gallant and meritorious services in the battle of Marye's Heights, Virginia, and major, March 2, 1867, for gallant and meritorious services in the battle of Rappahannock Station, Virginia. He received the brevet of major of volunteers, October 19, 1864, for gallant conduct during the whole campaign before Richmond, and especially in the battles of Winchester, Fisher's Hill, and Cedar Creek, Virginia.

Captain Witherell was transferred, on the consolidation of regiments, to the Nineteenth Infantry, March 31, 1868.

## CAPTAIN EDWARD E. WOOD, U.S.A.

CAPTAIN EDWARD E. WOOD (Eighth Cavalry) was born September 17, 1846, and is a native of the State of Pennsylvania. He enlisted September 8, 1862, in the Seventeenth Pennsylvania Cavalry, a regiment then being organized under the call for three regiments of cavalry made upon Pennsylvania just before the battle of Antietam.

After serving some time as a private, he was appointed commissary sergeant of Company C of his regiment. He was captured in a skirmish at Occoquan, Virginia, December 27, 1862, and was confined in the prison of Castle Thunder, Richmond. He was acting first sergeant of his company from the latter part of November, 1863, until April, 1864, when he was appointed first sergeant. He was made first lieutenant from first sergeant to fill the vacancy caused by the death of the first lieutenant at the battle of Meadow Bridge, May 12, 1864, and was mustered in July 22, 1864. From August, 1864, he was in command of his company until after the battle of Winchester, September, 1864, when he was appointed acting adjutant of his regiment. He served as acting adjutant until June, 1865. He then served on the staff of the First Cavalry Division, Army of the Potomac, as adjutant commissary of musters until the breaking up of the division organization caused by the muster out of the volunteer forces. He was honorably mustered out at Louisville, Kentucky, August 7, 1865. He served with the Seventeenth Pennsylvania Cavalry in the First Division, Cavalry Corps, Army of the Potomac, and was present at the campaigns, raids, battles, and skirmishes thereof, including Kilpatrick's and Sheridan's Richmond raids, Winchester, Five Forks, and Appomattox.

He was appointed cadet at the United States Military Academy, West Point, after competitive examination therefor in his Congressional district, June, 1866, and was graduated, June, 1870, with the standing of number six in a class of fifty-eight members. He was then commissioned second lieutenant in the Eighth Cavalry; first lieutenant July 31, 1873, and captain January 20, 1886. He was aide-de-camp to Major-General Schofield from June, 1879, to November, 1882, and has been assistant professor of French, and also of Spanish, at the United States Military Academy, and instructor in French, Spanish, and English.

## COMMANDER GEORGE WORTHINGTON WOOD, U.S.N.

COMMANDER GEORGE WORTHINGTON WOOD was born in the city of Dublin, Ireland, in May, 1843. He was appointed a midshipman from the State of Pennsylvania in 1859, and remained at the Naval Academy, Annapolis, until 1861. At the breaking out of the Civil War he was sent to the frigate "St. Lawrence," in the North Atlantic Squadron. He was present when that ship destroyed the privateer "Petrel," off Charleston.

In 1862 he was attached to the steam-sloop "Oneida," in the West Gulf Blockading Squadron, which ship was detailed on six different occasions to draw the fire of forts and batteries below New Orleans from the mortar-vessels which were then bombarding the forts. He commanded the after eleven-inch gun on one of these occasions, when it was disabled, and more than half its crew killed or wounded. Served at the passage of Forts Jackson and St. Philip, the destruction of the Confederate flotilla and transports, and the capture of the Chalmette batteries. Commanded howitzer in the landing party which forced the surrender of Natchez, May 12, 1862. Engagement with the Vicksburg batteries and passage up the river in June, 1862. Present at the engagement with the Confederate iron-clad "Arkansas," July, 1862, and in the same month with the batteries at Vicksburg on the passage of the fleet down the river.

Commander Wood was promoted to the grade of ensign in February, 1863, and served on board the frigate "Sabine" a few months of that year. He was attached to the steam-sloop "Dacotah," of the North Atlantic Blockading Squadron, after this, and on February 22, 1864, was commissioned a lieutenant. In 1864-65 he was attached to the iron-clad "Roanoke," at the mouths of the James and the Potomac, employed in guarding the prison camps. In February, 1865, Lieutenant Wood had charge of an expedition of ten boats and one hundred and fifty men, which entered Pagan Creek, a tributary of the James, and captured a torpedo-boat and outfit, designed for the destruction of the three-turreted "Roanoke." In the report of the Secretary of the Navy for 1865, we find the following reports:

"UNITED STATES STEAMER 'POWHATAN,'
"HAMPTON ROADS, February 7, 1865.

"SIR,—I have the honor to report that on Sunday, the 5th instant, Brigadier-General C. K. Graham sent an officer of his staff to inform me that he was now ready for an expedition to Pagan Creek and vicinity, in search of torpedo-boats, which expedition had been delayed in consequence of the ice, and asked my co-operation with two armed launches and a sufficient number of boats to land one hundred and fifty men. In compliance with this request, at 6 P.M., I despatched the steamer 'Delaware' with the two launches and the three cutters, all the available boats of this ship, and two boats from the 'Alabama,' having previously directed Captain Kitty, of the 'Roanoke,' to have three boats in readiness to join the expedition at Newport News at 8 P.M. The expedition returned to the ship this morning at 2 A.M., having succeeded in capturing a torpedo and a boat, and rebel naval officer, Ensign Heines. For further particulars I refer you to the enclosed letter of General Graham. Lieutenant George W. Wood, of the 'Roanoke,' was the senior naval officer engaged in this expedition, whose report will be forwarded to the department as soon as I receive it.

"I regret to add that one of the men of this ship, Svens Svendson, ordinary seaman, was accidentally wounded, seriously, but not dangerously.

"Very respectfully, your obedient servant,
"J. F. SCHENCK,
"Commodore, and Senior Officer present.

"HON. GIDEON WELLES,
"Secretary of the Navy, Washington, D. C."

Complimentary letter of Brigadier-General Charles K. Graham to Commodore J. F. Schenck:

"HEAD-QUARTERS NAVAL BRIGADE,
[No. 2.] "JAMES RIVER, February 6, 1865.

"COMMODORE,—I desire to express my thanks for the important assistance rendered by Lieutenant Wood, of the navy, and the officers and men under his command, on the banks of the James River and on Chuckatuck Creek, last night and this morning, and my approbation of the manner in which they subsequently searched the creeks and banks adjoining Jones's and Chuckatuck. Pagan Creek was likewise thoroughly examined for a distance of three miles above Smithfield by boats belonging to my own command. Lieutenant Wood had the good fortune to capture in Jones's Creek a torpedo-boat and a torpedo weighing seventy-five pounds, already adjusted; and Major Hassler, of this command, captured Ensign Heines, of the Confederate navy, who was the leader in the destruction of a schooner in Warwick River last fall, and a participator in destroying the tug-boat 'Lizzie Freeman,' off Pagan Creek, December last.

"I am also under obligation to Acting Master Eldridge, of the steamer 'Delaware,' and to the officers of the vessels stationed off Pagan Creek, for the assistance rendered by them.

"I am, very respectfully, your obedient servant,
"CHARLES K. GRAHAM,
"Brigadier-General.

"COMMODORE J. F. SCHENCK,
"Commanding United States Steamer 'Powhatan.'"

Commander Wood became a lieutenant-commander in 1866, and has since seen much sea-service on the North Pacific, South Atlantic, and other stations, besides practice-ship and navy-yard duty, and a torpedo cruise. He was promoted commander in February, 1878.

## LIEUTENANT-COLONEL AND BREVET COLONEL H. CLAY WOOD, U.S.A.

LIEUTENANT-COLONEL AND BREVET COLONEL H. CLAY WOOD (Adjutant-General's Department) was born in Maine May 26, 1832. He entered the regular service from civil life, having been appointed second lieutenant of the First Infantry June 27, 1856. He served on the frontier, and was at Fort Leavenworth in 1861. He was promoted first lieutenant May 10, 1861; transferred to the Eleventh Infantry May 14, 1861, and promoted captain October 24, 1861.

He served during the war of the Rebellion, and was ordnance officer on the staff of General Frémont in 1862. He participated in the Missouri campaign, and was engaged in the actions of Independence, Dug Spring, and battle of Wilson's Creek, where he was slightly wounded. He was subsequently ordered to duty in the provost-marshal's office at Washington City, where he remained until 1864. He was appointed major and assistant adjutant-general June 24, 1864, and on duty in the Adjutant-General's Office, at Washington, D. C., until September, 1867.

Colonel Wood was brevetted lieutenant-colonel March 13, 1865, for gallant and meritorious services in the battle of Wilson's Creek, Missouri, and colonel, the same date, for diligent, faithful, and meritorious services in the Adjutant-General's Department during the war.

He was assistant adjutant-general of the Third Military District of Georgia until January, 1868, and then transferred to the Department of the Lakes, and at various other stations since that time.

**BRIGADIER-GENERAL AND BREVET MAJOR-GENERAL THOMAS J. WOOD, U.S.A. (RETIRED).**

BRIGADIER-GENERAL AND BREVET MAJOR-GENERAL THOMAS J. WOOD was born on September 25, 1823, in Mumfordville, Hart County, Kentucky. His ancestors, for nearly two centuries, through colonial times, resided in Virginia, and migrated to Kentucky near the close of the eighteenth century, when the region in which they settled was a wilderness, infested by Indians, rendering it necessary for the pioneers "to fort." He entered the Military Academy July 1, 1841, and was at the Academy with many cadets who, subsequently as officers, achieved great distinction in the Mexican War, and more especially in the war for the suppression of "The Great Rebellion." First among these must always be named General Grant. He and T. J. Wood during one term occupied a room together; then was commenced an acquaintance and friendship which remained unbroken till the great soldier and ex-President departed this life. McClellan, Hancock, Stone, Gordon, Granger, W. F. Smith, and others who distinguished themselves in the national armies were also at the Academy with T. J. Wood.

He graduated July 1, 1845, and was promoted brevet second lieutenant of Topographical Engineers the same day. He was ordered to report for duty to General Zachary Taylor, in command of "The Army of Occupation," head-quarters at Corpus Christi, Texas. After a dreary winter, 1845-1846, passed under canvas at Corpus Christi, in March, 1846, the Army of Occupation marched to the Rio Grande, which brought on war with Mexico, and the battles of Palo Alto and Resaca de la Palma were fought, in which Lieutenant Wood was engaged. He then participated in the occupation of Matamoras, capture of Monterey, and was engaged in the battle of Buena Vista, in which four thousand five hundred American soldiers, under General Taylor, defeated and routed more than twenty thousand Mexican troops. Lieutenant Wood was transferred to the Second Dragoons, October 19, 1846, and promoted second lieutenant, December 2, 1846, and, as active operations on General Taylor's line ceased after the battle of Buena Vista, Lieutenant Wood was transferred, at his own request, to the army under General Scott, in the City of Mexico, and remained with that army until the close of the war, and was brevetted first lieutenant, February 23, 1847, for gallant and meritorious conduct in the battle of Buena Vista. He was promoted first lieutenant, June 30, 1851.

In the autumn of 1848 he accompanied his regiment to the Indian frontier of Texas. He was engaged on frontier service from the autumn of 1848 to the autumn of 1859. During this interim he was transferred from his old regiment, the Second Dragoons, to a captaincy in the First Cavalry, a new regiment added to the army in 1855. On leave from early in 1860 to March 30, 1861; visited every capital in Europe but Madrid and Lisbon. He reported to the War Department for duty; was ordered to Indiana to muster in the quota of that State; remained in Indiana on mustering duty from April, 1861, to October, 1861, and in the interval organized, equipped, mustered into service, and sent into the field forty thousand volunteers. In October, 1861, he was appointed brigadier-general U. S. Volunteers, and ordered to report to General W. T. Sherman.

General Wood commanded a division in the march to and capture of Corinth; then participated in the race to Louisville, and engaged at Perryville, October 8, 1862. He also participated in the Murfreesborough campaign, and was engaged at Stone River, December 31, 1862; in the battle of Chickamauga, September 19-20, 1863; in the battle of Missionary Ridge, November 25, 1863, when his division was the first body of troops to reach the crest; in the Atlanta campaign of 1864, and participated in all the important battles and actions of that campaign. At Lovejoy's Station General Wood was wounded, but never left the field. He succeeded to the command of the Twenty-fourth Army Corps, which he commanded in the battle of Nashville, Tennessee, December 15-16, 1864, and in pursuit of the retreating rebel army.

He was promoted major, First Cavalry, March 16; lieutenant-colonel, Fourth Cavalry, May 9, and colonel, Second Cavalry, November 12, 1861; appointed major-general of volunteers, January 27, 1865; and brevetted brigadier-general, U.S.A., for Chickamauga, and major-general for Nashville, Tennessee.

He served in various commands until mustered out of volunteer service, September 1, 1866. He was then ordered to the Indian frontier, but, on account of disability from wounds, was retired as major-general June 9, 1868, but subsequently changed to brigadier-general by law of March 3, 1875.

## MAJOR AND BREVET LIEUTENANT-COLONEL ALFRED A. WOODHULL, U.S.A.

MAJOR AND BREVET LIEUTENANT-COLONEL ALFRED A. WOODHULL, (Medical Dept.) was born at Princeton, N. J., April 13, 1837; he was graduated at that college in 1856, receiving the degrees of A.B. and A.M. in course, and in medicine at the Univ. of Penn. in 1859. He practised medicine in Douglas Co., Kan., from July, 1859, to Aug., 1861.

Immediately after the attack on Sumter he took an active part in organizing a company of mounted rifles for the Kansas militia, and was made its second lieutenant. He also qualified by examination for appointment as surgeon of Kansas volunteers. In Aug., 1861, he was examined by the Army Medical Board, New York, and was appointed assistant surgeon Sept. 19, 1861, and attached to Second U. S. Infantry. He also did duty with troops of all arms in Washington in the winter of 1861-62, and took the field with Second Infantry in March, 1862, remaining with that regiment, in the Army of the Potomac, doing duty on occasions with the other regiments of the Second Brigade of Sykes's division, until the last of Nov., 1862. He was present on the field with the command in all its operations during that period, including the siege of Yorktown, the battles of Gaines' Mill and Malvern Hill in the Seven Days, the camp at Harrison's Landing, the march to and participation in the battles of second Bull Run and Antietam, the affair at Shepherdstown Ford (where he acted as aid to the brigade commander), the skirmish at Snicker's Gap (with Sixth Infantry), and was several times commended in the official reports.

In December, 1862, he was temporarily in charge of a general hospital in Baltimore, and until November, 1863, was executive-officer to the medical director of the Middle Department, who at that time was charged with the management of forty thousand beds in general hospitals and their necessary staff, besides the medical control of Eighth Army Corps. From Nov., 1863, to May, 1864, he was on similar duty with the medical director of Department of Va. and N. C. at Fort Monroe, and early in May, 1864, took the field in the same capacity with the Army of the James. He remained in the field, as assistant to the medical director and for the greater part of the time as acting medical inspector, Army of the James, until May, 1865, and was present at the more important collisions with the enemy, including the surrender at Appomattox.

After a short hospital service near Bermuda Hundred he was—June, 1865—detailed in the Surgeon-General's Office to prepare a descriptive catalogue of the surgical section of the Army Medical Museum, containing at that time more than four thousand seven hundred specimens.

He was on board and other temporary duty at West Point a part of the summer and autumn, 1867, and, later, prepared at the Surgeon-General's Office a medical report upon soldiers' uniform clothing. He was recorder of

the Army Medical Board, New York, May to November, 1868.

He received the brevets of captain, major, and lieutenant-colonel, for "faithful and meritorious services during the war," to date from March 13, 1865; attained the rank of captain in the Medical Department July 26, 1866, and that of major October 1, 1876.

He was on duty at numerous posts in the West and different parts of the country to September, 1881, when he availed himself of a leave of absence for six months, and then served at various posts to May, 1891. He represented Medical Department, U.S.A., at the International Congress of Hygiene and Dermography, London, and was on special duty, studying the equipment and administration of the Medical Department of the British army, July to Dec., 1891. In charge of Army and Navy General Hospital, Hot Springs, Ark., from Feb., 1892. Lt.-Col. Woodhull was the gold medallist of the Military Service Institution, for the prize essay on " The Enlisted Soldier," 1886. While at Fort Leavenworth he lectured on military hygiene in the Infantry and Cavalry School.

Colonel Woodhull has published the following works: "Catalogue of the Surgical Section of the Army Medical Museum," 4to, pp. 664, 1866; " Medical Report upon the Uniform and Clothing of the Soldiers of the United States Army," 8vo, pp. 26, 1868; " Clinical Studies in the Non-Emetic Use of Ipecacuanha," 8vo, pp. 155, 1876; " On the Causes of the Epidemic of Yellow Fever at Savannah in 1876;" prize essay, " The Enlisted Soldier;" " Notes on Military Hygiene for Officers of the Line," 12mo, pp. 150, 1890; and occasional essays.

Lt.-Col. Woodhull springs from good American stock, being of the eighth generation from the first of the name who settled on Long Island in 1648, and having among his direct ancestors a signer of the Declaration (John Witherspoon) and military officers of the Revolution.

## CAPTAIN CHARLES A. WOODRUFF, U.S.A.

CAPTAIN CHARLES A. WOODRUFF (Subsistence Department) was born at Burke, Vermont, April 26, 1845. He enlisted in Company A, Tenth Vermont Volunteers, June 5, 1862, and served in the Army of the Potomac, with the First Brigade, Third Division, Third Corps, and First Brigade, Third Division, Sixth Corps. He was in the field continuously as private, corporal, and sergeant, until severely wounded at Cold Harbor, Virginia, June 3, 1864 (slightly wounded three times, June 1). He was then commissioned second lieutenant, but not mustered on account of wounds, and subsequently discharged for disability, wounds, August 18, 1865. He was pensioned, but surrendered the same from September, 1866. He was a cadet at the U. S. Military Academy from July 1, 1867, to June 12, 1871, when he was graduated and promoted second lieutenant, Seventh Infantry.

He served on frontier duty at Fort Shaw, Montana, from September 30, 1871, to January, 1872; at Fort Benton, Montana, to May 2, 1872; at Fort Shaw, Montana, to March 17, 1876, commanding mounted detachment, scouting and exploring country to Fort Colville, Washington, August 19 to October 19, 1873; acting regimental adjutant and acting assistant adjutant-general, District Montana, July to October, 1874; commanding company and mounted detachment at Camp Lewis, Montana, June 2 to October 19, 1875, guarding stage road and scouting; he was adjutant of the Montana Infantry Battalion on Yellowstone Expedition, from March 17 to September 5, 1876, and commanded the artillery in action against Sioux Indians, August 2, 1876, at the mouth of Powder River; he was on leave of absence to February 6, 1877; then at Fort Shaw, Montana, from February 6 to July 26, 1877, and adjutant of General Gibbon's Nez Perces Expedition to August 9, being engaged in the battle of Big Hole Pass, Montana, August 9, 1877, where he was thrice severely wounded.

He was promoted first lieutenant, Seventh Infantry, August 9, 1877; and was on sick-leave of absence from October 30, 1877, to May, 1878, when he was appointed captain, staff-commissary of subsistence, March 28, 1878. He was on duty in the commissary-general's office, Washington, D. C., June 4 to August 15, 1878; depot commissary at Fort Leavenworth, Kansas, August 22, 1878; acting chief commissary of subsistence, Department, Montana, August and September, 1879; and acting assistant adjutant-general, Department of Montana, August, 1879, to October 9, 1879; as chief commissary of the District of New Mexico, and post commissary of subsistence, Fort Marcy, New Mexico, to October 31, 1884; acting as engineer officer and acting assistant adjutant-general at various times during that period; chief commissary, Department of the Columbia, and purchasing and depot commissary of subsistence, Vancouver Barracks, Washington, November 17, 1884; on various staff duties, July 21, 1886, to May 14, 1889; with commanding general department during Chinese troubles at Seattle, Washington, to July 31, 1889; and as purchasing and depot commissary of subsistence at San Francisco, California, August 9, 1889, to present time, 1892.

## COMMANDER EDWIN TULLY WOODWARD, U.S.N.

COMMANDER EDWIN TULLY WOODWARD was born in Vermont in 1843, and appointed to the Naval Academy in 1859 from that State. Detached from the Naval Academy, May, 1861, and ordered to the U. S. frigate "Mississippi," Gulf Squadron, November 4, 1861, to January 24, 1862, garrison Ship Island; during this time was at the capture of Biloxi and Mississippi City in the steamer "Henry Lewis," January 25, 1862; gun-boat "Sciota," attack on and passage of Forts Jackson and St. Philip, Chalmette batteries, and capture of New Orleans. Mentioned in despatches by Fleet Captain Bell. Passage of Mississippi River to Vicksburg, capturing Baton Rouge, Natchez, and Port Gibson. Two attacks on Vicksburg under Admiral Farragut, passing the batteries both times. Engagement with rebel ram "Arkansas," above Vicksburg, and battle at Baton Rouge, when General Williams was killed, 1862. Extract from letter of Lieutenant R. B. Lowry, commanding gun-boat "Sciota:"

"You displayed great zeal, ability, and fitness for a naval officer, under the terrible fire of Forts Jackson and St. Philip, and the batteries of Chalmette, and before Vicksburg you displayed coolness and courage most commendable in any youth."

Sloop "Cyane," Pacific Squadron, 1863-64. Commissioned as lieutenant February 22, 1864; steam-frigate " Minnesota," North Atlantic Blockading Squadron, 1864-65; two attacks on Fort Fisher (in landing party); steam-sloop " Kearsarge," cruising after rebel ram " Stonewall," 1865-66. Commissioned lieutenant-commander July 25, 1866; Naval Academy, 1866-67; steam-frigate " Guerriere,"flag-ship South Atlantic Squadron, 1867-68. Steamers " Quinnebaug" and " Kansas," 1869. Ordnance duty, navy-yard, New York, 1869-71. "Canonicus" (iron-clad), North Atlantic Station, 1871-72. Receiving-ship " Vermont," 1873. " Brooklyn" (second rate), flag-ship South Atlantic Squadron, 1874-75; " Vandalia" (third rate), 1875-76; torpedo duty, 1877. Promoted commander February 2, 1878. Navy-yard, League Island, 1879-80. Commanding " Yantic," North Atlantic Station, 1881-82. During this time he received the thanks of the State Department. Commanding squadron of iron-clads, consisting of " Passaic," " Nantucket," and " Alarm," for instruction, 1884.

Received the following letter:

"NAVY DEPARTMENT,
"WASHINGTON, D. C., October 8, 1884.

"SIR,—The Department has received your final report of the 4th inst., in relation to the cruise of the monitors 'Passaic,' 'Nantucket,' and ram 'Alarm,' and your command, together with the reports of the commanding officers of the two last-mentioned vessels. The department desires to commend you for the manner in which you have carried out the spirit of the instructions to make the cruise one of practical instruction to both officers and men, and to state that you have commanded the squadron to its satisfaction.

"Very respectfully,
"EDWARD T. NICHOLS,
" Acting Secretary of the Navy.
"COMMANDER E. T. WOODWARD, U.S.N.,
" Commanding U. S. Monitor ' Passaic,'
" Annapolis, Maryland.
" Forwarded, October 9, 1884.
"T. M. RAMSEY,
" Commanding Station."

Commanding " Swatara," 1885-86, and temporary command of U. S. S. " Terror," 1888. Commanding U. S. S. " Adams," Pacific Station, 1889-90. Light-house inspector Tenth District, 1891-92.

## COLONEL GEORGE A. WOODWARD, U.S.A. (RETIRED).

COLONEL GEORGE A. WOODWARD was born in Wilkes-Barre, Pennsylvania, February 14, 1835. He graduated B.A. at Trinity College, Hartford, Connecticut, in June, 1855. In November, 1855, he removed to Milwaukee, Wisconsin, where he continued the study of the law, already begun, and was admitted to practice in December, 1856. He took an active part in military affairs, and served at different times as private in the Milwaukee Light-Guard and the Citizen Corps, as sergeant-major of the Light-Guard Battalion, and captain and judge-advocate on the division staff. In 1858 he was elected City Attorney of Milwaukee, and on expiration of term returned and entered upon the practice of his profession in Philadelphia.

Immediately after the attack on Fort Sumter he set about raising a company of volunteers for the war, and was mustered in as captain on the 27th of May, 1861. He was assigned to the Second Regiment of the Pennsylvania Reserves in June, 1861. He took the field with his regiment in July, 1861; was promoted to major April 2, 1862, and engaged at the battles of Mechanicsville, Gaines' Mill, and Charles City Cross-Roads (or Glendale), in which battle he was twice wounded; taken prisoner and confined in Libby Prison, Richmond, Virginia; promoted lieutenant-colonel February 20, 1863; commanding regiment, and engaged at the battle of Gettysburg, July 2-3, 1863; at close of Gettysburg campaign applied for honorable discharge on account of disability from wounds; withdrew that application at request of division commander, by whom was tendered the position of inspector-general of the division; pending consideration of such tender, received an appointment as major in Invalid Corps, accompanied by a letter from the provost-marshal-general explaining that no higher grade than that of major had yet been created in that corps, but that if, as was expected would soon be the case, higher grades should be authorized, his claim to higher rank would be duly considered; major, Invalid Corps, August 24, 1863, and lieutenant-colonel September 26, 1863; colonel December 4, 1863; colonel, Twenty-second Regiment Veteran Reserve Corps, to July 20, 1866, when he was honorably mustered out of the volunteer service; performed duty commanding the depot camp of the corps in Washington, and camps in Philadelphia, Columbus, and Cleveland; tour of inspection duty to Hartford, Connecticut, on returning from which found communication with Washington cut by enemy; reported for duty to General Cadwalader in Philadelphia, and by his orders proceeded to Washington, by sea, in command of five companies of convalescents organized from hospitals to assist in defence of Washington; being in Washington awaiting orders on the night of President Lincoln's assassination, volunteered his services, and acted as field-officer of the day in charge of the special guards established that night; accepted appointment as lieutenant-colonel, Forty-fifth Infantry, U. S. Army, September 18, 1866; assigned to duty superintending regimental recruiting service at Louisville, Ky.; superintended recruitment of and organized the Forty-fifth Regiment of Infantry, U. S. Army; ordered with it to Nashville, Tenn., April, 1867; on recommendation of his division commander was brevetted colonel for "gallant and meritorious services at the battle of Gettysburg." General Meade forwarding such recommendation with the following indorsement: "Respectfully forwarded, concurring in the recommendation that Lieutenant-Colonel Woodward be brevetted colonel for Gettysburg, and furthermore, that he be brevetted brigadier-general for distinguished good conduct in the field during the war;" in 1869 was retained as lieutenant-colonel Fourteenth Infantry; took post at Taylor Barracks, Louisville, Ky.; July, 1870, proceeded to Fort Randall, Dakota, and assumed command of regiment, establishing Camp Lovell; proceeded in command of regiment to Omaha, Neb., and then to Fort Sedgwick, Col.; in spring of 1871, in command of four companies, marched to Fort Fetterman, Wy. Territory; at Sidney Barracks, Neb.; Fort McPherson, Neb.; and Fort Cameron, Utah; promoted to colonel, Fifteenth Infantry, U. S. Army, Jan. 10, 1876; on sick-leave on account of breaking out of old wound in foot; retired for disability resulting from wounds March 20, 1879.

Received honorable mention in the official reports of Major-General McCall and Brigadier-General Seymour, for good conduct in the Seven Days' battles before Richmond ("Rebellion Records," Series I., Vol. XI., Part II., pp. 389, 404). Since 1887 has resided in Washington, D.C.

## REAR-ADMIRAL JOHN LORIMER WORDEN, U.S.N.
### (RETIRED).

REAR-ADMIRAL JOHN LORIMER WORDEN enjoys the distinction, unique in our service, of being placed upon the retired list, at his own request, upon full pay, the latter being done by special act of Congress. Admiral Worden's name will always be especially associated with the "Monitor," but he performed valuable service before the idea of the "Monitor" was conceived, as well as long after she went to the bottom.

Rear-Admiral Worden entered the navy as a midshipman from his native State, New York, in January, 1834, and served in the Brazils and the Mediterranean before going to the Naval School at Philadelphia. Promoted passed midshipman in July, 1840, and was in the Pacific for three years, after which he went to the Naval Observatory, at Washington. He obtained his next two steps in the same year, master in August, and lieutenant in November, 1846. He went out to the Pacific Station in 1847, and served there in the "Southampton," "Independence," and "Warren," coming home in the line-of-battle-ship "Ohio," in 1850. For several years afterwards he was on duty at the Observatory, and in the Mediterranean, at the navy-yard, New York, and as first lieutenant of the frigate "Savannah," Home Squadron.

On April 6, 1861, Lieutenant Worden reported at Washington for special duty connected with the discipline and efficiency of the naval service, but, finding that ships were being rapidly fitted for service, in consequence of secession movements, asked to be relieved from special duty, and applied for service afloat. On the 7th, at daylight, he was sent to Pensacola with despatches for the commanding officer of the squadron off that port, the orders to reinforce Fort Pickens, and reached there about midnight on the 10th. A heavy gale prevented him from communicating with the ships on the next day. But on the 12th he delivered his despatches at noon. At 3 P.M. left to return to Washington by rail. It was necessary to go via Montgomery, Alabama, and on the 13th, about 4 P.M., he was arrested at a station just south of the rebel capital, taken there, and detained as a prisoner until November 14. He was then paroled and ordered to report to the Secretary of War, at Richmond. He found that he was to be exchanged against Lieutenant Sharp, a Confederate who was confined on board the "Congress," at Newport News. By

flag of truce from General Huger to Admiral Goldsborough, this exchange was duly effected November 18, after Mr. Worden had been more than seven months a prisoner. On January 16, 1862, he was ordered to the command of the "Monitor." The story of this extraordinary engine of war, and its influence on our own fortunes and upon naval construction all over the world, has often been told, and cannot be told too often. In his battle with the "Merrimac," on March 9, 1862, Lieutenant Worden was severely injured, and was obliged to be removed as soon as the action was over, but not until complete success had crowned the efforts of one who was fighting an entirely novel and untried vessel, which had only come in the night before from a perilous voyage. He was made commander, July, 1862, and upon partial recovery was upon duty at New York, as assistant to Admiral Gregory, in superintending the construction of iron-clads. Commander Worden commanded the monitor "Montauk" from October, 1862, to April, 1863, in the South Atlantic Squadron. In her he attacked Fort McAllister, on the Ogeechee River, and on February 28, 1863, destroyed the Confederate privateer "Nashville," under the guns of that fort.

On April 7, 1863, he participated in the attack of the iron-clads, under Admiral Dupot, upon the defences of Charleston. In the mean time, February 3, 1863, he had been promoted to be captain in the navy. Commodore and superintendent, Naval Academy, 1868. Rear-admiral commanding European Station, 1872, and much other service.

**BRIGADIER-GENERAL JACOB ZEILIN, U.S.M.C.**
(RETIRED)

BRIGADIER-GENERAL JACOB ZEILIN is a native of Philadelphia, and was appointed a second lieutenant in the Marine Corps from Pennsylvania, October 1, 1831. After being stationed at the marine barracks at Washington, Philadelphia, and Gosport, Virginia, he made a long cruise in the sloop-of-war "Erie," from March, 1832, to September, 1837.

He became first lieutenant in 1836.

After serving at the Charlestown Barracks he made another cruise in the Brazils, in the "Columbus," 74. On his return served at the barracks at Philadelphia, Washington, and Norfolk, until the Mexican War, when he went to the Pacific in the frigate "Congress." He commanded the marines of the squadron, and was adjutant of the naval battalion at the capture of Santa Barbara, August 4, 1846; capture of San Pédro, August 6, 1846; capture of Los Angeles, August 13, 1846; assault and second capture of San Pédro, October 25, 1846; the relief of General Kearney, at San Bernardino, December 12, 1846; victory of San Gabriel, January 8, 1847; victory of La Mesa, January 9, 1847; bombardment and capture of Guaymas, October 20, 1847; capture of Mazatlan, November 8, 1847.

He was brevetted major for gallant conduct at San Gabriel and La Mesa, January 9, 1847. On January 28 of that year he was appointed military commandant of San Diégo.

He was commissioned captain September 14, 1847.

After being fleet marine officer of the Pacific Squadron until May, 1848, he had a round of shore-duty at Norfolk and at New York until June, 1852, when he went, as fleet marine officer, in Perry's Expedition to Japan. He was the second person to touch the shore at the formal landing of the naval forces at Yokohama, on July 14, 1853, and was one of those who received the silver medal presented by the merchants of Boston to the naval force that unsealed the empire of Japan.

Upon his return from this important and most interesting cruise, he was stationed at Norfolk, and in command of the barracks at the Washington Navy-Yard. He served in the frigate "Wabash," of the European Squadron, and then, from 1859 to 1862, commanded the marine barracks at Philadelphia and at Washington. In July, 1861, he was on detached duty with the marine battalion, and was wounded at the battle of Bull Run, July 21, 1861.

He was commissioned major in the Marine Corps, July 26, 1861,—a rank he had by brevet fourteen years before.

From November, 1862, to February, 1863, Major Zeilin commanded the marine barracks at New York. He was then ordered, on detached duty, to the command of the marine battalion at the siege of Fort Wagner, where he served during August and September, 1863.

He was then ordered to the command of the marine barracks at Portsmouth, but on June 30, 1864, was commissioned colonel commandant of the United States Marine Corps, and ordered to head-quarters at Washington.

Commissioned brigadier-general and commandant, March 2, 1867. Retired November 1, 1876.

General Zeilin's record shows thirteen years and eleven months of sea-service; thirty years and eight months of shore-service, and only four months unemployed.

## PAYMASTER GEORGE DE FOREST BARTON, U.S.N.

PAYMASTER GEORGE DE FOREST BARTON is a native of the city of New York, and was appointed an acting assistant paymaster in the navy in June, 1861, when only twenty years of age.

He reported for duty on board the "Monticello," one of the early-purchased steamers, a small, but fast and handy vessel. The "Monticello" was actively employed in Virginia waters and on the blockade at various points from the capes of Virginia to the Savannah River.

In August, 1861, the "Monticello" took part in the attack upon Forts Clark and Hatteras. After some hours' bombardment the enemy's flag was hauled down, when the "Monticello" was sent in by Flag-Officer Stringham to bring off the commanding officer. The pilot ran the vessel ashore, only a few hundred yards from the forts, and she was opened on at once, without rehoisting the flag in the forts. It was fortunate that the enemy had only solid shot, or the vessel must have been destroyed, as she was hulled fourteen times, but at last got off.

Next morning the forts were taken,—troops landed and occupied them,—one of the first Union successes. When the "Monticello" went out of commission, in the summer of 1863, Paymaster Barton was ordered to the new double-ender "Sassacus." In her he saw very active service, on the outside blockade, during which time she captured or destroyed several noted blockade-runners.

In the spring of 1864 the "Sassacus" was ordered into the Sounds of North Carolina, where she was destined to play a most conspicuous part. One of the most formidable of the rebel iron-clads, the "Albemarle," built at Plymouth, North Carolina, had recently played havoc with the squadron of small vessels in the Sounds, and was soon expected out again, while there were only wooden ships to place against her. She soon came down, and the "Sassacus," as previously arranged, rammed her at full speed, striking her on the starboard side, just abaft the casemate, the sharp prow of the "Sassacus" cutting its way in between the bars of railroad iron with which the "Albemarle" was plated. Then they attempted to push the iron-clad on to a shoal near by, but, in doing so, the vessels came together broadside on, and were held

in this position for some fifteen minutes, heavy firing being kept up almost muzzle to muzzle. The "Albemarle's" shot passed entirely through the wooden vessel, which had her boilers penetrated, with very great loss of life. At last they were separated, and the "Albemarle" steamed away up the river, pursued by the other Union vessels. At Plymouth she was afterwards destroyed by a torpedo at the hands of Lieutenant Cushing.

In the course of this engagement the "Bombshell" was captured by the "Sassacus." Paymaster Barton acted as signal officer and aid to the commander during this desperate fight. Soon after this he was appointed an assistant paymaster in the regular navy.

He served in the "St. Louis," and, after the war closed, in the store-ship "Supply," becoming paymaster in May, 1866. He served in the "Swatara," European Squadron, and in the "Portsmouth," of the Apprentice Squadron.

In 1869, Paymaster Barton resigned his naval commission, and has since then been engaged in business in New York.

He is an active member of the Military Order of the Loyal Legion, Commandery of New York, and has been treasurer, recorder, and is at present junior vice-commander of that Commandery.

### BREVET CAPTAIN EDGAR KETCHUM, U.S.A.

BREVET CAPTAIN EDGAR KETCHUM was born in New York City on July 15, 1840. He graduated at the College of the City of New York in July, 1860, and at the Columbia College Law School in the spring of 1862, then being admitted to practise law.

He was commissioned as second lieutenant, Signal Corps, U.S.A., to date from March 3, 1863.

Lieutenant Ketchum reported for duty at Signal Camp of Instruction, Georgetown, D. C., August, 1864. Subsequently reported in the field to chief signal officer, Department of Virginia and North Carolina, and was assigned to duty at Fort Signal Hill, near the extreme right of the Army of the James. A reconnoissance was made in December, 1864, by General Longstreet with a considerable force, and the forts at Signal Hill and Camp Holly were attacked, the skirmishing continuing during the whole day and evening. Lieutenant Ketchum was highly commended in the report of his superior officer for the "zeal and judgment displayed by him at that time."

Was ordered to accompany the expedition against Fort Fisher, North Carolina, under General A. H. Terry, in January, 1865. After landing in the surf, he assisted in establishing our line across the peninsula north of Fort Fisher, in order to sever communication between Fort Fisher and Wilmington.

On January 15, 1865, at the attack on Fort Fisher, was assigned to duty with General A. H. Terry as signal officer, kept up constant communication between Admiral Porter and General Terry during the seven hours of battle. During these seven hours, besides exposure to the ordinary risks of artillery and musketry, the signal officers were a mark for sharp-shooters, who used every effort to cripple the attacking force by preventing communication by signal between the army and navy.

The morning after the capture of the fort the large magazine exploded, causing the loss of more than two hundred men. Though in the fort, and about fifty feet from the magazine, Lieutenant Ketchum was not seriously injured.

In February, 1865, was on duty with General J. D. Cox, and took part in the capture of Fort Anderson during that month, and the battle of Town Creek, February 18, 1865, and the capture of Wilmington, February 22, 1865.

He was the first signal officer who arrived opposite Wilmington, and was shelled from the city the day before its capture.

After the capture of Wilmington, Lieutenant Ketchum was selected to proceed up the Cape Fear River on a gun-boat to open communication with General Sherman, who was believed to be in the vicinity.

On the march north from Wilmington was on the staff of General Terry as a signal officer.

After the battles of Bentonville and Averysborough was ordered to return to Virginia, and subsequent to the surrender of the Confederate armies Lieutenant Ketchum was assigned to duty at the Reserve Camp at Georgetown, D. C., and on August 12, 1865, was honorably discharged from the service of the United States.

He was made first lieutenant by brevet for gallant and meritorious services at the capture of Fort Fisher, and captain by brevet for gallant and meritorious services during the war. He was honorably mentioned by his superior officer for the faithful and efficient manner in which he performed his duties at Fort Fisher, and in the official record of his services on file in the War Department it is stated that, "while his career as an officer of this corps was comparatively brief, he not having served in that capacity but about one year, the memorable campaigns, hard-fought battles, and bloody skirmishes which occurred in the vicinity of Richmond and Petersburg during the last few months of the war, in many of which he took an important part and rendered valuable service, were sufficient to give him military renown surpassing that of many others who served a greater length of time;" and it is further stated that, "from the reports of his superior officers in the field, it is shown that he was a faithful, zealous, and reliable officer."

After leaving the service he returned to the practice of law in New York City, and is still so engaged. For three years he held the position of engineer, with the rank of major, in the First Brigade, First Division, National Guard of the State of New York, and was subsequently honorably discharged therefrom upon tendering his resignation.

He is a member of the Military Order of the Loyal Legion, the War Veterans of the Seventh Regiment, and Post Lafayette, of the Grand Army of the Republic.

## CAPTAIN AND BREVET MAJOR BENJAMIN F. RITTENHOUSE, U.S.A. (RETIRED).

CAPTAIN AND BREVET MAJOR BENJAMIN F. RITTENHOUSE was born in Berwick, Columbia County, Pennsylvania, December 15, 1839. He was brought up in the District of Columbia and Virginia, and in November, 1860, was appointed clerk in the Census Bureau. On June 20, 1861, he was appointed second lieutenant in the Fifth U. S. Artillery, to date from May 14. He was on recruiting duty in Pennsylvania and Kentucky from July 1 to November 1, and joined his battery (H, Terrill's) near Cincinnati, about November 7, and served with that battery in the march on to Nashville, Tennessee, the siege of Corinth, Mississippi, and in Buell's campaign in Mississippi, Alabama, Tennessee, and Kentucky. In July, 1862, he was promoted to first lieutenant, and in October ordered to join Battery D, of his regiment, serving in the Fifth Corps, Army of the Potomac. He served in this battery under the command of First Lieutenant Charles E. Hazlett, in the battles of Fredericksburg and Chancellorsville, Virginia, and Gettysburg, Pennsylvania, July 2. Lieutenant Hazlett was killed July 2, when the command of the battery devolved upon Lieutenant Rittenhouse, who commanded it on Little Round Top, during the remainder of the battle; also at Rappahannock Station, Mine Run, Wilderness, Laurel Hill, Po River, Spottsylvania, Guiney's Station, North Anna River, Bethesda Church, Virginia. On June 10, 1864, he became chief of artillery of Ayers's Second Division of the Fifth Corps, commanding three batteries at the siege of Petersburg, Virginia. On June 19 he was severely wounded and disabled for further field service.

He was brevetted captain to date from August 1, 1864, "for gallant and meritorious services at the battle of Bethesda Church and the campaign before Richmond," and brevet major, March 13, 1865, "for good conduct and gallant services during the war," and appointed captain in the Twentieth U. S. Infantry, to date July 28, 1866, but declined.

In November, 1864, he was ordered to Chicago, Illinois, on mustering duty, and in May, 1865, to Camp Parole, Annapolis, Maryland, to muster out paroled prisoners. In July he was ordered to join his battery, and in October was ordered with it to Fort Jefferson, Dry Tortugas, Florida; in May, 1867, he was transferred to Battery C, at Fort Monroe, Virginia; in May, 1869, graduated from the Artillery School, and was ordered to join Battery K, at Fort Sullivan, Eastport, Maine.

In May, 1870, he received his commission as captain in his regiment, to date from January 5, 1870, and ordered to join Battery L, at Fort Warren, Boston harbor; in September of the same year, he was ordered with his battery to Fort Adams, Newport, Rhode Island.

On October 7, 1874, he was placed on the retired list, on account of "wounds received in the line of duty;" in August, 1882, he was appointed secretary and treasurer of the U. S. Soldiers' Home, at Washington, D. C., and served in that position until March, 1890.

While stationed at Newport, Rhode Island, Major Rittenhouse studied law, and when he retired was admitted to the bar in that State.

Major Rittenhouse at present resides at Washington, D. C.

## CAPTAIN AND BREVET LIEUTENANT-COLONEL SAMUEL KLINGER SCHWENK, U.S.A. (RETIRED).

CAPTAIN AND BREVET LIEUTENANT-COLONEL SAMUEL KLINGER SCHWENK was born May 8, 1842, in Dauphin County, Pennsylvania, and is descended from the Von Schwenks of Germany, a noble family, several of whom served with distinction in the late Franco-Prussian war, and his ancestors, both paternal and maternal, participated in the war of the American Revolution. He was educated at the Dickinson Seminary, which he left in order to enlist in the service of his country during the war of the Rebellion. While at the seminary he instructed the Dickinson Cadets. On August 19, 1861, he was appointed a lieutenant in the Fiftieth Pennsylvania Infantry, and proceeded with the command to South Carolina; for actions at Beaufort, and twice at Port Royal Ferry, he received the thanks of Generals Stephens and Hunter. He was ordered with his regiment to Virginia, arriving there in time to take part in the battles of second Bull Run and Chantilly. At South Mountain he was wounded in the ankle. At Antietam he participated with his regiment in the battle, though scarcely able to walk, and was given command of the sharp-shooters on the front of the Ninth Corps, where he was pitted against the famous Palmetto sharp-shooters, whom he drove in and thereby opened connection with Hooker's Corps on the right, receiving therefor handsome recognition from Generals Willcox and Burnside. At Fredericksburg he again led the skirmishers, and reached out on the left until he joined hands with those of Franklin's grand division.

The Ninth Corps, to which his regiment was attached, was sent West in the spring of 1863, and at Blue Springs and Hough's Ferry, where the advance of Longstreet was met, Captain Schwenk performed one of those daring feats with which his name was often associated. He not only fought the enemy's skirmishers, gaining full information of the enemy's position and numbers, but in the end took prisoners a party sent out to demand his own surrender. "At Campbell's Station," says his brigade commander, General Cutcheon, "he behaved most bravely, and during the entire siege of Knoxville was especially distinguished for his coolness, prudent judgment, and determined gallantry, as well as professional skill in the construction of defences."

His most conspicuous acts of gallantry, however, were performed during the battles of the Wilderness, in 1864. At the battle of Nye River, on May 9, 1864, he is accredited with having "saved the day." The rebels were ascending a hill, and, if they had reached the crest, would have discovered the weakness of the Union forces confronting them; but Captain Schwenk, perceiving this, took the responsibility of ordering a charge with the bayonet, which his superior officers hesitated to do, and with part of a regiment repulsed the rebels from the crest and saved the brigade from a probable serious disaster. In one of the engagements before Spottsylvania Court-House he may be said to have gone into the fight as a captain of one company, and to have come out of it a commander of five regiments.

At the battle of Cold Harbor, after thirteen bullets had passed through his clothes harmlessly, he was struck in the side by one which passed through the vertebra, and he was carried from the field, as it was supposed, mortally wounded. He had, however, the benefit of eminent medical skill, the case being regarded as a remarkable one, and he survived, though many months elapsed before he was able to move about.

He was promoted major, and was at the retaking of Fort Steadman and final capture of Petersburg. For conspicuous gallantry before Petersburg, and in the assault on Fort Steadman, Virginia, he was brevetted lieutenant-colonel of volunteers March 23, 1865. On July 24, of the same year, he was brevetted colonel, and on the same day brigadier-general of volunteers. On July 28, 1866, he was appointed first lieutenant in the Forty-first Regular Infantry, and was in succession brevetted captain, major, and lieutenant-colonel in the regular army, for conspicuous gallantry and skilful and meritorious services at Nye River, Spottsylvania and Cold Harbor. He was stationed at Brownsville, Texas, in 1867, and was promoted to be captain in December, 1867, and on May 17, 1876, was placed upon the retired list of the army.

# INDEX.

| Name | PAGE |
|---|---|
| ALDEN, J., REAR-ADMIRAL U.S.N. | 5 |
| ALMY, J. J., REAR-ADMIRAL U.S.N. | 6 |
| AMES, L. S., CAPTAIN U.S.A. | 7 |
| AMMEN, D., REAR-ADMIRAL U.S.N. | 8 |
| ANDERSON, J., CAPTAIN U.S.A. | 9 |
| ANDERSON, R., BRIGADIER- AND BVT. MAJOR-GENERAL U.S.A. | 10 |
| ANDERSON, T. M., COLONEL U.S.A. | 11 |
| ANDREWS, G. L., COLONEL U.S.A. | 12 |
| ARNOLD, A. K., COLONEL U.S.A. | 13 |
| ARNOLD, I., JR., MAJOR U.S.A. | 14 |
| AUGUR, C. C., BRIGADIER- AND BVT. MAJOR-GENERAL U.S.A. | 15 |
| AUMAN, W., CAPTAIN U.S.A. | 16 |
| AVERELL, W. W., CAPTAIN AND BVT. MAJOR-GENERAL U.S.A. | 17 |
| AVERY, R., LIEUTENANT-COLONEL U.S.A. | 18 |
| BABBITT, L. S., LIEUTENANT-COLONEL U.S.A. | 19 |
| BABCOCK, J. B., CAPTAIN AND BVT. MAJOR U.S.A. | 20 |
| BADGER, O. C., COMMODORE U.S.N. | 21 |
| BAILEY, C. M., MAJOR U.S.A. | 22 |
| BAILEY, T., REAR-ADMIRAL U.S.N. | 23 |
| BAIRD, A., BRIGADIER- AND BVT. MAJOR-GENERAL U.S.A. | 24 |
| BARLOW, J. W., LIEUTENANT-COLONEL U.S.A. | 25 |
| BARNITZ, A., CAPTAIN AND BVT. COLONEL U.S.A. | 26 |
| BARRIGER, J. W., LIEUTENANT-COLONEL AND BVT. BRIGADIER-GENERAL U.S.A. | 27 |
| BARTLETT, H. A., MAJOR U.S.M.C. | 28 |
| BARTON, B. F., PAYMASTER U.S.N. | 48 |
| BATES, N. L., MEDICAL DIRECTOR U.S.N. | 29 |
| BECK, W. H., CAPTAIN U.S.A. | 30 |
| BECKWITH, A., COLONEL AND BVT. MAJOR-GENERAL U.S.A. | 31 |
| BELKNAP, G. E., REAR-ADMIRAL U.S.N. | 32 |
| BENHAM, H. W., COLONEL AND BVT. MAJOR-GENERAL U.S.A. | 33 |
| BENTEEN, F. W., MAJOR AND BVT. COLONEL U.S.A. | 34 |
| BENTLEY, E., MAJOR U.S.A. | 35 |
| BERGLAND, E., CAPTAIN U.S.A. | 36 |
| BERNARD, R. F., MAJOR AND BVT. COLONEL U.S.A. | 37 |
| BEST, C. L., COLONEL U.S.A. | 38 |
| BINGHAM, J. D., COLONEL AND BVT. BRIGADIER-GENERAL U.S.A. | 39 |
| BISHOP, J., COMMANDER U.S.N. | 40 |
| BLISS, Z. R., COLONEL U.S.A. | 41 |
| BLOODGOOD, D., MEDICAL DIRECTOR U.S.N. | 42 |
| BOGGS, C. S., REAR-ADMIRAL U.S.N. | 43 |
| BOWERS, E. C., CAPTAIN U.S.N. | 44 |
| BRACKETT, A. G., COLONEL U.S.A. | 45 |
| BRAINE, D. L., REAR-ADMIRAL U.S.N. | 46 |
| BRAYTON, M., COLONEL U.S.A. | 47 |
| BRECK, S., LIEUTENANT-COLONEL AND BVT. BRIGADIER GENERAL U.S.A. | 48 |
| BRECKINRIDGE, J. C., BRIGADIER-GENERAL AND INSPECTOR-GENERAL U.S.A. | 49 |
| BREESE, K. R., CAPTAIN U.S.N. | 50 |
| BREWERTON, H. F., CAPTAIN U.S.A. | 51 |
| BRICE, J. J., COMMANDER U.S.N. | 52 |
| BRIDGE, H., PAYMASTER-GENERAL U.S.N. | 53 |
| BRINKERHOFF, H. R., CAPTAIN U.S.A. | 54 |
| BRISTOL, H. B., CAPTAIN AND BVT. LIEUTENANT-COLONEL U.S.A. | 55 |
| BROOKE, J. R., BRIGADIER-GENERAL U.S.A. | 56 |
| BROOKS, H., COLONEL AND BVT. BRIGADIER-GENERAL U.S.A. | 57 |
| BROWNE, J. M., SURGEON-GENERAL U.S.N. | 58 |
| BRUSH, G. K., MEDICAL INSPECTOR U.S.N. | 59 |
| BRYSON, A., REAR-ADMIRAL U.S.N. | 60 |
| BURNHAM, H. B., LIEUTENANT-COLONEL U.S.A. | 61 |
| BURNSIDE, A. E., MAJOR-GENERAL U.S.A. | 62 |
| BURT, A. S., LIEUTENANT-COLONEL U.S.A. | 63 |
| BURTIS, A., PAY-INSPECTOR U.S.N. | 64 |
| BUTLER, E., LIEUTENANT-COLONEL U.S.A. | 65 |
| BUTLER, J. G., MAJOR U.S.A. | 66 |
| BATCHELDER, R. N., BRIGADIER-GENERAL AND QUARTERMASTER-GENERAL U.S.A. | 67 |
| BEARDSLEE, L. A., CAPTAIN U.S.N. | 68 |
| CALEF, J. H., CAPTAIN U.S.A. | 69 |
| CALLINAN, D. F., CAPTAIN U.S.A. | 70 |
| CAMPBELL, J., COLONEL U.S.A. | 71 |
| CANBY, E. R. S., BRIGADIER- AND BVT. MAJOR-GENERAL U.S.A. | 72 |
| CARLTON, C. H., COLONEL U.S.A. | 73 |
| CARMODY, J. R., PAYMASTER U.S.N. | 74 |
| CARPENTER, L. H., MAJOR AND BVT. COLONEL U.S.A. | 75 |
| CARROLL, H., MAJOR U.S.A. | 76 |
| CARROLL, S. S., MAJOR-GENERAL U.S.A. | 77 |
| CASE, A. L., REAR-ADMIRAL U.S.N. | 78 |
| CASEY, S., COLONEL AND BVT. MAJOR-GENERAL U.S.A. | 79 |
| CASEY, S., CAPTAIN U.S.N. | 80 |
| CASEY, T. L., BRIGADIER-GENERAL AND CHIEF OF ENGINEERS U.S.A. | 81 |
| CATLIN, I. S., COLONEL U.S.A. | 82 |
| CHIPMAN, H. L., LIEUTENANT-COLONEL U.S.A. | 83 |
| CLAPP, W. H., CAPTAIN U.S.A. | 84 |
| CLARK, J. C., JR., MAJOR AND BVT. COLONEL U.S.A. | 85 |
| CLEBORNE, C. J., MEDICAL DIRECTOR U.S.N. | 86 |
| CLEM, J. L., CAPTAIN U.S.A. | 87 |
| CLENDENIN, D. R., COLONEL U.S.A. | 88 |
| CLOSSON, H. W., COLONEL U.S.A. | 89 |
| CLOUS, J. W., LIEUTENANT-COLONEL U.S.A. | 90 |
| COATES, E. M., MAJOR U.S.A. | 91 |
| COE, J. N., CAPTAIN U.S.A. | 92 |
| COFFIN, G. W., COMMANDER U.S.N. | 93 |
| COLLINS, N., REAR-ADMIRAL U.S.N. | 94 |
| COLLUM, R. S., CAPTAIN U.S.M.C. | 95 |
| COMSTOCK, C. B., BVT. MAJOR-GENERAL U.S.A. | 96 |
| CONLINE, J., CAPTAIN U.S.A. | 97 |
| CONRAD, C. H., CAPTAIN U.S.A. | 98 |
| COOKE, A. P., CAPTAIN U.S.N. | 99 |
| COOPER, P. H., COMMANDER U.S.N. | 100 |
| CORBIN, H. C., LIEUTENANT-COLONEL U.S.A. | 101 |
| COTTON, C. S., COMMANDER U.S.N. | 102 |
| CRAIGIE, D. J., CAPTAIN U.S.A. | 103 |
| CRAVEN, T. A. M., COMMANDER U.S.N. | 104 |
| CROOK, G., MAJOR-GENERAL U.S.A. | 105 |
| CROSBY, P., REAR-ADMIRAL U.S.N. | 106 |
| CROWELL, W. H. H., CAPTAIN U.S.A. | 107 |
| CULLUM, G. W., COLONEL AND BVT. MAJOR-GENERAL U.S.A. | 108 |
| CUSHING, H. C., BVT. MAJOR U.S.A. | 109 |
| CUSHING, S. T., MAJOR U.S.A. | 110 |
| CUSHING, W. B., COMMANDER U.S.N. | 111 |
| CUSICK, C. C., CAPTAIN U.S.A. | 112 |
| CUSTER, G. A., LIEUTENANT-COLONEL AND BVT. MAJOR-GENERAL U.S.A. | 113 |
| DAGGETT, A. S., MAJOR AND BVT. LIEUTENANT-COLONEL U.S.A. | 114 |
| DAHLGREN, J. A., REAR-ADMIRAL U.S.N. | 115 |
| DANA, W. S., COMMANDER U.S.N. | 116 |
| DARLING, J. A., CAPTAIN AND BVT. MAJOR U.S.A. | 117 |
| DAVIS, C. H., REAR-ADMIRAL U.S.N. | 118 |
| DAVIS, J. C., COLONEL U.S.A. | 119 |
| DAY, H., COLONEL AND BVT. BRIG. GENERAL U.S.A. | 120 |
| DAY, S. A., CAPTAIN U.S.A. | 121 |
| DE RUDIO, C. C., CAPTAIN U.S.A. | 122 |
| DEWEY, G., COMMODORE U.S.N. | 123 |
| DILLENBACK, J. W., CAPTAIN U.S.A. | 124 |
| DIMMICK, E. D., CAPTAIN U.S.A. | 125 |
| DOUBLEDAY, A., COLONEL AND BVT. MAJOR-GENERAL U.S.A. | 126 |
| DOUGLASS, H., COLONEL U.S.A. | 127 |
| DRAYTON, P., CAPTAIN U.S.N. | 128 |
| DRUM, R. C., BRIGADIER-GENERAL U.S.A. | 129 |
| DRUM, W. F., LIEUTENANT-COLONEL U.S.A. | 130 |
| DUPONT, S. F., REAR-ADMIRAL U.S.N. | 131 |
| DURAND, G. R., COMMANDER U.S.N. | 132 |
| DYER, N. M., COMMANDER U.S.N. | 133 |
| EAKIN, C. P., CAPTAIN AND BVT. MAJOR U.S.A. | 134 |
| EINSTEIN, F. H. E., CAPTAIN U.S.A. | 135 |
| EDGAR, W. F., MAJOR U.S.A. | 136 |
| ERBEN, H., COMMODORE U.S.N. | 137 |
| EVANS, R. D., COMMANDER U.S.N. | 138 |
| EWING, E. S., CAPTAIN AND BVT. MAJOR U.S.A. | 139 |
| FARLEY, J. P., LIEUTENANT-COLONEL U.S.A. | 140 |
| FARQUHAR, N. H., COMMODORE U.S.N. | 141 |
| FARRAGUT, D. G., ADMIRAL U.S.N. | 142 |
| FEBIGER, J. C., REAR-ADMIRAL U.S.N. | 143 |
| FECHÉT, E. G., MAJOR U.S.A. | 144 |
| FIELD, E., CAPTAIN U.S.A. | 145 |
| FITZ GERALD, M. J., CAPTAIN U.S.A. | 146 |
| FLAGLER, D. W., BRIG.-GENERAL U.S.A. | 147 |
| FLOYD-JONES, DeL., COLONEL U.S.A. | 148 |
| FLUSSER, C. W., LIEUTENANT-COMMANDER U.S.N. | 149 |

## INDEX.

FOLGER, W. M., COMMODORE U.S.N. . . . 150
FOLTZ, J. M., SURGEON-GENERAL U.S.N. 151
FOOTE, A. H., REAR-ADMIRAL U.S.N. . . 152
FORNEY, J., LT.-COLONEL U.S.M.C. . . . 153
FORSYTH, J. M., COMMANDER U.S.N. . . 154
FRANK, R. T., LIEUTENANT - COLONEL
  U.S.A. . . . . . . . . . . . . . . . . . 155
FRANKLIN, S. R., REAR-ADMIRAL U.S.N. 156
FRANKLIN, W. B., COLONEL AND BVT.
  MAJOR GENERAL U.S.A. . . . . . . . . 157
FREEMAN, H. B., MAJOR U.S.A. . . . . 158
FREMONT, J. C., MAJOR-GENERAL U.S.A. 159

GAGELY, J. H., CAPTAIN U.S.A. . . . . 160
GARRETTY, F. D., CAPTAIN U.S.A. . . . 161
GETTY, G. W., COLONEL AND BVT. MA-
  JOR-GENERAL U.S.A. . . . . . . . . . 162
GHERARDI, B., REAR-ADMIRAL U.S.N. . 163
GIBBON, J., BRIGADIER- AND BVT. MAJOR-
  GENERAL U.S.A. . . . . . . . . . . . . 164
GIHON, A. L., MEDICAL DIRECTOR U.S.N. 165
GILBREATH, E. C., CAPTAIN U.S.A. . . . 166
GILE, G. W., LIEUTENANT-COLONEL AND
  BVT. BRIGADIER-GENERAL U.S.A. . . 167
GILLMORE, Q. A., COLONEL AND BVT.
  MAJOR-GENERAL U.S.A. . . . . . . . 168
GOLDSBOROUGH, L. M., REAR-ADMIRAL
  U.S.N. . . . . . . . . . . . . . . . . . 169
GOODLOE, G. C., MAJOR U.S.M.C. . . . 170
GORRINGE, H. H., LIEUTENANT-COMMAN-
  DER U.S.N. . . . . . . . . . . . . . . 171
GRANT, L. A., ASSISTANT SECRETARY OF
  WAR . . . . . . . . . . . . . . . . . . 172
GRANT, U. S., GENERAL U.S.A. . . . . 173
GREELY, A. W., BRIGADIER - GENERAL
  U.S.A. . . . . . . . . . . . . . . . . . 174
GREEN, J. G., COMMANDER U.S.N. . . . 175
GREENOUGH, G. G., CAPTAIN U.S.A. . . 176
GREER, J. A., REAR-ADMIRAL U.S.N. . . 177
GROESBECK, S. W., MAJOR U.S.A. . . . 178
GRUGAN, F. C., CAPTAIN U.S.A. . . . . 179
GUEST, J., COMMODORE U.S.N. . . . . . 180

HAINS, P. C., LIEUTENANT - COLONEL
  U.S.A. . . . . . . . . . . . . . . . . . 181
HALLECK, H. W., MAJOR - GENERAL
  U.S.A. . . . . . . . . . . . . . . . . . 182
HANCOCK, W. S., MAJOR-GENERAL U.S.A. 183
HARDIN, M. D., BRIGADIER-GENERAL
  U.S.A. . . . . . . . . . . . . . . . . . 184
HARRIS, H. T. B., PAYMASTER U.S.N. . 185
HARRIS, J. C., FIRST LIEUTENANT
  U.S.M.C. . . . . . . . . . . . . . . . 186
HARRIS, M. J., CAPTAIN U.S.A. . . . . 187
HARRISON, B., COMMANDER-IN-CHIEF . . 188
HARTZ, W. T., CAPTAIN U.S.A. . . . . 189
HASKIN, W. L., MAJOR U.S.A. . . . . . 190
HAY, C., CAPTAIN U.S.A. . . . . . . . . 191
HAZEN, W. B., BRIGADIER - GENERAL
  U.S.A. . . . . . . . . . . . . . . . . . 192
HEBB, C. D., COLONEL U.S.M.C. . . . . 193
HENDERSHOTT, H. B., CAPTAIN AND BVT.
  COLONEL U.S.A. . . . . . . . . . . . 194
HENRY, G. V., LIEUTENANT-COLONEL AND
  BVT. COLONEL U.S.A. . . . . . . . . 195
HENTON, J., MAJOR U.S.A. . . . . . . . 196
HESS, F. W., CAPTAIN AND BVT. MAJOR
  U.S.A. . . . . . . . . . . . . . . . . . 197
HEYWOOD, C., COLONEL AND COMMAN-
  DANT U.S.M.C. . . . . . . . . . . . . 198
HIGBEE, J. H., MAJOR U.S.M.C. . . . . 199
HOFFMAN, W., CAPTAIN U.S.A. . . . . . 200
HOLABIRD, S. B., BRIGADIER-GENERAL
  U.S.A. . . . . . . . . . . . . . . . . . 201
HOOKER, E., COMMANDER U.S.N. . . . . 202
HOOKER, J., BRIGADIER AND BVT. MA-
  JOR-GENERAL U.S.A. . . . . . . . . . 203
HORWITZ, P. J., MEDICAL DIRECTOR
  U.S.N. . . . . . . . . . . . . . . . . . 204
HOWARD, O. O., MAJOR-GENERAL U.S.A. 205
HOWE, H. L., CAPTAIN U.S.A. . . . . . 206
HOWELL, J. C., REAR-ADMIRAL U.S.N. 207
HOXIE, R. L., CAPTAIN U.S.A. . . . . . 208

HUMPHREYS, A. A., BRIGADIER AND BVT.
  MAJOR-GENERAL U.S.A. . . . . . . . 209
HUNT, H. J., COLONEL AND BVT. MAJOR-
  GENERAL U.S.A. . . . . . . . . . . . 210

INGALLS, J. M., CAPTAIN U.S.A. . . . . 211
INGALLS, R., BRIGADIER AND BVT. MAJOR-
  GENERAL U.S.A. . . . . . . . . . . . 212

JACKSON, J., MAJOR U.S.A. . . . . . . . 213
JACKSON, S., MEDICAL DIRECTOR U.S.N. 214
JENKINS, T. A., REAR-ADMIRAL U.S.N. 215
JEWETT, H., COLONEL U.S.A. . . . . . 216
JOCELYN, S. P., CAPTAIN U.S.A. . . . . 217
JOHNSON, J. B., CAPTAIN U.S.A. . . . . 218
JOHNSON, L., CAPTAIN AND BVT. LIEU-
  TENANT-COLONEL U.S.A. . . . . . . 219
JONES, D. P., CHIEF ENGINEER U.S.N. 220
JONES, W. H., MEDICAL INSPECTOR U.S.N. 221
JOUETT, J. E., REAR-ADMIRAL U.S.N. . 222

KAUTZ, A., CAPTAIN U.S.N. . . . . . . 223
KAUTZ, A. V., BRIGADIER - GENERAL
  U.S.A. . . . . . . . . . . . . . . . . . 224
KELLOGG, E. R., MAJOR U.S.A. . . . . 225
KELTON, J. C., BRIGADIER - GENERAL
  U.S.A. . . . . . . . . . . . . . . . . . 226
KENDALL, F. A., CAPTAIN U.S.A. . . . 227
KENNEDY, W. B., MAJOR U.S.A. . . . . 228
KERSHNER, E., MEDICAL INSPECTOR
  U.S.N. . . . . . . . . . . . . . . . . . 229
KETCHAM, R. B., BVT. CAPTAIN U.S.N. 482
KETCHUM, H. J., CAPTAIN U.S.A. . . . 230
KILPATRICK, J., CAPTAIN AND BVT. MA-
  JOR-GENERAL U.S.A. . . . . . . . . . 231
KING, R., MAJOR-GENERAL U.S.A. . . . 232
KRAMER, A., CAPTAIN U.S.A. . . . . . 233
KRESS, J. A., MAJOR U.S.A. . . . . . . 234

LANGDON, L. L., COLONEL U.S.A. . . . 235
LARDNER, J. L., REAR-ADMIRAL U.S.N. 236
LATCH, E. B., CHIEF ENGINEER U.S.N. 237
LEARY, P., JR., CAPTAIN U.S.A. . . . . 238
LEE, S. P., REAR-ADMIRAL U.S.N. . . . 239
LE ROY, W. E., REAR-ADMIRAL U.S.N. 240
LOCKWOOD, H. C., CAPTAIN U.S.A. . . 241
LOOKER, T. N., PAY-DIRECTOR AND EX-
  PAYMASTER-GENERAL U.S.N. . . . . 242
LORD, J. H., MAJOR U.S.A. . . . . . . 243
LOTT, G. G., CAPTAIN U.S.A. . . . . . 244
LUCE, S. B., REAR-ADMIRAL U.S.N. . . 245

MACKENZIE, R. S., BRIGADIER-GENERAL
  U.S.A. . . . . . . . . . . . . . . . . . 246
MACMURRAY, J. W., CAPTAIN AND BVT.
  MAJOR U.S.A. . . . . . . . . . . . . 247
MACOMB, D. B., CHIEF ENGINEER U.S.N. 248
MAIZE, W. R., CAPTAIN U.S.A. . . . . 249
MALLERY, G., CAPTAIN AND BVT. LIEU-
  TENANT-COLONEL U.S.A. . . . . . . 250
MANLEY, H. DE H., COMMANDER U.S.N. 251
MARIN, M. C., CAPTAIN U.S.N. . . . . 252
McCANN, W. P., COMMODORE U.S.N. . 253
McCAULEY, E. Y., REAR-ADMIRAL U.S.N. 254
McCAWLEY, C. H., COLONEL U.S.M.C. 255
McCLELLAN, G. B., MAJOR - GENERAL
  U.S.A. . . . . . . . . . . . . . . . . . 256
McCONIHE, S., CAPTAIN AND BVT. LIEU-
  TENANT-COLONEL U.S.A. . . . . . . 257
McCOOK, A. McD., BRIGADIER AND BVT.
  MAJOR-GENERAL U.S.A. . . . . . . . 258
McCREA, T., MAJOR U.S.A. . . . . . . 259
McCURLEY, F., COMMANDER U.S.N. . . 260
McDONALD, J., CAPTAIN U.S.N. . . . . 261
McDONALD, R., CAPTAIN U.S.N. . . . . 262
McDOUGALL, T. M., CAPTAIN U.S.A. . 263
McDOWELL, I., MAJOR-GENERAL U.S.A. 264
McGREGOR, C., COMMANDER U.S.N. . . 265
McKEE, G. W., MAJOR U.S.A. . . . . . 266
McPHERSON, J. B., BRIGADIER-GENERAL
  U.S.A. . . . . . . . . . . . . . . . . . 267
MEADE, G. G., MAJOR-GENERAL U.S.A. 268

MEARS, F., LIEUTENANT-COLONEL U.S.A. 269
MEIGS, M. C., BRIGADIER AND BVT. MA-
  JOR-GENERAL U.S.A. . . . . . . . . . 270
MELVILLE, G. W., ENGINEER-IN-CHIEF
  U.S.N. . . . . . . . . . . . . . . . . . 271
MERRIAM, H. C., COLONEL U.S.A. . . . 272
MERRITT, W., BRIGADIER AND BVT. MA-
  JOR-GENERAL U.S.A. . . . . . . . . . 273
MILES, E., LIEUTENANT-COLONEL U.S.A. 274
MILES, N. A., MAJOR-GENERAL U.S.A. 275
MILLER, F. A., LIEUTENANT-COMMANDER
  U.S.N. . . . . . . . . . . . . . . . . . 276
MILLIS, A., LIEUTENANT-COLONEL U.S.A. 277
MILLIS, W. H., CAPTAIN AND BVT. MAJOR
  U.S.A. . . . . . . . . . . . . . . . . . 278
MITCHELL, G., CAPTAIN U.S.A. . . . . 279
MIZNER, H. R., COLONEL U.S.A. . . . . 280
MIZNER, J. K., COLONEL U.S.A. . . . . 281
MORGAN, W. A., LIEUTENANT-COMMAN-
  DER U.S.N. . . . . . . . . . . . . . . 282
MORRIS, A., CAPTAIN AND BVT. MAJOR
  U.S.A. . . . . . . . . . . . . . . . . . 283
MORRIS, G. U., COMMANDER U.S.N. . . 284
MORROW, A. P., COLONEL U.S.A. . . . 285
MORTON, A., CAPTAIN U.S.A. . . . . . 286
MULLAN, D. W., COMMANDER U.S.N. . 287
MULLANY, J. R. M., REAR - ADMIRAL
  U.S.N. . . . . . . . . . . . . . . . . . 288
MURRAY, J. D., PAY-DIRECTOR U.S.N. 289

NICHOLSON, J. W. A., REAR-ADMIRAL
  U.S.N. . . . . . . . . . . . . . . . . . 290
NIXON, J. B., CAPTAIN AND BVT. LIEU-
  TENANT-COLONEL U.S.A. . . . . . . 291
NOBLE, H. B., CAPTAIN U.S.A. . . . . 292
NORRIS, B., COLONEL U.S.A. . . . . . . 293
NORTON, T. H., CAPTAIN AND BVT. MAJOR
  U.S.A. . . . . . . . . . . . . . . . . . 294
NORVELL, J. M., CAPTAIN AND BVT. MA-
  JOR U.S.A. . . . . . . . . . . . . . . 295

OBERLY, A. S., MEDICAL INSPECTOR
  U.S.N. . . . . . . . . . . . . . . . . . 296
O'KANE, J., CAPTAIN U.S.N. . . . . . . 297
ORD, E. O. C., MAJOR-GENERAL U.S.A. 298
OVERTON, G. E., CAPTAIN U.S.A. . . . 299

PAGE, J. H., LIEUTENANT-COLONEL U.S.A. 300
PALMER, I. N., COLONEL AND BVT. BRIGA-
  DIER-GENERAL U.S.A. . . . . . . . . 301
PARKER, D., LIEUTENANT - COLONEL
  U.S.A. . . . . . . . . . . . . . . . . . 302
PARKER, F. A., COMMODORE U.S.N. . . 303
PARKER, J. B., SURGEON U.S.N. . . . . 304
PATTISON, T., REAR-ADMIRAL U.S.N. . 305
PAUL, G. R., COLONEL AND BVT. BRIGA-
  DIER-GENERAL U.S.A. . . . . . . . . 306
PAULDING, H., REAR-ADMIRAL U.S.N. 307
PECK, G., MEDICAL DIRECTOR U.S.N. . 308
PENNINGTON, A. C. M., MAJOR AND BVT.
  COLONEL U.S.A. . . . . . . . . . . . 309
PENNOCK, A. M., REAR-ADMIRAL U.S.N. 310
PENNYPACKER, G., COLONEL AND BVT.
  MAJOR-GENERAL U.S.A. . . . . . . . 311
PENROSE, T. N., MEDICAL INSPECTOR
  U.S.N. . . . . . . . . . . . . . . . . . 312
PERKINS, G. H., CAPTAIN U.S.N. . . . 313
PHELPS, S. L., LIEUTENANT-COMMANDER
  U.S.N. . . . . . . . . . . . . . . . . . 314
PHELPS, T. S., REAR-ADMIRAL U.S.N. 315
PHILIP, J. W., CAPTAIN U.S.N. . . . . 316
POOLE, DE W. C., MAJOR U.S.A. . . . 317
PORTER, D. D., ADMIRAL U.S.N. . . . . 318
PORTER, FITZ-JOHN, COLONEL AND BVT.
  BRIGADIER-GENERAL U.S.A. . . . . . 319
PORTER, W. D., COMMODORE U.S.N. . 320
POTTER, E. E., CAPTAIN U.S.N. . . . . 321
POTTER, J. H., BRIGADIER-GENERAL
  U.S.A. . . . . . . . . . . . . . . . . . 322
POWELL, W. F., CAPTAIN U.S.A. . . . 323
POWELL, W. H., LIEUTENANT-COLONEL
  U.S.A. . . . . . . . . . . . . . . . . . 324
PREBLE, G. H., REAR-ADMIRAL U.S.N. 325
PRICE, C. E., MAJOR U.S.A. . . . . . . 326

# INDEX.

| Name | Page |
|---|---|
| Pulford, J., Colonel U.S.A. | 327 |
| Purington, G. A., Major U.S.A. | 328 |
| Quackenbush, S. P., Rear-Admiral U.S.N. | 329 |
| Ramsay, F. M., Commodore U.S.N. | 330 |
| Rawles, J. B., Major U.S.A. | 331 |
| Rawlins, J. A., Brigadier- and Bvt. Major-General, U.S.A. | |
| Rawolle, W. C., Captain U.S.A. | 332 |
| Ray, P. H., Captain U.S.A. | 333 |
| Reed, A. V., Captain U.S.N. | 334 |
| Remey, G. C., Captain U.S.N. | 335 |
| Remley, W. B., Colonel U.S.M.C. | 336 |
| Reynolds, J. F., Colonel U.S.A. | 337 |
| Rhoades, W. W., Lieutenant-Commander U.S.N. | 338 |
| Rice, E., Captain and Bvt. Lieutenant-Colonel U.S.A. | 339 |
| Ritner, I. N., Chaplain U.S.A. | 340 |
| Rittenhouse, B. F., Captain and Bvt. Major U.S.A. | 341 |
| Ritzius, H. P., Captain U.S.A. | 483 |
| Roberts, J., Colonel and Bvt. Brigadier-General U.S.A. | 312 |
| Robinson, J. C., Major-General U.S.A. | 313 |
| Rockwell, C. H., Commander U.S.N. | 314 |
| Rodenbough, T. F., Colonel and Bvt. Brigadier-General U.S.A. | 345 |
| Rodgers, C. R. P., Rear-Admiral U.S.N. | 346 |
| Rodgers, G. W., Commander U.S.N. | 347 |
| Rodgers, J., Rear-Admiral U.S.N. | 348 |
| Rodney, R. B., Paymaster U.S.N. | 349 |
| Roe, F. A., Rear-Admiral U.S.N. | 350 |
| Rogers, W. P., Captain U.S.A. | 351 |
| Romeyn, H., Captain U.S.A. | 352 |
| Rowan, S. C., Vice-Admiral U.S.N. | 353 |
| Rucker, W. A., Colonel U.S.A. | 354 |
| Ruger, T. H., Brigadier-General U.S.A. | 355 |
| Ruggles, G. D., Colonel and Bvt. Brigadier-General U.S.A. | 356 |
| Runkle, B. P., Major and Bvt. Colonel U.S.A. | 357 |
| Russell, A. W., Pay-Director U.S.N. | 358 |
| Russell, G., Major U.S.A. | 359 |
| Rutherford, R. G., First Lieutenant and Bvt. Captain U.S.A. | 360 |
| Sampson, W. T., Captain U.S.N. | 361 |
| Savage, E. B., Captain U.S.A. | 362 |
| Sawtelle, C. G., Lieutenant-Colonel and Bvt. Brigadier-General, U.S.A. | 363 |
| Saxton, R., Colonel and Bvt. Major-General, U.S.A. | 364 |
| Schenck, J. F., Rear-Admiral U.S.N. | 365 |
| Schley, W. S., Captain U.S.N. | 366 |
| Schofield, J. M., Major-General U.S.A. | 367 |
| Schwenk, S. K., Captain and Bvt. Lieutenant-Colonel, U.S.A. | 368 |
| Scott, W., Lieutenant-General U.S.A. | 484 |
| Scully, J. W., Major and Bvt. Colonel U.S.A. | 369 |
| Sears, C. B., Captain U.S.A. | 370 |
| Seeley, F. W., Captain | 371 |
| Selfridge, Jr., T. O., Captain U.S.N. | 372 |
| Shaw, R. G., Captain U.S.A. | 373 |
| Shepherd, O. L., Colonel and Bvt. Brigadier-General U.S.A. | 374 |
| Sheridan, P. H., General U.S.A. | 375 |
| Sherman, W. T., General U.S.A. | 376 |
| | 377 |
| Shippen, E., Medical Director U.S.N. | 378 |
| Shock, W. H., Chief Engineer U.S.N. | 379 |
| Shorkley, G., Captain and Bvt. Major U.S.A. | 380 |
| Shufeldt, R. W., Rear-Admiral U.S.N. | 381 |
| Shurly, E. R. P., First Lieutenant and Bvt. Captain U.S.A. | 382 |
| Simpson, E., Rear-Admiral U.S.N. | 383 |
| Simpson, J. F., Captain U.S.A. | 384 |
| Small, M. P., Lieutenant-Colonel and Bvt. Brigadier-General U.S.A. | 385 |
| Smedberg, W. R., Captain and Bvt. Lieutenant-Colonel U.S.A. | |
| Smith, C. H., Colonel and Bvt. Major-General U.S.A. | 386 |
| Smith, F. G., Major U.S.A. | 387 |
| Smith, F. R., Commander U.S.N. | 388 |
| Smith, H. E., Captain and Bvt. Major U.S.A. | 389 |
| Smith, J. E., Colonel and Bvt. Major-General U.S.A. | 390 |
| Smith, J. R., Colonel U.S.A. | 391 |
| Smith, M., Rear-Admiral U.S.N. | 392 |
| Snyder, J. A., Captain U.S.A. | 393 |
| Spear, J. C., Medical Inspector U.S.N. | 394 |
| Stanley, D. S., Brigadier-General U.S.A. | 395 |
| Stanton, O. F., Commodore U.S.N. | 396 |
| Steedman, C., Rear-Admiral U.S.N. | 397 |
| Stembel, R. N., Rear-Admiral U.S.N. | 398 |
| Sternberg, G. M., Lieutenant-Colonel U.S.A. | 399 |
| Stevens, T. H., Rear-Admiral U.S.N. | 400 |
| Stevenson, J. H., Pay-Inspector U.S.N. | 401 |
| Stewart, E., Paymaster-General U.S.A. | 402 |
| Stirling, Y., Commander U.S.N. | 403 |
| Stivers, E. J., Captain U.S.A. | 404 |
| Stone, E. W., Colonel U.S.A. | 405 |
| Stringham, S. H., Rear-Admiral U.S.N. | 406 |
| Sturgeon, S., Captain and Bvt. Lieutenant-Colonel U.S.A. | 407 |
| Sturgis, S. D., Colonel U.S.A. | 408 |
| Sumner, E. V., Major-General U.S.A. | 409 |
| Sutherland, C., Brigadier-General U.S.A. | 410 |
| Swaim, D. G., Brigadier-General U.S.A. | 411 |
| Swaine, P. T., Colonel U.S.A. | 412 |
| Swayne, W., Colonel and Bvt. Major-General U.S.A. | 413 |
| Sweeny, T. W., Brigadier-General U.S.A. | 414 |
| Sweet, O. J., Captain U.S.A. | 415 |
| Switzer, N. B., Colonel and Bvt. Brigadier-General U.S.A. | 416 |
| Tarbell, J. F., Paymaster U.S.N. | 417 |
| Taylor, A. H. M., First Lieutenant U.S.A. | 418 |
| Taylor, J. V., Medical Director U.S.N. | 419 |
| Terry, A. H., Major-General U.S.A. | 420 |
| Terry, S. W., Commander U.S.N. | 421 |
| Thatcher, H. K., Rear-Admiral U.S.N. | 422 |
| Thomas, G. H., Major-General U.S.A. | 423 |
| Thomas, H. G., Major and Bvt. Brigadier-General U.S.A. | 424 |
| Thompson, J. M., Captain U.S.A. | 425 |
| Tidball, J. C., Colonel and Bvt. Brigadier-General U.S.A. | 426 |
| Tilford, J. G., Colonel U.S.A. | 427 |
| | 428 |
| Townsend, E., Bvt. Brigadier-General U.S.A. | 429 |
| Tracy, A., Major and Bvt. Colonel U.S.A. | 430 |
| Tracy, B. F., Secretary of the Navy | 431 |
| Trenchard, S. D., Rear-Admiral U.S.N. | |
| Truxtun, W. T., Commodore U.S.N. | 432 |
| Tupper, T. C., Major U.S.A. | 433 |
| Turner, T., Rear-Admiral U.S.N. | 434 |
| | 435 |
| Upham, J. J., Colonel U.S.A. | 436 |
| Upton, E., Lieutenant-Colonel and Bvt. Major-General U.S.A. | 437 |
| Van Horn, J. J., Colonel U.S.A. | 438 |
| Van Vliet, S., Colonel and Bvt. Major-General U.S.A. | 439 |
| Vedder, S. C., Captain U.S.A. | 440 |
| Wainwright, J. M., Commander U.S.N. | 441 |
| Walke, H., Rear-Admiral U.S.N. | 442 |
| Walker, J. G., Commodore U.S.N. | 443 |
| Ward, G. S. L., Captain U.S.A. | 444 |
| Warren, G. K., Lieutenant-Colonel and Bvt. Major-General U.S.A. | |
| Watson, J. C., Captain U.S.N. | 445 |
| Webb, W. G., Major U.S.A. | 446 |
| Wheaton, C., Captain U.S.A. | 447 |
| Wheaton, L., Major and Bvt. Lieutenant-Colonel U.S.A. | 448 |
| Whipple, A. W., Major and Bvt. Major-General U.S.A. | 449 |
| Whipple, W. D., Colonel and Bvt. Major-General U.S.A. | 450 |
| White, C. H., Medical Inspector U.S.N. | 451 |
| White, J. C., Captain U.S.A. | 452 |
| Whitehouse, E. N., Paymaster U.S.N. | 453 |
| Whitside, S. M., Major U.S.A. | 454 |
| Wilhelm, T., Captain and Bvt. Major U.S.A. | 455 |
| Wilkes, C., Rear-Admiral U.S.N. | 456 |
| Willcox, O. B., Brigadier and Bvt. Major-General U.S.A. | 457 |
| Williams, W. W., Pay-Director U.S.N. | 458 |
| Wilson, B., Captain U.S.N. | 459 |
| Wilson, G. S., Captain U.S.A. | 460 |
| Wilson, J. M., Colonel U.S.A. | 461 |
| Wilson, T. D., Commodore U.S.N. | 462 |
| Wiltse, G. C., Captain U.S.N. | 463 |
| Wingate, G. E., Commander U.S.N. | 464 |
| Winslow, G. F., Passed Assistant Surgeon U.S.N. | 465 |
| Winslow, J. A., Rear-Admiral U.S.N. | 466 |
| Wise, W. C., Commander U.S.N. | 467 |
| Wister, F., Captain U.S.A. | 468 |
| Witherell, C. T., Captain and Bvt. Major U.S.A. | 469 |
| Wood, E. E., Captain U.S.A. | 470 |
| Wood, G. W., Commander U.S.N. | 471 |
| Wood, H. C., Lieutenant-Colonel and Bvt. Colonel U.S.A. | 472 |
| Wood, T. J., Brigadier-General and Bvt. Major-General U.S.A. | 473 |
| Woodhull, A. A., Major and Bvt. Lieutenant-Colonel U.S.A. | 474 |
| Woodruff, C. A., Captain U.S.A. | 475 |
| Woodward, E. T., Commander U.S.N. | 476 |
| Woodward, G. A., Colonel U.S.A. | 477 |
| Worden, J. L., Rear-Admiral U.S.N. | 478 |
| | 479 |
| Zeilin, J., Brigadier-General U.S.M.C. | 480 |

THE END.

www.ingramcontent.com/pod-product-compliance
Lightning Source LLC
Chambersburg PA
CBHW021425300426
44114CB00010B/652